CUBA IN TRANSITION

Volume 7

Papers and Proceedings of the

**Seventh Annual Meeting
of the
Association for the Study of the Cuban Economy (ASCE)**

Miami, Florida
August 7-9, 1997

(ISBN 0-9649082-6-3)

Cuba in Transition volumes may be ordered from:

Association for the Study of the Cuban Economy
José F. Alonso—ASCE Books
2000 Osborn Drive
Silver Spring, MD 20910-1319
Tel. 301/587-1664
Fax 301/587-1664
E-mail: asce@capacess.org

PREFACE

These Proceedings, from ASCE's Seventh Annual Meeting, contain a rich variety of analyses and discussion about the Cuban society and economy. They come to light at a time when the Cuban Government has decided literally to stop the timid reform process it had started during the past few years. Many of these reforms, including the licencing of selected independent work, the apparent dismantlement of the state farms *(sovjoses)* into quasi cooperatives, the licencing of small restaurants *(paladares),* and the legalization of the dollar, were expected to add dynamism to an almost paralyzed economy. In practice, however, despite their initial success, or more probably because of it, all of these reforms have been severely restricted, from the inception, by all sorts of impediments. Thus, their potential beneficial impact has been greatly curtailed.

It is not difficult to understand why this schizophrenic behavior. Individuals' economic success generates independence from the state, a situation that a government that practices totalitarian control can hardly afford. Sadly, the result of this "fear of flying" is an acute duality in which access to dollars makes the difference between achieving a minimum level of comfort and barely covering basic human needs. Also, as individuals endeavor to either comply or disregard governmental restrictions, all sorts of distortions creep in, reducing efficiency and productivity of resources used. Furthermore, the practice of paying peso salaries to Cuban workers in joint ventures while collecting much higher dollar salaries for their work from the foreign investor, not only distorts the labor market, but amounts to the government confiscating the surplus that has been earned by the worker. Karl Marx would have defined it as exploitation of the worker by the state.

ASCE's Seventh Meeting was very successful, mostly because of the enthusiasm and work of its members and their commitment to conduct serious analysis and discussion of the Cuban economy. I, together with the Board of Directors, want to express our strong appreciation to our past President, Jorge Pérez-López, and to José Alonso for the large amount of high quality work that has been done in preparing this publication. We are also very grateful to the North-South Center of the University of Miami for their support and co-sponsorship of the meetings and for the financial contributions to the meeting by several corporate sponsors.

Antonio Gayoso
President

TABLE OF CONTENTS

ASSOCIATION FOR THE STUDY OF THE CUBAN ECONOMY (ASCE)

Seventh Annual Meeting
University of Miami, Knight Center, Hyatt Hotel
August 7-9, 1997

Conference Program

Panel Discussion: The Current Situation

Luis Aguilar León, Georgetown University -Emeritus

Jorge Pérez-López, U.S. Department of Labor

Jorge Sanguinetty, DevTech Systems

Jaime Suchlicki, University of Miami

Roundtable: Non-Sugar Agricultural Trade

William Messina, University of Florida

James Ross, University of Florida

José Alvarez, University of Florida

Richard N. Brown, U.S. Department of Agriculture

Women

The Impact of the Transition on Cuban Women
Julie Marie Bunck, University of Louisville

Discussant: Alfred Padula, University of Southern Maine

La mujer cubana en el exilio: Su aporte económico y social y su visión sobre Cuba
Uva de Aragón, Cuban Research Institute, Florida International University

Discussant: Beatriz Casals, Casals and Associates

Self-Employment

The Cuban Self-Employed: Who Are They?
Ana Julia Jatar-Hausman, Inter-American Dialogue

Discussant: Ernesto Betancourt, International Development and Finance

Prospects for Cuban Entrepreneurs After Transition: A Comparative Analysis
Ricardo Tejada, U.S. Department of Labor

Discussant: Luis Locay, University of Miami

Roundtable: NGOs Working in Cuba

Oscar Brown Stamp, Canadian Cooperative Association

Christopher Gilson, Jr., Catholic Relief Services

Discussant: Luis Locay, University of Miami

Economic Policies, Human Capital, Growth, and Technological Change in Cuba
Manuel Madrid-Aris, University of Southern California

Discussant: Ricardo Martínez, Inter-American Development Bank

U.S. Policy Toward Cuba

A Proposal for U.S. Policy Toward Cuba
Carlos Seiglie, Rutgers University

Discussant: Eusebio Mujal-León, Georgetown University

Implications of the U.S. Economic Embargo for a Political Transition in Cuba
Juan J. López, University of Illinois at Chicago

Discussant: William C. Smith, University of Miami

Social Forces and the Process of Transition
Enrique Pumar, American University

Discussant: Benigno Aguirre, Texas A&M University

Foreign Assistance for a Democratic Cuba

Support for a Democractic Transition in Cuba
Robert V. Burke, U.S. Agency for International Development

Enfoque crítico del documento para la transición democrática
Maida Donate-Armada

Documento de programación de la cooperación internacional
Rolando Castañeda and George Plinio Montalván, Inter-American Development Bank

Discussants: Ernesto Betancourt, International Development and Finance and ErnestoHernández-Catá,
International Monetary Fund

Privatization and Reforms

Privatización: ¿Factor de unión y desarrollo o de conflicto social?
Alberto Luzárraga, Amerinvest Corp.

Discussant: Steven Escobar, U.S. Department of Commerce

Legal Foundations for a Successful Privatization in Cuba
Matías Travieso-Díaz and Alejandro Ferraté, Shaw, Pittman, Potts & Trowbridge

Discussant: Pamela Falk, City University of New York School of Law

Industrial Sector Issues

The Cement Industry
Teo Babún, Cuba-Caribbean Development Corporation, Ltd.

Discussant: James Powers, Lone Star Industries

Bioprospecting in a Post-Castro Cuba
Larry Daley, Oregon State University

"Power to the People: Assessing the Impact of Cuba's Nuclear Development Program and the Politics of
Modernization"
Jonathan Benjamin-Alvarado, University of Georgia

Discussant: Duane Fitzgerald, U.S. General Accounting Office

Roundtable: Reinstatement of the 1940 Constitution

José D. Acosta, OAS-Retired

Agustín de Goytisolo, Mesa, Rodríguez & Machado, P.A.

Néstor Carbonell-Cortina, Pepsico International

THE CUBAN ECONOMY IN MID-1997

Jorge F. Pérez-López[1]

In mid-1997, the Cuban economy remains in the doldrums. The economic downturn that began over a decade ago, and intensified in the 1990s, continues to batter the island. While the economic free fall of the early 1990s apparently ended sometime in 1994, positive economic growth recorded since then has not markedly improved the population's standard of living. As if the average Cuban citizen needed to be reminded, Minister of the Economy and Planning José Luis Rodríguez told a journalist in April 1997 that the "special period has not been overcome yet" and predicted that "in a reasonable time period, which may be a matter of a few years, Cuba will again reach [economic] levels achieved prior to the special period."[2]

These brief remarks focus on three issues: 1) economic policy developments during the last year or so; 2) macroeconomic performance; and 3) performance of certain critical sectors of the economy.

ECONOMIC POLICIES

Compared to the period 1993-94, when the Cuban government entertained some discussion of economic alternatives and introduced several reform measures, economic policymaking has been paralyzed in recent years. Hard line pronouncements by the leadership, coupled with an unyielding platform for the Fifth Congress of the Cuban Communist Party, evidence retrenchment and do not augur well for future reforms:

- In January 1997, speaking at the 9th Science and Technology Forum, Fidel Castro said: "We're going to maintain what we have in the form in which we have it, in spite of the measures, the openings we have had to make, etc. Renouncing our doctrine and our socialist cause would be giving ourselves up to fiends who wouldn't even want the whereabouts known of the remains of those who resisted them with unprecedented heroism, of those that they couldn't defeat for more than 35 years."[3]

- In March 1997, at a conference sponsored by *The Economist*, Carlos Lage restated to journalists that Cuba sought economic transformations "without altering its socialist essence."[4] A few weeks later, Lage told employees of the Ministry of the Economy and Planning that the establishment of private small and medium-sized enterprises—a long awaited change—was not a high priority of the government and could not be expected until state enterprises developed and became more efficient.[5]

---

1. These remarks present strictly the opinions of the author.

2. "Estamos aún en 'período especial,' dice ministro," *El Nuevo Herald* (25 abril 1997), p. 6A.

3. "The Forum serves to demonstrate the level of awareness, unity and integration in Cuba," *Granma International Electronic Edition*, no. 2 (1997).

4. Susana Lee, "We have initiated economic reforms within socialism," interview with Carlos Lage, *Granma International Electronic Edition*, no. 10 (1997).

5. "No habrá participación privada en la mediana empresea de Cuba a corto plazo, dice el gobierno," Notimex (1 abril 1997), Wold Wide Web.

- Meanwhile, General Raúl Castro stated in May 1997 that despite the complex circumstances, Cuba could still build socialism. He ominously warned that "Socialism is here to stay in this land, defended by the people's guns!"[6]

- Finally, the draft platform for the Fifth Congress of the Cuban Communist Party, scheduled to take place October 8-10, 1997, offers no hope of change in economic model: "In the midst of innumerable difficulties, the country has managed in recent years to halt its economy's free-fall and has adopted the necessary measures for initiating its recovery and finding new markets and economic trading partners. .... Today it is clearer than ever that the Revolution, the homeland and socialism are one and the same. There will be no restoration of capitalism in Cuba because the revolution will never be defeated. The country will continue intact and will continue to be socialist."[7]

Policy developments since August 1996 include passage of the long-expected legislation reforming the banking system and regulations limiting internal migration and further tightening activities of the self-employed.

Decree-Law 172, approved by the Council of State in May 1997, established the Banco Central de Cuba as an autonomous and independent entity and assigns to it traditional central banking functions. The Banco Nacional de Cuba, which had performed central and commercial banking functions since 1960, remains in existence, but its role is relegated to commercial banking. Decree-Law 173, approved by the

Council of State concurrently with Decree-Law 172, sets out a legal framework for registration and operation of commercial banks and financial institutions under the supervision of the Banco Central.[8]

In April 1997, Fidel Castro complained about pressures being placed on the public services infrastructure of the city of La Habana by "uncontrolled migration" from "the Third World countries of Cuba: Guantánamo, Granma, and others."[9] He complained that residents of La Habana no longer wished to do construction or police work, with migrants from other parts of the country temporarily coming to fill those positions and eventually settling permanently in La Habana. Castro equated internal migration with "social indiscipline" and linked it to increases in thefts and petty criminal behavior in La Habana. Decree 217, issued in late April 1997, required potential migrants to obtain authorization from the owners of the dwelling where they intended to reside and a document from urban development authorities certifying that the dwelling had space for the migrant and was is in adequate condition; violators would be subject to fines, prison sentences and eviction and return to their towns of origin.[10] Reportedly, more than 1600 migrants residing "illegally" in La Habana were expelled in May and returned to their towns of origin.[11]

The government has continued to hinder activities of the self-employed. Both Fidel Castro and Carlos Lage lashed at "irregularities" of self-employed workers and vowed to use the full force of the law to ensure that they paid all fees and taxes and did not engage in illegal activities. Regulations passed in May

---

6. "Socialism is here to stay," speech by Raúl Castro at the event marking the 36th Anniversary of the Proclamation of the Socialist Nature of the Cuban Revolution," *Granma International Electronic Edition*, no. 16 (1997).

7. "The Party of Unity, democracy and the human rights we defend," *Granma International Electronic Edition*, no. 21 (1997). See also Juan O. Tamayo, "Cuba chills talk of change," *The Miami Herald* (May 26, 1997), p. 20A and "Call to the 5th Congress of the Communist Party of Cuba," *Granma International Electronic Edition*, no. 16 (1997).

8. "Central Bank of Cuba established," *Granma International Electronic Edition*, no. 25 (1977).

9. "The consequences of neoliberalism affect Europe itself, not only the Third World," speech by Fidel Castro at the ceremony for the 35th Anniversary of the Young Communist League, *Granma International Electronic Edition*, no. 14 (1997).

10. "Entra en vigor decreto de migración en Cuba," *El Nuevo Herald* (12 mayo 1997), p 2B; "Capital en ruinas es meca que atrae a miles," *El Nuevo Herald* (14 mayo 1997), p. 6A.

11. "Desalojan 1600 de La Habana," *El Nuevo Herald* (28 abril 1997), p. 2B.

Table 1. Selected Cuban Economic Indicators (in million pesos, unless otherwise indicated)

	1989	1990	1991	1992	1993	1994	1995	1996	1997[a]
Gross domestic product (GDP)	19586	19088	16976	15010	12777	12868	13185	14212	
% growth	NA	-3.0	-10.7	-11.6	-14.9	0.7	2.5	7.8	4.0-5.0
GDP per capita (pesos)	1865	1795	1590	1394	1177	1174	1192	1275	
% growth	NA	-3.8	-11.4	-12.3	-15.6	-0.3	1.5	7.0	
Exports	5400	5415	2980	1779	1136	1331	1479	1966	2200
Imports	8140	7416	4233	2315	2036	2017	2772	3438	3830
Trade turnover	13540	12831	7213	4094	3172	3348	4251	5404	6030
Trade balance	-2714	-2001	-1253	-536	-900	-686	-1293	-1471	-1630
Hard currency debt (million U.S. dollars)	6200		6400		8785	9083	10504	11000[b]	
Budget deficit	1390	1958	3765	4869	5051	1421	766	569	461
% GDP	7.1	10.3	22.2	32.4	39.5	11.0	5.8	4.0	
Liquidity	4163	4986	6563	8361	11044	9944	9251	9200	8920
% GDP	21.2	26.1	38.7	55.7	86.4	77.3	70.2	64.7	
Average exchange rate (pesos per U.S. dollar)					78.0	95.0	32.1	19.2	
Sugar (million metric tons)	8.1	8.0	7.6	7.0	4.3	4.0	3.3	4.5	4.2[b]
World market price (cents/pound)	12.8	12.5	9.0	9.1	10.0	12.1	13.3	12.0	10.9[c]
Nickel (thousand metric tons)	46.6	40.7	33.3	32.4	30.2	29.9	42.9	53.7	
World market price (cents/pound)	603.9	402.0	370.3	318.2	240.8	287.2	373.0	340.0	343.2[c]
Oil (million metric tons)	0.7	0.7	0.5	0.9	1.1	1.3	1.5	1.6	64.4
World market price (dollars/barrel)	17.2	22.1	19.3	19.0	16.8	15.9	17.2	20.4	21.0[c]
Number of foreign tourists (thousands)	326	340	418	455	544	617	740	1000	1200
Gross income from tourism (billion U.S. dollars)	0.17	0.24	0.39	0.57	0.72	0.85	1.1	1.3	

Source: Banco Nacional de Cuba, *Economic Report 1995* and earlier issues; Economic Commission for Latin America and the Caribbean, *Cuba: Evolución Económica en 1996* and earlier issues; IMF, *International Financial Statistics;* Economist Intelligence Unit, various publications; articles in the Cuban press.

a. Plan
b. Estimated; for sugar, estimated production of 1996-97 zafra
c. First quarter 1997

1997 set limitations on the rental of rooms to citizens or foreigners, requiring a permit for such rental activities and payment of a tax.[12] While the government justified the regulations on the grounds that it was intended to keep a better control of internal migrants and foreign citizens, it appears that the objective was also to discourage the rental of space in private homes to foreign visitors and businessmen, forcing them to live in state-operated tourism hotels or rent more expensive space from state authorities.

MACROECONOMIC PERFORMANCE

Table 1 brings together available statistics on Cuban economic performance during 1989-96 and projections for 1997 from various sources. Most of the data are official Cuban government statistics; because their reliability is questionable, care should be exercised in using them.

According to Cuban official statistics, the gross domestic product (GDP) at constant prices grew from about 13.2 billion pesos in 1995 to 14.2 billion pesos in 1996, or by 7.8 percent, 56 percent higher than the 5 percent growth rate that had been anticipated.

---

12. "Cortan alas al negocio de alquilar viviendas," *El Nuevo Herald* (17 mayo 1997), p. 6A.

The corresponding growth rate in GDP per capita was 7.0 percent.

Thus, 1996 was the third consecutive year of positive economic growth (Cuban official statistics reported growth rates of 0.7 percent for 1994 and 2.5 percent for 1995). Cumulative GDP growth during 1994-96 was 11.2 percent and 5.3 percent in per capita terms, compared to declines during 1990-93 of 34.8 percent and 36.9 percent, respectively. That is, the 1994-96 "recovery" has regained only about one third of the ground that was lost in national production during 1990-93. GDP per capita in 1996 has been estimated at 1275 pesos, 31.6 percent lower than the 1865 pesos recorded in 1989.

As has become the practice in the 1990s, Cuba has not provided detailed statistics to support the GDP growth rate reported for 1996. Even the report by Minister of the Economy and Planning José Luis Rodríguez to the National Assembly of People's Power in the closing days of 1996, perhaps the most comprehensive account of the performance of the economy in 1996, presents sparse statistics that do not permit substantiation of the reported overall macroeconomic results.[13] Respected scholars have raised fundamental questions about the reliability of Cuban macroeconomic statistics for 1996 and, by extension, about those for earlier years and the Cuban system of national accounts at large.[14]

Cuba's 1996 merchandise trade deficit amounted to nearly 1.5 billion pesos, 13.7 percent higher than a year earlier. The value of merchandise imports grew by 24 percent, in part because of higher world market prices for imports of foodstuffs and of oil; according to Minister Rodríguez, foodstuffs imports were $118 million higher and oil imports $108 million higher than in 1995 because of higher world market prices. Meanwhile, the value of merchandise exports grew by nearly 33 percent, despite the fact that world market prices for Cuba's two main exports—sugar and nickel—were lower in 1996 than in 1995. According to Minister Rodríguez, external financing remains the main limitation on sustained recovery; in 1996, Cuba was forced to rely on short-term financing at very high interest rates. The hard currency debt at the end of 1996 has been estimated at about $11 billion, 4.7 percent higher than at year-end 1995.

One of the bright spots seems to be the domestic stabilization program. The budget deficit, which had ballooned to over 5 billion pesos in 1993 (nearly 40 percent of GDP[15]), has been reduced sharply since then, to 570 million pesos in 1996 (4 percent of GDP). Similarly, liquidity (currency in circulation) has also fallen steadily since 1993, to 9.2 billion pesos in 1996 (about 65 percent of GDP). The annual average unofficial exchange rate (recall that, officially, the Cuban peso is still valued at par with the U.S. dollar) fell in 1996 to 19.2 pesos/U.S. dollar from

---

13. "Economy grows by 7.8 percent," report on 1996 economic results and 1997 economic and social plan, presented to the National Assembly by Minister of the Economy and Planning José Luis Rodríguez, *Granma International Electronic Edition*, no. 2 (1997). The most detailed passage of the report dealing with sectoral output growth reads: "there was a 17.3 percent rise in agricultural production, including hunting, forestry and fishing, comparing well with the planned increase of eight percent; manufacturing grew by 7.8 percent, less than the 9.7 percent increase expected, basically due to financial difficulties. Construction, for its part, saw growth of 30.8 percent, compared to the planned increase of 21.6 percent." Not only are some critical sectors (e.g., services) missing altogether, but the relative weights of the sectors are not known. Along the same line, there is no information on how the sectoral growth indices mentioned by Rodríguez were produced and how output of joint ventures, of the self- employed and of agricultural cooperatives were recorded. The same is true for sales in agricultural markets outside of government control.

14. E.g., Marta Beatriz Roque Cabello and Arnaldo Ramos Lauzurique, "PIB: (Producto Interno Bruto)," in *Documentos del Instituto Cubano de Economistas Independientes*, pp. 1-5. Miami: Cuban Studies Association, 1997; and Carmelo Mesa-Lago, "¿Recuperación económica en Cuba?, *Encuentro de la Cultura Cubana*, no. 3 (Winter 1996/1997), pp. 54-61. See also Mesa-Lago, "The State of the Cuban Economy: 1995-96," in *Cuba in Transition-- Volume 6*, pp. 4-7. Washington: Association for the Study of the Cuban Economy, 1996.

15. The GDP series in Table 1 is reportedly at constant prices of 1981, while the budget deficit and liquidity figures are reportedly at current prices. Since time series of GDP at current prices are not available, the budget deficit/GDP and liquidity/GDP ratios in Table 1 combine current and constant price data. They should therefore be used only as measures of general trends rather than point estimates.

32.1 pesos/U.S. dollar a year earlier. While the strengthening of the Cuban peso *vis-a-vis* the U.S. dollar may be interpreted as an increase in the confidence of the population regarding the buying power of the peso, further research is needed to determine whether the strengthening of the peso reflects manipulation by the Cuban government through its network of Currency Exchange Houses.

Minister Rodríguez reported to the National Assembly highlights of the economic plan for 1997. Some of those highlights are:

- GDP growth rate of 4-5 percent;

- growth in exports of 12 percent and in imports of 11.5 percent; net income from tourism expected to increase by 50 percent compared to 1996;

- reduction in the state budget of 19 percent and of money in circulation of 3 percent;

- growth in domestic investment of about 9 percent, focused on the international tourism, sugar, nickel, electronics and fisheries industries; no increase over 1996 for investment in housing construction; and

- growth in agriculture of 4.6-5.6 percent, manufacturing of 6-7 percent, and construction of 4.1-5.1 percent.

Lest there be some doubt that the Cuban economy remains centrally planned, Minister Rodríguez described the following procedure for developing the 1997 projections:

> In June [1996], well ahead of time, the government drew up a set of directives for drawing the plan. At that time, based on the framework contained in those directives, discussion meetings were held in each enterprise, to evaluate the plan's potential from the grass roots upwards. On the basis of those meetings, the agencies and administrative councils in each province presented their planning proposals in September. These proposals were evaluated by the Ministry of the Economy and Planning and were submitted to the Executive Committee of the Council of Ministers, which defined the necessary priorities and adjustments that were subsequently worked out in detail with every entity and administrative council in a discussion process that, for the first time this year, permitted the plan to be structured in sectoral and territorial terms.

SECTORAL PERFORMANCE

Sugar: To date, the Cuban government has not released official information on the results of the 1996-97 *zafra*. Coming on the heels of a "successful"[16] 1995-96 sugar campaign, when 4.45 million tons of sugar were produced, the government had vowed to increase production by 20 percent, or to about 5.3 million tons. In early May, Fidel Castro admitted that the sugar campaign was in trouble— he blamed hurricane Lily, transportation problems, and the late arrival of imported supplies and inputs essential for the sugar industry—and the best scenario would be to match the previous year's production level.[17] Industry analysts are predicting a harvest of about 4.2 million tons.[18]

To finance the 1996-97 *zafra*, the Cuban government borrowed about $300 million in short-term loans at high interest rates.[19] Cuba was counting on a large harvest in 1996-97 to repay the loans and to fulfill delivery contracts it had already made.[20]

---

16. "Successful" in the sense that it reversed the downward trend in production that began in 1992. Production in 1995-96 was still substantially lower than the 7-8 million tons per annum produced in the second half of the 1980s.

17. Carlos Batista, "Zafra azucarera no superará la del 96," *El Nuevo Herald* (3 mayo 1997). See also "Pablo Alfonso, "Zafra parece encaminada al fracaso, dicen especialistas," *El Nuevo Herald* (24 abril 1997), p. 8A, and "Régimen cubano podría cerrar centrales ineficientes," *El Nuevo Herald* (13 mayo 1977), p. 1B.

18. Marc Frank, "Cuban sugar harvest is poor," *The Journal of Commerce* (June 9, 1997), p. 5B; and "Zafra termina con cifras en rojo," *El Nuevo Herald* (June 10, 1997), p. 6A.

19. "Zafra termina con cifras en rojo."

20. Larry Rohter, "Cuba Sees New Threat to Recovery: A Weak Sugar Harvest," *The New York Times* (May 18, 1977), p. 11.

Tourism: According to official statistics, over one million foreign tourists traveled to Cuba in 1996; gross revenues from international tourism were reported at $1.3 billion. Cuba reportedly had 27,000 rooms in 174 hotels suitable for international tourism. Construction is underway to increase the number of hotel rooms to 50,000 by the year 2000, when 2.5 million visitors are expected.[21]

For 1997, Cuban authorities expected 1.2 million tourists, a 20 percent increase over 1996.[22] These expectations may have to be tempered depending on how tourists respond to bombs that went off at two tourism hotels in La Habana—Hotel Nacional and Hotel Capri—in July, coinciding with the time when European tourists book their winter vacations.[23]

Foreign investment: Vice President Carlos Lage reported that at the beginning of 1997, there were more than 260 joint ventures with foreign investors: 45 of the joint ventures were in the tourism industry, 30 in oil prospecting, 5 in nickel mining, 33 in other mining activities, 85 in industry, and 12 in transportation and communications. Furthermore, 42 of the joint ventures were reportedly initiated after the coming into effect of the Helms-Burton legislation in the United States in March 1996.[24]

Cuba's response to the Helms-Burton Act was Law No. 80, the Reaffirmation of Cuban Dignity and Sovereignty Act, passed by the National Assembly in December 1996. The Helms-Burton "antidote" legislation establishes sanctions against those who facilitate the execution of the Act within Cuba, protects overseas businesspeople who have or wish to have commercial links with Cuba, updates Cuba's claims for damages resulting from the U.S. embargo and other U.S. policies, and expresses the willingness to negotiate "equitable compensation" with former U.S. owners of property, subject to conditions.[25] In the summer of 1997, Cuba mounted a diplomatic campaign to build support against the Helms-Burton Act and potential amendments to strengthen the Act being considered by the U.S. Congress, sending diplomatic representatives to over 20 countries in Latin America and Europe.[26]

There were significant developments regarding the long-standing joint venture agreement between Mexico's Grupo Domos and the Empresa Telefónica de Cuba, S.A. (ETECSA), in which Domos was reported to have pledged to invest $750 million. First, in early 1997, Grupo Domos withdrew from the joint venture, selling its participation to the Italian telephone company STET International; Domos had been notified by the United States that it would be subject to sanctions under the Helms-Burton Act for using properties confiscated from U.S. owners.[27] And second, in July 1997, the United States approved a private agreement between STET International and New York-based ITT whereby STET agreed to pay ITT approximately $25 million for the right to use the property in Cuba claimed by ITT. As a result of the agreement, STET is no longer subject to sanctions under the Helms-Burton Act.[28]

---

21. "Tourism Convention and annual COTAL Congress to be held in May," *Granma International Electronic Edition*, no. 13 (1997).

22. Rodolfo Casals, "Number of tourists to increase by 20 percent," *Granma International Electronic Edition*, no. 9 (1997).

23. Kevin G. Hall, "Cuban blasts leave investors wary, tourist industry jittery," *The Journal of Commerce* (July 15, 1997), p. 5A.

24. Lee, "We have initiated economic reforms within socialism."

25. Rodolfo Casals, "Helms-Burton: In effect for one year," *Granma International Electronic Edition*, no. 10 (1997). For the text of Law No. 80 see "Reaffirmation of Cuban Dignity and Sovereignty Act," *Granma International Electronic Edition*, no. 4 (1997).

26. "Anuncian acciones contra enmiendas a la Helms," *El Nuevo Herald* (6 junio 1997), p. 6A.

27. Andrés Oppenheimer, "Firm hangs up on Cuba deal," *The Miami Herald* (June 27, 1997), pp. 1C, 3C and Larry Rohter, "Mexican Conglomerate Abandons Cuban Phone Venture," *The New York Times* (June 30, 1997), p. D2.

28. Christopher Marquis, "ITT paid for confiscated Cuban properties," *The Miami Herald* (July 24, 1997), pp. 1C, 3C.

CONCLUSION

The attitude of the population toward the current economic situation is best described by a Cuban engineer who makes clay ashtrays and sells them to foreign tourists: "We are depressed *and* repressed."[29] The economy is operating at a very low level of capacity; government intervention in the economy has intensified; and, more importantly, there is nothing in sight that suggests a willingness on the part of the leadership to consider meaningful economic and political reforms that would lead the island out of the low growth trap in which it now lingers.

---

29. Juan O. Tamayo, "Sense of despair pervades Cuba as economy falters," *The Miami Herald* (August 2, 1997), p. 1A.

THE STRUCTURAL TRANSFORMATION OF THE CUBAN ECONOMY: A REPORT OF THE LAST TWELVE MONTHS

Jorge A. Sanguinetty

Over the last 38 years, quantitative and institutional information on the Cuban economy have typically been fragmentary and incomplete. The serious observer or investigator must reconcile his or her understanding of what is happening with reports that are vague and contradictory. That is why formal or scientific investigation of the Cuban economy is very difficult and must be reported with all sorts of caveats.

The latter statement is particularly valid when it comes to standard, generally quantitative, analysis of Cuba's economic activity during any given period. By standard economic analysis I mean, basically, the study of the evolution of the most important macroeconomic indicators for a year or longer. The traditional indicators are the Gross Domestic Product (GDP), its sectoral breakdown, and the aggregate levels of investment, consumption, external and internal savings, exports and imports, etc. The analysis of these indicators would include a description of their changes over time and a discussion of the causes of the changes.

In the Cuban case, however, the difficulties in carrying out standard macroeconomic analysis result from several conditions: (1) the statistical information is not reliable because Fidel Castro's government prefers to keep the public—and its own officers—in the dark about the real economic conditions of the country; (2) virtually all economic data are severely affected by an arbitrary and distorted price system; (3) the government does not seem to be gathering data on the economic activity of the self-employed and other

private forms of economic activity that contribute to the GDP; and (4) the government needs to hide the sources of funds that are dedicated to foreign covert operations and Castro's own personal finances. In addition, Cuban state enterprises—those that do not share ownership with foreign investors—are known for their faulty accounting systems. Finally, to the direct price distortions one must add the distortions introduced by an extremely overvalued exchange rate with which many official transactions are still carried out.

I base these propositions on my own experience in the Central Planning Board (*Junta Central de Planificación*, JUCEPLAN) between 1963 and 1966, first as an economist and then as Head of the National Investment Planning Department (*Departamento de Planificación Global de Inversiones*). One of my responsibilities was to estimate the actual levels of investment expenditures, which at the time had an order of magnitude of 20 to 25 percent of GDP. Though this is not the place to discuss this topic, it is necessary to say that my estimates were always produced under the most precarious conditions due to the lack of a proper statistical base. It was clear that the Cuban government was not particularly interested in national account statistics. There is no evidence that this situation has fundamentally changed since then.

The accompanying paper by Jorge Pérez-López[1] is a report of what I call standard analysis. It is also an excellent example of what an investigator can do, despite the data constraints mentioned above. In this report, however, I concentrate on the evolution of the Cuban economy from a qualitative, institutional or structural point of view. My main sources are: (1) individual accounts by former members of the Cuban public administration system; (2) reports from individuals still residing in Cuba whose identities cannot be revealed without jeopardizing their personal security, and (3) fragmentary and scattered reports by official and semi-official sources in Cuba.

BACKGROUND

Between 1960 and 1961, the Cuban economy was subjected to the structural shocks caused by massive expropriations of all forms of private enterprise, combined with the exodus of a large proportion of Cuba's best entrepreneurial and technical talent and with radical changes in international trade and financial relations.

Until the demise of the Soviet Union and the socialist bloc, the Cuban economy had the appearance of a typical socialist centrally planned economy, with almost no private economic activity except for some small farms. An essential characteristic of this economy was that it depended heavily on subsidies from the Soviet Union. The dependence on such subsidies gives rise to the argument that Cuba never achieved a socialist economy, at least not one operating at the typically mediocre levels of output of Cuba's partners in the socialist bloc.

The disintegration of the socialist bloc provoked the sudden and unexpected interruption of the subsidies, causing an economic trauma of enormous magnitude, this time out of the control of the Cuban government. Before, the Cuban economy can be said to have been in a state of structural equilibrium, with more or less stagnant levels of economic growth in per capita terms. The disappearance of the subsidies, however, caused such a disturbance to the economy that it has altered its structural equilibrium.

The Cuban government, unable—and perhaps unwilling—to adopt the policies necessary to engineer an economic stabilization and recovery has, in-

stead, implemented emergency measures that have caused some intended and some unintended results. Its main achievement seems to have been the stabilization of an economic subsystem that provides for the security of the top members of the government at the central level. The structural decay of the rest of the economy and the gradual loss of government control over parts of the population are among the most important unintended outcomes.

THE APPARENT ECONOMIC EVOLUTION IN THE LAST 12 MONTHS

Based on the several sources of information we have access to, the economic evolution of the Cuban economy in the last 12 months can be best summarized by sectors.

The sugar industry seems to continue to deteriorate and lose ground as the first source of income and foreign exchange for the country. At the time of this report, the Cuban government has failed to produce any official figures about the total output of sugar for 1997. In addition, there is no information available about production costs. Scattered but consistent reports, however, indicate that the industry has become a net loser of value added and of foreign exchange. Although the government insists that the main cause of the crisis in this sector is the lack of short-term credit, it seems that the major cause may be the lack of an effective management system and the lack of incentives to the workers in the fields and the sugar mills.

International tourism seems to have gained ground in absolute and relative economic importance vis-a-vis the sugar industry. Its net contribution to the Cuban economy, however, is constrained by the high dependence of the tourist industry on foreign imports as a result of the chronic crisis in agricultural and food production. Some estimates put the rate of gross foreign earnings to gross revenues at below 20 percent. The industry is also heavily dependent on foreign operators who, besides managing most tourist facilities in Cuba, also bring the visitors to the country. The main tourist attraction in Cuba seems

---

1. Pérez-López, "The Cuban Economy in Mid-1997," in this volume.

to be the widespread availability of prostitutes in the country and their low cost—a result of the predominantly low level of wages and the generalized lack of economic opportunities for young workers.

U.S. dollar remittances have become the most important source of foreign exchange to the Cuban economy. Grossly estimated at between US$500 and $800 million, the remittances are generated by an undetermined number of members of the exile community, in the United States and other countries, who send money to relatives resident on the Island. The remittances consist of physical transfers of cash to Cuba by individuals (called *mulas* in Spanish) who charge from 10 to 20 percent, depending on conditions (speed of delivery mainly). Since the volume of food distributed to the population remains very tight, it is plausible to assume that without the cash remittances Cuba could be suffering severe food and health crises, possibly in the form of scattered famine with epidemic events. Sources still residing on the Island estimate that the food distributed in Havana under the rationing system covers a maximum of 15 days per month. The food for the rest of the month must be purchased in the black market or in the U.S. dollar shops. The situation in the interior of the country and in the countryside seems to be more precarious because the availability of dollars is more constrained and the sources from which to obtain them are more limited.

As a result of Cuba's continuing inability to produce efficiently and deliver on time, the country continues to have difficulties in obtaining short-term credit in international markets, although some credit is still accessible at high interest rates and with Cuban collateral. It has recently become known that Castro himself has become a lender of last resort to the Cuban government. The funds involved belong to strategic reserves of unknown origin, balances that Castro manages as private accounts deposited in foreign institutions, and a Cuban bank expressly created for that purpose under the name of *Banco Financiero Internacional* (International Financial Bank).

MAJOR STRUCTURAL CHANGES IN THE CUBAN ECONOMY

Besides the changes of a quantitative nature that are taking place, Cuba is undergoing profound changes in the structure of its economy and in its economic management system. These changes have been taking place for many years and with the knowledge of a relatively small circle of Cuban officials. Such structural changes, as reported by recent defectors from the Cuban government, indicate that the Cuban economy has been evolving into four major interrelated economic subsystems or sectors.

The subsystem that holds the most economic and political power is the one administered by Castro himself, represented by enterprises such as Cubanacán and CIMEX, the Banco Financiero Internacional, Castro's monetary and physical reserves, and productive installations such as the cheese and yogurt factories. This economic subsystem operates outside the traditional public sector, as if it were Fidel Castro's manor or consortium. Its revenues come from tourism and the sale of imported goods to Cuban nationals who receive U.S. dollars through remittances from exiled Cubans, tips from tourists, payments for sexual services, and transactions in private, informal markets.

Castro's economy seems to have developed as a result of his own lack of trust in the economic system that he created and that never followed the strict discipline of a centrally planned system. Since Castro demanded loyalty instead of competence as the main criterion for promotion of individuals to executive positions (in the public enterprises or in government administration), the efficiency of productive activities in Cuba fell chronically, a phenomenon hidden by the Soviet subsidies for several decades. The main role of Castro's economic subsystem is to generate the resources necessary to guarantee the security of the government; the traditional planned economy, after the disappearance of the Soviet subsidies, could not be relied upon to maintain the minimum standard of living required for the personnel in the security police and in the armed forces.

A second economic subsystem is made up primarily of the foreign investors and entrepreneurs who operate in the tourist industry in partnership with Castro and possibly other Cuban officials who enjoy the grace of Castro and participate in the concomitant benefits. The foreign operators, as discussed already, bring marketing and managerial skills as well as some capital, the latter in limited amounts given the underlying lack of trust in Fidel Castro.

These two economic subsystems, Castro's and the foreign or mixed, may be the two most prosperous sectors of the entire economy. They benefit from each other's activity—the foreigners providing a large proportion of the foreign exchange earnings and Castro providing some property rights and contractual security on a case-by-case basis.

The presence of some privileged Cuban nationals in these two subsystems as possible stockholders or managers represents a form of clandestine privatization that is similar to the Sandinista *piñata* with one major difference: the Cuban *piñata* is taking place in a much larger country, involves greater volumes of wealth, and is being carried out long before the government is out of power. Some economic activities managed by the armed forces, especially in the production of food, can be included in one or both of these two systems since, on the one hand, they serve to support national security while, on the other hand, they are managed as private enterprises by the military.

The third economic subsystem, and possibly the one deteriorating at the fastest rate, is made up of the remains of the planned economy and public enterprises fully owned by the state. The entire sugar industry, with its agricultural and manufacturing branches, is the most important sector of this subsystem. Nevertheless, it is becoming apparent that Castro's investment priorities are neglecting this entire subsystem, since foreign resources are focused primarily on tourism and other foreign exchange-earning industries. The reason for this probably lies in the breakdown of the centrally planned apparatus and the government's inability to manage a sector that is widely scattered throughout the island. It seems that this sector is subjected to a policy of benign neglect, a condition that will have very negative effects on the

future prospects for an economic reconstruction of the Cuban economy.

A large proportion of the Cuban installed capacity in the traditional public sector is underutilized due to lack of parts and supplies. This condition was the basis for allowing self-employment in Cuba, a measure that the government reluctantly implemented due to the need to keep a degree of equilibrium between the total volume of salaries and the aggregate consumption and to avoid the further debasement of the Cuban peso. Self-employment then gave rise to what I propose is the fourth economic subsector—private but highly constrained, dedicated to those economic activities allowed under the law of self-employment but with the constraints already explicitly stated in the same law, the most important of which is the prohibition to hire workers.

This subsector is also made up of retired military personnel who perform some economic activities to make ends meet, especially through ventures such as *paladares*, improvised restaurants in regular residences that are limited in size by the government to four tables and are subject to very heavy taxation in U.S. dollars. This catch-all sector also includes workers of the third sector, since the rationed quotas are reported to be only sufficient to cover half the month's supply of food, requiring the additional contribution of black market activities, part-time (illegal) self-employment, some U.S. dollars received as remittances from exiled Cubans, or a combination of the above.

The picture that emerges upon observing the activities of these four economic subsystems is one of widespread corruption and uncertainty. Economic growth may be happening in subsectors one and two, and perhaps in four, though this is highly unlikely given the extreme constraints imposed by Castro and his reluctance to provide certain degrees of economic freedom, such as allowing the emergence of small enterprises, that could very well be compatible with his socialist rhetoric and would reduce the country's risk of a food crisis, even starvation. However, given that sector three is by far the largest of the four subsystems—composed of 80 or even 90 percent of the working population—the overall economy can be considered stagnant, possibly shrinking, and definitely in disarray.

CONCLUSIONS

For many years, several authors have question the socialist character of the Cuban "revolution." One of the earliest critics seems to have been Ernesto "Che" Guevara, who considered himself an orthodox Stalinist and was a strong advocate of central planning. René Dumont, an early admirer of Castro and an economic adviser on agricultural affairs, also questioned the socialist character of the Cuban system under Castro. The picture that appears after putting together the available pieces of this gigantic jigsaw puzzle that is Cuba under Castro's rule, leads one to doubt not only Cuba's socialism but also Castro's sincerity about his public utterances in this regard. The facts that have been accumulating over the years confirming the *sui generis* character of this system are many. Some important instances are the following: (1) the chronic lack of commitment and interest of the government in installing a reliable system of national accounts; (2) the abandonment of long-term planning at the very beginning of planning in Cuba in 1962; (3) the long-term dependence on Soviet subsidies and the parallel lack of effort to develop Cuba's internal economy; (4) the lack of productive discipline in Cuba's public enterprises; (5) the current breakdown of central planning to manage the Cuban economy; and (6) the surreptitious creation of private enterprises in the hands of Castro and some of his most intimate collaborators.

Ironically, many could argue in the future that socialism did not fail in Cuba because it was never really tried. It seems that if Castro had a real socialist agenda for Cuba, instead of his plans to export his revolution to other countries, Cuba would be better off today, even under the constraints of the U.S. embargo. This is not to say that a socialist economy would be better than a market economy, but simply that at least a socialist economic system would have provided Cuba with a level of economic mediocrity superior to what Castro actually achieved for his country.

Under the current conditions, Cuba cannot prosper until Castro lifts his own embargo from the Cuban workers and would-be entrepreneurs. This is a condition that those advocating a unilateral and unconditional lifting of the U.S. embargo fail to acknowledge—the most constraining element on the Cuban economy is Castro's own reluctance to liberalize, even within socialist canons. Under the current conditions, the lifting of the American embargo would only benefit Castro, since he is holding all the monopolistic powers that impede Cubans from enjoying the benefits of free domestic and foreign trade, free enterprise, private property, etc. In the meantime, Cuba's economy at large continues drifting towards unknown waters. With the exception of the minority of Cubans benefitting from the economic activities of subsystems one and two, most of the country seems to be following the fate of Congo under Mobutu Sese Seko, *mutatis mutandis*. Under these conditions, achieving stagnation would be an improvement.

CUBAN NON-SUGARCANE AGRICULTURAL TRADE PATTERNS: HISTORICAL PERSPECTIVES AND FUTURE PROSPECTS

William A. Messina, Jr., Richard N. Brown, James E. Ross and José Alvarez

HISTORICAL PERSPECTIVE[1]

Prior to 1959 the United States was clearly an important trading partner for Cuba. However, the historical trading relationship between the two countries has been far more dynamic than many people realize. For example, in the early 1930s, the United States was providing only slightly over half of Cuba's total import requirements while it was the destination for around 70 percent of Cuba's total exports. Both of these percentages increased steadily through the 1930s as Cuba's other major trade partners in Europe became increasingly embroiled in the developments and conflicts leading up to the Second World War.

Despite the shifts in trading partners which were taking place over this period, Cuba's mix of traded commodities remained fairly stable. Agricultural and food products typically represented between 25 and 30 percent of the value of Cuban imports during the 1930s and 1940s. Rice was consistently the most important single agricultural commodity imported although wheat flour, lard and vegetable oil were other significant import commodities. During the same period, agricultural products consistently represented more than 90 percent of the value of Cuban exports. Sugar clearly dominated the export mix, making up between 75 and 85 percent of total exports.

Trading relationships between Cuba and the United States were at their strongest during the years of

World War II because of the limitations in seaborne transportation given the hostilities. However, shortly after World War II, developments in the world marketplace caused some changes in Cuba's trade patterns. In 1947 the original GATT (General Agreement on Tariffs and Trade) was signed. In order to become a party to this agreement, Cuba had to suspend its Special Reciprocity Treaty with the United States and was forced to fall back on its 1927 tariff structure (with its subsequent revisions). This was an antiquated tariff structure which, in many cases, applied higher import duties to raw materials than to finished products. As a result, Cuba began to import fewer raw materials and more high-value processed products and the value of Cuban imports nearly doubled between 1946 and 1948. At the same time, increased competition in the post-war U.S. market drove down the value of Cuban exports somewhat, if not the volume. As a result, in 1948, Cuba registered a merchandise trade deficit with the United States for only the second time since 1902. Nevertheless, trade ties between Cuba and the United States remained strong through most of the 1950s.

It is worth noting that Cuba's commodity composition of trade in the late 1950s had changed very little since the late 1930s. Sugar continued to represent about 80 percent of total Cuban exports, tobacco and related products around seven percent, fisheries products one percent, other agricultural products 2

1. Summary of remarks by William A. Messina, Jr.

percent, minerals four percent and non-agricultural products approximately six percent. On the import side, agricultural products continued to represent about 29 percent of the value of Cuban imports.

During the 1950s Cuba had begun to expand their list of trading partners in an effort to seek more lucrative markets. As a result, in 1958 the United States was purchasing a somewhat smaller share of Cuba's exports—approximately 65 percent. Japan, and European countries made up most of the difference, with the Sino-Soviet bloc nations purchasing only about two percent of Cuba's exports. At this point in time, the United States continued to supply about 85 percent of Cuba's agricultural imports.

The value of U.S. exports to Cuba peaked in 1957 at slightly over $600 million, while the value of U.S. imports to Cuba peaked in 1958 at more than $500 million. With the imposition of the U.S. embargo, Cuba's pattern of trade changed rapidly and dramatically. By 1961, Cuba had completely shifted its primary trading partners with the Soviet Union and China purchasing over 70 percent of Cuba's exports and supplying about 65 percent of Cuba's import requirements.

With this as background, I would like to move on to our other speakers as they help us to assess Cuba's future prospects for non-sugarcane agricultural trade.

CUBA AS A POTENTIAL MARKET FOR U.S. AGRICULTURAL PRODUCTS[2]

For many years prior to 1960, Cuba was the number 1 or number 2 export market for U.S. agricultural products in Latin America. Similarly, the United States was the number 1 market for Cuban agricultural products. However, that all changed quickly in the late 1950's and early 1960's. Since 1961, U.S. policy has inhibited trade between the two countries. But the Cuban economy cannot function efficiently without a substantial volume of agricultural imports and exports. Cuba needs exports to provide the foreign exchange required to import food and inputs it can not produce.

Fidel Castro learned quickly in the mid-1960s, that import substitution policies often do not work very well, particularly when a tropical country, such as Cuba, has become accustomed to consuming temperate zone crops it can not grow efficiently, if at all. After the U.S. severed trade relations with Cuba, the former Soviet Union (FSU) stepped in and filled the void created by the 1961 change in the official U.S. policy toward Cuba.

By 1970, the FSU had become Cuba's foreign trade mentor and was committed to supporting the Cuban economy with oil for sugar barter deals, and other economic and financial aid packages. This assistance continued until the early 1990's when Socialism crumbled in Eastern Europe, and the Soviet Union no longer could subsidize the Cuban economy. Cuba's economy, as we all know has declined dramatically since then and this is now part of Cuba's history. But the U.S. trade embargo remains in place and is a bench mark for the following remarks.

So, how large is the potential market for agricultural products in Cuba today, tomorrow, next year, or five years from now, assuming either the embargo was never enacted, or the embargo is lifted? This obviously is where the fairy tale begins, because U.S. companies are still not allowed to trade or invest in Cuba directly. Nevertheless, U.S. businesses would like to know if Cuba could once again become an important export market for U.S. agricultural and non-agricultural products as it was before 1960.

If so, how large a market would Cuba be for the United States, and what agricultural products would Cuba likely buy from the United States? The answers to these and related questions depend to a considerable degree on the methodologies and assumptions used to develop estimates.

Methodologies

One approach to answering these questions is to assume that Cuba has production capabilities and import needs similar to those of other islands in the Caribbean. With that assumption one can develop a

---

2. Summary of remarks by Richard N. Brown

country proxy for Cuba for studying production, consumption and trade flows for a selected group of Caribbean countries which are still trading with the United States, and proceed from there. For example, a proxy of the Dominican Republic, Jamaica and Trinidad and Tobago was prepared for this analysis, because this proxy group has about the same population and non-sugar agricultural production base as Cuba. A second methodology is based on trends and market shares of total Caribbean, Cuban and U.S. agricultural trade over the past 40 to 50 years. Access to U.S., Cuban, FAO and other international data sources are needed to apply the later methodology.

Initial Findings

Preliminary results of some recent research conducted by the University of Florida, the U.S. Department of Agriculture, and others, suggests that U.S. agricultural exports to Cuba today could easily approximate $1.0 billion annually. But this is really a fairy tale because the U.S. has not had formal trade and diplomatic relations with Cuba since 1961. On the other hand, even if the embargo were lifted tomorrow, it could easily take 5 to 10 years to build a $1.0 billion market for U.S. agricultural products in Cuba. This of course depends on many factors too numerous to elaborate at this time. But let us assume the current figure is about $1.0 billion annually, and then see how well the proxy variables support this hypothesis.

Some Questions and Comments

Different methodologies can be used to develop trade estimates, but due to space constraints, as mentioned above, only some of the results will be mentioned at this time. For example:

- At $1.0 billion annually, how would Cuba compare with other foreign markets of the United States? Cuba would be among the top 10 or 15 export markets for the U.S. today, and it probably would have been among the top 10 to 15 export markets for the past 40 years.

- How has Cuba's share of Caribbean agricultural trade changed since 1961, and what would Cuba's imports likely have been in the mid-1990s, if Cuba had been free to trade with the United States? FAO time series data show that Cuba ac-

counted for about 40 percent of the total agricultural import trade of the Caribbean Islands (including Cuba) in the 1960s, 1970s and 1980s. However Cuba's trade has declined dramatically since 1989 when Cuba lost its Soviet assistance.

- How large was Cuba's market in the mid-1990s? Cuba's ability to import declined 50 percent or more between 1990 and 1995. But adjusted trade estimates suggests that the Caribbean Islands, with Cuba, would have imported $5 billion of agricultural products in 1995, $5.5 billion in 1996, and perhaps $6.0 billion in 1997. Cuba's 40 percent share would have totaled about $2.0, $2.2 and $2.4 billion respectively for these 3 years assuming the Soviet Union or some other benefactor was still supporting Cuba. Given the continued strong growth in non-Cuban Caribbean imports in 1996 and 1997, Cuba's 40 percent share of the total Caribbean Island market would have approached $2.5 billion per year sometime in 1998.

- How large would the U.S. share of the Cuban market be, given more normal diplomatic relations between the United States and Cuba since 1960? Even if the U.S. share of the Cuban import market dropped from highs of 60 percent or more per year in the 1950s, the U.S. would still appear to be marketing about $1.0 billion of product on a 40 to 50 percent share bases in the mid-1990s. By comparison, U.S. agricultural exports to the aforementioned three country proxy (Dominican Republic, Jamaica and Trinidad and Tobago), currently average $0.7 to $0.8 billion per year, which seems to support the conclusion.

- If Cuba were buying U.S. agricultural products today, would the product priorities be much different than in the 1950s? No, not likely, because Cuba would still need the same temperate zone grain, oilseed and livestock products it has been buying from Canada, Argentina and other countries since 1960.

- What are the primary products Cuba still needs from other countries? Cereals, animal feeds,

Table 1. Cuban Production of Selected Non-Sugarcane Agricultural Commodities, 1989 and 1993 to 1996 (in metric tons unless otherwise noted)

COMMODITY	1989	1993	1994	1995	1996
Citrus	825,655	644,446	504,491	555,353	N/A
Tobacco	41,606	19,892	17,084	25,000	33,100
Rice	563,381	226,213	226,095	222,838	122,000
Beans	14,107	8,819	10,771	11,472	15,000
Cattle (000head)	4,920	4,583	4,617	4,632	4,300
Pigs (000head)	1,292	558	587	N/A	N/A
Poultry (000birds)	27,904	14,367	13,935	N/A	N/A
Tubers & Roots	681,200	668,727	484,537	863,000	1.568,000
Potatoes	281,660	235,245	188,334	281,559	318,181
Vegetables	610,235	329,883	322,164	360,000	470,000
Tomatoes	259,955	127,757	95,876	138,590	N/A

Source: *Investment and Business Cuba, 1995-1996* and issue for 1996-1997; Consultores Associados; Ministry of Agriculture; *Granma International*; and Cuban government data.

beans, dairy and livestock products would still top the list. Cuba's list of imports however can be expected to be more diverse in the future as tourism expands and domestic demand increases. Additional insights in this regard can be obtained by observing how U.S./Caribbean trade has changed over the past 40 years.

IMPACT OF FOREIGN INVESTMENT ON NON-SUGARCANE AGRICULTURAL TRADE[3]

Production of important Cuban (non-sugar) agricultural export commodities and products dropped significantly beginning in 1989 following the loss of preferential markets in the Soviet Union and Eastern Bloc countries (Table 1). In particular, production of both citrus and tobacco declined by about one-third from 1989 to mid-1990.

Because of the lack of production inputs, such as fertilizers and farm chemicals, output of commodities for the domestic market also dropped. Production of rice, beans and livestock and poultry products also fell substantially. Even production of vegetables, especially tomatoes, plunged to about half the level of

the late 1980s. Only tubers and roots appeared to maintain their approximate production level.

Although some foreign investment had taken place earlier, it was not until 1993 that major foreign investment promotion in non-cane agriculture got underway. That year the principal government agencies in food and non-sugarcane agriculture, the Ministry of Agriculture and the Ministry of Food Industry, became aggressive in efforts to attract foreign investments in their respective areas.

Of the reported 260 economic associations signed by the end of 1996, less than 5 percent are agricultural projects. About the same number of economic associations have been formed in food processing (Table 2). During the past two years, information available indicates five new association agreements in food and agriculture have been entered into each year. Most of the economic associations in agriculture are pre-financing arrangements. Very few are joint ventures and none are enterprises formed entirely with foreign capital.

3. Summary of remarks by James E. Ross. For additional detail on the topic of foreign investment in Cuba's agricultural sector, see "Cuba: Overview of Foreign Agribusiness Investment," by James E. Ross and María Antonia Fernández Mayo, Department of Food and Resource Economics, International Working Paper Number IW97-10 (1997).

Table 2. Foreign Investment in Food and Agricultural Products in Cuba, by Number of International Economic Associations, 1991 to 1996

Investment	1991	1992	1993	1994	1995	1996	Total
Citrus	1[a]	1					2
Tobacco			1	1		1	3
AfricanPalm					1		1
Sunflowers						1	1
Rice					1		1
Fruit & Vegetables					1		1
Tomatoes & Cotton						1	1
Processed Foods			1	2	2	1	6
Beer, Rum & Mineral Water			1	1		1	3
TOTAL	1	1	3	4	5	5	19

a. International Economic Associations which have been terminated.

Early Cuban government efforts to attract foreign capital in agriculture focussed on citrus production and marketing. That was for a very good reason—of the exportable non-cane agricultural products, citrus fruit was the most affected by the loss of markets in Eastern Europe.

The first foreign investment arrangement was with the BM Corporation of Israel. In 1990 the BM Corporation entered into an international economic association with Cuba's Unión de Cítricos, which later became part of the National Citrus Corporation (NCC). The economic association was actually an agreement to renew and expand cooperative efforts which had begun in the 1960s but was ended when Cuba broke diplomatic relations with Israel. BM, through an economic association with NCC, agreed to manage a 38,750-hectare (96,000 acres) citrus plantation in Jagüey Grande, Matanzas province. The objective of the association was to increase productivity, improve the quality of the fruit, and find new markets for the citrus and citrus products.

In 1992 Ingelco S.A., a Chilean firm, entered into an economic association with NCC to produce 30 million liters of citrus juice annually at a processing plant in Jagüey Grande. Currently, citrus juice produced through this economic association is being sold under the brand name "Tropical Island."

In 1991 NCC entered into an economic association with a Chilean-owned firm, POLE S.A., to produce and export citrus. The operation involved 11,000 hectares (27,181 acres) of grapefruit on the Isle of Youth. Reportedly, the economic association agreement between POLE and NCC has been terminated.

In 1993 Lola Fruit S.A., a true joint venture involving firms in Greece and the United Kingdom in partnership with NCC, leased nine citrus plantations from NCC covering 31,000 hectares (76,601 acres). The objective was production and marketing internationally of oranges, grapefruit and limes. Reportedly, the joint venture arrangement was terminated in 1996.

Partly because of lower output but also as a result of the lack of markets, Cuba's fresh citrus export volume has fallen from the 1990 export level of 456,697 tons. Exports in 1991, 1992 and 1993 were: 107,300, 45,011, and 98,230 metric tons, respectively. Oranges accounted for more than half of all of the country's citrus exports during the decade before termination of Soviet aid and the loss of preferential markets in Eastern Europe. Grapefruit made up about 40 percent of the citrus exports and limes the remainder over that period. During the early 1990s, the ratio reversed. Fresh grapefruit exports have become larger than fresh orange exports, accounting for more than half to three-fourths of the value of all citrus trade. Trade data are not available for citrus con-

17

centrate, which might indicate an increase in exports of processed citrus products as a result of foreign investment.

From 1961 through 1990 Cuba's citrus exports were destined almost exclusively to the former USSR and former socialist countries of Eastern Europe. From 1981 to 1990 alone, the volume of citrus exports to these countries nearly doubled. Shipments were made at preferential prices and without the market demands of a competitive system. Therefore, little attention was given to quality, timeliness of delivery, economic efficiency and other factors important in a competitive market. Following the loss of preferential markets for Cuba's fresh citrus, exports shifted from Eastern Europe to Western Europe. The Netherlands became the dominant market for Cuba's fresh citrus during the 1990s. The United Kingdom, France and Germany have been other important markets.

With the loss of markets in Eastern Europe, according to data compiled by the U.S. Central Intelligence Agency, export earnings from citrus fell from $150 million in 1990 to $35 million in 1995—less than one-fourth of the level five years earlier. FAO data, however, show exports at $48 million rather than $35 million in 1995. Still a significant reduction from the late 1980s; and, whichever data are closer to actual export value, the loss of foreign exchange earnings is substantial. Some of the loss from fresh citrus exports may be offset by exports of processed citrus. Data, however, are not available to substantiate this possibility.

While the loss of markets in Eastern Europe made it necessary to think of foreign investment as a means of obtaining new markets for citrus, it was also true for tobacco products. The worldwide reputation of Cuban tobacco products and a knowledgeable consumer market have supported Cuba's efforts to attract foreign capital to this commodity sub-sector. Currently, the tobacco industry has drawn major resources from Spain, France, and the United Kingdom.

Cuba signed international economic association agreements in 1993 and 1994 with two state tobacco monopolies, Tabacalera of Spain and Seita of France. The two pre-financing agreements bound a large part of Cuba's tobacco exports. In 1996 Cuba signed a third economic association agreement involving tobacco; the Cuban Tobacco Union entered into a joint venture with Souza Cruz, a Brazilian subsidiary of the British-American Tobacco Company (BAT). Plans call for the production of five billion cigarettes per year at the joint venture factory, BrasCuba.

Tobacco as a percentage of total agricultural exports averaged 2.2 percent for the five years 1986 through 1990. For the next five years, 1991 through 1995, tobacco exports averaged 7.4 percent of total agricultural exports. The percentage has climbed steadily, reaching 9.4 percent in 1995. The value of tobacco exports, however, fell from $135 million in 1990 to $75 million in 1994 and 1995. The reduced value of exports was accounted for by both unmanufactured tobacco and tobacco products.

Spain, France, Switzerland, and the United Kingdom have been the major export destinations for Cuban tobacco during the past decade. Spain, alone, has accounted for more than 50 percent of Cuba's export market for tobacco. Except for Switzerland, the major market countries are also the countries entering into economic association agreements with Cuba. Cuban tobacco is well-known in foreign markets for its quality and aroma. With the world-wide trend toward cigar smoking, prospects are favorable for a viable and growing Cuban tobacco export market.

Cuban efforts to attract foreign investment in commodities for the domestic market have met with limited success. Cuba has, however, signed economic association agreements to produce African palm, sunflowers, rice, cotton, strawberries and vegetables, such as green peppers and tomatoes. Earlier this year, an economic association was formed to produce dairy products.

The Vice-Minister of Agriculture has said that Cuba wants to find new markets for timber, root crops, fruit, and cattle, and is ready to negotiate. In addition, the Ministry of Agriculture has announced that it is seeking financing or forms of economic association in accordance with Law No. 77 for the production of beans, bananas and pork.

In the interview with *Business Tips on Cuba* in August 1996, the Vice-Minister of Agriculture said that Cuba is more than satisfied under present conditions with the export levels of citrus and tobacco. Export data for fresh citrus and tobacco, however, do not support a reason for satisfaction. Citrus exports in 1995 were one-third the value of those in 1990. Tobacco exports in 1995 were about half of the value of tobacco exports in 1990. In addition to data on trade, citrus and tobacco production data show output levels substantially below those of the 1980s.

It can only be assumed that this satisfaction was based on the importance of citrus and tobacco trade relative to exports of other agricultural commodities. Data indicate that the value of citrus exports, as a percent of total agricultural export value, increased significantly from the 1990 level. In 1990 citrus exports accounted for 3.1% of total agricultural exports. Since 1990 there has been an upward trend and in 1995 citrus exports accounted for 6.0 percent, nearly double the significance of five years earlier.

Even more revealing is the change in importance of exports of tobacco products. In 1990 tobacco as a percent of the total value of agricultural exports was only 2.8 percent. By 1995 the relative value of tobacco exports had increased more than three times—to 9.4 percent of the total.

Some of the increase in these percentages can be accounted for by the substantial reduction in sugar exports and the corresponding drop in total agricultural exports. It appears, however, that foreign investment in non-sugarcane agriculture, particularly citrus and tobacco, has prevented Cuba's agricultural exports from falling even more than they might have without foreign investment.

Based on the information I have presented, my conclusions are:

- Data do not indicate that foreign investment has had heavy impact on the export of non- sugarcane agricultural commodities from Cuba.

- Data do indicate that foreign investment in citrus and tobacco has helped to increase the relative significance of these commodities in Cuba's total agricultural trade.

- Information does indicate that foreign investment in non-sugarcane agriculture, particularly citrus and tobacco, probably prevented the value of Cuba's agricultural exports from falling even more than it otherwise would have.

OTHER ISSUES AND FINAL COMMENTS[4]

The final formal presentation of this roundtable intends to make several summary observations on the future prospects for Cuba's non-sugar agricultural trade, with emphasis on citrus, other fruits, and vegetables. The bulk of this presentation follows the current realities as described in the previous discussions; that is, Cuba is in desperate need of investment capital in its agricultural sector and most of the little that has been invested by foreign firms so far falls under the Helms-Burton legislation.

Although sugar is not part of the topic, one needs to make a couple of brief comparisons with the non-sugar commodity sectors to set the discussion in the proper context of the Cuban agricultural economy. First, although the sugar sector needs heavy capital investment, such investment is not a significant element in most of the non-sugar commodity sectors. Examples include citrus and other fruits, and vegetables. The important elements in the latter groups are not in expensive industrial machinery and equipment as in the case of sugar, but in production inputs and, especially, in post-harvest technology and marketing expertise. Second, while almost all of the sugarcane land and mills represent expropriated properties with pending claims, the percentage of fruits and vegetable land and industrial facilities in this situation is far lower than in the sugar case. The importance of this issue is the potential for litigation under the

---

4. Summary of remarks by José Alvarez.

Helms-Burton legislation, with its obvious implications on foreign investment and thus future production and trade.

Let us move now to four observations we want to make concerning the potential for future changes in Cuba's agricultural exports. The first observation is that Cuba has a tremendous potential for increasing production of fruits and vegetables. After devoting the initial increases in production to supply the expanding tourist market, most of the best quality production would be devoted to the export market, and any remaining balance would be sold in the domestic market.

The second observation relates to current production. In recent months, increasing evidence suggests that agricultural production during 1996 is actually decreasing. Supplies at the new agricultural markets have decreased during 1996 and 1997. Recent statistics released by the Cuban government show that sales by the state sector in the agricultural markets during 1995 amounted to 11.5 percent of the total, while the corresponding figure for the first semester of 1996 was 24.7 percent. Private farmers' participation decreased from 83.4 percent to 71.5 percent, while UBPCs and CPAs together went from 5.1 percent to 3.8 percent during the same time period. The situation evidently has worsened during the last year and the state sector is trying to maintain an adequate level of supply at these markets. Although the reasons for this phenomenon are many and beyond the scope of this roundtable, the result may have translated into a decrease of agricultural exports for 1996-97, for which we have not found official statistics.

The third observation relates to the historical regulations of the U.S. Department of Agriculture concerning certification of agricultural products for import into the United States. The procedure includes validation of field research in the exporting country for each product, and many other bureaucratic steps that may take several years to complete. Therefore, even if the U.S. economic embargo is lifted tomorrow, it could easily be from three to five years before Cuba can export nearly any agricultural commodity to the United States—and perhaps longer. Under this scenario there would not be any immediate substantial changes in the direction of trade flows from Cuba from those delineated by my colleagues in their presentations. At this point, we must emphasize that the historical trade patters before 1959 illustrate commercial relations between the United States and Cuba and should not be taken as predictors of future events. Many changes have occurred in the U.S. since that time. A few examples include changes in market structures, the increasing importance of Mexico as a U.S. supplier, the recent North American Free Trade Agreement (NAFTA), and others.

The final observation relates to an announcement made last July 24. With the approval of the U.S. administration, ITT entered into an agreement with the Italian communications firm Stet International to receive $25 million for the use of ITT-claimed property in Cuba for the next 10 years. The transaction, according to State Department officials and even Senator Helms, is a victory for the Helms-Burton legislation.

Without debating the meaning of the words "victory" or "defeat," we believe that, if such an arrangement is copied by U.S. agribusiness firms, it could lead to substantial increases in Cuba's agricultural production and exports. Under that scenario, the impact of foreign investment on both sugar and non-sugar agricultural trade would be many times more important than the one discussed in this roundtable today.

WOMEN AND POST-COLD WAR SOCIALISM: THE CASES OF CUBA AND VIETNAM

Julie Marie Bunck

This paper compares the post-Cold War experiences of women in Cuba and Vietnam. The regimes in both of these countries suffered gravely from the collapse of the Soviet Union in 1991. The disappearance of the Soviet bloc and the subsequent economic slowdown forced the Cuban and Vietnamese leadership to sort quickly through various policies that might bring about recovery and rapid economic growth while averting the unraveling of socialism and communist- party rule. However, the two countries took markedly different paths.

Vietnam opted to embrace the market and carried out sweeping economic reforms, from privatizing state enterprises and agriculture to devaluing the currency, from drastically slashing subsidies to eliminating thousands of state firms, from opening the country to foreign trade and investment to laying off almost a million workers. The Cuban regime chose a more cautious and less costly approach of adjustment and limited reform. Enticed by the prospect of rapid economic development, the Vietnamese were prepared for a bold and risky move. Concerned at the possible wrench on their grip on power, the Cubans preferred to muddle along with incremental changes.

Given the cultural and structural differences between Cuba and Vietnam and their contrasting post-Cold War approaches to recovery, the experiences of wom-

en in each country raises important questions to which this paper advances partial answers. How similar were the experiences of women in Cuba and Vietnam throughout the prerevolutionary and revolutionary phases? In what ways has the post-Cold War period of reform affected women in each country? In other words, what have women gained and what have they lost?

WOMEN AND THEIR PREREVOLUTIONARY EXPERIENCES

Women in prerevolutionary Vietnam and Cuba wholly lacked equal rights and lived in sharply discriminatory societies. Women in Cuba, however, fared noticeably better than those in Vietnam. Cuban women received the right to vote in 1934. Rates of abortion and divorce in prerevolutionary Cuba ranked among the highest in Latin America. In education the percentage of female students from ages five to fifteen approximately equaled that of male students.[1] According to Cuba's 1953 census, the percentage of illiterate males (26 percent) exceeded that of illiterate females (21 percent).[2] The number of women working outside the home, attending school, and practicing birth control surpassed the corresponding percentages in nearly every other Latin American or developing country. Women served as judges, mayors, and cabinet members, and the Constitution of 1940 stood as one of the most progressive

1. José Moreno, "From Traditional to Modern Values," in *Revolutionary Change in Cuba*, ed. Carmelo Mesa-Lago (Pittsburgh: University of Pittsburgh Press, 1971), p. 479.
2. Julie Marie Bunck, *Fidel Castro and the Quest for a Revolutionary Culture in Cuba* (University Park: Penn State Press, 1994), p. 89.

in the Western Hemisphere with regard to women's rights.

Women in pre-revolutionary Vietnam, however, before and during French rule, enjoyed virtually no rights or privileges. Indeed, Vietnamese citizens in general enjoyed few rights. Law and society afforded women scant protection in the workplace and the home. In fact, throughout the colonial period, the French continued to recognize laws regulating the status of concubines and polygamy. In 1943, approximately 95 percent of the population and 98 percent of women could neither read nor write.

Moreover, traditional Vietnamese society—which might be characterized as patriarchal, authoritarian, and reliant on subsistence agriculture—wholly depended on the labor of wives, daughters, concubines, and female servants. Women lived narrowly circumscribed lives, usually confined to the home and the family rice paddies. Often, their lives did not extend far past the family plot. Prerevolutionary Cuban society, by contrast, offered broader horizons to its women. Cuba was more urban, literate, and commercial, and the roles of women were more varied and fulfilling.

REVOLUTION AND WOMEN IN CUBA AND VIETNAM

Perhaps the most important change for women in Cuba after the revolution was their rapid entry into the workforce. In 1959 women comprised only 17 percent of the workforce. By 1990 they made up 38 percent. Cuban women participated actively in the building of a revolutionary society—teaching peasants as part of the literacy campaign, promoting government goals, supporting child-care programs. Furthermore, throughout the 1960s and into the 1970s women's issues and objectives in Cuba, at least rhetorically, took on more visibility and importance.

In Vietnam, women's issues actually formed an important intellectual basis for the anti-colonial movement. While the French were by no means especially enlightened or progressive in governing Vietnam, they did openly support efforts to improve the lot of Vietnamese women in education and political rights. In fact, the French initiated most of the early efforts to improve women's condition in Vietnam's conservative Confucian society. Perhaps reflective of the role of women in French society, throughout France and its colonies gender was seen as an appropriate and acceptable topic of discourse, and progress in women's rights was one positive aspect of the history of French Indochina.

In promoting anti-colonial sentiments and fostering a revolutionary consciousness, Vietnam's Marxist intellectuals relied heavily on the language of gender. Indeed, as in so many other anti-colonial movements, Vietnamese revolutionaries turned the language and concepts of the colonizers back on the colonial hierarchy. Revolutionary intellectuals came to embrace the concept of gender as a code term for analyzing parallel conditions under colonialism. Intellectuals used debates regarding women as vehicles for arguing about colonialism. Inequality of women took on a second secret meaning: oppression of the whole society. The revolutionaries labeled the French and their Vietnamese supporters "Patrons" (males) oppressing and abusing women, who symbolized the victims of colonialism. Women's liberation, thus, became synonymous with colonial self-determination. Ultimately, as these double meanings became apparent, the French withdrew their support of women's rights.[3]

Throughout the fighting for independence, this use of gender to symbolize oppression appealed to and gained the support of Vietnamese women. Women hoped that revolution and liberation would mean political, social and economic equality. Despite all the gender-oriented language, however, not all Vietnamese Marxists were serious in advocating a change in the basic legal status of women. Many male revolutionaries—products of their culture—believed that women involved in the anti-colonial

---

3. Mary Ann Tetreault, "Women and Revolution in Vietnam," in *Women and Revolution in Africa, Asia, and the New World*, ed. Mary Ann Tetreault (Columbia: University of South Carolina Press, 1994), pp. 111-113.

movement should make traditional sacrifices and contributions. One Vietnamese Marxist, reminiscent of the writings of Che Guevara, wrote that women would provide to the anti-French movement "feminine strengths, such as virtue, patience, loyalty."[4]

Moreover, like the left in Latin America, including Castro's regime, Vietnam's Marxists expected all their followers to subordinate personal or private ambitions to the goals of the socialist state. After the Vietnamese defeated the French, the new leaders openly encouraged women to subordinate specifically female ambitions and goals to the objectives of the entire nation. Women were to pursue goals that prepared them educationally and politically to participate fully in a Marxist society.

In much the same way, the Cuban regime emphasized economic goals in many of its efforts on behalf of women. Fidel Castro clearly stated that he expected women to subordinate their personal goals to those of society as a whole. He declared: "women can be free only to the extent that they commit themselves first and foremost to the Revolution."[5] It may be that neither the Cuban nor the Vietnamese leadership, both overwhelmingly male, valued women's liberation on its own terms, apart from broader revolutionary goals. In the case of Vietnam this view reflected a long-ingrained communitarian ethic: one sacrifices not for one's self or even one's family or gender, but for the community or the nation as a whole.

It is highly revealing that polygamy, an institution under fierce rhetorical attack during the Vietnamese revolutionary movement, remained legal and untouched in the Socialist Republic of Vietnam until 1960. The Marxist regime justified polygamy on the grounds that the family in Vietnam's traditional patriarchal society formed the chief economic unit. In this unit women performed the bulk of the labor under male supervision. The idea was that the more wives, daughters, concubines, and female servants a male could dominate the more work could be performed and the more the family could produce.[6] Thus, for all the rhetoric promoting gender equality, the long process of dismantling the family farms really sounded the death knell for polygamy in Vietnam.

Once their revolutions began, both Cuban and Vietnamese leaders implored women to do more for the cause. And, the evidence suggests that many women participated fully and enthusiastically, viewing the revolutionary struggle as both their own personal battle for women's rights and, more important, as their duty to the larger whole. The Indochinese Communist Party created the Women's Union—still the largest women's organization in Vietnam—which mobilized women to work and to fight. The Castro regime organized the Federation of Cuban Women (FMC) primarily to promote revolutionary goals and to carry out various activities, such as the literacy campaign, teacher training programs, and child-care workshops.

The experiences of Vietnamese women may be contrasted with those of Cuban women. Indeed, on account of the decades of warfare in Vietnam, the revolution exacted a considerably higher price from Vietnamese women. Ho Chi Minh seized control of Hanoi in 1945, but the war against the French continued for another nine years. During that period Vietnamese women fought, gathered intelligence, transported supplies, and tended to the wounded. Many women died during the conflict, either in battle or by execution. In 1941, for example, the French executed Nguyen Thi Minh Khai, revered by the Vietnamese today as an anti-colonial heroine and martyr.

---

4. David Marr, *Vietnamese Traditions on Trial, 1920-1945* (Berkeley: University of California Press, 1981), pp. 242-243; see also Bunck, *Fidel Castro and the Quest for a Revolutionary Culture in Cuba*, p. 99.

5. Oscar Lewis, Ruth Lewis, and Susan M. Rigdon, *Four Women Living the Revolution: An Oral History of Contemporary Cuba* (Urbana: University of Illinois Press, 1977), p. xvii.

6. Tetreault, "Women and Revolution in Vietnam," p. 113.

After the partitioning of Vietnam in 1954, the intensified north-south conflict demanded even more sacrifices from Vietnamese women. According to one estimate, more than 250,000 women were killed between 1954 and 1965 alone.[7] Ultimately, by 1965, as the pool of males continued to diminish because of war casualties, the leadership recruited women to become even more deeply involved in the front lines of the conflict. Indeed, along with fighting and suffering from the ravages of war, Vietnamese women took a central role in farming, the so-called "feminization of agriculture." Although women had long performed most of the manual labor in Vietnam, they now actually managed the farm cooperatives. Vietnamese women, then, faced increasingly heavy burdens and extreme hardship between 1945 and 1975.

After 1975 how did the Vietnamese leadership reward Vietnamese women for their sacrifices? In various respects, it failed utterly to do so. The leadership was, and has remained, dominated by men. Indeed, the Vietnamese leadership never recognized seriously the vital contribution of women in the wars. Time and again, the leaders have opted to portray women solely as victims of the war, rather than as serious agents or contributors. For example, in the Museum of the Revolution in Hanoi, which boasts the most extensive collection of photographs and artifacts from the revolutionary period, little in the collection features or even includes women. One would not learn of the role women played by simply visiting the centerpiece museum in Hanoi.[8]

The War Crimes Museum in Ho Chi Minh City features a horrific collection of photographs of victims—piled corpses, mutilated bodies, crippled children. Yet, here again, while the museum prominently portrays women as victims, as it should, women are rarely, if ever, presented as soldiers, agents, or leaders. Moreover, Vietnamese memories of female contributions to the war efforts seem to have faded much more quickly than memories of male contributions. We know very few names of women involved—even in various recent memoirs by women themselves in the revolution.[9]

In the aftermath of the revolution women in Vietnam did gain considerable economic power, albeit a different type of power than that enjoyed by Cuban women. As more men entered the armed forces in the mid-1960s, and as the state seized more private family farms and converted them to state cooperatives, women virtually controlled the daily administration of agriculture, Vietnam's largest economic sector. Vietnamese women, like Cuban women, also rapidly joined the urban workforce. In fact, by 1991 women made up 52 percent of the population and 60 percent of the total workforce: in excess of 20 percentage points more working women than in revolutionary Cuba.

Several factors help to explain this remarkably high number. First, Vietnam lost so many males during the war years that throughout the 1970s and the early 1980s women seized millions of available positions and succeeded in holding them. Second, Vietnam was and remains an agricultural society. Indeed, 80 percent of the Vietnamese population continues to reside in rural areas.[10] Thus, women were poised to enter a field with considerable vacancies in which they or their ancestors had worked.

Perhaps most telling, within Vietnamese society the types of work that women began to do may not have been viewed as such a notable step forward. Hence, the door to the workforce may have swung open more easily than in many societies. In Vietnam, as in many other countries, rice- based agriculture was long considered fairly simple, menial, low-status work. And, Vietnamese society often relegated wom-

---

7. Le Han Danh, "The Long-Haired Army," *Vietnamese Studies* 10 (1966), pp. 61-62.

8. Women have their own museum in Hanoi—a much less known, less-touted museum. But, as Mary Ann Tetreault wrote, separate is not equal. See Tetreault, "Women and Revolution in Vietnam," p. 123.

9. See, for example, Truong Nha Trang's 1995 memoir.

10. Le Thi, "*Doi Moi* and Female Workers: A Case Study of Hanoi," in *Economic Reforms, Women's Employment, and Social Policies*, ed. Valentine M. Moghadam (Helsinki: World Institute for Development Research, 1995), p. 46.

en working outside the agricultural sector to support roles in light industry, services, and education.

Women also found that increased power in the agricultural realm both empowered and burdened them. On the one hand, the cooperatives offered to women decision-making capabilities and opportunities for social exchanges and relationships outside the family. It provided a chance to meet with, work with, and join forces with other women, a potentially potent means to dissent or, at least, to foment change.

On the other hand, Vietnamese women worked exceedingly long hours. Under the cooperative arrangements, the state paid men and women equally. But men did the heavy work—carrying loads, hauling water, maneuvering water buffalo. Because the largely male leadership classified this "male" work as more demanding, it permitted men to work fewer hours per day. So, while men and women received the same salaries, men enjoyed more time away from the workplace. Nevertheless, working women found that even men in revolutionary society were not ordinarily inclined to use their leisure time to maintain the house, cook the meals, and raise the children. Thus, the demands of the workplace added to, rather than replaced, the demands of the home.[11]

WOMEN AND EDUCATION IN CUBA AND VIETNAM

In the area of basic education, the gains of Cuban women and Vietnamese women are similar in certain respects, different in others. In Vietnam by 1985 women comprised about 50 percent of all primary students and 43 percent of all university students. Approximately 27 percent of university faculty and 11 percent of doctoral degree holders today are women. However, despite their level of education, women

faculty members, are rarely ranked above lecturer, and few universities employ female administrators.

Cuban women have fared better. While primary and secondary education has remained on par with Vietnam, Cuban women have accomplished more in higher education. In 1994 women accounted for 44 percent of the full professors and 65 percent of the assistant professors at the University of Havana. Moreover, women now hold ten of the sixteen deanships.[12] Given the regime's post-Cold War move to marginalize and diminish the influence of university education, however, the professional advances of women in education may not be quite so glowing if critically scrutinized.

WOMEN'S RIGHTS

As for women's rights, both revolutionary regimes have promised much, yet delivered little. The Vietnamese Constitution of 1980, like the Cuban Constitution, ensures women the right to vote, own land, and choose their own profession. It requires men to share equally with women the work of the home and protects women against domestic abuse. A pregnant woman can get a divorce, but her spouse cannot divorce her until one year after the baby is born, and each party after divorce is entitled to one-half of the common property.

While such provisions appear promising on paper, in reality, both the notion of a rule of law[13] and the court system in which such rights might be enforced remain weak and underdeveloped in revolutionary Vietnam. Corruption is rampant, people do not trust the courts, and those dispensing justice frequently consider an individual's revolutionary orientation before deciding a case. Thus, in practice, many laws regulating the rights of women go unenforced. The state often fails to honor labor contracts, and the

---

11. Tetreault, "Women and Revolution in Vietnam," p. 125.

12. Elena Díaz González, "Economic Crisis: Employment and Quality of Life in Cuba," in *Economic Reforms, Women's Employment, and Social Policies*, ed. Valentine M. Moghadam (Helsinki: World Institute for Development and Economic Research, 1995), pp. 139-140.

13. Michael Fowler has written of a rule of law as follows: "When the rule of law is supreme, the legal system guarantees individual rights and protects individuals from the actions of others and from abuse by the state. In a society that values law so highly, individuals can assert and defend their legal rights, and laws will define and limit the powers of the state." Michael Ross Fowler, *With Justice for All? The Nature of the American Legal System* (Upper Saddle River, N.J.: Prentice Hall, 1998), p. 7.

courts provide very limited recourse in labor and social matters.

Some exceptions do exist. For instance, the 1986 family law not only contemplates prison sentences for domestic violence, but actually establishes a mechanism for enforcement. It assigns to the women's union the responsibility of protecting women with shelter and support and reporting offenders. This provides an important sanctuary and a community structure that can give real practical meaning to an otherwise unenforced set of laws. To a large extent, however, vaunted legal undertakings have failed to upset traditional patterns of conduct toward women.

WOMEN IN POLITICS

In both Cuba and Vietnam women have never attained significant political power. Rhetoric to the contrary notwithstanding, both regimes have consistently excluded women from the center of important political discussion. In socialist societies such as Cuba in which the state controls virtually all resources and their distribution, political influence constitutes the only authentic form of power. Alternative forms of empowerment, such as the market, a free press, or autonomous artistic expression, are muted or nonexistent. The leaderships in both Cuba and Vietnam have quieted the voices of women, refusing to allow them a significant role in the political and economic decisions made on their behalf. In both societies, women have remained peripheral and politically impotent, despite their numbers in the workforce. Recently, the market in Vietnam has provided women with other mechanisms for empowerment. In Cuba, however, genuine power—power to shape their lives in positive ways—merely trickles down to women from the men who are in charge, or eludes women altogether.

In the case of Vietnam, the political role of women has steadily deteriorated since the revolution succeeded in unifying the country in 1975. While in 1965 women made up 17 percent of the Democratic Re-

public of Vietnam's central committee, women have never held that many central committee seats since. In 1946 women held only 2.5 percent of the seats—10 of 250 total seats - - of the first national assembly. By 1975 women made up more than 32 percent of the national assembly membership. Today that number has dropped to about 15 percent. Women today head 2 of 14 ministries, fewer than ever before since 1965, and they lead none of the major commissions.[14] Women serve neither on the politburo nor on the powerful party standing committee, newly established at the party congress in June 1996. Nor has a movement to reverse this trend yet surfaced among the men who run the country.

Vietnam's original leaders of the women's movement, the grand old women of the revolution, have largely disappeared from public life. For some years the sizeable women's union has drifted about, lacking vibrant leadership and clear purpose. Thus, to the extent that Vietnamese women once had substantive and symbolic influence in the political arena, it has been eroded over time.

Cuban women have not fared much better. No Cuban woman ever served on the secretariat, disbanded in 1991. Indeed, until 1991 only one woman—Vilma Espín, Raúl Castro's wife—served on the Political Bureau. Today, a mere three of the twenty-five-member politburo are women.[15] Women comprise only about 21 percent of the Party, 22.8 percent of the National Assembly, 16 percent of the Central Committee, and 10 percent of Cuba's ambassadors. Thus, the Castro regime has long overlooked the contributions women might make in each of the key policy-making institutions.

Why have women experienced such few successes in the political arena of these two avowedly revolutionary societies? Several explanations may shed some light. First, women joined the revolutions with idealistic and substantive goals. As the revolutions progressed and revealed themselves as elitist, isolated, and male-dominated, the idealism faded. Women

14. Arlene Eisen, *Women and Revolution in Viet Nam* (London: Zed Books, 1984), pp. 243-247.
15. Díaz González, "Economic Crisis: Employment and Quality of Life in Cuba," p.127.

became disillusioned and dropped away. They lost their drive and commitment, retreated from the public domain, and returned to private life. One might characterize this as a form of discreet, noncombative dissidence. An elite and self-selected group of men, perhaps more concerned with power than ideals and certainly confronted with more opportunities and fewer obstacles than their female revolutionary colleagues, have continued to control the state. Thus, the course of the revolution has moved from an ideals-oriented push for substantive change to a traditional male fight over power. Women in Cuba and Vietnam, with no record of winning that game, lost interest in playing it. Hence, they have retreated from the public to the private realm.

A second explanation focuses on the machismo of the regimes. As I have argued at more length elsewhere, the substantial disparity between the Cuban leadership's rhetoric and its actual policies toward women calls into question the notion that a chief objective of the Revolution was to ensure full equality between the sexes.[16] The governments in Cuba and Vietnam both had many opportunities to assure women equal access to political positions and leadership roles through fair, noncoercive measures. These regimes could have given women a voice in telling political decisions. In fact, however, the governments repeatedly failed to take the fundamental steps necessary to transform the rhetoric of equality into political reality.

For its part, the Castro leadership consistently concerned itself more with augmenting the size of the labor force than with achieving equality between the sexes.[17] Bringing women into the work force meant eradicating prerevolutionary attitudes that stressed the traditional role of women in the home. Traditional culture thus hindered the government's revolutionary goals. Hence, Cuban leaders created the FMC to mobilize women and to inculcate new attitudes throughout society that were more appropriate for the state's objectives.

The leadership itself, however, never relinquished its own traditional view of women's role in politics and society. Fidel Castro himself was perhaps too much the *caudillo*, the gun-carrying, jeep-driving, cigar-smoking *macho*, to revamp his own basic attitudes toward women. As Carlos Alberto Montaner observed: "[The government would have to] concoct a different mythology, adopt other manners, and castrate the revolution...[T]he revolutionary thing would be to eradicate the masculine accent, the machismo style which rules over Cuba's public life....But that would be like asking for a different revolution."[18]

Likewise in Vietnam, the regime certainly used seductive rhetoric in promoting women's issues. It certainly gained workers and fighters, but it displayed no commitment to truly empowering women. Few avenues provided women real access to the political arena. Alexis de Tocqueville, writing on the French Revolution, argued that France after the revolution appeared very much like France before the revolution. Culture—values, attitudes, beliefs, traditions—had changed very little. Similarly, in gender relations the term "continuity" describes modern Vietnam more appropriately than the word "revolutionary."

Crisis—especially after 1984 in Vietnam and 1991 in Cuba—further diminished attention to women's concerns. As economic difficulties became dire, both regimes turned to the tasks of consolidating and maintaining their power and averting economic disaster. With so few women in leadership positions

16. See Bunck, *Fidel Castro and the Quest for a Revolutionary Culture*, pp. 89-124.

17. See Bunck, *Fidel Castro and the Quest for a Revolutionary Culture*, p. 122; Susan Kaufman Purcell, "Modernizing Women for a Modern Society: The Cuban Case" in *Female and Male in Latin America*, Ann Pescatello, ed. (Pittsburgh: University of Pittsburgh Press, 1973), p. 259.

18. Carlos Alberto Montaner, *Secret Report on the Cuban Revolution* (London: Transaction Books, 1971), p. 91, cited in Bunck, *Fidel Castro and the Quest for a Revolutionary Culture*, p. 123. See also Ileana Fuentes, *Cuba Sin Caudillos: Un Enfoque Feminista Para El Siglo XXI* (Princeton: Linden Lane, 1994).

able to hold the regimes to their ideals and promises, gender issues naturally fell to the wayside.

It may also be the case that women themselves have continued to view their roles in fundamentally traditional terms. Polls in Cuba and Vietnam have revealed that women choose to subordinate politics to home and family. Le Thi, a noted revolutionary and the former director of the Women's Center in Hanoi, recently wrote an article in which she called on women to take on their "natural functions." She argued that men, naturally and appropriately, should manage the political affairs of state. Neither revolutionary Cuba nor revolutionary Vietnam has truly revolutionized the long-enduring view in those society's that men should control the public domain, while women occupy themselves with the private.[19]

WOMEN AND POST-COLD WAR SOCIETY

In the case of Vietnam, the economic transition has had a complex and contradictory impact on women. Since women continue to dominate the agricultural sector, the transition to the free market system has provided rural women with slightly more access to capital. Agricultural exports—primarily rice—earn much hard currency for Vietnam. By working in agriculture, women have independent, though limited, access to hard currency that they lacked when more doctrinaire Marxist policies were in effect.

At the same time, agricultural privatization dissolved the cooperatives and resurrected the family farms. Since the bonds forged in running the cooperatives have not always survived, this has deprived women of an important social and communication outlet. Many women are back to laboring within narrower confines. They have lost a key social role. Thus in agriculture, women are economically better off than before though they may be more socially isolated. Whether their role in the market will provide more opportunities to shape Vietnamese society than their role in the cooperatives did remains to be seen.

Second, as part of Vietnam's privatization the state laid off 900,000 workers and eliminated thousands of state enterprises.[20] Approximately 60 percent of those workers released from their jobs were women. At the same time, however, the private sector expanded and quickly absorbed virtually all of these workers. Thus, women found new opportunities. A recent study of one neighborhood in Hanoi revealed that women make up 64 percent of workers in newly-created enterprises. While the number of women in agriculture has actually been decreasing, the percentage of women in other sectors has increased steadily since 1988. Today women outnumber men in commerce, education, finance, and health care. In contrast to Cuba, however, Vietnamese women have not advanced in the higher professions. Women comprise a mere 6 percent of medical doctors and 4 percent of university professors.[21]

While the transition to the market has provided ample new opportunities for urban women, it may have further weakened their ability to secure equal pay and acceptable working conditions. Where in the past the state might pass laws and enforce them within state enterprises, now the state must try to police foreign firms doing business in Vietnam. Political corruption, ineffective judicial process, and the lack of an efficient regulatory state have opened new opportunities for skirting social laws.

In the private sector today women earn less than men working in the same job, keep long and irregular working hours, and lack most benefits provided in the state enterprises. Should the supply of labor no longer vastly exceed the demand, women may gain the economic clout necessary to ensure positive changes. And, should the legal system be strengthened and made more accessible, women may gain the practical ability to translate contractual and constitutional rhetoric into workplace reality. But, neither of these changes is likely to occur in the immediate future.

---

19. Le Thi, "Gender, Growth and Scientific Study on Women," *Vietnam Social Sciences* 4 (1992), pp. 6-9.

20. George Irvin, "Vietnam: Assessing the Achievements of *Doi Moi*," *Journal of Development Studies* 5:31 (June 1995), p. 727.

21. Le Thi, "*Doi Moi* and Female Workers," pp. 48-50.

Vietnam's economic transition has also triggered the migration of women to the cities. They come to find a job or sell produce. Many collect trash, perform domestic services, or work for little pay (20 cents a day).[22] Some bring their children with them; many resort to crime. As in Cuba, unprecedented numbers have been turning to prostitution.

Vietnam has also witnessed a phenomenal increase in the number of beggars—especially street children—which has led to crime, drug abuse, and child prostitution. According to a recent statistic, 50,000 children roam the streets of Vietnam's major cities. Moreover, the health of these children—indeed, of all Vietnamese children—remains a chief concern. Roughly 85 percent of Vietnamese youngsters have parasites, 70 percent have infections, and 27 percent suffer from glaucoma.

POVERTY

What has been the impact of the economic transition on the poorest groups in Vietnamese society? Some have argued that Vietnam's economic reforms increased the chasm between rich and poor. Illiteracy is on the rise as education has become increasingly inaccessible and privatized. Moreover, health care, which the Vietnamese state never provided on the level of other Marxist states, has also become increasingly out of reach. Unemployment has risen to around 12 percent. According to one estimate, 5 million rural workers remain unemployed and 3.5 million urban workers seek work.

Curiously, despite these statistics, poverty has not increased during the economic transition. The economy, of course, was performing abysmally before market reforms were implemented. According to a recent World Bank report, in 1984 approximately 75 percent of the population was poverty-stricken. In 1993 less than 55 percent remained so.[23] Thus, while relative deprivation may have risen in Vietnam, a rise in absolute poverty affecting a large segment of the population has not occurred. In fact, for several reasons

reforms have probably helped many Vietnamese citizens to lift themselves out of poverty.

First, national income has grown continuously throughout the late 1980s and early 1990s—and most of that growth was in the agricultural sector—historically the poorest sector. Thus, economic transition was not associated with a severe economic contraction, which generally harms the peasantry more than other social groups. Second, several features of the Vietnamese economy have cushioned the impact of reforms. Unlike in the industrialized, centrally planned economies, pre-transition Vietnamese firms provided few benefits to workers.

Moreover, a relatively large portion of the labor force worked outside the formal state sector. Thus, during transition Vietnam has avoided the heightened expectations that dogged other transition countries whose state sectors had long provided substantial benefits to their workers. Vietnam has not experienced a transition like those in Eastern Europe and the Soviet Union, in which severe economic contraction exacerbated the problems inherent in a collapsing welfare system.

Unlike the landless peasants of transition countries in Latin America, most peasants in Vietnam now own and farm their own land. And, given the staggering growth of the agricultural sector, the shift in terms of trade favored the peasantry since they produced the rice being exported. Finally, stabilization in Vietnam has been swift and effective. In this sense, the Vietnamese adopted a "shock-treatment" approach to economic transition, similar to that of Poland and quite different from the more gradual Chinese strategy.[24]

CUBAN WOMEN DURING THE PERIOD OF ECONOMIC ADJUSTMENT

Just as *doi moi* has had contradictory effects for Vietnamese women, so the much more limited adjustments in Cuba have also had positive and negative

---

22. Personal interview with Le Thi, Director of Hanoi's Women's Center, Hanoi, Vietnam (April 12, 1995).

23. *World Development Report 1996: From Plan to Market* (Washington: World Bank, 1996), p. 48.

24. George Irvin, "Vietnam: Assessing the Achievements of *Doi Moi*," pp. 741-742; *World Development Report 1996*, pp. 1-18.

repercussions. The leading drawback has been rising unemployment. In the late 1980s as the economic crisis in Cuba intensified, the Fidel Castro regime implemented a process of economic "rationalization" in which Castro announced that "nonessential" workers would be laid off, men who had concluded active military service would be guaranteed the best jobs, and workers would be assigned to jobs that the regime deemed most appropriate for their skills. In this process many women lost employment.

Some enterprises confronted women workers, many of whom could not afford child care, with new, longer and more erratic work hours.[25] In other instances the state simply decided that women had other home responsibilities and could be released more justifiably than men. The regime created the microbrigades to absorb excess workers and to construct houses. The microbrigades, however, largely excluded women. According to one estimate, by the summer of 1989 the program hired 33,000 workers, yet women accounted for only 6 percent of those hired.[26] Moreover, the state raised the cost and the minimum age of day care eligibility, which compelled still more women to stay at home.

With the regime still shunning the free market and intent on centralized decisionmaking, the women who retained their jobs often found the government reassigning them to different tasks. These work re-assignments undermined some of the previous gains women had made. In some instances, the government called on women to perform what had traditionally been seen as "women's work." In the national process of re-assigning workers, the regime called on women to work as teachers in day-care centers,

waitresses in restaurants, and maids and cooks in the tourism sector.[27] At the same time, the government reassigned many women to agriculture, primarily working in sugar.[28] In many cases women joined agricultural brigades, organized to grow food. Since these brigades were sex segregated, families were often split up and separated for anywhere from two weeks to two years.[29]

Nevertheless, the Cuban adjustment to post-Cold War realities has not been entirely negative for Cuban women. Despite the many obstacles, women continue to comprise approximately 35 percent of the Cuban workforce, roughly on par with the percentage of women in other labor forces in the region.[30] Although their occupations may often be menial, women continue to dominate the service sector, the most rapidly expanding part of the Cuban economy.[31] Women have thus been able to take advantage of the rapidly growing tourism industry, finding and holding more lucrative jobs than many Cuban men. By the same token, however, one unfortunate result of the expansion of tourism in Cuba has been the rapid burgeoning of the sex tourism industry. Prostitution provides thousands of young Cuban females, and some males, with fast access to hard currency, though with considerable health and psychological costs.[32]

Cuban women have also found adequate medical care to be in shorter supply in the post-Cold War era. Fewer medical facilities, tighter medical rations, and less available medicines have forced women to overlook basic health needs. Abortion, widely available to Cuban women in the 1980s, has become much more difficult to attain. In 1986 there were 91 abortions in

25. Lois M. Smith and Alfred Padula, *Sex and Revolution: Women in Socialist Cuba* (Oxford: Oxford University Press, 1996), p. 119.

26. Smith and Padula, *Sex and Revolution*, p. 119.

27. *Granma Weekly Review* (August 3, 1986, p. 1; February 21, 1988, p. 3; August 24, 1987, p. 8); and *Granma* (April 18, 1991), p. 2.

28. *Foreign Broadcast Information Service* (October 4, 1990), p. 4.

29. Smith and Padula, *Sex and Revolution*, p. 119.

30. According to Isel Rivero y Méndez, a full 53 percent of "economically active" women are virtually unemployed. Isel Rivero y Méndez, "Cuban Women: Back to the Future?" *Ms* (May-June 1993), p. 16.

31. The service sector alone accounts for more than half of the foreign direct investment in Cuba. See Carlos Lage, "La Economía Cubana," *Economía Cubana: Boletín Informativo*, 11 (Febrero 1995), p. 1.

32. See Julia O'Connell Davidson, "Sex Tourism in Cuba," in *Race and Class* 38:1 (July- September 1996), pp. 39-48.

Cuba for every 100 births. In 1993 that number had dropped to 56 for every 100, and the number has continued to plummet.[33]

The quality of Cuba's primary and secondary schools has also deteriorated as schools lack daily needs, such as books, pencils, erasers, and paper. The universities, likewise, cannot cover basic essentials, including books and computers. Day-care is no longer as accessible as before and services, such as laundries, have closed or raised prices. Indeed, the erosion of the Cuban standard of living has affected women more acutely and directly than men.[34]

In contrast to Vietnam, however, women in Cuba have retained a strong hold on the professions. Approximately 44 percent of the University of Havana's full professors and 65 percent of its assistant professors are women. Moreover, women make up roughly 58 percent of Cuba's medical doctors, despite the fact that in 1988 the Castro regime actually dropped medical school admission requirements for men in order to increase the number of male medical students.[35]

Nevertheless, a medical doctor in Cuba earns the equivalent of about three dollars a month: a disincentive to practicing a profession as opposed to opting for manual labor, prostitution, or child-rearing. Fur-

thermore, while the government has approved increasing numbers of licenses for self-employment in an attempt to alleviate unemployment and raise production levels, it has barred many professionals from self-employment. Given the high number of women among Cuba's professionals, they have been adversely affected by this regulation.

CONCLUSION

The post-Cold War crisis in Cuba and Vietnam has had a complex impact on women. The experiences of women in the prerevolutionary and revolutionary periods contained certain pertinent parallels, alongside a host of striking differences. The common denominator during the post-Cold War period seems to have been the contradictory nature of the changes. Progress in some areas has been tempered by backsliding in others. In general terms, Cuba's economic adjustment has been considerably less sweeping than Vietnam's market transition. While any findings at this early date must be tentative, the new economic policies seem to have opened fewer new opportunities for women in Cuba. While women remain outside the political center in both countries, the best hope for economic empowerment and personal independence may yet be found in the marketplace rather than in the tired rhetoric of supposedly revolutionary regimes long dominated by male elites.

---

33. Díaz González, "Economic Crisis," p. 137.

34. The recent legalization of various private enterprises, including laundries, has alleviated the burden somewhat.

35. Smith and Padula, *Sex and Revolution*, p. 90; Díaz González, "Economic Crisis," p. 133.

LA MUJER CUBANA EN LOS ESTADOS UNIDOS: ALGUNAS CONSIDERACIONES SOBRE SU APORTE SOCIOECONOMICO Y LAS MODIFICACIONES DE SU PAPEL

Uva de Aragón

Nos proponemos en este trabajo explorar los siguientes aspectos: 1) los niveles de educación y la participación en el mercado laboral de la mujer cubana en los Estados Unidos; 2) los campos en que la mujer en el exilio se ha destacado y aquellos en que su presencia es menos notable y por qué; y 3) plantear diversas hipótesis para un estudio futuro que analice con mayor profundidad los efectos del papel de la mujer cubana en Estados Unidos de cara a una Cuba futura.

En una conferencia dictada en el Museo de Arte y Cultura en 1984, el gran historiador cubano Leví Marrero hace un recorrido por los anales de nuestra isla en busca de las causas del éxito económico del exilio. Y concluye el tercer descubridor de Cuba (Marrero 1984, p. 36): "Lo que ha alcanzado (el cubano) no es obra de la improvisación y del azar, sino le viene al cubano de su larga experiencia, como hemos visto, en el ancho y competitivo campo de la economía liberal."

En un estudio más reciente de Thomas D. Boswell (1994) se comparan las características socioeconómicas de los cubanos con las de otros hispanos y con las de los norteamericanos. Basado en las cifras del censo de los Estados Unidos de 1990, el informe concluye que en los EEUU los cubanos trabajan más, ganan más dinero y son más educados que los puertorriqueños, dominicanos, mexicanos, centroamericanos y que los negros norteamericanos, aunque los índices se mantienen aún bastante por debajo de los de los blancos norteamericanos y de algunos otros grupos étnicos como los coreanos.

El estudio ofrece los factores a que se ha atribuido este éxito cubano: 1) la mayoría de los cubanos de la primera ola de exiliados eran de las clases altas y medias, con elevados niveles de educación y experiencia de trabajo; 2) el desarrollo paralelo de las economías de La Habana y de Miami permitieron a los primeros exiliados adaptarse fácilmente al medio económico de Miami; 3) muchos cubanos de las clases altas tenían experiencias anteriores y hasta contactos de negocio en los EEUU; 4) el gobierno americano invirtió más de un billón de dólares en ayuda a los cubanos a través del Cuban Refugee Program; 5) muchos latinoamericanos comenzaron a ver a Miami como la nueva capital del continente y comenzaron a invertir aquí; 6) el desarrollo de una economía de ghetto (economic enclave) en que los cubanos se ayudan unos a otros; y 7) que los cubanos se propusieron triunfar en los EEUU, ya que no pensaban regresar a Cuba mientras que el régimen de Castro estuviera en el poder (Boswell 1994, pp. 29-30).

El Dr. Lisandro Pérez (1986b) ofrece una explicación adicional como base de los logros de los cubanos. La ética de trabajo de la familia, más que los logros individuales, ha sido, según el autor, la clave del éxito cubano. Señala Pérez que las mujeres cubanas trabajan más no sólo que las mujeres de otros grupos hispanos, sino también que las norteamericanas. Debido asímismo a que las cubanas tienen la tasa de fertilidad más baja del país y a la presencia en la familia de personas mayores que con frecuencia ayudan en la crianza de los pequeños de la familia, inclusive las cubanas con niños pequeños trabajan más que todas las otras mujeres, incluyendo las americanas blancas o negras.

Estas afirmaciones no dejan de ser sorprendentes si consideramos que si bien la tasa de empleo femenino era alta en Cuba comparada con otros países de la América Latina de la época, según el censo de 1953, alcanzaba sólo el 13.7% de la población económicamente activa de 14 años o más. Para 1970, a pesar de los esfuerzos de la Revolución por incorporar a la mujer al mercado laboral, la cifra sólo había llegado al 18.5% de la población económicamente activa. En esa fecha, en Estados Unidos, ya 47% de las mujeres cubanas trabajaban. En 1980 y 1990 esa cifra se ha mantenido en 55%, que es superior al promedio nacional, y comparable a la tasa de los países industrializados de Europa y Asia (Bélgica 54%; Japón 57%, Suiza 56%, Portugal, 56 %; Inglaterra, 57%), y superior a la de España (42%) y otros países de la América Latina y a la de Cuba, que en 1988, era de 38%.

El aporte de las mujeres a la economía familiar no puede desestimarse. De acuerdo con las cifras del censo de 1980, el ingreso medio de la familia cubana en los Estados Unidos era de $18,245, el de otros hispanos de $14,712 y el de los norteamericanos de $19,917. En 1994, los cubanos ($27,038) continúan ganando más que los otros hispanos ($23,670), aunque no alcanzan el nivel de los norteamericanos ($36,966).

Sin embargo, cuando observamos ese ingreso medio en términos masculinos y femeninos, comprobamos que en 1979, que es la fecha más representativa con respecto al éxito económico de la primera oleada del exilio, pues no incluye a los refugiados del Mariel, y a muy pocos cubanoamericanos nacidos en EEUU, los hombres cubanos mayores de 15 años contaban con un ingreso medio de $14,168, comparado con $12,970 de otros hispanos y $17,363 de los norteamericanos. Las mujeres cubanas mayores de 15 años contaban con un ingreso medio de $8,982, en comparación a $8,923 de otras hispanas y $10,380 de las norteamericanas. Es decir, que aunque las cubanas

ganaban menos que los cubanos, al igual que las americanas ganaban menos que los norteamericanos, las cubanas ganaban en 1979, 86.5% con relación al promedio nacional, mientras que los hombres ganaban 81.6% del salario promedio nacional. En 1994 se agudiza esa diferencia, pues los hombres cubanos ganan, al igual que en 1979, 81.5% con relación al promedio nacional (y 78.9% en comparación con los hombres blancos), mientras que la entrada de la mujer ha ascendido a 95.0% con relación al promedio nacional y 93.6% con ralación a las mujeres blancas en EEUU. El ingreso de las cubanas se acerca grandemente al de las nortemericanas, todo lo cual confirma la teoría de que el aporte económico femenino no ha sido debidamente reconocido como un factor del éxito económico de los cubanos en Estados Unidos. Más allá de este reconocimiento, se precisa profundizar en las causas, características y consecuencias de este gran número de mujeres que trabaja y que aporta unas sumas considerables a los ingresos familiares.

Según el censo de los Estados Unidos de 1990, de 1,053,197 cubanos en EEUU, 51% (534,951) son mujeres y 49% hombres (518,246). Mientras la edad media de la mujer es 38.9 años, la del cubano es 37.0 años. (Sabemos que las mujeres viven más.) Sabemos asimismo que el 73% de las cubanas en EEUU han nacido en Cuba. (Más del 50% antes de 1959, que son las madres y abuelas de las nacidas en EEUU.)

¿Quiénes eran estas mujeres en Cuba? ¿Qué hacían? Con respecto a la primera ola migratoria, una mirada al último censo de Cuba con anterioridad al triunfo de la Revolución, nos permite hacer algunas especulaciones (Tabla 1). De las 256,440 cubanas que trabajaban en la isla en 1953, la mayor concentración estaba en las 87,780 de trabajadores de servicios, incluyendo 69,974 domésticas. El segundo sector más importante era el de las artesanas, operarias de fábrica, etc. (52,458), seguido por el de las profesionales, técnicas, etc., que alcanzaban 41,578, de la cuales 34,845 eran profesoras y maestras, 533 abogados y jueces, y 1,421 médicos. El cuarto sector era el de las oficinistas (35,645) y el quinto las trabajadoras de prendas de vestir (24,265). El resto trabajaba en una variada gama de ocupaciones.

Table 1. Ocupación de la Población Económicamente Activa de Cuba, de 14 Años y Más, 1953

Ocupación	Ambos Sexos	Varones	Porcentaje	Hembras	Porcentaje
Profesional, técnicos y afines	85,909	44,331	2.6	41,578	16.2
Gerentes, administradores y directores	93,662	88,619	5.2	5,043	2.0
Oficinistas y afines	141,329	105,684	6.2	35,645	14.0
Vendedores y similares	123,240	111,527	6.5	11,713	5.0
Agricultores, pescadores, etc.	807,514	795,715	46.4	11,799	4.6
Trabajadores en minería, canteras y afines	6,168	6,063	0.4	105	0.0
Trabajadores de conducción de medios de transporte	85,897	85,098	5.0	799	0.3
Artesanos, operarios de fábricas y afines	361,494	309,036	18.0	52,458	20.0
Trabajadores manuales y jornaleros, n.e.o.c.	72,609	63,761	3.7	8,848	3.5
Trabajadores de servicios y similares	160,406	72,626	4.2	87,780	34.2
Total	1,972,266	1,715,826	100.0	256,440	100.0

Source: *Informe General de Censos de Población, Viviendas y Electoral,* 1953.

Table 2. Cubanos en la Fuerza Laboral de los Estados Unidos, 1990

	Cubanos en los Estados Unidos				Cubanos nacidos en los Estados Unidos			
	Hombres	%	Mujeres	%	Hombres	%	Mujeres	%
Administradores y profesionales	67,037	22.5	56,121	24.1	11,853	24.2	12,842	27.8
Técnicos, vendedores y trabajadores administrativos	75,219	25.2	105,910	45.5	16,046	32.7	25,739	55.9
Servicios	38,144	12.8	31,826	13.7	6,927	14.1	4,982	10.8
Agricultores, silvicultores y pescadores	5,947	2.0	733	0.3	810	1.6	173	0.3
Artesanos y mecánicos	54,012	18.0	8,294	3.6	6,483	13.2	646	1.4
Operarios y trabajadores manuales	57,882	19.4	29,898	12.8	6,927	14.1	1,675	3.6
Total	298,241	100.0	232,782	100.0	49,046	100.0	46,057	100.0

Source: 1990 Census of Population, Persons of Hispanic Origin in the United States.

Veamos ahora en qué trabajan en 1990 las mujeres cubanas en Estados Unidos (Tabla 2). A simple vista vemos como ha aumentado el porcentaje de mujeres profesionales y administradoras y ha disminuido el de las que trabajan en industrias de servicio, factorías, etc. Esta tendencia se acentúa en las nacidas aquí y alcanza cifras muy similares a las que pueden observarse entre los anglosajones.

Comparemos también sus niveles de educación (Tablas 3 y 4). Fijémonos que en el censo de 1953 sólo un 0.8 % de la población femenina contaba con una educación universitaria, mientras este porcentaje se elevaba a casi el doble (1.5%) en la población masculina. En 1990, el porcentaje de la población femenina de origen cubano en Estados Unidos con títulos de

bachelors, masters, doctorados y con títulos profesionales, asciende a 14.9% (18.2% para los hombres). Con respecto a los nacidos aquí, es 25.7% para las mujeres y 28.1% para los hombres.

¿A qué conclusión llegamos? En primer término, parece obvio que muchas de las cubanas que vinieron en las primeras olas de refugiados ni tenían un nivel de educación tan alto como se presupone ni contaban con una "larga experiencia en el ancho y competitivo campo de la economía liberal." De todas formas, es fácil observar que la polarización entre los niveles de empleo y de educación ha ido disminuyendo, y que la diferencia con los hombres, en ambos aspectos—el de la educación y el del trabajo—se ha acortado, al punto que en algunos renglones, la mujer parece su-

Table 3. **Ultimo Grado o Año Aprobado en la Enseñanza Intermedia y en la Universitaria de la Población de 10 Años y Más, Según Sexo, 1953**

Sexoz	Población de 10 años y más	Grado o Año Aprobado					
		Ninguno	Enseñanza primaria	Bachillerato 1 a 5	Media 1 a 4	Universitaria	
						1 a 4	5 años y más
Ambos sexos	4,376,529	1,109,832	3,038,218	88,562	86,453	31,527	21,937
Varones	2,243,878	619,062	1,502,666	54,121	32,062	18,433	17,534
Porcentaje varones		27.5	67.0	2.4	1.4	0.8	0.7
Hembras	2,132,651	490,770	1,535,552	34,441	54,391	13,094	4,403
Porcentaje hembras		23.0	72.0	1.6	2.5	0.6	0.2

Source: *Informe de Censos de Población, Vividendas y Electoral,* 1953.

Table 4. **Nivel Educacional de los Cubanos en los Estados Unidos, 1990**

Personas de 25 años y más	Cubanos en los Estados Unidos				Cubanos nacidos en los Estados Unidos			
	Hombres	%	Mujeres	%	Hombres	%	Mujeres	%
Menos de 5° grado	27,937	7.5	34,307	8.6	1,016	2.5	1,141	2.8
5° a 8° grado	63,380	17.1	74,762	18.8	1,712	4.2	2,046	5.0
9° a 12° grado, no graduado	66,785	18.0	66,111	16.7	4,840	12.0	4,546	11.1
Graduado de "high school" (incluye aquellos con diploma de equivalencia)	66,313	17.8	80,843	20.4	8,225	20.0	9,151	22.3
Algún estudio universitario, no graduado	57,089	15.4	55,009	13.9	10,176	25.0	9,839	24.0
Associate degree, programa vocacional	9,643	2.6	10,572	2.7	1,473	3.6	1,620	4.0
Associate degree, programa académico	12,550	3.4	16,059	4.0	2,143	5.2	2,352	5.7
Bachelor's degree	36,876	10.0	34,987	8.8	7,263	18.0	6,849	17.0
Master's degree	12,379	3.3	13,555	3.4	2,361	5.8	2,535	6.2
Graduado de escuela profesional	14,294	3.8	6,646	1.7	1,338	3.3	834	2.0
Diploma de doctorado	4,261	1.1	3,871	1.0	411	1.0	185	0.5
Total	371,507	100.0	396,722	100.0	40,958	100.0	41,098	100.0

Source: 1990 Census of Population, Persons of Hispanic Origin in the United States.

perar al hombre (i.e., entre los nacidos aquí, hay más mujeres con *masters*).

Nos preguntamos ahora ¿por qué la mujer cubana salió a la factoría, a las tomateras, a las oficinas y a las aulas a trabajar? ¿Cambió su papel en la familia por esta incorporación al mundo laboral?

En un artículo publicado en 1979, Myra Marx Ferree concluye que, contrario a estudios anteriores que confirman un cambio de actitudes y de comportamiento en las mujeres relacionado con su trabajo en la calle, no hubo un cambio fundamental en el caso del aproximadamente cuarto de millón de cubanas

que llegaron a EEUU en la primera oleada de refugiados. Ferree arguye que los valores predominantes en las clases medias y altas cubanas dictaban que la mujer casada no trabajara, porque hacerlo era una señal de independencia de la autoridad masculina. Había una connotación de respeto y honor relacionada con que un hombre mantuviera a su familia y que la mujer estuviera dedicada a lo que por muchos años aparecía en los registros civiles como "sus labores." No eran pocos los casos, observamos nosotros, de mujeres con educación universitaria que dejaban de ejercer sus carreras al contraer matrimonio, o con la llegada del primer hijo.

¿Cómo pudieron, pues, las primeras exiliadas salir a trabajar sin causar la deshonra de sus maridos ni violentar sus roles tradicionales? Según Ferree, "en las circunstancias económicas en que las familias de inmigrantes se encontraron, el empleo de la mujer podía definirse no sólo como respetable sino como *una obligación a su familia*" (Ferree 1979, 37). No hubo conflicto, pues, entre el trabajo en la calle y el rol tradicional femenino. La mujer amplió así sus responsabilidades y compartió con el esposo el mantenimiento económico de la familia sin que ello provocara una división igualitaria de las labores domésticas ni una merma de la autoridad masculina. Además de su trabajo en la factoría o en la oficina, la amplia gama de obligaciones femeninas incluía la cena de sabor criollo, la ropa limpia doblada en los armarios, ayudar con la tarea a los hijos, llevar al médico a los viejos de la familia, y servirle el cafecito caliente al marido que discutía en la sala con los amigos cómo derrocar a Castro. En fin, que la mujer continuó haciendo lo que, en término acuñado por Isabel Larguía, se considera "el trabajo invisible."

Basándose en un estudio hecho en 1979 con un grupo de 122 mujeres en la zona de New Jersey, Ferree concluye que los roles tradicionales de la mujer no habían cambiado. Nosotros pensamos, sin recurrir en estos momentos a otras fuentes, que en las primeras generaciones, al menos, esas que vinieron ya adultas de Cuba, el rol de la mujer dentro de la casa continuó por varios años siendo muy similar al de la Cuba de 1959, al menos, de la puerta de la calle para dentro. No es posible, sin embargo, evitar la influencia de los tiempos y de la cultura norteamericana. Creemos, por tanto, que las mujeres, aún las mayores, han ampliado sus horizontes culturales y han desarrollado una mayor capacidad de tomar decisiones y de disfrutar la vida, sin necesidad de justificarse sólo como la sombra de un marido "que las representa."

El papel de la mujer, sin embargo, se ha ido modificando aún más en las generaciones posteriores, las que llegaron muy jóvenes a los Estados Unidos, y en las nacidas aquí. Debido a la influencia del medio ambiente norteamericano, y a su propia experiencia, las mujeres de la generación puente, inclusive las que no hayan alterado radicalmente sus conductas, en muchas ocasiones han trasmitido a sus hijas modificaciones de los valores tradicionales que han dado lugar a jóvenes mujeres cubanas más independientes que sus madres y abuelas. (Ejemplos: más libertad sexual, vivir con el novio, disfrutar la vida antes de casarse, no aguantar ciertas cosas al marido, no caer en las mismas trampas que la madre, manejo de su dinero.)

Queda por responder si los cambios en la correlación de niveles de ingresos y de educación entre hombres y mujeres que hemos observado anteriormente, ha influido de forma fundamental las dinámicas de pareja y de familia. A pesar de algunas hipótesis contrarias, nosotros creemos que sí y que ese proceso de cambio merece una mayor investigación de parte de sociólogos, psicólogos, politólogos y de todo investigador preocupado por el estudio de los cubanos fuera de Cuba.

Como muchas de sus antepasadas feministas de la república, que incluyeron en su lucha por los derechos de la mujer, su preocupación por la maternidad y la niñez, las cubanas en Estados Unidos continúan defendiendo sus papeles como madres. Como tales, han mostrado gran pragmatismo. El trabajo, el aprendizaje del inglés, el estudio y la unión familiar han sido los cuatro puntos cardinales de su vida. A ellas, madres y abuelas, les ha correspondido, además de colaborar dólar a dólar para la compra de la casita en Westchester, Hialeah o Union City, o para el pago del colegio de Belén, Lourdes, o Conchita Espinosa para los hijos, o para las compras semanales en Publix o en Varadero Supermarket, ayudar con los deberes escolares, ahorrar para traer los parientes de Cuba (o en muchos casos, como se vio durante el Mariel, ir físicamente en su busca) o para enviar medicinas y espejuelos a la isla, enfrentarse a los papeles de Medicaid, Medicare, HRS y otras agencias gubernamentales en busca de los mejores beneficios para los viejitos de la familia. En fin, esta "super" cubana ha seguido cumpliendo con el "canon de la mujer ángel" cuya obligación es cuidar de todos en el hogar (padres, suegros, marido, hijos, perros, gatos y matas) mientras trabaja en la calle más que su sus compañeras hispanas o norteamericanas. Además, naturalmente, de trasmitir valores culturales a hijos y nietos. Si se preocupó que los primeros aprendieran el inglés y fueran a "college," hoy se desvela porque los últimos conozcan el cuento de la Cucarachita Martina o el poema martiano de "Los zapaticos de rosa" y aprendan el español. En otras palabras, la cubana ha sabido integrar en su vida cotidiana lo tradicional y lo moderno, términos tantas veces antagónicos en las culturales patriarcales. (Virtud importante para el futuro de Cuba.)

Hay que destacar, por igual, que hay un gran porciento de mujeres cubanas divorciadas y que está por hacerse un estudio profundo de las causas de estos divorcios. Me atrevería a esgrimir la hipótesis de que mostrará una relación directa entre la modificación del rol femenino tradicional y la tasa de divorcio.

Hemos, hasta ahora, centrado nuestras observaciones en las mujeres anónimas, esas calladas heroínas del destierro cuyos nombres no recogerá jamás nuestra historia. El tiempo no nos permite en esta ponencia hacer mención, siquiera de forma incompleta, de las muchas mujeres que, a pesar de que vivimos en un mundo dominado aún por los hombres, han alcanzado logros y reconocimientos sin precedentes en casi todas las esferas de la cultura, la educación, la política, y el mundo de los negocios.

Y he dicho "casi" porque hay mundos aún vedados a la mujer. Al igual que las norteamericanas, las cubanas se tropiezan con un "techo" (glass ceiling) en el mundo empresarial que les es imposible romper. A no ser en sus negocios propios, muy pocas mujeres llegan a altas posiciones ejecutivas. Más difícil aún ha sido penetrar ciertas estructuras patriarcales cubanas. Las cubanas no están representadas en las juntas directivas de las asociaciones cívicas y políticas del la diáspora, aunque, naturalmente, haya excepciones que confirmen la regla. Basta mirar los diarios. Verán las fotos de mujeres en asociaciones de caridad (el canon del ángel se traslada de los espacios privados a los públicos) y las de los de hombres en las actividades empresariales o políticas. La presencia femenina entre los "dirigentes del exilio," con excepción de en el área de la lucha por los derechos humanos, ha sido y es nula.

Es importante señalar que en el último lustro se ha visto una creciente presencia de organizaciones femeninas que se han sumado al pionero Cuban Women's Club, formado originalmente por muchas liceistas, y cuya labor refleja en gran medida el estilo de las damas cubanas republicanas, y a la Coalición de Mujeres Hispanoamericanas (CHAW), más joven en creación y membresía, cuyos propósitos muestran una mayor aculturación a los Estados Unidos (i.e., sus objetivos subyacentes, "networking" y "empowering other women," son términos difíciles de traducir porque conllevan conceptos culturales de los Estados Unidos actuales).

También en los últimos años se han llevado a cabo varias conferencias importantes sobre la mujer, entre las que destaco *Espejos de la Mujer Cubana* en FIU en 1994 y *Pensando a Cuba en Femenino,* del Instituto de Estudios Cubanos, en 1995. Se han publicado asímismo varios libros que interpretan la problemática nacional desde perspectivas femeninas, como *Cuba sin caudillo* de Ileana Fuentes, que han resultado, además, éxitos de librería. En el mundo literario, las novelistas de más éxito en el momento actual, tanto en español como en inglés, son Zoe Valdés y Cristina García, cuyas narrativas reflejan el punto de vista femenino. En el ámbito académico norteamericano, las investigadoras de origen cubano han intensificado en años recientes los estudios de género, como lo muestra ampliamente éste y otros paneles similares en otras conferencias, como la de LASA que tuvo lugar recientemente en Guadalajara.

Me atrevería a decir que se gesta entre las cubanas en Estados Unidos un renacer del feminismo cubano que jugó tan importante papel en Cuba en la primera tercera parte de este siglo. Este feminismo incluye, como entonces, una defensa de la maternidad, de la familia, de los hijos, de los derechos de la mujer e intenta, por todos los medios, no confrontar, sino, para usar términos eróticomasculinos, *penetrar* las estructuras patriarcales. Más importante aún, formula una visión integradora de lo que debe ser la sociedad y de Cuba, como nación.

¿Podrá de forma alguna incidir este "pensar a Cuba en femenino" en el futuro de la isla o se sentirán los efectos de este movimiento solamente en las cubano-americanas que acabarán por borrar de su identificación el gentilicio primero, antes del "hyphen" o raya? Es una pregunta aún por contestar.

Una rápida referencia a las encuestas hechas durante los últimos años en FIU sobre las actitudes de los cubanos muestran, sistemáticamente, que menos mujeres que hombres quieren regresar a Cuba. Al mismo tiempo, las mujeres, más que los hombres, defienden la posibilidad de enviar medicinas, comida, de viajar libremente a y desde Cuba. Es decir, lo que muchos consideran una línea de apertura.

No cuestiono en momento alguno que el amor de las cubanas por la Patria sea menor (o mayor) que el de los hombres. Ni acepto que en la mujer prime el sentimentalismo por encima de los principios y las ideas. Pero para ellas los conceptos de Patria y familia van muy ligados. Al echar raíces en EEUU, el regreso a la Isla se les hace más difícil. Su preocupación por la familia, sin embargo, no se limita a esta orilla. Los viejecitos que han quedado atrás, los sobrinos que nunca se han conocido, el primo que escribe tras años de silencio, reclaman que las cubanas envíen paquetes o regresen de visita al pueblo cargadas de nostalgias, abrazos y regalos, cosa que con frecuencia su pareja acepta pero que no comparte por "cuestión de honor."

Quizás la mejor manera de entender la visión femenina de la Patria es a través de la literatura que la mujer nos ha dado, durante estas largas décadas de diáspora. Para ella, Cuba no es una abstracción sino una suma de elementos muy concretos, que pueden resumirse en el espacio privado de su casa, su patio, su pueblo. Ante el recrudecimiento del discurso homocéntrico dominante tanto en la isla como el exilio en las últimas décadas, la escritura femenina plantea un tenaz cuestionamiento de conceptos tradicionales y replanteamientos de la realidad social e individual, todo lo cual, naturalmente, sería tema de otro panel.

En momentos en que la definición de la identidad nacional ocupa gran parte del discurso político cubano, en la isla y en la diáspora, no es inútil insistir en la importancia de los estudios de género que reinterpreten nuestra historia, analicen el papel de la mujer en nuestra compleja realidad actual dentro y fuera de Cuba, y formulen una visión de futuro donde el yo femenino no sólo tenga su voz propia, sino forme parte esencial de un proyecto nacional de cara a la próxima centuria.

REFERENCES

Alvarez, Mercedes, Fernando González and Oscar Rodríguez. "La participación de la mujer en la fuerza de trabajo en Cuba: 1899-1970," *Revista de Administración de Salud* 5:4 (oct.-dic. 1979).

Boswell, Thomas D. *A Demographic Profile of Cuban Americans.* Miami: Cuban American National Council, Inc., 1994.

Informe General de Censos de Población, Viviendas y Electoral. La Habana: Oficina de los Censos Demográficos y Electoral, 1953.

Cruzada Educativa Cubana. *Premio "Juan J. Remos" (Mini-biografías de los que recibieron el preciado galardón de 1971 a 1983).* Nueva York: Senda Nueva Ediciones, 1984.

Employment and Earnings. Bureau of Labor Statistics, U.S. Department of Labor (1996).

Ferree, Myra Marx. "Employment without Liberation: Cuban Women in the United States," *Social Science Quarterly* 60:1 (June 1979).

González Pando, Miguel, ed. *Greater Miami: Spirit of Cuban Enterprise.* Fort Lauderdale, Fl.: Copperfield Publications, Inc., 1996.

Marrero, Leví. *Raíces del milagro cubano.* Guaynabo, Puerto Rico: Ediciones Capiro, 1984.

Martínez Guayanes, María A. "La situación de la mujer en Cuba en 1953," *Santiago* (Junio-Sept. 1974).

Pérez, Lisandro. "The Cuban Population of the United States: The Results of the 1980 U.S. Census of Population, *Cuban Studies* 15:2 (Summer 1985).

Pérez, Lisandro. "Cubans in the United States," *The Annals of the American Academy of Political and Social Science*, no. 487 (September 1986a).

Pérez, Lisandro. "Immigrant Economic Adjustment and Family Organization: The Cuban Success Story Reexamined," *International Migration Review* 20 (Spring 1986b).

Pérez, Lisandro. "Cuban Women in the U.S. Labor Force: A Comment," *Cuban Studies* 18 (1988).

Pérez-Stable, Marifeli. "Cuban Women and the Struggle for 'Conciencia,'" *Cuban Studies* 17 (1987).

Persons of Hispanic Origin in the United States. 1990 Census of Population, CP-3-3 (1990).

Prieto, Yolanda. "Cuban Women in the U.S. Labor Force: Perspectives of the Nature of Change," *Cuban Studies* 17 (1987).

Statistical Abstract of the United States, 1995. U.S. Department of Commerce, Bureau of the Census (1995).

PROSPECTS FOR CUBA'S ENTREPRENEURS AFTER TRANSITION: A COMPARATIVE ANALYSIS

Ricardo Tejada

The engendering of the spirit of entrepreneurship in a population is one of the most essential prerequisites for successful transition. The limited reappearance of self-employment in the Cuban economy has brought the question of the future of Cuban entrepreneurship under a new light. Almost immediately after economic reforms legalizing some forms of self-employment were passed, thousands of Cuban entrepreneurs, many from the informal sector, began official private economic activity. These entrepreneurs seemed to offer hope to those who believed that over three decades of almost uninterrupted repression of the private sector had all but killed Cuba's spirit of entrepreneurship.

But how useful will Cuba's diminutive new entrepreneurial class be to the economy in the long run and what are its odds of continued success in a transition economy? Some authors (e.g., Pérez-López 1995, p. 172) have argued that small pockets of private activity in centrally planned economies serve as "breeding grounds" for future entrepreneurs who will create the backbone of a modern economy. Others (e.g., Perry, Steagall and Woods 1995, pp. 98-99; Locay and Sanguinetty 1996, p. 320) are less optimistic and believe that lack of managerial and entrepreneurial skills will contribute to a very slow start for small business in Cuba. The question is impossible to answer with any degree of certainty, but it is possible to draw parallels with previous experiences in economies that have undergone processes of transition.

Cuba's reforms are not without historic precedent in a centrally planned economy. Similar attempts to

boost economies suffering from the inefficiencies of central planning have been implemented in a number of socialist countries. This paper will draw from the transition experiences of the Visegrad countries—the Czech and Slovak Republics, Hungary, and Poland—and examine their pre-transition experiments with the private sector. The paper will begin by looking at the different roles played by the private sector up to the point of economic liberalization. It will then analyze the development of small business relative to each country's starting conditions at the time of transition.

Data on the number of self-employed, owner-operated businesses, and registered entrepreneurs will be examined in order to assess the emergence of the "small" private sector, that is, the private sector composed of emerging small businesses rather than privatized companies formerly belonging to the state and maintaining a large number of their employees. Statistics on business registrations and the like are notoriously poor and often misleading. This is so because entrepreneurs often register without ever beginning economic activity or register two or more business "just in case." Also, business failures often fail to make it on the register. For these reasons, the statistics presented here should be considered a proxy for entrepreneurial activity and interpreted with care.

Despite the importance of the informal sector in the Visegrad countries as well as in Cuba, the paper will focus on the formal economy as a source of private entrepreneurship. The reasons for this are twofold. First, data for the informal sector are extremely unreliable and make analysis of this type guesswork at best. Second, the nature of the informal sector sets it apart from the legal private sector. Because informal entrepreneurship is, by definition, illegal (whether tolerated or not), the focus of those activities tends to be on short-run profits. There can be little room for concern for longer term investments and growth in such a volatile business sector. This said, many informal sector entrepreneurs in the Visegrad countries moved into the formal sector during the initial phases of transition. Also a great number moved from the legal private sector into the informal sector in order to avoid fees and taxes charged to registered entrepreneurs. These are further reasons to interpret the statistics put forth in this paper as indicators of the magnitude of entrepreneurial activity rather than point estimates.

SELF-EMPLOYMENT IN CUBA

On September 8, 1993, the Council of State approved Law-Decree No. 141. This was followed by regulations issued jointly by the State Committee for Labor and Social Security (CETSS) and the State Finance Committee (CEF). Together, these two documents acknowledged the importance of self-employment to the national economy and set out a list of 117 occupations, many previously performed by the informal sector, in which such activities could legally take place. Fees would be charged according to the type of occupation which included mechanics, hairdressers, taxi drivers, blacksmiths, and plumbers (EIU 1993, p. 13). However, these laws did not allow for hired labor and, more importantly, prohibited anyone with a university degree, especially physicians, teachers and researchers, and managers of state enterprises from taking up private activity. The decree and regulations further limited participation to those who were currently employed in a state work center, were retired or disabled, had been dismissed from the state sector or had been certified redundant by their employers, had suffered reduced hours as a result of the special period, or were homemakers (Pérez-López 1995, pp. 163-165).

A number of other market-oriented reforms took place in the period 1993-94. For example, also in 1993, the Cuban government legalized dollar holdings and transactions and announced the transformation of collectivized state farms into producer cooperatives. In the following year, farmers' markets were once again allowed to operate as were markets for handicrafts and surplus manufactured consumer goods. Reforms led to an surge in the number of small private restaurants or *paladares* and a large increase in the number of self-employed workers (Font 1997, p. 125).

The estimates for the total number of self-employed workers vary but they seem to have increased from about 70,000 at the end of 1993 to 150,000 a year later. By the end of 1995 approximately 208,000 workers held permits for self-employment. This would make one in every 20 members of Cuba's labor force a self-employed worker (Jatar-Hausmann 1996, p. 213). Most estimates of the informal sector put about the same number in similar but unlicensed activities.

More recently, the government has continued to increase the number of occupations authorized for self-employment but also increased the fees charged for such activities. This, together with bureaucratic barriers to entry, has caused a leveling off and even a reduction in the number of self-employed workers. By June 1996 the number of self-employed workers had fallen to 200,000. However, university graduates are no longer excluded from self-employment, a change brought about by pressure from traditional elites previously left out of the new opportunities in the private sector (Jatar-Hausmann 1996, p. 214).

Cuba's experimentation with a self-employed private sector is not without precedent in a centrally planned economy. Most of the Central and Eastern European economies which practiced central planning resorted to such measures in times of economic difficulty. In fact, Hungary and Poland began implementing reforms of this nature well before the historic transition of the late 1980s and early 1990s. The incentives for such reforms were not unlike those in Cuba in the 1990s: a desire to provide a boost to an ailing economy while hoping to preserve the socialist political order.

SELF-EMPLOYMENT IN THE VISEGRAD COUNTRIES PRIOR TO TRANSITION

The four Central European countries examined here had very different laws and regulations governing the private sector and private entrepreneurs prior to embracing market reforms. Each allowed private economic activities to some degree, but the restrictions placed on these entrepreneurial activities differed greatly. So did the number of years' experience that each country had in experimenting with the private sector. These differences meant that the starting conditions for the private sector at the time of transition were quite different.

As mentioned earlier, statistical coverage of private-sector activities was extremely poor in communist countries. Therefore, for years prior to 1989, it is difficult to assess the size and importance of this sector to the central European countries examined in this paper. This section attempts to provide a brief assessment of the extent to which private economic activities existed alongside the centrally-planned economies.

Czechoslovakia

Of the countries examined here, Czechoslovakia had the tightest control on private-sector activities. Private entrepreneurs were excluded from most sectors of the economy. In fact, virtually no private-sector reform took place after the Prague Spring invasion of Soviet and Warsaw Pact troops in 1968. In 1980, 99.8 percent of the workforce was employed in the socialist sector (Gawdiak 1988, p. 135). This meant that by 1989, the contribution of private firms to Czech GDP was very small, estimates ranging from less than 0.5 percent to 4 percent (OECD 1996, p. 18 and Borish and Noël 1996, p. 88). The same was true, of course, for the Slovak Republic. Prior to the Velvet Revolution in 1990, State Owned Enterprises dominated the enterprise sector. Prices, trade, and investment were controlled and private property had virtually no protection. This meant that, unlike Hungary and Poland which had relatively open private sectors, Czechoslovakia had virtually no experi-

ence experimenting with economic reform prior to economic liberalization.

As what later became the Czech Republic moved into the initial phases of economic and political transition, only about 8,000 sole proprietors existed. Because this was the extent of private-sector activity at the time, the number of commercially active persons in the Czech Republic could also be estimated at about 8,000.[1] However, the flowering of the private sector immediately following the shift to a market economy was quite remarkable. In the first year of transition, the private-sector contribution to GDP increased more than twofold. By 1994 the private sector was responsible for 56 percent of GDP and 65 percent of employment (see Table 1). Much of this increase in private-sector employment was generated by owner-operated and small-scale light manufacturing and service sector businesses. The number of sole proprietors in the Czech Republic jumped to about 925,000 in 1994 (excluding corporate bodies), a 115-fold increase in only five years (OECD 1996, p. 29). Much of this growth has come from the service sector which today accounts for 54 percent of the country's total output, up from 36 percent in 1990. Rough estimates now attribute 57 percent of industry, 90 percent of construction, and over half of transport to the private sector (Borish and Noël 1996, pp. 88-89).

Table 1. Private Sector Trends in the Visegrad Countries (Percent)

	1989	1990	1991	1992	1993	1994
Czech Republic						
GDP	4	11.5	16	25	44	56
Employment	16	20	30	40	59	65
Hungary						
GDP	20	20	30	50	55	60
Employment						
Poland						
GDP	28	31	42	47	52	58
Employment	47	49	54	57	59	61
Slovak Republic						
GDP			27	32	39	58
Employment			16	25	43	55

Source: Borish and Noël (1996, pp. 88, 94, 100, 111).

---

1. Although always low, estimates for employment in the private sector in the Czech Republic differ widely by source.

These trends suggest that the small-scale owner-operated private sector has been growing while large-scale state owned enterprises in the industrial sector have been declining as indicated by an increasingly smaller contribution to GDP. However, it must be noted that the split with the Slovak Republic helped the Czech Republic release many of the uncompetitive, heavy industrial enterprises of the former Czechoslovakia. Also, the Czech and Slovak Republics benefited from a relatively large industrial base, proximity to the industrial market economies of Central and Western Europe, and an early emphasis on rapid privatization.

The Slovak Republic has also experienced important growth in the private sector. Despite a significant slowdown in the rate of privatization following the initial efforts carried out while still a part of Czechoslovakia, the private sector's share of GDP grew to 58 percent in 1994 from 27 percent in 1991 (the first year for which data is available). Employment in the private sector in 1994 represented 55 percent of total employment, up from 16 percent in 1991 (see Table 1).

The growth in the number of Slovak sole proprietors has also been impressive. The number of private (small) companies grew from about 2,000 in 1989 to around 280,000 by the end of 1994. However, the number of small companies in operation per 100 inhabitants is significantly lower in the Slovak Republic than in the Czech Republic, 5.3 v. 9, respectively.

Hungary

In contrast to Czechoslovakia, Hungary had a well developed system of private self employment before 1989. In fact, Hungary had a longer history of experimenting with private-sector and market-based reforms than did other centrally-planned economies.

After a ban on private sector activity that lasted almost two decades, reforms in 1968 reactivated private sector economic activity. From the outset, these reforms resembled those which became predominant during the Soviet *perestroika* and went beyond those which have been adopted by the Cuban government. Among other reforms, farmers were allowed and en-couraged to sell produce directly to consumers rather than to the state sector.

In 1982, further reforms allowed the creation of numerous private and quasi-private firms. Self employment was legalized and limited partnerships were allowed providing that a number of legal and professional requirements were met. Table 2 shows the growth in private-sector employment in Hungary in the mid-1980s. While the bulk of private-sector reform in most CPEs translated into small family undertakings in the agricultural sector, significant increases in private activity were experienced in other sectors of the economy as well. The majority of activities in these sectors included repair and maintenance, passenger and goods transportation, building construction, retail trading, catering, and other services.

Table 2. Hungary: Active Earners by Sector of the Economy (Percent)

	State	Cooperative	Private
1980	71.1	25.5	3.4
1985	70.0	25.3	4.7
1986	70.5	24.4	5.1
1987	70.8	23.8	5.4
1988	70.4	23.5	6.1

Source: *Hungarian Statistical Yearbook 1989.*

In December 1989 the number of officially registered sole proprietors in Hungary was about 320,000. Hungary's flirtation with the private sector during the 1980s had increased its private-sector contribution to GDP to 20 percent in 1989-90. By the end of 1994 there were approximately 775,000 registered sole proprietors, an increase of about 140 percent over four years. Also by the end of 1994 nearly three-quarters of GDP was generated in sectors increasingly associated with the private sector—namely "non-material" services sectors (e.g., financial, legal, tourism, consulting services), industry, and trade. By the end of 1994, the private sector's contribution to GDP had grown to 60 percent.

The relatively slower rate of increase in the private sector relative to Czechoslovakia could be attributed to two factors: a more advanced starting point (a considerable number of private firms already existed in Hungary during the 1980s) and a more gradualist approach in the rate of privatization. However, Hungary's private sector as a share of the economy had reached a higher level than Czechoslovakia and, as will be examined later, Poland.

Regardless, the growth in private activities in Hungary can not be ignored. The number of registered firms increased by over 300 percent between 1990 and 1993 while the number of self-employed jumped from 427,500 to 801,700 in the same period. These trends depict a growth of over 400,000 new private firms since 1990 in a country with a population of only 10.3 million (Borish and Noël 1996, pp. 94-95). The vast majority of these firms are very small (under 20 employees), in the service sectors (such firms were responsible for 14.5 percent of industrial output in 1993), and are estimated to have contributed the most to the growth in GDP.

Poland

Although the role of private sector activities in the economy was at times quite small, Poland's communist regime never completely abolished them.[2] While the government loosened and tightened its restrictions on the private sector according to the political climate, the existence of the private sector was always legally guaranteed. Private entrepreneurs and small workshops were allowed to operate under the condition that their goods and services were sold to the state sector.

In the beginning of the 1980s, the Crafts Code was further liberalized and, in 1983, the pre-War Commercial Code of 1934 was reintroduced. This code, while amended to maintain many of the privileges of the state economy, provided a legal framework for corporate private business (Rostowski 1993, p. 3). Between 1981 and 1988, the number of small private firms operating in Poland doubled; by the latter year the private sector represented over 22 percent of total GNP (OECD 1996, p. 41). With the liberalization of the restrictions placed on private business, private economic activity began to satisfy many of the needs

that the Polish state sector was unable to fulfill. It has been estimated that by the late 1980s, privately generated incomes accounted for 35 to 45 percent of all incomes in Poland (Rostowski 1988).

The Polish post-transition experience in stimulating the private sector through self-employment, while impressive, does not seem to match the successes attained by the Czech Republic and Hungary. However, the economy has made long strides since full economic liberalization. One of the most important steps toward creating a competitive private sector in Poland was actually taken before the date associated with full economic and political transition. On January 1, 1989 the "Law on Economic Activity" came into force. This law effectively erased all restrictions on, and regulations of, private economic activity. The idea behind this law was to benefit from the gains of unrestricted private entrepreneurship and simultaneously do away with the fundamental ownership and management problems associated with the state sector. Private activity was expected to develop quickly thus eradicating the chronic shortages of goods and services in the economy. The resulting economic development would in turn ensure political stabilization and ensure the maintenance of communist power (Rostowski 1993, p. 3).

The failure of the communist government's last attempts at reforms may be attributed to the government's oversight in addressing profound macroeconomic problems generated by the state sector and the fact that a large portion of private sector activity continued to rely on arbitrage between controlled state prices and the free prices which the private sector was now free to charge (Rostowski 1993, p. 4). Nevertheless, the private sector's importance in the Polish economy increased significantly. By the time that full transition began, the Polish private sector had a strong head start.

According to official statistics the private sector in Poland accounted for 28 percent of GDP in 1989. This is a larger share than in any of the countries ex-

---

2. In fact, Poland was the only Eastern European centrally planned economy that never imposed the collectivization of agriculture but instead tolerated the existence of private property in rural sectors.

amined in this paper. Nearly half of the nation's employment was in the private sector. While agriculture played an important role in the Polish private sector prior to transition, there were an estimated 960,000 registered sole proprietors and 650,000 self-employed workers in the non-agricultural sectors of the economy in 1989.

Between 1989 and 1994 private sector share of GDP in Poland's economy increased to 58 percent and private sector employment to 61 percent (see Table 1). Private sector output increased almost 400 percent in U.S. dollar terms, from $16.4 billion in 1989 to $53.0 billion in 1994. The bulk of this growth has come from new private companies. In 1994, Poland had the highest number of owner-operated business in the Visegrad region (Borish and Noël 1996, pp. 100-101).

Output of the Polish private sector increased significantly in the years immediately following transition. Most of this output produced was in trade and industry. However, trends show strong private sector growth in services and a continued dominance in agriculture (Borish and Noël 1996, p. 101).

LESSONS FOR CUBA

Although the situation in Cuba today does not mirror the experience of any one Visegrad country prior to transition, there are a number of similarities which recall the Cuban experimentation with economic reform. Therefore, a number of parallels may be drawn. Were it not for the economic pressures placed on the island's economy following the ebb of Soviet support, the Cuban economy would most likely resemble that of Czechoslovakia prior to transition. Indeed, the tight controls placed on private entrepreneurs in Cuba, together with the government's constant tendency to restrict private economic activities, demonstrate a reluctance to reform not unlike that which was evident in Czechoslovakia.

However, many of the activities which have been legalized in the wake of the recent economic crisis and which are described in the previous section resemble those which appeared in Hungary and Poland prior to 1989. Like Hungary, Cuba has allowed self-employment in a number of service occupations. These

reforms have been instituted with the goal of relieving increasing pressures for labor shedding while helping to satisfy a demand for services which can not be met by the state sector. The reintroduction of farmers' markets also echoes the first reforms implemented in both Hungary and Poland.

Because restrictions are much greater in Cuba today, the growth of private entrepreneurial activity has not been as marked as that which occurred in these countries in the 1980s. Therefore, the entrepreneurial sector's contribution to national income, while unknown, is certainly only a fraction of that which characterized the Hungarian and Polish economies. Nevertheless, a legal private sector composed of profit-oriented entrepreneurs has been created and their contribution to small business know-how and the possible gains to the Cuban economic culture can not be ignored. But how important is previous experience with limited private entrepreneurship to entrepreneurs in a post-transition environment? Did experimentation with self-employment and a tolerance for entrepreneurship poise Hungary and Poland for a smoother transition than the more restrictive Czechoslovakia? This section will attempt to answer this question, at least in part, by examining the post-transition experiences of the Visegrad countries.

Despite an impressive record of private-sector and small-business growth, Poland and the Slovak Republic have arguably demonstrated the least spectacular results of the Visegrad countries. The Polish case is particularly interesting because the country had been experimenting with private sector reforms for some time prior to transition. While the importance of the private sector more than doubled in the first five years of transition, the strides do not seem to match those made by the Czech economy.

Why was the Czech Republic, and to a lesser extent the Slovak Republic, able to accommodate such a large growth in private entrepreneurship immediately after economic liberalization despite the almost complete absence of a private sector for over two decades? Does this suggest that situational factors outweigh attitudinal factors when it comes to the development of entrepreneurship?

Entrepreneurial talent forms the backbone of a successful market economy. Unlike the state and cooperative sectors prevalent in centrally-planned economies, the private sector can not be created. Instead it is the product of entrepreneurial talent and the economic culture that characterizes it. For the most part, such an economic culture was suppressed in the Visegrad countries as it is in Cuba today. Nonetheless, in Cuba, as in Hungary and Poland, small windows have been opened which have allowed entrepreneurs, in however limited a fashion, to enter the system and profit from their market activities. In every country where this has been the case, there has been an eager population of entrepreneurs whose activities have been limited by legal and physical (e.g., capital, inputs, etc.) constraints rather than talent.

There has always been a fear, with regard to centrally planned economies (CPEs), that decades of central administration and planning have changed the mentality of the population and erased the culture of entrepreneurship by reshaping its values, work ethic, and expectations. There is, however, no empirical evidence to suggest that the suppression of a market system and the controls placed on private-sector activities can achieve this. In fact, related empirical studies demonstrate the opposite, that is, that situational factors rather than attitudinal ones contribute principally to differences in economic behavior between residents of market economies and those of the former socialist economies (e.g., Shiller, Boyco and Korobov 1992, p. 127; Leff 1979, p. 46).

A recent paper on Cuba by Luis Locay and Jorge Sanguinetty (1996) supports this conclusion. The authors used data from the U.S. Current Population Survey to analyze the propensity for entrepreneurship observed in Cuban immigrants of various ages and who had lived under the two forms of government (Cuban central planning and the U.S. market economy) for varying portions of their lifetimes. These propensities for entrepreneurship were also compared to the overall U.S.-born labor force. The goal of the study was to assess the effects that years of socialism had had on the entrepreneurial skills of the Cuban population. The results generally indicated that the effects were minimal. While important biases, explained in the paper, can not be ignored and make it essential to interpret the results with care, there is no compelling reason to believe that Cuban entrepreneurs will find themselves at a particularly great disadvantage as a result of living under central planning.

These studies, when considered in combination with the experience of the Czech and Slovak Republics, seem to suggest that there are other factors which are responsible for the development of entrepreneurial skills and spirit. The private sector in the Czech Republic, and to a lesser extent in the Slovak Republic, quickly caught up to Hungary and Poland. It is as if the entrepreneurial spirit in these countries emerged from nowhere. This is especially evident when one considers the near absence of a private sector in Czechoslovakia at the outset of transition. This is perhaps because the most important incentives for entrepreneurship do not diminish the hope of a higher income and the desire for greater autonomy. The barriers which remain then are bureaucratic and, if they are dismantled or lowered substantially, the private sector in essence creates itself (Kornai 1992, pp. 433-434).

The existence of a private sector in a CPE, then, is not a prerequisite to the successful development of an entrepreneurial society and the growth of small business after transition. However, this should not be interpreted to mean that the presence of a private sector is not a boon to transition. Hungary's post-transition economy has benefited greatly from the private sector it inherited. For example, four years into transition, Hungary had the highest ratio of self-employed to economically active persons (outside agriculture), a sort of self-employment rate. Almost 15 percent of the active population was self-employed. The corresponding values for the other Visegrad countries (also outside agriculture) were: 9.8 percent in the Czech Republic, 9.6 percent in Poland, and 5.7 percent in the Slovak Republic (OECD 1996, p. 32).

Also, the greatest growth in small joint stock companies and partnerships has been in Hungary at about 10 per 10,000 inhabitants at the end of 1994. The Czech Republic has the second highest rate with about 7 per 10,000 inhabitants, followed by the Slovak Republic with around 4, and Poland with about 2.5.

For Hungary, these figures reflect the reform policies which began in the early 1980s and allowed the creation of several new forms of enterprises previously unknown in centrally planned economies. This experience consequently provided Hungary with a significant advantage in the transformation process to a market economy. Hungary has remained a clear leader in reform among the Visegrad countries, although the Czech Republic has pushed forward remarkably fast as well.

What does this mean for Cuba? While the suppression of entrepreneurship and the stifling of the Cuban private sector should not be a source of excessive worry to those concerned with the rooting and growth of small business after transition, the private sector which has recently emerged as a result of this latest wave of reforms will undoubtedly play a beneficial role in that transition. Provided, of course, that the Cuban private sector is indeed "here to stay." It is impossible to predict the future of the thousands of new entrepreneurs presently operating in Cuba today. Those who have pioneered private activities on the island undoubtedly possess a level of entrepreneurial spirit which will be of utmost importance in an economic transition. But the sweeping changes characteristic of a transition economy will shape and reshape the private sector in a Shumpeterian process of "creative destruction."

FURTHER LESSONS FROM THE VISEGRAD EXPERIENCE

If Czechoslovakia did not benefit from private sector reforms before 1989, what other policies or characteristics of the economy are responsible for the success of its entrepreneurial sector and what lessons might there be for Cuba? The reasons behind the success of the Czech and Slovak Republics are too numerous and complicated to be listed here. However, several deserve mention to place the success in context. The Czech and Slovak Republics have enjoyed a more stable macroeconomic environment than have Hungary and Poland: inflation rates have slowed, exchange rates have remained relatively sta-

ble and fiscal deficits have been kept in check. Also, geography and size play an important role as did a speedy move to privatize state industries. As mentioned earlier, the Czech Republic also benefited from the split with Slovakia in that it ridded itself of a great deal of its inefficient and unproductive industries.

But other reasons for the success of the two Republics, as well as for the other Visegrad countries, need to be examined. In doing so it is possible to draw important lessons for the success of small business in a transition economy.

Privatization and restitution can play a critical role in opening opportunities for small business. Privatization and the creation of new firms were closely linked in all Visegrad countries. For example, many entrepreneurs in the Czech and Slovak Republics utilized property and assets returned as part of restitution to set up new businesses. Also in the Czech and Slovak Republics, managers from state firms took advantage of the system of coupon privatization to set up their own firms. They then used the connections and sales and buying links from their former employers for their new enterprises. Hungary's diversified enterprise structure owes a great deal to privatization. The creation of new firms in the manufacturing, construction, and retail sectors has been most dynamic in the countries where privatization has made the greatest progress (OECD 1996, pp. 27-28).

An unambiguous set of property rights are a further requisite to an economic environment that encourages entrepreneurship. Legal reforms that establish clear and precise laws protecting private property, transfer of ownership, and restitution are vital. Tenancy laws that do not pose unnecessary restrictions on property owners, distort rental markets, or make repossession of mortgaged property difficult are also important.

A more difficult problem to overcome is a lack of available capital. In the Visegrad countries, this is the most often cited problem in the start-up of new businesses (OECD 1996, p. 47). This is a more difficult problem to solve as it is rooted in the role of the banking system. In Cuba, the problem may be slightly mitigated by a flow of capital from the United

States, both from the Cuban-American community and from investors in general. However, reform of the banking system, an acute and general problem in all transition countries, is of utmost importance to the private sector.

The list of problems and challenges is long. Business registration practices, commercial codes and contract enforcement laws, corporate structure and governance, are all issues which, unaddressed, present potential barriers to start-up business and entrepreneurs. Many of these barriers will indeed depend on a history of experience with a private sector. Here, a protracted and expanded private sector reform in Cuba could prove beneficial to post-transition entrepreneurs.

A final important component in the successful development of a small business community is cooperation between small enterprises in defending the sector as a whole. This cooperation usually takes the shape of small business membership organizations such Chambers of Commerce and Industry, business associations, and federations. Small enterprises are faced with numerous disadvantages such as decreased access to capital and information and diseconomies of scale in R&D and marketing. Business associations help to alleviate such problems through advisory services, promotional alliances and the like. In transition economies these organizations take on additional challenges brought about by the lack of developed regulatory and institutional environments.

The lesson to be drawn from the emergence of the entrepreneurial small business sector in the Visegrad countries is straightforward. While entrepreneurial tendencies can be suppressed over time as they have been in Cuba for over 35 years, the small businessman's spirit is difficult to kill. Despite a virtual ban

on all private sector activities, entrepreneurs in the Czech and Slovak Republics have fared well in the years immediately following the transition. The entrepreneurial sector developed almost overnight. The private sector in the Czech Republic has grown particularly fast and has now caught up and even passed its Visegrad counterparts. Many of the policies developed in these countries in the early stages of transition may be responsible for these successes and may hold the key for Cuba when it begins to move toward economic liberalization. These policies include rapid privatization, clear investment and property laws, as well as civil codes and governance.

Although this paper argues that the future for Cuba's entrepreneurs is not so bleak, there are numerous obstacles which will present great challenges to small business. It is true that a lack of experience and managerial skills will probably raise the volatility of initial start-ups and increase the failure rate of entrepreneurs, but this is part of a learning process that all former CPEs have been forced to endure. Perhaps here, Cuba will benefit from its years of experimentation with small private businesses. Shortage of capital could also strangle private sector growth. For this Cuba will need to rely on transparent investment laws, a speedy reform of the financial sector, and foreign investment, particularly from the Cuban-American community in the United States.

It would be foolhardy to expect a Cuban transition to mirror that of any of the former CPEs. However, given the limited tools for analysis available to those wishing to study the Cuban economy in a post-central planning environment, the experience of the Visegrad countries provides a useful point of comparison. It is, after all, the closest to the Cuban experience in the world today.

BIBLIOGRAPHY

Borish, Michael S. and Michel Noël. *Private Sector Development During Transition: The Visegrad* *Countries*. World Bank Discussion Paper No. 318. Washington: The World Bank, 1996.

Burant, Stephen R. ed. *Hungary: A Country Study*. Washington: Federal Research Division, Library of Congress, 1989.

Curtis, Glenn E. ed. *Poland: A Country Study*. Washington: Federal Research Division, Library of Congress, 1992.

Economist Intelligence Unit (EIU). *Country Report: Cuba* (Fourth Quarter 1993).

Font, Mauricio. "Crisis and Reform in Cuba," in *Toward a New Cuba? Legacies of a Revolution*, Miguel Angel Centeno and Mauricio Font, eds. Boulder: Lynne Rienner, 1997.

Gawdiak, Ihor, ed. *Czechoslovakia: A Country Study*. Washington: Federal Research Division, Library of Congress, 1988.

Jatar-Hausmann, Ana Julia. "Through the Cracks of Socialism: The Emerging Private Sector in Cuba," in *Cuba in Transition—Volume 6*. Washington: Association for the Study of the Cuban Economy, 1996.

Kornai, János. *The Socialist System: The Political Economy of Communism*. Princeton: Princeton University Press, 1992.

Leff, Nathaniel H. "Entrepreneurship and Economic Development: The Problem Revisited," *Journal of Economic Literature* 1 (1979).

Locay, Luis and Jorge Sanguinetty. "The Effect of Socialism on the Entrepreneurial Abilities of Cuban Americans," in *Cuba in Transition—Volume 6*. Washington: Association for the Study of the Cuban Economy, 1996.

Nyrop, Richard F. *Czechoslovakia: A Country Study*. Washington: Federal Research Division Library of Congress, 1981.

Organization for Economic Cooperation and Development (OECD). *Small Business in Transition Economies: The Development of Entrepreneurship in the Czech Republic, Hungary, Poland and the Slovak Republic*. Paris: OECD, 1996.

Organization for Economic Cooperation and Development (OECD). "The Emergence of Business Associations and Chambers in the Economies in Transition: Examples from the Czech Republic, Hungary, Poland, and the Slovak Republic," in *OECD Working Papers*. Paris, OECD, 1994.

Pérez-López, Jorge F. *Cuba's Second Economy: From Behind the Scenes to Center Stage*. New Brunswick: Transaction Publishers, 1995.

Pérez-López, Jorge F. "Cuba's Second Economy and the Market Transition," in *Toward a New Cuba? Legacies of a Revolution*, Miguel Angel Centeno and Mauricio Font, eds. Boulder: Lynne Rienner, 1997.

Perry, Joseph M., Jeffrey W. Steagall, and Louis A. Woods. "Small Business Development in Post-Transition Cuba," in *Cuba in Transition—Volume 5*. Washington: Association for the Study of the Cuban Economy, 1995.

Rostowski, Jacek. "The Decay of Socialism and the Growth of Private Enterprise in Poland," *Soviet Studies* (July 1988).

Rostowski, Jacek. *The Implications of Rapid Private Sector Growth in Poland*. Discussion Paper no. 153, London School of Economics Centre for Economic Performance. London, 1993.

Shiller, Robert J, Maxim Boycko, and Vladimir Korobov. "Hunting for Homo Sovieticus: Situational versus Attitudinal Factors in Economic Behavior," in *Brookings Papers on Economic Activity* 1 (1992).

Wilson, Sandra and Arvil V. Adams. *Self-Employment for the Unemployment-Experience in OECD and Transitional Economies*. Washington: The World Bank, 1994.

Wyznikiewicz, Bohdan, Brian Pinto, and Maciej Grabowski. *Coping with Capitalism-The New Polish Entrepreneurs*. Washington: The World Bank, 1993.

DEVELOPMENT STAGES OF THE "CUBAN EXILE COUNTRY"[1]

Miguel González-Pando

Since Cubans first began to flee their nation following the 1959 revolutionary takeover, the lost homeland has endured as the only constant throughout their diaspora—their common bond, the obligatory historical reference that lingers in their memory like bitter sugar on a child's palate. Cuba is, indeed, the shared past to which the emigrés, whenever they left, wherever they settled, could always relate. Not surprisingly, the "Cuban Exile Country" continues to be linked to its place of origin. Whether Cuban Americans or Cubans residing in other nations, nearly all emigrés define themselves in terms of Cuba, their collective homeland.

Over the years, most Cuban emigrés have insisted that they are political exiles even if their actual behavior in the United States contradicts the transient connotation of that definition. Much has changed in the internal dynamics of *el exilio* since 1959 and, evidently, this long-held sense of identity has begun to relent under the weight of time. But the emergence of a Cuban American generation represents a new phenomenon; until very recently, the majority considered themselves political exiles and, as such, reluctant emigrés. Among the older generation, most still do.[2]

From its onset, the political genesis of the Cuban exodus nurtured many self-defining characteristics that appear to set these emigrés somewhat apart from other Latin Americans coming to the United States. Unlike true immigrants, the early Cuban emigrés were well aware that they would lose in exile the socioeconomic status most of them had enjoyed in Cuba. Whereas immigrants are usually motivated by the "pull" this proverbial "land of opportunity" exerts upon them, the initial two waves of Cuban emigrés felt "pushed" by political conditions prevailing in Cuba at the time they left.[3] Truth be told, those Cubans did not come to the United States searching for the economic fortunes inherently promised by the American Dream; their exodus was a direct response to Castro's revolution and, once they settled abroad, they adamantly rejected being classified as immigrants. By the time other Cubans with somewhat different motivations and socioeconomic backgrounds later joined them in America, that initial exodus had already given their collective experience its lasting political imprint.

Through almost four decades, Cuban exiles have tried obsessively to stay abreast of developments back in their homeland. So much so that the emigrés, particularly those in South Florida, have continued to be

---

1. This paper summarizes Chapter 3 of the author's forthcoming book, *The Cuban Americans* (Greenwood Press).

2. The Cuban population in the U.S. climbed above the one million mark in 1990. Only six percent of it arrived before 1960; about a third arrived in the 1960s, 13 percent in the 1970s, and 20 percent in the 1980s. The remaining 28 percent were born in the U.S. but identify themselves as Cubans. See The Cuban American Policy Center, *A Demographic Profile of Cuban Americans* (Miami: Cuban American National Council, 1994).

3. The distinction between immigrants and refugees has been noted before. See Everett S. Lee, "A Theory of Migration," *Demography* 3 (1966), pp. 47-57.

influenced as much by the course of events on the island as by what actually transpires in their adopted surroundings. Not only have ensuing revolutionary measures triggered the exodus of additional waves, but each successive emigration has had an impact on the orientation of those already here. Time and again actions taking place in Cuba precipitate corresponding reactions among the exiles in the United States.

Such connection is so strong that events in the island determine the stages of development of the Cuban exile experience: survival (1959-1962), transition (1962-1965), adjustment (1965-1973), economic miracle (1973-1980), diversification (1980-1990), and post-Soviet era (1990 to the present).[4] These are not merely successive chronological periods; rather, they constitute true stages, for each has brought about a clear shift in the internal dynamics of the exile community and a new sense of collective direction.

THE SURVIVAL STAGE (1959-1962)

The Initial Exodus (1959-1961): Cubans began their Castro-era emigration the moment General Fulgencio Batista fled the island on New Year's morning of 1959 and a "provisional" revolutionary government took over the reins of the politically-troubled nation. The first exiles were hundreds of Batista's closest collaborators who feared reprisals from the regime that had ousted them. Soon after, they were joined in the United States by a massive exodus that originated within the nation's business and professional establishment but quickly enough included early defectors from Castro's own ranks. That initial exodus, therefore, embraced three distinct exile "vintages," the largest of which was the island's nonpolitical elite.[5]

The upper and middle classes were disproportionately represented in that initial wave. Because of political circumstances, the emigrés were mostly destitute upon arrival, but many of them were familiar with the United States, having often visited it for business or pleasure. In addition, because Cuban culture was highly Americanized, the members of this particular vintage were not complete strangers to America's way of life: To them the United States was not *terra incognita*. Precisely because of their familiarity with the United States, they "were the least given to believe that the American government would permit the consolidation of a socialist regime in the island."[6]

The demographic profile of the exiles who arrived between 1959 and 1962 confirms other characteristics associated with their high socioeconomic status in prerevolutionary Cuba. Most may have left empty-handed but not without considerable human capital. Their educational and professional backgrounds, in fact, placed them near the top echelons of society—in Cuba and in America as well. This initial wave was certainly the island's "cream of the crop"—many had studied English at Havana's private schools or had learned it at American summer camps, high schools, and colleges.

They were also older than most immigrants; hence, their cultural identity was rather defined by the time they left. The role that their identity as exiles has played on their American dynamics defies quantification; so do other defining traits displayed by this initial wave, such as pride, enterprising drive, adaptability, and a host of other psychosocial aspects that served them well in their new environment. Neither can the cultural "baggage" they brought be accurately measured by statistics. The same is true of their political idiosyncrasies. Perhaps there is something unique in the mind-set of all exiles that acts as a special in-

---

4. These stages of development were first published in 1996. See Miguel González-Pando, "Doing Business," *Greater Miami: Spirit of Cuban Enterprise*, ed. Miguel González-Pando (Ft. Lauderdale: Cooperfield, 1996), pp. 40-69.

5. E. F Kunz, "The Refugee in Flight: Kinetic Models and Forms of Displacement," *International Migration Review* 7 (1973), p. 137.

6. Nelson Amaro and Alejandro Portes. "Una Sociología del Exilio: Situación de los Grupos Cubanos en los Estados Unidos, " *Aportes* 23 (1972) p. 10.

centive to succeed.[7] If such be the case, the initial wave of Cuban emigrés had it in abundance. They were also heirs to an enterprising tradition honed by centuries of commercial contact with the outside world.

The Anti-Castro Struggle Among Early Exiles: Upon their arrival in the United States, the initial wave was driven by one all-consuming objective: to return to Cuba after toppling Castro's revolutionary government. They expected that, with the support of their powerful American ally, such an objective would be accomplished within a short period of time. This expectation was not the result of wishful thinking; rather, it was a most natural assumption given the geopolitical interest Americans had historically shown in its Cuban neighbors.

Truly, the odds against the survival of the revolutionary regime seemed formidable. By the summer of 1960, guerrilla groups linked to an incipient underground network had already surfaced in the Cuban mountains. More ominously, the U.S. government had begun to recruit and train exiles for paramilitary actions against Castro. Such internal and external threats, the exiles inferred, could not be effectively countered by the nascent regime.

By early 1961, right after the inauguration of President Kennedy, the emigrés' confidence in the liberation of their homeland reached a feverish pitch, as scores of Cuban exiles were being recruited by the Central Intelligence Agency (CIA) and sent to training bases in Guatemala and other locations.[8] This was supposed to be a covert operation, but pictures of the training camps were prominently displayed in the weekly tabloids (*periodiquitos*) published in the United States by exiles as well as in the *New York Times*. Despite President Kennedy's repeated denials, everyone was aware that a U.S.-sponsored invasion of the island would soon be launched.

The invasion fever sweeping the Cuban exile community became obsessive. A coalition of anti-Castro groups, the Consejo Revolucionario Cubano (Cuban Revolutionary Council), was brought together under the political and military control of the CIA, making the exiles nothing more than willing instruments of the United States. Although the relinquishing of authority did cause some friction among exile leaders, they were persuaded that this was an "unavoidable cost." The plans for the invasion continued at full speed.

The Need for Survival: While their attention remained focused on the liberation of Cuba, the exiles still needed to find the means to survive during what they assumed would be a temporary stay in America. Making ends meet meant accepting the first job that was offered. Since South Florida's strong unions maintained firm restrictions against the newcomers, Cubans were forced to take any jobs, even those traditionally held by Miami's African Americans.

Former Cuban entrepreneurs and professionals parked cars, washed dishes, drove taxis, waited on tables, delivered newspapers, and performed a variety of menial tasks for which they were overqualified. Unlicensed Cuban doctors and dentists, ever so careful not to be discovered by the authorities, saw patients in their own homes. Housewives who had never held a job in Cuba found employment as waitresses, maids, seamstresses, factory workers, and vegetable pickers in the fields. Thousands of exiles were able to go on the generous payroll of the CIA, which during the *Survival Stage* may have been one of Dade County's larger employers.

The challenge of survival was met with a strong sense of solidarity. Those who arrived earlier tried to ease the shock of the newly-arrived by offering them advice on how to find a job, to obtain a social security card, to enroll their children in school, to look for

---

7. That much has been suggested by Joel Krotkin in *Tribes: How Race, Religion and Identity Determine Success in the New Global Economy* (New York: Random, 1992).

8. Several authors have documented the Cuban exiles' anti-Castro war. See for example, Hugh Thomas, *Cuba: The Pursuit of Freedom* (New York: Harper, 1971); Juan M. Clark, *Cuba: Mito y realidad* (Miami-Caracas: Saeta Ediciones, 1990); Enrique Encinosa, *Cuba en guerra* (Miami: The Endowment for Cuban American Studies of the Cuban American Foundation, 1994).

housing, and to enlist in the federally-funded Cuban Refugee Program, where they could get free medical attention and bags of groceries.[9] The few fortunate enough to afford a car drove their Cuban neighbors to work, to the doctor, and to supermarkets. The spirit of community that characterized the *Survival Stage* was to prevail until today, as each new wave went through a similar process upon arriving in America. Survival, indeed, became the shared rite of passage into exile.

Settling in South Florida: The initial exodus settled primarily in and around Miami. There was a precedence for that. Throughout the island's brief history as an independent nation, South Florida's proximity to Cuba had made it the haven of choice whenever political troubles forced Cubans into exile. Moreover, Miami's quasi-tropical climate resembled Cuba's.

Those who had come in the past as exiles belonged to the more politically-active segments of Cuban society—for example, the opposition to General Gerardo Machado in the early 1930s and to General Fulgencio Batista in the 1950s. But not this time. This was a different type of exodus, far greater in numbers and consisting mostly of the well-educated upper and middle classes; unlike their predecessors, they brought their families and left everything else behind.

As more and more exiles came, they tended to settle in the then-depressed areas of Miami's southwest section, where rents were low. South Florida, a racially-segregated resort town catering mainly to winter tourists, had never witnessed such an incursion of often-destitute ethnics moving into "Anglo"[10] neighborhoods; these foreigners were very different from the free-spending Latin Americans who stayed in Miami Beach's hotels. Their sudden impact on the community was greeted with mixed emotions by the established residents, who perceived the newcomers as clannish and loud. Like most immigrants who come to America, the Cuban exiles met with some resentment.

The exiles, in fact, *were* clannish and loud. In those days, several families often pooled their resources and crammed into small apartments until each one was able to afford a place of its own. And they were also conspicuous. During the day, hundreds gathered downtown to share the latest news from Cuba and to exchange information about available jobs; at night, they visited with friends and sat on their porches seeking relief from Miami's heat. From the very start, the emigrés showed an all-consuming desire to stay in touch with each other and to keep alive their traditional way of life. By the end of the *Survival Stage*, an embryonic exile community was already emerging within Miami.

THE TRANSITION STAGE (1962-1965)

A Period of Hopelessness: Events involving Cuba—the Bay of Pigs Invasion and the Missile Crisis—jolted *el exilio* and left it in disarray. The *Transition Stage* thus began. Deep within their psyche, the exiles felt defeated in their cause and lost in a new land. The militant anti-Castro spirit that had so far lent coherence to the exile experience began giving way to painful introspection. During this period, commercial flights between Cuba and the United States were discontinued, leaving many of the relatives of the initial exodus stranded on the island.

Hopelessness about returning to Cuba was hard to accept. The invasion fiasco and the Soviet Union's involvement in the affairs of the Caribbean island had effectively consolidated Castro's regime; the United States had failed the exiles, not once, but twice. To make matters worse, they were forced to

---

9. In December 1960, the Eisenhower Administration created the Cuban Refugee Emergency Center to coordinate the relief efforts of voluntary agencies and to oversee resettlement. Some months later, President Kennedy created the more generous Cuban Refugee Program.

10. For lack of a better term, "Anglo" and "American" are used interchangeably throughout this paper to refer to the white, non-Cuban English-speaking U.S. population. Obviously it is a misnomer, for it includes Jews, Italian-Americans and other ethnics who, although American, are not Anglo.

recognize that Castro's international image had grown to mythical proportions as a result of his victories against American "imperialism," while the Cuban exiles, abandoned by their American ally and denigrated by the world press, had suffered a lasting defeat. It was time for the emigrés, albeit reluctantly, to come to terms with the prospects of a long stay in America.

That harsh realization could well have caused the exiles to follow the same fate as other immigrant groups and disappear into America's melting pot. Instead, after a period of soul searching, they emerged more determined to prevail. Thus challenged, the exiles still needed to find a new cause consistent with their battered convictions. Given the political nature of their exodus, the reluctant emigrés felt they could regain their collective self-worth only by somehow assigning a subliminal ideological justification to their commonplace struggle in America.

The End of the War Against Castro: For all intents and purposes, the exiles' struggle to liberate Cuba by force all but ceased during the *Transition Stage*. They lacked the resources to contend with Castro's growing military power, and without U.S. support, they knew any future action carried out by Cuban freedom fighters was doomed. The suddenness with which the United States implemented its turnabout left Cuban exiles in shock. In rapid succession, the CIA cut off the support it had been providing to Cuban freedom fighters, and the U.S. government began to persecute and prosecute exiles who tried to launch independent raids against Castro's regime. It was a sad finale to a struggle for which thousands of their comrades-in-arms had given their lives and tens of thousands languished in Cuba's jails.

By December 1962, when negotiations with the Cuban government for the return of the prisoners of the Bay of Pigs Invasion concluded and President Kennedy arrived in Miami to welcome the invasion veterans as heroes, the active phase of the struggle symbolically came to an end. From then on, group

after group of militant exiles were forced to accept that theirs was a lost cause, and many of their members reluctantly reoriented their lives in exile.

Resettlement Policy of the Cuban Refugee Program: From the moment the Cuban exiles began arriving, the official intention of the American government had been to relocate the newcomers throughout the country. That policy encountered much initial resistance, because most Cubans preferred to stay in South Florida in the hope that their exile would be a short-lived one. During the *Transition Stage*, however, thousands of exiles began to resettle in other communities across the nation.

For nearly all of those who left Miami during this period, their decision involved a tacit reordering of their personal priorities; the well-being of their family would now take precedence over the struggle to liberate their homeland. Anyway, most violent anti-Castro activities had all but stopped after the 1962 Missile Crisis; and South Florida's job market was saturated. Among those leaving were thousands of Cuban professionals, particularly lawyers and educators for whom secure employment as Spanish teachers in other states seemed to offer better prospects than hard-to-secure, dead-end jobs in South Florida. They were joined by former managers of American companies that had operated in Cuba, blue-collar workers attracted by higher-paying union jobs in the north, and disillusioned freedom fighters who joined the U.S. Army in the faint hope that a twist of fate might send them to fight Castro under the American flag.

Everywhere the exiles went, they carried with them an undying anticommunist spirit. They formed small colonies in New Jersey,[11] New York, Chicago, Boston, Washington, D.C., and other urban centers in the northeast as well as in dozens of cities of the Midwest and as far west as California.

Emergence of Little Havana: While some exiles were relocating throughout the nation, a counter

---

11. Exiles established a Cuban enclave in Union City, New Jersey, and much like Little Havana, it thrived. Small Cuban-owned businesses eventually dominated the commercial district of this so-called "Havana on the Hudson."

trend also ensued; a four-square-mile area in Miami's southwest section continued to attract new Cubans. It was during this period that the first Cuban businesses made their appearance on Flagler and Eighth streets, the area's main commercial thoroughfares. Although difficult to anticipate, in a few years Miami's *la saguesera*—as the early exiles mispronounced "southwest"—would emerge as the heart of the economically-viable exile enclave in South Florida; it would come to be known as "Little Havana."

The new Cubans settling in Miami were not coming directly from the island, since flights between the United States and Cuba were discontinued after the Missile Crisis. Once Miami became identified as the capital of the "Cuban Exile Country," it acted as a magnet to Cubans who had first gone to Spain and Latin America, as to some who had earlier been resettled elsewhere in the United States. Their common motivation was the desire to share life with their fellow Cubans, for inaccessible as the island actually was, it felt a lot closer from Little Havana.

During the *Transition Stage*, hundreds of Cuban-owned mom-and-pop shops that catered almost exclusively to an exile clientele dotted Little Havana's emerging landscape; and each opening was celebrated by the exiles as a collective victory. A rudimentary service network, partly underground, was also developing within the fledgling enclave. Doctors, dentists, and accountants saw their Cuban clients in their own apartments; electricians, roofers, plumbers, and other technicians offered cut-rate prices to fellow exiles.

Hialeah also attracted thousands of exiles and, although on a smaller scale than Little Havana, a Cuban enclave developed in this working-class community during the period. The exiles settling in Hialeah found employment at nearby Miami International Airport and in the textile and garment industries. The fact that these were nonunion companies made for a thriving industrial district, and the city of Hi-

aleah eventually emerged as the second-largest exile community in the United States.

THE ADJUSTMENT STAGE (1965-1973)

Beginnings of the Second Exodus—The Camarioca Boatlift: The *Adjustment Stage* started in September 1965, when Castro announced that any Cuban with family residing in the United States would be allowed to leave through Camarioca, a port located on the northern coast of Cuba. The Cuban leader also invited the exiles to come by sea to Camarioca to pick up their relatives who were left stranded in Cuba since commercial flights between the two countries were discontinued.

With this dramatic action, Castro probably intended to rid the island of political malcontents with close ties to the exiles. But by unleashing this demographic bomb, Castro also wanted to show that Havana, not Washington, exercised de facto control over Cubans entering Florida's seacoast borders.[12] Predictably, thousands of exiles sailed to Cuba, much to the chagrin of U.S. immigration authorities. In just a few weeks, about 5,000 Cubans made the trip to freedom before the United States halted the boatlift.

Although Cubans who left from Camarioca—as well as those who followed in the Freedom Flights—belonged mainly to the middle class that had supported Castro's initial revolutionary promises, a not-insignificant number of peasants and blue-collar workers also left during this second emigration wave. In contrast to their relatives who had left earlier hoping for a quick return to a free Cuba, this new wave did not entertain such illusions; they just wanted to get away from the Communist regime, not plot its destruction from across the Straits of Florida.

The Freedom Flights and the 1966 Cuban Adjustment Act: Soon after the beginning of the Camarioca Boatlift, President Lyndon B. Johnson announced that the United States would continue to welcome Cubans seeking freedom—as long as they sought it in an orderly, lawful fashion. The following month,

---

12. Since Camarioca, one of Castro's most effective tools has been the periodic encouragement of emigration. He has adroitly played this hand whenever he wanted to retaliate against the U.S. or relieve internal political pressures. Castro would use the "demographic bomb" again during the 1980 Mariel Boatlift and the 1994 rafter exodus.

the Johnson administration disclosed it had negotiated a "Memorandum of Understanding" with the Cuban government whereby close relatives of Cubans already in the United States would be allowed to emigrate into this country. In December 1965, the Freedom Flights were inaugurated.

Almost one year to the day of his first announcement, the American president also signed the Cuban Adjustment Act into law. With its passage, Cubans who lived in the United States were given the opportunity to "adjust" their legal status so that they could become American residents or naturalized citizens. Coming during the height of the Cold War, the Cuban Adjustment Act resonated with the prevalent anticommunist rhetoric of the time, even as it set a policy for treating Cubans differently from other immigrants, creating in effect a double standard.[13]

For the next eight years, planes loaded with Cubans would make the short daily trip from Varadero, Cuba, to Miami. About 300,000 Cubans had come to the United States by the time Castro discontinued the Freedom Flights in 1973.[14] This second wave was predominantly white, attesting to the fact that most were the relatives of those in the initial exodus. Because the revolutionary regime restricted the emigration of men of military age, females and older men were vastly over represented in this second wave. From a socioeconomic perspective, however, there were other marked differences. Whereas about a third of the earlier exiles had come from the professional and managerial ranks, less than a fifth of those coming between 1965 and 1973 belonged in that category.[15]

Cuban Exiles Turn to the Economic Arena: It was during the *Adjustment Stage* that most exiles were able to reconcile apparently clashing demands: the practical requirements of their new life and the devo-

tion to their old political agenda. Cubans managed this convoluted adjustment by subliminally elevating their commonplace ambitions to the realm of an ideological quest; they were intent in demonstrating the superiority of the capitalist system—of which they considered themselves self-appointed representatives —over Cuban socialism.

Finding a new direction consistent with their old ideological cause was an unconscious yet masterful stroke that allowed them to change behavior without dismantling their essential political values. But their new quest was not simply a matter of realism plus ideology; it was also motivated by a much deeper need to prove their self-worth. How else but by excelling economically in their new land could the exiles demonstrate they were really not "the scum of the Earth and worthless worms" that Castro called them? The disgrace and humiliation of their political defeat became the psychological impetus that fueled their efforts to prevail in the economic arena. Anticommunist ideals, practical imperatives, and psychological motivations were three elements that coincided at that difficult juncture; they produced a winning economic formula.

Self-Employment in the Informal Private Sector Economy: During the *Adjustment Stage*, many exiles gravitated toward the informal fringes of the private sector—a variety of professional, technical, and personal services rendered to other Cubans; a narrow range of marginal business activities requiring minimum start-up capital; and non-unionized garment and construction jobs. As soon as the enterprising exiles mastered entry level jobs, however, they began to talk their employers into restructuring hiring practices in the form of subcontracts.

This new arrangement, which became prevalent in the garment industry, proved to be mutually advan-

---

13. This preferential treatment lasted until the summer of 1994, when the Clinton Administration placed a de facto hold on the "open-arms" policy toward Cuban refugees.

14. U.S. agencies persuaded about half of the newly arrived Cubans to resettle outside of Miami.

15. Researchers often disagree on the precise socioeconomic extraction of the second wave. See, Silvia Pedraza-Bailey, "Cuba's Exiles: Portrait of a Refugee Migration," *International Migration Review* 19 (1985); and Juan M. Clark, "The Exodus from Revolutionary Cuba (1959-74): A Sociological Analysis," diss., University of Florida.

tageous: for the same amount of money, Cuban subcontractors took on the responsibility of hiring and accommodating workers in their living rooms and garages and delivering the finished goods on time. That rudimentary mode of self-employment often meant working longer hours, but the emigrés could enjoy the satisfaction of being their own bosses—even if their "workers" were actually relatives or friends. Self-employment also became widespread in the Cuban service sector, particularly in the construction trades. It is easy today to sneer at the underground network of "independent" tradesmen, unlicensed doctors, dentists and electricians, clandestine beauty shops, and door-to-door service workers that became increasingly prevalent in the *Adjustment Stage*, but that network provided much-needed income to thousands of uprooted professionals and technicians while rendering inexpensive benefits to the ever-expanding emigré population.

By this time, self-employment was the preferred mode for the entrepreneurial class that had been over represented in the initial exodus as well as for industrious Cubans whose lack of marketable skills severely limited other job opportunities. These aspiring businessmen *and* businesswomen pooled their family resources and continued to set up mom-and-pop stores along Eighth Street and Flagler Street. With hardly any need for capital to buy equipment and inventory, the exiles were able to open up groceries stores and cafeterias that offered culturally-differentiated products and services not available outside the Cuban enclave. They served a distinct market of fellow exiles.

The minimal risks of going into business were worth taking in those days when the Freedom Flights continued to bring an endless flow of Cubans from the island. To the exile entrepreneur, the newcomers provided two critical ingredients that fueled their developing businesses: a growing captive market and a source of cheap labor. The third ingredient, availability of financing, was the only bottleneck that kept the Cuban enclave from experiencing a true economic take-off.

Personal Style of Doing Business: The lack of investment capital with which to finance the growth of their small businesses was largely overcome by relying upon personal contacts. This style of conducting business was really an extension of a time-tested tradition brought from Cuba. When looking for a loan to start-up or expand a business, it seemed only natural that the exiles would rely upon their characteristic personal style.

Because the exiles had neither the track record in the Anglo community nor the collateral to secure conventional financing, they needed to locate, or being recommended to, a handful of Cubans already working for Miami's banks. That was how the practice of lending based "on moral character" became instituted, particularly at Republic Bank, a newly-established financial institution that attracted a Cuban management team around 1970. Taking advantage of such a practice, the enterprising exiles were able to expand the business base of their economic enclave, and Republic Bank was on its way to becoming the largest Miami-based bank some years later.

The personal style of doing business also proved effective in Latin America. The exiles' old contacts in that region offered a quick entry into the largely untapped import-export field. It was a perfect fit for the Spanish-speaking exiles. So much so that they packed their bags with samples and catalogues and headed south of the border by the hundreds. The strategy paid off: These international traveling salesmen returned to Miami with lucrative orders and contracts. Within a few years, they managed to establish countless small import-export businesses operating out of their homes and apartments—the incipient foundation of a thriving international market that would lead South Florida's economic development during the 1970s.

Diehard Exiles, Militant Students, and Terrorists: While by the mid-1960s most Cubans had actively abandoned the war against Castro, others tried to keep that struggle alive. In addition to the obvious economic imperatives and the hindrance of U.S. officials, diehard exiles faced obstacles of their own making. Lack of significant support from a largely-disenchanted emigré community, internal strife among the militant leadership and questions about some of their extremist tactics undermined several well-intentioned initiatives, while others were exposed as ill-conceived efforts or simple frauds.[16] Among the more bizarre of these initiatives was led by José Elías de la Torriente. On February 1970, the so-called *Plan Torriente* organized a major rally at a baseball stadium that was attended by about 40,000 Miami Cubans; shortly thereafter, a paramilitary commando operation on the island was staged under its auspices, but neither event succeeded in reviving the war against Castro.

During this period, the younger emigrés tried to keep the spirit of the anti-Castro struggle alive by involving themselves in protests designed to bring international attention to the Cuban issue. They founded the Federation of Cuban Students (FEC), an organization that soon had chapters in the United States, Puerto Rico and Costa Rica. The FEC published a monthly newspaper, *Antorcha*, and organized two student congresses. At the same time, another group of students founded Abdala in New York. Although it initially constituted a small study group, after 1972 the group broadened its scope to include non students and, for the next few years, served as the cradle for a new generation of militancy in exile.

During the *Adjustment Stage*, terrorist tactics also gathered new momentum, leading to what the exiles referred to as *la guerra por los caminos del mundo* (the war through the roads of the world). In the 1970s, frustrated diehard militants formed secret groups such as the Frente de Liberación Nacional (National Liberation Front), Acción Cubana (Cuban Action), Omega Siete (Omega Seven), Gobierno Cubano Secreto (Secret Cuban Government), and Jóven Cuba (Young Cuba), which revived the violent tactics against pro-Castro targets throughout the world; hundreds of explosions rocked Cuban embassies in Europe, Canada, Latin America, and the United States, and attacks against the Cuban regime's personnel abroad became commonplace. By 1974, the wave of terror reached its peak, and those allegedly linked to such activities—Orlando Bosh, Guillermo

Novo, Humberto López, and Luis Crespo—became heroes to many exiles.

By the end of the *Adjustment Stage*, terrorism was becoming more indiscriminate, as its targets then included exiles considered traitors to the anti-Castro cause; José Elías de la Torriente was the first of a series of exile victims. *La guerra por los caminos del mundo* was entering a new violent phase.

THE ECONOMIC MIRACLE STAGE (1973-1980)

Expansion of Miami's Cuban Enclave: Castro's suspension of the Freedom Flights signaled the onset of the *Economic Miracle Stage*, during which the once-displaced exiles finally put down roots in the United States. In South Florida, this period was fueled primarily by the business boom that began within the Cuban enclave. The shops in Little Havana flourished, leading to the establishment and expansion of countless restaurants, cafeterias, supermarkets, gas stations, book, record and hardware stores, private schools, appliance and furniture outlets, dry cleaners, pharmacies, clinics and doctors' offices, theaters, radio stations, funeral homes, and a whole gamut of services that could well have supported the population of a medium-sized city.

The exiles then extended the borders of their enclave into the middle-class neighborhoods of Westchester and the residential districts of Coral Gables and Kendall. Typically, the sections of Greater Miami to which they moved could be distinguished by the opening of new Cuban shops and the large number of cars parked outside their homes—clear evidence that the traditional concept of the extended family still prevailed. Another telling sign was the coming and going of pickup trucks and vans carrying construction supplies to convert garages into family rooms or to build new additions to accommodate relatives who had arrived from Cuba or to serve as offices for their businesses. Naturally, the small construction companies the exiles had started from the back of their trucks grew into aggressive firms.

---

16. For a unique insider's account of the anti-Castro war, see Enrique Encinosa, *Cuba en Guerra* (Miami: The Endowment for Cuban Studies of the Cuban American National Foundation, 1994).

The proliferation of the small-business sector and service network, as well as the boom linked to international trade, continued to drive the economic fortunes of the "Cuban Exile Country." Its prosperity was reinforced by three distinct developments: The entry of a younger generation into the professional ranks, the licensing of older Cuban professionals, and the return to Miami of many relocated exiles. By the end of the 1970s, as many as 40 percent of the Cuban population in Greater Miami may have settled previously in other American cities.[17]

The New Professional Class: Upon their arrival in America, the first generation of exiles had to face all sorts of hardships, but they always insisted that their children learn English, graduate from high school and attend college. Hence, the youngsters went to school in record proportions while their parents, lacking valid U.S. credentials, were forced to put on hold their professional careers or to practice underground. In the *Economic Miracle Stage*, however, those youngsters were completing their university education, and many of their parents were returning to school to obtain professional licenses. The gradual entrance of both generations into the professional ranks further boosted their prospects.

From the beginning, the parents' road to earning professional licenses in the United States was fraught with frustration, and not just because of their lack of English proficiency. Florida's politically-entrenched professional associations, for example, fought them every inch of the way. Not until the exiles started to flex their economic and political muscles, did former doctors, architects, lawyers, and other Cuban professionals could see their dream of practicing in America become, at long last, a reality.

For the younger generation, on the other hand, the educational path was much smoother.[18] Upon graduation, many of them returned to work in Greater Miami, or other areas of exile concentration. These young professionals were as eager to prosper as their parents, but they were better-prepared to compete for high-paying executive positions in mainstream businesses, take over and expand their parents' small shops, and challenge the "Anglo" establishment on its own turf. This bilingual generation, raised and educated in the United States, became known as "Cuban Americans."

Miami Emerges as the Gateway to Latin America. The embryonic import-export network started by the Cubans in the 1960s flourished during the *Economic Miracle Stage*. The expansion of Cuban firms involved in international markets triggered an unprecedented surge of related activities that broadened Miami's commercial base and bestowed a new economic identity on the city. It became the Gateway to Latin America.

The boom in international trade lured a growing number of multinational corporations, initiating a trend of moving their Latin American headquarters from New York, New Orleans, Mexico City or Caracas to Coral Gables and, later, to Miami. This development, in turn, attracted freight forwarders and insurance companies as well as out-of-state institutions specializing in financing import-export transactions. To cap the internationalization of South Florida, many wealthy Latin Americans, fearing their own country's political instability, brought large amounts of capital.[19]

Ethnic Politics in the South Florida Enclave: Since settling in South Florida the exiles had chosen to remain isolated from the political life of their adopted community. Even adopting U.S. citizenship, not to mention actually registering to vote, was often deemed a betrayal to their homeland. That attitude,

---

17. According to a recent survey conducted by *The Miami Herald*.

18. The author has long referred to this group as "the last generation." They are the *last generation* of Cubans old enough to remember pre-Castro Cuba.

19. The flow of billions of dollars from Latin America to Miami included both legitimately earned funds and drug monies. This capital provided further impetus to the economic Latinization of South Florida. Drug laundering schemes flourished during the period, and some Cubans became involved in illegal financial operations.

however, began to change with the emergence of a new Cuban American consciousness in the 1970s. Still, before breaking away from their self-imposed political marginality, Cubans needed to find a justification that would make sense in terms of their old exile mind-set. That rationale was provided by the argument that, as voters, they would be able to influence U.S. foreign policy toward Cuba.

During the *Economic Miracle Stage*, when Cubans still lacked the voting power to elect their own representatives, prominent exiles like Manolo Reboso and Alfredo Durán, who enjoyed impeccable anti-Castro credentials because of their participation in the Bay of Pigs Invasion, escorted "Anglo" politicians who were courting votes to Little Havana, Westchester and Hialeah. English-speaking politicians had to learn just enough Spanish to yell ¡*Viva Cuba Libre!* at political rallies in order to throw Cuban crowds into a frenzy. It was American ethnic politics as it had been traditionally practiced by first-generation immigrants.

In the early 1970s, Reboso and Durán were able to leverage their own political power among Cuban Americans into appointments for themselves to the City of Miami Commission and the Dade County School Board, respectively, thus becoming the first exile incumbents. In the case of Reboso, he was elected to the nonpartisan City of Miami Commission at the conclusion of his term. Durán, on the other hand, could not win the Democratic party's nomination to the School Board, his failure attests to the bias of registered Democrats against Cuban American candidates. That rejection, if anything, spurred the exiles to register—but as Republicans.

By the latter part of the 1970s, the old dilemma between competing allegiances to Cuba and the United States was finally overcome, opening the way to massive American citizenship and voter registration drives. During the decade, the number of Cubans who became American citizens more than doubled.[20] It would be misleading, however, to assume that all those who adopted U.S. citizenship had actually re-

placed their sense of identity as Cuban exiles for that of ethnic immigrants. Becoming American, in most cases, involved a rather pragmatic consideration. Since they were not about to return to their homeland, they wanted to take advantage of their full rights as citizens of the United States.

La Guerra por los Caminos del Mundo: The new wave of terrorism that resumed around 1970 reached its peak in the middle of the decade. By then, the attacks were not limited exclusively to pro-Castro targets such as Cuban embassies and consulates; among its victims were now several exile leaders who supported dialogue with the Cuban regime as well as others such as radio personality Emilio Milián who had publicly criticized these radical tactics.

In the three-year period between 1973 and 1976, more than 100 bombs exploded in South Florida. Debate over the appropriateness of these extreme tactics divided the exile community as well as the terrorists themselves. In 1976 the exile terrorists grew even bolder: In Washington, D.C., they killed Orlando Letelier, a former minister of Chile who was allegedly linked to Castro's regime; far more brutal was the blowing up of a Cubana de Aviación airplane off the coast of Barbados killing 73 passengers.

From then on popular opinion throughout the "Cuban Exile Country" turned against the indiscriminate spread of violence. The consensus at the time was that random terrorism had tarnished the image of the exiles' cause and had actually strengthened of Castro's regime. By then, moreover, there was increasing evidence that Castro's agents in the United States were behind some of the terrorist actions that were blamed on militant exiles. The violent "war through the roads of the world" had finally reached a dead-end.

THE DIVERSIFICATION STAGE (1980-1990)

The Controversial *Diálogo*: Once again, shock waves originating from within the island impacted the lives of Cubans living in the United States. The fuse that triggered it was set in November 1978,

---

20. Whereas in 1970 only 25 percent of the Cuban exiles were American citizens, by 1980 a majority (55 percent) was.

when Castro invited a group of exiles to meet with him in Havana. The unforseen consequences of that event soon turned it into a milestone that changed Cubans on both sides of the Florida Straits. Arguably, in the wake of this dialogue, the prosperous Cuban American community was stunned into a new era—the *Diversification Stage*.

The meeting between Castro and the exiles was supposed to follow a strictly humanitarian agenda, but its political implications soon overshadowed the professed goals of negotiating the release of political prisoners and the lifting of travel restrictions to the island. Upon returning from their meeting with Castro, the dialogue's seventy-five participants were denounced as traitors by a majority of their fellow exiles. Threats soon escalated into terrorist attacks against some of the exiles who had participated in the controversial talks.[21] Since then, the rift between supporters and opponents of the *Diálogo* has dominated the political debate among Cuban exiles.

The consequences of the agreement negotiated between Castro and the exiles were not any less significant on the communist island. As a result of the dialogue, the Cuban regime for the first time opened its doors to emigrés who wanted to visit their families back home. Thousands of Miami Cubans defied threats from hard-line exiles and descended in droves upon the island. The impact of the visitors ——and their gifts to family and friends—shook the communist regime to its ideological core. The exiles, whom Castro had repeatedly called *gusanos* (worms), were now welcomed as beneficent *mariposas* (butterflies) by their countrymen. To be sure, the Cuban population, tired of years of the severe hardships and shortages caused by the system's economic failures, were amazed at the contrast between their own ordeal and the exiles' success in America.

The Peruvian Embassy Incident: Given the widespread dissatisfaction with conditions in the island,

Cubans attempted to leave by whatever means they could. After one daring episode, in which a bus crashed through the gates of the Peruvian Embassy in Havana and a Cuban guard was killed, the government of Perú lodged an official protest against the communist regime's heavy-handling of the incident. An angry Castro retaliated by announcing he was retiring the security forces that surrounded the Peruvian Embassy.

Within a few days, over 10,000 Cubans crowded the embassy compound. The resulting spectacle embarrassed the *Máximo Líder* to no end, for the massive defections represented an obvious rejection of his regime—by a generation raised under Marxist slogans, no less. Trying to end such a damning display of disaffection, the regime offered safe-conduct to the refugees so that they could return to their homes while it negotiated their emigration. Peru, however, agreed to accept only one thousand refugees. It was then that Castro resorted once again to his old ploy—the demographic bomb.

In April 1980, just as he had done in 1965, Castro invited the exiles to come by sea and pick up, not only those who had originally sought asylum at the embassy, but anyone who wanted to leave. What followed was a reprise, albeit in a much larger scale, of the earlier opening of the port of Camarioca—although this time Mariel was designated the port of exit. As on the previous occasion, Cuban Americans sailed south to retrieve their loved ones. The Mariel Boatlift was underway.[22]

The Third Exodus—The Mariel Boatlift: The *Diversification Stage* may have actually started that moment in May 1980 when the first exiles sailed to the Cuban port of Mariel, and it certainly started off with a bang. About five months later, when this chaotic exodus finally concluded, some 125,000 Cubans had been brought into the United States in vessels owned or chartered by their fellow Cubans in exile.

---

21. Bombs exploded in Miami at the Continental Bank and at Padrón Cigars: their respective principals, Bernardo Benes and Orlando Padrón, had participated in the dialogue. *Dialogueros* were also victims of terrorist attacks in Jersey City and Puerto Rico.

22. In 1965 the Cuban government opened the port of Camarioca to exiles. Although only 5,000 refugees left with exiles at that time, this event led to the Freedom Flights which brought 300,000 Cubans to the United States between 1965 and 1973.

By then, the new refugees[23] had also managed to sink Miami into a deep crisis and to stigmatize the exiles who had brought them to America. Admittedly, the Mariel Boatlift cast a dark shadow over the image of the established exile community. Thereafter, *el exilio* would never be the same.

Demographically and ideologically, the refugees who arrived during the Mariel Boatlift appeared very different from the Cubans already in the United States. Whereas the two earlier waves were made up of older, mostly white emigrés who belonged to the upper and middle classes, the *Marielitos* were younger and represented a mix of races more typical of the island's multiracial population. Brought up under Cuba's socialist regime, the newcomers lacked their predecessors' business and professional experiences as well as their familiarity with free market economies.[24] To these differences in racial background and socioeconomic status, it is important to add the obvious contrast between the revolutionary political upbringing of the new arrivals and that of the established exiles. Moreover, unlike those who came in the first two waves, this new group was completely unfamiliar with Miami; they were clearly of a different vintage.

At first, Cuban Americans had reacted with enthusiasm to the incident at the Peruvian Embassy and the ensuing boatlift. The fact that these mostly young men, raised by the revolutionary regime, had turned their backs on communism was certainly cause for great celebration in Miami and the other exile colonies. But the festive mood lasted only a short while. As boat upon boat load of racially-mixed Marielitos made their way across the Florida Straights, the euphoria gave way to apprehension. After it was revealed that Castro had sprinkled the exodus with thousands of criminals and the mentally-ill, the exiles' mood turned to rancor.

The Post-Mariel Crisis: Within a few weeks of its on-set, the adverse repercussions of the boatlift had reached crisis levels. The housing shortage, unemployment and the crime wave unleashed by the newcomers upon South Florida prompted President Jimmy Carter to declare a state of emergency and to release $10 million to help local governments cope with the mounting crisis.[25] But that was hardly enough. By then, community leaders were up in arms, and Cuban Americans were blamed for bringing in the refugees.

For a while, it seemed as if the Cuban success story would be eclipsed by the *Marielitos'* penchant for getting themselves into trouble. A grim tent city appeared within the heart of once-quaint Little Havana, homeless peddlers roamed the streets, and violent crime engulfed South Florida. When police arrested the offenders, federal authorities confined these so-called excludables to prisons in other states, where they were to remain without hope of ever being released, even after serving their full sentences—unless they could be deported to Cuba. And Castro, of course, did not want to take them back. Facing such a dreadful legal limbo, the *Marielitos* who were confined at Fort Chaffee rioted, injuring scores of guards and setting fire to several buildings. Those housed at other federal penitentiaries soon followed suit.

U.S. officials had initially attempted to control the boatlift, but later they changed their position when President Carter himself reaffirmed this country's open-arms policy to Cubans seeking freedom. Toward the end of the summer of 1980, as the boatlift began to slacken, the Cuban regime finally closed the port of Mariel to the exiles, which effectively concluded this bizarre episode. Despite the damage that sensationalist reports had caused to South Florida's

---

23. To observe the prevailing terminology, Cubans who came in the first two emigration waves are referred to as "exiles" in this text; those who left during the 1980 Mariel Boatlift and the 1994 exodus are referred to as "refugees."

24. It was estimated that only 8.7 percent of the new arrivals, compared to 22.2 percent of the early exiles, had a managerial background.

25. At first, the *Marielitos* were processed by exile volunteers. That practice changed, however, after the federal government took charge and sent thousands to camps around the country: Eglin Air Force Base in Florida, Fort Chaffee in Arkansas, Fort Indian Gap in Pennsylvania, and Fort McCoy in Wisconsin.

image, and in particular to Cuban Americans, the worst was finally over; the troublemakers among the Mariel refugees, in reality, represented only a small minority, perhaps as low as 5 percent of the total. Once authorities had rounded them up, the post-Mariel crisis slowly faded away, but the damage had been done; the American press, and even the exiles themselves, echoed Castro's characterization of the entire batch of refugees as "worms and scum."

The "Cuban Exile Country" Matures and Diversifies: After a fleeting but chaotic interlude, the post-Mariel period was characterized by a consolidation of earlier trends toward a more diversified exile community, as evidenced by the appearance of new and often-contradictory developments: demographic shock, renewed leadership, political mobilization, economic maturity, and controversy over exile trips to the island.

Up to the *Diversification Stage*, the major thrust of Cuban business development in Miami had taken place within the ever-expanding boundaries of the enclave economy. Although by 1980 there were already over a dozen bank presidents and more than a hundred bank vice presidents born in Cuba, and the new U.S.-trained bilingual generation was being recruited by local enterprises as well as by multinational corporations, it was outside the mainstream economy where the exiles had concentrated their business efforts. That was to change drastically. In the 1980s, Cuban enterprises expanded beyond the enclave and began to challenge the "Anglo" business establishment on its own turf.

The growth of exile business outside the enclave proved rather successful in attracting the patronage of younger Cuban Americans (and even some "Anglo" customers) to a new breed of Cuban-owned supermarket chains, car dealerships, appliance stores, health maintenance organizations, etc. They managed to accomplish this feat by combining the traditional personal practices that had served them so well within the informal enclave economy with the ag-

gressive advertising and price discounting that were generally associated with large mainstream businesses. It was a winning strategy.

Cuban construction companies and developers, by now proficient in taking advantage of minority opportunities, began to vie with the biggest established enterprises for their share of government contracts and multi-million dollar projects. When South Florida's entrenched businesses realized the full potential of the exile economy, it was too late to stop the advance of the exiles; by then, Cubans not only enjoyed an almost-exclusive control of their thriving enclave, but were also making significant inroads into the rest of the South Florida market.

Cuban Americans Become a Political Force in South Florida: During the 1980s, the exiles fully discarded their earlier reservations about participating in American politics. Once that barrier was surmounted, the political enfranchisement of thousands of newly-registered Cuban American voters, as well as the reapportionment of new Hispanic districts, gave additional clout to the exiles. Cuban Americans quickly became adept at the art of using a political base to serve economic interests.

That combination of economic and political power proved very effective in furthering the aspirations of the "Cuban Exile Country." During the *Diversification Stage*, in fact, the exiles mustered sufficient political power to realize a goal that only a decade before had seemed highly implausible —influencing U.S. foreign policy toward Cuba. The creation of the Cuban American National Foundation (CANF) in the early 1980s stands as the best example of how the exiles managed to integrate political and economic power, and in so doing, avail themselves of a sophisticated lobby in Washington.[26]

Although primarily a politically-oriented group that advocates Cuban freedom, *la Fundación* helped articulate a sense of collective pride in what Cuban Americans have achieved. By reviving and refining the cru-

---

26. The Cuban American National Foundation's most dramatic accomplishment was its lobbying effort in favor of creating the U.S.-sponsored Radio Martí which broadcasts news and commentaries to Cubans on the island.

sading spirit that had driven the exiles in the 1960s, CANF and its chairman, Jorge Mas Canosa, have attracted considerable popular support and have emerged as formidable forces in the "Cuban Exile Country." The Cuban American National Foundation has also attracted scores of critics. Although no one appears to question its effectiveness, some perceive its political tactics as heavy-handed.

THE POST-SOVIET STAGE (1990-)
Renewed Hopes After Soviet Collapse (1990): After the disintegration of the Soviet Union and the suspension of the massive economic assistance it had been providing to the Cuban communist regime since the 1960s, Cuban society suffered a dramatic deterioration. Hope for the demise of the regime revived among the exiles, who became once again convinced that Castro's days were numbered. Those expectations drove Cuban Americans to recommit themselves to the struggle to liberate Cuba. They did so with novel strategies, but with the same passion of old.

The strategies often embraced by these groups were somewhat different from those of the early 1960s: Cuban Americans now recognized that for political change to take place in Cuba, it would have to be initiated by the opposition movement inside the island. Admittedly, this younger generation that is taking over the political agenda of *el exilio* has been more moderate than its predecessors and is more inclined to consider a wider range of approaches—a development that has revived the bitter political debate between moderate and hard-line exiles.

In the 1990s, the involvement of the "last generation" of Cubans, who came as youngsters and rebuilt their lives in America, surprised most observers, since it had been generally assumed that this generation of successful Cuban Americans had lost all interest in Cuba's political future. It is still too early to ascertain whether this constituency will demonstrate the same enduring commitment of its militant predecessors, but the new consciousness that younger Cuban

Americans have introduced in the anti-Castro movement seems to be spreading throughout the "Cuban Exile Country."

The Fourth Exodus: The Rafters (1994): In the early 1990s, the number of Cubans leaving the island began to increase noticeably. Their exodus seemed to follow the carrot-and-stick effects of two powerful forces: hope for a better life among exiles in the United States, and despair about worsening conditions on the island. But it is the latter, the near-collapse that Cuban society suffered after the disintegration of the Soviet Union, that appeared to be the determining factor in the new exodus.

From the perspective of the exiles, the latest wave of refugees seeking to escape Cuba's miserable conditions suggested that the Castro regime could be reaching its final phase. To be sure, economic activity in Cuba had dropped by about 40 percent since the collapse of the Soviet Union, a predicament that forced the communist regime to impose draconian measures that clearly undermined its popular support. It was no coincidence that human rights and dissident groups opposing Castro proliferated throughout the island and, for the first time, established working alliances with moderate exile political organizations.[27] The emergence of these loose coalitions linking opponents on both sides of the Florida Straights began to nurture a new kinship between Cubans who, although very dissimilar in backgrounds, experiences and even ideological visions of Cuba's future, shared a commitment to rid the island of communism.

Coupled with the continuing downward-spiral of the Cuban economy, the emboldened internal opposition added instability to the political climate on the island. Before conditions could reach a flash point, however, Castro again resorted to his time-tested ploy—the demographic bomb. In the spring of 1994, the communist regime reversed its three-decade-old policy of arresting anyone who tried to escape the island by sea; from then on, Castro an-

---

27. In 1996 more than one hundred independent unions and dissident groups came together in Cuba under an umbrella organization called Concilio Cubano, arguably the most recognized anti-Castro movement on the island.

nounced that Cubans would be allowed to leave in small vessels and makeshift rafts if they wished to embark for the United States.

The End of Open-Arms U.S. Immigration Policy toward Cubans: By the summer of 1994, as tens of thousands of *balseros* (rafters) took to the sea with the regime's overt encouragement, the Clinton administration negotiated an agreement with Cuba to put a stop to this new exodus. The new accord between the United States and Cuba suspended the preferential treatment that had been accorded to Cubans for three decades, provoking angry reactions among the exiles, who interpreted the de facto suspension of the open-arms policy toward Cubans fleeing the island as a first step toward normalization of relations between the two countries. In protest, exiles staged civil disobedience demonstrations throughout South Florida.

The 1994 immigration agreement also provided for the detention of those rafters who managed to reach American soil; from then on, all *balseros* were to be sent to the U.S. Navy Base in Guantanamo,[28] where they would have to stay indefinitely, unless they agreed to go back to the island from which they had risked their lives to escape. In a matter of weeks, the detainee population at Guantanamo reached 32,000 men, women and children. Six months later, however, the Clinton administration again shifted its position, allowing the Guantanamo detainee to qualify for entrance into this country.

New Crisis and the Tightening of the Embargo: The 1994 immigration accord gave credence to the notion that *el exilio*, as such, could be approaching its final phase. Although for different reasons, both Washington and Havana were under intense pressure to end the thirty-year-old U.S. trade embargo on Cuba and to normalize diplomatic and commercial relations. These speculations, however, proved premature. What derailed the fledgling rapprochement was Cuba's shooting down over international waters of two unarmed American airplanes belonging to Brothers to the Rescue. Four Cuban Americans lost

their lives in the incident, which dragged U.S.-Cuba relations to a confrontation level reminiscent of the bygone Cold War days.

In many ways, the genesis of this tragedy was somewhat predictable. Since the beginning of the recent *balsero* wave, Brothers to the Rescue planes had been engaged in humanitarian missions, carrying out thousands of rescue flights near or inside Cuban airspace in search of rafters adrift in the Straits of Florida. In 1995, however, the exile organization deviated from its original life-saving objective, and twice their airplanes actually intruded over Cuban territory to drop leaflets encouraging nonviolent rebellion. Truth be told, they seemed intent on provoking Castro, though peacefully. Finally, on February 24, 1996, Castro retaliated with a vengeance. He ordered the Cuban air force to shoot down two exile planes flying close to the island, thereby triggering an international crisis. President Clinton forcefully denounced the Cuban government for its criminal aggression and, reversing his personal opposition to the then-pending Helms-Burton Bill, promptly signed it into law. Enacted by the name of The Cuban Liberty and Democratic Solidarity Act, this piece of legislation tightened the U.S. embargo on Cuba even further— too much, according to its critics; just enough to force Castro out, according to its supporters. Its most controversial feature imposes sanctions on international companies doing business in Cuba.

What will happen in the wake of these developments is yet to be seen. In the short term, the once-hopeful prospect of forcing Castro into initiating a democratic transition have all but disappeared as a result of the latest incidents—which is not to suggest that the *Máximo Líder* had shown the slightest inclination to amend his totalitarian ways. Ironically, the hard-liners' position appeared to be validated by the belligerence of their nemesis, who at the same time cracked down against dissidents on the island with renewed ruthlessness. Once thing remains certain: given Castro's obstinate hold on power, *el exilio* can be expected to go on as long as the aging dictator continues to extend his thirty-eight-year old rule.

---

28. The Guantanamo Navy Base has operated on Cuban territory since it was ceded to the United States following Cuban independence in 1902. This last vestige of American imperialism on the island has remained a vexing presence often denounced by Castro.

CANADIANS IN CUBA:
GETTING TO KNOW EACH OTHER BETTER

Julia Sagebien

Even though Ottawa did not sever diplomatic relations with Havana in the 1960s, commercial and diplomatic exchanges between both countries were relatively minor until the collapse of the Soviet bloc. In the 1990s, Canadian business people, government officials and tourists have played a prominent role in the economic recovery of the Cuba. Canadians have, on the one hand, assiduously defended their sovereign right to trade with Cuba despite the renewed embargo tightening efforts of the United States government. On the other, they have maintained a firm commitment to bringing about economic, as well as political change in Cuba through engagement and dialogue. This work chronicles the highlights of the growing relation between Canada and Cuba in the 1990s and examines the challenges that Cuba poses to Canadian foreign and trade policy. It is divided into five sections: (1) Canada-Cuba foreign policy framework; (2) Canadian responses to U.S. extraterritorial measures; (3) up-date on trade and investment; (4) diplomatic demarches; and (5) conclusion.

FOREIGN POLICY FRAMEWORK

Canadian policy towards Cuba has been characterized as being *normal, active, promoting dialogue and engagement* and *balanced.*

Canadian Cuba policy is *normal* in the sense that it is similar to Canadian policy towards the rest of the Americas. The major difference between Canadian Cuba policy and that towards its other American neighbors is the dissonance of this policy with the United States' Cuba policy. For Canada, Cuba policy is symbolic of its ability to chart independent policy

vis-a-vis the United states. For example, Canada has a tradition of recognizing the "government of the day" and thus did not break relations with Havana in the 1960s as did most of the countries of the Americas at the instigation of the United States. One of the reasons why Ottawa has had more policy space in developing a more amicable Cuba policy is that Canada has a very small and inactive Cuban exile community which does not affect its electoral politics. In terms of the "morality" of maintaining diplomatic relations with Cuba, Cuba's human rights violations are seen in the spectrum of world-wide violations (e.g. Burma, China, etc.). In a manner similar to that expressed by Madeleine Albright in her assertion's regarding the objectives of U.S. policy towards China, Canadians believe that "engagement does not mean endorsement."

Canadian Cuba policy has been quite *active*, particularly in the 1990s. The two countries have enjoyed full diplomatic relations since 1945, however, in the 1990s there have been a number of high level official visits on both sides (Alarcón and Lage to Canada and Axworthy and Stewart to Cuba) and several provincial trade missions have taken place. Official aid to Havana was restored in 1994 and bilateral assistance was renewed in 1995 (aid had been cut in the 1970's as a protest over Cuban intervention in Angola). Canadian public and private agents have also provided economic restructuring advice particularly in taxes, fiscal management and central banking. Over 140,000 Canadians visited Cuba in 1996 (recently surpassed by Italians in terms of the largest country of origin). Commercial relations have also been quite active this decade. Canadians are likely the largest investors in Cuba given their numerous joint ventures in a variety of sectors and the presence of Sherritt International as a major player in the foreign direct investment sector of the Cuban economy. Canada-Cuba bilateral trade is increasing despite credit shortages and slowdowns in the Cuban economy.

Canada *promotes the notion of dialogue and engagement* in dealing with Cuba. The belief of the government of Canada and that of the majority of the concerned electorate is that this is the best policy to bring about economic and political liberalization. Canada has traditionally provided support for the yearly United Nations resolution to end the U.S. embargo, as well as for Cuba's renewed membership in the Organization of American States. In 1997 the governments of Cuba and Canada signed a Joint Declaration of Ministers of Foreign Affairs with the objectives of: being a confidence building measure; keeping channels open; and providing an umbrella programme for exchange of expertise (see Appendix A).

Canada has attempted to *balance* its Cuba policy. While there is support for trade, symbolic solidarity and mutual sympathy, the Department of Foreign Affairs and International Trade does not actively encourage business due Cuba's obvious political and commercial risk. There is little government backed credit and insurance. Canada has actively condemned human rights abuses and the lack of civil and political rights. The Embassy in Havana maintains an active human rights portfolio and remains in contact with dissidents, in and out of Cuban prisons. Canada has co-sponsored resolutions at the UN Human Rights Commission in Geneva criticizing Cuba's record, and it actively encourages establishment of civil society through efforts such as the Canada-Cuba Inter-Agency Project (non-government organization [NGO] steering organization).

The Canadian International Development Agency (CIDA), the government body which has handled the majority of Cuba assistance, has provided many different types of assistance to reflect this balanced policy. Bilateral assistance (government to government) has taken the form of, for example: (1) food aid; (2) the "Dialogue Fund"—for orderly fashion of policy implementation of the first 6 points of the Joint Declaration of Foreign Ministers 1997; (3) provision of C$5 million[1] for taxation reform spearheaded by Revenue Canada (Canada's IRS); and (4) C$4 million for paper for books and medicines. CIDA has also developed other programmes for economic planning and banking system reform, and for parliamentary, judicial, and legislative exchanges. New programmes on public sector management (C $2m) and on democratization are being put in place soon.

CIDA Inc., the department within CIDA that promotes private sector development had committed (though not necessarily disbursed) C$1.7 million by early 1997 for private sector ventures. CIDA's Institutional Cooperation branch has already committed C$6.2 million over 5 years for programmes in business and economics education, biotech and marine sciences. NGOs programme support is estimated at C$0.9 million committed and spent since 1994.

RESPONSE OF THE CANADIAN GOVERNMENT TO HELMS-BURTON

Canada and the United States have the largest trading relationship in the world, as well as the longest undefended border. In short, relations are excellent. However, since Canada did not break relations with Cuba in the 60s, there has been a fundamental conflict between Canada and the United States over Cuba for some time. While Cuba is just one of the U.S.-Canada disputes (others include lumber, salmon, press runs, etc.), conflict over the divergence of policies has generally been averted. In the mid 1990s, however, Helms-Burton has set them on a collision course.

Helms Burton is opposed by Canada on the grounds that: (1) it diverges from Canadian policy towards Cuba; (2) it is seen as magnifying the U.S.-Cuba problem rather than solving it; (3) it disrupts interna-

---

1. To convert Canadian dollars into U.S. dollars, multiply by 0.7

tional trade and investment and goes against the principles of international law; and (4) it sets a dangerous precedent of unilateral extraterritorial measures by the United States, which is seen in the broader context of general trade disputes.

Canadian moves to oppose Helms-Burton have included:

- support of the European Union's (EU) challenge at the World Trade Organization (WTO) even though there has been no Canadian participation in the EU-U.S. deal;

- application of Title III waivers to Canada. There is, however, concern over Canadian citizens already excluded from U.S. entry under Title IV;

- pursuit of the matter under NAFTA through ministerial consultations and the dispute settlement mechanism though no formal challenge has been presented yet;

- opposition at the OECD and OAS levels;

- lobbying with other U.S. trade partners with business interests in Cuba, especially Mexico and the European Union; and

- the Foreign Extraterritorial Measures Act (FEMA), which forbids compliance by Canadian firms with extraterritorial measures infringing on Canadian sovereignty. The law was first amended in 1992 to fight the Cuban Democracy Act (the Torricelli bill) and then amended again in 1997 as an "antidote" to Helms-Burton ("blocking" and "clawback" provisions). An example of the amended FEMA's implications in the fight against Helm-Burton's extraterritoriality can be seen in the Wal-Mart pajamas incident—the Cuban-made pajamas are back on the Canadian shelves despite a possible Helms-Burton violation and requests from Wal-Mart's head office to its Canadian subsidiary that the pajamas be withdrawn from the shelves.

The Canadian government's firm stance against Helms-Burton is not easy given that 80% of Canadian bilateral trade is with the United States; U.S. companies own a major portion of Canadian industry;

and one third of Canadian sugar imports come from Cuba and much of it used in confectionery products exported to the United States.

There has been a public outcry against Helms-Burton and a strong lobby to oppose the law. A 1996 survey reported that 71% of those surveyed supported the Canadian government's position. As a formal act of defiance of the U.S. legislation, twenty nine Canadian NGOs sponsored a "Boycott Florida Coalition."

UPDATE ON TRADE AND INVESTMENT

Canada is one Cuba's top three trade partners and Canada-Cuba bilateral trade has been rising in the mid-1990s after a sharp drop in the wake of the collapse of the Soviet bloc. In 1996, bilateral trade reached C$690.5 million (see Table 1). Most trade occurs on open account and trade efforts are constrained by limited credit. Canadian banks are keeping low profile in terms of financing Cuban trade while private financing and factoring companies have become very active in providing trade credit (at high interest rates rumored to be in the 16% annual range). The Export Development Corporation (EDC), the government body charged with assisting Canadian exporters, has had for some time two revolving credit lines totaling US$50 million. These lines are currently in arrears. There is some case by case credit cover by the EDC if there is either a guaranteed repayment flow or if a third party offshore guarantee is provided. The EDC has provided financing for some projects with clear repayment schedules such as the new terminal in the Jose Martí airport in Havana currently being constructed by the Quebec firm Intelcan.

Trade in services is poised for rapid growth given CIDA assistance for Cuba's reform process. Investment in infrastructure, construction and energy sectors is likely to become a priority area if the cost recovery issue can be overcome (e.g., toll highways). Service companies are interested in Cuba due to its potential market and to the fact that it is harder to build a trafficking case under Helms-Burton against service providers than it is towards traders and investors in products. While there might be some oppor-

Table 1. Canada-Cuba Trade (In million Canadian dollars)

	1995	1996	% change 1996/95	I Quarter 1996	I Quarter 1997	% change 1997I/96I
Canadian exports to Cuba	277.7	289.4	4.2	71.6	88.0	22.9
Canadian imports from Cuba	320.9	401.1	24.9	126.6	62.8	-50.3
Total bilateral trade	598.6	690.5	15.3	198.2	150.8	-23.9

Notes: Main Canadian exports to Cuba are machinery and mechanical appliances and foodstuffs; in 1996 (compared to 1995), there were increases in exports of vehicles, paper and food, and decreases in exports of cereals and fertilizers. Main Canadian imports from Cuba are nickel and sugar; Canadian imports of Cuban nickel in 1996 were higher than in 1995 by 33%. The decrease in Canadian imports from Cuba in the first quarter of 1997 compared to a like period in 1996 is mostly attributable to sharp drops in imports of sugar and nickel.

tunities in Cuba at this point, companies are aware that the real pay-off will only come with the end of the U.S. embargo and International Financial Institutions (IFI) moneys.

In terms of investment, there has been a renewed interest in Cuba despite nervousness over Helms-Burton. For example, the Cuba Growth Fund, an investment fund created in 1996 had, on paper, raised C$50 million by early 1997 for the purpose of investing in Canadian public companies doing business in Cuba and of making private placements in Cuba projects. As of mid-1997, the funds have not been secured even though a number of projects are under review. The major investment problem for the Fund and other investors such as Sherritt, is finding good "deals." There is concern over the capriciousness, control mania, and the ambivalent feeling towards foreign direct investment (FDI) of the Cuban government, as well as nervousness over the lack of an independent judiciary capable of resolving claims. Most Canadian business claims resulting form Cuba's nationalization process were settled in 1980-81 when Cuba paid US$875,000 in compensation. Discussions with five insurance companies regarding about US$10 million of claims are currently under way. Despite the risks and difficulties of investing in Cuba, Canadians are probably the premier foreign investors at this point. The official Statistics Canada figure is C$100m in FDI. However, government officials suggest that a total of C$300m is a more accurate figure.

Canadians are major investors in sectors such as resources and mining, tourism and biotechnology. In 1997, York Medical is continuing its efforts to commercialize Cuban biotechnology products. In re-

sources and mining, Sherritt International has the lead. The company raised C$675 million for overseas investment, primarily in Cuba in mining, energy, telecommunications, agriculture, tourism and transportation sectors. As of mid 1997, the company has not diversified much yet beyond mining. It has investments in hotel properties, agriculture (Sherritt green) and oil/gas. Sherritt is also reported to be looking at investment in the telecommunications industry. The company's second quarter 1997 results showed earnings of C$20.5m, total assets of C$1.4 billion, and cash and short term investment positions of C$320.7m. There are a number of other mining concerns such as Miramar Mining operating in Cuba. The latest large announcement has been KWT Resources (Quebec) with a C$300m investment for nickel mining in Moa.

In the tourism sector VANCUBA, a joint venture between Wilton Properties (Miramar Mining) and Gran Caribe is going ahead with its C$400 million project to open 11 hotels. Delta Hotels and Resorts has backed out of some management contracts citing business reasons rather than due to Helms-Burton. Journey's End has bought Commonwealth Holiday Inns management contracts in Cuba.

In terms of future bilateral trade patterns, exports to Cuba will depend on the continuation of economic recovery in Cuba and the provision of credit and investment in Canada. As far as imports from Cuba are concerned, nickel outflows are expected to remain steady and the sugar imports will depend largely on the success of the harvest for agricultural and financing reasons. FDI will depend on the progress of economic reform and on a more transparent legal framework. Priority sectors are likely to be energy and mining, telecommunications, construction and tourism. Since some Canadian companies are taking advantage of Americans not being there while others are waiting for them to arrive, the end of the U.S. embargo will be a mixed blessing for Canadian companies.

DIPLOMATIC DEMARCHES

The Canadian government is aware of fundamental questions surrounding Cuba's economic reform process such as: (1) How to insure that trade, aid and economic reform also result in political reform?; (2) What policy to pursue in order to best use carrots and sticks without linking trade and aid to human rights?; and (3) Will the reintroduction of market forces in Cuba provide the genetic material from which to make a market economy—or will it simply provide Castro with a vaccine against capitalism?

In 1997, Canadian diplomatic pressure on Cuba to accelerate the process of economic and political reform operates in two levels: (1) open lines of dialogue and clear communication to Cuban authorities that repression and paralyzed reform are not acceptable; and (2) formal "demarches" regarding assaults on microenterprises and dissidents (an on-going process). The Cuban response so far has been deemed not particularly "satisfactory". However, diplomatic pressure will be continuously applied. The view of the Canadian government is that at least the Cuban government is coming to the table and could learn from being exposed to other forms of governance.

There has been an increased awareness on the part of the Canadian government of the risks of its policy of rapprochement. For example, a CIDA request for proposal (RFP) on training in economic management states:

> There is a risk that recent reforms will not be maintained and strengthened and that Cuba could reinstate command-style economic planning. By automating MEP's [Ministry of Economics and Planning] economic planning information capacity the project could contribute to the perpetuation of state planning in Cuba.

The Canadian Government has so far been providing the tools for tax reform while not working on the

policy development side. More direct involvement on policy matters associated with aid projects is expected given the current wave of repression.

A number of changes in the Canadian diplomatic corps are also likely to affect the nature of Canada-Cuba relations. At the Canadian Embassy in Havana alone there has been a change in Ambassadors as well as in trade and political secretaries. Former Ambassador Mark Entwistle (Prime Minister Mulroney's former press secretary) who was very effective in increasing Canada-Cuba ties at all levels has been replaced by Keith Christie, a career diplomat who has been involved in a number of Canadian trade deals in Latin America. Mr. Christie is more bureaucratic and procedural in his approach. Guy Salese, the new trade secretary is considered to be a very pragmatic individual. He will put the emphasis on serving "ready, willing and able" clients and on the use of market intelligence. Nobina Robinson, who was also replaced as second secretary-political, was a very vocal critic of the Cuban government's human rights abuses and capriciousness in terms of reform.

There have also been changes in Ottawa in the personnel that covers the Cuban political and trade desks at the Department of Foreign Affairs and International Trade. The overall impact of changes in diplomatic corps is expected to be cooler, more formal and procedural relations; slowing down the flow of "gold-digging" companies; and more focus on results in terms of economic and political reforms.

Media coverage of Cuba in Canada is quite wide. Most articles cover progress of Helms-Burton and by-and-large support the Canadian position on sovereignty over trade and foreign policy. Nevertheless, there is broad coverage of contrary opinions in major dailies and magazines. There is increasing coverage of Cuba's harsh reality in terms of the state of the economy, of reform and of the severe treatment of dissidents. There are also frequent television and radio debates over the best Cuba policy *vis-a-vis* Canada's policy objectives and opposition from the U.S. Long-term Canadian residents of Cuba were negatively affected by Cuba's new housing law, and thus public opinion has been affected by the direct experience by

Canadian citizens of the dictatorial nature of the Cuban government.

CONCLUSION

Canadians and Cubans are "getting to know each other better." The dynamics of the "darker side" of the Cuban government is becoming more obvious to Canadians, thus policy and public opinion are being affected. Canadian government and commercial interests are presently stuck between a rock and a hard place: Helms-Burton and Cuban hard-liners. Nevertheless, neither Helms-Burton nor the resurgence of Cuban hard-liners has checkmated commercial interests. Opposition to Helms-Burton is based on its extraterritoriality, not on Cuba-Canada solidarity. Helms-Burton has, unfortunately, had a perverse effect—it has pushed Canadian policy over to the Cuban's anti-American camp and it has narrowed the leeway of policy options for the Canadian government.

Changes in Canadian diplomatic corps and in configuration of international opposition to Helms-Burton (EU-U.S. deal) as well as pressure on Clinton to both soften and tighten the law are bound to change the dynamics of the relationship. Nevertheless, Canadian commercial and diplomatic ties will continue to grow and the current policy framework is likely to remain much the same. A reversal of policy is not, however, unthinkable given Cuban intransigence in terms of political and economic reform, as well as domestic and international pressures.

In the final analysis, the long-term benefit of Canada's policy of rapprochement towards Cuba, as well as its general "good neighbor" policy towards the United States is that it qualifies Canada as probably the best possible arbiter between the two countries. The negotiator role is likely to gain importance with the end of the U.S. embargo. Though committed to encouraging change in Cuba by peaceful means, dialogue and engagement, Canadians want to make clear to Cubans as well as to Americans that they are not "patsies."

APPENDIX A

Joint Declaration of Ministers of Foreign Affairs of Canada and Cuba

1. Cooperation in the administration of justice and the judicial-legal system, including exchanges of judges and judicial training.

2. Exchanges between the House of Commons and the National Assembly, focusing on the operations of both institutions.

3. Exchange of experiences relating to the National Assembly's Citizens' Complaints Commission.

4. Broadening and deepening cooperation on the issue of human rights, including seminars of mutual interest, academic exchanges between officials, professionals and experts, sharing experiences and positions on the work of the specialized organizations of the UN.

5. Supporting the activities of Canadian and Cuban non-governmental organizations.

6. Continuation of macroeconomic cooperation, with an initial focus in the areas of taxation and central banking while studying other areas of Cuban economic policy reform.

7. Negotiate Foreign Investment Protection Promotion Agreement.

8. Further collaboration on narcotics interdiction.

9. Conversations on international terrorism and its prevention.

10. Negotiation of a Memorandum of Understanding between Health Canada and the Ministry of Public Health of Cuba.

11. The negotiation of an audio-visual co-production agreement.

12. The renewal of the bilateral sports cooperation accord.

13. The exploration of joint projects in health and environment.

14. The provision of food aid in response to Hurricane Lilli.

UPDATE ON FOREIGN INVESTMENT IN CUBA: 1996-97

María C. Werlau

Last year's paper presented at this conference[1] concluded that the argument for commercial engagement is fundamentally insupportable as a justification for foreign investment in Cuba under the current circumstances. Two primary factors were found to inhibit the feasibility of foreign investment as a vehicle of reform in Cuba. First, the island's distressed investment climate limits opportunities to attract a level of foreign investment that could have a meaningful impact on the economy and society as a whole. Second, because Cuba's peculiar *mode* of foreign investment has been designed to secure regime survival, its most significant reform-generating attributes remain, for all practical purposes, effectively suppressed. Perversely, its detrimental side-effects appear to mostly hinder, instead of bolster, the eventual establishment of a stable free-market democracy. In order to substantiate these points, last year's paper was divided into three parts. The first part established that Cuba's campaign to attract foreign investment had generated very disappointing overall results by mid-1996. The second part attributed this failure to Cuba's highly risky investment climate, which was described in certain detail. The third part illustrated how Cuba's mode of foreign investment—essentially joint venture enclaves subject to singular regulations—has limited multiplier and dispersion benefits which are incapable of fostering meaningful economic or socio-political reform. On this occasion, we will provide a brief update on the same fundamental aspects, which have again been found to substantiate our previous conclusion.

CUBA'S DRIVE TO ATTRACT FOREIGN INVESTMENT

The Campaign to Lure Investors: 1996-97

The Cuban government continues to court foreign investors. During the last year investment protection and economic cooperation agreements were signed with France, Grenada and Laos, bringing the total number of bilateral agreements to 21.[2] A number of business fairs and conferences were held in Havana covering a wide range of sectors from health products and tourism to investment opportunities in sugar.[3] Cuban officials continued to tour the world seeking to drum up business and covered a diversity of countries from the United States, Germany, France, and

---

1. See María C. Werlau, "Foreign investment in Cuba: The limits of commercial engagement," *Cuba in Transition—Volume 6* (Washington: Association for the Study of the Cuban Economy, 1996), pp. 456-495.

2. Agreements had been signed with: Italy, Russia, Spain, Colombia, U.K., China, Ukraine, Bolivia, Vietnam, Argentina, Lebanon, South Africa, Romania, Chile, Barbados, Germany, Greece, Sweden and Switzerland. Cuba reports thirty more bilateral agreements being negotiated. See *Economic Eye on Cuba* (17-23 February 1997, 3-9 March 1997 and 21-27 April 1997.) *Economic Eye on Cuba* is a weekly publication of the *U.S.-Cuba Trade and Economic Council, Inc.* (U.S.C.T.E.C.) For details on the *U.S.-Cuba Trade and Economic Council,* see Werlau, "Foreign investment in Cuba," p. 458.

3. *Economic Eye on Cuba* (21-27 April 1997, 25 November-1 December 1996, 26 May-1 June 1997, 3-9 March 1997); Joaquín Oramas, "Avance en el producto cubano, *Granma Internacional* (1997), edición digital.

Hungary to Belarus and Vietnam.[4] Likewise, a number of commercial delegations, such as from as China, Sweden, Laos and Jamaica, visited the island and groups of businessmen from Greece, Britain, France and others countries paid enthusiastic visits.[5] In the public relations' arena, Cuba's most visible successes appear to have been the January 1997 visit of Canada's Foreign Minister, Lloyd Axworthy, and the festivities for the 30th anniversary of the Cohiba cigar the following month. This first visit of a Canadian foreign minister since 1959 received wide media coverage and produced a joint declaration, which was regarded as a snub to the United States and a legitimizing boost to the Castro regime.[6] The Cohiba celebrations lasted over a week and culminated with a gala at Havana's Tropicana nightclub allegedly attended by 700 guests from 40 countries who paid US$500 each. The dinner featured an auction of especially-rolled Cohiba cigars and hand-crafted humidors—one signed by Castro. 200 journalists from 20 countries requested accreditation to cover the event, which received widespread international media coverage.[7]

Historic experience and the absence of tangible results, however, make it highly unlikely that a significant level of actual (direct) foreign investment will result from the apparent enthusiasm with Capitalism "a la cubaine." The primary focus of most business delegations to Cuba appears to be the development of trade opportunities and the exploration of *possible* investments. It seems that foreigners are more eager to tap into the island's dire need of a wide range of imports, despite the modesty of overall opportunities as a result of Cuba's lack of credit facilities and its depressed economy. Upon attempting to track down actual investment initiatives from the described contacts, one finds few concrete results. In turn, even optimistic coverage of the visits of French and British business delegations contain references to investors' concerns regarding such problems as Havana's water shortages, the need to totally renovate Cuba's citrus processing,[8] and the country's lack of import financing facilities.[9] While the President of the *U.S.-Cuba Trade and Economic Council* reported to the media that the past months have been very fruitful -with an increase in the Council's membership as well as in the number of companies involved in business- his personal comments are much less encouraging.[10]

Adding to Cuba's problems, a new trend seems to be emerging in the international media coverage on Cuba. Notwithstanding Cuba's publicity coups, the stream of enthusiastic stories on this "hot emerging market" seems to have dried out. Moreover, reports of a different twist are starting to gain ground. In March 1997 *Business Week* reported that Castro is counting on foreign companies to prop up Cuba through limited economic reforms, with the goal of keeping himself in power.[11] In July 1997 *The Economist* ran an article on free enterprise in Cuba, which

4. *U.S.-Cuba Trade and Economic Council,* electronic web page (11 July 1997); *Economic Eye on Cuba* (21-27 April 1997 and 9-15 June 1997).

5. *Economic Eye on Cuba,* several issues; Eloy Rodríguez, "Tercera visita del Consejo Nacional del Patronato Francés," *Granma Internacional* (30 abril 1997), ed. digital; Eloy Rodríguez, "Firma contratos misión empresarial británica," *Granma Internacional* (27 julio 1997), ed. digital; "Los griegos enfilan hacia el Caribe," *Granma Internacional* (2 junio 1997), ed. digital.

6. Axworthy was accompanied by the Secretary of State for American and African Affairs. Their visit took place on January 21-22, 1997. The Joint Declaration of the Ministers of Foreign Affairs of Canada and Cuba emphasized the mutual commitment and right to conduct international relations on the basis of the defense of international law and agreed to advance towards new bilateral initiatives and increased cooperation. *U.S-Cuba Policy Report,* 4:1 (January 31, 1997), pp. 7-8.)

7. Orlando Gómez Balado, "Festejos por el mejor habano del mundo, *Granma Internacional* (13 febrero 1997), ed. digital; *Economic Eye on Cuba* (17-23 February 1997).

8. Gabriel Molina, "Franceses dispuestos a llenar espacio en la economía cubana," *Granma Internacional,* ed. digital.

9. E. Rodríguez, "Firma contratos."

10. Rodolfo Casals, "Empresarios norteamericanos interesados en comerciar con Cuba," *Granma Internacional* (8 julio 1997), ed. digital; John Kavulich in telephone conversations with the author of April 12, 1997 and July 11, 1997.

11. "Castro's Capitalist," *Business Week* (March 17, 1997), p. 48 and "A touch of capitalism," *Business Week* (March 17, 1997), p. 50.

specifically cites the new free trade zones and states that Castro hates the result of "yielding to market forces." It declares the Cuban leader's regard for foreign investment as a "temporary" and "necessary evil," quoting a Castro supporter: "Our government hates people who make money."[12]

Yet, some foreign businessmen persist in making bullish predictions on Cuba. Ian Delaney, the chairman of Canadian company Sherritt International, told *Business Week* last March that Cuba is "the best investment opportunity in the world."[13] Peter Scott, Chairman of Beta Funds Limited, has called Cuba "the last embryo market ...in the process of recovery and undergoing a gradual transition to a market-based economy."[14] The President of the German Association of Travel Agents declared Cuba "the safest travel destination in Latin America."[15] And a Frenchman with a business in Cuba extols: "This is the seventh time I have encountered President Fidel Castro. He is an extraordinary person. ...the country is recovering extraordinarily. ...Every day I discover new clients and new things to do here."[16]

In the United States, a corporate campaign against unilateral economic sanctions has emerged involving General Electric, IBM, Exxon, Mobil, Citicorp, Allied Signal, Ingersoll Rand and Westinghouse. In alliance with the U.S. Chamber of Commerce the National Association of Manufacturers and the National Council for International Trade,[17] the Helms-Burton

legislation has become one of its targets.[18] In addition, a lobby to lift restrictions on the sale of food and medicine to Cuba was recently undertaken in Washington.[19] Nonetheless, the general mood of the U.S. business community appears to be one of continued caution. For example, in July of 1996 CBS aired a documentary in which the aforementioned president of the U.S.-Cuba Trade and Economic Council named several U.S. companies and declared: "There isn't a single CEO who doesn't want to return to Cuba as soon as possible." Yet, all but one of the companies responded to a letter of the Cuban American National Foundation disallowing any connections to the Council (Chrysler, General Motors, Ford, McDonalds, and ITT).[20] Most added strong statements denying business interest in Cuba and/or efforts to lobby against the embargo.[21]

To illustrate Cuba's seeming quandary, perhaps an anecdotal account might provide some lucid insight. In February 1997, an elite group of powerful Latin American businessmen (the "Group of 50") went on a visit to Cuba which featured a gala attended by Castro. Fidel was received as a star, posed for pictures and signed autographs. Notwithstanding the obvious enthusiasm, one of the attendees—the head of an industrial/banking conglomerate—admitted that most members of the delegation were not interested in doing any business in present-day Cuba, and were rather satisfying an alluring curiosity.[22] In sum, Cuba,

---

12. "Cuba: enterprise?: tax it," *The Economist* (July 5, 1997).

13. "Castro's Capitalist."

14. *Economic Eye on Cuba* (3-9 March 1997).

15. Rodolfo Casals, "Para los vacacionistas, Cuba es el país más seguro de Latinoamerica," *Granma Internacional* (7 mayo 1997), ed. digital.

16. This French businessman produces metallic parts for the construction industry in Cuba. See G. Molina, "Franceses dispuestos."

17. Newsletter of *The American Chamber of Commerce of Cuba in the United States* (April 23, 1997), p. 2.

18. "Empresas de EEUU lanzan campaña contra la ley Helms-Burton y las sanciones económicas," *Granma Internacional* (9 abril 1997), ed. digital.

19. Sherritt International was reported to have retained Malcolm Wallop, a former Republican Senator from Wyoming, to lobby on this behalf. *The U.S.-Cuba Policy Report*, 4:4 (April 30, 1997).

20. The exception is Archer Daniels Midland, whose former Chairman, Dwayne Andreas, has been a very vocal spokesman for lifting the embargo on Cuba.

21. "Credibility challenged: Cuba trade booster's comments on CBS rejected by companies," Press Release, *The Cuban American National Foundation* (September 26, 1996), with copies of letters from the cited companies.

22. Related in person to the author.

continues to be the focus of much curiosity, but actual commitments to invest foreign capital appear direfully lacking.

Results

Verifiable results, as in the past, are unavailable. Yet, despite the ambiguous and contradicting data emanating from Cuban government sources,[23] it becomes apparent that results are disappointing. By the end of 1996 fairly consistent statistics emerge from official sources of the *total* number of joint ventures and economic associations.[24] Although the Deputy Minister for Foreign Investment reported a total of only 236 in June 1997[25] most reports cite 260, said to be established in the following sectors: 30 in oil extraction, 38 in mining (5 of these in nickel), 45 in tourism,[26] 41 in hotel administration, 4 in real estate, 85 in industry, and 12 in transportation and communications. Only a few joint ventures are said to be more than 50% foreign owned, in no case more than 70% foreign owned.[27] This claim of 260 joint ventures up

to the end of 1996 is puzzling because in late 1995 both Minister Carlos Lage, Cuba's "economic czar," and the *Comisión de Estudios de la Economía Cubana* had claimed the existence of 270 joint ventures from 50 countries.[28]

Data on the number of joint ventures established in 1996 is more inconsistent. The Minister for Foreign Investment claimed that 80 were established after the enactment of the new foreign investment law in September 1995, 56 of these in 1996.[29] Notwithstanding, a later report from this same Minister cites 48 established in 1996[30] and the United Nations Economic Commission for Latin America (ECLA) report on Cuba of September 1997 refers to 46 joint ventures established in 1996.[31]

As in the past, reports from Cuba all fail to provide figures on foreign direct investment or to distinguish traditional joint venture investments from economic cooperation agreements, which typically don't entail direct capital infusions. A University of Havana pro-

23. Data is obtained from reports of Ministries, interviews and statements by different Ministers, the newspaper *Granma*, and other official and semi-official sources, such as academic centers. Cuba's reporting does not meet the standards of most countries; contrary to standard practice for the calculation of foreign direct investment, in addition to capital inflows, the data provided by Cuba appears to include diverse financial transactions, management contracts, production partnership arrangements, foreign contribution of assets, debt-equity swaps, exploitation contracts to service or expand deposits already mined, canceled deals and "announced" investments contingent on events that may never materialize. Discrepancies in figures provided by the government are exacerbated by conflicting information obtained from other national and international reports. See Werlau, "Foreign investment," pp. 462-463.

24. For purposes of simplification, we will use the term joint venture to refer to joint ventures and economic associations indistinctly.

25. "Cuba says few firms using old U.S. property," *Canadian Press*, Havana (June 18, 1997) and *Economic Eye on Cuba* (17-23 June 1997), p.1. (Minister Octavio Castilla is quoted.)

26. There is discrepancy with other reports provided by the same Minister for Foreign Investment which cite 20 joint ventures in tourism, including 17 hotels. See *Economic Eye on Cuba* (21-27 April 1997). The Minister of Tourism, in turn, reported 36 joint ventures in tourism—20 with joint capital, 16 management contracts. Orlando Gómez Balado, "Llegó el millón de visitantes," *Granma Internacional* (14 enero 1997), ed. digital.

27. *Economic Eye on Cuba* (25 November-1 December 1996), as reported by the Minister for Foreign Investment.

28. Magdalys Rodríguez, "Trabas al empresario interesado," *El Nuevo Día* (23 de noviembre de 1995); *Negocios en Cuba*, Suplemento del Mundo en Síntesis (semana del 19 al 25 de agosto de 1996), p.1. Adding to the confusion, the Ministry of Economy and Planning, however, reported 240 association agreements with foreign capital from 43 nations for the first semester of 1996. *Cuba: Economic Report*, First Semester 1996, Ministry of Economy and Planning.

29. *Economic Eye on Cuba* (25 November-1 December 1996).

30. Minister Ibrahim Ferradaz cited 48 joint ventures established in 1996 by December 1, 1996 for a total of 260. *Economic Eye on Cuba* (25 November-1 December 1996). In addition he reported the 1996 agreements as more complex and involving larger amounts of capital than those completed the year before and informed of an additional 100 joint venture agreements in the process of negotiation. *Economic Eye on Cuba* (3-9 March 1997). In another report, the Minister cited 42 association agreements with foreign investors from March to December 1996. Joaquín Oramas, "Turismo, zafra y níquel: ejes para el desarrollo," *Granma Internacional*, ed. digital.

31. United Nations Economic Commission for Latin America and the Caribbean (ECLA),"La evolución reciente de la economía cubana" (September 1997), p.139.

fessor acknowledged at an international conference: "It's difficult to quantify the flow of international capital into Cuba (...) committed disbursements have amounted to more than US$2.5 billion, of which what has actually been completed is unknown."[32]

One interesting and seemingly new development in the area of foreign investment is Cuba's participation in joint ventures abroad. One already began operating in Mexico and is said to have contributed capital to form BIOTEK, to produce soy milk substitute using technology developed by the Research Institute of the Food Industry of Cuba.[33] Another joint venture was announced in March 1997 between the government-operated Cuban Agriculture Equipment Research Institute and Mexico's Agroingeniería S.A., to produce in Mexico plowing equipment designed in Cuba to be sold in Mexico and other Latin American countries.[34] Cuba has also developed several joint investments with Vietnam. An agreement was signed by Cuba's government-operated Tecnoazur, Spain's Bilbao Vizcaya bank and "Vietnamese companies," to construct a sugar mill in Vietnam. Government operated companies of Cuba and Vietnam agreed to establish Bio Viet Nam Limited to produce and distribute the organic pesticide BIORAT in Vietnam and other Asian countries.[35] In May 1997 a US$8.5 million joint venture livestock and meat processing plant was inaugurated in Vietnam.

During the past year, it appears that indeed a few new joint ventures were established in Cuba, but none of those for which numbers are cited involve a large amount of capital and most announcements don't cite an amount at all.[36] Moreover, it's impossible to say if these represent capital infusions and/or if they have been included in figures previously "announced" or "committed/delivered" investments, as per data provided by the U.S.-Cuba Trade and Economic Council. For example, mining "investments" sound large, but it looks like capital expenditures are limited in scope in many of the announced deals, at least for now and particularly in relation to the required capital for project development in the exploitation phase. While firms from Canada, France, Great Britain, and Sweden are said to have invested more than US$200 million for seismic exploration in 19 of the 32 blocks in which the country has been divided, only a few wells are said to have been drilled and even fewer are producing.[37] Details on these investments are mostly unavailable and it is uncertain whether they will lead to continued investment. Some additional problems with announced foreign "investments" include:

- Valuation formulas are suspect; the terminology "valued at" chosen to cite some investment makes the amount of direct capital dubious;

- It is unclear whether foreign capital has actually been disbursed for many "deals";

- Reportedly, the proceeds of certain foreign investments (sale of Cuban assets) are diverted to special accounts subject to Castro's personal and

---

32. Omar Pérez Villanueva, Universidad de la Habana, Centro de Estudios de la Economía Cubana, *La inversión extranjera en Cuba: Peculiaridades*, paper presented at the LASA 97, XX International Congress, Guadalajara, Mexico, March 1997, p. 22.

33. *Cuba Monthly Economic Report* (July 1997), p. 3.

34. *Economic Eye on Cuba*, 1997 Monthly Chronology of Selected Commercial Activity (March 1997).

35. *Economic Eye on Cuba*, 1997 Monthly Chronology of Selected Commercial Activity (March and May 1997).

36. The author has compiled a partial list of 1996-97 joint venture deals in the form of an Addendum to this paper. This addendum is not included in this volume because of space restrictions. The addendum is available from the author. Ed.

37. A well in the Bay of Cardenas (Cupex IX) is said to be producing 3,750 barrels of oil a day, one at Puerto Escondido, 550 barrels a day. *Cuba Monthly Economic Report*, 1:3 (July 1997), p. 4.

arbitrary management ("the *Comandante*'s reserve");[38]

- Given the apparent nature of those investment agreements which grant joint ventures the rights to commercialize products of Cuban entities, capital infusions by the foreign partner for the development of these products seems improbable; and

- Foreign participation described as contributing technology and know-how[39] might indicate the sale of specialized equipment instead of a direct foreign investment.

Cuba has reported that 75% of the existing joint ventures and economic associations have initial capital of *less than* US$5 million.[40] In a hypothetical calculation, if the cited 260 joint ventures and economic associations each represented an average capital investment of US$2.5 million, the total foreign investment in Cuba could not exceed US$650 million. If the average investment were raised to the maximum US$5 million cited for 75% of the total, the amount would increase to only US$1.3 billion. Yet, by 1995, when the reported number of joint ventures was lower, Cuba was announcing foreign investment of US$2.1 billion. Moreover, government reports of US$2.2 billion in foreign investment through 1996[41] would represent an increase of a mere US$100 million from the figures it reported more than a year ago.[42] If 56 joint ventures had actually been established in 1996, the average investment would have been of a mere US$1.8 million.

To get an idea of the questionable and confusing nature of the available data, the following might be taken into account:

- The increase of US$50 million reported in Table 1 for Canadian investments includes investments made by Sherritt International and the purchase by KWG Resources, Inc. of a nickel option previously held by the South African company Gencor. Nonetheless, Sherritt's annual report cites only US$22.5 million in investments in Cuba in the fiscal year ending 12/31/96 and KWG's purchase was reportedly for US$10 million. Both total only US$32.5 million; the US$17.5 million shortfall is unaccounted for. Moreover, it is unlikely that KWG's option entailed a capital investment, which would mean that the shortfall in direct capital invested would actually increase

38. Related to the author in August 1997 by Jesús M. Fernández, who left Cuba in May 1996 after occupying very high level government positions, including dealing with Castro's "special reserve." *Cuba Monthly Economic Report*, a publication of DevTech Systems, Inc. published a Special Edition (August 1997) recounting Mr. Fernández's first-hand knowledge of the accounts. Mr. Fernández specifically cites a US$50 million payment for the "sale" of Havana Club rum distilleries to the French firm Pernod Ricard going directly to the *Comandante*'s reserve as well as estimated net earnings of US$10-15 million derived from several foreign investments involved in citrus, specifically citing joint ventures with Chilean investors. In 1993, Pernod Ricard obtained the rights to commercialize Havana Club rum internationally. Details of the financial arrangement involved have not been obtained as of the time of this writing.

39. As per at least one announced deal in which the Cuban part was said to be responsible for "assembling the equipment and implementing the investment." See "Modernizarán empresas francesas generación de la termoeléctrica Antonio Maceo," *Granma Internacional* (23 abril 1997), ed. digital.

40. Figures provided by the Minister for Foreign Investment. See *Economic Eye on Cuba* (3-9 March 1997); *Reuters* (November 5, 1996.)

41. *Economic Eye on Cuba* (21-27 April 1997).

42. The September 1995 issue of *Business Tips on Cuba* cites a Minister of Foreign Investment and Economic Collaboration, Ernesto Melendez, May 1995 report of 212 *economic associations* with firms from 53 countries with a "capital contribution of 2,100 million dollars, representing a 78% growth in relation to the same period of 1994." *Business Tips on Cuba*, 2:9 (September 1995), p. 6. One year later, this publication cites the Minister of Economy and Planning, José Luis Rodríguez, informing of 230 economic associations and *the same* amount of investment, US$2,100 million dollars. *Business Tips on Cuba*, 3:9 (September 1996).

by up to US$10 million even lower in direct investment.[43]

• We might extrapolate numbers cited for French joint venture investments to total investments. If the 39 French companies reported to be established in Cuba[44] (15% of 260 joint ventures) have US$10 million in committed/delivered investment, as per the above table, their average investment would be only around US$256 thousand. By applying this average investment to the 75% of joint ventures the government has cited as having investments below US$5 million, we end up with around US$49.9 million in total investment from 75% of all investors. This means that the remaining 25%, 65 foreign firms, would have invested around US$33.8 million each. In light of the reports the government has put out, this seems implausible.

• Table 1 shows committed/delivered Spanish investments of US$80 million, yet the total for direct Spanish investment in Cuba reported by Spain's Ministry of the Economy in late 1996 was equivalent to around US$11.2 million.[45] Yet, Cuba's Minister of Tourism reported that in 1996 alone Spain invested US$100million in just one industry—tourism.[46]

In fact, the total "committed/delivered foreign investment" in Cuba—*accumulated over time* from *all* investors from *all* countries—is estimated at no higher than US$869.9 million, as per data provided by the *U.S.-Cuba Trade and Economic Council*.[47] This data, it must be noted, includes "committed" investments, such as options for mining rights, rather than just direct invested capital. If, indeed, Cuba has US$869.9 million in direct investment, reported as "delivered" in Table 1, and we assumed a high return of capital of 33.3% per annum, a hypothetical 50/50 partnership would generate net earnings of US$289 million per annum—around US$145 million for each partner (the Cuban government and the foreign investor).[48] (Since the level of investment is presumably overstated and this assumed rate of return is very high, actual results would be lower unless a higher capital return ratio were factored in. It should be, for example, noted that Sherritt, Cuba's most notorious investor, reported a rate of return of 27% for its 1996 operations in Cuba.) Assuming our estimated revenue is for income derived from operations, the Cuban government will have additionally obtained approximately US$123.9 million in tax revenues for

---

43. KWG announced plans to invest US$300 million. (More details on this transaction are included in the Addendum referenced in footnote 36.) *CubaNews,* 5:7 (July 1997), p. 3. A media report cites 20 Canadian joint ventures by mid-1996 with investments totaling more than US$300 million. Juliett O'Neill, "Firms forced out won't have a headstart when communism falls, " *Southam Newspapers* (July 13, 1996), distributed by *CubaNet.*) Yet, if we hypothetically, took the ratio Cuba has cited of 75% of the joint ventures totaling *less* than US$5 million and pushed it to the very maximum of US$5 million for 15 joint ventures (75% of the total), we end up with US$75 million. This theoretically requires the five remaining Canadian companies to have invested US$45 million each. Yet, other than Sherritt's, no such large investments have been reported. Interestingly, a 1996 Canadian media report cites Canadian investments in Cuba as "hundreds of millions of dollars more" than the reportedly $390 million in two-way trade. Colin Nickerson, "Canada doesn't buy U.S. stance on Cuba," *The Boston Globe* (February 29, 1996.)

44. *Economic Eye on Cuba* (21-27 April 1997).

45. Spain's direct investment in Cuba was reported to have risen sharply in the first nine months of 1996, from 527 million pesetas (US$4.1 million) in relation to the same period in 1995. "Spain's investment rose sharply in 1996," *Reuters,* Madrid (November 26, 1996). The dollar equivalence was calculated at 128 pesetas to the dollar.

46. Armando Correa, "España nombraría embajador en Cuba por visita del Papa," *El Nuevo Herald* (12 agosto 1997), distributed by *CubaNet.*

47. Curiously, the *Council* reported US$705 million in committed/delivered foreign investment as of 4/1/97, 5% less than in 8/1/96. *Economic Eye on Cuba* (21-27 April 1997). The *Council* receives the official cooperation of the Cuban government and sends copies of its reports to Cuban officials, who have not advised of any discrepancies in the calculations of foreign investment. (As per John Kavulich, President of the *Council,* in telephone conversation with the author, 7/11/97).

48. A 3-year rate of return of capital is an assumed average minimum return for highly risky cross-border investments. This capital recovery ratio is reported for some foreign joint ventures in Cuba.

Table 1. Foreign Investment in Cuba (in million US$)

| Country | As of 8/1/96 | | Reflecting Changes as of 6/30/97 | |
	Announced	Committed/ Delivered	Announced	Committed/ Delivered
Australia		500		
Austria	0.5	0.1		
Brazil	150	20		
Canada	941	100	1191	150
Chile		69	30	
China	10	5		
Dominican Republic	5	1		
France	15	10		
Germany	10	2		
Greece	2	0.5		
Honduras	7	1		
Israel	22	7		
Italy	97	87	397[a]	
Jamaica		2	1	
Japan	2	0.5		
Mexico	2256	250	1806[b]	400[c]
Netherlands	300	40		
Panama	2	0.5		
Russia	25	2		
South Africa	400	15		5
Spain	350	125		80
Sweden	10	1		
United Kingdom	70	50		
Uruguay	0.5	0.3		
Venezuela	50	3		
Total	5301	751.9	5401	896.9
Net Change			+100	+145

Source: Conversations with John Kavulich, President, U.S.-Cuba Trade and Economic Council and adapted tables of August 1, 1966, January 27, 1997, and July 25, 1997 provided by the Council with the following statement: "Figures represent the amounts of announced, committed and delivered investments since 1990 by private sector companies and government companies from various countries to enterprises within the Republic of Cuba. ... Information compiled through the media and other public sources, individual discussions with company representatives, non-Republic of Cuba government officials, and Republic of Cuba-based enterprise managers and government officials.

a. $300 million increase attributed to STET's purchase of Domos' share in ETECSA.
b. $450 million decrease attributed to Domos' cancellation of $450 million expected investment in ETECSA.
c. $150 million increase attributed to Domos' alleged capital expenditures in ETECSA.

total revenues of US$268.9 million.[49] This amount, presumed as already overstated, cannot come close to compensating for the huge gap left by the loss of Soviet aid (estimated at around US$6 billion per annum).[50] In fact, even a University of Havana study has stated in circumspect language that "it has been reiterated that the development resulting from the absorption of foreign capital is inferior to what might be the actual needs of the country."[51]

Despite the obvious problems with Cuba's data, many media reports continue to pass on obscure data at face value. *The New York Times* reported in February of 1997 that, despite Helms-Burton, Canadian companies alone had "poured over half a billion dollars into nickel mines, luxury hotels and other businesses..."[52]

Performance and Notes on a Few Foreign Investments

A striking aspect of the stream of reports on Cuba's joint ventures is their almost complete absence of data on earnings performance. (Please see Addendum available from the author for a partial list of recent investments.) The only notable example of a foreign joint venture partner readily reporting earnings to the media is Sherritt, which, by its corporate nature, is compelled to make its audited statements available.[53] Almost all public references to joint ventures lack revenue/earnings data that would allow an assessment of results. Yet, it would seem that if joint ventures were generating attractive earnings, this information would be forthcoming.

Investment funds for Cuba might provide a more graphic appreciation of actual business opportunities

---

49. Assuming Cuba had a 50% share of every joint venture, earnings before taxes would total US$412.85 million and a 30% tax would net the state around US$123.9 million. This amount plus Cuba's estimated share of operating revenues ($145 million) equals $268.9 million.

50. Minister Lage indicated that Cuba's 1995 net income from foreign joint ventures was just US$114 million, representing 3% of the country's net income. Given the data we have, no significant improvement is likely to have occurred.

51. O. Pérez Villanueva, *La inversión extranjera en Cuba*, p. 22.

52. "Cuba's bridge to the U.S," *The New York Times* (February 16, 1997).

53. This, of course, does not mean that reports do not exist; if a diligent search in the country of origin of these investors were conducted, at least publicly traded company reports should be available. Many investments in Cuba, however, seem to come from privately-held businesses. For our purposes, a time-consuming investigation of this sort has not been possible.

in the island, but it looks like this activity is also very limited:

Beta Gran Caribe (B.G.C.), registered in the Dublin/Irish Stock Exchange and managed by *Havana Asset Management*, was the first investment company with an exclusive focus on the Cuban market.[54] In September 1996, more than six months after beginning operations, out of the 24 investment opportunities identified, only one investment was reportedly completed in the financial sector, two proposals were listed as approved and awaiting investment and six projects were being negotiated. By March 1997 it was reported that only around US$12.6 million, or 47% of the initial Swiss francs (CHF) 40 million (roughly US$27 million) raised for the fund had been invested.[55] In sum, the number and amount of investments—undertaken and under consideration—are modest.

The Herzfeld Fund, registered in the U.S., started operations in December of 1993 and began trading in May 1994. It seeks to invest in companies which could benefit from a free Cuba. The fund (of around US$8 million) is 63.3% invested mostly in U.S, Mexican and Panamanian securities (mostly stock) and placed 52 in a ranking of 85.[56] For the fiscal year ended June 1996 it posted a net investment income loss of .03% while its share price declined 7.26%.

Net asset value, however, gained 13.30%. Given the events of the past year and the unlikely lifting of the U.S. embargo, it is understandable why this fund—in size and performance—is, at least for the moment, of marginal importance.

The Cuba Growth Fund, Ltd., a Bahamas-based investment fund, issued a prospectus in January 1997 to raise C$370 million to invest in Canadian listed companies with substantial business interest in Cuba. (One source reported the Fund sought to raise US$365 million.[57]) In February 1997, Fund executives reported that approximately US$36 million in commitments from Canadian pension funds and other institutional investors had been obtained in one week.[58] Updated information on the closing and/or performance of the fund has not been found.[59]

The Tourism Industry

In April 1997 the Minister for Foreign Investment reported 20 joint ventures in tourism with a capital of US$605 million, including 17 hotels.[60] In June 1997, Cuba's Deputy Minister of Tourism reported that 36 hotels (30% of the 160 in operation) were under foreign management and that the tourism sector had 13 joint ventures valued at US$728 million covering 8,905 hotel rooms.[61] In September 1997 the Deputy Minister reported the tourism industry had 21 joint ventures with foreigners with foreign

---

54. The fund is registered in Guernsey, where costs and listing requirements are minimal. In February 1996 it placed around 1,000 units with investors, consisting of five ordinary shares and one warrant, the latter typically granting rights to purchase a share at a pre-established price. *The Cuba Report*, 6:1 (May 1997), p.4 and *Economic Eye on Cuba* (3-9 March 1997). The author's direct request to the company for information went unanswered.

55. 16% in finance (CHF6.4 million), 10% in real estate (CHF4 million), 11% in biotechnology (CHF4.4 million), 6% in mining (CHF2.4 million), and 4% in debt (CHF1.6 million). The reported investment in the financial sector is a 70% stake in Caribbean Finance Corporation (CFC) for CHF6 million (approx. US$4million),which started operating in July 1996, looking to develop financial services in Cuba, presumably in property development. It has deployed some CHF3.5 million -around US$2.4 million—in three short term loans. Investment figures for real estate are divergent; while *The Cuba Report* reports only two investments, *Economic Eye on Cuba* reports investments in several sectors. See *The Cuba Report* (May 1997), p.4 and *Economic Eye on Cuba* (3-9 March 1997).

56. Summary of *The Herzfeld Caribbean Basin Fund*, provided by Thomas J. Herzfeld Advisors, Inc.

57. *Economic Eye on Cuba*, 1997 Monthly Chronology.

58. *Economic Eye on Cuba*, 1997 Monthly Chronology.

59. The author's request to the company for information went unanswered.

60. *Economic Eye on Cuba* (21-27 April 1997). According to the President of FINTUR, the Republic of Cuba's company which finances production for the tourism industry, the 17 joint venture hotels had 8,336 rooms, of which 2,500 were operational, the remaining 5,836 in project or construction phase.

61. *Economic Eye on Cuba* (24-30 June 1997), p. 3.

capital invested of US$667 million and that 33 hotels out of 174 in operation under foreign management.[62] No explanation has been offered for the puzzling discrepancies.[63] In fact, reports on tourism joint ventures coming from different government sources are so contradictory and confusing that the actual number of joint ventures and the amount of capital invested in this sector is unclear. It is impossible to guess how much has been actually invested and what value Cuba may be assigning to management contracts or "economic association agreements," which typically imply that the foreign partner contributes management and know-how but no direct capital. Moreover, 15 "investments" in tourism have been said to not have the Cuban government as a partner.[64]

Officially, tourism was the country's largest U.S. dollar earner in 1995 and 1996[65] (see Table 2) and constitutes its fastest growing area. There are 211 non-hotel establishments catering to tourists, 360 retail stores selling products for U.S. dollars, 624 government-operated restaurants and cafeterias and 435 stores offering U.S dollar-priced prepared foods, thousands of privately-owned restaurants and cafeterias since they were legalized in 1994, and hundreds

Table 2. Tourism in Cuba, 1990-1996

Year	Tourists Number	% change	Earnings Amount (Million US$)	% change
1990	340,300	N/A	242.3	N/A
1991	424,400	19.8	387.4	37.4
1992	460,600	7.8	567.0	31.6
1993	546,000	15.6	720.0	21.2
1994	617,000	11.5	850.0	15.3
1995	745,000	17.2	1,000.0	15.0
1996	1,040,000	28.0	1,300.0	23.0

Source: Derived from data from Cuba's Ministry of Tourism, as reported in *The Cuba Report* 5:9 (February 1997).

Note: Country of origin of tourists in 1996: Italy, 185,000; Canada, 156,000; Spain, 113,000; Germany, 75,000; France, 61,000; Mexico, 36,000; England, 28,000; Colombia, 24,000; others, 362,000. See *The Cuba Report*, 5:9 (February 1997).

of bicycle-driven food carts and food kiosks established since 1996.[66]

The growth in tourism, however, is not without its problems. Official revenue reports are highly questionable, a problem compounded by Cuba's historic reporting of higher net revenues than more developed and presumably more efficient markets of the Caribbean.[67] Ministry of Tourism officials have uncovered problems such as corruption, poor marketing, inflexible pricing, and inelastic spending in respect of lower demand.[68] An occupancy level of

---

62. "Reconocen impacto de las explosiones en el turismo," *El Nuevo Herald* (24 de septiembre de 1997).

63. In another report of an earlier date, the same Minister for Foreign Investment cited different numbers: 45 joint ventures in the tourist sector by the end of 1996. *Economic Eye on Cuba* (25 November-1 December 1996). A *Granma* report cites 20 joint ventures plus 16 management contracts. Orlando Gómez Balado, "Llegó el millón de visitantes," *Granma Internacional*, via internet. For its part, the University of Havana's *Centro de Estudios de la Economía Cubana*, reports 20 joint ventures with foreigners plus 37 hotels under foreign management and 15 joint firms dedicated to tourism, mainly in nautical activities, and US$162 million in credits granted for the development of the nautical tourist sector. O. Pérez Villanueva, *La inversión extranjera*, pp. 13-14. Meanwhile, attendees of *The Economist's* "Fourth Roundtable on Cuba" were told by the government that 41 hotel management contracts are in effect with foreigners, for 11,000 rooms, of which one third is dedicated to international tourism. Susana Lee, "Hemos puesto en marcha una reforma económica dentro del socialismo," *Granma Internacional* (19 marzo 1997), ed. digital. ECLA, "La evolución reciente," p. 131, cites 20 tourism joint ventures and 39 hotels under foreign management.

64. Cuba's Ministry of Tourism, *Cuba Monthly Economic Report* (July 1997).

65. *Economic Eye on Cuba* (26 May-1 June 1997).

66. *Economic Eye on Cuba* (25 November-1 December 1996).

67. See Werlau, "Foreign investment," pp.471-472.

68. The government carried out a week-long inspection of 2,353 tourism industry facilities and 13 audits of the most important government-operated tourism corporations. Minister Carlos Lage reported that 20 government operated tourism employment agencies would be reorganized due to the discovery of corruption in Varadero. *Economic Eye on Cuba* (30 June-6 July 1997). Evidence of corruption reportedly included bribes (selling of jobs), falsification of documents and unauthorized payments. Michele Hergas, "En Cuba se paga por trabajar," *Habana Press* (Septiembre 15, 1997).

55.9% leaves many resources under-utilized[69] and only 10% of tourist visits is considered "repeat tourism," professedly due to the low quality of services.[70] In addition, the average daily expenditure per tourist has reportedly declined to a low of US$220, apparently due to the large number of underground services available for tourists.[71] As a result, the government has taken measures to combat these practices. Also, the risk factor in the tourist industry has risen significantly as of late and could dampen projection of continued growth. Several tourist facilities have been the target of terrorist attacks[72] and eight foreigners were killed in a July 1997 *Cubana de Aviación* accident which took 44 lives.[73] During a visit to Spain, Cuba's Vice Minister of Tourism acknowledged that tourism has suffered a decline due to recent bombings. In August 1997 tourism increased 2% despite projections of a 19.2% rise, and the first 15 days of September sustained a decline of 18.1%.[74]

In sum, given the puzzling statistics provided by the government, the only consistent conclusions about the tourism industry is that Cuba continues to attract increasing number of tourists and net revenues are not at desirable levels.

Free Trade Zones

Possibly, the most singular development in the area of foreign investment during the past year was the establishment of Free Trade Zones (FTZs). The Foreign Investment Law of September 1995 contained very general language authorizing the establishment of free trade zones and industrial parks. In June 1996, Decree Law 165 was signed, which authorized all forms of economic activity—assembly, manufacture, banking, financial services and warehousing, with incentives not available to ordinary joint venture investors.[75] The zones are to be regulated and overseen by the Ministry of Foreign Investment and Economic Development. Concessionaires, responsible for the development and operation of the zones, handle applications and negotiate for the provision of warehouses, factories, housing and commercial and other facilities.[76] The two companies awarded 50-year management concessions for the four existing zones are Republic of Cuba-controlled companies, mostly divisions of Cimex S.A. and the military. [77]

The Minister for Foreign Investment has declared that FTZs represent a significant relaxation in the requirements for foreign investment, particularly be-

---

69. ECLA, "La evolución reciente," p. 129.

70. *Cuba Monthly Economic Report* (July 1997), p. 2. According to official estimates, 68,000 visitors seek accommodations in private homes. *Cuba Monthly Economic Report*, 1:2 (June 1997), p.2.

71. *Cuba Monthly Economic Report*, 1:2 (June 1997), p.2.

72. In 1991, an exile group had taken credit for a mortar attack on a Varadero resort. Since April 1997 several bombs have exploded in Varadero and Havana hotels, one killing an Italian resident of Canada. Paul Simao, "Canadian tourists not put off by Cuban bombings," *Reuters* (September 18, 1997), distributed by *CubaNet*; "Reconocen impacto de las explosiones en el turismo, *El Nuevo Herald* (24 de septiembre de 1997); and Frances Kerry, "Explosions rock Havana hotels, bombs suspected," *Reuters* (July 12, 1997); Larry Rohter, "Cuba sees American link to hotel bombs," *The New York Times* (July 14, 1997); Larry Rohter, "On bombings at resorts, Cuba betrays its jitter," *The New York Times* (July 27, 1997).

73. The *Cubana* flight was en route from Santiago de Cuba to Havana; two Brazilians and six Spaniards died in the crash. "Cuban plane crashes with 44 aboard," *Associated Press* (July 12, 1997), distributed by *CubaNet*.

74. "Reconocen impacto de las explosiones en el turismo."

75. The Deputy Minister for Foreign Investment Octavio Castilla heads the Ministry's FTZ office. The Ministry has set up a commission on FTZs comprised of representatives from 10 ministries: Economy and Planning, Finance and Price, Foreign Trade, Labor and Social Security, Armed Forces, Interior, Transportation, National Bank, Customs and Science, Technology and Environment. Ley sobre zonas francas y parques industriales (FTZ law), Chapter IV, Article 2, *Prensa Latina* (junio 1996), via internet; *The Cuba Report*, 5:5 (September 1996), p. 7.

76. "Cuba: born free," *The Economist Intelligence Unit* (September 22, 1997).

77. "Cuba: born free," *The Economist Intelligence Unit*; *Economic Eye on Cuba* (28 April-4 May 1997). CIMEX corporation established in 1979, was the first private company in Cuba. O. Pérez Villanueva, *La inversión extranjera*, p.2. The Wajay concessionaire, Almacenes Universales, is a Cuban company reported to have the informal rights for the Mariel and Cienfuegos FTZs. See Eloy Rodríguez, "Zonas francas: Comienzan las operaciones," *Granma Internacional* (20 mayo 1997) ed. digital.

cause 100% foreign ownership will be authorized there.[78] Nonetheless, 100% foreign ownership and speedy approvals are customary in FTZs worldwide. Cuba's FTZs also offer:

- exemption from profit and payroll taxes for up to 12 years, 50% exception for 5 years thereafter; the exemption for service oriented companies is 5 years, with 50% thereafter for 3 years. These exemptions are renewable. More favorable tax incentives may be granted on a case- by-case basis.

- tax free repatriation of profits in hard currency.

- 25% of FTZ-produced goods may be sold in the internal market free of duty; incremental amounts shall be decided by the Ministries of Foreign Investment and Foreign Trade.[79]

- all products with 50% or more value added in the FTZs can be sold in the domestic (hard currency) market free of duty.

The first two FTZs opened in May 1997 near Havana (Berroa and Wajay)[80] and two more zones are set to open in the port of Mariel and in Cienfuegos[81] (see Table 3). Despite announcements of numerous approvals for FTZ operators in the Havana FTZs, in mid-1997 only seven foreign companies, which will provide combined employment for 150 workers, were reported to have been licensed.[82] The President of the U.S.-Cuba Trade and Economic Council, toured Cuba's FTZs in May 1997 and found seven operators (producing building materials, lamps, soft drinks, and housewares) with initial investments of less than US$1.5 million. These operators, he reported, are looking to eventually export to the Caribbean market, but all their current output had been previously contracted for the domestic Cuban market. Allegedly, they are being lured by an atmosphere of "everything is negotiable"—i.e. the terms of tax holidays, port status, regulations, etc.[83] For its part, *The Economist Intelligence Unit* reported that by September 1997 a dozen companies had established operations and around one hundred applications were being processed (30 involving industrial production); it called interest in the FTZs "hardly a mad rush."

Table 3. Specifications of Approved Free Trade Zones

Location	Size (hectares)	Warehousing (square meters)	Offices (square meters)
Berroa	244	41,616	4,200
Wajay	21	13,000	1,100
Cienfuegos	432	11,800	9,800
Mariel	533	7,000	9,800

Source: "Cuba: born free," *The Economist Intelligence Unit* (September 22, 1997).

Officially, the primary goals of the FTZs are to increase Cuban exports, generate employment and hard currency revenues, and acquire technology,

---

78. *Economic Eye on Cuba*, 28 April - 4 May 1997.

79. Cuban officials have stated that this is attractive to operators because many competing FTZs require the export of 100% of their production. E. Rodriguez, "Zonas francas."

80. *Almacenes Universales*, the concessionaire for the Wajay FTZ, announced the approval of 18 operators, four of them industrial—a soft drink plant financed with British capital, an Italian pasta company and two Spanish firms making plastics and furniture. The Berroa Valley concessionaire, *Havana in Bond*, was reported to have invested US$30 million in infrastructure to open the 600 acre warehouse complex, which is still partly under construction. It allegedly began operations with licenses to 55 commercial business and two industrial firms, with additional applications under study for 36 to 45 companies from countries such as Brazil, Italy, Mexico, Spain and Panama. Isabel Morales, "Mas de doscientas hectareas abiertas al mundo del comercio," *Granma Internacional* (8 mayo 1997), ed. digital and E. Rodríguez, "Zonas francas."

81. Wajay is near Havana's International Airport and at Valle de Berroa is east of Havana's port. Mariel is 43 km. from Havana and Cienfuegos is 250 km. southeast of Havana, adjacent to the Panama Canal.

82. Operators are: three from Spain, one each from Canada, Jamaica, Italy and Holland. Pascal Fletcher, "First Cuban free trade zone could open next week," *Reuters* (April 29, 1997); *Economic Eye on Cuba* (28 April-4 May 1997).

83. John Kavulich, in telephone conversation with the author, 5/12/97.

knowledge, and know-how.[84] Although a government source has said that the *primary* objective of the FTZs is to export,[85] it look as though existing operators are essentially producing for the domestic market. The cost of labor in Cuba is too high compared to other FTZs in similar locations in the Caribbean,[86] even though FTZ operators are free of the 11% payroll tax (labor utilization tax) typically paid by foreign investors.[87] Cuban workers in FTZs are reported to be earning 300 to 500 Cuban pesos monthly (equivalent to US$13.6 to US$22.7), but the Cuban employment agency is receiving an average of around US$450.00 per worker from the FTZ operators.[88] The high salaries payable to the state makes Cuba's FTZs improbable competitors in the export sector. Even Cuban officials have recognized strong competition from over 100 geographical neighbors and the handicap of inaccessibility to the U.S. market.[89] Competition is particularly strong from neighbors such as Mexico, Panama, Jamaica and the Dominican Republic, all experienced in the free-zone business and with access to the U.S. market; Puerto Rico will also soon be offering new incentives to attract industry.[90]

It is likely that FTZ operators in Cuba are primarily looking, at least in the short term, to fill a very hungry domestic demand for goods mostly unavailable in the island.[91] Although the purchasing power of the population is very limited,[92] remittances from abroad, said to be higher than the total wages of Cuba's entire labor force at current exchange rates,[93] account for increasing sales in dollar-only stores. (1996 revenues from all government-controlled hard-currency retail operations was estimated at US$750 million.[94]) Estimated between US$627 million[95] and US$800 million[96] for 1996, surpassing sugar and tourism, remittances have become the country's first source of hard currency revenues.

Cuba, meanwhile, is probably hoping to put its idle space to use in addition to adding assembly and/or production capacity that can create employment and bring in technology. Access to highly-skilled labor, prime geographic location, low capital requirements, the potential of quick returns, the ability to operate

---

84. FTZ law, Chapter I, Article 1.3; *The Cuba Report*, 5:5 (September 1996).

85. P. Fletcher, "First Cuban free trade zone."

86. Most FTZs in the Caribbean have been established for several years, if not decades, with similar incentives (zero or special customs, import and export duties, land and building taxes, fees for work permits, corporate or capital gains taxes, etc.) There are 33 FTZ industrial parks in the Dominican Republic—14 owned by the state, 17 managed by the private sector and 2 under mixed administration. In 1995 the average salary paid for workers employed three months or less was equivalent to around US$131 (RD$1,678.69), or US$0.57 an hour. Esther Hernández Medina, Employment Policies Coordinator, CIPAF, "A brief profile of free trade zones in the Dominican Republic," via Internet.

87. The FTZ Office Director has stated that labor costs will be only "a little over" the competition's, as the investor will be able to save in personnel training. E. Rodríguez, "Zonas francas."

88. John Kavulich, in telephone conversation with the author, 5/12/97.

89. Ibid.

90. "Cuba: born free," *The Economist Intelligence Unit*.

91. FTZs are normally attractive to companies looking to penetrate a market for which their goods, if produced in the country of origin, subject to conventional duties and taxes, would not be competitive.

92. Cuba's income per capita is currently the lowest in the Hemisphere, as per ECLA, "La evolución reciente." Pablo Alfonso, "Expertos: isla ocupa el último lugar en nivel de vida," *El Nuevo Herald* (28 de septiembre de 1997), distributed by *CubaNet*.

93. Pablo Alfonso, "$800 millones del exilio son la 1ra. fuente de divisas en Cuba," *El Nuevo Herald* (10 de septiembre de 1997), distributed by *CubaNet*.

94. *Economic Eye on Cuba* (5-11 May 1997).

95. As per the Cuban government, in *Cuba Monthly Economic Report* (July 1997), p. 1. This report alleges that substantial regional inequality in food consumption is closely related to the availability of remittances from the U.S. Citing government studies, 30 to 60% of the population of 9 provinces has access to dollars while less than 30% do in the remaining 5 provinces.)

96. P. Alfonso, "$800 millones del exilio," quoting ECLA.

without Cuban partners, and the absence of U.S. competitors can be assumed to be the main lures for investors. But Cuba's FTZs seem ambitiously large, spanning 1,250 hectares compared to 49 hectares in Panama's bustling Colón zone.[97] And it appears that capital for FTZ development has dried up. The FTZ director has acknowledged that the Cuban concessionaires of the Havana FTZs in operation are not planning to invest more capital; rather, they are looking for financing to continue developing to the planned levels. The Mariel and Cienfuegos FTZs, he reports, will need substantial foreign investment, as capital is unavailable in Cuba.[98] Moreover, the FTZ Director has given indications that FTZs are in experimental stage, stating: "We'll have to see if it's necessary to grant certain additional incentives or to decree complementary regulations to create a more adequate legal environment. This time frame will not be less than two or three years."[99] Unless dramatic changes are implemented, however, it is hard to imagine that Cuba's FTZs will turn into a success story. In the meantime, it seems that small enterprises eager to jump at opportunities in Cuba will be the ones taking the most advantage of this mode of investing.

THE INVESTMENT CLIMATE

Although in recent years there's been an upward trend in private investment in developing countries,[100] the competition to capture these funds is fierce. In Latin America, Chile—with a similar size population to Cuba's—received direct investment of US$5.02 billion just in 1996.[101] Poland, a transition economy of the former Soviet bloc, received over US$6 billion from 1990 to 1995.[102] Conversely, Cuba has failed to attract meaningful levels of foreign investment, ostensibly due to its very high country risk.[103] Furthermore, those who do invest in the island typically commit low amounts and require high capital return/recovery ratios. To compensate for its shortcomings, Cuba's investment authorizations are thought to include enticing inducements with the government promising potential investors returns of up to 80% a year.[104] A Vice President of Altamira Management Ltd., which holds 11% of Sherritt, has illustrated the simple logic behind investor interest in Cuba: "Cuba's assets are incredibly cheap, and the potential return is huge."[105] Investors willing to take the risk may well reap high short term payoff.

There are no noticeable positive developments in the island's investment climate. The condition of the Cuban economy remains critically distressed and its prospects for recovery almost nil. Sugar prices have declined worldwide, as Cuba's output remains seriously impaired. In fact, it has been reported that if the value of the sugar industry were correctly calculated, it would be negative.[106] The Minister of Economy and Planning recently provided a grim outlook of the Cuban economy: "The state of economic emergency continues. (...) the Republic of Cuba has been surviving on short term credits (...) building up a short term debt with excessively high interest rates. (...) The foreign investment process is going reasonably well, though not as well as the government

---

97. "Cuba: born free," *The Economist Intelligence Unit.*

98. FTZ Director, Octavio Castilla, quoted in E. Rodríguez, "Zonas francas."

99. E. Rodríguez, "Zonas francas."

100. Foreign direct investment reached a new height in 1995, increasing by 38% from the previous year to US$315 billion. *World Investment Report 1996*, UNCTAD, electronic overview. In 1996 private capital flows to developing countries alone totaled US$244 billion and made up more than 80% of long term financial flows to poor countries. *The Economist* (March 29 1997), p. 116, citing the World Bank's report *Global Development Finance.*

101. Philip Sanders, "Foreign Investment in Chile leaped 42% last year," *Bloomberg News* (January 28, 1997). Authorized investments totaled US$6.9 billion.

102. Values as of September 1995. U.S. companies have invested 30.5% of this total. "American vs. other foreign investors in Poland," Polish consulate in Chicago web page, updated 12/17/95.

103. See a more detailed explanation of country risk in Werlau, "Foreign investment," pp. 465-466.

104. "Castro's Capitalist," *Business Week.*

105. "Castro's Capitalist," *Business Week.*

106. "Castro's Capitalist," *Business Week*, p. 2.

would like."[107] Cuba's energy problems are particularly grave. Despite the increase in domestic oil prospecting and extraction (22 risk contracts for oil prospecting concessions have been completed with foreign companies) only 15% of the demand for oil fuel is being met locally.[108] In 1996 commercial energy usage rose 24% without a corresponding output increase (only 7%).[109] And, because Cuba's hard currency debt is in default since 1986, it remains fundamentally shut off international credit markets.[110]

The legal environment and foreign investment regime remain highly risky, although some modest advances occurred in the regulatory arena targeting the external sector as a means of rescuing the ailing economy. On May 28, 1997 two laws were issued that seek "to effectively contribute to the economic/financial transformations taking place in the country" (i.e. to encourage foreign business).[111] The banking sector was reorganized by splitting in two the function of the National Bank: (1) Decree Law 172 established a Central Bank to oversee and regulate financial institutions and carry out the traditional roles of regulating monetary policy; and (2) Decree Law 173 relegated the National Bank to financial intermediation and commercial activity and codified bank regulations in order to facilitate investment and trade. But the reforms are limited; the financial sector is far from reaching a modest or significant level of reform, both on the domestic and external sectors.[112] Foreign banks continue to be precluded from activities other than representative offices—of which there are 13—for the purpose of providing investments and serving foreign clients.[113]

In the FTZ law, the most significant element of reform is the establishment of 100% foreign-owned businesses, yet these remain of the traditional enclave type. The law disappointed those who had expected a relaxation in the labor regime characteristic of foreign joint ventures.[114] Only non-Cuban and non-residents of Cuba may be hired directly by the FTZ operators. Generally, although exceptions *may* be permitted, Cuban employees will be hired from the Cuban concessionaire-controlled employment agency.

Serious deficiencies in the normal conduct of business persist.[115] A business newsletter on Cuba recently acknowledged that "foreigners consider Cuba to be a very expensive place to develop and produce business." Adding to the already high costs, it cites Cuba announcement of mid-1997 that foreigners who re-

---

107. *Economic Eye on Cuba* (21-27 April 1997), citing highlights of interview given by Minister José Luis Rodríguez to Cuba's official business weekly *Negocios en Cuba*.

108. Joaquín Oramas, "Seguirán crecimientos en la industria del petróleo," *Granma Internacional* (28 julio 1997), ed. digital

109. *Cuba Monthly Economic Report* (July 1997), p.1.

110. Cuba owes approximately US$10 billion to Western creditors—European and Japanese banks—and has a huge debt with the former Soviet Union. A conversion of this debt must be worked out, but Moscow claims it amounts to 17 billion "transferable rubles." It was reported in the summer 1997 that once a conversion of the ruble debt is worked out, Russian companies would likely obtain equity in certain Cuban enterprises in lieu of the debt. Cuba still depends on an economic relationship with the former USSR; it conducted in 1996 trade of US$1.1 billion with Russia, of which 85% was barter, mostly sugar for oil. See "Cuban ambassador offers sweeteners," *Central European* (July/August 1997), p.9.

111. Francisco Soberón, the former National Bank President, assumed the Presidency of the new Central Bank. "Creado el Banco Central de Cuba," *Granma Internacional*; E. Rodríguez, "Firma contratos."

112. See Yosem Companys, "Institution building: A regulatory and supervisory framework for Cuba's financial sector reform," Yale University (March 29, 1997). A version of this paper is included in this volume. Ed.

113. *Economic Eye on Cuba* (9-15 June 1997).

114. The law established that Cuban FTZ concessionaires (companies of the Republic of Cuba or joint ventures between foreigners and these companies) may establish their own employment offices—apart from Cubalse—and may provide contracted Cuban nationals with U.S. dollar or U.S. dollar-based bonuses. *Economic Eye on Cuba* (28 April-4 May 1997). Although the Executive Committee of the Council of Ministries has the authority to provide special labor regulations for operators, it appears that only Cuban or joint ventures companies, not 100% foreign owned concessions, will be allowed to do this. *The Cuba Report* 5:5 (September 1996), p. 7.

115. See Werlau, "Foreign investment," pp. 465-480.

side in Cuba for more than 180 days must file income tax returns.[116] A University of Havana study, a telling source due to its origin, has detailed some of the problems business partners and potential investors confront:[117] 1) bureaucratic delays and slow completion of investment agreements; 2) highly cumbersome bureaucratic procedures for renting commercial space or obtaining transportation, telecommunications and personal services; 3) unfamiliarity with market techniques and a lack of historic entrepreneurial experience; 4) unavailability of qualified personnel for certain areas; 5) absence of economically sound reference points for the application of exchange rates and prices in the valuation of the assets of the Cuban partners; 6) problems with the employment regime, particularly doubts concerning the loyalty of the workers to the foreign partners; and 7) absence of local financing.

The climate for doing business does not seem to have improved much. Canada's Wilton Properties, which announced a US$400 million investment project in tourism in 1996, has allegedly pulled out of at least one of its projects (*El Viejo y el Mar*) for a number of reasons including problems with the Cuban partner.[118] Although Sherritt's Chairman, Ian Delaney, stated that large multinational companies have an advantage in obtaining access to the highest levels of government, allowing for the completion of agreements quickly, he acknowledged that Cuba "needed to do more to provide clear rules and regulations that would apply to small and medium-sized firms."[119] Sherritt is a prime example of the foreign investors who might benefit, at least in the short term, from the highly centralized and "flexible" nature of the

terms for investing, considered by Cuba as a lure to investors.[120]

But investors stay happy as long as arbitrary decisions of the Cuban state do not affect their best interests, as has been seen in several cases in the past years.[121] The recent falling out of the notorious joint venture investment by Mexico's Grupo Domos in Cuba's telecommunications company, ETECSA, is the most recent example. Apparently, Domos ran into problems obtaining financing for a portion of its share of ETECSA and was forced by the Cuban government to divest of its stock at a lower than market value. Allegedly, the stock was then sold by the government to the Italian company STET at a much higher price. Domos was said to be "studying its options to reclaim the $450 million it paid for the original investment" and has sued STET, claiming compensation for a minimum of $900 million. The Domos case is particularly poignant because from beginning to end it demonstrates the pitfalls of investors' "accessibility" to extremely centralized decision-making and the negotiation of agreements lacking in transparency and accountability. It might be noted that many foreign mining companies with operations in Cuba are not major industry players and at least one—Northern Orion—has been cited by market analysts as involved in investments in Cuba considered "speculative" and "highly risky."[122] Domos, for example, was less than an ideal partner; even the President of the U.S.-Cuba Trade and Economic Council admitted that its "problems stem in large part from the fact that they weren't a company with substantial assets going into the deal."[123] A little known company with limited experience in the telecommunications sector,

116. *The Cuba Report,* 6:1 (May 1997), p. 8.

117. O. Pérez Villanueva, *La inversión extranjera,* pp. 20-21.

118. The Cuban partner was allegedly playing games with cash flow and overbooking space by selling rooms to Europeans for more money than the Canadian hotel management firm, Delta, had sold to Canadian travel agents. (Anecdotal information from a confidential source.)

119. *Economic Eye on Cuba* (3-9 March 1997).

120. O. Pérez Villanueva, *La inversión extranjera,* p. 12.

121. See Werlau, "Foreign investment," p. 69 and footnote 78.

122. *The Cuba Report,* 5:9 (February 1997).

123. Larry Rohter, "Mexican conglomerate abandons Cuban phone venture," *The New York Times* (June 30, 1997).

was apparently chosen over European and Canadian competitors due to the close political relationship between Cuba and Mexico. Reportedly, the Domos deal, which granted Domos a 55-year monopoly on telephone services in Cuba, was put together with the intervention of former Mexican President Carlos Salinas de Gortari.[124]

Socio-political risks in Cuba remain high. Aside from recent bombings linked to the tourism industry, the media reported that in September 1997, several foreigners, including Spanish director Pedro Almodóvar and Swedish actress Bibi Anderson, were caught in a violent raid by Cuban security forces at a Havana discotheque. Those not carrying their identity documents were detained with many Cuban patrons. Social resentment against what foreigners represent apparently has not abetted.[125] While Havana University's MBA program graduated its first class in February, one of the graduates gripes: "I am studying about investing capital when Cubans cannot invest in Cuba. If you are a foreigner, you can invest. But if you are a Cuban, no."[126]

The condition of human rights in the island has not improved. Again, claims have been made against the government for utilizing telephone services to harass dissidents. (ETECSA, Cuba's telephone company, is a joint venture with foreign capital.[127]) The crackdown on dissidents initiated in late 1995 has been followed by successive waves of repression specifically targeted at independent journalists and dissidents who attain international media coverage.[128] In mid-July, for example, four dissident leaders who had distributed a joint paper to foreign media representatives were detained. All four remain in custody, accused of releasing false and inexact data about the Cuban economy with the intention of "negatively influencing internal and international public opinion and especially existing and potential partners and investors."[129]

As for the environmental impact of foreign investment, international awareness was raised during the United Nations June 1997 Earth Summit+5 meeting in New York, which Castro did not attend as expected. Exile environmentalists, in conjunction with Castro's daughter Alina Fernández, held a press conference which received international media coverage.[130] The damage caused by foreign investments in tourism and mining, specifically by Sherritt's joint ven-

---

124. For sources/details on the Domos investment, see Addendum referenced in footnote 36 available from the author and Werlau, "Foreign investment," p. 463, footnote 45.

125. A recent independent journalist's report from Cuba reads: "There are many tourism projects not lacking in cement, sand, gravel or any other construction material, all of which are nationally produced. ...while entire families from Camagüey languish in homes without maintenance, built more than 300 years ago. Meanwhile, tourists are provided with modern and comfortable buildings, in which they vacation happily. We don't know how long we can continue putting up with the situation to which the government subjects us." Carlos Manuel Guerra González (Patria Agency), "From Cuba: the other side of the coin," Camagüey (December 1996), distributed by *CubaNet*; slight translation modifications by the author.

126. "A touch of capitalism," *Business Week*.

127. For example, the Independent Press Agency for Oriente denounced government threats to one of its journalists to cut off telephone services and insinuated the monitoring of private conversations. "From Cuba: the government threatens independent journalists with canceling their telephone line" (October 21, 1996), distributed by *CubaNet*.

128. See for example, Press release from Havana from the Cuban Independent Press Bureau (June 27,1996), distributed by *CubaNet* and *Amnesty International Urgent Action Appeal* (July 18, 1997).

129. Those held form part of the *Internal Dissidents' Working Group for the Analysis of the Cuban Socio-Economic Situation* and are members of unofficial organizations: Marta Beatriz Roque Cabello, of the *Cuban Institute of Independent Economists*, René Gómez Manzano, of the lawyers' group *Corriente Agramontista*, Felix Bonne Carcassés of the *Corriente Cívica Cubana*, and Luis López Prendes of *Buró de Prensa Independiente*. The detainees were also accused of producing a letter to foreign businessmen warning them of the consequences of investing in Cuba under the one-party Communist government, of calling for the boycott of upcoming one-party elections and of involvement with leaders of terrorist groups based in the United States. See *Amnesty International Urgent Action Appeal* (July 18, 1997) and Pascal Fletcher, "Cuba explains arrests of four dissidents," *Reuters* (July 24, 1997).

130. Press conference held at Hyatt U.N. Plaza, New York, June 24, 1997 by the *Coalition for a Green and Free Cuba*, with the participation of Alina Fernández with Néstor Penedo and Andrés Solares of the A.M.A.C. (Asociación Medio-Ambiental Cubana).

ture plant at Moa Bay, was cited.[131] The Juraguá Nuclear Plant, which Cuba is actively seeking to complete with foreign financing, was also named as a potentially serious hazard.[132] On the other hand, foreign investment may bring some improvements to the environment. Sherritt reported the continued refurbishment and rehabilitation of two sulfuric acid plants at Moa Bay, with "considerable improvements in air quality," although still not meeting international standards.[133] Although the Moa joint venture has been criticized for its environmental impact, if foreign capital were not available, it is unlikely that the Cuban government, particularly at this time of crisis, would earmark important financial resources to protect the environment, which it recognizes is severely deteriorated.[134] Allegedly these mining facilities have historically been heavy polluters. Cuba, meanwhile, passed a new law on the environment,[135] but its potential consequences for foreign investors are unknown at this time. Nonetheless, reportedly it would regulate the environmental impact of foreign investments "which could become a potential source of income for the state."[136]

In the international arena, public sensitivity over ethical issues seems to be growing at the governmental and corporate levels, as witnessed recently by Nike in Indonesia and Unocal in Myanmar.[137] *The New York Times* recently reported on oil industry experts agreeing that "the threat of unilateral economic sanctions... has become a shadow over investment decisions stretching for Southeast Asia to West Africa to the Caspian Sea."[138] Meanwhile, the international outcry over Holocaust funds secretly kept by Swiss banks has bolstered the arguments of Helms-Burton proponents.[139]

The United States' Helms-Burton Law[140]

The international outcry and defiance against the Helms-Burton (HB) Law has not abetted. The European Union (EU) and several individual countries took steps to block the enforcement of U.S. judgments respective of HB measures range in intensity from mere discouraging language to "claw-back" provisions (allowing the recovery of legal awards) and the penalization of compliance.[141] For its part, Cuba passed a counter-measure—*Law of Re-affirmation of Cuban Dignity and Sovereignty*—declaring HB "null

---

131. Investments in the tourist industry were described as neglecting environmental considerations to reduce costs. Causeways to small keys have been constructed taking the cheapest routes which block water flows, exacerbate contamination, and destroy coastal and marine habitats. As a result, species such as the Cuban shrimp are reported to be disappearing. In Varadero beach too many and poorly constructed hotels are being built too close to the beach and with inadequate space between buildings. See *The State of the Cuban Environment* (June 1997), press kit distributed at 6/24/97 press conference in New York city by the *Coalition for a Free and Green Cuba*.

132. The Soviet-designed reactors are deficient even by Soviet standards and Juraguá is just 180 miles off the coast of Florida. *U.S.-Cuba Policy Report*, 4:3 (March 31, 1997).

133. Sherritt International Corporation, Annual Report 1996 (fiscal year ending 12/31/96).

134. *National Environmental Strategy*, presented by Cuba at the United Nations' Earth Summit+5, New York, 7/97.

135. Rodolfo Casals, "Tres nuevas leyes aprobó el parlamento," *Granma Internacional* (28 julio 1997), ed. digital.

136. "Cuba assesses damage, finds it extensive," *CubaNews* (July 1997), p. 11

137. The story covered Unocal's problems in Myanmar—where it has already invested US$1.2 billion to develop a natural gas field. Agis Salpukas, "Foreign energy, domestic politics: Burmese project tests Unocal resolve," *The New York Times* (May 22, 1997).

138. Referring to Unocal's problems in Myanmar, where it has invested US$1.2 billion to develop a natural gas field.

139. A piece authored by a legal expert states: "The Holocaust principle demanding restoration of stolen property from traffickers or custodians is high-minded: it loses none of its moral strength when the plundered are gentiles, not Jews. Indeed, the principle fits the controversial Helms-Burton law like a glove, and should become a bedrock of international law." "Applying Holocaust Principles to Cuba," TWT (2/4/97). Cited in *U.S.- Cuba Policy Report* 4:2 (February 28, 1997), p. 10.

140. For details on this issue, please refer to Werlau, "Foreign investment," pp. 472-473.

141. In October 1996 Mexico passed the "Act for the Protection of Commerce and Investment of Foreign Rules Contravening International Law," which does not penalize companies from withdrawing from Cuba nor revoke visas to American executives whose companies file HB suits against Mexican companies. *U.S.- Cuba Policy Report*, 3:10 (October 31, 1996). The EU took action in November 1996. Amendments to Canada's Foreign Extra-territorial Measures Act (FEMA) countering HB became effective in January 1997. France passed legislation in April 1997 to impose financial penalties on companies which ignore the EU's agreement to defy HB. "Amplía Francia legislación anti Helms Burton," *Granma Internacional* (16 abril 1997), ed. digital.

and void" and setting up commissions for Cubans to file claims against the U.S. for damages and injuries resulting from the embargo.[142] The Cuban government is warning embassies whose businesses are potentially endangered by HB that Cuban laws declare illegal any form of collaboration, direct or indirect, to assist in the application of the HB law."[143]

The U.S. State Department has issued letters warning of potential claims under the Helms-Burton law to several companies suspected of trafficking in confiscated U.S. properties. These include Canada's Sherritt,[144] the Israeli Group BM and a Panamanian company selling automobiles in Cuba, in addition to Mexico's Grupo Domos and CEMEX, both of which have reportedly ceased operations in Cuba.[145] More companies are vulnerable to Helms-Burton sanctions, including Title IV visa denials.[146]

Cuba's Minister for Foreign Investment has announced that the Helms-Burton law has not provoked the flight of any foreign investor and, instead, foreign investment has risen.[147] From the passage of the law in March 1996 to December of that year, 42 economic associations with foreigners were professedly established.[148] Meanwhile, the Deputy Minister for Foreign Investment Octavio Castilla report-

ed that only four joint ventures are linked to property formerly owned by U.S. firms.[149] But there are obvious signs that the law has indeed had a significant impact on foreign investment climate. A high official of Cuba's Foreign Ministry, Carlos Fernández de Cosío, acknowledged in January 1997 that as a result of the law, many people were afraid of investing in Cuba.[150] Minister Carlos Lage acknowledged the Act had "complicated" Cuba's relationships with some foreign enterprises and even Castro has admitted it has had "serious negative consequences" and has endangered foreign credits needed to reactivate main sectors of the economy, particularly sugar production.[151] Netherlands' ING-Barings Bank stopped financing Cuba's sugar harvest because of the HB law and one of its executives declared it would remain active in Cuba "in activities in line with the Helms-Burton law."[152] Spain denied the extension of US$15 million in pre-negotiated loans for Cuba's sugar harvest after uncovering "technical problems" in loan insurance risk analysis; one might assume that HB weighed in the decision.[153] Allegedly HB also contributed to Domos' problems by making alternative financing for its investment in ETECSA more difficult.[154] The law has also been cited as an impediment for Cuba to raise the financing to complete construc-

---

142. *U.S.-Cuba Policy Report*, 3:12 (December 31, 1996), p. 4.

143. Pascal Fletcher, *The Washington Post* (April 7, 1997), cited in the *Newsletter of the American Chamber of Commerce of Cuba in the United States* (April 23, 1997), p. 2.

144. Eleven persons affiliated with Sherritt are said to be barred from the United States. *The Cuba Report*, 5:11 (April 1997), p. 8.

145. Christopher Marquis, "Two firms face Helms-Burton sanctions," *The Miami Herald* (January 22, 1997) and *U.S.-Cuba Policy Report*, 3:5 (May 31, 1996). Before it sold its stake in ETECSA, executives of Grupo Domos had also received warning letters for denial of entry into the U.S.

146. These include Italy's Benetton, Spain's Sol Meliá, France's Pernod Ricard, Britain's ED&F Man and Tate & Lyle and Bancomext, Mexico's foreign trade bank. The latter has provided US$400 million in soft credits to Cuba since 1992, and has a cement plant joint venture with Cuba's Cement Producers. *Economic Eye on Cuba* (26 May-1 June, 1997); *U.S.-Cuba Policy Report*, 3:9 (September 27, 1996).

147. Eloy Rodríguez, "Califican de exitosa gira de ministro a Alemania y Francia," *Granma Internacional* (13 mayo 1997), ed. digital.

148. J. Oramas, "Turismo," and S. Lee, "Hemos."

149. "Cuba says few firms using old U.S. property," Canadian Press, Havana (June 18, 1997).

150. *U.S.-Cuba Policy Report*, 4:1 (January 31, 1997), p. 10, as per *The Washington Post* (January 25, 1997).

151. "Castro admits that Helms-Burton has hurt the Cuban economy," *El País* (September 18, 1996). Distributed by *CubaNet*.

152. *U.S.- Cuba Policy Report*, 3:9 (September 27, 1996), p. 8.

153. Javier Rodríguez, "Niega Cabrisas que haya razones técnicas en la cancelación de crédito español," *Granma Internacional*, 2:6 (20 febrero 1997), ed. digital.

154. Larry Rohter, "Mexican conglomerate abandons Cuban phone venture," *The New York Times* (June 30, 1997).

tion of the Juraguá nuclear plant in Cienfuegos.[155] Canadian banks remain nervous about lending to Canadian investors in Cuba and a drop in Canadian exports to the island[156] might also be attributed to limited financing alternatives. (The Canadian government is said to be offering seed funds to investors.[157])

Potential investors and other businesses are showing concern. Canada's then Ambassador to Cuba, Mark Entwistle, confirmed in January 1997 that investments from larger Canadian companies had leveled off since the passage of the law due to their asset exposure in the U.S. Although he reported that investments from medium-sized companies with no exposure in the U.S. were on the rise, their ability to invest can be assumed to be much more limited.[158] Beta Gran Caribe Fund has announced a policy to not "knowingly and intentionally" invest in property in respect of which there is significant risk of significant liability as a result of an outstanding claim certified by the U.S.[159] Several foreign companies, including the U.K.'s largest tour operator, Thomson Travel Group, have reportedly communicated with the

State Department to make certain that their business activities do not violate the HB Act.[160]

In August of 1996 President Clinton named Ambassador Stuart Eizenstat special representative to negotiate with allies on the issue of HB, to seek multilateral Cuba policies, specifically "concrete and specific measures to promote democracy in Cuba." Eizenstat initiated several rounds of foreign tours, visiting 12 countries. These efforts yielded several important successes despite a bleak start in Mexico City, where the envoy was pelted by eggs.[161] In November 1996 the EU issued a common position on Cuba focused on encouraging a process of transition to a pluralist democracy in Cuba and conditioning full cooperation with Cuba upon improvements in human rights and political freedom in the island.[162] In April 1997, shortly before initial papers were to be filed before a WTO dispute panel requested by the EU in February 1997, the U.S. and the EU announced their agreement to suspend the panel for six months,[163] with the EU reserving the right to reactivate the panel at any time if negotiations are unsuccessful. Terms

---

155. Cuba, which spends over US$1 billion annually to import oil, has renewed efforts to complete the plant, in which the former USSR had invested most of the US$1.1 billion to construct two 440 megawatt nuclear reactors. Construction which began in 1983, was suspended in September 1992 with the reactors 75% and 30% complete respectively. The Soviets are said to have demanded a $200 million payment to continue the project. Cuba has used an annual US$30 million Russian Federation grant to mothball the existing facility and is actively seeking foreign investors to complete the first reactor at a cost of US$750 million. Russia's Deputy Minister of Atomic Energy claimed the U.S. had rejected an offer made to Westinghouse Electric Corp—probably its Canadian subsidiary—to participate in the completion of the power plant and referred to the HB law as the legal impediment. The Minister of Nuclear Energy of the Russian Federation has announced that construction will resume in 1998 through a consortium. Companies from the U.K, Germany, and Brazil have allegedly expressed interest, although it appears financing is still being sought. See *Economic Eye on Cuba* (2-8 June 1997); Frank J. Gaffney and Roger Robinson, "Stop the Cuban Chernobyl," *The Wall Street Journal* (January 21, 1997); and *U.S.-Cuba Policy Report* 4:2 (February 28, 1997).

156. Professor John Kirk, Dalhousie University, Canada, in e-mail to the author of 7/28/97.

157. Ibid.

158. *U.S.- Cuba Policy Report*, 4:2 (February 28, 1997), p.8.

159. *The Cuba Report* 6:1 (May 1997), p. 8.

160. Michael Rannenberger, Director of the Cuba Office at the U.S. State Department, reported having received word from 12 companies of ceasing business in Cuba to comply with the H.B. law. (April 1997, in conversation with the author).

161. Steven Lee Meyers, "Cuba policy a big headache for top commerce official," *New York Times News Service,* Washington, 1996.

162. The Council of the European Union, Common position, Brussels, November 29, 1996. See *U.S.-Cuba Policy Report*, 3:12 (December 31, 1996).

163. On April 21, 1997, the EU approved the April 11 accord, which was cited as an "acceptable compromise." *U.S.-Cuba Policy Report*, 4:2 (February 28, 1997). The EU claims the extraterritoriality of the HB law whereas the U.S. categorically declares it would not recognize WTO jurisdiction over an issue of national security, hinting that bringing non-trade matters to the WTO jeopardized the legitimacy of the recently-created international body.

of the accord include:[164] (1) continued negotiations (sought to be completed by October 15, 1997) to develop agreed disciplines and principles for the strengthening of investment protection; (2) continued U.S. suspensions of Title III claims provision;[165] and (3) once an accord is reached, the Clinton Administration would seek a Congressional amendment to the HB law to provide the President with authority to waive Title IV (denial of visa) provisions.

In addition to the accord, the most threatening counter-sanctions, such as EU visa denials for U.S. executives, the freezing of U.S. assets and counter-suits,[166] have not materialized. Moreover, STET, the Italian company in a telecommunications joint venture with Cuba, recently completed a 10 year agreement with ITT to pay the latter US$30 million to use ITT's properties in Cuba. The accord relieves STET from penalties under the HB law and allows ITT to retain its US$130 million claim against the government of Cuba.[167] The U.S. government and HB supporters have claimed this as legitimizing of HB, a proof that the law is effective and acts as a disincentive to investment in Cuba. In turn, HB detractors, including the EU, claim it demonstrates that the law is toothless.[168]

Canada has taken the most active stance against HB. Its Ambassador to Washington declared that this was the most visible issue between the two countries and that Canada would not let go of its position on HB.[169] But, it appears that a coalition of 20 church, labor and relief groups from Canada which called for a tourist boycott of Florida—to punish its population of Cuban origin—was unable to attain any success. (Around 2 million Canadian tourists visit Florida, almost 13 times the 156,000 which visit Cuba.[170]) And, if push comes to shove, it would seem that Canadians will prioritize investments and trade with the U.S. Canada's annual trade with Cuba reportedly equals one day of its trade with the United States.[171] At this time no Canadian investors have been reported to have retreated from Cuba due to the law, but it seems that Canadian Foreign Extraterritorial Measures Act regulations which penalize these actions would be hard to enforce, as investors could cite other causes for leaving Cuba.

In sum, it looks like the international clamor against HB has not toned down in volume, but actual results to strike down the law are less forthcoming. All told, HB appears here to stay.

FOREIGN INVESTMENT'S IMPACT ON REFORM

Creation of Employment

As an element of empowerment, the overall impact of foreign investment on employment is relatively

---

164. *U.S.-Cuba Policy Report*, 4:4 (April 30, 1997) and *The Cuba Report*, 6:1 (May 1997), pp. 2-3.

165. On July 16, 1997, President Clinton suspend Title III claims for the third time. See Alison Mitchell, "Clinton again waives penalty on foreign companies in Cuba," *The New York Times* (July 17, 1997).

166. Mark Lawrence, "EU threatens retaliation unless U.S. waives Cuba sanctions," *Associated Press*, Brussels (July 12, 1996).

167. "ITT in deal for properties seized in Cuba in '61," *The New York Times* (July 24, 1997), p. A8; "ITT makes deal with Italian company," July 23,1997, *Associated Press*, distributed by *CubaNet*.

168. State Department Spokesman Nicholas Burns, in David Fox, "EU, US both claim victory in Helms-Burton twist," *Reuters*, Brussels (July 24, 1997), distributed by *CubaNet*. Also see Sue Pleming, "U.S. official asks Latin America to support Cuba moves," *Reuters*, Washington (July 28, 1997), distributed by *CubaNet*.

169. *U.S.- Cuba Policy Report*, 3 (October 31, 1996), p. 10.

170. See David Crary, "Groups urge boycott of Florida unless U.S. eases anti-Cuba bill," *Associated Press*, Toronto, (July 10, 1996). About 1.7 million Canadians spent US$1.8 billion in 1996 in Florida.

171. *U.S.- Cuba Policy Report*, 4:2 (February 28, 1997), p. 8. In 1995 Cuba's imports from Canada totaled US$200 million; exports from Cuba to Canada totaled US$234 million. As per official Canadian trade data, in *Cuba: Handbook of Trade Statistics, 1996* (Washington: CIA, Directorate of Intelligence, November 1996). Prof. Julia Sagebien, of Canada's Dalhousie University, claims that Canada's trade with Cuba equals half a day of Canada's trade with the United States. "Canadians in Cuba: Getting to Know Each Other Better," presentation at the VII Annual Meeting of the Association for the Study of the Cuban Economy, Miami, August 1997. A version of this presentation is included in this volume. Ed.

meaningless and, in some respects, even detrimental. Despite anticipation that Free Trade Zones would feature direct employment of workers, the actual terms of the legislation thwarted these hopes.[172] Moreover, FTZs have added very little employment—around 150 workers at present[173]—and a continued focus on the guaranteed pre-selling of their output to Cuban enterprises for domestic consumption leaves no expectation of large-scale production[174] or important levels of employment.

By 1996 it had been reported that all foreign joint ventures "officially" employed 60,000 workers.[175] Given that estimated foreign investment has not risen significantly, we might assume no material change in the number of workers employed by joint ventures. This represents a mere 1% of the workforce of 4.5 million.[176] (Direct employment in tourism is only 65,000 to 70,000 and indirectly 200,000 to 250,000,[177] but the number of workers employed in the foreign sector is unknown.)

This scenario reinforces our conclusion in last year's analysis: (1) with the unemployed said to be over a million (some estimate unemployment at around 50%, or 2.25 million), the number of workers employed in the foreign investment sector cannot significantly alleviate Cuba's grave unemployment crisis;

(2) given the conditions of the domestic and international labor markets, competitive market forces would likely make the cost of labor for foreign capital firms in Cuba much lower. Due to Cuba's singular labor arrangement, by arbitrarily fixing an artificially high price for labor, the state actually discourages and limits optimal employment by foreign capital firms; and (3) the limited number of jobs sought by a huge pool of workers in the foreign sector -the most desirable sector of the economy- instead of empowering the workers, actually reinforces the need to play by the government's rules.[178]

Generation of Hard Currency Earnings

Earnings derived from operations of foreign joint ventures had been estimated by June 1996 at roughly US$211 million.[179] Given the presumption that foreign investment has not risen significantly in the past year, it can be assumed that this scenario has not changed materially.

The tourism industry was officially reported as Cuba's largest dollar earner in 1996. Because revenues derived from foreign investment in tourism are not available, our conclusions must be based on overall data available for the industry. 1996 net revenues are noted inconsistently by different sources—reports range from 26% to 30-35%.[180] Yet, if tourism gener-

---

172. Only non-Cubans and non-residents of Cuba may be hired directly. The Executive Committee of the Council of Ministers has authority to provide special labor regulations for operators, but it appears that only Cuban or joint ventures operators will be allowed to hire workers from concession-managed employment agencies. See FTZ law, Chapter VIII, Section V and *The Cuba Report*, 5:5 (September 1996), p. 7.

173. The largest FTZ investor was a Canadian company producing building materials, reportedly employing 80 workers.

174. J. Kavulich, telephone conversations with the author, 5/12/97 and 7/11/97.

175. The number employed in joint ventures in the tourist sector is unknown. For the whole industry, in May 1997 the National Assembly of Cuba reported 130,000 employed (*Economic Eye on Cuba*, 26 May-1 June 1997) while the President of INTUR, reported 150,000 employed directly or indirectly at around the same date. *Economic Eye on Cuba*, 21-27 April 1997.

176. Employment as of 4/30/97, as reported by Cuba's National Tax Office (*Economic Eye on Cuba*, 2-8 June 1997).

177. The E.C.L.A. report (op.cit., p. 129) cites 65,000 employed directly and 200,000 indirectly, while Cuba's Deputy Minister of Tourism cited in September 1997 70,000 and 250,000 respectively. "Reconocen..." *El Nuevo Herald* (24 September 1997).

178. Despite very low wages, the material conditions of workers in the foreign enclaves is better than the rest. Workers are compensated with bonuses, gifts, transportation to work, meals, and in some cases dress. In the tourist sector, they receive tips and food served at the restaurants. These make jobs in this sector the most prized. Werlau, "Foreign Investment," p. 484.

179. Based on $751.9 million invested: $114 million from operations (Minister Lage's report for 1995) plus our calculation of $97.5 million in taxes of 30%. (Tips are not included, as it is very difficult to estimate a reliable number.) Telecommunications' payments made by U.S. companies constitute additional hard-currency earnings for Cuba.

180. Cuba had reported that costs per dollar of income dropped in the first half of 1996 to US$0.68 from US$0.73 (*The Cuba Report*, August 1996, p. 4), but these reports show costs ranging from US$0.65 to US$0.74. Data as per Cuba's Ministry of Tourism. *The Cuba Report*, Volume 5, No. 9, February 1997, p. 3; O. Pérez Villanueva *La inversión extrajera*, p. 14.

ated net revenues of 26% this would represent a mere US$338 million, which is low given the size of the population and the needs of the economy. Nevertheless, reported expenditures from these revenues totaled only US$84 million; these financed imports of US$66 million of food and agricultural and light industrial goods for the population while US$18 million was spent in the development of tourism.[181] (The latter is a strangely low sum in relation to the importance of this sector in the overall economy and Cuba's continued investment in new hotel rooms.) Even the government has recognized that 1996 revenue projections for tourism were not met.[182] While the number of tourists visiting the island in 1996 increased by 28%, earnings rose only 23%. From January to April 1997 the number of tourists increased 19% while gross earnings rose only 7%, officially due to a 6.7% decline in the average number of days of tourists' visits.[183] In fact, the Minister of the Economy reported a loss of US$3 million in the tourist industry for the first four months of 1997 (costs increased 1%), indicating that plans to improve efficiency/profitability have not materialized.[184] Analysts have traditionally estimated net revenues for tourism to be low due to a high dependence on imports, reportedly 70-80%,[185] hefty promotional discounts and mismanagement by the Cuban partners.

Plus, a low ratio of repeat tourism indicates that Cuba needs to dedicate expenditures to upgrade its services and facilities in order to remain competitive. In essence, without underestimating the importance to Cuba's deprived economy of tourism revenues tied to foreign capital, this does not appear to be a short-term answer to its predicament.

The disappointingly low level of revenues estimated from foreign investment, even from tourism, continues to make the wage retention arrangement of foreign capital firms the most lucrative source of hard currency earnings for Cuba from foreign capital enterprises.[186] (The new Free Trade Zones are also subject to this system.[187]) Wage retention generates the government a guaranteed income irrespective of whether these enterprises—joint ventures or economic associations—operate profitably or not, as state employment agencies continue to appropriate around 98% of the total value added of labor in the production process. In the case of specialized and highly-skilled workers, the confiscation rate is even higher.[188] Sherritt International Corporation, for example, is reported to be turning over to the Cuban government US$22 million per year for workers' salaries.[189] Just at its joint venture Moa Bay nickel-cobalt plant the wage retention scheme alone is estimat-

---

181. O. Gómez Balado, "Llegó ..." *Granma*, op.cit. (The inventory of hotel rooms has grown to 28,878 by 1996, at an annual average rate of 22.2% since 1990. According to official projection, the number will reach 50,000 by the year 2,000. N. Crespo and S. Negrón Díaz, "Cuban Tourism in 2007: Economic Impact," in this volume.)

182. O. Pérez Villanueva, *La inversión extrajera*, and *The Cuba Report*, February 1997, p. 3.

183. As per Republic of Cuba reports, *Economic Eye on Cuba*, 30 June-6 July 1997.

184. *Economic Eye on Cuba*, 30 June-6 July 1997.

185. *Cuba Monthly Report*, DevTech Systems, Vol. 1, No. 3, July 1997, p. 2. (The development of tourism requires substantial expenditures to remain competitive—promotional costs, personnel training, construction of new facilities, maintenance of existing facilities, and infrastructure development.)

186. A state-controlled employment agency hires the workers and charges the foreign capital firm salaries of an average of around US$450 per worker. The workers are paid average peso wages of around US$9. (Also see Werlau, op.cit., p.471.)

187. While the worker is earning 300-500 Cuban pesos, *Cubalse*—the state employment agency—is receiving approximately US$450 per worker from the FTZ operator. (J. Kavulich, telephone conversation, 5/12/97.)

188. The Cuban-Brazilian joint venture producing cigarettes is reported to pay the state employment agency US$3,000 per month for its manager, who in turn receives 380 pesos (US$17.3), at a confiscation rate of 99%, leaving the government US$35,792 in annual revenues. A mechanic at the plant receives 350 pesos while the employment agency gets US$916. Likewise, the employment agency is reported to receive US$2,700 for a geologist employed in Sherritt, while the geologist receives the equivalent of US$10—at a wage confiscation rate of 99.6%—providing the state a return of US$32,280 per year. (Charles Lane, "Canada Sly," *The New Republic*, August 6, 1996.)

189. *Cuba Monthly Economic Report*, July 1997, p. 3.

ed to leave the state at least around US$740.5 thousand per month, or US$8.9 annually (this without adding labor taxes and social security retention).[190] In 1995, before the existence of FTZs, earnings from wage confiscation in joint ventures are calculated to have totaled around three times the net earnings from operations. (With 60,000 workers in the foreign sector, wage conversion alone can bring around US$26.5 million per month, or US$317.5 million per annum. In addition, labor utilization taxes and social security contributions provide an estimated US$33 million per month, US$396.8 million per annum.[191]) Ostensibly, this situation hasn't changed much, with the exception of the FTZs, which will add to the state's appropriation of workers' salaries and benefits.

Meanwhile, the purchasing power of the workers is pitiful. The average monthly salary of 202.5 pesos (US$9.20) translates into US$2.19 per week, equal to US$0.44 a day or 5.5 cents an hour, which could well be the lowest in the world.[192] Economists in Cuba have estimated that, in order to buy goods at free market rates, workers on the average 202.5 peso per month salary have to labor 116 hours to purchase 1 kg. of powdered milk, 70 hours for 1 kg. of chicken, 13 hours for one lightbulb, and between 500-1,700 hours for a pair of shoes.[193] Some workers of joint ventures or under management contracts of foreign companies, subject to the same average peso salaries, are being reported as having access to hard-currency bonuses of a small percentage of their salaries. The sums involved are very low, but represent a sig-

nificant amount in Cuba.[194] Non-monetary benefits for workers of foreign joint ventures have endured: rewards such as meals, transportation, and uniforms. Moreover, material incentives for non-joint venture workers have been expanded; these can partly be attributed to the government's attempt to compensate for the special benefits of workers of the foreign sector. Last year, approximately one million workers, 25% of the labor force, had been estimated to be receiving some form of payment in dollars or convertible pesos as reward for meeting or exceeding work quotas. Presently, some 1.3 million workers—according to the government, one third of the workforce—are reportedly receiving bonuses for greater output. The problem is that these workers remain dependent on the state. Therefore, any material improvement in their situation—both the employed at joint ventures or exclusively by the state—is at the expense of even greater political compliance and economic dependence on the state. At the same time, the government continues to refuse allowing average Cubans, outside of the *nomenklatura*, to invest in joint ventures or even set up small or medium-sized businesses to supply even the tourist sector. Thus, by restricting the flow of revenues that foreign investment could generate workers and citizens, the government continues to prevent the emergence of independent economic agents potentially capable of diluting the formal power structure. While the most empowering hard currency earnings are those obtained directly by the population, through tips (in

---

190. The plant is reported to have 1,680 workers. "Castro's Capitalist," *Business Week*. The government employment agency is paid an average of US$450 per worker, while the worker earns the average salary of 202.5 pesos.

191. These are rough estimates based on the average salary of US$450, paid to workers as 202.5 Cuban pesos multiplied by 60,000 workers said to be employed in joint ventures. A 11% labor utilization tax on gross salaries and social security contributions of 14% of wages paid by the joint venture in hard currency but registered on behalf of workers in pesos at a one-to-one exchange rate, leaves the government, an estimated US$35.6 million and US $43.3 million per annum respectively.

192. A reported peso-dollar rate of 22 was used for this calculation. (Estimated US dollar hourly wages for garment workers in the spring of 1996 were: Pakistan .26, China .28, Bangladesh .31, Indonesia .34, India .36, Haiti .49, Egypt .63, Mexico 1.08, Honduras 1.31, El Salvador 1.38, Peru 1.39, Brazil 1.92, Taiwan 5.10, Britain 9.37, U.S. 9.56, Canada 9.88, Italy 14.32, Germany 18.43. Source: *The New York Times*, February 1, 1997.)

193. Study conducted by *Instituto Cubano de Estudios Sindicales Independientes* for year-end 1996, distributed by *CubaNet*, March 10, 1997.

194. At Suchel, the joint venture with British *Unilever PLC*, salespeople can earn one-third more than its Cuban executives. "A touch of capitalism," *Business Week* p. 50.

the tourist sector[195]) and informal services, the un-availability of reliable data, makes their difficult to assess.

In sum, hard currency earnings derived from foreign investment are not enabling a significant improvement in the economy with meaningful trickle down effects empowering of empower workers or citizens. In fact, due to the nature of the foreign investment regime, the conditions and terms for the generation of earnings appear to reinforce the vested interest both of the state and of foreign investors to preserve existing joint venture arrangements. These have been designed to maximize short-term benefits for the partners in the context of a command economy and a closed political system. Therefore, despite the peculiar deficiencies of Cuba's investment climate, foreign investors are rationally interested in the survival of the current Cuban government and its investment agreements for the minimum period required to secure capital recovery and indefinitely to generate a stream of profits. For the Cuban government any revenue generation, whatever it might be, fosters self-preservation at this time of profound crisis.

Multiplier Effects

More than three-quarters of joint ventures with foreigners involve investments no larger than US$5 million; these are concentrated in the export-oriented sector, in support businesses to foreign tourism or in extractive industries such as mining and oil exploration. Their relative size in the economy and their impact on overall domestic production are, consequently, insignificant. The highly risky investment environment appears to explain the limited initial capitalization (exposure) and the nature of the investments and the focus of investors on recovery instead

of reinvestment. All these factors restrict multiplier benefits to the local economy.

The multiplier effects emanating from worker remuneration remain very limited in scope due to wage confiscation, the low level of employment in joint ventures. The average size of the Cuban family is four. With 60,000 employed in joint ventures, roughly 240,000 people are calculated to depend on those jobs—around 2% of the population. For workers in tourism, with access to tips, a rough calculation which assumes that 40,000 are employed in tourism joint ventures shows around US$7.5 million per month in tips (US$187.5 per worker), a level which cannot have a significant impact on the economy. In terms of empowerment, advances are most perceived by the population in the informal and self-employed sectors, some of which service the foreign-generated economy. But the government has imposed steep taxes and fees to "redistribute" individual gains, canceling out most of their effect. And, with self-employment licenses totaling a scant 180,916 as of April 1997[196]—a 13% decline since January 1996[197]—multiplier impact is very limited. In fact, analysts have shown that the segregation of tourism from the rest of the economy limits the expansionary effect of the income multiplier. One elaborate study calculates that, due to Cuba's economic model, the country is losing several million dollars per day of economic impact from tourism. [198]

From the Cuban state's standpoint, the rationale for foreign investment continues to be the prioritization of political necessities over structural economic reform together with the extraction of immediate economic gains to alleviate the monumental economic crisis. From the standpoint of the investor, the high risk scenario continues to impose an essentially spec-

---

195. Although workers are required to turn over up to 75% of tips, receiving an equivalent sum in pesos calculated at the official one-to-one rate, non-compliance with this rule is reportedly high (although it may lead to termination of employment).

196. *Economic Eye on Cuba*, 2-8 June, 1997.

197. In September 1996, licenses numbered 184,922, down from a peak of 209,606 in 1996. Philip Peters, *Islands of enterprise: Cuba's emerging small business sector*, The Alexis de Tocqueville Institution, January 27, 1997.

198. N. Crespo and S. Negrón Díaz, "Cuba Tourism in 2007: Economic Impact," in this volume, elaborating on María Dolores Espino, "International tourism in Cuba: an economic development strategy." The study compares a simulation of Puerto Rico's and Cuba's tourism activity indicators for the year 2007. Data for Cuba is derived from official figures.

ulative and short-term rationale bent on fast capital recovery and the maximization of profits. This scenario is contrary to the economy's need for capitalization—that which enables the creation of domestic savings and spurs internal growth.

Dispersion of Development

Notwithstanding the FTZs' potential contribution to the development of a small industrial base, as designed, they merely provide another variant of selective capitalist "reform" in the context of the model of enclave economies favored up to now. While it had been reported that a non-Republic of Cuba company was discussing the possibility of managing one of the FTZs, a development which would be unique,[199] finally only government-controlled companies were authorized to run the four existing FTZs,[200] disappointing hopes for a small opening. In respect of empowerment, it will be interesting to observe if and how any potentially progressive elements are implemented, and, if they are, how the experience will be absorbed.

As for the dispersion impact of foreign investment discussed in our previous paper, a recent University of Havana study attributes to foreign investment a contribution in the promotion of efficient and competitive behavior and the creation of a new entrepreneurial culture.[201] These advances, however, are limited to a select group. The "demonstration effect on consumption"[202] or *"technocratic metamorphosis"*[203] (both discussed in more detail in last year's paper), do not appear to show any significant advances in respect of actual empowerment. Both state technocrats and the population at large have been kept firmly subjugated to state control while the operation of the new FTZs and the progression of activities related to foreign capital continue to indicate an extremely high concentration of resources in the state sector and the "privatization" of financial resources and capital among the ruling elite—especially the Armed Forces and the security police.[204] The dispersion effects of tourism are perhaps the most significant within the sector tied to foreign capital. But joint ventures and Cuban enterprises in the sector of tourism and leisure tend to be run by arms of the Armed Forces (FAR), CIMEX—a subsidiary of the secret security police—and Habaguanex, the city of Havana's joint-venture corporation.[205] Plus, its benefits are mitigated by its undesirable social costs—the most salient being prostitution, economic dualism and environmental damage—and the existing limitations of the traditional linkage between the tourist industry and the rest of the economy.

All in all, Cuba's enclave system of foreign joint ventures—captive to the *nomenklatura*, concessionary to foreigners, and lacking transparency and competitiveness—remains firmly in place. In fact, Cuba's brand of capitalism, designed to access foreign capital thru leadership-contained mechanisms (which we coined "coopted or distorted dispersion of development") harvests destructive societal aberrations which sabotage the eventual establishment of an appropriate framework to achieve social order and a rule of law. This scenario bolsters our original conclusion that, in a repressive regime, as long as individuals or groups remain suppressed, lacking the capacity to effectively implement change, empowerment seems independent of how foreign influence might alter their psychological disposition.

199. J. Kavulich, telephone conversation, 7/11/97.

200. *The Economist Intelligence Unit*, op.cit.

201. O. Perez Villanueva, *La inversión extranjera*, p. 18.

202. Michael Peters, *International Tourism*, Hutchinson Publisher, 1969; cited in G. Gunn, op.cit.

203. Term borrowed from James Shinn, "Engaging China: exploiting the fissures in the facade," *Current History*, Vol. 95, No. 602, September 1996.

204. A Canadian journalist has recently observed: "The new Cuban capitalist is more than likely an intelligence officer or army staffer," Brendan Howley, "Economic surge missing Cubans," *The Globe and Mail*, April 22, 1997, distributed by *CubaBrief*, Freedom House, March 1997.

205. Howley, "Economic Surge."

The dispersion effects of capitalist elements which might potentially challenge the prevailing economic and political order remain confined to this framework.

The Debate on Economic Determinism and Political Reform

A World Bank study has recently demonstrated that a state founded on effective institutions is essential for a prosperous economy; market friendly polices or reforms do not seem to work in their absence. In addition, it reveals that credibility in government weighs heavily in determining the level of foreign investment and economic growth a country effectively attains.[206] Even if a deterministic relationship between economic and political reform could be demonstrated, a relationship analyzed in last year's paper, Cuba's is far from attaining a level of economic reform that *could* eventually lead to political reform. This is poignantly illustrated in The Heritage Foundation's 1997 Index of Economic Freedoms, which evaluates key areas, such as trade, monetary and banking policies, taxation, government intervention, property rights, and regulatory environment. Cuba is ranked 148 out of 150 countries surveyed, just ahead of Laos and North Korea.[207]

Because in Cuba economic freedoms are perceived as subversive to the prevailing order, the imperative of regime survival overrides economic rationality and bars the establishment of a proper and enabling model, conceived on effective and credible institutions. As a result, the nature of foreign investment inherently limits and remains incompatible with stable and long-term economic growth and political stability.

CONCLUSION

The events of this past year buttress our previous conclusions. The October 1997 Party Congress is expected to reaffirm that the political necessities of the regime will continue to dictate the character of Cuba's economy, and, thus, of commercial engagement and foreign investment. As long as the ruling elite retains the means to impose power by force, this rationale will preclude meaningful economic and political development.

For the international community to promote a transition to a pluralistic democracy in Cuba, more realistic policy initiatives founded on the premise of "conditional engagement" ought to be pursued. These would condition economic ties to the dismantling by Cuba of reform-disabling mechanisms which assist in the containment of those forces which might bring about the eventual empowerment of the Cuban people.

---

206. "It's the government, stupid," *The Economist*, June 28, 1997, pp. 71-73.

207. Cited in *U.S.-Cuba Policy Report*, 3:12 (December 1996), p. 9.

CUBA: UNA PLENA REINSERCION INTERNACIONAL COMERCIAL Y FINANCIERA CON ESTABILIZACION RAPIDA, SIN RECESION Y CON CRECIMIENTO ALTO, ESTABLE Y SUSTENTABLE

Rolando H. Castañeda y George Plinio Montalván[1]

"Our subject has always thrived and advanced through controversy."

—Tobin (1996, p. 18).

"... the need for the state itself to manage the transition process was underestimated, and seemingly forgotten was the fact that there exist many different valid ways of conducting an efficient and sustainable market economy....Among its responsibilities, the state has to provide an essential public good—namely, a reasonable stable institutional and policymaking framework together with an adequate flow of information..."

—Berthelot (1997, p. 329).

"An important lesson of reform to date, both economic and political, is that market forces alone cannot always drive the restructuring process forward."

—World Bank (1996, p. 74).

Cuba enfrenta los demandantes retos de estabilizar su economía rópidamente sin recesión, así como alcanzar tasas de crecimiento económico altas, estables y sustentables para modernizarse y mejorar los niveles y calidad de vida de su población. Para lograr la estabilización rápida sin recesión debería lograr la convertibilidad del peso y eliminar la dolarización para terminar con las fuertes presiones inflacionarias "reprimidas" y las distorsiones, las confusiones en los incentivos, las conductas de ventajismo rentista, el tráfico de influencias y la corrupción que se originan de una tasa cambiaria en el mercado libre de CU$22 por US$1 (CU$=pesos cubanos) cuando la conversión oficial es de CU$1 por US$1. En contraste, para lograr una recuperación robusta y un crecimiento económico alto, estable y sustentable, Cuba necesita mantener una tasa de cambio real competitiva que estimule la expansión de las exportaciones de bienes y servicios, consolide y amplíe progresivamente la apertura y la competitividad de la economía.

En este ensayo se presenta una propuesta realista, es decir, con fundamentación técnica y legitimidad social, con medidas cambiarias, comerciales y financieras consistentes y efectivas, que se refuerzan mutuamente, tienen efectos sinérgicos y enfatizan distintos aspectos dentro de un paquete de medidas más amplio con un enfoque de equilibrio general encaminadas, *primero*, a eliminar la inconvertibilidad del peso y la dolarización de la economía que impiden la estabilización externa y, en *segundo* término, consolidar y ampliar progresivamente la apertura externa median-

---

1. Las opiniones aquí expresadas son de exclusiva responsabilidad de los autores y de ninguna manera reflejan sus vínculos institucionales. Este trabajo fue presentado originalmente por el primer autor en un Seminario de la Sede de Solidaridad de Trabajadores de Cuba en Caracas, Venezuela en setiembre de 1996 y febrero de 1997, y después ampliado y revisado conjuntamente. Los autores agradecen las observaciones de Rafael Núñez.

te la liberalización y desregulación de mercados, gradual y ordenada, pero integral, progresiva e incremental. Estas medidas buscan movilizar y coordinar la transición para dar energía y reforzar las fuerzas naturales de los mercados y que éstos funcionen mejor, contrarrestando las rigideces e imperfecciones (especificidad de algunos capitales, formas de organización y conductas después de casi 40 años de socialismo, rezagos e información imperfecta y asimétrica) existentes en los mismos y en los procesos de ajuste.[2]

La propuesta se basa en que es muy importante la consistencia general y la forma en que las políticas se diseñan y se ejecutan para realizar la apertura comercial y la reinserción internacional comercial financiera rápida y efectivamente y sin costos sociales innecesarios e intolerables. La propuesta se fundamenta en las ideas de Sachs, McKinnon, Williamson y Amsdem; la literatura reciente sobre los procesos de apertura externa; las experiencias de los antiguos países socialistas europeos y de Nicaragua en 1990-1996 y de Chile en 1973-1997; la apreciación que el papel de la política económica es muy importante; y el firme propósito que Cuba no tenga que experimentar más traumas ni costos sociales innecesarios.

En la discusión sobre el tema de inserción internacional comercial y financiera rara vez se repara en el hecho de que existen varias opciones para conducir este proceso que es continuo y que tales opciones no son igualmente óptimas ni correctas, lo que puede conducir a errores técnicos, a veces serios, en el proceso de inserción internacional comercial y financiera que en el mediano plazo pueden llevar a diferir y aún revertir el proceso. Del mismo modo, es necesario analizar con la mayor ecuanimidad y rigurosidad los factores que condicionan el resultado del proceso, los plazos en los que con realismo es posible esperar sus resultados y los instrumentos claves en este proceso.

El ensayo está organizado de la forma siguiente. En la primera sección se hace un breve examen del déficit comercial crónico, la moratoria y el elevado nivel de la deuda externa, el limitado y caro acceso a préstamos comerciales externos, así como la consecuente fuerte dependencia del exterior existente en la economía cubana. En la segunda sección se resume la experiencia de los antiguos países socialistas europeos, de Nicaragua y de Chile en la reinserción internacional comercial y financiera y sus implicaciones para el diseño, la gestión y manejo de las políticas públicas reformistas. También se presentan algunas consideraciones sobre los problemas aún pendientes. (*Ignorar las experiencias negativas recientes que han resultado en una fractura social es una invitación a que se repitan.*) En la tercera sección se resume la literatura económica reciente sobre la importancia de la apertura externa y la forma de hacerla, destacando algunos estudios empíricos. En la cuarta sección se analizan en detalle los objetivos, la estrategia con visión de largo plazo, los instrumentos y los posibles efectos de la propuesta para lograr una pronta y efectiva reinserción internacional comercial y financiera sin recesión y la progresiva orientación de la economía al exterior. Esta se basa en la liberalización de los mercados y la apertura al exterior, que permitan a Cuba lograr el despegue económico y utilizar el capital humano del país mediante los rigores del comercio y la competencia internacionales con economías más avanzadas, basada en mercados libres y la inversión privada para mantener la viabilidad económica del país y mejorar el nivel de bienestar de sus habitantes. Asimismo, en esta sección se comparan los posibles efectos de la estrategia propuesta con la eliminación inmediata de las restricciones arancelarias al comercio internacional y la flotación cambiaria que resultarían en la estabilización recesiva del sector externo con altas tasas de interés y tasas de cambio sobrevaluadas. En la quinta sección se indica cómo la propuesta se podría implantar y sus posibles implicaciones para el futuro y en la sexta se presenta el resumen de las principales conclusiones del ensayo.

---

2. *Liberalización* se entiende como cualquier medida que elimina o reduce en general controles y regulaciones al comercio exterior internacional y en especial a las exportaciones, así como las intervenciones en el mercado de cambios que impiden los efectos positivos de los incentivos económicos. *Apertura* se entiende como la importancia del comercio en la economía. En este sentido Cuba ha sufrido un notable cierre en el período 1989-1995, pues las exportaciones se redujeron del 28 por ciento del PIB al 12 por ciento.

LAS CONDICIONES INICIALES DE CUBA: EL DESEQUILIBRIO FUNDAMENTAL DE BALANZA DE PAGOS Y LA CONSECUENTE VULNERABILIDAD EXTERNA: LA FALTA DE COMPETITIVIDAD REFLEJADA EN EL DEFICIT COMERCIAL CRONICO, Y EN LA MORATORIA Y ALTO NIVEL DE LA DEUDA EXTERNA

En el caso cubano no se dispone de la información confiable necesaria para elaborar un análisis preciso de la evolución del sector externo; por ello éste deberá ser de naturaleza conceptual y especulativa. Desde los años 50, Cuba ha experimentado un déficit comercial que en años recientes se ha acentuado con el cierre al exterior. Las exportaciones de bienes se contrajeron de CU$5.4 mil millones en 1989, o aproximadamente el 28 por ciento del PIB, a CU$1.1 mil millones en 1993 o el 9 por ciento del PIB, aunque se recuperaron a CU$1.5 mil millones en 1995 o el 12 por ciento del PIB. Esta reducción refleja la disminución de los ingresos de Cuba que se originaban en términos de intercambio muy favorables con la antigua Unión Soviética, determinados por precios subsidiados para el azúcar y níquel (o sea, la causa de la "enfermedad holandesa" en la Cuba socialista), y el cambio del comercio de los antiguos países socialistas europeos hacia otros países que tienen estándares más altos para los productos que adquieren, pero la declinación también ha sido resultado del muy bajo nivel competitivo e ineficiencia productiva del país, aún en las actividades agrícolas e industriales del azúcar, el principal rubro de exportación de bienes. Cuba no administró prudentemente ni invirtió adecuadamente en la modernización del azúcar y, en consecuencia, no aumentó la productividad ni redujo los costos para mantenerse competitivo en el producto (una violación de la regla de Hartwick). La experiencia en 1989-1997 muestra una baja elasticidad efectiva de la oferta de exportaciones de bienes y una concentración en bienes y servicios primarios con inversión extranjera debido a políticas económicas inconsistentes, mal diseñadas, y aplicadas inflexiblemente, que han exacerbado los desequilibrios externos y se han reflejado en una marcada reducción del consumo por habitante.

Lo anterior hace suponer que una parte significativa del problema se debe a la sobrevaloración de la tasa de cambio del peso. Además, la política de contratar a los empleados a través de una entidad empleadora estatal y cobrar los salarios en dólares, más las respectivas contribuciones, a los inversionistas extranjeros que son mucho mayores que el nivel de salarios real del país (mayores a 22 a 1) impide un mayor uso de la mano de obra cubana, una de las ventajas comparativas del país. Las distorsiones en los precios relativos de las divisas y de la mano de obra constituyen obstáculos fundamentales para lograr el crecimiento. Adicionalmente, a nuestro juicio ha habido una dependencia excesiva de lo extranjero para determinar el crecimiento y muy poco de la adopción de medidas que estimulen lo nacional como la base del crecimiento. Un "apartheid" económico generalizado.

El gobierno de Cuba considera que, con los cambios de socios comerciales y otros de naturaleza cosmética, puede resolver la crisis (BNC, 1994, p. 12), la cual es sistémica. Los combustibles y los alimentos representan las dos terceras partes de las compras en el exterior. No hay políticas para enfrentar y corregir las causas de la crisis. Más aún, la reacción inicial del gobierno en 1989-1993 fue de fundamentalismo ideológico, es decir, de aislarse ante la desaparición del bloque socialista primero y de la Unión Soviética después. Esto ha sido reafirmado en el llamado al V Congreso del PCC de abril de 1997. Además, Cuba perdió el acceso al crédito comercial preferencial que provenía de los antiguos países socialistas europeos, pues anteriormente había dejado de recibir créditos comerciales de otras fuentes cuando se declaró en moratoria de la deuda externa en 1986, por no cumplir con los acuerdos previos después de haberla renegociado en tres ocasiones entre 1982 y 1985. Como se puede ver en el Cuadro 1 con niveles de deuda externa al PIB del orden de 5 veces. Los créditos comerciales para financiar la cosecha de azúcar de 1996 se estimaron a una tasa de interés del 15 por ciento, mientras que los préstamos del exterior fluctúan entre el 12 y el 20 por ciento (CEPAL, 1996, p. 203). El BNC reconoce que las tasas de interés que Cuba paga, ocasionalmente duplican las que prevalecen en los mercados internacionales y que los préstamos que recibe son poco flexibles (BNC, 1994, pp. 21 y 25). El

Cuadro 1. Cuba: Balanza de Pagos y Deuda Externa, 1971-1996

CONCEPTO	Promedio Anual			1986	1987	1988	1989	1990	1991	1992	1993	1994	1995	1996
	1971-75	1976-80	1981-85											
Balanza de pagos (US$ millones)														
Balanza en cuenta corriente							(4595)	(3624)	(1933)	(403)	(372)	(81)	(146)	
Balanza comercial							(4609)	(3666)	(2021)	(585)	(374)	(190)	(316)	
Exportaciones de bienes y servicios							5,562	5,605	3,270	2,309	1,989	2,246	2,944	
Bienes (FOB)	2,004	4,463	5,980	5,322	5,402	5,518	5,392	5,415	2,980	1,779	1,157	1,314	1,544	1,966
Servicios							170	190	290	530	832	932	1,400	
Importaciones de bienes y servicios							10,171	9,271	5,291	2,894	2,363	2,436	3,260	3,438
Bienes (CIF)	1,990	3,870	6,331	7,596	7,584	7,579	8,140	7,417	4,233	2,315	2,008	1,956	2,660	
Servicios							2,031	1,854	1,058	579	355	480	600	
Transferencias unilaterales privadas							20	50	100	200	315	529	600	
Servicio de factores							(6)	(8)	(12)	(18)	(313)	(420)	(430)	
Balanza de capital							5,700	3,700	1,900	402	388	79	143	
Transferencias unilaterales oficiales							3,000	1,000	500	50	50	200	208	
Inversiones extranjeras directas							100	150	250	350	54	563	800	
Otros capitales netos							2,600	2,550	1,150	2	284	(684)	(865)	
Balanza total							1,105	76	(33)	(1)	16	(2)	(3)	
Deuda Externa														
Deuda externa total en moneda convertible (en CU$ millones)	…	…		4,985	5,657	6,606	n.a.	n.a.	6,800	8,400	8,785	9,083	10,504	11,000
Bilateral oficial											4,047	3,992		
Multilateral oficial											438	503		
Abastecedores											1,867	2,058		
Instituciones financieras											2,406	2,501		
Otros créditos											27	29		

Fuentes: BNC (1995); CEPAL (1996); Economist Intelligence Unit, *Cuba Country Report 2nd quarter 1997* (London: EIU, 1997)

BNC atribuye la crisis comercial y financiera al embargo/bloqueo y a las presiones de EUA (BNC, 1994, p. 13) que sin dudas acentúan los problemas por los efectos de desviación de comercio hacia productos y socios comerciales más ineficientes.

La dolarización (o la tendencia a utilizar dólares como medio de intercambio, unidad de cuenta e instrumento para conservar valor)[3] y la depreciación del peso en el mercado libre se produjeron endógenamente como resultado de las deficientes gestión y políticas macroeconómicas aplicadas, que ignoran el dinámico y competitivo entorno internacional y están orientadas a mitigar la crisis existente en vez de a superarla. Así, la población se protegió de la creciente inflación y depreciación de la moneda nacional en el mercado negro, las que se acentuaron cuando el gobierno despenalizó la tenencia de divisas para estimular las remesas del exterior en agosto de 1993. O sea, la dolarización y la depreciación del peso son resultado de deficientes y tardías políticas macroeconómicas, la represión financiera y los factores institucionales existentes. Cuba actualmente recibe remesas del exterior por unos US$600 millones (CEPAL, 1996, p. 203).[4]

El sistema financiero cubano es muy rudimentario y pasivo. Los instrumentos monetarios se limitan básicamente al dinero en circulación y los depósitos en cuentas de ahorro con tasas de interés reales negativas en moneda nacional, así como cuentas de ahorro en divisas en la banca comercial que pagan un interés del

4 por ciento anual. Hasta 1996 sólo existían el Banco Nacional de Cuba, que cumplía algunas funciones de banca central y comercial, y el Banco Popular de Ahorro, que efectuaba las funciones de caja de ahorro para captar el ahorro personal y brindar pequeños créditos personales. El Banco Internacional de Comercio SA (BICSA) y el Banco Financiero Internacional realizan la mayoría de las transacciones externas. Las casas de cambio establecidas en setiembre de 1995 tienen funciones muy limitadas de intermediación cambiaria y están orientadas a la captación de divisas, ya que recibían divisas a CU$25 por US$1 y entregaban moneda convertible a CU$30 por US$1 (CEPAL, 1996, p. 200), mientras la tasa de cambio continúa a CU$1 por US$1 con lo cual se incentivan actividades buscadoras de rentas y la ineficiencia en la asignación de recursos. El Informe del BNC de 1994 es más amplio sobre las diversas instituciones financieras que se planeaban establecer que sobre las existentes.[5]

Cuba tiene una organización socioeconómica que determina una estructura no competitiva y rígida con un marcado sesgo antiexportador y paradójicamente muy dependiente del exterior, excluyente, que no permite resolver los problemas de la mayoría y conduce a la fractura social y la marginación en lo interno. Está basada en la confrontación más que en la colaboración, aisla de la verdadera situación internacional, y es inadecuada para reaccionar en forma suficiente y oportuna a la dinámica globalización comercial,[6] eludiendo acciones que pudieran signifi-

3. La dolarización dificulta seguir políticas monetarias y cambiarias independientes y magnifica los efectos inflacionarios de los déficits fiscales. No obstante, en un mundo crecientemente integrado algún grado de dolarización existirá como manifestación de la diversificación de los portafolios y de los efectos por histéresis de este fenómeno.

4. En la actualidad, la masa de ingresos monetarios recibida por los cubanos por su trabajo es menor que la masa de ingresos monetarios recibida de remesas de los cubanos emigrados o residentes en el exterior. Así, dado que hay unos 4.8 millones de cubanos en la fuerza laboral y éstos reciben un ingreso promedio mensual de 203 pesos, ello equivale a un ingreso total del trabajo de 11,700 millones de pesos al año. En cambio los ingresos por las remesas del exterior son de unos US$600 millones anualmente, que al cambio obtenido en las casas de cambio actualmente equivalen a ingresos de 13,200 millones de pesos al año. Tal vez esto explique por qué la tasa de cambio administrada en Cuba se ha apreciado respecto al tipo de cambio en el mercado negro previo a la despenalización de la tenencia de divisas.

5. Recientemente se establecieron la Financiera Nacional SA (FINSA) para proveer financiamiento de corto plazo al comercio exterior y el Banco Metropolitano SA para financiar proyectos prioritarios de inversión.

6. El proceso de "creación destructiva" generado por el rápido avance tecnológico e informático, y por las nuevas presiones competitivas de un mundo cada vez más integrado, ha acelerado el proceso de obsolescencia de ciertas actividades, habilidades, profesiones e instituciones.

car grandes beneficios para la población, pero que indudablemente conllevan riesgos y costos iniciales aunque mucho menores que el elevado costo a largo plazo del inmovilismo actual. "Más de lo mismo" nunca será permanente ni estable. No es una alternativa viable. Hay que realizar rectificaciones y modificaciones sustantivas en la estrategia y gestión del desarrollo del país, especialmente en el sector externo, con una visión de largo plazo. Existen muchas demandas económicas de la población, postergadas durante más de una década, que son evidentes en un país que ha experimentado una significativa involución económica; de acuerdo con un reciente informe de la CEPAL, "la inversión bruta no permitía satisfacer las ingentes necesidades de renovación del capital existente ... mientras el estado de la infraestructura, incluidas las viviendas, y de los bienes de capital sufrían un considerable y manifiesto deterioro" (CEPAL, 1996, p. 200). No es descartable que estos procesos se mantengan o acentúen en el futuro. En resumen, si la economía no se restructura, si no se sintoniza con los cambios que están ocurriendo a nivel mundial, se continuará quedando atrás.

LA EXPERIENCIA EN LA REINSERCION INTERNACIONAL DE LOS ANTIGUOS PAISES SOCIALISTAS EUROPEOS Y DE NICARAGUA EN 1990-1996. LA EXPERIENCIA CHILENA EN 1973-1997

"el consenso, el equilibrio macroeconómico y el gradualismo se han constituido en la trilogía valórica de la sociedad chilena de fines del siglo XX."

—Meller (1996, p. 309).

Las experiencias de los antiguos países socialistas europeos y de Nicaragua en 1990-1996 y de Chile en 1973-1997 son bastantes ricas en aciertos y errores cometidos en la gestión y política económica de estabilización y liberalización del sector externo, así como en la reinserción internacional comercial y financiera. Por ello hay un conjunto de lecciones útiles para Cuba cuyo objeto es evitar errores de política y los consecuentes costos sociales innecesarios en la reinserción internacional comercial y financiera. Cuba debe establecer políticas comerciales y de reinserción correctas que alienten el aprovechamiento de aquellas

con externalidades positivas y desalienten aquellas con externalidades negativas.

Diseño del Programa Ejecutado en Europa Oriental, Nicaragua y Chile

La política de liberalización inicial de las restricciones comerciales como elemento fundamental del programa de estabilización que se ha aplicado en los antiguos países socialistas europeos ha sido muy similar en general. No obstante, inicialmente hubo una amplia discusión y diferentes puntos de vista sobre el alcance y el ritmo de la liberalización tarifaria y sobre la posible dinámica de sus efectos. En cambio, en cuanto a la política cambiaria hubo marcadas diferencias entre los países que devaluaron y mantuvieron, al menos temporalmente, un régimen de cambio fijo y los que, desde el comienzo, flotaron su moneda, así como entre los que adoptaron una convertibilidad parcial de la moneda, principalmente para la cuenta corriente, y los que adoptaron una convertibilidad más amplia y generalizada.

Los antiguos países socialistas europeos han sido exitosos en reorientar sus exportaciones a nuevos mercados y en abrir sus economías al mercado mundial, pero han visto reducidos sus volúmenes de exportaciones. En general eliminaron las restricciones cuantitativas, fijaron bajas tarifas arancelarias para las importaciones, que actualmente a veces son inferiores al promedio de los países de la OECD y en el resto de los países no superan el doble de la OECD, mantuvieron algunos controles en forma de licencias para las exportaciones, e hicieron su moneda convertible para las transacciones de la cuenta corriente. También han sido exitosos en expandir las exportaciones de servicios. Sin embargo, varios países, entre ellos Polonia, Hungría y Rusia, que inicialmente bajaron los niveles arancelarios, posteriormente los han subido para protegerse de la competencia externa debido a que la tasa de cambio de su moneda se ha apreciado mucho por la entrada de capitales de corto plazo, perjudicando el objetivo estratégico de estimular al sector transable de la economía, lo que ha estado relacionado con el proceso utilizado de estabilización monetaria.

Sachs (1995, 1996b) considera que una vez que se liberan los precios, se eliminan las restricciones al comercio y la tasa de cambio se devalúa adecuadamente, el régimen cambiario debería ser fijo, al menos temporalmente, respecto a una moneda internacional y no basado en la flotación de la moneda nacional. Esto filtraría cambios que responden a movimientos especulativos y situaciones de muy corto plazo, permitiría una remonetización más rápida sin la espiral inflacionaria (tasa de cambio-salarios-precios-tasa de cambio), las inercias y las conductas especulativas que la flotación cambiaria desata y acentúa, aumentando la velocidad de circulación de la moneda, añadiendo al riesgo de la transición de sistema, los riesgos autogenerados e implícitos en las políticas adoptadas. Ese tipo de apertura también fomenta la debilidad del sistema financiero ya que los deudores piden más crédito para evitar la quiebra, y los bancos acceden a proporcionar nuevos préstamos y a renovar créditos incobrables para evitar la quiebra de las empresas con el fin de postergar sus propias pérdidas. Debido a la persistencia de altas tasas de interés, el riesgo de la insolvencia de las empresas productivas y de los bancos y entidades financieras aumenta y todo el sistema financiero se ve en problemas, aumentando el déficit fiscal consolidado a través del sector público financiero. En estos casos el sector bancario y el sector fiscal terminan haciendo transferencias a los prestatarios.

Una política monetaria restrictiva, a través de operaciones de mercado abierto, aumenta las pérdidas del banco central y el déficit fiscal, y pone en peligro la estabilidad financiera. La interacción entre empresas productivas, el sector financiero y el sector fiscal genera conductas especulativas perversas en que todos los agentes tienen incentivos erróneos, acrecentando la magnitud de los recursos involucrados y el nivel de riesgo, dándose la situación propicia a una quiebra generalizada y al resurgimiento del déficit fiscal, lo que puede paralizar, y aún revertir, el proceso de reformas.

Sachs compara el ajuste exitoso y más rápido realizado por Estonia, que también otros antiguos países socialistas (la ex-Checoeslovaquia, Polonia, Hungría y la ex-Yugoeslavia) utilizaron exitosamente, en contraste con Latvia, que flotó la moneda y tuvo un proceso de ajuste más inflacionario y depresivo, al igual que otros países que utilizaron el mismo régimen

cambiario (Bulgaria, Rumania, Ucrania y en general los países de la antigua Unión Soviética).

Fischer, et al (1996, pp. 61-63) encontraron que el régimen cambiario fijo o de ajustes periódicos tiene efectos positivos sobre la detención de la inflación y la recuperación económica más rápida, mientras la flotación cambiaria tiene los efectos opuestos. Como Milton Friedman señaló acertadamente varios años atrás, las teorías deben ser aceptadas por la correspondencia entre las predicciones y los hechos. Los hallazgos de Sachs y Fischer, et al son consistentes con los anteriores de Sargent (1982), Végh (1992), Rebelo y Végh (1995), y Sahay y Végh (1995). El Informe del Banco Mundial de 1996 sobre los países en transición si bien sostiene que Albania, Eslovenia, Latvia, Moldova y Vietnam han logrado estabilizar bajo un régimen cambiario flexible, reconoce que un régimen cambiario fijo podría lograr la estabilización más rápidamente y a un menor costo de crecimiento (World Bank, 1996, p. 39).

Nicaragua utilizó la tasa de cambio como ancla inicial y posteriormente devaluó marcadamente; a partir de entonces ha mantenido una tasa reptante. En general ha eliminado las restricciones no arancelarias y redujo las tarifas arancelarias a niveles entre el 15% y el 40%. Sin embargo, recientemente ha aumentado nuevamente las tarifas. Recibió amplios recursos del exterior en forma de transferencias y préstamos externos y ha utilizado las tasas de interés para movilizar capitales de corto plazo para financiar el déficit comercial.

Chile comenzó un proceso decidido de apertura comercial y financiera en 1973-1981, devaluando la moneda y manteniendo una tasa cambiaria competitiva hasta 1979 cuando decidió fijar el régimen cambiario, eliminó todas las restricciones cuantitativas a las importaciones, comenzó un proceso continuo de reducción y uniformación arancelaria paulatina preanunciada hasta llegar a una tarifa uniforme del 10 por ciento en 1979 y liberó la tasa de interés. La fijación cambiaria contribuyó a desatar una significativa crisis económica en el bienio 1982-1983, debido a que se hizo en el contexto de aumentos de los salarios reales. Tampoco existía un régimen de regulación y supervisión financiera prudente cuando se realizaron la liberalización financiera interna y externa, lo que contribuyó a la crisis (Meller, p. 199).[7]

A partir de 1983, Chile continuó su orientación hacia el exterior, aunque dada su experiencia anterior, aumentó temporalmente las tarifas arancelarias, comenzó la administración del régimen cambiario, de las tasas de interés y de los movimientos de capital para lograr un crecimiento estable y sustentable con la gestión y el mantenimiento de equilibrios macroeconómicos dinámicos basados en las exportaciones competitivas y en atraer un ahorro del exterior moderado. El gobierno chileno en 1984-1997 ha jugado un papel activo y pragmático muy importante en el diseño y aplicación de las políticas para tener un marco macroeconómico estable, creíble y predecible y una tasa de cambio competitiva que permita que la expansión de las exportaciones sea el motor del crecimiento económico y liberalizar la economía en forma gradual, pero progresiva, con lo cual Chile es una economía cada vez más abierta, eficiente y competitiva con base en al aprovechamiento de sus recursos naturales.

Durante el período 1984-1997, Chile ha utilizado el manejo de la tasa de interés para controlar las presiones inflacionarias y reducir gradualmente la inflación, así como los controles a los movimientos de capital para determinar su monto. También ha aplicado rigurosos mecanismos de control para asegurar y preservar la liquidez y la solvencia de las instituciones bancarias y financieras. Chile ha evitado que la estabilidad sea con base a altas tasas de interés y tasas de cambio sobrevaluadas que tienen efectos doblemente recesivos.

El gobierno chileno ha tenido una actitud proactiva en penetrar mercados internacionales mediante acuerdos intergubernamentales. Así ha tenido acceso al MERCOSUR, APEC, la Unión Europea y a acuerdos bilaterales con México y Canadá, por nombrar sólo algunos.

La Reinserción Todavía Pendiente en los Antiguos Países Socialistas Europeos, en Nicaragua y en Chile

Como consecuencia de la dinámica creada por la liberalización de las restricciones comerciales aplicadas en los antiguos países socialistas europeos, reforzada en algunos casos por el régimen de flotación cambiaria empleado y las estructuras de mercado deficientes y monopólicas con mercados laborales rígidos, estos países están revirtiendo parte de las políticas comerciales adoptadas inicialmente e imponiendo tarifas y hasta restricciones cuantitativas (European Bank, 1994, pp 107-116). El argumento que utilizan es que hay un período de aprendizaje y sofisticación (o de ajuste) requerido, que los deficientes mercados financieros y laborales hacen más lento y difícil. La debilidad de los mercados financieros está influenciada por la crisis del sector real, especialmente en los bienes transables. El sistema económico relativamente débil y la combinación de políticas erradas llevan a que cada vez que la economía crece cerca de su potencial, se genere una apreciación real y por consiguiente un balance comercial deficitario que requiere un ajuste monetario.

Nicaragua, a pesar de la ayuda externa masiva de alrededor del 15% del PIB, tendió prematuramente a tarifas muy bajas y a una flotación de la moneda, que han creado un entorno de tasas de interés muy elevadas y tasas de cambio sobrevaluadas y el sector privado ha demandado una mayor protección vía elevación de aranceles.

Chile aún requiere liberalizar su cuenta de capitales ya que persisten diversas regulaciones a los movimientos de capital a corto y largo plazo. También enfrenta la segunda fase de su desarrollo exportador basado en las exportaciones con mayor valor agregado. Actualmente, el 60% de las exportaciones se basan en recursos naturales, el 30% en recursos naturales procesados y 10% en productos industriales.

---

7. Nuestro análisis presupone que la liberalización financiera, en ausencia de un razonable nivel de supervisión y regulación bancaria, está asociada con una mayor probabilidad de que se produzcan crisis bancarias (BID, 1996, p. 140).

LA LITERATURA RECIENTE SOBRE LA ESTABILIZACION EXTERNA Y LA IMPORTANCIA DE LA APERTURA DEL SECTOR EXTERNO

En el mundo de la posguerra, cuando el comercio ha crecido mucho más en términos reales que la producción, especialmente a partir de 1980 cuando casi lo ha duplicado, y la integración internacional se está acentuando como consecuencia de los acuerdos para eliminar las barreras al libre comercio, la inversión directa y los flujos financieros, hay un consenso que los países en desarrollo tienen que insertarse en forma más amplia a la economía mundial. Para ello deben especializarse en las áreas en las cuales poseen ventajas comparativas, apoyadas en la dotación de recursos, y puedan desarrollar economías de escala, lo que requiere la gestión y el mantenimiento de balances o equilibrios macroeconómicos y posteriormente un régimen cambiario que mantenga la competitividad de las exportaciones, en especial ante "shocks" externos, y facilite las entradas de capital para complementar el ahorro interno.

La liberalización del sector comercial externo, tanto en términos de disminución de las barreras arancelarias como la eliminación de las restricciones no arancelarias, ha sido extraordinaria en los países en desarrollo. América Latina ha sido una de las regiones donde este proceso ha sido más sustancial (BID, 1996, p. 102). No obstante, la experiencia con las cuentas de capital es mixta y todavía existen múltiples controles al respecto, especialmente fundamentados en razones de la vulnerabilidad de las economías ante la volatilidad de dichos flujos.

La muy exitosa apertura de los países del este de Asia puso énfasis, en primer lugar, en la neutralidad, o sea en eliminar los sesgos contra las exportaciones, fijando un régimen cambiario competitivo y dando incentivos especiales a las exportaciones. Posteriormente, puso énfasis en la eliminación de los aranceles y las restricciones cuantitativas a las importaciones (Dean, et al, 1994, p. 96). Por otra parte, Amsdem (1994)

considera que la política de la apertura comercial unilateral aplicada en Europa Oriental fue muy rápida y drástica e implica una incorrecta política industrial con costos económicos y sociales muy elevados.

En lo referente al *régimen cambiario* hay cada vez más países que utilizan un régimen de tasas de cambio flexible, puro o administrado por la autoridad monetaria dentro de una banda, cuando la experiencia anterior era que en general los países utilizaban un régimen de cambio fijo. El propósito del régimen cambiario flexible es responder mejor a las modificaciones externas para mantener la competitividad, pero a expensas de tener mayores presiones inflacionarias por los ajustes cambiarios. El régimen fijo facilita una mayor disciplina financiera, un ancla y, por lo tanto, una mayor credibilidad de las políticas. Esto sugiere que la tasa de cambio puede utilizarse en forma distinta y desempeñar diferentes papeles en las etapas de estabilización y de crecimiento sustentable.

Végh presenta evidencia de una recuperación inmediata sin recesión cuando se utiliza la tasa de cambio fija como instrumento de estabilización *en economías con alta inflación*. Rebelo y Végh (1995) presentan evidencia de una recuperación inmediata con recesión posterior cuando se utiliza la tasa de cambio fija como instrumento de estabilización, así como de recesiones inmediata y posterior cuando sólo se utiliza la política monetaria restrictiva como instrumento de estabilización *en economías con inflación crónica* (inflación elevada y persistente). Sahay y Végh (1995) también encontraron que la devaluación y la fijación cambiaria han desempeñado un papel muy importante en los procesos de estabilización en las antiguas economías socialistas de Europa.[8]

En cuanto a la *secuencia* de las reformas referentes al sector externo, predomina el enfoque en la literatura que hay que lograr la estabilización primero para entonces comenzar los procesos de recuperación y crecimiento económicos (Fischer, et al, 1996b, p. 97 y 1996a, p. 230; Meller, 1996, p. 322). Adicionalmente que hay que realizar la liberalización comercial an-

---

8. "With regard to stabilization, an exchange rate anchor appears as the most effective nominal anchor in reducing high inflation, even if it may prove risky in the presence of inflation inertia or when programs lack credibility" (Sahay y Végh, 1995, p. 40).

tes que la liberalización de la cuenta de capital y que ésta sólo deber realizarse después que se haya establecido un sistema regulador moderno y eficiente (Edwards, 1995, p. 9 y Meller, 1996, p. 324). La liberalización de la cuenta de capital prematura, podría apreciar la moneda y dar la señal inadecuada al sector real, el cual tendría dudas razonables sobre la sostenibilidad de las políticas para alentar al sector transable, especialmente si se ve reforzada por una liberalización de los aranceles. La pérdida de competitividad hace necesaria la implementación de un severo ajuste en el gasto interno. También detendría, o aún revertiría, los ajustes y la reasignación de recursos y la modificación de conductas requeridos para una apertura comercial externa adecuada. Hay ramas que no son capaces de competir, pero hay sectores rezagados potencialmente competitivos. Adicionalmente, para conseguir todas las ventajas de la liberalización comercial se deberían liberalizar los mercados de trabajo para poder realizar y fortalecer los ajustes reales y lograr las modificaciones de las conductas requeridas.

En lo referente al sector externo, el Informe del Banco Mundial de 1996 sobre las economías en transición indica que en los países que liberalizaron más, la caída de la producción ha sido menor y la recuperación ha sido más rápida que en los países que liberalizaron menos. También que la liberalización externa debe ser simultánea con la estabilización y la liberalización interna y que deben eliminarse todos los controles comerciales lo antes posible (World Bank, 1996, pp. 28-29, 32).[9] Por su parte, el Informe sobre la Transición del Banco Europeo de 1994 aboga por una liberalización comercial gradual previamente anunciada, que sea creíble y que no esté sujeta a cambios de dirección o reversiones (European Bank, 1994, pp. 100).

UNA PROPUESTA PARA ESTABILIZAR RAPIDAMENTE, SIN RECESION Y LOGRAR LA REINSERCION COMERCIAL Y FINANCIERA CON UN CRECIMIENTO ALTO, ESTABLE Y SUSTENTABLE

En el contexto de una economía mundial muy dinámica, competitiva y cambiante, y crecientemente globalizada, es imprescindible que Cuba, siendo una economía pequeña, abandone su fundamentalismo ideológico y se reinserte plenamente en la comunidad internacional a la brevedad posible, potenciando las reformas que aumenten la flexibilidad y competitividad de la economía y que le permitan participar apropiadamente en los flujos de comercio, tecnología, inversión privada extranjera y financiamiento. Cuba tiene que alcanzar el objetivo estratégico de crecimiento sostenido del producto, sujeto a las restricciones de la capacidad productiva (crecimiento potencial) y de disponibilidad sustentable de divisas, mediante un manejo macroeconómico consistente, combinando pragmáticamente los objetivos estratégicos de estabilización y ajuste con los de crecimiento económico. Esta orientación de la política económica condiciona que el alcanzar los equilibrios macroeconómicos no se consiga a expensas de perjudicar las transformaciones necesarias para lograr el crecimiento económico sostenido. El énfasis en evitar una recesión es porque el período de ajuste en 1989-1997 ha sido muy duro y severo para la población, habiéndose reducido notablemente su ingreso y cuando hay recesión aumenta el desempleo y se reducen los salarios reales. La recesión pone en duda la viabilidad política y social de las reformas necesarias. En cambio una economía en expansión es la mejor vía para la solución de muchos problemas.

Dicha reinserción conllevará ajustes sustanciales en la estructura productiva del país, así como en el comercio exterior para tomar ventajas de sus recursos naturales y de la calidad de sus recursos humanos. El nuevo sistema de precios relativos estimulará las exportaciones; en consecuencia, la apertura externa y

---

9. "... on average, policymakers will maximize people's income by liberalizing as much as possible within the range left open by country specific constraints." "... Worldwide experience has shown that 'temporary' protection measures all too often become permanent and that frequent changes in trade policy are bad for firms that are developing foreign ties" (World Bank, 1996, pp. 29, 32).

la expansión de las exportaciones requieren de incentivos adecuados a los empresarios para que incorporen la tecnología moderna para enfrentar la competitividad internacional y conquistar los mercados externos. Una mayor apertura permitirá adoptar la estructura de precios relativos internacional y presionará y fortalecerá los ajustes para tener una mejor asignación de recursos y una producción más eficiente y competitiva. Así, las exportaciones de bienes y servicios se podrán convertir en el motor para expandir la producción nacional y con ello la capitalización y los niveles de empleo y de remuneraciones reales de los cubanos y permitirá servir la deuda externa una vez renegociada de manera ordenada. Sin embargo, será necesario adoptar medidas especiales que faciliten un mayor comercio exterior y la movilización de recursos externos y con ello la capitalización y la modernización del aparato productivo que es altamente dependiente de las importaciones. El aumento de las exportaciones tiene que estar apoyado de una ampliación, profundización y diversificación del sector financiero que sostenga la apertura hacia el exterior con nuevos instrumentos y facilidades.

Objetivos y Consideraciones Generales

Considerando la situación actual de Cuba, los objetivos iniciales que se pretenden son la efectiva y pronta eliminación de la inconvertibilidad externa del peso y de la dolarización existentes, o sea lograr la estabilización externa mediante una tasa de cambio que permita la convertibilidad del peso, y un régimen arancelario más competitivo, pero que no determine la desorganización total de la producción interna. La propuesta supone que en Cuba habrá una baja tolerancia política y social si se mantiene o aumenta la alta tasa de desempleo abierta y disfrazada actual, que debe ser del orden del 20 por ciento, dado el severo proceso de ajuste en 1989-1997. Posteriormente, una tasa de cambio real relativamente estable que mantenga y aliente la competitividad de las exportaciones, así como la progresiva liberalización de los aranceles y del régimen cambiario, contribuirán al crecimiento, a la progresiva apertura de la economía y al aumento de los niveles de eficiencia e inversión, lo que será un determinante fundamental del proceso y ritmo de desarrollo económico. Estas medidas de tipo macroeconómico deberían ser complementadas por otras

orientadas a la movilización de los recursos externos, referentes a: alentar las transferencias unilaterales del exterior; utilizar el financiamiento externo oficial, para lo cual se necesita renegociar la deuda externa de acuerdo con los términos del HIPC (Programa para Países Pobres Altamente Endeudados) y los reclamos por confiscaciones; alentar la inversión privada externa; y seguir una política de promoción de exportaciones. Asimismo, una medida que facilitaría y aceleraría la plena reinserción internacional comercial y financiera sería atraer el retorno de los cubanos del exterior.

Más que tener objetivos diferentes en cuanto a la liberalización y desregulación tarifaria, cambiaria y financiera, que son indispensables para reducir los costos de transacción y aumentar la transparencia en el sector externo, la propuesta es diferente y puede lucir controversial en lo referente a la utilización inicial de instrumentos como un régimen cambiario fijo y la protección temporal alta de la producción nacional, así como en cuanto a la amplitud inicial, el ritmo y la secuencia al implantar la liberalización y desregulación cambiaria, tarifaria y de movimientos de capital para endogenizar el crecimiento y desatar una dinámica virtuosa. La apertura gradual se basa en la situación depresiva del país y en la consideración que un ritmo más prudente y ordenado de cambios establece señales claras y coherentes a los agentes económicos para acumular riqueza; alimenta y desarrolla las fuerzas de mercado y su funcionamiento en mercados ausentes, segmentados o insuficientes; evita la paralización de la producción existente; y logra más pronto los resultados finales de estabilización externa y de apertura, mientras que la "gran explosión" no brinda señales claras y creíbles a los agentes, especialmente a los inversionistas en capital real y financiero. Además, la propuesta plantea avanzar y consolidar *simultáneamente* varios frentes esenciales (comerciales, cambiarios y financieros).

El diseño y aplicación de un paquete secuencial, gradual y ordenado similar fue utilizado por Yugoeslavia para estabilizar con éxito y rápidamente en 1994 en condiciones de bloqueo externo y de guerra y sin ninguna ayuda externa (Avramovic, 1997) y fue la base del éxito chileno en el período 1984-1997 (Meller,

1996, p. 324). El paquete propuesto creará expectativas de estabilidad que orientarán los mercados para hacerlos más estables. También la gradualidad se basa en la consideración que hay histéresis en los procesos de apertura externa que se deben alcanzar para retroalimentar el proceso de apertura y orientación externa (Rodrik, 1995, p. 2968).

Diseño de la Estrategia e Instrumentos Básicos Requeridos

El diseño de la estrategia con una visión de largo plazo y concentrándose en los elementos esenciales de las reformas se basa en las condiciones y características iniciales de Cuba indicadas anteriormente, en que la respuesta del sistema económico depende de las condiciones en que está, y en las experiencias recientes de Europa Oriental y de Nicaragua, así como de Chile en 1973-1997. Una espiral inflacionaria desatada por la dinámica de la flotación cambiaria y de la liberalización extrema de las restricciones comerciales en el contexto de un significativo excedente monetario, rigidez en los mercados laborales, escasos mecanismos de mercados y una estructura monopólica de los mismos, es inconsistente con la estabilización. Además, las reformas comerciales, cambiarias y financieras deben ser parte integral y consistente de un paquete mayor de políticas y de reformas institucionales coherentes para la transición hacia una economía de mercado que tengan la credibilidad, y vayan ampliando sostenida y progresivamente la mejor asignación de recursos de la economía y trasmitiendo los efectos de la orientación hacia el exterior, mejorando la flexibilidad de la economía ante choques externos y los niveles de vida de la población, generando de esta forma un juego de suma positiva, en el cual casi todos ganan y pocos pierden. De lo contrario los efectos de las liberalizaciones comerciales, cambiarias y financieras "tipo gran explosión," con reformas no esenciales o prematuras, podrían acentuar y verse acentuadas por las distorsiones e ineficiencias existentes y conducir a una crisis económica y financiera que conlleve al choque monetario como sucedió en varios antiguos países socialistas de Europa.

La propuesta, para lograr los objetivos indicados, consiste en la devaluación para restablecer la convertibilidad del peso y el establecimiento administrativo de una tasa de interés real positiva para modificar las expectativas, aumentar la demanda por los activos financieros nacionales en relación a los activos financieros internacionales, no sólo por los residentes sino también por los no residentes y extranjeros. Esto sería acompañado de la política monetaria restrictiva, una política fiscal austera y la ayuda externa que le den credibilidad a la nueva tasa de cambio y a la política de estabilización en general. De esta manera se sentarán las bases para la estabilización y la desdolarización. Ello se podría respaldar con un fondo de reservas internacionales con base en préstamos de los organismos internacionales o del sector privado y sujeto al dólar, al menos temporalmente, para lograr la desdolarización y la consolidación de un sostenido proceso de monetización o de inducción para aumentar la tenencia de activos financieros reales nacionales y dar un punto de referencia o *ancla* al tremendo ajuste que es necesario realizar en los precios relativos internos y en relación con los precios internacionales. Este esquema impondría restricciones a seguir una política monetaria expansionaria.

La devaluación supone que la economía no tiene una homogeneidad de grado 1 respecto al tipo de cambio y que sus efectos no son transferidos automática ni instantáneamente a los precios internos y que, en consecuencia, habrá un cambio relativo en los mismos y se generarán importantes incentivos para la producción de bienes transables. A su vez la devaluación requerirá políticas fiscales y monetarias que ayuden a validarla.

Después de la devaluación para corregir la marcada sobrevalorización del peso y la unificación de la tasa de cambio para todas las transacciones externas, se eliminarían todas las barreras no arancelarias, tales como cuotas, licencias previas (excepto las fitosanitarias, zoosanitarias y de seguridad), depósitos previos o pagos anticipados obligatorios de importación, y el monopolio estatal de las actividades de exportación e importación, pero se mantendrían controles sobre las transacciones de capital de corto plazo. Posteriormente a un período de estabilización inicial, la política cambiaria debería orientarse a mantener un tipo de cambio real competitivo suficientemente atractivo para estimular las exportaciones, mediante minidevaluaciones periódicas. La devaluación primero y el mantener una tasa de cambio real competitiva después que se ajuste por las alteraciones de la economía mundial, tienen por objeto estimular las exportaciones, para que hagan de motor primario del crecimiento económico, y bienes competitivos de las importaciones (bienes transables).

Como al principio no se podría pagar la deuda externa dado su elevado nivel y hay un proceso de histéresis en la apertura externa, la tasa de cambio se debería administrar manteniendo una subvaloración del peso, favoreciendo la capacidad exportadora del país para integrarlo adecuadamente a la economía internacional y favorecer la acumulación de reservas internacionales, así como aislándolo de las fluctuaciones externas en los términos de intercambio que podrían ser muy marcadas debido a la dependencia del país de los precios del azúcar y de otros bienes primarios, permitiendo mantener una política de interés real consistente con las metas de recuperación. Por años, Cuba tendrá que experimentar un superávit en la cuenta corriente de la balanza de pagos para enfrentar el servicio de la deuda externa renegociada.

Las medidas propuestas eliminarían la restricción externa de la economía, reintroducirían la competencia externa, tenderían a cambiar la estructura de precios y reorientarían la economía al exterior. Por ello debería haber una protección **transitoria** alta (aranceles ad-valorem del 100%) para las importaciones de bienes de consumo, a fin de facilitar que las empresas tengan un período de adecuación, se ajusten y familiaricen con los mecanismos de exportación, hagan los ajustes técnicos requeridos, y eliminen las rigideces propias del socialismo paternalista en la capacidad

gerencial, la gestión, tecnologías y equipos de producción, en la utilización de insumos[10] y el empleo, así como que se ajusten a las normas de los mercados occidentales. Las materias primas y los bienes de capital deberían tener aranceles bajos del 20%, excepto las utilizadas para las exportaciones que podrían estar exentas y se reintegrarían al momento de la exportación. También se debería reintegrar el IVA a aquellos bienes utilizados en la produc ción de las exportaciones. Varios productos transables de Cuba son subsidiados por los E.U., tales como arroz, oleaginosas, maíz, leche, etc.

Se debería definir que los aranceles se reducirían automáticamente, en fechas predefinidas y preanunciadas públicamente, hasta llegar a una tarifa uniforme del 10% en cinco años.[11] La protección temporal alta, armónica con la apertura al comercio internacional y con la experiencia chilena en 1973-1976, tiene por objeto reducir los costos de la disminución de la producción y de empleo del proceso de ajuste, especialmente en la etapa de estabilización y requeriría de una administración de aduanas efectiva. El surgimiento de nuevos agentes económicos eficientes que operan en un esquema competitivo abierto toma tiempo y conlleva ajuste, así como la eliminación d- muchas distorsiones que evitan la respuesta mercados laborales, financieros, etc. afectan la velocidad y la capacidad actividades potencialment- contribuiría a desaler- sumo de biene- una gran acu- nalizar las de mater-

---

10. En las economías socialistas se desarrolló la práctica de mantener altos finales.

11. Esto se podría realizar mediante el sistema *concertina*, o sea dismi niveles en vez de emplear el sistema *radial*, que sería disminuyendo en p reduce la protección efectiva en forma pareja a través del tiempo, lo cual e

12. Los niveles propuestos son inferiores a los actuales de Nicaragua y que mentos en la eficiencia y mejoras en la calidad de los productos por el aumento

Esta propuesta estaría en línea con las recomendaciones de McKinnon (1991), Williamson (1991, 1997)[13] y Amsdem (1994) para evitar la *catástrofe* ocurrida en las empresas estatales de los antiguos países de la Unión Soviética o una explosión, al menos en el corto plazo, de las importaciones que han estado reprimidas por tantos años. Una vez se cierre una empresa es muy difícil abrirla de nuevo y mucho peor es mantenerla artificialmente sin quebrar mediante préstamos suaves, lo que también perjudica y retrasa la sanidad y la reforma financieras. La propuesta también es consistente con la sugerencia precitada del Banco Europeo sobre el tema. Sin embargo, entendemos que aranceles altos y no parejos conducen a una asignación de recursos distorsionada que afecta la eficiencia y que promueven actividades buscadoras de rentas en vez de actividades productivas, pero el objetivo inicial es buscar una dinámica de crecimiento y facilitar ajustes en los sectores laborales de empresas que no son instantáneos.

Se descarta utilizar la flotación cambiaria porque puede retardar las decisiones de producción, reducir la inversión y producir efectos indeseables sobre el comercio, los movimientos de capital y la propia tasa de inflación por las incertidumbres y las inercias que desata y acentúa, aumentando la velocidad de circulación de la moneda, el casi colapso de algunas funciones del dinero, dando señales incorrectas o poco claras a los agentes económicos, y porque los cambios en la asignación de recursos entre los sectores transables y no transables requieren tiempo. Una entrada masiva de capitales de corto plazo por una apertura muy rápida de la cuenta de capitales tendería a apreciar el peso por encima de la tasa real de equilibrio, crearía burbujas especulativas (aumentos artificiales de precio de los activos reales, especialmente de los bienes que sesgarían los portafolios de los inversionistas de las ganancias rápidas de capital en bienes contra la acumulación de otros bienes de capital, y alentarían un fuerte endeudamiento externo y la inestabilidad cambiaria por razones coyunturales externas. Adicionalmente, una fuga de capitales, por temores o falta de confianza o por una percepción alta de riesgos, podría crear presiones indebidas en la tasa cambiaria.

Se deberían colocar valores denominados en dólares a más de un año con tasas de interés reajustables entre los cubanos residentes en el exterior para captación con propósitos de desarrollo. Cuba necesitará movimientos de capitales, especialmente en el proceso de la recuperación para complementar el ahorro interno, el cual será bajo inicialmente. Una tasa mayor que la internacional, de acuerdo a lo indicado anteriormente, debería atraer entradas de capital. Si los movimientos de capital fueran insuficientes se podría aumentar la tasa de interés o si fueran excesivos se podrían establecer encajes legales o impuestos, que tiendan a disminuir su rentabilidad. Para evitar influencias negativas sobre la estabilidad cambiaria y los niveles crediticios se debería exigir su registro en el Banco Nacional y establecer plazos mínimos (p.e. de 180 días) o encajes diferentes dependiendo del plazo.

Como lo demostraron las aperturas financieras externas de Sur América a principios de la década de los años 1980 y el llamado "efecto Tequila" en 1995, si la apertura no se diseña y aplica bien y produce una masiva entrada de capitales de corto plazo, el déficit en cuenta corriente alcanza proporciones insostenibles en el mediano plazo, revertiendo el flujo y causando una severa recesión o inclusive una crisis financiera. Además, esto produce un incremento artificial en el precio de las propiedades y de la tierra (burbujas especulativas), lo cual incentiva la especulación y el consumo. Hay que evitar la volatilidad y la vulnerabilidad innecesarias de la economía.

La liberalización y desregulación comerciales, cambiarias y financieras, que son *procesos y no simples*

---

n consensus recommended rapid elimination of quantitative restrictions on imports followed by the progressive re- tariff levels reached a uniform low rate in the range of 10 percent to 20 percent. I noted that there existed differ- he speed with which the tariff reduction should take place and about whether the pace of liberalization should conomics conditions or whether an adverse macroeconomic environment (low growth combined with large tify delay" Williamson (1997, p. 54).

acontecimientos, deberían concentrarse en los elementos esenciales para hacer el proceso sustentable y estarían encaminadas a alentar la competencia externa y la entrada de capitales. Esto debe realizarse a partir de un prudente y estricto marco de regulaciones y supervisión financieras que estimulen el crecimiento económico, el aumento de la productividad y facilite los procesos de privatización y gobernabilidad democrática.[14]

Este paquete de medidas esenciales y coherentes tenderá a aumentar la utilización de la capacidad productiva existente y a mejorar la productividad, y se basa en cuatro consideraciones fundamentales: (1) que el gobierno haya adoptado suficientes medidas adicionales para eliminar el déficit fiscal, o sea, la causa última de los desbalances internos y externos, lo cual también disminuiría las presiones sobre la tasa de cambio y la tasa de interés; (2) que el gobierno adopte medidas para incentivar el aumento de la producción liberando las pequeñas y medianas empresas, las profesiones, el trabajo por cuenta propia, la pequeña agricultura y las UBPC a fin de alentar la oferta que corrija al menos parcialmente las políticas e instituciones que limitan la tasa de crecimiento del país; (3) que se establezca un Estado de Derecho y un sistema judicial independiente, eficaz y confiable; y (4) que el gobierno adopte las medidas y los incentivos para permitir y alentar la activa participación de la comunidad cubana en el exterior, lo cual establecería un flujo de capitales y de recursos humanos talentosos hacia Cuba. La comunidad cubana en su conjunto tiene una serie de habilidades, destrezas y experiencias en el comercio exterior y en transacciones comerciales y financieras que los antiguos países socialistas europeos no tuvieron. La estabilización efectiva depende no sólo de controlar la demanda sino de estimular la oferta.

Con base en las políticas anteriores y solicitando los "waivers" relevantes, el gobierno de Cuba podría realizar una reincorporación efectiva a la Organización Mundial del Comercio (WTO), ya que su adhesión actual es más bien formal o simbólica. El gobierno de Cuba debería entrar en negociaciones inmediatas para tener un amplio acceso sin barreras al mercado de bienes agropecuarios, servicios turísticos y de capitales de EUA y su incorporación al Tratado de Libre Comercio de las Américas (ALCA) en o antes del año 2005. Cuba necesita buenos mercados para sus exportaciones y acceso adecuado a los mercados de capital, a fin de participar activamente lo antes posible en el sistema comercial y financiero internacional. En caso de que el país no progrese, habría una *fortísima presión* de la población para emigrar a los EUA, lo cual podría realizarse utilizando los vínculos familiares de los cubano-americanos. Ya en 1992 se había estimado que un millón de cubanos deseaba emigrar a los EUA (Bergner, 1992). A corto plazo, esa emigración sería una solución para el gobierno de Cuba, pero un problema para el gobierno de EUA como se observó con la crisis de los balseros en agosto-setiembre de 1994 y con la actual política migratoria. Adicionalmente, es absurdo que unos 20,000 cubanos tengan que abandonar a Cuba todos los años; a largo plazo es otra pérdida para Cuba y su capacidad de desarrollo.

Fortalezas, Debilidades y Posibles Efectos de las Políticas y Medidas Propuestas vis à vis la Liberalización Inmediata de las Restricciones Comerciales y la Flotación Cambiaria

La liberalización extrema de las restricciones comerciales y la flotación cambiaria desde un inicio desatan una dinámica inflacionaria y recesiva para la producción nacional por los efectos de la depreciación de la moneda nacional sobre el nivel de precios, que terminan con un choque monetario y altas tasas de interés para eliminar la inflación. Esto a su vez atrae movimientos de capital del exterior a corto plazo ("capitales golondrinas"), pero no es conducente a la formación de capital fijo ni al crecimiento. Dicha política tiende a estabilizar la economía, pero a altas tasas de interés que desincentivan la inversión al concentrar el ajuste en ésta y, a través del efecto de la entrada de capitales, a una tasa de cambio sobrevaluada que no fa-

---

14. "... a state too weak to supervise the financial system properly will jeopardize the functioning of the market" (Williamson, 1997, p. 54).

vorece la competitividad externa al deprimir el precio interno de los transables y desincentivar su producción. Esta política no es consistente con la estabilización ni dinámicamente con los objetivos propuestos. Además, los altos niveles de tasas de interés conducen a expectativas racionales de mayores inflaciones en el futuro. Esta política confunde la relevancia de los factores envueltos y desconoce la intensidad de la dinámica envuelta, desatando un equilibrio cuyas fuerzas se retroalimentan, no conducen al crecimiento y tienen histéresis o efectos difíciles de revertir.

Las desventajas de la liberalización prematura de las restricciones al comercio internacional, así como la flotación cambiaria para restablecer la convertibilidad y lograr la tasa cambiaria de equilibrio en el contexto de estructuras de mercado insuficientes y monopólicas, son la espiral, las inercias, las conductas especulativas y la histéresis inflacionaria transitoria o permanente que desatan cuando lo ideal es lograr anclas que tiendan a estabilizar rápidamente el sistema alrededor de los precios de equilibrio (tasas de cambio y de interés), evitar una recesión y otros costos involucrados en el proceso de ajuste. Los argumentos de Sachs (1995 y 1996b) para la fijación cambiaria después de una devaluación con credibilidad, o sea que la población la perciba como permanente y estable, son incontrovertibles. Además, es mucho mejor mientras más pronto se logra la estabilización externa y comience la recuperación dentro de un contexto de libre juego de las fuerzas de mercado. La evidencia empírica sugiere que cuando se logra exitosamente la estabilización le sigue de inmediato la recuperación (Rebelo y Végh, 1995, p 113).

Hay un doble error de utilizar la liberalización de las restricciones comerciales desde el inicio: (1) porque es un instrumento por excelencia apropiado para eliminar las distorsiones en los precios relativos, las ineficiencias en la asignación de recursos y las conductas rentistas, pero no para estabilizar la economía que es el principal objetivo inicial; y (2) porque la espiral y las inercias inflacionarias que desatan y acentúan, hacen que se utilice la política monetaria restrictiva para frenarlas en vez de facilitar la reestructuración y el crecimiento dentro de un marco estable, lo cual se evidencia en parte por los aumentos que conlleva en

las tasas de interés de largo plazo. En última instancia su interacción con la estabilización y sus efectos sobre la credibilidad son contrarios a la secuencia necesaria en las reformas. No todo se puede hacer a la vez (Avramovic, 1997). Lo que importa no es tanto *comenzar* todas las reformas a la vez sino *completarlas* simultáneamente (Berthelot, 1997, p. 342).

Otras Medidas para Reforzar la Plena Reinserción Internacional Comercial y Financiera

1. Promoción y flexibilización de las transferencias unilaterales

Problemas: Escasez de recursos externos; atraso y dificultad en mantener niveles de vida adecuados; costos humanos del ajuste.

Solución: Movilización de transferencias unilaterales.

Instrumentos: Permitir y alentar las remesas familiares e institucionales de entidades sin fines de lucro.

La entrada de transferencias unilaterales en efectivo, o remesas personales y de entidades no gubernamentales del exterior, se debería permitir libre de impuestos a la tasa de cambio de mercado. No se deberían imponer limitaciones a que las remesas personales se puedan utilizar para establecer pequeñas y medianas empresas o adquirir viviendas, para alentarlas y para que las familias en la Isla no tengan que depender permanentemente de sus familias o amistades en el exterior. Esta medida es muy importante no sólo para movilizar recursos externos sino por la importante contribución que podría hacer la recuperación de la producción interna y de las viviendas si se permite que las remesas puedan ser utilizadas en esa forma. Para un mayor estímulo a este flujo será necesario definir los derechos de propiedad.

Las organizaciones privadas, humanitarias y de desarrollo, de interés social y sin fines de lucro, aunque sean extranjeras o mixtas, se deberían permitir y alentar a que abran operaciones libres de impuestos sobre ingresos en Cuba. Con políticas novedosas será posible estimular y abrir espacios a la iniciativa, creatividad, generosidad, solidaridad y compasión de estas instituciones para incorporarlas en el proceso de recuperación nacional y en reducir los costos humanos del ajuste. Sin embargo, el envío de bienes se debería sujetar a los aranceles vigentes para evitar competencia desleal con los productores nacionales.

2. Promoción y flexibilización de la inversión privada

Problemas: Atraso tecnológico, organizativo y de gestión; escasez de recursos de inversión; dificultad de acceso a los mercados externos.

Solución: **Movilización de la inversión privada extranjera.**

Instrumentos: Código moderno para atraer la inversión privada extranjera. Entrar a MIGA, solicitar a OPIC e instituciones similares que actúen en Cuba. Promover tratados de doble tributación.

A fin de lograr el acceso y aplicación de nuevas tecnologías y formas organizativas y de gestión del exterior, la entrada a mercados internacionales, y la captación de recursos para financiar la recuperación y el crecimiento económico sustentable, se debería dictar una ley que aliente la inversión privada extranjera. Se debería comenzar con un estatuto provisional que modifique la ley existente de 1995 que es muy discrecional y que contiene importantes distorsiones como la prohibición a la libre contratación de mano de obra. El establecimiento de reglas uniformes y claras, la racionalización y la simplificación de los trámites y procedimientos, y el aumento de la transparencia deben ser elementos fundamentales de la nueva ley a fin de reducir los costos de transacción. No obstante, debería haber una severa restricción inicial para la adquisición de las empresas estatales existentes hasta que comience el proceso de privatización y se reestablezcan mercados financieros funcionales.

La nueva ley debería permitir nuevas inversiones en todos los sectores de la economía, salvo en los que no convienen a la seguridad del país, y brindar a las empresas extranjeras igual trato que a las nacionales. Esto podría considerarse una extensión de la Doctrina Calvo que establece la igualdad ante la Ley de los nacionales y los extranjeros radicados en el país, lo cual sería lo opuesto a lo que ha hecho el gobierno socialista de Cuba, que ha otorgado trato preferencial a los extranjeros. No se deberían contemplar incentivos, ni subsidios especiales, ni concesiones monopólicas. Se debería permitir la repatriación de ganancias desde un inicio, pero no del capital invertido que no se debería poder repatriar por tres años para evitar la especulación. La inversión extranjera se debería permitir mediante recursos financieros, nuevos equipos y plantas en todos los sectores productivos. Se debería garantizar la libertad de exportación, importación, comercio, industria y propiedad privada a las empresas extranjeras. No se debería alentar movimientos de capital de corto plazo para evitar la vulnerabilidad de la débil economía; todas las inversiones financieras deberían ser por un mínimo de seis meses. Se deberían garantizar los derechos fundamentales del trabajador cubano que han sido violados por el gobierno socialista. La aplicación y el cumplimiento de los cinco *Principios Arcos* orientaría un buen comienzo.[15]

Cuba debería entrar a MIGA y solicitar formalmente a la Overseas Private Investment Corporation (OPIC) y a otras instituciones similares de Europa para que comiencen sus operaciones de financiamiento y seguros en el país con el fin de reducir los riesgos no comerciales del inversionista extranjero. Además, debería comenzar discusiones inmediatas para lograr acuerdos bilaterales sobre doble tributación de manera que los inversionistas puedan acredi-

---

15. Principio I, **Respeto a la dignidad del pueblo cubano y a un proceso legal adecuado y justo;** Principio II, **Respeto a los derechos humanos básicos.** Igualdad de derechos y no discriminación ni exclusiones contra los cubanos en el acceso y uso de instalaciones, así como en la adquisición de bienes y servicios; Principio III, **Prácticas justas e igualdad de contratación y de empleo sin discriminación por razones políticas, sexo, raza, religión y edad;** Principio IV, **Promoción de prácticas laborales justas y del derecho de los trabajadores cubanos a sindicalizarse y a ser remunerados adecuadamente;** Principio V, **Mejoramiento de la calidad de vida de los trabajadores dentro y fuera de los centros laborales en áreas tales como: seguridad e higiene ocupacional, cultura y protección del medio ambiente.** Para un tratamiento más amplio de este tema y de las distorsiones en la legislación vigente sobre la inversión extranjera, ver Castañeda y Montalván (1994b).

tar los impuestos que pagan en Cuba en sus países de origen.

Cuba no debe seguir sólo una política unilateral de apertura de la economía, sino una política de acuerdos o tratados internacionales de forma que no sólo nos abramos al comercio internacional sino que también aseguremos que las otras economías se abran a nuestros productos. La política de liberalización gradual al comercio mundial, debería ser acompañada de una liberalización más rápida al comercio intrarregional, incluyendo servicios, inversión, propiedad intelectual. Estos acuerdos requerirán seguimiento, implementación y adecuación de los mismos a través de comisiones negociadoras.

3. Movilización de la cooperación financiera y técnica internacional

Problemas: Bajos niveles de ahorro e inversión para la pronta recuperación y el crecimiento elevado y sustentable; carencia de recursos humanos especializados.

Solución: **Movilizar asistencia financiera y técnica oficial.**

Instrumentos: Incorporarse a las entidades financieras internacionales. Solicitar préstamos y asistencia técnica oficial.

Dado los bajos niveles de ahorro interno y de desarrollo, Cuba necesita montos significativos de recursos externos netos (financiamiento externo) y en los términos más favorables posibles (menor costo de los recursos) para asegurar la recuperación y consolidación económica en el futuro próximo y tasas de crecimiento altas y sustentables posteriormente. El bajo nivel de ahorro interno del país es determinado por el bajo nivel de ingreso, el estancamiento económico, la represión económica-financiera existente y la carencia de instituciones financieras básicas e instrumentos de ahorro a largo plazo adecuados que fomenten y asignen el ahorro y faciliten la inversión, tales como: fondos privados de pensión, compañías de seguros, fondos mutuos, bonos, acciones, etc. Sin embargo, dadas las necesidades de inversión existentes en el país, lo más importante es movilizar un monto adecuado de recursos externos complementarios en vez de darle

prioridad a la concesionalidad de los recursos, la cual está tendiendo a desaparecer.

Cuba debería solicitar ser miembro asociado en los organismos financieros internacionales de desarrollo (FMI, Banco Mundial y BID) con objeto de recibir cooperación y asesoría técnica para entrenar personal y preparar planes detallados de las reformas y propuestas de préstamos para las etapas posteriores, mientras se determina su cuota de entrada en ellos de acuerdo con su nivel de ingreso. La cooperación financiera de los organismos internacionales facilitaría alcanzar los resultados necesarios y eliminaría la necesidad de imponer medidas más drásticas. La asistencia técnica podría ayudar en el adiestramiento rápido de gerentes, administradores, contadores, auditores, economistas y abogados. Asimismo, será necesario un programa inicial de emergencia alimentaria para atender la hambruna y la desnutrición infantil, que se superaría tan pronto se libere y desregule adecuadamente el agro.

Posteriormente, Cuba debería solicitar ser miembro regular en los organismos financieros internacionales de desarrollo (FMI, Banco Mundial y BID) con objeto de recibir cooperación financiera y técnica. Cuba podrá obtener significativos flujos positivos con propósitos de desarrollo, ya que no tiene deuda pendiente con ellos y además tiene condición de país altamente endeudado y de menor desarrollo relativo en el continente. Un programa de ajuste estructural discutido y apoyado por las instituciones financieras de desarrollo sería muy útil para negociar el nivel y los términos la deuda externa con los Clubs de París y de Londres con base en los términos del programa de apoyo a los Países Pobres Altamente Endeudados (HIPC) y tener así nuevamente acceso al crédito comercial y bancario internacional. La ayuda externa que se reciba debería dar preferencia a apoyar directamente el programa de estabilización; el establecimiento de un Estado de Derecho y un poder judicial independiente, eficiente y confiable; la renegociación de la deuda; la reconversión productiva de las pequeñas y medianas empresas privadas para que se capitalicen adecuadamente; financiar los programas de solidaridad e inversión social orientados a asegurar una calidad de vida adecuada durante el proceso de transición; obtener asistencia técnica temporal de los cubanos del exterior que decidan permanecer fuera del país; y expandir la infraestructura económica.

4. Renegociación de la deuda externa

Problemas: Acceso muy limitado y caro al crédito comercial externo; crisis y moratoria de la deuda externa desde 1986. Cuba es un país altamente endeudado.

Solución: **Normalización del acceso al crédito y pagos externos.**

Instrumentos: Renegociación del monto y términos de la deuda externa con base en los términos del HIPC.

El alto nivel de la deuda externa existente desalienta las inversiones, ya que implica un entorno negativo en términos de expectativas racionales de impuestos, devaluación y tasas de interés reales más elevados. Se debería diseñar una estrategia para reunir un grupo de países de apoyo a fin de renegociar, reduciendo el monto y los términos, y postergando el vencimiento y el inicio del servicio de la deuda externa con los Clubs de París y Londres que actualmente es inmanejable sin un proceso de reducción y redimensionamiento. Nicaragua ha tenido una excelente experiencia al respecto. Posteriormente, Cuba podría entrar en el Programa de los Países Pobres Altamente Endeudados (HIPC).

Dicha estrategia considerará que es imposible que el país pague el nivel actual de la deuda a la vez que estabiliza y reestructura la economía y que necesita apoyo en términos de líneas de crédito de corto plazo para atender posteriormente sus obligaciones. Hay que crecer para poder pagar la deuda renegociada. Si bien el gobierno no debería adoptar ninguna medida especial para pagar una deuda externa desproporcionada a la capacidad de pagos del país, en la actual economía mundial interdependiente el costo del no pagar es superior al del servicio de la deuda. Por ello se debería realizar un redimensionamiento ordenado y conveniente de la deuda renegociada y un esfuerzo coherente y serio de ajuste y de pagos para atraer nuevos créditos externos. Adicionalmente, se deberían autorizar operaciones de reconversión, dando preferencia a proyectos ecológicos, asistencia les y de

desarrollo municipal dirigidos a la población de bajos ingresos, pero se incluirían todo tipo de operaciones en nuevos proyectos de infraestructura o en la adquisición de las empresas estatales existentes que se expandan.

5. Relaciones con los ciudadanos expatriados

Problemas: Escasez de recursos humanos y financieros para desarrollar una economía de mercado.

Solución: **Atraer y reintegrar cubanos expatriados, movilizar sus recursos financieros, su iniciativa y su capacidad de gestión para administrar grandes empresas.**

Instrumentos: Código para la reintegración de los cubanos expatriados y facilitar la entrada de sus recursos financieros.

A todos los nacidos o antiguos residentes en el país, que deseen radicarse permanentemente en Cuba, se les debería permitir, libre de impuestos, la entrada de menajes domésticos, el recibo de pagos de jubilación del exterior, la entrada de capitales, así como el libre ejercicio profesional y de oficios. A tal efecto, se debería crear una Oficina Nacional de Retorno y la legislación sobre franquicias aduaneras y revalidación de títulos profesionales y técnicos especializados, que faciliten el regreso al país de los residentes en el exterior y su plena incorporación a la recuperación y desarrollo nacional. Se debería incentivar que entidades religiosas y los municipios estén muy activos en este proceso.

6. Estrategia y política de apoyo activo a las exportaciones

Problemas: Escasez de recursos externos.

Solución: **Aumentar las exportaciones de bienes y servicios.**

Instrumentos: Proactivismo en la promoción de exportaciones por concertación pública/privada (empresarios, sindicatos, representantes de la sociedad civil) y activismo del Estado en acceder a mercados internacionales altamente competitivos.

Cuba necesita reinsertarse activa y rápidamente en la economía mundial. Requiere un esfuerzo deliberado, sistemático e integrador de expansión de sus exportaciones de bienes y servicios que logre penetrar los mercados externos con precios rentables y competitivos que promueva la actualización, la eficiencia y el desarrollo tecnológico nacional, la orientación empresarial hacia una mentalidad exportadora hacia nuevos mercados, la continua capacitación de los trabajadores, la motivación del trabajo que tendrá ahora mayores incentivos materiales, así como el apoyo a la comercialización y mercadeo de la oferta exportable, tales como la participación en ferias internacionales y el apoyo de la cooperación técnica empresarial. Para ello se requiere una activa sinergia entre los sectores empresariales, gremiales y el gobierno y una institucionalidad de apoyo al sector exportador.

A tal efecto el gobierno, en concertación con el sector privado, debería establecer marcos legales apropiados, desarrollar una infraestructura científica y tecnológica con las universidades y centros superiores de estudios e investigación aplicada, así como una política de apoyo a la innovación de productos y procesos. Es necesario innovar, inventar y mejorar la calidad de los productos y servicios ofrecidos en el mundo, otorgando incentivos públicos para emprender actividades dinámicas e innovadoras y dando apoyo a la creación de nuevas empresas de alto nivel tecnológico con base a resultados verificables y utilizando indicadores de desempeño. Los incentivos fiscales (impositivos o de gastos públicos) deben ser estrictos, selectivos, acotados, limitados y decrecientes en el tiempo y con leves desviaciones de la neutralidad que privilegien las exportaciones no tradicionales, especialmente en rubros dinámicos. Costa Rica y Chile han aplicado con éxito imaginativas políticas selectivas e institucionales de promoción de exportaciones (BID, 1996, p. 104-105). También las políticas tecnológicas son muy convenientes.

Los sectores que se comentan a continuación tienen ventajas comparativas apoyadas en la dotación de re-

cursos, evidentes economías de escala, destrezas acumuladas, aprendizaje, especialización y podrían desarrollar y aprovechar externalidades dinámicas directas y de efectos barrio y manada. Pueden impulsar actividades que tienen un efecto de arrastre mediante eslabonamientos, tienen especial importancia para concentrar los esfuerzos de desarrollo institucional, la infraestructura de apoyo y las negociaciones de acceso a los mercados externos.

La producción agropecuaria y agroindustrial, el turismo, el níquel, la pesca y los servicios de escala internacional (marítimos y aéreos), se deberían establecer como actividades prioritarias y urgentes. El país tiene ventajas comparativas en estos sectores que son claves para la reactivación de la economía, la generación de divisas, y la elevación del nivel de vida de la población. El estado, con la activa participación del sector privado, sería responsable de determinar el marco institucional, coordinar recursos, controlar por vía de excepción y asegurar servicios básicos adecuados a estos sectores, pero muchos de ellos se brindarían directamente por el sector privado, fijando metas sectoriales indicativas y dando consistencia entre los marcos de políticas sectoriales y el programa global de equilibrios macroeconómicos dentro de un enfoque de crecimiento estable y sustentable.

El gobierno debería establecer la legislación forestal, pesquera y de aguas para dar al sector privado una mayor participación en su asignación y aprovechamiento y a su vez evitar la sobrepesca, la acidez, la salinización, la erosión, la desforestación y otros daños ambientales. Se debería involucrar a los usuarios, a través de asociaciones, en su manejo y financiamiento para promover una explotación racional de los recursos naturales renovables. Se debería mantener un fuerte papel del sector público en la extensión, investigación, y controles de calidad, fitosanitarios, zoosanitarios y de seguridad, a fin de elevar la competitividad en los mercados internos y externos y establecer una reputación para los productos nacionales en ellos. Adecuados controles sanitarios y fitosanitarios son imprescindibles para entrar al NAFTA.

IMPLANTACION DE LAS MEDIDAS DE LA PROPUESTA. SECUENCIA EN LA APLICACION E IMPLICACIONES PARA EL COMPORTAMIENTO DE LA ECONOMIA EN EL FUTURO

Al principio el énfasis debería ser en desarrollar un sistema estable, más neutral y más liberal sobre la asignación de recursos en vez de pretender establecer un sistema totalmente liberal de una sola vez. En general el proceso de reformas comerciales es más costoso y no es creíble si no se logra cierta estabilidad y se consolida de inmediato. El objetivo es desarrollar un proceso de reformas sostenidas que sea factible, creíble y crecientemente óptimo. Hay que tener una completa adecuación entre la situación inicial, los fines perseguidos y los medios.

En la situación actual de Cuba y con base en la escasa información disponible a mediados de 1997, la mejor forma de implantar el paquete de medidas propuesto con objeto de lograr la convertibilidad del peso y eliminar la dolarización, o sea para la *estabilización externa*, es realizar simultáneamente y tan pronto sea posible: (1) devaluar la moneda y fijar una tasa de cambio única, probablemente inferior a la tasa paralela actual de 22 pesos por dólar, para racionalizar el uso de los recursos externos y para mejorar la competitividad de la producción nacional; (2) fijar una tasa de interés real del 6 por ciento para los pasivos del sistema financiero (depósitos) y del 9 por ciento para los activos (préstamos), bajo el supuesto que la tasa de interés real internacional es del 3 por ciento, para hacer más atractiva la tenencia de activos monetarios nacionales y mejorar la asignación de recursos, así como para estimular una entrada de capitales moderada; (3) autorizar la convertibilidad parcial del peso para casi todas las transacciones de la cuenta corriente, brindando información e incentivos a los agentes económicos con base en precios internacionales más realistas, y para los movimientos de capital a largo plazo;[16] y (4) alentar la producción nacional median-

te la liberalización del trabajo por cuenta propia, las profesiones, los pequeños agricultores, las UBPCs y la autorización de la pequeña y mediana empresa.[17]

Estas cuatro medidas son fundamentalmente de saneamiento básico y sentarán las bases para después hacer una apertura decidida y progresiva al comercio y finanzas internacionales, manteniendo una tasa de cambio real competitiva que impida un nivel de equilibrio recesivo de un tasa de cambio sobrevaluada con altas tasas de interés que inducen un crecimiento económico y una formación de capital bajos. Adicionalmente, se adoptarán medidas para reincorporar a los cubanos expatriados al esfuerzo de recuperación y reconciliación nacional, se renegociará la deuda externa para normalizar la situación crediticia y de pagos externos del país, se movilizará financiamiento externo oficial, las remesas del exterior y las inversiones extranjeras. Esto se debería apoyar por la liberalización progresiva de las restricciones comerciales, de la convertibilidad del peso y de las restricciones financieras a los movimientos de capital, todo lo cual tendrá un impacto sustantivo en la asignación de los recursos, mejorará la eficiencia, dará gran dinamismo a la economía, y velará porque la expansión del sistema productivo se realice sobre bases sanas y sustentables.

RESUMEN Y CONCLUSIONES

Los problemas del sector externo de Cuba son mayores. Si no se introducen reformas profundas y amplias, se hará más difícil obtener el crecimiento necesario y los problemas de desbalances se empeorarán mientras la economía real se deteriora.

La literatura reciente destaca el papel importante que la apertura externa y la reinserción internacional comercial y financiera desempeñan como factores que impulsan el aumento de la productividad, la competitividad, la eficiencia y el crecimiento económico.

La inmediata liberalización de las restricciones comerciales y, en varios casos, la flotación cambiaria, se utilizaron para lograr más rápidas estabilización ex-

---

16. Calvo y Frankel (1991, p. 147) presentan razones de por qué la convertibilidad total debe establecerse *al final* de las reformas monetarias y cambiarias.

17. Es muy importante, de hecho imprescindible, alentar y expandir la oferta agregada como parte del proceso de ajuste y dinamización de la economía.

terna y reinserción internacional en los antiguos países socialistas europeos. Esta "liberalización externa prematura y apresurada", o sea disfuncional, creó una significativa reducción de la producción y una espiral e inercias inflacionarias e incertidumbres que fueron seguidas por una política de estabilización monetaria muy restrictiva, "choque monetario." El tipo de ajuste resultante, que atrajo una entrada de capitales de corto plazo, determinó una trampa de equilibrio para un crecimiento alto, estable y sustentable con tasas de cambio sobrevaluadas y tasas de interés muy altas, las que crearon un proceso interactivo y se refuerzan mutuamente. Esto ha tenido efectos perversos sobre el sector transable e indujo falta de credibilidad e interacciones negativas con el proceso de estabilización, o sea "fallas—o malos funcionamientos— del mercado" en las reformas en su conjunto; uno de los errores de política económica en la transición en los antiguos países socialistas europeos. También ha dificultado los procesos de privatización y restructuración, pues éstos se dan en un entorno recesivo y de mercados financieros restrictivos. En dicho contexto sólo contados agentes privados nacionales pueden participar en los procesos de privatización y restructuración productiva.

En 1973-1980 Chile tuvo un amplio proceso de liberalización comercial y financiera con fijación cambiaria desde 1979 que desembocó en una marcada y profunda crisis financiera en 1981-1983. Posteriormente, comenzó un proceso de liberalización y desregulación financieras progresivas e incrementales, de manejo de tasas de interés, cambiario y de los movimientos de capital externos, y con supervisión prudente de las instituciones bancarias y financieras, que han contribuido en forma significativa a un alto y sostenido crecimiento de la economía en 1984-1997.

El ensayo presentó una propuesta para endogenizar el crecimiento y desatar una dinámica virtuosa con políticas realistas y coherentes basada en los argumentos de Sachs (1995, 1996b) para emplear la devaluación con un régimen cambiario fijo o de ajustes periódicos para lograr la estabilización externa, en vez de emplear la flotación cambiaria. Dichos argumentos fueron comprobados por la evidencia de Fischer, et al (1996b). Asimismo, la propuesta utiliza los argumen-

tos de McKinnon (1991) en favor de que el proceso de apertura sea secuencial, gradual y ordenado con la liberalización comercial, siguiendo a la estabilización, pero precediendo a la liberalización financiera externa. Adicionalmente, se basa en las ideas de Williamson (1997) y Amsdem (1994) y en la exitosa experiencia chilena de 1984-1997 (Meller, 1996). Así las reformas se reforzarán, potenciarán mutuamente y tendrán efectos sinérgicos.

El diseño de la política propuesta pretende generar una economía de mercado competitiva y descentralizada que incentive la competencia, eficiencia e innovación, a fin de eliminar el desequilibrio externo, lograr la convertibilidad del peso y eliminar la dolarización. Evita la repetición de las experiencias recesivas de los antiguos países socialistas europeos basadas en un fundamentalismo excluyente, conducente a la fracturación, exclusión y tensión social. Sigue la experiencia chilena de 1984-1997 de manejo cambiario y de tasas de interés para mantener la competitividad externa y realizar la liberalización financiera externa gradual para atraer recursos externos complementarios. Cuba debería moverse primero de una economía prácticamente cerrada a una economía "semicerrada," después a una economía "semiabierta" y finalmente a una economía abierta. Si Cuba es capaz de eliminar realmente todos los sesgos contra las exportaciones en unos 5 años habrá realizado una gran transformación y será más efectiva que Nicaragua, los países de Europa Oriental y de la antigua Unión Soviética, en sus primeros 5 años de apertura.

El paquete propuesto de aplicar temporalmente una tasa de cambio fija después de la devaluación, hasta consolidar la estabilización, debe preceder la liberalización de las restricciones comerciales y la convertibilidad parcial en cuenta corriente. Dicho paquete será más efectivo para lograr rápidamente los resultados de la estabilización externa, evitar una recesión con inflación, alcanzar una recuperación económica robusta, y sentar las bases para realizar los procesos de liberalización progresiva de la convertibilidad del peso, del régimen tarifario y de la entrada de capitales. Esto a su vez tendrá efectos positivos sobre un crecimiento alto, estable y sustentable basado en la competitividad de la producción nacional. La experiencia de Yugoeslavia en 1994-1996 demuestra que *este tipo de estabilización se puede lograr aún en condiciones de bloqueo externo y de guerra*; el funcionario que diseñó esa política es un candidato popular a Presidente actualmente en dicho país.

El paquete propuesto es una autopista de alta velocidad algo apartada hacia el crecimiento sustentable vis à vis la liberalización de las restricciones comerciales y la flotación cambiaria inmediatas que constituyen un atajo cercano, pero largo, que se puede convertir en un "camino sin salida." Definitivamente, hay errores de políticas y reformas de apertura y de los procesos

de liberalización por el momento que se aplican y su ritmo, tanto por exceso como por defecto. O sea, no sólo hay respuestas insuficientes y tardías, sino también se han utilizado respuestas sobredimensionadas y prematuras. Albania es un caso trágico de estos errores cuya secuela es impredecible. Desde el punto de vista de política económica es necesario balancear el efecto credibilidad de una reforma rápida y clara con la probabilidad de que los cambios muy rápidos se reviertan debido a efectos y costos de los ajustes que se encuentran en el camino.

BIBLIOGRAFÍA

A. H. Amsden, J. Kochanowics and L. Taylor. *The Market Meets Its Match*. Cambridge, MA: Harvard University Press, 1994.

D. Avramovic."Lessons from the Transition: The Case of Yugoslavia 1994-96," en Louis Emmerij, editor, *Economic and Social Development into the XXI Century*. Washington: Inter-American Development Bank, 1997, pp 351-358.

Banco Interamericano de Desarrollo (BID). *Progreso Económico y Social en América Latina, Informe de 1996*. Washington: BID, 1996.

Banco Nacional de Cuba (BNC). Economic Report, 1994. La Habana: Banco Nacional de Cuba, 1995.

Y. Berthelot. "Lessons from Countries in Transition," en Louis Emmerij, editor, *Economic and Social Development into the XXI Century*. Washington: Inter-American Development Bank, 1997, p. 329-344.

M. Bruno y W. Easterly. *Inflation Crisis and Long-Run Growth*, National Bureau of Economic Research, Working Paper 5209. Cambridge, MA: The MIT Press, 1995.

J. Carranza, L. Gutiérrez y P. Monreal. *Cuba: La Restructuración de la Economía*. La Habana: Centro

de Estudios sobre América, documento preliminar, enero de 1995.

R. H. Castañeda and G. P. Montalván. "Transition in Cuba: A Comprehensive Stabilization Proposal and Some Key Issues," in *Cuba in Transition— Volume 3*. Washington: ASCE, 1993, pp 11-72.

Comisión Económica para América Latina y el Caribe (CEPAL). *Estudio Económico de América Latina y el Caribe 1995-1996*. Santiago de Chile: CEPAL, 1996.

J. M. Dean, S. Desai y James Riedel. *Trade Policy Reform in Developing Countries since 1985*, World Bank Discussion Paper No. 267, 1994.

R. Dornbusch. "Lessons from Experiences with High Inflation," *The World Bank Economic Review*, Vol. 6, No. 1 (1992), pp. 13-31.

W. Easterly. "When is Stabilization Expansionary?" *Economic Policy*, No. 22 (1996), pp. 65-107.

Economic Commission for Europe. *Economic Survey of Europe in 1994-1995*. New York: United Nations.

S. Edwards. "Introduction" in *Capital Controls, Exchange Rates, and Monetary Policy in the World*

Economy, edited by S. Edwards. New York, NY: Cambridge University Press, 1995.

European Bank for Reconstruction and Development. *Transition Report*, 1994 & 1995.

S. Fischer, R. Sahay and C. Végh. "Economies in Transition: The Beginnings of Growth," *The American Economic Review* (May 1996a), pp. 229-233.

S. Fischer, R. Sahay and C. Végh. "Stabilization and Growth in Transition Economies: The Early Experience," *The Journal of Economic Perspectives* (Spring 1996b), pp. 44-66.

P. Meller. *Un siglo de economía política chilena (1890-1990)*. Santiago de Chile: Editorial Andrés Bello, 1996.

S. Rebelo and C. A. Végh. "Real Effects of Exchange-Rate-Based Stabilization: An Analysis of Competing Theories," National Bureau of Economics Research, *Macroeconomics Annual 1995*. Cambridge, MA: The MIT Press, 1995.

D. Rodrik. "Trade and Industrial Policy Reform," in *Handbook of Development Economics*, Vol. III, edited by J. Behrman and T.N. Srinivasan (1995), pp 2925-2982.

J. Sachs. "Comments to Rebelo and Végh," *Macroeconomics Annual 1995*. Cambridge: The MIT Press.

J. Sachs. "The Transition at Mid Decade," *The American Economic Review* (May 1996a), pp. 128-133.

J. Sachs. "Economic Transition and the Exchange-Rate Regime," *The American Economic Review* (May 1996b), pp. 147-152.

T. Sargent. "The Ends of Four Big Inflation," in R. E. Hall, ed., *Inflation: Causes and Effects*. Chicago: University of Chicago Press, 1982, pp. 41-97.

R. Sahay and C Végh. *Inflation and Stabilization in Transition Economies: A Comparison with Market Economies*, IMF Working Paper, January 1995.

V. Thomas y J. Nash. "Reform of Trade Policy: Recent Evidence from Theory and Practice," *World Development Research Observer*, No. 6 (1991), pp 219-240.

J. Tobin. *Essays in Economics: National and International*, Vol. 4. Cambridge, MA: The MIT Press, 1996.

C. Végh. "Stopping High Inflation," *IMF Staff Papers*, Vol 39, No. 3 (September 1992), pp. 626-695.

John Williamson. "The Washington Consensus Revisited," en Louis Emmerij editor, *Economic and Social Development into the XXI Century*. Washington: Inter-American Development Bank, 1997, pp. 48-61.

World Bank. *From Plan to Market: World Development Report 1996*. New York: Oxford University Press, 1996.

CUBA'S TOURISM INDUSTRY

Charles Suddaby

For much of the world, Cuba is a relatively unknown tourism destination, and there remain many negative misconceptions. However, in spite of this, Cuba has experienced a tourism boom during the last eight or nine years, the likes of which have been rarely seen before. Take, for example, the growth in tourist arrivals which has increased from just over 300,000 in 1988 to more than 1 million in 1996, representing a compound annual growth of 16%, more than three times the level of global and Caribbean tourism growth. Significant as this may seem, it should also be noted that this has been achieved with virtually no travel from the vast U.S. market.

Unlike many of the Caribbean countries, Cuba has a substantial land mass, comprising 111,000 sq. km. and with a distance of approximately 1,250 km. from end to end. The country has a population of some 11 million people, making it by far the largest in the Caribbean (Dominican Republic and Haiti has population of approximately 7.5 million while Jamaica has 2.5 million). The country has diverse geographic regions, all with various tourism appeal, including an estimated 300 beach areas, mountains, tropical rain forests and arid flat lands. Similarly, the range of tourism attractors include an extensive supply of the traditional sun/sea/sand experiences, as well as world-class activities such as diving and fishing, while cultural and other attractions are still in the emerging stages.

The recent targeting of tourism as a key industry for the future development of the country has resulted in implementation of various legal and political reforms which are still evolving. However, the past growth in tourism and expectations for the future are impressive by any measure. While Cuba has many economic and social problems, it is evident that there is a huge level of interest in travel to the country. While competing to a great extent with tourism destinations elsewhere in the world and, more particularly in the Caribbean region, Cuba has many attributes which provide it with distinct advantages. In particular, the geographic diversity, enormous range of existing and potential attractions, cultural and architectural history and combination of educated workforce and low incidence of crime, make Cuba an appealing destination today. Future improvements to the infrastructure will continue to add to the appeal of the country, and it has the potential to become the dominant tourism destination in the Caribbean if made available to the U.S. market.

The following sections examine the recent evolution of tourism in Cuba and detail some of the key trends that have occurred.

TOURISM ARRIVALS

Exhibit 1 graphically portrays the increase in tourism arrivals to Cuba from 1988 to 1996, while Exhibit 2, compares the results for 1994, 1995 and 1996. As indicated, total tourism arrivals increased from 309,200 in 1988 to 546,000 in 1993, representing compound annual growth of 12%. In 1994, the number of arrivals increased to 619,200, representing growth of another 13%, while 1995 results show the total number of arrivals was 741,700, up by 20% over the year before. One of the reasons for the larger than average increase in 1995 was the result of hurricane damage to several other Caribbean islands in

Exhibit 1. Total Tourist Arrivals to Cuba
    Source: Cuban Ministry of Tourism

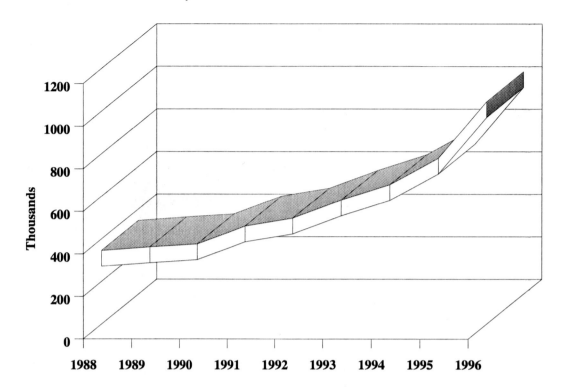

Exhibit 2. Total Arrivals to Cuba
    Source: Cuban Ministry of Tourism

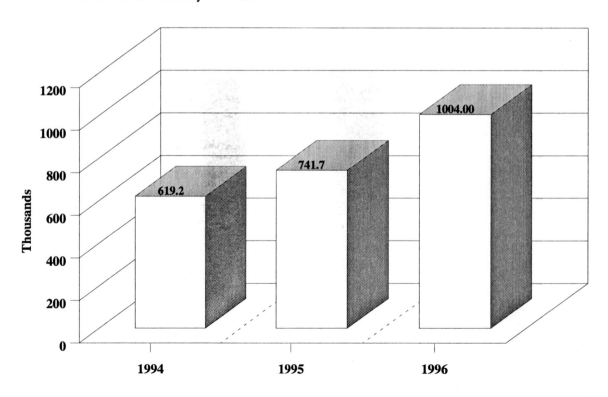

late 1994, causing demand to be redirected from these other destinations during the late winter and early spring periods of 1995. Visitation levels in 1996 reached 1,004,000 people, an increase of 35% over the previous year, placing it fifth on the list of most visited countries in the Caribbean, behind Puerto Rico (3.1 million), Dominican Republic (1.9 million), the Bahamas (1.6 million) and Jamaica (1.1 million).

An analysis of tourism arrivals indicates that in 1988, 56.0% of all arrivals came from Europe (173,000), followed by 17.2% from Canada (53,000), 11.3% from South America (35,000), 9.1% from Mexico (28,000), and 3.2% from each of the United States and 'Other' regions (Exhibit 3). Statistics for 1995 (data for 1996 was not available at the time of preparing this report) reveal that Europe's market share has declined, to 47.3% of total visitors, although the absolute number of arrivals continues to grow at a high rate, reaching 351,185 and reflecting annual average growth of 10.6% since 1988. Canada, which has historically represented the single largest source country for tourism to Cuba, has increased its market share from 17.2% to 19.4% of all arrivals, with the absolute number growing by an average of 15.4% annually, to a level of 144,113 in 1995. Other markets

represented 10,000 arrivals in 1988, but has since grown to 110,440 arrivals in 1995; this reflects average annual growth of 40.9% with the result that Other now represents 14.9% of all visitors to Cuba. South America has grown from 35,000 arrivals in 1988 to 83,157 in 1995 representing growth of 13.2% annually. South America now generates 11.2% of all tourist arrivals to Cuba. Mexico has demonstrated less aggressive increases, having grown to 31,838 arrivals in 1995, up from 28,000 seven years earlier. Mexico now represents 4.3% of all arrivals, down considerably from the 9.1% of all arrivals in 1988. As may be expected, the U.S. market is currently a nominal market for Cuba, with the annual level of visitation typically being in the 10,000 to 20,000 range. In 1995, the U.S. represented 2.8% of all arrivals in Cuba.

SEASONALITY

As may be expected in a Caribbean destination, the majority of visitors arrive during the colder months of the northern hemisphere, with the November through March period being the busiest. However, the success of Cuba in targeting the European market, which typically vacations during the summer, has resulted in strong visitation levels from this area in July and August.

Exhibit 3. Arrivals to Cuba, by Origin
Source: Cuban Ministry of Tourism

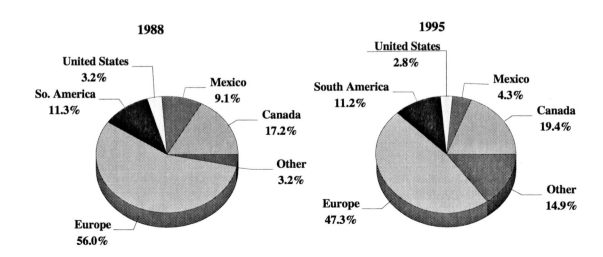

Exhibit 4. Average Length of Stay of Visitors to Cuba
           Source: Cuban Ministry of Tourism

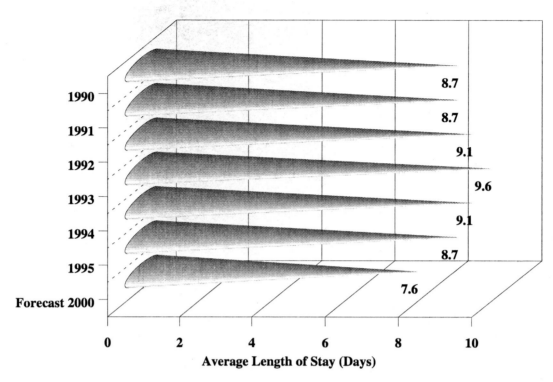

Visitation levels during the first half of 1994 and 1995 tracked very similar patterns; however, during the latter part of 1995, there was a dramatic increase in visitors, with individual months showing growth of 50% to 80% over the previous year. Results for 1996 show a similar pattern, particularly during the early part of the year, with 1996 far surpassing the prior two years' results.

AVERAGE LENGTH OF STAY

In Exhibit 4, we illustrate the average length of stay by visitors to Cuba over the period 1990 to 1995. As shown, the average stay increased from 8.7 days in 1990 to 9.1 days in 1992, before reaching a peak of 9.6 days in 1993. Since then, the typical visit has declined in duration, reaching 9.1 days in 1994 and 8.7 days in 1995. The Ministry of Tourism projects that at the end of the millennium, the average length of stay will have declined to 7.6 days.

At whatever point the U.S. embargo may be lifted, it can be expected that there will be a material change in the average stay. As evidenced in the Bahamas, for example, which is so close to the United States, the average length of stay is approximately 5.8 nights, with the U.S. market staying 4.7 nights in Nassau, 3.4 nights in Grand Bahama Island and 4.5 nights in Paradise Island. The average stay in Puerto Rico (where 70% of all visitors are from the U.S.) is 2.8 nights, and in the U.S. Virgin Islands (85% of visitors from the U.S.) is 4.4 nights. It is expected that in a post-embargo period, Cuba's average length of stay would decline quite significantly, and we estimate that it will likely reach 7.2 nights.

TOURIST EXPENDITURES

Information provided by the Ministry of Tourism indicates the average tourist expenditure per day has increased from $82.52 in 1990 to $170.25 in 1995. The graph in Exhibit 5 illustrates this trend. As indicated, there were substantial increases, of 28% and 29% in 1991 and 1992, respectively. However, there was virtually no improvement in 1993 (2%), while the following year saw an improvement of 9%, to $150.28. The average tourism expenditure in 1995, at $170.25, was 13% more than the year before.

Exhibit 5. Average Tourist Expenditure per Day ($US/Tourist Day)
Source: Cuban Ministry of Tourism

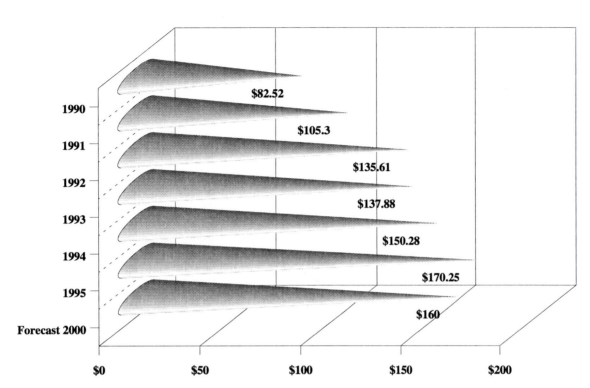

In its projection for 2000, the Ministry believes the average expenditure will decline to approximately $160.00. We believe this to be understated—if inflationary expenditures alone are achieved, and inflation is assumed to be 2% annually, then the average tourism expenditure in 2000 would be $188.00. Considering the recognition of Cuba as an inexpensive destination, the stated objective of the Ministry to increase prices of hotels to a more acceptable level, and the development of more modern hotels and resorts (such as the Meliá Cohiba, Meliá Las Américas and Sol Meliá, etc.), we believe the average expenditure will increase well beyond that indicated.

NUMBER OF HOTEL ROOMS

In a recent study, it was identified that there were approximately 34,000 hotel rooms in Cuba at the end of 1993, of which some 6,500 were operated by local municipalities for use by Cubans, as were a further 2,000 rooms under the control of Islazul (a hotel chain with properties targeted towards national tourism only). Since that time, a number of hotel rooms have been deleted from the supply, while others have been added. Because of the continual fluctuation in supply, in part due to the qualitative assessment of what really constitutes product suitable for international tourism, we provide a table (Table 1) that quantifies the number of hotel rooms, by geographic region, as provided by the Ministry of Tourism.

As shown in Table 1, the total number of rooms available has increased from 12,866 in 1990, to almost 27,000 in 1996. This represents annual average growth of 9.7%, a level below the rate of growth in tourism arrivals. The Ministry also anticipates there to be 49,556 hotel rooms available for international tourism in the year 2000, equating to further increases in supply each year of approximately 15%.

The inventory of hotel space is divided into different categories, according to quality levels. In keeping with the hotel industry elsewhere in the world, Cuba has adopted a star rating system, and the data in Tables 2 and 3 illustrate the segmentation of hotels and hotel rooms according to this star rating. It should be noted, and this is commented upon elsewhere in this report, the star rating system applied in Cuba is

Table 1. Number of Hotel Rooms, by Geographic Region

Region	1990	1991	1992	1993	1994	1995	1996	2000ᵃ
Havana	4,197	4,936	6,624	6,690	7,318	7,664	8,346	10,664
Varadero	4,145	5,614	5,622	6,641	7,151	7,273	8,675	14,773
South Coast	432	669	632	1,192	1,192	1,374	1,049	1,874
North of Camaguey	449	739	739	952	952	1,343	1,296	2,343
North of Holguin	816	1,079	1,043	1,000	1,235	1,594	1,632	2,594
South of Oriente	868	1,455	1,505	1,643	1,567	1,737	1,725	2,489
Canarreos	264	308	308	554	554	560	682	1,310
North of Ciego de Avila				458	678	821	1,521	5,621
Other	1,695	1,838	2,189	3,009	2,607	1,867	1,952	7,888
Total	12,866	16,638	18,662	22,139	23,254	24,233	26,878	49,556

a. Projected by the Ministry of Tourism

Table 2. Cuban Hotels by Star Rating, 1995

Hotels	Star Rating				
	2 Star	3 Star	4 Star	5 Star	Total
Havana	10	16	17	4	47
Varadero	6	9	18	2	35
South Coast	4	6	3		11
North of Camagüey	2	4	2		8
North of Holguín	4	4	4		12
South of Oriente	3	9	3	1	16
Canarreos		4	4		8
North of Ciego de Avila	1	1	2	1	5
Other	16	13	3		32
Total	46	64	56	8	174

Table 3. Cuban Hotel Rooms by Star Rating, 1995

Hotel Rooms	Star Rating				
	2 Star	3 Star	4 Star	5 Star	Total
Havana	825	2,689	3,011	1,821	8,346
Varadero	1,084	1,017	5,834	740	8,675
South Coast	149	266	634		1,049
North of Camagüey	58	668	570		1,296
North of Holguín	174	762	696		1,632
South of Oriente	190	943	290	302	1,725
Canarreos	1	131	551		682
North of Ciego de Avila	7	144	912	458	1,521
Other	937	962	53		1,952
Total	3,424	7,582	12,551	3,321	26,878

slightly more generous than in many other destinations, typically showing one full star above the quality that would be expected in the international markets.

Of the 26,878 hotel rooms available in 1996, 13% are categorized as 2-star, 28% as 3-star, 47% as 4-star, and just 12% as 5-star. Similarly, further analysis reveals that over two thirds of all 4-star hotels and all 5-star properties are located in either Havana or Varadero, the main destinations for tourists.

HOTEL COMPANIES

The principal hotel companies in operation in Cuba are Cubanacán, Gran Caribe, Gaviota, Horizontes and Marinas Puertosol. Cubanacán was the first of these to be formed, having been created in 1987 following the attempt by the Ministry of Tourism ('Intur') to apply 'private sector' management to certain hotels. Following recognition of the success of Cubanacán, a second company—Gaviota—was formed in 1989. In early 1994, Intur was dismantled and in its place, three new hotel companies were formed: Gran Caribe, Horizontes and Islazul.

The main hotel companies operate different quality hotels at different locations throughout the country. However, as a generalization, Cubanacán primarily operates 4- and 5-star hotels, with a concentration in Havana, Varadero, Santa Lucía, Guardalavaca, Granma and Santiago de Cuba. Gran Caribe operates primarily 4- and 5-star hotels in Havana, Varadero and Cayo Largo, while Gaviota operates 3- and 4-star products in Varadero, Sancti Spíritus and Guardalavaca. Horizontes is most well recognized for its 3-star hotels, with properties in Pinar del Río, Havana, Playas del Este, Matanzas, Varadero, Cienfuegos, Sancti Spíritus, Camagüey and Holguín.

SUMMARY

World tourism spending has been growing at a rate of over 12% annually over the last 45 years, while the number of tourists has grown by 4.4%. The World Tourism Organization projects international tourism arrivals will reach over 1 billion within the next thirteen years, with receipts reaching $1.5 trillion.

The Caribbean is one of the most well-established and popular sun destinations in the world. Tourist arrivals reached 14.7 million in 1995, an average increase of 4.9% annually, higher than the global average.

- Within the Caribbean, Cuba has significantly outperformed the majority of other destinations in terms of tourism growth. Annual growth over the last seven years has been 16.9% in Cuba, compared to 6.4% for Jamaica, 4.7% for the Dominican Republic, and 3.4% for Puerto Rico. The Bahamas recorded growth of less than 1%.

- The U.S. market represents the single largest source of tourism to the region, with some 7.3 million total visitors. Remarkably, Cuba's strong performance has been achieved in spite of the absence of this market.

- U.S. visitation levels to the Caribbean continue to grow, although this country's market share has declined. Stronger growth from other markets, particularly Europe, are expected to result in the U.S. share being approximately 51% in 1996, down from over 58% in 1988.

Cuba has tremendous diversity in its tourism product, offering a considerable variety of traditional sun/sea/sand experiences with historical and cultural attractions, sporting activities and forms of adventure tourism. The country is substantial in size, geographically close to the North American market, relatively crime free, and has a well educated workforce.

- Tourism arrivals have grown from 309,000 in 1988 to almost 1 million in 1996.

- In the last three years alone, tourism volumes have increased by 13%, 20% and 30% respectively.

- There are approximately 27,000 hotel rooms available today that cater to the international market. However, most of this product is characterized by Cuban 2-, 3- and 4-star quality that has limited appeal to the more discerning traveller.

- Our research has indicated that Cuba is still regarded as an inexpensive 'package' destination. This is a reflection of the initial tourism strategy of quickly penetrating source markets by offering low, all-inclusive prices, and the lingering impacts of this strategy.

- While some good quality hotels exist, the ability to leverage prices today is hindered by the lack of quality in product and services in other tourism sectors. Building high quality accommodations alone will not satisfy tourists if other aspects of the tourism experience are below acceptable levels; this includes food and beverage operations, retail facilities, recreational and entertainment activities, and other tourism infrastructure.

In our analysis of demand for higher quality hotel product in Cuba, we have measured growth in tourism in the Caribbean region, the likely performance of Cuba in this market, and the resultant demand for all types of hotel space as a result of the expected visitor levels. We then ascertained the extent of 4- and 5-star accommodations currently available in the Caribbean region, as well as the demand for such product. Utilizing Cuba's projected market share, we have then determined the number of new 4- and 5-star product which is supportable in the country.

- Caribbean tourism is expected to grow to 20.8 million visitors by 2003, with Cuba reaching 2.2 million. Under the assumption the U.S. embargo is lifted by 1999, Cuban tourism could reach 3.7 million by 2003.

- There are approximately 38,000 high quality hotel rooms in the Caribbean, and an equal number in Mexican resort areas. The competitive supply, representing some 76,000 rooms, operates at about 63%.

- Our projections indicate demand for this quality product will reach 24.8 million room nights in 2003.

- Based on Cuba's equal share of total tourism, this would indicate demand of 1.8 million room nights of demand for 4- and 5-star product in 1999, reaching 2.6 million by 2003.

- If the embargo were to be lifted by 1999, demand could reach 2.7 million room nights in 1999 and 4.5 million in 2003.

- On the basis that any new hotels would operate at 75% occupancy (the typical level at which cash flows generate good returns on investment), there would be a need for 3,700 new rooms of this quality by 1999, and 6,700 by 2003. If the embargo were to be lifted, the requirement is 7,100 new rooms by 1999 and 13,600 by 2003.

The determination of room demand is based on the assumption that there will be considerable improvement to the tourism infrastructure in Cuba. It also assumes that Cuba will attain its equal share of the available market; however, we believe that if the infrastructure improvements are made, Cuba has the potential to obtain more than its equal share. The amount of high quality rooms supportable in Cuba is much higher than the number of hotel and resort developments in process today, suggesting there is considerable market potential for new projects.

IMPACT OF THE HELMS-BURTON LAW
(THE CUBAN LIBERTY ACT) ON CUBAN TOURISM

Saturnino E. Lucio II and Nicolás Crespo

Whether one agrees or disagrees with the purpose, provisions, or probable consequences of the Cuban Liberty and Democratic Solidarity Act (the Cuban Liberty Act also popularly known as the Helms-Burton Law, particularly in Cuba) is beside the point. On March 12, 1996, President Clinton signed the Cuban Liberty Act into law, having previously been approved by the U.S. Congress by wide margins. The substantial support for the Cuban Liberty Act makes it highly unlikely that the U.S. policy towards Cuba will change in the foreseeable future absent some significant political changes in the Cuban Government. The Cuban Liberty Act is a reality and those persons affected by the new law will have to come to grips with its provisions and with how the new legislation will work in practice.

Numerous provisions contained in the Cuban Liberty Act condemn the government of Cuba for past and present violations of human rights and international norms of good conduct. One provision specifically condemns the attack by Cuban war planes of the two small civilian aircraft piloted by "Brothers to the Rescue," a Miami-based humanitarian organization. This incident appears to have triggered the overwhelming presidential and congressional bipartisan support for the Cuban Liberty Act.

The purpose of this paper is to analyze the Cuban Liberty Act in view of the tourism industry in Cuba. By necessity, other provisions which are not related to tourism are not discussed.

PROTECTION OF PROPERTY RIGHTS OF U.S. NATIONALS

The Cuban Liberty Act seeks to protect the property rights of U.S. nationals by making any person who "traffics" in the "property" of a "U.S. national" which was "confiscated" by the Cuban government liable in U.S. federal court. This provision of the Cuban Liberty Act takes effect on August 1, 1996, unless its operation is suspended for a six-month period by the President, which has occurred several times.

To "traffic" with respect to confiscated property of a U.S. national is a broadly defined term for purpose of Title III of the Cuban Liberty Act. It includes a person who "knowingly and intentionally" and "without the authorization of any U.S. national who holds a claim to the property": (i) sells, transfers, distributes, dispenses, brokers, manages or otherwise disposes of confiscated property; (ii) purchases, leases, receives, possesses, obtains control of, manages, uses or otherwise acquires or holds an interest in confiscated property; (iii) engages in a commercial activity using or otherwise benefiting from confiscated property; or (iv) causes, directs, participates in or profits from trafficking in confiscated property by or through another person.

Numerous limitations exist on this new "civil remedy," including the eight discussed below. It should be noted that some of the following "civil remedies," at the time of publishing this paper, are already a matter of the past.

First, there is a three-month grace period for anyone who is currently engaged in trafficking in confiscated property within which to discontinue such activities. In other words, past conduct by the persons involved in trafficking is immaterial.

Second, the amount in controversy has to exceed $50,000 and cannot, except in certain cases, involve Cuban residential property.

Third, only U.S. nationals with claims that have been certified by the Foreign Claims Settlement Commission (FCSC) may commence an action after August 1, 1996 unless this date is extended by the President; other types of U.S. nationals must wait two years before going to court.

Fourth, the claim must have existed in the hands of the claimant prior to the enactment of the Cuban Liberty Act, or, in those cases where the confiscation occurs after the date of the Cuban Liberty Act, the claimant must not have given value to acquire such claim.

Fifth, the claimant must show evidence of ownership of the property confiscated by the Cuban government. A court is required to accept as conclusive proof a claim that has been previously certified by the FCSC. That should not be a problem for the lawsuits that may be brought under the Cuban Liberty Act in the first two years, since only U.S. nationals who hold certified claims will be allowed to sue during that period of time. If a claim has not been previously certified by the FCSC, the federal court handling the lawsuit "may appoint a special master, including the FCSC, to make determinations regarding the amount and ownership of the claim. It is not mandatory that a special master be appointed by the federal court, and there is no guarantee that the FCSC will agree to act special master in connection with each case filed under the Cuban Liberty Act (or at what cost its services will be made available to the litigants). Also, there are no criteria to govern the determination of the special master, and it is not clear that any special master will relay on any special procedures customarily used by the FCSC in resolving claims.

Sixth, the claimant must pay a "uniform filing fee" in connection with the filing of the action, in a "level sufficient to recover the cost to the courts of actions" brought under the Cuban Liberty Act (whatever that is).

Seventh, the Cuban Liberty Act contains a statute of limitations period which provides that an action under Section 302 may not be brought more than two years after the trafficking giving rise to the action has been ceased to occur. It may be difficult in certain cases to determine when the "trafficking" has ceased for purpose of this limitation.

And **eighth,** any action commenced may be suspended or shall expire upon certification by the President that a "democratically" elected government in Cuba is in power.

Assuming one overcomes all these hurdles, a U.S. national may sue any person in federal court who has trafficked in confiscated property in Cuba which is the subject of his or her claim. That would appear to include any agency or instrumentality of the Cuban government, any Cuban official, and any other U.S. or foreign person. The amount which may be recovered by the claimant is the greater of: (i) the amount certified by the FCSC, if applicable, plus interest at the rate set forth by the law; (ii) the amount of the claim as determined by special master or by the FCSC, plus interest at the rate set forth by the law, or the fair market value of the confiscated property. Treble damages may also be recovered in certain cases.

EXCLUSION FROM THE UNITED STATES OF FOREIGN PERSONS WHO TRAFFIC IN CONFISCATED PROPERTY OF A U.S. NATIONAL

Another controversial provision is the "exclusion from the United States" of foreign persons who are involved in the trafficking of confiscated property in Cuba. The purpose of this provision is to isolate Cuba and to force foreign companies to choose between the United States and Cuba in terms of where they will be allowed to visit and do business. A related provision urges the President to enforce existing laws to deny visas to Cuban nationals who are considered by the Secretary of State to be employees of the Cuban government or the Communist Party of Cuba.

PROHIBITION ON INDIRECT FINANCING OF CUBA

The law provides that generally no loan, credit, or other financing may be extended knowingly by a U.S. national, permanent resident, or U.S. agency to any person for the purpose of financing transactions involving any confiscated property of any U.S. national (except for financing by the U.S. national owning such claim for a transaction permitted under U.S. law). This provision is simple to understand when applied to a transaction involving financing for the acquisition or improvement of a hotel in Cuba that is located on land confiscated from a U.S. national. A more difficult case is when the financing is provided for a typical trade transaction where the foreign buyer purchases products (e.g., agricultural crops such as sugar) grown and harvested in Cuba on land that was previously confiscated from a U.S. national. Equally difficult will be cases involving financing by banks in third countries of Cuban exports that bear a trade mark that in itself constitutes confiscated property. "Trafficking" is a term which is so broadly defined that it would appear to cover this indirect type of activity. Any person who violates this section may be punished by civil penalties as in the case of violations of the Cuban Assets Control Regulations, but does not appear to be amenable to suit by the owner of the claim except where a case can be established under the Cuban Liberty Act.

IMPLICATIONS

The Cuban Liberty Act does not expressly purport to prohibit a foreign person from conducting business with Cuba or traveling to that country. Similarly, the Act does not prohibit U.S. nationals from conducting business with Cuba and traveling to Cuba to the extent allowed by U.S. law. The Cuban Liberty Act permits the exclusion of foreign persons from the United States and makes U.S. nationals and foreign persons liable in U.S. federal courts if they are knowingly and intentionally: (i) trafficking in property confiscated by the Cuban government; and (ii) the property belongs to a U.S. national who does not

consent to the use of his or its property. Foreign nationals who are engaging in prohibited activities might well decide to run the risk of being sued in the United States, and if sued, to defend against any such liability on a number of grounds. Similarly, foreign nationals may take the risk that the U.S. Immigration and Naturalization Service will never seek to bar them from entering the United States.

Given the broad definition of "trafficking," it is clearly the case that many types of business dealings between Cuba and foreign nationals may be covered by the Cuban Liberty Act. The Cuban Liberty Act is directly aimed at foreign persons who currently own, manage, or otherwise make use of properties that were owned by U.S. nationals and confiscated by the Cuban government. Within that category are those properties which are the subject of certified claims before the FCSC and have been public knowledge for some time.

The Cuban Liberty Act is designed to increase the pressure on the Cuban government by restricting assistance to countries that would provide aid to Cuba, as well as forcing certain foreign persons to make a choice between doing certain kinds of business with Cuba or doing business with the United States. It is quite likely that there may be several court challenges to the Cuban Liberty Act, either based on the U.S. constitutional principles or treaty obligations previously undertaken by the United States. What may come from this jurisprudence cannot be gauged with accuracy at this point. Moreover, in the ever-changing ebb-and-flow of relations between Cuba and the United States, other incidents could arise which provoke further modifications of the embargo.

It does appear that the Cuban government is very apprehensive about the impact of the Cuban Liberty Act on its economy. What may eventually occur is a subject of speculation, but the U.S. appears to have drawn a "line in the sand" against Cuba and has now explicitly required foreign persons to essentially choose between the U.S. and Cuba. The obvious conclusion of the U.S. Congress and the President is that these foreign person will prefer to maintain their ties with the United States and consequently foreign investment in Cuba will cease or substantially decline. It is impossible to know whether a lack of foreign investment in Cuba will deprive the Cuban government of badly needed hard currency revenues, perhaps worsening living conditions on the island and fostering internal rebellion, or whether the Cuban Liberty Act will itself provoke liberalization towards foreign investment by the Cuban government in order to attract greater hard currency revenues. In either case, the United States is assuming that the Cuban Liberty Act may perhaps lead to the eventual democratization of Cuba.

THE REVERSE EMBARGO

Cuba's government has exploited the so-called U.S. embargo to present itself as a victim of imperialist U.S. policies. Noticeably, it has always referred to the U.S. Government as a separate entity, somehow divorced from the people of the United States. In contrast, the Cuban Government and the people of Cuba, they claim, are one and the same. There is, it is argued, a *tacit and permanent* mandate from the Cuban people to allow the Cuban Government to act on its behalf.

Perhaps this would explain the *implicit acceptance* of the deprivation of the Cuban people of any meaningful opportunity to visit the tourism installations in Cuba or to develop, invest in, own, manage, and enjoy the fruits of their work in the tourism industry. Perhaps it may also justify why foreigners and any of their foreign employees may own shares on their employers' equity and participate in their profits while the Cubans are not themselves allowed to do so. It seems that the Helms-Burton Law is used as an argument to perpetrate this inequity.

In a recent paper regarding the economic impact of tourism in Cuba,[1] the author calculates that Cuba was losing several million dollars each day of economic impact by continuing their obsolete system where "socialist state property and resources belonging to the people" are not owned by the Cuban people themselves, but only by the Cuban Government as a whole.

The Cuban Liberty Act has also been used by foreign companies to justify their declining interest in continuing to pursue doing business in Cuba.

Some that have tried have been discouraged by the great bureaucracy and the requirement that they prepare and submit hundreds of pages with worthless information that few read and fewer understand, have decided that they cannot afford to expend more time and money pursuing doing business in Cuba. It has been reported that such are the cases, in the hospitality industry, of Occidental Hotels, Paradores Nacionales and Thomson Vacations.

FUTURE EFFECT ON CUBAN TOURISM

The Effect on the Tourist

The great majority of tourists pouring into Cuban beaches and tourism centers are lured from their place of origin, mainly Canada, Mexico, Europe and South America, by attractive, glossy literature offering packages of 7-14 days at very reasonable prices. In some cases, the cost to the tourist is lower than similar package offered by destinations closer to home and even in locations a few hours driving time from their place of residence. Most of the tourists are not aware of the ongoing politics and are just looking for a reasonably-priced vacation on a beach with good climate and where they can rest with a cool drink in hand.

The recent acts of sabotage—in the form of explosions at several tourism hotels—caused a temporary scare that will probably fade in the near future. No significant number of cancellations has been noticed in the existing arrangements. The events will probably pass and will be forgotten as almost all the events in the world are, except by those who witnessed them or suffered their consequences. However if these explosions continue and become frequent and routine, then this is a factor that will likely adversely impact tourism in Cuba.

---

1. Nicolás Crespo and Santos Negrón Díaz, "Cuban Tourism in 2007: Economic Impact," in this volume.

Effect on Investors/Operators of Tourism Properties

Friends and foes of the Cuban Liberty Act have made extraordinary efforts to exaggerate its consequences or effects. The rhetoric used by friendly and unfriendly politicians and media in Europe, Latin America, and even in the United States and Cuba, distort, through their interpretation, the real extent of the law.

Important investors from Canada and Europe, mainly Spain and Italy, are presently involved in joint ventures, management agreements and other contractual relations in Cuba. They are taking the position that, in spite of the risk that the law might represent, for them it is good business sense to continue operating and investing in tourism in Cuba. Some of the countries have even enacted laws (anti-Helms-Burton legislation) that are intended to protect their nationals against the effect of the Cuban Liberty Act. An area of great concern, however, is the matter of entry visas into the United States that may affect some of the top executives.

In our considered view, the opportunities around the world are so great in the tourism industry, particularly in Asia and South America, that for large conglomerates or hotel chains the Cuban Liberty Act has created a nuisance if they wish to continue to be involved in Cuba. The time and resources necessary to do so do not compensate the potential legal repercussions that might affect the foreign investor. Nevertheless, most companies keep abreast of the Cuban situation through third country nationals and sometimes participating in fully hosted visits which do not violate U.S. law.

In a few cases, some politicians have exerted pressure on some European hotel chains to start or maintain a presence in Cuba and make announcements of upcoming investments in the island. Statistics compiled by U.S.-Cuba Trade and Economic Council from the media, other public sources, and discussions with company representatives, non-Cuban government officials, and Cuba-based enterprise managers and government officials indicate that of $5.5 billion of new investments promised by companies in 25 countries, only $736.9 million has actually been invested in Cuba. Mexico, Canada, Spain and Italy account for $562 million or 76 percent of the amount invested. So other countries appear to be insignificant investors in Cuba. Moreover, these figures refer to all types of investments and sectors of the economy, not just in the tourism industry.

Effect on the Non-Investor/Operator of Tourism Properties

Foreign companies operating under management and marketing contracts are responsible for the bulk of incoming tourism into Cuba. They make money by bringing plane loads of tourists who have bought prepaid packages in their country of origin. The printed literature and brochures are very attractive and eye-catching. They make and sell their own vacation packages or market them through Travel Agents and Wholesalers all over the world. Several major wholesalers are involved in Cuba, and Cuba depends substantially on them to market is tourism products.

As it happens in other markets, the wholesalers prefer Havana and Varadero destinations because they are easier to sell. The other destinations experience lower demand because they are not well known. Wholesalers have demanded higher commissions in order to promote and sell the less popular destinations. Parallel promotion is provided by the Ministry of Tourism and the several hotel holding companies, such as Cubanacán, Horizontes, etc. The quality of the printed material is also very good and the prices of the packages that include air transportation in Cubana Airlines are even more attractive.

In our view, the activity of the wholesalers does not seem to be affected by the Cuban Liberty Act, which does not explicitly bar the conduct of business with Cuba, but only that business which constitutes trafficking in confiscated property. Many of the same wholesalers operate also within the United States, although U.S. wholesalers are not permitted to operate in Cuba, at least directly.

Effect on Outside Operators, Travel Agencies, Consolidators, Wholesalers, Suppliers

It is the nature of the travel and tourism industries that it requires the formation of alliances, joint ventures and other type of arrangements for a more effective delivery of the product to the foreign purchaser of tourism services. Selling a service to a client may involved the participation of a string of persons and companies that perform the delivery of individual components of the service. Few worldwide organizations can afford to have an integrated organization of agents around the world who deliver all of the land services demanded and subsequently purchased by their clients.

Within the complexity of this web of persons and companies it is probable that a U.S. company may indirectly benefit from a tourism activity in Cuba. A U.S. company is not allowed to sell an airline ticket for traveling to Cuba, sell a vacation package to a resort in Cuba, or make reservations for hotels in Cuba unless licensed by the State Department. However, a U.S. company may have an equity interest in a foreign operator, agency, etc., and an agreement to deliver services in other parts of the world. The foreign operator, agency, etc., may operate in Cuba and funnel a corresponding share of its profits to the U.S. company. We are informed that it is legal if the U.S. company does not have control of the foreign operator and the foreign operator's business in Cuba does not represent a substantial portion of the parents organization's overall business.

A foreign non-U.S. supplier of products and materials to Cuba, who manufactures its own products or those of others that are not manufactured in the United States, has no problems with the Cuban Liberty Act even if it exports products to the United States. Jobbers, brokers, and suppliers who acquire products produced or licensed in the United States may encounter difficulties under U.S. law, however.

The quasi-clandestine method that Cuba employs to obtain products and materials demanded by foreign visitors has a further negative impact on the cost of delivering the tourism product. Reliable supplies are hard to obtain and sometimes only at a higher relative cost than would be available in a normally competing market. In addition, this erodes Cuba's reserves of foreign currency. Cuba is making great efforts to develop small industries to manufacture products to substitute for imports and reduce the leakage of hard currency. About $200 million has been earmarked for this purpose. Several joint ventures made with foreign companies are yet to produce results, however.

SUMMARY

Cuba's insistence in depriving the Cuban people of the opportunity to operate in a free environment may have an impact on future generations, through an effect economists refer to as the "Bangladesh Syndrome," which is a systematic and continuous impoverishment of the people and its means of subsistence. Nevertheless, Cuba appears to be succeeding in its growth strategy thanks to the concentration of resources and efforts in this single segment of the economy, while the Cuban government is counting on it as the salvation of the regime. This strategy may, in fact, succeed unless social unrest in Cuba expands and the *espíritu de un buen revolucionario* fades away by the pressures of hunger and deprivation and the realization by the Cuban people that they face a double standard rather than an egalitarian system. Moreover, many in Cuba can see all the fruits of a free society, particularly as travel increases in Cuba and there are more foreign visitors.

COMMENTS ON

"Cuba's Tourism Industry" by Suddaby and "Impact of the Helms-Burton Law on Cuban Tourism" by Lucio and Crespo

Artimus Keiffer

The movement of people is a major focus of study in Human Geography. Why movement takes place, where it is to, and when it happens are questions that geographers ask about cultural phenomena such as religious pilgrimages, sporting events, civil conflicts, economic and political changes, and tourism. In relation to the latter, which is today's topic of discussion, we ask why people leave their points of usual habitation to go to certain places to vacation and, out of a myriad of possible destinations, why.

Tourism has become the largest growing industry in the world. Many less-developed countries have taken advantage of their lack of an industrial landscape, persistent cultural traditions and unspoiled natural areas and are increasing their GNP by enticing visits from people from all parts of the world. As a result, some benefits have been derived for local residents of tourist destinations for the short term. Other benefits have come in the form of varying degrees of sustainable development, instituted for long-term economic growth. These policies are not always in the best interests of the people who live in certain areas, and are not always instituted with proper management techniques, means of enforcement or adequately funded.

The Caribbean, as a whole, has enjoyed an increased number of tourists, partially because of climatic conditions, available resort facilities and lower population densities. Tourist destinations are also affected by low pricing, all-inclusive amenities and relative isolation from the local populace.

TOURISM IN CUBA

As part of the Caribbean tourism market , Cuba has enjoyed considerable success in attracting tourists from Europe and Canada during its "special period"; the transition from a quota system to a global economic market. It has done this without even tapping the closest and largest market—the United States. As Mr. Suddaby points out:

> Cuba has tremendous diversity in its tourism product, offering a considerable variety of traditional sun/sea/sand experiences with historical and cultural attractions, sporting activities and forms of adventure tourism. The country is substantial in size, geographically close to the North American market, relatively crime free, and has a well educated workforce.

Cuba, admittedly, is unique even with the increase of tourism. The island already leads most other less-developed countries in quality of life and standard of living categories. This is indicated by, and not limited to, such measures as literacy rate, employment rate, number of doctors per 1000 people, low birth rates and death rates and caloric intake. Also, Cuba's population of 12 million residents is 60% African and is spread more or less uniformly across its land mass. It has a well trained military force, free access to educational and medical benefits, and most Cubans have adequate housing with decent, potable water and containerized sewage disposal. The shape of the island, its east-west positioning and its proximity to specific water and air currents helps dissipate various externalized source-point pollutants. Culturally, the island has distinct African-European influence and, because of its political and economic doctrine, there is a limited amount of both racism and sexism.

Being unique presents some endemic problems that affect its position in the tourism market such as: infrastructure maintenance, an economic embargo enforced by the United States, and the availability of capital to invest in long-term growth. As a result, these problems trickle down to the development of the tourism industry itself. This is manifested in the availability of tourist facilities, accessibility to tourism by Cubans, and, more specifically, the diverting of funds from human needs to development of the tourism industry.

As is pointed out, to maintain a supply for the demand, Cuba needs to double the number of hotel rooms available in the near future, and upgrade existing ones and meet projected increases in the number of tourists, their length of stay and their daily expenditures. Also, many misconceptions about conditions in Cuba exist and these need to be overcome through a well-funded marketing and advertising campaign if the "new" tourist is to be attracted.

The infrastructure itself needs major improvements to cope with continued development. Transportation, energy, water, sewage and solid waste disposal, to name a few, are in need of expansion or upgrade. With the Cuban economy still recovering from the fall of the its chief facilitator, the USSR, these improvements are slow in coming and being done in a piecemeal fashion.

HELMS-BURTON IMPACT

The economic embargo, supplemented by the Helms-Burton Law, has not had a tremendous affect on the overall quality of life in Cuba. Although certain products, such as medicine, foodstuffs and computers are rare, sufficient supplies of most durable and non-durable goods are imported from other countries, who, en masse, have ignored the provisions of Helms-Burton. As Messrs. Lucio and Crespo point out:

> The fans and foes of the law have made extraordinary efforts to exaggerate the consequences or effects of the

law.....and distort, through their interpretation, the real extent of the law.

And they add:

> in spite of the risk that the law might represent, for them it is good business sense to continue operating and investing in tourism in Cuba.....enacting laws that are intended to protect their nationals against the effect of the U.S. law.

The availability of capital to finance the tourist industry's expansion, maintain vital infrastructure, and keep the Cubans healthy and happy is a major issue, one that is necessarily complex in nature. Many U.S. companies would enjoy investing in our own "backyard" if the embargo were lifted and free trade was resumed. Since the future of trade and tourism between the U.S. and Cuba is an unknown variable, only possible projections can be offered as to how the entire Caribbean would be affected were the embargo lifted.

SUMMARIZING THE TWO PAPERS

Basing their assumptions on data from the Cuban Ministry of Tourism, both papers suggest that increased tourism, along with increased construction of tourist facilities will continue to have a major impact on the Cuban economy. Both authors also suggest that the lifting of the embargo will do much to make the tourism industry in Cuba a viable source of income and will provide profits and other benefits for the Cuban people. Again, both authors agree that despite the current problems in the Cuban economy, tourism is a good investment and will provide the basis for future economic development and growth in related industries.

DISCUSSION

As an economic/cultural geographer and an environmentalist interested in Latin America, I would like to stress a very important issue that I feel is neither stated in the papers nor represented by the statistics, but was of concern to me in my three visits to Cuba in the past year. The question of how increased development will affect the day to day living of Cubans and how that development will impact the environment, not just in the short term, but also in the long-term economic and political position of the island.

Obviously, increased tourism will have an affect on how people view their own position in relation to the rest of the world. I have already seen in one year an increase in the amount of consumer items available to some Cubans. Others, who are exposed to amenities provided for tourists, such as cable TV and international publications, are exposed to other points of view in regards to both international events and how events in their own country are relayed to others. A good case in point is the recent bombings in Cuba. According to my reports from the island, life pretty much went on as usual, even though the bombings were reported throughout the Cuban media. Media in Miami, however, suggested severe chaos in the city as a result of terrorist group activities.

Another element is the sharing of already scarce commodities with an increased number of tourists. Even though conditions in most parts of Cuba are tolerable, and basic necessities are available, increased tourism means that the government will have to divert items intended for the general population to tourist areas. An example of this is the availability of red meat on the island. In tourist areas, a varied menu of various meat dishes is available, but in the countryside, it is against the law to slaughter an animal for its meat, especially cattle. Roadblocks are set up in rural locations to check vehicles heading for urban areas to see if they are transporting illegal meat products to the city.

As tourism increases, what becomes of the environment? How will solid waste, which is currently burned, and sewage, which is largely untreated, be dealt with when the volume is doubled? As tourists crisscross the island in rented cars, how many more residents will have to walk, bicycle or wait in line to ride a crowed bus to get to their destination? The largest oil field in the country is located in the bay behind Varadero. Tourists are not fond of seeing or smelling resource extraction activities and the resultant imprint on the landscape.

Capitalism, as I have seen, is slowly encroaching on the island. Over the last year 24-hour gas stations, auto dealers and hamburger stands are making themselves seen. More international companies are displaying their logos and "diplo" stores are opening to sell the consumer goods demanded by successive waves of tourists from consumerized economies. In addition, more Cubans are opening and operating entrepreneurial efforts to help supplement their income. My favorite *parador* in La Habana is owned by an unemployed geologist; former dentists drive taxis; school teachers make sugar cane juice in roadside rests; and artisans must sell their pieces in competitive market squares. The legalizing of the American dollar has stimulated these activities, and how ironic this is that the very country that has economically blockaded the island supplies the only recognized usable currency.

All of this economic change is unequally distributed, yet another characteristic of capitalism. Working in the tourism industry is limited to those who have connections or who can speak a foreign language or who live in close proximity to a tourist area. In one respect, the limiting of regional employment opportunities to those who reside in the region has discouraged internal migration to areas where cash, in the form of tipping, is available. For instance, to work in Varadero, you must be from there or Matanzas or Cárdenas. All others need not apply.

Cuba is also different from other tourist destinations in its lack of crime and street begging. There are uniformed police on most corners and only recently has a rash of theft related incidents been reported. In the streets of Habana, many Cubans will tell you of their relative in the United States, but they will not ask you for money. Instead, they may just want to practice their English for when their visa is granted to go visit their relatives. Many elderly woman are delighted when I give them small bars of soap, a commodity that is rationed and not always available. Many children are excited when they receive a simple pen to do their homework.

CONCLUSION

It is amazing to me, and an accolade for the Cuban people, as to how many do so much with so little. The perception of Cuba, especially by Americans, is that Cuba is a dirty, vile place, full of filth and pestilence. Personally, I feel the Helms-Burton Law is a double edged sword. On one hand, it limits the amount of consumer items available in the country, especially the in the area of education, pharmaceuticals and other related technologies. On the other hand, if it were lifted tomorrow, how many Americans would see dollar signs in Cuba—the vintage cars, the native crafts, the cigars? Could we estimate that 500,000 people would invade Cuba immediately to strip them of items that could bring a small fortune in the United States? After the dust settles, what would be left? There would not be enough hotel rooms, food, energy, water and most other necessary items. Surely, some Cubans would be standing with a handful of cash, but what could they buy and where would they buy it?

The subject of tourism in Cuba is the topic of today's panel. As the industry expands, so must the facilities. As the facilities expand, more pressure is put on the people and the environment. The economic sanctions imposed by the United States, in this author's opinion, allow Cuba's tourism industry to expand in a more controlled setting and also, at the same time, protect it from becoming strained beyond its capabilities. I can only hope that given the papers presented today, which, in an economic sense, make their point, that the people, whose economy this association is studying, are not reduced to mere numbers and statistics. It is my opinion, that the ideals of capitalism as an economic system, should be administered in small doses, so Cuba will not endure yet another invasion to its historic shores. It is worth being a tourist in Cuba just to witness how a society *not* consumed with consumerization can be healthy, wealthy and wise.

CUBAN TOURISM, ECONOMIC GROWTH, AND THE WELFARE OF THE CUBAN WORKER

Joseph M. Perry, Jeffrey W. Steagall and Louis A. Woods

The recent boom in Cuban tourism is a classic example of maximization under constraints. Hampered by the tightened U.S. embargo and by the disappearance of substantial economic aid from the former Communist Bloc countries, the Cuban government has exploited one of the few growth sectors open to it. Joint ventures with companies from foreign countries that are willing to ignore the Helms-Burton strictures have provided the capital for the continuing construction of hotels and tourist attractions in popular resort areas such as Varadero. The number of tourists visiting Cuba annually has just passed the million mark, including some U.S. citizens who enter the island illegally from other foreign countries.

The expansion of tourist facilities has been encouraged by the passage of Law Number 77, which liberalizes Cuban investment opportunities. Foreign investors may now totally own enterprises in Cuba, in addition to engaging in joint ventures with Cuban businesspersons. The Cuban government still exercises indirect influence over such ventures by controlling the provision and remuneration of the labor force that they employ. Its policies clearly affect the economic impact of the tourism industry.

TOURISM AND ITS ROLE IN ECONOMIC DEVELOPMENT

Tourism is basically "an export industry that conveys domestic services and the experiences of domestic resources to foreign consumers in return for foreign currencies" (Woods, Perry and Steagall, 1991, p. 2). Instead of staying home and importing goods and services, however, tourists visit the exporting country and enjoy the experiences and activities on site. Tourist expenditures therefore enter directly into the domestic economy, through the firms and activities that cater to tourist wants.

From the point of view of the country providing the tourism experience, these dollars (or other currencies) are new monies that provide an additional stimulus to the domestic economy. They can help to reduce deficits in the current account of the balance of payments, they can generate government revenues, and, through the multiplier process, they can increase sales volume, employment, and income.

Measuring Economic Impacts

Measuring the impact of tourism on a given economy is conceptually a simple matter. Like a manufacturing plant or a dairy farm or a bank, a tourist attraction generates financial flows that move to other, interrelated sectors of the economy. These flows stimulate sales, output, employment, and income growth. There are additional induced increases that flow from the interaction. Spending in Sector A may affect economic activity in Sectors B and C. As Sectors B and C expand, they in turn stimulate the growth of Sector A, where the stimulus began. Interactions of this kind are probably best measured through input-output analysis, or through the use of multipliers derived from such tables.

Beyond this immediate level of impact, tourism can serve as an engine of longer-term economic development. If the tourism sector is closely interlinked with other sectors of the domestic economy, then its

141

growth can serve to support the continued expansion of those sectors. In addition, the expansion of tourism in a country will require a concomitant expansion in support industries, such as foreign exchange, transportation, lodging places, and security. Some developing countries have improved their domestic infrastructure by using foreign exchange generated by tourist inflows. Obviously, this is a two-way street, since tourism can only expand and succeed if an adequate infrastructure is in place, or grows with the industry.

Multiplier Estimation and Analysis

As tourist dollars move into an economy, their direct spending generates additional indirect and induced spending, resulting in an increase in economic activity that is a multiple of the original amount. The relationship between initial and final expenditure is commonly expressed as a multiplier, normally an adaptation of the 1930's Keynesian formulation. The multipliers used by most growth analysts are either derived from input-output tables (such as the RIMS II model of the U. S. Department of Commerce), or are derived in an *ad hoc* manner from economic theory. The formula for most simple *ad hoc* multipliers in economics is a fraction, with the adjusted initial spending impact expressed in the numerator, and the effect of leakages from the responding stream shown in the denominator. The initial multiplier model taught to most college sophomores, for example, is simply the reciprocal of the marginal propensity to save.

Multipliers are typically computed for four types of impacts resulting from tourist expenditures: sales, output, income, and employment (Pearce, 1989, 206-207). Less frequently used is a capital or asset multiplier, that measures the increase in the value of an economy's assets or stock of capital (Bull, 1991, 141). The most frequently cited and most frequently used of these four measures is the tourist income multiplier.

The range of values for tourism income multipliers varies with the economic structure and the degree of self-sufficiency enjoyed by a country. Since multiplier values are in part determined by leakages out of a responding stream, those countries with substantial import elements in their tourism sector (raw materials, services, absentee ownership of facilities) will find the tourist income multiplier depressed by those leakages. The higher the savings rate and the tax rates, the lower the multiplier. And the less integrated the economy (the weaker the sectoral linkages), the lower the multiplier. This last observation suggests that, from an input-output point of view, the tourist sector should ideally be heavily interrelated with other domestic economic sectors. If government policies inhibit the flow of tourist dollars, or reroute them to other sectors of the economy, the multiplier impact is clearly altered.

Empirical estimates of tourist income multipliers show a range of values from 0.18 for small towns in Wales to around 1.20 for an island center like Dominica. With few exceptions, however, the tourist income multipliers are less than one, reflecting substantial leakages (Pearce, 1989, 209). Espino (1994, 163) estimated the tourist income multiplier for Cuba to fall in the range of 0.74 to 0.84, based upon 1989 propensities to consume and import.

THE TOURISM INDUSTRY IN CUBA SINCE THE 1950S

The history of tourism in Cuba since the 1950s is a story of the death and the rebirth of a major industry. After the Revolution, the emerging socialist government decided that the ills of tourism were so great that the industry should be reduced or eliminated. The bright lights of Havana casinos were dimmed, prostitution declined, and the tourist inflows from the United States mainland disappeared. Changing attitudes and pressing financial needs two decades later lead to the revival of the industry, however. The major difference between the new Cuban tourism and its predecessor would be the conspicuous absence of legalized casino gambling.

Jenkins (1992, 142) provides a brief outline as he views policy changes at the time of the Soviet breakup:

> In order to break its dependence on sugar and develop more balanced foreign trading relations, Cuba needs to generate substantially greater export revenues. The key to the problem is being sought, almost

**Table 1. Cuba: Tourist Arrivals by Region of Origin, 1986-94
(percent of total arrivals)**

Region	1986	1987	1988	1989	1990	1991	1992	1993	1994
Americas	47.1	43.3	43.3	49.1	48.1	48.9	49.1	52.8	43.5
Europe	51.3	55.5	56.1	49.8	49.6	46.4	47.4	45.1	48.7
Africa	0.9	1.0	0.4	0.6	0.7	0.4	0.6	0.3	
Asia, East and South East/ Oceania	0.8	0.1	0.1	0.3	0.5	0.4	0.4	0.3	
Region not Specified						1.0	3.9	2.5	1.5	7.8
TOTAL	100.0	100.0	100.0	100.0	100.0	100.0	100.0	100.0	100.0

Source: United Nations, *Statistical Yearbook*, 1990/91 through 1994.

inevitably, in tourism. After two decades of spurning it as a source of foreign exchange — and despite bad memories of what tourism, prostitution, and gambling did to Cuba in the 1950s — the government made the decision in the late 1970s to open up the country to western tourism once again. The National Institute of Tourism (Intur), set up in 1959 to save the industry, was dusted off and set to renovating hotels, developing infrastructure, and attracting a new generation of tourists.

Although it had a ponderous, inexperienced, and inefficient bureaucracy, Intur was able to get the number of hard currency tourists visiting Cuba up from 78,000 in 1980—of whom 22,000 were from Canada and 35,000 from the United States—to 149,000 by 1986, despite the loss of the United States market when Reagan tightened travel restrictions. The main markets it succeeded in developing during this period were West Germany (23,000 in 1986), Spain (20,000), Mexico (13,000), Italy (11,000), and Argentina (7,000).

From the late 1970s until the late 1980s, Cuban tourism grew erratically and haltingly. Hard currency expenditures by visitors to the island totaled about US$16.7 million in 1977. By 1979, after a growth spurt, spending hit a level of US$87.6 million. A slump followed, with lower annual flows, until tourists again injected US$87.3 million into the economy in 1985. From that point forward, the trend was steadily upward. The average receipt per visitor from capitalist countries was estimated to be US$501 in 1982. This figure did not increase appreciably until 1988 (Espino, 1994, 156-157).

Tourism Patterns in Recent Years

The country mix of tourists visiting Cuba has changed only slightly over the past decade. As the data in Table 1 indicate, at least 90 percent of annual tourist arrivals in Cuba are from the Americas or Europe. Africa, Asia, and Oceania constitute minor sources of such flows. During 1996, Italian tourists constituted the largest national group visiting Cuba, with 185,000 persons. Canadian and Spanish tourists both numbered more than 100,000. Other major tourist sources included Germany, France, Mexico, England, and Colombia. Total expenditures by these tourists reportedly amounted to US$1.3 billion (DevTech, 1997, 2).

**Table 2. Cuba: Average Tourist Receipts per Arrival, 1984-94
(thousands of 1987 U.S. dollars)**

Year	Average Receipts
1994	$1,285.65
1993	$1,220.44
1992	$1,117.06
1991	$823.77
1990	$654.51
1989	$580.49
1988	$580.49
1987	$650.49
1986	$722.68
1985	$432.86
1984	$435.56

Source: Computed from data in United Nations, *Statistical Yearbook*, various issues, 1987 through 1994.

Assuming the validity of tourist receipt data generated by the United Nations (Table 2), there has been a clear increase in per capita tourist expenditures in Cuba. Since 1984, expenditures per tourist have increased at least threefold, albeit on a somewhat erratic trend.

Werlau (1996, 460) comments that "[t]he tourist sector has proven what is perhaps the most visible aspect of Cuba's push to attract foreign capital — both in terms of a growing number of tourist visits to Cuba each year and probably also in terms of investment. Since 1990 the number of visitors to Cuba — primarily from Canada, Spain, Italy, Germany, and France — has reportedly increased by 54 percent, and earnings by 75 percent; from January through June of 1996 visitors were said to have risen 46 percent in comparison to 1995."

While estimates of the level of tourist expenditure and the average expenditure per visitor may understandably vary, the underlying growth trend in tourism in recent years is undebatable. Tourists from developed countries have acquired an appetite for the delights of Cuban beaches and resorts, and are flocking there in increasing numbers.

LAW NUMBER 77

During the early 1990s, Cuba was still not attracting luxury tourists, who would leave greater amounts of foreign exchange in the country (Jenkins, 1992, 143). A joint venture law had been on the books since 1982 (Decree No. 50), but no joint ventures of any significance in tourism occurred until 1989. The subsequent inflows of capital were heartening, but fell far short of national needs. One impediment appeared to be the requirement that foreigners might not operate a wholly-owned enterprise in Cuba, but instead must always have a Cuban partner who possessed some of the equity.

Chapter XI of Law Number 77 establishes the ground rules for the hiring and compensation of Cuban workers by foreign or joint venture firms. Article 31 requires that the employees of such firms shall normally be Cubans or foreigners permanently residing in Cuba. Higher management positions and some technical positions may be filled by nonresident

foreigners, however, following pertinent immigration laws. Article 32 permits the establishment of an economic stimulus fund, generated from company profits, for the benefit of workers. Articles 33 and 34 establish an organ of the Cuban government as the official hiring agency for workers. This *entidad empleadora* receives payment from employers in hard foreign currency, and then pays the Cuban tourism workers in Cuban pesos.

The provisions of these articles establish the Cuban government as a monopsonist, or a single buyer of labor for the tourist industry (and other industries using foreign capital) at the national level. Since the *entidad empleadora* essentially serves as a single seller of labor to tourism facilities, the resulting situation is similar in many ways to bilateral monopoly. The opportunity for worker exploitation is evident. The arrangement is also clearly designed to generate additional foreign exchange for the government.

In addition to this wage arrangement, all such foreign enterprises are subject to Cuban taxation, generating even more government revenues: an income tax that takes away 30 percent of net income, an 11 percent tax for labor force utilization, a 14 percent social security tax, import duties, personal property taxes on automobiles, and documentary fees (Coto-Ojeda, 1995; Pérez-López, 1993, p. 234).

Miller, Glen, Jaspersen and Karmokolias (1997, p. 29) point out that joint ventures in developing countries "are often fragile and both difficult to negotiate and, once negotiated, to hold together." Those that succeed typically have developed an agreement that addresses potential conflicts, and that provides a means of resolving those conflicts or of exiting the agreement; and have established a good working relationship that is characterized by flexibility in negotiations and bargaining.

At this point in time, the effects of Law Number 77 are still uncertain and unproved. As time passes, the viability of this approach will be indicated by the permanence or departure of foreign investors. In any event, the Castro government retains control of the labor supply available to tourist attractions, and has the ability to control a substantial portion of the foreign exchange that flows through those attractions.

TOURISM IN CUBA TODAY

José Luis Rodríguez, Cuba's Minister of the Economy and Planning, reported in January that the Cuban economy had expanded by 7.8 percent, instead of the predicted 5 percent (1997, 1). He noted the role of foreign investors in the expansion, during which the number of "economic associations with foreign capital" rose from 212 to 260. As identified by government spokespersons, the primary sources of this growth were expansion in the tourism industry, continued growth in sugar and nickel production, and an increase in construction activity (DevTech, 1997, 1). Such optimistic figures may contain as much marketing as they contain truth. Sugar output figures are almost surely overstated, world sugar prices have dropped because of overproduction, the exact economic impact of tourism cannot be computed, and the country's trade deficit rose during 1996. Mesa-Lago (1996, 6-7) concludes that "the dramatic decline in the Cuban economy was halted in 1995-1996, at least temporarily, but the recovery has been sluggish to say the least."

Collis (1996, 453) describes recent and anticipated growth in Cuba's tourism industry:

> Between 1990 and 1994, Cuba's tourism grew more than 16 percent annually, compared with 4.7 percent for the Caribbean as a whole. By 1995 tourism ranked as Cuba's second highest gross foreign exchange earner ($1 billion for 1995) after sugar ($1.2 billion). Despite a brief downturn following the rafters exodus in mid-1994, tourist numbers grew again — to 745,000 — in 1995. Optimistically, the Cuban government announced it expects to have 50,000 hotel rooms (up from 23,255 in 1995), 2.5 million visitors and a gross revenue of 3-plus billion dollars by the year 2000. . . . The main tourist centers are Havana, Santiago de Cuba, Cayo Largo, Cayo Coco, and Varadero.

Calendar year 1996 is now a relative peak in this growth trend. The official Cuban statistics record 1,004,336 tourists arriving on the island, and "generating earnings" of US$1.3 billion. Government predictions are for 1.2 million tourists in 1997, creating earnings of US$1.75 billion. By the year 2000, tourist arrivals are predicted to exceed 2.5 million per year. A doubling of tourist volume in only four years will require a substantial expansion of tourist facilities and its supporting infrastructure (Casals, 1997, 2).

The urgency of the need for planning and adaptation is emphasized by the comments of Ignacio Vasallo, Secretary of the World Tourist Organization, at the end of his 1996 visit to Cuba (*Business Tips on Cuba*, 1996). Vasallo argued that Cuba was capable of sustaining tourism growth of 10 percent per year for the foreseeable future. In the worst case, he said, Cuba could count on a tourism growth rate double that of world tourism, which will grow by 3.5 to 3.8 percent per year in the near future. By the year 2005, Cuba could be the leading tourist destination in the Caribbean. And such growth inevitably places stresses upon the infrastructure and natural resources

THE POSITION OF LABOR IN THE CUBAN TOURIST INDUSTRY

Assessing the role of labor in the Cuban tourism industry requires data concerning employment levels, working conditions, and compensation. As is true of other economic sectors on the island, figures regarding the tourism industry are scanty, and are usually not subject to direct verification. Adequate data and anecdotal observations do exist, however, to paint a basic picture of labor conditions in the tourism sector.

Alfonso (1996, 11-13) lists the major categories of private-sector employment in Cuba as follows:

- *Trabajadores por cuenta propia*, such as paladares, taxis, beauty salons, and craft and mechanic shops. About half of the persons in this category were unemployed.

- *Trabajadores del sector mixto*, or *del sector de empresas mixtas*, which are the joint ventures involving foreign management and capital.

- *Trabajadores del sector campesino privado y cooperativo*, including farmers and members of cooperatives, producing such items as coffee and tobacco.

Other employed workers serve in state enterprises, 12 percent of whom are part-time. The estimated employment in each of the private sectors is as follows:

Trabajadores por cuenta propia con licencia	208,500
Trabajadores por cuenta propia sin licencia	190,000
Trabajadores del sector mixto	53,000
Sector campesino y cooperativo	271,857
Total sector no estatal	669,357

By this accounting, workers in the joint venture sector constitute only 7.9 percent of all private sector workers, and only 1.2 percent of the entire labor force. If the official labor force is 4.6 million, then subtracting the above figures from 4.6 million yields 3,930,643 persons who either work in state enterprises or are unemployed.

According to Rodolfo Casals (1997), about 130,000 Cuban workers are now employed in the tourism industry. Half of that number are directly employed by tourist enterprises such as hotels. The remainder presumably hold jobs that are created indirectly by tourist spending. In multiplier terms, these numbers suggest that the indirect and induced employment effects of tourist spending are equal to the direct effects. Again, assuming the correctness of this figure, tourism industry employees constitute only 2.83 percent of the total labor force. If all 130,000 tourism employees are included in Alfonso's total for the private sector, then they make up 19.4 percent of that total. Regardless of the accounting approach, Cuban workers associated with the tourism industry are a minor fraction of the total labor force.

Employees of the tourism sector are also treated differently from other workers in the Cuban economy. Córdova (1996, 365) lists three groups of workers in the economy with special compensation arrangements: "1) those working in strategic industries (like tourism, mining, ports, and the electric and power sector) who are allowed to receive part of their remuneration in dollars; 2) those active in other important but not so critical sectors who as an incentive may receive *convertible* pesos in specified quantities; 3) the rest of the labor force who continue to receive only Cuban pesos." Pérez-López (1993) confirms the special arrangements for tourism workers.

Córdova (1996, 365) points out that the government essentially circumvents the arrangement for workers in Group 1 who are in the tourism sector:

> Although those working in the tourism industry enjoy a special status, they are also adversely affected by other government measures. Foreign companies operating hotels for instance must pay their workers in dollars through a transfer of the corresponding amount to a government agency called Cubatec. The agency then pays the workers in pesos at the exchange rate fixed by the government. Such an arrangement represents a handsome profit for Castro and an infraction of Convention 95 of the International Labor Organization (ratified by Cuba) which in order to protect wages provides that they should be directly paid to the workers. It also constitutes an infringement of the principle of integrity regarding the amount owed to the workers.

Werlau's analysis (1996, 471) of labor conditions in the tourism industry is sobering. Joint ventures may officially pay workers a wage that is between US$400 and US$500 per month. Employers also foot the bill for a benefit package. Unfortunately, the workers get only a fraction of the official real wage when the Cuban government pays them in pesos. As a result, the employing enterprises add on other unofficial benefits ("bonuses, gifts, meals, automobiles, hard currency under the table"), further increasing the cost of labor. Transportation and uniforms also raise the wage bill. Not surprisingly, theft is a common problem. Werlau argues that, because of these additional costs, Cuban labor is expensive, relative to labor in other Caribbean countries. The differential could ultimately have an adverse effect Cuba's competitive position. As noted above, taxes imposed on the employing companies are also substantial.

With regard to working conditions, Werlau (1996, 472) notes that workers in the international tourist sector face more restrictions than other Cuban workers. They are "subject to longer probationary periods and work hours, more irregular schedules, shorter periods for challenging disciplinary decisions, and no right of appeal through usual judicial and administrative channels." Too, they are prohibited from saying or doing things that might tarnish the state's image. In essence, any labor conflict is quashed (Pérez-López, 1993).

In short, Cuban tourism workers are subject to the same kind of wage exploitation that the Cuban government imposes on employees of non-tourism joint enterprises. But they suffer additional restrictions on hiring, speech, and action. They receive, thanks to the largesse of their foreign employers, additional unofficial real income. As welcome as the additional dollars or food or other gifts may be, they cannot fill the gap between the wage payments they deserve and the small amounts of Cuban pesos that they receive.

PROSPECTS AND CONCLUSIONS

Some tentative conclusions emerge from the foregoing facts and analysis:

First, economic growth is continuing in Cuba, and tourism is one of the engines propelling that growth. Although the expansion of the tourism industry is beyond dispute, its precise role in recent Cuban economic growth cannot be adequately measured. As noted below, the multipliers associated with tourist spending simply cannot be determined at the moment. The size and timing of capital inflows associated with joint ventures are also uncertain. The facts are few: Tourist facilities have employed rising numbers of Cuban workers, presumably reducing the labor surplus recognized by the government in 1996. A large percentage of the foreign exchange left on the island by tourists flows to the Cuban government, through taxes and through expropriation under Law 77. There has undoubtedly been some induced growth in industries that support the tourism industry. Without adequate measures of sectoral linkages, such as an input-output table, the quantification of this growth becomes speculative.

Second, another discouraging conclusion is that the multipliers associated with the tourism industry in Cuba are either difficult or impossible to estimate at the present time, given the poor data available and the effects of Law Number 77. Good data concerning the marginal propensities to consume and to import are also lacking.

Third, Cuban workers who are employed in the tourism industry are exploited in several ways. They are screened and controlled more strictly than other Cuban workers. They are subject to dismissal without recourse, if they behave in inappropriate ways or make statements that are critical of the government. They are paid very low wages through the agencies established by Law Number 77. Not surprisingly, employers often provide unofficial and nominally illegal support to their workers through additional hard currency payments, use of resort facilities and equipment, and payments in kind, typically food. It is also no surprise that theft by employees is a problem at resorts. A policy intended to generate hard currency for government use has clearly exerted a strong adverse effect on the welfare of Cuban tourism workers.

Fourth, there are several wild cards in this analysis. The first is the continuing effect of the Helms-Burton Act on tourism growth. If foreign countries continue to battle with or ignore most of the strictures of Helms-Burton, then the expansion of tourism can continue over the near term. If the Clinton administration finally decides to enforce Helms-Burton, however, there may be a chilling effect on tourism growth. We are clearly dealing with an imponderable.

SOURCES AND WORKS CITED

Alfonso, Pablo (1996). "Apuntes Sobre la Situación Socio-Economica de Cuba." In *Cuba in Transition—Volume 6*. Washington: Association for the Study of the Cuban Economy, pp. 8-13..

Archer, B. H., and Christine B. Owen (1971). "Toward a Tourist Regional Multiplier," *Regional Studies*, Volume 5, pp. 289-294.

Bryden, John, and Mike Farber (1971). "Multiplying the Tourist Multiplier," *Social and Economic Studies*, Volume 20, pp. 61-82.

Bull, Adrian (1991). *The Economics of Travel and Tourism*. Melbourne, Australia: Pitman Publishing.

Business Tips on Cuba (1996). April. Posted on the Internet at ttp://www.tips.cu/1996/abril/ana-in.html.

Casals, Rodolfo (1997). "Number of tourists to increase by 20 percent." *Granma International* (March 12). Electronic edition posted at http://www.granma.cu/marz2/9marz4i.html.

Casals, Rodolfo (1997). "Havana: Latin American tourism capital." *Granma International* (May 13). Electronic edition posted at http://www.granma.cu/mayo3/18may3i.html.

Collis, David S. (1996). "Tourism/Ecotourism in Cuba." In *Cuba in Transition—Volume 6*. Washington: Association for the Study of the Cuban Economy, pp. 451-455.

Córdova, Efrén (1996). "The Situation of Cuban Workers During the 'Special Period in Peacetime.'" In *Cuba in Transition—Volume 6*. Washington: Association for the Study of the Cuban Economy, pp. 358-368.

Coto-Ojeda, Ramón (1995). "Cuba Revamps Foreign Investment by Enacting Law Number 77," *Commentary*, Autumn. Posted on the Internet by the law firm of McConnell Valdés at http://www.mcvpr.com/docs/cubarev.html.

Cumper, G.E. (1959). "Tourist Expenditures in Jamaica, 1958," *Social and Economic Studies*, Volume 8, pp. 287-310.

Daltabritt, M., and O. Pi-Sunyer (1990). "Tourism Development in Quintana Roo, Mexico." *Cultural Survival Quarterly*, 4, pp. 9-13.

DevTech Systems, Inc. (1997). *Cuba Monthly Economic Report*, 1:2 (March). Published by DevTech Systems, Inc., Miami, Florida.

Díaz-Briquets, Sergio, and Jorge Pérez-López (1994). "Cuba's Labor Adjustment Policies during the Special Period." In Jorge Pérez-López (Ed.), *Cuba at a Crossroads: Politics and Economics after the Fourth Party Congress*. Gainesville: University Press of Florida, pp. 118-146.

Espino, Maria Dolores (1994). "Tourism in Cuba: A Development Strategy for the 1990s?" In Jorge F. Pérez-López, editor, *Cuba at a Crossroads: Politics and Economics after the Fourth Party Congress*. Gainesville: University Press of Florida, pp. 147-166.

Jenkins, Gareth (1992). "Beyond Basic Needs: Cuba's Search for Stable Development in the 1990s." In Sandor Halebsky, John M. Kirk, Carollee Bengelsdorf, Richard L. Harris, Jean Stubbs, and Andrew Zimbalist, editors, *Cuba in Transition: Crisis and Transformation*. Boulder: Westview Press, pp. 137-151.

Mesa-Lago, Carmelo (1996). "The State of the Cuban Economy: 1995-1996." In *Cuba in Transition—Volume 6*. Washington: Association for the Study of the Cuban Economy, pp. 4-7.

Miller, Robert, Jack Glen, Fred Jaspersen, and Yannis Karmokolias (1997). "International Joint Ventures in Developing Countries." *Finance & Development*, 34(1), 26-29.

Oramas, Joaquín (1997). "Tourism, sugar harvest and nickel: bases for development." *Granma International* (May 19). Electronic edition posted at http://www.granma.cu/mayo4/19may6i.html.

Pearce, Douglas (1989). *Tourist Development* (2nd ed.). Essex, England: Longman Scientific and Technical.

Pérez, Louis A., Jr. (1975). *Underdevelopment and Dependency: Tourism in the West Indies*. El Paso, Texas: Center for Inter-American Studies, University of Texas at El Paso.

Pérez-López, Jorge F. (1993). "Cuba's Thrust to Attract Foreign Investment: A Special Labor Regime for Joint Ventures in International Tourism." *The University of Miami Inter-American Law Review* 24:2 (Winter), pp. 221-279.

Pérez-López, Jorge F., editor (1994). *Cuba at a Crossroads: Politics and Economics after the Fourth Party Congress*. Gainesville: University Press of Florida.

Pérez-López, Jorge F. (1995). *Cuba's Second Economy: From Behind the Scenes to Center Stage*. New Brunswick, N. J.: Transaction Publishers.

Rodríguez, José Luis (1997). "Economy Grows by 7.8 Percent." *Granma International* (January 14). Report on 1996 economic results and 1997 economic and social plan, presented to the National Assembly by the Minister of Economy and Planning. Electronic edition posted at http://www.granma.cu/ener2/2ene2i.html.

Rodríguez, Eloy (1997). "New directions for investment." *Granma International* (March 26). Electronic edition posted at http://www.granma.cu/mar4/11mar8i.html.

United States. Central Intelligence Agency (1996). *The World Factbook*. Electronic edition. Available at http://www.odci.gov/cia/publications/nsolo/factbook.

Weaver, David B. (1993). "Model of Urban Tourism for Small Caribbean Islands." *The Geographical Review*, pp. 134-140.

Werlau, María C. (1996). "Foreign Investment in Cuba: The Limits of Commercial Engagement." In *Cuba in Transition—Volume 6*. Washington, D. C.: Association for the Study of the Cuban Economy, pp. 456-495.

Williams, Allan M., and Gareth Shaw, editors (1988). *Tourism and Economic Development: Western European Experiences*. London: Bellhaven Press.

Woods, Louis A., Joseph M. Perry and Jeffrey W. Steagall (1991). "Tourism and Economic Development: The Case of Post-Independence Belize." Paper presented at the Fifth Annual Studies on Belize Conference, Belize City, Belize, C.A., September 3-6.

Woods, Louis A. (1985). "The Role of Free Trade Zones in the Caribbean Basin." Paper presented at the semiannual meetings of the Atlantic Economic Society, Washington, D.C., August.

Zimbalist, Andrew (1994). "Treading Water: Cuba's Economic and Political Crisis." In Donald E. Schulz, editor, *Cuba and the Future*. Westport, Conn.: Greenwood Press, pp. 7-21.

CUBAN TOURISM IN 2007: ECONOMIC IMPACT

Nicolás Crespo and Santos Negrón Díaz[1]

Our objectives in this paper are to carry out a study to evaluate recent trends in the tourism industry, analyze Cuba's perspectives and quantify the economic impact of tourism policy and activities on the island's economy. The task entailed not only an assessment of Cuba's specific conditions, but also positioning Cuba within the broader Caribbean context and the major trends and perspectives affecting the industry.

The economic impact of tourism is a key component of the study. In order to arrive at a conclusion, we analyzed the income and employment generating capacity of the industry and the fiscal resources which it generates. The conclusion arrived at in the study is that the operation of tourism, hotels, motels and other related assets represents a growing major contribution to both foreign currency income generation and employment in Cuba and that it will play a major role in the coming years based on the number of hotel rooms under development, the investment required and the potential impact on the economy during construction and operation.

Cuba's tourism industry is faced with challenges arising from new competitors and from a rapidly changing global tourism industry. This report suggests that Cuba could position itself to face these challenges successfully and generate major economic benefits for its economy through coherent demand and supply-side policies.

However, Cuba's tourism industry is not demand driven. The Cuban authorities determine what and when new supply will be developed, sometimes with unorthodox criteria. Demand for these products is expected to be created by the foreign operators and wholesalers.

Using the available official figures as the base for the tourism strategy, we attempt in this report to estimate the economic impact of the island's tourism industry ten years from today, in 2007, according to two scenarios. The first scenario assumes continuation of the current political and economic situation, perhaps with minor changes. The second scenario contemplates the complete elimination of political and economic barriers in a free capitalistic economy where American citizens and residents as well as Cuban citizens will be able to invest, operate, visit, and enjoy any of Cuba's tourism facilities.

The report suggests that there is an abysm between the two scenarios. However, it also indicates the tremendous opportunity that Cuba has to benefit all players, including the Cuban people, by improving its current political, economic and labor policies and allowing free enterprise and demand to lead the growth and success of its tourism industry.

TOURISM AND THE GLOBAL ECONOMY

International tourism has been a major contributor to the expansion of the world economy in recent years. According to the World Tourism Organiza-

---

1. The authors would like to thank the members of the Cuban Society of Tourism Professionals, particularly Marie L. Dexter, José A. González, Saturnino Lucio II, José A Menéndez, Margarita Navarrete, Roberto Pérez and Roberto Arencibia.

tion (WTO), international tourist arrivals increased by 3.6% in 1995 and by 4.5% in 1996, and will continue growing by 4.6% per year until the year 2010, while international tourist expenditures measured in U.S. dollars rose 13.1% in 1995 and 7.6% in 1996. Tourism expenditures will grow at a pace of 6-8% above inflation.

The Organization for Economic Cooperation and Development (OECD) points out that tourism is one of the three main sectors of trade in international services, as higher education, more leisure time and consistent growth of employment and personal income are inducing more people to travel and to explore new regions.

Although most European countries are highly industrialized economies where manufacturing, agriculture and services play a balanced economic role, the ratio of tourism expenditures (revenues) to the Gross National Product is quite significant in most of them: 6.6% in Austria, 4.5% in Spain and 4.1% in Greece. The world's top tourism destinations in 1996 were France, United States, Spain, Italy and China. International tourist arrivals in France reached 61.5 million, 44.8 million in the United States, 41.3 million in Spain, 35.5 million in Italy, and 26.0 million in China.

There is a clear consensus among world tourism organizations, travel industry associations and macroeconomic consulting firms regarding the future of tourism and world travel. Steady and sustained growth is anticipated for 1997 and the foreseeable future extending to the year 2000. In a revised forecast announced mid-1996, the WTO predicts that international tourists, which amounted to 566 million in 1995, will grow to 702 million in 2000 and to 1,018 million in 2010, while tourist international expenditures will climb from $393 billion in 1995 to $526.5 billion in 2000 and $620.5 billion in 2010.

In a report entitled *International Tourism Forecast to 2005*, The Economist Intelligence Unit came to the following conclusions:

- During the period 1995-2000 world tourism measured in terms of trips, real spending or nights abroad, will grow faster than in the period 1989-1995. The latter period was negatively influenced by the 1991-1992 world economic recession.

- During the period 2000-2005 the expansion of world travel will decelerate somewhat but still remain faster than in the period 1989-1996.

- Long-haul travel to the Caribbean, which grew at an average annual rate of 6.5% during the 1989-1995 period, will accelerate to 8.2% in the period 1995-2000, reflecting a 6.3% average annual growth rate.

- During the period 1995-2000 long-haul trips to the Caribbean will grow 8.2% per year, a rate which will be surpassed only by Australia/New Zealand (11.7%) and North America (9.8%).

- The Caribbean's share of total long-haul travel will increase, mainly due to significant rise in travel from European countries, especially Austria, Germany, Italy, Spain, the Netherlands and Switzerland, this compensating for a slight decline of travel to the region from Canada and the United States.

- Longer term trends in Europe and the United States should favor continued growth of travel to the Caribbean during 2006-2010, as growing incomes and increased leisure time enlarge the pool of potential travelers.

However, the ability to capture a rising share of this growing pool of travelers will depend on continued improvement in attractions, as competing locations around the world will be vying for a larger market share.

For a country to remain competitive in the international tourist market, its public authorities and the leading components of the private sector (hotels, recreational facilities, airlines, transportation systems, advertising agencies, etc.) must adapt to the challenges of the changing macroeconomic situation, environmental and security issues, higher emphasis on total quality of tourist services, diversification of tourist products and increasing competition among countries and destinations.

Quality of tourism has become a dominant strategic element. It means improved tourism supply, better educated staff and more efficient distribution of tourism flows both in time and space. Moreover, tourism has become a carefully planned economic activity that demands inputs from all sectors of society. For instance, the French government regards tourism as a separate economic sector with all the features of an industry. This has led to a complete reorganization of tourism activities in France, oriented by three priorities: a strategy to facilitate growth of French tourist products, the implementation of a policy to support tourist enterprises and full coordination of actions abroad.

THE CUBAN ECONOMY

For the purpose of this study we address the Cuban economy only with regard to the tourism industry and its ramifications into other activities.

As a result of the demise of the Soviet Union, significant changes occurred in all the countries of the Soviet bloc in Eastern Europe. The economic support provided by the Soviet bloc to Cuba dried up, forcing the Cuban government to declare a "special period" and to change its approach to the new situation. The full employment policy could not continue without the Soviet support.

The Cuban regime saw in the development of tourism an opportunity to use an enormous labor force, qualified, but idle. Even today, Cuba's work force is 45% unemployed or under-employed. Two principal advantages of the switch to tourism as a major economic activity are: 1) the tourism product is renewed every 24 hours with minimal additional investment; and 2) tourism is a labor-intensive industry whose workers in the majority perceive directly or indirectly incentive remuneration in addition to a base wage or salary. This is a unique change in Cuba after many years of repudiation of the "gratuity" or *propina* as counter-revolutionary.

Badly needed resources were dedicated to the construction and rehabilitation of tourism installations and lodging facilities. Several joint ventures with foreign hotel companies were arranged through diplomatic channels and directly. Many *carpet baggers* flocked to take advantage of the confusion and the lack of experience of the authorities on tourism matters. The vertical reporting and decision making system of the Cuban regime, on the other hand, provoked desperation, frustration, and great expense to the bonafide business person. However, once the relationship was established and a sense of trust developed, the subsequent negotiations became quasi/normal and effective for both parties.

Tourism in 1996 surpassed the sugar industry as a source of hard currency in Cuba. This is due to the dramatic increase in activity indicators in the tourism industry and to concurrent decrease in production in the sugar industry. The 1996 total tourism revenue amounted to $1.4 billion, while hard currency receipts from the sugar industry in the same period were about $1.2 billion.

Table 1 presents Cuban Ministry of Tourism statistics on number of available hotel rooms, visitors and total annual revenue received from tourism. Cuba's performance during the 1990-1997 period regarding growth in rooms inventory, visitors, and gross tourism revenue, although all following an upward trend, grew at different rates as indicated below: 18.45% average annual increase in the number of rooms, 31.61% average annual increase in the number of visitors, and 73.53% average annual increase in gross tourism revenue. These statistics are indicative of improved performance by Cuba as a tourist destination.

There is no doubt that the Cuban regime is committed to the further development of the tourism industry. Not only is Cuba committing substantial additional funds, including contributions by joint venture partners, but is also introducing new products to diversify the supply segments in preparation to an eventual opening to new markets, including North America and this region's enormous source of tourism demand. The goal regarding availability of hotel rooms in the year 2000 of Cuba's Ministry of Tourism is 49,556 rooms.

Table 1.   Cuba: Available Rooms, Number of Visitors and Gross Annual Revenue, 1990-1997

Year	Hotel Rooms Available	Annual % Change	Visitors (in 000s)	Annual % Change	Revenue (in $000s)	Annual % Change
1990	12,866	-	340	—	243	—
1991	16,638	29	424	25	387	59
1992	18,662	12	461	9	567	46
1993	22,139	18	546	18	720	27
1994	23,254	5	619	13	850	18
1995	24,233	4	742	20	1,100	29
1996	26,878	11	1,004	35	1,400	27
Est. 1997	31,878	18	1,200	20	1,675	20
Average Annual % Change		18.45		31.61		73.53

Source: Based on statistics of the Cuban Ministry of Tourism.

FUTURE GROWTH OF TOURISM ACTIVITY IN CUBA: 1997-2007

In an effort to analyze tourism industry activity in Cuba and its impact beyond the Cuban Ministry of Tourism's goal for the year 2000, we have considered two defined scenarios.

- *First Scenario*: Assumes the continuation through the year 2007 of current political and economic system, perhaps with minor changes of minimal impact.

- *Second Scenario*: Contemplates the complete elimination of political and economic barriers, both internal and external. A free capitalistic economy where American citizens and residents as well as Cuban citizens are able to invest in, operate, visit and enjoy any of Cuba's tourism facilities and to develop any enterprise to support the tourism industry in particular, and to satisfy the growing consumer demand for better products and services.

The two scenarios are defined in more detail in an accompanying box.

Why 2007? We believe that ten years from today is far enough into the future to achieve sufficient changes to modernize the obsolete planned economy and political system where government owns and exploits all resources in the Island, including its human resources. Moreover, we chose to project ten years into the future to avoid the analysis of the numerous variables, issues, theories, and suggestions for effect-

ing changes in Cuba. This way we do not cloud the purpose and methodology of our study with political issues.

Table 2 presents a comparison of the estimated growth of tourist arrivals to the Caribbean as forecasted by the World Tourism Organization versus ours through the year 2007. Cuba's share of the visitors to the Caribbean, 7.5% in 1997, will double by the year 2007 to 15.9%. This suggests that visitors to Cuba will not only grow in terms of number of persons—to an estimated four million by the year 2007—but that Cuba will penetrate the market more intensively than its fair market share. These projections do not contemplate the opening of the U.S. market. This means that Cuba continues taping the European and Latin American markets.

The projected growth in the number of hotel rooms (Table 3) reflects the Cuban Ministry of Tourism's goal of 50,000 rooms by the year 2000. In order to achieve this goal, Cuba will have to build more than 5,000 hotel rooms each year during the years 1997 through the year 2000. Our projection of new hotel rooms through 2007 averages 2,800 hotel rooms openings per year.

The rush to create a critical mass of tourism rooms is a priority in the Cuban Ministry of Tourism's strategy. It is obvious that in recent years Cuba has experienced difficulty in obtaining long range financing due, in part, to its failure to perform timely in on-going loans. Short term financing at a higher cost is a

Definition of the Two Scenarios

First Scenario	Second Scenario
According to article 15 of the Constitution of 1992, the following are socialist state property "belonging to all people":	Any Cuban may invest, own and operate hotels and any tourism asset. The government privatizes all its tourism assets.
a The land not belonging to small farmers or to cooperatives formed by them, the subsoil, the mines, the living and non-living natural resources, existing within the maritime economic zone of the Republic, the forests, the waters and the arteries of communication;	In the privatization, a formula to create capital in the hands of the people, is able to incentivize and reinstate the concepts of saving, investing, and ownership denied to the Cubans. Otherwise, very few Cubans would be able to acquire shares of the privatized enterprises.
b The sugar mills, factories and fundamental means of transportation, all enterprises, banks and installations nationalized and expropriated from the imperialist, large landowners and the bourgeoisie, as well as factories, enterprises and economic installations; and	The State would maintain the ownership of natural resources, such as rivers, waters, forests, etc. in order to preserve the ecological balance. However, within a sustainable development plan, could grant concessions under the best conditions to private persons and entities to develop them for tourism purposes.
c Scientific, social, cultural and sport centers fomented or acquired by the State and those that it will build, foment or acquire in the future.	The role of the State will be minimal and only for necessary regulatory and policing purposes.
The property of these assets may not be transmitted to natural or juridical persons, except in the exceptional cases in which their partial or total transmission may be destined to the development of the country and do not affect the political, social and economic bases of the State, subject to the prior approval of the Council of Ministers or its Executive Committee.	
The Cuban Government is the only entity in Cuba allowed to invest, own, operate all tourism assets. Joint ventures, leases, management contracts, and other form of contracting with foreigners are permitted but only with a government entity. Cubans are not permitted to own, operate, lease, manage similar assets.	Foreigners as well as Cubans will enjoy the same rights to invest, own, lease, develop and operate tourism assets.
The Cuban Government is the only entity in Cuba that is allowed to create industries to support the tourism activity.	Any Cuban or foreign person or entity may own, develop this type of industry or commerce.
The Cuban Government is the only employer of Cubans. A foreign entity has to obtain its personnel from a government agency. This agency pays the salaries of the employees and is reimbursed by the foreign enterprise in hard currency at the official rate of US$1 to 1 peso. The employee receives only pesos.	There is freedom to contract directly any person at freely agreed compensation. Private employment agencies could facilitate hiring by providing an ethical service. Unions of any form of association will provide assistance and protection to the labor groups without any dependence or influence from the government. Salaries would be stated in a convertible currency, perhaps the Peso, therefore avoiding the present inequity.
Current U.S. legislation precludes U.S. citizens and legal residents from investing, operating, leasing or doing any remunerative activity in Cuba. Travel restrictions prohibit expending money in Cuba or limits its quantity per day. Special license needs to be obtained from the State Department to justify traveling to Cuba. Cuban community travels to Cuba under tremendous stress caused by regulations, high prices, limitation of personal gifts and donations to relatives in the island, etc.	In our ideal scenario, all restrictions, internal and external are eliminated. Free travel for U.S. citizens and residents as well as for the Cuban community permits unrestricted visits. U.S. persons and entities may invest, develop, lease, operate, franchise, or any other method of commercialization in any tourism asset or activity with minimum necessity of regulatory legislation. Rights and taxation are equal for foreign and nationals.
The taxation system is designed to discourage the independent entrepreneur. You can only succeed if you violate the law by paying off the authorities that are supposed to control and collect your taxes. Examples are: the paradores, room rentals at private homes, and the independent professional services.	Taxes are levied to cover the expenses of regulation or to promote the business activities they are collected from. The new attitude is pro-business, which eventually will increase tax revenues and benefit all participants.

problem that Cuba has to manage promptly. Table 4 presents the estimated cost of new rooms additions at the time of their opening to the tourist public. Costs are calculated based on general information of the Cuban Ministry of Tourism adjusted by inflation. The cost of new properties will increase with the improvement in the quality of such new products. The planned addition of 22,678 new rooms during the

Table 2. Estimated Number of Visitors to the Caribbean and Cuba's Market Share, 1995-2007

Year	Visitors to the Caribbean (million)	Visitors to Cuba (million)	Cuba's Market Share (%)
1995	14.7	0.742	5.0
1996	15.3	1.004	6.6
1997	16.1	1.200	7.5
1998	16.8	1.440	8.6
1999	17.6	1.730	9.8
2000	18.4	2.000	10.9
2001	19.2	2.320	12.1
2002	20.1	2.640	13.1
2003	21.1	2.950	14.0
2004	22.0	3.240	14.7
2005	23.0	3.500	15.2
2006	24.1	3.770	15.6
2007	25.2	4.000	15.9

Source: Based on World Tourism Organization, *The Miami Herald.*

period 1997-2000 will have a total estimated cost of $1.901 billion at an average annual expenditure of $475 million. For the period 2001-2007 the addition of new rooms will grow at a slower rate. The addition of 19,444 new rooms is estimated to cost $1.904 billion, which represents an annual average investment of $272 million.

Table 5 presents simulations of gross revenues and earnings of Cuban tourism activities, compared with the estimated cost to develop the planned new room additions. We beg the reader's indulgence as it is obvious that the timing of the elements and activities in the chart are not concurrent. However, the chart demonstrates that the new rooms could be financed from the cash flow produced by the existing properties. It is expected that, due to more imminent needs of funds in other economic sectors, the Cuban Government would re-invest less than the totality of the cash flow in the tourism sector. This would cause short term borrowing and increase in the final cost of future units and in the operation of the existing units. The two levels of profits are used to provide a range of "normal results" in the industry. The esti-

Table 3. Cuban Hotel Rooms: Actual 1990-1996 and Estimated 1997-2007

Year	Number of Rooms	Year-to-Year Increase	Percent Increase (%)
1990	12,866		
1991	16,638	3,772	29
1992	18,662	2,024	12
1993	22,139	3,477	18
1994	23,254	1,115	5
1995	24,233	979	4
1996	26,878	2,645	11
1997	31,878	5,000	18
1998	37,778	5,900	18
1999	46,678	5,900	16
2000	49,556	5,878	13
2001	53,000	3,444	7
2002	56,000	3,000	6
2003	59,000	3,000	5
2004	61,500	2,500	4
2005	64,000	2,500	4
2006	66,500	2,500	4
2007	69,000	2,500	4

Source: Based on data from Cuban Ministry of Tourism and *Granma International.*

Table 4. Investments in New Hotel Rooms: Estimated 1997-2007

Year of Opening	Number of New Rooms	Million US$
1997	5,000	400
1998	5,900	486
1999	5,900	501
2000	5,878	514
SUBTOTAL 1997-2000	22,678	1,901
2001	3,444	310
2002	3,000	278
2003	3,000	287
2004	2,500	246
2005	2,500	253
2006	2,500	261
2007	2,500	269
SUBTOTAL 2001-2007	19,444	1,904
TOTAL 1997-2007	33,122	3,805

Source: Based on data from Cuban Ministry of Tourism and *Granma International.*

Table 5. Estimated Cash Flow from Operation of Existing Hotel Rooms vs. Investment Requirements for New Hotel Rooms, 1997-2007 (In million U.S. dollars)

Year	Gross Operating Revenue	Estimated Profits at 25%	Estimated Profits at 20%	Annual Investment Requirement
1997	1,675	419	335[a]	400
1998	2,065	516	413[a]	486
1999	2,559	640	512	501
2000	3,046	762	609	514
2001	3,640	910	728	310
2002	4,265	1,066	853	278
2003	4,911	1,228	982	287
2004	5,555	1,389	1,111	246
2005	6,180	1,545	1,236	253
2006	6,861	1,715	1,372	261
2007	7,500	1,875	1,500	269

Source: Based on data from Cuban Ministry of Tourism, *Granma International, Business Tips on Cuba.*

a. Insufficient cash flow.

Table 6. Cuba's Estimated Tourism Statistics, Year 2007

	First Scenario	Second Scenario	Increase in Units	Increase in %
Rooms	69,000	69,000		
Annual visitors	4 million	5 million	1 million	25
Annual tourism revenue	$7.50 billion	$11.25 billion	$3.75 billion	50
Annual room nights available	25.185 million	25.185 million	-	-
Annual room nights occupied	16.798 million	21.004 million	4.206 million	25
Annual occupancy	66.7%	83.4%	16.7%	25
Average number of days of stay	4.2 days	4.2 days	-	-
Expenditure per visitor	$1,875	$2,250	$375	20
Daily expenditure per visitor	$446	$536	$90	20
Direct number of employees	138,000	103,500	-34,500	-25
Indirect number of employees	130,000	180,000	50,000	39
Total number of employees	268,000	283,500	15,500	6

mates reflect results before payment of management fees and share of profits to join venture partners.

Table 6 presents our estimate of tourism statistics in the year 2007. They have been developed under the two defined scenarios and the difference in units and percentage of each activity indicator.

MEASUREMENT OF THE ECONOMIC IMPACT OF TOURISM IN CUBA

No matter how much disagreement we may find in regards to the significance of the contribution of in-

ternational tourism strategy to the solution of Cuba's economic woes—or as to the real intentions behind such a big push—there is no doubt about the fact that Cuban authorities have made a strong, concerted effort to expand both the supply and the demand sides of the tourism market.

Since we lack the basic data to do a cost benefit analysis of Cuba's bet on international tourism as a spearhead of economic development and a substantial source of foreign exchange, at least we may identify several qualitative elements that will determine Cuba's opportunity to come out favorably in this economic adventure. Tourist expenditures generate several benefits:

- Since they are classified as exports of services, they may improve the balance of payments of the country.

- Generate revenues for the government in the form of departure taxes, hotel occupancy rates, taxes on tourist expenditures, import duties, corporate repatriation (toll-gate) taxes, and so forth.

- Expand the income and employment opportunities of local citizens and induce a multiplier effect that benefits commercial, financial, industrial and service concerns all over the economy.

- Government revenues, business and personal income and savings, generated in tourism may be used to improve infrastructure (roads, airports, telecommunications, etc.) as well as economic infrastructure for all kinds of economic activities, which in turn contributes to overall economic development.

On the other hand, the development of tourism activity requires substantial expenditures to keep abreast with competing destinations in the world economy:

- Education and training of human resources to meet the high quality service standards of international tourism.

- Promotion and publicity costs that should compete in style and quality with those of world class destinations.

- The cost of capital to develop the portion of the supply side controlled by government (hotel construction, equipment, maintenance requirements, etc.).

- Expenditures abroad to attract foreign investors and foregone government income in case that tax incentives are used to attract foreign firms.

- Environmental costs of new tourism developments. Being essentially beach oriented in the Caribbean region, the building of tourist hotels sometimes is done at the expense of prime habitat for animals, some of them endangered species, coral reefs, water tables and underground waters.

- Tourism may be accompanied by undesirable social problems such as drug traffic, illegal gambling, illegal trading of commodities and prostitution.

Several important elements could be added to the benefit and cost lists just enumerated but the essential elements have been pointed out and the research problem is quite clear: How can we develop reliable data to conduct a cost-benefit analysis of Cuba's international tourism initiative, in order to evaluate its progress so far and project its future impact?

Given the severe budgetary constrains that the Cuban government faces, especially regarding hard currency, and the frantic pace of investment in tourism infrastructure and hotel facilities, it seems to be that a substantial portion of those operations are being financed by revenues obtained from tourism, given the high priority assigned to this economic activity in the present, critical phase of the Cuban economy. Any departure from this priority, which remains a strong possibility given Cuba's awesome set of social, health and housing needs (and the strong preference for military expenditures that has characterized the Cuban government since the inception of the Revolution), may slow down the pace of investment in tourism. It is estimated that tourism activity is contributing $300-$350 million in net revenues to the Cuban government, but such calculation seems to obey accounting costs and does not take into account the social environmental cost of such activity.[2]

In her research, María Dolores Espino has developed a very important argument in regards to the multiplier effect of tourism expenditure in Cuba: the present policy of keeping the tourism activity separate from

---

2. DevTech Systems, *Cuba Monthly Economic Report* (May 1997), p. 2.

Table 7. Economic Impact of Tourism in Cuba for 2007 Estimated on the Basis of Puerto Rico's Multipliers (million U.S. dollars, except number of employees)

	First Scenario	Second Scenario	Increase
Employment Multipliers			
Gross Revenue	7,500	11,250	3,750
Direct Employment	114,225	171,337	57,112
Indirect Employment	203,320	304,979	101,659
Induced Employment	239,700	359,550	119,850
Production Multipliers			
Gross Revenue	7,500	11,250	3,750
Production Generated in the Rest of the Economy	7,650	11,475	3,825
Income Multipliers			
Type I	8,325	12,487	4,162
Type II	18,525	27,787	9,262

the rest of the economy hinders both the expansionary effect of the income (we may add *and the employment*) multiplier and discourages linkages between tourism and other industries.[3] It seems that Cuba lacks an input-output matrix that may allow to calculate reliable income and employment multiplier effects. Using data for 1988, Espino makes several mathematical calculations that lead her to the conclusion that "the total impact of tourist expenditures on the Cuban economy is probably not much larger than the direct income and employment that these expenditures create." Of course, this remains a preliminary statement until harder, much more detailed data is available. Using Puerto Rico's employment, production and income multipliers for tourism hotels,[4] derived from the 1982 input-output table, the impact of economic impacts of the two scenarios can be calculated. As is clear from Table 7, the differences in the two scenarios is vast in all categories, with the second scenario providing much more positive results.

The cost of Cuba's tourism is very difficult to quantify, given the lack of specific, item by item, figures. Cuba has developed hotel and hospitality training schools, has invested substantially in international promotion and publicity campaigns, especially in Canada and several European countries, and has established at least 20 mixed enterprises and several joint ventures with foreign companies to develop tourism facilities. The broad, vague figures that Cuban authorities use to describe their strategic actions should not be taken at face value, but they are the only information available, unless further research discovers ways to gather more detailed and trustworthy information.

Environmental costs are difficult to calculate even in open, democratic societies, where sometimes both the government and private companies share the same nondisclosure tactics. We may guess that international environmental organizations making research in Cuba may come out with information about the environmental cost of developing tourism

---

3. María Dolores Espino, "International Tourism in Cuba: An Economic Development Strategy?" In *Cuba in Transition*, p. 216. Miami: Florida International University, 1991.

4. The production multiplier indicates how much production (defined as intermediate plus final sales) is needed to satisfy one dollar of final demand concerning any industry included in the input-output matrix. The employment multiplier shows the direct and indirect employment generated in the economy for each direct employment created in a particular sector or industry. The income multiplier shows the direct and indirect income generated by a unit of final deman required from a particular sector.

activity at the apparently unsustainable rate that Cuba has been following lately.

Finally, the social cost of tourism have been widely discussed be Gert Oostindie,[5] Jaime Suchlicki,[6] and other researchers and some policy statements by Cuban government officials show a deep concern for the socially undesirable effects of economic dualism, which clearly discriminates against persons not having access to dollars and depresses the incentive to work of persons locked in the traditional socialist sector of the economy.

In sum, the economic assessment of Cuba's international tourism strategy is a major task that faces nearly impossible obstacles, but should be a top priority in any research of the economic future of the country. On the basis of available information, there is no way of telling if the strategy is going to prevail in the future, but it is quite obvious that the Cuban government has engaged in a high risk but potentially rewarding business adventure. The short-run success of the strategy so far seems to be based on low prices, given the low salaries prevailing in Cuba, but such competitive advantage may gradually disappear in the future if local economic conditions improve and workers begin to demand higher benefits for their efforts. In the long-run, Cuba will need to upgrade significantly the quality of its tourism services and facilities in order to remain competitive in the tourism market, even if it retains some degree of cost advantage in regards to salaries and wages.

International tourism is a major accelerator of economic and political change and an effective promoter of knowledge about other cultures. In the long-run, Cuba's enclave approach to tourism may become a limiting factor, especially if other types of tourism activity—ecotourism, cultural tourism and adventure tourism—which have been highly successful in many other Caribbean destinations, are adopted as strategies to boost tourism expenditures. Such new trends require wider closer interactions of tourists with the local social and cultural environments, which will translate into much higher income and employment multiplier effects that will increase the economic returns of tourism for the Cuban government and for the population in general. If economic rationality prevails, the future development of tourism in Cuba may be not only a spearhead of economic development and significant source of foreign exchange, but also influence in the promotion of political change towards the free exchange of ideas and democracy,

SUMMARY HIGHLIGHTS

A market assessment and economic impact analysis identified key factors about Cuba's competitive market position, forecast of future hotel supply and demand trends, and economic impact of tourism in Cuba. The forecast results contained herein are solely the product of the author and participants in the study and is significantly based on official information derived from publications and the Cuban Ministry of Tourism. In this study we only compare two economic scenarios limiting ourselves to the minimum in our critique of the official data and activity indicators that are neither consistent nor reliable.

The number of tourist arrivals to Cuba increased by 262,300, or 35%, between 1995 and 1996, to a total of 1,004,000 in 1996. The Cuban Ministry of Tourism estimates an increase of 196,000 in 1997 to a total of 1,200,000 visitors, which represents an increase of 20% over the previous year. Furthermore, by the year 2000 the official estimate of visitors at 2,000,000 represents a 20% annual increment in the number of tourist arrivals. Our estimates and professional experience indicate that by the year 2007, Cuba will double its number of tourist arrivals and will reach the 4,000,000 level.

Total visitor expenditures in 1996 at $1.4 billion, increased $300 million, or 27 percent over 1995. Total visitor expenditures for 1997 is estimated at $1.675 billion by the Cuban Ministry of Tourism. Accord-

---

5. Gert Oostindie, "A Loss of Purpose: Crisis and Transition in Cuba," paper presented at the 1995 Utrecht University Conference entitled *Societies of Fear*, 34 pages.

6. Jaime Suchlicki, "Cuba: A Current Assessment" (1997).

ing to the study results, we projected visitor expenditures to grow to $3.046 billion in the year 2000 and $7.5 billion in the year 2007.

According to official estimates, 68,000 visitors seek accommodations in private homes in a semi-clandestine way. While this practice is legitimate in other countries, the Cuban authorities consider it as "unfair competition against the hotels" and has initiated a tax system that may eliminate many of the underground hoteliers. Another entrepreneur that is opposed by the authorities and might be soon listed within the endangered species is the *buquenque*, an intermediary, ad lib travel agent, or broker that procures clients to the private homes. Although it is estimated that these activities represents about $20 million, we are not considering them significant enough to affect our estimates and calculations.

We consider that Cuban citizen residing in Cuba have no significant impact in the growth of participants or users of the tourism facilities. Under the first scenario they will continue being excluded from the tourism facilities as they are today.

The hotel room supply in Cuba, particularly in the tourism sector, increased by 2,645 new hotel rooms in 1996, or 11%, to a total of 26,878. For 1997 the Cuban Ministry of Tourism is planning to develop 5,000 new hotel rooms. This effort, if sustained, would make a reality of the Ministry's goal of operating 50,000 hotel rooms by the year 2000. An average of 5,900 new hotel rooms per year would need to be constructed between 1997 and the year 2000 in order to meet this ambitious goal. We estimate that an annual average of 2,500 to 3,000 new hotel rooms will result in an inventory of approximately 69,000 hotel rooms in the year 2007.

To calculate the average hotel occupancy in Cuba from the official activity indicators is a difficult task. Our review of a substantial number of official documents, publications, speeches, press releases, etc. do not reveal reliable national data. Only the individual hotel enterprises publish sporadic data, mainly when it is good news. The properties operated by recognized quality international operators normally enjoy occupancies ranging between 75 and 90 percent, and

in a few cases even higher. Our best professional estimate indicates that at a national level, occupancies have been approximated 64% in 1987, 73% in 1995, and 75% in 1997. These occupancy rates will decrease as a result of the aggressive new hotel room construction announced by the Cuban Ministry of Tourism. They will level off after this construction fever subsides. In our annual projections through year 2007 we assumed occupancy rates of 66.7%.

The gross cost of development of a new hotel room in the four and five star category was estimated by the Cuban Ministry of Tourism at US$80,000. This is a moderate figure by international standards, particularly in resort locations. Our estimate of the investment required to meet the planned increase of hotel rooms inventory goal of 50,000 rooms in the year 2000 amounts to $1.9 billion. This represents an increase of 22,678 hotel rooms during the period 1996-2000. In addition, our estimate of growth for the period 2000-2007 at 10,444 new hotel rooms requires an additional $1.9 billion of investment.

The Government of Cuba is becoming one of the largest hotel owning companies in the world. Without analyzing Cuba's motivations and peculiar foreign investor arrangements and its labor, political, and social ambiguities, it seems to be able to continue supporting its tourism industry growth. With a current base of 174 hotels and 26,878 hotel rooms it seems to be able to produce enough cash flow to support the ambitious development program, as it is shown in this paper.

Comparing the current situation with a hypothetical second scenario that contemplates a free enterprise economic system where Cubans as well as any foreign national have equal rights to travel, use the tourism facilities, own, invest, manage, or any other form of economic activity, without internal or external restrictions, we can reach the following conclusions:

• Cuba, by maintaining its present socialist political and economic system is shortchanging the Cuban people from the opportunity to invest and benefit from the exploitation of its national resources. The monopolistic system precludes, the Cuban people from enjoying and benefiting from the economic multipliers and their ripple effect that their work might create.

- This situation is critical in the tourism industry because of its particular intensive labor characteristics.

- Our analysis of the tourism activity indicators for 2007 and a simulation using the Common-

wealth of Puerto Rico's income and employment multipliers demonstrate a substantial lack of economic benefits in the tourism activity in Cuba when we compare the two scenarios.

To conclude, by maintaining the status quo, Cuba is reducing its potential gain from international tourism by at least several million U.S. dollars per day.

REFERENCES AND CREDITS

Cuban Ministry of Tourism

Granma and *Granma International*

Business Tips on Cuba

Prensa Latina

World Tourism Organization

Phoenix Hospitality and Consulting Corporation

Cuban Society of Tourism Professionals

The Economic Planning Group of Canada

The Miami Herald

Executives of foreign hotel companies operating in Cuba

Former functionaries of the tourism activity in Cuba

Non-U.S. hospitality industry executives

Andre Mas, France

Pablo Sanz, Spain

Carlo Miroglio, Italy

Charles Suddaby, Canada

Nicolas Behard, United Kingdom

Also special thanks to Rita

TRANSICION Y RECUPERACION ECONOMICA EN CUBA

Gerardo González

El tema de la transición en Cuba ha ocupado un lugar prominente en la cubanología a partir del desencadenamiento de la crisis económica en la isla y de los procesos de reconversión capitalista en Europa Oriental. Desde entonces se han sucedido innumerables análisis sobre las circunstancias, la orientación y el momento específico en que el cambio debe ocurrir.

Más allá de cualquier afinidad ideológica y a pesar de la obstinación del liderazgo cubano a rechazar la posibilidad de una transición, hay que reconocer que los cambios que se han dado en el contexto nacional e internacional obligan a Cuba a producir una profunda transformación sistémica de su ordenamiento económico, político y social como condición para colocar al país en la senda del desarrollo económico y la prosperidad. Para que esta tranformación—independientemente de su orientación—pueda tener lugar sin grandes traumas sociales y alcance sus objetivos debe partir de un proceso de recuperación que revierta la crisis económica y logre reestablecer los equilibrios macroeconómicos.

Los resultados económicos que el país comenzó a exhibir desde 1995 han sido tomados con mucho optimismo tanto por el gobierno de la isla como por observadores extranjeros, al considerarlos como el inicio de la recuperación económica.[1] Este trabajo pretende dar una lectura diferente al significado de los resultados alcanzados y tratará de demostrar cuán lejos está el país de la recuperación económica, así como enumerar y analizar sucintamente cuales son—a nuestro criterio—las condiciones y metas necesarias que deben alcanzarse para que la recuperación sea un hecho irreversible.

RECUPERACION ECONOMICA: OBJETIVOS Y CONDICIONES

La literatura económica se ha referido a la recuperación como el proceso a través del cual se reestablece la capacidad de acumulación de un país, es decir, supone la paulatina utilización máxima de las fuerzas productivas,[2] la mejoría de las condiciones para la inversión y la realización, la utilización máxima de las capacidades productivas instaladas y en general el progresivo reestablecimiento de los equilibrios macroeconómicos.[3] Si bien es un concepto ampliamente

---

1. Carlos Lage, "Intervención en la segunda reunión con los dirigentes de las entidades que operan en divisas," *Granma* (12 de diciembre de 1996).

2. Las fuerzas productivas es el conjunto formado por la fuerza de trabajo, los medios de trabajo (bienes de capital y herramientas) y los objetos de trabajo.

3. Los análisis sobre las crisis y las recuperaciones o expansiones económicas son tan antiguos como el propio capitalismo, en definitiva, el objeto de estudio de la mayoría de dichos análisis, dado que ha sido la formación socioeconómica predominante y porque el sistema socialista no había experimentado crisis económicas de las características de la cubana que pudieran servir para un esfuerzo teorizador, sin negar la existencia de relevantes análisis sobre la naturaleza y funcionamiento de los modelos económicos en los países socialistas. Para tener una aproximación más cercana al debate sobre la crisis y la recuperación se deben consultar: Samin Amin y otros, *Dinámica de la crisis global* (México: Siglo XXI, 1983); Rosa Luxemburgo, *La acumulación de capital*, (Barcelona: Editorial Grijalbo, 1978) y Ernest Mandel, *El capitalismo tardío* (México: Editorial ERA, 1979).

aceptado y aplicable a cualquier realidad económica, no es menos cierto que está referido únicamente a una noción cuantitativa del problema de la crisis, es decir, se refiere a la posibilidad de reestablecer el *crecimiento económico*, obviando dimensiones cualitativas que son abarcadas en el concepto de *desarrollo económico*.

Desarrollo económico es un concepto mucho más vasto que el de crecimiento al vincular la expansión de la base material con el *bienestar* de la población, ya que además de considerar el desarrollo de la acumulación productiva, entendido como el *progreso* de las fuerzas productivas que permite el crecimiento de los bienes y servicios, incluye un cambio institucional—calificado como *modernización*—y una adecuada política distributiva, que corresponden al aspecto cualitativo del concepto. Dicho en pocas palabras, el crecimiento económico es una condición necesaria pero no suficiente para alcanzar el desarrollo, el cual implica *modernización, progreso y bienestar*.[4] La dinámica entre crecimiento y desarrollo supone que el primero debe ser sostenido y sustentable, lo cual es sinónimo de economía estructuralmente sólida, menos vulnerable a cambios en el mercado mundial.

Las circunstancias, características y duración de la crisis cubana obligan a plantear el problema de la recuperación desde la perspectiva del concepto de desarrollo económico.

La crisis económica cubana es el resultado de una crisis estructural y de una crisis de inserción. Es una crisis estructural porque las actuales estructuras económicas son incapaces de garantizar la reproducción ampliada de la economía,[5] a pesar de los esfuerzos desarrollados por el gobierno para provocar una diversificación productiva que se ajustara a las necesidades de la acumulación y a las exigencias de la economía internacional contemporánea. La dimensión estructural de la crisis se refleja, igualmente, en el agotamiento del modelo de desarrollo por vía extensiva que ha prevalecido hasta entonces, que se expresa en la incapacidad de la economía de generar el ahorro necesario para garantizar su reproducción, lo cual obliga al país a invertir una proporción creciente de recursos, mayormente externos, para obtener los mismos resultados en la producción. Cuando hablamos entonces de una dimensión estructural de la crisis estamos reconociendo la existencia de causas internas en su generación.

La crisis cubana tiene a su vez una dimensión exógena—crisis de inserción—derivada de la pérdida de su principal partner: la Unión Soviética y el campo socialista europeo en general. Desde entonces, Cuba no ha podido estabilizar un nuevo sistema de relaciones económicas externas. Un agravante en los esfuerzos por buscar alternativas de inserción en el mercado mundial ha sido el reforzamiento de las expresiones internacionalizadoras del bloqueo o embargo norteamericano.[6]

Por lo tanto, la economía se enfenta al reto de buscar su viabilidad como consecuencia de la pérdida de sus mercados concesionarios que precipitó la crisis del modelo de desarrollo por vía extensiva. El reto exigía, en primera instancia, un ajuste de la economía a las nuevas circunstancias para pasar a la construcción de un nuevo modelo de desarrollo económico que se basara en la eficiencia y en la competitividad (acumulación por vía intensiva) y que garantizara la reinserción de la economía en un mercado mundial que es mucho más exigente sobre todo para el mundo subdesarrollado y para el caso concreto de Cuba, ade-

---

4. El debate sobre los conceptos de desarrollo y crecimiento ha sido muy extenso. Para una mejor aproximación a las distintas posiciones en torno a estos conceptos se deben leer: G. Myrdal, *Teoría económica y regiones subdesarrolladas* (México: Fondo de Cultura Económica, 1962); A. Gunder Frank, *El subdesarrollo del desarrollo* (Madrid: IEPALA, 1991); y M. Blomström y B. Hettne, *La teoría del desarrollo económico en transición*, (México: Fondo de Cultura Económica, 1990).

5. Por reproducción ampliada nos referimos al proceso de acumulación productiva y a la satisfacción de las necesidades crecientes de la población.

6. Para un mejor análisis del diagnóstico de la crisis, cfr. Gerardo González, "Cuba y el mercado mundial," en Jorge Rodríguez Beruff (comp.), *Cuba en Crisis* (San Juan: Universidad de Puerto Rico, 1995) y Julio Carranza, "Cuba: los retos de la economía," en *Cuadernos de Nuestra América*, No. 19 (julio-diciembre de 1992).

más, sin solidaridades y con un entorno de hostilidad por parte de la principal potencia mundial.

Sin embargo, la percepción y actuación del liderazgo cubano frente a la crisis ha sido diferente. Consideran que la fuente de la crisis es solamente externa y a la reinserción de Cuba en el sistema económico internacional como un acto exclusivamente de política exterior y no como el resultado de profundos cambios económicos internos. De esta forma han confiado en una recuperación económica basada solamente en la combinación de medidas de ajustes interno, reformas no sistémicas y medios políticos e ideológicos. Sólo decidieron aplicar algunas transformaciones emprendedoras cuando la crisis llegó a niveles intolerables y amenazaba con convertirse en una crisis social y política.

En resumen, el gobierno cubano ha tratado de enfrentar la crisis sin abandonar el proyecto socialista, instrumentando políticas reactivas, no sistémicas y sin una lógica coherente. Han sido políticas reactivas porque fueron tomadas sólo cuando la situación económica fue extremadamente crítica y como respuesta a acontecimientos producidos, particularmente de carácter político. No han sido sistémicas y sin una lógica coherente debido a lo anterior y porque no responden a un programa estratégico explícitamente formulado.[7]

La renuencia a enfrentar la crisis acorde a sus causas gestoras y obviando los cambios políticos y económicos que se han dado en el contexto internacional ha prolongado excesivamente la misma, provocando el agotamiento de las fuerzas productivas, principalmente la fuerza de trabajo y los bienes de capital.

La fuerza de trabajo se encuentra desmotivada laboralmente desde el momento que ha sufrido un deterioro significativo de su nivel de vida y observa que su esfuerzo laboral no es suficiente para garantizar su reproducción y la de su familia, por lo que ha tenido que adoptar soluciones individuales como pasar a puestos de trabajo de mayor remuneración pero con exigencias técnicas por debajo de su preparación o emigrar al reconocer que las mayores posibilidades de prosperidad económica y movilidad social se encuentran en los ámbitos externos.

Los bienes de capital han ido sufriendo una depreciación moral, no solamente por la obselencia tecnológica de muchas de las plantas industriales, sino también por la poca explotación que han tenido en los últimos años dada la carencia de los recursos productivos, piezas de repuestos, etc, necesarios para su funcionamiento.

Es evidente que a medida que pase el tiempo, la crisis económica va dejando huellas indelebles e imponiendo la necesidad de transformaciones más profundas. De la misma forma que un enfermo de cáncer no se puede curar con sedantes, la recuperación económica no será posible con medidas parciales y sin una visión integral de la economía. Por lo tanto, la recuperación es un complejo proceso que abarca la estabilización macroeconómica y una reestructuración de la economía, la cual debe emprenderse paralelamente al proceso de búsqueda de la estabilización y ser el resultado de un conjunto de medidas y políticas coherentes, de aplicación secuencial y con una visión sistémica (integral) de la economía que tenga en cuenta las causas estructurales y de inserción que originaron la crisis, que tienda a resolver las desproporciones macroeconómicas existentes y propicie un crecimiento y desarrollo por vía intensiva, es decir, con altos niveles

---

7. La despenalización del uso de las divisas, la expansión del auto empleo y la creación de las Unidades Básicas de Producción Cooperativa (UBPC) fueron en respuesta a las manifestaciones de descontento social que se produjeron en la capital en el verano de 1993. La liberalización del mercado agropecuario y de productos industriales, el lanzamiento y aplicación de un sistema tributario, la eliminación de algunas gratuidades y el incremento de los precios de algunos productos fueron en reacción al incremento de los signos evidentes de descontento social que tuvieron su máxima expresión en los sucesos del 5 de agosto de 1994 y en la crisis de los balseros. Todo ello como resultado de un agravamiento de la crisis cuya mayor expresión fueron los pobres resultados obtenidos en las zafras azucareras de 1993 y 1994.

de eficiencia y productividad.[8] Dicha reestructuración debe llevar implícito el diseño de un nuevo modelo de desarrollo económico que exprese nuevas formas de concebir, conducir y organizar la economía.

Igualmente, la meta de la recuperación no puede estar fijada en los niveles existentes en los años precrisis. En aquellos momentos el país disfrutaba de una relativa bonanza y estabilidad económica sustentadas fundamentalmente por los cuantiosos recursos provenientes del campo socialista europeo que garantizaban a su vez el funcionamiento del modelo económico extensivo. Aún en esas condiciones el ideal del bienestar de la población no había sido alcanzado al permanecer muchas necesidades sin satisfacer. Por lo tanto, las aspiraciones de la recuperación tienen que estar ajustadas a las nuevas realidades doméstica y externa a las que Cuba se enfrenta y ser compatibles con las necesidades tanto nacionales como personales del sujeto económico y social cubano.

LOS RESULTADOS ECONOMICOS[9]

A diferencia del pálido crecimiento económico de 1994 que fué básicamente inflacionario y garantizado por una determinada reanimación de algunos servicios no productivos, el crecimiento de 1995 y 1996 tuvo un componente más sólido ya que fue el resultado de un comportamiento favorable en diversos sectores productivos. Algunos de estos resultados fueron (Tablas 1 y 2):

- Las actividades agrícolas reportaron un crecimiento acumulado de 21.5% en relación a 1994. La producción con mejores resultados fue el tabaco con un incremento en los dos años del 82%

respecto a 1994. Las viandas y hortalizas mostraron igualmente resultados alentadores, con crecimientos sostenidos hasta alcanzar en 1996 un nuevo record de producción con 2.2 millones de toneladas.[10]

- El sector industrial creció acumuladamente un 14.2% a pesar del desplome de la zafra azucarera de 1995. Una de las producciones que más creció fue la del níquel con un total acumulado del 95.1%, y un nivel de producción en 1996 de 55,800 toneladas superior a la cifra más alta alcanzada en los años precrisis que fue de 46,592 toneladas en 1989.

- La generación de electricidad creció un 7% logrando cerrar 1996 con una potencia eléctrica disponible del 62%.

- El turismo continuó su paso ascendente generando ingresos superiores a los mil millones de dólares.

- Las exportaciones crecieron un 53% y las importaciones un 55%.

Los resultados mencionados muestran que, al menos, se detuvo la caída en espiral de la economía cubana, pero están lejos de confirmar que son el inicio de la recuperación económica. Las razones son las siguientes:

1. Como se observa en la Tabla 3, el crecimiento alcanzado estuvo sustentado básicamente en el comportamiento de dos sectores: el comercio, restaurantes y hoteles, cuyo dinamismo está basa-

---

8. Para una mejor aproximación a las cuestiones de la coherencia, integralidad y secuencialidad de la reestructuración, cfr. Julio Carranza, Luis Gutiérrez y Pedro Monreal, *Cuba: La reestructuración de la economía. Una propuesta para el debate* (La Habana: Editorial de Ciencias Sociales, 1995).

9. El análisis de la evolución de la economía cubana es una tarea muy compleja dada la poca disponibilidad de datos, las dudas que existen sobre su confiabilidad y las contradicciones que existen entre las diferentes fuentes, por lo que siempre va a existir la posibilidad de un margen de error. En este trabajo aceptamos el reto al basarnos en las estadísticas oficiales y asumir que las mismas son confiables, ya que discutir su veracidad implicaría otro artículo.

10. La información de la producción de viandas y hortalizas es un ejemplo de las contradicciones en las cifras sobre el estado de la economía cubana, que se dan, incluso, en las esferas oficiales. Según el informe sobre los resultados económicos de 1996 brindado por José L. Rodríguez, Ministro de Economía y Planificación, al Parlamento a finales de diciembre del propio año la producción de viandas y hortalizas fue de 2 millones 200 mil toneladas (es la que brindamos en nuestro trabajo), sin embargo, 3 semanas después salió un artículo en *Granma Internacional* (14 de enero de 1997) sobre la producción agropecuaria basado en una entrevista realizada al viceministro de agricultura Alcides López que señalaba que la producción de viandas y hortalizas en 1996 fue de 1 millón 700 mil toneladas.

Tabla 1. Estadísticas Seleccionadas de Cuba

	1989	1990	1991	1992	1993	1994	1995	1996
Producto Interno Bruto (millones dólares)	19585.8	19008.3	16975.8	15009.9	12776.7	12868.3	13185.0	14213.4
PIB (% crecimiento)	0.7	-2.9	-10.7	-11.6	-14.9	0.7	2.5	7.8
Exportaciones (millones dólares)	5399.2	5415.0	2961.5	1780.0	1136.9	1314.2	1577.0	2097.4
Importaciones (millones dólares)	8139.7	7416.6	4149.0	2236.0	2037.6	1956.1	2660.0	3545.8
Cantidad Turistas (miles)	326	340	422	460	544	817	740	1000
Ingresos Turismo (millones dólares)	...	189.0	290.0	530.0	720.0	850.0	1100.0	1400.0
Déficit Fiscal (millones pesos)	1390.0	1958.0	3765.0	4869.0	5050.6	1421.4	775.0	570.01[a]
Oferta Monetaria (millones pesos)	4163.0	4986.0	6663.0	8361.0	11044.0	9939.7	9062.0	9250.0

... Datos no disponibles

Fuentes: Informes sobre los resultados económicos de 1995 y 1996 presentados al Parlamento cubano por José L. Rodriguez, Ministro de Economía y Planificación, *Granma* (27 de diciembre de 1995) y *Granma Internacional* (2 de enero de 1997); CEPAL, "Cuba: Evolución Económica durante 1995" (3 de junio de 1996).

a.   Cifra estimada

Tabla 2. Algunos Indicadores de Producción

	Generación de electricidad GWH	Cemento Millones Ton.	Níquel Toneladas	Azúcar Millones Ton.	Viandas Miles Ton.	Hortalizas Miles Ton.	Cítricos Miles Ton.
1990	15,025	3.3	41,100	8.0	410.0	193.2	1,016.0
1991	13,247	1.8	33,900	7.6	419.0	196.9	826.0
1992	11,538	1.1	32,500	7.0	507.8	206.1	787.0
1993	11,004	1.0	30,200	4.3	388.2	156.4	644.0
1994	11,967	1.1	26,900	4.0	338.6	128.8	505.0
1995	12,589	1.4	42,693	3.3	1,219.0	469.8	573.6
1996[a]	13,218	....	55,800	4.5	1,568.0	610.3	....

... Datos no disponibles

Fuentes: Las mismas de la Tabla 1.

a.   Cifras preliminares

do principalmente en la actividad turística, con una participación alrededededor del 23% del Producto Interno Bruto (PIB) y el manufacturero que representa entre el 26% y el 27% del PIB. Pero dentro de este sector, la industria azucarera tiene una participación cercana al 25%, equivalente a cerca del 10% del PIB. Ello significa, que las posibilidades de crecimiento y desarrollo del país dependen de bases muy débiles ya que una caída del precio del azúcar, una recesión mundial o algún desastre natural podrían revertir la tendencia expansionista de la economía.

2.   Por otra parte, Cuba posee una ventaja contable que le posibilita reflejar niveles no despreciables del PIB. En el cálculo del PIB se incluyen activi-

dades como la educación, la salud pública, el deporte, la cultura, el arte, los servicios comunales y otros servicios personales, además de computar exclusivamente su valor agregado, uno de cuyos principales componentes es el salario. En Cuba estas actividades emplean a cerca del 30% de la fuerza laboral cubana y en algunas de ellas (educación y salud, por ejemplo) se pagan altos salarios de acuerdo a los estándares cubanos. Ello implica que si bien no son sectores con posibilidades de altos crecimientos, ayudan a garantizar de una manera estable entre un 20% y un 27% del PIB.

3.   El crecimiento logrado entre 1994 y 1996 ha sido sobre bases extensivas, es decir, con la utili-

Tabla 3. Producto Interno Bruto por Actividad Económica
(precios constantes de 1981)

	1990 Millones de Pesos	%	1993 Millones de Pesos	%	1994 Millones de Pesos	%	1995 Millones de Pesos	%	1996 Millones de Pesos
Producto Interno Bruto	19,008.3	100	12,776.7	100	12,868.3	100	13,185.0	100	14,213.4
Agricultura, caza, silvicultura y pesca	1,756.3	9.2	924.9	7.2	879.4	6.8	915.5	6.9	...
Explotación de minas y canteras	91.6	0.5	96.4	0.8	97.5	0.8	152.1	1.2	...
Industria manufacturera	4,640.2	24.4	3,103.61	24.3	3,340.6	26.0	3555.7	27.0	4,306.0a
Construcción	1,508.1	7.9	385.7	3.0	383.9	3.0	412.1	3.1	...
Electricidad, gas y agua	454.6	2.4	335.2	2.6	350.0	2.7	384.2	2.9	
Transporte, almacenamiento y comunicaciones	1,202.3	6.3	733.3	5.7	708.7	5.5	748.4	5.7	...
Comercio, restaurantes y hoteles	4,936.3	26.0	2,936.4	23.0	2,935.2	22.8	2984.8	22.6	...
Establecimientos financieros, bienes inmuebles y servicios a empresas	603.2	3.2	513.4	4.1	492.4	3.8	483.8	3.7	...
Servicios comunales, sociales y personales	3,815.7	20.1	3,747.8	29.3	3,680.6	28.6	3548.4	26.9	...

... Datos no disponibles

Fuentes: Las mismas de la Tabla 1.

a. Cifra preliminar

zación masiva de recursos en detrimento de mayores niveles de eficiencia. Ello pudiera demostrarse con la desproporción entre el incremento de las importaciones en relación con las exportaciones, que resultó en una ampliación del desequilibrio financiero externo. Ciertamente, la recesión económica obliga a la utilización de cuantiosos recursos materiales y financieros para revertir la tendencia, pero no tenemos información para valorar que nivel de las importaciones responden a esa necesidad lógica y cuanto a manejo ineficiente de la economía. Sin embargo, el dato de que en 1996 el consumo de energéticos creció un 24%, es decir, 3 veces más que el crecimiento de la economía, puede ayudar a mostrar las debilidades de dicha expansión.[11]

4. El primer peldaño para iniciar y consolidar un proceso de recuperación económica es la estabilización macroeconómica que se logra con la solución del desequilibrio financiero interno median-

te la reducción del exceso de oferta monetaria, la recuperación del poder de compra del peso cubano y el incremento de la oferta de bienes y servicios. Como veremos a continuación, esta problemática no ha sido superada.

¿CUAN LEJOS ESTA LA ESTABILIZACION MACROECONOMICA?

Uno de los graves problemas que ha tenido la economía desde el inicio de la crisis ha sido el exceso de liquidez acumulada (exceso de oferta monetaria) originado por el desbalance entre los ingresos y gastos de la población, que ha generado, entre otras consecuencias, la pérdida del interés por el trabajo en la fuerza laboral cubana.

La liquidez comprende tanto el ahorro monetario en banco como el que tiene la población a su disposición físicamente, es decir, el que está en circulación. Ambos representan la posibilidad real de la población para enfrentar cualquier tipo de gasto. En las condiciones cubanas, ese dinero rota en ciclos que comien-

11. "Informe sobre los resultados económicos de 1996" presentado al Parlamento cubano por José L. Rodríguez, Ministro de Economía y Planificación, *Granma Internacional* (2 de enero de 1997).

Tabla 4. Comportamiento de la Oferta Monetaria

	1989	1990	1991	1992	1993	1994	1995	1996
Oferta Monetaria (MMP)	4163.0	4986.0	6663.0	8361.0	11044.0	9939.7	9062.0	9250.0
Rotación (Veces)	4.7	3.8	2.5	1.8	1.2	1.3	1.5	1.5
Rotación (Días)	77	96	146	203	304	281	243	243

Fuentes: Las mismas de la Tabla 1.

za con la salida de las arcas del Estado en forma de diferentes tipos de ingresos: salarios, pagos por seguridad y asistencia social, pagos por la producción a los campesinos cooperativizados o independientes y otros y después regresa al Estado a través de la adquisición de bienes y servicios y otras formas recaudatorias.[12]

Para garantizar un funcionamiento normal de la economía la estabilización macroeconómica requiere llevar la oferta monetaria a un nivel equivalente al 30% de los ingresos anuales de la población, que de acuerdo a las condiciones en los años precrisis, representaría un poco más de 3 mil 500 millones de pesos. Es decir, esa cifra posibilita que el dinero rote al menos nueve meses al año y el ciclo transcurrido para que entre y salga de las arcas del Estado no deba exceder los 43 días. Por lo tanto, teniendo en cuenta lo acumulado al cierre de 1996 habría que extraer de la circulación algo más de 5 mil 700 de millones de pesos. Ello se puede lograr por dos vías no excluyentes: el incremento de la oferta de bienes y servicios y el uso de palancas fiscales, de precios y el control de gastos.

La segunda vía fue la opción exclusiva de política que adoptó el gobierno cubano para el saneamiento de las finanzas internas y que posibilitó que entre mayo de 1994 (momento de mayor liquidez acumulada) y diciembre de 1995 se extrajeran de la circulación más de 2 mil 800 millones de pesos.[13] Sin embargo, a partir de 1995 estas medidas comenzaron a mostrar signos de agotamiento como mecanismo de eliminación del desequilibrio financiero interno ya que cerca del 60% del exceso de oferta monetaria extraída de la circulación entre 1994 y 1995 se debió al aumento de la oferta y de los precios de los cigarros, tabaco y bebidas alcohólicas, productos que han disminuído su demanda en la población, por ejemplo, la venta de cigarros bajó de 16.8 millones de paquetes mensuales en el segundo semestre de 1994 a 7.3 millones en 1995 y 4.5 millones en 1996.[14] Todo ello ha dado como resultado que 1996 cerrara con un incremento ligeramente superior de la liquidez acumulada en comparación con igual período de 1995, tal y como lo refleja la Tabla 4.

El control de gasto fue parte de la política desplegada para disminuir el exceso de oferta monetaria y que llevó al déficit presupuestario a 570 millones de pesos en 1996 después de haber alcanzado más de 5 mil millones de pesos en 1993, donde la partida de *subsidios por pérdidas a las empresas* fue la que más se redujo: de cerca de 5 mil 500 millones de pesos en 1993 a casi 1 mil 400 millones de pesos en 1996. Sin embargo, no parece ser que dicho esfuerzo haya tenido el impacto esperado, lo cual demuestra que la solución

---

12. Recordemos que en Cuba el Estado es el gran empleador con el 97% de la fuerza laboral ocupada, por lo que la gran mayoría de la población depende de los ingresos provenientes de dicha fuente. Además, como no existe un sistema impositivo suficientemente abarcador y estructurado, la vía virtualmente exclusiva que el Estado posee para captar el dinero de la circulación es a través de la venta de bienes y servicios. En una economía de mercado, la institución que se toma en cuenta como punto de partida y de llegada para medir el nivel de rotación del dinero es el banco (ya sea privado o estatal) que es en definitiva el depositario de dicho dinero.

13. En mayo de 1994 había una liquidez acumulada de alrededor 12 mil millones de pesos, equivalente a un ciclo de rotación de un año de duración y a 18 meses de salario.

14. Una combinación de altos precios, priorización de los gastos por parte de los consumidores, una campaña nacional antitabaquismo y una ley bajo estudio que prevee limitar el espacio a los fumadores hacen pensar en una reducción mayor en el consumo de esos productos no esenciales. "Desenfrenada la liquidez del peso en Cuba" por Carlos Batista de la Agencia France Press en La Habana, *El Nuevo Día*, Puerto Rico (26 de marzo de 1997).

del problema de la liquidez acumulada no puede ser viable con medidas parciales, sino como resultado de políticas integradas y sustentadas en una concepción sistémica del problema.

La pérdida del poder de compra del peso cubano está vinculada al aumento del exceso de oferta monetaria, por lo que la reducción de la liquidez acumulada que se alcanzó en 1994 y 1995 contribuyó a detener la pérdida del valor de compra de la moneda nacional y revalorizarla en algo, uno de cuyos indicadores para medirlo es la tasa de cambio. Si tenemos en cuenta que en agosto de 1994 llegó a estar en una relación de 1.00 USD=150.00 pesos cubanos, lo alcanzado en 1995 y 1996 es alentador pero quizás aún insuficiente de lo que la economía requiere para su estabilización (Tabla 5). Decimos "quizás aún insuficiente" basado en una observación empírica porque a pesar del incremento de las posibilidades de compra en moneda nacional con las medidas de liberalización del mercado adoptadas a partir de 1993, todavía sigue siendo el dólar la moneda que garantiza la satisfacción de las necesidades básicas de la población. Además, un problema a resolver es determinar cual debe ser el poder de compra mínimo que debe alcanzar el peso en las nuevas condiciones para que permita estimular el interés por el trabajo y la eficiencia.

Una de las variables estratégicas para asegurar la establización macroeconómica es el incremento del consumo personal. Según lo anunciado por las autoridades cubanas, en 1996 el consumo personal creció un 4% apoyado por el incremento del número de trabajadores incluídos en los planes de estimulación material y salarial directa (830,000 trabajadores en 1996 contra 635,000 trabajadores en 1995) y por el aumento en la adquisición de productos y servicios en dólares, al contabilizar más de 627 millones de dólares en 1996 frente a 530 millones en 1995.[15]

Estos resultados, sin embargo, no son suficientes para apoyar un esfuerzo estabilizador, ya que cuantitativamente están lejos de satisfacer mínimamente las necesidades más apremiantes de toda la población cuba-

Tabla 5. Tasa de Cambio del Dólar en Relación al Peso (pesos por dólar)

1990	7
1991	20
1992	35
1993	60
Junio 1994	100
Julio 1994	110
Agosto 1994	150
Septiembre 1994	80
Octubre 1994	50
Diciembre 1994	45
Enero 1995	40
Abril 1995	35
Julio 1995	30
Agosto 1995 (1ra. Quincena)	25
Agosto 1995 (2da. Quincena)	8
Septiembre 1995	25
Diciembre 1995	25
Junio 1996	25
Julio 1996	21
Septiembre 1996	19
Octubre 1996	15
Diciembre 1996	20

Fuentes: Observación personal y entrevistas realizadas a personas residentes en Cuba.

na. Por ejemplo, lo adquirido en dólares representa solamente $57.27 USD de productos por persona en el año, es decir, $4.77 USD mensuales. Otro ejemplo: el área de consumo priorizada por la población es la alimentación, donde invierte alrededor del 80% de sus ingresos. Según las cifras oficiales disponibles, a pesar del incremento de las producciones de viandas y hortalizas y de la dinamización en la comercialización de los productos agropecuarios por la existencia del mercado libre, la población consumió en 1995 un promedio mensual de una libra de dichos productos por persona.[16]

Por otra parte, el incremento del consumo no es equitativo por la existencia de una diferenciación en

---

15. "Informe sobre los resultados económicos de 1996."

16. *Bussiness Tips on Cuba*, no. 3 (marzo de 1996).

Tabla 6.   Gastos del Presupuesto del Estado

Partidas de Gastos	1990 Millones de Pesos	%	1993 Millones de Pesos	%	1994 Millones de Pesos	%	1995 Millones de Pesos	%	1996 Millones de Pesos
Educación	1,620	11.4	1,385	9.5	1,334	9.4	1,410	11.5	...
Salud Pública	937	6.6	1,077	7.4	1,061	7.5	1,088	8.9	...
Defensa	1,149	8.1	713	4.9	651	4.6	727	5.9	...
Seguridad Social	1,164	8.2	1,452	10.0	1,532	10.8	1,573	12.8	...
Administración	453	3.2	4113	2.8	354	2.5	375	3.1	...
Vivienda y Servicios Comunales	383	2.7	260	1.8	316	2.2	291	2.4	...
Cultura y Arte	201	1.4	173	1.2	160	1.1	158	1.3	...
Ciencia y Técnica	124	0.9	125	0.9	121	0.9	133	1.1	...
Deportes	117	0.8	104	0.7	106	0.7	103	0.8	...
Asistencia Social	96	0.7	94	0.6	94	0.7	154	1.3	...
Subsidio por Pérdidas	2,975	20.9	5,434	37.3	3,447	24.3	1,790	14.6	1,400[a]
Gastos Inversiones	2,886	20.3	2,038	14.0	2,683	18.9	3,195	26.1	...
Otros	2,108	14.8	1,299	8.9	2,319	16.4	1,248	10.2	...
TOTAL	14,213	100	14,567	100	14,178	100	12,245	100	...

... Datos no disponibles

Nota: En **Otros** están computados "Otros gastos de la actividad empresarial," "Ayuda económica a las UBPC" y "Reserva."

Fuentes: Las mismas de la Tabla 1.

a.   Cifra estimada

las posibilidades adquisitivas de la población cubana, así por ejemplo, los 830,000 trabajadores con acceso a fuentes de estimulación adicional representan solamente el 23% de la fuerza laboral cubana, además, los que tienen acceso a las divisas no es el espectro mayor de la población. La información brindada por las autoridades cubanas de que entre el 30% y el 60% de la población tuvo acceso a la divisa en 9 provincias durante 1996 hay que tomarla con cautela, porque no refleja la frecuencia de dicha tenencia, es decir, alguien puede recibir algunos recursos financieros en divisas de una manera coyuntural en un momento dado y ello no significa que tenga una fuente permanente que es en difinitiva la condición que le permitiría satisfacer regularmente sus necesidades.[17]

El análisis hasta aquí presentado demuestra que el país está aún lejos de alcanzar la estabilización macroeconómica, por lo que es muy prematuro asegurar que los resultados obtenidos a partir de 1994 son el inicio de la recuperación.

Como ya habíamos mencionado, la estabilización es el resultado del equilibrio financiero doméstico que se alcanza extrayendo el exceso de circulante y evitando a su vez su reproducción. Ello se logra mediante un conjunto de medidas integradas y simultáneas que tienda a la solución del déficit público y sus mecanismos de financiamiento y el incremento de la oferta de bienes y servicios.

La solución del déficit público y sus mecanismos de financiación

La solución del déficit público debe ser el resultado tanto de una reducción de los gastos como de un incremento de los ingresos del presupuesto. ¿Donde radican las principales áreas de reducción y aumento respectivos? Empezaremos primeramente por el lado de los gastos.

Analizando la Tabla 6 observamos que las principales partidas de gastos corrientes son: *educación y salud pública* que absorben alrededor del 20% de los gas-

17. "Informe sobre los resultados económicos de 1996."

tos, los *subsidios por pérdidas a las empresas* que representan cerca del 15% y la *seguridad y asistencia social* con cerca del 14% de los gastos del presupuesto.[18] Es decir, que entre el área empresarial y el área social están concentradas las principales fuentes de los gastos con casi un 50% de los mismos.

Una de las condiciones del éxito de los procesos de estabilización y de reestructuración es la necesaria legitimización que los mismos deben tener en el amplio espectro de los sectores sociales y una de las bases de dicha legitimidad es la garantía del apoyo estatal a los servicios sociales básicos.[19] Si bien se podría pensar en alternativas de reducción de gastos en las áreas sociales sin que se afecten las condiciones de acceso de la población a los mismos, en aras de no afectar las aspiraciones de amplios sectores, el foco debe estar concentrado en el área empresarial con la disminución drástica de los subsidios por pérdidas.

Haber llevado el subsidio por pérdidas a la cifra de 1 mil 400 millones de dólares en 1996 no necesariamente tiene que haber sido el resultado de un incremento de la eficiencia empresarial. Hay que tomar en cuenta que la reducción del subsidio a las empresas se produjo en el contexto de paralización total o parcial de varias industrias por la falta de insumos, por lo que si las empresas no funcionan no generan gastos o estos están reducidos a la mínima expresión. Por ejemplo, la industria azucarera y agricultura cañera—las cuales absorben aproximadamente el 60% de los subsidios por pérdidas—enfrentaron la zafra 1994-95 con el 40% de los centrales inactivos. Por otra parte, la no existencia de una tasa de cambio realista que permita traducir los precios internacionales a la moneda nacional distorsiona la contabilidad del país al no permitir calcular con veracidad los costos de producción, por lo que se pueden estar reflejando

pérdidas menores o incluso ganancias no correspondientes con la realidad.

Descargar al Estado de partes considerables de la carga financiera que resulta del apoyo a un sistema empresarial mayoritariamente ineficiente sin que ello redunde en una afectación de la capacidad productiva del país puede ser solamente el resultado de una reestructuración profunda del sistema empresarial que incluya la privatización total o parcial de algunos sectores o empresas en las que el Estado ha demostrado incapacidad para conducir de una forma eficiente, no solamente en términos monetarios sino también en términos de servicios a la población o en aprovechamiento de las capacidades instaladas.

La reestructuración empresarial debe incluir, además, el redimensionamiento y el otorgamiento de una real autonomía a aquellas empresas que se mantengan bajo la égida estatal. El redimensionamiento implicaría llevar el tamaño de las empresas a una dimensión que le permita competir en las condiciones existentes en los mercados internacionales, es decir, lograr que sus gastos de producción sean iguales a los precios de importación.

La mayoría de los especialistas e instituciones internacionales toman en cuenta el número de empleados como indicador para medir el tamaño de las empresas. De acuerdo a una tipología de las Naciones Unidas basada en dicho indicador, el 88% de las empresas cubanas serían consideradas como *"grandes empresas."*[20] Aquí está focalizado uno de los problemas medulares que explica el comportamiento no eficiente de un amplio espectro del cuerpo empresarial cubano, habida cuenta de que si bien la política de pleno empleo practicada por la Revolución tuvo una innegable justificación social, económicamente generó subutilización de la fuerza de trabajo causante, entre

---

18. Es necesario hacer algunas precisiones. Las partidas de *educación y salud pública* han mantenido por los años una participación similar en los gastos del presupuesto. La participación de los *subsidios por pérdidas* se ha visto reducida, ya que en los años precrisis representaba entre un 20% y un 25%. Algo diferente ha ocurrido con la *seguridad y asistencia social* que antes de 1989 solamente tenían una participación en los gastos presupuestales del orden del 9%-10%.

19. El análisis de las condiciones para la legitimidad de un proceso de transición en Cuba será abordado en el artículo ya aludido que se titula: "¿Se encuentra Cuba en transición?."

20. La clasificación utilizada por las Naciones Unidas para medir el tamaño de las empresas es la siguiente: microempresa—menos de 10 ocupados; pequeña empresa—10 a 49 ocupados; mediana empresa—50 a 99 ocupados; grandes empresas—más de 100 ocupados.

otros factores, de los bajos rendimientos y productividad sectorial conocidos.

Por lo tanto el redimensionamiento implicaría la eliminación de la fuerza de trabajo excedente, proveyéndole las condiciones necesarias para que puedan emplearse en el sector privado. La ampliación del trabajo por cuenta propia a partir de 1993 son partes de esas condiciones pero aún insuficientes por cuanto el desarrollo de la actividad privada ha estado constreñida por obstáculos de carácter económico y administrativos.

Ante todo debe asegurarse que el derecho a emplearse privadamente sea una garantía constitucional a la que todo cubano tenga acceso, sin que para ello sea necesario la autorización de las autoridades locales, provinciales o nacionales. A su vez, para que el área privada sea una fuente efectiva de empleo, ingresos y de producción se debe pasar de la simple forma de prácticas laborales individuales a la creación de pequeñas y medianas empresas. La experiencia internacional ha demostrado que las pequeñas y medianas empresas han sido componentes esenciales en las dinámicas productivas nacionales y en la satisfacción de las necesidades de la población. Una experiencia similar en Cuba podría ser el centro del proceso de privatización aludido anteriormente.

Cuando hablamos de otorgar real autonomía a las empresas estatales nos referimos a la concesión de prerrogativas que le provea a las empresas de amplias responsabilidades sobre sus ingresos y gastos e implica que el Estado renuncie al control totalmente centralizador que ejerce actualmente sobre las empresas en Cuba que, entre otros efectos, desmotiva el interés y la preocupación por los resultados productivos y la eficiencia en general.[21] Por supuesto, esta política descentralizadora sería un proceso de mediano y largo plazo en la que poco a poco el Estado le iría traspasando facultades decisionales a las empresas, ya que no es posible de la noche a la mañana eliminar toda una cultura paternalista y verticalista muy enraizada en las mentes de los empresarios cubanos que los lleva a pedir autonomía pero a su vez no desean desprenderse de la protección estatal cuando la situación económica de sus respectivas empresas no es favorable.[22]

Otra fuente de gastos que podría ser factible de reducción son los subsidios a los productos de primera necesidad que se comercializan por el Estado.[23] La vía de reducción es cambiando la concepción del subsidio: en vez de subsidiar a los productos se debe subsidiar a las familias de más bajos ingresos.

La reestructuración empresarial ayudaría a resolver igualmente el problema del déficit público por el lado de los ingresos. Como se puede observar en la Tabla 7 la fuente principal de ingresos son las empresas y unidades presupuestadas con más del 80% de la recaudación, sin embargo la mayoría de dichos ingresos provienen del *impuesto de circulación* cobrado fundamentalmente de la venta de cigarros, tabacos y bebidas alcohólicas. Solamente entre un 10% y un 15% de los ingresos corresponden a los aportes de la ganancia, es decir, son vinculados a la eficiencia empresarial.

La estructura de los ingresos no puede viabilizar la solución del déficit presupuestario y sus posibilidades de reproducción ya que como hemos visto se está verificando una reducción paulatina del consumo de cigarros, tabacos y bebidas alcohólicas, por lo tanto es necesario que los *aportes de la ganancia* de las empresas privadas y estatales sean la fuente principal de los ingresos lo cual sería factible con un lógico incremen-

---

21. Para conocer la percepción del empresario cubano sobre los efectos que provoca el sistema de dirección económica centralizada, cfr. Gerardo González, *Possibilities and Realities of Cuba's Integration into the Caribbean: Perceptions of Cuban Entrepreneurs.* The North-South Agenda, Paper 26 (Coral Gables: University of Miami, North-South Center, May 1997).

22. Los problemas vinculados a la autonomía empresarial en Cuba fueron ampliamente investigados en un estudio no publicado titulado *Autonomía empresarial y participación de los trabajadores en Cuba* realizado por Haroldo Dilla y Gerardo González con el apoyo de la International Development Research Centre de Canadá.

23. No hay cifras precisas de lo que se desembolsa por este concepto. Generalmente, estos vienen incluidos en la partida de *otros*.

Tabla 7.   Principales Ingresos del Presupuesto del Estado

Partidas de Ingresos	1990 Millones de Pesos	%	1993 Millones de Pesos	%	1994 Millones de Pesos	%	1995 Millones de Pesos	%	1996 Millones de Pesos
Impuesto de Circulación	5,017	40.9	3,310	34.8	5,097	40.0	5,500	48.0	...
Aportes de la Ganancia	1,404	11.5	1,400	14.7	1,865	14.6	...	...	2,156[a]
Aportes de la Amortización	2,752	22.5	1,287	13.5	1,134	8.9	...	...	...
Otros aportes de las empresas y unidades presupuestadas	1,465	12.0	1,516	15.9	2,331	18.3	...	...	...
Impuestos y derechos de la población	131	1.1	414	4.4	572	4.5	...	...	...
TOTAL	12,255		9,516		12,757		11,470		...

... Datos no disponibles

Nota: El **TOTAL** de cada columna no refleja la suma de las distintas partidas ya que se han considerado solamente los ingresos que se obtienen a través de distintas formas recaudatorias.

Fuentes: Las mismas de la Tabla 1.

a.   Cifra estimada

to de la eficiencia productiva, alcanzable con la reestructuración del sistema empresarial ya mencionada.

Podría pensarse en una mayor participación de los *impuestos y derechos de la población* a tenor de la experiencia de otros países en los que esta partida tiene un peso significativo en la recaudación presupuestaria vía los impuestos a los ingresos. Sin embargo, en las condiciones cubanas podría ser sólo una posibilidad de largo plazo ya que dado la pérdida del poder adquisitivo del Peso y el congelamiento de los salarios nominales no sería política ni económicamente aconsejable recargar el ya sufrido "bolsillo" del consumidor con nuevos impuestos, a pesar de que el actual Sistema Presupuestario de la isla tiene contemplado tal posibilidad con un *impuesto sobre los ingresos* y un *impuesto suplementario para la seguridad social*. En la actualidad el *impuesto sobre los ingresos* se está aplicando solamente al trabajador por cuenta propia y aquellas personas que obtienen otros ingresos suplementarios. Según cifras oficiales, por este concepto se recaudaron en 1995 106 millones de pesos y en 1996 192 millones de pesos.[24]

Incremento de la oferta de bienes y servicios

Este sería el otro componente de política para reducir o eliminar el exceso de oferta monetaria y evitar su reproducción, pero a su vez uno de los más difíciles

de lograr en el corto plazo dado la profunda recesión que atraviesa la economía cubana.

Cuando hablamos de incremento de la oferta de bienes y servicios estamos apuntando al hecho de que el consumo personal tiene que jugar un papel determinante en las posibilidades reproductivas de la economía cubana, lo cual implica necesariamente la solución de la contradicción latente entre acumulación y consumo, es decir, reestablecer las proporciones adecuadas entre ambos destinos del producto final. Históricamente la participación del consumo personal en el producto final ha manifestado una tendencia decreciente en favor de los crecientes volúmenes de recursos destinados a la acumulación productiva. Por otra parte, de las disponibilidades para el consumo se ha destinado prácticamente más de la mitad al consumo social, lo que indudablemente ha limitado las posibilidades del consumo personal.

A simple vista, la solución de dicha contradicción en el corto plazo no parece ser viable habida cuenta de que para revitalizar la economía se necesita un fuerte y sostenido proceso de acumulación que indiscutiblemente le restaría recursos a la revitalización del consumo personal. Pero el asunto no es insoluble si se enfrenta de una manera integral.

24. *Business Tips on Cuba*, No. 6 (junio de 1997).

En primer lugar, habría que hacer una lectura diferente al concepto mismo de acumulación, el cual se ha manejado de una forma parcial por los dirigentes cubanos. Cuando se habla de acumulación no se refiere exclusivamente al proceso de reproducción de la base material, sino también incluye la reproducción de la fuerza de trabajo, en definitiva, uno de los factores productivos más estratégicos con los que cuenta un país por ser el único capaz de absorber y trasmitir habilidades y conocimientos y de manejar y manipular todos los demás factores. Por lo tanto, si a ese recurso no se le garantiza su reproducción y la de su familia—que es decir la satisfacción de sus crecientes necesidades—no se estaría propiciando el incentivo para lograr su involucramiento intensivo y por lo tanto eficiente en la producción. Dicho en otras palabras, el consumo personal debe convertirse en una de las variables estratégicas más determinantes en los próximos años, lo cual no significa sacrificar los planes de desarrollo, pero si adecuarlos a las nuevas realidades.

Para reestablecer las proporciones adecuadas entre la acumulación productiva y el consumo personal sin sacrificar las metas del desarrollo se debe garantizar una tasa de acumulación constante y sostenida mediante el incremento del rendimiento de los fondos básicos (bienes de capital) y de la productividad del trabajo. Teniendo en cuenta las experiencias de los NIC's, hay que lograr que este componente intensivo responda, por lo menos, por el 30% del incremento de la producción. A su vez, se debe propiciar un incremento anual del consumo personal del 5% o al menos proporcional al incremento del PIB.

El incremento de la oferta de bienes y servicios no debe ser solamente en términos de valor. Cuando el incremento del consumo va correspondiéndose con la liquidez acumulada pero no satisface las necesidades en valores de uso, se produce un "gap" entre la demanda material y la oferta monetaria que ejerce igualmente una presión inflacionaria.

Pensamos que el Estado no debe ser el único responsable que garantice los incrementos del consumo personal, sino que debe tener una participación activa la pequeña y mediana empresa privada nacional y la inversión extranjera en esa esfera.

Sin ánimo de ser exhautivo, hemos señalado simplemente algunos de los componentes de política que deben ser adoptados dentro del proceso de estabilización macroeconómica partiendo de las condiciones actuales de la economía y la sociedad cubana. Por supuesto que un proceso de esta magnitud requeriría la aplicación de otras políticas en otras esferas de una manera integrada y coherente. Sin embargo, habría que retener la premisa de que cualquier decisión que se aplique no puede desconocer las desproporciones que existen con respecto a la distribución de los ingresos: el 85% de la población tienen un percápita de ingresos de $150 pesos o menos mensuales cuando el costo de la canasta básica supera los $300 pesos; el 13% de los ahorristas atesoran el 84% del dinero depositado en las cuentas bancarias.[25]

El factor tiempo es otro elemento que merecería una consideración en el proceso de lograr la estabilización macroeconómica. Como se observa en el análisis que realizamos, en las condiciones presentes la búsqueda de la estabilización requeriría de una dinámica secuencial, es decir, paso a paso, para ir acomodando la economía a las nuevas condiciones y evitar a su vez grandes traumas sociales, además de que algunas de las medidas como el incremento de la oferta de bienes y servicios requieren en si mismo de un período de tiempo mayor. No obstante, si la economía y todos sus factores siguen depauperándose, la opción de la terapia de choque no debe ser descartada.

EL LARGO CAMINO DE LA REESTRUCTURACION ECONOMICA[26]

La solución del desequilibrio financiero interno es una condición necesaria pero insuficiente para garantizar la recuperación económica del país, ya que el desequilibrio financiero no es la causa sino la mani-

---

25. Cfr. "Desenfrenada la liquidez del peso en Cuba" e "Informe sobre los resultados económicos de 1996." Para el cálculo del costo de la canasta básica tuvimos en cuenta los precios del mercado estatal y del mercado libre de los siguientes productos: manteca, aceite, pan, café, leche, frijoles, detergente, jabón, mantequilla, pollo, carnes y huevos.

festación de fenómenos económicos de carácter estructural imposibles de corregir exclusivamente con medidas de ajuste monetarias y financieras. Su no solución dejaría intactas las condiciones para la reproducción de problemas financieros similares. A su vez, la recuperación económica es impensable con una desestabilización en su punto de partida.[27] Por lo tanto, la estabilización debe ser la antesala y a su vez parte integrativa de un programa de reestructuración económica que en el mediano y largo plazo garantice la recuperación económica del país.

Dado que en las condiciones de la economía cubana el sector externo sigue siendo factor clave para su reproducción ampliada, uno de los objetivos medulares del programa de reestructuración es la solución del desbalance financiero externo. Ello es posible a través de un adecuado equilibrio entre el incremento de los fondos exportables en bienes y servicios y la sustitución de importaciones.

Las nuevas condiciones en que Cuba debe desarrollar sus relaciones externas la hacen partícipe del llamado desafío exportador, cuyo éxito o fracaso está directamente relacionado con el comportamiento de la competitividad externa del país, entendiendo por ella la capacidad para mantener o extender su participación en los mercados internacionales y lograr al propio tiempo que no se afecte el desarrollo interno, lo cual demanda una mayor productividad y la incorporación del progreso científico-técnico.

Esta competitividad está, por otra parte, íntimamente asociada al tipo de bienes que se exportan ya que no todos los patrones de especialización internacional participan en igual medida en las corrientes más dinámicas del intercambio comercial a nivel mundial. El éxito de la especialización escogida dependerá de su correspondencia con los núcleos más dinámicos del intercambio internacional. En relación con esto, los bienes que se comercializan mundialmente se han

clasificado de acuerdo con su desempeño en los últimos 15 años en: *productos dinámicos* (su participación en el comercio mundial se ha incrementado), *productos estancados* (su participación virtualmente no ha variado), y *productos en retroceso* (su participación ha disminuído). Los rubros más dinámicos se concentran en manufacturas de alto contenido tecnológico, consideradas "industrias de punta," en tanto que los rubros regresivos están constituídos por los productos primarios y de poca elaboración.

La característica de la situación actual a nivel mundial es la polarización entre los renglones dinámicos (52% del comercio mundial) y los regresivos (38% del comercio mundial) y la disminución del peso de aquellos que pueden considerarse como *estancados*. De hecho puede afirmarse que el dinamismo del primer grupo tiene altas posibilidades de perdurar ya que está inducido por las tendencias mundiales en tecnología, consumo y el comercio. Este esquema de análisis lo aplicamos a Cuba, dando como resultado de que más del 50% del perfil exportador de la isla está conformado por productos considerados *en retroceso*, mientras que los productos considerados *dinámicos* representan alrededor del 34%.[28]

Hoy en día no es posible concebir el desarrollo sustentado en un patrón cualquiera de especialización internacional, sino sobre la base de aquellos modelos a partir de los cuales avanzan dinámicamente las corrientes principales del intercambio. Por tal motivo, las posibilidades de desarrollo económico de Cuba son bastante precarias si se siguen sosteniendo básicamente sobre sectores primarios de exportación.

En este contexto, las debilidades de la estructura industrial actual requieren ser evaluadas rigurosamente y proyectar una industrialización sustentada en aquellas ramas que tengan mayores perspectivas de desarrollo y competitividad en el mercado mundial y a su vez permita la sustitución selectiva de aquellos bienes

26. Nuestra intención en este epígrafe no es exponer un programa de reestructuración detallado ya que ello implicaría un trabajo más extenso. Simplemente señalaremos algunos de los objetivos y políticas esenciales que debería comprender dicho programa.

27. Carranza, Gutiérrez y Monreal, *Cuba: La reestructuración de la economía.*

28. En el caso de Cuba consideramos productos en retroceso al azúcar, níquel, cítricos, pesca y productos agropecuarios; productos estancados: confecciones y tabaco; productos dinámicos: turismo y medicamentos.

Tabla 8. Distribución de las Asociaciones Económicas por Sectores

	1988-1990	1991-1993	1994	1995	1996[a]	TOTAL
Agrícola	-----	5	3	2	-----	10
Minería	-----	11	17	-----	5	33
Petróleo	1	20	4	-----	5	30
Industria	-----	31	12	13	29	85
Turismo	1	13	16	4	11	45
Transporte	-----	-----	1	4	3	8
Construcción	-----	11	10	1	-----	22
Comunicaciones	1	1	1	-----	1	4
Otros	-----	12	10	7	-----	29
TOTAL	3	104	74	31	54	266

Fuentes: Tercera y Cuarta Conferencias sobre Cuba organizadas por la revista *The Economist* (abril de 1996 y marzo de 1997).

a.   Cifras preliminares

y servicios cuyos costos de producción domésticos sean inferiores a los del mercado mundial. Por supuesto, ello requiere una modernización tecnológica de la dotación industrial instalada, algo solamente concebible a largo plazo dada la escacez de recursos financieros.

La inversión extranjera es el recurso imprescindible para garantizar el esfuerzo diversificador de la estructura productiva y exportadora cubana. Su afluencia ha apoyado grandemente los resultados económicos obtenidos en los últimos dos años, cuando precisamente los sectores que han recepcionado la mayor cantidad de inversiones como la minería, la industria y el turismo—tal y como muestra la Tabla 8—son los que han exhibido los mejores resultados. Pero aún es insuficiente el volumen inversionista: si bien se han creado entre 1988 y 1996 unas 266 asociaciones económicas con un aporte de capital superior a los 2 mil 500 millones de dólares esta cifra es muy pequeña si la comparamos con los $15 mil millones de dólares que recibió Viet Nam entre 1990 y 1995.[29]

Hay tres razones que han impedido una entrada masiva de capital extranjero en Cuba: una administrativa, una económica y otra política. La administrativa está relacionada con las restricciones de carácter legal y sectoriales impuestas a los inversionistas, como por ejemplo, la imposibilidad de realizar contratación libre de personal o la aceptación exclusiva de inversiones para generar fondos exportables, cuando algunos potenciales inversionistas muestran interés en desarrollar producciones para el mercado interno. La restricción económica está dada por lo poco atractivo que resultan algunas industrias o sectores por su pobre competitividad dado en muchos casos por su obsolecencia tecnológica y los altos costos que implicarían su posible reconversión.[30]

Las razones políticas están vinculadas a la extraterritorialidad del embargo o bloqueo aplicado por los Estados Unidos a Cuba que ha ahuyentado a no pocos inversionistas, reforzada con la promulgación de la controversial Ley Helms-Burton. Indiscutiblemente, cualquier modelo de desarrollo que se implemente estará condicionado por las consecuencias derivadas de estas presiones, que por demás dificultan la reinserción de Cuba en el sistema económico internacional, elevan los costos de la recuperación económica y alejan cualquier posibilidad de transición inmediata.

---

29. Carlos Lage, "Intervención en la 4ta. Conferencia sobre la economía cubana organizada por The Economist," La Habana (marzo de 1997) y *Granma* (30 de septiembre de 1995).

30. Fernando Zalacaín, "La economía cubana en transición," *Boletín de Economía*, no. 3, Unidad de Investigaciones Económicas, Universidad de Puerto Rico (enero-marzo de 1996).

Es imprescindible la solución de dos nudos gordianos para el reestablecimiento del equilibrio financiero externo. Uno es el acceso al mercado financiero internacional que es una fuente decisiva para el financiamiento de la recuperación. En la medida que la economía cubana vaya mostrando signos reales de recuperación mejorará la confianza de los prestamistas, pero sobre todo Cuba tendría que aprovechar la renovación de sus posibilidades externas para plantearse alternativas renegociadoras de su deuda externa cifrada en 10 mil 400 millones de dólares.[31]

El otro problema a resolver es la alta dependencia del petróleo importado. Cuba necesita para su funcionamiento de alrededor de 11 millones de toneladas anuales, de las cuales un poco más de 5 millones se destinan a la generación de energía eléctrica. Esta dependencia la hace vulnerable frente a las variaciones que se producen en el mercado petrolero mundial.

El país requiere disminuir su dependencia externa del combustible importado o al menos reducir su vulnerabilidad. Dos alternativas complementarias y a largo plazo se pueden manejar: garantizar una base financiera sólida para la adquisición del combustible incrementando los fondos exportables y producir una reconversión tecnológica de la planta industrial que posibilite la introducción de tecnologías de consumos energéticos más eficientes.

---

31. En esta cifra no está computada la deuda con la ex Unión Soviética. Cfr. "Nuevo banco central será eje de reformas" por Pascal Fletcher de la Agencia Reuter en La Habana, *El Nuevo Herald* (15 de junio de 1997).

ALGUNOS APUNTES SOBRE LA
TEORIA DE LA TRANSICION SOCIAL

Martha Beatriz Roque Cabello

Como un ejercicio mental el lector debe imaginar a alguien con trastornos de la personalidad, tratando de que no se mueva una pelota que lo obsesiona, a la vez que quiere mantenerla escondida. Para ello la mete en una caja, pero no la ajusta y decide en períodos cortos de tiempo cambiarla de lugar. A pesar de su obstinación, cada vez que la desplaza para un sitio más seguro, la pelota se mueve.

*****

El Instituto Cubano de Economistas Independientes ha venido trabajando un poco más de un año en la Teoría de la Transición Social. Se han elaborado varios documentos que fundamentan el conjunto de situaciones en las que se basa este pensamiento. Ahora es imprescindible reseñar la presencia en nuestra sociedad de un proceso evolutivo, partiendo del hecho que muy pocos refutan la idea de que la transición hacia la democracia en Cuba es algo que deberá ocurrir más temprano que tarde.

Aceptar que aquí se hacen reformas económicas tiene para muchos una connotación política que implica al menos "simpatías" hacia el sistema. Sin embargo para el Gobierno cubano reconocerlo constituye prácticamente una derrota a su inmovilismo, a la forma tan cómoda que ha venido decidiendo el futuro de este pueblo, omnipotentemente, con el control total de la vida de sus habitantes.

Los que aspiran a que se ejecuten cambios profundos, se niegan a admitir que las propias contradicciones en que ha caído el sistema en su afán de retener el poder, han propiciado que comience una transición, no de

la forma efectiva que todos anhelamos, sino gradual y autónoma.

Reconocer que se está transitando aunque de una forma muy lenta, tiene a su favor el llevar implícita la consideración de que son efectivas las acciones de la oposición (interna y externa) y de todos los que en el mundo cooperan de una forma u otra a resolver el problema cubano. Por eso este es un momento en que se hace necesario cambiar el lenguaje.

Si se analiza que las medidas que se han implantado han sido en contra de la voluntad gubernamental, que no responden a un programa y se han ido destilando gota a gota, se podrá asegurar que se va allanando el camino. Es que precisamente la falta de sistematicidad y de pautas a seguir para mantener la forma novedosa de totalitarismo con rasgos de economía de mercado, ha llevado al Gobierno a violar sus propias leyes y lo tiene envuelto en estos momentos en toda una serie de contradicciones que no le ha permitido hacer un movimiento más, a pesar que los ha anunciado.

En algunas ocasiones parece que amaga con retirar espacios a los que ha accedido, pero no se decide a hacerlo. Las personas viven con la incertidumbre de si lo que se ha permitido hoy, mañana será prohibido, pero mientras tanto, aprovechan los intervalos para respirar algún aire de independencia económica y van presionando para obtener su total ruptura con el aparato estatal.

Hay que evaluar que para la dirección del país se hace harto difícil poder salir de la crísis con un pueblo que constantemente está descartando lo establecido. Esto tiene un costo. Esa persistente violación ha ido debilitando, y seguirá haciéndolo, la forma en que el poder gubernamental controla la sociedad, la economía y de hecho la política.

Es imposible predecir si los efectos de esta indudable pérdida del papel preponderante del Estado traerán consecuencias positivas o negativas para la sociedad, pero en ello jugarán un papel importante los que quieren corregir el camino que debe tomar el país. Sin exclusiones de ningún tipo, desde los defensores de los derechos humanos, hasta la iglesia. No se puede negar que tanto uno como los otros, han podido con su tesón lograr un poco de empuje para abrirse paso en la maltrecha sociedad civil.

Desde los años 80 para acá, han cambiado mucho los valores y los objetivos esenciales de la sociedad cubana. Para ejemplificar esto, se pondrá un grupo social, digamos los trabajadores. En aquella época, cualquier persona vinculada laboralmente al Estado, ya fuera obrero, técnico o profesional, veía en el trabajo una forma de asegurar el futuro e incluso obtener algunas prebendas. Ser trabajador destacado o internacionalista, implicaba poder tener acceso a un bono para adquirir efectos electrodomésticos, autos, motocicle-

tas, ir de vacaciones a los ex-países socialistas o disfrutar en algún centro turístico nacional. Existía un interés personal por superarse y hasta de llegar a obtener título universitario, por lo que el objeto primordial era esforzarse.

De esto ya poco queda. El trabajador promedio actual es un holgazán, que aspira a estar emplantillado en algún lugar donde tenga acceso a bienes materiales, que lo ayuden a vivir a partir de inventar ingresos adicionales, porque el salario es demasiado poco para las necesidades de la familia. Ya no le interesa ser el mejor, mucho menos superarse y tampoco trabajar en su profesión. No compra acciones para el futuro sino que trata de resolver el presente. Si algo lo estimula es poder llegar a tener alguna independencia económica, como los que trabajan por cuenta propia y sobre todo el acceso al dólar.

Esto significa que el Estado ha empezado a perder de alguna forma el control absoluto que tenía sobre el trabajador. En la actualidad no pagan la cotización del sindicato, el aporte a las Milicias de Tropas Territoriales y con certeza se puede afirmar que de forma mínima concurren a la guardia del CDR. No obstante, se mantienen en los centros de trabajo las acciones coercitivas, como la que indica este cartel:

ATENCION

TODOS LOS TRABAJADORES DEBEN PARTICIPAR EN EL DESFILE EL PROXIMO 2 DE DICIEMBRE. UNA VEZ TERMINADO EL MISMO PODRAN RETIRARSE HACIA SUS DOMICILIOS.

LOS JEFES SERAN LOS RESPONSABLES DE CONTROLAR LA ASISTENCIA DE SUS TRABAJADORES EN LOS PUNTOS RESPECTIVOS.

Cualquier sector social que sea sometido a análisis tiene las mismas características. Dentro de los propios trabajadores algunos han ganado más espacio. Entre ellos, por sólo citar uno, están los artistas. Las deserciones en el extranjero ocurrían una tras otra, dejando prácticamente sin figuras conocidas los principales medios de difusión. El Gobierno se vio forza-

do a permitir la libre contratación en el extranjero y el retorno al país de estos trabajadores del arte. En la actualidad en Venzuela, Colombia y México está representado este movimiento independiente.

La crísis económica coopera también a esta transición, porque ha empujado al Estado a privatizar, aunque sea en parte, algunas empresas. Es un proceso lento, pero contribuye a debilitar los fundamentos del sistema, donde la nacionalización ocupó un lugar fundamental y se hizo política con ella. Como no hay opciones diferentes al incremento de la inversión extranjera, tendrán que tratar de aumentar este tipo de negocio. (Quedaría para un estudio aparte el explicar por qué se utiliza la palabra "tratar," pero conviene señalar que no está vinculado solamente a los obstáculos del llamado "bloqueo," sino que tiene mucho más que ver con la propia burocracia del sistema, que convierte en un infierno los intentos de cualquier empresario extranjero de establecerse aquí.)

Con conciencia de la posibilidad de verse obligado a un cambio, la dirección política del país ha venido llevando a cabo una "piñata" de los puestos claves en estas empresas, denominadas gerencias, repartiéndolas entre militares en retiro y personas de alta confianza, que irán acumulando algunos conocimientos de mercado.

Los defectos con que se están haciendo las transformaciones, adulterando las reglas de la economía de mercado, han sido portadoras de la corrupción. Cabe señalar que no significa que éste se haya manifestado después de este período, pero sí ha llegado a alcanzar su mayor apogeo.

Unir criterios es un "arte" extremadamente difícil. Dentro de la oposición cubana no ha sido una excepción; pero si la continuidad del sistema político del país dependiera de lo que todos podemos hacer en común, bien valdría la pena comenzar a reconocer públicamente que Cuba ya está en transición y esto significa que sin que el Gobierno lo admita se ha comenzado el paso de un modo de organización de la economía a otro que será completamente diferente. ¡Es cierto!, todo marcha a una velocidad no deseada, de forma caótica y no dirigida. Es un desafío abrumador para los que tanto hemos esperado. Pero de hecho reestructurar la base institucional del sistema social y desarrollar la sociedad civil es algo que sólo podrá alcanzar después de algunos años. Serán muchas las variables que influirán en la definitiva transición; la forma en que se ha hecho en diferentes países así lo explica, pero hay un factor específico: "el efecto de los cambios políticos que se deben producir al mismo tiempo," que es sin lugar a dudas el que mayor tiempo acapara, entre los que desean la democratización cubana.

El mensaje fundamental de la teoría de la transición social es éste que aquí hemos trasmitido. Si se comprende todos estaremos de acuerdo en que ya no hay marcha atrás. La más ínfima medida, negativa o positiva, resultará un escalón más en el ascenso hacia una nueva forma del quehacer social. Incluso pueden mantenerse inmóviles las decisiones y esta masa poblacional ahora en movimiento, las empujará el siguiente paso. No debemos descartar dos factores con los que hay que contar: la historia de la nación cubana y su geografía.

PROPUESTA PARA EL REORDENAMIENTO DE LA ECONOMIA CUBANA: ASPECTOS INSTITUCIONALES Y FINANCIEROS

Rodolfo A. Carrandi

El propósito del estudio consiste en determinar, para uso del Gobierno Provisional, las acciones institucionales y financieras necesarias, para la transformación de la economía estatizada de Cuba a una economía de libre iniciativa. La premisa es que Cuba es viable económicamente.

En las opciones para el reordenamiento de la economía de Cuba que se exponen en el primer capítulo, se selecciona un cambio rápido y el modo de privatización de los medios de producción. La transición rápida tendría la ventaja de hacer visible los problemas de la economía, principalmente empleo, oferta de bienes y servicios y por consiguiente, la adopción de acciones para resolver los mismos.

El Plan de Reordenamiento de la Economía Cubana se describe en el segundo capítulo, que contiene los objetivos específicos y la misión del Gobierno Provisional. En el tercer capítulo se esboza un Programa de Desarrollo Económico que contiene políticas de carácter taxativo, como la fiscal, e indicativas en cuanto a las sectoriales. La industria azucarera, por necesidad, quedará reservada para intereses privados radicados en el país. El cuarto capítulo comprende el tratamiento de la deuda externa y otros tópicos de importancia.

OPCIONES PARA EL REORDENAMIENTO DE LA ECONOMIA DE CUBA

En base a estudios y experiencias de la Europa del Este se han formulado dos tésis relacionadas con el tiempo de la transformación de una economía centralizada a una de mercado. Estas son: en forma gradual y en forma inmediata.

Vinculada con la transformación a una economía de mercado, está la cuestión de como proceder a la privatización con las fórmulas de subasta pública o de distribución de certificados (*vouchers*) a la población adulta, para ser utilizados en la adquisición de acciones de empresas industriales. También se han formulado alternativas como autogestión de las empresas por los trabajadores. El sector agrícola no ha sido tratado en profundidad.

El otro tema que se presenta en el proceso es la restitución de bienes confiscados y en su defecto, el pago de compensaciones.

Tiempo de Ejecución del Plan
Para Cuba se recomienda en cuanto al proceso de la transformación, un cambio rápido, con la excepción de la agricultura, que se diferirá hasta la terminación del ciclo de producción en progreso. Se justifica que la acción de la fase de transición sea de carácter inmediato a fin de quebrantar las estructuras políticas, institucionales y administrativas actuales, ya que además la permanencia de estructuras paralelas entorpecerían el proceso del logro del objetivo de mediano plazo, relacionado con el desarrollo del país, que se explica en el próximo capítulo.

La transición rápida tendría la ventaja de hacer visible los problemas de la economía—principalmente empleo, oferta de bienes y servicios y precios—y por consiguiente, la adopción de acciones para resolver los mismos.

Privatización

Para el caso de Cuba se recomienda un modo que permita otograr a la población una participación en la propiedad de los medios de producción. De acuerdo con los requisitos que se especifican en el siguiente capítulo, se propone:

- En relación con la privatización de los medios de producción relacionados con servicios a las personas, comercio y pequeñas industrias proceder a la venta, en condiciones financieras equitativas, a los obreros y empleados de los mismos, y la constitución de compañías por acciones de las empresas industriales de envergadura, ingenios, gran minería, complejos turisticos y hoteles, refinerías de petróleo y servicios públicos como telecomunicaciones y energía.

- Para la producción agrícola brindar a los asociados en las cooperativas, la elección de permanecer en las mismas o individualizar sus parcelas. En cuanto a las fincas estatales y unidades básicas de produccion cooperativa, de acuerdo con los suelos y actividades, se crearán unidades de producción que permitan la explotación en forma intensiva. Las unidades de producción serán vendidas al personal de las fincas también en condiciones financieras satisfactorias.

- Autorizar el libre ejercicio de las profesiones y oficios.

En esta forma los medios de producción no se distribuirán en forma generalizada, ni amorfa, y se evitaría el supuesto riesgo de vender las empresas a la precios rídiculos que se derivaría de una subasta de los mismos.

El mecanismo de control, indispensable para asegurar que no se dilapiden los bienes, o no ser explotados en forma eficiente, se ejercerá por medio de la supervisión bancaria, teniendo como indicador el pago oportuno del servicio del préstamo. En las compañías por acciones, el indicador será la rentabilidad financiera. En ninguna forma se impondrán restricciones que aten el hombre a la tierra o al centro de trabajo.

Condiciones Necesarias para el Funcionamiento de la Economía de Mercado

Las condiciones necesarias para el funcionamiento de la economía de mercado serán satisfechas en la forma siguiente: **Derechos de propiedad**—quedarían definidos claramente. Como se explica más adelante se adoptarían medidas jurídicas que posibiliten el traspaso de los medios de producción. **Apoyo político**—los beneficiarios del proceso de privatización brindarían su apoyo político, al otorgárseles la posibilidad de poseer y explotar los medios de producción para su propio beneficio. **Mercado financiero**—el proceso de privatización generará recursos para capitalizar sendos bancos del estado, uno para la industria y otro para la agricultura así como para la creación de la banca comercial.

Las acciones que queden en poder del Estado de las compañías a ser constituídas, servirán para establecer un fondo de pensiones y jubilaciones privado, que junto con las contribuciones de los trabajadores, serviría de instrumento para el funcionamiento de una bolsa de valores. El fondo de pensiones y jubilaciones liberaría al gobierno de esta responsabilidad fiscal.

La función crediticia, al contar con disponibilidades de recursos para el financiamiento de capital de trabajo e inversiones, quedaría establecida. Además, se producirían los efectos siguientes: **Precios y salarios**—se fijarían a nivel de las unidades de producción. **Proceso de inversiones**—la atracción de inversionistas o búsqueda de los mismos se daría a nivel de las propias empresas. La actividad del gobierno se limitaría a empresas de envergadura, especialmente en minería, telecomunicaciones y energía, para su posterior venta a intereses privados. **Eficiencia**—las empresas que no se desempeñen en forma eficiente, medida por su capacidad de pago para cumplir con los compromisos financieros contraídos, se verían obligadas a reorganizarse o vender los medios de producción.

Las propuestas sobre restitución o compensación de bienes confiscados se describen más adelante y se hacen en función de procurar, en la mayor medida posible, la incorporación de los expatriados al proceso de reconstrucción del país.

Inserción en la Comunidad Financiera Internacional

Un requisito esencial para el proceso de reconstrucción de Cuba es su inserción en la Comunidad Financiera Internacional. Entre ellos se encuentra la reincorporación de Cuba al Fondo Monetario Internacional (FMI). Para la solicitud de incorporación al Fondo, como señala Pujol,[1] se requiere contar con suficiente apoyo político de los miembros. La admisión al Fondo es un requisito para la aceptación en el Banco Mundial y por extension a las instituciones afiliadas que integran el grupo, como la Corporación Financiera Internacional.

Con respecto al Banco Interamericano de Desarollo, se requiere ser miembro de la Organización de Estados Americanos (OEA). No se ha adoptado el procedimiento para la readmisión de Cuba a su seno.

No es necesario abundar sobre las ventajas de la incorporación de Cuba el sistema financiero internacional. Una de ellas sería la del Club de Paris, en el caso de reestructuración y refinanciamiento de la deuda externa.

En las tres organizaciones básicas mencionadas Cuba deberá suscribir y pagar las quotas de capital. Para el financiamiento de estos aportes podrían destinarse los fondos congelados por el Gobierno de Estados Unidos.

Tipo de Cambio

En Cuba circulan tres monedas: el peso, el peso convertible—que aparentemente no tiene aceptación —y el dólar.

En cuanto al tipo de cambio la condición inicial en el proceso de transformacion será, con certeza, de incertidumbre. La autoridad monetaria tendrá, ademas de adoptar un criterio sobre el tipo de cambio, que establecer políticas sobre las tasas de interés tanto activas como pasivas y todo ello en el contexto de las perturbaciones que deben esperarse en la balanza de pagos. El propósito de la política sería el de crear las condiciones para llegar a establecer un tipo de cambio fijo.

La condición de incertidumbre obligaría a considerar un tipo de cambio flexible, aceptando los riesgos de sus fluctuaciones. No debería entorpecerse la circulación del dólar ni tampoco establecer el control de cambios y su derivado que son las cuotas y permisos de importación. El peso sería la unidad de cuenta para todas las transacciones y su registro.

Política Fiscal

El objetivo será el de mantener un presupuesto balanceado, ya que no se darían las condiciones para financiar un déficit fiscal al no existir un mercado financiero para colocar obligaciones del Gobierno. La política fiscal no deberá permitir subsidios a las empresas. La administración pública deberá dimensionarse en función a los servicios necesarios a prestar.

Conforme con esto se mantendrá el sistema de salud pública y el sistema de educación vigentes, hasta tanto la evolución del país permita la introducción de modificaciones en la forma de prestar estos servicios. La tarea principal sería la de estructurar y poner en vigor de inmediato un sistema tributario simple que grave a las empresas y a las personas así como tarifas aduaneras. Interinamente y para efectos de recaudación de impuestos sería necesario considerar un mecanismo de utilidad presunta de las empresas, como modo de percibir ingresos de forma inmediata.

PROPUESTA PARA EL REORDENAMIENTO DE LA ECONOMIA CUBANA

En base al diagnóstico de la situación económica de Cuba y la opción recomendada para la reconstrución del país, se formula el Plan para el Reordenamiento de la Economía Cubana. Se da énfasis a los aspectos institucionales y financieros. El Plan ha sido diseñado para uso de un Gobierno Provisional en Cuba.[2]

---

1. Joaquín P. Pujol, "Membership Requirements in the IMF: Possible Implications for Cuba," *Cuba in Transition* (Miami: Florida International University for the Association for the Study of the Cuban Economy, 1991). Como nota de interés, a Cuba, según expresó Pujol, se le asignó, al constituirse el FMI, una cuota igual a las Nueva Zelandia, Noruega y Chile. La cuota de Cuba era superior a las de Grecia y Egipto.

2. Sobre un Gobierno Provisional hay una elaboración de José D. Acosta que contiene un "análisis juridico-formal que parte de ciertos presupuestos de caracter político." El Gobierno de Unidad Nacional, como lo denomina, sería gobierno de facto, al fin. José D. Acosta, "El Marco Jurídico-Institucional de un Gobierno Provisional de Unidad Nacional en Cuba," *Cuba in Transition—Volume 2* (Miami: Florida International University for the Association for the Study of the Cuban Economy, 1992).

Objetivos

El Plan está dirigido al logro de los objetivos siguientes: (1) establecer un sistema de libre concurrencia al mercado; (2) reintegrar el país a la comunidad financiera internacional; (3) preparar al país para un proceso de modernización; y (4) sentar las bases para la ejecución de un Programa de Desarrollo.

El Plan se adaptaría a las condiciones prevalecientes, y reconoce las modificaciones que se han producido en la tenencia de la vivienda urbana y en la organización para la producción agrícola. El Plan asimismo, otorga el derecho a los obreros de participar en la propiedad así como en la gestión de las empresas.

Cambio de Estructuras: Será necesario un cambio en las estructuras de poder y relaciones económicas, por lo cual se procederá a: (1) abolir la constitución política comunista, disolver la Asamblea Popular, las siete organizaciones de masas, la Unión de Jóvenes Comunistas y otras existentes; (2) incautar los bienes en usufructo por el Partido Comunista y sus organizaciones. El funcionamiento del Partido Comunista es sufragado por el Estado; (3) disolver los ministerios que son superfluos en una economía de mercado. De los 21 ministerios, nueve no serían necesarios; (4) liquidar operativa y financieramente las empresas del Estado relacionadas con los negocios de importación, exportación, y distribución; y (5) derogar las regulaciones que impiden el libre movimiento de personas, bienes y capital.

Requisitos Políticos: El Plan supone un escenario de solución política que de lugar a la instalación de un Gobierno Provisional que se ajuste a los requisitos básicos siguientes: (1) regirse por principios constitucionales democráticos generalmente aceptados; (2) observancia de todos y cada uno de los preceptos de la Declaración Universal de los Derechos del Hombre; y (3) cumplimiento de los compromisos internacionales contraídos y sometimiento de los diferendos a arbitraje cuando no se llega a acuerdos.

Dada las circunstancias, el Gobierno Provisional deberá asumir las funciones ejecutivas y legislativas. La misión del Gobierno consistirá en: (1) establecer un régimen de libertades públicas; (2) mantener la paz y tranquilidad social; (3) poner en vigor los arreglos institucionales y financieros para el reordenamiento de la producción; y (4) preparar al país para la celebración de elecciones municipales y generales.

Estrategia del Plan: La estrategia para la reestructuración económica comprenderá dos fases: Una fase inicial para reordenar el sistema de producción y distribución hacia una economía de mercado y una segunda fase para sentar las bases de la ejecución de un programa de desarrollo. Las dos fases, aunque nítidamente separadas, podrán llevarse a cabo en forma paralela.

El proceso del reordenamiento de la producción se cumplirá en un período breve. Consistirá básicamente en mantener los mecanismos de distribución y el pago de salarios en los primeros días del Gobierno Provisional y simultáneamente publicar los decretos de ordenamiento de la producción, divulgando su alcance y contenido a los interesados, en una etapa de preparación para el cambio. El conjunto pretende atraer la inversión real, en oposición a la inversión financiera, que de lugar a la creación de nuevos empleos.

Traspaso de los Medios de Producción: El medio para sentar las bases para un proceso de modernización y diversificación consistirá inicialmente en la venta de los medios de producción a los obreros y empleados y constitución de sociedades por acciones. Una premisa es que Cuba cuenta con los elementos de organización en la administración, así como recursos humanos, que harían viable el plan de ordenamiento de la producción.

Tomando en cuenta a las características de los sectores productivos y actividades, se adoptarán las siguientes modalidades para el traspaso de los medios de producción: (1) venta a los obreros y empleados de: pequeños negocios de venta al detalle y de prestación de servicios; industrias pequeñas y medianas; pequeña minería; hoteles y hospedajes; (2) constitución de compañías por acciones: industria azucarera; empresas industriales grandes; refinerías de petróleo; empresas eléctricas y de teléfono; flota mercante; ferrocarriles; transporte aéreo y complejos turísticos y grandes hoteles; (3) sistema de cooperativas: industria de pesca; transporte por carretera de carga y pasajeros. Con respecto a las fincas estatales y cooperativas, al concluir el ciclo agrícola en progreso, se dará la opción a los obreros de formar cooperativas o individualizar las explotaciones, siempre por medio de venta de las unidades de producción.

Condiciones de Traspaso: Las condiciones de traspaso en cuanto a la venta, se formalizarán mediante contratos de préstamo y de acuerdo a la tasación de los bienes. Según las características, riesgos y rentabilidad, el valor del préstamo, en relación con la tasación, habrá que variar. El propósito además es que las empresas cuenten con un capital inicial propio que les permita ser sujetos de crédito. Una proporción de las acciones de las compañías se distribuirá a los obreros y empleados. El Estado sera poseedor de la mayoría de las acciones.

Resultado Financiero del Traspaso: El traspaso de los bienes de producción mediante venta y constitución de empresas por acciones, dará lugar a una tenencia de instrumentos financieros en poder del Estado, respaldados por bienes raíces, equipamiento y existencias. El monto de estos títulos permitirá absorber yerros de cálculo y servirán como base de recursos financieros para la creación de la banca oficial y privada, lo cual se trata más adelante, y para dotar de un patrimonio al fondo de pensiones y jubilaciones.

Mecanismos Institucionales

Banco Nacional de Cuba: El mecanismo principal para llevar a cabo la fase inicial del proceso de transformación sería el Banco Nacional de Cuba, que cuenta con oficinas en todo el territorio del país, debiendo organizarse en tres departamentos básicos: banca comercial, financiamiento agrícola y financiamiento industrial. El personal del Banco Nacional de Cuba asignado al financiamiento agrícola, industria y comercio, en la fase de transición, constituirán los núcleos para integrar las instituciones financieras privadas y del Estado.

Se autorizaría al Banco Nacional de Cuba, en la fase inicial, a otorgar anticipos en forma de préstamos a las industrias y agricultura para financiar básicamente sueldos y salarios y compra de materias primas y capital de trabajo permanente. También se autorizará a hacer anticipos al Gobierno Central y Municipios para pagos de sueldos y gastos de funcionamiento.

Bolsas de Trabajo: La reducción del aparato estatal, de las fuerzas armadas y los criterios de eficiencia económica, originarán un desempleo abierto. El Gobierno Provisional, por tanto, estará obligado para mantener la tranquilidad social a hacer pagos por desempleo. Además será necesario disponer de un mecanismo de información sobre empleo y desempleo. Para cumplir con ambos propósitos, se crearán las Bolsas de Trabajo, que tendrán a su cargo la administración del pago por desempleo y proporcionar información sobre necesidades de adiestramiento y oportunidades de empleos.

Ministerio de Hacienda: Los anticipos fiscales para pago de sueldos al personal y jubilados podrá constituirse en una emisión monetaria inorgánica, al no haber un respaldo del mecanismo de recaudación de impuestos. Será necesario que el Ministerio de Hacienda examine de inmediato los dispositivos de transferencia de recursos financieros por las empresas al Estado, para su captación y ponga en vigor un sistema impositivo simple de carácter interino, basado inclusive en la rentabilidad presunta de las empresas, con carácter retroactivo a la fecha de transformación, así como un arancel de aduanas.

Riesgos del Proceso de Transformación

Los riesgos del proceso de transformación que se pueden identificar, son los siguientes:

• Datos de las empresas y censos agropecuarios— Para minimizar este riesgo y disponer de información, se ha previsto que en la inscripción de los establecimientos, en las oficinas del Banco Nacional de Cuba, se incluirá información básica para su tabulación y análisis.

• Capacidad gerencial—Las debilidades que se encuentran deberán superarse por medio de programas intensivos de adiestramiento organizados por los Bancos del Estado. Se establecerá además que estos bancos participen en la administración de las empresas por acciones. Para ciertas empresas y negocios la gestión puede ser contratada con terceros.

- Sistema de distribución y almacenaje—Las compras, almacenaje y distribución de bienes de consumo, daría lugar a un trastorno inicial, agravado por el hecho de no contarse con reservas de alimentos y dificultades de transporte. Sin embargo la liberalización del comercio y de los precios, unido a la importación de alimentos, aliviaría el problema de suministros, hasta tanto se restablezca la producción.

- Comercio exterior—Es de esperar una perturbación en las exportaciones y además habrá que hacer desviaciones para abastecer el consumo interno.

Instituciones Financieras

Una vez establecido el sistema de libre concurrencia será necesario para la reactivación económica y ejecución de un Programa de Desarrollo Económico, el crear instituciones financieras públicas y privadas. Los títulos financieros en poder del Estado producto del proceso de transformación servirán de base para el establecimiento de las siguientes entidades:

Instituciones del Estado: Se crearán sendos Bancos del Estado: El Banco Agrícola y el Banco Industrial, que actuarán también como agentes financieros del Gobierno para canalizar la asistencia financiera oficial y fomento de las actividades productivas.

Instituciones Privadas: Se constituirán los siguientes sistemas financieros: Banca Comercial—Por medio de la venta a intereses privados de las cuentas de depósito del público y la cartera de préstamos comerciales creadas en el Banco Nacional de Cuba. Sistema de Ahorro y Préstamos—También se crearían estas asociaciones, vendiendo a intereses privados la cartera de préstamos de vivienda y del Banco de Ahorro Popular. Sistema de Seguros—Para el sistema deberán dictarse las regulaciones y normas de seguro y reaseguro. No hay una base en Cuba para la constitución de toda la gama de un sistema de seguro y reaseguro. Bolsa de Valores—También deberán dictarse en primera instancia las regulaciones y normas necesarias

para la operación de la bolsa de valores. Fondo de Pensiones y Jubilaciones—Con la cartera de acciones en empresas y contribuciones de los empleados se constituirá un fondo de Pensiones y Jubilaciones de carácter privado. La cuantía del Fondo se determinará en función de un estudio actuarial. Es de esperar que los recursos del Fondo sirvan de medio para el funcionamiento de la bolsa de valores, que facilite la inversión a largo plazo.[3]

Demanda de Recursos Financieros

Las reservas del país serían mínimas y por tanto insuficientes para financier las importaciones necesarias para mantener el aparato de producción y se confrontaría la cuestión de la provisión de alimentos a la población. A fin de mitigar esta situación se tomarían las siguientes acciones:

- Obtención de Recursos Externos—Cuba debería gestionar la obtención de un préstamo puente del Gobierno de los Estados Unidos, por medio del Departamento del Tesoro, para apoyo de balanza de pagos, hasta se que se puede contar con financiamiento del Fondo Monetario Internacional (FMI). También se daría prioridad a procurar del Gobierno de Estados Unidos la provisión de alimentos para seis meses de necesidades, en base al programa de ayuda conocido como PL-480. Los fondos generados en la moneda nacional, por la venta de los productos al consumidor, se utilizarían para el fomento de la producción agrícola.

- Recursos Internos—El Banco Nacional de Cuba, la única fuente de crédito disponible en la etapa de transformación, evitará que el financiamiento a las industrias y al sector agrícola encubra ineficiencias y limitaría su financiamiento al capital de trabajo, incluyendo la importación de materias primas, repuestos y equipos, relacionados con la producción. El objetivo sería evitar que la actividad crediticia provoque un proceso inflacionario. La política de financiamiento tiene

---

3. La función del fondo de pensiones deberá quedar separada de la asistencia social, o sea el "safety net" inicial, y ella debidamente regulada. No se autorizará que los recursos financieros del fondo se destinen a la compra de títulos del gobierno para financiar el deficit presupuestario en cuenta corriente.

también relación con los gastos del Gobierno, por lo cual deberá producirse una estrecha colaboración entre el Ministerio de Hacienda y el Banco. La situación económica de Cuba obliga a atraer el ahorro externo y por ende la inversión, que como se dijo, debe consistir en inversión real, en oposición a la de carácter financiero. Como ello es esencial para hacer viable el proceso de reordenamiento de la economía deberán adoptarse políticas y gestionarse financiamientos.

Cuantificación de Demanda de Recursos Financieros: Para la cuantificación de la demanda de recursos pueden brindarse los siguientes datos, que son de carácter indicativo:

- Administración pública—El personal profesional y técnico de los sistemas de salud pública y educación es elevado y la población jubilada de 1,200,000 personas. A esto debe agregarse, en la fase de reconstrucción, a cerca de un millón de desempleados a los cuales será necesario brindarles un mínimo de seguridad.

- Agricultura—Será necesario a corto plazo reponer el parque de tractores y equipo agrícola. La población ganadera vacuna deberá duplicarse sobre el número actual de 4,900,000 cabezas.

- Industria—El costo unitario de crear un empleo industrial es elevado y guarda relación con el tipo de industria y la tecnología a emplear. Este costo puede oscilar entre un importe mínimo de tres mil dólares por empleo como ejemplo, para maquiladoras, a una cifra del orden de cien mil dólares. Como la creación de nuevos empleos estará dado por los sectores industriales y de servicio, al haber agotado la agricultura sus posibilidades, la magnitud de las inversiones serán de gran envergadura. Sólo como referencia puede inferirse que la creación de 500,000 empleos, a razón de diez mil dólares por cada uno, demandaría recursos de inversión por cinco mil millones de dólares.

- Energía y comunicaciones—La generación de energía atómica y la ampliación de las comunicaciones telefónicas exigirán inversiones cuantiosas.

- Parque automotor—Se requiere renovar y añadir unidades en un número apreciable al parque automotor destinado al transporte de carga y pasajeros.

La Sección IX, "Análisis Especifico Industrial," contenido en la publicación de la Fundación Cubano-Americana, contiene cifras indicativas de requerimientos de inversion para algunos sectores claves.[4] Las estimaciones de inversión hechas son como sigue: (a) telecomunicaciones: $2,456 millones en un período de 10 años; (b) energía eléctrica: Entre $190 millones a $360 millones en un período de 5 años; (c) transporte: A corto plazo, o sea, en un período de 5 años las necesidades ascenderían a $1,710 millones desglosados en la siguiente forma—transporte público: $360 millones; ferrocarriles: $1,350 millones. A largo plazo se precisarían $4,510 millones para infraestructura vial; (d) para construccion de viviendas, reparaciones de viviendas y edificios públicos el importe estimado para los primeros años sería $1,000 millones. En el estudio citado no se hizo una estimación de las demandas de inversión en el sector de agua potable y alcantarillado sanitario,

Fuentes de Recursos Financieros

La cuantificación somera de los ingresos fiscales necesarios para el funcionamiento del Gobierno y los niveles de inversión requeridos para la reactivación y modernización de la economía evidencian que la contribución de cada cubano en la Isla y en el exterior es esencial, no habiendo lugar para el reclamo de intereses, que pierden trascendencia ante la magnitud del esfuerzo a realizar. Esfuerzo que a su vez significará oportunidades para todos.

Inversión Privada: La piedra angular sería la atracción de la inversión privada. Consistente con una economía de mercado, donde el criterio de eficiencia debe prevalecer, no se otorgarán incentivos, ni se im-

---

4. *The Cuban Economy: Blueprint for Reconstruction* (Miami: The Endowment for Cuban American Studies, Cuban-American National Foundatiom, Octubre 1992).

Cuadro 1. Actividades Económicas y su Financiamiento

Demanda	Posibles Fuentes
Reactivación económica	
1. Agricultura; insumos importados	Organismos regionales e internacionales
2. Industria; materias primas y repuestos	Organismos regionales e internacionales
Desarrollo económico	
1. Agricultura; equipamiento	Organismos regionales e internacionales, préstamos de proveedores
2. Industria; expansión	Generación interna de fondos; inversión privada
3. Energía y comunicaciones; expansión	Usuarios, inversión privada, proveedores, organismos regionales e internacionales

pondrán restricciones al libre movimiento de capitales. No será necesario, por consiguiente, emitir una ley de inversiones. La única concesión podría consistir en la afiliación de Cuba a la Agencia Multilateral de Garantía de Inversiones, del Grupo del Banco Mundial, para cubrir el riesgo político de la inversión extranjera.

Asistencia Financiera Bilateral y Multilateral: Cuba debe reintegrarse a la comunidad financiera internacional. Para la admisión en los organismos regionales y multilaterales de financiamiento y cooperación técnica será necesario cumplir con requisitos formales y de índole financiera. En los primeros organismos se encuentra el Banco Interamericano de Desarrollo y en los segundos el Grupo del Banco Mundial y el Fondo Monetario Internacional. Cuba mantiene su vinculación con los organismos especializados de Naciones Unidas.

De inmediato deberá invitarse al país a una misión técnica del Fondo Monetario Internacional para sentar las bases de incorporación al sistema monetario internacional y examinar la política de la nación. Si es necesario deberá gestionarse colaboración para fortalecer el sistema de estadísticas y de cuentas nacionales.

La dificultad para Cuba consiste en que al no ser miembro de estos organismos no tiene asignado cupos de financiamiento. Las disponibilidades de recursos del Gobierno de Cuba congelados por Estados Unidos, por alrededor de noventa millones de dólares, se emplearían para el pago de cuotas a los mencionados organismos internacionales.

Por fuerza será necesario lograr el concurso y apoyo del Gobierno de Estados Unidos con tres propósitos:

obtener asistencia financiera de emergencia; agilizar la incorporación de Cuba a los organismos internacionales y regionales; y cooperar en el logro de la participación de los países de la Unión Europea y Japón en la reconstrucción del país. Para ello será necesario contar con un plan concreto de trabajo.

Una vez cumplidos los requisitos de admisión a los organismos multilaterales y regionales, se solicitarán préstamos y colaboración para la formulación de estudios sectoriales para su posterior financiamiento. Las acciones aquí descritas deberán llevarse a cabo en forma simultánea e individualizada, para mantener el control y evitar la imposición de políticas y concesiones. Estas operaciones de financiamiento se caracterizarían en la forma que se muestra en el cuadro 1.

Otros Requerimientos: Como complemento habría que gestionar con los bancos de exportación e importación el otorgamiento de préstamos y garantías para equipamiento agrícola y la reposición del parque automotor del país. Se procederá a la emisión de bonos para ser ofrecida a los cubanos en el exterior, por unos cien millones de dólares. Para ello habría que cumplir con los requisitos de la Comisión de Valores de Estados Unidos (SEC) y designar a un agente financiero.

PROGRAMA DE DESARROLLO ECONOMICO

En correspondencia con el Plan para el Reordenamiento de la Economía y ante una coyuntura interna desfavorable y una externa no propicia, se hará necesario formular un Programa de Desarrollo Económico que permita superar los problemas existentes y sentar las bases para lograr un crecimiento sostenible. En el sector público, el Programa será dirigido por el

Ministerio de Economía con el concurso del Banco Central de Cuba y los bancos del Estado.

Fundamentos del Programa

El programa se fundamenta en el principio de que Cuba es viable económicamente, dado por su tamaño territorial y de población, recursos naturales y posición geográfica. La historia económica de Cuba, la capacidad empresarial demostrada y la condición de Isla, define el criterio básico de libre comercio y libre movimiento de capitales. La estrategia global se aparta de modelos rígidos de sustitución de importaciones o fomento de exportaciones como políticas de crecimiento, debido a los costos sociales que impone el primero y la exigencia de regímenes autoritarios que demanda el segundo modelo.

Como no puede separarse la acción política de la economía, el Programa de Desarrollo conjuga los dos conceptos basados en que la dirección de la economía es una función propia de los partidos políticos. El espacio para actuar de los partidos políticos, los profesionales, técnicos y obreros, dependerá de la respectiva competencia y dedicación y el respeto a la ley, que es fundamento de la democracia. El Programa, su ejecución, sus ajustes, es responsabilidad de la actual generación. Un compromiso con la que sería el Proyecto Cuba, como voluntad nacional.

Políticas Sectoriales

El Programa de Desarrollo se guiará por políticas de carácter indicativo. Estas se enumeran a continuación:

- Producción Agrícola—En base al tamaño geográfico, calidad de suelos, los hábitos alimenticios de la población, la política aspira a satisfacer la demanda de consumo interno y obtener excedentes para exportación. La explotación agrícola sería intensiva y en adición dirigida a fomentar la agroindustria, incluyendo la producción de materias primas y aprovechamiento de sub-productos.

- Producción de Azúcar—Dada la ventaja comparativa, el rol vital que juega en la economía y las características de su mercado, la industria azucarera quedaría reservada para intereses privados radicados en el país. Con el propósito de lograr

una actividad contínua y no estacional, el criterio para su explotación será el de eficiencia y aprovechamiento máximo de los sub-productos de la caña.

- Industria—La política industrial descansará en el pilar de la agroindustria. En el campo industrial, el desarrollo tecnológico y la organización global de la economía, abre posibilidades para la inversión privada.

- Servicios—Los servicios, especialmente el turismo, deberán ser un factor de creación de empleos y generación de divisas. Su desarrollo descansará en el turismo familiar, de clase media, que procura actividades recreativas sanas.

Política Energética

El supuesto básico de la política energética es que el petróleo es un recurso natural no renovable, sujeto a un precio de cartel, manipulable, para impedir la investigación y el desarrollo de fuentes alternativas de energía. Por tanto la política debe dirigirse al empleo de fuentes primarias tales como energía nuclear, biomasa y solar. El propósito de la política sería reducir la dependencia del petróleo a través de un esquema de producción, conservación y diversificación de fuentes de energía.

Política Impositiva

Los siguientes criterios guiarían la política impositiva: (a) principio de neutralidad—No se utilizarán para promover inversiones u otros objetivos sociales. De acuerdo con lo anterior no se emplearán mecanismos de transferencias implícitas. El subsidio por la parte del gasto fiscal será directo y por tanto transparente; (b) universalidad—El impuesto será universal. La universalidad se vincula directamente al derecho político ejercido por medio de representantes electos; (c) aranceles de aduana—Los derechos de aduana serían consistentes con la política de libre comercio y se aplicará en forma recíproca a los socios comerciales; (d) repatriación de utilidades—En forma igual a la política de libre movimiento de capitales no se gravará la repatriación de utilidades.

RESTITUCION/COMPENSACION DE BIENES

El proceso de confiscaciones en Cuba se extendió hasta convertir en propiedad estatal a casi la totalidad de los medios de producción y bienes raices. Además de los bienes físicos hubo quebrantos por pérdidas de activos financieros, como bonos del Gobierno en poder del público, los ahorros en fondos de retiro, todo acorde con una economía donde funcionaba el crédito. En el Anexo 1 se hace, como punto de referencia, un examen de la experiencia en los países de Europa del Este. En Alemania del Este se actuó con generosidad. En Hungría y la antigua Checoeslovaquia se han impuesto restricciones.[5]

Caso de Cuba

En base al examen que se hace en el Anexo 2, en la situación presente de Cuba pueden identificarse las siguientes situaciones:

- Vivienda Urbana—En general en Cuba se han vendido las viviendas a los ocupantes y ha habido otras modalidades como las construcciones dentro del systema de ayuda mutua y esfuerzo propio. Los derechos se limitan a la edificación ya que la tierra continúa siendo propiedad del Estado. La exepción son los bienes inmuebles traspasados al Partido Comunista.[6] Dentro de esta generalizacion es de destacar que en todas las localidades se establecieron zonas congeladas para el usufruto de los dirigentes, conocidos como la *nomenklatura*. Un punto relevante consiste en los derechos adquiridos en la materia de vivienda.[7]

- Propiedad Rural—No se han otorgado derechos en las fincas estatales, ahora Unidades Básicas de Producción Cooperativa, que representan el 83% del área agrícola. Se han hecho obras que han alterado físicamente la propiedad, tales como plantaciones permanentes, consolidación de áreas y especialización de actividades. La in-

certidumbre con respecto a la restitución de estas propiedades es la edad de los empresarios originales y su capacidad financiera para explotar las empresas agrícolas. El tiempo transcurrido es un factor adverso.[8]

- Sector Azucarero—Los arreglos anteriores de la industria azucarera dados por el colonato, han perdido vigencia al haberse perdido la cuota azucarera de Estados Unidos, que daba lugar a una rentabilidad financiera aceptable. La cuota azucarera representaba un subsidio a Cuba que era apoyado por otros sectores del mencionado país. Como la eficiencia debe ser la norma del sector azucarero y dada su importancia económica, debe por necesidad, quedar reservada para intereses radicados en el país. La restitución, sobre todo a intereses en el exterior vinculados al negocio azucarero, no sería prudente.

- Sector Industrial—El equipamiento y las edificaciones originales son obsoletos. Las industria establecidas en los años 1950s, se financiaron en muchos casos, con préstamos de la banca oficial. En principio la restitución debería condicionarse a casos calificados de empresarios con capacidad financiera para explotar las industrias.

- Comercios—El remanente del proceso de confiscaciones en este grupo consiste en edificaciones, con una utilidad limitada, hasta tanto se recupere el ingreso de la población. La restitución también debería limitarse a casos calificados.

Intereses Foráneos: Otro antecedente que complicaría un proceso de restituciones de propiedades es el caso de intereses extranjeros, que aparentemente no

---

5. Más información sobre las características de los esquemas de restitución y compensación en algunos países de Europa Central se encuentran en el trabajo de Rolando H. Castañeda y George Plinio Montalván, "Economic Factors in Selecting an Approach to Confiscation Claims in Cuba," *Cuba in Transition—Volume 5* (Washington: Association for the Study of the Cuban Economy, 1995).

6. Información sobre los arreglos y términos de venta de las viviendas urbanas aparece en "Private Property Rights in Cuba: Housing," *Boletín de la Sociedad Económica* 15 (1991).

7. Como se dice en el documento *Apoyo para Una Transición Democrática en Cuba*, Informe Presidencial emitido en Washington (28 de enero de 1997), "el propiertario de una vivienda que haya adquirido derechos a bienes previamente expropiados esperará que un gobierno de transición, en búsqueda de soluciones...preste la debida atención a los derechos adquiridos..."

8. Información sobre el sistema de tenencia de la tierra aparece en "Private Property Rights in Cuba: Farmland," *Boletín de la Sociedad Económica* 16 (1992).

se presenta en los paises del desaparecido bloque socialista ya que el Gobierno de Estados Unidos aceptó deducir del Impuesto sobre la Renta las pérdidas incurridas por sus ciudadanos en Cuba. La restitución o compensación de estos casos, sería gravada, convirtiéndose en una transferencia de recursos financieros al mencionado gobierno.

También es posible que se planteen demandas de grupos organizados. Uno de ellos es el "Cuban Claims Associates" que registró reclamaciones en Washington. Asimismo el régimen de Castro ha formalizado arreglos de compensación con España y probablemente con otros países. El admitir un tratamiento preferencial a intereses foráneos no sería equitativo.

Compensación de Bienes Confiscados

Para una mejor comprensión de la materia de la compensación resulta apropiado incorporarla en el contexto de la deuda externa. Como definición y para efectos de este trabajo, la deuda externa comprende las compensaciones derivadas de las reclamaciones por propiedades confiscadas; préstamos externos; e inversiones. Esta clasificacion obedece al efecto en la balanza de pagos por pagos de intereses y dividendos, repatriación de capitales y amortizacion de préstamos. No estarían presentes otras partidas como royalties, reaseguros y transferencias.

Las Confiscaciones: Previamente coresponde destacar que en forma arbitraria se hace una distinción entre las propiedades confiscadas a no nacionales y nacionales, lo cual se origina en el derecho reconocido a un país de expropiar a extranjeros, sujeto a la condición de adecuada compensación. En Cuba la confiscación fue generalizada y por consiguiente no habría lugar para hacer esta diferencia y por tanto el tratamiento debe ser idéntico. Un fundamento para este alegato sería la doctrina del jurista argentino Calvo: el extranjero es igual al nacional ante la ley.

La Compensación: José F. Alonso y Armando M.Lago, en el modelo economico sobre las perspectivas en

una Cuba democrática post Castro, que contiene tres escenarios, estimaron el valor de las propiedades confiscadas para incorporar el correspondiente flujo financiero al modelo.[9] La hipótesis del estudio de Alonso y Lago fué el de la compensacion, sin que ello implique que hayan tomado una posición sobre el tema de la restitución o la compensación. El valor estimado de las compensaciones a ciudadanos de Estados Unidos, incluyendo intereses acumulados ascendería a $5,364 millones a agosto de 1993. Con respecto a los ciudadanos cubanos la valuación se estimó entre $6,924 millones y $6,733 millones. Con la capitalización de intereses el valor alcanza a $20 mil millones, a mediados de 1993.

Surge del trabajo de Alonso y Lago que en el escenario de una privatización parcial, el servicio de estas obligaciones no sería factible; parcialmente en el segundo, al darse preferencia a las compensaciones a cuidadanos americanos. En el tercer escenario, la factibilidad se daría en el año t-10, aunque implicaría una menor tasa de crecimiento en la recuperación económica. La capitalización de intereses producto de las reclamaciones supone que en Cuba no sucedió nada y por tanto procede el reconocimiento del lucro cesante.

Opción para las Estimación de las Compensaciones: La proposición contraria es que en Cuba aconteció algo y para establecer el valor actual de las propiedades confiscadas, tanto urbanas como las de producción, podría emplearse el metodo de flujos descontados de fondos. Con este método, de hacerse el cómputo en base a los precios al momento del cambio, se puede anticipar que el resultado final sería irrisorio para los casos de producción de bienes para el consumo interno y viviendas debido a que la población sencillamente no tiene capacidad de pago. El cálculo reflejaría que en Cuba hubo acaecimientos. Ello obedece a que los salarios, particularmente, estan fijados a nivel de subsistencia que incluye las distorsiones en el pago de la renta de la vivienda y por los servicios a la población.

---

9. José F. Alonso y Armando M. Lago, "A First Approximation of the Foreign Assistance Requirements of a Democratic Cuba," *Cuba in Transition—Volume 3* (Washington: Association for the Study of the Cuban Economy, 1993).

Para rectificar esta anomalía podrían emplearse para los costos los precios de frontera que no daría solución al problema, ya que la población no tiene capacidad de pago, aunque puede anticiparse que si tendría una disposicion a pagar, condicionada, desde luego a la eventualidad de una recuperación económica rápida. Para los productos de exportación, que sería otro extremo, puede esperarse que los resultados sean positivos y por ello, como se dijo, habría que acudir a los precios de frontera para superar las discrepancias. Se considera que el estudio de Alonso y Lago aqui citado es sustancial y podría servir de base para la toma de decisiones en materia de restitución de bienes y en su defecto la compensación.

El tema de las compensaciones esta vinculado directamente a la atención del servicio de la deuda externa de Cuba, de lo cual se informa a continuación.

Préstamos Externos: La deuda externa de Cuba en moneda convertible se estimaba en $10,552 millones de los cuales $4,100 millones estaban en mora.[10]

Inversiones Extranjeras: Los importes comprometidos y desembolsados de la inversión extranjera, según el estudio de Maria C. Werlau, ascendían a $751,900,000. Esta cifra, sin hacer calificaciones sobre su orígen y naturaleza, se emplea para el cómputo de las obligaciones financieras en moneda extranjera.[11] No obstante es de mencionar que estas inversiones son en esencia, de caracter financiero, y por tanto no dan lugar a ampliaciones de la capacidad instalada y que en su caso son esfuerzo interno.[12] El riesgo político asumido por los inversionistas es elevado y de ello el amparo de los acuerdos a nivel de gobiernos sobre protección de inversiones. La capacidad juridica para contratar de una de las partes es cuestionable.

Impacto Finaciero de la Deuda Externa Total

El cómputo de la deuda externa que tendría que enfrentar Cuba sería de $36 mil millones. Una consecuencia de reconocer las compensaciones sería el de crear una deuda interna a residentes en el exterior, que limitaría la capacidad de endeudamiento del país. Otro efecto en cuanto a la factibilidad de reconocer estas obligaciones por compensación a extranjeros y nacionales es que para su atención deberán generarse exportaciones. Sería un caso de "transfer," término relacionado con las reparaciones de guera impuestas a Alemania en 1921 por $31 mil millones (132 mil millones en marcos oro), para lo cual debería contarse con un excedente de exportaciones. Escapa al alcance de este trabajo el examen del tema, ya que se menciona con el solo propósito de llamar la atención sobre las complejidades que tal reconocimiento de obligaciones significan.[13] Luis Locay, en sus comentarios especificos al trabajo de Alonso y Lago hace referencias al concepto de "transfer" y señala que la compensación, en la manera que fue formulada, es simplemente una transferencia de riqueza al exterior.[14]

Hay otra implicacion que conviene recordar. Era uno de los aspectos que complicaba la solución política de los problemas de Cuba a la terminación de las hostilidades en 1898: la deuda de guerra registrada por España en la "Cuenta Cuba," que excedía al valor de la propiedad raíz de la Isla.

Principio de Solidaridad: Como no existe la opción de la autarquía y necesariamente deberá rescatarse el crédito público de la Nación, habrá que acudir a la búsqueda de apoyo en el exterior. Alberto Martínez-Piedra y Lorenzo L. Pérez han argumentado en forma

10. Gabriel Fernández, "Hard Currency Debt," *Cuba in Transition—Volume 6* (Washington: Association for the Study of the Cuban Economy, 1996), table 1, p. 47.

11. Maria C. Werlau, "Foreign Invesment in Cuba: The Limits of Commercial Engagement," *Cuba in Transition—Volume 6* (Washington: Association for the Study of Cuban Economy, 1996), Table 2.

12. Un examen de las inversiones muestra que estan relacionadas con la exportación de bienes y turismo. Solo un proyecto es para consumo domestico: bicicletas, de acuerdo a un arreglo con China.

13. Charles E. Staley, "The Transfer Problem and the Optimun Amount of Foreign Investment," *International Economics: Analysis and Issues* (Englewood Cliffs: Prentice-Hall, 1970).

14. Luis Locay, "Comments on Alonso and Lago, 'A First Approximation of the Foreign Assistance Requirements of a Democratic Cuba,'" *Cuba in Transition—Volume 3* (Washington: Association for the Study of the Cuban Economy, 1993).

persuasiva sobre el asunto de la deuda externa y el principio de solidaridad. Aunque los conceptos por ellos formulados se dirigen a los problemas de la deuda externa convencional y con el enfoque de que se trata de casos de liquidez, este pensamiento como se demuestra, es aplicable al caso de Cuba y mas aún cuando evidentemente se puede calificar como de solvencia.[15] El principio de solidaridad demandaría que la reduccion de la deuda externa, dentro de los esquemas existentes, se extienda a las demandas de compensaciones por propiedades confiscadas, tanto por los extranjeros como por los nacionales cubanos.

Conclusion Preliminar

La solución de las confiscaciones se plantea en términos simplificados de restitución de los bienes, sin calificaciones y en su defecto proceder a compensaciones monetarias. La restitución de la propiedad raíz urbana, que sería la existente no sería factible ya que daría lugar a un desalojo masivo de la población que la colocaría en una situación de precariedad insoportable.

El examen hecho demuestra que no se podría proceder a la restitución de las viviendas urbanas, debido a hechos que han dado lugar a la creación de derechos para los ocupantes. La restitución en los otros sectores pudiera hacerse en casos calificados, sujeto a que presenten un plan de trabajo factible, para la modernización de las empresas y reconozcan la participación de los trabajadores en el capital accionario.

Estos hechos derivarían la proposición de otorgar algún tipo de compensación. Ello, dado el tiempo transcurrido, obligaría a reconocer derechos a herederos y sucesores, siempre incorporando la carga que pesaba sobre los bienes confiscados.

Otro factor que implica la proposición, es el hecho que los cubanos radicados en el exterior procurarían convertir la compensación e inclusive la restitución, a monedas extranjeras con repercusiones negativas para la economía del país. Lo significativo de proponer algún tipo de compensación es que equivaldría a un tipo de reparación de guerra que el país no podrá satisfacer y crearía rentistas radicados en el exterior, originando una salida cuantiosa de divisas.

Sin embargo es necesario por un lado reparar en la medida de lo posible las injusticias cometidas contra ciudadanos cubanos tanto en la Isla como expatriados, asi como a extranjeros, y más importante procurar la incorporación de todos los ciudadanos al proceso de reconstrucción de la Isla. También es de interés preservar valores y tradiciones y, por tanto, sería apropiado restituir los bienes y asegurar el desarrollo de instituciones tales como fundaciones, entidades mutualistas y asociaciones de beneficencia culturales y de educación. Finalmente, el derecho de propiedad debe quedar nítidamente establecido, al ser una condición necesaria para el funcionamiento de una economía de mercado.

En base al examen hecho y considerando que Cuba presenta una situación de calamidad pública y el interés nacional, se recomienda decretar en primera instancia que todos los inmuebles del país, incluyendo tierras, edificaciones e instalaciones, así como los bienes muebles, son propiedad de la Nación y en segunda instancia establecer que no se admitirán reclamaciones de ningún tipo. Sobre esta base es que podrían dictarse normas para restitución de propiedades.

Alternativa de Restitución de Bienes Confiscados

La compensación por bienes confiscados, como se ha procurado demostrar, no sería factible financieramente. Por consiguiente en el caso de Cuba quedaría solamente la alternativa de la restitución de bienes, que dado el tiempo transcurrido y las condiciones del pais, deberá hacerse en forma calificada y que no den lugar a la creación de expectativas y por tanto a incertidumbres sobre la propiedad de la tierra. El pragmatismo es lo que debería gobernar el proceso, dentro de la proposición básica de rescatar el crédito público de la Nación. No se alentaría la presentacion de solicitudes de restitución. Dentro de ello se tomaría la iniciativa de proceder a la devolución de los bienes

---

15. Alberto Martínez-Piedra y Lorenzo L. Pérez, "External Debt Problems and the Principle of Solidarity: The Cuban Case," *Cuba in Transition—Volume 6* (Washington: Association for the Study of the Cuban Economy, 1996).

que se ajusten al esquema que se detalla en el Anexo 3 de este trabajo.

OTROS TEMAS

En esta sección se examinan temas específicos que deberían ser de atención por el Gobierno Provisional.

Deuda con la Banca Internacional—La razonalidad de esta deuda se establecerá en términos de la contribución al desarrollo del país, el beneficio a la población cubana y eliminación de los términos onerosos de contratación. El reconocimiento de la deuda se basará en el valor de mercado previo a la disolución de la Unión Soviética. En esta cuestión con la comunidad financiera internacional, el Gobierno Provisional adoptará en las negociaciones de la deuda una posición firme, aunque flexible.

Deuda con el ex-Bloque Soviético—La deuda con el ex-Bloque Soviético es definitivamente cuestionable, para no decir espurea, expresada originalmente en una moneda no convertible, que además respondía a un sistema de trueque y provisión de bienes y servicios, para fines políticos. No obstante es de interés para Cuba el mantener relaciones comerciales con Rusia y los otros estados que integraban la Unión Soviética, así como con los países de la Europa del Este. De acuerdo con este interés la deuda sería examinada de acuerdo a su origen, en relación con alimentos, materias primas para la producción, equipos agrícolas e industriales, armamentos militares, pagos de asesores, sostenimiento de tropas soviéticas en Cuba, contribuciones para el aparato de represión y propaganda y transferencias a terceros países, valorando las exportaciones y las importaciones para uso estrictamente civil, a precios internacionales y competitivos en cuanto a calidad. En base a todo ello se establecerá el saldo de la deuda. En otro orden se cuantificará el perjuicio en crecimiento económico ocasionado a Cuba, como resultado de su condición de satélite de la desaparecida Unión Soviética.

Reservas de Oro—El Gobierno Provisional deberá exigir la devolución de las reservas de oro de Cuba, que fueron trasladadas en depósito a la desaparecida Unión Soviética.

Bienes del Estado—El Gobierno Provisional deberá tomar posesión de una serie de bienes dispersos en todo el país, entre los que se encuentran: depósitos y almacenes de materias primas y materiales, equipos y repuestos; edificios, equipos y vehículos asignados al Partido Comunista; instalaciones de recreación y esparcimiento para uso exclusivo de la clase dirigente; residencias que están sólo a la disposición de los jerarcas; residencias de la tropas y asesores extranjeros; empresas comerciales establecidas en el exterior; cuentas bancarias personales en el exterior; cuentas bancarias en el exterior del aparato de inteligencia y propaganda; embarques de importación y exportación en tránsito; y activos financieros congelados por potencias extranjeras. Para la preservación de estos bienes se organizará un grupo de trabajo en el Ministerio de Hacienda, que se constituirá en la Dirección de Bienes del Estado, encargada del registro, clasificación y disposición de los mismos.

Anexo 1
RESTITUCION Y COMPENSACION DE PROPIEDADES CONFISCADAS: EXPERIENCIA DE EUROPA DEL ESTE

ALEMANIA DEL ESTE

Política adoptada—Compensación y restitución, calificada como de forma generosa.

Regulaciones—Se acepta sólo reclamaciones de propiedades confiscadas después de 1949.

Número de Reclamaciones—Hasta el final de 1990: 500,000; En 1991: 700,000. Integradas por tierras, viviendas y 10,000 por empresas.

Observaciones sobre el proceso—Calificado como un desastre. Resentimientos sobre los reclamantes que habían escapado del país.

Acciones—Prioridad de compensaciones sobre restituciones. Creación de un fondo de compensación.

Efecto sobre la privatización—Desaliento y paralización de nuevas inversiones. Demoras en la transferencia de empresas al sector privado. Incertidumbre sobre derechos de propiedad de la tierra.

HUNGRIA

Política Adoptada—Compensación por medio de bonos (vouchers).

Regulaciones—Limitado a los que perdieron propiedades después de 1949, y a ciudadanos húngaros al tiempo de la confiscación, descendientes de estos, o sus esposos. Las reclamaciones no deben de exceder US$ 70,000 individualmente. Se espera que el costo final exceda a mil millones de dólares.

Número de Reclamaciones—Reclamaciones esperadas de tierras cultivables: 800,000; Reclamaciones esperadas por otros bienes: 30,000.

Observaciones sobre el proceso—Los húngaros expatriados, un tercio de la población total, que espera-ban reclamar predios rurales o villas en Budapest, se han resentido. El esquema adoptado se considera el único compromiso que podía ser asumido.

Efecto sobre la privatización—El propósito fundamental es buscar una solución al tema de derechos de propiedad.

CHECOESLOVAQUIA[16]

Política adoptada—Basada en el criterio moral de la justificación de la restitución.

Regulaciones—Limitado a pequeños negocios y viviendas nacionalizadas después de 1948. La tierra e industria serán objeto de otra ley. No se incluyen reclamaciones de emigrados, unos 500,000, a no ser que regresen y fijen su residencia en el país, antes del 30 de septiembre de 1991. Si las reclamaciones son por una vivienda, el reclamante debe negociar con el ocupante de la misma. Si no es posible la restitución, se hará una compensación en efectivo, mil dólares, y el resto en bonos.

Número de reclamaciones—Unas 600,000.

Observaciones. sobre el proceso—El esquema no se considera viable.

Efecto sobre la privatización—Los propósitos consisten, en clarificar el derecho de propiedad para facilitar la privatización de los pequeños negocios a fin de crear una clase media propietaria, y acelerar las políticas de reforma. Las propuestas de inversión de los emigrados, no deben mezclarse con reclamaciones de restituciones.

Fuentes: "The Compensation and Restitution of Property Confiscated by Communist Governments to Former Owners: The Example of Eastern Europe," Sociedad Económica de Amigos del País, *Interim Report* 1 (1991).

---

16. Hubo una separación constituyéndose dos Repúblicas, la Checa y Eslovaquia.

Anexo 2
RESTITUCION Y COMPENSACION DE PROPIEDADES CONFISCADAS: CASO DE CUBA

La restitución de la propiedad confiscada o compensaciones tiene relación directa con reparar injusticias, un valor moral. También tiene vinculación con el derecho de propiedad que posibilite junto con el contrato, el funcionamiento de una economía basada en la iniciativa y propiedad privada. No obstante, el tratamiento de la cuestión no debe vincularse al establecimiento de una economía social de mercado, particularmente en el caso de Cuba.

Alemania, Hungría y Checoslovaquia han adoptado medidas que comprenden restitución, compensación o una combinación de ambos. El examen que se hace en el Anexo 1 evidencia que los esquemas adoptados impiden el desenvolvimiento económico y en el caso de compensaciones es altamente cuestionable su viabilidad financiera.

RESTITUCION DE BIENES
Propiedad Urbana—Se han creado derechos, al haberse otorgado contratos de venta de vivienda. La excepción son las viviendas en mal estado. Las viviendas y edificios requieren de reparaciones y reemplazos de instalaciones.

Propiedad Rural—No se han otorgado derechos en las fincas estatales. En estos predios se han producido cambios físicos, incluyendo plantaciones permanentes.

Ingenios Azucareros—Se hicieron inversiones en mejoras y ampliaciones, construcciones nuevas y se eliminaron un número de doce unidades.

Industrias—El equipamiento y las edificaciones originales son obsoletas. En particular es de señalar que las industrias establecidas en la década de los cincuenta se financiaron, en muchos casos, con préstamos de la banca oficial.

Conclusiones: De lo expuesto surge que la restitución de bienes confiscados no debiera adoptarse como una norma general.

COMPENSACION POR BIENES CONFISCADOS
No se estima que un país empobrecido esté en capacidad de absorber el costo de la compensación, limitado inclusive a bienes físicos. Los siguientes factores de órden financieros y administrativos, en adición apoyan esta proposición:

• Para las unidades de vivienda, el precio actual esta en función del nivel de ingreso de la población, del cual se deriva la renta. El precio sería superior al costo de transacción de la tramitación de reclamaciones.

• Para la propiedad rural—fincas estatales—cualquier precio razonable sería imposible de financiar. Un precio del equivalente de 500 dólares por hectárea arrojaría un total de cinco mil millones de dólares, o sea cinco mil dólares por habitantes, como deuda nacional.

• La rentabilidad de la industria azucarera dependía del subsidio implícito en la cuota azucarera de Estados Unidos. De excluirse este factor, el valor de un ingenio como negocio en marcha, no sería significativo.

• Para la industria, solo el valor residual de la tierra sería relevante, sin incluir los gravámenes que pesaban sobre la empresa. En menor medida esto es aplicable a los comercios.

Anexo 3
CUBA: ESQUEMA DE RESTITUCION DE PROPIEDADES CONFISCADAS

Viviendas: Sin condiciones respecto a propiedades: (a) ubicadas en zonas congeladas de las ciudades y que por consiguiente han sido asignadas a los miembros de la *nomenklatura*[17]; (b) ocupadas por extranjeros; o (c) puestas a disposición de legaciones y entidades extranjeras.

Edificaciones: Condiciones: Demostración de capacidad para renovarlas, si fuere el caso, asi como para operarlas y mantenerlas. Comprenderían las pertenecientes a: (a) asociaciones mutualistas, colegios profesionales y gremiales, fundaciones y centros educativos; (b) comercios por departamento y similares; o (c) oficinas bancarias.

Industrias: Condiciones: Presentación de un plan de negocios, incluyendo el componente financiero y sujeto a distribuir una proporción del capital existente para: (a) el fondo de jubilaciones y pensiones; y (b) a los obreros y empleados.

Casos Especiales: (a) Ingenios Azucareros: Participación en el capital accionario; (b) Medios de Difusión (prensa escrita y de televisión): Podrían precisar de un subsidio temporal hasta tanto puedan generar ingresos por publicidad.

Patrimonio Familiar: Dentro del esquema de restitucion se procuraría crear un patrimonio familiar representado por bienes físicos, como viviendas, para familias que hayan sufrido quebrantos de envergadura.

---

17. Las zonas congeladas que son controladas por el Ministerio del Interior han sido extendidas a la playa de Varadero y probablemente a otros complejos turísticos.

LIBERALIZATION AND THE BEHAVIOR OF OUTPUT DURING THE TRANSITION FROM PLAN TO MARKET

Ernesto Hernández-Catá[1]

Recently a number of empirical studies have begun to analyze the evolution of output during the transition from planned to market economy in the countries of Central and Eastern Europe and the former Soviet Union.[2] A number of important conclusions emerge from the analysis of the reform process, some of which are illustrated in Table 1 and Chart 1: (i) In its early stages, the process of liberalization and macroeconomic stabilization involves a large fall in output in virtually every country in the area.[3] (ii) Initially, the fall in output tends to be particularly steep in those countries where the liberalization effort is relatively strong. (iii) After a number of years, however, the countries where liberalization was strong and early show the highest rates of output growth, and the smallest cumulative declines in output. (iv) There has been considerable underutilization of industrial capacity in the early stages of transition. (v) Although price decontrol initially results in a burst of inflation, over the medium term there is a negative correlation between growth and inflation, and also between liberalization and inflation.

There is relatively little disagreement about these "stylized facts," but a unified model that could explain them has not yet been provided. The empirical models estimated by Aslund, Boone and Johnson (1996) and Fischer, Sahay, and Végh (1996) illustrate several of the conclusions just noted, including in particular the inverse relation between output and inflation, and the medium-term positive association between output and liberalization. But these models cannot account for the fact that the initial fall in output is inversely correlated with the degree of liberalization (see Table 1). In fact, these models are unable to explain the relation between the time pattern of output during the transition and the timing and intensity of liberalization. In contrast, De Melo, Denizer, and Gelb (1996), De Melo and Gelb (1996), and Selowsky and Martin (1996) provide extensive empirical analysis of these factors, albeit without a formal theoretical background.

The purpose of this paper is to specify and estimate a model that explains the behavior of output during the transition and its relation to the process of liberalization and stabilization, both in terms of the time profile of the key variables and in terms of differences among countries. In explaining the changing relationship between output and liberalization over time,

---

1. The author would like to thank Robert Corker, David Coe, Martha De Melo, and Ratna Sahay for their very helpful comments on previous drafts and Yutong Li for her assistance. This paper was originally published in *IMF Staff Papers* and is reprinted by permission.

2. See Aslund, Boone, and Johnson (1996), De Melo, Denizer, and Gelb (1996), De Melo and Gelb (1996), Fischer, Sahay, and Végh (1996), Havrylyshyn (1995), and Selowsky and Martin (1996).

3. In contrast, China and Vietnam never experienced a contraction of output, for reasons that include the relatively small size of the industrial state sector in these countries and hence the comparatively less burdensome task of restructuring; a considerably lower degree of integration in the CMEA; and the fact that central planning mechanisms in China and Vietnam had been less deeply ingrained than, for example, in the countries of the former Soviet Union. On this issue, see De Melo and Gelb (1996).

Table 1. The Changing Relation Between Output Growth and Liberalization

Country groups	Liberalization index 1991	% change in real GDP 1989-91	Liberalization index 1993	% change in real GDP 1991-93	Liberalization index 1995	% change in real GDP 1993-95	% change in real GDP 1989-95
1 Advanced reformers	0.75	-15	0.84	-4	0.89	9	-11
2 High intermediate reformers	0.37	-18	0.76	-21	0.76	7	-32
3 Low intermediate reformers	0.10	-13	0.59	-27	0.69	-27	-53
4 Slow reformers	0.07	-5	0.32	-17	0.44	-22	-37
5 Countries affected by conflicts	0.29	-18	0.49	-40	0.59	-14	-58
6 Correlation coefficients between	-0.35		-0.29		+0.61		+0.31
7 liberalization and growth	-0.03		+0.59		+0.39		-0.35

* Growth rates and liberalization indexes are averages for country groups. The liberalization indexes are weighted averages of three liberalization indexes developed by De Melo, Denizer and Gelb (1996a, pages 32-33) for each of the countries listed below: (i) for internal prices and competition; (ii) for external markets; and (iii) for private sector entry, including privatization. Annual values for each of these indexes were derived through an extensive consultation process involving: proposed rankings by the authors based on their knowledge and on country reports; consultations with World Bank and other country specialists followed by a further evaluation by senior Bank experts from a wider cross-country perspective; and adjustments based on the EBRD's (1994) transition indicators.

Line 1: Slovenia, Poland, Hungary, Czech Republic, and Slovak Republic.

Line 2: Estonia, Bulgaria, Lithuania, Latvia, Albania, Romania, and Mongolia.

Line 3: Russia, Kyrgyz Republic, Moldova, and Kazakstan.

Line 4: Uzbekistan, Belarus, Ukraine, and Turkmenistan.

Line 5: Croatia, Macedonia FYR, Armenia, Georgia, Azerbaijan, and Tajikistan.

Lines 6 and 7: The correlation coefficients are between the growth rates and the liberalization indexes in the last year of the relevant subperiod; they are derived from individual country data. Line 6 excludes (and line 7 includes) the countries affected by regional conflicts.

the model emphasizes two elements: (i) the distinction between "old" goods and "new" goods and (ii) the role of underutilization of capital during the early phase of the transition. Inflation also is an important variable in the model. Indeed, macro-stabilization is seen as a critical element in bringing about the recovery of economic activity, both by reducing the chaos and uncertainty associated with hyperinflation and by reinforcing liberalization.

The empirical part of the paper relies extensively on the liberalization index constructed by De Melo, Denizer, and Gelb (1996a) for the countries of Central and Eastern Europe and the former Soviet Union. The results show that the doubts expressed by Aslund, Boone, and Johnson (1996) concerning the usefulness of these indexes in explaining output growth do not appear to be valid. Also, this paper confirms the De Melo-Denizer-Gelb intuition that economic recovery depends on the *duration* as well as the *intensity* of the liberalization process. Finally, it illustrates the key role of transitional unemployment of capital in explaining the fall in production in the

early stages of the transition, and it confirms the hypothesis that there has been considerable under-reporting of output in the official statistics, particularly in the countries of the former Soviet Union.

A SIMPLE TWO SECTOR, FULL EMPLOYMENT MODEL

The simplest version of the model, presented here for illustrative purposes only, assumes full utilization of productive capacity and no net capital accumulation. Domestic output is produced by two types of firms: *type-B firms* typically produce the "old" goods they were required to produce under the central planning system but for which demand falls as the state order system is dismantled and the economy is liberalized. *Type-A firms* produce "new" goods and services which they are increasingly able to sell for a profit as the economy is liberalized, and for which there is growing demand by consumers and by other firms that are increasingly free to purchase what they wish in free markets. It should be stressed that the two types of enterprises should not be classified rigidly in terms of the economic sector to which they belong

199

Chart 1.   Formerly Planned Economies: Evolution of Output During the Transition[1]
(real GDP, 1989=100)

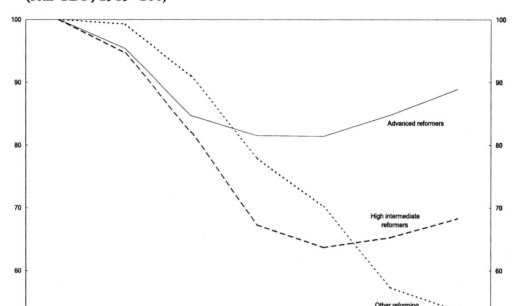

1/ See footnote to Table 1 for classification of countries. Excludes countries affected by conflicts.

(i.e., industry vs. services, or privatized vs. state-owned firms). Rather, enterprises are categorized as type-A firms to the extent that they have structured or restructured their production and modified their technology (defined in broad terms to include management, product design, and marketing) with the intention of selling at a profit in the market.

In each sector, a production function relates output to the amount of capital used in the sector.

$$Q = Q_A + Q_B = \alpha_A K_A + \alpha_B K_B \qquad (1)$$

where Q is output, K is the capital stock, α_A and α_B are output/capital ratios and the subscripts A and B refer to the new goods- and the old goods-producing sectors, respectively. The marginal product of capital is expected to be higher in sector A than in sector B, and thus $\alpha_A > \alpha_B$. The rate of decline of the capital stock in sector B relative to its pre-reform level is assumed to be proportional to a measure (L) of the degree of liberalization, i.e.,

$$K_B / K_o = 1 - \lambda L \qquad (2)$$

where K_o indicates the aggregate capital stock just prior to the beginning of reforms.

Conceptually, the variable L should capture the degree of privatization and market access, elimination of state trading monopolies, and liberalization of domestic prices and external trade. It is defined so as to range between zero and one, L = 1 representing a fully liberalized market economy. The parameter λ indicates the extent to which the output of old firms contracts as the economy is liberalized—i.e., as L rises—and should also range between zero and one. As explained below, another relevant factor in this context is the extent to which the reduction in subsidies, centralized credits, and budgetary transfers associated with anti-inflationary macro-policies help to enforce hard budget constraints on type-B firms and force them either to cut production or to restructure and transform themselves into type-A industries.

If new enterprises are able to put in place immediately all the capital released by old enterprises, and assuming no net capital accumulation (i.e., K = K_o at all times), equations (1) and (2) can be combined into an equation for the aggregate output of the economy:

$$Q = \alpha_A \lambda L K_o + \alpha_B (1 - \lambda L) K_o = [(\alpha_A - \alpha_B) \lambda L + \alpha_B] K_o \qquad (3)$$

Assuming that before the transition starts output is produced by type-B firms only, the pre-transition level of output will be $Q_o = \alpha_B K_o$. Thus, dividing through by Q_o in equation (3) provides a simple equation for the ratio of current to pre-reform output.

$$Q / Q_o = (\alpha_A / \alpha_B) \lambda L + (1 - \lambda L) \qquad (4)$$

In this simple full employment model, total output always rises as the economy is liberalized as long as the marginal productivity of capital is higher in the new goods-producing sector A than it is in the old goods-producing sector B. Thus, this model explains why several years after the beginning of the transition output fares better in those countries where liberalization is relatively advanced. But it is unable to account for the initial decline in output that has accompanied liberalization in all the countries of Eastern Europe and the former Soviet Union, let alone for the fact that, *initially*, the drop in output tends to be steeper in those countries where the liberalization effort was the strongest.

A MODEL WITH TRANSITIONAL UNEMPLOYMENT OF CAPITAL

In this section, the assumption of zero net investment is retained[4] but the assumption that the capital released by type-B enterprises can be immediately used by type-A enterprises is relaxed. Instead, it is assumed that this process takes time, not only because new firms must go through a learning process, but because much of the capital released by old firms must be extensively restructured to be effectively usable by type-A enterprises. This is the case even for those formerly type-B enterprises that transform themselves into type-A enterprises through restructuring (it takes time to shift production from peri-

scopes to microscopes). It will now be assumed that only a fraction of the capital stock released by type-B enterprises can be put in place by type-A enterprises in any given year—the rest remaining temporarily unused—and that this fraction increases gradually as the process of economic liberalization matures.[5] This hypothesis can be formulated by assuming that, in any given year, the ratio of capital put in place by type-A enterprises to the capital released by type-B enterprises is an increasing function of the number of years that has elapsed since the beginning of the transition.

$$K_{At} = X_t \lambda L_t K_t \qquad (5)$$

where the gradual restructuring variable X_t is an increasing function of the difference (τ) between the current year (t) and the first year of reform ($s + 1$), and takes on values ranging between 0 and 1.

Using equations (1) and (2) and substituting for K_{At} from equation (5) yields an equation for total output in the economy:

$$Q_t = \alpha_A \lambda X_t L_t K_t + \alpha_B (1 - \lambda L_t) K_t \qquad (6)$$

Assuming that $K_t = K_o$ at all times (no net capital accumulation) and that $Q_o = \alpha_B K_o$, and dividing equation (6) through by K_o yields an equation for the growth of aggregate output measured from its pre-reform level:

$$Q_t / Q_o = \alpha \ \lambda \ X_t L_t + (1 - \lambda L_t) \qquad (7)$$

where $\alpha = \alpha_A/\alpha_B$ is the ratio of marginal products. Equation (7) has two terms. The first one reflects the growth of output of type-A firms and is positively related to: (i) the intensity of liberalization in the current year (L_t); (ii) the duration of the reform process

---

4. This is a major simplification, but one which allows the analysis of important aspects of the reform process (such as changes in unused capacity) to proceed within a tractable model, and without requiring data on net fixed capital formation which are unavailable in many of the relevant countries and are of dubious quality where available. The assumption of zero net capital formation is probably not very unrealistic in the context of the early transition from plan to market (say the first six to eight years). It is, of course, unsuitable for the longer term when the growth of capacity (as opposed to changes in its degree of utilization) play the more important role in explaining growth.

5. The model could be extended by allowing a fraction $1-\gamma$ of the old firm's initial capital stock to be hopelessly obsolete. In that case, the right-hand side of equation (5) would have to be multiplied by γ, i.e., by the fraction of the initial stock of capital that does not have to be discarded and is potentially usable by new firms.

(τ, which is captured by the variable X_t); and (iii) the extent to which the marginal product of capital is higher in type-A firms than in type-B firms (α). Initially, the output of type-A enterprises is zero or negligible, but it increases over time because, as the reform process matures, new firms increasingly absorb the productive capacity idled as a result of past liberalization. The second term, $(1 - \lambda L_t)$, reflects the contraction in the output of type-B firms resulting from liberalization in the current period.

As τ and X rise over time, equation (7) converges toward equation (4) and the response of output to liberalization becomes unambiguously positive. For small values of τ, however, the effect of liberalization on *aggregate* output can be negative because for some time the initial response of type-A firms is smaller than the contraction in the output of type-B firms induced by liberalization. Thus, in this model transitional unemployment of capital is an important reason for the transitional contraction of output.[6] (The underlying relationship between liberalization and output is illustrated in Chart 2.)

INTRODUCING INFLATION

In addition to liberalization, inflation has had a major influence on the evolution of output during the transition. The countries that have experienced relatively high inflation have registered a relatively large drop in output because the uncertainty and the chaotic conditions created by high inflation seriously complicate business decisions in general and encourage investment of effort and resources in unproductive activities directed only at seeking protection from price increases. Conversely, the elimination of hyperinflation should be expected to raise productivity by improving confidence and predictability and

by discouraging wasteful activities. In addition, a substantial drop in inflation (following the initial and unavoidable price surge associated with decontrol) presupposes the implementation of measures that also help to enforce hard budget constraints and encourage inefficient enterprises to adjust. These measures—which include the reduction or elimination of budgetary transfers, subsidies and directed credits to inefficient enterprises—contribute to the fall in inflation, to restructuring, and also to a better allocation of financial resources.

In the model presented above it was assumed that output in each sector depended only on the stock of utilized capital, and that the marginal product of capital in each sector was constant. It will now be assumed that the marginal productivity of capital in sector j is the sum of a fixed component α_j and a component that is inversely related to the excess of actual cumulative inflation (π) over a threshold level of inflation at or below which price changes cease to have detrimental effects on economic activity (π^*):

$$\alpha'_j = \alpha_j - \beta \, (\pi_t - \pi_t^*) \qquad j = A, B \qquad (8)$$

Substituting for α_A and α_B from equation (8) into equation (1) yields:

$$Q/Q_t = \alpha_A K_{At} + \alpha_B K_{Bt} - \beta \, (\pi_t - \pi_t^*) \, K_t \qquad (9)$$

Using equations (2), (5), and (9), assuming no net investment (as before) and zero excess inflation in the initial period, and dividing through by K_0:

$$\overline{Q} = \alpha \lambda X_t L_t + (1 - \lambda L_t) - \beta/\alpha_B \, (\pi_t - \pi_t^*) \qquad (10)$$

where $\overline{Q}_t$ is the ratio of output in year t to output in the base year.

---

6. Other explanations have been given for the decline in output, including the collapse of export markets following the dissolution of the U.S.S.R. in 1991, the loss of transfers from the Union in some former Soviet Republics and the negative multiplier effects of anti-inflationary financial policies—although the results obtained in this paper suggest that this latter hypothesis is unconvincing. (See Anderson, Citrin, and Lahiri (1995) for an examination of various explanations.) In addition, there are reasons to believe official GDP figures overestimate the fall in output in the countries of the former Soviet Union by a considerable margin. This issue is examined below.

ESTIMATION RESULTS

In estimating equation (10), the De Melo-Denizer-Gelb weighted index[7] was used as a measure of liberalization, and the adjustment variable X was approximated by the logarithmic-reciprocal function:

$$X_{it} = \exp(-\theta / \tau_i)$$

where $\tau_i = t - s_i + 1$ is equal to one plus the difference between the current year (t) and the first year of major reforms (s_i) in the ith country; X_{it} is the share of the capital stock released by old firms that is put in place by new firms in country i in year t; it equals zero for $\tau = 0$, increases monotonically with τ, and approaches 1 as τ tends to infinity. The function X has an inflection point at $\tau = \theta/2$, where θ is a fixed parameter. (The estimation results for an equation using an alternative functional form with similar characteristics to approximate the variable X is reported in column F of Table 2a.)

The estimated equations also include a set of dummy variables (described in more detail below and in Annex 1) to control for the effects on economic activity of regional differences, armed conflicts, and other exogenous factors. Equation (11), which is similar to equation (10) but incorporates a vector of dummy variables D_{it} and a specific formulation of the variable X, was estimated using pooled time series/cross-section data for the period 1990-95 for the 26 former communist countries listed in Table 1.

$$\overline{Q}_{it} = c - \lambda L_{it} + \alpha \lambda L_{it} \exp(-\theta / \tau_i) - \beta/\alpha_B \pi + \delta D_{it} \quad (11)$$

where, $\overline{Q}_{it}$ is an index of real GDP based 1 in 1989, and $c = 1 + \beta \pi^*/\alpha_B$ is a constant term. The regression results are shown in Tables 2a and 2b, and the data and sources are described in Annex 1. All equations were estimated using heteroskedasticity-consistent estimators of the variance-covariance matrix which correct for any bias in the standard errors (and therefore in the t-ratios) that might result from the heteroskedastic residuals that appear to be present in some of the equations as indicated by White's test. (See Table 2a.)

Regional dummy variables were included for the countries of the former Soviet Union and the Baltic region, for the Visegrad countries (Poland. Hungary, and the Czech and Slovak Republics), for the former Yugoslav Republics (Slovenia, Croatia, and Macedonia FYR), and for the other countries of Eastern Europe (Bulgaria, Romania, and Albania). The DFSU variable had been included by Aslund, Boone, and Johnson (1996) in their cross-section regressions under the heading of "Ruble Area" dummy. This is a misnomer, however, since most of the Baltic and former Soviet Republics left the ruble area at various times beginning in 1992. Accordingly, a proper ruble area variable was constructed with values equal to one for each original member of the ruble area before the introduction of a national currency (or the introduction of a general-use coupon as legal tender), and to zero otherwise. The coefficient of this variable was expected to be negative in view of the propensity of some countries to export inflation to other members of the ruble area in 1993-93 and of the conflicts between Russia and certain other countries regarding the use of ruble correspondent accounts held with the Central Bank of Russia by other central banks. Another variable (Dcom) was introduced to capture the length of time a country has operated under a communist system, as suggested by Ickes (1996). Its coefficient was expected to be negative because the length of this period should be associated with more deeply entrenched central planning mechanisms and a more distorted economy.

---

7. The application of the model underlying equation (10) raises a particular problem on the case of the three former Yugoslav Republics included in the sample. In these countries, economic liberalization had started as early as 1965; by 1989 the process was already quite advanced and the De Melo-Denizer-Gelb index already had reached 0.41. This would make for higher level of productivity and per capita output in these countries compared with all the other countries in the sample, but it would not affect the *growth* of output in the 1990s relative to a base period in 1989—and this is what is measured by the dependent variable $\overline{Q}$. To avoid the bias that would have resulted otherwise, the liberalization variables for the three former Yugoslav Republics was defined in terms of deviations from the level of that variable in 1989.

The dummy variable Dwar was introduced to capture the direct or indirect economic effects of regional conflicts in several countries at various points during the sample period, and the variable Dnr was used to test whether economic activity in those countries rich in natural resources had been relatively less affected by the problems of industrial restructuring than in other countries in transition. Finally, a variable (Dfixed) proposed by Fischer, Sahay, and Végh (1996) was used to capture the (presumably) positive effects on economic activity of fixed exchange rate systems.

In column (A) of Table 2a, all the coefficients have the expected signs and are significantly different from zero,[8] with two exceptions. First, the variable representing the number of years in which the country has been under communist rule (Dcom) has the wrong sign, perhaps because the impact of that variable is already reflected in the liberalization index, as suggested by the results presented in Annex 2. Second, the coefficient of the ruble area variable is insignificantly different from zero. These two dummy variables are dropped from the other regressions presented in Table 2, with minor effects on the results.

It is noteworthy that coefficients of inflation and of the two liberalization variables (L and LX) are significant in spite of the collinearity among these three variables. This suggests that Aslund, Boone, and Johnson's (1996) finding that the (cumulative) liberalization variable becomes insignificant when they add two dummy variables (DFSU and Dwar) to the list of regressors probably reflected an insufficiently complete specification (the authors were limited in terms of degrees of freedom as they were using cross-section data only). In a comment addressed to Aslund, Boone, and Johnson (1996), Ickes (1996) argued that the use of the *cumulative* liberalization index is inappropriate because if two countries have achieved exactly the same degree of liberalization, the one that started the process earlier would achieve a higher score. However, this seems to miss the point that, in explaining the evolution of output during the transition, both the *intensity* and the *duration* of the process of liberalization matter. Indeed, De Melo, Denizer, and Gelb (1996) used the *cumulative* liberalization index precisely to summarize these two dimensions of the process in a single number. This point is also recognized by Selowsky and Martin (1996) who used current and lagged values of the noncumulative liberalization variables to capture the effect of duration. The present paper also uses the *actual* rather than the cumulative liberalization index, but it models explicitly the interaction between the intensity of liberalization, the duration of the transition process, and the evolution of output.

In columns (A) through (D) the coefficient of the gradual restructuring variable $(\alpha\lambda)$ ranges approximately between 0.9 and 1.2, and the coefficient of the (unmodified) liberalization variable (λ) ranges between 0.3 and 0.4. On that basis, the range of estimates of α falls between 2.6 and 3.6 — i.e., new enterprises are roughly 2½ to 3½ times more productive than old enterprises. Of course, these results must be interpreted with caution because the estimates of α seem vulnerable to changes in specification, because there are serious problems with the output data (see below), and also because there may be questions about the liberalization variable which, although it was based on the careful judgment of World Bank experts, was not derived from direct measurement.[9] It should also be noted that the present model imposes the same ratio of marginal productivities and the same speed of restructuring to all countries. Thus, the estimated coefficients reported in Table 2 are averages of individual country coefficients that in fact may differ significantly among each other in ways that are not fully captured by the dummy variables included in the regressions.

---

8. All statements about significance are based on one-tailed t-tests and a 1 percent confidence interval. With an infinite number of degrees of freedom, a positive value of t larger than 2.33 has a probability of 1 percent. This applies approximately to the equations reported in Table 2, where the number of degrees of freedom is 156.

9. It is noteworthy, however, that the De Melo-Denizer-Gelb liberalization index is strongly correlated to the share of the private sector in the economy and also to the EBRD and the IMF measures of institutional development. See Aslund, Boone, and Johnson (1996).

Table 2a. Estimation Results for Output in 26 Transition Countries, 1990-95[a]

Explanatory variable	Parameter	(A)	(B)	(C)	(D)	(E)	(F)[b]	(G)[c]
Constant	c	0.92	1.07	0.97	1.05	196.0	1.06	0.37
		(14.9)	(32.0)	(45.2)	(64.1)	(10.5)	(60.7)	(3.5)
Liberalization	$-\lambda$	-0.34	-0.39	-0.30	-0.34	-0.20	-0.42	-0.28
index (L)		(8.0)	(9.8)	(8.5)	(7.5)	(-3.5)	(7.3)	(5.9)
Gradual restructuring	$\alpha\lambda$	1.21	1.03	1.05	0.90	3.99	0.67	0.99
variable (L X)		(4.4)	(4.4)	(5.3)	(5.3)	(10.0)	(4.4)	(4.3)
Inflation (π)	β/α_B	-0.04	-0.04	-0.04	-0.04	...	-0.04	-0.03
		(11.6)	(12.0)	(16.4)	(13.5)		(13.6)	(9.1)
Time trend (t)		...	...	...	...	-0.10	...	...
						(10.5)		
Under-recording		...	...	...	...	..	..	0.63
proxy (Φ)	φ							(6.9)
productivity ratio	α	3.6	2.7	3.5	2.6	19.5	1.6	3.6
adjustment coefficient	θ	12	11	11	11	13	12	13
crossover point	$\theta / \ln(\alpha)$	9.4	11.3	8.8	11.3	4.4	16.9	10.2
long-term gain from full								
liberalization	$(\alpha-1)\lambda$	87%	64%	75%	56%	378%	26%	72%
R squared, adjusted		0.819	0.812	0.818	0.891	0.859	0.889	0.911
Standard error[d]		11.2%	11.4%	11.2%	8.7%	9.9%	8.8%	7.8%
White heteroskedasticity test		16.0	14.1	16.0	82.1	78.2	63.6	82.5
Log likelihood ratio		175	171	174	225	205	223	241

a. The dependent variable in all equations is the ratio of real GDP in year t to real GDP in 1989. T statistics are in parenthesis.
b. In column (F) the variable X is equal to $\tau / (\tau + \upsilon)$. In all other equations X = exp $(-\theta / \tau)$.
c. In estimating equation (G) the ratio Φ is added to the set of explanatory variables which yields an estimate of the coefficient φ. In addition, each of the other explanatory variables is multiplied by the ratio Φ. The parameters $-\lambda$ and $\alpha\lambda$ are obtained by dividing the coefficients of L and L X, respectively, by φ.
d. In percent of the mean of the dependent variable.

The results shown in columns (A) through (D) of Table 2b confirm that armed conflicts have had a large adverse effect on output, reducing cumulative growth from 1989 to 1995 by 11 to 16 percent in the countries affected relative to the other countries in the sample. However, other results, discussed below, suggest that conflicts may have affected *measured* output more severely than *actual* output. The regional variables also had appreciable effects: other things equal, cumulative growth may have been raised by 3 to 9 percent in the Visegrad countries, lowered by 1 to 7 percent in the other countries of Central and Eastern Europe, and raised by 5 to 7 percent higher in the countries with abundant natural resources. The results in columns (A) and (B) imply that, other things equal, output may have been about 10 percent lower in the countries of the former Soviet Union and the Baltic region, but the results discussed below suggest that this may have been partly a statistical mirage.

Column (C) shows the results of replacing the regional dummy DFSU by a set of subregional dummy variables. The estimated coefficients of these variables suggest that, *ceteris paribus*, output may have been 6 percent lower in the Transcaucasian countries, 4½ percent lower in the Baltic countries, but almost 5 percent higher in the former Soviet Republics of Central Asia relative to other countries in the sample.[10] However, the standard errors of these estimates are relatively high. The estimated coefficients of other variables do not change much in comparison with columns (A) and (B), except that both the size and the t ratio of the war dummy coefficient falls, perhaps because it now competes with the dummy variable for Transcaucasia, a region including three

10. The precise composition of these country groups is provided in Annex 1.

Table 2b. Estimation Results for Output in 26 Transition Countries, 1990-95[a]

Dummy variable	(A)	(B)	(C)	(D)	(E)	(F)	(G)
Dwar	-0.16	-0.16	-0.12	-0.11	-0.12	-0.12	-0.06
	(7.7)	(7.1)	(6.3)	(4.0)	(3.3)	(4.2)	(2.3)
Dnr	0.05	0.07	0.05	...	...	...	..
	(2.6)	(3.8)	(2.6)				
Dfixed	0.03	0.02	0.01	0.03	0.04	0.03	0.02
	(1.6)	(1.0)	(0.8)	(2.0)	(2.2)	(2.0)	(1.4)
DrubleA	-0.01	...	...	...	...	...	...
	(0.5)						
Dcom	0.003	...	...	...	...	...	...
	(2.9)						
DFSU	-0.10	-0.11	...	-0.19	-0.28	-0.18	0.00
	(3.6)	(3.8)					
DVisegrad	0.06	0.05	0.09	0.03	0.05	0.04	0.08
	(2.8)	(2.4)	(3.1)				
DYugoslavia	-0.01	-0.05	0.04	0.09	-0.03	0.13	-0.03
	(0.2)	(1.5)	(1.3)				
DotherCEE	-0.05	-0.07	-0.01	-0.07	-0.10	-0.07	-0.05
	(1.6)	(2.3)	(0.2)				
DBaltic	...	...	-0.05	-0.11	-0.18	-0.11	-0.03
			(1.4)				
DTranscaucasia	...	...	-0.06	-0.14	-0.18	-0.13	-0.02
			(2.0)				
DCentralAsia	...	...	0.05	-0.01	-0.03	-0.01	0.07
			(2.2)				

a.   See footnotes to Table 2a. The coefficients of regional variables shown in columns (D) through (F) are calculated as averages of the estimated coefficients for the relevant individual country dummies. T statistics are shown in brackets.

countries that were seriously affected by armed conflicts during the period. In column (D), the regional dummies are replaced by a set of country dummies. The results broadly confirm those discussed above for regional aggregates but also indicate that, other things equal, output was particularly weak in Georgia, Moldova, and Lithuania, and particularly strong in Poland and Slovenia.

Columns (E) and (F) illustrate the sensitivity of the results to two kinds of changes in specification. In column (E), the inflation variable is dropped and replaced by a time trend—which might be loosely justified on the ground that the productivity of the inherited stock of capital diminishes over time. The coefficient of the trend variable turns out to be significantly negative and the signs and significance of the other coefficients are unchanged, suggesting that the inflation variable may, to some extent, be picking up

the effects of gradual obsolescence of old plant and equipment. However, the estimated size of α is not credible. When both inflation and the time trend are included in the equation the first variable is highly significant, while the latter is not. When both variables are dropped from the equation, the other variables remain correctly signed and significant, but the overall explanatory power of the equation drops substantially.

Column (F) shows the effects of using an alternative gradual restructuring variable of the form:

$$X_{it} = \tau_i / (\tau_i + \upsilon) \tag{12}$$

where υ is the number of years required to achieve half of the adjustment.[11] The results are not drastically altered, except that the productivity gap between type-A and type-B goods is substantially narrower than in the other equations.

---

11. X was also approximated by other functional forms, including the square root of t and the logarithm of t, with similar results but larger standard errors.

Finally, the coefficient of the variable Dfixed suggests that output may have been 1 to 4 percent higher in the countries that adopted a fixed exchange rate, but the coefficient of this variable was not significantly larger than zero in most regressions. Some qualifications are in order, however. First, it is possible that the positive impact of fixed rate regimes on output occurs *indirectly* through the inflation variable. This conclusion is supported by Fischer, Sahay, and Végh's finding that countries with fixed rates have experienced relatively low inflation, and by the results in Table 2 which show a strong, inverse correlation between output and inflation. It is also consistent with the fact that the coefficient of the fixed rate dummy rises (and its standard error falls) when the inflation variable is omitted from the equations. Second, however, these results do not necessarily confirm Fischer, Sahay, and Végh's claim that nominal exchange rate anchors *per se* improve economic performance. It is possible that the causality runs in reverse order, and that those countries that had achieved a sufficiently high degree of institutional development and political consensus for stabilization found it possible to peg the exchange rate.

AN INTERPRETATION OF THE RESULTS

Chart 2 illustrates the effect of liberalization on the production of type-A and type-B goods during the transition. The sectoral breakdown of output between new and old firms—which is, of course, unobservable—is derived by simulating equation (A) in Table 2,[12] where the variable X is equal to the logarithmic-reciprocal function $\exp(-\theta/\tau)$. The proportion of available capital put in place by type-A firms is zero for $\tau = 0$, rises gradually with the passage of time, and approaches 1 asymptotically as τ increases. In the first two years, the contraction of aggregate production is much steeper for the strong reformer than for the slow reformer because the pace of liber-

alization is faster, and therefore the fall in the output of old goods is sharper in the former country. In the third year, however, positive growth resumes in the strong reform country reflecting the gradual pickup in the output of new goods as the liberalization process matures. In the slow reform country, the fall in output initially is less abrupt but it is more prolonged, while the recovery is much slower because the growth in the output of type-A goods is relatively low and the share of the less productive type-B enterprises in total output remains much higher. Beginning in the sixth year, output in the strong reformer exceeds output in the weak reformer by a margin that rises as liberalization takes hold.

Table 2a provides estimates of several key parameters of the model, including the number of years required for output to return to its pre-reform level (the *crossover point*). Except in equations (E) and (F), output is estimated to return to its initial level after approximately 9 to 11 years, although for a particular country the period can be shorter or longer depending on the sum of coefficients of the corresponding dummy variables. Abstracting from the effects associated with dummies, the number of years required for output to return to its pre-reform level is equal to the adjustment parameter θ divided by the logarithm of the relative productivity ratio α.[13] It is therefore independent of the level of L_t although, of course, the earlier liberalization starts the sooner will recovery be complete.

The *long-run level of output*, however, does depend critically on the intensity of liberalization. Setting X = 1 in equation (10)—i.e., assuming completion of the restructuring process—and ignoring the effects of high inflation yields an expression for the long-term rate of growth of output relative to the base year:

---

12. It is important to note that the simulations underlying Chart 2 are intended to capture the impact of liberalization on output with other variables remaining unchanged. If the impact of inflation in 1989-95 were taken into account, the fall in output would be larger in both countries, and particularly in the slow reform countries (typically, strong reformers also have succeeded in bringing down inflation more quickly than slow reformers). The simulations underlying Chart 2 use actual data for a strong reformer (the Czech Republic) and a slow reformer (Belarus) from 1989 through 1995; and projections thereafter.

13. This result holds for the logarithmic-reciprocal version of X_t. In the case of the ratio form used in equation (F) of Table 2a, the number of years needed for output to return to its initial level is equal to $(\theta - \alpha)/(\alpha - 1)$.

Chart 2. Simulated Impact of Liberalization on theOutput of Old and New Firms (share of 1989 output)

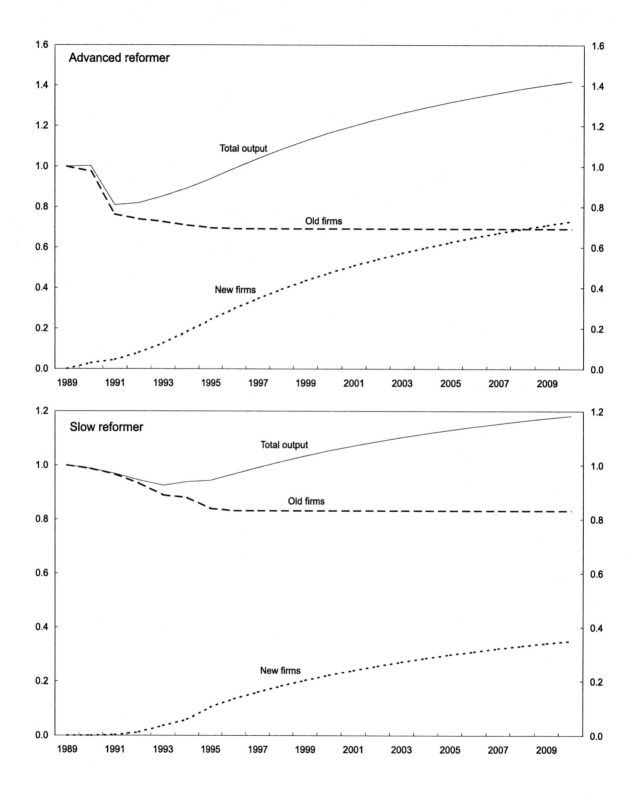

Chart 3. Simulated Path of Output: Full vs. Partial Liberalization[1]
(share of 1989 output)

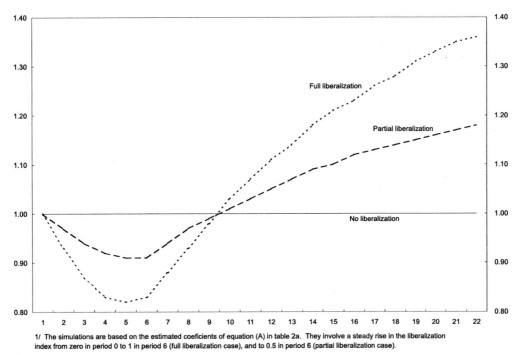

1/ The simulations are based on the estimated coeficients of equation (A) in table 2a. They involve a steady rise in the liberalization
index from zero in period 0 to 1 in period 6 (full liberalization case), and to 0.5 in period 6 (partial liberalization case).

$$\overline{Q}_t - 1 = (\alpha - 1) \lambda L_t \qquad (13)$$

If liberalization is complete (L = 1) the percentage deviation between long-term and base-period output is simply $\lambda (\alpha - 1)$; in Table 2 this deviation is estimated to range between 56 percent and 87 percent.[14] Chart 3 illustrates the relation between long-term growth and liberalization by comparing two countries that achieve full liberalization (L = 1) and partial liberalization (L = 0.5), respectively. These levels are assumed to be attained in five years, after which no further changes in liberalization take place. The chart confirms that output falls during the period of liberalization[15] (as L rises from zero to its steady-state level) and that the fall is steeper in the country that achieves complete liberalization. After the contraction ends, however, output rises much faster in the country that achieves full liberalization, and that country attains a much higher level of output in the long term.

Chart 3 does not imply that everyone will benefit from full liberalization. Some may prefer to forgo the substantial, long-term output gains for the sake of avoiding the short-term contraction of output—for example, if they are old and care little about the next generation, or if liberalization means the end of the political and economic privileges they enjoyed under the old regime. But the large dividend paid by full liberalization makes the concept of a short-term sacrifice for a long-term gain appear quite attractive, particularly in view of the evidence that increased economic liberalization also is associated with greater political freedom. The picture in Chart 3 also suggests that some consumption-smoothing would make sense. It might be argued that private consumption and the social component of government spending could be prevented from falling too sharply during the period of output contraction by running fiscal deficits financed by issuing domestic bonds and thus crowding-out domestic investment temporari-

---

14. Excluding the outliers in columns (E) and (F).

15. Except, of course, if there is no liberalization, in which case output never changes.

ly—after all strong, productivity-led growth is likely to occur anyway as a result of restructuring—or by borrowing from abroad. However, it remains to be seen how far this policy can be pushed without leading to an unsustainable accumulation of debt and eventually to a financial crisis, particularly in situations where initially low credibility is likely to boost the cost of borrowing.

TESTING FOR THE UNDER-RECORDING OF OUTPUT

As indicated earlier, it has been strongly suspected for some time that the official national accounts data in the countries in transition underestimate the output of new enterprises and therefore total output by a substantial margin, and that the degree of overestimation is particularly large in the countries of the former Soviet Union. In recent papers, Kauffmann and Kaliberda (1995) and Dobozi and Pohl (1995 and 1996) have observed that electric power consumption, a good proxy for output in most developed market economies, has declined significantly less than real GDP since the beginning of reforms, and that while the gap between the two variables has been relatively small in Central and Eastern European countries, it has been very large in the countries of the former Soviet Union (see Table 3).

Table 3. Cumulative Changes in Real GDP and Power Consumption, 1989-94 (in percent)

	Real GDP (Official)	Power Consumption
All reforming countries	-40.9	-28.2
Former Soviet Union	-50.5	-33.4
War countries	-75.2	-45.5
Central and Eastern Europe	-19.7	-17.0

Source: Kauffmann and Kaliberda (1995).

The authors do not find any convincing explanation for these results[16] other than an indication that the

official GDP statistics overstate the true fall in output because of: (i) attempts by enterprises to avoid high taxes and residual state orders to supply goods at regulated prices; and (ii) the failure of official national accounts systems to keep up with the growth of new activities, particularly in the small-scale service sector. They proceed to construct indexes of power consumption that they regard as more reliable indicators of the evolution of actual output than the official GDP numbers.

In order to correct at least in part for the under-recording of output by the official data, it was assumed that the ratio of officially measured output (Q) to true output (Q^T) was proportional to the ratio Φ of measured output to power consumption.

$$Q/Q^T = \varphi \, \Phi \qquad (14)$$

where φ is a positive parameter and the ratio Φ is calculated on the basis of the power consumption data provided by Kauffmann and Kaliberda (1995) as explained in Annex 1. It is therefore possible to express the official output index used in the regressions as a function of the ratio of output to power consumption and the unobservable level of true output:

$$\overline{Q}_{it} = \varphi \, \overline{\Phi} \, \overline{Q}_{it}^T \qquad (15)$$

where bars on top of the variables indicate indexes based in 1989. Since the right-hand side of equation (11) seeks to explain *true* output, it can be substituted for $\overline{Q}_{it}^T$ in equation (15). This provides a simple way to correct for the underestimation of output in the official GDP numbers: to multiply the constant term as well as each explanatory variable in equation (11) by the ratio $\overline{\Phi}_{it}$ and to run the regression using the transformed variables.[17] The results are shown in column (G) of Table 2a.

The coefficient of the variable $\overline{\Phi}$ is significantly positive and suggests that, on average, almost two thirds of the gap between changes in measured real GDP and changes in power consumption reflect under-re-

---

16. Indeed, they note that the large rise in electricity prices that has occurred in these countries should have led to a *fall* in the ratio of power consumption to GDP.

17. For an alternative way to adjust for under-reporting, see Selowsky and Martin (1996).

cording of output. This would mean that the average contraction of real GDP in the countries of the former Soviet Union during 1989-94 would have been a little less than 40 percent, compared with more than 50 percent indicated by the official estimates. The results in column (G) also show a drop in the coefficient of the war dummy compared with previous equations, perhaps because the incentive to under-report production is relatively high in war situations. Finally, it is noteworthy that the sum of co-efficients of the dummy variables for the FSU countries drops to zero, suggesting that the major difference between countries of the former U.S.S.R. and other reforming countries—other than those differences already captured by other explanatory variables in the model—has been the under-reporting of output.

SOME CONCLUSIONS

The results presented in this paper indicate that the transition from central planning to a growing market economy is almost unavoidably arduous—*un mauvais moment à passer*. It is also probably fairly long, taking as much as a decade, or more. This is not particularly surprising given the extraordinarily difficult circumstances inherited from the old regime, including heavily distorted price systems and trade patterns, and overly large industrial sectors often unprofitable at the new, much freer structure of relative prices. In particular, the results suggest that it takes considerable time to restructure the capital stock inherited from the previous system and use it in the productive process. While this process of restructuring takes place, part of the usable capital stock is temporarily unemployed, leading to a contraction of total output.

During this period of transitional unemployment, the structure of the economy changes: the old firms cut production as the economy is liberalized, releasing resources that are used partially and gradually by the new enterprises. Thus, an aggressive policy of liberalization will lead to a comparatively rapid contraction of the old enterprise sector and a relatively sharp initial drop in total output. But it will also make room quickly for the new, more profitable enterprises, and set the stage for a much higher level of income in the medium term.

For those countries that have embarked audaciously in the process of liberalization, the light at the end of the tunnel is now clearly visible. The worst is over as much of the old sector has disappeared or transformed itself, and the new sector gradually increases its share in the economy. As a result, most countries of Central and Eastern Europe, the three Baltic countries, Mongolia, and some countries of the former Soviet Union, like Armenia, Georgia and the Kyrgyz Republic, experienced positive growth in 1995 and probably also in 1996. It is true that measured real GDP remains well below 1989 levels in many countries, but this gap is probably exaggerated by the official data which, as suggested by the empirical results presented in this paper, underestimate the true level of production by a wide margin, particularly in the countries of the former Soviet Union. Moreover, the prospects for growth among the strong and early reformers appear to be quite good, because from now on new investment will go into the new enterprises and contribute rapidly to economic expansion.

In those countries that have been slow in adjusting, the contraction of the old industrial sector has been relatively gradual. But the bad news is that much of this sector remains in place, and much of the unavoidable task of liberalization and restructuring remains ahead. Output in these countries is still falling, even though many of them, like Azerbaijan, Uzbekistan, and Turkmenistan, have been blessed with a wealth of natural resources. For these countries, and also for those like Cuba and North Korea, where centralized control is still the principal mechanism of resource allocation, the advice is to move on as soon as possible with full liberalization. The alternative path—to support the monuments to inefficiency built by the old regime—promises nothing but blood and tears.

The empirical results of the model strongly confirm the finding of previous studies that there is a close association between price stabilization and the resumption of growth. The results also confirm that armed conflicts have hindered economic activity in various countries in transition (although this may have been more a feature of the data than of reality) and that regional differences have been of some importance. However, there is no clear evidence that the counties of the former Soviet Union have performed significantly worse than the average after controlling for differences in the timing and intensity of liberalization, price stabilization and under-reporting of output. In particular, the evidence does not support the hypothesis that membership in the ruble area con-

tributed to an exceptionally difficult transition. Finally, the results provide some—but not much—support for the view that fixed nominal exchange rates have contributed directly to a relatively strong performance of output, although they may have contributed indirectly to this result by helping to bring down inflation.

Annex 1
DEFINITIONS AND SOURCES OF VARIABLES USED IN THE REGRESSIONS

F = index of political freedom. From De Melo, Denizer, and Gelb (1996b).

L = weighted liberalization index, from De Melo, Denizer, and Gelb (1996a). Unpublished data for 1995 were provided by Martha De Melo.

π = cumulative inflation rate. Equal to the natural logarithm of the ratio of consumer prices in the current year to consumer prices in the base year. Derived from annual rates of inflation published by the European Bank for Reconstruction and Development (1996b).

$\overline{Q}$ = real GDP index (1989 =1). Derived from annual growth rates published by the European Bank for Reconstruction and Development (1996b).

$\overline{\Phi}$ = Index of the ratio of officially recorded real GDP to electrical power consumption. Based on data published by Kauffmann and Kaliberda (1995) and rebased to equal 1 in 1989. Data for the Czech Republic and Armenia were constructed on the basis of power consumption data provided by Dobozi and Pohl (1995), and data for the three former Yugoslav Republics were set equal to the average for Central and Eastern European countries. The ratios of output to power consumption were assumed to remain unchanged in 1995 from their 1994 values.

s = assumed first year of the liberalization process in the late 1980s or early 1990s. Defined as the first year in which the de Melo-Denizer-Gelb liberalization index measured 0.1 or more: 1992 for Uzbekistan, Azerbaijan, Turkmenistan, and the Kyrgyz Republic; 1991 for Albania, Mongolia, Russia, Moldova, Armenia, Georgia, Kazakstan, Belarus, Tajikistan, and Ukraine; 1990 for the Czech and Slovak Republics, the three Baltic countries and Romania; 1989 for Poland, Hungary, Bulgaria, and the former Yugoslav Republics.

τ = age of the reform process, in years. Equal to t - s + 1.

t = time, in calendar years

Dwar = Dummy variable to capture the effect of armed conflicts. Equal to 1 in all years for Armenia and Azerbaijan (Nagorno-Karabakh conflict and, in the case of Armenia, natural gas blockade); for Georgia (fighting between the government of Georgia and Abkhazian rebels; between the government and South Ossetian rebels; and between the government and rebels loyal to former President Gamzakhurdia); and for Tajikistan (civil war). Equal to 1 in 1991 and 1992 for Croatia (Yugoslav civil war) and Macedonia (indirect effects of the sanction on Serbia); and to 1 in 1992 for Moldova (Trans-Dniestr conflict). Equal to zero otherwise.

Dfixed = Dummy variable for countries on a fixed exchange rate regime: Poland since January 1990, Hungary since March 1990, the Czech and Slovak Republics since January 1991, Estonia since June 1992, Croatia since October 1993, Macedonia since January 1994, Latvia since February 1994, and Lithuania since April 1994. Equal to 1 multiplied by the proportion of months in every year in which these countries were on a fixed exchange rate; equal to zero otherwise.

DrubleA = Dummy variable equal to 1 for every country of the former Soviet Union before the introduction of a national currency or a generalized coupon as legal tender, prorated by the number of months in the year in which the ruble was not used as the predominant currency; equal to zero otherwise.

Dcom = Number of years during which a country was under a communist government. Equal to the difference between the initial year of reform in the late 1980s or early 1990s (s) and the following years: 1948 for Bulgaria, the Czech and Slovak Republics, Hungary, Poland and Romania; 1946 for Albania; 1945 for the former Yugoslav Republics, Moldova, and the Baltic countries; 1924 for Mongolia; and

1918 for the other countries of the former Soviet Union. In the regressions presented in Annex 2, the beginning of communist rule was dated 1949 in China and 1954 in Vietnam. The beginning of reforms in these two countries was dated 1978 and 1986, respectively.

The following regional dummy variables were set equal to 1 for the countries listed below and to zero otherwise.

DBaltic = Estonia, Latvia, and Lithuania.

DCentralAsia = Kazakstan, Kyrgyz Republic, Tajikistan, Turkmenistan, and Uzbekistan.

DFSU = all countries of the former Soviet Union and the Baltic region.

DotherCEE = other Eastern Europe: Albania, Bulgaria, and Romania.

Dnr = countries rich in natural resources: Azerbaijan, Kazakstan, Russia, Turkmenistan, and Uzbekistan.

DTranscaucasia = Armenia, Azerbaijan, and Georgia.

DYugoslavia = Croatia, Macedonia FYR, and Slovenia.

DVisegrad = the Czech and Slovak Republics, Hungary, and Poland.

Annex 2
EXPLAINING ECONOMIC LIBERALIZATION

The relation between economic liberalization and political freedom, as measured by the Freedom House index, has been illustrated by De Melo, Denizer and Gelb (1996c). The results presented in this annex indicate that the intensity of liberalization is also related (inversely) to the length of time that a country has been under communist rule (Dcom). A cross-section regression for the 26 countries listed in Table 1 for the year 1994 gave the following results:

$$L = 0.77 + 0.064\ F - 0.008\ Dcom$$
$$\quad (3.9) \quad (3.4) \qquad (3.3)$$
$$\bar{R}^2 = 0.746 \qquad\qquad SE = 0.116$$

The coefficients of other variables that might have influenced the authorities' decisions regarding economic liberalization—such as armed conflicts, per capita income, the share of industry in GDP, and population density—were insignificantly different from zero.

The regression results are quite similar if the equation is run for 1993 or 1995. Also, it is noteworthy that the results are even stronger if China and Vietnam are added to the regression.

$$L = 0.74 + 0.067\ F - 0.007\ Dcom$$
$$\quad (6.6) \quad (5.5) \qquad (4.8)$$
$$\bar{R}^2 = 0.747 \qquad\qquad SE = 0.111$$

REFERENCES

Anderson, Jonathan, Daniel A. Citrin, and Ashok K. Lahiri (1995), "The Decline in Output," Chapter II in *Policy Experiences and Issues in the Baltics, Russia, and Other Countries of the Former Soviet Union*, IMF Occasional Paper No. 133 (Washington: International Monetary Fund).

Aslund, Anders, Peter Boone, and Simon Johnson (1996), "How to Stabilize: Lessons from Postcommunist Countries," *Brookings Papers on Economic Activity* 1.

De Melo, Martha, Cevdet Denizer, and Alan Gelb (1996a), "From Plan to Market: Patterns of Transition," Policy Research Working Paper Number 1564 (Washington: World Bank).

De Melo, Martha, Cevdet Denizer, and Alan Gelb (1996b), "Patterns of Transition from Plan to Market," *The World Bank Economic Review*, Vol.10 (September).

De Melo, Martha, and Alan Gelb (1996c), "Transition to Date: a Comparative Overview," Chapter 3 in *Lessons from the Economic Transition in Central and Eastern Europe in the 1990s*, ed. by Salvatore Zechini (Boston: Luwer Academic Publishers).

Dobozi, Istvan, and Gerhard Pohl (1995a), "Real Output Decline in Transition Economies," *Transition*, Vol. 6 (January-February).

Dobozi, Istvan, and Gerhard Pohl (1995b), "How Much has Output Declined in Eastern Europe and the Former Soviet Union," (Washington: World Bank).

Dobozi, Istvan, and Gerhard Pohl (1995c), "Update of Electricity-Based GDP Estimates for Eastern Europe and FSU" (unpublished, Washington: World Bank).

European Bank for Reconstruction and Development (1994), *Transition Report*, 1994.

European Bank for Reconstruction and Development (1996a), *Transition Report Update*, (April).

European Bank for Reconstruction and Development (1996b), *Transition Report*, 1996, *Infrastructure and Savings*.

Fischer, Stanley, Ratna Sahay, and Carlos A. Végh (1996), "Stabilization and Growth in Transition Economies: The Early Experience," *The Journal of Economic Perspectives*, Vol.10 (Spring).

Havrylyshyn, Oleh (1995), "Economic Transformation: The Tasks Still Ahead," Per Jacobsson Foundation.

Ickes, Barry W. (1996), "Comment" on Aslund, Boone, and Johnson, (1996)," *Brookings Papers on Economic Activity*, 1, pp. 298-305.

Kauffmann, Daniel and Aleksander Kaliberda (1995), "Integrating the Unofficial Economy into the Dynamics of Post-Socialist Economies: A Framework of Analysis and Evidence." (unpublished: Washington: World Bank).

Selowsky, Marcelo and Richard Martin (1997), "Policy Performance and Output Growth in Transition Economies," *Papers and Proceedings of the American Economic Association* (May).

GROWTH AND TECHNOLOGICAL CHANGE IN CUBA

Manuel Madrid-Aris[1]

This empirical paper is purposely written to be simple and straight forward. It has two main goals. The first is to provide a descriptive analysis of the historical patterns of growth, international trade, factor accumulation and human capital in Cuba during the post-revolution period. The second is the estimation the rate of technical progress or total factor of productivity (TFP) in Cuba during the period 1963-1988, and to compare it with other world regions.

The literature dealing with economic growth, technological change and human capital is vast and growing at a fast rate. It is widely known that the importance of changes in TFP in explaining why some countries grow more rapidly than others, or why some specific industries of a country grow faster than others for a given period of time. But empirical estimations of TFP of centrally planned economies are rarely seen. This can be explained because of the lack of good and reliable data, which makes this type of research a lengthy if not unattainable task. As result of the lack of empirical studies relating growth and technological change, Cuba's economic growth still challenges economists. Hence, many questions could be asked, such as: Is the increased per capita income in Cuba a consequence of better educated labor force, which could have led to a high rate of technological change (TFP), or is it the result of increased investment resulting from Soviet subsidies? How much is the contribution of the different factors (la-

bor, capital, TFP) to total Cuban economic growth and to the growth of some specific sectors of the Cuban economy? Is Cuba's rate of technological change lower or higher than of capitalist economies? The research underlying this paper is directed to answer these questions.

The paper is organized as follows. The first section provides a brief overview of the Cuban economy, including some macroeconomics indicators, productive structure, international trade, and human capital indicators. The intent of this section is to give some background of Cuba's economy to have a better understanding of Cuba's initial economic conditions and its process of economic growth during the period 1960-1988. The second section contains a brief review of the literature dealing with economic growth, technological change and human capital. The third section is the core of the paper. It tries to explain growth and technological change in Cuba; technological change is estimated using the traditional methodology to estimate TFP (Solow, 1957). The contribution of factors to Cuban economic growth is also estimated. The fourth section contains an econometric estimation of the economy of scale of the Cuban economy and of some economic sectors (agriculture and industry). The fifth section compares Cuban technological change with other world regions. The last section contains some conclusions.

---

1. I would like to thank the many people in Cuba who helped me collect some of the data used in this research. The views expressed, opinions and conclusions reached in this paper are those of the author, and do not necessarily reflect those of the institutions with which the author is affiliated.

Table 1. Macroeconomic Indicators (in percent)

	Economic Growth	Per Capita Growth	Investment as a % of GMP	Soviet Subsidies as a % of GMP	Exports as a % of GMP	Imports as a % of GMP
1960-1964	1.9	-0.2	0.14	0.08	0.15	0.19
1965-1969	3.6	1.7	0.19	0.07	0.14	0.21
1970-1974	10.0	8.2	0.17	0.07	0.18	0.23
1975-1979	3.4	2.2	0.28	0.18	0.34	0.40
1980-1984	5.7	5.1	0.30	0.33	0.44	0.52
1985-1988	1.3	0.3	0.31	n.a.	0.40	0.60
AVERAGE	4.4	3.2	0.28		0.28	0.36

Source: Rodríguez (1990), Brundenius (1984), Mesa-Lago and Pérez-López (1985) and author's estimates; Soviet subsidies figures come from Central Intelligence Agency (1984, p. 40 and 1989, p. 39).

Note: Economic growth has been estimated with Gross Material Product (GMP), since statistics on the Gross Social Product (GSP) are not as accurate as GMP. See Mesa-Lago and Pérez-López (1985).

THE CUBAN ECONOMY: A BRIEF OVERVIEW

Cuba's economic history is directly linked to agricultural production and its international trade is mainly related to sugar production. The revolution has had to constantly struggle with the need to diversify the economy and build an industrial base against the need to increase sugar production in order to accumulate capital required to industrialize and diversify the economy. By 1959, 80% of Cuba's export revenues came from sugar. Although the Cuban revolution has tried to carry out plans for agricultural diversification, industrialization and export diversification, it has not accomplished enough in these areas given that the Cuban economy is still highly dependent on sugar as much as thirty years ago.

As will be shown below, the failure of the industrialization plans is reflected in the fact that the percentage of Cuba's total industrial production output as share of Gross Material Product (GMP)[2] has basically remained the same over a twenty-five year period. On the other hand, construction's share has increased steadily and agriculture's has decreased over the years.

Macroeconomic Indicators

Despite its smallness, dependence on sugar monoculture, lack of natural resources and energy resources, Cuba sustained a good economic growth during the period 1960-1988. Cuba was able to grow at a steady annual rate of 4.4% during this period. Statistics show that during the period 1960-1988, per capita income increased at an average annual rate of 3.2%. Cuba increased considerably the rate of investment, which went from 15% of the national product in 1960 to 30% in 1988 (Table 1). Huge amounts of resources were invested in agriculture and education.

Table 1 shows that the highest rate of economic growth was achieved when the investment rate was decreasing. It is apparent that between 1960 and 1964 there were no increases in per capita income. On the other hand, during the period 1964-1988 income per capita increased at a considerable rate. Note that Soviet subsidies rose considerably through time, reaching a higher share of national product than investment for the period 1980-1984. In other words, it can be assumed that most of the Cuban investment during this period was realized by using Soviet subsidies. This clearly shows that the Cuban economy was losing saving capacity.

---

2. Cuba's national income accounting system is different from the Western concept of Gross National Product (GNP). Cuba uses the Soviet system of Global Social Product (GSP) and Gross Material Product (GMP), which is also called "gross product." For a detailed explanation of the Cuban national income accounting system, see Brundenius (1984, p. 19-40) and Mesa-Lago and Pérez-López (1985).

Table 2. **Sectoral Shares and Sectoral GMP Growth Rate (in percent)**

	Industry GMP as a % of GMP	Industry Output Rate of Growth	Agriculture GMP as a % of total GMP	Agriculture Output Rate of Growth
1963-1969	0.65	2.2	0.24	5.0
1970-1974	0.69	11.4	0.19	0.7
1975-1979	0.65	2.6	0.18	4.0
1980-1984	0.66	5.9	0.16	1.9
1985-1988	0.68	1.8	0.14	0.7
AVERAGE	0.67	4.7	0.19	2.7

Source: Rodríguez (1990) and *Anuario Estadístico de Cuba,* various issues.

Table 3. **Structure of Cuban Exports (in percent)**

	1957	1970	1975	1980	1987
Sugar	80.0	76.7	89.8	83.6	74.3
Tobacco	5.9	3.1	1.8	1.7	2.0
Minerals	5.7	16.7	4.7	4.8	6.6
Others	9.3	3.5	3.7	9.9	17.1
TOTAL	100.0	100.0	100.0	100.0	100.0

Source: Central Intelligence Agency (1984, 1989); Rodríguez (1990); and author's estimates.
Note: Other exports include fish, citrus, fruits, minerals, and rum.

Table 4. **Structure of Cuban Imports (in percent)**

	1965	1970	1975	1980	1986
Foodstuffs	25.2	20.0	19.0	17.1	10.4
Raw materials	2.9	4.7	3.9	4.3	4.0
Fuels and lubricants	9.8	8.7	10.0	20.5	33.5
Mach & transportation equipment	15.4	28.1	24.2	35.1	30.8
Others	46.7	38.5	42.9	23.1	21.3
TOTAL	100.0	100.0	100.0	100.0	100.0

Source: Central Intelligence Agency (1984, p. 33 and 1989, p.31).

Industrial and agricultural production are the main economic sectors in Cuba's economy, accounting for more than 80% of the total GMP or about 60% of Gross Social Product (GSP). Table 2 shows the share of total GMP and their rate of growth for the period 1963-1988: agriculture's share has been decreasing over time, while industry's share has remained constant over the last 25 years.

International Trade

Cuba's main exports are sugar and sugar derivatives (Table 3). These accounted, during the 1980's, for approximately 77% of total exports. Recently, mineral exports (mainly nickel) have replaced Cuba's second chief export, tobacco. Tobacco exports accounted for 10% of total exports in 1960, but for only 2% in 1987.

The concentration of international trade on sugar exports makes Cuba's economic output extremely vulnerable to world sugar prices, which have dramatically fluctuated over the years. During the revolution, some stability was attained by Russian guaranteed

fixed prices, which were often higher than world prices.

With respect to Cuba's imports, statistics show the degree of the nation's dependency on imports. This dependence is clearly evident in a continuous trade balance deficit for more than 32 years. This constant international trade deficit contributed to Cuba's reliance on Soviet financing. Following the so-called "end of the cold war," with the disintegration of the Soviet Union, Cuba no longer receives Russian financing for the trade deficits.

Note that Cuba's imports statistics are not very accurate because some of their strategic goods imports—such as weaponry—were supplied free of charge at least during 1962-1970. Foodstuffs were, on average, the most important imports between 1963-1975, accounting for about 20% (

4). Fuel imports increased considerably from 1960 to 1986, accounting for one third of total imports in recent years. Also note that the share of machinery and transportation equipment imports increased at a rate of more than 4% a year during the last 20 years. Cuba's dependency on imported technology for machinery and transportation equipment is clear. Table 4 shows the failure of the Cuban industrialization program adopted as the main goal of the government after 1959.

Education and Human Capital

Investing in human capital is a concept widely used by economists, which basically describes the process of improvement of the quality of the labor force. Thus, human capital is referred to as the level of education of the labor force. Improvement of the quality of the labor force is basically accomplished by education and training. Since there is no accurate data concerning the rate of change of education of the Cuban labor force, for purposes of discussion in this paper, it is assumed that human capital changes at the same rate than the enrollment rate change.

Table 5 contains data of enrollment in Cuba between 1958 and 1985. With respect to education, Cuba considerably increased the rate of enrollment, thus increasing its human capital during this period. It is clear from Table 5 that human capital accumulation has been quite rapid. Hence it could be concluded that the Cuban government was successful in achieving a high rate of improvement of human capital.

Table 5. Students Enrolled by Level of Education (per 1,000 inhabitants)

	Primary	Secondary	Higher	Other	Total
1958	106.1	13.0	3.8	1.0	123.9
1980	163.6	120.0	15.6	28.5	327.9
1985	143.0	151.0	21.5	18.5	334.0

Source: Zimbalist and Brundenius (1989, p.168).

Improvements in the educational attainment of the labor force, as happened in Cuba, should contribute positively to output through efficiency gains, which should be reflected in the rate of technical change or TFP. Thus, the important issue to be examined in this paper about human capital is how human capital improvement contributed to Cuban economic growth. The two crucial questions regarding human capital that we will try to answer in the coming sec-

tions are: How much did the educational effort contribute to economic growth under a centrally planned economy? Is there any economic return from the investment directed to improve Cuban human capital during the period 1962-1988?

LITERATURE REVIEW

Many theories have been developed by economist over the years to explain economic growth and development. These usually try to pinpoint what are the determining factors that contribute to growth and development.

Old political economist such as Adam Smith and J.S. Mill considered education as an important factor for economic growth and development. But investment in human capital was for the most part ignored in discussions of economic growth until the mid-1950s. In the 1960s work by T.W. Schultz (1961, 1963), Denison (1962), Mincer (1958, 1962) and Becker (1964), began to focus more and more attention on the role of human capital in economic growth and technological change and to determine the returns from education and the proportion of the rate of growth of output due to investment in education.

In 1980, the World Bank showed renewed interest in the development of human capital (Wheeler, 1980). The results of Wheeler's comparison of 88 developing nations suggested that education, health and nutrition contributed to growth of output not only directly, but also indirectly, by increasing the rate of investment and by lowering the birth rate. Wheeler also found that, on the average, an increase in the literacy rate from 20 to 30% caused national income (GDP) to increase by 8 to 16%.

The finding that general investment has less effect on growth rates when it is not supported by educational investment has been confirmed by studies carried out by Jamison and Lau (1982) and Psacharopoulus (1984). An empirical study by Mankiw, Romer and Weil (1992), using an augmented version of the Solow model (1956)—adding accumulation of human and physical capital—also found that the presence of human capital accumulation increases the impact of physical capital accumulation. Decades earlier, Schultz (1963) had also expressed puzzlement over a residual he was finding when measuring the increases in production over time and determined that the missing piece was the investment in human capital via education.

The neoclassical growth model was mainly defined by Solow (1956). His model focuses on capital accumulation and the quality of labor for economic growth. But, Solow's model had the shortcoming in that it did not explain the link between growth and technological change, which was seen as exogenous in his framework, which obviously could result from level of education of the work force among other factors.

The new endogenous growth theorists, starting with Paul Romer (1986) and Robert Lucas (1988), have tried to find the determinant factors that drive economic growth, such as human capital, new technologies, economies of scale, and international trade. Much empirical work has been carried out lately to find out what factors are important for economic growth. Barro (1991) studied 98 countries for the period 1960-1985, concluding that faster growth is associated with a higher rate of investment by either private or government sector, a lower share in GDP of government consumption spending, higher school enrollment rates, greater political stability, and lower fertility rates.

UNDERSTANDING CUBAN GROWTH AND TECHNOLOGICAL CHANGE

Capital, labor, human capital and technical progress are in general the four principal sources of growth of aggregate output. Based on extensive data collected for this study, the traditional methodology (Solow, 1957) will be applied to the Cuban case to have a better understanding of its economic growth.

Conceptual Points

Consider the traditional production function:

$$Y_t = F(K_t, L_t, t) \qquad (1)$$

$$Y_t = A(t)G(K_t, L_t) \qquad (1')$$

where Yt, Kt, and Lt are the quantities of aggregate real output, physical capital and labor, respectively, at time t, and t is an index of chronological time. The

second equation (1') is the traditional neoclassical growth model, which is a specific case of the first one. Since A varies with time and independently of K and L, technological change is by assumption disembodied, where a Hicks neutral technological change is assumed. This is the basic Solow (1957) model.

The growth rate of output (GDP or GMP) can be expressed in the familiar equation of growth accounting by taking natural logarithms of both sides of equation (1) and differentiating it totally with respect to t:

$$\frac{dLnYt}{dt} = \frac{\partial lnF}{\partial lnK}(Kt, Lt, t)\frac{dlnKt}{dt} + \frac{\partial lnF}{\partial lnL}(Kt, Lt, t)\frac{dlnLt}{dt} + \frac{\partial lnF}{\partial t}(Kt, Lt, t) \qquad (2)$$

Here $\frac{\partial \ln F}{\partial \ln K}$, $\frac{\partial \ln F}{\partial \ln L}$ are the elasticities of output with respect to capital and labor at time t and $\frac{\partial \ln F}{\partial t}$ is the instantaneous growth rate of output holding the inputs constants, or equivalent to the rate of technical progress, which is normally known as total factor productivity.

Note that the factor A(t) of equation (1') represents the rate of technical progress, which may contain many elements such as: (1) capacity of people to create or to adopt new technologies; (2) capacity of the people to achieve a better way of combining means of production (Schumpeter's view); (3) the efficiency of incentives or markets to innovate; (4) several possible forms of cost reduction (Harberger, 1990); (5) the efficiency of energy use; and (6) catch-up growth.

For the above mentioned facts, it is important to understand the determinants of TFP, especially when they are aggregated for the whole economy, and try to find an explanation to better understand this "black box" called A(t). Endogenous analysis of TFP has been a widely used technique to find the determinants and quantifying the facts that that generates technological change, such as, education, foreign trade and economy of scales. In general, technological change is considered to be mainly embodied in the labor, thus, it is assumed that education is the main determinant of technological progress.

In the present research we will be applying a Cobb-Douglas function to estimate the total factor of productivity for the entire Cuban economy and by sectors (agriculture and industry). Thus:

$$Y_t = A_t K_t^{\alpha} L_t^{\beta} \qquad (3)$$

Equation (4) is the discrete approximation of the time derivative obtained after taking natural log and then differentiating equation 3:

$$\frac{\Delta Y}{Y} = \frac{\Delta A}{A} + \alpha \frac{\Delta K}{K} + \beta \frac{\Delta L}{L} \qquad (4)$$

Where, $\frac{\Delta Y}{Y}, \frac{\Delta K}{K}, \frac{\Delta L}{L}$ are the rate of growth of output, capital and labor respectively in annual basis. The constants α and β are the elasticities of output with respect to capital and labor respectively. The factor $\frac{\Delta A}{A}$ represents the rate of technical progress or TFP.

Hence, we have to keep in mind that when equations (2) or (4) are used to measure technical progress over time, three basic assumptions are implicit. In general constant return to scale are considered, together with neutrality of technical progress[3] and profit maximization with competitive output and factors markets.

As we know, not every quantity on the right side of equations (2) or (4) can be measured directly. In fact only the growth rate of output, capital and labor are directly measured. Hence, the elasticity of output with respect to labor and capital must be estimated. This forces us to assume perfect competition, which implies that firms will set return on capital equal to marginal product of the capital, which implies that the elasticity of output with respect to capital (α) can be measured as the capital income in total output (GDP or GMP). Thus, the elasticity of output with respect to labor is considered as the labor share in total aggregated output.

Another alternative to using equation (1) to measure technical progress is the direct econometric estimation of the aggregate production function. Such direct estimation, does not require any assumption beyond that of the functional form.

Estimating the Stock of Capital and Factor Shares

It is common practice to build the time series for capital stock based on perpetual inventories using investment time series Others use the rate of growth in investment as a proxy for the rate of growth in capital.[4] Since there are no estimates of the stock capital for the Cuban economy, a capital stock time series was constructed. The key assumption of the methodology used to estimate the stock of capital is that the capital-output ratio is constant for short period of time.[5] Thus, the stock of capital is determined by:

$$K = \frac{I}{(\hat{Y} + \delta)} \qquad (5)$$

Where $\hat{Y}, \delta$ are the rate of growth of output and the depreciation rate, respectively. This equation is used to estimate the stock of capital at the beginning of the period (1960). The following years stock of capital is basically the initial stock of capital plus gross investment minus depreciation. The stock of capital series was calibrated with the depreciation figures obtained from the Cuban national account statistics in conjunction with our estimates. The annual rate of depreciation considered for the whole economy and the industry sector was 4.5%, which corresponds to the average value of depreciation in similar income economies. Depreciation for agriculture was considered as 3.5%. Sensitivity analysis was conducted using a higher rate of depreciation (6%) to analyze how sensitive are the TFP estimates, without detecting much variation in the TFP obtained.

---

3. A function with neutral technical change takes the form $Y = A(t) f(K, L, t)$. In a specific case of a Cobb-Douglas, it would be expressed as $Y_t = A \cdot e^{\lambda t} K_t^{\alpha} L_t^{\beta}$.

4. Victor Elias (1993) argues that using investment rate of growth instead of capital rate of growth leads in most of the cases to a difference of less than 20% for the two estimates. In our case using investment rate of growth as a proxy for the rate of change of the stock of capital leads to results that differ by greater than 200%. I recommend the creation of the capital stock series, which leads to more accurate results.

5. For a further explanation and example of this methodology, see Harberger (1976, pp. 132-155).

The estimation of the factor shares of labor in total output was estimated from Cuba's national accounts.

Total Factor Productivity for the Cuban Economy

Using equation (4), the TFP in Table 6 were estimated for the Cuban economy. Table 6 shows that productivity changes have been decreasing through time, achieving negative values after 1980. On the other hand the rate of investment increased considerably from 1963 to 1988. This results are contrary to what any economist would expect. Empirical applications to capitalist economies shows that increases in investment and human capital and a lower rate of population growth leads to higher TFP. Hence, we would expect a higher TFP for Cuba, but we have found the opposite results.

Table 6.   TFP Estimates for the Cuban Economy

	TFP (%)	Output Rate of Growth (%)	Investment Rate of Growth (%)	Investment/ GMP
1963-1970	1.0	4.4	3.2	0.18
1971-1980	0.8	5.9	18.3	0.26
1981-1988	-1.7	3.8	4.9	0.31
Average (63-88)	0.22	4.5	9.3	0.25

Table 7 shows that Cuban TFP contribution to economic growth is very low (only 3%). The contribution of investment to economic growth is very high (75%). Hence, Cuba's economic growth has been basically driven by increased investment, which is the result of the Soviet subsidies (Table 1). In other words, TFP results shows that Cuba was not able to take advantage of the investment in human capital to increase efficiency by cost reduction or productivity increase, specially during the 1980s.

Sectoral Total Factor of Productivity

To better understand the previous results, a sectoral analysis of TFP was conducted. The sectoral results obtained are shown below. Table 8 shows that agricultural TFP has been negative for the period 1963-1988. Hence, there was complete technological stagnation in the Cuban agricultural sector under the Cuban centrally planned economy. During this peri-

Table 7.   Aggregated Sources of Growth and Factor Contribution to Growth

	Growth Rate (%)	Contribution to Output Growth	Factor Contribution (%)
Output (1963-1988)	4.5		
Source of Output Growth (1963-1988)			
Capital	5.8	3.3%	72%
Labor	2.0	1.1%	25%
TFP	0.2	0.1%	3%

od, agricultural output growth was basically driven by increased investment. Note that the investment rate in the agricultural sector was much higher than in the industrial sector and the whole economy. Again, the only possible explanation is that agricultural output was the result of increased investment. It could be concluded that the negative agricultural TFP led to the widely known actual level of underdevelopment in agriculture (low yields and low level of productivity).

In sum, the large amount of investment in the agricultural sector has been mainly wasted and Cuba's agricultural sector has been consuming the stock of capital, without any productivity achievement. It seems an irony, because Cuba's industrial development strategy was oriented toward getting resources from agriculture to develop an industrial base. But, reality shows that agriculture has been a big consumer of resources, without any positive result. While Cuba's main exports are based on agricultural products, agriculture was not able to achieve any positive level of technological change.

One possible explanation for this technological stagnation is the lack of markets and economic incentives, which are impossible to be implemented in a centrally planned economy. In sum, it is possible to conclude that Cuban centrally planned agricultural economic policies were totally inefficient in their attempt to force some technological change during the period 1963-1988. Again, it can be concluded that Cuba was not able to take advantage of the investment in human capital which could have led to an

Table 8.   TFP Estimates for Agriculture

	TFP (%)	Agriculture Output Rate of Growth (%)	Agricultural Investment Rate of Growth (%)	Agricultural Investment as Share of Agricultural TMP
1963-1970	-1.9	3.8	8.0	0.28
1971-1980	-1.2	2.7	10.3	0.35
1981-1988	-2.4	1.7	5.6	0.48
Average (63-88)	-1.5	2.7	8.1	0.37

Table 9.   TFP Estimates for Industry

	TFP (%)	Industry Output Rate of Growth (%)	Industry Investment Rate of Growth (%)	Industry Investment as share of Industry GMP
1963-1970	1.4	5.2	13.2	0.06
1971-1980	0.7	4.6	25.6	0.11
1981-1988	-0.4	4.3	6.0	0.19
Average (63-88)	0.6	4.7	15.0	0.12

increase in TFP and eventually to an increase in agricultural output.

Table 9 shows that TFP in the industrial sector was moderate for the period 1963-1980. But again, TFP was negative for the period 1981-1988. Looking at Table 2, it seems contradictory that at the same time imports of capital goods such as machinery and transportation equipment were increasing, TFP was decreasing. Table 9 shows that the ratio of investment over output in the industrial sector was very low compared with the agricultural sector. This clearly shows that the right amount of investment, avoiding over investment, makes people more productive, achieving higher rates of technological change. Again, during the 1980s Cuba was not able to take advantage of the investment in human capital which could have led to an increase in TFP.

The rates of growth of the different factors and their contribution to economic growth can be seen in Tables 10 and 11. Some could argue that the negative TFP during the 1970s and 1980s could be attributable to business cycles fluctuations. But in the case of Cuba this is not possible, since this period is considered as the golden era of the Revolution due to the high rate of economic growth achieved. Moreover, during this period, Cuba was receiving the largest amount of subsidies from the Soviet Union, which

isolated Cuba from world business cycles (see Table 1).

Looking the results in Table 11, it is difficult to explain why the massive investment in physical and human capital led to low TFP in the seventies and eighties. One explanation could be the very well known Latin American proverb "*escoba nueva barre bien*" (a new broom always cleans well). In other words, during the first years of Castro's regime, the vast majority of the population was excited about the revolution and communism. This initial excitement created high incentives for people to work hard and be productive and innovative, which could have led to the positive level of technological change observed during the 1960s. Then, as people tired of the regime, as the result of unfulfilled expectations and lack of gains from communism, they relaxed in their creativity and stopped working hard. Consequently, TFP decreased to negative levels.

ECONOMETRIC ESTIMATION OF ECONOMY OF SCALE

It could be possible that Cuba's economy does not show constant return to scale (CRTS) as a whole. To verify the assumption of CRTS, in this section a Cobb-Douglas production function will be estimated econometrically to test the hypothesis of constant re-

Table 10. Rates of Growth of Factors

| | Rate of Growth (%) | | | | | | | | |
| | Overall Economy (%) | | | Agriculture (%) | | | Industry (%) | | |
Years	Labor	Capital	TFP	Labor	Capital	TFP	Labor	Capital	TFP
1963-1970	1.2	4.5	1.0	1.3	8.8	-1.9	1.2	5.1	1.4
1971-1980	2.1	6.8	0.80	0.7	6.9	-1.2	2.3	5.5	0.7
1981-1988	2.6	6.1	-1.7	0.7	5.6	-2.4	3.9	4.1	-0.4
Average (63-87)	2.0	5.8	0.2	1.1	6.7	-1.5	2.5	4.9	0.6

Table 11. Contribution of Factors to Economic Growth

| | Contribution of Factors (as % of total economic growth) | | | | | | | | |
| | Overall Economy (%) | | | Agriculture (%) | | | Industry (%) | | |
Years	Labor	Capital	TFP	Labor	Capital	TFP	Labor	Capital	TFP
1963-1970	18	67	15	16	107	-23	16	66	18
1971-1980	22	70	8	11	108	-19	27	65	8
1981-1988	37	87	-24	18	144	-62	51	54	-5
Average (63-87)	25	72	3	17	106	-23	31	61	8

turn to scale considered previously and to verify the elasticities of labor and capital to real output. Thus:

$$Y_t = A \cdot K_t^\alpha \cdot L_t^\beta \qquad (6)$$

applying natural logs to equation (6), we obtain the linear equation:

$$\ln Y_t = \ln A + \alpha \ln K_t + \beta \ln L_t + \varepsilon \qquad (7)$$

Estimating equation (7) with time series data for the period 1962-1988, yields the results in Table 12. Note that econometric estimation of equation (6) could lead to a multicollinearity problem (see Boskin and Lau, 1992; Harberger, 1996). Our data was tested for multicollinearity, without finding any problem. Null hypothesis tests for CRTS were conducted, which led us to accept the hypothesis of existence of CRTS for the industrial sector and the Cuban economy as a whole.

Results from Table 12 show that the elasticity of capital (0.52) and of labor (0.54) to output for the overall economy are close to the average value of factor share to total output considered in the previous section, which average 0.51 and 0.49. In sum, it can be concluded that the results previously obtained by us-

Table 12. Regressions Results (1962-1988)

	Ln A	α	β	$\alpha+\beta$	N	R^2
Y_t-Agriculture	2.56	0.37	0.11	0.48	27	0.94
Y_t- Industry	-2.64	0.71	0.38	1.09	27	0.98
Y_t-Cuban Economy	-3.89	0.52	0.54	1.06	27	0.97

ing the indirect method are good estimates of TFP for the Cuban economy.

CUBA'S TECHNOLOGICAL CHANGE COMPARED TO OTHER REGIONS

Table 13 provides a comparative historical analysis of Cuba's rate of technical progress during this period with respect to other regions. Estimates in Table 13 show that on average during the period 1963-1988, Cuba performed much worse than most of the capitalist economies.[6] In sum, it seems that under a centrally planned economy, the rate of technological change (TFP) is significantly lower than in capitalist economies.

CONCLUSIONS

Some general conclusions can be drawn from the above analysis. First, that the Cuban economy as a whole, as well as the industrial sector, exhibited con-

Table 13. GDP Growth and Contribution of Factors to Economic Growth

Countries	GDP (%)			TFP Contribution to Growth (%)			GMP(%)	TFP(%)
	1950-73	1973-80	1980-89	1950-73	1973-80	1980-89	1963-1988	1963-1988
Cuba							4.4	3 (0.2)
Chile	3.42	3.39	2.9	51 (1.75)	44 (1.48)	26 (0.74)		
Latin America	5.79	5.20	1.34	42 (2.43)	23 (1.20)	-97 (-1.30)		
Asia	7.73	7.51	7.64	51 (3.93)	31 (2.31)	54 (4.09)		
Advanced	5.34	2.23	2.56	69 (3.26)	47 (0.93)	47 (1.20)		

Source: Hofman (1993, pp. 128-130.)

Note: Figures in parenthesis represent the value of TFP.

stant return to scale during the period 1962-1988. Second, that the Cuban agricultural sector exhibited decreasing return to scale during the same period. Third, that TFP for the Cuban economy has been decreasing through time, turning negative during the 1980s. Fourth, that the average rate of change in technical progress (TFP) of the Cuban economy over the period 1963-1988 is very low (0.2%), this value being much lower than for most capitalist economies that were growing at rates similar to Cuba's. Fifth, that the agricultural sector showed a very high negative rate of technical change; thus, there was a complete technological stagnation in this sector.

With respect to the agricultural sector it can be concluded that: (1) Cuban centrally planned economic policies were totally inefficient in promoting technological change in agriculture; (2) human resources were used in an inefficient manner; and (3) there was over investment in agriculture, which possibly led to an even lower TFP. Our results show that Cuban government agricultural planning has been very poor and inefficient, a finding that has been validated by other studies (e.g., Mesa-Lago, 1981, pp. 24-25). According to Mesa-Lago, this poor planning is the result lack of manpower, its lack of knowledge and expertise, and the lack of maintenance controls; for example, because of lack of maintenance controls, equipment breakdowns depleted the locomotive fleet by 50% (Mesa-Lago, 1981, p. 26). Obviously all

these facts are reflected in the negative TFP estimated in the present study.

With respect to the industrial sector, it can be concluded that the change in TFP has also been decreasing, but in this case the average value for the period of 1962-1988 is positive (0.6). The gains in productivity during the 1960s could be considered reasonable, but again TFP is negative during the 1980s. It seems ironic that the largest lack of capital was in this sector, which was able to achieve a moderate level of technological change during the period 1962-1988.

These research results clearly show that Cuba's growth during 1963-1988 was basically the result of capital accumulation rather than from productivity gains. Moreover, considering the large amount of Soviet subsidies given to Cuba during the 1970s and 1980s, at first glance one might conclude that Soviet dependency created inefficiency, because during this period of lack of capital (lower level of investment), technical progress was higher. Cuba's experience is contrary to capitalist economies, where an increase of physical and human capital create increases in technological change. Cuba's special case could be partially explained by the lack of economic incentives to innovate and by a centrally planned investment policy which was totally inefficient in allocating resources.

The main conclusion from this empirical analysis is that Cuba's development strategy has been a com-

---

6. Similar results were found by Poznanski (1985) when comparing the technological performance of the Soviet bloc countries with respect to the U.S. and Western Europe. See Poznanski (1985) for plausible explanations for the poor technological performance of centrally planned economies.

plete failure. The progress in Cuba was much like Russian growth in the past—it was obtained by massive, often wasteful, capital accumulation rather than by productivity growth. In other words, the Cuban centrally planned development strategy has consumed large sums of the capital received through Soviet subsidies; these subsidies have been mostly wasted, without any improvement in technological change. Hence, it could be concluded that the main problem with a centrally planned economy is the lack of the right economic incentives and price systems. The lack of these elements do not allow for technical progress, leaving centrally planned economies behind those of capitalist countries.

It can also be concluded that most of the investment in education has not had any economic return, especially those investments in human capital related to agricultural activities. In other words, a large amount of money has been wasted in the creation of human capital which has not been very productive under the Cuban centrally planned system.

TFP estimates for Cuba compared to other countries (Table 13) show that if Cuba maintains a centrally planned economy, it will have a very difficult time catching up with the rest of the world. To correct this path, Cuba should consider some policies that make use of the markets and economic incentives to encourage technological change.

Many important topics were not considered in this paper, such as a the role of the public sector through its actions and its expenditures in the process of technological change. Finally, additional research is needed linking Cuba's international trade and public policy with technological change, in order to arrive at a better understanding and quantification of the determinants of the low level of Cuban technological change and their effects.

REFERENCES

Barro, Robert, J. "Economic Growth in a Cross Section of Countries," *Quarterly Journal of Economics* (May 1991), 407-444.

Barro, R., and X. Sali-i-Martin. "Convergence Across States and Regions," *Brookings Papers on Economic Activity* (1991).

Becker, G.S. *Human Capital.* New York: Columbia University Press, 1964.

Boskin, B., and L. Lawrence. "Capital, Technology and Economic Growth." In Landau, Ralph, Nathan Rosemberg and David Mowery, *Technology and the Wealth of the Nations.* Stanford: Stanford University Press, 1992.

Brundenius, Claes. *Revolutionary Cuba: The Challenge of Economic Growth With Equity.* Boulder: Westview Press, 1984.

Central Intelligence Agency. *The Cuban Economy: A Statistical Review.* Washington, 1984, 1989.

Denison, E. "United States Economic Growth," *Journal of Business*, 35 (1992), 357-394.

Denison, E. *Trends in American Economic Growth, 1929-1982* .Washington: Brookings Institution, 1985.

Domínguez, Jorge. *Cuba: Order and Revolution.* Cambridge: The Belknap Press of the Harvard University Press, 1978.

Elias, Victor. "The Role of Total Productivity in Economic Growth." In Special Issue on Economic Growth, Universidad de Chile, Departamento de Economía, Santiago, Chile, 1993.

Fischer, Stanley. "Growth, Macroeconomics and Development." In Olivier Blanchard and Stanley Fischer, eds., *Macroeconomics Annual 1991.* Cambridge: MIT Press, 1991, 329-379.

Grossman, G. and H. El Hanan. *Innovations and Growth in the Global Economy*. Cambridge: MIT Press, 1993.

Harberger, A.. *Project Evaluation*. Chicago: University of Chicago Press, 1976.

Harberger, A. *Reflections on the Growth Process*, UCLA manuscript, 1990.

Harberger, A. *Reflections on Economic Growth in Asia and the Pacific*, UCLA manuscript, August 1996.

Hofman, Andre. "Chile's Economic Performance in the 20th Century: A Comparative Perspective." In Special Issue on Economic Growth, Universidad de Chile, Departamento de Economía, Santiago, Chile, 1993.

Jiménez, Georgina. *Hablemos de Educación: Recopilación de Artículos, Comentarios y Reportajes sobre Educación*. La Habana: Editorial Pueblo y Educación, 1985.

Jorgenson, Dale W. and Z. Griliches. "Issues in Growth Accounting: A Reply to F. Denison," *Survey of Current Business*, 52:5, Part II (1972), 65-94.

Jorgenson, Dale W., Frank M. Gollop, and Barbara M. Fraumeni. *Productivity and U.S. Economic Growth*. Cambridge: Harvard University Press, 1987.

Kim, J.I., and Lawrence Lau. "Economic Growth of the East Asian Newly Industrializing Countries," *Journal of the Japanese and International Economies* (1995), 235-271.

Krugman, Paul. "The Myth of Asia's Miracle," *Foreign Affairs* (Nov/Dec 1994), 62-78.

Landau, Ralph, Nathan Rosemberg and David Mowery. *Technology and the Wealth of the Nations*. Stanford: Stanford University Press, 1992.

Lau, L. and Jong-Il Kim. *The Sources of Economic Growth of the Newly Industrializing Countries on the Pacific Rim*. Stanford University: Center for Economic Policy Research #295, 1992.

Levine, R. and D. Renelt. "A Sensitivity Analysis of Cross-Country Growth Regressions," *American Economic Review*, 82:4 (September 1992), 942-963.

Lucas, Robert. "On the Mechanics of Economic Development," *Journal of Monetary Economics* 22 (1988), 3-42.

Mankiw, G., D. Romer, and D. Weil. "A Contribution to the Empirics of Economic Growth," *Quarterly Journal of Economics* 57:2 (May 1992), 407-43.

Mesa-Lago, C. *The Economy of Socialist Cuba: A Two Decade Appraisal*. Albuquerque: University of New Mexico Press, 1981.

Mesa-Lago, C. "Cuba's Economic Counter-Reform: Causes, Policies and Effects. In *Cuba After Thirty Years: Rectification and the Revolution*, ed. by Richard Gillespie. London: Frank Cass Company Ltd., 1990.

Mesa-Lago, C. and J. Pérez-López. *A Study of Cuba's Material Product System, Its Conversion to the System of National Accounts, and Estimation of Gross Domestic Product per Capita and Growth Rates*. World Bank Staff Working Papers No. 770. Washington: World Bank, 1985.

Mincer, Jacob. "Investment in Human Capital and Personal Income Distribution," *Journal of Political Economy* (August 1958).

Mincer, Jacob. "On-the-job Training: Costs, Returns and Some Implications," *Journal of Political Economy* 70:5 (October 1962).

Pérez-López, Jorge. *Measuring Cuban Economic Performance*. Austin: University of Texas Press, 1987.

Psacharopoulus, G. *Returns on Education*. San Francisco: Jossy Bass-Elsevier, 1973.

Psacharopoulus, G. "The Contribution of Education to Economic Growth." In *International Comparisons of Productivity and Causes of Slowdown*, edited by J.W. Kendrick. Cambridge: Ballinger Press, 1984.

Rodríguez, José Luis. *Estrategia del Desarrollo de Cuba.* La Habana: Editorial de Ciencias Sociales, 1990.

Romer, Paul. "Human Capital and Growth: Theory and Evidence." NBER Working Paper #3173, 1989.

Romer, Paul. "Endogenous Technical Change," *Journal of Political Economy* 98 (1990), 71-102.

Schultz, T. W. "Investing in Human Capital," *American Economic Review* (March 1961).

Schultz, T. W. *The Economic Value of Education.* New York: Columbia University Press, 1963.

Schultz, T. W. "Education Investment and Return." In *Handbook of Development Economics*, Chapter 13, H. Chenery and T.N. Srinivasan, eds. New York: North Holland, 1988.

Solow, Robert M. "A Contribution to the Theory of Economic Growth," *Quarterly Journal of Economics*, 70 (1956), 65-94.

Solow, Robert M. "Technical Change and the Aggregate Production Function," *Review of Economics and Statistics*, 39 (1957), 312-320.

Solow, Robert M. "Investment and Technical Progress." *In Mathematical Methods in the Social Sciences*, Kenneth J. Arrow, Samuel Karbin and Patrick Suppes, eds. Stanford: Stanford University Press, 1960.

Wheeler, D. "Human Resource Development and Economic Growth in LDC's: A Simulation Model," World Bank Staff Working Paper No 407. Washington: World Bank, 1980.

Young, A. "A Tale of Two Cities: Factor Accumulation and Technical Change in Hong Kong and Singapore." In *Macroeconomics Annual 1992.* Cambridge: MIT Press, 1992.

Young, A. "The Tyranny of Numbers: Confronting the Statistical Realities of the East Asian Growth Experience," *Quarterly Journal of Economics* (August 1995), 641-680.

Zimbalist, Andrew and Claes Brundenius. *The Cuban Economy: Measurement and Analysis of Socialist Performance.* Baltimore: The Johns Hopkins University Press, 1989.

IS U.S. FOREIGN POLICY TOWARD CUBA JUSTIFIABLE?

Mauricio Solaún

Allow me to make a very brief general statement to introduce our topic to be followed by the presentations and discussions. A fundamental question facing us is: is U.S. foreign policy *vis-a-vis* Cuba justifiable? In my opinion, it is not.

Naturally during almost four decades since the Revolution, U.S. and Cuban policies have varied. But since the outset, Fidel Castro's principal objective has not changed: remain in power at any cost, including war; define the United States as the great enemy; develop a violent system of control to impede the growth of viable internal opposition.

Many years have passed. Since 1959, the United States has been governed by 9 presidents—Republicans and Democrats—yet it has been impossible to normalize U.S.-Cuban relations. For one simple reason: Fidel Castro and his core followers have not wished to do so.

Remember the case of Jimmy Carter, who sought a rapprochement with Castro and moved to establish diplomatic relations with him. As a sequel to the liberalization of ties—which included allowing visits from the United States and to the island—in 1980 there was an explosion of Cuban refugees. Fidel Castro laughed at Carter's noble intentions of receiving over 100,000 refugees in Florida, sending to the U.S. about 15,000 hardened criminals and mental patients among them. In his memoirs Carter interpreted this crisis as a factor that contributed to his not being reelected. In any case, it is noteworthy that the Cuban Government supported the Soviet invasion of Afghanistan, which took place about this time.

A crucial turning point in the relations was the Missile Crisis of October 1962. Before then, the American objective was the overthrow of the Cuban regime because of its political-military alliance with the Soviet Bloc and commitment to expand its sphere of influence.

But the result of this direct United States-Soviet Union confrontation was very significant: you will recall, part of the resolution of the crisis consisted of the acceptance of the continuation of Castro's rule by the American government. And although this was contingent upon conditions, in fact, since then Democratic and Republican Administrations have considered it the U.S. policy. This has meant that the anti-Castro movements, outside and inside Cuba, have not been accorded belligerent status. Since the 1960s, the U.S. Government has very substantially assisted several groups seeking to overthrow their governments, and has deployed American troops to change governments in the Caribbean and Central America, but not against Fidel Castro.

Indeed, after the Missile Crisis the American Cuban policy, with exceptional departures, had these components:

- isolate Castro;
- avoid other Cubas;
- generously give residence to Cubans wishing to settle in the United States; and
- maintain an economic embargo.

One thing is certain, of course: Castro is still in power though his wings and international projection have been severely cut.

It is impossible to isolate Cuba. Leaders of other nations wish to have contact with it. Castro himself continues to be an international guest, though in the new post-Communist climate in Western and Latin nations, he has been scolded and even asked to allow free elections during international visits. This was the notable case last November in his visit to Chile, where Salvador Allende's widow herself publicly asked him to do so.

Another item of the agenda is the refugee policy, a latent problem for all U.S. Administrations. This has been the humanitarian side of the U.S. policy: welcome into the United States those dissatisfied with conditions in Cuba. Politically, however, the migration option (recently altered by the Clinton Administration) contributed to defuse the spirit of internal protest, as hopes are placed on an alternative future in foreign lands already densely populated by Cuban contacts.

Thirdly, the "avoidance of other Cubas" has lost relevance with the collapse of the Soviet Bloc. Only in Colombia does a large guerrilla movement operate at this time; in Peru less so. Other issues of U.S. national or security interests have gained paramount importance—for instance, drug trafficking.

Finally, the U.S. embargo. We must keep in mind that the embargo is not a blockade and that total embargoes can only be achieved by war. Other countries have maintained economic ties with Cuba all along. In fact, the purpose of the Helms-Burton act is to tighten an ineffective embargo.

But interestingly, the embargo's origin was tied to U.S. policy to unseat Castro. In January 1962 —the same year of the October Missile Crisis—the Eighth Consultative Meeting of OAS Ministers of Foreign Affairs in Uruguay adopted an unprecedented resolution: it excluded Cuba from the regional body, and authorized member states to take those steps that they considered appropriate for their individual or collective defense; the regional body gave the green light to any of the member states, including the United States, to overthrow Castro. And the American response was to decree a suspension of commercial relations with Cuba, declaring the embargo in February 1962. (In January of the previous year diplomatic relations had been suspended and a more partial embargo declared.)

It is thought provoking that on November 27, 1962, aware that as a result of the Missile Crisis the United States had changed policy and would not seek to overthrow Castro, the Consejo Revolucionario de Cuba, the entity that had been formed with U. S. Government backing to lead the liberation of Cuba, after the end of the U.S. naval blockade of the island during the Missile Crisis stated:

> We warn again that the diplomatic isolation and economic embargo, by themselves, won't overthrow the Communist regime of Cuba, nor reduce its expansive force of perturbation and contagion ... The crisis of Cuba can only be resolved by armed force, exercised by Cuban democrats and those [foreigners] who desire the survival of freedom in the Americas.

Five months later, José Miró Cardona, upon resigning as president of the Consejo, wrote:

> I have sustained and sustain that the goal of isolating [Cuba] proposed by those who fear armed action is criminal. The economic suffocation that is exercised by ... embargo, prolonging the suffering of a people that has arrived at the unbearable limits of its resistance, to provoke an internal rebellion, cannot be justified if the time of its ending is not preestablished. To promote or intent an insurrectional movement determined by desperation, without coordinating it with armed action projected from abroad, of a people dominated by terror would lead: 1) to relive the dark page of Budapest [i.e., the unsuccessful 1956 revolt in Hungary]; 2) to create the myth of Fidel Castro's invincibility; and 3) to promote negotiations for a coexistence that has just been repudiated in the [Organization of American States].

These words have been forgotten especially by a Cuban-exile community that blindly seeks revenge, and does not know better in its frustration *vis-a-vis* the collective madness of the clique that rules Cuba led by Fidel Castro's pathological personality. Economic embargoes are, usually, relatively ineffective tools—their success depends partly on their psychological impact on the targeted rulers, and Fidel Castro obviously has felt that he is above yielding.

Obviously the embargo has posted costs: it is more expensive to ship merchandise to Cuba from China or England that from Miami; the Cuban economy could benefit from added American investment, etc. After the fact, the embargo has acquired a reasonableness of its own as a negotiating chip, though a total embargo—an economic blockade of Cuba—is unviable.

Cuba's economic problems, however, do not rest on these partial shortcoming, but rather on the nature of its economic regime, which has proved unviable in all continents of this world when the balance has been tallied. Suppose that as a consequence of increased economic hardship there were an uprising in Cuba that is actually suppressed by the Castro gang who remains in power. What then?

To conclude, does this mean that U.S.-Cuba relations can be normalized? Castro's enemies need not fear: as long as he is the political sovereign, I don't think so.

I have recalled that after the Missile Crisis, the U.S. has basically followed policies of coexistence with the Cuban regime. Relations have turned friendlier (as initially with Carter) and more hostile (as under Reagan). But the path to normalize, stabilize, them has not been sustained because the Cuban rulers have not wanted to do so.

A principal impediment to achieving normal relations is Castro's messianic-apocalyptic self-identity as a warrior who must perpetually fight and hold power against his enemies: the United States of America and his countrymen who happen to disagree with him. The crux of the problem is Fidel Castro, the indomitable pirate, troublemaker, who has appropriated as his personal fiefdom the island. Given his mind-set it has been impossible to establish civilized relations with him. As with criminal elements, I cannot envision relations with him without a military component. The ineffective alternative is isolating him. Paradoxically, the more international interaction with his regime, the greater the propensity toward internal opposition in Cuba, and the more the pathological side of his cruel and absurd policies is exposed.

Must or should we be at Fidel Castro's caprices?

THE POLITICAL ECONOMY OF
TRADE SANCTIONS: THE CASE OF CUBA

Carlos Seiglie

In any discussion of the effects of economic sanctions it should be clear that sanctions are *potentially* harmful or costly to not only the target nation, but also the sanctioning countries. The *potential* harm will be dependent on the degree of substitution in trade and capital markets, i.e., on "fungibility." Even if sanctions impose harm on the target nation they may not alter the policy which motivated the sanctions. Some have argued that sanctions might even backfire because they can serve to increase support for the regime if the population "rallies around the flag." Therefore, the effectiveness of sanctions as an instrument to invoke change is constrained by the openness of the international goods and capital markets, as well as by the political markets in both the sanctioning and target nations. Consequently, any analysis of the effectiveness and usefulness of the U.S. embargo on Cuba should take these factors into account.

This paper aims to do so by extending a model by Kaempfer and Lowenberg (1988) to account for transnational responses which results in a country being in both an *internal* and *external* political equilibrium. This is developed by applying this more generalized model to the case of U.S. sanctions towards Cuba. I argue that the embargo against Cuba is ineffective because it cannot be sufficiently tight to cause political change in Cuba. For example, even though Cuba has been denied access to U.S. capital markets for three decades it still is one of the most heavily indebted countries in Latin America. It is estimated that at the end of 1995, Cuba owed $10.5 billion in

hard-currency debt. Of this total, $4.5 billion was owed to the Paris Club comprised of official government creditors, $2.9 billion to the London Club composed of commercial bank creditors and $2.4 billion in the form of trade credits. It should be noted that these figures would be much higher if not for the fact that Cuba has not paid on its debt obligations for the past 10 years and as a result has not been borrowing in the international capital markets. In addition to these figures, which support the fact that Cuba has had ample access to world capital markets during the period of the U.S. embargo, we must note that Cuba's debt to the former Soviet Union (assumed by Russia) has been estimated to be in the range of $6 to $34 billion.

In fact, if embargoes or sanctions were an effective tool in reducing the income of rulers or citizens of a country we should observe that historically countries would invest in "sanction preventing" measures or some type of "insurance" to protect against the harm from these. The reason that there is no need to do so is because if sanctions increase the damage to the economy of the sanctioned country, the willingness to pay by individuals in the country for the scarcer commodities increases and therefore, creates an incentive on the part of other sovereign countries to not participate in the sanctions. In other words, sanctions create rents and these rents induce other nations to circumvent the sanctions and supply the target country with the scarcer commodities. As they supply the target country, these rents are dissipated and the previous harm is reduced. In the short run, it requires tighter and more costly measures by the sanctioning leader to continue to impose harm, but this again increases the target country's willingness to pay and potential rents that other nations can capture. Eventually, the political market imposes a level of sanctions which has little effect and are just purely for the domestic consumption of political groups who receive utility from the sanctions per se. These sanctions will have no relationship to the level of sanctions required to influence the "offending" policy of the target country. In other words, the level of sanctions a country imposes is not related in any systematic way to some "optimal" level.

MARKET FOR SANCTIONS IN THE UNITED STATES

Although for concreteness we concentrate on Cuba, an analysis of the influence that lobbies have on foreign policy in general is straightforward using the framework presented. This influence by pressure groups is readily seen in the U.S. policy towards Haiti (the Congressional Black Caucus playing a dominant role), Ireland and Israel. In order to illustrate how the level of sanctions towards Cuba is established, several groups in the U.S. affected by sanctions on Cuba are highlighted.

The first group is the organized Cuban-American community which is denoted by O. The most powerful of these political lobbies is the Cuban-American National Foundation. This lobby is reminiscent of the China lobby of the 1950's which blocked changes in the United States' China policy until President Nixon's opening towards China.

The second group is the unorganized Cuban-American community, U. Note that the Cuban-American population is less then 4/10 of one percent of the U.S. population which implies that its electoral influence outside of Florida is very small.

The third are business groups, both domestic and foreign subsidiaries, who are in favor of sanctions (because they benefit) and which are denoted by B, and finally a group opposed to sanctions (because they lose or they ideologically support the regime), denoted by C. This latter group can be viewed as consumers of the products from Cuba who now are forced to pay a higher price for Cuban imports (e.g., cigars) or vacations and supporters who share the ideology of the regime.

Each individual member of a group has the following utility function and solves the maximization problem:

$$\underset{S}{\text{Max}} \; U_1^i(Y_1^i, S) \tag{1}$$
$$\text{subject to } Y_1^i(S; A),$$

where Y denotes income, S the level of sanctions, A the level of the offending policy of the "sanctioned" nation, the subscript denotes country 1, and individual i is a member of group O, U, B, or C.

I allow for some individuals to value sanctions on "moral" grounds and therefore their utility function is dependent on S directly.

If $i \in O$, then it is assumed that $\dfrac{\partial Y_1^i}{\partial S} = 0$ and $\dfrac{\partial U_1^i}{\partial S} > 0$. (2a)

If $i \in U$, then it is assumed that $\dfrac{\partial Y_1^i}{\partial S} < 0$ and $\dfrac{\partial U_1^i}{\partial S} \geq 0$. (2b)

If $i \in B$, then it is assumed that $\dfrac{\partial Y_1^i}{\partial S} > 0$ and $\dfrac{\partial U_1^i}{\partial S} = 0$. (2c)

If $i \in C$, then it is assumed that $\dfrac{\partial Y_1^i}{\partial S} < 0$ and $\dfrac{\partial U_1^i}{\partial S} \leq 0$. (2d)

The interpretation of equation (2a) is that the organized Cuban-American community's level of income is unaffected by sanctions but that they value sanctions directly on "moral grounds." Equation (2b) states that the unorganized Cuban-American community's income is reduced by sanctions and that some members, but not all, may value sanctions on "moral grounds." The reason that U's income is reduced should be interpreted that sanctions requires them to send remittances and medicine to Cuba to support family members. Implicit in this assumption is that their utility function includes the utility of family members in Cuba, i.e., that they have altruistic preferences. I assume this is being captured by the reduction in utility as income falls in order to simplify the notation involved in explicitly introducing altruism in their preferences. Finally, equations (2c) and (2d) imply that firms producing commodities and services similar to Cuba's are made better off by sanctions (e.g., the U.S. sugar cane producers) and therefore, they will support them; that consumers are made worse off indirectly by the higher transactions cost they must incur and that ideological sympathizers are directly made worse off since sanctions enters as an argument in their utility function.[1]

It is important to note that the Cold War environment helped increase the political support for sanctions. The reason is that the opposition's influence was diluted by groups who argued that the policy towards Cuba helped contain Soviet influence in Latin America and Cuba's promotion of revolution in the hemisphere. With the end of the Cold War, this group's argument that Cuba poses a threat to national security is no longer considered very plausible.

For the members of each group, the total change in utility from an incremental change in sanctions is

$$\frac{dU_1^O}{dS} = \frac{\partial U_1^O}{\partial S} > 0, \tag{3a}$$

$$\frac{dU_1^U}{dS} = \frac{\partial U_1^U}{\partial Y_1^i}\frac{\partial Y_1^i}{\partial S} + \frac{\partial U_1^U}{\partial S} \lessgtr 0, \tag{3b}$$

$$\frac{dU_1^B}{dS} = \frac{\partial U_1^B}{\partial Y_1^i}\frac{\partial Y_1^i}{\partial S} > 0, \tag{3c}$$

$$\frac{dU_1^C}{dS} = \frac{\partial U_1^C}{\partial Y_1^i}\frac{\partial Y_1^i}{\partial S} < 0. \tag{3d}$$

If we group all those who gain from sanctions, their marginal willingness to pay for an incremental tightening of the embargo is:

$$P_S = D^i(S,A) = \sum_i \frac{dU_1^i}{dS} > 0, \tag{4}$$

with $\partial D^i/\partial S < 0$ and $\partial D^i/\partial A > 0$ and where $i \in$ O, B, and some members of U.

For all those who lose from sanctions their marginal willingness to pay to forego an incremental tightening of the embargo is:

$$P_S = D^j(S,A) = -\sum_j \frac{dU_1^j}{dS} > 0, \tag{5}$$

with $\partial D^j/\partial S > 0$ and $\partial D^j/\partial A \geq 0$ and where $j \in$ C and some members of U.

Equating the demand for sanctions to the supply of opposition against sanctions leads to the political equilibrium level of sanctions in country 1. This is shown graphically in Figure 1. We depict this equilibrium at a level of sanctions of S where the initial demand for sanctions is D_1^i.

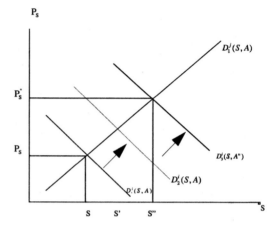

Figure 1: The Sanctioning Country -1

MARKET FOR LIMITED REFORMS IN CUBA

We can similarly derive the political equilibrium in the target country, Cuba. In this case the political conflict is over the level of a policy which we denote by A. This policy can be interpreted as the degree of openness of the political and economic system i.e., whether to maintain a state planned economy and one party rule (a high level of A) or to permit free market reforms and plurality in the political system (A = 0). Recently, Cuba seems to be interested in re-integrating into the world financial markets and has been engaging in debt-equity swaps with foreign corporations. For simplicity, we continue to denote the initial demand (support) for policy A in country 2 by

---

1. In order to simplify the notation, it is assumed that some individuals have preferences over S, but more directly we should introduce as an argument the level of utility of certain groups on the island towards whom they feel an affinity.

D_1^i and opposition to the policy by D_1^i. These demands are derived when groups for and against the policy in country 2 solve the following maximization problem:

$$\underset{A}{\text{Max}}\ U_2^i(Y_2^i, A)$$
$$\text{subject to } Y_2^i(A; S),$$
(6)

where the subscript denotes an individual who is a member of country 2.

We continue to make similar assumptions regarding how policy A impacts on the income of country 2, Cuba, namely some groups benefit, $\partial Y_2^i / \partial A > 0$ (bureaucracy, communists, *maybe* small farmers) with others losing $\partial Y_2^i / \partial A < 0$. As for sanctions, they are assumed to have an adverse effect or no effect on the level of income of particular members of the different groups in Cuba. We could actually envision that sanctions may be preferred by some individuals if their income is increased, as is possibly the case if managers of state enterprises experience an increase in the terms of trade for their products. Similarly, this potential reduction in foreign competition in commodities and capital serve to increase *rents* which can be captured by some individuals. Introducing these considerations strengthen our results, but for simplicity we assume that in the aggregate total income is reduced. Figure 2 depicts the political equilibrium in country 2 at a level of the offending policy of A.

It is important to note that the political equilibrium depicted in Figures 1 and 2 are equilibrium at the domestic level of interactions. A Nash equilibrium at the international level is some (A^*, S^*) combination such that if we denote the country by k $D_k^i(A^*, S^*) = D_k^j(A^*, S^*)$, k=1, 2. In addition, no member of a group can do better in the domestic political market given the level of the policy chosen in the other country's political market.

To illustrate this notion of two-level equilibrium, i.e., domestic and international, let us assume we are

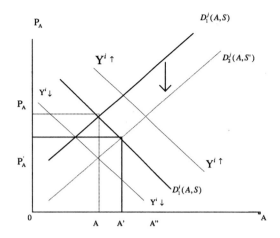

Figure 2: The Sanctioning Country -1

initially in a Nash equilibrium at S in country 1 and A in country 2. Then assume that a group in favor of sanctions in the U.S. is able to exert more influence politically, e.g., by better controlling free-riding by group members. Then demand shifts outwards to D_2^i from D_1^i. The new level of sanctions imposed by country 1 would rise to S'. But this would not be a Nash equilibrium at the international level. Country 2 which previously had a policy of A has suffered a reduction in income. This leads to a fall in the willingness to pay of group j as indicated to D_2^j. Now there are two potential effects on group i, namely their income can fall or it can rise because they may capture additional rents. If their income falls their willingness to pay falls and the new demand curve is labeled $Y^i\downarrow$. In this case the domestic equilibrium level of the policy continues to be A. If this group's income actually rose, then demand would increase to that labeled $Y^i\uparrow$ and the actual level of the offending policy will actually *increase*. If we factor in a "rally around the flag" effect which reduces free-riding by members of group i then their demand can shift out even more as this group feels its sovereignty is being jeopardized and the domestic equilibrium level of the offending policy is even greater.[2] In any case we are not guaranteed that even if the income of group i

---

2. Kaempfer and Lowenberg (1988) introduce a political effectiveness function, E, which is a function of S into the demand functions of each group, i.e., into P_A and P_S to incorporate this effect.

falls we will attain a movement towards the objective of A = 0, namely democratic reforms. Kaempfer and Lowenberg show that if the income of group i is reduced the optimal policy for a sanctioning country is to selectively use sanctions which hurt the prime beneficiaries of regimes to a much greater extent then it does group j, the internal opposition. Ideally, we would want the opposition's income to not be reduced at all.

Although this is a domestic equilibrium, Kaempfer and Lowenberg fail to consider that it is not an international equilibrium as earlier mentioned. To see how we arrive at this Nash equilibrium, let us assume that the sanctions actually increased the level of A to A". This would lead to a further shift in demand in country 1, the US to D_3^i and the equilibrium level of sanctions increased to S". In figure 1, I assume that the opposition against sanctions by the supporters of the regime (their demand curve D_1^j) is unchanged as A increases. It could be possible that the demand could shift in either direction. For example, the more hard-line policy could become an embarrassment and their willingness to support the regime falls, in which case sanctions would become tighter than S", i.e., the equilibrium is to the right of it. Conversely, this hard-line policy may evoke greater sympathy in which case the equilibrium would be to the left of S". The other possibility is that the two-level Nash equilibrium would entail a fall in income of supporters of

the regime in country 2, Cuba, and a resulting moderation in policy, i.e., a reduction in A. In this case, the demand for sanctions in country 1 falls and so would the level of sanctions. Eventually, the Nash equilibrium would be restored.

CONCLUSION

The basic conclusion from the application of this model to Cuba is that sanctions, including the embargo, have no relationship to some optimal policy which would lead the regime to open up the political process. In fact, it has been shown that the opposite effect can actually occur, i.e., the regime becomes more recalcitrant. I have not introduced a third country (the rest of the world) but doing so would strengthen this result further. This reinforcement comes from the fact that if the U.S. embargo raised rents, other countries have a strong incentive to not participate in the embargo and attempt to capture these rents, thereby rendering the embargo ineffective. The fact that we find no other nations participating in the embargo and continuing to have good relationships with Cuba is in fact a sign of the benefits they receive from the U.S. unilateral policy. Therefore, any request from the U.S. to other world nations to participate in the embargo will not be heeded. Furthermore, the failures of multinational embargoes in provoking change in Haiti and Iraq leaves little optimism that this policy instrument is effective.

REFERENCES

Bayard, Thomas O., Pelzman, Joseph and Pérez-López, Jorge. "Stakes and Risks in Economic Sanctions," *The World Economy* 6 (March 1983) 73-87.

Eaton, Jonathan and Engers, Maxim. "Sanctions," *Journal of Political Economy* 82 (October 1992) 899-928.

Kaempfer, William H. and Lowenberg, Anton D. "The Theory of International Economic Sanc-

tions: A Public Choice Approach," *American Economic Review* 72 (September 1988) 786-793.

Losman, Donald L. *International Economic Sanctions: The Cases of Cuba, Israel, and Rhodesia.* Albuquerque: University of New Mexico Press, 1979.

Porter, Richard C. "International Trade and Investment Sanctions: Potential Impact on the South African Economy," *Journal of Conflict Resolution* 23 (December 1979) 579-612.

Polachek, Solomon W. "Conflict and Trade: An Economics Approach to Political International Interactions." In *Economics of Arms Reduction and the Peace Process*, ed. by Walter Isard and C. Anderton. Amsterdam: North-Holland, 1992.

Seiglie, Carlos. "International Conflict and Military Expenditures: An Externality Approach," *Journal of Conflict Resolution* 32 (March 1988) 141-161.

Tullock, Gordon. "The Paradox of Revolution," *Public Choice* 11 (Fall 1971) 89-99.

IMPLICATION OF THE U.S. ECONOMIC EMBARGO FOR A POLITICAL TRANSITION IN CUBA

Juan J. López[1]

Does the U.S. embargo against the Castro government, and in particular the Cuban Liberty and Democratic Solidarity (LIBERTAD) Act of 1996, help, hinder or is irrelevant for the probability that a political transition will take place in Cuba? This is the main question this work seeks to answer. As Przeworski (1986, 48) observes, questions about possibility are theoretical and necessarily involve propositions that are counterfactual. I will address this key query using a combination of theory, comparative analyses, and available data.

Whether the United States should maintain its economic embargo on the Castro government has been controversial for a long time. But after the LIBERD-TAD Act (commonly known as the Helms-Burton law) became law in March 1996, the degree of contention has reached an unprecedented degree of intensity.

The main justification on the part of the U.S. government for the establishment and implementation of the Helms-Burton law is that it will promote a transition to democracy in Cuba. A key mechanism by which the Helms-Burton suppose to contribute to a transition is by tightening the economic embargo and thus reducing the hard currency available to the Castro government. This reasoning was emphasized by President Bill Clinton when he signed the Helms-Burton bill as well as by congressional supporters of the measure.[2] The same justification has been repeated over time by officials of the Clinton administration.[3]

The Helms-Burton law has four titles.[4] Title I seeks to strengthen international sanctions against the Castro government. Among of the clauses of Title I is the instruction to U.S. executive directors of international financial institutions to oppose loans to Cuba and Cuban membership until a transition to democracy occurs in the island. Title II mandates the preparation of a plan for U.S. assistance to transitional and democratically elected governments in Cuba.

---

1. This is a revised version of a paper prepared for presentation at the Seventh annual meeting of the Association for the Study of the Cuban Economy. I thank William C. Smith, Juan M. del Aguila and Jorge Pérez-López for comments on the original draft. I am solely responsible for the contents of this article.

2. White House press release on March 12, 1996. President Clinton, who had opposed the Helms-Burton bill while its supporters sought to obtain congressional approval, decided to back it and sign the bill after the Cuban air force shot down two small, unarmed U.S. civilian aircrafts in international waters on February 24, 1996, killing the four men that piloted the planes.

3. For example, see the declaration by Michael Ranneberger, Director of Cuban affairs at the State Department, that appeared in Armando Correa, "EU protegerá activistas en Cuba," *El Nuevo Herald* (1 March 1997).

4. The U.S. policy toward the Castro government is not limited to provisions under the Helms-Burton Act. For example, the U.S. government maintains a "track-two" policy of seeking to strengthen independent organizations in Cuba. The "track-two" policy was stipulated in the Cuban Democracy Act (known as the Torricelli Bill) signed into law by President Bush in October of 1992.

Title III of the LIBERTAD Act enables U.S. nationals to sue in U.S. courts those who "traffic" in properties that were confiscated by the Castro government from U.S. citizens or businesses. Trafficking is understood as buying, selling, leasing, marketing or otherwise benefiting from expropriated assets.[5] President Clinton allowed Title III to become law, but under a provision of the LIBERTAD Act, the president has the authority to waive enforcement of Title III for periods of six months. Title III has never been enforced since Clinton has always deferred enforcement.

Title IV also targets firms that traffic in properties confiscated from American nationals. Title IV denies entry into the U.S. to corporate officers and main shareholders, and their spouses and children under eighteen years of age. Foreign firms that traffic in confiscated properties can avoid the sanctions by divesting from such properties. Thus far, this aspect of the law has only been applied to the two largest foreign investors in Cuba: Grupo Domos (from Mexico)[6] and Sherritt International (from Canada). Warning letters have been sent to a number of other firms.[7]

Title III and IV have engendered widespread, strident criticism of the Helms-Burton law, especially from Mexico, Canada, and Western European countries, claiming that the Helms-Burton law violates trade accords and is an infringement on the sovereignty of other countries by its "extraterritorial" attempt to apply U.S. laws to foreign enterprises.[8] The LIBERTAD Act has been condemned in assemblies at the UN, at the OAS, and in other international fora. Countries of the European Community were about to suit the U.S. at the World Trade Organization (WTO) over the Helms-Burton law until an agreement was reached between the U.S. and EC countries to postpone taking the case to the WTO.[9] The U.S. government has found itself in conflict with its main trading partners and has risked undermining the authority of the WTO over the Helms-Burton Act maintaining that the law is conducive to a democratic transition in Cuba.[10] Yet the claim that the Helms-Burton law helps a transition to democracy has been reproached by prestigious academics, government officials, Cuban dissidents and other personalities. According to Jimmy Carter, the Helms-Burton law is an obstacle to a transition to democracy in Cuba.[11] Carl-Johan Groth, the special investigator for Cuba of the UN Human Rights Commission, in his 1996 report to the Commission, concluded that outside pressure like the U.S. embargo only helped worsen the human rights situation in Cuba.[12] Eloy Gutiérrez-Menoyo, a Cuban exile who heads an anti-Castro group called Cambio Cubano, agrees with Groth.[13] Elizandro Sánchez Santa Cruz, one of the best known dissidents living in Cuba, thinks that the U.S. should discard the Helms-Burton law and follow the policy of the European Com-

---

5. The value of American properties seized by the Castro government was about $2 billion at the time of the expropriations in 1960. There are now about 1,000 claimants who are entitled to file suit under the Helms-Burton law. Arthur Gottschalk, "Putting Pressure on Cuba: U.S. Puts Embargo Ultimatum in the Mail," *Journal of Commerce* (13 June 1996).

6. Subsequently, Grupo Domos divested from its business in Cuba.

7. Elena Moreno, "EEUU y UE Reconocen Fallaron sus Métodos Respecto a Cuba," *CubaNet News* 2 (February 1997).

8. For example, see the article by Tom Raum, "Allies criticize U.S. sanctions on trade with outlaw nations," *The Miami Herald* (29 June 1996).

9. According to the terms of the agreement made public, the EC pledged to adopt rules to inhibit new investment in confiscated property, and the U.S. promised to seek congressional approval to waive Title IV of the Helms-Burton law and to continue to suspend Title III. Under the LIBERTAD Act, the Executive forfeited its foreign policy power to change the provisions of the Act without congressional approval. Christopher Marquis, "U.S., Europeans strike deal on Helms-Burton," *The Miami Herald* (12 April 1997).

10. The U.S. position has been that if the WTO rules against it concerning the legality of the LIBERTAD Act, the U.S. would disregard the ruling on grounds of national security.

11. "Robaina llama a la 'unión sagrada' de los cubanos," *El Nuevo Herald* (19 January 1997).

12. Robert Evans, "Update from Geneva," *Reuter* (22 April 1996).

13. Voice of America (5 March 1996).

munity of promoting investment in Cuba while pressuring for political changes.[14] Mesa-Lago (1995, 197) believes that the U.S. embargo is counterproductive for a democratic transition in Cuba. Gunn concurs with Mesa-Lago and argues that the Helms-Burton law will end up sabotaging the prospects for a transition to democracy within Cuba.[15]

Despite the high degree of political and academic controversy that the Helms-Burton law has engendered, arguments in favor as well as against the policy have paid little or no attention to theoretical works on transitions to democracy and to comparative evidence in evaluating the impact of the law on the likelihood of a political transition in Cuba. In this article, I seek to demonstrate that theory, comparative analyses, and data indicate that at this juncture in Cuban history, the U.S. economic embargo and the LIBERTAD Act in particular help bring about the demise of the Castro dictatorship. In the discussion, I will address a number of other related issues that have also been at the center of political and academic debates.

THE CASTRO REGIME TYPE AND MODES OF TRANSITION

Linz and Stepan (1996, chaps. 3 and 4) argue that the type of nondemocratic regime has a major effect on the available modes of political transition. Pacted, negotiated, relatively peaceful transitions (ruptura or reforma pactada) are possible in authoritarian regimes, e.g., the type of dictatorships that existed in South America and Spain, and in mature post-totalitarian regimes, e.g., the type of regime in the Soviet Union in the 1980s. By contrast, negotiated transitions are impossible under totalitarian, early post-to-

talitarian, frozen post-totalitarian, and sultanistic regimes. A fundamental reason is that under these types of dictatorships there are no regime softliners (blandos) with sufficient power and autonomy over time to contain the regime hardliners and conduct negotiations with members of the moderate opposition. If regime softliners emerge who might negotiate a pact with democratic moderates, such regime softliners do not last for long in positions of authority; they are eliminated or demoted.

If one uses the categories of Linz and Stepan, the Castro regime seems to be a mixture of frozen post-totalitarian and sultanistic regimes.[16] In a frozen post-totalitarian regime there is persistent tolerance of some civil society critics of the regime, but almost all control mechanisms of the party-state endure and do not evolve (e.g., East Germany and Czechoslovakia in 1989).[17] The essence of sultanism is unrestrained personal rulership. Political power is directly related to the ruler's person, and all individuals, groups and institutions are permanently subject to the unpredictable and despotic intervention of the sultan. In sultanistic regimes influential figures in the regime derive their importance by being on the personal staff of the sultan. There is absolutely no room on the sultan's staff for someone who would publicly negotiate the demise of the sultan.[18]

According to Linz and Stepan (1996, chap. 4), the most likely path of regime transition in frozen post-totalitarian regimes is mass uprising, and the most likely domestic causes for the demise of a sultanistic regime are assassination of the sultan or revolutionary upheaval by armed groups or civil society. O'Donnell (1989, 73) coincides with Linz and Stepan in per-

---

14. "Castro debe iniciar la transición, dice disidente cubano," *El Nuevo Herald* (17 December 1996).

15. Peter Zirnite, "US-Cuba: Clinton Finally Comes Down Hard on Cuba," InterPress Third World News Agency (12 March 1996).

16. The Castro regime seems to be quite similar to Romania under Nicolae Ceauçescu. Linz (1990) classifies Romania as a mixed type of totalitarianism and sultanism.

17. A frozen post-totalitarian regime also includes some limited spaces for a market economy and features associated with totalitarian regimes (but in a somewhat deteriorated form) like an official guiding ideology and routine mobilization of the population. Linz and Stepan (1996, chap. 4). For a characterization of the Castro regime that points to features of frozen post-totalitarianism see Edward González (1996, ix). The regime in Cuba is portrayed as being in a state of stasis, with limited market reforms, the Communist Party monopolizing power, and without feasible political alternatives.

18. For clear sultanistic features of the Castro regime see Baloyra (1993).

ceiving the unavailability of a peaceful, negotiated mode of political transition from sultanistic regimes. In O'Donnell's view, caudillos-führers are highly paranoid and have a compulsion to eliminate any source of power independent of their whims, particularly the softliners. Softliners may emerge, but they cannot move too far toward liberalization without being removed from their leadership positions by the caudillo. The only possible modes of political transition are the death of the supreme leader or the leader's overthrow. There has never been a transition initiated by a caudillo.[19]

Castro and other hardliners dominate, insist on the retention of one-party rule, and oppose political liberalization.[20] Fidel is unwilling to relinquish any of his power and would not accept a negotiated political transition. The lesson he drew from the demise of communism in Eastern Europe is that political liberalization leads to disaster for the dictatorship (González and Ronsfeldt 1994, ix-xi; Centeno 1996).

Thus, given the nature of the dictatorial regime in Cuba, one should not expect the emergence of softliners with sufficient power over time to be able to negotiate a transition to democracy. Hence, the possibility of a peaceful, negotiated political transition in Cuba is impossible under the current regime.

Some critics of the U.S. economic embargo maintain that tightening the embargo is detrimental for political reformers within the regime because a confrontational U.S. policy toward the Castro government gives hardliners among the ruling elite a convenient pretext to repress regime reformers who favor dialogue with dissidents; thereby U.S. policy hinders the possibility of a peaceful transition to democracy.[21]

Hardliners have launched attacks on potential reformers after the Helms-Burton became law. The best known recent assault by hardliners took place at the V Plenum of the Central Committee of the Communist Party of Cuba in March 1996.[22] In the speech given by Raúl Castro, he attacked academics in Cuba who have published with scholars in the U.S., specifically targeting the Center for American Studies in Cuba for allegedly falling into a trap laid by foreign Cuba experts. According to Raúl, academics in the U.S. served the U.S. policy of promoting "fifth columnists" to generate subversion. Raúl stated that, "the party cannot tolerate officials who act on their own; ... we must strive to maintain our revolutionary purity." After Raúl's speech, the director of the Center for American Studies was fired and replaced with an academic with solid hardline credentials. Copies of the speech were distributed to all academic centers, and teams of "inspectors" were sent to academic centers attacked in the speech.[23]

While one can see attacks by hardliners on apparent softliners after U.S. measures to strengthen the embargo, the causal relation between the two factors is spurious. When have hardliners in Cuba allowed softliners to flourish? Do hardliners need any externally generated pretext to crack down on reformers when hardliners feel it is necessary? Both theory and evidence point to the false causal relation between U.S. policy and repression of regime reformers. True to its sultanistic nature, Fidel Castro has through time repressed potential challengers within the regime. Back in the 1960s, he repressed members of the pre-1959 communist party, the Popular Socialist Party, during the "microfraction" crisis because Castro perceived Moscow-oriented communists to be a potential challenge to his authority. Since 1980,

---

19. Baloyra (1993, 38) also makes the observation that no peaceful transition has ever taken place in a caudillo-led regime.

20. For the very unlikely emergence of viable softliners under the Castro regime and the rooting out of potential regime softliners during 1990-91 see del Aguila (1993).

21. For example, see Gunn (1994, 140).

22. At the meeting, Fidel Castro maintained that, "socialism has no alternative in this country; the revolution has no alternative." *CubaHoy* 2, no. 142 (27 March 1996).

23. Mimi Whitefield and Juan O. Tamayo, "Raul Castro's attack on intellectuals stirs backlash," Knight-Ridder News Service (12 April 1996).

mechanisms of control have been strengthened, and there have been widespread substitutions of personnel, as Fidel Castro launched a campaign to resist infringement on his authority (Baloyra 1993, 49-51). In the mid 1980s, the "maximum leader" implemented an attack on individuals and ideas favorable to perestroika, resulting in the dismissal of high-ranking personnel (Domínguez 1993a, 105).

NORMAL INTERNATIONAL RELATIONS AND POLITICAL TRANSITION

In their dispute with the U.S. over the Helms-Burton law, officials from Western European countries have repeatedly argued that the way to achieve political reforms in Cuba is to have more trade with the Castro government.[24] The same position is advocated by some scholars. For example, Mesa-Lago and Fabian suggest that internal democratization could be encouraged by a policy of dialogue-bargaining and openings in trade; that the hostile U.S. approach has failed to change Cuba for more than three decades (Mesa-Lago and Fabian 1993, 370). Some who advocate this line of thinking assume that normal international relations could allow foreigners to travel to Cuba, exercise freedom of speech, make contacts with people and strengthen the opposition, eventually pushing the Castro government toward political liberalization. Moreover, there is the belief that regime elites would be willing to exercise some political flexibility for the sake of maintaining economic relations with foreign countries.

It should be kept in mind that the U.S. economic embargo is not a blockade. Practically every country in the world has normal relations with Cuba. Mexico and Canada never broke off their diplomatic and economic relations with the Castro government. In addition, the U.S. economic embargo has not precluded contacts between people in the U.S. and those in Cuba. Thousands of Cuban exiles have been going to visit their relatives in Cuba over the years; there have been visits and contacts between scholars in the U.S. and academics in Cuba. In addition, the Cuban Democracy Act, a U.S. law established in 1992, pushed for a "track-two" policy of fostering personal contacts between the two countries and seeking to help nongovernmental organizations in Cuba.

Raúl Castro has denounced the track-two U.S. policy as a "rotten carrot" and exhorted Cubans to resist it. Referring to the tack-two policy, Castro said, "we are not (sitting) with our arms crossed, we are ready and prepared to reply in this politico-ideological area, to confront it in every dimension."[25] Foreigners that have met with persons considered dissidents by the Castro government have been expelled from Cuba and the Cubans contacted have been repressed.[26] A new tactic being used by the regime to curtail contacts between dissidents and foreign visitors is to banish dissidents to the provinces, away from Havana.[27]

The often heard criticism of the embargo, that it has lasted since 1962 and Castro is still in power (which I will address below) can be turned into a critique of the effectiveness of normal relations in achieving political change in Cuba. Have normal relations between Cuba and countries in Western Europe and Latin America been effective in fostering a political transition in Cuba? The answer is negative whether one takes a long-term perspective (1960s to the

---

24. Thomas W. Lippman, "U.S. Allies to Seek Reforms in Cuba," *The Washington Post* (17 August 1996).

25. Reuters News Service (18 November 1995).

26. For example, Susan Bilello, an official of the New York-based Committee to Protect Journalists was expelled from Cuba in June 1996 after being arrested and interrogated by Cuban security for "fomenting rebellion." Ms. Bilello was in Cuba meeting with Cubans attempting to practice independent journalism. All of her notebooks, personal papers, and film were seized. Hector Palacio Ruiz, president of the Partido Solidaridad Democrático, was jailed after talking to Swedish journalists in December 1996. And envoys from the U.S. and Europe reaching out to dissidents are being harassed by Cuban authorities; see Christopher Marquis, "Havana placing bumps in foreign envoy's way," *The Miami Herald* (4 April 1997).

27. Juan O. Tamayo, "Banishment wears down Cuban dissidents," *The Miami Herald* (5 September 1996).

present) or one looks at the results of normal international relations in the post Cold War period.[28]

Over the years, officials from various countries and international organizations have asked ruling elites in Cuba to respect human rights and move the country toward democracy. Felipe González, the former prime minister of Spain, had a close and supportive bilateral relation with the Castro government. His attempts to convince Castro to introduce democratic reforms were unsuccessful (Mesa-Lago, 1995, 194). The list of foreign dignitaries that have recently tried to get the Cuban government to respect human rights and/or to carry out political reforms is extensive, including for example: Jakob Kellenberger, chancellor of the Swiss Confederation; José María Aznar, current prime minister of Spain, and Carlos Menem, president of Argentina.[29]

Fidel Castro joined twenty-two other heads of state of Latin American nations plus Spain and Portugal at the sixth Iberian-American Summit held in Viña del Mar, Chile during November 10-11, 1996. The focus of the conference was democratic governability. At the summit, the heads of state, including Castro, signed a final declaration document, the "Declaration of Viña del Mar." The declaration has three parts. The first is a reaffirmation of democracy. It states that democracy has to be representative and commits the signatories to support political pluralism, freedom of speech and of association, free, regular, and transparent elections, and respect for human rights.[30]

After returning to Cuba from Chile, in a speech to the Havana leadership of the Communist Party, he sneered at what he called "recipes" for democracy and maintained that in Cuba the Communist Party is enough.[31] As could be expected, harassment, beatings, and imprisonment of peaceful dissidents and independent journalists by Cuban authorities have continued to this day.[32]

Given the precarious situation of the Cuban economy, one could expect that this would be an appropriate time to test the willingness of the Castro regime to enter into negotiations with foreign countries to bargain internal measures of political liberalization for external economic assistance. In December 1996, the European Community officially made respect for human rights and indications by the Castro regime of political liberalization a prior condition for the establishment of an economic cooperation accord with Cuba. The EC policy is binding on its fifteen members. Since 1994, EC officials had been telling Cuban authorities that reaching an economic cooperation agreement with Cuba depended on respect for human rights and political reforms.[33] A cooperation agreement with the EC would facilitate trade, investments and aid. EC governments no longer protect private investments in Cuba nor offer entrepreneurs

---

28. Even after the political and economic consequences for Cuba of the lost of support from Soviet Bloc countries in the 1990s, the Castro regime has proven to be unyielding to international pressures for significant respect for human rights, not to mention other demands for political liberalization.

29. *Cuba al día* (June 1994) and the Chronology of Cuban Events, 1994, Information Resources Branch, Radio Martí Program. José Miguel Vivanco, executive director of Human Rights Watch/Americas, in an article published in 1996, states that while Europe's dialogue with Cuba has led to the periodic release of some political prisoners European Union policy toward Cuba has had no effect whatsoever on the repression of basic liberties by the Castro regime. Christopher Marquis, "Rights group: EU economic policy in Cuba unjustified," *The Miami Herald*, 21 September 1996.

30. *CubaHoy*, 2, no. 200 (12 November 1996).

31. "Castro again rejects world pleas for reform," *The Miami Herald* (26 November 1996).

32. Reports of human rights violations come from Cuba on a daily basis by independent journalists, see CubaNet on the internet. The Inter-American Commission on Human Rights, an agency of the OAS., issued a report in 1997 stating that the Cuban government systematically tramples civil rights and political freedom, among other abuses. Pablo Alfonso, "Report cites abuses of rights in Cuba," *The Miami Herald* (30 April 1997).

33. Chronology of Cuban Events, 1994, Information Resources Branch, Radio Martí Program, (26 January 1994).

insurance for their exports to the island.[34] At the sixth Iberian American Summit in Chile in November, 1996, José María Aznar offered Fidel Castro to get the EC to improve relations with Cuba if Fidel took some step toward democracy. Castro flatly rejected Aznar's offer declaring that he has no intention to democratize his regime.[35] Both Fidel and Raúl Castro have reiterated that their government would never negotiate better relations with the U.S. on conditions of changes in Cuba's domestic policies.[36]

ECONOMIC CRISES AND TRANSITIONS: THEORY AND COMPARISONS

Major theoretical works on transitions to democracy concur in that dictatorships tend to fall when faced with crises. Przeworski (1991, 57) observes that splits in the authoritarian power bloc are induced by signs of an imminent crisis, including signs of popular unrest. Softliners, who emerge from divisions in the ruling elite, usually initiate political liberalization (the start of a transition process).[37] Huntington (1991, 593) argues that when an authoritarian regime confronts seemingly unsolvable problems (usually of an economic nature) and/or when the regime resorts to increasing repression, reformers within the regime are more likely to emerge. This is so because softliners conclude that it is desirable to seek a graceful exit from power, given the costs of staying in power.[38]

In a recent cross-national, statistical study involving 139 countries from 1950 to 1990, Przeworski and Limongi (1994, 11) found that authoritarian regimes are more likely to survive when their economies grow and more likely to be destabilized when they face economic crises. Scholars of Eastern European politics observe that a key factor underlying the pressures that caused the fall of communism in Eastern Europe was the deterioration of the economies in Eastern European countries. Decline in the population's standard of living decreased people's tolerance for the regimes. As their situation grew worse, the population became increasingly aware of the failure of their own regimes to provide an acceptable level of prosperity. The economies of Czechoslovakia, Romania, and other Eastern European countries experienced a declining trend in average annual GNP growth from 1970 to 1990. In East Germany, average annual rates of growth went on a downward course from 1970 to 1980 and stagnated afterward until the collapse of communism (Linden 1993, 28-30). In Hungary, the drying up of external resources increased internal tensions (Bruszt 1990, 383). In Czechoslovakia, one of the causes of the collapse of communism was the perception of an approaching economic crisis. The growing public awareness of economic stagnation stimulated the opposition (Judt 1992, 96-97). In Romania, the impoverished economic conditions contributed to the popular mood that led to the uprising in December of 1989 (Brown 1991, 209). The connection between deterioration of economic performance and transitions to democracy is also observed in Latin America. Economic decline and drops in standards of living predated the wave of democratization in the region during the 1980s (Remmer 1992, 10-12).

---

34. Juan O. Tamayo, "Europeans get tough in policy on Cuba," *The Miami Herald* (3 December 1996); Steven Lee Myers, "Europe's Call for Rights in Cuba Wins U.S. Approval," *The New York Times* (4 December 1996); Pablo Alfonso, "UE quiere mover a Cuba hacia la democratización," *El Nuevo Herald* (4 December 1996).

35. *CubaHoy* 2, no. 200 (12 November 1996).

36. For Raúl's comments see Reuters News Service (18 November 1995). For Fidel's position see Mesa-Lago (1995, 196-97).

37. Liberalization is the process of allowing individuals to have certain rights. These rights include: freedom of speech, of movement, and of association, and the right to a fair trial under rules of preestablished laws. Liberalization is a matter of degree, rights can be granted by the dictatorship to a lesser or greater degree (O'Donnell and Schmitter 1986).

38. Huntington also points to factors that induce the emergence of regime softliners by making them believe that democratizing would produce benefits for their country: (a) reduction of U.S. or other sanctions against their regime, and (b) opening the door to economic assistance and I.M.F. loans. These two factors are relevant for Cuba since by law the U.S. embargo would be lifted upon democratization and Bill Clinton's "Support for a Democratic Transition in Cuba," (discussed below) commits U.S. assistance to transitional and democratic governments in Cuba.

Two ways in which economic crises seem to contribute to the demise of authoritarian regimes are: (a) by fostering opposition to the regime among ordinary citizens—people blame the government for their increased poverty and withdraw support or acquiescence; and (b) by reducing the benefit stream to direct supporters and coalition allies (Geddes 1995, 27).

By contrast, when an authoritarian regime is perceived as successful, e.g., in terms of economic performance, softliners are less likely to be able and willing to launch liberalization (O'Donnell and Schmitter 1986, 16). There is no empirical evidence to support the hypothesis that economic development generates democracy. Countries under authoritarian regimes are not more likely to experience a transition to democracy as they reach higher levels of economic development (Przeworski and Limongi 1994, 6-9).

Applying the theoretical discussion to the situation in Cuba leads to the following conclusions.

If one were to assume that a negotiated, peaceful political transition is possible in Cuba (like in Spain or Poland, for example), then an economic crisis helps to increase the probability of a negotiated transition by fostering the emergence of softliners able and willing to lead such transition. The U.S. economic embargo hurts the Cuban economy (as will be seen below). Thus, the argument by critics of the embargo that lifting the embargo would help a peaceful transition in Cuba is self-contradictory.

Yet, as analyses of regime types and modes of transition indicate, a negotiated transition is extremely unlikely or impossible under the Castro regime. Hence, the economic crisis in Cuba should stimulate some regime elites to take political reformist positions, but such positions cannot be made public, doing so

would result in demotion or elimination. A hypothesis that can be derived is that the combination of the Castro regime type with economic crisis produces latent softliners.[39] A practical question is whether such covert political reformers would help to bring about the end of the Castro regime in the event of a political transition pushed from below. Intuitively, the answer seems positive.

When softliners emerge in authoritarian regimes, some are proto-democratizers who, confronting the choice between democracy and the status quo or an even more repressive dictatorship, prefer democracy.[40] Other softliners come to prefer democracy over other possible alternatives when confronted with pressures from below and the incapacity to repress social forces effectively. These softliners do so because they engage in wishful thinking and entertain the illusion that they will be able to win elections (Przeworski 1991, chap. 2). Geddes (1995, 2) observes that transitions to democracy from single-party regimes tend to take place due to exogenous shocks rather than internal splits. A highly visible popular opposition is an exogenous shock that tends to persuade cadres of the dictatorship to desert the regime based on a cost-benefit analysis of staying with the dictatorship.

In Cuba, there are signs that the regime is distressed about inadequate support among regime cadres. The economic crisis seems to be having a negative impact on support within the regime.

A recent report from the "Central Commission of Cadres," created two years ago to help the Council of Ministers evaluate the work of the top levels of the *nomenklatura,* stated that problems with salaries continue to impair the motivation of cadres.[41] It has been documented that the standard practice of the Castro regime over time has been to grant all sorts of

39. In the Soviet Union, Gorbachev was able to find allies within the Communist Party and the bureaucracy, people that supported glasnost. Yet these same people were there in the pre-Gorbachev period, indicating that latent political reformers existed under the orthodox mantle of the pre-1985 period.

40. The usual first choice for softliners is a liberalized dictatorship. The typical initial project of softliners is not to establish democracy but to liberalize as a way to ease pressures confronting the regime and thereby save the dictatorship.

41. "Raúl Castro arremete contra dirigentes políticos," *El Nuevo Herald* (10 April 1997).

privileges, including material ones, to the ruling elite, especially top officers of the party, the government bureaucracy, the military and the state security apparatus (Clark 1992, chaps. 22 and 23). In meetings to discuss the party's platform for their national congress to be held in the fall of 1997, Communist Party members in Havana report that a surprising number of cadres are openly criticizing the platform. Traditionally such meetings have been to merely rubber-stamp the platform. Members say that the platform does not mention solutions to the economic problems that Cubans face every day. According to one party member, "People are saying they don't see the government admitting anything wrong or taking any real steps to get us out of our crisis; they are at the end of their ropes, depressed."[42] The regime also appears to be having problems with the motivation of the Committees for the Defense of the Revolution, (CDR). In a meeting of CDR leaders in Santiago de Cuba in April 1997, CDR leaders were criticized by the national leader of the CDR for abandoning their mission of maintaining surveillance of their blocks and neighborhoods.[43] Most ominous of all for the regime are indications of concern over the loyalty of military officers.

Title II of the Helms-Burton law calls for the U.S. government to prepare a plan of assistance to transitional and democratic governments in Cuba. Following this directive, the Clinton administration released in January 1997 a plan titled, "Support for a Democratic Transition in Cuba." The document pledges the U.S. government to help Cuba in various ways, e.g., technical and financial assistance to rebuild the economy, the infrastructure, and democratic institu-

tions. In addition, the document declares that the U.S. is willing to return to a democratic government the Naval Base at Guantanamo (a carrot to Cuban nationalism) and that the armed forces in Cuba could play a positive role in the transition. In reference to militaries in former communist countries, the document makes the point that their core professional interests need not be threatened by democracy, that the armed forces in such countries have withdrawn from non-military functions like internal security and economic activities. Moreover, an offer is made of military-to-military cooperation with the U.S. armed forces to a Cuban military that is supportive of a civilian democratic government.

With the deterioration of the Cuban economy, a key role for the Cuban military has been to run agricultural and business enterprises, e.g., department stores and tourist resorts.[44] According to a colonel in the Cuban air force who defected to the U.S. in 1994, there is a lot of discontent among professional officers in the Cuban military because they have been forced to work in the agricultural sector.[45] An official of the Cuban government disclosed that fifty percent of the armed forces is dedicated to agricultural activities.

After Clinton made public the "Support for a Democratic Transition in Cuba," the Castro government conducted a national campaign to have military officers sign a document supporting the Castro regime and repudiating U.S. policy toward Cuba.[46] Contingency plans for the death of Fidel Castro, disclosed in a document of the Cuban government, call for the

---

42. Juan O. Tamayo, "Will Albright make a move on Cuba policy?" *The Miami Herald* (19 June 1997).

43. Tomás Regalado, "Redoblan la vigilancia a los cubanos," *Diario Las Américas* (30 April 1997).

44. Cathy Booth, "The Surprising Emergence of Raul," *Time*, 144, no. 20 (14 November 1994).

45. Huntington (1991) indicates that in Romania, military disaffection was promoted by Ceauçescu's policies weakening military professionalism and corrupting the officer corps. From this perspective, the Romanian experience seems replicated in Cuba. The military in Cuba is involved in business enterprises in the dollar sector of the economy, and some of these firms have become quasi-private. The Cuban government acknowledges that there is widespread corruption among its ranks. See for example, Tomás Regalado, "Comunismo cubano admite corrupción amplia del gobierno," *Diario Las Américas* (26 March 1997). For a report of corruption among top ranking members of the state security apparatus (the Ministry of the Interior) see, "Impugnados por corrupción dos altos funcionarios militares cienfuegueros," *CubaNet News* (1 August 1997).

46. Armando Correa, "Ejército cubano no asusta a Castro ni a Clinton," *El Nuevo Herald* (20 April 1997).

arrest of more than one hundred military officers, who are under investigation.[47]

The bombings in major tourist hotels in Cuba in 1997 has kindled the question of possible involvement of dissident military or security personnel in Cuba, given the extreme security measures of the government and the expertise and coordination involved in the bombings. Whoever was responsible for these acts, their occurrence points to a deterioration in the effectiveness of the security apparatus. These events had not occurred in Cuba for a very long time.

TRANSITION FROM BELOW IN CUBA

In cataloging possible scenarios of political change in Cuba, Suchlicki (1992, 25-26) considers highly improbable that: (a) Fidel Castro will turn power to somebody; (b) that he will be overthrown by a military coup; or (c) that he will be assassinated.[48] In Suchliki's view, it is a lot more likely that the Castro regime will fall as the result of a Romanian-type transition, in which as the economy continues to deteriorate or stagnate popular revolt will spread with the military, or most of it, siding with the population.[49] I agree with Suchlicki's opinion. But assigning this scenario a high probability can be questioned on a number of grounds.[50]

One possible argument against the likelihood of a transition from below is that the Castro regime still enjoys considerable support. A variant of this assertion, but with the same implication, is that Cuba is different from Eastern European countries in that communism in Cuba is the result of a national revolution rather than an imposition by Soviet power.[51] The underlying assumption in these arguments is that legitimacy is an important factor in explaining the endurance of the Castro regime.[52] Yet to use the notion of legitimacy to account for the survival of dictatorships is tautological.[53]

Another argument, similar to the legitimacy one but not quite the same, is that the Castro regime enjoys some significant degree of support due to feelings of nationalism.[54] In this view, the U.S. embargo, rather than increasing the possibility of a transition from below, actually makes it less likely. The reason is that the embargo produces a rallying around the flag effect. The idea is that pressure from the U.S. on the Cuban government helps Castro to stay in power by fostering among people support for the regime because of nationalism.[55]

While it is true that the Cuban government uses the embargo, and measures to tighten it like the Cuban

---

47. Frank Calzón, "Los funerales del Líder Maximo," *El Nuevo Herald* (24 January 1997).

48. Removal of Fidel by a military coup is considered to be practically impossible, in part due to the organizational structure of the armed forces and to the nature of counterintelligence. Elimination of Castro by assassination is also given a low probability because of the tight security surrounding him.

49. The perception that substantial popular revolts can occur in Cuba as a consequence of the poor state of the economy is shared by top generals in the Cuban military and by dissidents leaders in Cuba. Pablo Alfonso, "Plan abre vía a militares cubanos," *El Nuevo Herald* (6 February 1997) and "Elizandro Sánchez ve cambio inminente en Cuba," *El Nuevo Herald* (19 January 1997).

50. The view that a deterioration of the economy increases popular discontent and can lead to a political transition in Cuba is held by a number of scholars, e.g., Mesa-Lago (1995, 250).

51. A case could be made that, as in Cuba, in the Soviet Union communism was the result of a national revolution, or one could argue that in both Cuba and the Soviet Union communists imposed their rule by force after the national revolutions.

52. Domínguez (1993b, 97-98) argues that an important factor explaining why the Castro government has not fallen is that, in contrast to countries in Eastern Europe, the Cuban regime enjoys legitimacy among the population.

53. For an explanation of this point see Przeworski (1986, 50-53). Dictatorships can survive without legitimacy; they can do so by the threat of force. What matters for the stability of a dictatorship is not the legitimacy that the regime may have but the presence or absence of preferable alternatives.

54. The arguments are similar in the sense that both assume that popular support is an important factor for the survival of the regime. They differ in the source of motivation for the support.

55. This argument is made quite frequently, e.g., Domínguez (1995, 698); Schulz (1994, 2); González (1996, 79-80); and Alejandro Portes, "Under Helms-Burton: Cuba struggles but it's not vanquished," *The Miami Herald* (25 November 1996).

Democracy Act and the Helms-Burton law, to stir up nationalism, the effectiveness of these efforts is questionable.[56] It is a big assumption to believe that because an authoritarian government tries to equate itself with the flag people will fall for it and support the regime out of nationalism. The government attempts might work on some people, but on how many? Making what difference for regime support? In Romania, Ceausescu tried to use nationalism as a pillar of support for his government, but his appeal to nationalism was depleted and came to fall on deaf ears (Eyal 1990, 155).

There are a number of indicators raising doubts about the effectiveness in Cuba of the rally around the flag government efforts. One is the disjuncture between the government and nationalism that ensues from "tourist apartheid" and from the privileged treatment given to foreign investors.[57] Foreign capitalists are given generous concessions to invest in Cuba while the possibility of Cubans to develop their own private enterprises is severely restricted by the government (Gonzalez and Ronsfeldt 1994; Centeno 1996).[58] Castro and other hardliners oppose going beyond quite limited market reforms in Cuba's internal economy as they open the country to enclaves of foreign investment.[59] Evidence also suggests that people are unswayed by efforts on the part of the Castro government to blame the U.S. for problems in Cuba. Reports indicate that people do not pay attention to official declarations against the U.S., trying to fuel the flames of confrontation.[60]

Even if one discards notions of popular support as important for the survival of the regime, a transition from below can be seen as a remote possibility because civil society is weak and the means of repression in the hands of the state are strong.[61] This is the view of several scholars, e.g., González and Ronsfeldt (1994, 36); Centeno (1996); and Schulz (1994).

In an unprecedented coalescing of opposition groups inside Cuba, Concilio Cubano was formed in October of 1995. It is an umbrella association that at its inception brought together 130 organizations of various types, e.g., political, environmental, professional, labor unions, and human rights groups. Its central goal has been to push for a peaceful transition to democracy. Concilio formally petitioned the Cuban government for permission to meet for its first conference on February 24-27, 1996, appealing to a provision in Cuba's Constitution that recognizes the right to free association. The government denied permission and launched an intensive campaign of repression against members of Concilio.

---

56. Ricardo Alarcón, president of the National Assembly, stated that the Helms-Burton is very useful for the Castro regime in ideologically motivating young people. Larry Rohter, "Cuba taking a harder line," *The New York Times* (31 March 1996).

57. The term apartheid tourism is used to depict the fact that foreign tourist receive luxury treatment that is off-limits to the Cuban population. The worst measures of apartheid lasted until 1993, but still the general population is not allowed into hotels, resorts, beaches, and other tourist areas.

58. For a description of obstacles put by the state on Cuban private entrepreneurs see Ulises Cabrera, "Crónica de un cuentapropista," *APIC* (14 August 1996) and Juan O. Tamayo, "Cuban inspectors crack down on home businesses," *The Miami Herald* (27 March 1997).

59. According to Brown (1991, 127), in the German Democratic Republic and Romania, two regimes very unreceptive to perestroika, the state's refusal to reform antagonized the population to the point of open rebellion.

60. José Rivero García, "La Verdad Desnuda" *CubaPress* (2 March 1996). See also the declaration of the Partido Liberal Democrático de Cuba (8 April 1997), distributed by *CubaNet*. Cubans that have recently left the country report a growing pro-U.S. feelings among Cuba's youth because of the U.S. strong stand against the Castro dictatorship. "Cuba en la VI cumbre iberoamericana," *Revista Contacto* (November 1996). It is revealing that one of Fidel's nicknames in Cuba is Armando Guerra Solo.

61. A weak civil society is seen as one in which independent associations have few members and meager resources.

Despite the constant repression against dissidents and independent journalists in Cuba, the regime has not destroyed them.[62] New independent organizations are emerging all the time. The number of independent organizations, e.g., political, professional, labor unions, is increasing. For example, during the past two years, the number of independent news agencies grew from one to eight, and the number of reporters from a handful in Havana to several dozen around the island.[63]

A common argument is that measures taken by the U.S. to strengthen the economic embargo, i.e., the Cuban Democracy Act of 1992 and the LIBERTAD Act of 1996, have a negative impact on the strength of the opposition in Cuba because such U.S. policies give the Cuban government a pretext to increase repression, and the government does so, e.g., Mesa-Lago and Fabian (1993, 369-370) and Schulz (1994, 2). Yet the Cuban government has intensified repression whenever the regime have felt pressure from the opposition, regardless of whether or not measures to intensify the U.S. embargo were in place. The wave of repression against members of Concilio Cubano started on February 15, 1996. At this time, the Helms-Burton bill seemed to be going nowhere in the U.S. Congress, as Bill Clinton opposed the measure, and there was the impression that Clinton wanted to ease relations with Cuba. Yet one could argue that at the time of the crack down on Concilio, the Cuban Democracy Act of 1992 was in force. But in 1991 there was another surge of repression in Cuba against dissidents and human-rights activists. In May 1991, in reference to the fall of communism in Eastern Europe, Fidel Castro declared that if a single concession is made to "reactionaires" all sorts of concessions are demanded until they ask for your head (Domínguez 1993a, 123-125). The regime did not need any pretext of U.S. policy to justify repression. The campaign launched by Castro in 1991 against opponents in civil society was motivated by a desire to avoid the experiences of Eastern European countries, not because of an intensification of hostility on the part of the U.S. against the Cuban government. In May of 1991, President Bush said in an address transmitted over Radio Martí that the United States had no aggressive intentions toward Cuba and pledged that the U.S. would not invade Cuba.[64] Thereafter, until 1992, Bush systematically opposed bills introduced in Congress that would tighten the U.S. economic embargo on Cuba (Domínguez 1994, 171-172). In 1991, Cubans did not fear an aggression on the part of the United States (Domínguez 1994, 170-172).

At the level of the general population, there has been a positive association between deterioration of the economy on one hand and discontent and criticism of the Cuban government on the other.[65] The Cuban government has experienced an "exhaustion of ideology."[66] Linz and Stepan (1996, 49) argue that in post-totalitarian regimes, faith in official ideology as a foundation of legitimacy declines among the population, and regime authorities increasingly resort to performance criteria as the basis of support. From this perspective, a current weakness of the Castro regime is that economic performance in Cuba is quite poor. Survey data show widespread popular dissatisfaction with micro economic conditions (Baloyra 1994 and González and Ronfeldt 1994).

---

62. An important phenomenon is happening. Recent reports indicate that people are coming out to defend dissidents as the latter are being attacked by government repressive forces. Mercedes Moreno, "La solidaridad del pueblo con los periodistas," *Buró de Prensa Independiente de Cuba* (13 February 1997). Manuel David Orrio, "Defienden vecinos a sindicalistas independientes," independent journalist in Cuba (17 February 1997). In a meeting of leaders of the CDR's, some participants stated that the population is attacking the Committees. Tomás Regalado, "Redoblan la vigilancia a los cubanos," *Diario Las Américas* (30 April 1997).

63. Elise Ackerman, "Guerrilla Journalism: The Underground Press Fights for an Audience," *The Washington Post* (9 March 1997).

64. This was the first time since Castro took power that a U.S. president made such a pledge to the Cuban people.

65. According González and Ronsfeldt (1994, xiii, 55 and 57), if the Castro regime is to survive, it will need to improve economic performance at the micro level.

66. On the crisis of ideological legitimation in Cuba see Horowitz (1995) and Baloyra (1993 38).

If one were to compare the strength of civil society in Cuba today with that of civil societies in East Germany, Czechoslovakia and Romania, on the eve of their transitions from below, the civil society in Cuba does not seem weaker. These three Eastern European countries, but specially Romania, had dictatorships similar to the Castro regime. Czechoslovakia and the GDR had frozen post-totalitarian regimes and Romania had a mixed type of totalitarianism and sultanism.

In Romania, before the start of the revolt that toppled Ceauçescu, the opposition was minuscule. One estimate is that there was one dissident for every two million people (Brown 1991, 210). With a population of about twenty-three million people, that would have been approximately twelve dissidents. In June 1989, there were only two independent organizations, neither of which had publicly known leaders. Dissidents worked alone or almost alone (Linz and Stepan 1996, 352). Although sectors inside the Ceauçescu government, members of the Communist Party and of the Securitate, seem to have played an important role in his overthrow, the initiative came from below. The mass uprising triggered the actions regime cadres took against the Ceauçescu dictatorship (Verdery and Kligman 1992, 120-121).

Czechoslovakia had not experienced political liberalization when its velvet revolution started (Judt 1992). The foremost dissident group was Charter 77, whose members were often jailed. None of the groups that emerged in 1988 and 1989 besides Charter 77 could be considered an organized political opposition. In 1989, the hard-core of opposition groups consisted of about sixty people, with approximately five hundred supporters and collaborators (Linz and Stepan 1996, 319 and 321). The umbrella organization, Civic Forum, was not formed until November 1989, when the regime was about to collapse (Linden 1993, 32).

East Germany's dissident umbrella organization, Neues Forum, was also formed in the heat of the revolution (Linden 1993, 32). As late as months preceding the collapse of communist rule in East Germany, there was a high degree of repression against members of independent groups and others who challenged the regime (Naimark 1992, 81-82).

It is estimated that in Cuba today there are several thousand overt dissidents.[67] Whatever the correct figure for Cuba, there are now more overt dissidents in Cuba than there were in Romania and possibly in Czechoslovakia and in East Germany as well.

In transitions via dictatorship breakdown, the military is the ultimate support for the regimes. If the military refuses to use force against the opposition when the latter takes to the streets, the regime falls. Opposition to the regime normally has to be widespread before the military deserts the regime (Huntington 1991). The growing disbelief in ideology among government cadres in post-totalitarian regimes, a feature of the regime in Cuba, increases the probability that cadres in the repressive apparatus will let the regime collapse rather than fire on the democratic opposition in times of crisis (as occurred in the velvet revolutions of East Germany and Czechoslovakia) (Linz and Stepan 1996, chap. 4).[68] The likelihood that the military will accept a democratic outcome is greater when the military has had little or no involvement in repressing the population, as is the case in Cuba (O'Donnell and Schmitter 1986, 28).

AN OVERVIEW OF THE ECONOMIC SITUATION

Economic growth in Cuba had been declining since 1986, but it was not until the fall of communism in Eastern Europe that the Cuban economy plummet-

---

67. One estimate is 5,000. Steve Fainaru, "Nine Months Later, Cuba Dissidents Still in Disarray," *The Boston Globe* (12 November 1996). Elizandro Sánchez, one of Cuba's best known dissident, say that there are "thousands." Anita Snow, "Bruised by Crackdown, Cuban Opposition Vows to Fight On," *Associated Press* (24 March 1997).

68. Interview data indicates that among the coercive staff of the communist dictatorship in East Germany in 1989 there was a sharp erosion in the belief in the legitimacy to use force against protesters. This fact seems to explain why protestors in East Germany were not shot when they challenged the regime (Linz and Stepan 1996, 323).

ed. From 1989 to 1993, Cuba's Global Social Product decreased by 45 percent (Mesa-Lago 1996). Eighty-four percent of Cuba's trade was with the Council for Mutual Economic Assistance, and Cuba lost socialist economic aid of more than $6 billion annually (Mesa-Lago 1995, 187). The loss of Soviet Bloc markets represented a decline in Cuba's exports from $5.4 billion in 1989 to an estimated $1.7 billion in 1994. Imports dropped from $8.1 billion to $2.5 billion in the same period.[69] Mesa-Lago (1996) estimates that in 1985 Cuba's GDP per capita was US$334, similar to that of Haiti, and in 1996 the Cuban GDP per capita was US$61, the lowest in the world.

Cuba stopped servicing its hard-currency debt in 1986. As of June 1997, the hard-currency foreign debt of Cuba was about $11 billion.[70] As a consequence of the foreign debt situation, Cuba's external financing consists mostly of costly, short-term loans.

One of the consequences of Cuba's foreign debt is the disruption of trade. Firms in foreign countries have refused to continue trading with Cuba or have threatened to suspend deliveries to Cuba because of arrears in payments.[71] Among the essential goods Cuba needs to import are fuel and food. Cuba needs to import fuel supplies to cover 50-80 percent of its needs (Mesa-Lago 1995, 187). Data from Cuba's Central Planning Board indicate that in 1989 Cuba imported 79 percent of the grains it consumed, 99 percent of beans, 21 percent of meat, 44 percent of fish, and 38 percent of dairy products.[72]

The decline of the Cuban economy at the macro level after 1990 made the standard of living of the population a lot worse than usual, e.g., greater shortages of food and fuel and a decrease in the availability of transportation (Mesa-Lago 1993, 181-184 and 187; Domínguez 1995, 691). Other consequences of the poor economic performance have been deterioration in government services, a sharp increase in unemployment, and reduction of state subsidies for consumer goods and public services.[73]

Since 1994, the tumble of the economy stopped. From the low level in which the economy found itself in 1993, the government reported 0.7 percent growth for 1994, 2.5 percent for 1995, and 7.8 percent for 1996. Cuban officials estimate that the growth rate for 1997 will be 4 percent. These growth data are more indicative of a trend than of actual growth because of the unreliability of the data. At an annual growth rate of 4 percent, it would take until 2005 for Cuba to attain the economic levels of 1989.[74]

The economic growth since 1994 has not meant improved living conditions for the population. Carlos Lage, a vice-president of Cuba's Council of State and the top official in charge of the economy, in a speech at the V Plenum of the Central Committee of the Communist Party in March 1996, said that, despite the economic recovery, ordinary Cubans should expect to continue living with the austerity that has been the main feature of life since the collapse of communism in Eastern Europe.[75] The Central Workers Union (CTC), the government controlled

69. Data from the Economist Intelligence Unit. Don C. Becker, "Cuba," *The Journal of Commerce* (8 February 1996).

70. Nelson del Castillo, "Débil la relación económica cubana con el Caribe," *Diario Las Américas* (16 June 1997). This foreign debt figure does not include the 21 billion rubles owned to the former Soviet Union.

71. "Cuban debt discord sours Japan trade mission," *Reuter News Service* (24 November 1995). Chronology of Cuban Events, 1994, Information Resources Branch, Radio Martí Program, 22 March and 1 November. Cuba's officially declared trade deficits have been increasing. In 1994, the deficit was $624 million; in 1996 it was $1.7 billion.

72. Dalia Acosta "Food Shortfall Continues" *InterPress Third World News Agency* (23 September 1996).

73. The problem of unemployment has resulted from a reduction in public employment and the inability of a very limited private sector to absorb a significant number of the unemployed.

74. Edward González, "U.S. Can Better Dispose of Castro by Helping the Moderates in Cuba," *Los Angeles Times*, home edition, Business section (3 March 1996).

75. Larry Rohter, "Cuba taking a harder line," *The New York Times* (31 March 1996).

labor union, declared in September of 1996 that the growth of the economy in 1995-96 had not meant a significant improvements in the consumption of basic foodstuff for the general population.[76] There are indications that living conditions for the populace have deteriorated in comparison with 1995.[77]

Sugar production does not promise to be a solution to Cuba's economic quagmire. Attracting foreign capital seems to be a necessary element to make headway in Cuba's economic performance (Mesa-Lago 1995, 187, 191 and 201-203). Tourism accounts for a large share of all foreign investment in Cuba. Foreign earnings from tourism have recently surpassed foreign income from sugar.[78]

In 1989, the Cuban government started a campaign to attract foreign investment, mostly in the form of joint ventures in which state enterprises are the majority shareholders. Foreign investment has been allowed primarily in enclaves oriented toward exports and in the tourist industry.[79] Using official figures, foreign investment "committed/delivered" as of August 1996 was about $752 million.[80] Risk analyses published for foreign investors, e.g., by Euromoney, rank Cuba as one of the riskiest countries in the world. Thus, the type of private investments in Cuba must typically be in projects that require small investments, that offer high profits and that make possible quick rates of return on investments.[81] Ibrahim Ferradaz, Cuba's foreign investment minister, stated in 1996 that more than 75 percent of joint ventures and economic associations with foreign firms in Cuba involved investments no larger than $5 million.[82] The

business climate in Cuba inhibits a sufficient level of foreign investment to make a significant difference for economic growth. Foreign joint ventures employ only 1.3 percent of the working age population (Werlau 1996).

Yet foreign investment provides hard currency to the regime. The Cuban government is receiving about US$212 million in annual income, including tax revenues, from foreign investment. The state's most important source of revenue from foreign investment comes from wage confiscation. The system of super exploitation of workers employed in joint ventures nets the state approximately an additional US$361 million a year. Foreign firms cannot hire workers directly. The state provides the work force through a special employment agency. On average, the state receives from foreign investors US$450 a month per worker while the government pays workers in Cuban pesos the equivalent of approximately US$10 a month (Werlau 1996).

THE EFFECT OF THE U.S. EMBARGO ON CUBA'S ECONOMY

Given the large amount of economic aid that Cuba received from the Soviet Bloc countries, the U.S. economic embargo did not pose a major problem for Cuba (Mesa-Lago 1995, 197). The U.S. economic embargo has come to have an important negative effect on the Castro regime only after the end of nonmarket economic relations between Cuba and Eastern European countries.

The Helms-Burton law has curtailed hard currency income to the Cuban government in at least the fol-

---

76. Dalia Acosta "Food Shortfall Continues" *InterPress Third World News Agency* (23 September 1996).

77. At the end of 1996 and the beginning of 1997, several sources reported increased shortages of food in the rationing system, price increases for food in the market system, worsening electricity and cooking gas shutoffs, and increases in prices for public utilities. For example, see Juan O. Tamayo, "Cubans fear a recurrence of 'old days'," *The Miami Herald* (25 September 1996); Ulises Cabrera, "La verdad sobre la falsa revalorización del peso cubano," *APIC* (26 November 1996).

78. Frances Kerry, "Cuba tourism sector tries to stamp out prostitution," *Reuters News Service* (12 December 1995).

79. Baloyra (1994, 33) and Frank Calzón, "Is Canada aware of evil in cutting deals with Cuba?" *The Miami Herald* (15 April 1996).

80. Cuban government data on foreign investment in Cuba are inflated. According Jorge Pérez-López, UN data shows that foreign direct investment into Cuba from 1990 to 1994 was $60 million; see Werlau (1996).

81. Some of the incentives given by Cuba to foreign investors are: total or partial exemption of taxes on profits and customs duties and free repatriation of profits.

82. "Cuba woos small, medium foreign businesses," *Reuter News Service* (25 November 1996).

lowing ways: (a) decreasing new investment in Cuba by non-U.S. firms; (b) getting some firms which had investments in Cuba to divest; and (c) solidifying the maintenance of the embargo (since lifting it now requires congressional approval); thus significantly decreasing the possibility that American investors and tourists will expend their money in Cuba.

Carlos Lage acknowledges that the Helms-Burton has slowed down foreign investment in Cuba.[83] According to Canada's Ambassador to Cuba Mark Entwistle, the Helms-Burton law has had a "chilling effect" on investment decisions in Cuba by Canadian businessmen.[84] Following the passage of the Helms-Burton law, a trade delegation that was scheduled to travel to Cuba from the Caribbean Export Development Agency lost half of its participants due to cancellations.[85] Foreign firms have canceled, frozen or quietly deferred plans for investment in 17 hotels in Cuba.

Two firms that have ended their business in Cuba after the signing of the LIBERTAD Act are the Spanish firms Occidental Hoteles and Paradores Nacionales.[86] Cemex, a Mexican company, also left Cuba just days before its top executive was to receive a U.S. State Department letter warning him that he might be violating provisions of the Helms-Burton law.[87] Cemex has four cement production plants and eight distribution sites in the United States and its CEO wanted to avoid losing his ability to come into the United States. According to Archibald Ritter, professor of economics of Carlton University in Canada, Irving Corporation pulled out of Cuba in August

1995 largely because of concerns over the liability in the U.S. that the Helms-Burton bill presented. Irving Corporation owns property in the U.S. (In 1995, the bill was being considered in the U.S. Congress.)[88] Other companies that have reportedly abandoned Cuba after the passage of Helms-Burton law include the Canadian sugar trading house Redpath, the South African mining company Gencor, and Mexican companies PEMEX and Grupo Vitro.[89] The Mexican firm Grupo Domos, the largest foreign investor in Cuba, decided to divest from its share in the Cuban telephone company ETECSA. Domos had been singled out by the U.S. government in applying Title IV of the Helms-Burton law. Domos executives and their families were barred from entry into the U.S. Moreover, Domos was short $300 million to complete the original deal with the Cuban government, and apparently Domos could not find a partner willing to invest in ETECSA because potential investors were afraid of being subject to sanctions under the Helms-Burton law.[90]

Despite the problems that Cuba has in attracting foreign investment due to political and economic problems unrelated to the U.S. embargo, it is to be expected that if the United States were to lift its embargo there would be a number of American firms willing to invest in Cuba.

Before the Cuban air force shot down the civilian planes on February 24, 1996, killing three American citizens and one U.S. resident, the Clinton Administration gave the impression that it wanted to ease relations with the Cuban government. There was the

83. *Time News Service* (7 March 1996) and *CubaHoy* 2, no. 142 (27 March 1996).

84. Pascal Fletcher, "Canada sees 'chill' effect of U.S. law on Cuba," *Reuter News Service* (8 May 1996).

85. *Cuba Brief* (12 April 1996).

86. Juan González Yuste, "Una cadena de hoteles española se retira de Cuba," *El Periódico* (12 June 1996) and Juan O. Tamayo, "Foreign Firms Delay Plans for Cuba Hotels," *The Miami Herald* (14 June 1996).

87. "Cemex leaves Cuba to avoid U.S. sanctions," *Reuter News Service* (9 May 1996) Cemex operated a cement plant in Cuba that once belonged to the U.S. company Lone Star Industries and had a contract to market cement produced in Cuba.

88. *The Journal of Commerce* (6 March 1996).

89. *Cuba Brief* (12 April 1996). U.S. Assistant Secretary for International Affairs, Jeffrey Davidow, reported to Congress in July 1996 that, because of Title IV of the LIBERTAD Act, a significant number of firms that were doing business involving confiscated U.S. properties were ending those business deals (Werlau 1996).

90. "Mayor inversionista anunciaría su retirada de Cuba a fin de mes," *El Nuevo Herald* (3 March 1997).

expectation that the U.S. economic embargo was going to be lifted or at least weakened. This perception prompted a surging trend of American entrepreneurs traveling to Cuba to scout business deals. Between 1994 and 1996, about 1,500 representatives of American firms went to Cuba, and according to an official of the Cuban government, more than 100 U.S. companies signed nonbinding letters of intent with state enterprises to do business in case the U.S. embargo ended.[91]

Besides increases in foreign direct investment going into Cuba if the U.S. embargo is lifted, such an event would also increase hard currency earnings for the Cuban government from American tourists. It is estimated that an end of the embargo could quickly double the number of tourists going to Cuba. When Clinton seemed to be considering lifting or weakening the embargo, there were plans in the shipping sector to dock four cruise ships simultaneously in Havana. Under the embargo, ships calling on Cuba have to wait six months before making a port stop in the United States; thus, Cuba currently hosts only one cruise ship a week.[92] The U.S. Trading with the Enemy Act prohibits Americans from going to Cuba as tourists; the fine can be up to $55,000 per violation.

Despite measures to strengthen the embargo, the U.S. is the largest source of humanitarian aid to Cuba.[93] The European Union sends Cuba about $20 million a year in humanitarian aid.[94] The Clinton administration allowed the delivery of $140 million in humanitarian aid to Cuba during Clinton's first term.[95]

CONCLUSIONS

It is a tragedy. Under the Castro regime, the only kind of political transition that can be reasonably expected is a transition in which the initiative comes from below. It is not a matter of preferring a transition from below among alternative transition paths. It is that the regime type leaves no choice. A negative aspect of a transition via collapse in Cuba is that such transition can involve violence. At best, the transition could be relatively non-violent like those in the German Democratic Republic and in Czechoslovakia. But the end of the Castro regime most likely will be like the Romanian case. The sultanistic features of the Castro regime virtually preclude a nonviolent transition.[96] It is unrealistic to believe that a peaceful, negotiated transition is possible under the Castro regime, regardless of whether there is a U.S. embargo or not.

The weakness of civil society in Cuba today and the strength of the repressive apparatus are not factors that preclude a transition from below. A mass uprising could erupt, spread and obtain the support of significant sectors of the armed forces and possibly of members of the security forces and other regime cadres. The current strength of the overt opposition in civil society in Cuba is not less than in other countries with similar dictatorial regimes that experienced political transitions initiated from below. Moreover there are theoretical reasons and indications of evidence to expect that regime cadres may be willing to join the people in the event of a popular uprising.

Objections to the U.S. embargo, and to the Helms-Burton law in particular, may be raised on several grounds, e.g., in terms of violations of international

---

91. Werlau (1996, 458-59) and Mimi Whitefield, "Bill Puts Damper on Foreign Investments Initiatives," *The Miami Herald* (1 April 1996). On October 7, 1995, senior executives from more than 40 major U.S. corporations, including Sears, Hyatt Corporation, General Motors, Samsonite Luggage, Kmart, Tandy Corporation, the Gap, Lowes, Rockwell and Harley-Davidson dined with Fidel Castro in Havana. Chronology of Cuban Events, 1995, Information Resources Branch, Radio Martí Program.

92. Don C. Becker, "Cuba," *The Journal of Commerce* (28 February 1996). Frances Kerry, "U.S. travel executives meet Cuban tourism minister" *Reuter News Service* (12 December 1995).

93. U.S. Department of State, "The U.S. embargo and healthcare in Cuba" (14 May 1997).

94. "Cuba-Europe: EU Rejects Washington Deal," *InterPress Third World News Agency* (4 September 1996).

95. Steve Fainaru, "Nine Months Later, Cuba Dissidents Still in Disarray," *The Boston Globe* (12 November 1996).

96. Sultanistic characteristics make a violent transition most likely, see Linz and Stepan (1996, 357).

or U.S. laws. This article has limited itself to an analysis of the impact of the embargo on the possibility of a political transition in Cuba. This relationship is the main justification on the part of the United States for the Helms-Burton law and already presents enough complexity and controversy to warrant an article devoted solely to it. Other implications of the U.S. embargo can be the subject of other works.

The U.S. embargo is conducive to a political transition in Cuba. Even if it were possible for a transition to be negotiated between softliners and members of the opposition inside Cuba, the U.S. economic embargo would help promote the emergence of softliners by contributing to the economic plight. In the scenario of a transition from below, the embargo, and the LIBERTAD Act, also help bring about the demise of the Castro dictatorship by increasing the economic pressures that promote covert opposition within the regime and make a mass uprising more likely.

Theory and evidence from comparative studies indicate that poor economic performance is conducive to the demise of dictatorships. Concurrently, evidence from Cuba indicates that the economic crisis is undermining the ability of the dictatorship to survive by increasing discontent among regime cadres and in the general population.

The test of the effectiveness of the U.S. embargo is not its power to paralyze the Cuban economy but its capacity to reduce the financial resources available to the regime to distribute benefits to regime cadres and sustain mass acquiescence, i.e., to ease pressures within and below the regime arising from the deterioration of economic conditions. In fact, the embargo is currently reducing the amount of hard currency that the Cuban government is able to obtain.

Domínguez (1995, 691) has raised a challenging question. There has been a severe deterioration of the Cuban economy at the macro level as well as in the living conditions of the population for about six years now. So, why has the Castro regime not fallen, despite the extraordinary suffering that afflicts the Cuban people? How long does it have to take for the Castro regime to fall under current conditions? How bad does the economic situation have to get before there is a mass uprising? An answer to these questions is in terms of probabilities.[97] While the Castro dictatorship has managed to survive thus far, the likelihood that it will fall is greater the longer its economy continues to deteriorate or stagnate.[98] The issue is not one of a threshold; it is one of probability. Evidence from Cuba indicates that as the economy stagnates discontent with the regime is greater among the population and among cadres. Thus, the political dynamics seem to be moving in a direction conducive to a political transition. The correct notion does not seem to be that if after a certain number of years of serious economic problems or after reaching a given point of economic deterioration the dictatorship has not fallen then it can be concluded that the regime is invulnerable to economic crises.

An alternative to maintaining the embargo is to lift it. It is an illusion to believe that ending the embargo will lead to greater respect for human rights in Cuba or encourage a negotiated political transition under the Castro regime. The failure of normal international relations between Cuba and countries in Latin America and Western Europe to achieve political liberalization or respect for human rights supports this conclusion. The foremost goal of the ruling elite is to perpetuate itself in power. The strategy of the dictatorship apparently is to obtain enough foreign exchange from its international transactions to muddle through while refusing to allow political liberalization. The Castro government is not willing to pay the price of respect for human rights for better international economic relations.

Lifting the embargo would not mean that the Castro government would allow significant market-oriented

---

97. A finding by Przeworski and Limongi (1994) is that the probability that a dictatorship will fall is greater when the dictatorship experiences an economic crisis.

98. Geddes (1995, 25) observes that, contrary to military regimes of the South American type, political transitions in single-party regimes require further and deeper economic shocks.

economic reforms nor that there would be a dramatic improvement in economic performance. The Cuban government has refused to move beyond quite limited market reforms while engaging in economic relations with countries other than the United States. Yet lifting the embargo would help the Castro regime to survive. Besides handling a political victory to the Cuban government, the end of the embargo would increase the financial resources available to the regime with which to ease the pressures it confronts arising from Cuba's economic situation.

The end of the embargo would make a political transition less likely. The likelihood that Fidel would die of natural causes while in office would be greater.

The current regime could last for an additional decade. Under the best outcome in this scenario, after Fidel dies a different type of regime could emerge in which a negotiated transition becomes possible. But the emergence of such a regime is not assured after the death of Fidel. It is possible that his younger brother, Raúl, the second in command in Cuba, could be able to maintain the current regime. In any event, anyone willing to bet on helping the Castro regime survive for the sake of a possible negotiated transition at some point in the distant future must not lose sight of the fact that people in Cuba have been living in hell for a long time.

REFERENCES

Aguila, Juan M. del. 1993. "The Party, the Fourth Congress, and the Process of Counter-Reform." *Cuban Studies* 23.

Baloyra, Enrique A. 1993. "Socialist Transitions and Prospects for Change in Cuba." In Enrique A. Baloyra and James A. Morris, eds., *Conflict and Change in Cuba*. Albuquerque: University of New Mexico Press.

_____. 1994. "Where Does Cuba Stand?" In Donald E. Schulz, ed., *Cuba and the Future*. Westport: Greenwood.

Brown, J. F. 1991. *Surge to Freedom: The End of Communist Rule in Eastern Europe*. Durham, North Carolina: Duke University Press.

Bruszt, Laszlo. 1990. "1989: The Negotiated Revolution in Hungary." *Social Research* 57, no. 2 (Summer).

Centeno, Miguel Angel. 1996. "Cuba's Search for Alternatives." In Miguel Angel Centeno and Mauricio Font, eds. *Toward a New Cuba? Legacies of a Revolution*. Boulder: Lynne Rienner Publishers.

Clark, Juan. 1992. *Cuba: Mito y Realidad. Testimonios de un Pueblo*. 2nd ed. Miami: Saeta Ediciones.

Domínguez, Jorge I. 1993a. "The Political Impact on Cuba of the Reform and Collapse of Communist Regimes." In Carmelo Mesa-Lago, ed., *Cuba After the Cold War*. Pittsburgh: University of Pittsburgh Press.

_____. 1993b. "The Secrets of Castro's Staying Power." *Foreign Affairs* (Spring): 97-107.

_____. 1994. "U.S. Policy toward Cuba in the 1980s and 1990s." *The Annals of the American Academy of Political and Social Science* 533 (May): 165-176.

_____. 1995. "Why the Cuban Regime Has not Fallen." In Irving Louis Horowitz, ed., *Cuban Communism, 1959-1995*. 8th ed. New Brunswick: Transaction Publishers.

Eyal, Jonathan. 1990. "Why Romania could not avoid bloodshed." In Gwyn Prins, ed., *Spring in Winter: The 1989 revolutions*. Manchester, U.K.: Manchester University Press.

Geddes, Barbara. 1995. "Games of Intra-Regime Conflict and the Breakdown of Authoritarianism." Paper presented at the annual meeting of the American Political Science Association, Chicago.

González, Edward. 1992. *Cuba Adrift in a Postcommunist World*. Santa Monica, CA: RAND.

_____. 1996. *Cuba Clearing Perilous Waters?*. Santa Monica, CA: RAND.

González, Edward and David Ronsfeldt. 1994. *Storm Warnings for Cuba*. Santa Monica: RAND.

Gunn, Gillian. 1994. "In Search of a Modern Cuba Policy." In Donald E. Schulz, ed., *Cuba and the Future*. Westport: Greenwood Press.

Horowitz, Irving Louis. 1995. "Castro and the End of Ideology." In Irving Louis Horowitz, ed., *Cuban Communism, 1959-1995*. 8th ed. New Brunswick: Transaction Publishers.

Huntington, Samuel P. 1991. "How Countries Democratize." *Political Science Quarterly* 106, no. 4 (Winter): 579-616.

Judt, Tony R. 1992. "Metamorphosis: The Democratic Revolution in Czechoslovakia." In Ivo Banac, ed., *Eastern Europe in Revolution*. Ithaca: Cornell University Press.

Linden, Ronald H. 1993. "Analogies and the Loss of Community: Cuba and East Europe in the 1990s." In Carmelo Mesa-Lago, ed., *Cuba After the Cold War*. Pittsburgh: University of Pittsburgh Press.

Linz, Juan J. 1990. "Transitions to Democracy." *The Washington Quarterly* 13, no. 3 (Summer): 143-164.

Linz, Juan J. and Alfred Stepan. 1996. *Problems of Democratic Transition and Consolidation: Southern Europe, South America, and Post-Communist Europe*. Baltimore: The Johns Hopkins University Press.

Mesa-Lago, Carmelo. 1993. "The Economic Effects on Cuba of the Downfall of Socialism in the USSR and Eastern Europe." In Carmelo Mesa-Lago, ed., *Cuba After the Cold War*. Pittsburgh: University of Pittsburgh Press.

_____. 1995. "Cuba's Economic Policies and Strategies for the 1990s." In Irving Louis Horowitz, ed., *Cuban Communism, 1959-1995*. 8th ed. New Brunswick: Transaction Publishers.

_____. 1996. "The State of the Cuban Economy: 1995-96." In *Cuba in Transition—Volume 6*. Washington: Association for the Study of the Cuban Economy.

Mesa-Lago, Carmelo and Horst Fabian. 1993. "Anologies Between East European Socialist Regimes and Cuba: Scenarios for the Future." In Carmelo Mesa-Lago, ed., *Cuba After the Cold War*. Pittsburgh: University of Pittsburgh Press.

Naimark, Norman M. 1992. "Ich will hier raus": Emigration and the Collapse of the German Democratic Republic." In Ivo Banak, ed., *Eastern Europe in Revolution*. Ithaca: Cornell University Press.

O'Donnell, Guillermo. 1989. "Transition to Democracy: Some Navigation Instruments." In Robert A. Pastor, ed., *Democracy in the Americas. Stopping the Pendulum*. New York: Holmes & Meier.

O'Donnell, Guillermo and Philippe Schmitter. 1986. *Transitions from Authoritarian Rule: Tentative Conclusions about Uncertain Democracies*. Baltimore: The Johns Hopkins University Press.

Przeworski, Adam. 1986. "Some Problems in the Study of Transition to Democracy." In Guillermo O'Donnell, Philippe C. Schmitter and Laurence Whitehead, eds., *Transitions from Authoritarian Rule: Comparative Perspectives*. Baltimore: The Johns Hopkins University Press.

_____. 1991. *Democracy and the Market: Political and Economic Reforms in Eastern Europe and Latin America*. New York: Cambridge University Press.

Przeworski, Adam and Fernando Limongi. 1994. "Modernization: Theories and Facts." University of Chicago, Chicago Center on Democracy, Working Paper # 4 (November).

Remmer, Karen L. 1992. "The Process of Democratization in Latin America." *Studies in Comparative International Development* 27, no. 4 (Winter): 3-24.

Schulz, Donald E. 1994. "Introduction." In Donald E. Schulz, ed., *Cuba and the Future*. Westport: Greenwood Press.

Suchlicki, Jaime. 1992. "Possible Scenarios of Change in Cuba." In *Cuba's Transition to Democracy*. Miami: The Endowment for Cuban American Studies.

Verdery, Katherine and Gail Kligman. 1992. "Romania after Ceauçescu: Post-Communist Communism?" In Ivo Banak, ed., *Eastern Europe in Revolution*. Ithaca: Cornell University Press.

Werlau, María C. 1996. "Foreign Investment in Cuba: The Limits of Commercial Engagement." In *Cuba in Transition—Volume 6*. Washington: Association for the Study of the Cuban Economy.

SOCIAL FORCES AND THE POLITICS OF TRANSITION: LESSONS FROM THE CUBAN EXPERIENCE

Enrique S. Pumar

Rule by one has innumerable times been reproached for the contradiction which is supposed to lie in the purely quantitative disproportion between the one-ness of the ruler and the many-ness of the ruled.

— Georg Simmel[1]

Unlike most, if not all, of the research on the breakdown of authoritarian rule, the Cuban case affords us the unique opportunity to investigate the transactions between a daring opposition, the *desgaste* of authoritarian politics, and the contention of the island's future in the international arena as they unfold. Skeptics may view my summation of the regime's capacity to rule and the challenges it faces from the mounting opposition as grossly exaggerated. These critics insist that the anfractuous recent history of the opposition abates their capacity to grasp media attention or the hearts and minds of the populace. Furthermore, the crisis of the early 1990s demonstrates the resilience of the ruling elite. As for international mindfulness, any discussion of the island's future is a de facto consequence of its hostility with the United States. Even the inevitable question of "transition to what?" begs one of Yogi Berra's most favorite predic-

ament, that it "is hard to make predictions, especially about the future."

This paper takes issue with this quizzical perspective and argues that actions by the opposition are precipitating the regime's demise. Moreover, the future of pluralism depends on how the various social forces opposing the regime relate to one another during this period of transition. Building on the intellectual foundations laid in new social movement and regime transformation theorizing, I will demonstrate how the framing tactics of *the disgruntled opposition*, coupled with the dire economic and social situation in the island, are eroding the social base of support for the regime.[2] The fact that some observers may overlook the weight of framing options reflects either the extent to which they analyze Cuba's contentious repertoires with, as Charles Tilly would say, "alien eyes," or their overestimation of the invincibility of authoritarian rulers.[3]

One of the most relevant lessons to be learned from the Cuban case is that peaceful defiance and avocation of *antisystem frames are among the most successful tactics during the process of transition in any authoritar-*

---

1. Georg Simmel, "Subordination Under an Individual," in Kurt H. Wolff, ed., *The Sociology of Georg Simmel* (New York: Free Press, 1950), p. 201.

2. For a good illustration of this literature see, Guillermo O'Donnell, Philippe C. Schmitter, and Lawrence Whitehead, eds., *Transition from Authoritarian Rule: Prospects for Democracy* (Baltimore: Johns Hopkins University Press, 1986); Enrique Laraña, Hank Johnston, and Joseph R. Gusfield, eds., *New Social Movements* (Philadelphia: Temple University Press, 1994); and Doug McAdam, John D. McCarthy, and Mayer N. Zald, eds., *Comparative Perspectives on Social Movements* (New York: Cambridge University Press, 1996).

3. Charles Tilly, "Contentious Repertoires in Great Britain, 1758-1834," in Mark Traugott, ed., *Repertoires and Cycles of Collective Action* (Durham: Duke University Press, 1995), pp. 15-42.

ian situation.[4] Antisystem frames alter the rules of the game that govern state-society relations, corrode popular expectations about the efficacy of the government, and promote an increasing number of political opportunity structures by challenging existing norms of political toleration and demanding further change. In the final analysis, the delegitimizing effects of an alternative construction of reality proposed by challengers demonstrate the contradiction between the rhetorical claims of universal accountability, i.e., "esta revolución es del pueblo," and the regime's disdain for political toleration.

Analyzing the Cuban predicament from this perspective generates several consequential hypotheses for the study of regime change and the field of social mobilization in general:

1. Political mobilization under authoritarian rule is prompted by the erosion of political authority rather than by institutional openings. This means that disequilibration of authoritarian rule is not necessarily marked by political liberalization from above.

2. The content of *sociation* among actors in a civil society is autonomous for it makes use of materials and symbols, i.e., mobilizing frames, of protest that reflect their interests and operations as conditioned by structural holes embedded in particular state-society relations.

3. Challengers to authoritarian regimes maneuver different repertoires of contentions; but with the passing of time, frame of meanings—of which antisystem frames are a part—tend to predominate.

4. The survival of an authoritarian ruler depends on inter-network ties among challengers and in particular strong ties between *disgruntled opposition and skeptical supporters* of the regime.

In developing my argument, I will first explain the notion of repertoires and frames and discuss their significance to the Cuban situation. Then, I will map the contending social sectors in Cuba's political scene. I assess the capacity of different groups to take advantage of the increasing weakness of the regime and to outline their repertoire. This section also stresses that the absence of a meaningful coalition among the different sectors comprising the dissident political scene has guarantee the survival of the regime thus far. Lastly, I will demonstrate how the cascading actions of internal opposition are weakening Castro's rule. In short, the Cuban case offers some theoretical as well as practical challenge since the transition is not developing according to the prediction of observers. I will conclude by summarizing the implications of my argument.

REPERTOIRES, FRAMES, AND THE POLITICS OF OPPOSITION

Repertoires and frames are interchangeable strategies of popular protests. These tactics go a long way in explaining the behavior of the opposition during the transition from authoritarian rule. Yet, many political sociologists rarely focus their attention on the role of the opposition during these situations. Rather they concentrate on the repression/toleration calculus of the ruling elite[5] or on the capacity of the regime to overcome structural crises.[6] In the case of Cuba, both of these trends are dominant the literature.[7]

---

4. The notion of antisystem frame comes from Mario Diani, "Linking Mobilization Frames and Political Opportunities in Italy," *American Sociological Review*, Vol. 61, No. 6 (December 1996), pp. 1056-57.

5. See Robert R. Kaufman, "Liberalization and Democratization in South America: Perspective from the 1970s," in Guillermo O'Donnell, Philippe C. Schmitter, and Laurence Whitehead, eds., *Transition from Authoritarian Rule: Comparative Perspectives* (Baltimore: Johns Hopkins University Press, 1986).

6. See John Sheahan, "Economic Policies and the Prospects for Successful Transition from Authoritarian Rule in Latin America," in *ibid*, pp. 154-164.

7. For an appeal to adopt a more "holistic understanding" of events in Cuba beyond the focus on economic decision, see Benigno E. Aguirre, "A Skeptical View of the Announced Demise of Castrism," in *Cuba in Transition—Volume 3* (Washington: Association for the Study of the Cuban Economy, 1993), p. 148.

A convenient definition of repertoires has been proposed by Tilly. For him, these are "the established ways in which pairs of actors make and receive claims bearing on each other's interests."[8] Frames, on the other hand, are the cultural artifact and symbolic meaning manipulated by actors who desire to justify and dignify collective action and social mobilization.[9] Simply put, repertoires encompass action-oriented tactics against the regime such as strikes, insurgencies, or urban sabotages. Frames depict the social construction of reality for the purpose of delegitimizing government institutions and practices.

This dichotomy begs three theoretical questions. First, when are those who disagree with authoritarianism more likely to employ repertoires or frames to articulate their grievances? Second, what prompts the choice between one tactic, the other, or both? Third, what are the effects of either strategy in the organizational game plan of detractors of the regime?

An analysis of the Cuban situation today offers some striking conclusions to these queries. A history of the opposition's tactics to confront the Castro regime reveals a significant transformation in the course of action of the opposition. This point is illustrated below, by distinguishing between the first and second waves of opposition. In the early 1970s, the number of subversive strikes against the regime began to decrease substantially as the anti-system frame became the preferred mode of dissent among internal and external foes. Several factors contribute to this pattern. First, the longer authoritarian governments stay in power the more sophisticated their security and repressive apparatus become. With the accumulated experience of ruling, governing elite also learns the "tricks of the game." With time, political leaders realized that the means to sustain are different from the ones they used to win control of the state. Second, since authoritarian regimes monopolizes the means

of communication, it can indoctrinate the populace on how opponents' action-oriented repertoires are impeding their efforts on behalf of the people. Third, from a public relations point of view, it is not in the best interest of detractors to sustain a menacing campaign against a regime, especially if it is one they cannot win in the interim.

Contrary to the stimulating conclusions drawn by Diani's study of the Northern League in Italy,[10] the opportunity structure that leads to the predominance of anti-system frames among opposition groups derives from the current cost associated with exploiting the contradictions inherited by the regime's attempts to institutionalize its rule and its efforts to quiet discursive dissent over time. Diani's case study takes place in a democratic setting, hence concealing this insight. However, when the state remains autocratic after a process of institutionalization is in place, even some supporters question the efficacy of governing institutions, the prospects for political participation, or the absence of rules governing political succession. Another source of contradictions is the repetitive exercise of political repression despite constitutional norms guarantee the articulation of a popular political voice.

The choice between repertoires and frames is an area that remains unexplored by proponents of social movement theories. This is partly because many of the historical grounded studies of this form of social mobilization deal with a single movement or coalition.[11] Once we consider a situation with multiple groups, each with their choice of repertoire, frames, or both, the choice of strategies among them will have *contentious* consequences on the other, as well as on the incumbent. For this reason, the possibility of a network between two or more opposition groups will depend in part on the choice of tactics. Groups that embrace similar tactics will have a better chance

8. Charles Tilly, 1995, *op. cit.*, p. 27.

9. This definition derives from the work of Sidney Tarrow, "Cycle of Collective Action: Between Moments of Madness and the Repertoire of Contentions," in Traugott, ed., *Repertoires and Cycles of Collective Action*, p. 94.

10. Diani, *op. cit.*, pp. 1056-57.

11. For an illustration, see Mayer N. Zald and John D. McCarthy, eds., *Social Movements in an Organizational Society* (New Brunswick: Transaction Publishers, 1987).

Table 1.   Repertoires of Contention among Social Forces[a]

| | Skeptics | Outsiders | | Disgruntled |
		Duros	Blandos	
Cohesion	low	high	high	high
Competitiveness	high	low	low	high
Setting	internal	external	external	internal
Distinctiveness	low	high	high	high
Goals	reforms	change	reforms	change
Strategy (main)	gradual liberalization	breakdown	democratization	democratization

a.   The criteria used to compare the different ideological positions are taken from Robert Dahl, "Patterns of Opposition," in Dahl, ed., *Political Opposition in Western Democracies* (New Haven: Yale University Press, 1966), p. 332.

of collaborating with one another, for strategies are a reflection of political inclinations.

To summarize, two structural conditions seem to expedite the choice of strategy among opposition: the longevity of power of the governing elite and the apparent contradictions throughout the routine of governance by authoritarian governments. When multiple groups of dissenters compete to depose a regime, intra-organizational networks are more likely among clusters of actors with similar strategic outlooks and shared visions. The experience of the Cuban opposition shows that there is a great deal of coordination and contacts but no formal ties among various cliques.

MAPPING THE CUBAN POLITICAL STRUCTURE

Table 1 compares the social forces that are part of the political spectrum in Cuba today.[12] It focuses on groups that promote a forward- looking solution to the island's trouble, even if that solution is not democratic in the short term. One such sector are the *skeptic supporters,* which are not formally part of the opposition, but play an important role in the future either because of their access to political power, or for their determination to introduce reforms. The table leaves out any representation of hard-core supporters of the regime (i.e., the military, members of the in-

ternal security apparatus, or old cadres) who participated in the insurgency against Batista and generally have remained loyal to Castro since he grasped political power. These supporters owe allegiance to the ruler out of conviction, patronage, and their stake in the survival of Castroism.

The First Wave: The opposition to the Cuban revolution is perhaps one of the most vocal and indefatigable any Latin American regime has faced. Its history falls into two distinct phases. The first ten years after the revolution, the detractors of the regime manifested their repertoire in the form of what Traugott calls "barricades."[13] This tactic of political opposition was never very successful, as the events in Escambray or the Bay of Pig fiascos remind us. On the one hand, the shortcomings of these operations could be attributed to early revolutionary euphoria or to popular faith on the official rhetoric promises of future panacea. On the other, these tactics tried to match the regime militarily. Authoritarian rules with firm control over the armed forces possess a comparative advantage to avert violent confrontations. At an ideological level, the regime also had a relatively easy time offsetting the appeal of the early opposition, since Castro managed to stigmatize early detractors as foreign-funded mercenaries backed by the tradi-

---

12. The tendency to group the opposition into factions follows Alfred Stepan's "On the Tasks of a Democratic Opposition," *Journal of Democracy,* Vol. 1, No. 2 (Spring 1990), pp. 41-49.

13. See Mark Traugott, "Barricades as Repertoire," in Traugott, *op. cit.*, pp. 47-48.

tional elite wanting to procreate a tarnished republican policy of the past.[14]

Besides the intolerant ideology and exclusionary politics of the regime, three other reasons triggered the polarization between supporters and opponents of the Castro government. First, the timing of the coming to power of the revolutionary elite provided its rivals with the ammunition to claim that policies based on a Marxist-Leninist ideology were not warranted for the nation. By the end of the 1950s, through a combination of Cuba's integration into the world economy, its dependent development relation with the United States, and its populist policies backed by every government since at least 1940, afforded the island with the third-highest standard of living in the hemisphere. Even sympathetic observers of the revolution have noted the relative success of republican politicos.[15]

More importantly, Cuba's location and its proximity to Florida made it a transit hub for visitors and immigrants alike. This factor is politically relevant because it contributed to the deepening of transculturation and provided a sense of distorted regional identity.[16] Popular culture and expectations were closer to the North than to the South or the rest of the Caribbean. Whatever the fate of the revolutionary initiatives, they were measured against the developmental experiences of the United States or nations throughout Western Europe.[17] The cultural affinity with Western values forged popular suspicions about the intentions of the new allies of the revolutionary

regime during the Cold War, principally the Soviet Union and China.

A third triggering factor was the degree of intra-elite cleavages experienced during Castro's consolidation of power. During the early years of the revolution, Castro first formed a coalition government with moderates who had opposed Batista, only to maneuver them out of power soon thereafter. Fewer than a handful of his ministers came from other groups who had fought side by side with the 26th of July movement. Castro's alliance with the Cuban Communist Party and his embrace of socialism alienated several former associates.[18] This political brinkmanship made strange bedfellows out of moderate Batista supporters and dismayed former revolutionaries. As Simmel predicted some time ago, "common enmity is one of the most powerful means for motivating a number of individuals of groups to cling together."[19]

In short, the first wave of dissent was dominated by a sector that could be called the opposition from abroad. As its name indicates, these opponents took refuge in the United States. They also recruited most of the sector's members from the upper and middle classes. Two of the accomplishments of this sector are that it has managed to survived until today and that it has changed its repertoire from violent confrontation to peaceful provocation. At present, its biggest leverage is the capacity to steer American foreign policy towards Cuba and its endowment to mobilize the Cuban exile community living in the United States. However, its influence is undermined by its unyielding image and its splits along ideological

---

14. A detailed history of this period can be found in Hugh Thomas, *Cuba: The Pursuit of Freedom* (New York: Harper and Row, 1971), pp. 1214-1384.

15. A good overview of the political economy of the 1950s in Cuba can be found in James O'Connor, *The Origins of Socialism in Cuba* (Ithaca: Cornell University Press, 1970).

16. For a discussion of transcultural Cuban identity, see Gustavo Pérez-Firmat, *The Cuban Condition* (Cambridge: Cambridge University Press, 1989).

17. It is interesting to see that in a recent manifesto published by four opposition leaders within Cuba, they compare Cuba's standard of living prior to the revolution with those of Spain and Italy while making references to Western Europe. The document in question will be further discussed below. See Vladimiro Roca, Martha Beatriz Roque, René Gómez Manzano, and Felix A. Bonne Carcasés, *The Homeland Belongs to Us All* (Washington: Freedom House, 1997).

18. Eloy Gutiérrez Menoyo, Húber Matos and Carlos Franqui are particular illustrations.

19. G. Simmel, "Subordination under an Individual," in Wolff, *op.cit*, p. 192.

and generation lines. In general, three points of contention divide this group into *duros* and *blandos:* position with regard to the U.S. embargo; political aspirations in post-Castro politics; and the question of whether increased communication or alienation is the best mean by which to topple the regime.[20]

The *duros* tend to support the embargo, the isolation of the regime, and follow a Machiavellian approach to the overturn of the revolution. The majority are professional and business leaders; few come from academia. This attitude is also popular among a generation of Castro's peers who believe that he betrayed the Cuban nation. Two celebrated institutions that represent the hard-liners are The Cuban American National Foundation and Of Human Rights, both of which are very effective lobbying Cuban-American organizations in Washington, D.C.[21] While most of the public attention has been focused on the Cuban American National Foundation, Of Human Rights has tirelessly defended the political aspirations of individuals inside the island and the freedom of political prisoners. It also publicizes political essays and manuscripts authored by internal dissidents.

The *blandos* support democratization through a careful rapprochement with the regime. They have few illusions about the political role of exiles once Castro is gone. Another aim of this group is to deter a violent transition of power. They too support the political freedom of dissidents but believe that those would be better secured if the American government were to gradually relax its embargo on the island. For them, the embargo has lost its forte and may event be assisting Castro to blames the United States for his regime's missteps. According to this group, a policy of national reconciliation is what Castro fears most.[22]

The soft-liners consist of baby boomers, young academics, and some professionals. They travel frequently to the island and therefore have numerous contacts with dissidents and skeptic supporters of the regime. The most vocal groups among the blandos are the Institute for Cuban Studies, the Cuban Committee for Democracy, and Cambio Cubano.[23]

The Second Wave: Events in 1967-68 triggered new waves of dissent against the regime. Externally, these years marked the aftermath of the death of Che Guevara, the Prague uprising, the Breshnev Doctrine, and worldwide student protests. Inside Cuba, the crushing of the microfacción, Cuba's own version of the Cultural Revolution, and the beginning of a rapprochement between Castro and the Soviets alienated many former government supporters. Unlike the earlier opposition, this group evolved tediously and attracted intellectuals and professionals with previous close ties to the revolution.[24] Today, this sector, which I named the disgruntled opposition, comprises several groups that advocate a wide variety of concerns and grievances against the state, ranging from the environment to human rights issues. This faction derives some of its leverage from having organized an alternative press with frequent contacts with international media outlets and from its residency in the island.

Several structural factors have recently propelled the proliferation of groups within the disgruntled opposition. After the crisis of the early 1990s, the regime today has embarked on economic policies that try to imitate the Chinese development model whereby regulated foreign investment is sought without the state giving up the reigns. For skeptics supporters behind the push for more market deregulation, the vac-

---

20. A good synthesis of the various political position among Cubans today can be found in Manuel Ramos de Zayas, "Who's on First?: The Cuban Political Ballgame," *Apuntes Postmodernos*, Vol. 1, No. 2 (Spring 1991).

21. For a critical overview of the Cuban American National Foundation and the *duros* see, Carla Anne Robbins, "Dateline Washington: Cuban-American Clout," *Foreign Policy*, No. 88 (Fall 1992), pp. 162-182

22. An example of this position is Marifeli Pérez-Stable, "Cuba en los albores del Siglo XXI," *Apuntes Postmodernos*, Vol. 6, No. 2 -Vol 7, No. 1 (Spring/Fall 1996), pp. 49-53.

23. See Stan Yarboro, "The New 'A' List," *South Florida* (July 1994).

24. Gustavo Arcos of the Cuban Committee for Human Rights and Elizardo Sánchez of the Comisión Cubana de Derechos Humanos y Reconciliación Nacional are good examples.

illation of the regime in implementing these reforms causes concerns and discontent. This group realizes that there are fundamental differences between Cuba and China in terms of market size and abundance of natural resources which makes inapplicable this development strategy. Critics of the regime have reached similar conclusions. Martha Beatriz Roque, a leading figure within the unofficial Cuban Institute of Independent Economists, has offered the following assessment:

> El Gobierno toma una serie de medidas que pueden constituir un paliativo en el corto plazo, pero que en definitiva, no solucionarán la crisis, ya que todas ellas van encaminadas a mantener el centralismo estatal, la propiedad social, y la distribución de acuerdo a los principios socialistas.[25]

Yet, the shared preoccupation has not produced enough grounds for coalition between these two cliques. The risks of joining the opposition encompass not just the chance of physical repression but in addition silencing and marginality from potent decision-making. In addition, there are sharp differences between these two factions as to whether reforms should come from within or outside ruling circles. Observers who have recently visited the island and contacted many of reformers report of a growing discontent within this group regarding the pace of economic reforms. This point of contention has made many of this reformers *skeptic supporters* of the regime.

Another significant factor promoting today's discontent in Cuba are the unintentional consequences of economic change. Tourism, for example, has created a market for prostitution and a secondary market for goods and services, two activities the revolution is alleged to have eradicated. There is also a small but burgeoning informal sector. With the legalization of self-employment, the government has also opened a Pandora's box, for these *trabajadores por cuenta pro-pia* are providing the same services—but of better quality and more efficiently—than the state used to render. Hence, the state bureaucracy is becoming obsolete and in the eyes of many, rent-seeking and repression are perhaps the two state functions that seem to work effectively.

Finally, the need to replace old revolutionary cadres with younger, more professional leaders is creating new tensions between core supporters and the *skeptics*. Promotion of new leaders was prompted by attempts to provide appearances of democracy and to calm the evident disillusionment of the youth. However despite the benefits core supporters continue to enjoy after leaving office (including the appointment of many to head state-run corporations and joint ventures), this move is creating some friction that only the presence of the Castro brothers, particularly Fidel, seem to ease. Ironically, like the exiled community, these two brands of supporters evidently disagree about the extent of change necessary to resolve the current quagmire on the island.[26] So far, the regime has reluctantly sided with those pushing for reform, but last year Communist hard-liners managed to persuade Raúl to order an internal security investigation into the practices of the growing semi-autonomous "think tanks" where reformers tend to congregate, a sign of the precarious political atmosphere between these two factions.

One conclusion that can be drawn from this mapping of the political discourse regarding Cuba is that contrary to popular perception, emerging forces of dissent have the capacity to cluster together around a core set of values. However, unsustainable intra-organizational ties among the wide political spectrum are guaranteeing the longevity of the regime. Wide-ranging and growing dissident factions within civil society have demonstrated their willingness to cooperate and organize interlocks, as the case of *Concilio Cu-*

---

25. Martha Beatriz Roque, *La Crisis Económica en Cuba: Cuba Vista Desde Dentro*, Buró de Información del Movimiento Cubano de Derechos Humanos (1996).

26. For a penetrating discussion of the different factions within the governing elite see Juan O. Tamayo's analysis in *The Miami Herald* (September 4, 1997).

bano clearly shows.[27] The principal opposition groups also consort on the futility of action-oriented repertoires.

POLITICAL DECAY AND OPPORTUNITY STRUCTURES

This section investigates the relationship between the frame activities of two networks within the disgruntled opposition and how they are contributing to the incumbent's political decay. The groups in question are Concilio Cubano and the more recently formed, Grupo de Trabajo de la Disidencia Interna para el Analisis de la Situación Socioeconómica Cubana (or the Cuban Dissidence Task Group). First, I briefly discuss the socioeconomic context in which dissidence activities take place.[28]

The process of transition from the current authoritarian rule is already underway in Cuba. According to Schmitter, the breakdown of authoritarianism is characterized by "the launching of the process of dissolution of an authoritarian regime." [29] Although, there are no reliable public opinion polls on the island that could confirm this trend, such indicators as the massive number of sympathizers who defect or emigrate, the innumerable calls for unity by the ruling elite, the defiance of the opposition, and the gradual experimentation with market-oriented economic reforms substantiate this assertion. In one respect, the pattern of political change in Cuba today, however, is distinct from the one that unfolded throughout the rest of Latin America in the late 1980s. Cuba's transition is marked by political decay rather than liberalization.[30]

In practical terms, the implication of this situation is that the regime is arbitrarily choosing when, how, and how much to change while it desperately searches for a way out of the current economic conundrum. In addition, it has decided to arbitrarily champion its own brand of socialism rather than embark on a political opening. Still, the government has not found a solution to the persistent challenges it faces from the growing organized opposition in the island. The recent call to abstain in the next voting by the disgruntled opposition could potentially turn the current economic crisis into one of governance. In short, the sociopolitical environment in Cuba for the last eight years has been one of diminishing expectations, popular anger, and an ongoing crisis.[31]

Two networks that have taken advantage of this situation are Concilio Cubano and the Cuban Dissidence Task Group. Concilio is an umbrella organization founded in October 1995 with the purpose of representing the diverse opposition groups throughout the island. Today, it encompasses 101 organizations with critical perspectives on every political contending issue. One of its most audacious moves was to send a letter to Fidel Castro asking for permission to hold a peaceful national assembly.[32] That event was scheduled for February 24, 1996 but the meeting never took place because the regime used the downing of the Hermanos al Rescate's plane to suspend this meeting and jail the organizers.

The most significant defiance Concilio brings to politics is the exposition of official double standards with regards to political representation and the rules

---

27. One of the early documented sources of this cooperation among diverging groups inside Cuba can be found in Christopher Kean, *Diez Días en Cuba* (Washington: Of Human Rights, 1992).

28. A more thorough investigation of these events and their effects can be found in any of the annual ASCE publications, *Cuba in Transition*.

29. See Guillermo O'Donnell and Philippe C. Schmitter, *Tentative Conclusions about Uncertain Democracies* (Baltimore: Johns Hopkins University Press, 1986), p. 6.

30. The concept of political decay derives from Samuel P. Huntington, *Political Order in Changing Societies* (New Haven: Yale University Press, 1968), p. 86

31. For the first time in three decades, frustrations are turning into sabotage. Raúl Rivero, a journalist with the independent agency Cuba Press, recently told journalists in Miami that since the explotions in the hotel Capri and Nacional, there are rumors of other bombs throughout the country and that in the city of Havana "hay muchos policías en todos los lugares y también un clima de tensión," *El Nuevo Herald* (July 23, 1997), p. 6A.

32. This letter and other documents of the *Concilio* are available in the World Wide Web at www.fiu.edu/~fcf.

of the game governing political assembly.[33] In its letter to Castro, the organization defends its right to hold the aborted meeting on the basis of Article 54 of the Cuban Constitution and on the Universal Declaration of Human Rights, of which Cuba is a signatory. Furthermore, it refers to Jose Martí to endorse its call for freedom of expression and describes itself as an association of different groups representing divergent criteria and issues, alluding to the intransigence of the Cuban Communist Party.

This sends a very clever message for delegitimization. It supports Concilio's right to freedom of assembly on the same premises than the ruling party and confronts the regime on its own terms. Moreover, it denies any opportunities by officials to claim that this organization is subversive. Finally, by appealing to constitutional grounds and cultural icons like Martí, it opens a window of opportunity for others to follow the same course of action and escalate their demands.

Abroad, the continued arrests, detentions, and contempt for unofficial political mobilization has damaged relations with international investors, donors, and political associates. Concilio has placed the ruling party in the shameful position of defending repression against peaceful and conciliatory efforts behind coexistence and change. In the public sphere, the regime symbolizes conservatism while Concilio has emerged as a progressive reformer.

A more recent network of dissidents challenging the legitimacy of the governing elite is the *Cuban Dissident Task Force* organized by Vladimiro Roca, Martha Beatriz Roque, René Gómez Manzano, and Felix A. Bonne Carcassés to draft a document entitled *The Homeland Belongs to Us All* (or *Homeland* hereafter). This document was published on June 27, 1997 and, like the case of Concilio, shortly after publication the four leaders were incarcerated.[34] The purpose of the manuscript is to present a counterhegemonic interpretation of the Cuban reality as discussed in "The

Party of Unity, Democracy and the Human Rights We Defend," a report drafted by the Cuban Communist Party as a working platform for its upcoming Fifth Congress.

The infrastructure laid out in *Homeland* is a message of unity, tolerance, and reconciliation. As James C. Scott demonstrates in his recent book *Domination and the Art of Resistance*, hidden meanings are the infrapolitics of subordinate political actors.[35] By making their manifesto public, Roca, Roque, and their associates seem to be inviting the Cuban nation to an open political dialogue transcending ideological lines. As the title clearly states, this document departs from the assumption that there is only one homeland regardless of ideology. This discourse is a clear contradiction of the long official policy in Cuba of deporting its vocal opponents and encouraging popular *actos de repudio* against anyone who does not publicly patronize the state. In addition, the fact that it was presented to the public at all demonstrates the courage of these dissidents. The timing of this publications is also significant, for it was made public at about the same time the remains of Che Guevara were scheduled to return to the island. In effect, the publication of *Homeland* and subsequent detentions of dissidents seem to cast a shadow on this event and on the celebration the Communist Youth Festival currently underway in Havana.

Homeland deconstructs the prevalent political reality in Cuba by asserting five discursive claims challenging the elite rhetoric. These are: First, the Cuban government distorts the meaning of nation by narrowing the space for political dissent and stigmatizing their opponents as enemies or wreckers of the revolutionary social well-being. Second, the continuous references to certain historical events in order to legitimize the revolutionary process reflects an intentional mobilization of bias which obscures the historical reality. Third, the argument that the unity of the

---

33. Sidney Tarrow has asserted: "Collective action embodies claims in dramatic ways that show others the way." See his *Power in Movement* (New York: Cambridge University Press, 1994), p. 97.

34. According to *El Nuevo Herald* of July 30, 1997, the police has arrested more than 50 dissidents and suspects.

35. James C. Scott, *Domination and the Art of Resistance* (New Haven: Yale University Press, 1990), especially pp. 183-201.

political elite leads to national unity makes for a circular argument. The imposition of a single party leads to errors of judgment in public policy and fosters an image of associating the regime with autocratic leaders worldwide. Fourth, the main objective of the state is not to serve the populace but to dominate. Fifth, the government's economic policies impose limitations on the people it is supposed to serve resulting on inefficiency.

More importantly, the antisystem frame discussed in *Homeland* also undermines official arguments about the revolution being under siege since it calls attention to the ruling dogmatism and wavering support for state policies. They also bluntly associate Castro's rule with some of the most dictatorial governments of this century by contending: "The Cuban Communist Party, in imposing a single party system, places itself in the unenviable company of Stalin, Mussolini, Hitler, Franco, Trujillo, Pol Pot and Sadam Hussein, among others."[36]

Antisystem frames such as those discussed in this paper deepen the ongoing political decay in Cuba in several ways. As the government attempts to depict the crisis of the island in technical, economic terms, dissidents continue to invalidate this depiction by introducing a political dimension. Discussion of the contradictions between rhetoric and practices moves the state to take actions that produced embarrassing results and violate norms of democratic behavior. On the other hand, if the states chooses to overlook or tolerate criticism from civil society, it may be perceived as weakening thus further escalating demands from below. Finally, dissident groups have contributed to the transparency of the regime substantiating recurrent human rights violations and other accounts of repression.

CONCLUSION

As the discussion in this paper demonstrates, the opposition to the Castro regime has become more sophisticated and, in many respects, effective with the passing of time. Under adverse and dangerous circumstances, the internal opposition has highlighted the cleavages between rhetoric and official conduct. By making their claims in the public sphere, they have also challenged the regime to eliminate or else tolerate escalating demands from other dissident groups. Today, the provisions advocated by dissidents have become the performance criteria the international community employs to measure the accountability of the Castro regime. On its part, the government has been left with no choice but to admit the arrest of dissidents and tacitly concede the weight of the opposition.[37]

In sum, the Cuban case offers two insightful conclusions for the study of regime change. First, antisystem frames are effective means to undermine the legitimacy of authoritarian regimes and open opportunities for further political actions. The reluctance to admit open dissent seems to have the opposite effect. Second, perhaps one of the reasons for the duration of authoritarian regimes is the unsustainable cross sectional ties among its adversaries and skeptic supporters.

---

36. *Homeland,* p. 3.

37. See "Cuba admite arresto de opositores," *El Nuevo Herald* (July 18, 1997).

CUBA: COOPERACION INTERNACIONAL DE EMERGENCIA Y PARA LA RECUPERACION

Rolando H. Castañeda y George Plinio Montalván[1]

"Llegaron los días difíciles actuales en que predominan las carencias materiales, se produce una indeseada diferenciación social y aumentan las ilegalidades ..... La lista de los problemas es enorme. Las limitaciones en alimentación, vestido, calzado, medios de higiene y medicamentos; los apagones y la carencia de combustible doméstico; las graves dificultades en transporte, vivienda y servicios comunales, han puesto a prueba la voluntad heroica de nuestro pueblo, que resiste con abnegación y estoicismo esas penurias."

> — *El partido de la unidad, la democracia y los derechos humanos que defendemos*, documento oficial para el V Congreso del Partido Comunista de Cuba, PCC, mayo de 1997.

CONTEXTO

El Partido Comunista de Cuba (PCC), que de acuerdo con el artículo 5 de la constitución política del país es la (única) "fuerza dirigente superior de la sociedad y del Estado, que organiza y orienta los esfuerzos comunes hacia los altos fines de la construcción del socialismo y el avance hacia la sociedad comunista," ha convocado el V Congreso para realizarse del 8 al 10 de octubre de 1997. En el documento de convocatoria para dicho congreso, se indica lo siguiente respecto del documento arriba citado:

> Aspiramos a que el análisis y el debate popular de este documento, abierto a toda consideración y propuesta de los militantes y de las masas, se convierta en un proceso esencialmente participativo, de reafirmación

y enriquecimiento de nuestros valores, posición y principios revolucionarios.[2]

Sin embargo, a pesar de que el "proyecto" del PCC es extenso, las propuestas del Comité Central para hacerle frente a la situación de extrema pobreza y vulnerabilidad externa en que se encuentra sumido el pueblo de Cuba que ellos mismos describen, se limitan a las frases siguientes:

> Sin renunciar a su rumbo socialista, Cuba debe *reinsertarse en la economía mundial*, dominada por las transnacionales, caracterizada por el intercambio desigual, y en mercados internacionales inundados de productos donde la competencia es cada vez más difícil ... Nuestra apertura económica conlleva la creación de empresas mixtas y otras formas de asociación con el *capital extranjero*... Objetivos estratégicos permanentes ahora decisivos son: ahorrar en todo, rebajar costos, lograr *mayor eficiencia* en la producción y los servicios.

> Las tareas concretas están claras. Continuar la batalla alimentaria. Alcanzar el mejor resultado posible en cada zafra, y una labor óptima en la siembra y cultivo de la caña. Lograr un salto en la construcción y una mayor explotación de instalaciones turísticas. Obtener la utilización más eficiente de portadores energéticos, sustituir importaciones e *incrementar exportaciones*. Avanzar en la aplicación de la política tributaria y el

---

1. Los puntos de vista aquí expresados son de exclusiva responsabilidad de los autores y de ninguna manera representan sus vínculos institucionales.

2. "Convocatoria al 5º Congreso del Partido Comunista de Cuba," *Granma Internacional*, Edición Digital (16 de mayo de 1997).

saneamiento de las finanzas internas" (el énfasis es nuestro).

No existe ningún detalle de cómo se lograrían los objetivos expuestos y prácticamente todo el resto del documento está dedicado a una reinterpretación de un siglo y medio de historia de Cuba, particularmente a los presuntos esfuerzos continuos por parte de Estados Unidos para apoderarse de la isla, así como a la necesidad de defender la continuación de un fundamentalismo socialista que ya ha sido abandonado por su fracaso en todos los países del mundo con excepción de Corea del Norte y que se ha convertido precisamente en el obstáculo principal a la reinserción de Cuba en la economía mundial y al mejoramiento de las condiciones de vida de los cubanos.

OBJETIVO DEL DOCUMENTO

"El hombre no puede vivir de la historia, que es lo mismo que vivir del cuento; se necesitan bienes materiales, satisfacer su espiritualidad y —de hecho— poder mirar para el futuro con expectativas, pero además, un espacio que todos conocemos como libertad."

— *La Patria es de todos*, Grupo de Trabajo de la Disidencia Interna, La Habana, 28 de junio de 1997.

En oportunidades recientes, altos funcionarios del gobierno de Cuba tales como el vicepresidente Carlos Lage y el ministro de economía y planificación José Luis Rodríguez se han referido al muy limitado acceso de Cuba a los flujos de financiamiento externo como el obstáculo principal —además del embargo/bloqueo estadounidense— al desarrollo económico de Cuba.

En vista de que el PCC ha invitado a la amplia consideración de este tema, *¿qué tendría que hacer Cuba para reinsertarse en la economía mundial, qué tipo de ayuda podría recibir de la comunidad internacional para ello y cuáles serían las condiciones para recibir dicha ayuda?*

En el presente documento, se esbozan áreas y sectores específicos, así como montos indicativos o primeras aproximaciones, para las acciones recomendadas (i.e., donaciones, cooperaciones técnicas, préstamos de inversión, créditos de recuperación económica, préstamos de ajuste estructural, préstamos de reforma sectorial, etc.) partiendo de la situación actual de *penurias* parcialmente descrito por el PCC, y tomando en consideración la experiencia de la cooperación internacional en los casos de Chile, Nicaragua, Perú y los países del ex bloque socialista, los mandatos y áreas de acción prioritaria de las principales agencias de cooperación internacional y los trabajos anteriores presentados por los autores en ASCE.[3] En otro trabajo para la reunión de 1997, se presentó con mayor detalle una estrategia para lograr una plena reinserción de Cuba en la economía mundial.

Es importante señalar que para que se materialice la cooperación de la comunidad internacional como la expuesta en este trabajo, ello requerirá satisfacer condicionalidades que representarían cambios profundos en la ideología económica y política vigente actualmente en la isla. Ello es ineludible, ya que estas condicionalidades se derivan de los propios mandatos de las agencias financieras internacionales y para que los préstamos sean repagables. Previo a cualquier negociación de la deuda externa para reducir el servicio de

---

3. Por ejemplo, véase Castañeda y Montalván, "Cinco áreas de acción estratégicas para lograr el milagro económico cubano: Una rápida recuperación con un alto y sustentable crecimiento con equidad e inclusión social," *Cuba In Transition—Volume 6* (Washington: ASCE, 1996), pp. 219-233; y "Transition in Cuba: A Comprehensive Stabilization Proposal and Some Key Issues," *Cuba In Transition—Volume 3* (Washington: ASCE, 1993), pp. 11-72. Asimismo, en varios trabajos presentados por otros investigadores en las conferencias de ASCE, se hace referencia a la cooperación financiera y técnica que podría recibir Cuba para su reconstrucción y para apoyar la transición hacia una economía de mercado en el contexto de una democracia representativa. Por ejemplo, José F. Alonso y Armando Lago, en "A First Approximation of the Foreign Assistance Requirements of a Democratic Cuba," *Cuba in Transition—Volume 3* (Washington: ASCE, 1993), pp. 168-219, hacen varios supuestos acerca del monto total de cooperación financiera internacional que Cuba podría recibir de USAID, el BID, el FMI y el Banco Mundial bajo diferentes hipótesis que incluyen en su modelo. Ernest Preeg, en el trabajo "A Five-Year Projection for a Restructured Cuba," *Cuba in Transition—Volume 3* (Washington: ASCE, 1993), pp. 153-167, también hizo varios supuestos acerca del financiamiento externo total que recibiría Cuba en un período de cinco años comenzando en el momento en que se levanta el embargo/bloqueo de EUA.

la deuda y obtener capital fresco de los gobiernos que integran el Club de París, se requiere la adopción de un programa económico con el Fondo Monetario Internacional. Por otra parte, en la reunión celebrada el 26 de junio de 1997, los cancilleres de los países integrantes de la Unión Europea ratificaron su decisión de **no** proporcionar ayuda económica a Cuba hasta tanto se realicen importantes modificaciones en los ámbitos político y económico. La solución para mejorar la calidad de vida del cubano e insertar al país en la economía internacional debería basarse en un crecimiento estable con equidad, abandonando el *statu-quo* del socialismo real, que ha atrapado a Cuba en el atraso económico y social en un mundo muy dinámico y competitivo, sin que ello signifique retornar a la situación de los años 1950, ya que las realidades de Cuba y del mundo han cambiado significativamente, ni la implantación de una solución de corte neoliberal, que nunca parece haber estado en las aspiraciones del pueblo cubano como lo demuestran los acontecimientos políticos en los años 1930 y los principios fundamentales y la orientación de la constitución de 1940.

También es importante subrayar que el objetivo principal de la cooperación internacional en este período, más que proveer capital, es dejar sentadas las condiciones para que el sector privado, nacional y externo, inviertan para reactivar los sectores productivos, así como en ciertas áreas de infraestructura y de servicios públicos. El flujo de capital privado debería exceder con creces la ayuda de la comunidad internacional descrita en este documento. De hecho, el motor del despegue y crecimiento de la economía cubana será indudablemente el sector privado, tanto nacional como de inversionistas extranjeros, dentro de un marco de competencia y libre concurrencia.

Cumpliendo con el principio de contribuir a la más amplia discusión participativa de los ingentes problemas de Cuba y sus posibles soluciones, este es un intento por iniciar un diálogo entre todos los cubanos, que es imprescindible y a la vez inevitable para lograr un proyecto de nación. El documento ha sido enviado a organizaciones cubanas, tanto en Cuba como en el exterior, con objeto de que el mismo sea examinado por todos. Por ejemplo, en cuanto al gobierno de

Cuba se refiere, fue enviado al presidente de la Asamblea Nacional del Poder Popular directamente y a través de la Sección de Intereses de Cuba de la Embajada Suiza en Washington, D.C.

También estaba siendo enviado al *Grupo de Trabajo de la Disidencia Interna*, formado por dirigentes de grupos de profesionales independientes en Cuba: Félix Bonne Carcassés, ingeniero, presidente de la Corriente Cívica Democrática; René Gómez Manzano, abogado, presidente de la Corriente Agramontista; Vladimiro Roca, licenciado en ciencias políticas y presidente del Partido Socialdemócrata de Cuba; y Martha Beatriz Roque Cabello, economista, presidente del Instituto Nacional de Economistas Independientes y coordinadora del Grupo de Trabajo. Estas personas estaban elaborando un ayuda memoria de reacción al documento, que iba a ser incluido como Anexo I, con sus comentarios y sugerencias, tal como lo haría responsablemente un gobierno que estuviera verdaderamente comprometido a lograr niveles crecientes de bienestar del pueblo de Cuba y dispuesto a considerar e implantar las reformas, el proceso de estabilización y los profundos cambios en los planos político, jurídico y económico que se requieren para lograr la recuperación del país. Lamentablemente, el pasado 16 de julio estas personas fueron detenidas por Seguridad del Estado simplemente por mantener una discrepancia pacífica, lo cual es otra manifestación más de la verdadera intolerancia del actual gobierno de permitir la libertad de expresión a los cubanos y su desperdiciadora renuncia a que todos contribuyan a la solución de los problemas nacionales.

Otras agrupaciones a las cuales se está enviando este documento incluyen *Concilio Cubano*, la *Plataforma Democrática Cubana*, la *Fundación Nacional Cubano-Americana y otras dentro y fuera de Cuba*, **dado que el objetivo fundamental es promover el diálogo más amplio posible sobre los problemas que aquejan a la sociedad cubana y, tal vez lo que es más importante, las posibles vías de solución "con todos y para el bien de todos."**

LA SITUACIÓN ACTUAL
El producto interno a precios de 1981 se contrajo de CU$19,585.5 millones (CU$=pesos cubanos) en

1989 a CU$12,868.3 millones en 1994, o sea, una disminución del 34.3 por ciento. La producción cayó en 2.9 por ciento en 1990, 10.7 por ciento en 1991, 11.6 por ciento en 1992 y 14.9 por ciento en 1993, experimentando una recuperación del 0.7 por ciento en 1994, del 2.5 por ciento en 1995 y del 7.8 por ciento en 1996. Las exportaciones, que promediaron cerca de CU$6,000 millones anuales entre 1981 y 1985, cayeron a menos de CU$2,000 millones anuales cada año de 1992 a 1996, o sea a un tercio del nivel previo. Lógicamente ello repercutió en las importaciones, que también se redujeron a la tercera parte del período anterior. Por lo tanto, el nivel y calidad de vida se ha deteriorado considerablemente, especialmente a partir de 1991, lo que se manifiesta en las escaseces alimentarias, el alto grado de hacinamiento habitacional y el deterioro en la provisión de los servicios sociales.

Cuba tiene un significativo excedente monetario. La circulación monetaria, definida como el efectivo en circulación y los depósitos en las cuentas de ahorro, aumentó de CU$4,152.5 millones en 1989 a CU$9,939.7 millones en 1994, es decir, una expansión del 139.4 por ciento. La relación entre dichos activos monetarios y la producción real pasó del 21.2 por ciento en 1989 al 77.2 por ciento en 1994. Dado que los precios oficiales o controlados se han mantenido prácticamente fijos, ello explica la fuerte presión inflacionaria "reprimida" a los precios oficiales vigentes. El Informe del Banco Nacional de Cuba (IBNC) correspondiente al año 1994 no presentó cifras sobre la inflación en los años recientes, ni sobre el circulante y los depósitos en cuentas de ahorro denominados en "pesos convertibles" que comenzaron en diciembre de 1994.

El déficit fiscal aumentó del 7 por ciento del PIB en 1989 a cerca del 40 por ciento del PIB en 1993, pero se redujo al 3.6 por ciento en 1995 y a 2.4 por ciento en 1996. Por otra parte, Cuba se declaró en moratoria de su deuda externa en 1986. Según el IBNC la deuda externa, excluyendo la contraída con el antiguo bloque socialista, ascendía a US$9,082.8 millones en 1994. Esto compara con las exportaciones de bienes y servicios de US$1,314 millones en ese año e implica relaciones de la deuda al PIB y de servicio de la deuda muy superiores al promedio latinoamericano. Se estima que la deuda externa en moneda convertible alcanzó US$11,000 millones a fines de 1996, en tanto que las exportaciones totalizaron US$1,966 millones.[4]

Luego del inmovilismo del período 1989-julio de 1993, Cuba comenzó un cauteloso proceso de reformas económicas a partir de agosto de 1993, orientado a superar los problemas anteriores a la crisis, pero agudizados por ella, tales como el alto nivel de la deuda externa, y por otros que han sido resultado de las erróneas políticas económicas adoptadas durante de la década de los 90, tales como el déficit fiscal, el excedente monetario y la dolarización. El gobierno está realizando un esfuerzo por mantener los niveles de empleo y los servicios de salud, educación y seguridad social, los cuales son elevados para el nivel de producción del país.

Cuba tiene un sistema económico y político muy centralizado. Los mecanismos de mercado, de propiedad privada de los medios de producción y de descentralización de decisiones son parciales y limitados, ya que las reformas económicas adoptadas a partir de 1993, a veces tienen efectos perversos y empobrecedores por la forma en que se están aplicando, especialmente la dolarización y la inversión privada extranjera.

Las fuerzas del mercado sólo se utilizan en los sectores agrícola, artesanal y los servicios personales. La

---

4. Julio Carranza, del Centro de Estudios de la Economía Cubana de la Universidad de La Habana, estima que la deuda externa alcanzó a fines de 1996 un total de US$12,000 millones y que la relación de deuda externa al PIB pasó de 26.7% en 1990 a 71.5% en 1996. Sin embargo, dado que la deuda fue contraída mayormente en marcos alemanes, yenes, francos suizos, pesetas y otras monedas que se han depreciado frente al dólar estadounidense, el total puede ser inferior al estimado por Carranza. Se estima que la deuda contraída con los países del desaparecido bloque socialista, actualmente reclamada por Rusia, tiene un valor equivalente a entre US$20 y 25,000 millones. En el caso de Nicaragua, una vez que el país inició su proceso de reformas y se reintegró a la economía mundial, el gobierno de Rusia condonó aproximadamente un 95% de la deuda de dicho país.

propiedad privada de los medios de producción está limitada a la agricultura, la artesanía y el trabajo por cuenta propia; todas estas actividades fueron ampliadas parcialmente en 1993 y 1994, pero muy reguladas, controladas y con elevados impuestos, los cuales fueron aumentados a niveles prácticamente confiscatorios desde mayo de 1996 y, más recientemente como resultado de la aprobación de una ley de arrendamiento de viviendas, habitaciones o espacios aprobada el 15 de mayo de 1997. Sólo existen pequeños propietarios individuales u organizados en cooperativas que ocupan el 14.9 por ciento de la tierras agrícolas (3.4 por ciento y 11.5 por ciento, respectivamente) y en el área de servicios y artesanías (trabajo por cuenta propia). Entre junio de 1996 y comienzos de 1997, el número de personas registradas como cuentapropistas en las 160 ocupaciones autorizadas se *redujo* de 208,000 a 171,860 (seguramente para evadir los impuestos y otros controles), aunque se estima que hay al menos 250,000 adicionales trabajando clandestinamente y que dicha cifra está creciendo rápidamente. La descentralización de las empresas, especialmente las que efectúan el comercio con el exterior, parece ser una respuesta a los cambios ocurridos en el comercio exterior en general y especialmente con los antiguos países socialistas que ahora se efectúa con empresas y no con los gobiernos.

El sistema político está muy centralizado en Fidel Castro, quien es Presidente de la República, Comandante en Jefe de las Fuerzas Armadas, Primer Secretario del Partido Comunista, Presidente del Consejo de Estado y Presidente del Consejo de Ministros. De hecho, el artículo 74 de la constitución política establece que el "Presidente del Consejo de Estado es jefe de Estado y jefe de Gobierno." Personalmente Castro detuvo los experimentos liberalizadores previos al Tercer Congreso del Partido Comunista de 1986 con el llamado Proceso de Rectificación de Errores y Tendencias Negativas y las propuestas aperturistas del IV Congreso del PCC de octubre de 1991. La Asamblea Nacional del Poder Popular, que es el órgano legislativo, se reúne en período ordinario de sesiones sólo dos veces al año por espacio de tres días para discutir una amplia agenda de trabajo. Así no puede haber una fiscalización efectiva del Poder Ejecutivo. De acuerdo con el informe de 1996, "la subordinación al

poder político de la totalidad del quehacer social cubano, la práctica política del régimen y del ordenamiento jurídico en que dicha práctica se sustenta, el carácter excluyente de toda concepción política distinta y la ausencia de garantías efectivas para que las personas hagan valer sus derechos frente al Estado, permiten considerar a la Comisión Interamericana de Derechos Humanos que *se trata de un sistema político totalitario*".

En cuanto al sector judicial, la constitución política establece en el artículo 121 que "Los tribunales constituyen un sistema de órganos estatales, estructurado con independencia funcional de cualquier otro y *subordinado jerárquicamente a la Asamblea Nacional del Poder Popular y al Consejo de Estado,*" es decir, que establece una relación de *dependencia* con respecto al poder político. En cuanto a las limitaciones a los derechos civiles y políticos, basta citar el artículo 62 de la constitución:

Ninguna de las libertades reconocidas a los ciudadanos puede ser ejercida contra lo establecido en la Constitución y las leyes, ni contra *la existencia y fines del Estado socialista, ni contra la decisión del pueblo cubano de construir el socialismo y el comunismo. La infracción de este derecho es punible* (el énfasis es nuestro).

Es evidente que dichos criterios escapan del ámbito jurídico para situarse en el campo político.

Por otra parte, de acuerdo con el Decreto-Ley Nº 81 de 1984, se establece que para ejercer la abogacía se requiere pertenecer a la Organización Nacional de Bufetes Colectivos y para ingresar a dicha organización se requiere "tener condiciones morales acordes con los principios de nuestra sociedad," lo que en la práctica se utiliza para excluir a quienes discrepan del sistema político vigente.

Con respecto al código penal vigente, la falta de libertad de asociación, expresión y reunión resultan de las figuras penales más frecuentemente utilizadas para caracterizar actividades ilegales, que son las de "propaganda enemiga," "desacato," "asociación ilícita," "clandestinidad de impresos," "peligrosidad," "rebelión," "actos contra la seguridad del Estado," etc. Junto con estas imprecisiones que se prestan para todo tipo de arbitrariedades, el Decreto Nº 128 de 1991, que complementa el código penal, establece la declaración del estado peligroso predelictivo, el cual debe decidirse en forma sumaria.

De acuerdo con el Informe del Relator Especial de las Naciones Unidas de 1996, Cuba tiene en la actualidad 294 prisiones y campos de trabajo correccional, con un estimado de entre 100,000 y 200,000 presos de todas las categorías. El Informe de la Comisión Interamericana de Derechos Humanos de 1996 señala que "las graves condiciones a las que, diariamente, es sometida la población carcelaria en Cuba sobrepasan ampliamente a las que dan cuenta de las violaciones de otros derechos consagrados en la Declaración Americana."

Por último, en cuanto a la situación laboral de los trabajadores en un país cuya constitución política comienza diciendo que "Cuba es un Estado socialista de trabajadores, ..." (Artículo 1º), un informe reciente de Naciones Unidas señala de la manera siguiente la contradicción entre los postulados ideológicos del sistema y la operación práctica del mismo, en relación con los trabajadores en empresas de capital extranjero:

... en particular por la falta de todo tipo de negociación colectiva y por la arbitrariedad que supone el que la contratación, el pago de salarios, la terminación de contratos y otros aspectos del vínculo laboral no se realice en forma directa entre la empresa y el empleado, sino a través de una entidad empleadora designada por el Gobierno. Los mismos criterios discriminatorios por motivos ideológicos que rigen en otros ámbitos pueden también ser aplicables en el marco de estas empresas, con lo que el control gubernamental sobre los trabajadores queda asegurado. ... los salarios no son pagados directamente a los trabajadores, sino a la empleadora gubernamental que los devenga en moneda fuerte y posteriormente paga al trabajador en moneda nacional. La diferencia entre los salarios pagados por la empresa y los efectivamente pagados al trabajador por la entidad empleadora se estima que es

considerable, lo que permite al Estado obtener sustanciosos beneficios en detrimento de lo que el trabajador hubiera podido percibir. Además, la ley establece que cuando las empresas mixtas o las empresas de capital totalmente extranjero consideren que un determinado trabajador no satisface sus exigencias en el trabajo pueden solicitar a la entidad empleadora que lo sustituya por otro, sin que exista ninguna protección legal.[5]

Estas preocupaciones han sido recogidas en los "Principios Arcos," los cuales han recibido el respaldo de organizaciones cubanas dentro y fuera de la isla, así como de instituciones de otros países.

El fundamentalismo o la línea dura del socialismo económico ha prevalecido sobre el pragmatismo o el reformismo por casi 37 años. Hubo una amplia y detallada discusión en los años 1960 que culminó con la *Gran Ofensiva Revolucionaria* que confiscó y estatizó las pequeñas y medianas empresas comerciales e industriales en 1968. También hubo un proceso de apertura y mayor racionalidad económica en 1975-1985 con el *Sistema de Dirección y Planificación de la Economía*, que terminó abruptamente con el *Proceso de Rectificación de Errores y Tendencias Negativas* en 1986, cuando se eliminaron los mercados libres campesinos, los mercados artesanales, el mercado de viviendas, los bonos y otros incentivos materiales a los trabajadores, y el cálculo económico a nivel de las empresas.

El Proceso de Rectificación se realizó cuando todos los otros países socialistas (tanto en Europa como en Asia, excepto Corea del Norte) estaban en algún proceso de apertura y reforma económica. También dicho proceso demostró fehacientemente que las reformas económicas en Cuba no son irreversibles. La dirigencia cubana basó la Gran Ofensiva y la Rectificación en la "corrupción prevaleciente" en la sociedad, pero realmente se debió al enriquecimiento de individuos y funcionarios en un sistema empresarial que tiene dos o más precios diferentes para un

---

5. Naciones Unidas, *El disfrute de los derechos económicos, sociales y culturales*, A/50/663 (24 de octubre de 1995), p. 20. El artículo 45 del Decreto-Ley Nº 45 del 3 de junio de 1996 sobre creación de zonas francas y parques industriales reafirma esta práctica laboral discriminatoria y explotadora del trabajador cubano.

mismo bien, uno en el mercado oficial y otro en el mercado libre o en el negro ("clandestino").

Los altos niveles de gastos sociales se han podido mantener en el período 1959-1997 debido a que se ha obtenido una fuente de financiamiento independiente del nivel de ineficiencia del aparato productivo de la economía. En la década de los 1960 los gastos sociales se pudieron mantener principalmente por el excedente generado por el uso de las tierras ociosas de los latifundios y la eliminación de las remesas de ganancias al exterior por las empresas confiscadas; en 1970-1985 por el endeudamiento externo y la ayuda externa del desaparecido campo socialista; en 1986-1991 por la ayuda soviética; y más recientemente, en 1992-1996, por la inversión extranjera y las remesas del exterior. Esto ha creado una fuerte dependencia del exterior.

Actualmente las remesas de cubanos en el exterior—que se estima están entre US$650 y 800 millones para 1996—constituyen el estímulo principal de la economía, ya que son superiores al valor de las exportaciones de azúcar (US$673 millones en 1996), a los ingresos netos del turismo y, lo que resulta verdaderamente increíble, al valor total de los ingresos salariales de la población cubana (alrededor de US$525 millones en 1996).[6] Ello a pesar de que el gobierno de Estados Unidos ha impuesto restricciones a las remesas procedentes de ese país.

La dirigencia política considera que los problemas principales del país tienen origen externo: el injusto orden internacional, la caída del bloque socialista, la desaparición de la Unión Soviética, y el recrudecimiento del embargo/bloqueo norteamericano, primero por la Ley Torricelli de octubre de 1992 y después por la Ley Helms-Burton de octubre de 1996. Reiteradamente ha ignorado la fragilidad y vulnerabilidad del sistema económico que ha desarrollado.

Cuba tiene indefiniciones y postergaciones de políticas, así como instituciones precarias e incompletas; la economía tal cual existe es muy débil y vulnerable y se considera que puede colapsar en cualquier momento.

RESUMEN DE ÁREAS Y TEMAS CLAVES DE POLÍTICA ECONÓMICA

Los temas macroeconómicos centrales[7]

Débil capacidad de formulación de políticas económicas y financieras: Por años la política económica en Cuba ha estado subordinada a las concepciones del "hombre nuevo" y de la organización social comunista. Concretamente en los últimos años las políticas e instituciones económicas y financieras del gobierno han sido principalmente erróneas en su diseño y por su insuficiente aplicación cuando son correctas en las áreas de estabilización, incentivos para aumentar la producción a mediano y largo plazo, movilizar recursos externos, insertar internacionalmente al país, lograr niveles adecuados de inversión y ahorro nacionales, etc. En el futuro el gobierno deberá adoptar políticas e instituciones que promuevan el crecimiento y evitar políticas que lo obstruyan. Un crecimiento alto y sostenido es la condición indispensable para que la población alcance mayores niveles de ingreso, empleo y bienestar, así como garantice condiciones apropiadas de vida a la población más vulnerable, lo que conducirá a una sociedad más integrada a mediano y largo plazo y permitirá un apoyo mayoritario al proceso de transforma ción hacia una economía más participativa.

El gobierno deberá crear efectos positivos sobre el crecimiento emprendiendo políticas e instituciones en las siete áreas que se identifican a continuación, pero también deberá evitar efectos negativos sobre el crecimiento, tales como malgastar fondos en proyectos de inversión sin ningún valor económico, en bu-

---

6. De acuerdo con el informe sobre los resultados económicos de 1996 y el plan económico y social para 1997 presentado por José Luis Rodríguez, ministro de economía y planificación, ante la Asamblea Nacional del Poder Popular en diciembre de 1996, el salario promedio en Cuba para 1996 fue de CU$203 mensuales lo cual, a la tasa de cambio obtenida en las casas de cambio en el país (CU$23/US$1), resulta en un **salario anual promedio del trabajador cubano equivalente a US$105.** En la actualidad, se estima la fuerza de trabajo en alrededor de 5 millones de personas.

7. Si bien no nos referimos al requerimiento de la democracia política en el trabajo, consideramos que ésta es imprescindible para realmente despolitizar y racionalizar las decisiones económicas.

rocracias sobredimensionadas, y manteniendo impuestos confiscatorios y regulaciones que distorsionan las decisiones de asignación presente y futura de recursos (ahorro e inversión).

Los países exitosos económicamente son los que analizan permanentemente cómo están, o sea evitan la autosatisfacción y conocen integralmente y con exactitud su realidad, así como qué medidas deben adoptar para reaccionar frente a las nuevas realidades, tendencias y los cambios económicos y sociales. Cuba no ha enfrentado aún seriamente el proceso modernizador y globalizante en marcha en el mundo contemporáneo que le permita atender sus urgentes necesidades económicas y sociales. Además, un elemento clave de la modernidad es incorporar a *todos* los ciudadanos—no únicamente los que comparten la ideología del partido que ejerce el gobierno—al proceso de desarrollo.

Necesidad de saneamiento y estabilización: Como se indicó anteriormente, Cuba tiene un significativo excedente monetario en relación con su nivel de actividad económica y nivel de precios, lo que se debe en parte a la represión y al escaso desarrollo institucional financiero, y es agravado por la dolarización y la segmentación financiera, y se genera principalmente por el elevado déficit fiscal (ver sección siguiente). Asimismo, terminar con la dolarización y el excedente monetario acumulado por varios años de déficit fiscales y de deficientes políticas monetarias y cambiarias, mediante un paquete coherente de medidas de reforma monetaria, devaluación y régimen cambiario fijo, de que el banco central actúe independientemente para mantener la estabilidad económica y el tipo de cambio, y garantizar un sistema de regulación y supervisión financieras prudentes.[8] Con ello se logrará la estabilización y se evitará el choque monetario y la consecuente recesión que han sufrido los antiguos países socialistas europeos. Entonces se podrá iniciar un proceso gradual, pero integral y progresivo, de liberalización, desregulación e institucionalización para lograr la ampliación, profundización y

diversificación de la economía de mercado, que es tan importante para el crecimiento económico y la privatización de la economía.

El saneamiento y la estabilización, o sea, restaurar el balance del nivel de precios (equilibrio interno) y de la tasa de cambio (equilibrio externo) y eliminar el racionamiento, las colas y las escaseces actuales, son requisitos indispensables para la recuperación rápida y el crecimiento sustentable a mediano y largo plazo mediante una relación adecuada entre la disponibilidad y la demanda efectiva de recursos. Sin embargo, la razón de ser de la estabilización es el establecimiento de condiciones que faciliten un crecimiento sostenido, la orientación de la economía hacia el exterior y el comercio internacional, la institucionalización y la privatización. También crearán un ambiente propicio para la reunificación de la nación cubana, una concertación nacional económica y social, y el fortalecimiento de la democracia participativa.

La estabilización supone un programa inicial de muy corto plazo, rápido y efectivo—de unos seis meses—destinado a detener la inflación, ahora reprimida, antes que se liberen los precios y se restablezca parcialmente la libre convertibilidad externa. Estas medidas iniciales serían simples y fáciles de implantar, y se complementarían por otras aplicadas al manejo de la política monetaria y fiscal, a efectuar reformas institucionales y jurídicas, a atraer recursos del exterior y a reestructurar el aparato productivo, que requieren más tiempo para ejecutarse.

El éxito de la estabilización en el primer año se puede determinar por una tasa de inflación anual del 30% al 40%, un nivel del déficit fiscal del 3 por ciento del PIB financiado por medios no inflacionarios, el mantenimiento de tasas de interés positivas elevadas en términos reales (cercanas al 6%), un nivel de déficit en la cuenta corriente financiado con inversión privada y movimientos de capital de largo plazo y el mantenimiento de un tipo de cambio real competitivo.

8. El Decreto-Ley No. 72 del 28 de mayo de 1997 sobre la creación del Banco Central de Cuba representa un primer paso, si bien tímido, en la dirección correcta, ya que no es independiente, por cuanto tiene la facultad de *proponer* y, una vez aprobadas, dirigir la aplicación de las políticas monetaria y cambiaria.

Débil gestión financiera del sector público: Como se indicó anteriormente, es imprescindible superar la insostenible situación de déficit significativos del sector público. A tal efecto, las finanzas públicas se deberán balancear inicialmente con el aumento de los precios y las tarifas de las empresas públicas, la reducción de los subsidios y los gastos innecesarios (militares, políticos, administrativos), la racionalización de los gastos sociales, así como el establecimiento de impuestos. En la nueva estrategia de crecimiento basada en una economía de mercado, el estado tiene un rol central en establecer las políticas e instituciones que garanticen la estabilidad macroeconómica, facilitar la acumulación de capital humano de los más pobres, asegurar la existencia de un marco regulador para la promoción de la competencia tanto en servicios básicos como en la economía como un todo, facilitar y desarrollar directamente la infraestructura básica cuando tiene un elemento de bien público, garantizar el cumplimiento de los derechos de propiedad, mejorar la planificación y el suministro de los servicios públicos, y desarrollar e implementar medidas encaminadas a reducir la extrema pobreza.

La política fiscal austera pretende reducir el exceso de demanda agregada y que el sector público tenga fuentes propias de financiamiento (presupuesto balanceado de gastos corrientes y de capital, incluyendo financiamiento por deuda interna y externa hasta un límite del 3% del PIB), con lo cual se eliminaría la causa principal de los desbalances internos y una de las causas más importantes de los desbalances externos. Si no se controla el déficit fiscal, una vez se liberen los precios, se podría desatar una espiral inflacionaria de precios/salarios/tasa de cambio.

Reducción del papel del estado y racionalización de las empresas públicas: La expansión y el mejoramiento de la infraestructura económica y de la calidad del capital humano son dos áreas que requieren de una profunda reestructuración del estado, de manera de racionalizar el gasto público, promover la participación de la iniciativa privada en estas áreas y dar lugar a este tipo de gastos en el presupuesto público (más efectivos y menos costosos). En particular, se requiere reducir la participación del sector público en las actividades que pueden ser desarrolladas por el sector privado en un marco de competencia y eficiencia. Algunos países latinoamericanos han desarrollado esquemas que promueven la participación del sector privado en actividades que hasta ahora sólo las realizaba el sector público (tales como: teléfonos, electricidad, gas, agua y saneamiento), así como en los servicios de educación, salud y seguridad social, y en obras de infraestructura, principalmente a través de concesiones, desarrollando para este propósito un marco regulador apropiado para permitir al sector privado invertir en las mismas.

Necesidad de un sistema apropiado de incentivos que promueva una asignación más eficiente de los recursos: En 1997 Cuba tiene niveles de ingreso por habitante sustancialmente inferiores a los de 1985 y es necesario incentivar conductas que estimulen la producción de bienes y servicios. Cuba con un régimen de comercio muy distorsionado y mercados de bienes no-competitivos, tiene mucho que ganar con la adopción prácticas competitivas y con la liberación del comercio a través del tiempo. Para ello requiere incentivos adecuados que promuevan la eficiencia, la competitividad externa y el crecimiento económico. Por el lado de los bienes y servicios no financieros se requiere que los precios internos de los bienes transables (los bienes exportables y bienes que compiten con las importaciones) se asemejen a los precios en los mercados internacionales y que los servicios públicos sean eficientes y a precios que reflejen los costos marginales de producción. En particular, la inserción internacional con la eliminación de las barreras no arancelarias y aranceles cuya tendencia es a ser bajos y uniformes es la vía para lograr incentivos adecuados. A través de las señales entregadas por estos incentivos se promueve una estructura de producción y de consumo que le permitirá a Cuba beneficiarse plenamente de las amplias oportunidades que brinda el comercio internacional.

En el área de servicios no financieros, es necesario establecer y desarrollar un marco regulador que promueva la iniciativa privada, la competencia y la eficiencia en sectores de infraestructura básica, tales como: telecomunicaciones, electricidad, agua y saneamiento, puertos, aeropuertos y transporte de carga y de pasajeros. Los significativos avances tecnológicos recientes y la creación de un marco regulador que promueva la libre concurrencia y la competencia permitirán mejorar la eficiencia en estas áreas, lo que estimulará la inversión, al mismo tiempo que permitirán liberar al sector público para concentrar su actividad en áreas prioritarias donde tiene un rol central.

En el área de servicios financieros se requiere en el área bancaria establecer requerimientos mínimos de capital, una regulación prudencial y una supervisión adecuada que promuevan la libre concurrencia y competencia y que al mismo tiempo eviten el abuso de activos riesgosos y los seguros implícitos y explícitos de depósitos. Una vez que se haya avanzado en estos requisitos se debe proceder a eliminar paulatinamente los controles a las tasas de interés.

En los mercados de factores productivos se requiere liberar el mercado laboral para facilitar el ajuste de la economía, la competitividad de los bienes transables y promover la creación de empleos, especialmente para los grupos laborales con menores calificaciones y destrezas cuyas posibilidades de empleo se ven generalmente reducidas por prácticas y políticas laborales que limitan su ingreso al mercado del trabajo o que distorsionan en contra de su uso. Las reformas del mercado de trabajo implican reformas institucionales, jurídicas, de políticas y el establecimiento de sistemas de información sobre dicho mercado. En el caso de la agricultura es necesario realizar un proceso de regularización de la tenencia de la propiedad de la tierra.

El proceso de liberalización tiene como objetivo establecer y lograr el funcionamiento apropiado de mercados libres y competitivos, utilizados como mecanismos principales en la asignación de recursos, ayudados a su vez por la reducción y eliminación de obstáculos indebidos al sector privado, tales como: prohibiciones, controles y restricciones que no cumplan una función económica positiva.

La amplitud y profundidad de la propiedad socialista, la centralización y complejidad burocrática en las decisiones económicas, la organización monopólica y oligopólica de la producción, y la estructura de precios muy distorsionada, dificultan los procesos de desregulación, apertura y privatización, propios de

una auténtica y radical solución, como lo están haciendo muchos países latinoamericanos, los antiguos países socialistas en Europa Oriental, la Unión Soviética, China y Vietnam y como lo han hecho con éxito los países del Asia Oriental y Chile.

La liberalización y la privatización están orientadas a aumentar la flexibilidad, la eficiencia y la capacidad de adaptación en asignación de los recursos existentes, así como la aplicación de tecnologías ampliamente conocidas conformando la base fundamental de apoyo para el fomento de la inversión y el ahorro. A medida que se consoliden estos procesos habrá un mayor nivel de inversión y ahorro y mayores tasas de crecimiento económico.

Estas aperturas fomentarían la existencia y desarrollo de un aparato productivo eficiente y competitivo, en consonancia con el entorno internacional globalizado altamente competitivo que prevalece hoy día. La liberalización deberá ir acompañada de un trabajo decidido de organización y desarrollo de mercados, sobre todo en la agricultura y servicios, para que el agricultor y el trabajador por cuenta propia se beneficien directamente de la expansión de la producción. La liberalización requiere una normatividad apropiada y transparente, mejor que la prevaleciente antes del gobierno socialista, la cual mostraba una serie de sesgos y preferencias monopólicas, en favor de la industria del azúcar y laborales, y de las que se han utilizado en los antiguos países socialistas de Europa Oriental, de la Unión Soviética, China y Vietnam.

Desde el principio de su historia republicana, lamentablemente Cuba se vio afectada por una tradición de corrupción generalizada, lo que llevó al establecimiento del Tribunal de Cuentas a mediados de siglo. En la era socialista dicha tradición se ha mantenido y quizás profundizado, evidenciado por la frecuente destitución de altos funcionarios por cargos de corrupción, así como la condena de la dirigencia política a las prácticas generalizadas de *sociolismo* o favoritismo y el robo a las empresas del estado y a las empresas mixtas con capital extranjero. Es evidente que en Cuba la corrupción es un fenómeno que está arraigado en los valores de la sociedad y en los sistemas y las prácticas que determinan las relaciones humanas, incluidas las relaciones entre individuos y su interacción con sus gobiernos y los funcionarios públicos. Por ello es imprescindible tomar en consideración el sistema educativo y los medios de comunicación en cualquier estrategia de combate a la corrupción. En cuanto a las acciones respaldadas directamente por la cooperación internacional, será necesario establecer, desde el comienzo de la transición, mecanismos que aseguren alta responsabilidad y probidad en la gestión y administración públicas mediante sistemas modernos y competitivos de adquisición de bienes y servicios, construcción de obras, y enajenación de bienes del estado, así como el establecimiento de sistemas modernos y transparentes de control y auditoría y de participación y fiscalización ciudadana.

Liberalización de la pequeña y mediana empresa y del trabajo por cuenta propia: La amplitud, profundidad y persistencia de los desbalances internos y externos de la economía y los principales factores de la crisis sistémica (la propiedad socialista y la regulación a la iniciativa privada) hacen difícil el proceso de estabilización sin recesión. La capacidad de respuesta de los agentes económicos a las medidas macroeconómicas tradicionales no es igual en una economía socialista extrema. Por ello la importancia de emprender desde el inicio algunas reformas estructurales complementarias (institucionales y de liberalización y desregulación de los mercados para actividades claves) para establecer un marco favorable a la economía de mercado y sanear el funcionamiento de la economía. Así, se busca consistencia entre las medidas de tipo macroeconómico y la creciente capacidad de respuesta a las mismas por los agentes económicos, mediante indispensables reformas microeconómicas estructurales, tales como: desregulación, desmonopolización y privatización. Esto hará posible que las metas de estabilización y transformación se alcancen a plenitud.

Los efectos inmediatos de la política de estabilización (reducción del déficit fiscal y del excedente monetario, tasas de interés reales positivas y crédito restrictivo) son recesivos y deben desalentar la inversión privada. Por ello es muy importante tomar medidas para contrarrestar estas tendencias, alentando desde el principio la producción agrícola y de los trabajadores por cuenta propia mediante la desregulación de sus actividades, eliminando prohibiciones, controles, restricciones e impuestos confiscatorios, así como autorizando la micro, pequeña y mediana empresa en todas las actividades. Las experiencias de China y Vietnam con estas medidas fue muy exitosa y debe utilizarse. También merecen especial consideración las propuestas de economistas en *cuasi*-ONGs cubanas (por ejemplo, el trabajo de Carranza, Gutiérrez Urdaneta y Monreal en el Centro de Estudios sobre América, en La Habana) u otras similares para producir un cambio inicial positivo sin crear el caos generalizado en el sector estatal, que ha sido el éxito de China y Vietnam en comparación con Europa Oriental.

Si bien la búsqueda de crecimiento durante el proceso de estabilización pudiera reducir su efectividad, el caso de Cuba envuelve la rehabilitación imprescindible de la oferta agregada. Cuba tiene un amplio potencial de recuperación por los recursos no utilizados y los asignados y utilizados ineficientemente en la agricultura y en el trabajo por cuenta propia, además del potencial para lograr incrementos en productividad con tecnologías conocidas y fácilmente disponibles mediante la micro, pequeña y mediana empresa. Seguir con una subutilización innecesaria de la capacidad productiva y con el estancamiento o la caída de la producción, podría aumentar los costos sociales a niveles intolerables, y generar conflictos y tensiones distributivas inmanejables que podrían detener el proceso de transformación como ha sucedido en varios países de Europa Oriental o aún revertirlo.

Movilización de recursos externos y liberalización del sector externo: Cuba enfrenta una severa crisis del sector externo caracterizada por déficit crónicos de balanza de pagos, moratoria de la deuda externa, tasas de interés muy elevadas para los créditos comerciales externos, vulnerabilidad extrema del sector externo, etc. La promoción de un robusto y sólido crecimiento de las exportaciones es básica en cualquier estrategia de recuperación y desarrollo, la cual debe orientarse al principio a la utilización de la capacidad instalada del turismo, la industria azucarera, y de otros productos tradicionales (tabaco, cítricos y níquel). Es necesario diseñar una política económica dirigida desde el inicio a aumentar las exportaciones de bienes y servicios, atraer la inversión extranjera, los préstamos externos oficiales, y las remesas y transferencias del exterior, y renegociar de la deuda, permitiendo así una mayor capacidad de importaciones y un mayor nivel de actividad económica con la capacidad instalada. Ello permitiría superar el principal cuello de botella que Cuba enfrenta actualmente y recuperaría el nivel de la producción, disminuyendo los costos de la estabilización.

Se debería ajustar (devaluar) y fijar inicialmente un nivel cambiario para que las exportaciones sean competitivas el cual se iría ajustando paulatinamente después para que las exportaciones se puedan expandir sostenidamente. No se debería permitir la libertad de entrada y salida de capitales de corto plazo, ni las flotaciones cambiarias, ni tasas de interés muy elevadas en términos reales, que determinarían un bajo crecimiento con estabilidad. Al hacerlo la tasa de cambio quedaría fijada por debajo del nivel de competitividad externa, debido a que es imposible atender desde el inicio la elevada deuda externa y a que tasas de interés reales muy altas atraerían una gran entrada de capitales de corto plazo que tendería a sobrevaluar la moneda y a desalentar las exportaciones y que pondrían en una situación muy riesgosa a las empresas productivas que se endeuden, así como las instituciones financieras que le presten.

Con sistemas de tipo de cambio fijo o deajustes períodicos, la integración a los mercados de capitales internacionales reduce de manera significativa la efectividad de la política monetaria. Para maximizar los beneficios netos de la integración a los mercados internacionales de capitales, se debe evitar, a través de un manejo macroeconómico prudente, que fuertes ingresos de capitales de naturaleza especulativa y muy volátiles resulten en una caída de la tasa de ahorro interno, una aceleración de la inflación y una caída pronunciada e insostenible del tipo de cambio real, al financiar aumentos en los niveles de consumo más que en los niveles de inversión.

Mayores tasas de inversión y de ahorro nacional: Cuba tiene niveles de inversión y ahorro nacional muy bajos, que es indispensable aumentar significativamente para lograr un crecimiento alto y sustentable. El aumento en la tasa y en la eficiencia de la inversión privada depende fundamentalmente de un ambiente macroeconómico estable y de marcos institucionales, derechos de propiedad y reglas impositivas, claros y predecibles. También se requiere de un sector financiero bien capitalizado y sujeto a una regulación y supervisión adecuada, que por su solvencia y eficiencia sea capaz de canalizar eficientemente recursos financieros desde grupos con superávit netos de fondos hacia grupos demandantes netos de ellos. Para esto último, se requiere que existan los incentivos para que se desarrolle un sistema bancario y financiero con una capacidad para evaluar proyectos y medir su riesgo adecuadamente. Asimismo, que establezca las bases para ampliar, profundizar y diversificar el sistema financiero que facilite el ahorro e inversiones de alta rentabilidad y un crecimiento alto y sustentable.

Con la introducción de un programa de reformas estructurales, sin embargo, la estructura de incentivos cambia continuamente, lo cual introduce una gran incertidumbre con respecto a cuál va a ser la estructura permanente de incentivos. En estas circunstancias no es de sorprender que algunos inversionistas preferirán esperar hasta tener una idea más clara de la evolución probable de los precios relativos, antes de comprometer recursos de inversión. Esta respuesta lenta de la inversión es una característica muy común de la mayoría de los programas de reformas estructurales, y especialmente de programas de reformas que comienzan (y a veces que terminan) con poca credibilidad y, por consiguiente, con poca viabilidad política. De ahí la importancia de emprender programas de reformas con objetivos y programas claramente definidos y aplicados decididamente.

Por ello es necesario alentar la inversión privada decididamente, mediante un nivel de tributación bajo a las empresas, incentivos tributarios para ganancias reinvertidas, regímenes temporales de depreciación acelerada, un régimen tributario que ajuste las ganancias de capital y los ingresos por intereses por la inflación, que no tema a los subsidios implícitos a la inversión a través de la privatización de empresas vendidas por debajo de su valor real, etc.

Para lograr un aumento sostenible en la tasa de inversión es necesario también lograr aumentos sostenidos en las tasas de ahorro nacional. Una vez que la economía comienza a crecer, se presenta una dinámica virtuosa porque una mayor tasa de crecimiento deberá resultar en una mayor tasa de ahorro.

Reforma de los sectores sociales

Necesidad de implantar una profunda reforma educativa en todos los niveles: Con la crisis de los años 90, la educación—sector en el cual el gobierno de Cuba invirtió sustanciales recursos y logró importantes avances en la reducción del analfabetismo, en la tasa de escolarización en todos los niveles, así como en la enseñanza superior en varias ramas científicas en el período 1960-90—no ha escapado del deterioro general del país. Aún cuando la tasa de escolarización a nivel de primaria se ha mantenido, ha habido una declinación significativa en los niveles de secundaria y superior, y todo parece indicar que la tasa de deserción en esos dos niveles se ha disparado como consecuencia de la dolarización y las distorsiones existentes que brindan incentivos erróneos. Por ejemplo, en la actualidad un docente tiene un salario mensual promedio de 250 pesos, que equivale aproximadamente a US$11 al tipo de cambio que se obtiene en las casas de cambio en el país; el salario mensual promedio de un médico es 350 pesos, o aproximadamente US$15. En cambio, los que trabajan directa o indirectamente en el turismo o con empresas extranjeras—muchos de ellos en trabajos que no requieren formación académica (por ejemplo, mozos, maleteros, taxistas, mensajeros, etc.) tienen la posibilidad de ganar mucho más directamente en dólares por vía de propinas, venta de mercancías o servicios directos. Otro importante desincentivo a la educación secundaria y superior es la restricción legal a las ocupaciones en las que se puede trabajar por cuenta propia, ya que el peso ha perdido su valor monetario. Además, la educación en Cuba está altamente politizada—tal como se puede notar en el contenido del *Expediente Acumulativo Escolar,* que se requiere que tenga cada alumno y que se toma en consideración para efectos de empleo—tanto desde el punto de vista organizativo como sustantivo.

Debido a lo anterior, se necesita llevar a cabo una profunda reforma educativa en Cuba, junto con las otras reformas indicadas en este documento, a fin de:

(a) mejorar la eficiencia interna (reducir la repitencia y la deserción a niveles primario y secundario) y la externa (relacionando más directamente la enseñanza con las exigencias del mercado de trabajo en un mundo competitivo, especialmente a niveles secundario y superior) estableciendo normas de calidad para la enseñanza y evaluación de desempeño educativo rigurosas; (b) despolitizar la educación vía reforma curricular, la modernización de textos junto con su impresión y distribución, y la certificación de escuelas y docentes; y (c) liberalizar el sector, permitiendo la participación de grupos religiosos y del sector privado, siempre que se cumpla rigurosamente con la normatividad establecida. Además, será necesario rehabilitar las escuelas primarias y secundarias públicas e introducir sistemas de recuperación de costos a nivel superior. Asimismo, en vista de que nos encontramos en un mundo en que la riqueza está cada vez más determinada en función del conocimiento y la información, sería importante llevar a cabo un proyecto para garantizar el acceso a computadoras, sistemas de información y al Internet, a todos los alumnos de las escuelas en Cuba.

Salud, saneamiento y medio ambiente: El sector de salud en Cuba se ha caracterizado por haber logrado mejoras significativas en las condiciones de salud de la población, comparables hasta principios de la década de los 90 a los de los países industrializados, pero a un costo que en 1993 representó el 11.7% del PIB. A pesar del alto costo y de la grave crisis que atraviesa el país, se destaca el crecimiento del 7% de las asignaciones para la salud pública en el presupuesto aprobado para 1997. El reto para una reforma del sector salud es mantener el estado actual de la salud a un costo sustancialmente menor, mediante la reducción de personal no médico, de servicios ambulatorios (por ejemplo, visitas médicas a domicilio) y de los altos costos administrativos del ministerio de salud pública. En cuanto a opciones de financiamiento, éstas deberían ser objeto de estudio y la realización de proyectos piloto, pero en cualquier caso se debería instituir un proceso de privatización gradual de servicios médicos, comenzando tal vez por los servicios de médicos de familia y en hospitales, a ser financiados con un seguro de salud a través del cual el Estado le garantice un paquete de servicios básicos a toda la población.

Existe un diagnóstico de la situación del sector de agua potable y saneamiento realizado en 1994 por técnicos cubanos, con la participación de especialistas de la Organización Panamericana de la Salud (OPS), en el cual se plantea la necesidad de inversiones por un total de US$1,390 millones, así como reformas que incluyen el establecimiento de tarifas para servicios. Tal como es el caso en otros sectores (por ejemplo, carreteras), el plan supone la participación de capital privado en estos servicios, pero seguramente bajo las modalidades actuales que rigen la inversión extranjera.

De acuerdo con el diagnóstico, en 1993, *nominalmente*—porque se reconoce que "estas coberturas están asociadas a redes de acueducto y de alcantarillado con un elevado porcentaje en estado técnico regular o malo"—las coberturas de servicio intradomiciliario de agua alcanzaron 83% en el área urbana y 30% en el área rural (versus un promedio general de 78% para América Latina), mientras que las coberturas de alcantarillado fueron de 40% y 5% respectivamente (versus el promedio general para América Latina de 48%).

Aún cuando una primera parte de las inversiones en rehabilitación—aquellas que están en la situación más crítica y representan mayores peligros para la salud pública—podrían ser financiadas como parte de un Programa de Emergencia, será necesario previo a la aprobación de un programa más amplio a nivel nacional de rehabilitación, desarrollo operacional y soporte, realizar los estudios y elaborar y poner en vigencia las disposiciones legales para reformar el sector, establecer un marco regulador apropiado, determinar las modalidades de prestación de servicios y especificar la participación del sector privado.

Seguridad social: Cuba requiere crear un sistema de pensiones privadas mediante fondos de cuentas individuales en vez de un sistema público de reparto para estimular el esfuerzo y el trabajo personal, al asociarlos con los resultados de la jubilación. Este sistema también podría ser muy efectivo para vincular a los asociados con las inversiones que realizan y facilitaría

recursos de largo plazo para el financiamiento de las inversiones privadas. Además, se requiere modificar las edades mínimas de jubilación y crear mecanismos transparentes de regulación y supervisión de los fondos de previsión para asegurar niveles mínimos de rentabilidad y reducir el riesgo de las carteras.

El sector público y la reforma institucional

La modernización del estado y el fortalecimiento de la sociedad civil son procesos complementarios sin los cuales no será sustentable el proceso de reforma económica y social. Basado en otras experiencias, los lineamientos fundamentales de una estrategia serían: (a) reforma del marco legal y regulatorio; (b) adecuada secuencia de implantación de un programa selectivo, con objeto de lograr sustentabilidad de las reformas; y (c) logro de una concertación política efectiva de respaldo a las reformas.

Tal como ha ocurrido en todos los sistemas de gobierno socialistas, el estado cubano está extremadamente sobredimensionado. Más del 90% de los ingresos del estado provienen de un gran número de empresas públicas, aunque en su conjunto éstas arrojan pérdidas operativas significativas. Hacia fines de la década de los 80, el empleo en el sector estatal era de más de 3.5 millones de personas, de una fuerza de trabajo menor a 5 millones. No hay datos disponibles sobre el número de personas empleadas en el gobierno central, pero éste cuenta con 26 ministerios además de varias agencias. La reforma del estado cubano debería enfocarse al establecimiento de un papel rector, racionalizando la administración pública y la intervención del estado en la economía.

En cuanto al poder ejecutivo, será necesario: (a) implantar un sistema de administración financiera integrada, incluyendo administración tributaria, aduanas, presupuesto público, seguridad social, así como el fortalecimiento de las entidades encargadas de la supervisión y control de la administración financiera; (b) establecer un servicio civil profesional, incluyendo programas de capacitación, para mejorar la efectividad en el funcionamiento del sector público; (c) fortalecer la capacidad de formulación y ejecución de políticas públicas; y (d) establecer y fortalecer la capacidad institucional y normativa del estado a fin de que pueda desempeñar funciones de regulación de manera transparente y eficiente.

El ejercicio de la democracia requiere de un poder legislativo capaz de forjar consenso político en relación con el proceso de reformas económicas y sociales. La Asamblea Nacional del Poder Popular se reúne sólo dos veces al año mayormente para aprobar los proyectos propuestos sin modificaciones importantes y adolece de debilidades técnicas e institucionales, además de una falta general de credibilidad.

Con objeto de mejorar el funcionamiento del poder legislativo en Cuba, ya sea de la Asamblea Nacional del Poder Popular o de un órgano sucesor a consecuencia de las profundas reformas constitucionales requeridas, será necesario: (a) capacitar a grupos de parlamentarios en áreas técnicas y de políticas públicas; (b) establecer sistemas para mejorar y realizar control de calidad del trabajo legislativo, incluyendo el desarrollo de sistemas de información; y (c) establecer una organización parlamentaria profesional.

Con relación al poder judicial, en primer lugar será necesario realizar profundas reformas—o reemplazar completamente—la constitución política, al código penal y a otras leyes a fin de garantizar la total independencia del sistema jurídico del poder político, garantizar las libertades constitucionales sin limitaciones políticas, así como para promover una administración eficiente e imparcial de la justicia con el objetivo principal de establecer un verdadero Estado de Derecho en Cuba. Por otra parte, será imprescindible modernizar el marco jurídico general, incluyendo áreas de alta prioridad tales como códigos de bancarrota, empresas, seguridad social, inversión extranjera, propiedad intelectual, laboral, tributario, presupuestario, comercial y electoral.

BOSQUEJO DE UN PROGRAMA OPERATIVO DE SEIS AÑOS
Consideraciones

El programa operativo que aquí se esboza es un primer planteamiento de trabajo que podrá ir perfeccionándose a medida que se establezca el proceso necesario de consultas con autoridades cubanas. Este programa no incluye actividades relacionadas con el mantenimiento de la seguridad pública, defensa y fuerzas armadas en general ni en los ámbitos estrictamente políticos, a no ser que estén directamente vinculados con el proceso de reformas de los sectores económico y social y/o con la reactivación de la economía. Es decir, se restringe principalmente al tipo de cooperación técnica y financiera provisto por los organismos financieros y técnicos internacionales.

Membresía en instituciones financieras internacionales (IFIs): El gobierno de Cuba se retiró del Fondo Monetario Internacional (FMI) y del Banco Mundial (BM) en 1962 y, como nunca ratificó el convenio constitutivo del Banco Interamericano de Desarrollo (BID), tampoco es miembro de dicha institución. Por lo tanto, para acceder al financiamiento externo de dichas instituciones y de los gobiernos que integran el Club de París, en caso de que en una primera instancia tomara un tiempo considerable determinar y acordar las cuotas de suscripción, Cuba debería considerar solicitar ser miembro asociado en dichas IFIs con objeto de recibir cooperación financiera y técnica para entrenar personal y preparar planes detallados de las reformas y propuestas de préstamos para las etapas posteriores, mientras se determina su cuota de entrada en ellas de acuerdo con su nivel de ingreso. La cooperación financiera de las IFIs facilitaría alcanzar los resultados necesarios y eliminaría la necesidad de imponer medidas más drásticas. La cooperación técnica podría ayudar en el adiestramiento rápido de gerentes, administradores, contadores, auditores, economistas y abogados. Asimismo, será necesario un programa inicial de emergencia alimentaria para atender la hambruna y la desnutrición infantil, que se superaría tan pronto se libere y desregule adecuadamente el agro, así como para rehabilitar la infraestructura social en estado crítico.

Como se ha señalado anteriormente, se estima que a fines de 1996 la deuda externa en moneda convertible de Cuba—excluyendo la contraída con la Unión Soviética y reclamada por Rusia, el estado sucesor—era de aproximadamente US$11,000 millones. Además, el país se declaró en moratoria de su deuda externa en 1986. En meses recientes ha habido contactos informales por parte de las autoridades cubanas con miembros del Club de París (deuda bilateral oficial), pero se requiere tener previamente un programa económico aprobado por el FMI para convocar una reunión de comité consultivo. Aún cuando será imprescindible renegociar y reestructurar la deuda externa, Cuba tiene la ventaja de no tener saldos deudores con las IFIs y un saldo de apenas US$100 millones con el Eximbank de Estados Unidos. Ello significa que *un gobierno cubano dispuesto a comprometerse a llevar a cabo el proceso de reformas requerido —y que, de hecho, comenzara a implantar medidas en ese sentido— podría recibir a muy corto plazo la ayuda de la comunidad internacional.* Incluso en la medida en que Cuba califique para la Asociación Internacional de Fomento (véase abajo) podría participar en el Programa para Países Pobres Altamente Endeudados (Highly Indebted Poor Countries—HIPC—Debt Initiative), que representa un compromiso por parte de todos los acreedores de actuar en forma concertada y coordinada para reducir la deuda externa a un nivel sustentable, para lo cual se requiere que el país se haya abocado a un proceso de reformas estructurales y de políticas sociales.

Un programa de ajuste estructural aprobado por las IFIs, particularmente el FMI, sería condición necesaria para negociar el nivel y los términos de la deuda externa con los Clubs de París (deuda bilateral oficial) y de Londres (deuda con instituciones financieras) con base en los términos del HIPC y tener nuevamente acceso al crédito comercial y bancario internacional. La ayuda externa que se reciba debería dar preferencia a apoyar directamente el programa de estabilización, la renegociación de la deuda y la reconversión productiva de las pequeñas y medianas empresas privadas para que se capitalicen adecuadamente; financiar los programas de solidaridad e inversión social orientados a asegurar una calidad de vida adecuada durante el proceso de transición; obtener asistencia técnica temporal de los cubanos radicados en el exterior que decidan continuar residiendo fuera del país; y expandir la infraestructura económica.

Respecto de la oportunidad de los primeros desembolsos de un programa de financiamiento externo: Con frecuencia se plantean interrogantes respecto del tiempo que requiere la preparación, negociación, aprobación y firma del contrato y determinación de elegibilidad para las operaciones de las IFIs. Es cierto

que la adecuada preparación y consideración de un proyecto de financiamiento externo requiere típicamente entre uno y dos años. Pero bajo ciertas condiciones, especialmente cuando se trata de una situación de emergencia como la del caso de Cuba, es posible comenzar los desembolsos de financiamiento externo a muy corto plazo. Por ejemplo, en el caso de Bosnia y Herzegovina, el acuerdo de paz fue firmado el 21 de noviembre de 1995 y el primer desembolso de un crédito del Banco Mundial de recuperación de emergencia tuvo lugar el 29 de febrero de 1996, es decir, escasamente 3 meses a partir de la firma de los tratados de paz en Dayton. Incluso la situación descrita se produjo antes de la aceptación de Bosnia y Herzegovina como país miembro del Banco Mundial, lo cual se decidió el 1º de abril de 1996 con retroactividad al 25 de febrero de 1996.

Con objeto de ganar tiempo, sería conveniente formar un *grupo consultivo* bajo el liderazgo de una de las IFIs para desarrollar un programa de financiamiento externo de mediano plazo (por ejemplo, 6 años). Dicho grupo debería diseñar, desarrollar y coordinar no sólo el programa de financiamiento externo, sino también un programa de cooperación técnica internacional de las IFIs y de los miembros del Club de París. El grupo consultivo podrá ofrecer asistencia y asesoramiento a las autoridades cubanas, quienes carecen de experiencia con dichas instituciones. La aprobación por el grupo consultivo de un programa de políticas económicas y reformas estructurales contribuirá indudablemente a producir un entorno favorable para la renegociación de la deuda, la resolución de reclamos externos, así como para obtener capital adicional de agencias de crédito a la exportación, instituciones financieras y proveedores. Además, las transferencias de recursos de las IFIs probablemente tendrán el efecto de aumentar la confianza de parte de los inversionistas, resultando de esta manera en una expansión de la inversión privada extranjera.

Relacionadas con préstamos subsidiados (AIF y FOE): En diciembre de 1959, al determinarse las suscripciones a las acciones de capital autorizado del BID, el monto asignado a Cuba fue de US$36.840.000, que la colocaba en quinto lugar entre los países de América Latina después de Argentina, Brasil, México y Venezuela —que integran el Grupo A en dicha institución— y superior a las suscripciones asignadas a Chile, Colombia y Perú, países miembros que en la actualidad integran el Grupo B.[9] Casi 40 años después de creado el BID, Cuba probablemente formaría parte del Grupo D, correspondiente a los países miembros de más bajo PIB per cápita (o de menor desarrollo relativo).

No obstante la penosa implicación de lo anterior, lo importante, en cuanto a las condiciones financieras de los préstamos se refiere, radica en la probable elegibilidad de Cuba para préstamos concesionarios. En el caso del BID, si se clasificara a Cuba en el Grupo C, tendría acceso mucho más limitado a préstamos concesionarios que si clasificara, al menos temporalmente, para el Grupo D, incluyendo recursos del Fondo para Operaciones Especiales (FOE). En el Grupo del Banco Mundial, el nivel de producto per cápita actual para establecer elegibilidad para créditos de la Asociación Internacional de Fomento (AIF) es alrededor de US$1,000. En el caso de AIF, algunos países, incluyendo China, son considerados prestatarios "mixtos", es decir, son elegibles para obtener una combinación de financiamiento de los recursos de AIF y préstamos a tasas de mercado del Banco Mundial. No se cuenta con información confiable de cuentas nacionales para Cuba, pero una estimación basada en información oficial correspondiente a 1994 es que el PIB per cápita a precios corrientes en 1996 era de aproximadamente CU$1,780 pesos que, al tipo de cambio paralelo (obtenido en las casas de cambio) representaría menos de US$100. Por consiguiente, puede afirmarse que, a lo menos, Cuba sería un prestatario mixto.

Estos préstamos concesionarios son créditos subsidiados hasta el punto de que alrededor del 85 por ciento del préstamo resulta ser una donación. En el caso del FOE, los préstamos típicamente son a 40 años de plazo de amortización, con un período de gracia de 10 años, una comisión de crédito anual del 0.5 por ciento anual, y una tasa de interés de 1 por ciento anual durante el período de gracia y 2 por ciento durante el plazo de amortización. En el caso de AIF, el plazo de amortización es de 35 a 40 años, con un período de gracia de 10 años y no se cobra interés, sino más bien un cargo por servicio de 0,75 por ciento anual.

Relacionadas con la aprobación de los préstamos por un gobierno de transición: La aprobación de la contratación de empréstitos es normalmente función del poder legislativo. Ello significa que las operaciones a las cuales se refiere este documento requerirían, al menos hasta que se modifique la organización estatal cubana, la aprobación de la Asamblea Nacional del Poder Popular la cual, de acuerdo con el artículo 69 de la constitución política "es el órgano supremo del poder del Estado" y, según el artículo 75, incisos (d) y (e) tiene las atribuciones de aprobar los planes nacionales de desarrollo y el presupuesto público.

El programa de emergencia

Fondo de Inversión Social de Emergencia (FUNDACUBA): El objetivo central de esta operación es mantener y mejorar los servicios sociales básicos durante el período de estabilización y ajuste económico, hasta tanto los ministerios de línea sean restructurados y tengan la capacidad para servir de manera efectiva como entes rectores y los municipios tengan la capacidad proveer servicios sociales de acuerdo con sus nuevos mandatos. Asimismo, y no menos importante, este proyecto sería diseñado para tener un impacto significativo de generación de empleos temporales.

Con objeto de atender la situación precaria de infraestructura y servicios sociales básicos en el país, se recomienda establecer la Fundación Cuba (FUNDACUBA) como agencia semiautónoma de financiamiento (no de ejecución) temporal (mandato de cinco años, no renovable) de proyectos de los siguientes tipos: (a) proyectos de *infraestructura social*, tales como la rehabilitación de centros médicos, escuelas y sistemas de agua y alcantarillado; (b) proyec-

---

9. En el caso del Banco Mundial, la suscripción de Cuba fue establecida en US$35 millones, igual que las de Colombia y Chile y muy superior a la de Venezuela (US$10.5 millones).

tos de *infraestructura económica*, tales como pavimentación y señalización, rehabilitación de edificios, parques y espacios públicos, drenaje y caminos vecinales; y (c) proyectos de *servicios sociales*, tales como alimentación y medicamentos para niños de edad preescolar (población de 930,000) y personas mayores de 65 años (población de 965,000). Para promover la transparencia y eficiencia de sus operaciones, FUNDACUBA debería preparar y divulgar un listado estandarizado de proyectos que financiará, así como un manual operativo y los procedimientos (simplificados) de contratación y licitación.

Considerando la necesidad de creación de empleos temporales con remuneración basada en el costo en pesos de una canasta familiar de consumo mínimo, se establece como meta para cada uno de los dos primeros años de operación la generación de 300,000 empleos con un promedio de seis meses de duración, con una reducción en los tres años restantes a medida que los proyectos de rehabilitación hayan concluido.

FUNDACUBA debería consistir fundamentalmente de una junta directiva independiente, un equipo de personal reducido y de alto calibre y debe ser estrechamente auditado por los donantes externos. Los proyectos a ser financiados por FUNDACUBA deberían ser ejecutados por contratistas privados nacionales, ONGs independientes, entidades religiosas, municipalidades u otras agencias públicas. La metodología para la aprobación de los proyectos debería ser de amplio conocimiento; los criterios incluirían focalización hacia los municipios más necesitados que identificarían los proyectos, así como recuperación de costos, particularmente para el mantenimiento y operación de proyectos de agua potable y alcantarillado.

Alimentación escolar: A pesar de los esfuerzos por mantener los servicios sociales y la alimentación básica de niños y ancianos en la severa crisis de los años 90, se ha incrementado la desnutrición en todos los grupos incluyendo los niños de edad preescolar y primaria. Los requerimientos nutricionales de niños en edad preescolar serían atendidos a través del proyecto de FUNDACUBA. Para los alumnos de las escuelas primarias, se sugiere estudiar alternativas basadas en criterios de disponibilidad y costo de insumos locales, con el objetivo de establecer un programa que aporte

por lo menos un 30% de los requerimientos diarios de calorías y proteínas de los niños entre 6 y 11 años. En la práctica, este programa debería ser manejado por las municipalidades y comunidades; de esta manera, presentará diversas modalidades, las cuales van desde el suministro de un desayuno en la escuela consistente en un envase de leche enriquecido con vitaminas y proteínas, al de la atención en cocinas escolares o en casas familiares designadas por la comunidad o en centros comunitarios en donde además de la alimentación para los menores, se proporcionaría ayuda alimentaria a ancianos, minusválidos y otros grupos vulnerables. La meta para los alumnos de escuelas primarias debería ser alcanzar en los primeros meses la distribución de 1 millón de raciones diarias.

Las cooperaciones técnicas

Cuba requiere urgentemente ayuda conceptual, ideas frescas y asistencia para reorganizar su economía y su gobierno. A través de la cooperación técnica internacional el país puede obtener rápidamente la transferencia de conocimientos y habilidades que le faltan en la actualidad, particularmente para la formación de banqueros, gerentes, contadores, auditores, economistas y abogados de empresas. Dada la gran diversidad de fuentes de cooperación técnica, sería conveniente desarrollar un paquete de proyectos integrado, quizás bajo la coordinación de un organismo internacional como el PNUD, para evitar duplicaciones y promover la complementariedad entre proyectos. *Se estima que una importante fuente de recursos humanos para prestar cooperación técnica son los cubanos expatriados.*

En general, las cooperaciones técnicas pueden ser de tres tipos: (a) donaciones, o cooperaciones técnicas no reembolsables, provenientes de las IFIs, de otros grupos multilaterales como la Unión Europea y de las agencias de cooperación bilaterales, ya sea directamente o a través de fondos establecidos en las IFIs y que no están directamente relacionadas con una operación de préstamo; (b) las que son paralelas a préstamos y se tramitan conjuntamente con un préstamo pero no forman parte del costo de la operación; y (c) las que son parte de un préstamo, es decir, constituyen una categoría de inversión y figuran en el contrato correspondiente. Existe un híbrido, que son las de recuperación contingente: éstas cooperaciones técnicas se financian cuando existe una posibilidad razonable de que conducirán a una operación de préstamo en cuyo caso se convierten en parte del préstamo (categoría *c*); si ello no ocurre, la cooperación técnica se convierte en no reembolsable (categoría *a*). Se considera que la mayoría de los proyectos de cooperación técnica para Cuba que se sugieren en el cuadro que sigue cabría bajo de la categoría *a* o serían híbridos.

Un factor esencial para el crecimiento de la agricultura cubana es la regularización y la seguridad de la tenencia y propiedad de la tierra, que a menos que se atiendan adecuadamente, pueden dificultar o impedir las reformas económicas de ese sector comentadas en este documento. Esto es especialmente importante dada la sustancial modificación de la propiedad de la tierra con las dos reformas agrarias ocurridas en 1959 y 1963 con sus complejidades y contradicciones, así como posteriormente con la constitución de las Unidades Básicas de Producción Cooperativa (UBPC) en 1993. Por ello, es necesario un programa de regularización de la tenencia de tierra, de manera que los programas de producción e inversión en el sector puedan reanudarse con prontitud, con su correspondiente catastro y otorgamiento de títulos para consolidar y garantizar los derechos de propiedad.

A tal efecto deberá elaborarse un proyecto de ley destinado a establecer, consolidar y garantizar los derechos de propiedad de la tierra bajo la premisa que las pequeñas y medianas propiedades deben ser transferidas a los agricultores que las estén ocupando y explotando, y que se deberá compensar a los antiguos propietarios y que las grandes unidades deberán ser privatizadas por un procedimiento que garantice empleo al mayor número de trabajadores en forma eficiente. El concepto principal que respalda las medidas que se proponen es que tiene que separarse los temas de regularización de la tenencia y propiedad de la tierra y los de compensación por confiscaciones previas. El segundo tema, no menos importante, es reconocer que la tenencia y propiedad debe ser concedida a quienes las hayan ocupado por años, previo pago al menos de los impuestos o derechos de adquisición correspondientes.

Es un hecho que, aún cuando existen proyectos de restauración, éstos se concentran en unas pocas manzanas por lo cual, en su mayor parte, tanto La Habana Vieja como Trinidad se están derrumbando, poniendo en peligro estas áreas designadas por la UNESCO como Patrimonio de la Humanidad. Uno de los proyectos de cooperación técnica sugeridos se concentraría en el establecimiento de un marco regulador para la restauración de áreas históricas y monumentos nacionales, la rehabilitación de techos y el desarrollo de planes de restauración de La Habana Vieja y, además, en la ciudad colonial de Trinidad, como primer paso de carácter urgente para la recuperación de estos Monumentos a la Humanidad. Se considera que se requiere aproximadamente US$3 millones para realizar una primera rehabilitación de los techos de los edificios de La Habana Vieja, lo cual permitiría proteger las estructuras básicas por varios años más, hasta que se puedan ejecutar obras de restauración de acuerdo con un plan integrado de desarrollo urbano que también sería elaborado como parte del proyecto sugerido.

Las operaciones de reformas estructurales, de políticas económicas y reforma del estado

El programa de ajuste estructural en general, y los programas de préstamos sectoriales de apoyo, deberán estar insertos dentro de un marco de referencia derivado de la teoría y la práctica del diseño e implementación de programas de reformas de políticas e instituciones orientados a aumentar el crecimiento y el empleo, así como a reducir la pobreza.

La teoría económica y la evidencia empírica sugieren ciertos requisitos para lograr un crecimiento sostenido del producto y del empleo con reducción de la pobreza. Este consenso, unido al éxito de países que han implementado este tipo de políticas e instituciones y el hecho que en años recientes un grupo cada vez más grande de países en desarrollo hayan iniciado cambios en sus políticas económicas e instituciones que siguen un patrón similar, le ha dado un gran impulso a los procesos de reformas.

En el cuadro que sigue se presenta un listado de las operaciones sugeridas, sus objetivos, montos indicativos en forma de rango y su programación durante un período de seis años.

Cuba: Cooperación Internacional de Emergencia y Para la Recuperación

Operación	Objetivo de la Operación	Monto Indicativo (En US$ Millones)	Año 1	Año 2	Año 3	Año 4	Año 5	Año 6
1. Programa de Emergencia (incluye ayuda humanitaria)								
a. Fondo de Inversión Social de Emergencia (FUNDACUBA)	(a) Mantener y mejorar los servicios sociales básicos, especialmente a preescolares (930.000) y ancianos (965.000), durante el período de ajuste y estabilización; (b) Generar 300.000 empleos temporales en cada uno de los dos primeros años; y (c) Rehabilitar la infraestructura social y económica en estado crítico.	300 - 450	X	X	X			
b. Alimentación y salud escolar	Apoyo a la producción y distribución de alimentos (30% de los requerimientos diarios de vitaminas y proteínas) y atención médica básica (medicamentos, vacunas) en todas las escuelas primarias con la activa participación de ONGs independientes y entidades religiosas.	150 - 250	X	X	X			

2. Cooperaciones Técnicas (Todas estas operaciones de asistencia técnica incluirán asesorías, entrenamiento, pasantías y equipamiento básico. Los estudios que se realicen deberán definir los objetivos, organización, equipamiento, personal y operación de las unidades o entidades que se establezcan o modifiquen. Se anticipa que la mayoría de estos proyectos representarían donaciones, es decir, tendrían carácter no reembolsable.)

Operación	Objetivo de la Operación	Monto Indicativo (En US$ Millones)	Año 1	Año 2	Año 3	Año 4	Año 5	Año 6
a. Fortalecimiento y modernización del Ministerio de Finanzas orientado a establecer un sistema de administración financiera del estado	(a) Apoyo para instalar un sistema de administración financiera integrada para el gobierno central y el sector público que proporcione información adecuada y oportuna para tener una visión completa y permanente de la situación de los ingresos y egresos del estado y para la toma de decisiones públicas; (b) Apoyo para modernizar y fortalecer las funciones de presupuesto, tributación (incluyendo aduanas), control del gasto corriente y de inversión, y renegociación y administración de la deuda pública (interna y externa); y (c) Apoyo para establecer una unidad que coordine la renegociación de la deuda externa y los nuevos préstamos externos y actúe como entidad de enlace administrativo y técnico y mantenga contacto permanente con las instituciones financieras internacionales.	5 - 15	X	X	X			
b. Catastro y registro nacional de tierras y propiedades	Apoyo para elaborar: (a) un proyecto de ley para establecer, consolidar y garantizar los derechos de tenencia y propiedad de la tierra; (b) un proyecto de ley para establecer un marco regulador para establecer y mantener un catastro y un sistema de información geográfico (SIG); (c) implantación del SIG, incluyendo diseño conceptual, diseño de base de datos, conversión de datos, seminarios y talleres de capacitación; y (d) un programa de regularización de la tenencia de tierra con su correspondiente catastro y titulación de predios.	5 - 7	X	X	X			

Cuba: Cooperación Internacional de Emergencia y Para la Recuperación (continued)

Operación	Objetivo de la Operación	Monto Indicativo (En US$ Millones)	Año 1	Año 2	Año 3	Año 4	Año 5	Año 6
c. Tribunal de Cuentas	Apoyo para elaborar, instalar y poner en funcionamiento un sistema moderno de revisión, control y auditoría independiente, moderna, adecuada y oportuna de todos los procedimientos y decisiones de adquisición de bienes y servicios corrientes y de capital por el gobierno central y el sector público, para mantener elevados niveles de ética pública y combatir decididamente la corrupción.	3 - 5	X	X	X			
d. Evaluación y compensación de reclamos al Estado	Apoyo para el establecimiento y funcionamiento por un período que no debería exceder de 5 años, de un mecanismo autónomo de evaluación de reclamos y determinación de compensación por propiedades expropiadas a ciudadanos cubanos.	5 - 7		X	X	X	X	X
e. Estudios fiscales y públicos	Apoyo técnico para realizar estudios y redactar proyectos de ley cuyos objetivos son: (a) eliminar los subsidios y reducir los gastos corrientes innecesarios (militares, políticos, administrativos), racionalizar y focalizar los gastos sociales, y establecer impuestos; (b) promover una profunda reestructuración del estado y del gasto público dando lugar a la participación de la iniciativa privada en el gasto público para que sea más efectivo y menos costoso.	0.6 - 0.9	X					
f. Racionalización de las empresas del Estado	Apoyo para: (a) aumentar los precios y las tarifas de las empresas públicas; (b) establecer una entidad temporal e independiente para la racionalización, restructuración, valoración y venta de las empresas públicas del estado; (c) definir y establecer los marcos regulatorios y de supervisión en servicios básicos (tales como: energía eléctrica, petróleo, agua potable, alcantarillado, telecomunicaciones, correos, puertos, aeropuertos) que promuevan que las empresas que se privaticen o se les otorgue concesiones provean los servicios en forma eficiente, confiable y a bajo costo; y (e) financiamiento de 40-50 becas de estudios en reconocidos centros universitarios para funcionarios a ser empleados por entes reguladores y de supervisión de monopolios naturales privatizados.	5 - 7	X	X				
g. Estadísticas económicas y financieras	Apoyo técnico para diseñar el mejoramiento o el establecimiento de un sistema de generación y publicación de estadísticas económicas y financieras básicas (de producción y precios nacionales y sectoriales, monetarias, financieras, fiscales, de balanza de pagos y de comercio exterior) para conocimiento y toma de decisiones de los agentes económicos.	3 - 5	X	X	X	X		
h. Mejoramiento de la capacidad de análisis, diseño y gestión de políticas económicas	(a) Apoyo para establecer y mantener políticas macroeconómicas y sectoriales compatibles con los objetivos de alcanzar y preservar la estabilidad económica y lograr un crecimiento alto, estable y sustentable; y (b) financiamiento de 40-50 becas de estudio en reconocidos centros universitarios para un primer grupo de funcionarios jóvenes que posteriormente estarán a cargo del análisis y diseño de políticas macroeconómicas y profesores universitarios.	3 - 5	X	X	X	X		

Cuba: Cooperación Internacional de Emergencia y Para la Recuperación (continued)

Operación	Objetivo de la Operación	Monto Indicativo (En US$ Millones)	Año 1	Año 2	Año 3	Año 4	Año 5	Año 6
i. Modernización de la seguridad social	Apoyo para el establecimiento y puesta en marcha de: (a) una Oficina de Normalización Previsional a cargo del Sistema Nacional de Pensiones que reduzca el déficit previsional público; y (b) una Superintendencia de Administradoras Privadas de Pensiones.	1 - 2		X	X	X		
j. Reforma del sector salud	(a) Apoyo a la reestructuración del sistema de salud pública tal que Estado cumpla un papel rector y regulador; (b) realización de estudios y preparación de un plan para que el Estado compre un paquete de servicios básicos de salud para toda la población; y (c) financiamiento de proyectos piloto a nivel municipal para ensayar el mecanismo de compra de servicios básicos de salud.	5 - 7		X	X	X	X	
k. Modernización del sector agua potable y alcantarillado	Apoyo para: (a) Desarrollo y puesta en vigencia de un marco regulador y de supervisión reformado para el sector que promueva que las empresas del sector tengan autonomía, provean los servicios en forma eficiente en cuanto a cantidad y calidad, en forma confiable y a bajo costo y que haya participación comunitaria en la toma de decisiones; (b) saneamiento financiero de los proveedores de servicio existentes; y (c) diseño de un plan maestro y un préstamo de inversión estratégica en el sector.	1 - 1.5	X	X				
l. Desarrollo del sector turismo	(a) Desarrollo y puesta en vigencia de un marco regulador reformado para el sector; y (b) reestructuración y fortalecimiento de la entidad nacional de turismo, instalación de sistemas y procedimientos operativos, capacitación.	5.0 - 8.5		X	X			
m. Aspectos jurídicos e institucionales para la conservación del medio ambiente	Apoyo para: (a) establecer la legislación básica para la conservación del medio ambiente; (b) el establecimiento y la puesta en marcha de una entidad rectora y revisora de estudios ambientales, de medidas mitigadoras y de su activa fiscalización; y (c) la elaboración de un plan estratégico ambiental de mediano y largo plazo y su concertación con la sociedad civil.	2 - 5		X	X			
n. Restauración de monumentos nacionales	(a) Desarrollo y puesta en vigencia del marco regulador, lineamientos y reglamentaciones para la restauración de áreas históricas y monumentos nacionales; y (b) rehabilitación de techos en La Habana Vieja y Trinidad.	4 - 6	X	X	X	X		
o. Asamblea Constituyente y Consejo Supremo Electoral	Apoyar: (a) la realización de una asamblea constituyente con la más amplia participación y sin restricciones por razones ideológicas, que prepare un proyecto de constitución; y (b) el establecimiento de un Tribunal Supremo Electoral independiente, con sistemas y procedimientos eleccionarios transparentes, eficaces y ejecutados y procesados eficientemente.	3 - 6	X	X				

Cuba: Cooperación Internacional de Emergencia y Para la Recuperación (*continued*)

Operación	Objetivo de la Operación	Monto Indicativo (En US$ Millones)	Año 1	Año 2	Año 3	Año 4	Año 5	Año 6
p. Modernización del Poder Legislativo	Financiamiento de: (a) pasantías para conocer experiencias sobre procesos de modernización legislativa en otros países; (b) introducción de sistemas automatizados de estenografía, votación electrónica y consulta legislativa; (c) apoyo a la reorganización del poder legislativo; (d) establecimiento de un centro de información legislativa y un centro de atención al público; (e) establecimiento de una oficina técnica de asuntos económicos; y (f) capacitación del personal en el uso de sistemas de computación.	10 - 15			X	X	X	
q. Modernización del Poder Judicial	Apoyo para la: (a) preparación de nuevos códigos en las áreas penal, laboral, comercial, de bancarrotas, de tributación, de presupuesto, anti monopolio y de empresas; (b) diseño de una operación de modernización del poder judicial y para el establecimiento de un Estado de Derecho, incluyendo reorganización del sistema judicial, de la administración de justicia y rehabilitación de la infraestructura penal.	10 - 15	X	X				
r. Oficina Nacional de Retorno	Apoyo para el establecimiento de una Oficina Nacional de Retorno y la legislación sobre franquicias aduaneras y revalidación de títulos profesionales y de especialización técnica, que promuevan el regreso al país de los cubanos expatriados y su plena reincorporación a los procesos de reconstrucción y desarrollo nacional. Adicionalmente, brindar una prima de instalación como incentivo monetario para reclutar y facilitar el retorno de 2,000 profesionales, técnicos especializados y pequeños empresarios cuyas destrezas sean críticamente requeridas para el proceso de reconstrucción.	21 - 26	X	X				

3. Operaciones para la Recuperación Económica y Reformas de Políticas

Operación	Objetivo de la Operación	Monto Indicativo (En US$ Millones)	Año 1	Año 2	Año 3	Año 4	Año 5	Año 6
a. Crédito para la Estabilización, Recuperación Económica y Ajuste Estructural	Apoyar el programa de estabilización inicial (reducir la inflación y establecer la libre convertibilidad del peso) y realizar las reformas básicas iniciales en la economía en los sectores globales claves (fiscal, comercial, financiero, cambiario y laboral) para restablecer un sistema general de incentivos a la producción basado en la libre iniciativa, la competencia y el mercado.	300 - 450	X	X	X			
b. Reforma y Modernización del Sector Público (Poder Ejecutivo)	(a) Consolidar el proceso de instalación de un sistema de administración financiera integrada, fortalecer la administración tributaria y el sistema de aduanas; (b) diseñar y apoyar el establecimiento de un servicio civil profesional y la restructuración y reforma del poder ejecutivo; (c) apoyar el establecimiento y fortalecimiento de los mecanismos de regulación; y (d) apoyar el saneamiento financiero, restructuración y privatización de empresas del estado.	50 - 80		X	X	X	X	

291

Cuba: Cooperación Internacional de Emergencia y Para la Recuperación (continued)

Operación	Objetivo de la Operación	Monto Indicativo (En US$ Millones)	Año 1	Año 2	Año 3	Año 4	Año 5	Año 6
c. Reforma del Sector Financiero e Inversiones	Consolidar, ampliar y profundizar las medidas de reformas iniciales en el sector financiero adoptando políticas e instituciones, tales como: establecimiento de una superintendencia bancaria y otra de instituciones financieras para la definición, aplicación y supervisión de normas prudenciales para la capitalización, la liquidez y la disciplina crediticia y de inversiones de las instituciones bancarias y financieras; así como ampliar la participación privada en la banca comercial.	400 - 600			X	X	X	X
d. Reforma del Sector de Comercio Exterior	Consolidar, ampliar y profundizar las medidas de reformas iniciales en los sectores cambiarios y comerciales para consolidar un mercado de libre convertibilidad (comercial y financiera para movimientos de capital a largo plazo). También para lograr la eliminación del monopolio estatal del comercio exterior y la simplificación de los procedimientos para actividades de comercio exterior; el establecimiento de una estructura arancelaria baja y uniforme; barreras zoosanitarias, fitosanitarias y de seguridad razonables; una política flexible de contratación laboral por empresas extranjeras; y una política de incentivar el sector exportador.	400 - 600			X	X	X	X
e. Reforma del Sector Judicial y de la Administración de la Justicia	(a) Preparación y/o revisión completa del marco jurídico del país; (b) desarrollo e implantación de un sistema judicial moderno; (c) desarrollo e implantación de un sistema administrativo eficiente, incluyendo establecimiento de estándares de transparencia, de habilidades técnicas y gerenciales; (d) desarrollo de programas de capacitación; (e) establecimiento de sistemas de información jurídica; y (f) rehabilitación de la infraestructura penal, priorizando las instalaciones para jóvenes infractores.	35 - 60		X	X	X		
f. Reforma del Sector Agropecuario y Agroindustrial	Apoyar un marco institucional y de políticas apropiado para el crecimiento sustentable del sector agropecuario, tal como: eliminación de controles de precios a la producción y comercialización de bienes agropecuarios; garantizar la tenencia de la tierra; mejorar la prestación de servicios públicos de investigación y transferencia de tecnología moderna; información de precios y mercados; y la ampliación de mercados y ferias agropecuarias.	80 - 120			X	X	X	
4. Préstamos de Inversión								
a. Programa de rehabilitación de viviendas y lotes con servicios	(a) Desarrollar las políticas de vivienda, aclarando las funciones de las entidades públicas en este sector; (b) apoyar al establecimiento y/o fortalecimiento de sistemas financieros privados para promover préstamos a la vivienda con respaldo hipotecario; (c) mejorar la calidad sanitaria de las soluciones habitacionales existentes que afectan a las familias de bajos ingresos y que habitan en condiciones de hacinamiento o insalubridad; y (d) reducir el déficit habitacional mediante el apoyo (p.e. contribución al pago inicial de hipotecas) a la construcción de 50,000 soluciones habitacionales por año con aproximadamente 100 m2 de superficie.	220 - 300		X	X	X	X	

Cuba: Cooperación Internacional de Emergencia y Para la Recuperación (*continued*)

Operación	Objetivo de la Operación	Monto Indicativo (En US$ Millones)	Año 1	Año 2	Año 3	Año 4	Año 5	Año 6
b. Programa de reforma y mejoramiento educativo	(a) Desarrollar e implantar una política educativa que incorpore al sector privado, garantizando la educación primaria y secundaria moderna y no doctrinaria para toda la población; (b) mejorar la eficiencia externa o relevancia de la educación 1-12 grados; (c) mejorar la eficiencia interna del sistema educativo a nivel primario y secundario; y (d) apoyar la rehabilitación de escuelas de nivel primario y secundario, la instalación y equipamiento de bibliotecas y el desarrollo de centros de computación y conexión al Internet en escuelas, en colaboración con el sector privado.	80 - 120		X	X	X	X	X
c. Programa nacional de saneamiento	(a) Rehabilitar las redes existentes de agua potable y alcantarillado, las plantas de tratamiento y las de potabilización; (b) instalar medidores en todos los predios; (c) preparar un plan maestro para la expansión del sistema, con participación del sector privado.	100 - 160		X	X	X	X	
d. Programa de microempresas y cuentapropistas	Desarrollar un programa de apoyo a los microempresarios y cuentapropistas para: (a) proveer crédito, capacitación, asesoría y asistencia técnica directamente a asociaciones de microempresarios y cuentapropistas o a instituciones que proporcionen servicios individuales a los mismos; y (b) establecer y fortalecer a las mencionadas instituciones en los procesos de canalización y manejo de crédito, capacitación y asesoría en gerencia, administración y contabilidad, para que así desempeñen un papel más activo y efectivo en los servicios que brindan y puedan atraer y servir mejor un mayor número de microempresarios y cuentapropistas.	80 - 150			X	X	X	X
e. Programa de infraestructura vial, puertos y aeropuertos	(a) Mejorar la calidad, la capacidad estructural y la señalización del sistema de carreteras, incluyendo la carretera central, las autopistas y otras carreteras; (b) establecer sistemas eficientes de mantenimiento; (c) fortalecer institucionalmente a las entidades encargadas del sistema de carreteras y la autoridad vehicular; (d) preparar un plan maestro para la modernización de los puertos y aeropuertos principales del país, incluyendo carga, descarga y almacenaje; y (e) establecer un marco regulador que facilite la participación del sector privado en la operación y mantenimiento de la infraestructura portuaria, aeroportuaria y de carreteras.	150 - 200			X	X	X	X
f. Programa nacional de energía	(a) Preparar un plan maestro para el desarrollo de fuentes de energía, convencionales y no convencionales, para satisfacer la demanda en una economía con altas tasas de crecimiento; (b) establecer un marco regulador y de supervisión para el sector; (c) rehabilitación de las plantas eléctricas y las líneas de transmisión y distribución; (d) instalación de medidores en todos los predios del país; y (e) saneamiento financiero de las empresas eléctricas y posterior privatización.	170 - 250		X	X	X	X	

Cuba: Cooperación Internacional de Emergencia y Para la Recuperación *(continued)*

Operación	Objetivo de la Operación	Monto Indicativo (En US$ Millones)	Año 1	Año 2	Año 3	Año 4	Año 5	Año 6
g. Programa de fortalecimiento municipal	(a) Financiar proyectos prioritarios de inversión básica para el desarrollo de los 169 municipios del país (reposición, mejoramiento, ampliación, construcción, equipamiento y rehabilitación de establecimientos e instalaciones de educación, salud, saneamiento, vialidad urbana y rural, electrificación y telefonía); y (b) desarrollar la capacidad institucional de los municipios para asignar autónomamente los recursos de inversión, así como para planificar, evaluar, diseñar y ejecutar proyectos de inversión en concordancia con los objetivos de desarrollo económico y social del país.	20 - 30			X	X	X	X
TOTAL ESTIMADO		2,600 - 3,900						

COMMENTS ON

"Cuba: Cooperación Internacional de Emergencia y para la Recuperación" by Castañeda and Montalván

Ernesto Hernández-Catá

There are many things in this paper that I agree with, particularly as regards the broad economic strategy. For example, I agree that international cooperation in Cuba's transition should help to create the condition for private investment, both Cuban and foreign; that private foreign investment flows should exceed flows of official development assistance by a wide margin; and that the engine of recovery of the Cuban economy must be the private sector. I am happy that we agree on these rather basic things because there are a number of more specific, but nevertheless important points of economic policy on which I disagree. In several cases the disagreements reflect the authors' misunderstanding of the experience of transition in other former communist countries. I will mention five points.

First, the authors are right in that a substantial monetary overhang probably remains in Cuba in spite of the government's restrictive monetary/fiscal policy in 1994-95 and the relatively high inflation in free and black markets during those years. The authors state that the solution to this problem is "a coherent package of monetary reform" (I am not sure exactly what that means) and the establishment of a fixed exchange rate *vis-a-vis* the dollar (that may or may not be desirable, but it is not clear how it is going to absorb the excess demand for money). I think it is im-

portant to be clear on this point: the only sure way to get rid of the overhang—and at the same time to eliminate a major source of resource misallocation—is to eliminate price controls. The experience of Eastern Europe and the former Soviet Union strongly suggests that price liberalization leads only to a *temporary* (and unavoidable) jump in the price level, and *not* to a sustained inflationary process; and that much is to be gained by liberalizing fully and as soon as possible. Therefore, a recommendation to stabilize first and then only to "initiate a gradual process of liberalization" is, I believe, an invitation to waste precious time.

Second, there is another lesson from the transition in other centrally planned economies that the authors should bear in mind: what they call a "monetary shock"—by which, I assume, they mean the tight monetary policy implemented by certain countries in transition to avoid hyper-inflation—is *not* the cause of the recession suffered by many of these countries. I believe I have shown in a recent paper[1] that such a recession is mostly the result of the overriding need to restructure the hopelessly inadequate economy inherited from the old regime and to replace the output of socialist junk goods by the production of goods and services that people want to buy freely. In fact, the overwhelming empirical evidence indicates that the

---

1. "Liberalization and the Behavior of Output In the Transition from Plan to Market," in this volume.

countries that ran a tough anti-inflationary policy from the start, like the Czech and Slovak Republics, Poland, Estonia and Latvia, have been the first ones to come out of the recession and are now experiencing above-average output growth. Those that chose to disregard the need for a disciplined monetary policy like Ukraine and Belarus, are now paying the price.

Third, for the reasons I just mentioned, I take exception to the suggestion that under-utilization of existing capacity in the state sector is "unnecessary," or that it justifies in any way the adoption of a "Chinese" or "Vietnamese" model, as opposed to an "Eastern European" model. The reason why China and Vietnam avoided a period of output decline after the beginning of reforms is that their industrial sectors were very small compared to those in most Central, Eastern European or former Soviet states, and that China and Vietnam aggressively liberalized their large agricultural sectors (contrary, for example, to what was done in Russia and Ukraine).[2] I would add one important fact: in Russia, in the Baltic countries and in most of the countries of Central and Eastern Europe you can now vote freely for the candidate of your choice and you can criticize the government as strongly as you wish.

Fourth, Castañeda and Montalván write that "the success of stabilization can be determined by a an annual inflation rate of 30% to 40%." This I find extraordinarily unambitious by the standard of this region. Consumer price inflation this year is running below 20% in virtually all the countries of the Western Hemisphere with the notable exception of Venezuela. And in most of the major countries of the region, including Argentina, Brazil, Canada, Chile, Perú and the United States, inflation is in the single digits. What I find difficult to understand is how, with inflation considerably above that prevailing among its major trading partners and a fixed nominal exchange rate against the U.S. dollar, will Cuba succeed in maintaining a "competitive real exchange rate" as the authors recommend.

Fifth, perhaps the answer to the puzzle is the authors statement in the paper that there should be an initial devaluation large enough to ensure initial competitiveness and that the exchange rate will then be "adjusted gradually" to allow "a sustained expansion of exports." But if we have learned one lesson from the currency crisis in Mexico, the Czech Republic, the Philippines, and more recently Thailand, it is that once they are on a fixed exchange rate, the authorities tend to fall asleep until the crisis comes. In the words of Carmen Reinhart, fixed exchange rate systems (and their close cousins like *tablitas*) carry in themselves the seeds of their own destruction, because as soon as they are announced speculators anticipate the sequence of real exchange rate appreciation and mounting current account deficits and, at the first opportunity, they attack the currency. This is not what Cuba's new central bank will need at a time when its reserves probably will be exhausted.

A fixed exchange rate at the beginning of the transition is much too dangerous. Cuba should float until the peso finds its proper level in foreign exchange markets. Then, there is room for a serious debate on exchange rate policy in the longer term—on whether Cuba (like Canada) could maintain a stable relation between its currency and the dollar without surrendering its ability to adjust the exchange rate when its competitive position is threatened by asymmetric shocks, or whether it should peg to the U.S. dollar (like the Bahamas and other tourist-based Caribbean economies). But the authors do not see it that way. They state that exchange rate floating "should not be tolerated," and they go on to say—to end on a surrealistic note—that neither should the "free entry and exit of short term capital nor very high real interest rates be tolerated." This is a rather remarkable statement coming from people who are willing to accept real interest rates of around 6% as a sign of a successful stabilization program.

---

2. Of course, the relatively small size of the industrial sector in Cuba augurs well for a *relatively* mild adjustment process *provided that* the other sectors are aggressively liberalized—which does not mean that the new government will not have to deal with some white elephants.

ENFOQUE CRITICO AL DOCUMENTO: APOYO PARA UNA TRANSICION DEMOCRATICA EN CUBA

Maida Donate-Armada

Las relaciones Cuba-Estados Unidos han estado presente en el discurso político de los cubanos, desde mucho antes de alcanzar la independencia de España. Por las más diversas y contradictorias razones—omisión o injerencia—los cubanos han responsabilizado al poderoso vecino geográfico, con los desaciertos y errores que han cometido como gobernantes y gobernados. En buen cubano diríamos que los Estados Unidos han sido, daltónicamente, el *totí*[1] histórico de la política cubana.

Desde enero de 1959 hasta la fecha, las acusaciones se han hecho cada vez más violentas y delirantes. En la Isla, con la misma enérgica vehemencia conque se condena *la política injerencista estadounidense*, se exige imperativamente a los Estados Unidos ser su socio comercial. En el exilio, a la vez que se reconocen los beneficios del Plan de Ajuste Cubano, se lamenta la falta de fuertes acciones militares, económicas y políticas ante el gobierno de La Habana, y alternativamente, se es cubano-americano o americano de origen cubano, según se presenten las circunstancias.

La falta de análisis crítico de los cubanos de sus propias acciones políticas, de sus errores económicos y sus fracasos sociales, que han llevado a la nación cubana a la situación actual, se trata de encubrir con arengas y monsergas paralizantes en las que se repite la culpabilidad de los *yanquis*, en uno u otro sentido, y se apela al sacrificio individual en aras del beneficio colectivo, ya sea la libreta de racionamiento o la necesidad de rechazar la ayuda familiar desde el exterior y apoyar el embargo comercial. En aras de un futuro planteado en términos humanamente imposibles de alcanzar, ya sea el *comunismo redentor* o la conversión de la sociedad de *proletarios en propietarios*. Además, el sacrificio exigido debe transitar al futuro por la muerte o los derramamientos de sangre de una *inevitable* confrontación civil.

Tales enfoques son el soporte del círculo vicioso en el que se encuentra la sociedad cubana presente, y son las disyuntivas políticas que se le han estado presentando al pueblo cubano. Los gritos de los extremos de la política cubana, no han dejado oir otras voces que, obviamente, enfocan la cuestión desde una perspectiva más sensata, acorde con los cambios políticos, económicos y sociales posteriores a la desestructuración del socialismo en Europa del este, el fin de la guerra fría y de la correlación de fuerzas en el ámbito internacional.

El 28 de enero de 1997, cumpliendo con un requerimiento de la Ley Helms-Burton, bajo el sello del Presidente de los Estados Unidos, William J. Clinton, se dió a conocer el documento *Apoyo para una Transición Democrática en Cuba*. Desde el principio, este documento adquirió independencia de la Ley que lo patrocinó por el punto de equilibrio que logra en el análisis de la problemática cubana. No es un docu-

---

1. El *totí* es un pequeño pájaro negro que gusta comer el arroz de los sembrados. En el refranero popular se dice: *"Todos los pájaros comen arroz, pero el totí es el que tiene la culpa."*

mento programático, es un documento para pensar en soluciones. Quizás el mérito esté en que da esperanza de futuro a una salida civilizada a la actual crisis, reconociendo el papel protagónico a los casi once millones de cubanos que residen en la Isla y participación activa en la recuperación económica y social de su país, a los cubanos que viven en el extranjero.

Dicho documento ha provocado airadas reacciones críticas de parte de los cubanos, unas dirigidas al injerencismo *plattista* norteamericano en las cuestiones internas de Cuba. Otras, ponen en duda su validez porque *en los Estados Unidos cuando se hace una propuesta de Ley para otorgar ayuda económica a otro país, se adjunta un protocolo en el que se describe hasta el más mínimo detalle, los gastos y la relación costo-beneficio, y este documento no tiene ese anexo.* (sic).

La reacción al documento, externamente contradictoria, pero reflejo de la relación amor-odio que tienen los cubanos con los americanos, me hizo reflexionar sobre la estructura y los diferentes tópicos que se abordan en él. Reflexiones que se enriquecieron con la lectura de otro documento elaborado por el Grupo de Trabajo de la Disidencia Interna Cubana: *Cuba: Una propuesta sensata. Plataforma de Trabajo para la Transición.* Los resultados de esas reflexiones son los que presento a la consideración de los lectores.

¿A QUE DEMOCRACIA ASPIRAMOS LOS CUBANOS?

Hay consenso en la necesidad de cambios de la realidad cubana hacia formas democráticas de gobierno que garanticen y respeten la libertades civiles y políticas de los ciudadanos, y estimulen el desarrollo económico y la prosperidad de la nación. Pero, la historia de Cuba nos muestra que los cubanos no hemos sido practicantes del principio básico de toda democracia: el balance entre el derecho a gobernar de la mayoría y el respeto al derecho a la oposición de la minoría.

La vida política republicana se ha caracterizado por el uso de la violencia para acceder o mantenerse en el poder, para dominar y someter a la minoría que no piense como los que gobiernan. Tampoco los cubanos han sido escrupulosos en la administración de los fondos públicos. La eficiencia en la administración

del erario es el gran reto para cualquier gobierno democrático, porque en las sociedades abiertas, es lo que permite garantizar el desenvolvimiento de las inversiones económicas, el incremento del nivel de vida de la población y el desarrollo de programas sociales en el marco de las instituciones democráticas.

Los cubanos hemos usado y justificado el uso de la violencia política en nombre de la democracia y la restauración de las libertades a través de toda su historia. No hemos aprendido la lección de que las revoluciones y los cambios violentos nunca han traído democracia, porque rompen de manera abrupta las estructuras y los valores de las instituciones de la sociedad civil, destruyen la confianza de los individuos en las formas pacíficas de gobierno y facilitan el acceso al poder de personas, que de otra manera, no hubieran ascendido en la escala social. Ninguna revolución se ha desarrollado dentro de los marcos de la ética y la moral. La revolución cubana no es la excepción.

El primer intento cubano de autogobierno terminó en 1906 con la segunda intervención de los Estados Unidos, a solicitud del primer presidente elegido democráticamente por el pueblo. Después de tres presidentes controversiales, el quinto presidente electo, Gerardo Machado, devino en un dictador que fue derrocado por la violencia. La experiencia de la Revolución del 30, debió de ser suficiente para que los cubanos no optáramos nunca más por ese tipo de solución política.

Sin embargo, tras el breve período en que se elaboró y aprobó la Constitución de 1940, por una asamblea en la que estuvieron presentes representantes de todas las tendencias políticas existentes en el país, no fue posible contener la tradición de violencia política como manera de resolver las divergencias entre gobierno y gobernados. En 1952, Fulgencio Batista, el primer presidente que fue elegido (1940-1944), bajo los principios de la Constitución del 40, dió un golpe militar inconstitucional, al que también se le respondió con mayor violencia política.

La revolución de 1959, amplió las pulsiones de violencia política de los cubanos más allá de las fronteras nacionales. Primero, las luchas fueron entre los propios cubanos y trajo como consecuencia una diáspora de alrededor de un millón de personas, que en los albores del siglo XXI, con independencia de la edad, sexo, condición social, incluso de activismo político, están sancionadas a *salida definitiva del país* y a engorrosos y vigilados trámites de regreso temporal a su propio país, si no quieren seguir las normas de voluntarismo de un gobierno que accedió al poder por la vía violenta y que ha perpetuado a una persona como máximo-líder-dirigente de la nación por casi cuarenta años.

Paulatinamente, ese voluntarismo político para consolidarse en el poder, siguió un esquema militarista que ha involucrado a gran parte de la población civil, e intentó llevar la idea de la *guerra perpetua* hasta otros países de América Latina, Africa y Asia.

Esta experiencia militarista de las tres últimas décadas, ha sido vivida de manera diferente por los cubanos de la Isla y los de la diáspora. En la diáspora, la militarización de la sociedad cubana ha sido causa, entre otras razones, para el desplazamiento geográfico y es uno de los referentes por los que se está *en contra de*. La han vivido como espectadores y ha estado enmarcada entre los avatares de la vida cotidiana bajo estructuras de instituciones democráticas en una sociedad abierta, que les ha garantizado el desarrollo personal.

En la Isla, esta manera de gobernar enajenó el trabajo como medio de vida y trajo la consecuente depauperación de las condiciones de vida de la población. El militarismo totalitarista al que han estado sometidos, hasta cierto punto ha vacunado a los cubanos, contra la violencia política como vía de cambio. Es un hecho que la mayoría de los ciudadanos cubanos mayores de 16 años, que hayan residido en el territorio nacional posterior al triunfo de la revolución, tienen algún tipo de instrucción militar. También es un hecho, que la inconformidad y la desconfianza con el gobierno han ido aumentado progresivamente durante todos estos años. Si en la Isla no han habido más acciones de violencia para lograr cambios políticos, no ha sido por falta de entrenamiento ni de acceso a las armas. Tampoco por fidelidad al socialismo y a Fidel Castro.

De una parte, los cubanos están hartos de los proyectos de cambio donde las metas de libertad, democracia y prosperidad estén por alcanzar a través de acciones de sangre y violencia. Porque esas *guerras necesarias* han llevado a la nación cubana a la situación actual. En otro sentido, hasta ahora no ha habido una propuesta de futuro real sin transitar por interminables rendiciones de cuenta. En otras palabras, la mayoría de los cubanos en la Isla quieren cambios que conlleven los ajustes políticos y socio económicos, que permitan la normalización de la vida en el país a través de acciones civilizadas.

Si tenemos en cuenta que la población residente en Cuba que tiene entre 16 y 59 años de edad,[2] sólo ha ejercido sus derechos laborales y electorales bajo el socialismo, y representan el 63 por ciento de la población con derecho al voto, podemos comprender por qué los discursos basados en la recuperación del *pasado*, han perdido receptividad y capacidad movilizativa. En nombre de ese *pasado*, demonizado o evangelizado, según el orador, a la población cubana menor de 60 años, se les secuestró el presente y se les suprimió la posibilidad de proyectar el futuro, individual y nacional.

Desde mi punto de vista, el documento del Presidente de los Estados Unidos, propone a los cubanos, pensar soluciones alternativas a la violencia; así como, la necesidad de atemperarse a la realidad política contemporánea y enfocar el problema a través de transacciones políticas. En este documento la administración vigente del *amigo-enemigo* histórico de los cubanos, hace un llamado a la cordura política, y expresa sus puntos de vista sobre las posibilidades de futuro en una Cuba democrática.

En una tónica muy parecida, el Grupo de Trabajo para la Disidencia Interna, sin tener acceso al texto

---

2. Los que ahora tienen 16 años nacieron en 1981 y aprendieron a leer cuando se estaba debatiendo sobre la perestroika, la glasnost y el derrumbe del campo socialista. Los que ahora tienen 59 años, en las elecciones de 1958 no tenían edad para votar, y los que participaron en la lucha contra Batista, lo hicieron en edades de la adolescencia tardía y la juventud temprana.

completo del documento citado, coincide con el planteamiento clave—el cambio en Cuba tiene que ser realizado por los cubanos: *"la autodeterminación del pueblo cubano es un derecho soberano y nacional de los ciudadanos de Cuba que debe ejercerse libre de toda interferencia por parte de gobiernos de otros países... el momento, la naturaleza y el rumbo de la transición en la Isla tienen que ser determinados por el propio pueblo de Cuba."*[3]

¿NEGOCIACION? ¿CON QUIEN Y QUE?

El camino cubano hacia la democracia no puede ser a través de un cambio violento, porque no traería democracia, sino todo lo contrario, haría al país social y políticamente ingobernable, profundizando la situación de caos existente y, precisamente, de lo que se trata es de acabar con el caos en el que hoy se encuentra la sociedad cubana.

Existe consenso en que la salida a la crisis cubana es la negociación. El problema está en quiénes son los que tienen que negociar y qué es lo que habría que negociar. La respuesta más sensata, que cae por su peso: son los propios cubanos los que tienen que negociar sus discrepancias y desacuerdos, porque, en buena lid, son los principales y únicos responsables de los destinos de Cuba.

Para los Estados Unidos, Cuba es un país más de Latinoamérica, cuyos ciudadanos han constuído una fuerte corriente migratoria por razones de desestabilización económica, política y social de su país, como consencuencia de una revolución socialista, que rompió el área de influencia política en el continente, en medio de la guerra fría. Para las administraciones estadounidenses, la idea de negociar el problema cubano no es nueva ni ha sido excluyente de otras acciones durante todos estos años. Siempre ha estado en las agendas como un asunto de relaciones exteriores de la nación americana. La posibilidad de negocia-

ción se ha considerado, más o menos, según las variaciones que se han presentado en el contexto político internacional, en especial en relación con América Latina.

Por ejemplo, en mayo de 1980, en la ciudad de Santa Fe, antes de las elecciones presidenciales de noviembre, los asesores en materia de política exterior del que fue electo Presidente de los Estados Unidos, Ronald Reagan, redactaron un documento, *A New Inter-American Policy for the Eighties*,[4] en el que se hacía énfasis en la necesidad de limitar la influencia soviética en la región. Analizaban los fracasos de la política respecto a Cuba del Presidente saliente, James Carter, y proponían centrar la atención en el diferendo USA-URSS.

En el momento en que se redactó ese documento, en Nicaragua los sandinistas habían ascendido al poder, Jamaica, Granada y Panamá eran fuertes aliados políticos de Fidel Castro. Otros países del Caribe mostraban simpatías por la revolución cubana y establecían vínculos comerciales con Cuba, que intentaba aprovechar la coyuntura para expandir su influencia política en la región. En el orden interno, el gobierno cubano, después de la fallida zafra de los 10 millones de toneladas de azúcar, había iniciado la institucionalización del país bajo el esquema de los países socialistas de Europa del Este. A la vez que admitía a los representantes de la Comunidad Cubana residente en el exterior, principalmente en Estados Unidos. Se había celebrado el I Congreso del Partido Coumnista, los militares cubanos estaban participando en las guerras de Angola y Etiopía, y estaba en pleno apogeo el éxodo de Mariel.

Unos meses antes de concluir el período presidencial de Ronald Reagan, en agosto de 1988, en la misma ciudad de Santa Fe, el mismo grupo de asesores, excepto L. Tambs, redactó otro documento: *Santa Fe*

---

3. Presidente de los Estados Unidos, William J. Clinton, *Apoyo para una Transición Democrática en Cuba* (Washington, 1997), p. 3.

4. *A New Inter-American Policy for the Eighties*, ed. Lewis Tambs, foreword by Ronald F. Docksai (Committee of Santa Fe for the Council for Inter-American Security, Inc., May 1980). [Committee of Santa Fe: Lewis Tambs, L. Francis Bouchey, Roger N. Fontaine, Ph.D., Ambassador David C. Jordan y Lt. General Gordon Summer, Jr.]

II: A Strategy for Latin America in the Nineties.[5] En este documento se hicieron tres propuestas sobre la política a seguir con Cuba:[6]

- Propuesta número 8: Estados Unidos debe sostener conversaciones de alto nivel con la Unión Soviética, con el objetivo de obtener la retirada militar soviética de Cuba.

- Propuesta número 9: En cuanto estas conversaciones alcancen una conclusión, o al menos arriben a una etapa promisoria, Estados Unidos debe iniciar conversaciones con (Fidel) Castro o su sucesor, a fin de estar preparados para una Cuba post-Castro.

- Propuesta número 10: Puesto que el castrismo está acabado, en bancarrota y ha fracasado como un modelo para el desarrollo y la libertad, Estados Unidos debe expandir las transmisiones de sus medios de comunicación hacia Cuba como un medio de educación cívica para crear un régimen democrático. Tan pronto como sea posible se deberá poner al aire la Televisión Martí, con programas diseñados para enseñar los elementos de la cultura democrática.

Los principales argumentos en los que los asesores basaron sus propuestas fueron:

- Hacia fines de siglo, Castro estará próximo a sus 75 años de edad. La próxima administración [de Estados Unidos], debe estar preparada para la futura crisis "porfirista" en Cuba, que bien puede ocurrir durante su mandato.

- En el frente doméstico, la intención de Castro de crear una revolución permanente de estilo stalinista fracasó claramente. La economía continúa dando tumbos a medida que se va quedando más y más rezagada.

- A diferencia de las otras economías dirigidas del Este, el líder cubano impide todo indicio de verdadera reforma. Hablar de la perestroika—y

mucho menos del glasnost—está estrictamente limitado dentro de Cuba.

- La oposición interna está creciendo dentro de Cuba. Radio Martí ha resquebrajado con éxito el monopolio de Castro sobre la información y la propaganda.

- Los activistas de derechos humanos, antes totalmente desconocidos, han logrado dirigir, por primera vez, la atención del mundo hacia el deplorable récord que el régimen tiene en ese frente.

- Los militares están cada vez más inquietos debido a sus pérdidas en Angola.

- El régimen está cada vez más a la defensiva, y esa actitud continúa aumentando al costo de su aventurerismo en el extranjero sin un beneficio patente en favor del pueblo cubano.

- El futuro bajo Castro, según él mismo lo ha admitido, es igualmente sombrío.

Los asesores de Reagan afirmaron que el fracaso total de Castro, del que sólo se tenía en ese momento, una vaga comprensión fuera de Cuba, era el hecho fundamental y relevante que la nueva administración de Estados Unidos debía tener en cuenta en la elaboración de un nuevo enfoque hacia *esta isla esencial* (sic).

Añadieron:

> Estados Unidos debe estar preparado para conversar con los detentadores claves del poder, especialmente los militares cubanos que han pagado lealmente un precio muy alto por las ambiciones globales de Castro...La nueva administración debe re-pensar su enfoque total respecto a la alianza soviético-cubana.

> La nueva administración debe tomar la iniciativa en cuanto al futuro del régimen cubano. Es de vital importancia que se inicien conversaciones de largo alcance mientras Castro mantenga aún su control. Estados Unidos debe evidenciar su deseo de normalizar rápidamente sus relaciones con una Cuba desovietiza-

---

5. *Santa Fe II: A Strategy for Latin America in the Nineties*, edited by L. Francis Bouchey et al (Committtee of Santa Fe, August 1988). [Roger N. Fontaine, Ph.D., Ambassador David C. Jordan y Lt. General Gordon Summer, Jr.]

6. *Santa Fe II: A Strategy for Latin America in the Nineties*, pp. 35-37.

da, una normalización que incluiría el levantamiento del embargo comercial. Las conversaciones serían incondicionales, directas y al más alto nivel, sin la participación de intermediarios cuestionables.

El objetivo es restaurar a Cuba como un miembro libre e independiente de la comunidad internacional y, en particular, del hemisferio occidental, para que finalmente concluyan los treinta años de guerra entre cubanos y estadounidenses.[7]

Para esa fecha el ámbito político internacional era diferente al de 1980, se había realizado la cumbre de Reykjavik entre Reagan y Gorbachev y habían comenzado los cambios políticos y económicos en Europa del Este que desestructuraron el campo socialista, especialmente el tratado militar del Pacto de Varsovia. En América, Jamaica, Granada y Panamá ya no eran aliados del gobierno cubano y la revolución sandinista apuntaba a ser derrotada a través de las urnas.

En Cuba había aumentado la audiencia de las trasmisiones de Radio Martí, las guerras de Angola y Etiopía estaban finalizando, dejando una mala memoria entre la jerarquía militar cubana. Se cerraban breves pero exitosas modalidades de libre mercado que habían dado a la población una cierta esperanza de mejora de sus condiciones de vida. Después del III Congreso del Partido Comunista, se había convocado a un delirante *proceso de rectificación de errores y tendencias negativas*, mediante el cual, el gobierno cubano con Fidel Castro a la cabeza, continuaba destrozando, minuciosa y eficazmente, el más mínimo rastro de racionalidad económica. Fue la época cuando el máximo líder intentó ordenar a los científicos cubanos reinventaran una "vaca doméstica," es decir, la chiva, y se le ocurrió la idea de que la población criara pollitos para el autoconsumo en azoteas, balcones y bañeras, y se comenzó a hablar del *período especial para la guerra en tiempo de paz.*

De entonces acá, han ocurrido una serie de hechos que han hecho, cada vez más evidente para la opinión pública nacional e internacional, el fracaso total y la crisis del gobierno de Castro, entre otros:

- El silencioso encausamiento militar a más de dos mil oficiales del Ministerio de las Fuerzas Armadas (MINFAR) por *perestroikos* que terminó con la prisión de una parte de ellos y la separación de todos de las filas del ejército cubano.

- La causa No. 1 en julio de 1989, que culminó con los fusilamientos del General Arnaldo Ochoa y el Coronel Antonio de la Guardia junto a otros dos oficiales del MINFAR y del Ministerio del Interior (MININT) y las condenas a varios oficiales de alta graduación.

- La detención, enjuiciamiento y posterior muerte en la cárcel del entonces Ministro del Interior, General José Abrahantes.

- La desestructuración del MININT y su intervención por oficiales del MINFAR.

- Carlos Aldana, el ideólogo del partido comunista, quien dirigió las conversaciones internacionales para la terminación de la guerra de Angola, jugó un papel importante en la proyección y análisis de los planteamientos que hizo la población cuando se convocó el IV Congreso del Partido Comunista, y orientó acciones contra la disidencia interna, especialmente contra algunos intelectuales (el caso más sonado fue el de María Elena Cruz Varela), fue separado de sus cargos bajo la acusación de *poseer una tarjeta de crédito que no había usado.*

- Ricardo Alarcón, el diplomático de carrera más conocido popularmente, dentro y fuera de las filas del partido comunista, con mayor experiencia acumulada en la esfera de las relaciones internacionales, en particular con Estados Unidos, cesó en sus funciones de canciller para ocupar la presidencia del órgano parlamentario cubano, por decisión del máximo líder. El cargo de canciller lo ocupó Roberto Robaina, cuya experiencia y conocimientos sobre política internacional era obviamente nula.

---

7. Cabrera, Enriqueta, *Respuestas a Santa Fe II* (México: Publicaciones Mexicanas, S.C.L., 1989), pp. 214-216.

- Las sanciones a los militantes del partido *por cuestiones ideológicas* y el rechazo de los jóvenes a pertenecer a las filas de la organización juvenil comunista, se incrementaron.

- La disidencia y la oposición abierta crecen cada día más y están dando evidencias de su presencia dentro de Cuba. El aparato represivo tiene la moral resquebrajada, salvo en los casos de disidentes y opositores muy conocidos, ya no puede funcionar como sistema porque no puede identificar al *enemigo*.

- Se restringieron los contactos que tenían intelectuales y académicos oficiales con instituciones académicas y culturales extranjeras, especialmente de Estados Unidos. Por ejemplo, la desintegración del equipo de trabajo del Centro de Estudios de América (CEA), cuyos investigadores estaban autorizados a mantener intercambio personal con homólogos en el extranjero.

- Los militares, que son la base real de la permanencia en el poder de Fidel Castro, están siendo presionados y enfrentados por sus familias, en particular por sus hijos, a una realidad sin salida en la que ellos están contra la espada y la pared.

La movilidad de los cuadros en las estructuras del aparato político-militar cubano durante los últimos años, puede ser indicador (entre otros) de que Fidel Castro está interesado en que no se personalice a posibles negociadores de la transición democrática. En otras palabras, en el aparato de gobierno ha habido personas que han dado algún indicio de estar interesados en hallar soluciones pacíficas y racionales a la situación del país; pero, de un lado, la perspicacia del aparato político represor del gobierno cubano, y del otro, las suspicacias de las organizaciones opositoras del exilio, han hecho posible que Castro haya mantenido el juego que tanto le conviene a sus afanes de poder: lograr la incomunicación y la atomización del pensamiento político entre los cubanos.

Recientemente, Alexander M. Haig Jr., General retirado del Ejército de Estados Unidos y ex Secretario de Estado, afirmó a Gil Dorland en una entrevista para *The Miami Herald*: "Castro es irrelevante. De hecho, está políticamente muerto. No es cuestión si se va o no, sino de cuándo lo hará."[8]

Desde mi punto de vista, antes de hablar de las particularidades de cómo sería la ayuda monetaria internacional a una transición democrática en Cuba, habría que plantear el tema de la negociación de la cuestión cubana en dos planos, uno nacional y otro internacional.

En el plano internacional se ha dirigido la discusión sobre el sí o no al embargo comercial, la Ley Torricelli y, últimamente, a la Ley Helms-Burton. Ese es un punto muy específico que se debería tratar como lo que es: un asunto de relaciones políticas internacionales entre dos países. Sobre el cual, cada cubano puede tener su opinión al respecto. Ese no es el eje del asunto que los ciudadanos cubanos tenemos que negociar con el actual gobierno de la nación.

El gobierno de Cuba no tiene por qué utilizar como pretexto una legislación extranjera, para coactar los derechos ciudadanos al pueblo cubano, y actuar fuera de las normas civilizadas que reconoce el estado de derecho. En el plano nacional, la discusión debe centrarse en:

- Amnistía general para todos los presos de conciencia y por razones políticas.

- Eliminación del concepto "delitos de conciencia" y de ambigüedades tales como "propaganda enemiga" del código penal cubano.

- Restauración de los derechos civiles y las libertades políticas a todos los cubanos sin distinción de sexo, raza, creencia religiosa, filiación política o de cualquier otra índole.

A MODO DE CONCLUSION

Al margen de cualquier otra posible consideración, propongo:

1. La violencia política no es la salida a la crisis de la sociedad cubana actual.

---

8. Dorland, Gil, "Al Haig on Latin America," *The Miami Herald* (June 22, 1997), pp. L1, L6.

2. La negociación política debe ser entre los cubanos y centrar la discusión en: (a) amnistía para los presos políticos y de conciencia; y (b) incluir a todos los cubanos en un amplio diálogo nacional sobre la salida a la actual crisis de la sociedad cubana.

3. Hay que llamar la atención internacional sobre la ausencia de derechos civiles y libertades políticas del pueblo cubano, al margen de cualquier diferendo del gobierno de Cuba con los Estados Unidos.

PRIVATIZACION EN CUBA: ¿FACTOR DE UNION Y DESARROLLO O DE CONFLICTO SOCIAL?

Alberto Luzárraga

La privatización de la economía cubana, proceso inevitable que a pesar del régimen ya está en marcha, es un tema que no obstante haber sido estudiado desde diversos aspectos sufre de cierto soslayo en cuanto al problema básico que implica: la aceptación de que para llevarla a cabo hay que llegar a una concertación de intereses, donde todos los involucrados van a tener que ceder en algo.

Hay muchos puntos de vista pero usualmente enfatizan un aspecto de la cuestión que suele ser jurídico, económico o político. Tal vez sea útil plantear los extremos a fin de definir el problema. Para el jurista a ultranza, debe primar la subsanación de las injusticias y la vuelta al "status quo" anterior; para el economista que sólo enfoca en la eficiencia y la productividad lo que debe primar es el mejor resultado económico; y para el que considera la política como el arte de obtener la mayor popularidad con el mínimo de problemas la privatización se acomodaría a esa premisa.

No hay duda de que en un arreglo del devenir cubano hay que hacer justicia, ser eficientes y obtener un consenso de la población respetando las ideas siempre que no sean impuestas, patentemente nocivas o absurdas. El problema es de grado y de definir los límites mínimos que cada factor social puede y debe aceptar. Los países progresan cuando los ciudadanos saben que usualmente es imposible obtener la sociedad ideal que cada cual define para sí, pero que sí es posible vivir en una situación muy aceptable aunque siempre se aspire a mejorar alguna cosa.

Los cubanos lo sabemos también, pero sufrimos de dos traumas, el del exilio y el de la tiranía.

El exiliado tiende a guiarse instintivamente por la nostalgia, y sueña con un cambio rápido que haga volver a Cuba la prosperidad y la libertad, pero su vida diaria no depende de ello. Es una aspiración más espiritual que material. El cubano residente en la isla sueña también con la misma Cuba pero tiene la natural aprensión de un futuro que desconoce.

El régimen ha explotado esta aprensión presentando al exilio como un conjunto de codiciosos sin corazón que sólo quieren recobrar sus propiedades y para ello gestionan embargos y legislación revanchista.

Sabemos de sobra que no es así, pero es fácil distorsionar cualquier posición cuando se controlan los medios de comunicación; aparte de que en ocasiones algunos sectores del exilio inconscientemente ayudan al régimen tomando posturas que no son muy realistas ni ponderadas.

Los países del antiguo telón de hierro que han tomado el camino de la reforma han pasado y están aún pasando por diversos traumas pero han llegado a un mínimo de convivencia. Los que han vuelto de dictaduras de derecha a regímenes democráticos tales como Chile, Argentina o España han hecho lo mismo, aceptando cosas que parecían imposibles antes del cambio. ¿Quién iba a pensar que Santiago Carrillo volviese a España o que el ejército chileno aceptase volver a sus cuarteles sin disparar un tiro o que Gorbachev cediese el puesto a Yeltsin?

En todos los casos el cambio político ha ido acompañado de un cambio económico potenciado por la privatización. Sin duda ha sido tal vez el factor más importante, puesto que sin propiedad privada no hay libertades políticas, pero el cambio de la propiedad estatal a la propiedad privada no se ha desarrollado en el vacío.

Según de que país se tratase, de 40 a 70 años habrían transcurrido y al hacer los cambios se hizo necesario tomar en cuenta no sólo lo que sería teóricamente ideal, sino lo que parecía ser factible en el contexto jurídico, económico y político del momento vivido.

Cuba no va a ser una excepción. Los seres humanos reaccionamos en forma parecida ante problemas similares y a lo que debiéramos aspirar como cubanos es a hacerlo mejor que los que nos antecedieron en el proceso, lo cual no significa copiar irreflexivamente, sino **crear** con un espíritu que sea justo y cubano.

Tal vez seamos unos románticos pero creemos que Cuba tiene algo que aportar al proceso de organización social del siglo XXI. Al fin y al cabo experiencias no nos faltan. En un siglo hemos tenido capitalismo colonial, capitalismo clásico, períodos de social democracia y despotismo marxista.

Las posiciones extremas del exilio adolocen de una cierta inconsistencia conceptual. Se sueña con la restauración de la Constitución del 40 en su integridad, pero se hace poco caso al hecho de que fué una Constitución social demócrata con una serie de ideas que son anatema al esquema neo-liberal hoy en boga. Lo cual no quiere decir que estas ideas sean necesariamente incorrectas, pero sí que van a sufrir un rudo ataque de ciertos sectores que aportarían capitales sólo si se les complace en lo que ellos estiman que es un esquema económico consecuente con sus aspiraciones.

El exilio no ha enfocado este problema en forma sistemática, dejándolo para después o adhiriéndose totalmente al sistema en boga, sin reflexionar a fondo sobre lo que convendría o no convendría hacer en un momento dado y en unas circunstancias difíciles.

Los cubanos de la isla a veces también son inconsistentes en cuanto a pretender que se mantenga un alto nivel asistencial del Estado (por encima de la educación y la salud), pues ello implicaría el control de buena parte de sus vidas y un nivel de tributación que pudiera ser asfixiante.

Debe pensarse que en una Cuba libre habrá que remunerar adecuadamente a los que presten los servicios y como bien sabemos el Estado paga con los recursos extraídos a los gobernados. Mantener un servicio de salud y de educación de primera son dos aspiraciones legítimas pero probablemente absorberían la mayor parte del presupuesto o en su defecto tendrían que ser pagados en parte y directamente por los ciudadanos.

Una sociedad libre y progresista resuelve estos problemas encarándolos con un espíritu práctico, cívico, patriótico y lo más importante: espíritu de **virtud y de verdad**. Los grandes pensadores, desde Tocqueville que dijo que América es grande porque es buena hasta Montesquieu que hacía residir las bases del Estado y de la libertad en la virtud, lo han identificado claramente.

En Cuba ha faltado totalmente la virtud al nivel oficial por 40 años. Antes de Castro también teníamos nuestros fallos que es preciso reconocer, aunque sin caer en las diatribas y difamaciones del presente régimen que engorda todos los vicios pasados para disimular los suyos.

La privatización va a ser el tema neurálgico del concierto social y puede ser fuente de concordia o de nuevas luchas y seria discordia según se maneje. De aquí el título de este trabajo. El objetivo es intentar definir las contrapartidas que los cubanos debemos manejar, las cosas que las diversas tendencias deben ceder y los mínimos por los que es razonable luchar y no ceder. Y hablamos de mínimos porque los conciertos sociales se hacen a base de eso y no de pasar la cuenta íntegra al opositor. Presentamos estas premisas básicas bajo el título de contrapartidas porque lo son. Ninguna funciona sin una reciprocidad de la otra parte involucrada en el quehacer de la reconstrucción.

Hemos omitido las formulaciones exclusivamente técnicas porque después de meditar sobre soluciones a diversos problemas, llegamos a la conclusión de que el exceso de detalle provoca más confusión que claridad.

Hay muchos datos sobre la situación actual que ignoramos (las estadísticas no son confiables) y asimismo ignoramos las circunstancias de tiempo y situación económica y social al momento de implementar las reformas. Creemos pues, que lo más útil es comenzar a pensar en cuáles principios debemos acoger para lograr reconstruir, que en propuestas demasiado específicas. Así pues, este trabajo sólo pretende lo siguiente: estimular la reflexión. Y después de reflexionar, debemos poner de nuestra parte. Para arreglar a Cuba, hay que contar primero que nada con buena voluntad y segundo, como dijo Agramonte, "con la verguenza de los cubanos," pues verguenza nos ha de dar ver a nuestro país sumido en la miseria y la destrucción física y moral mientras los demás progresan.

EL ASPECTO JURIDICO

No existe duda de que para que un país funcione y prospere tiene que existir respeto por la ley y las instituciones que ésta crea y ampara. Perdemos el tiempo ideando soluciones económicas "brillantes" si no hay voluntad de aceptar que existen límites razonables a la conducta humana. Este asentimiento de la voluntad a la norma jurídica es en cierta forma un fenómeno psicológico, pues la efectividad de la ley sólo depende en parte de la capacidad de forzar su cumplimiento a través de los medios legítimos (tribunales, etc.). La verdadera efectividad surge del convencimiento social de que es mejor vivir bajo la ley, pues la alternativa es la barbarie.

La característica básica de la ley para que sea aceptada es que sea justa y que se dirija al bien común. Este es el aspecto esencial y hay que convenir que el bien común con frecuencia no equivale ciento por ciento al bien individual.

Para llegar a un acuerdo justo hay que estar dispuesto a conceder ciertas cosas y a mantener unos mínimos. En los contratos consensuales que encontramos en la vida cotidiana, los cubanos sabemos que este principio es cierto y lo aplicamos sin mayores dudas. En general no hemos sido así en la contienda política, guiándonos frecuentemente por la pasión sectaria aunque hemos tenido etapas de gran lucidez de pensamiento. Veamos cuales son las principales contrapartidas jurídicas que los cubanos deben negociar.

Primera contrapartida jurídica: Después de casi 40 años de arbitrariedad el pueblo cubano está deseoso de vivir bajo un sistema en que la ley no refleje el capricho o la ideología de un sector de la población. Pero, para que el sistema no resurja viciado hay que empezar por reconocer que se violó el Estado de Derecho y las Leyes de la República de Cuba. La República es nuestro país y no la Revolución de Castro, que constituye sólo un episodio de su historia. Enunciaríamos así la contrapartida: *Hay que aceptar que en muchas cosas se actuó injustamente y estar dispuesto a subsanar las injusticias en la medida de lo posible.* El pueblo cubano de la Isla tiene que superar su aprensión y enfrentar este reto en forma inteligente y constructiva.

Segunda contrapartida jurídica: Qué cosas son posibles es un tema legítimo a discutir. Aquí es útil insertar el preámbulo de la ley Húngara de "Compensación Parcial por Daños Causados por El Estado."[1] Dice así:

> En el interés de estabilizar las relaciones de propiedad, crear las condiciones necesarias para la seguridad de las empresas y una economía de mercado, el Parlamento guiado por el **principio de constitucionalidad**, y teniendo en cuenta el **sentido de justicia y la capacidad de la sociedad**, ha dictado la siguiente ley para remediar los daños ilegalmente causados por el Estado a las propiedades de los ciudadanos.[2]

Obsérvese que la ley habla del principio de constitucionalidad y de la necesidad de hacer justicia, pero específicamente se refiere a la **capacidad** de la sociedad. La mayor parte de las reclamaciones datan de actos realizados hace más de 40 años y se rechaza el concepto de intereses moratorios o compensación total. El artículo 4 de la Ley fija como suma máxima 5 mi-

---

1. Ley #25 de 1991.

2. El énfasis es nuestro.

llones de florines húngaros por cada propiedad o cada afectado.[3] La compensación ciertamente no es amplia pero responde a las posibilidades del país. La de Checoeslovaquia asciende aún a menos.[4]

Lo anterior significa que el exilio debe entender que Cuba (país mucho más endeudado y en mucho peores condiciones económicas que Hungría y Checoeslovaquia) no va a ser capaz de pagar grandes indemnizaciones y ciertamente no podrá hacer frente a las exigidas por la Ley Helms-Burton. Que sean debidas nadie lo duda. Que sea pagada una suma importante a cada afectado casi todos los que hacen cálculos realistas lo reputan económicamente imposible. *La contrapartida para el exilio es aceptar que el principio de legalidad se debe sustentar pero que en muchos casos la indemnización podrá ser muy modesta porque no hay para más.*

Tercera contrapartida jurídica: En el supuesto de que exista incapacidad para indemnizar siempre se puede restituir, también en la medida de lo posible. Este principio es de los que crean conflictos en cuanto se menciona. Algunos de los confiscados sueñan con la restitución absoluta y los usuarios de sus bienes en Cuba temen la desposesión. Ambas cosas son exageraciones. La realidad es que en la práctica hay cosas restituibles en las cuales se puede conceder la posesión y el dominio y cosas en que sólo se puede restituir el dominio.

Ejemplos: Tomemos una empresa extranjera (confiscada por Castro) que requiere grandes aportaciones de capital para poner sus equipos e instalaciones en capacidad de competir internacionalmente. Obviamente se puede y debe restituir tanto el dominio como la posesión pues lo contrario sería torpe. ¿Para que incurrir en indemnizaciones, dejar de percibir los capitales y conservar una empresa ineficiente? El poseedor que es el Estado ve en la posesión de la empresa no un bien de uso sino una carga que no puede afrontar.

Tomemos en cambio el caso que tanto preocupa en Cuba, la vivienda habitación. Aquí la solución preferida en la Europa Oriental es restitución si la propiedad está deshabitada. En defecto de lo anterior se estipula el retorno del dominio, pero no de la posesión quedando el que habita la casa en calidad de inquilino con derecho de permanencia y un alquiler controlado y módico.

El dueño con el dominio y sin la posesión está obligado entonces a mantener la propiedad y repararla. El dueño no cuenta con un activo que produzca una renta razonable y el inquilino ya no es dueño. El negocio en sí no es muy atractivo para nadie. Las implicaciones económicas de este sistema son previsibles pero por ahora valga decir que jurídicamente la solución es aceptable. Se respeta la propiedad original y se ampara al poseedor actual porque para él este bien no sólo lo usa diariamente, sino que no puede sustituirlo dada la crisis habitacional.

El tratamiento de la propiedad agrícola en dichos países se ha acomodado también a las circunstancias, tomando en consideración una diversidad de casos y dando soluciones adecuadas. Por ejemplo, si la propiedad estaba poseída por una cooperativa se designan lotes de tierras a los cooperativistas y se sacan a subasta. Se dá una opción al reclamante que podría ejercer el derecho de concurrir a la subasta ofreciendo la compensación que se le debe como parte del precio o por el contrario se reputa que acepta la compensación. (Un buen ejemplo de este enfoque es el art. 21 de la ley 25 de 1991 dictada por la República Húngara y su reglamento, decreto 104/1991.)

¿Se nos dirá que existen críticas jurídicas y se señalarán inconsistencias y defectos? No cabe duda y en

---

3. El florín húngaro se cotizaba a 192 por dólar el 18 de julio de 1997. A esa tasa, la compensación es aproximadamente US$26,000. Sin embargo, el art. 13 de la ley 25 de 1991 establece que para las propiedades agrícolas se establecerá una equivalencia de 1 corona de oro por cada 1000 florines, suponemos que con el laudable fin de proteger la compensación contra los efectos de la devaluación.

4. Este país como otros ha intentado restituir en la medida de lo posible, y privatizar a través de subastas y la creación de fondos mutuos de acciones de compañías privatizadas. Se intentaba auspiciar la inversión en fondos diversificados y así bajar los riesgos. La idea es buena pero el tema se presta a toda clase de maniobras. Se requiere cautela y contar con personal experimentado en finanzas para dictar buenas leyes, regular efectivamente el mercado de fondos mutuos y dar garantías a los inversionistas.

esto consiste el colofón de la tercera contrapartida: *Será necesario aceptar muchas soluciones jurídicas que en la teoría más pura no son las más correctas pero que responden a situaciones de hecho que hay que enfrentar con justicia.* Se actúa justamente cuando la solución consiste en lo siguiente: *Los principios se mantienen pero no se fuerzan situaciones insostenibles, ni se reconocen derechos de propiedad emanados de actos ilegales.*

Cuarta contrapartida jurídica: La restitución o la indemnización son optativas. Se escoge una u otra. El aceptar cualquiera de las dos equivale a dar saldo y finiquito a cualquier reclamación.

La seguridad jurídica exige que las reclamaciones se resuelvan y se ponga término a una situación de inestabilidad. Lo más probable es que con o sin Ley Helms los tribunales americanos se inhiban de conocer de reclamaciones cubanas una vez que Cuba sea libre. La sección 302.8.d ya establece que las sentencias de los tribunales americanos no serán ejecutables contra un gobierno de transición o un gobierno electo democráticamente En dichas circunstancias lo más práctico para un tribunal americano es remitir el pleito a la jurisdicción de origen donde se pueden practicar las pruebas.

Como es sabido, la ley Helms también faculta al Presidente para suspender los pleitos de los cubano-americanos.[5] Ya lo ha hecho en circunstancias menos favorables, de modo que se puede prever que dicho comportamiento se repita. Quiere decir que lo que ofrezca el gobierno cubano a los cubanos será discutible y recurrible en Cuba. Corresponde pues al gobierno cubano dictar leyes que estimulen la inversión y el retorno de capital y a los exiliados el reconocer las límitaciones económicas que el gobierno enfrentará. La contrapartida es: *Para el exilio, aceptar menos de lo justo, a cambio de estabilidad y oportunidad. Para el gobierno cubano, aceptar que lo que no pueda pagar como indemnización debe suplirlo creando un Estado de Derecho que permita producir legítimamente la riqueza que el país perdió.* En definitiva las grandes pérdidas

se enjugan con ganancias y no reclamando a quien no puede pagar.

Quinta Contrapartida Jurídica: *El proceso de privatización tiene que ser llevado con arreglo a derecho.* El gobierno no puede dar preferencias a unos cubanos respecto a otros basándose en ideologías o lealtades, ni liquidar activos en forma privada y no transparente. Repetir la llamada "piñata" organizada en Nicaragua por los Ortegas, donde antes del cambio se repartieron entre la "nueva clase" las mejores casas, etc., sólo crearía en Cuba nuevas disensiones y entorpecería el desarrollo.

Por otra parte, organizar las transferencias sin crear incompatiblidades entre los funcionarios del gobierno y el acceso a cargos o posiciones accionarias en las empresas subastadas tambien sería fuente de corrupción. El proceso debe evitar "negocios previos" entre los que venden y los inversionistas, sancionándose severamente qualquier infracción, por quien sea, de las reglas que se dicten. Las subastas de propiedades deben efectuarse con avalúos previos, balances de las empresas y reglas para que los precios mínimos de salida en cada subasta y el sistema de pujas y puestas sean razonables, abiertos a todos y supervisados por auditores independientes o subastadores que ofrezcan las garantías necesarias (incluso fianzas) respecto a la transparencia de su gestión.

La legislación de Europa Oriental ha acogido estas ideas de sentido común estableciendo incompatibilidades entre los cargos de gobierno y los de las empresas vendidas.[6]

El exilio por su parte debe aceptar que este proceso implicará la suspensión o no aplicación de las garantías a la propiedad e indemnizaciones y recursos judiciales en caso de expropiación que el artículo 24 de la Constitución del 40 concedía. El art. 24 o la regla de igual contenido que lo suceda tendrá que ser aplicado de la privatización en adelante. No existe otra forma pacífica ni práctica de hacerlo pues de lo contrario no

---

5. Ver: Sección 306.b y 306.c

6. Ver art. 8 de la ley # 44 de 1992 de la República Húngara sobre la Venta, Utilización y Protección de Activos Temporalmente Poseídos por el Estado.

existiría seguridad jurídica. Estos principios también han sido acogidos por otras legislaciones.

Además el exilio debe cooperar con su capacidad profesional al saneamiento del proceso y abstenerse de proponer transacciones que no sean correctas. La legislación de privatización debe sancionar fuertemente cualquier intento de cohecho directo o indirecto.

Sexta Contrapartida Jurídica: El proceso de privatización tiene que abrir una esperanza y camino a los cubanos residentes en la isla, procurando que su participación sea la mayor posible. Se reconocerá el principio de que es necesario el capital extranjero, pero se intentará proteger en todo lo posible que la propiedad pase a manos de cubanos residentes en la isla. Esto implica reserva de las indemnizaciones para aquellos que residan en Cuba permanentemente, sin importar que se hayan exiliado o no. Lo que se pretendería es que el producto de lo pagado se gaste o invierta en Cuba y no en el exterior. Asimismo será necesario un sistema para financiar la compra por los empleados de lotes de acciones de las empresas privatizadas, mediante créditos suaves a largo plazo amortizados con deducciones salariales, o métodos que produzcan un resultado similar.[7]

Los cubanos sin capital tendrán que aceptar que grandes empresas inviertan en Cuba, como ya lo hacen, sujeto claro está al respeto de una legislación laboral y fiscal justa y puesta al día. Sin embargo, el exilio deberá reconocer, aceptar y estimular el retorno de la propiedad privada a nuevos empresarios nacionales y en su caso apoyar la participación a los trabajadores en los beneficios de la reconstrucción. Existen multitud de esquemas en el mundo desarrollado que son idóneos para lograr este objetivo. La participación accionaria pagada en efectivo es sólo es uno de ellos, existen otros que proporcionan resultados semejantes con menor compromiso de capital.

En todo caso es preciso que la mentalidad propietaria sustituya a la mentalidad proletaria, y que la práctica de la empresa privada dé un mentís a las distorsiones y mentiras de tantos años de propaganda y explotación. Una Cuba que sólo sea campo fértil para la inversión de los cubanos exiliados no residentes o la inversión extranjera, no logrará a la larga estabilidad ni paz social. *La contrapartida jurídica consiste en que los residentes de la isla deben aceptar una legislación que fomente la inversión y los cubanos del exilio acepten que ciertas protecciones al cubano residente son inevitables y justas, si se quiere un cambio perdurable.*

Séptima contrapartida jurídica: El proceso implicará un cambio radical en la legislación tanto Constitucional como complementaria. En otras ocasiones hemos analizado el tema del cambio Constitucional y legislativo que será necesario.[8] La Constitución vigente, que data de 1976 con reformas en 1990, no es un documento susceptible de reforma ni adaptación para promover un cambio. Se inspiró en la Constitución Estalinista de 1936 y no fué creada para limitar el poder sino para consolidar la hegemonía de un partido y un sistema. Carece de la división de poderes y funciones que garantizan que el poder no se concentre arbitrariamente, ya que supedita el Poder Judicial al Legislativo y ambos al Ejecutivo.[9] Además no contiene un sistema de control de la Constitucionalidad de las Leyes en tanto en cuanto, que en forma absurda, hace a la Asamblea del Poder Popular juez y parte, al encomendarle la revisión de la Constitucionalidad de las leyes que ella misma aprueba.

Los derechos individuales son enumerados profusamente para ser luego limitados en su ejercicio utilizándose diversos métodos, tales como el monopolio de los medios de comunicación, de los sindicatos y prácticamente todas las formas de asociación.

Como si fuera poco, la legislación complementaria hace caso omiso de las llamadas garantías y establece

---

7. Además de Checoeslovaquia, tanto Hungría como Polonia han reservado las indemnizaciones a los ciudadanos **residentes en el país** y han estimulado asimismo la participación popular en las privatizaciones, a través de cupones, fondos mutuos, etc.

8. Ver: Alberto Luzárraga "Cuban Constitutional Law: Present and Future. An Analyis of the Changes Needed to Restore the Rule of Law." New York University School of Law. Seminar held on April 21, 1997.

9. Ver artículos 75 y 121 de la Constitución de 1976 modificada en 1992.

delitos tales como la "diseminación de propaganda enemiga," "abuso de la libertad religiosa," "salida ilícita" y muchos otros (cuya lista sería muy larga de enumerar) que contradicen las llamadas Garantías Constitucionales. Dichas leyes permanecen porque no hay control Constitucional de la legislación, ejercido a través de un tribunal constituciuonal independiente, como los que existieron en Cuba desde 1903.

Tampoco hay garantías electorales ni división de partidos, concentrándose el poder en uno sólo por expreso mandato Constitucional. Consecuente con esa lógica el sistema permite la concentración de cargos en personas reputadas fieles al régimen dándose el inaudito caso de que en Cuba se pueda ser juez y diputado al mismo tiempo.[10]

En fin, los cambios tendrían que ser tan radicales que el documento actual quedaría irreconocible. Mejor es empezar de nuevo y aquí viene la pregunta clásica. ¿Se restaura la Constitución del 40 o se convoca a una nueva Asamblea Constituyente? La respuesta no es tan difícil. De hecho muchos artículos de la Constitución del 40 requieren una puesta al día. Por ejemplo, el sistema semi-parlamentario de gobierno que instituyó es un híbrido que merece justas críticas técnicas y que en la práctica no funcionó muy bien debido a defectos conceptuales. Las garantías sociales referentes al empleo asistencia médica y educación, con seguridad van a provocar un debate y comparaciones. Será necesario además, asegurarse de que lo que se prometa se cumpla.

En cuanto a indemnizaciones y privatizaciones ya señalamos los problemas jurídicos que ocasionaría permitir el planteamiento constante de recursos judiciales. Quiere decir que en la práctica un gobierno de transición no podrá implementar dicha Constitución, tal como fué promulgada, por muy buenas intenciones que tenga. Lo que sí podrá hacer es inspirarse en sus principios y restablecer en toda la medida de lo posible el Título IV que consagra las garantías individuales. Esto pudiera hacerse con un Estatuto Constitucional provisional que rija las relaciones entre los gobernantes y gobernados, mientras se debate

el futuro legal y jurídico de Cuba y se dan los pasos para organizarlo.

Dentro de ese esquema debería existir un Tribunal Constitucional de modo que el Gobierno de transición esté sujeto a algún control respecto a su gestión. Asimismo el gobierno de transición deberá marcarse un tiempo para su función e hitos que deberá cumplir, como por ejemplo, tantos meses para un censo electoral, idem para la organización del Poder Judicial, etc.

¿Como calza lo anterior con la privatización? Es esencial. Habrá inversión de calidad en función de las garantías proveídas. Cuanto menos garantías menor será la calidad del inversionista. A pocas o ninguna el inversionista queda desplazado por el especulador que sólo busca un lucro rápido como sucede ahora en Cuba. *Resumido, un elemento básico de la contrapartida consiste en lo siguiente: Para volver a la empresa privada hay que evitar aferrarse a esquemas ideológicos o nostálgicos.*

La Constitución de 1976 no es idónea para desarrollar un país libre y dinámico; intentar modificarla es perder el tiempo y mostraría precisamente una aferración a un sistema ideológico fracasado. La Constitución del 40 fué un gran documento para su época pero no es totalmente aplicable al momento actual, aunque muchos de sus principios y artículos sí lo son. La Constitución del 40 provee una base de referencia apoyada por una jurisprudencia valiosa sobre su aplicación. Utilizar esta parte de nuestro acervo político y jurisprudencial no es nostálgico sino práctico. Pretender por otra parte que más de cincuenta años no han pasado y que la Constitución del 40 se puede implementar con sólo ligeros cambios sí sería nostálgico e impráctico, ya que la simple modificación de la parte orgánica constituiría una reforma integral a la Constitución según esta misma lo define en su artículo 286.

Es evidente que mientras se organiza el país y se sientan las bases de una democracia se hace imprescindible dinamizar la economía y privatizar. Esto requiere

10. Ver artículos 75 y 125 de la Ley de Organización del Poder Judicial dictada por el actual gobierno.

una base jurídica que hay que proveer tan pronto como sea posible. Los otros elementos de la contrapartida son:

- *Aceptar que esta base jurídica va a ser dictada por un gobierno de transición, es una conclusión inevitable que debe ser entendida por el exilio.* Si será razonable exigir que las garantías del Título IV de la Constitución del 40 sean implementadas en toda la extensión posible, particularmente las que se refieren a la propiedad, concediéndose protección efectiva y real al inversionista respecto a todos los actos jurídicos que realice desde la promulgación de los "estatutos constitucionales" en adelante. La creación de un control judicial del ejecutivo tan pronto como se pueda organizar un Tribunal Constitucional serio, será también una exigencia razonable. Hay que cambiar la mentalidad de "ordeno y mando" que permea la mente de los funcionarios, por la de "cumplir y hacer cumplir" las leyes para utilizar la frase feliz de la Constitución del 40.

- *Por su parte el pueblo residente en la isla debe aceptar la triste realidad de que no ha tenido Constitución por 40 años sino un triste remedo de lo que significa esa palabra, y aplicarse a aprender de Cívica y Constitucionalidad a marchas forzadas.* No hay duda de que en el aspecto técnico existen personas en Cuba con formación teórica adecuada, pero nos referimos al pueblo porque la defensa efectiva y plena de la libertad y de los derechos Constitucionales no es cosa sólo de abogados sino de ciudadanos.

Entender que no hay libertad política sin instituciones que se respeten, y que no hay libertad personal sin propiedad privada es un supuesto indispensable para la convivencia y el desarrollo, no sólo económico sino también personal y social.

EL ASPECTO ECONOMICO

La privatización está de moda en el campo económico. Hablar de intromisión estatal en cosas que puede y debe hacer el ciudadano es hoy en día un anacronismo. Una concepción sana del Estado es la que proclama Juan Pablo II en su encíclica "Centessimus Annus" donde hace resaltar el principio de subsidiariedad, mediante el cual el Estado suple la falta de actividad privada en ciertos campos y actúa como árbitro y poder equilibrador de las relaciones entre los diversos factores sociales. Se reconoce asimismo la legitimidad y utilidad social de los beneficios que generen las empresas, siempre que exista la conciencia de que operan dentro de una sociedad donde el bien común es el objetivo primario. Esta concepción encaja perfectamente bien con las aspiraciones de libertad y desarrollo del individuo que preconizan diversas escuelas económicas, aunque sin duda choca con las concepciones radicales del "Darwinismo Económico" que resucita el viejo axioma de que el hombre es el lobo del hombre.

Hoy en día se postula que la llamada "economía de mercado" es el método más idóneo para llegar al resultado apetecido, i.e. la consecución de la libertad. Por nuestra parte preferimos el término de **economía de libre empresa o de economía de libre actuación y contratatación**. Esta preferencia se basa en que el término mercado, enfatizado al máximo como hoy se acostumbra a hacer, distorsiona la realidad. A veces se exagera tanto que tal parece que el mercado es un organismo viviente e independiente de la voluntad humana, cuando sólo refleja los millares o millones de actividades personales que lo conforman. En realidad cuando existen estos millares de individuos que concurren al mercado es cuando mejor funciona, pero no siempre es así.

Hay mercados intervenidos, hay mercados monopolizados o oligolipolizados, hay mercados cohechados y hay mercados artificiales. Existen leyes antimonopolio en los países desarrollados precisamente por esto, así como sanciones criminales por fraude mercantil y por soborno, por idénticas razones. La manipulación reciente del mercado de futuros del cobre donde se descubrieron cohechos y trasnacciones ilícitas por cantidades masivas es sólo un episodio de los muchos que han ocurrido recientemente y que han sido difundidos ampliamente por los medios de comunicación.

Por último hay cosas que están fuera del comercio de los hombres y que no son vendibles ni comprables. Son valores espirituales que se deben al ser humano por su simple condición de tal, valores que no son susceptibles de ser tasados a un precio pero que por eso mismo son más importantes.

Lo anterior no es razón para dejar de creer en la eficacia de los mercados. Deben ser estimulados y regulados sólo con vistas a que funcionen real y efectivamente y no para asfixiarlos. Lo que pretendemos es señalar que existe causa suficiente para nuestra preferencia de términos, porque el mercado no es un ídolo, ni un ente viviente, es algo creado por empresarios individuales que concurren a él para contratar libremente. Como creación humana al fin, a veces sufre por las acciones de los hombres y se precisa de la intervención de otras personas para arreglar los desperfectos causados, aunque los apologistas casi fanáticos del mercado digan que siempre se arregla sólo.

La esencia de la libertad es pues que existan empresarios y mercados donde los individuos puedan contratar sin trabas indebidas. Sin estos requisitos no hay mercados. Por trabas debe entenderse, no sólo las que pongan las autoridades, sino también las más sutiles que pueden surgir de concentraciones exageradas de poder económico y comercial. Para el caso cubano vale resaltar la ausencia de ciertos elementos que se dan por sentados en otras sociedades. No hay en la Cuba actual concepción de empresa, ni de libre contratación porque nunca en los últimos 40 años han existido empresarios libres ni leyes que les permitieran actuar como tales. Esta situación es tan típica en los regímenes que vuelven de la tiranía estatizante, que uno de los primeros pasos de los países de Europa Oriental fué dictar leyes sobre la libertad de empresa.[11]

En estas circunstancias, hablar del mercado como si fuese el maná caído del cielo que resuelve todos los problemas automática e inmediatamente es tan ilusorio que casi resulta engañoso. Es la experiencia de Rusia, Polonia, etc., donde la retórica se adelantó en mucho a los resultados. Se puede hablar de una economía de libre empresa y contratación que produzca mercados libres, pero hay que explicar que son y como se llega a ellos. No se puede suponer una cultura económica donde no ha existido más que el capricho y la orden arbitraria. El haber hecho poco caso a este simple hecho, y exagerar lo que se puede obtener a corto plazo, es en buena parte la causa de muchas sorpresas políticas recientes en diversos países de Europa Oriental.

Los antaño responsables por la destrucción de la economía, los enemigos de la libertad política y empresarial, han vuelto al poder (adoptando un barniz de libertad), por la torpeza política, debilidad conceptual y falta de vocación didáctica de los que piensan que las transformaciones económicas se hacen solamente con leyes y reglamentos. Esta formación mental es la causa de que con frecuencia se apliquen teorías concebidas en gabinetes de estudio por extranjeros no comprometidos con la realidad social del país, que pueden permitirse el lujo de opinar, insistir en sus ideas y luego marcharse sin asumir las responsabilidades.

Dicha torpeza ha producido esquemas de aplicación festinada de ideas muchas veces buenas, con los consecuentes abusos y concentraciones de riqueza dudosamente adquirida. Los que quedan fuera del "reparto" de bienes del Estado lo resienten y votan por los que con su tiranía pasada hicieron posible tal estado de cosas. ¿Enigmas de la conducta humana? No ciertamente; esto es previsible y debemos pensar en como no se reproduce en Cuba.

Privatización—Cómo y cuándo: Hay dos escuelas básicas, la del "shock" y la del gradualismo y una tercera que vive escondida dentro de ambas, que llamaríamos la del sentido común. La escuela del "shock" preconiza la necesidad de actuar de inmediato para resolver problemas de décadas, antes de que el gobierno de transición a la economía libre agote el capital político de que dispone frente a la población. El postulado es aparentemente razonable, pero adolece de exceso de énfasis en su planteamiento. Los que plantean el tema son usualmente producto de sociedades occidentales y, subconscientemente, entienden por capital político el asentimiento prestado por una po-

11. Ver Ley #5 de 1990 de la República Húngara, Ley #105 de 1990 de la República Checa y Ley de 23 de Diciembre de 1988 promulgada por Polonia.

blación a un gobierno electo democráticamente en un país que goza de instituciones tradicionales y fuertes.

En las transiciones que examinamos, tal asentimiento obviamente no existe, lo que existe es un sentimiento de alivio y de esperanza de que las cosas mejorarán, pero no hay concreción de pensamiento respecto a cómo se logrará la mejoría ni a través de que instituciones y leyes. Imposible que exista, no hay base educativa ni experimental.

El "shock" es pues esencialmente oportunista. Sus proponentes dirían: "Actuemos mientras podamos pues después se cerrarán las puertas de una sociedad acostumbrada al anquilosamiento y la inercia y las reformas serán imposibles."

Además, se piensa que el "shock" quiebra las bases del poder político del estado socialista en tanto que transfiere las nóminas y las inversiones fuera de la esfera de control de los que dirigían el sistema anterior. El peligro del shock es la secuela de resentimientos y negocios turbios que deja tras sí, debido a la festinación con la que frecuentemente se actúa para enfrentar problemas muy complicados que usualmente requieren estudio a fondo. La rapidez lleva al error conceptual, y la subasta o entrega inmediata de empresas frecuentemente no se hace en las condiciones más ventajosas para la sociedad. Su ventaja es mover el proceso adelante y mostrar a la población que existe otra forma de hacer las cosas.

El gradualismo por su parte pretende escoger los momentos y estudiar las situaciones. Teóricamente también es razonable. Hay problemas industriales y agrícolas donde se puede hacer más daño que bien si no se ponderan las soluciones. Pero tiene el peligro de la inercia y la consolidación de posiciones de los que regentean las empresas, con la eventual resistencia al cambio y uso de la demagogia para mantener sus cargos.

La realidad es que ambas posiciones tienen riesgos y ninguna satisface plenamente desde un punto de vista práctico. Por ello es que ninguno de los dos modelos puede presumir de pureza. Se hacen cosas oportunistas y cosas graduales porque así vienen las circunstancias. El arte de este proceso consiste en

mezclar las dosis convenientes y suministrarlas en el tiempo adecuado.

¿Cómo actuar ante esta disyuntiva en el caso cubano?: Con el sentido común y la mezcla de soluciones, sin importar lo que digan los teóricos a ultranza. Pero existe un asunto a resolver "a priori" que está íntimamente ligado al asunto de la privatización: se trata de la moneda. Seríamos partidarios de una flotación monetaria inmediata porque habrá que privatizar en términos de dólares.

Además, Cuba no es país que toleraría aún por un corto plazo las distorsiones y abusos de un control de cambios, ya que puede preverse que habrá una buena cantidad de dólares por concepto de turismo, remesas familiares e inversión. Aceptado lo anterior, lo mejor será sincerar la tasa de cambio del peso desde el primer momento y dejar que la población se acostumbre a ganar y ahorrar en una moneda que tiene un valor real. En este caso el "shock" no lo es tanto porque de hecho el dólar sería la moneda de curso para las operaciones importantes, en tanto el peso adquiera estabilidad y merezca la confianza de la población. En cierta forma el gobierno actual ha comenzado ya a andar por ese camino con la creación peculiar del peso convertible.

Volvamos al tema. Hay asuntos que se prestan al "shock" y temas en los que es puede resultar dañino. Ejemplos de lo primero son el turismo y la empresa familiar y de servicios personales. El turismo, como industria de servicios que requiere atención y esmero y que crea muchos empleos de inmediato, es el tipo de actividad donde existe poco riesgo en privatizar rápidamente; sabida la poca aptitud del Estado para los negocios de servicios y que el producto a vender en buena parte consiste en la naturaleza. El mismo nivel de riesgo existe en permitir la industria familiar y de servicios personales. Pero es que en estos ejemplos en realidad no hay "shock" puesto que no se deja a casi nadie sin trabajo, ni se restringen sus ingresos o la capacidad de aumentarlos.

El "shock" se produce cuando hay que racionalizar empresas con alta empleomanía, que requieren asimismo inversiones importantes en equipos para mantenerse técnicamente al día y capaces de competir en precio y calidad. En este caso, la privatización frecuentemente se convierte en un problema de reconversión industrial debido a que el Estado, durante su gestión, no ha mantenido las empresas a un nivel técnico que las haga viables. En otros casos podrá existir un panorama mezclado, con empresas totalmente ineficientes dentro de un giro, que son prácticamente chatarra y algunas que pueden mejorarse y hacerse aptas para competir a nivel internacional.

En estas situaciones el "shock" es inevitable ya que el Estado, de por sí quebrado, mal puede sostener empresas que por sus pérdidas aumenten el déficit estatal. La solución conlleva rebajas de personal y cierre de empresas, problemas muy serios en una economía postrada que no genera empleos suficientes. Junto a ésto existen los costos de mitigar sus efectos, o sea pagar una prestación social que al menos provea una subsistencia digna a las personas desplazadas, y/o los costos de volver a entrenarlas en otra profesión u oficio. Estos costos, que son por cuenta del Estado, recargan sus presupuestos y aumentan los déficits.

Probablemente la industria azucarera, la mayor empleadora de personal en Cuba necesite una reconversión a fondo. Tendrá que hacerse en forma tal que el Estado no acabe manteniendo en su cartera sólo las empresas permanentemente deficitarias e ineficientes para las cuales será imposible encontrar compradores u operadores privados. Esta industria es un ejemplo clásico de los problemas del "shock," puesto que es evidente que no se puede actuar sin contar con un plan bien pensado, que provea oportunidades de empleo a los desplazados de empresas ineficientes. El tema azucarero se agrava además por el carácter dual de la industria ya que su rama agrícola plantea problemas de más lenta solución y de mayor conflicto social que la rama industrial.

En general el asunto agrícola es de los que no se adaptan muy bien a soluciones rápidas y requiere un volumen de trabajo preparatorio importante así como educación y legislación especial.

Financiamiento del "shock": Hablar de "shock" sin discurrir en como se financia es o una simpleza o una majadería. Sin embargo la literatura económica está plagada de verdades de Perogrullo sin desarrollo ulte-

rior. En este tema se abusa de enunciar lo obvio sin decir cómo se hace, y cuáles son sus consecuencias inevitables. Es una verdadera disyuntiva: si el estado continúa manteniendo empresas que den pérdidas, yerra en el método de cumplir una obligación social, i.e. crear empleo. Pero cerrar empresas y sumir a una parte importante de la fuerza de trabajo en la desesperanza tampoco es aceptable.

A nivel estatal, la solución parcial que se ha dado a estos problemas es la de gestionar créditos para efectuar la reconversión industrial y la transición. Los créditos supuestamente deben emplearse en re-entrenar la fuerza de trabajo, pagar indemnizaciones o prestaciones sociales a los dados de baja, etc. El Estado pudiera entonces pasar las empresas restructuradas a la empresa privada dándole la oportunidad de crear fuentes de trabajo que generen beneficios y paguen impuestos con los que amortizar los créditos.

Sin embargo, estos créditos por necesidad provienen de instituciones multilaterales (no son aptos para la empresa privada) y tienen tres problemas. Primero, usualmente son insuficientes, segundo frecuentemente los plazos de pago son demasiado cortos, no dando tiempo a que se generen los ingresos fiscales necesarios para su amortización y finalmente su tramitación es lenta, no teniendo muchas veces la virtud de ser oportunos. En adición los créditos vienen acompañados de una serie de condiciones financieras respecto a la política fiscal, política de precios, déficits públicos, tasa de cambio, etc. Se pretende con estas medidas que el Estado no caiga en la solución ilusoria de crear dinero e inflar para pagar sus deudas.

Las condiciones mencionadas, en términos de asegurar una gestión económica que garantice el pago del crédito son lógicas, pero el sistema tiene trazas de ser cambiado y ampliado en forma radical.[12] El problema de las condiciones financieras, consiste en su aplicación, y en el precio de independencia política que es aceptable pagar por un crédito, dado que los créditos no son nunca suficientes y que las necesidades sociales se multiplican y se presentan con urgencia.

La concepción tradicional y jurídicamente correcta es que la aceptación de un crédito conlleva la firma de un compromiso para actuar en la forma convenida.

El quebrantamiento de las condiciones impuestas origina la suspensión de los desembolsos y nuevas negociaciones para que la política de emisión monetaria para financiar el gasto público (siempre la culpable más inmediata) se restrinja.

Esta y no otra, es la historia de las negociaciones con el Fondo Monetario y de otras instituciones multilaterales con los países endeudados que sufren además desajustes internos. La realidad se dramatiza por ambas partes con frecuencia, pero la experiencia demuestra una cosa: las soluciones permanentes no se generan con créditos ni contratos, que a lo más son ayudas temporales y parciales, sino por la voluntad de una sociedad de apartarse de un camino irracional y educarse en que consiste buen gobierno, a fin de crear uno que deje trabajar y producir a sus ciudadanos. Esta labor corresponde a cada sociedad, que tiene que aprender por el método empírico: prueba, error y tiempo para enmendarlo. Es por ello, que la labor de educar a la población en lo que se aspira a hacer y en las dificultades del proceso es vital. Sólo un gran cociente de solidaridad social logra disminuir al máximo el flujo y reflujo de los problemas, y evita que los sectores desafectos entorpezcan el proceso de tal manera que lo retrasen o lo hagan imposible de momento. Rusia ha sido un buen ejemplo, que sólo lentamente va saliendo de sus problemas a pesar de la gran riqueza del país.

Soluciones: Se basan en dos principios:

- La privatización tiene que ser enfocada no sólo como un método de devolver la propiedad a la gestión privada, sino también como un método de promover y financiar la reconstrucción del país.

- La sociedad como un todo tiene que involucrarse en el proceso, y no solamente en un plano teórico sino en forma comprometida, contribuyendo con su trabajo, ahorro y pago de impuestos.

El primer principio supone que las propiedades del Estado que sean susceptibles de venta en subasta pública tienen que ser bien vendidas, de forma que existan ingresos con los cuales sea posible financiar, en parte, las múltiples cargas a las que el gobierno habrá de hacer frente.

La reserva por el Estado de paquetes accionarios en algunas de las empresas puestas a la venta para su ulterior liquidación, preferiblemente cuando las empresas accedan a la Bolsa de Valores y sus acciones hayan cobrado un valor respetable, es un método idóneo. Se ha seguido con éxito en Argentina, Chile, Venezuela y Brasil y la venta de los paquetes no liquidados en primera instancia siempre ha sido extraordinariamente rentable.

Cuba tiene empresas interesantes que bien pudieran entrar en este modo de operar. Ejemplos son: todas las de servicios públicos donde el Estado tiene que dar la concesión, turísticas, de recursos naturales, etc.

---

12. Se vislumbran cambios notables. El *New York Times* de Julio 15 de 1997, publica un artículo donde se anuncia que el Fondo Monetario va a comenzar a conceder créditos para procurar el "buen Gobierno." Argentina sería el primer caso y el crédito se condicionaría a que existiesen mejoras institucionales tales como tribunales eficientes, mejorías en la educación, salud, sistema fiscal, etc. Como casi todas las teorías peligrosas de concentración del poder esta modalidad tendría una base aparentemente lógica, que pudiera enunciarse así: "Los malos gobiernos crean riesgos para los inversionistas y prestamistas; riesgos que no son solamente fiscales sino que afectan a toda la sociedad y sus instituciones. Procuremos pues gobiernos a nuestro estilo que es el bueno." Faltaría saber que hace al Fondo competente para ser maestro de ciencias sociales a nivel mundial y que competencia tiene sobre materias educativas, jurídicas o de sanidad. Una cosa es exigir condiciones que inciden directamente sobre la capacidad de generar recursos para pagar un crédito puramente financiero y otra conceder créditos a fin de "comprar" la facultad de actuar como juez en materias sociales. Sea que el Fondo actuase directamente o pasase esos trabajos a terceros (léase consultores a quienes habrá que remunerar) tendremos el caso de que los ciudadanos pagarían impuestos para liquidar deudas cuya condición es que otras personas (no electas) evalúen el trabajo de los gobiernen. Se rompe así el primer principio de buen gobierno, a saber: responsabilidad y actuación directa y transparente de los funcionarios ante los electores, con quienes deben discutir lo que conviene a su sociedad y no lo que estime conveniente una burocracia internacional que no vive en esa sociedad ni rinde cuentas de su gestión sea buena o mala. Cada sociedad tiene que aprender a pedir cuentas a quienes deben rendirlas y pueden ser echados de sus cargos. El hecho de que este proceso tome tiempo y sea traumático es parte del aprendizaje de la libertad. Lo propuesto concentra el poder, crea demasiadas excusas y traslada la responsabilidad a quienes ni la asumen ni rinden cuentas. ¡Flaco servicio al buen gobierno!

Manejando bien los activos de primera y extrayendo de su venta el máximo, se pueden allegar recursos muy considerables. En cierta forma la privatización tiene que ser vista como lo siguiente: la liquidación de los malos negocios en la forma menos costosa posible; la venta de los buenos negocios al mejor precio posible; y en buena parte la financiación de lo primero a través de lo segundo.

Dentro de este esquema cabe lo que señalábamos anteriormente sobre indemnizaciones y restitución. Se debe indemnizar en la medida de lo posible, tal como hacen las legislaciones de la Europa Oriental o sea sin quebrar al Estado (no hay otra salida); y se debe restituir con criterio de función social o sea a quien pueda poner el activo a producir en forma rentable y asegure así la creación continuada de empleos. Si el dueño antiguo no es capaz de asegurar este resultado le cabe la opción de elegir la indemnización o asociarse con alguien que tenga mayores recursos para acceder a la subasta de los activos. En este caso utilizaría sus cupos de indemnización como parte del precio, autofinanciando así la indemnización.[13]

La contratación de créditos con las instituciones multilaterales debe hacerse en condiciones sensatas. Si los plazos de amortización son de imposible cumplimiento es mejor no aceptar el crédito. Si las condiciones de política a seguir son tan estrechas que no permiten un campo de acción legítimo será también mejor no aceptar. Cuba ha vivido con tan poco por tanto tiempo, y tiene tantas posibilidades que no puede ni debe hipotecar su futuro político ni económico por el Bíblico plato de lentejas. Aunque las ayudas facilitarían el proceso de reconstrucción recuérdese que nunca serán suficientes en cantidad ni oportunidad.

Las soluciones parciales tienen un precio que no puede ser exagerado, ni tampoco pueden conllevar la aceptación de un sistema de paternalismo tal que retrase una vez más el desarrollo político e institucional de la isla. Ya llevamos casi cuarenta años sujetos a diversos "sabios" domésticos y extranjeros y es hora de que se aplique el principio de "vox populi vox Dei."

Lo anterior nos lleva nuevamente al tema jurídico/financiero. Para salir adelante, aún sin ayudas multilaterales de importancia, hace falta contar con un sistema legal que dé garantías tales al inversionista, que lo que no se supla por una fuente entre por la vía preferida de la inversión privada. Una buena legislación mercantil y seriedad en su aplicación (buen sistema judicial) haría de Cuba un destino muy atractivo para las inversiones, fomentando así la flotación de emisiones de títulos valores que financiarán la reconstrucción y serían el verdadero motor de ésta. Igualmente, el sistema fiscal debe proporciar estímulos a la reinversión de las utilidades de las empresas mediante desgravaciones fiscales.

Una legislación de Bolsa moderna y dinámica permitiría además canalizar parte del ahorro popular a valores bursátiles, potenciando así la participación accionaria de los empleados en las empresas; y haría más interesante la creación de fondos de retiro que inviertan parte de sus activos en valores. Una vez que este proceso de contribución al retiro e inversión de los productos en títulos valores cobra impulso, se convierte en una máquina de movimiento perpetuo. El capital generado por las empresas que lanzan emisiones permite la creación de nuevos empleos y de personas que ahorran y contribuyen a sus fondos de retiro. El ahorro a su vez genera nuevo capital, parte del cual se invierte en acciones. Dicho ahorro debe ser estimulado, desgravándose por completo los pagos por concepto de intereses. Las ganancias de capital también deben ser desgravadas a ciertos niveles populares y gravadas a una tasa preferente a otros niveles, a fin de estimular la inversión.

El dinamismo bursátil facilitaría resolver el problema de las indemnizaciones, pues la creación de nuevas empresas con salida a Bolsa hace que los que reciban cupones de indemnización puedan invertirlos en empresas con crecimiento. Todo esto se ha ensayado ya

---

13. El detalle sobre las cantidades a indemnizar y los métodos específicos, no son objeto de este trabajo. Un estudio de la legislación y circunstancias de la Europa Oriental nos ha llevado a la conclusión de que hay demasiadas variables propias de cada nación y economía para pretender dar una indicación siquiera razonable.

con buenos resultados en Europa Oriental, pero confiamos en que puede ser mejorado en Cuba, dada nuestra proximidad a los mercados de capitales y la capacidad de gestión financiera de muchos cubanos, que conocen bien el medio por haber trabajado en él.[14]

El principio de comprometer a la sociedad tiene dos vertientes una general y otra específica. En general significa la necesidad de explicar al pueblo que aunque el desastre lo gestó un sector de la sociedad nos afectó a todos dentro y fuera de Cuba. Y que a todos nos toca colaborar en la solución, pagar nuestra parte del costo de la reconstrucción y beneficiarnos de sus resultados. Frente a los desastres no cabe un individualismo exagerado donde cada cual pretende lo máximo. Los ciclones afectan por igual a los buenos y a los malos, no son justos. En sentido específico comprometer significa que tiene que existir una aportación tangible de cada cual. No se trata de un compromiso retórico.

Método: Un fondo para la reconstrucción debe ser organizado, y nutrirse de los ingresos producto de las ventas por concepto de privatización, un impuesto especial ad valorem aplicable solamente sobre artículos de uso suntuario (se controla así el consumismo demencial, tan frecuente en las transiciones) y un recargo modesto al impuesto sobre la renta, aplicado al exceso sobre cierto nivel de ingresos.

El objetivo debe ser no sólo recabar fondos, sino crear un ambiente de solidaridad donde a medida que los beneficios del cambio llegan a ciertos sectores de la población, sean revertidos precisamente en entrenar al elemento humano que hará posible el cambio. Con ésto explicamos el propósito del fondo: educar, buscar empleo a los desplazados y durante ese período cubrir sus sueldos. Los beneficiados a su vez pagarán impuestos al fondo cuando estén empleados y sus ingresos lleguen a un nivel adecuado.

En términos económicos la contrapartida que tenemos que aceptar es: *solidaridad nacional o cada cual por su cuenta.* La primera produce la capacidad de enfrentar los múltiples problemas que explicamos con un espíritu inteligente y práctico. La segunda nos puede conducir a ser nuevamente manipulados, explotados y sujetos tal vez a una nueva tiranía que no por más sutil deja de ser menos peligrosa.

EL ASPECTO POLITICO

Por alguna razón a lo largo de su historia, Cuba ha sido país de contrapuntos, desfases y reacciones sorprendentes. La última colonia en separarse de España, fué la primera en incorporar ciertos adelantos como el cable trasatlántico con Europa, y los ferrocarriles. Fué a su vez el conflicto colonial más notable de finales del siglo XIX. Sufrió el ataque de una fuerza expedicionaria desmesurada relativa su población y emergió devastada de la guerra del 95, para recuperarse con rapidez vertiginosa.[15]

Abundando en sorpresas, en el siglo XX Cuba se incorpora sorpresivamente tarde al comunismo internacional, cuando la decadencia de este sistema ya se había gestado como consecuencia de la segunda guerra mundial. Y este pequeño y sorprendente país se dedica a ser punta de lanza del comunismo y a inmiscuirse en cuanta trifulca existía en la guerra fría y casi logra hacerla caliente en 1962. No contentos con el abrazo tardío al marxismo, los dirigentes actuales y parte de la población que acogió la Revolución, con entusiamo entonces juvenil, continúan aferrados a él (por razones de una auto-defensa mal concebida), aún después de que el sistema creó una situación nacional que ni a Marx le parecería justificable.

---

14. Para información detallada sobre la legislación de Europa Oriental, ver la ley #44 de 1992 sobre Co-Propiedad e Inversión Accionaria de Empleados en Empresas; la ley #54 sobre Venta de Activos del Estado, ambas de Hungría; la ley de 26 de Febrero de 1991 sobre Venta de Activos y el decreto sobre uso de Cupones de Inversión de Septiembre 6, 1991, ambos de Checoeslovaquia; y la ley de Fondos Nacionales de Inversión de Abril 30 de 1993 de Polonia.

15. De 1895 a 1898 España envió a Cuba una fuerza expedicionaria de casi 225,000 hombres respondiendo a la promesa del Ministro Cánovas del Castillo: "hasta el último hombre y la última peseta." Si observamos que Cuba tenía entonces una población de apenas un millón y cuarto de almas se puede constatar la intensidad del esfuerzo y sus consecuencias. Los cubanos insurrectos destruyeron la base agrícola azucarerera que financiaba ese esfuerzo, pues de Cuba salían los recursos para pagar la guerra.

Sin duda que los personajes cuentan y mucho en la historia de un país, pero a los cubanos tal parece que nos gusta estar "enredados entre las patas de los caballos" para utilizar una metáfora tan guajira como cubana. En nuestra próxima edición nacional debutaremos en el mundo del esquema neo-liberal. ¿Lo abrazaremos con entusiasmo desmedido o lo intentaremos "cubanizar"? La pregunta tiene mucho que ver con el tema de este trabajo, porque la privatización se ha convertido en uno de los puntos neurálgicos del sistema liberal y porque sabemos que volver a la economía de empresa en Cuba no es cuestión de ideología, es cuestión de supervivencia. Así planteado el asunto, el quehacer político cubano va a tener que sortear un difícil campo ideológico.

Ensayemos a dibujar algunas tendencias y los problemas y aportaciones que pueden plantear:

Nostálgicos pre-1959. Tal vez esta tendencia pudiera pecar de exagerar un poco el pasado, pero básicamente sería cubana y bien intencionada. Su parte positiva sería contrarrestar tantos años de mentiras y distorsiones. No vemos que ofrezca ningún problema importante a no ser que se dedique a exigir una vuelta prístina al estado anterior, lo cual sería utópico.

La Revolución Frustrada. (edición # ?) No sabemos el número de la edición porque hay demasiadas. Pudiera plantear un sistema de socialismo a medias, sin comunismo pero con un estatismo axfisiante. Privatizaría a regañadientes conservando lo más posible del "statu quo" y enderezaría su artillería de grueso calibre a resaltar las injusticias y distorsiones del sistema neo-liberal, mezclando una buena dosis de exageración con marxismo recalentado. Tendría resonancia entre muchos que conservan añoranzas de los 60s y 70s. También hay nostalgia socialista.

El neoliberalismo puro. Pretendería ser la solución de todos los problemas con tal de que se deje hacer. Su énfasis sería económico, apoyaría privatizar todo rápidamente (si es barato aún mejor) y no estaría mayormente preocupado por los problemas sociales. Se dirá que éstos los resuelve el mercado. Esta mantra (que por su repetición constante, se parece un tanto a las cansonas consignas marxistas de que la culpa de todo la tiene el imperialismo) tiene sus peligros pues

puede ser explotada por la Revolución Frustrada y crear una confusión conceptual entre la empresa privada y el darwinismo económico.

El nuevo invento cubano. Con suerte e imaginación (esto último sí nos sobra) pudiera surgir un híbrido de todas las posiciones anteriores que sea la resultante de un equilibrio de fuerzas o de un concierto social. Sus características generales serían: libertad de empresa y la mayor participación posible del individuo en la reconstrucción y en la empresa donde trabaja. En lo político y social este sistema sería abierto y conservaría nuestras tradiciones jurídicas y políticas importando sólo aquéllo que tenga valor probado y no lo que supuestamente "hace todo el mundo." Cuba fué un país abierto en lo económico y avanzado en doctrina social. Estas tradiciones pueden y deben mantenerse sin mezclarlas con extremismos ideológicos de cualquier tendencia. En lo económico permitiría la inversión extranjera, asegurando de que el respeto a la propiedad y a una gestión honesta sea absoluto. Asimismo el sistema sería partidario de privatizar y eliminar la ingerencia estatal en la economía.

¿En que se diferenciaría pues de los esquemas neo liberales y de la Revolución Frustrada? En que tendría un contenido de nacionalismo moderado e inteligente, transido de sentido común y al mismo tiempo estaría muy consciente de las exigencias sociales que plantea una transición y el mundo que se avecina.

Expliquémonos. Cuba está descapitalizada y por tanto lo están la inmensa mayoría de los cubanos. Proteger la creación de empresas controladas por nacionales de Cuba y la acumulación de la propiedad en manos de cubanos sería un objetivo razonable que estaría justamente en el medio de la tendencia socialista y la neoliberal. El lograr ésto sin caer en demagogias ni restricciones inoperantes no es sencillo, pero puede hacerse pues existen múltiples esquemas de *estímulo fiscal y administrativo* aptos para lograr ese resultado. Pensamos que con un poco de "ventaja" inicial, el cubano se incorporará rápidamente a la competencia pues es naturalmente apto para hacerlo.

Si unimos a ésto el favorecer la participación de la empleomanía en la empresa a base de paquetes accionarios, representación en las directivas, etc., bien pudieran surgir empresas muy ágiles y creativas capaces de competir con cualquiera. Se trataría de estimular y hacer que la gente invierta, pague su inversión, trabaje y la vea crecer y dar resultados.

Nada de regalar acciones, porque "yo soy pobre y tú eres rico"; al contrario: "te doy oportunidad de que me acompañes en el proceso productivo en igualdad de riesgos, salvadas las diferencias cuantitativas." ¿Créditos suaves para comprar acciones? Seguramente que sí, pero hay que pagarlas y mientras tanto están dadas en garantía. De igual forma hay que tratar las cuestiones sociales. Servicios sí, buenos servicios, rotundo sí, pero hay que pagarlos y remunerar bien a los que los proveen. El ciudadano tendrá que asumir parte del costo si el presupuesto nacional no puede absorber todo lo que se pretende.

Por otra parte, nada de considerar al hombre como otra mercancía más, como una máquina sólo apta para producir o consumir, siendo desechable cuando decrece o desaparece esa aptitud. En los países que sufrieron el marxismo, se explotaron los resentimientos creados por esa forma de obrar durante muchas décadas y se vendió una solución falsa. Pero sin embargo, se dejó en la mente de buena parte de la población la conciencia de que en una sociedad debe existir preocupación por las aspiraciones del individuo y una participación mayor del mismo en las actividades sociales. En buena medida, la Revolución Cubana al principio se nutrió del entusiasmo ingenuo del pueblo de Cuba por una utopía que escondía una tiranía.

¿Qué tiene que ver todo lo que antecede con la privatización? Tiene que ver absolutamente en todo, pues privatizar no es sino redistribuir el poder económico de un país con las consecuencias sociales que ello implica. Disyuntiva: ¿Se privatiza concentrando la propiedad y creando un ejército de asalariados no interesados en las empresas; o se crea un ejército de pequeños empresarios y de empleados accionistas en las grandes empresas que son necesarias en ciertos giros?

El diseño adoptado decidirá el futuro de los conflictos sociales en Cuba. En el supuesto de un proletariado enorme y pocos dueños, es previsible un sindicalismo fuerte y presiones continuas sobre el porcentaje de la creación de riqueza que corresponde a cada sector. El grado de sensibilidad social y la historia del sindicalismo en Cuba hace que este resultado sea probable, una vez que el período inicial de aceptar cualquier trabajo en cualesquiera condiciones, haya pasado. Esta sensibilidad hará proclive a la fuerza de trabajo a ser movida por planteamientos irredentistas y nacionalistas extremos, que en definitiva retardarán el progreso y la recuperación, aunque puedan ser objetivamente correctos. No hay nada peor que crear fama de difícil o impredecible.

En el supuesto de un diseño participativo, habrá dificultades sin duda, pues concretarlo es complicado pero siempre se contará con la ventaja de ofrecer soluciones creativas, alternas y llenas de esperanza que serán difíciles de criticar. El arte del diseño consistirá en crear participación obrera y dejar campo a la legítima libertad de acción que la gerencia requiere. Asimismo, las diferencias en las aportaciones de capital y de riesgo a correr tienen que ser reconocidas, acordándoles las protecciones pertinentes. No se llegará a nada práctico con un esquema ilusorio, repleto de derechos para los trabajadores y ninguna protección para el capital de riesgo porque nadie lo aceptará como base para hacer nada importante.

Finalmente, la asociación tiene que ser libre. No se puede forzar a nadie a ser socio de nadie. Lo que sí puede hacerse es dar estímulo a esas asociaciones y aquí hay mucho campo para la política económica y fiscal.

Cuba no puede enfrascarse en una nueva lucha de clases, ni apuntarse irreflexivamente a la última moda, ni reaccionar con exceso ante peligros vislumbrados que pueden o no concretarse. O tenemos inteligencia para crear un país pequeño pero de calidad o seremos una mera isla caribeña apta para vacaciones, vicios, industrias extractivas o industrias de poco valor agregado.

El diseño participativo tal vez no agrade al liberalismo puro. Se alegará que dificulta la gerencia y el manejo de las empresas, pero pensamos que bien estructurado tendrá a su favor resultados muy importantes: eficiencia, buena voluntad, creatividad, espíritu de empresa. Creemos que todo ésto vale más que la simple mano de obra barata o el control absoluto del 100% del capital accionario y todos los puestos del consejo de dirección. *En definitiva lo que haría triunfar un diseño de ese tipo serían los resultados, que dependen del elemento humano y su dedicación.*

El reto para Cuba será este: producir diversidad de artículos y servicios de buena calidad a precios competitivos, pero sin que este resultado se base en la creación de una isla factoría. Dadas las condiciones de daño a la moral, a la educación libre y a los hábitos sanos de trabajo creadas por el régimen, que todo lo anterior es una aspiración elevada y difícil, ¿quién lo duda? Pero el tema es el siguiente: ¿Entramos en otros 20 años de conflictos sociales agudos o intentamos algo nuevo y más sensato?

El tiempo lo dirá. Por nuestra parte pensamos que si Cuba produce esta vez un cupo de políticos inteligentes y patriotas, una buena parte del camino tendrá que ser andado por la vía de crear una economía de empresa con preocupaciones sociales, a fin de lograr por fin la Cuba "con todos y para el bien de todos" con que soñó Martí.

LEGAL FOUNDATIONS FOR
A SUCCESSFUL PRIVATIZATION PROGRAM IN CUBA[1]

Matias F. Travieso-Díaz and Alejandro Ferraté

This paper describes the legal bases for a privatization program in Cuba during its free-market transition.[2] An adequate legal framework will be necessary to remove Cuba's state-owned enterprises ("SOEs") from state control and allow the resulting private entities to function efficiently. Recent examples of successful privatization programs from which one can draw guidance for Cuba are found throughout the world, particularly in Eastern Europe and Latin America.

The management of SOEs in state-dominated economies, such as Cuba's,[3] suffers from a number of shortcomings that prevent the effective operation of the enterprises.[4] Basically, SOEs are used by the government to further its social and political goals. The

state's lack of concern for their efficient operation renders the SOEs uneconomical and, in most cases, incapable of functioning without financial aid.[5]

The main goals sought in privatizing state-owned enterprises are to improve their efficiency and increase their productivity.[6] Other potential goals of privatization programs include reducing the size of the government, providing a "jump start" for the economy, increasing worker ownership in the nation's assets, and raising revenues for the state.[7]

Few, if any, sectors of the economy are so vital that they need to remain under the ownership and control of the state. The experience of those privatization programs that have been implemented in a compre-

---

1. This paper is a condensed version of the paper presented at ASCE's Seventh Annual Meeting in August 1997.

2. A commonly used definition, and the one used in this paper, applies the term "privatization" to the transfer or sale of any asset, function or activity from the public to the private sector. ERNST & YOUNG, PRIVATIZATION: INVESTING IN STATE-OWNED ENTERPRISES AROUND THE WORLD 29-34 (1994) [hereinafter PRIVATIZATION AROUND THE WORLD]. This definition encompasses "joint public-private ventures, concession leases, management contracts, as well as some specialized instruments, such as build-own-operate-transfer (BOOT) agreements." Id. Outsourcing of government functions and services (e.g., water supply) is also included in this definition. See Richard M. Phillips & Marian G. Dent, Privatizing Eastern Europe: A Challenge for the Nineties, in JOINT VENTURES AND PRIVATIZA-TION IN EASTERN EUROPE 448-49 (Practicing Law Institute Commercial Law and Practice Course Handbook Series No. 575 (1991) for other, broader and narrower, definitions of the term "privatization."

3. Private ownership of income-producing property in Cuba is limited to small plots of land in the hands of farmers, and the assets of joint ventures between state enterprises and foreign venturers. CONSTITUCION DE LA REPUBLICA DE CUBA (1992), published in Gaceta Oficial (August 1, 1992), arts. 19-23 [hereinafter "1992 CONSTITUTION"].

4. See, e.g., Jozef M. van Brabant, PRIVATIZING EASTERN EUROPE: THE ROLE OF MARKETS AND OWNERSHIP IN THE TRANSITION 23-26 (1992).

5. Horst Brezinski, The Autonomous Sector in a Society of Shortage, in PRIVATIZATION AND ENTREPRENEURSHIP IN POST-SOCIALIST COUNTRIES: ECONOMY, LAW AND SOCIETY 33 (Bruno Dallago et al. eds., 1992).

6. Mary M. Shirley, The What, Why, and How of Privatization: A World Bank Perspective, 60 FORDHAM L.REV. 23, 25-27 (May 1992).

7. PRIVATIZATION AROUND THE WORLD, supra note 4, at 10-13. See also, van Brabant, supra note 9, at 188-189; Jan Winiecki, Polish Mass Privatization Programme: The Unloved Child in a Suspect Family, in MASS PRIVATIZATION: AN INITIAL ASSESSMENT 48 (1995).

hensive manner shows that even instrumentalities carrying out traditional governmental functions—including those which Cuba cites as the main accomplishments of the 1959 Revolution, such as education and health care—can be successfully transferred to the private sector.

A factor that may complicate the prospects for privatization in Cuba is the existence of a large number of claims by U.S. nationals, Cuban Americans, and Cubans living in the island for the expropriation of their assets after the Cuban Revolution.[8] Cuba has failed to provide compensation to any of these groups, thus they all have outstanding claims against the state, and may seek restitution of the confiscated assets in lieu of compensation or other remedies.[9]

The outstanding expropriation claims will need to be addressed early in Cuba's transition to a free-market society. The Cuban government will need to resolve the claims to restore full relations with the United States, foster political stability, and encourage foreign investment. To the extent that any expropriation claims are resolved through restitution of the assets to their former owners, privatization of those properties will automatically occur.[10] This paper assumes that the enterprises subject to privatization are those against which no outstanding property claims exist, or that claims against those properties have been denied or resolved through non-restitutional means.

Enterprise privatization, once decided, can be total (i.e., the complete transfer of ownership and control of the SOE to private parties) or partial, with the state retaining an ownership interest and/or a degree of control over the enterprise. Common methods used for the outright sale of an SOE include: auction, negotiated sale, tender, stock offering, stock distribution, voucher or coupon privatization, and management / employee giveaway or buyout. Partial privatization methods include joint ventures, build-own-operate-and-transfer (BOOT) agreements, leases, and management contracts.[11] These privatization options are summarized below.

ALTERNATIVE METHODS FOR THE PRIVATIZATION OF STATE-OWNED ENTERPRISES

This section describes the methods most commonly used to privatize SOEs. The privatization method chosen often depends as much on the political and economic climate prevailing in a country as on the characteristics and condition of the enterprises. It is not unusual for a privatization effort to start under one method and are completed under another, as political conditions change.

Gradual Versus Rapid Privatization

A privatization program may be designed to occur gradually, or to take place as rapidly as the circumstances permit. Gradual privatization is used in countries which seek to retain a centrally-planned economic system. China and Vietnam, for example, are implementing gradual privatization programs de-

---

8. See, e.g., Matías F. Travieso-Díaz, *Some Legal and Practical Issues in the Resolution of Cuban Nationals' Expropriation Claims Against Cuba,* 16 U. PA. J. INT'L BUS. L. 217 (1995); Matías F. Travieso-Díaz, *"Alternative Remedies In A Negotiated Settlement Of The U.S. Nationals' Expropriation Claims Against Cuba,"* 17 U. Pa. J. Int'l. Bus. L.659 (1996); Matías F. Travieso-Díaz, *Legal and Practical Issues in Resolving Expropriation Claims,* NEW YORK L.J., February 20, 1996.

9. Cuba may need, for political reasons, to provide comparable remedies to claimants living in the island to those given to Americans and Cubans living abroad. See, e.g., Matías F. Travieso-Díaz and Steven R. Escobar, *Cuba's Transition to a Free-Market Democracy: A Survey of Required Changes to Laws and Legal Institutions,* 5 DUKE J. COMP. & INT'L L. 379, 412 (1995) [hereinafter LAWS AND LEGAL INSTITUTIONS]; Rolando H. Castañeda and George P. Montalván, *Economic Factors in Selecting an Approach to Expropriation Claims in Cuba,* presented at the Shaw, Pittman, Potts & Trowbridge Workshop on Resolution of Property Claims in Cuba's Transition, Washington, D.C. 16 (January 1995).

10. This paper does not address the issue whether restitution of SOEs to their former owners should be favored by the Cuban government as a way to bring about the rapid privatization of SOEs.

11. PRIVATIZATION AROUND THE WORLD, *supra* note 2, at 17-18.

signed to unfold over long periods of time.[12] Such programs have proved to be slow, awkward and bound by political constraints. Nonetheless, even these limited efforts have been beneficial in driving the management and workers of SOEs toward profit-seeking activities, resulting in increased productivity.

A rapid privatization program is one whose goal is to turn SOEs over to the private sector as quickly as practicable. Rapid privatization methods attract private investors and foster the re-emergence of a domestic enterprise sector. They are, therefore, the most appropriate methods for handling the transition from a state-controlled to a free-market economy. The discussion in the remainder of this paper assumes that Cuba will seek to implement one or more rapid privatization methods.

Full Privatization

Full privatization is used when the state no longer wants to retain any ownership or control over an SOE. Full privatization is particularly appropriate in the case of commercial enterprises that provide no essential services to the public and have no perceived security or strategic importance, hence there is no reason for continued state involvement in them.

Direct Sale of the SOE: Selling state-owned enterprises allows the state to draw income from the sale of the companies or their assets.[13] On the other hand, the sale of SOEs tends to concentrate ownership in the hands of a few individuals or corporations, often foreign, which may cause public resentment if it is

the exclusive way of dealing with all state-owned enterprises. Therefore, SOE sales are often coupled with other methods as part of the overall privatization program.

Preparation of Enterprises for Eventual Sale: Before an SOE is offered for sale, a feasibility study should be conducted to determine whether the enterprise can be sold as an ongoing concern, or should be liquidated.[14] Assuming the enterprise is salable, it should be prepared for the sale.[15] This preparation requires: (1) conversion of the state-owned enterprise's accounts and financial records into a form that meets international accounting standards and allows the preparation of reliable financial statements; (2) writing a report identifying any potential problems with the sale; (3) engagement of advisors to help address legal issues relating to the sale and to prepare the necessary legal documents; and (4) appointment of an economic/financial advisor to valuate the company's assets and liabilities and perform other financial analyses.[16]

The enterprise may also have to be restructured to make it more attractive to potential purchasers. Structural changes include refinancing or writing off debt, eliminating unprofitable lines of business, reducing the number of employees, hiring new managers, and disposing of assets and liabilities that make the enterprise more difficult to sell.[17]

Negotiated Sale: In a negotiated sale, sometimes called a private sale, the SOE negotiates directly with

---

12. Fan Liufang, *China's Corporatization Experiment*, 5 DUKE J. COMP. & INT'L. L. 149 (Spring 1995); Matthew D. Bersani, *Privatization and the Creation of Stock Companies in China*, 1993 COLUM. BUS. L. REV. 301 (1993); Andrew Xuefeng Qian, *Riding Two Horses: Corporatizing Enterprises and the Emerging Securities Regulatory Regime in China*, 12 UCLA PAC. BASIN L. J. 62 (Fall 1993); FREEHILL HOLLINGDALE & PAGE, VIETNAM: A BUSINESS GUIDE 103 (1991). China has coupled the limited opening of SOEs to private ownership with a grant of increased operational autonomy to its SOEs. BARBARA LEE & JOHN NELLIS, ENTERPRISE REFORM AND PRIVATIZATION IN SOCIALIST ECONOMIES 7-9 (1990). *See* Steven Mufson, *Profit Motive Praised for Chinese Firms*, WASHINGTON POST, Sept. 12, 1997, at A27.

13. Farid Dhanji & Branko Milanovic, *Privatization, in* 2 THE TRANSITION TO A MARKET ECONOMY: BROAD ISSUES 30 (Paul Marer and Salvatore Zecchini, eds., 1991) [hereinafter TRANSITION TO A MARKET ECONOMY].

14. United Nations, ACCOUNTING, VALUATION AND PRIVATIZATION 14 (1993) [hereinafter ACCOUNTING].

15. United Nations, LEGAL ASPECTS OF PRIVATIZATION IN INDUSTRY 35-36 (1992) [hereinafter LEGAL ASPECTS OF PRIVATIZATION] at 42-43.

16. *Id.* at 43.

17. ACCOUNTING, *supra* note 14, at 14-15.

a potential buyer towards the transfer of the enterprise's assets or stock.[18] The advantages of a negotiated sale include speed and flexibility.[19] A private sale may allow the seller to impose certain requirements, such as asking prospective buyers to submit a proposed management or restructuring plan to ensure successful performance of the enterprise after the sale.[20]

On the other hand, it is difficult to obtain a fair price in negotiations with a single buyer, and the state may receive a lower price than the enterprise would command in a competitive environment. There is also a potential lack of transparency in the transaction, which may create the possibility (or the public perception) of fraud.[21]

Auctions: Public auctions are an effective way to sell quickly small, commercially viable companies. A drawback of this method is that auctions seldom realize the full value of the enterprises. Therefore, the auction sale of SOEs is not effective in maximizing receipts by the state.[22] Auctions should be preceded by the pre-qualification of bidders to ensure they are capable of operating the enterprise.[23]

Tenders: A tender is similar to an auction except that it is a formal process, conducted under pre-established rules and timetables. In a tender, the state solicits sealed bids from potential buyers. Bids are received up to a certain date, after which the bids are opened; the highest responsive bid wins. The competition between investors produced by the secret bidding process may enable the state to obtain a higher price for the SOE than what would have been obtained at an auction.[24] On the other hand, there are significant costs and delays associated with the formal tender process, which tend to offset some of its benefits.

One important advantage of the tender method is that the transfer of ownership occurs through a transparent process, thereby protecting the government from charges of secret deals or favoritism.[25]

Stock Offerings: Offering stock of an SOE for public sale allows the government to raise capital and spread ownership of the enterprise among many investors, including local ones. Stock offerings, however, are only effective in promoting domestic ownership when there is a functioning local capital market. In the case of countries like Cuba, with non-existent or poorly established capital markets, privatizing SOEs through this method will require selling the shares in international markets and vesting stock ownership in foreign investors.[26]

Another problem with stock offerings is the dilution of ownership interests it produces, which complicates management oversight. This problem can be alleviated, however, by selling a large block of shares to a single purchaser, to ensure there is at least one share-

18. PRIVATIZATION AROUND THE WORLD, *supra* note 2, at 20. These negotiations are often brokered by an investment bank or other financial intermediary. *Id.*

19. VAN BRABANT, *supra* note 4, at 221.

20. This approach was frequently followed in the privatization of SOEs in East Germany. Wendy Carlin, *Privatization and Deindustrialization in East Germany, in* PRIVATIZATION IN CENTRAL AND EASTERN EUROPE 137(1994) [hereinafter PRIVATIZATION IN CENTRAL AND EASTERN EUROPE].

21. *Id.* at 221-222.

22. PRIVATIZATION AROUND THE WORLD, *supra* note 2, at 19-20.

23. For example, the auctions conducted in Chile during the second phase (1975-1983) of its privatization program did not require bidders to undergo pre-qualification procedures. As a result, some enterprises were sold to purchasers lacking adequate financial bases or technical and managerial expertise. The absence of rigorous pre-qualification criteria was one of the factors that contributed to the bankruptcy or renewed privatization of about 70% of the enterprises privatized in Chile during the second phase. Helen Nankani, 2 TECHNIQUES OF PRIVATIZATION OF STATE-OWNED ENTERPRISES 17, 21 (1988).

24. *Id.*, at 21.

25. Carlos E. Martínez, *Early Lessons of Latin American Privatizations*, 15 SUFFOLK TRANSNAT'L L.J. 468, 493 (1992).

26. Nankani, *supra* note 23, at 22-23.

holder with enough of a stake to ensure the enterprise is managed properly.[27]

Management/Employee Buyouts or Giveaways: The management/employee buyout or giveaway method allows the SOE managers and/or workers to acquire all or a portion of the shares in the enterprise. This method has the advantage of giving managers and workers a direct stake in the success of their enterprise, and thus may improve the employees' productivity.[28] On the other hand, leaving the old management in control risks a continuation of the pre-privatization methods of operating the enterprise. This tendency and the likelihood that the enterprise will suffer from early financial problems due to lack of operating capital make buyouts and giveaways risky.[29]

Voucher or Coupon Privatization: Also known as mass privatization, voucher or coupon privatization involves the sale or giveaway to private citizens of "vouchers" representing the right of ownership in, or the right to buy, shares in an SOE.[30] This method can, in theory, produce a rapid privatization of an SOE, but yields little or no compensation to the state.[31] Furthermore, the wide dispersal of the owner-ship of the company allows the existing managers to maintain control over the enterprise until the shareholders organize themselves.[32]

Partial Privatization Methods

Under partial privatization methods, the state maintains some degree of ownership and/or control of the SOEs. Maintaining government ownership of the enterprise assuages criticism over selling a country's "patrimony" to a privileged few or to outsiders. In addition, partial privatization methods are sometimes used to prepare SOEs for an eventual privatization by introducing improved management and technology that will make the enterprise more attractive for potential investors.

Joint Ventures: In a joint venture, the private investor and the state-owned enterprise contribute assets to a new entity under a joint venture agreement.[33] The private partner usually supplies technology (and capital) unavailable in the host country, and the government usually provides labor and physical resources.[34] Joint ventures can take different legal forms, ranging from simple trade agreements to jointly-owned companies.[35]

---

27. This approach has been used in New Zealand, where the government extracted a control premium by selling sizable blocks of shares to strategic investors. Stephen Franks, *Rigorous Privatization: The New Zealand Experience*, 28 COLUMB. J. OF WORLD. BUS. 85, 92 (1993).

28. Id.

29. ACCOUNTING, *supra* note 14, at 11. One of the best known instances of management/employee "buyouts" occurred in Hungary. When that country enacted laws that permitted management and employees to initiate the privatization of their enterprises, many managers "spontaneously" privatized their companies, confiscating their assets and becoming owners, or selling the enterprise to foreign investors and becoming managers in the new firms. BARBARA LEE AND JOHN NELLIS, ENTERPRISE REFORM AND PRIVATIZATION IN SOCIALIST ECONOMIES 11 (1990).

30. PRIVATIZATION AROUND THE WORLD, *supra* note 2, at 23-24.

31. *Id.* Stanley Fischer, *Privatization in East European Transformation*, *in* THE EMERGENCE OF MARKET ECONOMIES INN EASTERN EUROPE 237 (Christopher Clague and Gordon C. Rausser eds. 1994) [hereinafter EMERGENCE].

32. PRIVATIZATION AROUND THE WORLD, *supra* note 2, at 23-24. *See also* Saul Estrin, *Economic transition and privatization: the issues*, *in* PRIVATIZATION IN CENTRAL AND EASTERN EUROPE, *supra* note 20, at 26-27.

33. PRIVATIZATION AROUND THE WORLD, *supra* note 2, at 24.

34. Martínez, *supra* note 25, at 498.

35. ACCOUNTING, *supra* note 14, at 11. Joint ventures between SOEs and foreign partners have been permitted in Cuba since 1982 after the Cuban government issued its first foreign investment code, known as Law 50. Matías F. Travieso-Díaz and Alejandro Ferraté, Recommended Feature of a Foreign Investment Code for Cuba's Free-Market Transitions 21 N.C.J. INT'L & COMM. REG. 511, 516 (1996) [hereinafter RECOMMENDED FEATURES]. Joint ventures with foreign investors may continue to play an important role in Cuba's free-market transition, provided the proper legal and regulatory conditions are set in place for their operation. In addition, joint ventures may provide the springboard for the privatization of many Cuban SOEs. See below.

Leases and Concessions: In these arrangements, the lessee or concessionaire pays a fee in exchange for the right to operate a facility or provide a service, keeping the proceeds from the operation. Leases are generally granted for the exploitation of natural resources and the use of manufacturing facilities, while concessions refer to a public services or other public activities.[36] The lease/concession method has certain advantages, including making it easier for the government to achieve enterprise efficiency without needing to transfer ownership of the asset to the private sector.[37] However, since the lessee or concessionaire generally has no incentive to invest in the assets beyond what is necessary to ensure a return for the period of the lease or concession, it may be difficult to ensure that the value of the assets will be maintained past the term of the lease or concession.[38] Another problem is the need to price out any improvements made during the term of the lease or concession once it has terminated and the improvements are conveyed to the state.[39]

Management Contracts: In a management contract, the government hires a private firm to operate a public facility or provide a service.[40] Management contracts are often used in developed countries to provide local government services such as public transportation, garbage collection, street cleaning, etc.[41] Management contracts are also starting to be used for industrial facilities in developing countries.[42]

Management contracts require intensive monitoring, since they are subject to the problems associated with the separation of ownership and control.[43] Management contracts must be accompanied by the deployment of an effective oversight mechanism by the state.[44]

SURVEY OF PRIVATIZATION METHODS THAT COULD BE USED IN CUBA

This section seeks to explore the applicability to Cuba of methods commonly utilized to implement the rapid privatization of SOEs. The discussion in this section is intended to be illustrative and does not cover in detail all, or even a significant portion of, Cuba's SOEs. Nor is it our objective to develop a blueprint or proposal for a privatization program in Cuba. Rather, our aim is only to examine how the various privatization techniques could be applied to the Cuban situation.

---

36. PRIVATIZATION AROUND THE WORLD, *supra* note 2, at 25-26.

37. Martínez, *supra* note 25, at 497.

38. LEGAL ASPECT OF PRIVATIZATION, *supra* note 15, at 53. Another problem that may arise is that of asset stripping by the lessee. VAN BRABANT, *supra* note 4, at 218.

39. *Id. at* 218-219.

40. PRIVATIZATION AROUND THE WORLD, *supra* note 2, at 26. Management contracts have some similarities with leases, such as control over the operation of the assets, but there are several marked differences between both methods. In a lease, the lessee assumes total control over the leased assets, and also exposed to financial risk if the enterprise is not profitable. In a management contract, the management contractor's authority is limited by the terms of the contract, yet it is paid its management fee regardless of whether or not the enterprise is profitable. CHARLES VUYLSTEKE, 1 TECHNIQUES OF PRIVATIZATION OF STATE-OWNED ENTERPRISES 36-37 (1988). In Poland, SOEs were given the option of entering into management contracts (with both insiders and outsiders) during an interim restructuring period before full privatization. The goal was to improve the enterprise's performance in expectation of its future privatization. ROMAN FRYDMAN, ANDREJ RAPACZYNSKI, JOHN S. EARL ET AL., THE PRIVATIZATION PROCESS IN CENTRAL EUROPE 199 (1994) [hereinafter PRIVATIZATION IN CE].

41. ACCOUNTING, SUPRA note 14, at 9.

42. Sri Lanka, for example, has successfully transferred many SOEs, particularly textile mills, to the private sectors through management contracts. NANKANI, *supra* note 23, at 132.

43. The delegation of a management responsibility to a private firm also requires that the owner (in this case the state) expend resources to monitor the managers' performance, lest the manager fail to discharge its duties appropriately or use the firm's resources for its own, rather than the owner's, profit. *See* Larry E. Ribstein, Business Associations 4-5 (1990). Constraints placed on the state, such as limited resources and bureaucratic entanglements, may impede proper monitoring of the manager's efforts.

44. VAN BRABANT, *supra* note 4 at 219-220.

General Considerations

Political Factors: In addition to the legal factors described in this section and throughout the paper, there are political considerations that may dictate in a given country whether, when and how particular enterprises will be privatized. Many strategies can be followed to carry out the privatization process; each has inherent political risks as well as potential benefits. Cuba's privatization process will accompany the restructuring of an entire political, economic and social system. Therefore, privatization of SOEs in Cuba is likely to elicit the political scrutiny, and often opposition, that is common in post-Socialist environments.[45] Like the recent privatization processes in Eastern European countries, Cuba's privatization will involve a variety of government actions including the breaking-up of state-owned enterprises, the search for new owners, the transfer of state assets to the private sector, and the closing of unproductive operations.[46] These actions will inevitably lead to political reactions that must be taken into account in choosing the privatization model.

There are also macroeconomic transformation processes that will need to take place during the transition period, which will influence the privatization program. While a discussion of those processes is beyond the scope of this paper, recent studies suggest that the economic changes must result in the rapid, and most likely painful, liberalization of the economy if the transition is to be successful.[47]

Important Privatization Decisions: An early, "large-scale" privatization of state-owned enterprises would quickly eliminate state control of Cuba's SOEs in a short time and allow for immediate access to the country's productive assets by the private sector. However, such a massive change could have signifi-

cant short-term consequences, including unemployment, increased interest rates and high inflation. The concurrent privatization of a large number of SOEs may also prove infeasible due to the lack of the necessary external financing.[48]

Alternatively, the government could take the less risky political route of privatizing at first only a few large, relatively successful enterprises, to showcase the positive effects of privatization. If the initial privatization of a few large enterprises is successful, the positive political impact of this success could be great. On the other hand, if the privatization of those enterprises runs into difficulties or yields disappointing results, these setbacks could discredit the privatization process and erode public support for the project.

A political strategy that might prove viable over the long run would be to seek foreign investors with the necessary capital resources, technology, and know-how for the privatization (early or late) of major SOEs, and to find ways of turning over other enterprises, particularly medium and small ones, to local entrepreneurs. For, if the privatization of Cuba's SOEs is to be successful, a balance may need to be eventually struck between foreign and local participation in the process.

Privatization Method: In addition to the decisions as to the timing, scope and sequence of the privatizations, Cuba's leaders will need to choose for each enterprise from among the many available methods of privatization, a decision that may have an impact on what results are achieved and affect public perceptions. The choice of privatization method will involve several balancing acts, including choices between economic efficiency and political expediency.[49] Thus, for example, political considerations may dic-

45. David Gordon, *Privatization in Eastern Europe: The Polish Experience,* 25 L. & Policy in Int'l Bus. 520 (1994).

46. *Symposium: Economic, Legal, and Political Dilemmas of Privatization in Russia: Privatization in East Europe: Another Case of Words That Succeed and Policies That Fail?* 5 Transn. L. & Contemporary Problems 8 (1995) [hereinafter SYMPOSIUM].

47. *See* Ernesto Hernández-Catá, "Liberalization and Behavior of Output During the Transition from Plan to Market," in this volume.

48. Simon Johnson and Gary W. Loveman, *Starting Over in Eastern Europe: Entrepreneurship and Economic Renewal,* IAC (SM) Newsletter Database Central European Business Ltd. Business Europa, Harvard Business School Press, June 1, 1996, available in LEXIS Nexis Library, 3.

49. SYMPOSIUM, *supra* note 46, at 11.

tate that Cuba's government award long term concessions for the operation of critical enterprises such as the electric power company to avoid selling the company to a foreign investor, even though a sale might be more beneficial than a concession from the financial standpoint.

Role of Enterprise Managers and Employees: Cuba's privatization program will also have to find a role for the managers and employees of the enterprises to be privatized so they have an incentive to strive for the economic success of the newly-privatized companies. In fact, the property interest (if any) which employees and managers will have in the privatized enterprise should be settled before Cuba proceeds to make the SOE available to potential private buyers.[50]

One approach, sometimes described as "external privatization," turns over the SOE to outside agents, including foreign investors, institutions, and even the public at large, leaving the SOE managers and employees without a stake in the new enterprise. At the other extreme there is an "internal privatization" model which transfers ownership of the enterprise to its workers and/or managers. Internal privatization could provide a means of shifting away from state-run management while allowing for Cuban participation in the newly privatized enterprise. However, internal privatization will not yield the same level of revenues for the state as an external sale.[51] In addition, since the transfer of ownership to the managers and employees excludes the general population from the opportunity to buy into the new company, it

may be perceived by the population as no less arbitrary than the external method of privatization.[52]

The privatization program could also provide some form of employee-ownership programs.[53] Allowing employees to acquire an interest in the privatized enterprise may quiet political resistance to privatization, but may also result in gridlock as managers, employees and investors compete for control and influence over decisions.

Classification of Cuba's SOEs for Privatization Purposes

For analytical purposes, it is possible to classify the state-owned economic resources in Cuba into three main categories:

* Assets subject to joint ventures between the state (or one of its agencies, instrumentalities, or wholly-owned companies) and a foreign investor

* Co-operatively held property or enterprises in which the co-operative members have perpetual or time-defined rights to exploit the resource in question (typically, agricultural land)

* Wholly state-owned and operated enterprises.

The most appropriate methods for dealing with each type of economic entity are likely to be different. Therefore, in the discussion that follows, each type will be addressed separately.

Privatization of Enterprises Subject to Joint Ventures

Cuba's efforts in the last few years have succeeded in attracting a certain amount of foreign investment.[54] Foreign investment in Cuba has bolstered discrete

---

50. For a discussion of the importance of selecting privatization models which meet political objectives and the interests of enterprise managers and employees, see Igor Filatochev, Robert E. Hoskisson, Trevor Buck, Mike Wright, *Corporate restructuring in Russian privatizations: implications for U.S. investors*, California Management Review (January, 1996) available in LEXIS Nexis Library, at 9.

51. Farid Dhanji and Branko Milanovic, *Privatization in Eastern and Central Europe: Objectives, Constraints and Models of Divestiture*, Working Papers, Country Economics Department, World Bank 1991, at 17.

52. Id.

53. *Id.* at 10.

54. It has been estimated that between 1990 and January 1997, $707 million of foreign investments were committed or delivered to Cuba. EIU Country Reports (Cuba) April 11, 1997, available in LEXIS, Nexis library. This relatively low figure would imply that, despite some notable exceptions, the international investor community has been slow to enter into significant long term commitments in the island.

economic sectors, particularly tourism. Cuban officials have pointed to foreign investment as one of the mechanisms on which the government relies to overcome the country's economic crisis.[55] An example of the role of foreign investment is the exploration and production of oil. Having depended heavily on Soviet oil supplies and Soviet technical assistance in oil exploration, the national oil company, CUPET, found itself after 1989 limited by inadequate technology and lack of financing. CUPET sought to solve this deficiency through several joint ventures, such as the formation of an oil prospecting company jointly owned between France's *Total Compagnie Européenne* and *CUPET*. Likewise, *Mexpetrol*, a Mexican-based group of public and private companies, has entered into a joint venture with CUPET to renovate the Soviet-constructed Cienfuegos oil refinery.[56]

As will be further discussed below, the Cuban government may be able to raise capital and "jump start" its privatization program by selling its interest in some of the SOEs subject to joint ventures to the foreign participant in the venture, or to other foreign investors. Since foreign investors are already part owners in these enterprises, turning the enterprises totally over to foreigners should have limited political impact. Using the oil industry as an example again, the privatization of the oil joint ventures (and similar ventures engaged in mining projects) could be ac-

complished by a renegotiation of the terms of the agreement to grant the foreign venturer a sole concession or lease to explore and exploit the property for a period of a specified number of years, subject to the payment to the state of increased concession fees, an undertaking by the concession holder to improve the physical facilities for the extraction and processing of the oil or minerals, and the pertinent technology transfers that will permit the state or another licensee to assume operation of the properties once the concession is over.

Summary Overview of Current Foreign Investment Regime in Cuba: It was not until the collapse of socialism in the Soviet Union and Eastern Europe and the attendant steep decline in the Cuban economy that Cuba actively sought to attract foreign capital.[57] In order to draw investment to the island, the government liberalized certain restraints on its investment practices.[58] Amendments to the Cuban Constitution in 1992 eliminated important restrictions on foreign investment, permitting property ownership by mixed enterprises and the transfer of state property to joint ventures with foreign capital.[59]

These constitutional amendments signaled the institution of a less restrictive foreign investment regime.[60] Indeed, the entire Cuban economy, with the exception of health care, education, and the military sector, was declared open to foreign investment in

---

55. *See* MATIAS F. TRAVIESO-DIAZ, THE LAWS AND LEGAL SYSTEM OF A FREE-MARKET CUBA—A PROSPECT FOR BUSINESS (Quorum Books, 1996) [hereinafter LAWS AND LEGAL SYSTEM], Chapter 5, for a detailed discussion of Cuba's foreign investment program. *See also*, Jorge Pérez-López, *A Critical Look at Cuba's Foreign Investment Program*, paper presented at the 1995 Meeting of the Latin American Studies Association, Washington, D.C. (Sep. 1995) 1-4 [hereinafter CRITICAL LOOK]; *see also* Carmelo Mesa-Lago, *Cuba's Economic Strategies for Confronting the Crisis, in* CUBA AFTER THE COLD WAR 200-203 (Carmelo Mesa-Lago ed., 1993) [hereinafter CONFRONTING THE CRISIS].

56. GARETH JENKINS & LILA HAINES, CUBA: PROSPECTS FOR REFORM, TRADE AND INVESTMENT 121(1994) [hereinafter CUBA PROSPECTS].

57. GILLIAN GUNN, CUBA IN TRANSITION—OPTIONS FOR U.S. POLICY 34 (Gillian Gunn, ed., 1993) [hereinafter CUBA IN TRANSITION].

58. *Id.* at 32. In order to make itself more attractive to possible trading partners, the Cuban government began in 1989 to form business-oriented Sociedades Anónimas (SAs). SAs are state-owned enterprises, organized like corporations and acting in many respects like private companies (e.g., they hold foreign exchange in offshore accounts, serve as trading partners to foreign investors, and can hire and fire at will).

59. *See* 1992 CONSTITUTION, *supra* note 3, art. 23.

60. CARMELO MESA-LAGO, ARE ECONOMIC REFORMS PROPELLING CUBA TO THE MARKET? 17 (1994) [hereinafter MESA-LAGO ON ECONOMIC REFORMS].

1994. However, the main sectors where significant foreign investment has taken place are still limited to tourism, mining, oil exploration, construction, and agro-industry.[61]

The most commonly used format for foreign investment has been the formation of joint ventures between the foreign party and a Cuban enterprise, which is either an existing state instrumentality or a "private" company (S.A.) formed by the Cuban government. Over 270 such ventures have been established in the last seven years.[62]

On September 5, 1995, Cuba's National Assembly of People's Power (the country's highest legislative body) enacted a new foreign investment law, known as Law No. 77 of 1995 (Law 77).[63] Some of these changes in Law 77 represent potentially significant improvements over previous legislation and, if fully implemented, could help liberalize the investment climate.

Law 77 retains several forms of business organization already allowed by Cuban law (joint ventures, production agreements, and joint accounts), and creates a new form of investment vehicle, the "enterprise with wholly foreign capital," which is a company formed by foreign investors without Cuban equity participation. Such companies can be established in two different ways: either by the foreign individual or entity registering in its own name with the Chamber of Commerce of Cuba, or by setting up a wholly-owned Cuban corporation as a subsidiary of the for-eign entity.[64] The law contains an express guarantee against uncompensated expropriation of the property of foreign investors.[65] The state also promises to "protect" the investor against third-party expropriation claims, to the extent such claims are in accordance with Cuba's laws and the rulings of Cuba's courts.[66]

The present state of Cuba's foreign investment program is not unlike that which existed in Central and Eastern European countries, such as Hungary, the former Czechoslovakia, and Poland, prior to their transition to free-market economies.[67] Like the socialist governments in those countries, Cuba's leadership still imposes significant constraints on foreign investment in order to control the investment process.[68] Thus, although the new foreign investment law creates a somewhat improved framework for investment in the island, Cuba's transition to a free-market economy will require a far greater liberalization of the country's foreign investment regime than this law provides.

Case Study of Privatization of SOEs Subject to Joint Ventures—Cuba's Tourism Industry: Cuba's tourism industry has become the engine driving the country's economy. It is a rapidly growing industry in Cuba and is said to have already replaced sugar as the number one source of income for the country.[69] Foreign investors play an increasingly influential role in Cuba's tourism industry. The success of the tourism joint ventures has often been based on the satis-factory exchange between the foreign investor's man-

---

61. *See generally*, CUBA PROSPECTS, *supra* note 56.

62. Robert P. Walzer, *Cuba Trade Official Sees '97 Tourism Income Up 16%*, WALL ST. J., JUNE 5, 1997, at A1.

63. LEY NUMERO 77 DE LA INVERSION EXTRANJERA, *published in* Gaceta Oficial, Sep. 6, 1995.

64. *Id.*, art. 15(2). However, no instances of enterprises wholly-owned by foreign investors have been reported since the new law was enacted. This is not surprising, since upon enactment of Law 77 President Castro warned that very few businesses would ever be authorized to operate as 100% foreign-owned ventures. Douglas Farah, *Socialist Cuba Alters Course to Spur Foreign Investment*, WASHINGTON POST, Sep. 6, 1995, at A25.

65. Law 77, supra note 63, art. 3.

66. *Id.*, art. 5.

67. For example, until 1988 foreign investors could only operate in Hungary as minority partners in joint ventures with domestic enterprises. ZBIGNIEW DOBOSIEWICZ, FOREIGN INVESTMENT IN EASTERN EUROPE 45 (1992).

68. See, e.g., MESA-LAGO ON ECONOMIC REFORMS, *supra* note 60, at 17.

69. *Cuba Sees 18% Tourism Rise Despite Hotel Blasts*, ASSOCIATED PRESS, July 21, 1997.

agement know-how and capital resources and Cuba's supply of physical facilities and cheap labor.

Cuba's tourism industry currently includes many joint ventures with foreign investors. For example, the state-owned enterprise *Cubanacán* runs over a dozen hotels under joint ventures with foreign contractors, including a joint-venture with the Spanish group, *Sol Meliá*. Many of these agreements are based on management contracts, including those with foreign investors such as *LTI-International Hotels* of Germany, a subsidiary of the German air charter group *LTU*, and the Amsterdam-based group, *Golden Tulip*. Cuba's agreement with *LTI* requires that *LTU* manage the Tuxpan hotel in Varadero. The contract with *Golden Tulip* has the Dutch company managing the *Hotel Caracol* in Santa Lucía and providing marketing and sales services.[70]

Potential Privatization Methods: The portion of the tourism industry subject to joint ventures with foreign investors lends itself well to a "private sale" privatization method in which the state sells all or most of its interest in the enterprise to the private investor, leaving perhaps a minority interest in the hands of the workers. Typically, the SOEs subject to joint ventures are already organized as *sociedades anónimas*, so the initial phase of the transformation has already been achieved. Thus, the only major step remaining for a full privatization is the transfer of the residual equity in the venture. Whether Cuba chooses a private sale to liquidate the state's interest in tourism joint ventures will depend, among other things, on the perceived political risks of allowing complete foreign domination of the industry. Since tourism-related facilities are not critical to the running of the Cuban economy (as opposed to, for example, public utilities), they perhaps could be sold to foreigners without raising the concerns that might be present for more sensitive industries. Thus, Cuba

may well decide to privatize much of the tourism industry by selling the state's interest in a private sale to the joint venture partner or, if that should fail, through a stock sale to other investors.

Enterprises Subject to Cooperative Arrangements

Cuba's reforms allowing the creation of cooperative farms may provide a starting point for the eventual privatization of agribusiness. In 1992, approximately 144, 000 private farmers developed 22% of Cuba's cultivable land and 34% of its pasture land.[71] In 1993, the Cuban government enacted Law-Decree No. 142 establishing a form of agricultural cooperative known as the Basic Units of Cooperative Production ("UBPCs").[72] Art. 1 of the law states that the UBPCs will be based on the following principles:

• the linking of the man to the land;

• the self-sufficiency of the worker's collective and their families, with a cooperative effort, and the improvement of their living conditions;

• the worker's earnings will be rigorously related to the production achieved; and

• to develop the autonomy of management and to administer their resources with the objective of achieving self-sufficiency in the productive process.

Although the members of the cooperatives are assigned a share of machinery and equipment, they do not receive title to the land they farm.[73] When Cuba proceeds towards decentralization of these cooperatives, it will need to transform its property laws by conveying title to the lands of the cooperative farmers.

Case Study—Citrus: Approximately 90% of Cuba's citrus output is produced by thirteen SOEs (the rest is produced by private interests). These SOEs are un-

---

70. CUBA PROSPECTS, *supra* note 56, at 86-88.

71. *Id.* at 96.

72. Law-Decree No. 142, *published in* Gaceta Oficial, September 20, 1993.

73. José Alvarez and William A. Messina, Jr., *Cuba's New Agricultural Cooperatives and Markets: Antecedents, Organization, Early Performance and Prospects, in* CUBA IN TRANSITION: PAPERS AND PROCEEDINGS OF THE SIXTH ANNUAL MEETING OF THE ASSOCIATION FOR THE STUDY OF THE CUBAN ECONOMY 175, 178 (Aug. 1996) [hereinafter ASCE-6].

der the control of the Junta Central de Planificación (JUCEPLAN).[74] Joint venture agreements have aided in stemming the almost 40% decline in citrus production that took place between 1989 and 1993.[75] For example, the British company *Sims & Co.* has created a joint venture with Cuba by supplying Cuban fruit to two major British supermarket chains. Cuba's citrus company, the National Fruit Corporation, also maintains a joint venture with the Greek company, *Lomar Shipping,* under the name *Lola Fruit, S.A.*, by exporting its citrus to Europe.[76]

Cuba's citrus industry has also employed the management contract models prevalent in its tourism industry. For example, the Israeli Company, *Grupo BM,* manages a lime plantation of 115,000 acres in the Matanzas province. The citrus fruit industry has also benefited from Chilean capital and foreign fertilizer for its product export.[77]

Implementation of the 1993 Cuban legislation in the citrus industry has allowed the creation of cooperatively run farm units providing a measure of autonomy for farmers.[78] Since many citrus groves have already been turned over to cooperatives, a logical step in the privatization process would be to give title to the land to the cooperative farmers, probably subject to a long-term mortgage in favor of the state and certain restrictive covenants on the alienability and use of the land for a limited period of time. Also, the farmers' limited experience in making market-based decisions requires that agricultural privatization be managed, at least initially, by an experienced participant in the joint venture with access to international markets and technology. (This participant can be, if appropriate, the joint venture partner that holds an existing management contract.) Such a manager should be required to commit to acquiring a signifi-

cant stake in the output of the agricultural enterprise to ensure international market access for the harvest and bind the manager to the venture in order to avoid the "shirking" of responsibilities.

Enterprises Under Total State Ownership and Control

Enterprises under total ownership and control by the state comprise the majority of the non-agricultural business activities in Cuba. Also under total state control are a number of agencies and instrumentalities that carry out public or public/private functions (e.g., the ports). Clearly, no single formula would suffice to meet the needs of every type of SOE. The discussion that follows provides examples of approaches that could be applied to important categories of enterprises.

Large SOEs: Some of the large, state-owned SOEs could be attractive to foreign investors and could be sold off through a tender process, that is, through an offer to sell the stock of the company (after its transformation into a *sociedad anónima*) to pre-qualified bidders. The Cuban national carrier Cubana de Aviación might be sold in that manner, and so could the rum refineries, cigar manufacturing facilities, and other industrial and commercial enterprises. As an intermediate step to full privatization, these SOEs might have to be run under management contracts for a period of time in advance of the privatization in order to improve their efficiency and make them more attractive acquisition targets.

Medium and Small-Sized Enterprises: There are a large number of medium and small industrial and commercial enterprises throughout Cuba. Many of these are insolvent or uneconomical to operate due to obsolete equipment or technologies, need for expen-

---

74. Joseph M. Perry and Louis A. Woods, *Cuban Citrus Production in a Post-Transition Economy, in* CUBA IN TRANSITION: PAPERS AND PROCEEDINGS OF THE FIFTH ANNUAL MEETING OF THE ASSOCIATION FOR THE STUDY OF THE CUBAN ECONOMY 383, 384 (Aug. 1995) [hereinafter ASCE-5].

75. William A. Messina, Jr. *et al., Cuba's Non-Sugar Agriculture: Current Situation and Prospects,* ASCE-6 at 17.

76. Perry and Woods, *supra* note 74, at 383-85.

77. Id.

78. The UBPCs in the citrus industry must still purchase inputs from the State and sell a portion of the harvest to SOEs or joint-venture. Messina *et al., supra* note 75, at 18.

sive repairs, high production costs, and general inefficiency. Those enterprises proved to be uneconomical should be liquidated and their assets sold to the public or to foreign bidders.

The transition government, through a newly-created Privatization Agency (see below) should determine which medium-sized and small enterprises would likely be salable. Those could be offered for sale at public auctions. The auctions should be conducted following the Czech model, with an initial round open only to Cuban nationals, and a second round open to foreign investors as well as Cuban nationals if the first round fails to yield a satisfactory bid. The main problem to be encountered by Cuban nationals wishing to participate in these auctions will likely be the non-availability of credit to finance their acquisitions; a source of credit for such entrepreneurs should be established in advance of the auctions.

Enterprises Providing Public Services: There are a number of SOEs that provide essential public services: energy, bus and rail transportation, postal service, water supply, garbage collection and disposal, airports, ports, and the like. While each of these presents a different picture in terms of financial and physical condition, they bear in common the need to ensure that the services are provided reliably and at as low a cost as possible to the population. To ensure

this result, the transition government should concession out through competitive bidding the provision of these services to qualified foreign bidders.

Some of the enterprises—e.g., the power companies—may be amenable to a sale through a tender process. However, given the political sensitivity of turning ownership of public utilities to foreigners, the actual sale may need to be postponed by several years. In the meantime, the terms of the concession agreement should require the concession holder to make the necessary capital investment to upgrade, expand and modernize the facilities.[79]

A Special Case—The Sugar Industry: Cuba's sugar industry has suffered a spectacular decline since the demise of the Soviet Union, a formerly reliable trading partner that supported Cuba's industry through favorable trading of oil for sugar .[80] The industry is significantly distressed, after a number of years of decreasing sugar cane production, deteriorating physical plant, and poor labor productivity. This has been true even after the conversion of state farms into UBPCs.[81] Cuba claims to seek foreign investment in its sugar industry, but has made no moves to privatize the basic components of the industry.[82]

The establishment of cooperatives in the sugar plantations may allow the use of the same transitional

---

79. As part of the concession of public utilities and other enterprises providing public services, the transition government may enter into Build-Own-Operate-Transfer (BOOT) type arrangements with foreign investors. BOOT projects are typically government concessions for large projects (typically, infrastructure development projects) built and financed by the private sector. PRIVATIZATION AROUND THE WORLD, *supra* note 4 at 25. Under such a concession, the private investor operates the project long enough to recover its investment and obtain a return by charging user fees. At the end of the term, ownership and management of the enterprise are turned over to the government.. *Id.* Malaysia has implemented an aggressive BOOT program which has resulted in the construction of billions of dollars worth of projects, including highways and submarine pipelines. The government expects to build airports, free-trade zones, railway and road projects, and water supply and treatment facilities through BOOT concessions. Matthew L. Hensley & Edward P. White, *The Privatization Experience in Malaysia: Integrating Build-Own and Build-Operate-Transfer Techniques with the National Privatization Strategy*, 28 COL. J. OF WORLD. BUS. 71, 79 (1993).

80. Oscar Echevarría, *Cuba and the International Sugar Market*, ASCE-5 at 363, 364-65; CONFRONTING THE CRISIS, *supra* note 57, at 214-15.

81. *Havana Mum on Sugar Harvest Outcome*, CUBANEWS, June, 1997, at 2; *Descalabro en la Zafra*, CUBA NEGOCIOS, June 1997, at 2, 3; *Sugar Cooperatives in Deep Trouble*, CUBANEWS, May, 1997, at 8. Some recent estimates place the 1997 zafra at no more than 3.5 million tons. Roger Fontaine, *Cuba Begins to Slide Back Economically*, WASHINGTON TIMES, July 15, 1997 at A12.

82. Investment in sugar is still limited to the prefinancing of sugar crops and loans towards acquisition of fuel, fertilizers, herbicides, spare parts, and other inputs rather than the transfer of ownership or control of productive assets. *See Sugar Slump Blights Improving Cuban Economy*, REUTERS, Jul. 21, 1995; *Dutch ING Financing 20 Pct. of Cuban Sugar*, REUTERS, Apr. 4, 1995. However, some of this financing may be disappearing due to concerns over U.S. actions against foreign investors in Cuba. *ING Withdrawal May Involve Bank Acquisition*, CUBANEWS, September, 1996, at 3.

model for the sugar cane production as was discussed earlier with respect to the citrus industry. However, sugar—unlike citrus—is a highly processed product that requires significant industrial operations. The sugar mill portion of the industry will require massive capital investment to repair and upgrade existing facilities, provide modern harvesting and transportation equipment, and generally reduce production costs. These needs leave little choice but to sell the mills to foreign investors, either through private sales or auctions. The "capitalization" schemes used successfully in Bolivia, where part of the proceeds of the sale are earmarked for financing improvements in the SOE, may work well in the case of Cuban sugar mills. The state may decide to "package" several facilities to be sold jointly to improve marketability, and may need to sell some of the plantations together with the mills. Whatever the means, the sale of the sugar industry components to the private sector should occur quickly, since the state is unlikely to have the means to undertake the complete overhaul that the industry requires.

LEGAL FOUNDATIONS OF CUBA'S PRIVATIZATION PROGRAM

Whatever methods are chosen for carrying out Cuba's privatization program, their success will require the existence and effective administration of four types of laws and attendant regulations: (1) laws, like the Constitution, providing the fundamental legal underpinnings for the program; (2) laws governing the conduct of the program itself; (3) laws on subject areas which either relate to privatization (e.g., foreign investment) or which would be important to private parties participating in the privatization of SOEs (e.g., bankruptcy); and (4) laws whose application could result in financial benefits or penalties for a party acquiring an interest in a privatized SOE (e.g., environmental laws). We will discuss each of these categories of laws separately.

Laws Providing Fundamental Support for Privatization

Constitutional Law Provisions: Some countries have included in their constitutions a requirement that the state retain ownership of certain areas of the economy, such as mineral rights. A privatization program in those countries will necessarily be limited in scope and may be less likely to succeed than those in countries with no limitations on the sectors open to privatization.[83] Since the constitution generally determines the scope of private sector participation in the economy, Cuba's Constitution should explicitly declare the economy to be open for private investment, and impose few (if any) restrictions on the types of state-owned enterprises eligible for privatization.[84] In addition, the Constitution will need to expressly authorize the privatization of SOEs and the conveyance of state-owned property to the private sector.[85]

Property Rights Laws: Clearly defined property rights are the foundation of free-market economies and provide an incentive for foreign and domestic investment in privatized enterprises.[86] The existence of well-defined property rights is a also a pre-condition to the establishment of a system of enforceable contractual relationships.[87] Well defined property rights are also critical for the privatization process itself, because in order for an SOE to be sold, leased, concessioned, or even given away, the bundle of property rights associated with the property must be defined and parsed out. Property rights should also be enforceable through an effective dispute resolution system.[88]

---

83. Martínez, *supra* note 25, at 497.

84. LAWS AND LEGAL INSTITUTIONS, *supra* note 9, at 407-408.

85. As noted earlier, Cuba's current Constitution prohibits the transfer of title of state-owned property to private parties. 1992 CONSTITUTION, *supra* note 3, art. 15.

86. *See* Michele Balfour & Cameron Crise, *A Privatization Test: The Czech Republic, Slovakia and Poland,* 17 FORDHAM INT'L L.J. 84, 87-88 (1993).

87. Paul H. Brietzke, *Designing the Legal Frameworks for Markets in Eastern Europe,* 7 TRANSNAT'L LAW 35 (1994).

88. LEGAL ASPECTS OF PRIVATIZATION, *supra* note 15, at 15.

In particular, establishing adequate property rights to real estate is critical to privatization:[89] without such rights, private ownership of agricultural land cannot be implemented, urban land cannot be transferred, and any type of transaction involving land cannot be consummated.[90]

Enforceable intellectual property rights will also have to be established in order to disperse through the private sector the property rights now vested in the state. Cuba should, therefore, quickly accede to international conventions on intellectual property rights, or adopt interim laws based on internationally-recognized standards, before it initiates the privatization process.[91]

Another set of laws affecting property, contract laws, are essential to a successful privatization program.[92] Some of the elements of contract laws that are crucial to privatization include: rules to determine when a contract has come into existence; and what type of contract it is; rules to determine when a breach of the contract has occurred; rules for the establishment and dispensation of remedies; rules to determine the measure of damages; and rules regarding the validity of certain types of clauses or contracts.[93]

Laws Governing the Resolution of Expropriation Claims: One of the legal problems that needs to be addressed by Cuba as a condition to a successful privatization program is the resolution of outstanding property expropriation claims. As noted above, Cuba has outstanding expropriation claims by many hundreds of thousands of its nationals, both in the island and abroad, as well as claims by almost six thousand U.S. nationals whose assets in Cuba were expropriated without compensation during the early years of the Revolution.[94] It is imperative to establish a framework for the resolution of these claims before the privatization process gets fully under way.[95]

Procedures to resolve conflicts between owners of privatized enterprises and expropriation claimants will also have to be established. Germany provided a straightforward solution: successful claims against already privatized property did not result in restitution, but entitled the claimant to compensation from the government.[96] This method, however, may only be feasible to the extent funds can be made to finance such a compensation program, or if alternative compensation methods acceptable to the claimants are provided.

Whatever methods and procedures are used, they must set a firm deadline for raising expropriation claims; any claims raised after the deadline would be disallowed, and the property would remain in the hands of the new owner.[97] Although imposing deadlines may leave some expropriation claimants with-

---

89. A dependable property registry must be established from the outset, since it is a necessary component of a system where land is alienable. See CHERYL W. GRAY, WORLD BANK DISCUSSION PAPERS VOL. 209, EVOLVING LEGAL FRAMEWORKS FOR PRIVATE SECTOR DEVELOPMENT IN CENTRAL AND EASTERN EUROPE 5 (JULY 1993) [hereinafter EVOLVING LEGAL FRAMEWORKS].

90. VAN BRABANT, *supra* note 4, at 218.

91. The Agreement on Trade-Related Aspects of Intellectual Property Rights (TRIPs Agreement) of the Uruguay Round of the GATT may provide an adequate model for Cuban interim intellectual property laws. The TRIPs Agreement establishes minimum standards for the protection of patents, trademarks and copyrights, although several important aspects of intellectual property are not addressed. Tara Kalagher Giunta & Lily H. Shang, *Ownership of Information in a Global Economy*, 27 GW INT'L L. & ECON. 327, 336-338 (1993-1994).

92. Balfour & Crise, *supra* note 86, at 88-89; LEGAL ASPECTS OF PRIVATIZATION, *supra* note 15, at 23.

93. Id.

94. See *note 8, supra*, and associated text.

95. Stanley Fischer, *Privatization in East European Transformation, in* THE EMERGENCE OF MARKET ECONOMICS IN EASTERN EUROPE 230-231 (Christopher Clague & Gordon C. Rausser, eds., 1994). *Id.*

96. *Germany: Why Unification Has Made the Road to Economic Integration Difficult,* EUROMONEY SUPPLEMENT, July 7, 1991 (no page citation available).

97. *See* LEGAL ASPECTS OF PRIVATIZATION, *supra* note 15 at 18.

out remedy, it avoids holding the privatization program hostage to conflicting property claims.

Laws Governing the Privatization Process

Laws Permitting the Preparation of SOEs for Privatization: Before an SOE can be privatized, its legal status must be changed from public to private and its affairs must be set in order.[98] Typically, this process requires the transforming the enterprise into a state-owned corporation;[99] legislation must be enacted to permit such a change. The enterprise's pending litigation, administrative or judicial proceedings, and other liabilities should be settled or assumed by the state, so investors will not be deterred by potential liabilities.[100] Other legislation dealing with the specific problems of an enterprise or industry sector (e.g., telecommunications) may also need to be enacted.

Enterprise Transformation Laws: Transformation laws are the rules governing the privatization of SOEs. They define the types of enterprises eligible for privatization, identify which parties can initiate a privatization, establish the procedures by which privatization can take place, and nominate the agencies responsible for overseeing the privatization processes.[101] The countries that have not formalized these matters in a law generally have not had successful privatization programs.[102]

Power to Initiate Privatization: The transformation laws must define who has the power to initiate the privatization of an SOE. In Poland, the Privatization Law allowed the Minister of Privatization to "transform the enterprise upon the joint request of the managing director and the worker's council" (after consultation with a general assembly of all employees).[103] Under this system, the employees maintained an effective veto power which often blunted the privatization efforts.[104]

The negative Polish experience provides an important lesson. Employees or managers of SOEs should not be given the right to initiate privatization, or have express or effective vetoes over the disposition of the enterprises.

Likewise, transformation laws that allow the "spontaneous" privatization of SOEs, such as those enacted in Hungary, should be avoided.[105] "Spontaneous" privatization transfers de facto ownership of the enterprise to the current managers, which often means simply changing the name of the state-owned enterprise, rather than carrying out a true change in organization.[106] Transformation laws that permit spontaneous privatizations often also create business environments ripe for fraud, or at least questionable transactions involving the newly privatized enterpris-

---

98. Martínez, *supra* note 25, at 488.

99. Paul Marer, *Transformation of a centrally-directed economy: ownership and privatization in Hungary during 1990, in* PRIVATIZATION AND ENTREPRENEURSHIP IN POST-SOCIALIST COUNTRIES 179 (Dallago et al., eds. 1992).

100. Martínez, *supra* note 25, at 488.

101. *See* PRIVATIZATION AROUND THE WORLD, *supra* note 2, at 49.

102. *Id.*

103. PRIVATIZATION IN CENTRAL EUROPE, *supra* note 40, at 204.

104. *Id.* The enterprise's employees and other interested parties often had to be, in effect, bribed by the Polish government to agree to privatization. The Polish government offered them, among other inducement, preferential sales of shares in the newly privatized companies, exemptions from certain taxes, and reductions on excess wage taxes. *Id.* Another privatization method, conceived as an exceptional measure, allowed the Prime Minister to initiate the transformation without consent from the managing director, employees or other interested parties, although the Privatization Minister had to solicit their opinion. *Id.*

105. Hungary is not the only country that experienced spontaneous privatizations. Spontaneous privatizations have also been recorded in Russia and Ukraine. Simon Johnson, Heidi Kroll & Santiago Eder, *Strategy, Structure, and Spontaneous Privatization in Russia and Ukraine, in* CHANGING POLITICAL ECONOMIES: PRIVATIZATION IN POST-COMMUNIST AND REFORMING COMMUNIST STATES (Vedat Milor, ed., 1994).

106. In Hungary's "spontaneous" privatizations, the existing managers gained control of the enterprise and continued the old ways of doing business. Michael Mandelbaum, *Introduction, in* MAKING MARKETS: ECONOMIC TRANSFORMATION IN EASTERN EUROPE AND POST-SOVIET STATES 180-182 (Shafiqul Islam & Michael Mandelbaum, eds. 1993).

es.[107] In addition, managers turned into owners are also more likely to strip the enterprise of its assets.[108]

The most common, and probably most efficient, way to transform Cuba's state-owned enterprises is to keep the state as interim owner of the enterprise until the privatization has been accomplished through one of the methods described earlier. There are several good reasons for having the state remain in control. First, the state may be able to preserve the enterprise as a going concern, rather than allowing its assets to be "stripped" for short-term gain.[109] Second, the state may have to retain ownership of some enterprises to fulfill its governmental functions.[110] Finally, and probably most importantly, the state, as interim owner, can more easily settle the enterprise's outstanding obligations and make it ready for privatization.[111]

Responsible Agency: Transformation laws often nominate a body (ministry or independent government agency) to be responsible for the implementation of the privatization program.[112] The policy-making and implementation functions of such an agency should be separated to assure that the privatization program does not get bogged down in political debate, and to avoid corruption and the misuse of political influence.[113]

Following the examples in Poland, Eastern Germany and elsewhere, an independent governmental body ("Privatization Agency") should be established in Cuba to implement the privatization program and supervise its day-to-day operation. The functions of the Privatization Agency include:

- Guiding the transformation of state-owned enterprises into private ones.

- Retaining consultants and determining the best privatization methods.

- Obtaining independent valuations of the enterprises to be privatized and marketing the eligible enterprises to suitable prospective buyers.

- Initiating and following through the tendering process in those instances in which the SOE is to be sold through competitive bidding.

- Selling some enterprises (usually small concerns) through auctions or other mechanisms.[114]

Privatization Rules: In addition to establishing the Privatization Agency and defining its functions, the transformation law must set out the rules that will govern the privatization process. One of the key concepts that must be implemented through these rules is that of "transparency". A high degree of transparency deflects any suspicions that could build up and impede progress in privatization.[115]

Other Provisions of Transformation Law: Other basic features of the transformation law include:

- Provisions that authorize the government to sell the SOEs or dispose of their assets, assume their

---

107. In Hungary, the managers of spontaneously privatized enterprises used them as captive customers or suppliers for companies they had set up on the side. Another practice was to sell the enterprise at below market prices in exchange for job security and job-related financial considerations. *Id.* at 181-182.

108. *See* Eva Voszka, *Spontaneous Privatization in Hungary, in* PRIVATIZATION IN THE TRANSITION TO A MARKET ECONOMY 97 (John S. Earle et al, eds., 1993).

109. Ronald Daniels & Robert Howse, *Reforming the Reform Process: A Critique of Proposals for Privatization in Central and Eastern Europe*, 25 N.Y.U. J. INT'L L. & POL. 27, 37 (1992).

110. *Id.*

111. *Id.*

112. LEGAL ASPECTS OF PRIVATIZATION, *supra* note 15, at 32.

113. Phillips & Dent, *supra* note 2, at 490-91.

114. LEGAL ASPECTS OF PRIVATIZATION, *supra* note 15, at 33.

115. V.V. Ramanadham, *The Monitoring and Regulatory Aspects of Privatization, in* PRIVATIZATION AND AFTER 11 (V.V. Ramanadham, ed., 1994) [hereinafter PRIVATIZATION AND AFTER].

liabilities, and apply the proceeds to state needs (e.g., external debt reduction)

- Provisions that grant the state the power to give warranties or indemnities to purchasers of SOEs.

- Provisions to ensure that accounting standards are adhered to and that there is a tendering or bidding process.[116]

Laws to Regulate Newly Privatized Enterprises: Once state-owned enterprises are privatized, new laws and regulations will have to be drawn to regulate the areas of the economy controlled by the private sector. Post-privatization regulation of the private sector should not be excessive; overregulation could, if carried to extremes, virtually expropriate again the privatized enterprises.[117] Care must be taken in drafting the regulations affecting newly privatized sectors of the economy to avoid placing unfair and stifling requirements which may affect the viability of the enterprises and the competitiveness of the economy as a whole.

Other Laws Indirectly Supporting A Privatization Program

Business Organization and Governance Laws: Cuba needs to enact a Companies Law (perhaps as a part of an updated Commercial Code) that authorizes the formation of the types of companies that are likely to result from privatization (i.e. corporations). Cuba could use as a model for this purpose the business organization forms used in Latin America, which are also similar to those used in the United States.[118]

Special provisions regarding business governance in the context of privatization will need be included in Cuba's Companies Law. The provisions include those granting voting rights or seats on the board of directors to employees participating in the privatization of the company, establishing "special" shares giving veto power to the government, regulating the exercise of such veto power, and defining the governance regime after the enterprise becomes part of the private sector.[119] It will also be important to provide for the separation of ownership and control in publicly held corporations, and the prevention of oppressive conduct by some owners against others in closely-held corporations and other forms of business associations.[120] The Companies Law should also deal with subjects such as voting rights, voting agreements, allocation of power between shareholders and directors and other corporate governance rules.[121]

Securities Laws: The privatization program may eventually contribute to the development of a securities market in Cuba, once the market is established.[122] At that time, the government could give a boost to the stock market by placing shares of privatized companies in the market.[123] The market could also provide an "exit route" for foreign investors who wish to sell the shares they acquired in the privatization program.[124] The creation of a securities market and entities to supervise it would be a necessity if the privatization program includes the distribution of SOE shares to the citizenry, as has occurred in Cen-

---

116. Zelijko Bogetic, *Is There a Case for Employee Ownership?* in THE TRANSITION FROM SOCIALISM IN EASTERN EUROPE 88 (Arye L. Hillman & Branko Milanovic, eds. 1992).

117. This is known as "creeping expropriation," a process in which there are regulatory measures that have the effect of impairing the economic viability of an enterprise. ALAN C. SWAN & JOHN F. MURPHY, CASES AND MATERIALS ON THE REGULATION OF INTERNATIONAL BUSINESS AND ECONOMIC RELATIONS 785-787 (1991).

118. Id.

119. EVOLVING LEGAL FRAMEWORKS, supra note 89, at 7.

120. *See* LARRY E. RIBSTEIN, BUSINESS ASSOCIATIONS 103 (1990).

121. *Id.* at 103-169.

122. *See* Balfour & Crise, *supra* note 86, at 90.

123. Martínez, *supra* note 25, at 490.

124. *See* LEGAL ASPECTS OF PRIVATIZATION, *supra* note 15, at 24.

tral and Eastern Europe.[125] Before such a market is developed in Cuba, however, securities laws must be issued regulating the operation of the market and protecting the rights of market participants.

Competition Laws: Competition laws will be necessary to remove the barriers to entry imposed by the existence of monopolistic or oligopolistic SOEs. To do so, however, it is important to establish competition laws early in the game to prevent anticompetitive behavior to arise.

The competition laws should address the problems of monopolies, trade restraints and restrictive business practices created by privatized enterprises, and should contain provisions that:

- Allow the government to implement measures to avoid the abuse of monopoly power.

- Regulate the merger of enterprises, to prevent the creation of enterprises with market dominance.

- Regulate agreements by enterprises that fix prices or divide markets either by product or geographically.

- Regulate anti-competitive provisions in agreements to prevent undue influence over weaker competitors by stronger ones.[126]

Bankruptcy Laws: Bankruptcy and bankruptcy procedures in centrally-planned economies such as Cuba's do not exist, since the state prevents companies from becoming bankrupt.[127] Once the privatization process commences, however, bankruptcy laws will be necessary to deal with insolvent enterprises, and to provide an orderly process for paying creditors out of

the remaining assets of the enterprises.[128] In addition, the bankruptcy laws must provide mechanisms for closing inefficient state-owned enterprises and restructuring enterprises with potential for recovery.[129]

Foreign Investment Laws: Cuba's privatization program should be wide open to foreign investors. For the reasons discussed above, suitable laws to promote and regulate foreign investment must be enacted in Cuba. One important aspect of foreign investment laws directly related to foreign investment in privatized SOEs is the existence of international commitments to protect and promote foreign investments. These international commitments include Bilateral Investment Treaties, accession to multilateral conventions such as MIGA and ICSID, and membership in regional conventions.

Dispute Resolution: An impartial and effective judiciary is essential to the success of the privatization program, especially with regard to foreign investment. Foreign investors are less likely to participate in the privatization program if they are not confident that the courts will enforce their rights, enforce contractual agreements, and give effect to foreign judgments.[130] The dispute resolution process is itself amenable to privatization. Private means (such as arbitration) for the resolution of commercial disputes may be an effective alternative to traditional dispute resolution mechanisms, such as the courts.[131] This is particularly true if the courts lack experience with the complex issues that arise from the privatization of SOEs.

Labor Laws: In the context of privatization, the labor laws must include provisions to address the following:

---

125. *See* OECD, MASS PRIVATIZATION: AN INITIAL ASSESSMENT 24 (1995). The distribution of shares to the citizenry is usually associated with voucher privatization schemes, which were carried out in the former Czechoslovakia, Lithuania, Mongolia, and Russia, among others. *Id.* at 18.

126. LEGAL ASPECTS OF PRIVATIZATION, *supra* note 15, at 28.

127. LEGAL ASPECTS OF PRIVATIZATION, *supra* note 15, at 24.

128. Id.

129. EVOLVING LEGAL FRAMEWORKS, *supra* note 89, at 11.

130. Martínez, *supra* note 25, at 486.

131. EVOLVING LEGAL FRAMEWORKS, *supra* note 89, at 15.

- Occupational health and safety (minimum standards)

- Compensation for loss of employment (contractual damages or statutory provisions)

- The transfer of employees of the former state-owned enterprises to the newly privatized companies. Provisions must be included to determine which employees will be transferred to the newly privatized enterprise and who will pay compensation to those employees who lose their jobs. This is important because foreign investors are less likely to invest in enterprises that inherit a bloated work force

- The power and structure of labor unions

- The creation and maintenance of pension plans and tax regimes that make them attractive to employers and employees.[132]

The right balance between employer's and employee's rights and obligations will be a critical component of the privatization program. If the labor laws tilt too far in favor of the employees, investors, particularly foreign investors, will be hesitant to invest in privatizing companies with expensive labor benefits, hurting the privatization program as a whole. The German "social market economy," for example, with laws that provide for short work weeks, strong labor unions, high severance payments, worker participation in important management decisions, generous worker benefits and high capital gains taxes, scared some U.S. investors away from privatized East German enterprises.[133]

Tax Laws: The privatization of SOEs also requires the existence of a comprehensive Tax Code that addresses both any unique treatment of newly privatized enterprises and accommodates increased private participation in the economy. One aspect of taxation requiring serious attention is the avoidance of double taxation of foreign investors, which if occurring could adversely affect the privatization program.[134] Elimination of double taxation should be a legislative priority for a government considering the privatization of its SOEs.

Environmental Laws: One of the most serious obstacles encountered in the Eastern European privatization programs were the huge environmental liabilities accrued by the state-owned enterprises.[135] These liabilities complicated the privatization of state-owned enterprises in Europe, often blocking the sale of SOEs.[136] In particular, the environmental liabilities often hindered foreign investment in these enterprises.[137]

Absent a massive infusion of foreign economic assistance for this purpose, Cuba will have to adopt a legal framework during the privatization process that shifts the cost of cleaning up contaminated SOEs to those who acquire them. The drawback of such a system is, obviously, the potential to discourage investment in the privatization of SOEs. The government, however, may consider a cap on the extent of liabilities. This middle-of-the-road approach recognizes the limited resources and limited options available in the resolution of this issue.

Whatever method is chosen, the applicable legislation should clearly define what the liabilities consist

---

132. LEGAL ASPECTS OF PRIVATIZATION, *supra* note 15, at 29.

133. Anthony Gardner, *Why So Timid in Eastern Germany?*, N.Y. TIMES, March 8, 1992, at 13.

134. LEGAL ASPECTS OF PRIVATIZATION, *supra* note 15, at 27-28.

135. Randall S. Thomas, *The Impact of Environmental Liabilities on Privatization in Central and Eastern Europe*, 28 U.C. DAVIS L. REV. 165, 167 (1994).

136. Francis S. Kiefer, *Air Clears Up in Eastern Germany*, THE CHRISTIAN SCIENCE MONITOR, March 19, 1992, at 12.

137. Sam Loewenberg, *Pollution Often Part of Package Deal with Eastern Block Firms*, L.A. TIMES, August 28, 1994, at D3. The absence of environmental regulation in the former communist states resulted in the production of extreme amounts of pollution by inefficient state-owned enterprises. Foreign investors in former state-owned enterprises usually do not discover the extent of the environmental hazards associated with the assets they have purchased until after they have purchased them. *Id.*

of and the what the standards of environmental quality are. These guidelines should define the environmental obligations of SOEs and the steps investors have to take to achieve compliance with environmental regulations.

CONCLUSIONS

There is no single or preferred recipe for privatizing Cuba's SOEs. It is not even necessary in every case that ownership pass at once from the state to a private party: interim devices such as management contracts, leases, and concessions can be used to bridge the gap between state and private ownership and allow the state time to better prepare itself for the eventual divestiture of the enterprise.

Several important policy decisions must be made, however, at the outset of Cuba's privatization program. These include, for example, whether managers and employees of SOEs will be allowed to acquire significant interests in the enterprises. If managers and employees become majority (or even significant minority) shareholders in an enterprise, sale of the enterprise to private parties may become difficult or impossible.

Another important decision is whether the state wishes to maximize hard currency receipts from the disposition of SOEs, which would point to the sale of all or part of most enterprises to foreign nationals. On the other hand, to the extent that the state wants to maximize enterprise ownership by Cuban nationals, stock issuances to the public, "voucher" privatizations, or auctions from which foreigners are excluded would be appropriate.

Still another key decision will be whether the state will proceed as quickly as possible with the privatization process or whether it will seek to minimize the short-term effects on the work force by keeping in state hands as long as possible enterprises that should be liquidated as economically not viable, or whose transfer to the private sector would likely entail massive layoffs of personnel. Related to this decision is that of building sufficient to popular support for the privatization program to make it politically viable. This may require time.

Equally important will be the enactment of legislation that shapes the privatization process or bolsters it indirectly by creating the necessary legal infrastructure. Privatization touches on, and is affected by, many areas of the law. Accordingly, for Cuba's privatization program to succeed, it must be accompanied by comprehensive legal reforms that propel the country into a modern, free-market system of laws.

THE IMPLICATIONS OF GOOD GOVERNANCE FOR THE RECONSTRUCTION OF CUBA

Lorenzo L. Pérez[1]

This paper reviews some of the recent economic literature on the role of government in market economies and in economies in transition from central planning to a market structure, and draws implications for the reconstruction of Cuba. After an introductory section which defines governance, the paper discusses how governments have a distinct role to play in advancing good economic performance, overcoming market failures, and promoting equity. Based on the public choice and rational expectations literature, it then discusses the analytical reasons of why the public sector should play a secondary role to the private sector in economic activity. The next section identifies specific areas of government influence where the international experience provides guidance to what constitutes good governance. The final section draws general conclusions and implications for Cuba.

DEFINING GOVERNANCE

For purposes of this paper it is useful to use the definition of governance of the Development Assistance Committee (DAC) of the Organization for Economic Cooperation and Development (OECD). The DAC defines governance as the use of political authority and the exercise of control in a society in relation to the management of its resources for social and economic development.[2] The DAC distinguishes three aspects of governance: (1) the form of political regime; (2) the processes by which authority is exercised in the management of a country's economic and social resources; and (3) the capacity of government to formulate and implement policies and discharge government functions. The first aspect of governance falls outside the purview of this paper.[3] The economic aspects of this definition encompass the management of public resources as well as the establishment of an economic and regulatory environment supportive of private sector activities.

Governance is an essential element of what North defines as "institutions," which are a key determinant of an economy's performance through time.[4] Tanzi

---

1. The views expressed here are those of the author and do not necessarily represent the official views of the International Monetary Fund.

2. *DAC Orientations on Participatory Development and Good Governance* (December 1993).

3. In their comments on this paper at ASCE's Seventh Annual Meeting, Roger Betancourt and Ricardo Puerta argued that the paper should specify what type of political regime was being assumed in the analysis. Betancourt noted that there is an interaction between good governance and regime type and that the omission of this consideration is an important flaw of the paper. It is obvious that there is a relationship between governance and regime type, but I do not believe that the paper is flawed because it does not address the question of what type of political regime is necessary for the implementation of the practices being recommended. I would argue that the paper should be read as a proposal of the measures and practices that countries would need to adopt to improve governmental practices to promote economic development.

4. Douglas North, "Economic Performance Through Time," *American Economic Review* (June 1994). North defines "institutions" as the humanly devised constraints that structure human interaction, being made up of formal constraints (e.g., rules, laws, constitutions), informal constraints (e.g., norms of behavior, conventions, self-imposed codes of conduct), and their enforcement characteristics." North stresses the importance of institutions in defining the incentive structure of economies.

has noted that the collapse of the centrally planned economies and the failures of the welfare state in mixed economies have brought about an in-depth re-evaluation of the role of the public sector in an environment that is much more pro-market than was the case in recent decades.[5] At the extreme some economists argue in favor of a minimalist state, in which the government should have very limited functions. This view is essentially justified by giving little importance to the possibility of the existence of market failures such as the existence of externalities, public goods, monopolies, and informational deficiencies. However, the retreat of the state from many activities, could lead to many problems such as the growing incidence of crime, the growth of poverty, and a progressively more unequal income distribution.

Adopting a pragmatic approach to what is the appropriate focus of governance, Guitian has observed that "the establishment of an appropriate boundary between the roles, responsibilities and activities of the public and private sectors in the economic areas remain complex, dynamic, and elusive endeavor as ever."[6] It remains complex because there are many areas where both sectors interact closely and there exist no hard and fast criteria to determine precisely where public action takes off, or should take off, and private activity begins, or should begin. The interaction between the role of the public and private sectors is dynamic because it varies over time with society's preferences for public services and its willingness to finance them. Already in Cuba the interaction between the public and private sectors is beginning to change, from a rigid central planning model to one where the private sector begins to play a role in some economic activities. It is difficult in any country to gather a firm consensus about how far should government participate and interfere in the economic progress or to keep at all times the demand for public services in line with social willingness to pay for them. Nevertheless, every society needs to lay down some demarcation between the government and the rest of the economy as the basis of design and implementation of economic policy.

The World Bank's *World Development Report 1997* analyzes the role of the state in a changing world.[7] It concluded that the determining factor behind the contrasting developments among the various regions of the world has been the effectiveness of the state. An effective state is vital for the provision of goods and services, as well as the rules and institutions, that allow markets to flourish and people to lead healthier, happier lives. However, the World Bank stresses that contrary to what many recommended 50 years ago, the state is central to economic and social development, not as a direct provider of growth but as a partner, catalyst, and facilitator.[8]

ROLE OF GOVERNMENTS

Governments have key roles to play in the economy.[9] There are areas of action which are generally recognized as belonging within the purview of government, such as **defense, justice administration and public works**. But, governments also have an important role to play at the macroeconomic level by adopting **sound macroeconomic policies** to create the basis for price and external stability, sustained economic growth, and high employment conditions. Markets by themselves do not necessarily ensure appropriate levels of investment, particularly in infrastructure, human capital, and research and development. Regulation of financial institutions to enhance their soundness and safety can increase the effectiveness of this important sector of the economy.

Government policies can increase the microeconomic performance of the economy to offset the presence

5. Vito Tanzi, "Government Role and the Efficiency of Policy Instruments," *IMF Working Paper*, WP/95/100 (October 1995).

6. Manuel Guitian, "Scope of Government and Limits of Economic Policy," in Mario Blejer and Teresa Ter-Minassian, editors, *Macroeconomic Dimensions of Public Finance* (1997).

7. *World Development Report 1997: The State in a Changing World* (Washington: World Bank, 1997).

8. *World Development Report 1997*, p. 1.

9. For a discussion of areas of government action see Joseph E. Stiglitz, "Role of Government in the Contemporary World," in International Monetary Fund, *Conference on Income Distribution and Sustainable Growth* (June 1995).

of **market failures**. Governments can play an important role in maintaining and encouraging competition, which not only enhances the efficiency and innovativeness of the economy, but ensures that the benefits get passed on to consumers. On the environmental front, markets by themselves do not necessarily ensure adequate protection of the environment, which is crucial for using resources on a sustainable basis (e.g., beaches for tourism activities). The protection of health and safety of a country's citizens are important determinants of living standards and requires government regulation, for example, on the use of toxic pesticides which though they increase agricultural productivity, at the same time can increase the incidence of cancer.

Concerns about **equity** also call for government action. Even well-functioning market economies may yield outcomes in which large proportions of the population live in poverty. Research has shown that investment in human resources is a key ingredient for economic development and for ensuring a minimum level of opportunity for all members of a society so that they can share in the benefits of economic growth. In this process the government can play a key role. Imperfections in capital markets imply that many poor individuals will not be able to invest in their own education or in that of their children at an efficient level, or that it may be very difficult for them to maintain an adequate level of health care. Policies that enhance the accessibility of education and health to all thus can both increase equality and promote overall economic growth and efficiency.

Stiglitz has pointed out that what goes under the rubric of equity policies should really be thought of as policies to enhance living standards far more broadly.[10] This is particularly true of social insurance type of programs where it is more difficult for markets to provide (or to provide at a very high individual cost) insurance against many of the most important risks individuals face. It is these market failures which at least in part explain the role of government in pro-

viding unemployment insurance, disability insurance, and health insurance (particularly for the aged).

FACTORS THAT LIMIT THE ROLE OF GOVERNMENTS

Notwithstanding the above, in recent decades there has been a growing realization that the role that government can play in the economic area is limited, and that it is easier to have the wrong economic policy to prevent the economy from performing efficiently than the correct policy to guarantee that it will. As noted by Guitian, **public choice theory** has developed a methodology to analyze governmental behavior based on the tools of market economies.[11] In the process this theory has contributed strongly to the skepticism with regard to the efficiency of government action and to what extent government institutions can represent the interests of the majority in a society. Public choice theory has also influenced the economics of regulation by focussing on the political elements in regulatory policy. Two main conclusions of this literature are that governments should concentrate in the provision of public goods in their activities and that, more generally, markets represent a more efficient alternative to other governmental endeavors. This literature emphasizes that there is a need to reform the incentive and institutional structures in government to reduce the costs of policy activism and increase government accountability.

While the public choice perspective questioned the role of government, the literature on **rational expectations** has focussed on the role of government policy. It has shed light on the boundaries within which policy can be expected to be helpful. For this purpose, it has stressed two basic interrelated points on the economic policy front. First, unpredictable or erratic policies, because they are hard to diagnose correctly can be very disruptive for the private sector, and second, policy should be thought of as involving the selection of well designed, stable rules of the game. Appropriate policies—interpreted as those that lay out stable norms are necessary for good eco-

---

10. Stiglitz, "Role of Government in the Contemporary World."

11. Guitian, "Scope of Government and Limits of Economic Policy."

nomic performance but to be sufficient to generate good economic behavior require their internalization in the behavior of economic agents.

Incorporation of the nature of policy into the behavior of private economic agents will reflect its stability which, provided it is progressively confirmed, will endow policy with another necessary characteristic: **credibility.** Policies that establish conditions for sustained economic development require credibility from economic agents. However, policy plans may need to be adapted, for example, because the attainment of economic objectives may require policy variations. Useful though these adaptations may be at times, policy adaptations run counter to credibility and carry, therefore, a cost. On the other hand, inability to alter policy when circumstances clearly call for adaptation can also impair the credibility of its stance and durability. The point is that governments in formulating and implementing their policies need to keep in mind the importance of maintaining credibility on their policies in order to be effective.

These analytical developments as well as the empirical evidence has moved authorities in developed countries to try to replace government activism with stable, credible policies and to the abandonment of counter cyclical policy formulation as a major goal. In developing countries views have undergone radical changes in recent decades. The change in views has involved taking government out of the production and distribution of goods and services which are not clearly public in nature and focussing it instead on the provision of a framework where entrepreneurship can develop, market forces thrive and competition prevail. The change of view has been more drastic in the formerly centrally planned economies as they move to a market based system. In these economies in transition, more fundamental questions arise regarding establishing the boundary between private and public activity.

PROMOTING GOOD GOVERNANCE PRACTICES

The empirical evidence across many countries identifies a number of practices and institutions useful to formulate stable, credible, and good government policies. In general they go in the direction of what Dhonte and Kapur have categorized as going from a patriarchal or centrally planned system to a rule of law socio-political system.[12] The patriarchal system relies on the authority of the patriarch (e.g., the communist party or the head of state) to enforce "law and order" and on "far-sightedness or enlightment" to ensure predictability. The ruler's discretion is unrestricted in principle. The rule of law system is basically Hayek's formulation that government in all its actions is bound by rules fixed and announced beforehand—rules which make it possible to foresee with fair certainty how the authority will use its coercive powers in given circumstances and to plan one's individual affairs on the basis of this knowledge.[13]

Dhonte and Kapur note that in a patriarchal system, the ruler's fiat is the organizing principle of activity and the system cannot achieve complete investor confidence, no matter how benevolent it is or appears to be. Predictability in this system is always subject to the limitations imposed by the ruler's retained right to prey on economic output or arbitrarily alter the allocation of resources. For this reason, such a system can be effective as a means of implementing centralized initiatives, but much less so when it comes to creating a suitable framework for mobilizing decentralized initiatives. It also tends to attract investors who demand a very quick payback on their investments or less desirable investors. In contrast, Dhonte and Kapur believe that a market system preordains the rule of law by ensuring three basic conditions: free entry to markets, access to information, and the objective sanctity of contracts.

---

12. Pierre Dhonte and Ishan Kapur, "Towards a Market Economy: Structures of Governance," *IMF Working Paper*, WP/97/11 (December 1996).

13. F.A. Hayek, *The Road to Serfdom*, Fiftieth Anniversary Edition (Chicago: University of Chicago Press, 1994), cited in Dhonte and Kapur, "Towards a Market Economy."

If the rule of law system is going to substitute for a paternalistic system, there are a number of areas where government action would be fruitful:[14]

- Efforts to decontrol prices, liberalize the exchange and trade system, and create a money market where interest rates are market-determined can be identified as key measures that need to be implemented to permit the process of sustainable growth to start. In general, any reform that promotes competition will help reduce the incentives for corruption. The incentives to make payoffs in regimes characterized by multiple exchange rates, quotas, and credit controls are well documented. The experience of the former republics of the Soviet Union shows that efforts should be made to avoid the development of networks of informal and nontransparent arrangements between governments and vested interests. For example, in certain countries preferential treatment has been given to enterprises that have been privatized, or are still under government control, to the detriment of competition and the discouragement of investment. To the extent that the possibility for economic rents is eliminated, the quality of governance is improved.

- Early in the transition process there is a need for judicial and regulatory reform to clarify property rights; provide a legal basis for the enforcement of contracts and civil prosecution, particularly bankruptcy laws; and provide an appropriate framework for private sector activities. Well-designed regulatory systems can help societies influence market outcomes for public ends. Regulation can help protect consumers, workers, and the environment. It can foster competition and

innovation while constraining the abuse of monopoly power.[15]

- The implementation of strong macroeconomic policies while prices are liberalized. The reduction of inflation can also indirectly improve governance. The lowering of inflation can help clarify the incidence of taxation and the factors that affect resource allocation and income distribution. Stabilization creates more appropriate conditions for investment.

- The rationalization of the public sector and the enhancement of the competencies of all branches of government—executive, legislative and judicial—to facilitate economic decision-making are important steps that need to be taken. A special effort has to be made to reduce the role of the public sector, particularly in the production of goods and services through privatization, liquidation, and restructuring. However, the process of privatization needs to be transparent and closely monitored because the possibilities for corruption are high. The success of a privatization process is enhanced if the acquiescence of employees is obtained and a broad-based ownership is generated. Soft budget constraints should be avoided for the remaining public sector enterprises for fiscal reasons and to avoid unfair and inefficient competition.

- Public sector accountability needs to be strengthened through the promotion of transparency in financial transactions, such as inclusion of extra budgetary transactions and implicit subsidies in the budget, improvements of central bank accounts, bank supervision, and external audits of government and public enterprises which can

---

14. In recent years the international community has placed an increased emphasis on the need to promote good governance on economic efficiency and growth considerations. What follows reflects the main conclusions reached by international organizations in this area. In addition to the already mentioned *World Development Report 1997*, see the declaration of "Partnership for Sustainable Growth" adopted by the Interim Committee of the International Monetary Fund in its September 1996 meeting and the governance guidance note of the IMF published in the *IMF Survey* (August 5, 1997).

15. The *World Bank Development Report 1997* notes that the regulatory reforms initiated in the 1980s resulted in sustained private investment in Chile's telecommunications industry, increased service quality and competition, and declining prices. By contrast, dysfunctional regulation of the Philippine telecommunications industry—long privately owned—resulted in underinvestment and poor and high-priced service.

identify areas of poor governance. Civil service reform will be a major issue particularly as low pay levels provide a major incentive for payoffs and secondary incomes. Although this is a difficult problem, linking pension and other benefits to the elimination of corruption have worked in some countries (i.e., a public official only gets his or her pension if he or she retains good standing).

• A modern tax system needs to be adopted with an appropriate combination of direct and indirect taxes, with due concern for tax administration, efficiency, and equity considerations. Government investment should emphasize basic infrastructure and human capital needs to address some of the market failures and equity concerns discussed above. Investment in education is becoming increasingly important as changes in technologies have increased the skill premium. In industrialized countries the changes in technologies themselves have reduced the relative incomes of unskilled workers who have more of a need to acquire better skills. In this context, government has a vital role to ensure access to education which both enhances equality and economic efficiency.[16] The philosophy in many developed countries is that society should provide individuals with the opportunities and resources with which to attain a decent standard of living—provided the individual exercises individual responsibility.

• Mono-banking systems of centrally planned economies where the central bank serves the function of the monetary authority as well as acts as a commercial bank need to be reformed. Commercial banking functions need to be separated from the functions of the old state banks and a new central bank structure created to encompass monetary, exchange, research, gathering and processing of statistics, and supervisory functions of the financial system. Also, there is a need to establish legislation to permit the establishment of private commercial banks with clear prudential regulations in line with international practice.

IMPLICATIONS FOR THE ECONOMIC TRANSFORMATION OF CUBA

An analysis of the changes being implemented in Cuba to promote investment and economic growth in recent years is beyond the scope of this paper.[17] Some reforms have been attempted such as the liberalization of agricultural markets and the opening of some sectors to foreign investment. However, the reforms have been much too timid and in some cases they have been reversed. Key reforms remain to be implemented. For example, the price mechanism is not permitted to play a role and Cuba still has a rationing scheme for basic consumer goods which promotes black market activities. There are serious limitations to private property and the possibility of the self-employed hiring workers is a matter of serious debate within the Cuban political power structure. A recently-approved foreign investment code exhibits many characteristics of the paternalistic system where the government reserves the right to change the rules of the game.

Overall, the process of rationalizing the public sector is at a very infant stage and its structure is not conducive to public sector accountability. It is clear that many changes need to be made before governance practices in Cuba begin to resemble the practices recommended in this paper. In these circumstances, it is not possible to avoid skepticism about the possible

16. See Stiglitz, "Role of Government in the Contemporary World."

17. For a discussion of the role of government, public sector management, and the legal framework existing in Cuba and how it would have to change in post-Castro Cuba see Ernesto F. Betancourt, "Governance and Post-Castro Cuba," *Cuba in Transition—Volume 4* (Washington: Association for the Study of the Cuban Economy, 1994). Roberto González-Cofiño, in his comments on this paper at the Seventh Annual Meeting of ASCE, noted that the United Nations also has developed criteria for good governance which includes, among others, legitimacy, freedom of association, accountability, transparency of governmental actions, and cooperation between government and civil society. He observed that Cuba did not meet these criteria.

progress that Cuba can make in economic development unless governance practices are changed.

A reform government in Cuba would need to speed reform by making decisions that widen people's options, articulate the benefits of the reforms clearly, and ensure that policies are inclusive. To be effective it would need to pay attention to the needs of businesses and workers and work in partnership with them in designing and implementing policy. The political process would need to be opened to allow for the participation of political candidates who stand for economic reforms of the type advocated in this paper without their views automatically excluding them from the political process.

COMMENTS ON

"The Implications of Good Governance for the Reconstruction of Cuba" by Pérez

Roger R. Betancourt

This paper provides the beginnings of a discussion on a topic that is both of the utmost importance and that has been somewhat neglected until recently. It should be viewed as a collection of subtopics for further discussion rather than as a definitive assessment of any particular item. With this view in mind, I offer the following three criticisms to warn about potential pitfalls in some of the arguments presented.

1. Lorenzo makes an assumption at the beginning of the discussion that, in my opinion, throws out the baby with the bathwater. Namely, he is going to discuss good governance independently of regime type. In any area where there is an interaction between good governance and regime type, this assumption makes the subsequent discussion flawed. One such area is taxation. It has been recently shown by McGuire and Olson (*Journal of Economic Literature*, 1996) that in a prototype market economy with an autocratic government the tax rate will be higher than in the same prototype market economy with a majority rule government. The level of taxation alters incentive structures in a society and good governance in terms of providing incentives will be affected by the regime type. Another such area are growth promoting policies. In a recent paper, Azariadis and Lahiri (1997) show that in a democracy where a high ability government generates higher growth by investing more in infrastructure, but requires more taxes to exist, the

voters will choose a low ability government, and implicitly the lower level of growth, at low levels of income. If good governance includes taking into account the wishes of the governed, as it should, discussions of growth promoting policies have to take into account regime type. Finally, good governance in terms of monetary policy usually includes some discussion of Central Bank independence. This concept is a bit of a contradiction in terms in an authoritarian regime. At the very least, it needs to be articulated not asserted as if it made sense, which was done in the presentation by Lorenzo as well as elsewhere at the meetings by others. In a democracy, on the other hand, it is impossible to discuss good governance in terms of monetary policy without a substantive and thorough discussion of Central Bank independence. Again the assumption that regime type does not matter flaws the subsequent discussion of good governance with respect to monetary policy.

2. The level of generality at which the topics are addressed in the paper needs to be brought down to far more concrete terms before arguments can be evaluated or suggestions become useful. I will illustrate with an aspect of the discussion of the role of government in the economic system. Government intervention is justified by the existence of market failures and some economists are characterized as extreme "minimalists" who

give little importance to these market failures. What some of these so called extremists could reply is that the same fundamental characteristics that give rise to market failures lead to government failures when governments intervene in the usual way, especially when informational problems are the source of the market failures. In the case of lending to economic agents that are small in size, for example small farmers in developing countries, it has been shown that the usual mechanisms for government intervention, such as subsidized loans to the formal economic system, make matters worse by increasing the interest rates faced by small borrowers in the informal sector due to information failures (Hoff and Stiglitz, *Journal of Development Economics*, 1996). What is needed is not a labeling of positions but an understanding of what mechanisms work under what circumstances.

3. Finally, in drawing implications for the reconstruction of Cuba it is indispensable to assess what initial conditions one is referring to in any instance, which is not done in the paper. Again we can illustrate with an example. The most fundamental characteristic of the economic system in Cuba today, as it affects ordinary citizens, is the dollarization of the economic system started in 1993 when the dollar effectively became legal tender. Much has been made of the argument that the revolution, just like most centrally planned systems, has made criminals of every citizen by forcing them to break the law in all the ordinary transactions needed for survival. The imposition of any exchange rate system by a transition government without allowing the dollar to remain as legal tender requires making criminals again of people who have been made criminals for just about everything else over the last four years except for this activity. Good governance implies that in designing the exchange rate system this serious problem raised by the initial conditions be faced squarely in the face and addressed.

THE WELFARE STATE AND ITS ETHICAL IMPLICATIONS: A VIABLE ALTERNATIVE FOR POST-CASTRO'S CUBA?

Alberto Martínez-Piedra

More than fifty years ago the distinguished Austrian economist Friedrich Hayek in his brilliant book *The Road to Serfdom* wrote the following statement: "The coming of socialism was to be the leap from the realm of necessity to the realm of freedom. It was to bring 'economic freedom,' without which the political freedom already gained was 'not worth having.' Only socialism was capable of effecting the consummation of the age-long struggle for freedom, in which the attainment of political freedom was but a first step."[1] Recent events in the former Soviet Union and other socialist states have proven that the freedom from necessity so much promised by the defenders of centralized economic policies never materialized. The irresponsible promises of increased wealth and the elimination of poverty lured many well intentioned people, including not a few intellectuals, into the socialist camp without realizing that they were being led into what Hayek called the High Road to Servitude.

It was believed by many that the triumph of Cuba's socialist revolution in 1959, under the guise of political and economic freedoms, meant the dawn of a new era of economic affluence that would bring about prosperity and welfare to all Cubans. At least, this was the expectation of the great majority of the Cuban population during the early months of the revolution. It took some time before the average Cuban became aware that Castro' socialism led to the

opposite of freedom, to what Hayek called the High Road to Servitude. It is to be hoped that the results of almost forty years of Castro's radical socialism (communism) will open the eyes of the remaining believers in utopian socialist policies and make them see the fallacy of such policies which have been mainly responsible for the economic inefficiencies and the debasement of individual freedoms that have plagued Cuba since the advent of the revolution. But, is democratic socialism and the Welfare State a viable alternative to the radical socialism of the left introduced by Castro and his followers in the fateful year of 1959?

The Cuban people will have to make important decisions as to the type of economic and political regime that will be established after the end of Castro's socialist regime. It is almost certain that the cry for freedom will prevail and a pluralistic democratic system will be installed. But, in the area of economics the decision may not be as clear cut and generalized as some persons might be inclined to believe. Given the bad experience of radical socialisms of the left all over the world, the free enterprise system seems to be the natural heir, but there still may be those who believe that democratic socialism or some type of Welfare State might be the optimum solution to Cuba's ills. After all, they claim, it would be very difficult if not impossible to dismantle all the social contributions of the Castro regime without creating future political

---

1. Friedrich Hayek, *The Road to Serfdom* (Chicago: The University of Chicago Press, 1944), p. 25.

upheavals that could endanger the very basis of the democratic system. Some version of the Welfare State might be the best solution.

Thus, the pertinent question that has to be raised by Cubans after the fall of Castro is whether it is more fitting for the wellbeing of Cuban society to establish a free enterprise system or, on the contrary, accept the concept of a comprehensive State Welfare scheme, following the model of democratic socialism. Would it be fair to state that the economic programmes and policies of the Welfare State would have the same disastrous economic consequences as those applied by radical socialisms of the left as in the case of Castro's Cuba? Or, are the social programmes of the Welfare State more in accordance with Cuba's needs, where the majority of the population has already become totally dependent on the State, than a return to a capitalism that, according to its critics, would only bring an abuse of freedom, a different type of exploitation and further economic injustices? These are some of the questions that we will attempt to answer in this brief presentation. Although we realize the difficulties that a deep analysis of such a complex topic would entail, we do hope that the brief comments included in this paper will give ground for further study.

This paper will be divided into four major parts with an introduction and a final conclusion. First we will discuss the basic principles and objectives of the Welfare State in order to determine how valid were the expectations of all those who believed firmly in the bounties of the Welfare State. To do this, we will examine in the second part the effects of the social policies carried out by the major industrialized countries in Western Europe; in particular those countries which were preponderantly under socialist influence and which guaranteed all citizens "freedom from want" and the promise that the State would provide social services, security and employment for everybody. The example of what has happened in these countries after many yeas of State organized public assistance will help us determine the success or failure of these policies and how valid were the optimistic expectations of the believers in the modern Welfare State. The third part will limit itself to a brief examination of the Cuban case, indicating how effective have the social policies of the Castro regime been in eliminating poverty and guaranteeing employment and security for all Cubans. The ethical implications of the Welfare State and specifically its effects on the ethics of work and leisure will be the topic of the fourth part. Finally, we will assess whether the Welfare State is a viable alternative to Castro's socialist regime or, on the contrary, the Cuban people would be better off with a responsible free enterprise system.

PRINCIPLES AND OBJECTIVES OF THE WELFARE STATE

Otto von Bismarck has been credited with inventing the Welfare State when he set about wooing workers with "Sanitized Socialism."[2] He introduced compulsory accident and sickness insurance in 1881 but "the Bundesrat forced employers and employees to foot the bill, rather than vote the Reich Government new powers of taxation."[3] The German Chancellor sponsored a Welfare State that was not financed by the government but by employers and employees. It covered accident, unemployment and old age insurance. A far cry from a Welfare State that relies heavily on government financed assistance.

In the modern era it was Lord Beveridge who many years ago in his famous book *Full Employment in a Free Society*[4] left no doubt as to the role of the Welfare State in the twentieth century when he wrote that: "Full employment cannot be won and held without a great extension of the responsibilities and powers of the State exercised through organs of the central Government. No power less than the State can ensure adequate total outlay at all times, or can control, in the general interest, the location of industry and the use of land."[5] He further stated that: "Social Security today can be made the subject of a defi-

---

2. Brian Reading, *The Fourth Reich* (London: Weidenfeld and Nicolson, 1995), p. 38.

3. Reading, *The Fourth Reich*, p. 38.

4. This book is a sequel to the Report on Social Insurance and Allied Services made to the British Government in November 1942.

nite Plan and of legislation to give effect to the Plan. It lies wholly within the power of each National Government; once a decision has been made to abolish Want by comprehensive unified social insurance as the principal method, once a few issues of equity between older and newer contributors have been settled, the rest is administrative and actuarial detail: the Plan should be as definite as possible, so that every citizen, knowing just what he may expect from social insurance, can plan his personal spending and saving to suit his special needs."[6]

"Freedom from want" through Government controls was the main objective of the Beveridge Report. It recommended that the State should pay to all workers subsistence incomes whilst they are unemployed and allowances granted to children so as to ensure that no child need ever be in Want. Furthermore, among other things, all persons should receive medical treatment without charge when sick if they do not have the means to pay the doctor or the hospital.[7]

In a similar way the prominent British economist Professor A.C. Pigou in his book *The Economics of Welfare* defended the basic principles of the Welfare State and the need for government planning. He stressed that "...any given annual transfer of resources from the relatively rich to the relatively poor are likely to increase the national dividend" and that "there is little doubt but that plans could be devised, which would enable transferences involving a very large amount of resources, to be made with results advantageous to production."[8] However, in the case of the incurable and other permanently mentally and physically unfit no transference of resources would be necessary. Real cure is practically impossible and, thus, no transference of resources would render them more efficient to society. In such cases, the State would have the right to restrict their propagation for the welfare of society.[9]

During the years that followed the Second World War, the trend toward the Welfare State seemed irreversible. "Freedom from want" and the guarantee of security for everybody, together with drastic income redistribution policies, became the main objectives of the numerous Plans introduced by many European socialist governments in the sixties and seventies. The utopian promises of "Freedom from want" which preceded the introduction of such sweeping government measures were challenged from the very beginning by such prominent economists, among others, as Friedrich Hayek,[10] Wilhelm Roepke,[11] Colin

5. William H. Beveridge, *Full Employment in a Free Society* (New York: W.W. Norton & Company, 1945), p. 36.

6. Beveridge, *Full Employment in a Free Society*, p. 38.

7. Beveridge, *Full Employment in a Free Society*, p. 17.

8. A.C. Pigou, *The Economics of Welfare* (London: Macmillan and Co., 1952), p.758.

9. With respect to the incurable, Pigou categorically states the following: "The fact is that, in the economic, as in the physical, sphere, society is faced with a certain number of incurable. For such persons, when they are found, the utmost that can be done is to seclude them permanently from opportunities of parasitism upon others, of spreading their moral contagion, *of breeding offspring of like character to themselves.* The residue of hopelessly vicious, mentally defective, and other unfortunates may, indeed, still be cared for humanely by society, when they come into being, and it would be wrong to neglect any method of treatment that might raise the lives of even a few of them to a higher plane. But our main effort must be, by education and, still more, *by restricting propagation among the mentally and physically unfit, to cut off at the source this stream of tainted lives.* To cure them in any real sense is beyond human power. The same thing is true of those persons who suffer from no inherent defect and have lived in their day the life of good citizens, but whose powers have been worn out by age or ruined by grave accident. Here again from the point of view of investment, the soil is barren." Pigou, *The Economics of Welfare,* pp. 745-746. Italics are mine.

10. Hayek, *The Road to Serfdom.*

11. With reference to the Welfare State, Roepke says the following: " Its essential purpose is no longer to help the weak and needy, whose shoulders are not strong enough for the burden of life and its vicissitudes. This purpose is receding and, indeed, frequently to the detriment of the neediest. Today's welfare state is not simply an improved version of the old institutions of social insurance and public assistance. In an increasing number of countries it has become the tool of a social revolution aiming at the greatest possible equality of income and wealth. The dominating motive is no longer compassion but envy." See Wilhelm Roepke, *A Humane Economy* (Chicago: Henry Regnery Company, 1960), p. 156.

Clark,[12] Ludwig von Mises,[13] and Bertrand de Jouvenel.[14]

There is no doubt that the idea of the Welfare State had its historical origin in the era between the old preindustrial society of the early XIXth century and the highly developed industrial society of the mid XXth century. The abuses of early capitalism which brought about the miserable living conditions of the average worker in the major industrial cities of Europe, particularly in England, cried for justice and the need for remedial measures. The new working class, no longer subject to the bonds which held them together in the past, became, using Marxian terminology, the exploited proletariat. As Roepke has stated: "An unforeseen vacuum arose, and with it a need for assistance; only with the greatest difficulty could this need have been satisfied without State aid."[15]

The need for government assistance during the predominance of an uncontrolled *laissez faire-laissez passer* capitalism became rather obvious in view of the pitiful state in which the working classes found themselves during the early stages of the industrial revolution. However, as capitalism evolved and the state of the workers improved substantially, the system of State organized public assistance with its restraints and controls rapidly became redundant.[16]

It seems paradoxical that now, when the advanced industrialized countries have overcome the early abuses of an unrestrained capitalism, the principle of the Welfare State has become so generalized. Under the pretext of welfare a larger and larger number of persons are treated, economically speaking, as infants who need the protection of the State in all areas of their daily lives. Granted that it is not only a legitimate right but a grave duty of the State to come to the assistance of the needy, especially when their incomes fall below the subsistence level, but it is quite another matter when that same State for the purpose of redistributing income and in the name of economic equality taxes a large part of private income into the coffers of the Welfare State. As the process of redistribution of income is very often done with considerable waste and at the expense of individual responsibility, it is wrong to assume that every extension of State provision for the masses can be equated to an increase in progress. There is no doubt that the State should play a subsidiary function, for example, granting assistance to those in need as a substitute for self insurance but it does not have to become the Father Christmas in charge of the distri-

---

12. Colin Clark, "Welfare and Taxation," as quoted by Roepke, *Welfare, Freedom and Inflation*, p. 20.

13. Ludwig von Mises once wrote that "it is a serious blunder to consider socialism, planning or the welfare state as solutions to the problem of society's economic organization which would be different from that of communism and which would have to be estimated as 'less absolute' or 'less radical.' Socialism and planning are not antidotes for communism as many people seem to believe. A socialist is more moderate than a communist insofar as he does not hand out secret documents of his own country to Russian agents and does not plot to assassinate anticommunist bourgeois. This is, of course, a very important difference. But it has no reference whatever to the ultimate goal of political action." Ludwig von Mises, *The Anti-Capitalist Mentality* (Princeton: D. van Nostrand Company, Inc., 1956), p. 64.

14. When Bertrand de Jouvenel claims that the consequence of policies geared toward redistribution of income is to expand the role of the State, he poses the question as to which of the two phenomena predominates. He then asks "...whether what we are dealing with is not a political even more than a social phenomenon. This political phenomenon consists in the demolition of the class enjoying 'independent means' and in the massing of means in the hands of managers. This results in a transfer of power from individuals to officials, who tend to constitute a new ruling class as against that which is being destroyed. And there is a faint but quite perceptible trend toward immunity for this new class from some part of the fiscal measures directed at the former." Finally, he adds: "Such immunity has always been afforded to the international bureaucracy." See Bertrand de Jouvenel, *The Ethics of Redistribution* (Cambridge: Cambridge University Press, 1951), pp. 77-78.

15. Wilhelm Roepke, *Welfare, Freedom and Inflation* (Alabama: University of Alabama Press, 1964), p. 36.

16. Roepke, *Welfare, Freedom and Inflation*, p. 36.

bution of "goodies" as if that were the normal way of satisfying needs.[17]

The all embracing socialization of income expenditure and the fact that the modern Welfare State has become a permanent institution distributing welfare and security in all directions seems to give credence to the statement made during the last last century by the French economist Frederic Bastiat: "la grande fiction a travers laquelle tout le monde s'efforce de vivre aux depans de tout le monde." Such policies carried out in the name of social security can easily lend themselves to abuse and dangerous excesses. They can seriously threaten the stability of the economy, the State and society and, in the end, can even destroy freedom itself, not to mention the sense of personal responsibility and the spontaneity of human relations.

It is perfectly natural and legitimate for men to desire security but it is quite another thing when it becomes an obsession. To give in to this obsession will lead, in the long run, not only to the loss of freedom and human dignity but also to the loss of that security that men are so eager to obtain. Security tends to recede farther and farther into the distance the more desperately and passionate it is pursued.[18]

Thus, it is fair to state that the greatest danger posed by the Welfare State is in the area of freedom. As the power and control of the government increases, people become more and more dependent on the State. In fact, its power can acquire such gigantic proportions that men and women can easily lose their individuality and become mere pawns in the hands of government bureaucrats: a high price to be paid in exchange for greater security. As someone once said, the best place to be totally secure, where all your basic needs are taken care of, is in the county jail.

Would it not be better for a person to make provisions against the changes and chances of life by his own resources than to depend on government sources for assistance? A person who becomes dependent on the State and refuses to take the necessary precautions for a rainy day is, *de facto*, shifting the burden of responsibility on the shoulders of someone else, in this case the government. But, the State's generosity depends on the resources of those who have the capacity to give. The State is a simple intermediary who, through taxation or inflation, takes away money from the more productive sectors of society and distributes it to almost anyone who clamours for it. The stronger is the cry for assistance from individuals or groups, the more is the government inclined to give in to their demands, especially in democratic societies where the vote is all powerful.

It is undoubtedly true that the vicissitudes of life cannot be totally solved without a minimum of compulsory provision by the State. This is especially true in the case of old-age pensions, sickness insurance and unemployment relief. But, it should also be recognized that the help extended to the poor and helpless should be a supplement made available when individual and group provision are inadequate and never looked on as the normal method of anticipating misfortunes.[19]

The effectiveness of the Welfare State in solving some of the problems of a post modern society can best be determined by analyzing the effects of its various policies on the economies of those industrialized nations of Europe that wholeheartedly embraced its basic postulates. The experience of Western Europe can help us identify some of the major difficulties re-

---

17. Pope Pius XI in his famous encyclical *Quadragesimo Anno* # 79 clearly reaffirms the principle of subsidiarity when he states categorically the following: "...just as it is wrong to withdraw from the individual and commit to the community at large what private enterprise and industry can accomplish, so, too, it is an injustice, a grave ill and a disturbance of right order for a larger and higher organization to arrogate to itself functions which can be performed efficiently by smaller and lower bodies. This is a fundamental principle of social philosophy, unshaken and unchangeable, and it retains its full truth today. Of its very nature the true aim of all social activity should be to help individual members of the social body , but never to destroy or absorb them."

18. Roepke, *Welfare, Freedom and Inflation*, p. 15.

19. Roepke, *Welfare, Freedom and Inflation*, p. 24.

lated to the Welfare State and the dangers of an over mighty State when it becomes the main dispenser of assistance and the distributor of wealth.

THE EUROPEAN EXPERIENCE

After years of Welfare State initiatives many European countries are beginning to realize that the utopian ideals of the Welfare State—among them freedom from want—did not materialize. On the contrary, there are already signs of possible economic and social upheavals in the near future if present trends continue. The costs of the Welfare State have become too high even for the industrialized countries to afford. Governments no longer have the financial means to maintain the same level of public expenditures without running into serious economic difficulties.

In many European countries peace time budget deficits are at an all time high. Together with the rise in unemployment rates, they threaten the political and social stability of the continent. Drastic austerity measures, although unpopular, will have to be taken in order to reduce government expenditures and, thus, alleviate the heavy burden that is affecting negatively the already battered government deficit. Privatization of bankrupt State-owned enterprises and increased incentives for the private sector to invest must be carried out also if sustained economic growth is to be attained. A stagnating Europe does not fare well neither for the future of the European Union nor for a unified European currency, the Euro. If the European governments are not able to cut their deficits to 3% of gross domestic product (GDP), the European Union will become another utopia for future historians to discuss.[20]

Already, a new type of Euro-socialism is raising its head in some European countries. Whether it succeeds or not will depend on the successful application of economic reforms that will do away with traditional forms of protectionism, subsidies and social programmes which are hampering economic growth and development. The abuses of the Welfare State which operated under the assumption that there was no limit to the power of the State as the distributor of wealth and dispenser of "free goodies," is becoming more and more apparent as the years go by. This is especially true in the case of France but other members of the European Union are not exempt from the same or similar adverse effects of a bankrupt Welfare State.

With the dawn of the XXIst century, it is the traditional *dirigism* of the French State which poses the most serious threat to the free enterprise system. The over-educated technocrats in Paris with their centralist policies and all sorts of economic controls, have helped foster the Welfare State that is now causing the social commotion that is threatening the economic and political foundations of a country already in the verge of bankruptcy. The French government can no longer afford the huge public deficits and the impressive social programmes that it has provided so generously to the French people during the last few years. Drastic cuts in the Welfare State must take place if the country is to avoid the disastrous consequences of a bankrupt nation. It is a job that no government, whether French or otherwise, will find easy to perform. It will require a lot of tact so as not to antagonize the working class whilst, at the same time, carrying out the needed reforms leading towards the liberalization of the economy from unnecessary expenditures, excessive controls and unproductive traditional subsidies. The recent strikes in France by truck drivers and railway workers which forced the government to give in to their demands, is another example of the difficulties involved when attempting to enforce reform policies that run counter to popular opinion or the power of organized labour.

As a result of the disenchantment with the center-right parties for their dismal failure to reduce unemployment and cut taxes, the union of the left has

---

20. For a more comprehensive study of these matters see: F. Sturzenegger, "Understanding the Welfare Implications of Currency Substitutes," *Journal of Economic Dynamics and Control* 21 (1996), pp. 391-416; Guillermo Tabellini, "Money, Debt and Deficits," *Journal of Economic Dynamics and Control* 10 (1986), pp. 427-442; Andrés R. Domenech and C. Molina, "Macroeconomic Reforms in OECD Countries," *European Economic Review* 40:9 (1996), pp. 1683-1702.

gained substantial ground in the French political scene. With the recent victory of the socialists, allied with the communists, it is doubtful that the new French government will apply the tough reforms required in order to meet the challenge of an aging population and alleviate the fiscal and financial stresses that affect the public sector and which, to a large degree, are the effect of an overextended social security system. This is especially true if the socialists keep their campaign promises to reverse the goal of cutting the budget deficit, to reduce the work week from 39 to 35 hours and to curtail the privatization of state-owned enterprise whilst, at the same time, proposing to create 700,000 youth jobs, half of them in the public sector and half in the private sector.[21]

According to some experts, the big battle between state direction and the free market system is being fought in France. The election results clearly indicate that, at least for the time being, the battle has been won by the left and those who favour a bankrupt Welfare State. The socialist victory, however, may turn out to be a Pyrrhic one for France as the grievous problems related to the budget deficits will not disappear with demagoguery and unattainable promises. As a recent editorial in *The Economist* said rather bluntly when stressing the need for a reduction of France's public deficit: "This (a reduction of the public debt) has to be done, despite the pain, if the euro is to replace the franc. But it would have been necessary anyway if France's economy is eventually to revive."[22]

Due to the brevity of this presentation we will limit ourselves to a few indicators which clearly show the economic difficulties experienced by the majority of the European countries and the near state of bankruptcy in which the "generous" policies of a misunderstood Welfare State has led them to: 1) unem-

ployment rates and the public deficit as a percentage of GDP; 2) the fertility rates and the aging of the population; and 3) the near bankruptcy of the public pension schemes.

Unemployment Rates and Public Deficits

The rise in unemployment rates constitutes one of the major problems facing the Western European economies during these final years of the twentieth century. Austria, France, Germany, Italy and Spain had unemployment rates above 10% in 1996. Spain leads the group with 22.1%, followed by Belgium (12.6%), France (12.4%), Ireland (12.4%), Italy (12.1%) and Germany (10.3%). In 1996, the growth in employment was negative in Germany (-1%) and only 0.1% in both France and Italy.[23] The outlook for 1997 and 1998 is not significantly better. The hardest hit by unemployment were the young between the ages of 15 and 24.

The need for free market reform and austerity measures is quite evident when any given country reaches unemployment rates above 10%, one fourth of its work force is on the State payroll and government spending represents no less than one half of the GDP. The tax load is already so heavy that in certain countries tax revenues represent almost 50% of GDP. Under such circumstances the need for cuts in social programmes which are no longer indispensable should become the top priority of any government if total bankruptcy is to be avoided: a situation which, if it occurs, will be disastrous for employment and particularly damaging to the less privileged sectors of society.

To believe that the solution to the unemployment problem lies in more social give-outs and in cutting the work week even more—as it has been suggested in France by the socialists—is pure folly and only

21. The socialist government of Juppe hopes to cut down the deficit budget by 0.4 percentage points but not enough to meet the Maastricht target of 3%. The plan is to cut the budget deficit to 3.2 or 3.3% of GDP, primarily through an increase in corporate taxes but there is no guarantee that the deficit will shrink even more in 1998. Corporate tax rates will increase from 36.6% to 41.6%. These are the highest rates in Europe, excluding Germany where they stand at approximately 45%. This move by the French socialists will please their communist allies but will not fare well with the business community. See *The Economist* (August 1, 1997), pp. 41-42.

22. *The Economist* (May 24-30,1997), p. 13.

23. International Monetary Fund, *World Economic Outlook* (May 1997).

postpones the day of reckoning. The same applies to policies which propose that the government impose controls on layoffs. Such policies of "social protectionism accessible to all" will only aggravate an already alarming situation and instead of limiting inequalities, as their sponsors suggest, will eventually lead to the country's ruin.

To make matters worse, for the new socialist government in France to promise that it will create 350,000 new government jobs for the young when France already has one of the highest rates of government workers among the industrialized countries, will only put more pressure on an already overburdened public debt.

In the name of social and economic security for everybody, the proponents of the Welfare State are enlarging the role of the State bureaucracy and heaping increased responsibilities on the government without realizing that there is a limit to what they can overburden the average taxpayer with without destroying incentives and private initiative. When total tax revenues are already at a very high level and the budget deficit in many countries is well above 3% of GDP, there is not much more room for an increase in government expenditures.[24] The hope that a sharp rise in economic growth might provide the solution to the unemployment problem does not seem to be materializing in most European countries. The expectation that the growth rate will not rise above 2.5% in 1997, as in the case of France, will dash all hopes that the dole queues will be shortened.[25]

Fertility Rates and the Aging Population

According to the United Nations population estimates, the world's average fertility level in 1990-1995 was 3.0 births per woman. The world's average, however, conceals the disparity between the major areas and countries of the world. Fertility rates vary

from 1.6 in Europe to 5.7 in Africa, and from 1.2 in Italy to 8.8 in the Gaza Strip.[26]

For the more developed countries the average fertility rate during the period 1990-1995 was 1.69 children per woman, a figure well below the 2.1 rate required for long term replacement of generations. In Western Europe, nine countries had average fertility rates of 1.5 or less, among which can be included Italy (1.2), Spain (1.3), Germany (1.3), Austria (1.5), Greece (1.5) and Portugal (1.5). Another six countries (Belgium, Denmark, France, Netherlands, Norway, and Switzerland) had fertility rates of 2 or less than 2.

Fertility rates in Eastern Europe did not fare much better. Between 1980-1985 and 1990-1995 fertility rates in every country of Eastern Europe, including the Baltic nations, declined on the average from 2.1 to 1.6. The decline in the Russian Federation was especially acute, from 2.1 to 1.5. These low fertility rates in Western and Eastern Europe (1.5 and 1.6 respectively) contrast sharply with the much higher rates in Asia (3.0), Africa (5.8) and Latin America and the Caribbean (3.1).

On the other hand, during the period 1990-1995, Western Europe had an average life expectancy of 76.7 years. In Eastern Europe and the Baltic countries the average life expectancy was 72 years. The Russian Federation experienced the lowest life expectancy (66.5). The low life expectancy in Eastern Europe and in the Baltic States was mainly the result of an extremely poor health situation which was the main contributor to the high mortality rates. However, the general decline in population that occurred in Eastern Europe and the Baltic States was due also to international migration which was estimated to be +1.4 million during the same period 1990-1995.

Societies become older either when fertility rates decline so that fewer children are born or when life ex-

---

24. In Western Europe, budget deficits as a percentage of GDP vary but very few countries are expected to meet the requirements of the Maastricht treaty. At this point only Luxembourg does so.

25. *The Economist* (May 24-30, 1997), p. 21.

26. Population Division, Department for Economic and Social Information and Policy Analysis, United Nations Secretariat, *World Population Prospects: The 1996 Revision* (annex tables) (New York: United Nations, 1996). The demographic statistics in this section originate from the same source.

pectancy increases. Aging affects many societies in our contemporary world but, in a particular way, the industrialized nations of the world. Europe, in particular, is suffering from the phenomenon of an aging population, a phenomenon which seems to characterize the consumer oriented societies of our post modern age.

The continuous increase in life expectancy together with the sharp declines in the fertility rates experienced by the majority of the Western European countries, have the potential for creating, at a not too distant future, a real social and economic debacle. An aging population not offset by a dynamic and hard working younger generation will have to depend increasingly on the State to solve their most basic needs once they reach the retirement age. The age distribution of the population increasingly will take the form of a cylinder or even an inverted pyramid instead of the traditional shape of a pyramid. If this tendency is not reversed, a decreasing number of young people will have to maintain an ever larger older generation incapable of working for their livelihood. Assuming that the younger generation is no longer willing or capable of assisting the retired and elderly population, the State will have to come in, but this can only be done through increased taxation or inflation.

In principle, the individuals themselves are the ones who should be responsible for taking the necessary precautions for their old age by making adequate provisions for retirement. However, this is not always the case for a variety of reasons.[27] As a result, it has become necessary for the State to provide public supported schemes. The trouble is that the burden of supporting the aged has become an issue of conten-

tion as the proportion of the working population declines and the needs of the elderly increase.[28]

Retirement Plans and Public Pension Schemes

For the most part, public schemes for providing for retired persons are of a pay-as-you-go (PAYG) type.[29] Generally, the coverage is comprehensive but it can also be supplemented by funded schemes operated by the private sector. In the early stages of a PAYG system, the benefits of a small number of beneficiaries can be covered with relatively low payroll contribution taxes on the working population. But, as the number of elderly and retired persons increase, benefits paid out tend to exceed contributions, requiring increases in payroll taxes or budget transfers. Otherwise, the increase in benefits would have to be financed through inflation.

As the proportion of the elderly and retired persons increases whilst, at the same time, the proportion of the younger working population decreases, insurmountable fiscal stress will be placed on the government in order to finance public pension schemes and other assistance programmes. Such an outcome will surely have dire consequences for the political and economic stability of the affected nations. As a recent report of the International Monetary Fund clearly states: "A failure to address the resulting fiscal stresses, coming on top of an already burdensome fiscal situation, could inflict serious macroeconomic and structural damage, both on the domestic economy and in the case of large industrial countries through international linkages, on the world economy."[30]

The compulsory retirement age varies between countries in Europe. France has probably the lowest compulsory retirement age in the continent (60 years for both men and women). But, there is a growing de-

---

27. The Welfare State with its promises of "Freedom from Want" and other policies geared toward a greater dependency on the State and a diminished reliance on personal effort and initiative are in no small degree responsible for the increasing lack of interest in providing sufficient savings for retirement.

28. In addition, the political strength of the elderly increases as their numbers grow, a fact that, in democratic societies, is not easily ignored by politicians who are desperately looking for votes in order to be elected.

29. A standard PAYG system levies payroll taxes on the working population, while paying benefits to the retired, but usually without the close person-based relationship between individual contributions and benefits that characterizes fully funded schemes. See International Monetary Fund, *Aging Population and Public Pension Schemes*, Occasional Paper 147 (Washington: IMF, 1996).

30. International Monetary Fund, *Aging Population and Public Pension Schemes*, p. 1.

mand for reducing the retirement age to 55 with full pension rights. In certain cases there might be a justification for such a move,[31] although experience tends to indicate that early retirement so generously granted by the State has had very little, if any, effect in creating new jobs for the young. According to data compiled by the Organization for Economic Cooperation and Development (OECD), the percentage of young people (both men and women) between the ages of 15 and 24 that were actively employed in 12 member countries declined from 53.6% in 1972 to 45.8% in 1995.[32] The high proportion of young people between the ages of 20 and 24 that do not attend school nor are actively employed is another clear symptom of the grave crisis affecting the industrialized nations. In some countries like Spain and Italy the proportion is well over 25%. In Belgium, France, Greece, Ireland and the United Kingdom the proportion is between 20% and 25%.

To meet the demands of an early retirement, payroll contribution taxes will have to be increased to meet the extra demands posed by a social security system that is already in near bankruptcy. Such demands will surely have a negative impact on the level of employment as costs per unit of production will tend to increase and make the firms less competitive in a world geared towards greater economic globalization. This, in its turn, will make foreign investments less attractive.

Recent studies by international institutions have warned the industrialized nations that if the present trend continues the number of pensioners will so outnumber the economically active population that by the year 2025 there will be only 1.5 persons actively employed for every retired person. At present in France there are only 1.6 economically active individuals for every retired person dependent on the social security system. Twenty years ago the proportion was 3 active persons per retired person. Such a trend,

as mentioned above, if not reversed can only lead to chaos.

For many years we have been hearing about the problems related to what is called the dependency ratio. But by dependency ratio it was meant the number of children fifteen years of age or younger dependent on the economically active population (between fifteen and sixty four years of age). The greater the number of children in relation to the economically active population, the larger would be the dependency ratio and, as a result, it could easily be concluded that the standard of living would be higher if the birth rate were lower. Thus, the argument was used to justify population control policies that would reduce birth rates and lower the dependency ratio. Very little. if anything, was said about the aging of the population. if anything, was said about the aging of the population and a dependency ratio which relates the older retired persons with the economically active population.

It now turns out to be that one of the greatest dangers to the economic and social stability of the industrialized countries is the aging of the population and the dangerously high elderly dependency ratios.[33] Although it may be true that simple arithmetic would give credence to the fact that, in the short run, each additional baby means less goods to go around, it is also true that as the population grows older each person in the labour force has a larger number of elderly to support and let us not forget that the cost of supporting a retired person is much greater than supporting a child.

Given the extremely low fertility rates characteristic of most European countries and the significant rises in life expectancy, the short term demographic outlook leaves no doubt that by the year 2030 elderly dependency ratios will have reached 49.2% in Germany, 48.3% in Italy and almost 40% in France and the United Kingdom, more than double than what

---

31. Certain types of physical labour or any kind of work that requires much stress could fall into this category, but the argument that, by reducing the retirement age, the young will find new sources of employment seems to be false.

32. OECD, *Statistics on the Economically Active Population* (1996).

33. The elderly dependency ratio is defined as population aged 65 and over as a percent of the population aged 15-64. See International Monetary Fund, *Aging Population and Public Pension Schemes*, p. 4.

they are today.[34] As of 1995 they were 22.1% in France, 22.3% in Germany, 23.8% in Italy and 24.3% in the United Kingdom. Barring unexpected immigration changes the projected elderly dependency ratios are not unrealistic. Political realities in Europe tend to indicate that net immigration flows will fall to zero by the year 2005. Europe is now paying the consequences of a limited vision of population trends which ignored the long run consequences of low fertility ratios and high elderly dependency ratios.

How governments will be able to meet the increasing demands for welfare and other types of assistance is the real challenge that the defendants of the Welfare State will have to face sooner or later. Mere promises of Freedom from Want and other generous offers of free assistance for the elderly and other "generous" pension plans are not enough. If France and other European countries hope to reduce their deficits to approximately 3.3% of GDP by the end of 1997, they will have to tighten the economic screws much more than they are inclined to do. And even so, the goal of 3.3% may not satisfy the more rigorous Germans who insist on keeping the deficit at 3% of GDP as a condition *sine qua non* for the adoption of the Euro. The present policies of the Welfare State do not augur well for the future of the Euro.[35]

THE CUBAN EXPERIMENT WITH SOCIALISM

For over forty years Cuba, under the aegis of a radical socialism of the left (communism), has experienced the effects of an economic and social policy that has led the country into what the French writers Jean Francois Fogel and Bertrand Rosenthal call, *"une vitrine sociale vide."*[36] The Cuban *nomenklatura* with

Castro at the helm promised the Cuban people a new era of prosperity and freedom from the injustices of the past.[37] The results have been, to say the least, frustrating.

The euphoria and optimism that prevailed during the first year of the revolution is well known to all those familiar with Cuban history. It did not take long, however, for that optimism to turn into disillusionment as the promises of political freedom and economic well-being faded into the background. Instead of liberty and affluence, the Cuban people began to experience scarcities of all types and had to go through the constraint of queuing for the basic necessities of life.

It is ironical that Castro who had promised Cuba's "independence" from the United States had to turn to the former Soviet Union for help when his economic policies turned out to be a total failure. The government's attempts to industrialize and become less dependent on the sugar industry, major economic objectives of the revolution, did not materialize and Cuba had to rely more than ever on foreign assistance and sugar exports for its survival. It was only the huge subsidies provided by Moscow which kept the economy going and the country's social security system in operation.

In spite of the economic difficulties of the Castro regime, the government doesn't cease to claim successes in what it considers the greatest accomplishment of the revolution: the social security system. To dignitaries visiting Cuba, the country's social security system, together with the advances in general education and health, are presented as the prime legacy of the regime.

---

34. International Monetary Fund, *Aging Population and Public Pension Schemes*, p. 4.

35. For an interesting approach to the future of the European Union see Jacques Groothaert, *L'Europe aux miroirs* (Bruxelles: Editions Labor, 1996).

36. Jean Francois Fogel and Bertrand Rosenthal, *Fin de Siecle a La Havanne* (Paris: Editions du Seuil, 1993), p. 501.

37. The *nomenklatura* has been defined the following way by the Russian specialist Michael Voslensky: "La nomenklatura est cette 'troupe dintellectuels' dont la 'profession est la direction' et qui 'de ce fait se trouve dans une situation particuliere par rapport a ceux charges du travail d'execution' Staline a mis en place cette 'nouvelle aristocratie'—l'appareil—et lui a appris a regner. La classe dominante de l'URSS, la 'nouvelle classe' c'est la Nomenklatura'" See Michael Voslensky, *La Nomenklatura: Les Privilegies en U.R.S.S.* (Paris: Pierre Belfond, 1980), p. 99.

According to Castro's centralized economic system, income equality, freedom from want and welfare were to be guaranteed to all Cubans. This was to be ensured by introducing price and wage controls intended to satisfy merit wants, as defined by the ruling bureaucracy. Following the example of other socialist countries, the social safety net introduced in Cuba by the revolutionary government in 1979 and its subsequent regulations provided, among other things, unemployment compensation, pensions, health coverage, old age retirement, disability payments, housing and food benefits to all Cuban workers and their families. It is one of the most comprehensive social safety nets in the world, a fact that has been internationally recognized.

It was believed during the early stages of the revolution that high growth rates together with price stability would raise the general living standards of the population and eliminate poverty. Under those circumstances, unemployment compensation and social assistance would be reduced to a minimum. Unfortunately for Cuba, the economy did not grow according to expectations and productivity fell, causing all types of problems for the average Cuban as shortages began to appear. This brought about an increase in social security claims in addition to larger subsidies. To make matters worse, the aging of the Cuban population, resulting from a sharp drop in fertility rates, meant a sharp rise in the old age dependency ratio, all of which imposed a heavy financial burden on the government budget. The cost of both social security benefits and consumer and producer subsidies totaled over one fourth of GDP.

As long as the former Soviet Union was willing to subsidize the island with trade subsidies and foreign assistance, the Cuban government was able to pursue an extensive free-of-charge safety net which, otherwise, it would not have been capable of maintaining. The cost would have been too high, given the country's available resources. However, after the collapse of the Soviet regime, the situation began to deteriorate even more and the Cuban government found it very difficult, if not impossible, to continue with such an elaborate safety net system. It was forced to make cutbacks in its various social welfare programmes as, for example, reductions in food subsidies and in the level of services. The same applied to unemployment compensation and pensions schemes which were far too "generous," given the resources available on the island.

Cuba's budget deficit began to increase significantly during the latter part of the 1980's, a reflection of a deteriorating economic situation caused, primarily, by the sharp reduction in assistance from the former Soviet Union and its East European allies. By 1994, the budget deficit reached 12.8 billion pesos. As Cuba's economy continued to disintegrate, the country's fiscal deficit augmented, reaching 32.7% and 33.5 % of GDP in 1992 and 1993, respectively. Due to the series of drastic measures taken by the government with respect to prices and in the fiscal area, the budget deficits as a percentage of GDP began to decline. According to data presented by the Banco Nacional de Cuba, the deficit fell to 3.5% of GDP, a drop of 46.1% with respect to 1994. It was expected to fall to 3% in 1996.[38]

Social security payments amounted to 1.2 billion pesos in 1989 and represented 7.8% of total budget expenditures. These payments, both in absolute and relative terms, rose steadily since 1989, reaching 12.4% of total budget expenditures in 1995.

As a result of the "austerity" measures taken by the Cuban Central Bank, the amount of subsidies decreased sharply and serious shortages of both imported and domestically produced goods began to appear. As these shortages increased and consumers were unable to spend their government incomes because of the sharp fall in supplies, a flourishing black market began to develop—a black market which was mostly supplied by government warehouses. However, the transactions were performed at high prices and, as wages remained the same, consumer purchasing power and the standard of living deteriorated to a near subsistence level.[39]

---

38. Banco Nacional de Cuba, *Informe Económico* (mayo de 1996), p. 14.

Official publications of the Cuban government leave no doubt as to the precarious economic situation in which the country finds itself. Between 1989 and 1993, Cuba experienced a persistent downward trend in its economy, creating with it enormous strains on its already overburdened government budget. According to Cuba's National Bank, in 1995 the country's GDP grew by 2.5% with respect to 1994, a slight recovery from previous years. It was expected that the growth rate would increase to 5% in 1996 in relation to 1995.[40]

For Cuba to meet its internal obligations, in addition to its already enormous external debt—which in 1995 amounted to 10.5 billion pesos in freely convertible currency[41]—is not going to be an easy task, especially if the government persists in maintaining a safety net system as "generous" as the present one which the government quite clearly cannot afford. Even Castro himself admitted that there is a deficit of 500 million pesos in social security every year and that it will become necessary for the workers to make a contribution to social welfare. He suggested the possibility of workers contributing between 5% and 7%, given the fact that in the past they had not contributed anything for social security. This, Castro claimed, must change.[42]

The main problem facing Castro's communist government with respect to its welfare system consists in the need to slash its bloated bureaucracy to a level more in accordance with the country's resources. The same applies to a series of subsidies and price controls which are jeopardizing the system and putting an extraordinary burden on the public deficit. But, to liberalize the market and reduce the size of the bureaucracy will affect adversely the interests of the ruling elites—the *nomenklatura*—and, thus, will have the staunch opposition of the hard core members of the communist party.

The truth of the matter is that Cuba cannot afford to have a Welfare System of the size and amplitude of the one now in existence. The heavy fiscal burden imposed on the productive structure is compounded by the waste and misallocation of resources that inhibit the incentive to work and save. For example, old-age pensions are costly, offer inadequate protection in times of inflation and are often riddled with inequities. In reality, the low retirement age and short service period is another way of providing unemployment compensation.

In socialist countries, the health care system is characterized by waste and misallocation of resources, a consequence of the absence of incentives and information necessary for cost efficient use. Cuba is no exception. The ease with which disability payments are distributed in Cuba lends itself to all sorts of abuse and in many instances has become also another form of unemployment relief. This indicates, among other things, the lack of ethical principles on the part of those who issue the medical certificates and make the payments of millions of pesos without any compensating work.

Between 1994 and 1995, pensions for disability increased by approximately 28% and the cost of the pensions granted as a result of the laxity in issuing medical certificates increased every year from 1987 to 1993.[43] The number of workers that have been dis-

39. José F. Alonso, Ricardo A. Donate-Armada and Armando Lago, "A First Approximation Design of the Social Safety Net for a Democratic Cuba." In *Cuba in Transition—Volume 4* (Washington: Association for the Study of the Cuban Economy, 1994).

40. Banco Nacional de Cuba, *Informe Económico*, p. 3.

41. Lorenzo Pérez and Alberto Martínez-Piedra, "External Debt Problems and the Principle of Solidarity." In *Cuba in Transition—Volume 6* (Washington: Association for the Study of the Cuban Economy, 1996).

42. See an exclusive interview with Castro in "Castro's Compromises," *Time* (February 20, 1995), p. 59. With respect to education and public health, he said in that same interview that he does not want "to cut back education and public health because we cannot destroy the system we have created. We do not want to have private medicine because we have created a health system which has rendered extraordinary results, and we do not want to destroy it. It would be a historic crime to do so."

43. Marta Beatriz Roque, "Un logro que tiende a desmoronarse." In *Cuba in Transition—Volume 6* (Washington: Association for the Study of the Cuban Economy, 1996), p. 112.

charged for disability reasons has become so large that in Guantánamo, for example, 50% of retired persons were laid off on account of total disability.[44]

In 1995 the economically active population of Cuba had reached approximately 4.3 million people, out of which 3.7 million were employed by the State and 640,000 by the "private" sector. In relation to total employment, the percentage of workers employed by the State in 1994 and 1995 (84.1 % and 79.6%, respectively) fell to 76% in 1996. Whether this trend will continue or not is open to debate although it is very doubtful that Castro's socialist government will permit further privatization of employment.[45]

Given the worsening demographic trends—low fertility rates and an aging population—the proportion of the economically active population of Cuba will tend to decline in relation to the total population. The claims on social security payments must unavoidably have to increase. With a life expectancy of 74 and the low retirement age of 60 for men and 55 for women, the government will have to provide pension payments, on the average for 15 or 20 years, something which it will find increasingly difficult if not impossible to finance.[46] The situation would become worse if the habit of easily granting disability payments continues.

The French authors Fogel and Rosenthal were right in declaring that the Castro regime has little to offer except an "empty show window." Even its much talked about socialist Welfare State is turning out to be a disappointment, riddled with waste and incapable of providing sufficient protection for the elderly and the destitute. Perhaps, this failure of Castro's socialist experiment with a social security system which promised an economic safety net for all Cubans, is best expressed by Vito Tanzi when he says the following concerning the social security systems of countries under socialism: "Perhaps ironically, countries that have lived for decades under *socialism* are experiencing a *social security crisis* of major proportions. The inherited social security systems impose a heavy burden on these countries' productive structure, provide insufficient protection for the elderly and the indigent, induce waste and misallocation of resources, inhibit incentives to work and to save, and are vulnerable to considerable abuse."[47]

Cuba should learn the lesson from former socialist countries which have had such a bad experience with their social security schemes. Not only have they proven to be uneconomical by placing such a heavy burden on public budgets which led them to the brink of bankruptcy but also they have undermined the ethical foundations of a free society based on individual responsibility, productive work and respect for the dignity of the human person.

THE ETHICAL IMPLICATIONS OF THE WELFARE STATE

Respect for the dignity of the human person constitutes the basis of any free society. For freedom to flourish, the individual must find a fertile ground where he can develop his personality and sense of responsibility to the fullest. It is precisely in these areas of freedom and personal responsibility where the Welfare State is doing the greatest harm. Respect for human dignity implies that, as far as possible, men are expected to provide for themselves the necessities of life through their work and personal savings and insurance. In case of need, voluntary group aid, in accordance with the principle of solidarity, should avoid the need for a constant reliance on the government for material assistance. Government assistance should be considered as a last resort and limited to those cases of hardship that cannot be solved at the local level. Only such an attitude is proper for mature and responsible human beings.

---

44. Marta Beatriz Roque, "Un logro que tiende a desmoronarse," p. 112.

45. Banco Nacional de Cuba, *Informe Económico*, p. 19. The Bank recognizes the benefits of small private businesses for the Cuban economy, in particular because they provide extra goods and services to the Cuban population.

46. Marta Beatriz Roque, "Un logro que tiende a desmoronarse," pp. 112-113.

47. Vito Tanzi, editor, *Fiscal Policies in Economies in Transition* (Washington: International Monetary Fund, 1992), Chapter 14.

The Welfare State is not well known for its support of personal responsibility, of dedication to work and much less of transcendental values. On the contrary, the very concepts of freedom, work, and personal responsibility tend to erode gradually in the face of a powerful State bureaucracy that encroaches more and more on the individual rights of man and makes him lose the value of the virtue of work. These are characteristics that, in the longer run, do not fare well for a healthy sustained economic growth and much less for the development of the traditional Christian values of man. Dependency and security are not good substitutes for personal effort and freedom.

The process of increased dependence on the State, together with the centralization of decision making taking place in the Welfare State, is having a deteriorating effect on man's basic values. Man's will to self assertion slackens as he becomes more dependent on the State and is less inclined to practice personal effort. His search for security at the hands of the State can only be attained at the cost of personal freedom and at the expense of somebody else who is the one who has to pay for the "generosity" of the government, either by way of taxation or, in the last Instance, through inflation. As Roepke reminds us: "...the modern Welfare State makes it more and more its business to distribute welfare and security in all directions now in favour of this group, now in favour of that group- it must degenerate into an institution which is morally rotten and which must, therefore, finally destroy itself."[48]

The Welfare State, if permitted to expand indefinitely will destroy the very dignity of the human person by obliterating personal initiative and annihilating whatever remains of work ethics. Self reliance and voluntary mutual assistance will fade into the background as man becomes more and more dependent for his personal needs on government handouts. His sense of personal responsibility weakens and with it

the ethics of work. As a result, the very foundations of a free society are threatened. However, can it be said that the Welfare State is sponsoring a new "culture of work" where dependency and reliance on government "generosity" takes precedence over the practice of personal effort and the rewards of an honest day's work?[49]

The dignity of the common labourer, as that of any other member of society, is closely linked with the ethics of work. If the often excessive subsidized unemployment compensation schemes, together with the overly generous pension plans and early retirement programmes become the general norm, the very idea of work as a virtue may lose its significance. In such a case, in the eyes of the younger generation, work itself runs the risk of becoming obsolete or, at least, an unbearable burden that, if possible, should be avoided at all costs or, as far as possible, substituted by the "generosity" of the government. In certain ways something similar is occurring with respect to the concept of leisure.

The development of science and technology together with a commendable work ethics have made it possible for man to increasingly enjoy the benefits of leisure. Ironically, this triumph of man' ingenuity and technological capabilities has become a victory for mankind but also a source of present and future problems. Accepting that technology is a basic coefficient of economic progress and, thus, mainly responsible for permitting man to enjoy more time dedicated to leisure, would it not be appropriate to raise questions concerning human leisure and its relationship to the transcendental goal of man?[50]

In fact, one of the greatest dangers to a free society may lie in a false interpretation of the term leisure which, interestingly enough, the Greeks and the Romans related to the concept of education. According to Aristotle, "we occupy ourselves in order that we

48. Roepke, *Welfare, Freedom and Inflation*, pp. 42-43.

49. For an interesting but controversial approach to the "culture of work" see Miguel Martínez-Echevarría, "Los cambios en la cultura del trabajo," *Nuestro Tiempo*, Pamplona, Universidad de Navarra (enero-febrero, 1997).

50. José Luis Illanes, *On the Theology of Work* (Dublin, Ireland: Four Courts Press Limited, 1982).

may have leisure,"[51] but, he added, this is not enough, it is necessary "to be at leisure the right way."[52]

As man cannot remain idle for idleness is the mother of all vices, he must use his time of leisure "the right way" which means that he must convert it into something good and make it an essential means toward his own perfection. It is important that he use the time dedicated to leisure in a fruitful way. Mere physical activity, no matter how important, is not enough. Much less activities that lead us away from the development of the human spirit and tend to debase our cultural and spiritual heritage.

Just as work is a fundamental dimension of human existence on earth, in a similar way, leisure has an essential dimension, complementary to work; a dimension that is clearly stated in the Book of Genesis. As commanded by God, man must rest from his daily toils and by so doing he participates in the plan of God and shares in the work of creation. Consequently, man is not free to do as he pleases during his time for leisure. His freedom does not authorize him to perform activities that run counter to God's plan.[53]

The faculty of leisure belongs to the fundamental faculties of the human soul, the same way as the gift of contemplation and the possibility of raising man's heart to higher values is the force that transcends the material world and permits us to establish contact with the supernatural.[54] Thus, a purely humanistic approach to the use of leisure time is not sufficient.[55] There is the need for man to accept the existence of transcendental values, something which is not easy to accept in our materialistic consumer oriented society.

The denial of the reality of the transcendental will affect negatively man's faculty of leisure. By such a denial, he will tend to use that faculty improperly as his activities will be directed toward objectives that may very easily run counter to his own perfection in accordance to God's Plan. The consequence of such an attitude would be disastrous for the future well-being of humanity.

But what, specifically, has leisure to do with the Welfare State? No one can deny that the time dedicated to leisure has increased significantly during the present century but this is not a phenomenon that can be attributed exclusively to the Welfare State. As mentioned earlier, it is the result of man's spirit of initiative and his capacity to put to good use the gale of continuous innovations that have revolutionized the world. This, in its turn, is mainly the result of man's freedom, condition *sine qua non* for man's prosperity and integral development.

However, the Welfare State has contributed to an increase in leisure time by, among other things, fostering social policies that easily provide early retirement pensions, a lower retirement age and reduce the work week even though, economically speaking, these policies may not be the most appropriate for a healthy and viable economy.[56] Another matter is the question as to how the extra free time will be used: a question that the Welfare State has not been able to deal with in a satisfactory manner. The good use of free time will depend to a large degree on the education and values which the new generations will receive and it is precisely in this important aspect that the Welfare State cannot be taken as an example.

---

51. Aristotle, *The Ethics of Aristotle*, The Nichomachean Ethics (Baltimore, Maryland), Book Ten, Chapter Seven, p. 304.

52. Aristotle, *The Politics* (London: Penguin Books), Book VIII, 1337b23, p.455.

53. Aristotle a few centuries before the advent of Christianity had already said: "If we need both work and leisure, but the latter is preferable to the former and is its end, we must ask ourselves what are the proper activities of leisure. Obviously not play; for that would inevitably be to make play our end in life which is impossible." To be at leisure proper attention must be given to education and the pursuit of virtue. See Aristotle, *The Politics*, pp. 455-456.

54. Joseph Pieper, *El Ocio y la Vida Intelectual* (Madrid: Ediciones Rialp, S.A., 1970), p. 50.

55. Pieper, *El Ocio y la Vida Intelectual*, p. 66.

56. Politically speaking it might be a "good" policy in order to gain the support of large sectors of the population. However, the "goodness" of a policy is not always determined by the number of votes it can master, even though the politicians might not find it "politically correct" to accept such a premise.

Given the type of education young people are receiving in public schools financed by the State, it is doubtful that the value of work and/or the proper use of leisure time will be encouraged and much less the reality of the transcendental and the beauty of the "good" things in life. A centralized educational system in which the very distinction between good and evil tends to be taught in a fuzzy if not irrelevant way should not be taken as a model for the formation of future generations. Ethics would become a relative concept and, as a result, relativism would reign supreme in human relations. As the title of a recent revival of a Broadway musical announces: "Anything Goes."

Thus, the negative consequences of a powerful bureaucratic controlled State are not limited exclusively to the sphere of economics. They also tend to affect in a negative way not only man's attitude towards work but also his entire approach towards the use of his time of leisure; an important aspect of his daily life which is acquiring increasing relevance in our rapidly advancing technological age.

Under the Welfare State, all the "unbought graces of life," as Edmund Burke defined leisure, as well as other refined pleasures are strangled by the choking grip of the State.[57] Lacking a proper cultural and spiritual education, as is often the case in a publicly controlled educational system, man tends to use his easily acquired free time in those activities that momentarily please him, such as video games, etc., but which do not fully satisfy his most intimate desires. Eventually, the well known law of diminishing returns sets in compelling him, in order to avoid boredom, to search for new and stronger emotions such as drugs and other types of activities that will leave him even more dissatisfied than ever. A materialistic culture, institutionalized by a State bureaucracy and based on conspicuous consumption, is unable to provide any other answer to the use of free time except by way of physical enjoyment and/or evasion.

Undoubtedly, the increased time available for leisure is a victory for humanity but at the same time it can become a problem. As mentioned earlier, an improper use of leisure can easily lead to boredom; a symptom of an existential void which has become the collective illness of our modern culture.[58] Narrower and narrower grows the scope for a cultivated way of life and rarer and rarer becomes the climate in which true liberalism, variety, true community and *noblesse* can thrive. As Roepke would say: "Therein lies one of the causes of the deadly boredom which seems to be a distinguishing feature of the radical Welfare State; and this result of the Welfare State cannot be taken too lightly."[59] A culture that has been able to overcome many of the dire necessities of life has, nevertheless, been unable to cope with the problem of boredom.

Never in the history of mankind has there been so much time for leisure and, consequently, for the exercise of freedom. But, it is precisely in this area of freedom that lies the core of the problem. Man can use his freedom for good or for evil. This applies to the activity of leisure just as much as to any other activity that he performs but to exercise it properly requires certain criteria on the meaning of freedom itself. Freedom certainly does not give man the license to do whatever he pleases or what is even worse give the State or an ever growing and ever more powerful bureaucracy the right to influence public opinion in such a way that they are able to mold the minds of the young in ways that are not propitious for the development of human virtues; virtues without which freedom cannot prosper.

---

57. Roepke, *Welfare, Freedom and Inflation*, p. 46.

58. The French writer Albert Camus in his novel *La Chute* has portrayed in an excellent manner that superficial life that only tries to run away from boredom: "Je ne peut supporter de m'ennuyer et je n'apprecie dans la vie que les recreations". and "Je vivais donc sans aute continuite que celle, au jour le jour ... J'avancais ainsi a la surface de la vie, dans les mots en quelque sorte, jamais dans la realite. Tous ces livres a peine lus, ces amis a peine aimes, ces villes a peine visites, ces temmes a peine prises! Je faisais des gestes par ennui, ou par distaction." Albert Camus, *La Chute* (Paris: Gallimard, 1989), pp. 64 and 55.

59. Roepke, *Welfare, Freedom and Inflation*, p. 47.

The Welfare State, in spite of its promises of increased freedom and a better life, does not have an answer to the challenges posed by leisure and boredom. To manipulate or condition the man's attitude toward leisure through public education and/or State organized means of communication that promise newer and more sophisticated material goods is definitely not the answer. Such psychological pressures on the part of State controlled institutions will de facto restrict even more man's freedom of options.

To rely on a generalized public education void of any transcendental values, will only increase the chances of a more generalized boredom. The policy makers of the Welfare State will soon find out that education is not enough to make a man virtuous as Jean Jacques Rousseau had preached. Without the development of human virtues, no society can really progress. It is sufficient to take a close look at not a few of the political and socioeconomic experiments of the XXth century to realize the veracity of this statement. The price that had to be paid in lives and suffering is too staggering to believe in the redeeming value of an education not accompanied by the development of human virtues.

Obviously the possibility of not using leisure time properly is not an exclusive phenomenon of the Welfare State. It can and also happens in a society that is operating under a free market system. But, the compulsive power of a centralized State, together with the degree of dependency and erosion of freedom which it directly or indirectly fosters, aggravates and adds a new and more dangerous dimension to the dangers of a misused leisure.

CONCLUSIONS

There is nothing objectively wrong with carrying out social programmes that have as their objective the establishment of a safety net for the protection of those affected by adversity. On the contrary, it is a widely accepted principle by all well intentioned people that there is a certain percentage of the population that cannot be abandoned to events over which they have no control and which often plunges them into undeserved misfortune. Under those circumstances it is a moral obligation for society to provide for them. But another thing is to believe that every extension of

State provision for the masses will bring about a new era of progress for all.

The truth of the matter is that social programmes that try to guarantee the security of everybody, as those advocated by the Castro regime, affect adversely the very masses that they try to protect. Cuba is a perfect example. The data presented in this paper clearly indicate that the Cuban government was no longer able to sustain the heavy fiscal burden imposed on the budget by an overextended social security system and had to cut back on many of the programmes that it could no longer finance. Subsidies, pension plans and other types of social assistance were among the first to suffer as the economy deteriorated from both external and internal disequilibria. For example, in both 1992 and 1993, the fiscal deficits were over 30% of GDP, the rates of economic growth were -11.5% and -14.9%, respectively and the external debt had reached over 10.5 billion pesos in 1995. A slow recovery began in 1994. It should be stressed, however, that the lack of assistance from the Soviet Union was not the only culprit of Cuba's economic collapse, as it is often implied. Much of the blame must be placed also on inefficient socialist central planning and overextended social programmes which have proven to be totally counterproductive and particularly harmful to the less privileged sectors of society.

As in the case of most if not all socialist countries, Cuba's overextended social security system had adverse implications for equity, allocative efficiency and external competitiveness, affecting adversely the neediest sectors of the population. The cost of social security benefits in addition to various producer and consumer subsidies were too heavy a burden for the country to maintain and, as a result, inflationary forces set in which raised the general price level, devalued the currency and made a joke of the pension plans that were supposed to offer protection for retirement and old age. Adjustments for inflation are not sufficient to meet the injustices of inflation and, anyhow, they generally are granted only to those whose pensions are at a minimum.

But the real tragedy is the impact that such a social security system has had, not only on the stability of

369

the economy but on the very foundations of Cuban society. Freedom of initiative, responsibility and spontaneity in human relations have all been sacrificed on the alter of an elusive security. Old age pensions, for example, have contributed to the lack of incentives to work and save. Service period necessary for eligibility has been shortened due to the fact that contributory periods, such as maternity, studies and military service have qualified as service years. Eligibility for disability has been eased to ridiculous proportions. As already mentioned, in Guantánamo the number of persons applying for disability was exceptionally high; approximately fifty five per cent of all pensions. Although a portion of these pensions may serve a genuine need, in many cases they are the result of unethical deals and may be considered as a form of hidden unemployment compensation. The same applies to health related schemes. The entire system is riddled with abuses of this sort, contributing even more to the skepticism that already abounds in Cuba.

In spite of Castro's claims that Cuba's health care system is one of the best in the world, all sorts of deficiencies are quite apparent. Gross waste prevails and misallocation of resources are frequent occurrences due primarily to lack of information related to cost-efficient use. Such problems characterize also the pharmaceutical industry where products are dispensed freely but at highly subsidized prices. Abuse is clearly reflected in the way that health care services serve to justify sick pay and disability disbursements in exchange for gratuity payments.

Thus, Cuba's overextended and bankrupt social security system has not been able to provide the Cuban people with the safety net that the revolution had so insistently promised. Scarcities, queuing and a crippling dependency have been the result. But, to make matters worse, it has also brought with it many other adverse effects, in particular the slackening of labour discipline and the gradual loss of the ethical standards of the work force. It is difficult to estimate how many hours of hard work have been lost through waste and corruption but they must have been many. The image of well-being that the Cuban regime has tried to present to the outside world quickly disap-pears when the reality of what has happened, in terms of freedom, responsibility and ethical standards, is honestly and objectively analyzed.

For man to wish for security is a natural inclination but to obtain it at the price of freedom is a tragedy. Cubans, under the leadership of Castro, were forced to forfeit their freedom with the expectation of gaining security without realizing that, in the end, they would also lose their much sought after security as the value of money inevitably eroded and their incomes in devalued Cuban pesos became increasingly meaningless. The Cuban people are already experiencing the demoralizing effects of an erosion of the value of money and a devalued currency; a currency which they are forced to accept but which they would willingly exchange for the dollar or any other hard currency.

Given the bad experience of Cuba's ineffective social security system, would it be fair to say that a Welfare System *a la European* would be the solution to the islands's social problems after the fall of Castro? The acceptance and implementation of either a responsible free market system or of a democratic socialist regime is a choice that the Cuban people will have to make in the years to come once the Castro regime has passed into the realm of history.

The various models of Welfare States that have prevailed in Europe have all relied heavily on government centralization and the application of social security systems that have tried to protect the citizenry from the uncertainties of the free market system. The results have been varied but, particularly in the area of social security and other assistance schemes, the outcomes have been, and correctly so, the object of severe criticism.

The state of near bankruptcy in which the social security systems of many of the partners of the European Union find themselves is becoming increasingly apparent as the difficulties to attain a monetary union and a common currency, the euro, tend to increase. According to the Maastricht Treaty, governments must keep their annual budget deficits below 3% of the country's GDP and total debt below 60% of GDP if they want to participate in the European

Monetary Union. But most countries cannot meet these standard, including France and Germany, pillars of the European Union, that have budget deficits of approximately 4.2% and 3.4%, respectively.

To meet Maastricht standards, countries have to apply strict budget cutting measures in order to bring about the required deficit reductions. However, this has met, especially in France, with the stiff opposition of workers and recipients of government benefits who threaten strikes and social disorders. Not only do they not want reductions in government expenditures for welfare but, to make matters worse they are demanding a cut in the work week and an earlier retirement age. These demands are made in spite of the fact that the French already have such protections as subsidized education, national health care, a guaranteed minimum income and long term unemployment benefits. A social security system which is already overburdened with expenditures will not be able to meet such demands without serious economic and social consequences.

The aging of the European population, mainly the result of prevailing low fertility rates, is another problem threatening the viability of the social security system in the years to come. How is the present "generosity" of the Welfare State going to be maintained if the elderly dependency ratio continues to increase, the proportion of economically active persons within the total population continues its downward trend and the unemployment rates are in the two digit range? This is matter of extreme importance that cannot be ignored or brushed aside easily and needs the attention of all those that are interested in the well-being of society. A solution has to be arrived at but it is not going to be found within the existing parameters of the Welfare State.

The apparently irresistible insistence of the Welfare State to extend public providence to an increasing number of people who could provide for themselves if not placed under the protection of the State, must stop. Public assistance should be a subsidiary and temporary function of the State and only granted to those persons who cannot provide for themselves. It should not become the rule and much less an excuse to please the broad masses of voters. Apart from well deserved exceptions, unemployment compensation, under whatever form it may take, is not a good substitute for honest work. The virtue of work must be encouraged and not the opposite, as Welfare States often do by granting excessively early retirement plans and other compensations that cannot be economically or ethically justified.

The example of Europe in this area of social security is far from perfect. Only now are we beginning to see the consequences of a European fiscal socialism that burdens the population with the highest possible level of taxation and destroys personal initiative, savings and the ethics of work.

What is the solution to Cuba's ills after the fall of Castro's radical socialism of the left, in the last instance, is for the Cubans themselves to decide. However, given the total disaster of socialism in the former Soviet Union and its allies, it is difficult to visualize that the Cuban people would choose, as a model for the country's economic reconstruction, socialist central planning, even if it is of the more "moderate" Welfare State type. The West European socialist model with its overextended welfare plans and excessive central decision making policies would be a poor substitute for the radical socialism of the Castro regime which is already bankrupt. Apart from everything else, Cuba, a relatively poor and less developed country, could not afford the size and extension of a welfare system which is already taking most of the rich industrialized countries of the European Union to the brink of bankruptcy.

If by capitalism is meant an economic system which recognizes the fundamental and positive role of business, the market, private property and the resulting responsibility for the means of production, as well as free human creativity in the economic sector, then there is no doubt that the Cuban people are much better off by choosing a free market economy. But this freedom must be circumscribed within a strong juridical framework which places it at the service of human freedom in its totality, and which sees it as a particular aspect of that freedom, the core of which is ethical and religious.[60]

Let us never forget that the roots of socialism and the Welfare State can be traced to the abuses of an unrestrained individualism. The economic liberalism of the so-called Manchester School with its almost exclusive reliance on a purely egotistic self interest was greatly responsible for the development of the opposite extreme, socialism and the Welfare State. Thus, a healthy society should avoid the extremes of both a centralized Welfare State and the abuses of an economic system based on a false freedom that ignores man's social responsibilities and the common good. The potential dangers of an unrestrained free market system and the greed of unethical capitalists were already mentioned by Adam Smith, the founder of the English Classical School of Economics. Let the Cuban people heed the warnings of this great eighteenth century economist and avoid the greed and abuses of post Soviet Russia "capitalists." Hopefully, it will never be said of Cuba what the controversial billionaire financier George Soros, whose philanthropy sustained thousands of scientists and scholars after the collapse of communism, said of Russia: "I think that Russia has moved from the excesses of the Soviet System to the excesses of laissez faire capitalism, or, more appropriately robber capitalism."[61]

Let me conclude with an optimistic note, quoting from Seneca, the Latin philosopher of the first century who, wrote the following:

"Senabilibus aegrotamus malis ipsaque nos in rectum genitos natura, si emendari velimus, invat."

"The illnesses that we suffer are not incurable, and for us, born for the good, our very nature helps us by simply wishing that we be cured."

---

60. John Paul II, *Centesinus Annus*, #42.

61. "A Financier Who Promoted Free Markets in Russia Censures Its 'Robber Capitalism,'" *The Washington Post* (June 21, 1997).

COMMENTS ON

"The Welfare State and Its Ethical Implications: A Viable Alternative for Post-Castro's Cuba?" by Martínez-Piedra

Roger R. Betancourt

This paper raises a question in its title and proceeds to provide an answer in a very scholarly fashion. The origins of the welfare state are amply documented together with its shortcomings as it has developed in Europe. Worthwhile ethical distinctions are made with respect to the tension between security and freedom. The punchline is that there is no moral or ethical imperative to provide security to those who do not need it, especially at the expense of freedom. Therefore, whether or not one views this as an ethical implication of the welfare state the answer to the question is no. On the other hand, Martínez-Piedra stresses that there is a moral obligation for any system to provide means of sustenance at a decent level for those who are unable to take care of themselves. Hence, if capitalism or the free market is adopted one should avoid its excesses and provide a safety net for "the truly needy" so that a post-Castro Cuba would have what one could call "capitalism with a human face."

One would have to be very callous to argue with this objective. Unfortunately, the paper is not very insightful in guiding us on how to accomplish this objective. Identifying the truly needed is difficult and the moral hazard problems associated with helping the truly needed are ignored. For instance, with respect to mental illness the term *enablers* is now well established, at least in the more popular part of the literature. These individuals help the mentally ill but at the same time enable them to continue with manifestations of their illness whereas withdrawal of their support leads the mentally ill to suppress these manifestations just as the healthy do. Most of the recent literature on targeting of the poor recognizes the difficulty in reaching the poorest of the poor, many of whom would fall under this category of the truly needed. Therefore, we conclude by urging Martínez-Piedra to examine the difficulties in providing for the truly needed next year with the same careful attention that he devoted to the evils of the welfare state this year.

CUBA'S CEMENT INDUSTRY

Teo A. Babún, Jr.

Cuba was the first country to produce cement in Latin America, on July 7, 1895, two years before Brazil. The Cuban cement industry now bears the scars of its politics. The nation's cement makers have to use some of the Western world's most outdated equipment, and are producing at low levels of capacity utilization only 90 miles from one of the world's most cement-hungry nations, the United States, which refuses to trade with Cuba. Gray cement production in Cuba was 1.08 million tons (Mt) in 1994, compared to 1.05 in 1993, but 3.79 in 1989. Statistics on Cuban production and imports of cement for the period 1950-1996 are provided in an Appendix.

This bizarre situation has arisen as a by-product of the Cold War, when the United States and the Soviet Union staged a power struggle in Cuba that brought the world to the brink of nuclear apocalypse. However, the roots of Cuba's problems effectively date back several centuries. Spanish colonies were established on the island in the early 1500s, with the Spanish dominating trade in sugar, leather and copper over four centuries.

Cubans struggled for a hundred years for their independence from Spain, and the decisive battle for their freedom was fought in 1895, the same year as the inception of the cement industry in Cuba. The freedom-fighters were led by Antonio Maceo, Máximo Gómez and José Martí, and the latter's name and image is celebrated throughout the world as Cuba's national hero.

After the United States invaded Cuba in 1898, a series of governments followed, culminating in the dictatorship of Fulgencio Batista from 1934 to 1958.

Castro and his guerrillas took over power in 1959 and realigned Cuba's politics to parallel those of the Soviet Union. The country's three cement plants were nationalized by Castro under the administration of the Unión de Empresas de Cemento (UEC).

The United States has since waged an economic war against the island, partly in revenge against the nationalization of the extensive pre-Revolutionary American assets on the island, including Lone Star's massive facility at Mariel, and partly through its concern over the state's communist politics.

Cuba's economy has taken a beating over the last three decades, and has suffered acutely since 1989, due to the collapse of the Soviet Union and the effective drying-up of Soviet aid. Trade links with former Soviet-aligned states have also weakened considerably. Cuba has had to reform trade ties with its South American neighbors, which amounted to only five per cent of exports in 1989, but which are now at close to 40 percent.

With no hard currency to pay for foreign equipment, the Cuban cement industry has become a veritable time capsule, with virtually no new equipment being installed over the last seven years. Plants have had to innovate, cannibalizing components from older inoperable kilns, as well as machining their own components.

STRATEGIC INSTALLATIONS

The collapse of Cuba's traditional ally and paymaster has led the government to water-down its isolationism, and led the Executive Committee of the Council of Ministers to issue Agreement of Administrative

Control No. 2712 in October 1993. This ten-year agreement authorized the Unión de Empresas de Cemento to form a mixed company with Cemex SA of Mexico. The two organizations set up a new company, Empresa Mixta Cementos Curazao NV (EMCC), based in Curacao, with shares split equally, and the Mariel plant being sold to the new company.

The formation of Cementos Curazao was partly necessary to circumvent the trade embargo against Cuba. For the operation of the new plant, the UEC formed a new organization in 1994, the Empresa de Asistencia Técnica y Servicios, which is responsible for the administration of raw materials, workforce and technical matters at the plant. Cemex provided the bulk of the technical personnel for the organization. The EMCC also exclusively authorized Cemex to export cement from the Mariel plant, and from Cuba's five other plants.

Faced with the uncertainty that its executives would fall under the sanctions of the Helms-Burton (Libertad) Act, in May of 1996, Cemex notified the U.S. government that it had withdrawn from Cuba and was no longer in business there.

Details of the equipment and operating techniques of Cuba's six cement factories are given below. Cement plants in Cuba are regarded as strategic installations and as such are presently off limits to foreigners.

MARIEL (RENE ARCAY)

Lone Star Cement Corporation of the United States focused its attention on Cuba after noting that the island was drawing considerable cement imports at the beginning of the 1900s. The imports occurred even with the operation of South America's first cement plant, "Fábrica Cuba," which started production on July 7, 1895, and which closed in 1910, and the El Almendares factory, both in Havana.

Lone Star sent an engineer to prospect for a suitable site in Cuba, and the Mojica property, adjacent to the port of Mariel and about 40 kilometers West of Havana, was bought for 10 million pesos. Two cement kilns were assembled on the site and were put into operation in 1918. The Allis Chalmers "Vulcan" kilns were each 52.6 meters long and had a production capacity of 450 tons per day (td). Lone Star con-

trolled the company, Compañía Cubana de Cemento Portland (CCCP), which operated the plant, named "El Morro."

At this time, Lone Star had a domestic cement production monopoly, and decided to install a third kiln. The government subsequently decided to award CCCP a market monopoly guarantee, which lasted for four years and which allowed the company to install another three kilns at the site, although they were subsequently moved and reinstalled in Brazil in 1931-34.

Between 1945 and 1951, Lone Star installed another three kilns on the Mariel site, and brought total production from the plant to 0.33 million tons per annum (Mta). Faced with the prospect of losing its monopoly on Cuban cement production, Lone Star attempted to acquire the plant which was under construction near Santiago de Cuba.

The Mariel plant was nationalized by Revolutionary Resolution No. 3, on October 24, 1960 and renamed "René Arcay." The plant takes its revolutionary name from the organizer of the strike of April 9, 1958, who was killed by a self-made bomb which exploded in his own hands. Production levels at the plant decreased in 1961, as the combined effects of poor quality kiln refractories and the U.S. embargo began to bite.

In 1973, Centunion de España was contracted to supply two KHD Humboldt-Wedag dry-process cement kilns for the site at Mariel. The newest kilns at the site are fitted with planetary coolers and each has a clinker production capacity of 0.74 Mta. Raw material is crushed by a 750 ton-per-hour (tph) Centunion hammer mill, before being dried to eight per cent moisture content, and ground by two KHD closed circuit ball mills. Clinker is ground in two 16 meter-long 165 tph ball mills and is stored in four Claudius Peters silos, each with 10,000 ton capacity. The plant is adjacent to its own cement loading quay and supplies cement to barges by conveyor at a maximum rate at 300 tph. The first of the new kilns entered service at the end of 1979 and the second at the end of 1981. The installation of the new kilns effectively changed Mariel from being the oldest operating cement plant in Cuba to the most modern, and made it the most attractive target for foreign investment and capital participation.

Table 1. Selected Available Production History, René Arcay Plant, in Thousand Metric Tons

Year	Bulk	Bagged	Total
1983	500	511	1011
1989	460	483	943
1992	470	224	694
1993	316	188	504
1994	389	235	624

MARTIRES DE ARTEMISA

The plant is situated 90 kilometers West of Havana and, with Mariel, supplies Havana with the majority of its cement. The site was first used in 1919, when a lime works was set up by Manuel Domínguez Morejón, with limestone being extracted from the quarry using pickaxes. In 1952, a horizontal lime kiln was commissioned, and two more lime kilns, commencing in 1958 and 1959, brought the site's total number to six.

Starting in 1954, Morejón, together with "Papo" Batista (son of the dictator) and General Luis Robaina Piedra organized the acquisition and setting up of a 2.74 meter diameter by 99.1 meter long Unax FLS wet-process rotary cement kiln from the American Cuban Manganese Company (ACMC). The kiln started operation on September 18, 1957, and produced 1,873 tons of clinker in its first month of operation. Other equipment in use at this time included a Folax clinker cooler, two Unidan slurry ball mills of 26 tph capacity and a St. Regis bagging machine.

In 1959-1960, the plant was nationalized by Castro's new government, and took the "Mártires de Artemisa" name after the martyrs commemorated by the town. Starting from 1961, the cement plant suffered periodical closure due to lack of spare parts.

An increase in construction in the 1970's led to an increase in cement demand, and in 1973, Fives Lille-

Cail signed a contract to expand cement production at Artemisa from 0.2 Mta to 0.6 Mta. New equipment installed at the plant included a 400 tph Dragon hammer mill, a three chamber 3.4 meter by 14.7 meter long ball mill for slurry, a 4.4-4.8 meter diameter by 151 meter long wet-process rotary kiln with a production capacity of 1250 tons per day (tpd), a five-chamber grate cooler with 39.1 square meter surface area, a tubular ball mill with 64 tph capacity at 3200 blaine, two four spout packing machines and a weighbridge for cement trucks.

The new kiln started production in February 1976, with a monthly production of around 17,000 tons. Pozzolanic cement production (PP250) started at the plant in 1984, with tuff trucked from Mariel each day. It is estimated that 40 percent of the plant's output is in the form of PP250, which has a tuff content of around 20 percent. The kiln started to burn Cuban crude oil as fuel in 1990. Cement is bagged at the plant using FCB bagging equipment, and is transported to Havana on trucks, in (decidedly ancient) powder tankers and by rail.

Table 2. Selected Available Production History, Mártires de Artemisa Plant, in Thousand Metric Tons

Year	Bulk	Bagged	Total
1983	60	446	506
1989	300	356	656
1992	305	157	462
1993	299	109	408
1994	287	103	390

CIENFUEGOS (CARLOS MARX)

One Cuba's most modern cement plants is located 15 kilometers Southeast of Cienfuegos, on Cuba's Caribbean coast. The Cuban government decided that the planned construction growth in the 1980's warranted the construction of another cement works, and the Cienfuegos site was chosen for four main reasons: the high quality of both limestone and marl in the area, its central location, the pre-existence of an industrial development zone, and the possibility of exports to South America through the nearby port.

A Cuban trade mission was sent to the former East Germany in September 1972, and a contract was signed in March 1973 for the supply of all equipment for a dry-process cement plant. Construction work on the plant commenced in January 1974, and the first kiln was commissioned in February 1980. Both Castro and the reviled former leader of East Germany, Erich Honecker, attended the inauguration of the plant in May 1980.

Limestone is crushed at the quarry in a 600 tph double impact hammer mill before being conveyed 2.5 kilometers to the plant. Two roller mills, each with 230 tph capacity, are installed at the plant and are used prior to a drying stage. The raw material was originally thought to have a moisture content of 6 percent, but when it was discovered that it was closer to 27 percent, a rotary drier 5 meter and 35 meter long was commissioned. Raw material leaves the 200 tph drier with a moisture content of around 8 percent.

The works operates three dry-process kilns, each 4.6 meter diameter and 69 meter long, with a rotation velocity of 1.8 rpm and an individual clinker production capacity of 1500 tpd. Each kiln line is fitted with an electrostatic precipitator, and clinker from the kilns is transferred to one of three grate coolers, each with a surface area of 62 square meters.

Cooled clinker is fed into the three SKET two-chamber ball mills, each 4 meter diameter by 12 meter long. The plant also has storage for 5850 tons of gypsum and 8200 tons of pozzolanas. The milled cement is subsequently packed by the three 14-sprout rotary packers, each with a capacity of 2000 50 kilogram bags per hour. In 1992, the Carlos Marx plant commenced production of CC-200 cement, which consists of up to 60 percent pozzolana. The plant also manufactures PP250 and P450 cement.

SIGUANEY

The plant is situated almost exactly in the center of the country, between Sancti Spíritus and Ciego de Avila. Geological exploration in the area of the plant commenced in 1950, although it was not until after the revolution that a contract for the new plant was signed. Prerovsky Strojirny of Czechoslovakia sup-

Table 3. Selected Available Production History, Carlos Marx Plant, in Thousand Metric Tons

Year	Bulk	Bagged	Total
1983	NA	NA	NA
1989	445	252	697
1992	520	145	665
1993	501	147	648
1994	416	182	598

plied four wet-process rotary kilns to the site, each 3.5-4 meter diameter and 126 meter long.

The kilns are supplied with slurry after the quarried limestone has been crushed by the two 210 tph double shaft hammer mills and further milled in five 40 th open-circuit 14 meter long ball mills. The kilns have grate coolers, and three two-stage closed-circuit 40 tph cement mills are used. Three 14-sprout rotary packers are used to pack the cement, at a maximum rate of 1200 bags per hour.

The establishment of an energy efficient dry-process cement factory at Cienfuegos inevitably has led to a reduction in the output of the relatively inefficient kilns at Siguaney. To counter this mid-1980s trend, the plant has experimented with alternative fuel sources, including peat and rice husks, apparently with some success. However, the National Energy Commission suggested the use of Cuban crude oil as an energy source in 1986, even though there were known to be problems with the potential use of the fuel in terms of its high viscosity, low ignition point, high sulfur content and transport problems. In 1987, Cuban crude oil was used experimentally as a fuel for the first time in two Siguaney's kilns, and since 1991, crude oil has been used exclusively to fuel the kilns at the site. Siguaney is also the site of Cuba's white cement production.

NUEVITAS (26 DE JULIO)

The plant is located on Cuba's northern coast, 550 kilometers East of Havana. The plant has its roots in the 1929 construction by Lone Star Cement, of a quay on the Bahía de Nuevitas as well as eight silos and bagging machines with a capacity of 6000 bags per day. Bulk cement was transported from the plant

Table 4. Selected Available Production History, Siguaney Plant, in Thousand Metric Tons

Year	Bulk	Bagged	Total
1983	127	410	537
1989	351	222	573
1992	194	124	318
1993	105	154	259
1994	184	130	314

Table 5. Selected Available Production History, 26 de Julio Plant, in Thousand Metric Tons

Year	Bulk	Bagged	Total
1983	120	420	540
1989	180	373	553
1992	280	148	434
1993	257	44	301
1994	263	57	320

at Mariel for redistribution to the eastern provinces via the facility at Nuevitas.

During the construction boom of the 1960's, it was decided to build a cement plant at Nuevitas and equipment was ordered from the former East Germany. The first kiln line to be completed, in 1968, consisted of a wet process kiln, 3.6 meter diameter and 150 meter long, with a 0.2 Mta clinker production capacity. On April 9, 1968, the plant, named after the day on which Castro's rebels assaulted the Moncada Barracks in 1953, was opened by Fidel Castro himself.

By April 1973, another line was ready for production at the plant. This line consists of a second 0.2 Mta wet-process kiln, with tandem slurry and clinker mills, and another cement bagging machine. On July 19, 1973, the third and last production line was commissioned, with a third kiln, a fourth slurry mill and a fourth clinker mill.

In 1979, cement transfer stations were installed permitting bulk-cement barges of 5000 ton capacity to be loaded on the Bahía de Nuevitas. Electrostatic precipitators were fitted between 1987 and 1989.

In 1989, the use of Cuban crude oil as a fuel was started at the plant, as a means of deal with Cuba's low levels of hard currency. By 1993, Cuban crude oil had replaced the former sources of energy completely. The plant currently has an installed capacity of around 0.6 Mta.

SANTIAGO DE CUBA (JOSE MERCERON)

The plant supplying Santiago de Cuba (Cuba's second city and Capital of the Revolution) with cement, currently called "José Mercerón," was constructed in

1955. Imports from Puerto Rico, largely from a plant in Ponce, were the main source of cement prior to the establishment of the works. An international group of investors and business people, realizing that there was sufficient demand at the Eastern end of the island for cement production, set up the Compañía Industrial y Comercial Marlex to build the plant, and in 1953 Cementos Nacionales SA was formed to operate it.

By the start of the production at the plant in 1955, the Cuban national family Babún owned 79 percent of the shares in the facility, and Cementos Ponce of Puerto Rico, under the direction of the Ferré family, 21 percent. However, Cementos Ponce provided technical help and operators for the plant until 1960, giving it more influence over the operation of the plant. Starting in May 1955, the plant was initially operated only as a grinding station, with clinker from Ciment D'Obourg in Belgium and from Puerto Rico being ground in two Fellner & Ziegler three-chamber cement mills, each with a capacity of 16 tph.

By November 1955, the plant was ready to produce clinker of its own. A Hazamag 250 tph double-rotor hammer mill was used to crush the raw materials and two Fellner & Ziegler paste mills used to prepare raw materials for the kiln. The wet-process kiln, also manufactured by Fellner & Ziegler, is 3.6 meter diameter by 130 meter long, with a clinker production capacity of 408 tpd. The cement is packed using a Haver & Boecker packer with a capacity of 1200 bags per hour.

A second wet-process kiln was put into operation in May 1957, and this effectively ended Puerto Rican cement imports into Cuba. The kiln was manufactured by Allis Chalmers, with a diameter of 4 meters and a length of 160 meters, and has a clinker production capacity of 680 tpd. The kiln feeds into a Fuller grate cooler and clinker is subsequently milled in an Allis Chalmers three-chamber ball mill.

A further expansion at the plant was planned for 1958, but the revolutionary struggle disrupted industry and communication, forcing the postponement of development. However, after the completion of the revolution and the nationalization of Cementos Nacionales in 1960, the government ordered a new kiln line from Industrial Export of Romania.

The new line, which started production in 1968, consisted of extra paste mills, compressors for cement conveying, a further wet-process kiln with diameter of 3.6 meters and length of 150 meters and two 2.6 meter diameter by 13 meter long, 25 tph cement mills.

Table 6. Selected Available Production History, José Mercerón Plant, in Thousand Metric Tons

Year	Bulk	Bagged	Total
1983	108	445	553
1989	376	240	616
1992	299	18	317
1993	127	153	280
1994	199	155	354

WHITE CEMENT IN CUBA

The use of white cement has a long history in Cuba. In 1912, 5000 tons were imported from France, and by the mid 1980s, around 30,000 tons were being imported annually. In 1986, the feasibility of producing white cement at the Siguaney plant was studied, and the search for suitable raw materials started.

Very pure white limestone was selected from the quarry at Guayos, 20 kilometers from the plant. Feldspar from Macagua and gypsum from Punta Alegre were also selected for use in the first experimental batch of production. In October 1986, kiln No.2 at Siguaney was used to produce white cement for the first time in Cuba, and based on this successful test run, the Onoda Cement Company of Japan

was contracted to equip a 0.1 Mt white cement production line at the plant.

Equipment supplied included four raw material feeders with conveyors and an elevator, two 2,000 ton clinker silos, conveyor belt systems and a special burner from Onoda for the kiln. Siguaney's kiln No.4 has been designated for white cement production since July 1989 and now produces at close to capacity. Around 55,000 tons of white cement raw material slurry is produced each year, converting to some 31,000 tons of clinker and then to 30,000 tons of white cement.

Changes to the raw mix composition, with the elimination of imported fluorite, Macagua feldspar and siliceous sand, and the introduction of kaolin from Gaspar, near Ciego de Avila, have significantly reduced costs of production. The raw mix changes have also led to a product with increased whiteness: 90 percent compared to the original 86 percent.

CONCLUSION

Until the precipitous downturn of the "special period," cement had enjoyed a prominent place among industries with the fastest rates of growth in Cuba. The most significant growth occurred after 1970 when several important factories were built and existing ones were expanded.

Moreover, the growth in cement production promoted rapid expansion in the allied industry of construction materials. Crushed rock production jumped from 2.5 million cubic meters (3.3 million cubic yards) in the late 1960's to 47.6 (62.2) in the late 1980's. In the same period, the production of concrete blocks grew from 18.6 million units to 45 million.

The pre-fab industry, almost non-existent until then, reached a level of four million square meters (43 million square feet) of annual capacity 10 years ago, enabling it to produce a large amount of commodities, from simple railroad ties to complicated engineering structures. Pre-fab for housing in 1986 was theoretically capable of producing enough structural pieces to build 40,000 dwellings a year, a figure far above the actual number of new housing units.

Geological formations contributed strongly to the growth in cement production. Among the critical factors behind the expansion of the cement industry are the abundance of raw materials such as limestone, clays, gypsum and silicates, the even distribution of the population and the development of the transportation network. (On the other hand, the lack of energy deposits is a significant problem.)

Of the six cement plants currently operating, three were built after 1959 and the others have all undergone expansion and repeated improvement. They are located conveniently near the country's oil refineries, thermoelectric plants and major power transmission lines, as well as close to the main cities, industrial cores, ports and railroad lines.

Total annual production capacity of the factories is about 5 million metric tons. The leading plants are "René Arcay" (formerly "El Morro"), built in 1918 in Mariel, 27 miles West of Havana, and the "Carlos Marx" in Cienfuegos, which began production in 1980. Their combined nominal output equals 60 percent of national capacity.

As in many other industries, however, real production never attained capacity. In 1989, to cite a good year, production was 75 percent of capacity; worse, average output for the 1980's was only two-thirds of installed capacity.

More important however, is the energy factor. It requires one barrel of oil to manufacture a ton of cement, resulting in a process in which oil consumption accounts for 60 percent of the cost of production. Furthermore, the cement industry consumed 12 percent of the electricity in the country in 1989. Given the scarcity and rationing of electrical power across the country, the industry has to limit its consumption and thus, its output.

The sudden elimination of huge quantities of Soviet oil supplies after 1989 pushed the industry to its worst crisis. Lacking this crucial ingredient and faced with a shortfall in electrical energy, production plunged to one-fifth of the normal level in four short years.

After the industry hit bottom, a concerted effort by the government to build new hotels and produce cement for export seemed to help turn it around. But in 1995, after a second consecutive year of growth, production reached 1.38 million tons, 31 percent more than in 1993, but 23 percent below 1994. Projections for 1996 were 1.8 million tons, 30 percent above 1995, but equal to the production level in 1994.

Following renewed trade relations between the United States and Cuba, the cement industry will benefit in three ways; the currently run-down plants will almost certainly be privatized, and will experience a boost in investment; through a cement-intensive hotel and tourism led construction boom and through being able to export to the cement hungry U.S. market.

REFERENCES

CubaNews

Cemco United, Inc.

Holmer Bank Inc.

International Cement Review

Dr. José Oro

Un Estudio Sobre Cuba (University of Miami Press, 1963)

APPENDIX

Cuban Cement Production and Imports, 1950-1996
(In metric tons)

Year	Production	Imports	Total
1950	1,860,300	672,006	2,532,306
1951	2,246,200	1,022,184	3,268,384
1952	2,462,700	894,335	3,357,035
1953	2,384,600	631,301	3,015,901
1954	2,470,800	1,078,919	3,549,719
1955	2,493,700	1,519,879	4,013,579
1956	2,445,500	1,188,476	3,633,976
1957	3,915,788	960,171	4,875,959
1958	4,270,758	124,564	4,395,322
1959	3,973,098	50,994	4,024,092
1960	3,536,863	0	3,536,863
1961-82	NA	NA	NA
1983	3,160,000		3,160,000
1984	3,000,000		3,000,000
1985	3,300,000		3,300,000
1986	3,125,000		3,125,000
1987	3,525,000		3,525,000
1988	3,750,000		3,750,000
1989	3,790,000		3,790,000
1990	3,225,000		3,225,000
1991	3,100,000		3,100,000
1992	2,890,000		2,890,000
1993	1,050,000		1,050,000
1994	1,800,000		1,800,000
1995	1,380,000		1,380,000
1996	1,800,000		1,800,000

BIOPROSPECTING IN A POST-CASTRO CUBA

Larry Daley

The intent is—in post-Castro Cuba—to establish bio-prospecting laboratories in the rain-forests of eastern Cuba and fund them through a combination of commercial, international agency and U.S. based federal grant funding for visiting researchers. The task of these laboratories will be to seek pharmacologically, medically, and agriculturally useful biochemicals among the exceptionally diverse plant, and fungal flora, and the fauna of Cuba.

What is proposed here differs from anything the present government does. This is because this project is designed to be run by free people, independent researchers, and funded by a combination of private pharmaceutical and agro-business sources, competitively funded U.S. granting agencies and private foundations.

The expected benefits include those associated with rain forest preservation and restoration, cleaner water, preservation of biological diversity, reduction of erosion. The political stabilization of the area and increased welfare of the local inhabitants is also an expected outcome. The areas designated for this use are the mountain heights between the Guamá and the Bayamo valleys which are biologically very diverse and steeped with Cuban history and deserve to be clean and free and forested again (Enamorado, 1917).

FUNDING

This should not be thought of as a government funded project. A free and democratic Cuba will have enough demands on public funding. Thus, contemplated sources of bioprospecting funding include:

Private Companies

Bioprospecting can be a source of great profits as the history of Syntex corporation has shown. In varying levels of detail, some authors have discussed the returns from the bioprospecting (Katzman and William, 1990; Lesser and Krattinger; 1994; Hodson *et al.*, 1995 Moran, 1996) and have come up with positive estimates. One paper (Simpson, 1997) believes it would be negative. However, while the authors of the above papers are certainly interested parties, Simpson's analyses seems to also to be partisan where ethical and ecological considerations are given greater weight than potential profits. In my view Simpson, although he does make some convincing points, underestimates the efficiencies of modern screening technologies. He seems less aware of both biochemical diversity which he assumes to be more repetitive than the vast mass of literature on "natural products" plant biochemicals would suggest. It would seem that further and more formal economic studies should be made using whatever real life data is available; Lesser and Krattiger (1994) have made a good start.

International Funding

Another source of economic returns is international agency funding to compensate for such things as fossil fuel burning in the more highly developed countries (e.g. Gass and von Loesch, 1996; Putterman, 1994). The situation of Cuba adds other political and environmental recovery reasons to supplement fund (Díaz-Briquets, 1996). In my view one of the most urgent reasons to seek to seek to retain Cuba's forests, aside from the erosion and diminishing the peak run offs (Díaz-Briquets, 1996), is the potential contribution to political stability of remote areas (see below). This political consideration may also attract funding.

Visiting Scientists

A third source of funding is the renting of facilities to visiting scientists. Contact has been already made with scientists who in their research visit the areas selected. It is common for many U.S. university-faculty to seek and obtain this kind of funding for sabbaticals and summer terms. Research facilities such as Cold Springs Harbor in the United States and "La Selva" in Costa Rica supplement their funding in this way.

Protection of Migratory Birds

There is U.S. funding support for the protection of migratory birds and the protection of non-migratory species. This area may be one of the last areas on earth where a significant and well-loved bird, the ivory-billed woodpecker, survives. This funding would be directed at the maintenance of shade coffee, which makes an excellent migratory bird habitat (Rice *et al.*, 1996). The funding is to compensate for the loss of production associated with the shade—as opposed to the sun coffee production—method. The area in Cuba under consideration has old coffee groves. These groves could be maintained in this use with this funding support, until the coffee bushes age and become less productive, and trees that provide the shade grow very large and the area starts to return to forest.

POLITICAL REASONS TO RESTORE THE RAIN FOREST

In the past it has proven politically destabilizing to permit the destruction of forest by allowing slash and burn agriculture. This leads not only to the destruction of the forest but also to heart-breaking human misery. Having seen this first-hand it is hard to think of this situation dispassionately. Slash and burn agriculture as done in the Sierra Maestra was labor intensive and the ambition to cut large swaths of forest and keep the crops weed-free required much work, thus promoting excessively large family size.

The area was remote from most schools, and from the law. To feed their large families these children frequently just worked their parents holdings and did

not attend school; thus as they grew up these children only knew slash and burn agriculture. Repeating the cycling these children at a very early age also started families. This situation rapidly generated large numbers of illiterate, easily influenced, poor and desperate people, often called Montunos (people of the forest and the mountain), unaccustomed the rule of law. As families grew young men and women in search of their own lives, and independence from their families were always ready to seek more forest to cut. In these circumstances all who owned rain forest and wished to hold their land had to cut forest or it would soon be filled with squatters. It was a constant struggle just to maintain trees along the water courses. Erosion and flooding became more prevalent.

Then came the revolution of 1956-1959. In the morass of things that followed, Sorí Marín—defender of the Montunos—and possibly some of the Montunos of the area were executed. Life in the mountains grew even harsher, and much land in the mountains was abandoned (Díaz-Briquets, 1996).

In the present phase of transition, there is a lack of fuel, people in cities like Bayamo have no way except to use firewood to cook. I understand that this is again generating pressure on the forests, especially since in misguided attempts to "improve" and centralize agriculture there are now few trees on the plains (Díaz-Briquets, 1996). Even the live fence post trees (*Gliricidia spp.*), which would normally provide a considerable amount of cuttings for replanting or firewood (64 Kg of green-wood /year/tree in Sri Lanka, Allen and Allen, 1981 pp. 300-302) are gone. Such live fences must be replanted to spare the forest.

CUBAN RAIN FORESTS AS A SOURCE OF PHARMACEUTICALS

Rain forests are increasingly important sources of valuable pharmaceuticals and other bioactive products, and each different rainforest is a source for different bioactive compounds. In the rain forest, water and temperature do not limit growth; here interaction between species determines survival. The plants, animals, and fungi found in these areas are in relentless competition, species form and break alliances for defense, and to attack or exclude other species. Pathogens rapidly adapt, attacking any specie that

GLOSSARY OF TERMS AND CONCEPTS

Biochemical diversity: The root of diversity is the complexity of life's biochemistry (Castri and Younes, 1996). Each species of life be it plant, animal, fungi, and microorganism shares basic biochemical functions of DNA, RNA and enzymes (e.g. Taiz and Zeiger, 1991; Voet and Voet, 1995). Simple observation tells us that these basic biochemical functions give different results. One readily distinguishes between a fly and a human, poison ivy and a palm tree, a cow and a pig.

Yet, it is not always possible to tell life forms apart so readily. Take for instance edible mushrooms and deadly *Amanita phaloides*, the death angel mushroom (Klein, 1979 p. 173). Biochemicals—in this case the complex cyclopeptides found in this deadly fungus—make a mayor difference between these species. An extract containing these cyclopeptides, and a very supportive mother, allowed Nero to become Emperor of Rome. Even today, one thousand nine hundred and forty three years after Nero, some wild mushroom pickers, do not always make the distinction between species of mushrooms. These pickers dying regrets very forcefully make the point that biochemical differences between species do matter.

Even closely related species have different biochemistry, a classical case is the massive tristeza disease disaster of citrus crops which occurred about forty years ago South America. This financial and agricultural disaster was a direct result of the mandated use of the sour-orange rootstock instead of the tristeza tolerant root stock such as rough lemon, sweet orange (Pratt, 1958). The biochemistry of the sour orange rootstock is such that the rootstock does not thrive when infected with tristeza. The infected rootstock does not provide sufficient water and minerals to the upper part—the grafted sweet orange bearing part—of the tree. Thus the tree sickens, saddens, and dies.

Bioprospecting: Bioprospecting is the search among the diversity of life's millions organisms—and the many millions if not billions of biological compounds found in these organism—for biochemicals of use to humanity especially for pharmaceutical and agricultural uses (Rouhl, 1997). Bioprospecting is—like prospecting for minerals—a game of numbers. A way to measure, to assay, the desired activity called a screen (see below) is set up, and thousands of relatively crude samples—each containing many biochemicals—are processed through the screen to find one or more that works. The more species one examines, the greater the chance is that one will find the desired activity. Some times each sample is fractionated, usually by some chromatographic technology, into different groups of biochemicals before this assay this screen is performed.

Diversity: Diversity is a much bandied about word which in the common use and in the press. Is commonly given a fuzzy meaning evoking images of verdant beauty and forests and falling rain with dedicated, usually hirsute, almost mad, ecologists struggling to protect this treasure against evil despoilers of nature. Somehow, per-

haps because many ecological activists talk little about biochemistry and pharmacology the word diversity has become a mantra, a word of sacred content, pregnant with symbolism, but seemingly without precise meaning. However, there is hard science, much international political maneuvering, great commercial value and interest behind all this talk of diversity (Dudenhoefer, 1997; Castri and Younes, 1996; Gass and von Loesch, 1996; Hodson, *et al.*, 1995; Katzman and Cale, 1990; Lesser and Krattinger, 1994; von Loesch, 1996; Moran, 1996; Putterman, 1994).

Diversity within species: Diversity also exists within species. We all know the commercially significant difference between a Leghorn and Barred Plymouth Rock chicken or between a green Granny Smith and Red Delicious apple. Here the colors tell us that the different feathers or the different colored peels are biochemically different. These intra-specific differences can have tremendous commercial significance in such circumstances as disease or pest significance. For instance, presence of *Septorium* resistance in wheat strains (Kronstad, personal discussions, 1996) is critical to the profitability of crop in the Willamette Valley.

Economic consequences of diversity: Ignoring these difference, this diversity of plant materials, has led to massive crop failures. Thus, diversity and its ownership is matter of great concern for crop breeders and agricultural development agencies (Gass and van Loesch, 1996; van Loesch, 1996). Diversity is based upon variability in biochemistry and that variability in biochemistry extends below the species level to distinguish the individual plant or clone.

Germplasm: Germplasm refers to the living organisms that carry the diversity of life. Germplasm is defined as "the genetic donors: DNA sequence information, DNA, RNA, and protein sequences, cells, seeds, propagules, clones, plants organisms, etc., which are available or potential sources of variation in genetic composition" (Feng, *et al.*, 1994). The biochemistry of each individual plant varies not only with their genetic composition germplasm, but with the season, and the part of the plant: leaf, seed root etc, which have different biochemical components. (See discussion of site for screening below.)

Pharmaceutical interests: For a plant scientist the preservation of plant and animal germplasm is very significant. However for human medicine, as diseases constantly emerge, change, and acquire resistance to older treatments, it is essential to find new biochemicals that can act as new drugs, and antibiotics, etc. For these reasons bioprospecting is an active field; and there is a continual search, not only among the plant and animal kingdoms, but also among the bacteria and the fungi for new drugs and antibiotics. Scientists seek biochemicals in living organisms for several reasons: (1) there is vast number of biochemicals in living organisms; (2) there is a tradition of finding pharmaceuticals in this way; (3) many biochemicals have very complex chemical structures and chirality that are either too difficult to synthesize or simply cannot be made in the laboratory; and (4) the synthesis of a biochemical in a living organisms—as opposed to making it in the laboratory—mean that such biochemicals generally are not harmful to the cells in which they live (Gerwick, personal communication, 1996).

Rain forest: A rain forest is a heavily forested area of high rain fall where species diversity is high, trees grow tall and then branch out at different heights generating two or three separate canopies. Fallen trees decompose and rot to support a large number of other organisms. In family legends, I was told as a child that large white grubs were found inside these fallen giants. Grubs that last century the Cuban Insurgents, the Mambises, ate when there was nothing else to eat. There are large numbers of species of trees, lower story and epiphytic vegetation, and associated fungi, microorganisms and fauna. The value of the rain forest is in its biochemical diversity. "The immense biological diversity of tropical forests is difficult to comprehend. For example, ten selected 10-hectare plots in Borneo contain 700 species of trees and 1 hectare of tropical Peru contained 300 tree species. By comparison, 700 species of trees occur in all of North America" (Skole and Tucker, 1993).

Screening Today the screening process is highly automated. Automation is very necessary because one could expect a positive result from about 1/12,000 samples (*e.g.* Lesser and Krattinger, 1994). This new technology with its great sensitivity and through-put discovers new biochemicals, with new agricultural, biological and pharmacological activities at a much faster rate than ever before. Through use of anecdotal, traditional folk medicine, information the proportion of active biochemicals to inactive biochemicals can be enhanced considerably (Moran, 1996). Such information is available for a good number of Caribbean plants (Robineau, 1991).

Still each screen usually only determines one or few activities, thus for each activity it is usually necessary to set up a new screen. Since the array of biological materials screened for one purpose will almost certainly contain many other activities, the same array of biological materials can, and should, be run through other screens. This is a game of numbers and endless research.

Site: Today much of the screening research is done in separate academic and governmental centers far from the source of the materials. Although one way to make the screening process more effective is to establish on site centers of investigation (Putterman, 1994). Such on site laboratory centers might help reduce scientific unemployment, were post-Castro Cuba to follow the German Reunification model and decrease the number of scientists staffing at government laboratories.

Synthetic genes: A synthetic gene is one designed by man and made on a machine: on a DNA synthesizer. Synthetic genes, although used for basic experiments, are seldom if ever used in bioengineering, instead genes are taken from a living system. To be useful in bioengineering a DNA sequence must efficiently guide the generation of an RNA sequence. That RNA sequence must efficiently guide the synthesis of a protein; and the protein, the enzyme, made in this process must work better than the natural enzyme.

Synthetic genes have difficulties (Chen, personal communication, 1997) because the sequences designed by man rarely function as well as evolved genes found in living organisms. Natural genes have been honed by evolution over many millions of years. For instance to my knowledge, despite massive research effort, no synthetic gene for ribulose bis-phosphate carboxylase (the very critical enzyme of carbon fixation and the enzyme on which all life on earth depends) has proven to be more efficient than the natural enzymes. Difficulties with synthetic genes are that they often: (1) yield proteins alien to the cell and thus these proteins are broken down by cell proteases; (2) generate an insoluble protein which precipitates in the cell, and does not function; (3) generate an enzyme or structural protein that does not fold to the correct conformation and not thus have the appropriate catalytic action; (4) generate synthetic RNA codes from the introduced DNA that are not compatible with host's protein synthesis apparatus and little if any of the new protein will be made; and (5) do not work as well as very efficient natural genes.

Thus to date synthetic genes are a laboratory tool, not a way to bioengineer new and better living beings. On the other hand a DNA sequence from nature, say from a Cuban rain forest tree, will have evolved to maximum efficiency for its function in that plant.

Transformant bioengineering technology: Not so long ago plant breeders were limited to diversity within the same species or species closely related enough to interbreed. Then, if a crop had a new disease and there was no related plant with a resistant gene, "it was simply too bad." Farmers had to live with the disease. For example Gross Michel variety of bananas are very hard to breed (Tempany and Grist, 1958, p. 172). Long ago, Panama, Cuba and many other countries' banana crops were attacked by "El Mal de Panama" *Fusarium oxysporium f. cubensis (Fusarium cubense* E.F. Smith) Snyder and Hansen (Cook, 1939, pp. 245-250). Cuba lost a major crop. Eventually with much difficulty and expense resistant varieties were bred using traditional methods and genes from the Cavendish variety (Cook, 1939, p. 250; Tempany and Grist, 1958, p. 172,).

Now that bananas can be transformed, bioengineered, even to produce vaccines (Strobel, 1995, personal communication), introduction of a pathogen resistant gene is not as difficult. Now a gene can be taken—not only from one plant to a related plant—but also genes can also be moved to crop plants from unrelated plants that would never cross, even from animals and from fungi. This is what makes tropical and semitropical forests so important. These forests are full of plant diseases and insects. To survive under these conditions these plants have had to evolve resistance to them. This resistance, almost always, involves biochemicals.

becomes too numerous. Species diversity is the rule. New species, with new ways of survival, arise. Older species adapt and fight back. Much of the competition and many alliances are carried out using bioactive biochemicals.

The intense biochemical competition between host, pathogen, parasite and herbivores produces many bioactive products. To be most effective, a bioactive product should attack an important biochemical pathway of pest, pathogen, etc. without harming the host species. Many biochemical pathways are general and are common throughout life. Thus, other organisms can produce bioactive products harmless to man, but active against man's pathogens; when such products are found, they have pharmaceutical potential. One of the more famous bioactive products obtained from forest is taxol (Baskin *et al.*, 1994; Stierle, *et al.*, 1993), a compound—extracted from northern forest trees—used for cancer treatment. More pertinent to Cuba, for example, are the trees of the Annonacea family. These trees and their fruit have a number of useful and potentially useful bioactive materials such as parviflorin which has remarkably selective cytotoxicity against certain human solid tumor cell lines (Hoye and Zhixiong, 1996). Many other examples exist: e.g. thionin proteins, which are found in tropical as well as temperate climate plants. Thionins were once thought of as merely interesting redox proteins. Now thionins can be used to bioengineer fungi and bacteria resistant plants (Carmona *et al.*, 1993; Daley and Theriot, 1987; Molina, *et al.*, 1993). New ways of purification, new automated screening assays, and increasingly efficient biotechnological production methods have made the search for bioactive products much more economically viable.

Access to Rain Forest Bioactive Products

Seeking the bioactive products of the rain forest is not easy. Collections of seasonal products is difficult because climatic and heat conditions frequently make long stays difficult. Then there are difficulties with the local legal and business environments and legal barriers against export of germplasm. This paper explores a plan to avoid some of these difficulties by taking advantage of the opportunity to plan now for

access to the rain forest of Cuba when Castro falls (Díaz-Briquets, 1996).

Influence of Geology and Isolation on Genetic Diversity

Genetic diversity of flora and fauna (germplasm) and regional divergence of germplasm determine each rain forest's products. More prolonged geological isolation, and greater diversity of habitats favor more unique arrays of component germplasm (Borhidi, 1991; Leon and Alain, 1946-1953, 1974; Schultes and Raffauf, 1990; Skole and Ticker, 1993; Terborg, 1992; Victorin and Leon, 1944). This enhances the potential of a particular rain forest to harbor distinctly different kinds of commercially valuable products. Cuba is such a place (Borhidi, 1991).

About 38 million years ago, less than 100 miles south of what is now the United States, great geological changes occurred (MacPhee and Iturrralde-Vinent, 1994). The Greater Antilles Ridge arose from the sea, and in the next twenty or so million years, this ridge first joined then separated from South America, forming the Greater and Lesser Antilles. The westernmost islands that would become Cuba were separated from the rest of this complex by the rejuvenation of the Oriental Fault of which the Deep of Bartlett (also known as the Cayman Trench) forms a part. After this, with the exception of air and avian borne seed, the ancient South American Oligocene plant and terrestrial animal germplasm speciated and diverged in isolation to become unique Cuban species. At this time, large mammals such as giant rodents and enormous ground sloths roamed the coalescing islands that form Cuba today (MacPhee and Iturrralde-Vinent, 1994). Arriving much later in Cuba than in other areas of the Americas, Paleo-indians eventually wiped out this megafauna. However, some believe that even the ground sloth survived in neighboring Haiti until the time of William the Conqueror or perhaps later (Walker *et al.*, 1964). While the megafauna became extinct, the vegetation and many smaller animals, including some mammals survived, and could still be living in the rain forests of Cuba near the selected site (Walker, et al., 1964; Barbor, 1944).

Human Health and Living Conditions in the Eastern Cuban Rain Forest

In most of the world the surviving rain forests, especially those that are most diverse, are frequently not easily accessible, and are unhealthy and dangerous, which make these areas more expensive to survey for bioactive products. Cuba's rain forests are free from poisonous snakes. Reservoirs of yellow fever and malaria were wiped out after the United States helped liberate Cuba from the Spanish (1898) and controlled the infected mosquitoes that spread these diseases. The general area is very scenic, relatively cool and healthy, and readily accessible from Jamaica, the Cayman Islands and various cities, ports and towns on the eastern Cuban plains. There should be little difficulty recruiting appropriate staff.

Rain Forest Regeneration

It is a commonly held misconception that all rain forests, such as described by Skole and Tucker (1993) for Amazonia, once cut do not re-grow because the soils degenerate. Personal experience shows that does not occur as intensely in the limestone and ancient igneous rock derived 'laja' soils of the mountains of eastern Cuba. Cuban rain forest is resilient. As long as 'cayos' of rain forest persist, fungi, primitive vascular plants, tree ferns, etc. regenerate from wind born spores. Angiosperm seeds are frequently dispersed by birds, wind and water from undisturbed sections of the forest. Other angiosperms are spread on the coats or in the droppings of cattle, pigs and horses that replace, in this respect, the extinct megafauna. Today in Cuba, the guásima (*Guazuma ulmifolia* Miller.) or bastard cedar or West Indian elm tree (Fors, 1956) still grows in Cuban pastures. While once dispersed by the extinct megafauna (Mabberley, 1993, p. 255), this tree is now dispersed by cattle that eat the seed and pass the seed in their droppings. Underground roots spread from adjacent undisturbed land or survive for years in cultivated fields; for it is a constant struggle to maintain pastures of trees and crop fields free of lianas, to stop the formation of the "bejuquero".. Thus, if left undisturbed, tropical rain forests can rapidly re-expand their range. For instance, the valuable Cuban fine wooded Leguminosae *Lysiloma latisiliqua* (sabicú) grows five feet in the first year (Fors, 1956; Jiménez

Aguilla, *et al.*, 1991). Recolonialization is even faster for tree species such as yagrumas (*Cecropia peltata* and *Didymopnax morototoni*), which yield poor lumber, yet have bioactive potential because of their complex association with ant colonies (Copeland and Moiseff, 1997). However, a word of caution, as Gómez-Pompa points out that eco-system recovery, may mask diversity loss (Rice *et al.*, 1997, p. 2.) so there is not that much time to lose

Historical Events that Promoted Survival of Cuban Rain Forest

Growing in very complex and intermingled habitats on cave riddled limestone and igneous based mountains, rain forests still exists in areas of eastern Cuba. Some of this rain forest was cut back for coffee plantations in the early and middle 1800s, mainly by French immigrants displaced from Haiti. However, this activity ceased and the rain forest again closed in on these holdings during the prolonged struggle of the Cubans to free themselves from Spain (Enamorado, 1917). These wars were of considerable intensity and duration. By the end of the nineteenth century, after freedom from Spain, Cuba's small population was reduced by at least one third. Between the turn of the century and the 1950s, the expanding population gradually pushed back the rain forest. The rain forests range was to a few small areas in the middle of the island and somewhat larger areas of the old eastern province of Oriente (Marrero, 1955).

The expansion of farming into this area was halted by the revolts (1957-1959) against Batista's dictatorship. Then Castro's government converted large amounts of this area to military zones, and displaced the traditionally rebellious montuno, mountain population, to exile or towns and collective farms on the plains. The rain forest area, a traditional refuge of disaffected populations for five centuries, is now laced with military roads constructed first by Batista and then greatly expanded by Castro, despite continued landslides, and only sporadically populated between military garrisons.

THE COMING CHANGE IN CUBAN BUSINESS ENVIRONMENT

Despite the present Cuban government's desperate attempt to survive, its power is slipping away and a much more open and democratic government can soon be expected to replace it. The new Cuban government will need to rely heavily on the very successful Cuban exile business community of the United States to redevelop the economy. Thus, a free Cuba can be expected to have a business environment much more like the United States, than other countries which have rain forest resources, but also insular business methods less favorable to U.S. investment and licensing procedures.

The Effects of This Change on Cuban Rain Forests

As the Castro government loses its tight control over the population, the mountain land will again be open to development (Díaz-Briquets, 1996). Additional pressures on the rain forest will arise because this is also a mineral rich area with proven deposits of manganese, copper, silver and gold (e.g. Simons and Straczek, 1958; Oro, 1992 and personal memories). It is necessary to plan to protect the rain forests now. If plans are not in place, there will be little time to make them when Castro's fall triggers a rush to repopulate the area and clear the rain forests for agriculture.

Satellite Imagery

This is our first step. At present, satellite imagery is the only certain way to access information on the Cuban rain forests. Ground and air access to Cuba's rain forests is extremely limited. It is necessary for our purposes to determine how much of the Cuban rain forest remains, and if and where the rain forest has re-expanded. The Cuban government's data and concern for rain forest survival are not considered reliable. Castro's government has built strategic military roads, strong points and dams, with concurrent damage to ecology (Díaz-Briquets, 1997). Although we do not have on ground or over flight information, and no U.S. company representative can go into the area, commercial satellite data can readily provide information on the extent and health of the rain forest using standard techniques.

The plan is to use available satellite image data to survey the present extent of the rain forest (Cohen and Spies, 1992). Locations have already been found using United States Board on Geographic Names 1963 data and computerized versions of this same data provided by the Defense Mapping Agency. Only when this data is known, can plans be developed to contact and reach exploration and preservation agreements with those holding title to the critical areas before Castro falls. This will allow the new Cuban government to stay the final destruction of its unique rain forests (Díaz-Briquets, 1996, 1997), while legitimizing the rights of private industry to seek and utilize the bioactive compounds from these areas. Thus, our first step is to map, by remote sensing, the critical, most germplasm rich, potential sources of pharmaceuticals and bioactive substances in the eastern Cuban rain forest.

ANNOTATED BIBLIOGRAPHY

Allen, O.N. and Allen, E.K. 1981. *The leguminosae: A source book of characteristics, uses and nodulation.* Madison: University of Wisconsin Press, 812 pp. This is used as an example of reference text illustrating both the botany and the bioactive products of just one family of tropical plants, many of them rain forest trees.

Barbor, T. 1944. "The solenodons of Cuba." Proceedings of the New England Zoological Club 23, 1-8. Locates the almiquí in old Oriente Province, near Bayamo among other places.

Baskin, T.I., Wilson, J.E., Cork, A., and Williamson, R.E. 1994. "Morphology and microtubule organization in *Arabidopsis* roots exposed to oryzalin or taxol." *Plant Cell Physiol.* 35, 935-942. This paper illustrates the way bioactive products affect all life. Taxol, a bioactive plant and fungal product, is a useful treatment for cancer in humans.

Borhidi, A. 1991. *Phytogeography and vegetation ecology of Cuba*. Budapest: Akademiai Kiado, 857 pp. (Translation of a Hungarian flora of Cuba.)

Carmona, M.J., Molina, A., Fernández, J.A., López-Fando, J.J., and García-Olmedo, F. 1993. "Expression of the a-thionin gene from barley in tobacco confers resistance to bacterial pathogens." *Plant J.* 3, 457-462. Example of thionin action and bioengineering. Transfer of *Pseudomonas* resistance from barley to transgenic tobacco.

Castri, F. di and Younes, T. (eds). 1996. *Biodiversity, science and development*. Wallingford, England: CAB International.

Cohen, W.B. and Spies, T.A. 1992. "Estimating structural attributes of Douglas-fir/western hemlock forest stands from Landsat and SPOT imagery." *Remote Sens. Environ.* 41, 1-17. This is an example of the use of satellite imagery to determine forest stand structure and "wetness" of forest.

Copeland, J. and Moiseff. 1997. "Ants on *Cecropia* in Hawaii." *Biotropica* 29,128-132. Although this paper deals with non-native species in Hawaii, where neither the ants nor its host trees are native, there is a good review of this complex and potentially useful plant-insect relationship.

Cook, M.T. (translated by José L. Otero). 1939. *Enfermedades de las Plantas Económicas de Las Antillas*. San Juan: University of Puerto Rico Monograph, Series 2. Number 4.

Daley, L.S. and Theriot, L.J. 1987. "Proteins-similar to purothionin from tomato (*Lycopersicum esculenta*), mango (*Mangifera indica*), papaya (*Carica papaya*) and walnut (*Juglans regia*). Purification, protein redox activity, and effect upon proteolytic activity." *J. Agric. Food Chem.* 35, 680-687. First demonstration of thionins in tropical species. This work continues successfully in more applied, but still unpublished form in laboratory of the author.

Díaz-Briquets, S. 1996. "Forest policies of Cuba's socialist government: An appraisal." *Cuba in Transition—Volume 6*, 425-437.

Díaz-Briquets, S. 1997. *The Environmental Legacy of Socialism in Cuba*. Manuscript in submittance.

Dudenhoefer, D. 1997. "Costa Rica conference focuses on nexus between business and biodiversity conservation." *Diversity* 13, 7-8.

Enamorado, C. 1917. *Tiempos Heróicos: Persecución*. La Habana: Imprenta y Papelería de Rambla, Bouza y Cia., 255 pp. Prize winning book, written by a general of the Cuban wars against Spain, a diplomat and scholar who, in later years was very interest in plant germplasm. The book is placed in, and describes in detail, the extent of the rain forests of the area in the middle and late nineteenth century and provides firsthand details on Cuba's eastern rain forests' vegetation and rivers not available elsewhere.

Feng, W., Ning, L. Daley, L., Moreno, Y., Azarenko, A. and Criddle, R. S. 1994. "Determination of effective temperature minima for CAM carboxylation in diverse plants by scanning microcalorimetry." *Plant Physiology and Biochemistry* 32, 319-330.

Fors, A. J. 1956. *Maderas Cubanas*. La Habana: Ministerio de Agricultura, 162 pp. This book describes many of the rain forest trees' growth habits, etc. in considerable detail. The author also wrote the present Cuban government forestry manual. Fors, A. J. 1966. *Manual de Silvicultura*. La Habana: Publicaciones INRA, Havana, 237 pp.

Gass, T. and Loesch, H. von. 1995. "Genetic resources targeted as a priority for new CGIAR thrust in Eastern Europe and NIS states." *Diversity* 12(4), 3.

Hodson, T.J., Englander, F., and O'Keefe, Hsu.1995. "Rain forest preservation, markets, and medicinal plants: Issues of property rights and present value." *Conservation Biology* 9, 1319-1321.

Hoye, T. and Zhixiong, Y. 1996. "Highly efficient synthesis of the potent antitumor annonaceous acetogenin (+)-parviflorin." *J. Amer. Chem. Soc.* 118, 1801-1802. The first paragraph of this paper reads: "The annonaceous acetogenins are a rapidly growing class of natural products that have received considerable attention. Many members (of this plant family) possess a variety of biological effects including potent cytotoxic, antitumor, and pesticide activities. parviflorin, a relatively rare C_{35} bis THF acetogenin, was isolated by McLaughlin et al. both from *Asimina parviflora* Duanl and from *Annona bullata* Rich. Parviflorin showed remarkable selectivity in its cytotoxicity against certain human solid tumor cell lines."

Jiménez Aguilla, M., Calzadilla Zaldívar, E., Renda Sayous, A., Sánchez Rodón, J., Torres Torres, J., and Casate Tenrero, C. 1991. "Los sistemas agroforestales: Alternativa para manejo integral de los suelos montañosos de Cuba," *10th Proc. World Forestry Congress* 3, 28-34. These authors report growth of replanted native trees in prepared terraces in igneous based soils on the foot hills below (less than 700 feet elevation) the rain forests of eastern Cuba. For instance, the rapid growing, highly prized, native rain forest timber source *Lysiloma latisiliqua* (sabicú, jigüey) is reported to reach a mean height of almost 12 feet in 27 months.

Jiménez Arrellanes, A., Mata, R., Lotina-Henssen, B., Anaya Lang, A.L., and Velasco Ibarra, L. 1996. "Phytogrowth-inhibitory compounds from *Malmea depressa* (syn. *Guatteria leiophylla*)." *J. Nat. Prod.* 59, 202-204. This paper is used as an example of studies that could be done in Cuba, since the species studied is related to naturally occurring Cuban species *Guatteria Blainii* and *Guatteria Moralesii*.

Katzman, M.T. and Cale, W.G. Jr. 1990. "Tropical forest preservation using economic incentives." *Bioscience* 40, 827-832.

Klein, R.M. 1979. *The Green World*. New York: Harper and Row.

León, H. and Alain, H. 1946-1953, 1974. *Flora de Cuba*. Koenigstein: Otto Koeltz Science Publishers. Part of the classic life work on Cuban flora

(description of plants) of the monk Hermano León (see also Victorín and León below). Since these authors belong to a religious order, their first name is given as Hermano which translates to Brother in English and Frere in French, thus initials, are B., F. or H., depending on the language of the citation.

Lesser, W.H. and Krattiger, A. F. 1994. "The complexities of negotiating terms for germplasm collection." *Diversity* 10, 6-10.

Loesch, H. von. 1996. "World Bank official warns of future 'Scientific Apartheid.'" *Diversity* 12(4), 5.

MacPhee, R.D.E. and Iturralde-Vinent, M.A. 1994. "First tertiary land mammal from Greater Antilles: an early Miocene sloth (Xenarthra. Megalonychidae) from Cuba." *American Museum Novitates*, number 3094, 1-13. Although the dating of this find is subject to scientific discussion, the description of the geological development of the Antilles, by virtue of the two authors' contacts in present day Cuba, is very useful for the purposes described here.

Marrero, L. 1955. *Geografía de Cuba*. La Habana: Alfa. 736 pp. This book contains a large number of aerial photographs of the rain forests of eastern Cuba as they existed in the late 1940s and 1950s, and thus is very useful for comparisons with data on present extent of rain forest to be obtained in this proposed project. In addition, very complete rainfall and some soil information is provided for all areas including the rain forests.

Mabberley, D.J. *The plant-book*. Cambridge, England: Cambridge University Press.

Moran, K. 1996. "Compensating forest-dwelling communities for drug discovery: The work of the Healing Forest Conservancy." *Unasilva* 47, 40-46.

Molina, A., et al. 1993. "Inhibition of bacterial and fungal plant pathogens by thionins of types I and II." *Plant Science* 92, 169-177. Example of range of activity of thionin proteins.

Oro, J.R. 1992. *The poisoning of paradise*. Miami: Endowment for Cuban American Studies.

Pratt, R.M. 1958. *Florida Guide to Citrus Insects, Diseases and Nutritional Disorders*. Gainesville, Florida: Agricultural Experiment Station.

Putterman, D.M. 1994. "Trade and the biodiversity convention." *Nature* 371, 553-554.

Rice, R.A., Harris, A.M,. and McLean, J. 1996. *Proceedings 1st Sustainable Coffee Congress*. Washington: Smithsonian Migratory Bird Center, National Zoological Park. A compendium of the relationship between different types of coffee growing practices and bird habitat, with rain forest recovery aspect included.

Robineau, Lionel. 1991. *Towards a Caribbean Pharmacopoeia: Scientific Research and Popular Uses of Medicinal Plants in the Caribbean*. Santo Domingo, Dominican Republic and Universidad Nacional Autonoma de Honduras: Enda-Caribe. This is a very catholic source of data varying from the traditional medicine traditions to scientifically reviewed publications.

Rouhi, M. 1997. "Seeking drugs in natural products." *Chemical & Engineering News* 75(14) (April 7, 1997), 14-29. An interesting article that, among other things, discusses the changes in bioprospecting practices in recent years, a number of successful and promising enterprises in this field, and the effectiveness of different biosprospecting practices

Schultes, R. E. and Raffauf, R.F. 1990. *The healing forest. Medicinal and toxic plants of Northwest Amazonia*. Portland, Oregon: Dioscorides Press. Richard Evans Schultes is Jeffrey Professor of Biology and Director of the Botanical Museum of Harvard University and a very well known medicinal plant explorers. This book illustrates the great number of bioactive materials found in rain forests. One should keep in mind that, although some species and genera overlap, the flora of Cuba is different from that of Amazonia. Thus Cuba's flora with its large number of endoge-

nous species is another rich source of bioactive compounds.

Simons, F.S. and Straczek, J.A. 1958. *Geology of manganese deposits in Cuba*. U.S. Geological Survey Bulletin 1057. This bulletin contains maps of the site area.

Simpson, R.D. 1997. "Biodiversity prospecting." *Resources* 126, 12-15

Skole, D. and Tucker, C. 1993. "Tropical deforestation and habitat fragmentation in the Amazon: Satellite data from 1978 to 1988." *Science* 260, 1905-1910. This paper describes a similar application of remote sensing technology to what we propose.

Stierle, A., Strobel, G. and Stierle D. 1993. "Taxol and taxane production by *Taxomyces andreanae* an endophytic fungus of pacific yew." *Science* 260, 214-216. The first report of the finding of the cancer treatment drug, taxol, in an endophytic fungus. This reference shows bioactive compounds can be found in complex associations of different organisms and documents the established competence of one of the author's associates to search for bioactive compounds.

Taiz, L. and Zeiger, E. 1991. *Plant Physiology*. Redwood City, California: Benjamin/Cummings.

Tempany, H. and Grist, D. H. 1958. *An introduction to tropical agriculture*. London: Longmans, Green and Co. This old but still useful book gives and idea of how difficult breeding of some tropical crops could be before biotransformation greatly expanded the sources of genetic diversity available to breed each crop plant species.

Terborgh, J. 1992. *Diversity and the tropical rain forest*. New York: Scientific American Library. A less specialized approach to the general aspects of rain forest diversity and value. The lush illustrations and quality of this book are a reflection of the great popular interest in rain forest conservation.

United States Board on Geographic Names. 1963. *Cuba*, 2nd edition. Washington: Office of Geography, Department of the Interior. 619 pp. Locates many of the smaller rivers and population centers in great detail, giving latitude and longitude, allowing precise localization for SPOT imagery. An updated version is available on CD disks from the Defense Mapping Agency.

Victorín, F.M. and León, F. 1944. *Itineraires botaniques dans l'ile de Cuba*. Montreal: Botanical Institute of the University of Montreal. 410 pp. A classic reference on Cuban vegetation.

Voet, D. and Voet, J. G. 1995. *Biochemistry*, 2nd edition. New York: John Wiley & Sons, Inc.

Walker, E.P., Warnik, F., Lange, K.I., Uible, H.E., Hamlet, S.E., Davis, M.A., and Wright, P.F. 1964. *Mammals of the World*. Baltimore: The John Hopkins University Press, Baltimore. In volume 1, p. 483, describes ground sloth remains found in Hispaniola and Puerto Rico associated with human pottery, bones of man, and domestic pig. Pp. 104-105 of the same volume describe the almiquí (*Solenodon cubanus*). Volume 2, pp. 1033-1035 describe and illustrate *Capromys spp.* the jutías.

FUNDAMENTO CONSTITUCIONAL
DE LA TRANSICION EN CUBA

José D. Acosta

En la segunda Conferencia celebrada por la ASCE en 1992, presenté un documento sobre "El Marco Jurídico-Institucional de un Gobierno Provisional de Unidad Nacional en Cuba" en el que sostuve mi opinión en el sentido de que el retorno a la democracia reprentativa desmantelada en Cuba en 1959 requeriría el reconocimiento, en alguna medida razonable, de los derechos surgidos en razón de la sustitución ilegítima de la Constitución de 1940, que regía en el país en aquel momento. Mi competidor en Cuba y querido colega (Salaya y Casteleiro) el Dr. Agustín de Goytisolo, comentarista de mi documento, formuló en aquella oportunidad su opinión de que los principales Títulos de la Carta de 1940 no planteaban grandes problemas de reimplementación. Ese comentario constituyó un programa de trabajo que los dos nos propusimos mantener vigente en ASCE.

El año pasado mi también competidor y querido colega (Bufete Zayas, Morán y Valdés Rodríguez) el Dr. Alberto Luzárraga organizó dos paneles en la Conferencia de ese año para examinar el problema desde la otra cara de la medalla: la necesidad de que cualquier gobierno que pretenda iniciar la transición hacia la democracia debe lograr, como cuestión previa, el reconocimiento general, por parte de la ciudadanía, de que el mismo ha reconquistado el Estado de Derecho, es decir, esa situación en la que todos consideran que los daños jurídicamente tutelados por el sistema legal que encarnaba la democracia en Cuba en 1959 tienen en una medida razonable la protección del nuevo sistema establecido.

Este año se me ocurrió que para adelantar los esfuerzos de ASCE en este campo, habría que iniciar un examen a fondo de cada uno de los Títulos de la Constitución de 1940 para medir las posibilidades de su reimplementación y determinar las dificultades que ello plantearía, habida cuenta de las necesidades y realidades sociales, políticas y económicas que limitan sustancialmente la esfera de acción de un gobierno provisional de transición hacia una democracia plena, retomando así el tema donde lo dejó mi colega Goytisolo.

Para ello, he logrado la cooperación del Dr. Goytisolo, que gestionó y obtuvo la participación de un número significativo de especialistas cubano-americanos de fuera de Cuba que iniciaran esa tarea. El resultado de las gestiones del Dr. Goytisolo fue mayor que el que nos imaginamos inicialmente, y fue así como este año de 1997 este tema requirió el tiempo disponible, sin interrupciones, de dos sesiones de trabajo de la Conferencia de agosto pasado. Por eso, me limité a declarar abierto el panel a la exacta hora señalada, y de inmediato solicitar al Dr. Goytisolo que continuara él presidiendo este panel, con un resultado excelente.

Cuando me dirigía hacia la sala asignada, la señora Ruth Montaner, representante en Miami del Grupo de Trabajo de la Disidencia en Cuba, me facilitó gentilmente copia del profundo documento titulado "Constitución y Cambio Democrático en Cuba." El documento fue preparado en la Habana, en junio de este año, por el Dr. René Gómez Manzano, Presidente de la Corriente Agramontista, una de las organizaciones representadas en el Grupo de Trabajo de la Disidencia en Cuba, distinguido abogado de profesión, y por consiguiente, posiblemente la persona de mayor autoridad profesional en el país para examinar el problema constitucional de la transición desde el punto de vista jurídico. El documento constituyó para mí, la primera opinión seria, de dentro de Cuba, sobre la problemática constitucional de la transición y refleja un importantísimo aporte a ese tema.

Profundamente impresionado por el documento, consulté rápidamente al Dr. Jorge Pérez-López, Presidente del Comité de la Conferencia, sobre las posibilidades de su inclusión en ese evento. Jorge me sugirió que introdujera brevemente el documento en la apertura del panel lo que hice gustosamente.

Al final de mi intervención, sin embargo, la señora Ruth Montaner me explicó que consideraba apropiado consultar al Dr. Pablo Llabre, representante en Miami de la Corriente Agramontista, de la que fue co-fundador, antes de incluir el documento en la memoria de la Conferencia de este año. Así lo hice y el Dr. Llabre accedió gentilmente a que el documento se publicara bajo el nombre de su autor, con la simple aclaración de que el mismo sólo refleja la opinión profesional del autor en la fecha de su preparación y que no involucra a ninguna de las organizaciones a que el mismo pertenece en Cuba.

Si más demora, se anexa el texto original. El que suscribe hace sólo constar su profunda satisfacción como cubano y como abogado por esta sesuda y bien fundada opinión de un abogado cubano residente en Cuba y actualmente en prisión junto con los otros tres miembros del Grupo de Trabajo de la Disidencia Interna en Cuba, con mis seguridades al Dr. Gómez Manzano de que su valioso aporte será tomado muy en cuenta en los futuros trabajos de ASCE sobre este tema.

CONSTITUCIÓN Y CAMBIO DEMOCRÁTICO EN CUBA

René Gómez Manzano[1]

En 1810, el bayamés Joaquín Infante redactó su proyecto de ley fundamental para la isla de Cuba. No obstante, la primera Constitución que rigió en la isla fue la española de 1812, promulgada en la ciudad de Cádiz. Más de medio siglo más tarde, en abril de 1869, los independentistas que seis meses antes habían dado comienzo a la Guerra de los Diez Años eligieron democráticamente a sus representantes, los que se congregaron en el poblado de Guáimaro y aprobaron la carta magna que con ese nombre es conocida, en cuya redacción desempeñó un papel fundamental el insigne libertador y jurista camagüeyano Ignacio Agramonte. Fue ésta la primera constitución cubana que tuvo vigencia real. Nota distintiva de este documento jurídico (que lo diferencia de otros similares aprobados en los restantes países de Iberoamérica en análogas circunstancias) es el hecho de que aun en medio de las dificilísimas condiciones de la insurrección. sus autores se plantearon el establecimiento de un Estado de Derecho, en el que fueran respetados los derechos humanos.

Años más tarde, ya al final de aquella contienda, fue promulgada la Constitución de Baraguá, de efímera vigencia. Durante la Guerra de Independencia (1895–98), rigieron sucesivamente las leyes fundamentales de Jimaguayú (1895) y La Yaya (1897).

En 1901, durante la Primera Intervención Norteamericana, se convocó una Convención Constituyente, que elaboró la constitución de ese año, la cual, a pesar del apéndice foráneo de la tristemente célebre Enmienda Platt, rigió el establecimiento de Cuba como Estado independiente internacionalmente reconocido, el 20 de mayo de 1902. Este código político se caracterizó por plasmar, en su parte dogmática, los principios del liberalismo; en su parte orgánica, se inspiró en las experiencias de la gran democracia norteamericana. Su breve período de vigencia fue accidentado: en 1928, bajo la dictadura del general Gerardo Machado, fue objeto de una reforma general encaminada a permitir la prolongación del mandato de éste, lo que concitó el rechazo de la nueva oposición. En medio de la gravísima crisis económica del treinta, la actuación de los antimachadistas condujo al derrocamiento del régimen en 1933, y abrió un paréntesis de gobiernos provisionales que se prolongó hasta 1940.

ASPECTOS ESENCIALES DE LA ADOPCION DE LA CONSTITUCION DE 1940: SU VIGENCIA

Al término de la cuarta década del siglo, bajo la presidencia del jurista doctor Federico Laredo Brú, las fuerzas políticas del país convinieron en buscar una salida a la crisis institucional a través de la convocatoria de una convención constituyente, lo que se llevó a efecto por medio de unas elecciones que fueron consideradas las más pulcras realizadas dentro de la etapa republicana. Virtualmente todas las tendencias estuvieron representadas en ese cónclave democrático, incluyendo a los comunistas, que, de acuerdo con la vo-

---

1. Este documento refleja sólo la opinión profesional del autor y no involucra a ninguna de las organizaciones a que el mismo pertenece en Cuba.

tación obtenida, pudieron contar con una bancada no muy grande, pero que si demostró ser muy activa.

La carta magna elaborada por los asambleístas de 1940 ha sido considerada la más progresista de su tiempo. En ella, junto con el reconocimiento pleno de las libertades formales que siempre había proclamado el Estado cubano, se dictaron normas encaminadas a procurar el imperio de la justicia social, que pudiéramos calificar como de carácter socializante; en el plano orgánico, se prohibió la reelección presidencial, que había gravitado negativamente en toda la vida política nacional y—más concretamente—había sido causa de graves crisis durante los mandatos de Tomás Estrada Palma, Mario García-Menocal y Gerardo Machado.

Siempre resultaría poco cuanto se dijera en elogio de este verdadero monumento jurídico, que no en balde ha sido y es considerado con justicia como un real logro nacional. El profesor Ramón Infiesta, comparándolo con su similar de 1901, señala las ventajas que en su opinión posee, aunque refiriéndolas al tiempo en que él escribía ("en nuestro tiempo"). En ese contexto, la califica de "popular y cubana," "instructiva y cívica," "progresista" y programática.[2]

No obstante sus múltiples perfecciones, este código político presenta distintos defectos, que fueron señalados ya por el propio profesor Infiesta. Según este catedrático, las críticas que se enderezan a la Constitución de 1940 son "ordinariamente" las siguientes:

- "es demasiado extensa" (lo cual califica el autor como "inevitable");

- "es casuística" (lo que—en opinión de Infiesta—"es un defecto más grave que el anterior"); y

- "su técnica es defectuosa" (lo que puntualiza señalando que "ofrece, en general, cierto descuido en la nomenclatura," así como que "no faltan contradicciones ni omisiones" y que "el más somero análisis de las Disposiciones Transitorias

plantea dudas insalvables acerca de su naturaleza y viabilidad."[3]

Casi doce años rigió ese texto democrático, progresista y socializante; al producirse el golpe de estado encabezado por el general Batista en marzo de 1952, aquél fue remplazado por unos Estatutos Constitucionales. A raíz de tomar posesión las nuevas autoridades victoriosas en las elecciones generales espurias de 1954, el régimen autoritario imperante proclamó el restablecimiento de la Constitución. El carácter eminentemente formal de su vigencia (que, aunque si la dificultó, no impidió la perpetración de violaciones de los derechos fundamentales, incluyendo numerosos asesinatos extrajudiciales) dio lugar a que los luchadores antibatistianos enarbolaran como bandera el texto fundamental de 1940. Obviamente, con esto no se pretendía su vigencia formal (la cual databa de 1955), sino la aplicación real de sus principios y preceptos. Esto incluía el respeto escrupuloso de los derechos fundamentales, el ejercicio real de la soberanía popular mediante elecciones verdaderamente libres y la promulgación de las leyes complementarias que se requerían para poner en práctica algunos de.sus preceptos sociales (y, de modo especial, una ley de reforma agraria que hiciese realidad la proscripción del latifundio).

EL ESTABLECIMIENTO DEL GOBIERNO REVOLUCIONARIO: LA LEY FUNDAMENTAL DE 1959

Esos objetivos declarados no se llevaron a la práctica tras el triunfo revolucionario de 1959. Aunque en los primeros días se proclamó solemnemente el "restablecimiento" de la Constitución del 40, esto no pasó de ser un mero formalismo. De hecho, en febrero de aquel mismo año se dictó la Ley Fundamental, la cual, en su parte dogmática, recogía el texto casi íntegro de aquélla, pero en su parte orgánica establecía un sistema autoritario que—entre otras cosas—incurría exactamente en los mismos vicios tan criticados en los Estatutos Constitucionales de 1952: un Presidente de la República que nombraba a los mi-

---

2. Ramón Infiesta, *Derecho Constitucional*, 2ª edición, La Habana, 1954, p. 143.

3. Ibíd., pp. 140–42.

nistros y que—a su vez—era elegido por el Consejo de Ministros, y una supuesta carta magna que podía ser libremente reformada por este propio órgano, con el único requisito de la aprobación de los dos tercios de sus miembros. Veamos como sonaba la crítica de esos aspectos de los Estatutos en boca del propio doctor Fidel Castro, en su autodefensa conocida como *La Historia me Absolverá*: "El artículo 2 dice: 'La soberanía reside en el pueblo y de este emanan todos los poderes.' Pero luego viene el artículo 118 y dice: "El Presidente de la República será designado por el Consejo de Ministros." Ya no es el pueblo, ahora es el Consejo de Ministros. ¿Y quién elige el Consejo de Ministros? El artículo 120, inciso 13: "Corresponde al Presidente nombrar y remover libremente a los ministros, sustituyéndolos en las oportunidades que proceda." ¿Quién elige a quién por fin? ¿No es éste el clásico problema del huevo y la gallina que nadie ha resuelto todavía?"[4] Y unas líneas más adelante agregaba el hoy Comandante en Jefe: "Hay en los Estatutos un artículo que ha pasado inadvertido pero es el que da la clave de esta situación y del cual vamos a sacar conclusiones decisivas. Me refiero a la cláusula de reforma contenida en el artículo 257 y que dice textualmente: Esta Ley Constitucional podrá ser reformada por el Consejo de Ministros con un quórum de las dos terceras partes de sus miembros. Aquí la burla llego al colmo. No es sólo que hayan ejercido la soberanía para imponer al pueblo una Constitución sin contar con su consentimiento y elegir un gobierno que concentra en sus manos todos los poderes, sino que por el artículo 257 hacen suyo definitivamente el atributo más esencial de la soberanía que es la facultad de reformar la ley suprema y fundamental de la nación..."[5] *Mutatis mutandis,* estas ardorosas palabras del doctor Castro Ruz son perfectamente aplicables a la Ley Fundamental de febrero de 1959.

Ni siquiera el Poder Judicial (generalmente respetado en los anteriores cambios revolucionarios) quedó indemne: se suspendió la inamovilidad de que, en virtud de un precepto supralegal, gozaban sus funcionarios, y se llevó a cabo una amplia purga. Es cierto

que, después de pasado ese proceso, los tribunales continuaron disfrutando de cierta autonomía y siguieron estando integrados por jueces de carrera; pero también es verdad que, en el plano político, fueron despojados de la mayor parte de sus funciones de control, al eliminarse los recursos de inconstitucionalidad en todas aquellas materias que más esencialmente interesaban a las nuevas autoridades. Cabe—no obstante—hacer la salvedad de que—en esencia—ese control judicial de la constitucionalidad había perdido casi toda virtualidad desde el mismo momento en que, al dictarse la Ley Fundamental, las reformas de su texto sólo requerían de la aprobación por los dos tercios de los miembros del Consejo de Ministros, lo que nunca resultaba difícil para un régimen que desde el principio había dado sobradas muestras de una notable vocación de unanimidad.

Por consiguiente, ya desde 1959 la carta magna de la República perdió su condición de texto garante de la seguridad jurídica; prueba al canto: las incontables medidas "nacionalizadoras" que, sin indemnizar a derechas a los antiguos dueños, condujeron de hecho a la eliminación de la propiedad privada y sentaron las bases de la involución económica que ha sufrido Cuba, se llevaron a cabo "constitucionalmente."

Estimo que, en la práctica, ninguno de los tres objetivos fundamentales arriba señalados fue cumplido.

Fueron violados los derechos fundamentales, comenzando por el más importante: el derecho a la vida. La Constitución de 1940 proscribía virtualmente la pena de muerte; la última ejecución judicial databa de los años de la Segunda Guerra Mundial. Sin embargo, con el advenimiento del nuevo régimen, cambió radicalmente esta situación. En la carta magna de la República siguió figurando un artículo en el que se hacía referencia a la supuesta prohibición del castigo capital, pero, con el transcurso del tiempo, se fueron agregando más y más excepciones a ese enunciado teórico. La situación se vio agravada por la circunstancia de que esas causas salieron de la jurisdicción de las cortes ordinarias (compuestas por honestos profe-

---

4. Fidel Castro, *La Historia me Absolverá*, Oficina de Publicaciones del Consejo de Estado, La Habana, 1993, p. 98.

5. Ibíd., p. 99.

sionales de carrera) para caer en la de los llamados "tribunales revolucionarios," integrados mayoritariamente por guerrilleros carentes de instrucción jurídica, los que dieron muestras de una gran proclividad a privar de la vida a quienes comparecían como acusados por delitos graves. También fueron menoscabadas las libertades de reunión, de asociación y de libre emisión del pensamiento, e incluso las de religión y de libre entrada y salida del territorio nacional.

En lo que respecta al ejercicio real de la soberanía popular por medio de elecciones libres, baste decir lo siguiente: ¡El pueblo cubano tuvo que esperar la friolera de más de diecisiete años para poder participar en un proceso con visos de elecciones!... No cabe negar que, en un principio, el Gobierno Revolucionario contó con un apoyo ampliamente mayoritario de la ciudadanía, supongo que nadie pretenda desconocer que como fruto de la política seguida por el nuevo régimen, ese respaldo comenzó a erosionarse rápidamente. Lo cierto es que, de manera típicamente orwelliana, la promesa formal inicial de efectuar comicios en un plazo de seis meses fue remplazada por la pasmosa consigna de "¿Elecciones para qué?" Fue sólo en 1976 que el régimen realizó el proceso que el mismo bautizó como "de institucionalización," con lo cual—como es obvio—estaba reconociendo implícitamente que, por lo menos hasta ese momento, había hecho caso omiso de las sabias enseñanzas de Lincoln, y había mantenido un gobierno de hombres, y no de instituciones.

De los mencionados tres puntos que abarcaba la consigna del restablecimiento de la Constitución de 1940 durante la lucha antibatistiana, el único que fue objeto de determinadas medidas del nuevo Gobierno fue el de la promulgación de leyes complementarias; esto se refiere especialmente a la realización de la reforma agraria, la cual (crasa omisión de los gobernantes democráticos) no había sido iniciada en más de un decenio de regímenes *de jure*, a pesar de que el artículo 90 del texto supralegal declaraba la proscripción del latifundio. A mediados de 1959 se promulgó

la Ley de Reforma Agraria, en la que se anunció la entrega de tierras a los campesinos; no obstante, lo que primó en la práctica fue la estatización de las tierras expropiadas, de modo que alguien podrá tal vez decir que se cumplió con la letra del precepto constitucional (afirmación que discuto, pues lo que se hizo fue crear un inmenso latifundio estatal), pero nunca con su espíritu, que estaba orientado al fortalecimiento del colonato criollo y del campesinado pequeño y medio en general.

LA "CONSTITUCION SOCIALISTA" DE 1975

Con esos antecedentes, se llega a la proclamación, el 24 de febrero de 1976, de la llamada "Constitución socialista," a la cual dedicaré un buen espacio porque la misma constituye la base de la situación que, en este terreno, presenta Cuba hoy. Es bueno aclarar que, aunque generalmente ese cuerpo supralegal es conocido como la Constitución de 1976 (que es el año de su entrada en vigor), en realidad es más correcta (por ser el de su elaboración) la referencia al de 1975, que propuso en su momento el prominente jurista católico, doctor Raúl Gómez Treto.[6] En la promulgación de esta nueva carta magna alcanza su culminación el proceso de ruptura con los antecedentes del desarrollo constitucional de nuestra Patria. Esto comprende casi todos los aspectos de la elaboración del texto supralegal.

En primer lugar, se abandonó la tradición de que esos documentos fundamentales fuesen elaborados por asambleas constituyentes democráticamente electas. Así había sucedido no sólo en 1901 y 1940, sino también—como ya vimos—en 1869 (durante la violenta ofensiva de las fuerzas integristas conocida como la "Creciente de Valmaseda"), en 1895 e incluso en 1897 (o sea: en plena Guerra de Independencia). Precisamente el último proceso de elección de una asamblea constituyente efectuado en Cuba (el de 1940) constituyó un ejemplo de libertad, pureza y pluralismo: cada uno de los partidos que compitieron estaba obligado a proclamar los principios que propugnarían sus delegados en la asamblea de modo que

---

6. Raúl Gómez Treto, "El concepto marxista de la Constitución y el sistema jurídico-normativo de la sociedad constituida en Estado," *Revista Cubana de Derecho*, Nº 31, p. 17.

el elector podía votar con pleno conocimiento de causa. Independientemente de los defectos consustanciales a toda obra humana, el formidable resultado de ese trabajo de conjunto ha quedado para la admiración de los cubanos y de todos los hombres libres de hoy y de mañana: una constitución progresista, defensora de los derechos del ciudadano, afiliada a las doctrinas de la tripartición de poderes y de la no re-elección, pluralista, respetuosa de la representación y de los derechos de las minorías, así como de la autonomía de la Provincia y del Municipio; en resumen: profundamente democrática.

Según lo demuestran los hechos, ese sistema para re-dactar leyes fundamentales no resultó del agrado de los comunistas llegados al poder. Así vemos que, en lugar de una asamblea constituyente soberana, se constituyó, mediante acuerdo del Buró Político del Partido Comunista y del Consejo de Ministros, de fecha 22 de octubre de 1974, una Comisión Mixta del propio Partido Comunista y del Gobierno. Nada—pues—de elecciones, sino meros nombramientos. Nada de pluralismo: sólo los declaradamente gobiernistas tenían derecho a participar. Nada de divulgar los nombres de los encargados de la importantísima tarea: salvo el Presidente, los miembros de la Comisión quedaron condenados a un virtual anonimato, pues sus nombres fueron dados a conocer en publicaciones especializadas apenas en aquel momento. Nada de divulgar el desarrollo de los debates (si es que los hubo): el proceso vivo de creación quedó sumido en el secreto...

Lo que sí organizó el régimen castrista fue un proceso asambleario en el que participaron masivamente los ciudadanos. Creo que se trató—en esencia—de una mera formalidad. El problema no radica en que se hiciera caso omiso de las sugerencias formuladas: resulta evidente que, en un proceso al que asisten millones de personas, necesariamente tenían que surgir al menos algunas ideas aceptables para los jefes. El problema radica en que, en un país que no es libre, nada

puede ser libre. Por consiguiente, esas asambleas, convocadas por el Partido Comunista, encabezadas por sus militantes y vigiladas por los inevitables agentes de la policía política, difícilmente podían entrar a cuestionar aspectos medulares del texto. Por lo demás, lo voluminoso de este hacía virtualmente imposible un análisis profundo y sistemático. Como si todo esto fuese poco, se sabía de antemano que correspondería a los propios comunistas el estudio y la valoración de las propuestas que se formulasen.

No caben dudas de que la postura asumida por la alta dirigencia del país era—en esencia—la de aprobar lo elaborado por la Comisión Mixta. Léanse, si no, las palabras pronunciadas por el doctor Fidel Castro el día 24 de febrero de 1975, en el acto de recibir el Anteproyecto de Constitución de manos de sus redactores: "En la dirección del Partido y del Gobierno se discutirá artículo por artículo y de esa discusión surgirán ideas, algunos cambios y lo mismo ocurrirá cuando se discuta con todo el pueblo. Pero cualesquiera que sean las pequeñas modificaciones que nosotros le introduzcamos, me parece que lo esencial del Anteproyecto va a permanecer."[7]

Obviamente, después de estas palabras del Máximo Líder no eran de esperarse modificaciones sustanciales al trabajo de la Comisión Mixta, que seguramente—tal y como resulta usual en los países del llamado "socialismo real"—efectuó su trabajo bajo el estrecho control del Secretariado del Partido. En todo caso, el papel futuro del propio Comandante en Jefe quedaba plenamente garantizado en el Anteproyecto, como con elegancia admirable lo expuso el señor Blas Roca, presidente de la Comisión, en el acto de entrega de dicho documento, del que afirmó que "puede tomar en cuenta determinadas realidades políticas que se manifiestan en este período de transición; y, para no producir situaciones ficticias en el desempeño de cargos y ejercicio de poderes, consignar fórmulas que tengan en cuenta el papel real que

---

7. "Palabras del doctor Fidel Castro Ruz en el acto de entrega del Anteproyecto de Constitución" (24 de febrero de 1975), *Revista Cubana de Derecho*, Año 5, Nº 11, pp. 53–54. (Énfasis mío. - R.G.M.).

la historia de nuestro proceso revolucionario ha conferido a determinadas personalidades."[8]

Ciertamente, los frutos arrojados por la larga "discusión popular" fueron bastante magros, a juzgar por las propuestas de modificación a las que específicamente se refirió el propio señor Blas Roca en el acto de presentación del tema ante el Primer Congreso del Partido Comunista. En esa ocasión, el destacado dirigente marxista-leninista aludió únicamente a cuatro materias que fueron objeto de proposiciones dignas de que él las mencionara específicamente; a saber: el preámbulo de la Constitución, los símbolos nacionales, el nombre del Estado (al que algunos exaltados habían propuesto denominar "República Socialista de Cuba") y el señalamiento de que el idioma oficial era el español (aspecto que—por cierto—fue rechazado con el fútil pretexto de que esa es la única lengua que se habla en el país). Como se puede apreciar, nada sustancial. En esa propia oportunidad, el veterano dirigente comunista aludió a la actividad de la Comisión Preparatoria Central del Congreso del Partido (que fue la encargada de preparar la versión final del documento); sobre este particular, señaló el señor Roca: "se acogieron, total o parcialmente, modificaciones propuestas al preámbulo y a 60 de sus 141 artículos, la mayoría de forma, ordenamiento o redacción."[9]

En definitiva, el Primer Congreso del Partido Comunista de Cuba (organización que se ufana de su carácter selectivo y a la que—por ende—pertenece una neta minoría de la población adulta) se autoconcedió la potestad constituyente y aprobó la propuesta que le sometió la Comisión de Constitución y Poder Popular del propio Congreso, la cual—por cierto—sesionó durante un solo día (el 19 de diciembre de 1975, al que el diario oficial *Granma* denominó "el día de trabajo de las comisiones en el primer Congreso").[10] Fue así que, el 20 de diciembre de 1975, los 3116 delegados al Congreso, amén de escuchar los saludos de ocho de las "delegaciones fraternales," aprobó por unanimidad, junto con otros cinco documentos, el Proyecto de Constitución.[11]

Faltaba una última etapa: la celebración de un referendo en el que cada ciudadano podría votar en pro o en contra de la aprobación de ese documento. Los castristas exhiben con orgullo los resultados de ese proceso, y así lo acaban de reiterar en el llamamiento que han emitido con vistas al V Congreso de su Partido.[12] En ese plebiscito el número de los que votaron a favor excedió en más de cien veces el de los que lo hicieron por la negativa, lo que justifica plenamente las palabras del profesor Héctor Garcini, cuando hablaba de "una mayoría rayana en la unanimidad."[13] En efecto: es evidente que se trató de una manifestación más de esa extraordinaria vocación de unanimidad que es consustancial al sistema comunista y a los regímenes totalitarios en general, y que tanto admira y asombra a quienes, por vivir en países libres y democráticos, desconocen los sutiles mecanismos internos del totalitarismo.

A fuer de sincero, debo señalar mi criterio de que hacen mal los castristas en sentirse tan ufanos, máxime cuando todo aconteció en Cuba, la patria de la Condesa de Merlín. Por ello, si se me permite hacer una pequeña digresión, relataré aquí la famosa anécdota del plebiscito que organizó entre sus esclavos la bellísima criolla, el cual es harto ilustrativo de los inesperados resultados que pueden arrojar las instituciones democráticas en sociedades que no son libres: En una ocasión se encontraban reunidos en la finca azucarera

---

8. "Algunas consideraciones sobre el Anteproyecto de Constitución" (documento elaborado por la Comisión Mixta y dado a la publicidad en el acto de entrega del Anteproyecto, el 4 de febrero de 1975), *Revista Cubana de Derecho*, Año 5, Nº 11, p. 49. (Énfasis mío.-R.G.M.)

9. "Discurso de Blas Roca al Primer Congreso del Partido Comunista de Cuba," al presentar el Proyecto de Constitución, *Revista Cubana de Derecho*, Año 5, Nº 11, p. 63. (Énfasis mío. - R.G.M.)

10. Diario *Granma*, 20 de diciembre de 1975, p. l. (Énfasis mío. - R.G.M.)

11. Diario *Granma*, 21 de diciembre de 1975, p. 1.

12. Ver: Suplemento del diario *Granma*, mayo de 1997, p. 7.

13. Héctor Garcini Guerra, "Constitución del Estado Socialista Cubano," *Revista Cubana de Derecho*, Año 5, Nº 12, p. 103.

de la aristócrata numerosos amigos, la conversación derivó hacia la política, uno de los contertulios, apoyado por algunos otros, inició un apasionado elogio de los referendos, que él consideraba la expresión suprema de la democracia. "ya que tanto les agradan, ¿entonces por qué no organizamos uno?," preguntó la condesa, y mandó reunir de inmediato a la dotación de su ingenio. Una vez congregados los infelices siervos, la pícara cubana les anunció que a partir del siguiente día estarían obligados a iniciar las labores una hora más temprano y a terminarlas una hora después de lo acostumbrado, que la comida sería más escasa, que las cantidades de caña cortadas tenían que aumentar y que los castigos serían más severos; acto seguido les pidió que, si estaban de acuerdo con sus propuestas, lo expresaran alzando las manos. Los exaltados partidarios de los referendos contemplaron con asombro que las draconianas medidas propuestas por la dueña fueron aprobadas por unanimidad.

Retornando a 1976, debo señalar que los resultados obtenidos por el régimen no hicieron más que reflejar las condiciones anómalas en que se llevó a cabo ese proceso: sin participación de personas discrepantes en la elaboración del proyecto, sin debates pluralistas acerca de las bondades o desventajas de éste, sin una información balanceada y objetiva, con la población sometida a un verdadero bombardeo propagandístico encaminado a hacerle creer que—en la práctica—la única opción real era la de votar sí, y convencida por los hechos de que la menor manifestación de oposición estaba preñada de potenciales peligros de todo tipo y destinada de antemano al fracaso, sin la presencia de observadores oposicionistas o siquiera imparciales.

¿Cuáles son los aspectos fundamentales de ese documento que obtuvo el apoyo casi unánime de la población cubana? He aquí algunos de sus rasgos esenciales:

- Enunciado de los derechos fundamentales que es netamente más imperfecto que el de la Constitución de 1940 y el de la Ley Fundamental de 1959.

- Subordinación del disfrute de los mismos a la condición general de que no sean ejercidos "con-tra la existencia y fines del Estado socialista, ni contra la decisión del pueblo cubano de construir el socialismo y el comunismo."

- Eliminación pura y simple de derechos humanos internacionalmente reconocidos, tales como el de libre entrada y salida del territorio nacional.

- Restricción considerable o subordinación de algunos otros de los sí reconocidos a condiciones específicas (así—por ejemplo—se declaraba "ilegal y punible oponer la fe o la creencia religiosa a la Revolución; al proclamar la libertad de palabra y prensa," se aclaraba que ello era únicamente "conforme a los fines de la sociedad socialista," se reconocían "los derechos de reunión manifestación y asociación" pero sólo para distintos "sectores del pueblo trabajador," lo que implícitamente presuponía su no reconocimiento a categorías enteras de ciudadanos; se subordinaba la libertad de creación artística a que "su contenido no sea contrario a la Revolución").

- Declaración del principio de igualdad de los ciudadanos, pero sin incluir las ideas políticas o religiosas entre los criterios de discriminación prohibidos.

- Proclamación del Partido Comunista de Cuba (partido único) como "fuerza dirigente superior de la sociedad y del Estado."

- Ratificación de la virtual proscripción de la propiedad y de la libre iniciativa privadas.

- Proclamación del marxismo-leninismo como doctrina oficial del Estado y fundamento de su política educacional y cultural; y de la "formación comunista" como uno de sus objetivos fundamentales.

- Proclamación de la concepción monista del Estado ("la unidad de poder y el centralismo democrático," según el texto constitucional), lo cual se tradujo en la creación de la Asamblea Nacional del Poder Popular como órgano supremo de poder estatal integrado por casi medio millar de diputados (cifra que, en las condiciones de Cuba, determina que no se reúna de manera sistemática y que su actuación sea eminentemente simbólica).

- Existencia del Consejo de Estado y del Consejo de Ministros como cuerpos formalmente subordinados a la Asamblea Nacional del Poder Popular.

- Centralización de la máxima autoridad en la persona del primer mandatario, que es simultáneamente Presidente del Consejo de Estado, Presidente del Consejo de Ministros y Comandante en Jefe de las Fuerzas Armadas (amén de ostentar, en el plano partidista, el cargo de Primer Secretario).

- Establecimiento de un sistema de elecciones indirectas (excepto para los delegados a las asambleas municipales).

- Posibilidad de que un cubano (incluso por nacimiento) sea privado de su ciudadanía mediante simple decreto del Consejo de Estado.

- Eliminación de la independencia formal de los tribunales, y subordinación de los mismos a los órganos supremos del Poder Estatal.

- Proclamación del "deber internacionalista" de ayudar en las guerras que califica como "legítimas."

- Supresión definitiva del control de la constitucionalidad de las disposiciones legales por un órgano jurisdiccional independiente.

- No inclusión de disposiciones encaminadas a prohibir o limitar la reelección.

- Eliminación del habeas corpus como institución constitucional.

- Mención, por sus nombres, de un país extranjero y de un ciudadano vivo.

En cuanto a los criterios que tienen sobre el texto de esa superley los teóricos marxistas cubanos, puedo citar al doctor Vicente Rapa Álvarez, para el cual, "los principios fundamentales del nuevo orden constitucional" son—en esencia—los siguientes:

1. "La sociedad y el Estado son dirigidos por la clase obrera."

2. "Se reconoce la posición dirigente del Partido Comunista en la sociedad en el Estado."

3. "Los órganos representativos... son elegibles..., pero los representantes del pueblo... También están obligados a rendir cuenta de su labor a sus electores, sus mandatos pueden ser revocados por éstos."

4. "Las masas... ejercen el poder estatal no sólo por medio de sus representantes, sino directamente mediante las elecciones de éstos, la revocación de sus mandatos y el control de su actividad."

5. "El principio de la legalidad socialista posee fundamental importancia."

6. "El centralismo democrático del Estado es otro de los fundamentos cardinales."

7. "Finalmente, la política exterior del Estado se fundamenta en el internacionalismo proletario y la solidaridad combativa, la igualdad de derechos, soberanía e independencia."[14]

Por su parte, el magistrado Fernando Alvarez Tabío recalca que "nuestra Constitución no pretende ocultar el hecho de que las libertades públicas que consagra, están restringidas para las minorías que tratan de perjudicar los intereses de las mayorías,"[15] y Domingo García Cárdenas—a su vez—señala en primer término, entre los "principios constitucionales," el de la "unidad de poder," y aclara que "el Estado socialista tiene como uno de sus fundamentos la existencia de un solo poder," al que define como el "poder de la clase obrera y sus aliados." Acto seguido, precisando el concepto, señala que "la unidad de poder en el funcionamiento de los órganos estatales socialistas, por diferentes que sean sus actividades, se expresa básica-

---

14. Dr. Vicente Rapa Álvarez, "Acerca de la Constitución de 1975," *Revista Cubana de Derecho*, Año 3, Nº 6, pp. 131–32.

15. Fernando Álvarez Tabío, *Comentarios a la Constitución Socialista*, Ediciones Jurídicas, La Habana, 1981, p. 227.

mente en que las demás instituciones son creadas y se subordinan a las instituciones representativas."[16]

LA REFORMA CONSTITUCIONAL DE 1992

En 1992, la "Constitución socialista" fue objeto de una reforma general. Este proceso tuvo una diferencia con el de 1975: si entonces la responsabilidad de redactar las normas supralegales recayó en la Comisión Mixta, primero, y posteriormente en el Buró Político y el Secretariado del Partido Comunista, en la Comisión Preparatoria Central del Primer Congreso de dicha organización política y en este propio cónclave, lo cierto es que en 1992 la labor de modificar la carta magna recayó en la Asamblea Nacional del Poder Popular.

Esta reforma estuvo motivada fundamentalmente por la necesidad de adecuar el contenido de la constitución a las nuevas realidades surgidas (la extinción del llamado "campo socialista" y de la Unión Soviética, con la consiguiente desaparición del multimillonario subsidio que se recibía; la necesidad—por ende— de propiciar algunas inversiones extranjeras; el deseo de introducir determinadas regulaciones nuevas, tales como las relativas al estado de emergencia; y la pertinencia de realizar algunos gestos de supuesta apertura para hacer menos impresentable el sistema imperante). Sobre este punto, Félix Pérez Milián, funcionario del Comité Central del Partido Comunista, en su artículo titulado "Motivos para una reforma," después de aludir a "instituciones que están presentes en la mayoría de las constituciones modernas" y que resultaba conveniente incluir en la superley cubana, añade: "Todo ello contribuiría grandemente a ajustar nuestra Carta Magna a la práctica internacional generalmente aceptada."[17]

El primer aspecto que hay que destacar al hacer alusión a esa reforma, es la circunstancia de que—en mi opinión—se llevó a cabo con infracción de lo dispuesto en el último párrafo de la ley de leyes, que era (y continua siendo) del siguiente tenor: "Si la refor-

ma es total o se refiere a la integración y facultades de la Asamblea Nacional del Poder Popular o de su Consejo de Estado o a derechos y deberes consagrados en la Constitución, requiere, además, la ratificación por el voto favorable de la mayoría de los ciudadanos con derecho electoral, en referendo convocado al efecto por la propia Asamblea."

Como puede apreciarse son tres los casos en que resulta obligatorio convocar a un plebiscito para que la reforma sea constitucionalmente válida. Pues bien: afirmo que en esa oportunidad concurrían todos y cada uno de esos tres supuestos, pese a lo cual las autoridades del país tuvieron a bien no celebrar el referendo ordenado por su propia ley. Veamos en los párrafos siguientes las razones de esta afirmación mía.

En primer lugar, parece que no caben dudas de que la reforma fue total. Esto—en mi opinión—se pone de manifiesto en el hecho de que sólo uno de los doce capítulos de la carta magna quedó sin sufrir modificación alguna; también resulta ilustrativa la circunstancia de que el Gobierno publicó oficialmente y divulgó el texto íntegro de la Constitución ya modificada, cosa que no hizo con ocasión de la anterior reforma de la superley. Para los que gusten de datos cuantitativos, baste señalar que de las 142 partes de que constaba la versión de 1975 (el preámbulo y los 141 artículos), fueron afectadas (es decir: sufrieron alguna modificación o fueron abrogadas) 79, lo que representa el 56%; además, fueron incorporados al texto 6 preceptos enteramente nuevos. El propio general de división Juan Escalona Reguera, que en aquel momento se desempeñaba como Presidente de la Asamblea Nacional del Poder Popular, calificó de "numerosas" las propuestas de modificación.[18]

En segundo lugar, me parece innegable que la reforma—entre otras cosas—se refirió también a la integración y facultades de la Asamblea Nacional del Poder Popular o de su Consejo de Estado. Esto está dado por la circunstancia de que, mientras que ante-

16. Domingo García Cárdenas, *La organización estatal en Cuba,* Editorial de Ciencias Sociales, La Habana, 1981, pp. 20–2l.

17. Dr. Félix Pérez Milián, "Motivos para una reforma," *Revista Cubana de Derecho,* Nº 7 (1992), p .3.

18. Dr. Juan Escalona Reguera,"En torno a la Ley de Reforma Constitucional" (discurso pronunciado ante la Asamblea Nacional del Poder Popular el 10 de julio de 1992), *Revista Cubana de Derecho,* Nº 8 (1992), p. 6.

riormente los diputados eran "elegidos por las Asambleas Municipales del Poder Popular," ahora lo son "por el voto libre, directo y secreto de los electores"; además, dada la forma en que se llevaba a cabo antes esa elección (repito: "por las Asambleas Municipales del Poder Popular"), resulta evidente que la Constitución establecía implícitamente que la circunscripción electoral fuese el municipio; sin embargo, con la reforma, esa disposición perdió su rango supralegal (sólo se ordena la votación directa, pero sin especificar en la propia carta magna si ese proceso se lleva a cabo por municipios o —digamos— por provincias o nacionalmente). En virtud de lo señalado, parece evidente que el mencionado órgano supremo del Poder Estatal se integra ahora de manera distinta de la que establecía la superley de 1975.

En tercer lugar, estimo que tampoco cabe negar que la reforma se refirió también a los "derechos y deberes consagrados en la Constitución." En este sentido puedo señalar que:

- Se modificó el texto del artículo 54 (referente a la libertad de religión).

- Se adicionó el nuevo e inquietante "derecho de combatir por todos los medios... contra cualquiera que intente derribar el orden... establecido..."

- Se incluyó, dentro de las motivaciones por las que el ciudadano tiene derecho a no ser discriminado, la de las creencias religiosas.

- Se concedió a los electores el derecho de votar directamente por los diputados a la Asamblea Nacional y por los delegados a las asambleas provinciales.

- Se incluyó un nuevo capítulo relativo al "estado de emergencia"; en el mismo se dispone —entre otras cosas— que la ley "determina los derechos y deberes fundamentales reconocidos por la Constitución, cuyo ejercicio debe ser regulado de manera diferente durante la vigencia del estado de emergencia."

En virtud de lo señalado en los tres párrafos precedentes, me parece evidente la veracidad de la afirmación que hacía al inicio de esta sección acerca de que la reforma de la carta magna que se llevó a cabo en 1992 se hizo con total infracción de las normas constitucionales entonces vigentes, al no haberse celebrado el referendo que ordenaba el texto de 1975.

¿Pero qué dicen sobre este importantísimo particular los jurisconsultos comunistas? El ya mencionado Pérez Milián en su aludido artículo (publicado antes de realizarse la reforma), se apoya en opiniones de "un grupo de juristas" (cuyos nombres no señala) para argumentar que "podrían modificarse sin dicho requisito" (la celebración del referendo) todos los capítulos de la Constitución, excepto los números V y VI. A lo anterior añade que "otro grupo de juristas" (que tampoco enumera) estima que también esos dos capítulos (que versan, respectivamente, sobre la igualdad, y sobre los derechos, deberes y garantías fundamentales) podrían ser objeto de reformas, siempre que éstas "no limiten, restrinjan o eliminen el ejercicio de esos derechos y deberes." A lo anterior agrega que la inclusión de "una nueva atribución" de la Asamblea Nacional o el Consejo de Estado, o de "cualquier nuevo derecho o deber" de los ciudadanos, "puede comprenderse como no sujeto al requisito del referendo." Resumiendo su argumentación, y refiriéndose a la cláusula de reforma, señala: "Si nos ajustamos a la letra del mencionado artículo 141 de la Constitución, y aunque resulte discutible, a partir de una interpretación estricta de la letra de dicho precepto, puede ser aceptable la interpretación que desarrollamos en los párrafos anteriores." Para finalizar alude a que "pudiera pensarse por algunos que aun cuando los cambios que se propongan técnicamente no requieran de su ratificación mediante un referendo, éste debe realizarse de todas maneras porque el texto actual fue aprobado en un evento de esta naturaleza." Y concluye: "Todo ello es posible: depende de una decisión política del más alto nivel de dirección del país."[19]

Otro argumento que se ha esgrimido (al menos en contra del carácter total de la reforma) es el formula-

---

19. Dr. Félix Pérez Milián, "Motivos para una reforma," *Revista Cubana de Derecho*, Nº 7 (1992) pp. 5–7.

do por el profesor Juan Vega Vega, en su libro *Derecho Constitucional Revolucionario en Cuba* (publicado en 1988; o sea: cuatro años antes del proceso que estamos analizando). En él se asevera que "en los países socialistas la reforma parcial es la única posible en la práctica," y argumentando en base a la carta magna soviética de 1977, explica: "Como se mantiene e incluso se desarrolla en la nueva Constitución el régimen socialista, no se puede hablar ciertamente de reforma total; en realidad lo que cambia es cierto número de artículos o se adicionan otros o se realizan modificaciones estructurales."[20]

Hasta aquí lo publicado antes de la reforma. A raíz de realizarse ésta, el único trabajo que he tenido a la vista ha sido el del general de división Juan Escalona Reguera, el cual consiste en las palabras que él, en la condición de Presidente de la Asamblea Nacional del Poder Popular que entonces ostentaba, dirigía ese órgano el día 10 de julio de 1992, con ocasión de iniciarse el debate sobre la reforma constitucional. En esa oportunidad, plantea que las propuestas de modificación se habían realizado sobre tres bases, las cuales enunció—en esencia—del siguiente modo: 1) "no se trata de hacer una nueva Constitución"; 2) se requiere "dar debida respuesta a los acuerdos y resoluciones del V Congreso del Partido"; y 3) "la tarea que nos corresponde, por tanto, es realizar las modificaciones indispensables, y sólo las indispensables, para dar cumplimiento a esos objetivos."[21] Acto seguido, el general Escalona agrupó los distintos tipos de enmiendas que se proponían y explicó sucintamente su contenido.

Sobre la importantísima cuestión de si se requería o no celebrar una consulta popular para aprobar definitivamente las reformas, el Presidente de la Asamblea despachó el tema de la manera siguiente: "Para los que en alguna ocasión han planteado dudas sobre si estas modificaciones—que proponemos—requieren o no de un referendo posterior a la aprobación, por el voto nominal de los dos tercios de los miembros de la Asamblea, señalamos que no se refieren a cambios en "la integración y facultades de la Asamblea Nacional del Poder Popular o de su Consejo de Estado, como pueden apreciar en el proyecto que les ha sido entregado, y además añadir, para dejar esclarecido definitivamente este aspecto, que tampoco les hemos propuesto cambios referidos a derechos y deberes consagrados en la Constitución actual, que son los requisitos que fija el artículo 141."[22]

Como se ve, ni una sola palabra acerca de si la reforma es total o no (que es el primero de los tres supuestos en que se debe celebrar el referendo, según el precepto supralegal últimamente mencionado): sobre este importantísimo punto, apenas existe la aseveración antes mencionada de que—supuestamente—"no se trata(ba) de hacer una nueva Constitución." Sobre las otras dos cuestiones, sería imposible pedir mayor poder de síntesis: la argumentación (de algún modo hay que llamarla) consiste—en esencia—en la mera afirmación de que no se está en el segundo ni en el tercer supuesto contemplado en la cláusula de reforma.

Pienso que, como es usual en los países del llamado "socialismo real," la posición que tienen ante el problema los estudiosos de esta temática en Cuba no podemos tanto conocerla por lo que éstos dicen, sino inferirla de lo que callan: el hecho cierto es que, a pesar de la evidente importancia extrema de la cuestión, en las publicaciones especializadas cubanas brillan por su ausencia otros enfoques o criterios, y tras los pronunciamientos del general Escalona y la consiguiente decisión de la Asamblea Nacional de aprobar definitivamente las reformas sin convocar a referendo, se ha hecho el silencio sobre el asunto.

Después de haber observado lo señalado en los párrafos precedentes, mantengo mi posición del principio de esta sección acerca de que la reforma general de la carta magna que se llevó a cabo en 1992 se hizo con total infracción de las normas constitucionales entonces vigentes. Si tenemos en cuenta que el Gobierno

---

20. Juan Vega, *Derecho constitucional revolucionario en Cuba,* Editorial de Ciencias Sociales, La Habana, 1988, p. 307.

21. Dr. Juan Escalona Reguera, "En torno a la ley de Reforma Constitucional," *Revista Cubana de Derecho,* Nº 8 (1992), p. 6.

22. Ibíd., p. 12.

cubano cuenta con juristas competentes (que saben lo antes expuesto) y está integrado por políticos habilísimos (que—precisamente por serlo—no ignoran que la victoria del *sí* en un nuevo referendo hubiera significado un gran apoyo para el régimen), entonces no podemos menos que pensar (a falta de otra explicación lógica) que la no convocatoria del plebiscito representó una decisión deliberadamente adoptada por los dirigentes cubanos, y motivada por la fundada prevención de enfrentar en las urnas un resultado desfavorable, que hubiera deslegitimado al régimen. Evidentemente, había corrido mucha agua desde 1976...

Ese año, en un proceso al que pueden hacérsele todas las objeciones que ya formulé y algunas más, el régimen cubano puso en vigor la "Constitución socialista." Con ello sentó lo que—con buena voluntad—pudiéramos llamar "la legitimidad de 1976." Dieciséis años más tarde, ante la imperiosa necesidad de reformar ese texto supralegal y ante el temor de enfrentar un mayoritario rechazo popular, lo violó deliberadamente al modificarlo, y—por ende—se colocó fuera de su propia legalidad.

Otro aspecto que estimo muy conveniente destacar es la extraordinaria celeridad con que se aprobaron las reformas a la carta magna: la sesión de la Asamblea Nacional del Poder Popular que decretó la modificación o abrogación del preámbulo y 78 artículos de la Constitución vigente, así como la inclusión de 6 nuevos preceptos, duró apenas tres días (del 10 al 12 de julio de 1992). Hasta donde sé, esta realidad es digna de figurar con pleno derecho en el *Libro de Records Guinness*. Otro aspecto que vale la pena señalar (y que recogió la prensa cubana en el tono laudatorio que la caracteriza cada vez que trata sobre el funcionamiento de los órganos estatales nacionales), es el de que no en todos los casos las reformas aprobadas habían sido objeto de estudios previos, pues no faltaron lo que el órgano oficial de los comunistas cubanos denominó "nuevas formulaciones hechas al calor de las discusiones."[23]

Por último, debo señalar otro aspecto inusitado de todo este proceso, el cual considero muy ilustrativo del modo en que funcionan los órganos legislativos de los países comunistas en general (y de Cuba, en particular), y que es el hecho de que, una vez que la Ley de Reforma Constitucional fue aprobada por la Asamblea Nacional del Poder Popular, ese mismo órgano designó una "Comisión de Estilo" encargada de "trabajar en la Ley aprobada."[24]

Pero bien: ¿Cuáles son las características esenciales de ese nuevo texto que las autoridades cubanas presentan como su actual Constitución? En su esencia, se trata de lo mismo que el documento original: se repiten casi todas las características básicas que unas páginas antes le señalaba a la versión del 75, con algunos cambios; a saber:

- Se eliminó, del precepto referido a la libertad de religión, el planteamiento de que se prohíbe "oponer la fe o la creencia religiosa a la Revolución."

- Se incluyó, dentro de las formas de discriminación expresamente prohibidas, la motivada por las "creencias religiosas" (pero continúa ausente la debida a las ideas políticas).

- Se flexibilizaron algo las disposiciones referentes a los fundamentos económicos del Estado.

- Se reconoció "la propiedad de las empresas mixtas, sociedades y asociaciones económicas," pero sigue sin aceptarse que el ciudadano común cuente con posibilidades empresariales.

- Junto al ideario marxista-leninista (o simplemente marxista, según el precepto de que se trate), se invoca también la doctrina martiana.

- Se estableció la elección directa para los diputados a la Asamblea Nacional del Poder Popular y para los delegados provinciales.

- Se eliminó la mención constitucional a un país extranjero.

---

23. Diario *Granma*, 11 de julio de 1992, p. 1.
24. Diario *Granma*, 13 de julio de 1992, p. 5.

Otras de las novedades más importantes del nuevo texto son las siguientes:

- Proclamación del "disfrute de la libertad política" como uno de lo fines del Estado cubano.

- Inclusión de un inquietante derecho de los ciudadanos a "combatir por todos los medios... contra cualquiera que intente derribar el orden político, social y económico establecido"..., con lo cual—al parecer—se pretende "legalizar" los tristemente célebres actos de repudio.

- Adición de un nuevo capítulo relativo a la extranjería.

- Inclusión de otro nuevo capítulo que versa sobre el estado de emergencia, situación que puede ser declarada unipersonalmente por el Presidente del Consejo de Estado.

- Referencia constitucional a los nuevos órganos locales denominados consejos populares y remplazo de los antiguos comités ejecutivos provinciales y municipales por órganos de administración.

En relación con este último punto, es digno de ser señalado el hecho de que (cosa no usual en la Cuba de hoy) en una monografía publicada dentro de la isla (y a pesar de la evaluación general positiva que—como era de esperar—se hace del sistema), aparecen varios señalamientos críticos. En particular, sobre este tema de la administración local establecida en 1976, se afirma que "después de más de tres lustros de funcionamiento, es posible apreciar en el subsistema de gobiernos municipales tanto sus logros como sus lados flacos, así como que muchas de las soluciones propuestas en el diseño original han devenido virtualmente parte de los problemas."[25]

Como observación final al proceso de reforma constitucional llevado a cabo en 1992, cabe destacar que, a pesar del carácter "martiano" que, en insólita conjunción con el de "marxista-leninista," los comunistas cubanos le asignan a su partido (lo que incluso aparece reflejado en el artículo 5 de la versión actual de la carta magna), en esta última no se observa ni uno solo de los rasgos que nuestro Apóstol estimaba necesarios. El profesor Infiesta, que estudió monográficamente el tema, señala lo siguiente: "Atento a tales guiones, creo que la Constitución inmediata para una Cuba liberada de la Metrópoli que Martí meditaba se hubiese organizado conforme a estas bases:

1. una forma de gobierno democrático de separación de poderes, aparentemente de tipo presidencial;

2. una amplísima formulación de libertades civiles, de sustancia individualista;

3. un sistema de sufragio basado en la obligatoriedad del voto y la frecuente consulta popular; y

4. un Poder Judicial de función destacada.[26]

RESUMEN DE LA SITUACION CONSTITUCIONAL DE LA CUBA ACTUAL

Como resultado de todo lo antes expresado, estimo que la Constitución de la República que actualmente exhibe el Gobierno cubano es totalmente inidónea para ser la carta magna de una futura Cuba democrática.

Lo anterior no excluye—desde luego—que en una primera etapa (que considero que, por definición, tendría que ser breve) la misma se mantenga en vigor en aras de procurar una salida negociada a la honda crisis nacional. No obstante, parece indudable que en esa situación, para que pueda hablarse de apertura democrática, sería indispensable que fueran abrogados o modificados distintos artículos entre los que puedo señalar, como mínimo, sus números 3 (párrafo segundo), 5, 6, 9 (inciso a, plecas 1ª, 4ª y 6ª), 12, 14, 15, 16, 32 (párrafo segundo), 39 (incisos a, c y ch), 53, 54, 62 y 67.

Insistiendo en lo expuesto anteriormente acerca de la inidoneidad de la carta magna actual para avanzar

---

25. Haroldo Dilla, Gerardo González y Ana Teresa Vincentelli, *Participación popular y desarrollo en los municipios cubanos*, Centro de Estudios sobre América (CEA), La Habana, 1993, pp. 33–34.

26. Dr. Ramón Infiesta Bages, *Martí, constitucionalista* (conferencia), Editorial El Siglo XX, La Habana, 1951, p. 33.

con ella por el proceso de la democratización, debo expresar que—en mi opinión—ello se debe:

- **A su esencia:** ya que, si nos atenemos a la precisa definición de Thomas Paine ("Una constitución no es un acto de un gobierno, sino de un pueblo que constituye un gobierno"), entonces se hará evidente el hecho de que el mencionado documento—en puridad—no es una, constitución propiamente dicha.

- **A su génesis:** ya que no fue redactada por una asamblea libremente elegida.

- **Al menoscabo de los derechos humanos:** lo cual incluye el absoluto desconocimiento de algunos de los que han sido internacionalmente reconocidos.

- **Al sistema económico obsoleto que mantiene:** el cual impide el desarrollo de las fuerzas productivas y determina que el país continúe sumido en el estado de verdadera postración en que se encuentra.

- **A su carácter partidista:** en lo que se destaca la declaración del Partido Comunista (único legalmente existente) como "fuerza dirigente superior de la sociedad y del Estado."

- **Al tipo de Estado monista y autoritario que establece:** en el que no se prohíbe la reelección del Jefe de Estado, y no hay cabida siquiera para una administración de justicia formalmente independiente.

- **Al carácter obsoleto del sistema estatal que ha creado:** que no se ajusta a los principios democráticos internacionalmente reconocidos (y sí al sistema tradicional de los países comunistas) y que teóricamente centraliza la actividad del Estado en una representación nacional hipertrofiada, la cual, en virtud de ello mismo, no puede reunirse de manera sistemática, es incapaz de ejer-

cer un verdadero control y tiene un carácter eminentemente simbólico.

- **A la manera inconstitucional en que fue aprobada:** ya que—como he señalado—las reformas de 1992 no fueron sometidas a la consulta popular que se requería.

En razón de lo antes expresado, el Grupo de Trabajo de la Disidencia Interna Cubana, en la Plataforma que dio a la publicidad en agosto de 1996 y puntualizó en el mes de septiembre del propio año, ha planteado la necesidad de que—en definitiva—se ponga en vigor otra Constitución, para lo cual dicha principal coalición de la oposición pacífica del interior de la isla plantea que "resulta indispensable dar al pueblo la posibilidad de elegir democráticamente a sus delegados; sin perjuicio de someter posteriormente el proyecto a referendo."[27]

Un aspecto a señalar es el de que muchos opositores al régimen castrista, así como otras personalidades independientes, propugnan que, ante la total inidoneidad de la carta magna que hoy impera en el país, se restablezca el imperio de la Constitución de 1940. Un ejemplo de ello lo tenemos en monseñor Carlos Manuel de Céspedes y García-Menocal, quién afirma que ella "ofrece una base jurídica robusta, capaz de sostener ese postulado, imprescindible también irrenunciable (el del "Estado de derecho").[28]

Al estudiar esta cuestión, debo señalar ante todo que—en principio—nada tengo que oponer a esa propuesta; todo lo contrario: ya he señalado mi aprecio por las muchas excelencias de aquella carta magna, que, por encima de cualquier otra consideración, tiene la indudable legitimidad de haber surgido de un inobjetable proceso democrático. En ese contexto, no puedo menos que afirmar tajantemente que, si las únicas opciones posibles fueran las de mantener el texto supralegal que exhibe actualmente el gobierno comunista o restablecer la Constitución de 1940, entonces apoyaría sin la menor vacilación la segunda

---

27. "Ampliación de la Plataforma del Grupo de Trabajo de la Disidencia Interna" (Punto 5), editado en computadora, La Habana, septiembre de 1996, última página.

28. Carlos Manuel de Céspedes G., *Promoción humana, realidad cubana y perspectivas*, Fundación Konrad Adenauer, Caracas, 1996, p. 67.

variante. No obstante lo anterior, parece innegable que sería improcedente que el restablecimiento de la vigencia de ese texto supralegal—en su caso—se produjera por decreto; por el contrario: las reglas del libre juego democrático harían necesario que tal decisión fuese tomada por acuerdo de una legítima representación nacional.

Ahora bien: ¿Resultaría posible hoy restablecer la Constitución del 40 *tel quel*? Me parece evidente que la respuesta tiene que ser negativa. Gústenos o no, es un hecho innegable que en estos casi cuarenta años de régimen marxista-leninista se han producido transformaciones enormes en lo económico, lo político y lo social, las cuales harían hoy inaplicables toda una serie de preceptos de la referida superley. Esto, unido a las deficiencias que desde un inicio se le señalaron a la misma, conduce a que, en el supuesto más favorable para los partidarios más fervientes del restablecimiento de la mencionada carta magna, éste sólo podría producirse después de una reforma general de su texto.

Sin pretender agotar el tema, y señalando únicamente las objeciones más obvias e importantes que pueden hacérsele a su articulado (sin tomar en consideración las Disposiciones Transitorias), puedo aludir a los preceptos siguientes:

Art. 4:   Contiene la enumeración de las antiguas seis provincias, lo cual—como es lógico—no se ajusta a la realidad cubana de hoy.

Art. 9:   Al establecer que los ciudadanos están obligados "a servir con las armas a la Patria", no contempla el caso de los objetores de conciencia ni la posibilidad de que estos presten un servicio social sustitorio.

Art. 15:   Dispone la pérdida de la ciudadanía de "los que adquieran una ciudadanía extranjera." Es evidente que esto no se ajusta a la realidad de la Diáspora que ha producido más de un millón de exiliados que son tan cubanos como los que residimos dentro de la isla y a los que debe reconocérseles el derecho a mantener, junto a la ciudadanía extranjera, su condición de cubanos por nacimiento.

Art. 26:   Al regular las detenciones (en su párrafo segundo), no contempla la obligación de que el actuante informe al detenido de sus derechos, ni de que se comuniquen a algún ser querido de éste los particulares de la detención.

Art. 37:   Los derechos de reunión, desfile y asociación aparecen enunciados de manera global en un solo precepto, que alude a su disfrute "conforme a las normas legales correspondientes." Es evidente que no están reflejadas aquí las tendencias jurídicas más modernas y democráticas, que hacen innecesario el permiso previo para asociarse o para reunirse (al menos, en lugares privados).

Art. 41:   La cantidad de derechos individuales cuyo disfrute puede ser suspendido, parece demasiado amplio. Por una parte, las tendencias más modernas se inclinan a reducir ese número, cuando no a prohibir por completo el desconocimiento—siquiera temporal—de los derechos ciudadanos. Por otra parte, los preceptos cuya suspensión se autoriza abarcan aspectos que no tenían por qué figurar allí. Ejemplos: la presunción de inocencia; la obligación de respetar a los detenidos; la separación de los detenidos políticos y comunes, así como de los reos y los ciudadanos en prisión provisional; la prohibición de los juicios en rebeldía; el derecho a no declarar contra uno mismo ni contra el cónyuge o parientes cercanos; y la prohibición de que se fuerce a alguien a declarar.

Art. 43:   Lo preceptuado en el párrafo octavo sobre la pensión para la mujer divorciada no se ajusta a las disposiciones actuales.

Art. 44:   Es obsoleta la alusión que contiene el párrafo segundo a que la igualdad de los hijos legítimos y naturales no se extiende al terreno de la herencia.

Art. 48: Deben ser derogadas las disposiciones sobre el pago de matrícula que contienen los párrafos tercero y cuarto.

Art. 52: Entre otros aspectos objetables, establece que el sueldo de un maestro primario no sea inferior a la millonésima parte del presupuesto, lo que era ya inaplicable (por irreal) antes de 1959.

Art. 53: Sólo se concede autonomía a la Universidad de La Habana (único centro de enseñanza superior que existía en 1940), ignorando a los otros creados antes y después de 1959.

Art. 65: Alude a "los seguros sociales" (así, en plural), desconociendo la nueva situación actual la existencia de un sistema único nacional de seguridad social.

Art. 81: El reconocimiento del mutualismo que contiene resulta obsoleto, al no ajustarse a la realidad de hoy, representada por la red nacional de salud pública.

Art. 112: Las disposiciones sobre las prestaciones de seguridad social a los empleados del Estado, la Provincia y el Municipio son anacrónicas, como lo es el límite de $2400 por año que se fija para ellas.

Art. 115: Son válidas aquí las objeciones que se hicieron al número 65, por las mismas razones.

Art. 120: La integración del Senado con ciudadanos elegidos a razón de nueve por provincia conduciría a la hipertrofia de esa cámara, debido a que el número de provincias se ha más que duplicado.

Art. 123: Análoga observación puede hacerse para la Cámara de Representantes: la elección de un miembro de ese cuerpo colegislador por cada 35,000 habitantes o fracción, llevaría a que el mismo contase con más de trescientos integrantes, lo que parece evidentemente excesivo en un país de las dimensiones del nuestro.

Art. 128: Al fijar el quórum de las cámaras (la mitad más uno de sus miembros), este precepto no establece procedimiento alguno para el caso de que no se cumpla ese requisito.

Art. 133: Las disposiciones del párrafo final del inciso a) para los casos de empate entre candidatos a la Vicepresidencia de la República son anfibológicas. De la lectura del precepto no queda claro si el elegido para ocupar ese cargo deberá ser o no quien haya figurado en la misma candidatura que el seleccionado como Presidente.

Art. 134: Este artículo enumera, en sus incisos a), b), g), h), i), j), l) y r), toda una serie de materias sobre las que puede legislar el Congreso. Esta relación no sólo es casuística: también parece innecesaria (en un país unitario como Cuba, en el que no hay que distinguir entre las potestades legislativas del centro y de las partes componentes) y, hasta contraproducente (pues pudiera dar pie a la interpretación de que el Congreso no está facultado para legislar sobre otras materias;

Art. 140: El método establecido para la elección del Presidente de la República (que es análogo al de los Estados Unidos) parece inadecuado. Puede comprenderse el empleo de un sistema como se ve en un país federal, pero no en una república unitaria como Cuba. En caso de que se fragmente la votación popular, es perfectamente posible que ocupe la primera magistratura un ciudadano que haya obtenido una cantidad ínfima de votos (incluso menos que otro u otros candidatos) y que se haya limitado a ganar la primera mayoría en la provincia más poblada.

Art. 148: Aparte de las objeciones que pueden hacérsele al sistema de sustitución presidencial, no se puntualizan los casos en que entraría en funciones ese mecanismo fundamental: se prevén las posibilidades de "ausencia, incapacidad o muerte" del primer mandatario, pero no se especifica cómo se declarara la existencia de las dos primeras.

Art. 160: Se mencionan distintos ministerios que ya no existen con ese nombre (lo cual sucede también en los números 74 y 80).

Art. 170: Parece excesiva la disposición del párrafo tercero, que reserva la administración de justicia al Poder Judicial. Esto implica la prohibición del arbitraje, lo cual es inadecuado, pues desconoce una libertad de los particulares y pone trabas innecesarias a la libre empresa.

Art. 180: El nombramiento de los Magistrados del Tribunal Supremo depende en demasía del Presidente de la República, lo que objetivamente conspira contra la real independencia de aquéllos. Es cierto que se establece que para cada designación se constituya un "colegio electoral" de nueve miembros, pero tres de ellos son de libre designación del Jefe de Estado, lo que hace pensar que al menos uno de los que figuren en la correspondiente terna sea un aspirante preseleccionado por el primer mandatario, quien posteriormente podrá nombrarlo y presentarlo a la aprobación del Senado.

Art. 182: Entre los asuntos de que conoce el Tribunal de Garantías y Sociales figuran—según el inciso f)—"los recursos contra los abusos de poder." Contradictoriamente, en los numerales 218 y 246 se le otorga jurisdicción en esa materia al pleno del Tribunal Supremo de Justicia,

Art. 198: Se alude casuísticamente a "los tribunales de las fuerzas de mar y tierra," olvidando las del aire.

Art. 204: Este precepto, que disponía que fuesen apelables las sentencias de los jueces correccionales, es obsoleto.

Art. 207: La prohibición de que los miembros del Poder Judicial figuren como candidatos a cargos electivos, parece tener un alcance de-

masiado limitado, pues no se proscribe su pertenencia a partidos políticos en general.

Art. 212: La declaración de que las facultades que la Constitución no otorga al Municipio queden reservadas al Gobierno Nacional parece contradictoria con la del inciso h) del número 213 del propio texto supralegal.

Art. 213: La prohibición al Municipio de que.grave el comercio, las comunicaciones y el tránsito intermunicipales, tiene un alcance limitado en demasía: la Constitución no prohíbe expresamente, con carácter general, las aduanas interiores.

Art. 282: Se admite la posibilidad de que el Poder Legislativo delegue en el Consejo de Ministros algunas de las que el número 134 de la propia Constitución define como "facultades no delegables del Congreso."

Además de lo anterior, pudiéramos señalar distintas omisiones importantes de la misma (incluso en lo tocante a la regulación de los derechos humanos, que—obviamente—es su porción que conserva mayor actualidad). Esto—claro está—no se debe fundamentalmente a deficiencias intrínsecas del propio texto, sino más bien al notable desarrollo que se ha experimentado en este terreno en los últimos años. Entre esas omisiones, pudiera mencionar—por ejemplo—las siguientes:

- No se establece la preeminencia (o la simple vigencia) de las normas internacionales sobre derechos humanos (tales como las contenidas en las declaraciones Universal y Americana, o las de los distintos tratados que rigen en ese campo).

- No se contempla la existencia de un *ombudsman* o "defensor del pueblo."

- No se establece un recurso de amparo u otra vía análoga para la protección general de los derechos humanos.

Además, existe una serie de derechos que los códigos más modernos recogen expresamente y que no figuran en la Constitución del 40; a saber:

- El derecho a hacer todo lo que no está prohibido y a no hacer lo que la Ley no ordena, lo que incluye el derecho a desarrollar cualquier actividad económica y a adquirir toda clase de bienes.

- El derecho a la defensa.

- El libre acceso a las fuentes de información (en particular, a los archivos y registro estatales).

- La libertad de contratación.

- El derecho a la propia imagen;

- El derecho del reo a que el sistema penitenciario le garantice condiciones mínimas para la extinción de su sanción en circunstancias decorosas.

- El derecho a no tener que declarar sobre la propia ideología, religión o creencias.

- La prohibición de que un juez pueda serlo en distintas instancias del mismo asunto.

- La prohibición de la prisión por deudas.

- El derecho de los particulares a ser indemnizados por perjuicios irrogados por servidores públicos en el ejercicio de sus cargos (en especial, en caso de error judicial).

- El derecho a no verse limitado en el disfrute de la propiedad por causa de actividad o delito político.

- El derecho de todos a la protección de la salud, así como a vivir en un medio ambiente sano.

- La protección de los ancianos, los minusválidos y otras categorías de ciudadanos discapacitados.

- La defensa de los consumidores y usuarios.

- La prohibición de que la enseñanza propague tendencia política partidista alguna.

Estimo que la carta magna de 1940 (analizada en un plano más general) omite también otros aspectos de importancia, tales como los siguientes:

- Una mención expresa al Estado de Derecho, a la democracia participativa y al pluralismo.

- El reconocimiento declarado de los principios de independencia y colaboración de los poderes del Estado, así como del de no injerencia de cada uno en las actividades de los otros.

- La proclamación de la libertad de empresa como fundamento de la actividad económica de la Nación, así como de la promoción de la inversión de capitales nacionales y extranjeros.

- La declaración de que la existencia de un "partido único" es incompatible con el sistema democrático, y el reconocimiento expresodel estatuto de la oposición y de los derechos de los partidos no gubernamentales.

- La proclamación de que el Estado está al servicio de la persona humana.

- La prohibición de prácticas legislativas inadecuadas, tales como las llamadas leyes-retrato (aplicables a una sola o pocas personas), las denominadas leyes-remache (que cohonestaban los cómputos iniciales de los comicios, reduciendo virtualmente a la nada las garantías establecidas en la legislación electoral) y las conocidas como perchas (disposiciones totalmente ajenas a las ideas centrales de un proyecto legislativo dado).

- La proscripción del nepotismo.

- El establecimiento de los principios generales del sistema tributario (tales como el de su igualdad, su progresividad y su carácter no confiscatorio, así como la prohibición de la doble tributación interna).

- La fijación de la mayoría de edad.

- Los principios generales de las leyes (fecha en que entran en vigor; inadmisibilidad de que se alegue su ignorancia, ineficacia de la renuncia a las mismas, etc.).

- La limitación y el control de las contribuciones a las campañas electorales (lo cual puede incluir el aporte del Estado al financiamiento de las mismas).

- La audiencia a los ciudadanos en el proceso de elaboración de las disposiciones administrativas que les afecten.

- Los principios fundamentales de la actividad de los legisladores (tales como su no sujeción a mandato imperativo, su derecho a no declarar sobre informaciones que reciban con motivo del ejercicio de sus cargos y la posibilidad de que pierdan su mandato por inasistencia sistemática e injustificada a las sesiones).

- El mantenimiento de un registro nacional de personas a cargo de las autoridades apartidistas encargadas de realizar las elecciones.

- El principio de que las leyes del trabajo (y las relaciones laborales en general) están inspiradas en la armonía y la colaboración entre el capital y el trabajo).

- La prohibición de armas nucleares, químicas y biológicas.

- La supervisión de los productos alimenticios, químicos, farmacéuticos y biológicos por parte del Estado.

- La declaración expresa de la vigencia de las leyes y demás disposiciones anteriores que no contravengan lo dispuesto en la Constitución.

En aras de la justicia, me parece conveniente repetir que la generalidad de los señalamientos arriba formulados surge del notable desarrollo que se ha experimentado en la materia constitucional en los últimos años, por lo que aun aquellos que compartan por entero mis planteamientos no deben de culpar de esas omisiones a los asambleístas de 1940, quienes realizaron una labor destacadísima para las circunstancias de tiempo y lugar en las que actuaron.

No obstante, lo que sí resulta evidente es que, si se admite que, antes de poner nuevamente en vigor—en su caso—la Constitución de 1940, habría que modificar los aspectos arriba señalados (o al menos una parte de ellos, unidos quizás a algunos otros que no he mencionado) para atemperarla a los tiempos actuales, entonces no cabrá dudas de que lo que se está debatiendo—en esencia—es una simple cuestión de nombre, pues, en cualquier caso, el texto que quedaría sería una carta magna esencialmente nueva.

CONCLUSIONES

En virtud de todas las razones que he expresado a lo largo del presente trabajo, estimo que, una vez que se haya iniciado en nuestra Patria el inevitable proceso del cambio democrático, será necesario proceder a la elaboración de una nueva constitución, que tome en cuenta todas las realidades actuales de nuestro país y los progresos alcanzados en el mundo (y—en particular—en los países de nuestro mismo idioma y entorno cultural) en el terreno supralegal.

Cabría destacar que, al formular esa proposición, no estoy propugnando nada diferente de lo que hizo la propia generación del 40, la cual, menos de cuatro decenios después de haber sido adoptada la carta magna de 1901, no optó por restablecerla con las reformas necesarias, sino que prefirió la elaboración de un nuevo texto (y ello a pesar de que—como es obvio—las diferencias existentes entre las sociedades de la Cuba del inicio del siglo y la de 1940 eran muchísimo menores que las que se observan entre esta última y la de hoy, 77 años más tarde).

Esto parece ser el sino de los países que han sufrido grandes conmociones politicosociales, como lo demuestran (por sólo citar algunos de los más importantes) los casos de Alemania, Francia, Italia y España, todos los cuales se han dado nuevas constituciones (en los tres primeros casos, después de pasar por la terrible experiencia de la Segunda Guerra Mundial; y en el último, al extinguirse el franquismo).

Lo mismo podemos decir de los países que a partir de 1989 han logrado salir del llamado "socialismo real" en la Europa Central y Oriental. Por razones obvias, ése es el caso de los muchos que han nacido como Estados independientes tras la disolución de las federaciones de las que formaban parte (la Unión Soviética, Checoslovaquia, la antigua Yugoslavia); en situación análoga se encuentra la llamada "República Democrática Alemana" (desaparecida al integrarse a la RFA). En estos casos parece "natural" que se hayan adoptado nuevas constituciones, aunque no resulta ocioso señalar que no tengo noticias de que alguno de los Estados bálticos que habían gozado con anterioridad de vida democrática independiente (Estonia, Letonia y Lituania) haya restablecido la vigencia de la constitución existente antes de su anexión a la URSS.

También han adoptado nuevas constituciones la generalidad de los que han mantenido la misma condición de estados independientes que tenían antes de la gloriosa caída del Muro de Berlín: Albania (abrogación de la antigua superley comunista en 1991, y—pese a no haberse adoptado otra integralmente diferente—promulgación de leyes constitucionales nuevas entre abril de 1991 y marzo de 1993); Bulgaria (1991); Polonia (nueva Constitución en 1997; aunque desde 1992 la carta magna de 1952, que con las numerosas enmiendas que había sufrido continuaba rigiendo, había sido adicionada con una llamada "Pequeña Constitución"); y Rumanía (1991).[29]

La consabida excepción que confirma la regla está representada—y ello sólo en parte—por Hungría: de manera análoga a lo que sucedió en Polonia entre 1992 y 1997, en el país magiar continua formalmente vigente la Constitución de 1949, aunque la misma fue objeto de reformas integrales en 1989 y 1990. Cabe destacar que incluso en este Estado centroeuropeo se ha llevado a cabo, entre los años de 1994 y 1996, un proceso para la promulgación de una carta magna esencialmente nueva, el cual ha fracasado por razones que el señor Arato, especialista en la materia, se atreve a calificar como "bizantinas."[30]

Como colofón de todo lo antes expresado, estimo que está en lo cierto el Grupo de Trabajo de la Disidencia Interna cuando, en el documento intitulado *La Patria es de Todos*, publicado en junio de 1997, plantea que, "si se reconocieran otras corrientes ideológicas además de la que propugna el Partido Comunista, se debería convocar a una Asamblea Constituyente, que modifique ante todo la actual Constitución vigente, pudiendo tomar como base la Constitución de 1940, con el fin de posteriormente realizar elecciones multipartidistas."[31]

---

29. Ver *In the Public Eye (Parliamentary Transparency in Europe and North America*, editado por International Human Rights Group, U.S.A.,1995; y asimismo la *East European Constitutional Review*, Vol. 3, Nº 3–4, Summer-Fall 1994, p. 2.

30. Ver reportes especiales de Andrew Arato, en la *East European Constitutional Review*, Vol. 3, Nº 3–4, Summer-Fall 1994, pp. 26–32; así como Vol. 5, Nº 4, Fall 1996, pp. 31–39.

31. *Boletín Especial*, Grupo de Trabajo de la Disidencia Interna (para el Análisis de la Realidad Socioeconómica Cubana), editado en computadora, La Habana, junio de 1997, última página.

LA CONSTITUCIÓN DE 1940: SIMBOLISMO Y VIGENCIA

Néstor Carbonell Cortina

Ante la crisis terminal del régimen de Castro, la Constitución del 40 cobra de nuevo actualidad. Numerosos movimientos y sectores del exilio abogan por su restablecimiento, en la medida de lo posible. Y los líderes del Grupo de Trabajo de la Disidencia Interna en Cuba, en su contundente documento "La Patria es de Todos," se han manifestado a favor de una transición a un estado de derecho, basada en los principios de la Constitución del 40.

LEGITIMIDAD CONSTITUCIONAL

Esta posición del exilio y de la disidencia es, a mi juicio, certera y trascendental. Si queremos ponerle fin a la tiranía y cerrar el ciclo tenebroso de la usurpación, tenemos que encontrar, después de Castro, una fórmula de convivencia con visos de legitimidad. Y esa fórmula no es la Constitución totalitaria de 1976, aunque se le hagan remiendos.[1] Ni es otra Ley Fundamental espuria, impuesta sin consentimiento ni debate durante la provisionalidad.

No, la única que tiene historia, simbolismo y arraigo para poder pacificar y regenerar el país antes de que se celebren elecciones libres, es la Carta Magna de 1940. Ella fue el leitmotiv de la lucha contra Batista, y no ha sido abrogada ni reformada por el pueblo, sino suspendida por la fuerza.[2]

Es evidente que durante la provisionalidad no todos sus preceptos serán aplicables, y habrá que resolver situaciones de hecho con un criterio de realismo práctico y equidad. Esto podría lograrse mediante disposiciones transitorias que dejarían sin efecto, temporalmente, los artículos de imposible cumplimiento, tales como los que se refieren a los órganos de elección popular y algunos de los preceptos que conforman el régimen económico y laboral.[3]

Lo importante es tener una base constitucional que haya sido legitimada por la voluntad soberana del pueblo y que permita encauzar armónicamente la transición a la democracia representativa. Podrá después el Congreso o los delegados electos a una Asamblea Plebiscitaria reformar o actualizar la Constitución del 40, supliendo sus deficiencias y podando sus casuísticos excesos.[4]

Interesa recalcar que esto no le compete al gobierno de facto provisional que se constituya a la caída de Castro. La suplantación o reforma de la Carta del 40 por ukase o decreto, sin mandato expreso de la nación, podría ser el preludio de una nueva usurpación con otras caras.

---

1. Uno de los fallos o errores de los países de Europa del Este, que vino a retrasar su recuperación en la fase postcomunista, fue el haber prolongado la vigencia de sus Constituciones totalitarias. Ver Juan J. Linz y Alfred Stepan, *Problems of Democratic Transition and Consolidation* (Baltimore: The Johns Hopkins University Press, 1996), p. 331 (caso de Hungría).

2. La doctrina de la intangibilidad constitucional fue consagrada en el artículo 36 de la Constitución Argentina de 1994, que dice: "Esta Constitución mantendrá su imperio aun cuando se interrumpiere su observancia por actos de fuerza contra el orden institucional y el sistema democrático. Estos actos serán insanablemente nulos…"

3. Las disposiciones transitorias deberían ser adoptadas, con carácter excepcional, por un gobierno provisional de unidad nacional y referidas posteriormente al Congreso o a una Asamblea Plebiscitaria para la acción que proceda.

La defensa del principio de la legitimidad constitucional es de vital importancia para evitar decepciones y retrocesos. No olvidemos nunca lo que nos aconteció a principios de 1959 cuando figuras representativas de la ciudadanía, incluyendo elementos de la clase togada, proclamaron que la revolución era fuente de derecho—no para restablecer la Constitución del 40 como se había prometido, sino para aniquilarla.

En lo personal, recuerdo claramente la respuesta indirecta que Castro le dió al artículo que publiqué en el *Diario de la Marina* en Cuba el 8 de marzo de 1959. En dicho trabajo, titulado "La Nueva República," abogué por el imperio de la ley y por el pleno restablecimiento de la Carta del 40. A los cinco días, en un discurso que pronunció en el Palacio Presidencial, Castro sentenció lo siguiente: "Nos hablan… de la ley, pero ¿de qué ley? …Para la ley vieja ningún respeto; para la ley nueva todo el respeto."

Y en cuanto a la Constitución del 40, Castro aseveró que el Consejo de Ministros era el poder constituyente, y que si algún artículo resultase inoperante o demasiado viejo, el Consejo de Ministros (es decir, Castro) podría transformarlo, modificarlo, cambiarlo o sustituirlo.[5] Fue así que nos quedamos sin Constitución, a merced de la voluntad omnímoda de un tirano megalómano.

De cara a esta trágica experiencia, hay que aferrarse en el mañana a los principios inmutables de nuestra Carta, porque sin ellos no seremos más que yunque: postrados indefensos en la ignominia, y expuestos a los martillazos implacables de los mandamás de turno.

SIGNIFICACION HISTORICA DE LA CARTA DEL 40

¿Qué representa la Constitución del 40 en nuestra evolución histórica e institucional, y cómo se llegó a elaborar y promulgar? La Carta del 40 es la obra cumbre de la República. Dando amplias muestras de madurez política y patriotismo, los delegados a la Convención Constituyente cerraron una década de convulsiones revolucionarias e inseguridad jurídica, y le dieron a Cuba una Constitución previsora y avanzada, sin injerencia extraña. Una Constitución que no es de nadie y es de todos, porque es patrimonio de la nación.

Después de la reforma constitucional de 1928, viciada de origen, y de la prórroga de poderes de Machado que dió lugar a la Revolución de 1933, Cuba se rigió por leyes constitucionales sin base legítima. Pero a lo largo de todo el período de provisionalidad, y aun después de las elecciones generales de 1936, la ciudadanía no dejó de reclamar una Constituyente que plasmara las reformas políticas, económicas y sociales que se estaban perfilando en la conciencia nacional.

¿Cómo cristalizó ese gran anhelo popular? En 1939, el Presidente de la República, Federico Laredo Brú, resuelve mediar entre los jefes de la oposición y el entonces coronel Fulgencio Batista para sentar las bases de la convocatoria a una Convención Constituyente. En una histórica reunión convocada por Laredo Brú en la finca Párraga en el Wajay, Ramón Grau San Martín, Batista, Mario García Menocal, Joaquín Martínez Sáenz y Miguel Mariano Gómez acordaron sellar, en principio, el llamado Pacto de Conciliación que culminó en la Constituyente.

---

4. El ilustre constitucionalista cubano, Dr. Gustavo Gutiérrez Sánchez, reconoció que la Constitución del 40 era demasiado casuística o reglamentista en algunas partes, pero consignó que no había reglas invariables para determinar lo que era y no era materia constitucional. Dijo Gutiérrez: "La norma jurídica es unas veces constitucional por su carácter institucional medular o básico, y otras, porque los pueblos la han incorporado a la Constitución buscando la garantía de su permanencia, como se observa en no pocas Constituciones de gran prestigio científico. 'Mediante esta forma constitucional—escribe Hans Kelsen, el gran maestro de la filosofía constitucional moderna—pueden ser reguladas otras materias jurídicas, diversas de las que corresponden al concepto de Constitución en el sentido material y riguroso de la palabra.'" [Este es el caso de la enmienda constitucional norteamericana No. XVIII, que prohibió la fabricación, distribución y venta de bebidas alcohólicas.] Gustavo Gutiérrez Sánchez, *Constitución de la Republica de Cuba* (La Habana: Editorial Lex, 1941), pp. 60, 61.

5. Fidel Castro, *Discursos para la Historia* (La Habana: Imprenta Emilio Gall, 1959), Tomo 2, pp. 75, 76.

En elecciones libres y honestas, en las que cada uno de los partidos formuló públicamente su programa constitucional, ganó la coalición oposicionista comandada por Grau San Martín, obteniendo 42 de los 77 delegados electos. La coalición gubernamental, bajo la jefatura de Batista, quedó en minoría con 35 delegados.[6]

La Convención, que presidió Grau San Martín gran parte del tiempo, contó con una representación amplia, distinguida y variada de la nación. En ella intervinieron estadistas como Orestes Ferrara, José Manuel Cortina y Carlos Márquez Sterling; intelectuales como Jorge Mañach y Francisco Ichaso; libertadores como Miguel Coyula; juristas como Ramón Zaydín y Manuel Dorta Duque; internacionalistas como Emilio Núñez Portuondo; parlamentarios como Santiago Rey Pernas, Rafael Guas Inclán, Aurelio Alvarez de la Vega, Miguel Suárez Fernández, Pelayo Cuervo Navarro y Emilio Ochoa; líderes obreros como Eusebio Mujal; industriales como José Manuel Casanova; líderes políticos y revolucionarios como Ramón Grau San Martín, Carlos Prío Socarrás, Eduardo Chibás y Joaquín Martínez Sáenz.

Y representando al equipo comunista, descollaron, entre otros, un sagaz líder sindical de acerada dialéctica, Blas Roca, y dos polemistas e intelectuales de alto vuelo, Juan Marinello y Salvador García Agüero.

¿COMO SE FORJO EL CONSENSO NACIONAL?

En nuestra Constituyente hubo que superar un gravísimo incidente en plena sesión inaugural, provocado por turbas enardecidas que trataron de disolver el Pacto de Conciliación. Es entonces que Cortina lanza, desde la tribuna, su célebre apóstrofe para dominar la situación: "¡Los Partidos, Fuera! ¡La Patria, Dentro!"[7]

En las sesiones subsiguientes no se produjeron alteraciones del orden, pero hubo que trabajar afanosamente para armonizar, en lo posible, criterios antagónicos y posturas divergentes. Las transacciones son esenciales en toda democrática Constituyente. Sólo se sorprenden de ello los teorizantes, quienes piensan que las Constituciones son documentos de academia o fórmulas de gabinete, y no pactos sociales de ancho espectro, que surgen muchas veces del seno mismo de enconadas controversias.

La Constitución de los Estados Unidos, modelo de democracia, fue el producto de grandes transacciones entre los delegados que abogaban por un gobierno nacional con amplios poderes federales, y los que insistían en una confederación de estados que tuvieran plena autonomía. Y el sistema electoral que se acordó, de representación proporcional en la Cámara y representación igualitaria en el Senado, fue el resultado del llamado "Great Compromise" entre los estados grandes y los estados pequeños. Esta fórmula salomónica, que no figuraba en ningún texto, vino a romper el impasse que a poco liquida la Convención de Filadelfia.

En la Constituyente cubana del 40, en la que estuvieron representados todos los partidos y corrientes ideológicas del país, hubo que encontrar puntos de convergencia que sirvieran de puente entre dos tendencias político-filosóficas extremas. De un lado, el "laissez-faire" individualista que abanderó, entre otros, Orestes Ferrara—devoto fervoroso del viejo liberalismo que surgiera de la Revolución Francesa. Y del otro extremo, la tesis colectivista defendida, principalmente, por el triunvirato de Roca, Marinello y García Agüero.

La mayoría centrista trató de balancear los derechos individuales y sociales, y los llevó al texto constitucional para que no naufragaran en los cambios de go-

---

6. Según el Dr. Carlos Márquez Sterling, los delegados a la Constituyente fueron 77, y no 81, como afirman algunos comentaristas, quienes no han tomado en cuenta las renuncias de varios convencionales que fueron sustituidos al constituirse la Asamblea. Ver el prólogo de Márquez Sterling en el libro de Néstor Carbonell Cortina, *El Espíritu de la Constitución Cubana de 1940, Principios y Doctrina* (Madrid: Playor, S.A., 1974), p. 24.

7. Ver *Diario de Sesiones de la Convención Constituyente*, Tomo I (La Habana), Sesión Primera (Inaugural), 9 de febrero de 1940, pp. 9-13.

bierno. La tesis mayoritaria favoreció la acción tutelar del Estado, pero sólo para suplir la iniciativa individual cuando ésta sea insuficiente y para limitarla cuando sea anti-social.[8]

Francisco Ichaso esbozó esta tesis en su réplica a Ferrara. Dijo Ichaso: "El señor Ferrara ha entonado un hermoso himno al viejo liberalismo…, que no hace otra cosa que producir en todas partes la ruina de la libertad… Me ha preocupado mucho la despreocupación del Estado… ese cruzarse de brazos, ese mantenerse indiferente ante los problemas cotidianos… Esto no es postular la hipertrofia del Estado… Es, sencillamente, darle un poco de intervención en cuestiones vitales de las que dependen la estabilidad y el progreso social."

Diversos factores contribuyeron a zanjar las hondas desavenencias y a darle feliz término a la misión constituyentista. Entre ellos sobresale la labor de la Comisión Coordinadora que presidió Cortina. Esta Comisión, que agrupó a 17 de los líderes más prominentes de la Convención, tuvo a su cargo el estudio y conciliación de los distintos dictámenes, y la elaboración y defensa, en la asamblea plenaria, de la mayoría de los preceptos que fueron aprobados.

La otra clave del éxito fue el ascenso a la presidencia de Carlos Márquez Sterling, que se produce cuando Grau, al perder la mayoría, renuncia a su cargo en la Convención. Con gran autoridad y destreza, Márquez Sterling agiliza los debates (sólo se habían aprobado cuatro títulos cuando él asumió la presidencia), y logra clausurar las sesiones dentro del plazo fijado de tres meses.

Uno de los grandes beneficios de la Constituyente del 40 fue la lección cívica que le impartió al pueblo de Cuba. Como señalara Márquez Sterling, "la radio llevó a todos los hogares de la nación los debates de sus delegados, creando un gran fervor patriótico y acrecentando la fe del pueblo en sus destinos. Nunca estuvieron más identificados los cubanos con sus instituciones políticas como en 1940."[9]

DEBATES MEMORABLES

Para aquilatar los logros de la Constitución del 40, no basta con estudiar su frío y extenso articulado. Hay que bucear en las profundidades de los debates para traspasar la letra de los preceptos, a veces defectuosa, y llegar a la médula de la argumentación o espíritu constitucional.

Veamos algunos ejemplos, comenzando con la invocación a Dios en el preámbulo, que provocó una ardiente polémica. García Agüero y otros se opusieron enérgicamente a la invocación, alegando que la Constitución se hacía tanto para los creyentes como para los no creyentes. Prevaleció la tesis de Coyula, quien sostuvo que Cuba era un país creyente, aunque no siempre practicante, y que debíamos llevarlo "por el camino de la ilusión que alienta y no por el de la fe perdida que destruye y envilece."[10]

El título cuarto de la Constitución, que recoge con extraordinaria amplitud una vasta gama de Derechos Individuales, fue el que suscitó los debates más intensos. Los convencionales del 40 no sólo garantizaron las libertades fundamentales de expresión, locomoción, asociación y cultos. Recordando vivamente un pasado de violencias y arbitrariedades, reforzaron también el habeas corpus y establecieron disposiciones adicionales para proteger la integridad personal, la seguridad y la honra de los detenidos, y para evitar los desafueros de la llamada "ley de fuga."

Bajo el rubro de las garantías individuales, los convencionales incluyeron los dos pilares en que descansa la libertad de empresa: la contratación y la propiedad privada. A la contratación la protegieron contra

---

8. A juicio de la Comisión Internacional de Juristas, entidad consultiva del Consejo Económico y Social de las Naciones Unidas, la Constitución de 1940, "en cuya redacción colaboraron prácticamente todos los sectores representativos de la opinión política cubana, se caracteriza por traducir un raro equilibrio entre las estructuras republicanas, liberales y democráticas y los postulados de justicia social y promoción económica." *El Imperio de la Ley en Cuba* (Ginebra: Comisión Internacional de Juristas, 1962), p. 87.

9. Carlos y Manuel Márquez Sterling, *Historia de la Isla de Cuba* (New York: Regents Publishing Company Inc., 1975), p. 222.

10. Andrés Mª Lazcano y Mazón, *Constitución de Cuba* (Con los Debates sobre su Articulado y Transitorias en la Convención Constituyente) (La Habana: Cultural, S.A., 1941), Tomo 1, pp. 3-14.

la retroactividad de las leyes civiles, y a la propiedad privada contra la intervención confiscatoria del Estado.

Movido y trascendental fue el debate que originó el artículo 24 sobre la confiscación de bienes. Blas Roca, entre otros, pretendía que se prohibiera únicamente la pena de confiscación, no los decretos u otras medidas gubernamentales de carácter confiscatorio, como las que preconizaron Marx y Lenin para minar y destruir el sistema de la propiedad privada.

En apoyo de su ponencia, Blas Roca invocó el artículo 43 de la Constitución cubana de 1901, que sólo se refería a la pena de confiscación, y pidió que, en homenaje a los convencionales de 1901, se respetera la integridad de ese texto.

Consciente de la táctica de Blas Roca, y viendo que algunos delegados incautos se sumaban al "homenaje" propuesto, Cortina pide la palabra: "… Yo creo que el homenaje que se rinda a los Constituyentes de 1901 no tiene que consistir en repetir todo lo que ellos hicieron, sino en mantener el mismo espíritu de previsión y de alto patriotismo que inspiraron sus palabras…"

"Lo que se trata en el precepto que defendemos es que quede prohibida en toda forma la confiscación… Que no se pueda imponer la confiscación por razones políticas, cuando un partido determinado suba al poder o lo crea conveniente a sus intereses."

"Queda perfectamente aclarado que no es lo mismo el concepto de 1901 que el que nosotros mantenemos; que el de 1901 habla de la confiscación como pena exclusivamente, y nosotros pretendemos que la confiscación no se imponga bajo ningún concepto y por ninguna causa."[11]

Prevaleció en la Constituyente la tesis de Cortina, pero, para desgracia nuestra, permitimos en 1959 que se violara impunemente esta prohibición constitucional, y dejamos que arrasara el huracán vandálico del castro-comunismo.

La Constitución reconoce también, como derecho fundamental, la profesión de todas las religiones, sin otra limitación que el respeto a la moral cristiana y al orden público.

Se opusieron airadamente a la limitación de la moral cristiana los delegados que le daban un sentido confesional y dogmático al concepto. La palabra sosegada y culta de Jorge Mañach aclaró la situación.

Dijo Mañach: "Lo que estamos tratando de establecer… es la necesidad de que los cultos religiosos… sean normados por un sentido moral. Pero la palabra moral es muy vaga… Hay muchas morales. Tenemos que elegir alguna, y la… que elegimos es la moral tradicional cubana, la que informa nuestras costumbres… Esa moral está representada por la figura de Jesucristo."

Agregó Mañach: "Y hasta aquellos autores que, como Renán, Strauss o Papini, han escrito los libros más negativos acerca de Cristo como divinidad, no han podido menos que ponderar y situar en su lugar histórico la significación moral, la ejemplaridad moral de Cristo."[12]

La libertad de asociación está garantizada en la Constitución, pero se declara ilícita la formación y existencia de organizaciones políticas contrarias al régimen de gobierno representativo democrático… o que atenten contra la soberanía nacional.

Los proponentes de este precepto sostuvieron que la libertad tiene que defenderse frente a los que, a su amparo, tratan de destruirla. Los partidos que se consideren agredidos o discriminados injustamente pueden recurrir ante los tribunales para ampararse.

El debate apasionado que este precepto provocó estuvo salpicado de buen humor. En su réplica a Blas Roca, que se oponía vigorosamente a esta pragmática, José Manuel Casanova le hizo estas preguntas: "¿Y cree S.S. que hay libertad en Rusia y duda de que exista aquí la libertad? ¿Cree S.S… que podría mani-

---

11. Lazcano y Mazón, *Constitución de Cuba*, p. 339.
12. Lazcano y Mazón, *Constitución de Cuba*, pp. 519, 520.

festarse en el Parlamento de Rusia con la libertad con que se produce aquí…?"

Contesta Ferrara: "¡Sí podría decirlo [en Rusia] el señor Roca… [pero] una sola vez…!"[13]

Precisa reconocer que las agudezas de Ferrara, irónicas y penetrantes, sirvieron para tonificar las discusiones en la Constituyente y desinflar las vaporosas peroratas.

PRINCIPIOS FUNDAMENTALES

Dejaré para otra oportunidad la reseña de los grandes debates que se suscitaron en la Constituyente del 40. Me limitaré ahora a hacer algunas consideraciones generales sobre los principios que informan sus preceptos fundamentales.

En la sección sobre la *Familia*, los convencionales del 40 defendieron la estabilidad del matrimonio, rechazando propuestas peligrosas que bordeaban el amor libre. Sometieron el matrimonio por equiparación a la decisión del juez, basada en la equidad. Asimismo, establecieron la igualdad absoluta de derechos para ambos cónyuges, y abolieron las calificaciones sobre la filiación para que no pesara sobre los hijos ningún estigma de ilegitimidad.

En lo que respecta a la *Cultura*, los constituyentes del 40 abogaron por la educación integral del cubano. Ordenaron la creación de un Consejo Nacional de Educación y Cultura, libre de sectarismo. Protegieron la enseñanza privada y reconocieron el derecho a impartir la educación religiosa, reiterando en los debates que Estado laico no quiere decir Estado ateo.

En su afán de dotar a la educación pública de un presupuesto adecuado, los convencionales se extralimitaron, estableciendo condiciones como la de "la millonésima" para el sueldo de los maestros, que son inaplicables e impropias para una Constitución.

El título sobre el *Trabajo*, que le dió rango constitucional a múltiples conquistas obreras, colocó a Cuba a la vanguardia del progreso social. Inspirados en las corrientes nacionalistas y justicieras en boga, los convencionales les otorgaron a los trabajadores cubanos

numerosas prerrogativas para mejorar sus condiciones de vida y garantizarles un mínimo decoroso de seguridad social.

Ahora bien, a la luz de la experiencia y de las circunstancias actuales, algunas de esas prerrogativas, como el descanso retribuido de un mes y la jornada semanal de 44 horas de trabajo equivalentes a 48 en el salario, parecen excesivas por incosteables.

Excesivo es también el casuismo reglamentista de éstos y otros preceptos de la Carta del 40. Si la Constitución de los Estados Unidos pecó por omisión (le faltó nada menos que el "Bill of Rights"), la cubana pecó por exceso—signo infalible de nuestra idiosincracia. Muchas son las virtudes de los cubanos, pero éstas no incluyen el sentido del límite. En nuestro caso, lo bueno y lo malo suelen venir en demasía.

En una futura Constituyente habría que simplificar y liberalizar los títulos correspondientes al Trabajo y a la Economía Nacional a fin de que las disposiciones constitucionales, (que prohiben, entre otras cosas, el despido compensado), no obstaculicen la urgente tarea de privatizar empresas estatales y atraer inversiones nacionales y extranjeras.

No es fácil podar el tupido follaje del Estado Benefactor ("Welfare State"). Europa, con Alemania y Francia a la cabeza, no ha podido lograrlo todavía. La Cuba democrática del mañana tendrá necesariamente que hacerlo, pero con mucho tino, mitigando los inevitables desajustes de la transición con una generosa red de protección social o "safety net" para ayudar a los desplazados y desamparados.

En el título correspondiente a la *Propiedad Privada*, se reconoce y garantiza este fundamental derecho en su más alto concepto de función social. Guiados por el espíritu que encierra este precepto, los convencionales del 40 proscribieron el latifundio, estableciendo criterios flexibles para fijar el máximo de extensión de tierra para cada tipo de explotación. Pero limitaron cuidadosamente la intervención estatal, rechazando por confiscatorio el impuesto progresivo sobre la tierra. Y en caso de expropiación, le otorgaron al pro-

---

13. Lazcano y Mazón, *Constitución de Cuba,* pp. 582, 583.

pietario el máximo posible de derechos, incluyendo el pago previo de la indemnización en efectivo, fijada judicialmente, o la restitución de la propiedad cuando no se cumplan los requisitos establecidos.

Estos principios son esenciales para restaurar la confianza y acelerar la reconstrucción económica del país. El gobierno provisional que se constituya después de Castro deberá ratificarlos, adecuando su aplicación a las experiencias recientes en los países de Europa del Este y a las realidades imperantes en la Cuba liberada.

Bajo el título de los *Organos del Estado* (cuyos preceptos sólo podrán entrar en vigor después que se celebren elecciones libres), los convencionales introdujeron el llamado sistema semiparlamentario, que desde 1930 Cortina y otros colegas trataron de implantar.[14] El propósito que perseguían era atemperar los poderes excesivos del Ejecutivo, es decir, el cesarismo de nuestros Presidentes, otorgándole al Congreso la facultad de interpelar y censurar a los ministros, y de provocar cambios de gabinete bajo ciertas condiciones e intervalos de tiempo.

Los que critican este sistema por no ser parlamentario puro se olvidan que hasta las repúblicas más maduras y cultas han tenido que regular el parlamentarismo desenfrenado. Francia tuvo 26 gobiernos durante los 12 años de la Cuarta República, hasta que regresó De Gaulle en 1958 y estableció un régimen híbrido, que algunos llaman semiparlamentario y otros semipresidencial.

Italia, por su parte, que ha reorganizado sus gobiernos 55 veces desde el fin de la guerra, está a punto de aprobar una reforma parlamentaria a la francesa.[15]

En Cuba, los fallos de nuestro sistema semiparlamentario, que rigió a medias durante sólo 12 años de gobiernos constitucionales, no fueron realmente orgánicos, sino funcionales—producto de viejas corruptelas

y de hábitos presidencialistas arraigados. Esos fallos son superables, a mi juicio, con una buena dosis de democracia, experiencia y probidad.

Entre los otros avances y logros de la Constitución del 40 se encuentran: el sufragio directo sin voto acumulativo; la Carrera Administrativa; las Comisiones de Conciliación Obrero-Patronales, presididas por un funcionario judicial; la Autonomía Municipal; el Banco Nacional; el Tribunal de Garantías Constitucionales y Sociales; el Tribunal de Cuentas y el Tribunal Superior Electoral.

No todas estas instituciones funcionaron a cabalidad, ya sea por defectos de forma o de fondo, o por falta de leyes complementarias. Pero subsanando las deficiencias que hubiere, dichas instituciones podrían ser sólidos puntales de la Cuba vigorosa y libre del futuro.

CONCLUSIONES

En resumen, la Constitución del 40 ha sido pisoteada y abolida por un régimen tiránico que prometió restablecerla. Pero no ha muerto. Su espíritu vive como expresión genuina de la voluntad soberana del pueblo de Cuba. Muchos de sus preceptos, que recogen experiencias dolorosas de nuestro pasado y aspiraciones vehementes de nuestro pueblo, pueden llegar a tener aplicación, renovándolos y adaptándolos a las realidades presentes en una democrática Constituyente.

Hay que evitar nuevas emboscadas o engaños después de Castro. Ni continuismo embozado, ni vacío desestabilizador. La Carta Magna del 40, en su esencia, es nuestra mayor garantía de paz con justicia y libertad. Es nuestra base legítima para estabilizar a Cuba y encauzar la transición a un estado de derecho. Es el único puente institucional que tenemos para unir a la República del mañana con las tradiciones de nuestra historia, el tesoro de nuestra cultura y las glorias inmarcesibles de nuestra Patria.

---

14. Ver José Manuel Cortina, *Presidentes y Parlamentos* (La Habana: J. Arroyo y Cia., 1931).

15. Polonia y otros países de Europa del Este, al iniciar la etapa postcomunista, adoptaron un régimen semipresidencial parecido al implantado por De Gaulle en Francia. En cuanto a España, el ex-Presidente del Gobierno, don Leopoldo Calvo Sotelo, afirmó lo siguiente en carta a este autor de fecha 12 de febrero de 1997: "A mí la fórmula semipresidencialista de la V República Francesa me parece inteligente y eficaz. Aunque la Constitución Española de 1978 implantó un sistema parlamentario, hay en ella rasgos presidencialistas que han tenido su eficacia."

EL TRIBUNAL CONSTITUCIONAL Y SU ORGANIZACION: UNA PROPUESTA DE REFORMA

Alberto Luzárraga

Las Constituciones tienen un propósito esencial: restringir el poder y encauzarlo por vías predeterminadas. La Carta Magna, Bill of Rights, Fueros de Vizcaya o de Aragón son antecedentes de esta función en la que se limitaba al soberano y se le hacía reconocer que su poder no era absoluto. Este reconocimiento estaba transido del sentimiento cristiano de la igualdad de los hombres ante Dios según lo desarrolló la patrística en sus glosas y comentarios al Derecho De Gentes, originalmente concebido por los romanos. De ahí, fórmulas tales como la usada ante el rey una vez que juraba los fueros del Señorío de Vizcaya: "y sabed Señor que cada uno de nos vale tanto como vos y todos juntos valemos más que vos."

La limitación al poder es natural al hombre y la sociedad. Sabemos que somos frágiles y que es necesario precaver. Con el fortalecimiento del estado moderno esta aspiración debió enfrentar nuevos desafíos. Las leyes se multiplicaron debido a la complejidad de las relaciones humanas y los jueces y tribunales aumentaron en número y diversidad, con las inevitables diferencias en la calidad de las personas y de los criterios de aplicación de la ley.

Al mismo tiempo se comenzaron a dictar Constituciones que organizaban el funcionamiento del Estado y las relaciones de éste con los ciudadanos. El juez se vió ante una disyuntiva: su deber era aplicar las leyes promulgadas y votadas por las autoridades competentes pero a veces esas leyes contradecían los derechos que la Constitución concedía a los ciudadanos o no respetaban la separación de poderes entre los órganos del Estado.

La primera Constitución moderna fué aprobada por los Estados Unidos en 1787 y puesta en vigor en 1789, una vez que la ratificaron los Estados de la Federación. El problema apuntado no tardó en presentarse y el Presidente del Tribunal Supremo en aquél entonces, (1803) magistrado John Marshall razonó que si bajo el artículo 6 de la Constitución ésta era la ley fundamental del país, tenía que primar y por lo tanto, provocar la anulación de otras leyes que contradijesen sus preceptos. Sus colegas en el Tribunal Supremo aceptaron la tesis y así surgió la famosa decisión de Marbury vs. Madison y el comienzo del Derecho Constitucional moderno.

Desde entonces los sistemas se han perfeccionado y evolucionado. En materia Constitucional existen varios sistemas. En el sistema Inglés el Parlamento es soberano y puede hacer lo que quiera en teoría, pero no lo hace puesto que conculcar derechos establecidos significaría su remoción por el voto. En el sistema americano existe la llamada "revisión judicial" mediante la cual los tribunales pueden declarar una ley inconstitucional y suspender su ejecución en tanto el Tribunal Supremo confirma o no la sentencia del juez o Tribunal. Es por ésto que se le ha llamado sistema de *jurisdicción difusa* pues aunque la resolución final compete al Supremo, los jueces inferiores pueden conocer y resolver sobre asuntos de Constitucionalidad.

Contrapuesto a este sistema existe el llamado sistema de *jurisdicción concentrada* creado por la escuela austríaca de la que su máximo expositor es el profesor Kelsen. Para esta escuela la jurisdicción difusa es un sistema demasiado amplio. Bajo su concepción, existe un Tribunal Constitucional que conoce *exclusivamente* de cuestiones Constitucionales y que además es el *único facultado* para hacerlo.

Kelsen lo llama "legislador negativo" porque su función es decir la ley sí se ajusta a la Constitución en cuyo caso no hay efectos; o no se ajusta, en cuyo caso la ley se anula. El sistema no admite la suspensión de la ejecución de la ley en tanto no exista una declaración de inconstitucionalidad.

Y en fin, existen los sistemas híbridos que crean un Tribunal especializado para decidir asuntos de constitucionalidad; pero conceden a los jueces o tribunales ordinarios la facultad de no aplicar la ley vigente en casos de duda (donde deben consultar al Tribunal Constitucional) o en aquellos casos en que la Constitución es específica y legisla y establece un derecho que la ley aplicable al caso "sub judice" contradice o vulnera.

Todos los sistemas coinciden en dos principios fundamentales: respeto a las decisiones del Tribunal e independencia absoluta de éste, no sólo de los poderes Ejecutivo y Legislativo del Estado sino incluso del Poder Judicial, pues se configura usualmente como Tribunal Especial.

BREVE HISTORIA DEL TRIBUNAL CONSTITUCIONAL EN CUBA

En el caso cubano se ha seguido el sistema de *jurisdicción concentrada* con modificaciones, de modo que nunca existió un sistema austríaco puro.

Sí podemos decir con orgullo que fuimos uno de los primeros países en implantar el control judicial de la legislación, pues la primera ley estableciendo el Recurso de Inconstitucionalidad data del 31 de Marzo de 1903 o sea al año escaso de establecerse la República y plasmó el recurso autorizado por el artículo 83 de la Constitución de 1901. Esta ley fué substituída por la del 31 de Mayo de 1949 que desarrolló los principios contenidos en los artículos 182, 183 y 194 de la Constitución del 40. Ambas leyes facultaron al Tribunal Supremo para ser el único que podía decidir sobre estas cuestiones. En realidad al dictar nuestra primera ley nos adelantamos al sistema austríaco que sólo surgió como escuela en los años 20.

Los constituyentes del 40 arrastraban el recelo justificado de que la Constitución no se cumpliera en la práctica y abrieron una gama muy amplia de recursos de inconstitucionalidad, creando así un sistema complicado. Asimismo, la Constitución creó el Tribunal de Garantías Constitucionales y Sociales pero no lo diseñó como Tribunal independiente sino como una Sala del Tribunal Supremo, integrada por quince magistrados para decidir cuestiones constitucionales y de nueve para cuestiones sociales. Esta última atribución ambigua de cuestiones "sociales" creó muchos problemas según veremos.

Fueron errores técnicos. La falta de independencia del Tribunal hizo que no fuese plenamente capaz de controlar al Poder Judicial si no aplicaba la ley o violaba la Constitución. Una de las facultades de un Tribunal Constitucional debe ser la de anular sentencias de cualquier órgano del Poder Judicial (aún del Tribunal Supremo) si en casos sometidos a ellos se ha violado la Constitución. Por ejemplo, supongamos que un juez o tribunal haya negado arbitrariamente a la parte recurrente el derecho a practicar pruebas y que por ello se la coloca en estado de indefensión, violándose así las garantías procesales establecidas por la Constitución. En este caso el Tribunal Constitucional anularía la sentencia que confirmase esa decisión aunque fuese emitida por el Tribunal Supremo.

Ahora bien, bajo el sistema establecido por la Constitución del 40 imaginemos al Tribunal Supremo terminando de dictar una Sentencia que confirma la de un juez subalterno y constituyéndose después en Tribunal Constitucional a fin de conocer sobre la anulación de sus propios actos. El absurdo no requiere mayor explicación.

Otro error de envergadura fué ocasionado por el artículo 182.f que incluyó dentro de la competencia del Tribunal "las cuestiones de legislación social que la Constitución y la ley sometan a su consideración." La ley orgánica de 1949 en su artículo 13 incluyó en esta definición las reclamaciones por despidos, retiros, descanso retribuído, excedencias, escalafones sindicación, contratos de trabajo, etc. No contenta con una lista detallada añadió: "y en general todas las que versen sobre cuestiones de carácter social y de relaciones entre patronos y obreros." Esto creó un volumen tal de asuntos que de hecho el Tribunal de Garantías se convirtió en un Tribunal Laboral, con el consiguiente retraso del desarrollo de las cuestiones puramente constitucionales.

Aunque sin duda hubo buenas sentencias, aparentemente el tema constitucional no cobró suficiente importancia en la conciencia popular ni en el Tribunal en sí. Este efecto se palpó a raíz del 10 de Marzo cuando por una votación de 10 contra 5 el Tribunal de Garantías (por sentencia #127 de 17 de Agosto de 1953) desestimó el recurso interpuesto por 25 ciudadanos contra los Estatutos Constitucionales promulgados por Batista; sin que esta decisión conllevase el mismo grado de censura popular que el golpe del 10 de Marzo y sin que se resintiese el funcionamiento del tribunal que siguió operando como si no hubiese faltado a su razón esencial de ser.

Es justo sin embargo reconocer que el voto de la minoría declaró que la Ley Constitucional de 4 de Abril de 1952 "es inconstitucional y no podrá aplicarse en ningún caso ni forma, debiendo ser derogada....por quebrantar los principios de soberanía popular innatos en el pueblo cubano....violar el contenido total de la Constitución de 1940 que no ha sido derogada, su articulado, su esencia, sus principios y razón de ser, y en suma por no provenir de órgano legitimado para hacerlo."

En cuanto a los recursos admitidos por la Constitución, la ley de 1949 al desarrollarlos creó diversos problemas debido a algunas fallas de rigor científico. El proyecto de ley original sufrió modificaciones poco felices en el Senado y la ley finalmente aprobada adolecía de defectos técnicos al extremo de que algún autor comentó que ciertos de sus preceptos eran inconstitucionales. Sea ello o no cierto, constituyó un adelanto y los defectos eran fácilmente subsanables. De lo que no cabe duda es de que la Constitución y por ende la ley complementaria de 1949 no hicieron la distinción técnica entre el recurso de *amparo constitucional* y el *recurso de inconstitucionalidad puro*.

Esta distinción es muy útil porque el amparo permite a la persona afectada instar para que se proteja su derecho sin que la sentencia tenga que anular la ley, sino solamente los actos específicos que afectaron sus

derechos. Por el contrario el recurso de inconstitucionalidad anula la ley para todos y es radical en sus efectos, pues no matiza aquellas situaciones en que la inconstitucionalidad puede surgir de circunstancias especiales del caso y no de la ley en sí.

La ventaja del amparo para la parte actora es obvia. Cuando se trata de anular una ley "erga omnes" las cosas se complican pues el Estado tiene interés en preservar la seguridad jurídica y por ello usualmente se hace parte en el proceso e impugna los argumentos del actor. La consecuencia es que una controversia relativamente simple puede convertirse en un pleito muy complicado, aunque en la práctica ésto se evitaba restringiendo la causa de pedir. Otras legislaciones civiles han ampliado los efectos del amparo, facultando al Tribunal para que de "motu proprio" pueda suscitar la cuestión de inconstitucionalidad y anular la ley "erga omnes" una vez que haya dictado sentencia sobre el caso particular. En este caso estaría actuando sobre una base de equidad, pues habría percibido que en el caso planteado la violación de derechos constitucionales se basaría no en las circunstancias del caso, sino en la esencia de la ley impugnada.

No sólo carecía la Constitución de esta distinción útil sino que abría la puerta a recursos muy peligrosos desde un punto de vista político y de seguridad jurídica. Nos referimos al llamado recurso por 25 ciudadanos establecido por el artículo 194.b de la Constitución del 40 y desarrollado por la ley del 49 bajo el título de "acción pública." Según este recurso cualesquiera 25 ciudadanos en pleno disfrute de sus derechos podían impugnar la constitucionalidad de cualquier ley aún sin que en lo personal hubieran sufrido daños.

Se trataba de un recurso formal que por su naturaleza tenía que ser extremadamente técnico y por ende fuera del alcance de 25 ciudadanos comunes. Era pues un recurso para abogados, pero posible con sólo allegar 25 firmas de cualesquiera personas. Por ello se prestaba a ser usado con fines políticos simplemente para entorpecer la labor legislativa o ganar notoriedad. Tenía su mérito libertario (de hecho la impugnación de los estatutos de Batista se basó en este recurso) pero hubiera sido mejor ponerlo en manos de un funcionario del tipo de un "ombudsman" o defensor del pueblo, que recibiese la instancia de los 25 ciudadanos. Otra alternativa hubiera sido restringirlo a temas constitucionales de contenido orgánico.

Sin embargo el sistema de consulta de jueces y Tribunales ordinarios al Tribunal de Garantías en caso de dudas sobre constitucionalidad de leyes (artículo 182.b, Constitución del 40) sí merece aplauso, ya que tendía a crear uniformidad de criterio y mejor comprensión de la Constitución. Además recalcaba que la aplicación y cuidado de que se cumpla con la Constitución es una función que compete a todo el Poder Judicial, aunque sólo pueda decidir en forma vinculante el Tribunal Constitucional.

En resumen, es justo decir que la Constitución del 40, en términos de apertura y de facilitar la defensa de los derechos individuales, tuvo la preocupación de hacerlo, lo hizo, y fué generosa hasta llegar a la si se quiere exageración; pensando seguramente los constituyentes que cuantas más vías quedasen abiertas, mejor. Como apuntamos este error era subsanable en la práctica mediante la jurisprudencia. Los errores esenciales fueron: no hacer independiente al Tribunal y recargarlo con cuestiones laborales que claramente competían a Tribunales del Trabajo, creados especialmente para esos menesteres.

RECOMENDACIONES PARA EL FUTURO

No cabe duda de que la pieza central de un sistema de limitación del Poder tiene que ser el Tribunal Constitucional. Aceptada esta premisa es lógico dotarlo del máximo de independencia y prestigio. Si la Constitución es la Carta Fundamental y por ello merece un lugar especial, el Tribunal es la concreción viviente de la Constitución.

El Tribunal debe ser respetado profundamente y respetarse a sí mismo. Sus decisiones tienen que estar bien fundadas y deben desenvolver la Constitución *y no crear ni descubrir nuevos derechos u obligaciones so pretexto de interpretación,* lo cual debe quedar bien claro en la ley Orgánica que lo autorice.

Procesalmente, la ley que lo habilite tiene que ser clara y los recursos sencillos y asequibles al común de los letrados y/o ciudadanos. La Constitución del 40 tenía un gran precepto en su artículo 194 al decir: "en todo recurso de inconstitucionalidad el tribunal resolverá siempre el fondo de la reclamación" y más adelante abundaba en igual idea estableciendo que si existiesen defectos de forma en el planteamiento del recurso, se concediese un plazo para su subsanación. Se trata de resolver problemas y no de echarlos a un lado mediante argucias procesales. Igualmente la denegación de admisibilidad de un recurso tiene que hacerse como se hacía, por resolución fundada. El ciudadano debe saber por qué no se acepta su recurso.

Los principios enunciados conllevan las recomendaciones siguientes:

1. Separación del Tribunal del resto del Poder Judicial. Monopolio de la facultad de decidir que es o no es Constitucional. Restricción de su función a esos asuntos exclusivamente, incluyendo conflictos entre los órganos del estado. Obligación de decidir siempre sobre el fondo de la cuestión. Facultad de anular leyes o resoluciones administrativas, sentencias judiciales y/o sus efectos cuando vulneren la Constitución. Facultad de suspender, previo cumplimiento de los requisitos del caso, la ejecución de actos o de sentencias firmes.

2. Vinculación de todo el Poder Judicial a la salvaguarda de los Derechos Constitucionales. Los jueces estarían obligados a aplicar la Constitución cuando ésta es específica y a suscitar la cuestión de constitucionalidad cuando estimen que la ley aplicable contiene una vulneración clara y general de derechos constitucionales, pudiendo en esos casos suspender el proceso y elevar los autos al Tribunal Constitucional. Asimismo se mantendría el sistema de consulta para aquéllos casos en que sólo existiesen dudas.

3. Reglas procesales simplificadas para aquéllos casos en que la intervención del Tribunal necesite hacerse rápidamente, pues de lo contrario se producirían perjuicios irreparables. Condena en costas y hasta multas a las partes, acompañada de reprensión a los letrados y pérdida de honorarios por el uso frívolo de este vía expedita.

4. El recurso continuaría sujeto a un trámite de admisibilidad (que no significa estimación favora-

ble) a fin de determinar si merece o no ser admitido a trámite. El recurso sería admitido o denegado mediante resolución fundada. Se mantendría así nuestra tradición jurídica que no admite la simple denegación sin causa explícita que rige en otros sistemas. Asimismo se facilitaría la subsanación de defectos formales.

5. El Tribunal no conocería de los hechos en asuntos que se suscitaran dentro de actuaciones judiciales. No es un Tribunal de apelación. Solamente conocería de las cuestiones constitucionales que puedan afectar las actuaciones judiciales y hacerlas susceptibles de anulación por violar garantías constitucionales.

6. Habilitación del recurso de amparo. Conservación del recurso de inconstitucionalidad puro abierto a los ciudadanos en caso de daños efectivos sufridos por el actor. Habilitación del recurso de inconstitucionalidad formal dentro de un sistema de control como el descrito con anterioridad.

7. Nombramiento de magistrados por un sistema que bien pudiera ser similar al de ternas consagrado por la Constitución del 40 en su artículo 180, añadiendo la confirmación del Senado. Los magistrados serían inamovibles y habría que decidir si el cargo es vitalicio o por un período considerable de tiempo, aunque limitado. En los comienzos nos inclinaríamos por un sistema de tiempo limitado, que a su vez podría sufrir reducciones en el término, en el caso de los primeros nombramientos, suponiendo que éstos hayan sido hechos por un gobierno de facto. Tal vez se pensará que un gobierno de facto no debe hacer nombramientos pero si acepta auto-restringir sus poderes nombrando a un Tribunal Constitucional ello sería un paso de avance y no de retroceso. Los así nombrados organizarían el sistema y deberían ser ratificados en sus cargos o cesar en ellos de acuerdo con lo que determine el órgano competente establecido por un régimen democrático.

8. Dotación amplia de recursos para organizar Salas y remunerar Magistrados a fin de que el despacho de asuntos sea expedito. El pueblo debe apreciar que la justicia es rápida y efectiva si se pretende que respete sus instituciones.

9. Sanción (incluída como precepto constitucional) de separación del cargo e inhabilitación vitalicia para desempeñar un cargo público a todo miembro del Poder Ejecutivo o las fuerzas del orden (Policía o Ejército) que rehuse directa o indirectamente acatar lo dispuesto por una Sentencia firme o un mandamiento del Tribunal, expedido con arreglo a derecho. Igual sanción se aplicará a aquéllos que coadyuven directa o indirectamente a dicha resistencia. Este requisito draconiano es necesario en el período de transición. Una generación más tarde tal vez no sea necesario.

10. Remuneración adecuada para los magistrados que deben percibir un buen sueldo en función de la importancia de su cargo. Prohibición de actividades y afiliaciones políticas durante el ejercicio de su cargo. Idem respecto a afiliaciones comerciales. Inmunidad para los magistrados respecto a pleitos, reclamaciones, indemnizaciones, etc. planteadas por terceros con motivo de actos realizados o sentencias expedidas durante el ejercicio del cargo.

COMENTARIOS SOBRE EL ARTÍCULO XVII SOBRE HACIENDA PÚBLICA DE LA CONSTITUCIÓN DE 1940 DE CUBA

Lorenzo L. Pérez[1]

El Artículo XVII de la Constitución de 1940 contiene cuatro partes: la primera trata sobre los bienes y las finanzas del estado; la segunda sobre el presupuesto; la tercera sobre el Tribunal de Cuentas; y la cuarta sobre la economía nacional. Los comentarios que ofrezco en este panel son desde el punto de vista económico y no desde un punto de vista legal o más concretamente constitucional. He analizado este artículo de la constitución para tratar de evaluar cuales son sus implicaciones para el funcionamiento de una economía moderna de mercado.

COMENTARIOS GENERALES

En materia de hacienda pública, una constitución debe proveer términos de referencia generales sobre materias fiscales y reguladoras pero debe evitar provisiones muy específicas que tal vez sean adecuadas para cierto momento histórico pero que pudieran convertirse obsoletas en otro momento. La razón de esto es que lo que puede lucir perfectamente razonable en un momento puede ser perjudicial en otro y hacer un cambio en una constitución siempre es difícil. Un ejemplo moderno de este tipo de problema es la constitución de 1988 de Brasil que contiene muchos artículos específicos en materia económica que reflejaron el momento histórico que se vivía a la salida de una dictadura militar. Cambios en estas materias implican una reforma de la constitución que re-

quiere difíciles procedimientos de votación en el congreso.

Normas sobre las operaciones de hacienda publica deben hacerse por medio de leyes generales y no entrar en mucho detalle en una constitución. De hecho, Cuba tenía una ley general de presupuesto que trataba de hacer esto. Desafortunadamente no tuve oportunidad de analizarla durante la preparación de este trabajo.

Un último comentario general tiene que ver con la importancia de la integridad de las personas que ejercen funciones dadas por una constitución y sus leyes. Es importante crear en Cuba un respeto al orden jurídico para que las intenciones de la legislación sean cumplidas. La triste historia de Cuba es un buen ejemplo de la importancia de este punto.

COMENTARIOS ESPECIFICOS

En mi opinión, el Artículo XVII es innecesariamente detallado y contiene una serie de provisiones que son mejor tratadas por legislación específica. Además, algunas provisiones de este artículo reflejan una filosofía económica del estado que está bastante pasada de moda. El estado se ve como promotor de actividades económicas claves que casi siempre resultan en una provisión de subsidios de los que se benefician sectores individuales de la economía con detrimento del

1. Estos comentarios se ofrecen de forma personal y no necesariamente representan las opiniones oficiales del Fondo Monetario Internacional. Le estoy agradecido a mis colegas del Fondo, José Luis A. Ruíz, Héctor Elizalde y Víctor Thuronyi por sus sugerencias en las materias tratadas aquí.

bienestar nacional. Más adelante daré ejemplos específicos.

Los párrafos 251 y 252 de la **primera parte del Artículo XVII** contienen provisiones generales sobre el patrimonio del estado y la venta de sus activos. En general se cubren temas apropiados para una constitución, tales como: maneras de llevar a cabo una subasta pública y cómo el congreso debe aprobar ventas de activos por leyes extraordinarias. Los párrafos 253 y 254 también tratan de los procedimientos legislativos para la concertación de empréstitos y la garantía estatal de cualquier empréstito que implique responsabilidad económica para el tesoro nacional. Este tema también es materia constitucional en muchos países. Por ejemplo, en los Estados Unidos la constitución especifica que la autoridad para aprobar empréstitos reside en el congreso. El congreso ejercita esta obligación aprobando periódicamente aumentos en el límite de la deuda pública. En Francia, sin embargo, las leyes presupuestarias que incluyen la autoridad de aprobar empréstitos tienen un carácter orgánico que es casi-constitucional (o sea de una importancia mayor que leyes ordinarias). Al mismo tiempo se puede decir que los temas de los párrafos 253 y 254 también se pueden tratar como parte de una ley de presupuesto general. En cuanto a que si los aumentos de los topes de deuda deban requerir las dos terceras partes de los votos de cada cámara del congreso como lo exige la constitución de 1940, habría que decir que no se puede dar una respuesta técnica sobre el asunto. Sin embargo, sí se puede decir que esto sería inusual y probablemente poco práctico.

La **segunda parte del Artículo XVII** trata sobre las prácticas presupuestarias y exige que las operaciones de ingresos y gastos sean incluídas en presupuestos anuales. Hay mucho que se puede apoyar en esta parte de la constitución, sobre todo el requerimiento específico que las operaciones presupuestarias sean aprobadas por ley. Sin embargo, el párrafo 255 deja la puerta abierta para muchos gastos fuera del presupuesto, creando fondos especiales para programas sociales, obras públicas, promoción de actividades para el sector agrícola y otros, y asignando ciertos recursos para fines específicos. El punto no es que estas actividades no deban recibir apoyo presupuestario, sino

que este tipo de gasto debe estar directamente en el presupuesto y sujeto a una revisión anual por el congreso. Al mismo tiempo, el poder ejecutivo debe tener la oportunidad de proponer anualmente cómo se deban usar los recursos del estado para facilitar el manejo macroeconómico de las finanzas públicas. Estando estas operaciones en el presupuesto se promueve la transparencia en las finanzas públicas y se pone directamente la responsabilidad de velar por la salud de ellas en el ejecutivo y en el congreso.

El párrafo 256 prevé que la ley podrá crear asociaciones obligatorias de producción y de profesionales para promover el interés común de los productores manejadas por reglamentos democráticos. Me imagino que este párrafo estaba dirigido más que nada a la industria azucarera pero me parece que refleja una mentalidad corporatista de la economía que no estaría de acuerdo con una economía de mercado y, de todas formas, no parecería ser materia de la constitución.

Los párrafos 257 (transacciones fuera del presupuesto y creación de nuevos impuestos); 258 (la preparación del presupuesto por el poder ejecutivo y la aprobación por el congreso); 259 (pago de la deuda flotante); y el 260 (autorización adicional para gastar por razones de guerras y desastres nacionales) son demasiados específicos y se meten en temas que son mejor tratados por leyes presupuestarias. Por ejemplo, hay un requerimiento en el párrafo 257 que exige que si un impuesto va a ser eliminado tiene que ser substituido por otro o por un corte de gasto. Es deseable que se requiera legislación para eliminar un impuesto y que se sigan prácticas presupuestarias conservadoras que exijan que se tomen medidas para que la eliminación de un impuesto no tenga un impacto negativo en el resultado presupuestario. Pero también es fácil de vislumbrar situaciones que no se tenga que compensar necesariamente por la eliminación de un impuesto.

La **tercera parte del Artículo XVII** trata sobre el Tribunal de Cuentas y también es muy específico, entrando en temas que mejor son tratados en legislación ordinaria. Por ejemplo, el tema de la composición del Tribunal de Cuentas es tratado con un detalle exhaustivo. La definición de los términos de referencia es apropiada en términos generales pero tiene un error serio en mi opinión. El Tribunal de Cuentas se crea como un organismo independiente que responde solo a la ley que lo crea. De esta forma el Tribunal de Cuentas se puede convertir en un cuarto poder del gobierno lo cual no es práctico ya que el mismo Tribunal de Cuentas pudiera ser arbitrario en su actuación. Esto último ha ocurrido en países de América Latina que tienen este tipo de tribunal y donde se han creado crisis políticas debido a las actuaciones del tribunal. Sería más apropiado que el Tribunal de Cuentas reportara al congreso, que podría usar los informes del Tribunal de Cuentas para asegurarse que el poder ejecutivo no cometa impropiedades presupuestarias. Además, el poder ejecutivo debe tener su propia agencia de auditoría externa, independiente del Tribunal de Cuentas. Esto no está vislumbrado en la constitución de 1940.

La **cuarta parte del Artículo XVII**, que trata sobre la economía nacional, identifica cómo la función primordial del estado (párrafo 271) la promoción de la agricultura y de la industria; determina que parte de los beneficios de un aumento del valor de la propiedad por causa de acción del estado sea cedida al estado en una proporción a ser determinada por ley (párrafo 273); determina que la siembra y la cosecha azucarera sean reguladas por ley; y el párrafo 278 prohíbe la imposición de impuestos en materias primas que van a ser usadas en exportaciones manufactureras. En mi opinión, estos párrafos son innecesariamente intervencionistas. Este tipo de asuntos no deben formar parte de una constitución por razones económicas ya que bajo esas banderas se pueden cometer muchos errores en política económica (e.g., párrafos 271 y 278) o se prestan a abusos (párrafo 273).

Por último, el párrafo 280 estipula que los bancos comerciales tendrán representación en la junta directiva del banco central. Esta modalidad de junta directiva de un banco central no es la mejor para garantizar un banco central independiente cuyas funciones principales deben ser la protección del valor de la moneda y de las reservas internacionales del país.

INSTITUTION-BUILDING:
FINANCIAL SECTOR REFORM IN CUBA

Yosem E. Companys

Although financial reform is a difficult first step for achieving economic prosperity, the theoretical and empirical literature demonstrate that it is also a powerful tool for propelling economic growth. However, the reform process is also filled with a myriad of potential quagmires that can jeopardize both long-term and short-term economic development in transition economies.

In recent years, Cuba has begun to pursue financial reform in an effort to achieve economic revitalization. The Cuban government has made it clear that it will not abandon socialism, but it has realized that a greater level of decentralization is essential for its financial system to play a more modern and active role in ensuring efficiency in and adequate capital flows to the most productive sectors of its economy.[1] However, the complex nature of financial reform demonstrates that Cuba needs to answer several policy questions before embarking on this task: First, how does its tradition, history and culture fit into the financial reform equation? Second, what kind of financial system does it want to establish? How much private ownership is the government willing to allow? And third, how can the current institutional framework be used to carry out the financial reform program? What new institutions need to be established to support a strict regulatory and supervisory framework in the country?[2]

It is not clear how many of these questions Cuba has answered before embarking on financial reform.

---

1. "We don't deceive anyone. We are not offering our foreign partners a transition to capitalism. Cuba is and will continue to be a socialist country," Carlos Lage, Vice-President of the Council of State, as quoted in a January 27, 1995 address at the World Economic Forum in Davos, Switzerland. See Travieso-Díaz and Escobar (1995, p. 386). Previously, Lage (quoted in Mesa-Lago 1994, p. 65) has also stated that, "[w]e have no need to create a [new] economic model because the one we want and are defending is the socialist one." Before the National Assembly, at the end of 1993, Fidel Castro, President of the Council of State (quoted in Mesa-Lago 1994, p. 65), declared, "I have some convictions I will never resign: I do believe in socialism [and] the better I know capitalism, the more I love socialism...it has more solutions to our problems than capitalism... We must make socialism efficient and not destroy it... The steps backward we must take now should not discourage us because, tomorrow, we will be taking steps forward...this is nothing new...back in 1917, Lenin suggested [it]."

2. I will use the definition of regulation and supervision as stated by Castañeda and Montalván (1996, p. 6): "**Regulation** is the joint group of laws, rules and procedures established within a country to provide investors, depositors and financial institutions with transparent information regarding the economic risk in which they incur, while at the same time ensuring the security of the financial system and of any of its agents in order to prevent malpractice, corruption, fraud and embezzlement. The regulations include criteria and requirements for the entrance of new institutions wishing to operate in the system, accounting procedures and statements of financial condition, limits for the concentration of loans and limits to the exposure of individuals or related groups, minimum capital requirements, conditions of liquidity, collateral, classification and provisioning of reserves for liquidity and for financial losses from dilapidated assets, as well as the frequency and content of auditing. **Supervision** refers to the monitoring of and following-up on financial institutions by the respective authorities, as well as enforcing compliance to regulation and policy in order to prevent excessive risk taking and general incompetence."

Nevertheless, Cuba seems to be firmly riding on the financial reform bandwagon. However, its efforts have been gradual, emphasizing institution-building the most while paying the least attention to the development of new financial instruments.

Mehran et al (1996, p. 3) state that financial reform can be visualized as an economic triad consisting of institution-building, financial instrument development and price liberalization. They say:

> Analytically, it is useful to conceive financial sector development as a balanced development of the triangle of institutions, instruments and markets. The first element includes the establishment of banks and other financial institutions, as well as of infrastructure, such as the payments system. The instrument leg refers to the development of a range of financial instruments available to market participants to invest and trade. Development of the third component, markets, presupposes the free operation of the price mechanism across financial markets. Without price flexibility, financial markets do not mature either to support trade and investment or to conduct economic policy.

Given the realities of the Cuban financial system today and its early stages of development, this essay will focus on the first elements of financial reform: the institutional framework—including effective regulation and supervision—as well as existing or emerging financial infrastructure. Meanwhile, discussion of the other two arms of the triad will be limited since little change has occurred in these areas.

The essay will argue that the Cuban government needs to proceed faster in the development of financial institutions and their supporting regulatory and supervisory mechanisms in order to achieve an economic transformation within the economy: a transformation from classical socialism to what could be called a market-oriented socialist system, where the economy functions with a little of its own logic.[3] Under such a system, the development of a pro-competitive and efficient institutional framework is pivotal for achieving the emergence of a dynamic private sector. Furthermore, the essay will draw considerably from the experience of the recent reform economies—particularly from that of China and Eastern Europe—in order to apply the lessons from these countries to the Cuban case. By means of this analysis and through a thorough study of Cuba's existing institutional framework, the paper expects to prove that existing institutions are insufficient to revitalize Cuba's economic performance and to stimulate sustained growth and development. Thus, the essay encourages the Cuban government to continue reforming its financial system via a process that emphasizes further institutional reform and the development of new infrastructure and improved financial instruments. Although the third triad—price liberalization—will not be discussed in this essay, the author does understand that it is an important piece of the reform process and will recommend its gradual implementation, but only after a strong institutional framework has been firmly established.

THE ONSET OF FINANCIAL REFORM IN CUBA

The Banco Nacional de Cuba (BNC) continues to operate today as Cuba's chief central, commercial and development banking institution. As such, it is responsible for issuing credit and currency, financing capital investment, and handling all of the country's international transactions. In addition, the BNC has

---

3. I prefer the term "reform economy" to "transition economy", since the former refers to any economy engaging in a process of self-reform while the latter relates to an economy making a direct switch from one economic system to another. Carranza et al (1995, p. 7) allude to this fact: "In the context of a socialist economy, we must understand that economic reform is not just a change in the central planning mechanism, but rather modifications to the foundations of the system, which imply a change to new economic elements... The history of socialist economic reform demonstrates that the more radical experiments have been exceptional such as the so-called New Economic Mechanism (NEM), applied in Hungary in 1968, and more recently to the Vietnamese economic reform process. On the other hand, 'the deepening' of reform in countries like Hungary and Poland, towards the end of the 1980's, constituted an important challenge to the central planning mechanism, but their political evolution quickly placed these experiences on the road of the so-called 'post-communist' transitions rather than on that of the socialist reform economies." The author believes that Cuba falls in the latter category since it seems to be pursuing limited reform towards a system of "market-oriented socialism." Likewise, China and Vietnam would fall under the same category.

the authority to approve or reject all joint venture proposals, and is responsible for both overseas payments and the restructuring and renegotiation of Cuba's external debt (Triana Cordoví and Plasencia interviews; "Cuba Opens" 1996; EIU 1995-96, p. 30). However, with growing decentralization, it is becoming increasingly harder for the BNC to satisfy its growing demand for specialized financial services. As a result, Cuban scholars and leaders seem to agree that in order to satisfy the growing demand for these services, the government will need to formally institutionalize a two-tier banking system similar to those established by the economies of Eastern Europe, communist East Asia, and the former Soviet Union (Echevarría Vallejo (1996, p. 22; Soberón Valdés 1995, p. 8; Triana Cordoví and Plasencia interviews). This legal framework would clearly limit the role of the BNC's influence in the economy, as well as recognize the benefits that private-owned financial intermediation can bestow upon a developing economy.

Although between 1978 and 1984 the Cuban government had set the groundwork for financial sector reform, a period of economic retrenchment in later years had slowed down institution building progress. In fact, the BNC granted only two licenses to financial institutions in the decade that followed the passage of this law. However, growing decentralization in Cuba during the early 1990's has led to an increased emphasis on the establishment of new financial institutions, including the licensing of a new holding company—Grupo Nueva Banca, S.A. (GNB)—to provide specialized financial services to the emerging private sector. In addition, the government has laid the groundwork for the establishment of the Banco Central de Cuba (Central Bank of Cuba, CBC). Although the CBC is still pending approval from the Council of State, it is expected to become operational sometime in 1997. Finally, in a limited effort to engage in directed development, the government will reorganize the BNC into two policy

banks—the Banco Agro-Industrial y de Comercio (BAIC) and a second bank keeping the same name. The Cuban government's principal objective with the reform is to better access foreign capital in order to provide loans for the prefinancing and financing of large-scale agricultural and industrial ventures on the island (Triana Cordoví interview). The BPA, the BAIC and the BNC will remain as independent banks, but similar to other existing financial institutions, will be subjected to the CBC's direct regulation and supervision. These institutions are discussed in greater detail below.

Banco Popular de Ahorro (BPA)

Although the BPA was created as an independent retail bank during the 1978 to 1984 economic reform period, it still maintains a departmental character and is subject to the BNC's direct control. Officially, the BPA's purpose is to promote savings by collecting deposits, carry out day-to-day banking transactions for Cuban citizens, issue credit to private individuals at commercial terms, and act as the government's accident and fire hazard insurance provider (BNC 1995, p. 28; Soberón Valdés 1995, p. 12). However, from 1983 up to the early 1990's, the bank was relatively backwards, lacking the financial infrastructure required to perform many of these transactions. Thus, recent reform will seek to modernize the bank so that it may gradually emerge from its private banking role and become a universal commercial bank in the near future (BNC 1995, p. 28; Soberón Valdés 1995, p. 12). Moreover, during the economic crisis of the early 1990's, the BPA became an extremely important tool for extracting excess circulation from the economy since 60% of the island's deposits at the time were in this bank. Its success has helped the BPA expand into a network of 275 branches throughout the island.[4]

Banco Financiero Internacional, S.A. (BFI)

Founded in November 1984, the BFI is a financial institution operating solely with convertible currency in commercial banking activities. Its goal is that of

---

4. There is some dispute over the exact figures. According to Babún (1996, p. 191), the BPA has already established close to 275 branches throughout the country. Other sources indicate that the number is 249. Thus, to be conservative, I assume that the "true" figure is between 225 and 275, depending on what is defined as a "branch." BNC (1995, p. 28); Soberón Valdés (1995, p. 12).

providing financial advice, preparing prefinancing arrangements on large-scale foreign investment, as well as raising capital with which to finance joint venture projects. At the same time, the BFI offers conventional banking services such as term deposits, current accounts and letters of credit (Babún 1996, p. 192). Finally, the bank also provides exchange services at market rates.[5] The BFI has grown significantly since it was established in 1984, and now possesses a correspondent relationship with 200 banks worldwide, as well as a total branch network of 14 or 15 throughout the island.[6] According to the island's policy-makers, this institution has become the "bank of choice" for financing joint ventures in Cuba.[7]

Cuba's Future Policy-Lenders

According to Mehran et al (1996, p. 14), "the separation of policy lending from commercial lending has become a critical issue" in economic development since it can serve as a transitory step for the commercialization of state-owned banks. In countries like China and Cuba, however, the legislation does not clearly distinguish or separate commercial lending from policy lending. Nevertheless, the success of public financial institutions (e.g., government-owned development banks) in countries like Japan, Korea, and Taiwan demonstrate that such institutions are vital towards the success of a directed credit policy.[8] Most of these countries have been more successful than others in the world because of their emphasis on institution building, bank supervision and regulation. In China, where the government initially relied on the formation and subsequent development of specialized banks, it is too early to evaluate their per-

formance (Mehran et al 1996, p. 4). Mehran et al (1996, p. 14) define policy lending in any of the following five ways:

1. *Power and Infrastructure Investment Loans.* These are financially sound investments, but are generally risky in the short-term as a result of their size and long-term repayment periods.

2. *Fixed Asset Loans.* These are provided to state-owned firms to enhance their technological capability.

3. *Rural Development Loans.* These loans are granted for the development of agriculture, rural areas, and for the alleviation of poverty. These loans usually entail significant risk.

4. *Working Capital Loans.* These type of loans are generally risky in reform economies due to the relatively large numbers of loss-making enterprises.

5. *Subsidized Sector Loans.* Any loan granted to a subsidized economic sector such as health or education.

In the case of Cuba, as in China, there is no strict definition for a policy lending bank as of yet and may encompass any of the definitions set out by Mehran et al. In addition, no real policy lending institution exists in Cuba at the time. However, the Cuban government expects to create some soon when it transforms the BNC's remaining 214 branches and agencies into the Banco Agro-Industrial y de Comercio (BAIC). In addition, the BNC will continue to oper-

5. "The bank provides exchange services among freely convertible currencies, at the rates prescribed by the market at large, most notably the NYSE and other applicable exchange-rate authorities." Babún (1996, p. 192).

6. BNC (1995) provides contradictory information on the BFI. On page 28, it states that the BFI possesses 14 branches, while on page 29 it says that the BFI possesses 15. In any case, the Cuban government foresees the opening of 7 more offices in the near future.

7. Triana Cordoví and Plasencia interviews. Babún (1996) states that in Cuba "the two dominant banks are the Banco Financiero Internacional (BFI), which commenced operations in 1984, and the Banco Internacional de Comercio (BIC), which opened in 1994."

8. During the early stages of Japan's industrialization drive, for instance, the Ministry of International Trade and Industry (MITI)—which controlled foreign exchange and exerted considerable influence over the banking sector's capital financing—pursued a strategy of "picking the winners," and thus, provided preferential interest rates, low-cost financing and government-guaranteed loans to "winning" industries. Prestowitz (1988). Similarly, in South Korea, the government created development institutions which exerted direct control over available credit and planned investment in strategic economic sectors. Datta-Chaudhuri (1990). In both cases, however, the government disciplined producers by setting minimum production and profitability requirements in order to prevent moral hazard problems and to ensure the economy's efficient growth and development.

ate in a much more limited and streamlined fashion. Although the BAIC's organizational structure has yet to be revealed publicly, the institution will be expected to serve in the near future as a policy lender in government projects (BNC 1995, p. 28; EIU 1996-97, p. 32). However, the Cuban government expects the BAIC to naturally evolve into the leading provider of commercial banking services on the island (BNC 1995, p. 28; Plasencia interview). Meanwhile, the BNC will maintain its current responsibility of financing the country's existing external debt. In addition, the bank will be expected to provide state-owned enterprises with the essential capital to develop strategic sectors of Cuba's nascent modern economy (BNC 1995, p. 28).

Despite the success of such institutions in several East Asian economies, Mehran et al (1996, p. 14) caution other countries considering implementing similar institutions with which to finance their economic development for two reasons. First, unrestrained policy lending can prove extremely inflationary. Second, governments usually find it difficult to regulate the commercialization of the state-owned banks while simultaneously supervising policy lending activities. Nevertheless, the success of the East Asian model demonstrates that policy lending—under the right set of conditions—can assist a country to dramatically bolster its economic growth and development.

Grupo Nueva Banca, S.A. (GNB)

In an attempt to expand the number of financial services available to foreign investors and liberalized firms on the island, the Cuban government has established the GNB, a holding company for a network of recently-created financial institutions. Although its creation has paved the way for the establishment of an independent national banking system, however, the GNB remains controlled by the Cuban government. Currently, the GNB has a majority stake in each of the recently created institutions, which are—in the order of their founding—BICSA, FINSA, CADECA, Banco de Inversiones, S.A., and Banco Metropolitano, S.A. (EIU 1996-97, p. 32). These institutions—as well as their holding company—shall be under the regulatory authority of

the CBC, which will be responsible for their supervision ("Cuba Opens" 1996; Plasencia interview). The section that follows outlines the major aspects of each of these institutions, and explains the role they play or will play in Cuba's economic development:

Banco Internacional de Comercio, S.A. (BICSA): Similar to BFI, BICSA was established in January 1994 with a share capital of $10 million as a merchant bank operating in Cuban pesos and in convertible currency. Its objective is to secure financing arrangements with foreign lenders for Cuban institutions and joint ventures. However, it also offers a wide range of conventional banking services, such as term deposits, current accounts, letters of credit and exchange transfers (Babún 1996, p. 192). Due to similarity in scope of operation, BICSA is already considered a dominant player in the industry and is currently BFI's most direct competitor (Triana Cordoví, Plasencia and Mulet interviews; Soberón Valdés 1995, p. 12; BNC 1996, p. 28).

Financiera Nacional, S.A. (FINSA): In April 1995, the Cuban government established FINSA as an export-import bank. Its purpose since then has been to provide working capital and short-term finance on a fee basis to Cuban enterprises. In addition, this institution provides financial advice and lends support in arranging lines of credit as well as leasing and factoring agreements. All its operations are undertaken in convertible currency (Triana Cordoví and Plasencia interviews; Soberón Valdés 1995, p. 12; BNC 1995, p. 28; BNC 1996, p. 28).

Casas de Cambio, S.A. (CADECA): CADECA was established in October 1995 as a network of currency exchange houses. Currently, CADECA consists of 16 to 20 foreign exchange houses whose principal clients are the nearly one million tourists who visit Cuba each year, the 72 state-owned enterprises that already operate in foreign currency, and private citizens who have access to foreign exchange.[9] In addition, by setting prices based on supply and demand, CADECA has helped to diminish black market activity in foreign currency transactions (Echevarría Vallejo 1996, p. 24; Soberón Valdés 1995, p. 12; BNC 1995, p. 28; Plasencia interview).

Banco de Inversiones, S.A.: Banco de Inversiones, S.A. was created in August 1996 to provide financial advice and investment banking services to both national and foreign enterprises. The bank's main objective is that of attracting and fostering investment in Cuba. As a result, the investment bank will seek to establish itself rather quickly in the international capital markets in order to carry out highly-specialized transactions, such as brokerage, derivatives and debt-to-equity swaps. By gaining access to the international markets, the Cuban government hopes the bank can secure capital for medium- and long-term development finance operations. In addition, the bank may help deal with enterprise and financial restructuring by providing the technical expertise and advice needed for this to occur (BNC 1995, p. 29; BNC 1996, p. 29; U.S.-Cuba Business Council 1996, p. 8; Plasencia interview).

Banco Metropolitano, S.A.: Banco Metropolitano, S.A. was founded in June 1996 in the Vedado neighborhood of La Habana. The bank was created as a result of a divestiture of the BNC's international branch. Its purpose is to provide banking, stock brokerage services and financial advice to foreign companies, personnel and diplomatic corps residing in Cuba. The bank performs its financial transactions—such as checks and deposits—in both national and convertible currency ("Cuba Opens" 1996; BNC 1996, pp. 28-29; Plasencia interview; Babún 1996, p. 193).

The GNB-owned institutions continue to operate within largely segmented financial markets; nevertheless, their profitability has improved enormously during their short time of existence. For instance, BIC-SA has grown to become a major competitor of the

BFI with a superb average return on equity of 127.8% and an average return on total assets of 9.41% (BICSA 1996, p. 15). Whether this success continues will depend largely on the successful development of the economy. As was mentioned earlier, the simultaneous success of enterprise reform and continued liberalization will be critical to these efforts.

Although economic deepening has helped to recover positive profit margins in some firms, 69% of the country's enterprises as of May 1994 were operating with losses (Carranza Valdés et al 1995, p. 28; Mesa-Lago 1994, p. 50). The extent to which this problem has been solved is unknown since most available research within and outside of Cuba provides relatively little information on this regard. Thus, the problem of bad loan portfolios in Cuba will not be addressed in this paper. However, considering the common traits and characteristics shared by pre-1989 Cuba with the reform economies in Eastern Europe, the former Soviet Union and communist East Asia, one can safely assume that bad loan portfolios continue to constitute a widespread problem within the island's financial sector. As a result, it is fair to say that the development of the GNB's institutions, as well as that of other financial institutions within the country, will largely depend on their ability to effectively deal with this problem.[10]

Banco Central de Cuba (CBC)

By divesting its commercial branches, the Cuban government expects to transform the BNC into a truly independent central bank. Although the CBC's future institutional role in the economy has yet to be defined, the existence of an independent central bank

---

9. BNC (1996, p. 28) states that there are 14 CADECA offices in Ciudad de la Habana, 1 in Varadero and 1 in Santiago de Cuba. However, another source (EIU 1996-97) states that there are 20 such offices throughout the country. The recent opening of offices in Holguín and Villa Clara may account for the difference.

10. An example of another group that has actively participated in Cuba's financial sector development is Grupo ACEMEX. Founded in 1974 as a group of financial companies that specialize in shipping and financial activities, Grupo ACEMEX's scope of activities has gradually been expanded to meet the growing demands of the recovering economy. Among the services provided by Grupo ACEMEX's financing institutions are providing credit for prefinancing and short-term financing, engaging in factoring and leasing agreements, as well as managing the financial activities of the Group's private companies. Since its creation, "the ACEMEX Group has arranged credits for its clients amounting to $612.0 million, of which approximately $89.0 million were directly provided by its financing institution." Brochure for Acemex Management Company n.d., pp. 1, 16.

will help to vastly improve the resource allocation process on the island.

Based on the financial sector's current demands, most experts agree that the CBC's role will be that of overseeing the monetary flows within the liberalized sectors of the economy in order to stifle its inflationary pressures, stabilize the exchange rate, and help curtail the government's fiscal deficit (Soberón Valdés 1995, p. 9). To ensure the fulfillment of this objective, the Cuban government is expected to empower the CBC with various financial instruments—such as interest rate manipulation—with which to stabilize the economy.

However, the Cuban government is conscious that it will need to instill confidence in the financial system in order to succeed. For instance, to establish its credibility in the public eye, the CBC will need to engage in strict supervision of the enterprise and financial sectors. In this manner, the CBC can minimize the risk of widespread insolvency, while strengthening the economy's deposit base currently at nearly 5.4 million accounts. (Echevarría Vallejo 1996, p. 23; Soberón Valdés 1995, p. 8). As such, the CBC is expected to emerge as the regulatory and supervisory authority of the commercial sector. However, to ensure enforcement of the CBC's policies, the Cuban government will need to confer upon it broad powers such as that of removing bank managers based on negligence, lack of compliance or lack of preparation. Strict enforcement of the CBC's policies would prevent the resurgence of capital inadequacy and preempt the need of taking over the bank's management (Roe 1995, p. 17). As a result, the CBC can help to create a more efficient supervisory and regulatory mechanism that in turn can expand and improve financial intermediation, lead to greater financial deepening in the economy, instill confidence in the payments system, and in turn, pro-

mote economic development on the island (Soberón Valdés 1995, p. 9).

Foreign Financial Institutions in Cuba

By prohibiting foreign financial institutions from operating branches on the island, the Cuban government has greatly inhibited their activities in the financial sector. As of June 1994, foreign banks have only been allowed to establish representative offices in Cuba, with the purpose of identifying prospective investors to whom they can offer specialized financial advice regarding new investment opportunities. Thus, a local presence entitles foreign banks faster access to the Cuban market, which in turn allows them to discern high-return investment opportunities particularly in the growing joint venture market (EIU 1996-97, p. 33). The opening of a local office is a strategic decision for a foreign bank since it provides new business contacts and prepares the groundwork for the eventual establishment of a fully-operational branch on the island.[11]

To date, approximately thirteen banks have taken advantage of this opportunity (BNC 1996, p. 29). For example, even before 1994, a prominent European financial institution engaged in trade finance had established offices in Cuba via subsidiaries to perform very limited financial services ("Cuba's Pre-Revolution Banking" 1995). In 1994, International Nederladen Bank (ING Bank of Holland) became the first foreign bank to open two offices in Havana: first, a subsidiary by the same name, and later a 50% owned subsidiary—the Netherlands Caribbean Bank, N.V. from Curaçao—to perform trade finance as well as other banking services.[12] On November 20, 1995, licenses were granted to the Société Générale de France and to Banco Sabadell from Spain (Soberón Valdés 1995, p. 11). Some other banks which have established representative offices in Cuba are Havana International Bank Ltd., the National Bank of Canada, Fransabank S.A.L. of Lebanon, Banco Nacional

---

11. Although the Cuban government rules out the possibility for foreign banks to open representative branches on the island in the near future, many foreign banks are optimistic that it will happen soon. Plasencia interview; Soberón Valdés (1995, p. 10); "Cuba's Pre-Revolution Banking" 1995.

12. Netherlands Caribbean Bank is 50% owned by ING Bank of Holland and 50% owned by Grupo Acemex, a Cuban shipping company. "Cuba's Pre-Revolution Banking" 1995.

de Comercio Exterior from México, and the Banco Exterior de España and Banco Bilbao de Vizcaya (BBV), both from Spain (BNC 1996, p. 28). Other foreign commercial, investment and merchant banks have expressed interest in opening representative offices on the island.[13]

With scarce credit available to Cuba as a result of the US trade embargo, many foreign financial institutions have begun providing private financing in exchange for conventional bank loans. Some examples are the Guernsey-based Beta Gran Caribe—which will provide capital for trade financing and leasing facilities—as well as the Cayman Islands-based International Financial and Investment Holdings Company Ltd.—which according to a company announcement possesses "substantial expertise in the financial services sector in Cuba" ("New Financing" 1996). Although these foreign institutions have a small capital base and are offering very limited amounts of financing, their presence is helping to fill the credit gap the Cuban financial sector is currently facing. In addition, some of these institutions, as is the case with the Curaçao-based offshore bank created by ING Bank of Holland along with ACEMEX Group's financing institution has guaranteed the Cuban government's access to other banking services such as fund transfers, deposits, currency exchange, letters of credit as well as banking and financial advice.[14] As a Canadian lawyer with business interests in Cuba said recently: "When banks are pulling back and government-supported credits are drying up, offshore merchant banking is increasingly a growth area providing one of the only avenues available for for-

eigners doing business in Cuba" ("New Financing" 1996).

With the passage of Decree Law No. 165 on June 6, 1996, the possibility for foreign banks to open fully operational branches on the island became very real. This law allowed the establishment of a series of special economic zones (SEZ) in Mariel, Cienfuegos and La Habana.[15] Among its concessions, the law authorized foreign banks to freely operate in these trade zones subject to their respective countries' laws and regulations (Rúa del Llano 1996, p. 7; Plasencia interview; U.S.-Cuba Business Council 1996, p. 8). However, the government has been slow at implementing the law partly due to the complex bureaucracy in the country and partly because the trade embargo obstructs corporations which operate in Cuba from exporting their goods and services to the United States.

Nevertheless, it is unknown at this point to what extent this law will actually help to liberalize Cuba's financial sector. In China, for instance, the SEZs gave freedom to branches of foreign banks to offer specialized financial services that could attract foreign investors. Although these were not allowed to conduct business throughout the whole country, the branches of foreign banks in China were allowed to set interest rates according to the market conditions of the given region in which they operated. In addition, the Chinese government also allowed ITICs to proliferate in these areas. These institutions, as was mentioned earlier, helped to access international funds to promote further foreign investment and economic growth in the country (Mehran et al 1996, pp. 9, 11). Such

---

13. Recently, however, foreign banks have begun to shy away from the opportunity of establishing representative offices in Cuba. Despite reassurances from the BNC, foreign banks are concerned with Titles I and II of the LIBERTAD Act. Title I prohibits US entities from financing transactions that involve expropriated property. Title II goes further and states that those who engage in a commercial activity that utilizes or benefits from expropriated property will be subject to legal action in the United States. A Canadian banking official said that he interpreted the bill to mean that "a bank supplying services to a trafficker could also be vulnerable to litigation." U.S.-Cuba Business Council (1996, p. 7); *Intervención* (1996, p. 8).

14. Brochure for Acemex Management Company, Ltd., n.d., p. 16.

15. Although Special Economic Zones (SEZ) vary from country to country depending on its legal framework or the economic sectors which they encompass, they are in general defined as geographically determined, tax exempt areas where the government of the host country grants special concessions to selected export-oriented enterprises. These concessions can be in the form of taxes, tariffs, labor regulations and the like. As stated in Caves (1996, pp. 220-221: "[t]he government can thereby relax onerous regulations that it does not wish to repeal outright." See also Mañalich Gálvez (1996, p. 94).

broad financial and economic freedoms led many to proclaim that "[p]arts of China, like the coastal areas, can take the road of free-market authoritarianism."[16]

However, one can safely assume that even when fully operational, the SEZs in Cuba will not be considered such an integral piece for the success of financial reform as they have been in China because of the difference in size between both countries (Mehran et al 1996, pp. 9, 11).[17] The SEZs in Cuba will more likely generate results similar to those achieved by smaller communist nations such as Vietnam. Nevertheless, by allowing the establishment of foreign banks in the SEZs, Cuba will be able to attract greater foreign investment and prepare the local financial sector for the future entrance of these banks in a fully competitive financial environment.

Future Reform

As the last section has demonstrated, the institutional aspects of Cuba's financial sector reform are still in their incipient stages. However, as a result of the crisis of the early 1990s, the Cuban government has been able to establish a blueprint for future reform that will nonetheless allow the financial sector greater freedom at promoting economic growth and development than the monobank system that had preceded it. However, Cuba's financial sector is still afflicted by such grave problems as insufficient capitalization, little or no public confidence and support, excessive segmentation, poor regulation and supervision, a high proportion of bad loans, poor sav-

ings instruments, a lack of modern techniques and technology, and inexperienced managers. Thus, if the Cuban government hopes to successfully carry out its economic reform agenda, it will require further institutional change. Coupled with a stronger institutional framework, the establishment of a strict supervisory and enforcement mechanism will help to create an efficient financial sector and a budding enterprise sector with which to prevent economic stagnation and massive social dislocation. Achieving this objective will require the Cuban government to improve its financial infrastructure while implementing further reform in a gradual fashion, taking into account the growing private sector's financial needs. In this way, Cuba may ultimately avoid the fate of the other reform economies, which as Jeffrey Sachs has stated, "succumbed to an extreme financial crisis during the reform period."[18]

RECENT EFFORT AND PROGRESS

One way in which the government has attempted to improve the resource allocation process is through the passage of laws that seek full financial transparency.[19] As McKinnon (1991) has demonstrated, the establishment of a national tax system is a requirement for economic decentralization since tax revenue helps to fill the deficit created by the simultaneous income reduction caused by reduced profit confiscation. Decree Law No. 73, for example, established a national taxation system, which has required many state-owned enterprises to submit income statements for taxation purposes (Pérez interview; Carranza et al

16. Antonio Chiang, a Taiwanese magazine publisher, as quoted in "Chinese Communism" (1996, p A6).

17. Although officials at the BNC have stated otherwise, Carlos Lage has repeatedly stated that Cuba will not allow foreign banks to operate on the island. In a recent speech to the Council of Ministers, Lage (1996) said the following: "This [financial sector reform] is not a matter of bringing in foreign banks to operate in Cuba; there are branches of foreign banks in Cuba which are involved in a sort of promotion of investments or promotion of financing. But the operation of banks in Cuba is the terrain, the province of the Cuban state, which with the restructuring uses, in some cases, private forms of organization, while the ownership is absolutely in the hands of the state." Also, Plasencia interview.

18. Sachs, as quoted in Castañeda and Montalván (1996, p. 1).

19. An area of dispute in the economic study of Cuba is the degree to which the island government has achieved financial transparency. Babún (1996) states: "Unconfirmed reports suggest that BIC may be quite large, with income of about $100 million on revenue of about $2 billion. However, these banks are private companies; hence, it is not possible to obtain financial information on them." As the author will show in this section, Babún is correct in noting that the degree of financial transparency in Cuba is limited. However, recent reform is helping to overcome this problem. BICSA's 1995 Annual Report—audited by the prestigious accounting firm Ernst & Young—states that the firms' total operating income for 1995 was $13 million, growing from $4 million the year before. The bank's total assets amount to approximately $156 million. BICSA (1996).

1995, p. 47). However, the reform stopped short of founding an independent auditing agency, which could have objectively examined the accuracy of these statements. Instead, the Ministry of Finance and Prices has been made the de facto tax collection agency, although it is unknown to what extent they actually ensure compliance with present tax law.

Based on the information I obtained from senior managers of Cuban enterprises, little or no on-site supervision takes place in Cuba. On the contrary, the Ministry of Finance and Prices depends almost solely on bank and enterprise disclosure. Considering the Eastern European experience with bank disclosure, such a practice could open the door to false accounting and tax evasion.[20] For example, in Cuba, failing state enterprises are allowed to deduct their losses, which sometimes perpetuates their poor financial condition despite the continuance of government support via preferential credit and subsidies (Pérez interview). In addition, most Cuban tax examiners do not have adequate loan appraisal capabilities. To the Cuban government's credit, the Ministry of Finance and Prices is painstakingly trying to increase their capabilities so that they may more adequately fulfill their tax collection duties.

Furthermore, the Cuban government claims it is currently improving the country's so-called "financial fundamentals," such as instituting uniform accounting guidelines and procedures. To prove this fact, 1995 was the first year in which Cuba provided the international community with an annual income statement on the BNC's financial strength. For the reader's review, a copy of the income statement has been attached. In addition, the Ministry of Finance and Prices has been put in charge of training financial sector personnel in order to guarantee that they possess the technical skills necessary to administer credit and manage economic information (Soberón Valdés 1995, p. 10). As Francisco Soberón Valdés—

the President of the BNC—recently told foreign investors, the problem is as follows:

> We are in the complex process of redefining our entire enterprise sector. Our system of payment orders is deficient, and does not allow a dynamic flow of financial transfers across all sectors of the economy. Our entrepreneurial accounting procedures are also deficient and we are undertaking a huge effort of instituting a uniform and accurate accounting system based on recognized and established international standards. We are also in the process of restructuring and automating our banking system (*Intervención* 1996).

Based on Calvo et al. (1993, p. 10), these changes should constitute a positive first step towards the better macroeconomic management of the economy since they will help Cuban banks to objectively assess both the borrower's creditworthiness and the investment risk behind a given venture. In addition, the reform will reduce the unnecessary burden currently placed upon foreign investors of having to reconcile Cuba's system of payment orders with Western-style banking. These reforms are expected to create a banking system that operates under globally recognized accounting rules and procedures (Triana Cordoví interview).

Increased financial transparency, however, will also require stronger supervision and enforcement mechanisms to guarantee compliance with the law. For example, one may assume that the successful implementation of Cuba's auditing mechanisms and tax structure will largely depend on ensuring the compliance of the newly independent financial institutions and state enterprises managed by the Ministry of the Armed Forces (MINFAR, from its Spanish name, *Ministerio de las Fuerzas Armadas Revolucionarias*), since their influence and power in Cuban economic activity is significant. As such, securing the MINFAR's compliance with this system would probably assure the compliance of non-MINFAR managed state enterprises as well.[21] Although the enforcement

---

20. Eastern Europe's reform experience has demonstrated that weak accounting rules and poor supervision disguise the quality of loan portfolios, which allows enterprises to have apparent profits and pay taxes despite their true situation. Roe (1995, pp. 15, 18, 26).

21. For an extensive review of the MINFAR's influence over Cuba's economic activities, see Pérez-López (1995a), Mesa-Lago (1994) and Amuchastegui (1995, p. 5).

of rules is obstructed by the inexperience of the regulators who created them, compliance can also be achieved by granting strong enforcement powers to the CBC's supervisors to remove managers and to allow fresh capital injections, as well as by using external auditors to complement the Ministry of Finance and Prices internal staff (Roe 1995, p 38).

Improving Financial Sector Efficiency

In Cuba, most equipment used for effecting financial transactions is Eastern European or Soviet for which replacement parts are no longer available. As a result, Cuba's financial sector now possesses a backwards and outdated infrastructure, and is in desperate need of modernization. However, the Cuban government has already begun to pursue a massive effort towards modernizing its financial infrastructure. As Soberón Valdés (1995, p. 12) has indicated: "We are undertaking a massive effort to modernize the operational efficiency of our banking system by installing computers and by linking its branches via an electronic network of data transfer. This effort is taking place at a rapid pace." In addition, since banking personnel lack the skills to engage in specialized financial transactions, the Cuban government is seeking to improve the professional and technical capacity of its staff (Triana Cordoví interview).

Currently, Cuba's banking staff is well-qualified by international standards. Most of the NBS's employees have accounting and economics degrees. However, with exception of the recent-graduates that studied under the special University of Havana-sponsored MBA program, most lack the knowledge and necessary skills to provide specialized financial services for a market-oriented socialist system.[22] Thus, Cuba faces the arduous task of training and developing the managers, bankers, accountants, auditors and financial analysts of the future; those that will effectively manage the complex activities of the NBS and who will be responsible for ensuring its long-term credibility.[23] At year end 1995, 85 specialists had been trained. By 1996, the government expects to have trained 350 more (BNC 1996, p. 27). However, how do you change an educated population's mindset quickly enough to absorb the sudden changes occurring as a result of the country's current financial reform? As the Cuban government is learning, this transformation is a difficult one since it includes changing the Cuban people's attitude towards risk and the acceptance of responsibility. Such are the challenges the legacy of central planning is posing to Cuba's economic development.[24]

Besides seeking to improve its organizational capacity, the BNC is also attempting to improve the speed of its payments system via an ambitious modernization program (Echevarría Vallejo 1996, p. 17; Mehran et al 1996, pp. 38-39). Lage (1996) stated in a speech to the Council of Ministers that by the end of

---

22. "To change the mind-set, Havana University has launched an MBA program. Its first 50-member class, which graduated in February, was chosen from 800 applicants. The courses range from accounting to foreign trade. But there are ideological ironies. Gripes one MBA student: 'I am studying about investing capital when Cubans cannot invest in Cuba. If you are a foreigner abroad, you can invest. But if you are a Cuban, no." DeGeorge (1997, p. 50).

23. According to Pérez-López (1994, p. 295), "[w]hat thirty-odd years of socialism have done, however, is to erode market-oriented skills of managers, accountants, auditors, etc." Travieso-Díaz and Escobar (1995) argue that Cuba is ill-prepared to handle the growing demands of a decentralized economy, lacking even the legal professionals required to regulate it. While Luis Salas reports that there were only 700 professional judges in Cuba in 1991, Czechoslovakia—a country of comparable population—had about 1,600 at the start of their transition in 1989. Thus, according to Travieso-Díaz and Escobar (1985, p. 384), currently the "[l]aw practice in Cuba is constrained not only by the inadequate number and qualifications of the legal professionals, but also by the judiciary's lack of independence, the prohibition against the private practice of law, and the expectation that defense counsel in criminal cases will put the interests of the state before those of their clients."

24. Soberón Valdés (1995, p. 10) said that the island currently lacks the skilled personnel to perform specialized financial services, but that the Cuban people have the educational base and the willingness to learn quickly. Also Triana Cordoví and Plasencia interviews. However, Murrell and Wang dispute his optimism; as quoted in Pérez-López (1994, p. 295) they say that: "The ability to function efficiently within a particular set of market institutions comes about as a result of market activity rather than being endowed or learned quickly through formal education. Therefore the lack of market institutions under communism leads to a dearth of both market-oriented human skills and organizations that can function in the market environment."

440

June 1996, the Cuban government expected to have automated 303 banking units and have installed 5,000 computers in the country. According to the government, the BPA's 500 branches are currently being modernized as well (EIU 1996-97, p. 32). The government expected to have modernized 71% of its branches by year end 1996, and to have installed 8,000 computers in all of its 700 banking branches throughout the island by year end 1997. The results of this program are yet to be seen (Lage 1996; BNC 1996, p. 27). However, the need for modernization is evident from the photographs on the following page, which demonstrate that while banks that cater to foreign investors such as BICSA and the Banco Metropolitano, S.A. already have state-of-the art equipment, the BNC and the BPA continue to perform its financial transactions in a manual fashion.[25]

Given the difficulties in purchasing U.S.-manufactured equipment and after surveying several branches of the BNC in Pinar del Río and Havana, I am skeptical that the government's modernization program is pursuing as quickly as it claims. Nevertheless, upon completing the modernization drive, the Cuban government should have finished installing an extensive banking network via computerized links from its branches to a national data center in Havana (BNC 1996, p. 27). This change by itself will result in dramatic increases in the efficiency of financial transactions versus what had existed during the pre-reform monobank dominated system.

STRENGTHENING THE FINANCIAL SECTOR TO FUEL FUTURE ECONOMIC GROWTH

As we have seen, the Cuban government is tackling important challenges by undertaking financial sector reform while engaging in a difficult economic transformation. In the financial realm, the government's new economic development strategy has sought to reform the monobank system in order to create a more efficient and financially strong banking system that can effectively channel credit to the most strategically important and productive sectors of the econ-

omy. To accomplish this goal, the Cuban government will continue engaging in budgetary restraint by further reducing subsidies, streamlining enterprises, and providing a more active role for the financial sector to attract capital and foster investment on the island (Soberón Valdés 1995, p. 8; Echevarría Vallejo 1996, p. 18). Therefore, the Cuban government will need to continue deregulating and decentralizing the economy, while enforcing tighter rules to govern its banks and state-owned enterprises.

To fulfill this objective, it is imperative that the Cuban government establish a strong CBC as quickly as possible so that it can effectively implement monetary policy in order to facilitate the macroeconomic regulation of the economy (Soberón Valdés 1995, p. 7). As such, its focus will need to be achieving capital adequacy, fully establishing uniform accounting guidelines and procedures, limiting large exposure in the banking system's loan portfolios, and ensuring the effectiveness of its supervisory and enforcement powers, while inhibiting itself from intervening in situations of enterprise or bank failure (Roe 1995, p. 16). Considering the challenges that lie ahead, I have included some institutional recommendations which the Cuban government should consider while engaging in financial sector reform:

- *Demonopolization.* The Cuban government has already partially demonopolized its tourism sector. Nevertheless, most of the country's other strategic economic sectors continue to be dominated by one or two large industrial interests. This situation needs to be changed to allow greater competition within these sectors, including the banking sector (Dunning 1993, pp. 336-339).

- *A legal framework which prohibits state banks from lending to state enterprises.* State enterprises should gradually become subjected to a system of self-financing, while the emerging private sector

---

25. "Cuba Opens" (1996). In addition, BICSA is already connected to an international consortia of firms founded in 1973 called the Society for Worldwide Inter-bank Financial Telecommunication (SWIFT), which has established an international clearing system for the banking sector. See Dunning (1993, p. 271); Mulet interview.

should be given greater access to available credit (McKinnon 1991).

- *Establishment and subsequent enforcement of laws that prevent predatory pricing and unfair competition.* This legal framework and its compliance will just help to encourage the development of the independent NBS and the emerging private sector, which will in turn allow the economic reform process to take root.

- *The formation of private capital markets similar to the agropecuario markets, wherein private enterprises and cooperatives can access credit.* This policy will help to create independent financial intermediaries as well as small private commercial banks. However, strict regulation and supervision will be required to prevent the formation of credit cartels and intimidation via high interest payments. These markets should provide a sorting mechanism for "young" private enterprises as well as a method by which the Cuban government can better understand the true size of real interest rates in the economy.

- *Finally, to increase credit access in the economy as a whole, further financial reform needs to eradicate the segmentation of household savings.* By doing so, implementation of a personal income tax will help to reduce consumption levels and increase government revenue for investment.[26]

However, these recommendations by themselves will not improve the resource allocation process nor the flow of financial transactions within the Cuban economy. Instead, these recommendations will require a strong, but flexible regulatory and supervisory framework that can quickly adapt to the changing realities

of the emerging private sector. In this way, a reform government can exercise sound judgment to correct market failures as they occur, in order to maximize long-term economic output and profitability.

Moreover, institution-building becomes one of the most important steps for achieving such development, since without it there can be no regulatory mechanism with which to safeguard the emerging private sector. This process, however, needs to reflect the country's culture and history, as well as its already existing institutional framework. It is very convenient for skeptics to recommend that Cuba privatize all of its state property to foreign interests and adopt a Western-style institutional framework with which to regulate the nascent market-economy.[27] Their argument usually relies on the economic efficiency achieved by such market economies as Japan and the United States.[28] However, the reality is that these global economic powers did not build their institutional frameworks overnight, but rather did so over many decades, creating new regulations depending on the particular set of internal and external circumstances that prevailed at the time. Thus, Cuba needs to continue pursuing a strategy of gradual financial sector reform, whereby as the private market grows and strengthens, the institutional framework changes to accommodate to the needs of its economic actors.

According to BICSA (1996, p. 10), signs of further reform continue emerging. The Cuban government, for the first time since the onset of the Revolution, has a firm commitment to decentralizing financial activity to help continue fostering the country's economic growth and development. Besides the creation of the CBC in the next few months, the Cuban government plans to continue creating new specialized

26. Pérez-López (1994, p. 296). For a more in-depth discussion of pro-competitive policies, see Dunning (1993).

27. Pérez-López (1994, p. 296) argues that "a thriving market economy does not emerge spontaneously as a result of 'letting capitalism happen': it requires a special set of institutional arrangements that most countries in the world do not have. Moreover, he argues (p. 299) that "[c]are must be exercised not do away with the noxious socialist institutions until replacement institutions that support and nurture the market are in place."

28. The author makes reference to the works of Carlos Fernández, Raúl M. Shelton, Fernando A. Capablanca and Jorge Salazar-Carrillo, all of which seem to advocate a radical eradication of existing socialist institutions and their subsequent replacement with Western-style institutional frameworks. All of these works were included in *Cuba in Transition—Volume 4* (Washington: Association for the Study of the Cuban Economy, 1994).

financial institutions and licensing more foreign financial entities to establish representative offices on the island. This further decentralization—coupled with lessened market segmentation—will expand Cuba's current institutional environment and lead to greater competition and efficiency in the economy as a whole. Finally, the sector's continued modernization will help establish a strong regulatory and supervisory framework that ensures fair and efficient credit allocation as well as promotes productive economic activities throughout the island.

REFERENCES

Amuchastegui, Domingo. "More Banking Changes." *Cuba News* (November 1996), p. 5.

Babún, Teo. *Business Guide to Cuba*. Miami: The Miami Herald Publishing Company, 1996.

Banco Internacional de Comercio, S.A. (BICSA) *1995 Annual Report to its Shareholders*. La Habana, 1996.

Banco Nacional de Cuba (BNC). *Informe Económico, 1994*. La Habana, August 1995.

Banco Nacional de Cuba (BNC). *Informe Económico, 1995*. La Habana, August 1996.

Brochure for Acemex Management Company, Ltd. No date.

Brochure for Banco Internacional de Comercio, S.A. No date.

Calvo, Guillermo A., Kumar, Manmohan S., Borensztein, Eduardo, and Masson, Paul R. *Financial Sector Reforms and Exchange Arrangements in Eastern Europe*. Washington: International Monetary Fund, 1993.

Carranza Valdés, Julio, Gutiérrez Urdaneta, Luis; and Monreal González, Pedro. *Cuba: La restructuración de la economía. Una propuesta para el debate*. La Habana: Editorial de Ciencias Sociales, 1995.

Castañeda, Rolando H. and Montalván, George Plinio. "Cuba: Estabilización sin recesión ni choque monetario." *Cuba in Transition—Volume 6*. Washington: Association for the Study of the Cuban Economy, 1996.

Caves, Richard. *Multinational Enterprises and Economic Analysis*. Cambridge: Cambridge University Press, 1996.

"Chinese Communism's Secret Aim: Capitalism." *New York Times* (October 18, 1996), pp. A1, A6.

"Cuba Opens New Bank." *Cuba News* (June 1996), p. 5.

"Cuba's Pre-Revolution Banking System." *The Cuba Report* 3:9 (February 1995).

Datta-Chaudhuri, Mrinal. "Market Failure and Government Failure." *Journal of Economic Perspectives* 4:3 (Summer 1996).

DeGeorge, Gail. "A Touch of Capitalism: Castro Tries to Keep the Wolf at Bay through Careful Injections of Private Enterprise." *Business Week* (March 17, 1997), pp. 50-52.

Dunning, John H. *The Globalization of Business*. London: Routledge, 1993.

Echevarría Vallejo, Oscar U. "Elementos para un rediseño del sistema financiero." *Economía Cubana: Boletín Informativo* 27 (July/August/September 1996), pp. 16-31.

Economist Intelligence Unit (EIU). *EIU Country Profile: Cuba (1995-96)*. London: The Economist Intelligence Unit Limited, 1995.

Economist Intelligence Unit (EIU). *EIU Country Profile: Cuba (1996-97)*. London: The Economist Intelligence Unit Limited, 1996.

Fernández, María del Carmen. Private interview held at ING Bank of Holland, La Habana, Cuba, February 11, 1997.

Intervención del Compañero Francisco Soberón Valdés, Ministro-Presidente del Banco Nacional de Cuba ante el Consejo Empresarial Mexicano para Asuntos Internacionales (CEMAI). Ciudad de México, D.F., 9 de mayo de 1996.

Lage, Carlos. *Speech Given by Carlos Lage, Secretary of the Executive Committee of the Council of Ministers, During the 5th Plenum of the Central Committee of the Communist Party of Cuba, Held in the Palace of the Revolution, on March 23, 1996, Centennial Year of Antonio Maceo's Death in Combat.* 1996.

Mañalich Gálvez, Isis. "Cuba y las zonas económicas especiales en el mundo." *Cuba: Investigación Económica* 2:2 (abril-junio 1996), pp. 93-130.

McKinnon, Ronald I. "Financial Control in the Transition from Classical Socialism to a Market Economy." *Journal of Economic Perspectives* 5:4 (Fall 1991), pp. 107-122.

Mehran, Hassanali; Quintyn, Marc; Nordman, Tom; Laurens, Bernard. *Monetary and Exchange System Reforms in China: An Experiment in Gradualism.* Washington: International Monetary Fund, 1996.

Mesa-Lago, Carmelo. *Are Economic Reforms Propelling Cuba to the Market?* Coral Gables: North-South Center, University of Miami, 1994.

Mulet, Abelardo. Associate Director, Banco Internacional de Comercio, S.A. (BICSA). Private interview at BICSA's headquarters, La Habana, Cuba, February 18, 1997.

"New Financing Source." *Cuba News* (October 1996), p. 5.

Pérez, Víctor. President, Interaudit. Private interview held at Interaudit, La Habana, Cuba, February 18, 1997.

Pérez-López, Jorge F. "Economic and Financial Institutions to Support the Market." *Cuba in Transition—Volume 4*. Washington: Association for the Study of the Cuban Economy, 1994. Vol. 4, 1994.

Pérez-López, Jorge F. *Cuba's Second Economy: From Behind the Scenes to Center Stage.* New Brunswick: Transaction Publishers, 1995a.

Pérez-López, Jorge F. "Cuba's Socialist Economy Toward the Mid-1990s." *The Journal of Communist Studies and Transition Politics* 11:2 (June 1995b).

Pérez-López, Jorge F. "Odd Couples: Joint Ventures Between Foreign Capitalists and Cuban Socialists." *The North-South Agenda*, paper 6. Coral Gables: North-South Center, University of Miami, November 1995c.

Plasencia, Sergio. Vice-President, Banco Nacional de Cuba (BNC). Private interview held at the BNC, La Habana, Cuba, July 4, 1996.

Prestowitz, Jr., Clyde V. *Trading Places.* New York: Basic Books, Inc., 1988.

Roe, Alan. *Financial Sector Reform in Transitional Socialist Economies.* Washington: International Bank for Reconstruction and Development, 1995.

Rúa del Llano, Manuel. "Foreign Investment in Cuba." Paper prepared for delivery at the workshop "Foreign Investment in Cuba: Past, Present, and Future," sponsored by Shaw, Pittman, Potts & Trowbridge and Oceana Publications, Washington, D.C., January 26, 1996.

Soberón Valdés, Francisco. "Reformas en la Banca." *Cuba al Día* (November 1995).

Travieso-Díaz, Matías F., and Escobar, Steven R. "Cuba's Transition to a Free-Market Democracy: A Survey of Required Changes to Laws and Legal Institutions," *Duke Journal of Comparative & International Law* 5:2 (1995).

Triana Cordoví, Juan. Director, Centro de Estudios de la Economía Cubana (CEEC). Private interview at the CEEC, La Habana, Cuba, July 1, 1996.

U.S.-Cuba Business Council. *Cuba Bulletin* 33 (July 1, 1996).

AVOIDING MANAGERIAL HUMAN CAPITAL LOSS IN TRANSITION II SUGAR FACTORIES

Willard W. Radell

In the decade after 1958, hundreds of thousands of Cubans left Cuba. Among those who exited were many highly skilled workers who had managed Cuba's 161 sugar factories. Although the physical capital left behind remained intact, the human capital embodied in each of the emigrants was lost to the Cuban sugar industry forever.

Revolutionary leaders found it easy to label those who left as *gusanos,* without whom Cuba would be better off. By the 1970s Cuban government leaders had recognized the loss implicit in the emigration of so many skilled workers, but continued to view the economic value of factory managers as somewhat suspect, as if the managers were getting away with something by being administrators.

Cuba's transition to socialism and its brief period of relatively free post-revolutionary emigration offers a unique opportunity to gauge the impact of a loss of human capital on industrial productivity. Cuba is an unusually rich laboratory for serious research on industrial managerial productivity because there are few countries that have had revolutions, periods of free emigration, and adequate data on industrial management and performance at the factory level of a major industry. The exodus of over 90% of Cuban sugar factory managers within a decade of the revolution set the stage for a very large scale "natural" experiment on the value of retaining experienced managers.

If postrevolutionary sugar factories that retained experienced managers operated significantly more effi-

ciently than those that lost all their pre-revolutionary managers, then it can be concluded that managerial experience does have measurable value. In this study it is found that those mills that had pre-revolutionary managerial "holdovers" operated more efficiently than those that lost all experienced managers. The implication is that by losing managerial talent in the sugar mills Cuba suffered a massive capital disinvestment that hobbled economic development in the early stages of Transition I—the transition from capitalism to socialism. Now, as Cuba is poised for Transition II—the transition from socialism to marketism (if not capitalism), a crucial question is will the Transition II leadership make the same mistake by driving out the old managers who are tainted by service to the old regime?

EMIGRATION OF MANAGERIAL CAPITAL

If human capital is defined as the "stock of skills and productive knowledge embodied in people" (Eatwell, 1987, p. 682), then management could be viewed as a specialized form of human capital that could be defined as the stock of experience in how to organize production to achieve predictable outcomes. While many human capital studies have focused on the value of formal education and systematic on-the-job training, Arrow has identified ordinary experience on the job, *learning by doing,* as a significant contributor to productivity (Arrow, 1962). The value of that kind of experience has been empirically measured by Lazonick and Brush, Lundberg, and others, and is known as *the Horndal effect* (Lazonick and Brush, 1985).

In most studies of the Horndal effect, stable enterprises with no significant changes in personnel, technology or capital are compared to others that make significant changes. Factories that are left alone and whose owners do not "invest" in greater productivity, are found to have annual rates of labor productivity growth on the order of two percent. Somehow, without new investment or radical restructuring, workers and managers find ways to do their jobs better, even if left alone. Usually, with Horndal and human capital studies, researchers are comparing baseline productivity of factories to which no physical capital has been added to others with greater rates of productivity growth stemming from changes in either the human or inanimate capital stock. What makes a study of Cuban sugar factories different is that all factories suffered a massive loss of human capital between 1958 and 1968. Thus, mills that lost every manager in a decade are being compared to others that retained a few of their experienced managers.

When managers exit an enterprise, they take with them their embodied skills, knowledge, and experience. Most organizations are "learning organizations," in that skills are accumulated as personnel gain more experience in organizing and executing production. At the margin, managers and workers continually learn to make improvements to solve problems like "tramp iron" in the cane feed stream (Germinsky, 1989). Perversely, Cuba's sugar factories became "unlearning organizations," between 1958 and 1968, as managers and other workers joined the exodus that would decimate Cuba's population.

For Cuba, as a whole, the population loss to emigration was over 10% between 1960 and 1995, with the emigration wave of the 1960s weighted disproportionately toward professional workers as "many tens of thousands of university professionals, administrators and technicians, [were] forever lost to contributing toward Cuba's advance (Romeu, p. 297). According to Pedraza (1995, p. 314),

> This initial exodus over-represented the professional, managerial, and middle classes, 31 percent, as well as the clerical and sales workers, 33 percent. Likewise,

the educational level of these refugees was remarkably high.

Of Cuban men who came to the United States from 1960 and 1964, about 64% had "managerial, ... professional, technical, sales, or administrative" occupational classifications, while between 1965 and 1971 about 45% declared "middle class" job status. Female Cuban émigrés also had high numbers in the "white collar" and technical categories. (Pedraza, 1995 p. 325).

Although the aggregate effect of Cuba's loss of managerial and entrepreneurial capital and the "... consequent loss of productive and investment capabilities (Sanguinetty 1995, p. 22)" is very great, it is very difficult to quantify. For most of the migrants, the data do not exist that would tell how their choice to exit Cuba affected productivity, costs, and performance in the enterprises they left behind. Fortunately, in the case of Cuba's sugar factories, there are data that allow us to infer the negative impact of losing managers by detecting the positive effect reaped from the few managers who had not left by 1966.

MEASURING MANAGERIAL EXODUS

Researchers of the Cuban economy, both inside and outside Cuba, are afflicted with a paucity of good data. The sugar industry is no exception, as the Cuban government routinely suppresses release of operating data that are commonly available for sugar factories in most of the world. Fortunately, in 1972, the Cuban government released **Manual Azucarero de Cuba 1971** for the first time since its general publication was discontinued in 1963. The **Manual Azucarero de Cuba, 1971** published data for the 1966 and 1967 zafras, mill by mill, allowing comparison to the prerevolutionary operating experience of individual factories. For this study, the Cuban 1966 and 1967 data were compared to the prerevolutionary years of 1956 and 1957. Factory "mastheads" from the 1958 **Gilmore Manual Azucarero de Cuba** (Meyers, 1958) were compared to factory mastheads from the 1971 **Manual** to draw conclusions on the magnitude of the exodus and to discover any obvious changes in factory management. Changes in management titles were noted and a count was made of how many managers from 1957 were still working in each factory in 1967.

Table 1. Managers Listed For Factory, "Elena" (Post-Revolutionary, "Juan M. Quijano")

Pre-Revolutionary		Post-revolutionary	
Pre-Rev. Title	Name of Manager	Name of Manager	Post-Rev. Title
Presidente	Gerardo Fundora Fernández	Juan Bellocq Miranda	Administrador
Vice-Presidente	Carlos Fundora Fernández		
Tesorero-Administrador	C. P. Jorge Fundora Fernández		
Jefe de Oficina	Réne D. Duque Acevedo	Réne D. Duque Acevedo	Jefe de Oficina
Jefe de Fabricación	Clemente Pérez Rodríguez	Arístides Casas Rendón	Jefe de Fabricación
Jefe de Maquinaria	Manuel Prego	Manuel Prego	Jefe de Maquinaria
Jefe Químico	José Antonio Arana García		
		Juan Hernández Fundora	Jefe de Laboratorio
Jefe de Campos	Bonifacio Carmona Ferrera		
		Silvio Falcón Domínguez	Jefe de Agronomía
Electricista	Antonio Ramírez		

A striking result of the examination of factory mastheads was the absence of "executive" personnel in the revolutionary period. Consistent with the belief of the early revolutionary politicians that top-level managers were parasites, most top executive positions were eliminated. Thus, all executive and financial managerial positions (Personal Ejecutivo) listed in pre-revolutionary factory rosters were absent in 1967. For example, Table 1 shows the pre- and post-revolutionary positions listed for the small pre-revolutionary factory, *Elena (Juan M. Quijano)*. Table 1 reflects the socialist take-over of the factory in that all the executive positions were eliminated, leaving only the administrative positions (Personal de Administración). It can also be seen that of the nine managers working at *Elena* before the revolution, only two, Réne D. Duque Acevedo and Manuel Prego, were still there in 1967, when the mill became known as *Juan M. Quijano*. For all Cuba's sugar factories only 69 managers from the pre-revolutionary era remained as managers in 1967. The magnitude of "Transition I" can be assessed by considering that, of the approximately 2000 named pre-revolutionary executives and administrators, only about 70 remained after a decade of revolution.

Statistical Results

The next step in the study was to see if there was a statistically significant link between an indicator of individual factory performance and the number of managers retained (holdovers). The measure selected (one of many possible) was lost time, defined as the percentage of time during the *zafra* that a mill was not grinding. Lost time increases as industrial and agricultural sugar operations break down or as coordination between the two fails. Lost time increases as production becomes more intermittent, a condition that usually leads to higher unit costs. As Payne (1982, p. 151) notes:

> Steady operation is the critical factor in maintaining steam usage efficiency. A reliable cane supply must be available so that the processing rate, once set, can be held with minimum fluctuation. A stop-and-go situation means excess and shortage of steam.

Lost time was predicted in a model using the number of managers retained, factory size (measured as daily cane grinding capacity), lost time in a pre-revolutionary year, grinding days in a pre-revolutionary year, and grinding days in the year for which the lost time was being measured. The rationale for including pre-revolutionary lost time as an independent variable was to capture geographic and mill idiosyncrasies that would have nothing to do with the number of managers lost or retained. For the same reason, pre-revolutionary grinding days were included in the model. Results from the regression analysis can be seen in the equation at the bottom of the next page for the 147 mills for which all the necessary data were available.

The model reveals that for each experienced pre-revolutionary manager retained, a sugar factory could expect to have a 1.5 percentage point reduction in lost time. Although extrapolation is somewhat tenuous, for the average mill that lost about ten managers, the imputed increase in lost time from a failure to retain experienced managers is on the order of magnitude of fifteen percentage points. The implicitly higher production costs associated with that excess lost time would have made many mills produce sugar at unit costs above the prices at which the sugar could be sold (even at preferential prices).

Another interesting feature of the model is the high tolerance values. Tolerance is the percentage of the variation in an independent variable that cannot be "explained" by variation in all of the other independent variables. With the simplest interpretation, the high tolerance values tell us that there is no serious multicollinearity in the model. The high tolerance value on HOLD shows that the number of managers who stayed had nothing to do with the size of the factory, how long the harvest was before or after the revolution, or how much lost time was characteristic at that mill before the revolution. Thus, it cannot be said either that only the weaker or the stronger of the managers left Cuba between 1957 and 1967. The high tolerance values on prerevolutionary lost time and mill capacity show that size of factory was not related to lost time before the revolution, but the significance of the capacity variable in the model shows that size was related to lost time in Transition I. Since the tolerance values are high for DAG56 and DAG66, it is clear that with almost identical physical

capital in 1966 as in 1956, there was no correlation between days of operation in the two years. The reality behind that curious result must have given sugar industry managers many somber thoughts as they prepared to attempt a ten million ton harvest in 1970.

Summary of Lessons from the Regression Analysis

A number of conclusions can be derived from the analysis of the factory data before and under the Cuban revolution.

1. The Cuban Revolution "caused" increases in lost time in the sugar factories. In the aggregate, lost time in 1966-67 was 10.6 percentage points higher than lost time in 1956-57. Although some of that excess lost time must have been caused by parts and fuel shortages, political turbulence, and misguided economic policy, much of it can be attributed to the loss of experienced managers.

2. Mills with greater lost time before the revolution were likely also to have greater than average lost time eight years into the revolution.

3. Retention did not vary significantly from province to province. Separation of the data by province showed that the holdovers were distributed evenly across all provinces.

4. Retention did not vary significantly by size of mill. Managers of small sugar factories were no more or less likely to stay in Cuba than their counterparts in the huge mills.

$$AVLT6667 = 24.359 - 1.552(HOLD) + .001(CAP) + .057(DAG66) + .449(AVLT5657) - .203(DAG56)$$

(tail prob.)	(.000)	(.029)	(.000)	(.003)	(.000)	(.000)
(tolerance)		.997	.882	.880	.995	.995

R^2 = .425   n = 147   SEE = 6.004

where,

AVLT =	Average (mean) percentage lost time for 1966 and 1967
HOLD =	Number of pre-revolutionary factory managers listed for the 1967 harvest
CAP =	Rated daily cane input capacity (metric tons)
DAG66 =	Days from beginning to end of harvest in 1966
AVLT5657 =	Average percentage lost time in 1956 and 1957
DAG56 =	Days from beginning to end of harvest in 1956

Table 2. Mean Capacities of Cuba's Best and Worst Performing Sugar Factories

Date of Published List	Mean Capacity Best List	Mean Capacity Worst List	t-test: Difference of Means	Probability Difference is Random
19 February 1991	2599	7622	3.4	.007
14 March 1991	2346	6658	3.9	.004
5 April 1991	2622	7527	3.8	.004
8 May 1991	2438	7206	3.7	.004
6 June 1991	2634	6315	3.4	.007
17 September 1991	2530	6984	4.8	.000

Source: Lists: *Granma* (dates listed); Capacities: Ahlfeld, (1990, pp. C49-C51). Note that the mill capacities used from F. O. Licht differ somewhat from those given by Pérez-López (1991, pp. 241-245).

5. While mill capacity did not correlate with lost time before the revolution, it did after the revolution.

6. Larger factories had disproportionately more lost time after the revolution.

7. Losses to the Cuban economy from emigration of managers and technicians were significant.

8. Individual managers' productivity was significant enough to be detectable, measurable, and significant.

SOCIALISM, MILL SIZE, MANAGERIAL RETENTION, AND TRANSITION

One of the most persistent problems in Cuba's revolutionary sugar factories has been the chronic underperformance of the largest sugar factories. Over three revolutionary decades there have been frequent complaints in the Cuban press about the poor performance of the largest mills ranging in size from about 7,000 metric tons of daily capacity at *Héctor Molina Riano* (*Gómez Mena*) and *Grito de Yara* to the relative giants above 10,000 tons like *Brasil* (*Jaronú*) and *Antonio Guiteras* (*Delicias*). Cuba's smallest mills in the provinces of La Habana, Pinar del Río, Matanzas, Villa Clara, Granma, Guantánamo, and Cienfuegos were the subjects of very few complaints over the revolutionary years. A study of the 1984 harvest campaign found that the largest mills were over-represented in published lists of poorly performing mills and that the smallest mills were over-represented in published lists of the best performing sugar mills (Radell, 1987).

The pattern of systemic problems with larger sugar factories persisted into the eve of the collapse of the CMEA. Table 2 shows results from lists of 10 best and 10 worst factories reported in the newspaper, *Granma*. Average capacities of mills on the lists were computed and a t-test was done on the differences of mean values. Table 2 shows the probabilities that the differences in mill capacities, on the order of 4500 metric tons for the year (September 17, 1991 entry), were random. A study by the author (not used here) did the same analysis for Louisiana sugar factories and found no systematic difference between the industry leaders and the industry laggards. For Cuba it can be asserted with better than 99% certainty that the larger mills have performed more poorly than the smaller mills.

Persistent inferior performance of larger mills is a Transition II management issue because in the transition period resources cannot be directed equally to all sugar factories if optimal results are expected. It would be tempting to close down most of the smallest sugar factories under the assumption that these mills are sub-optimal by international standards (Alonso and Lago, 1993, p. 180). While scaling up or closing sub-optimal plants must be part of the long range planning for Transition II, that will work better after five to seven years of stabilization of the industry. The problem with the strategy of closing sub-optimal mills early in Transition II is that, although outside Cuba the smallest mills tend to have the highest unit costs, in today's Cuba, the smallest mills are likely to have the lowest unit costs. That condition will persist well into Transition II and must be planned for. A strategy that closes the smallest mills using international economies of scale arguments will not succeed in reducing Cuba's aggregate sugar production unit costs until the later stages of Transition II.

The reasons why Cuba cannot quickly approach international sugar factory sizes have much to do with the nature of the revolutionary economic system. Under socialism, Cuban managers were forced to respond to many constraints that distorted their own resource allocation decisions. To respond to the fixed input allocations characteristic of socialism without the variable price structure characteristic of capitalism, Cuban factory managers had to get very good at managing shortages, lacks, gaps, and (ironically) surpluses of some inputs. The fixed price system created strong incentives for employees to misappropriate factory property and this situation also had to be managed. The broad statement of Sanguinetty (1995, p. 22) that "the more centralized the government is, the worse the information glut it creates and the more serious become the deviations from a market system," applies precisely to the Cuban sugar industry. The information required and resources available were just barely adequate to keep small sugar factories operating efficiently. Managers of the smallest mills needed to be able to work around myriad irrational allocation errors and surprises. The small sizes of their mills made it possible for them to manage the logistical nightmare that is a *zafra* without abundant resource inputs.

The managers of large factories had no chance to practice the craft of "good" management. For them, the best that could be done was to mitigate the inefficiency. For large factories under socialism, the normal symbiotic link between agricultural and industrial operations turned against efficient operation. When that link between field and factory is poorly managed and coordinated, the basis for "...general efficiency of the agro-industrial activity" is eroded (Alvarez and Peña Castellanos, 1995, p. 361). Large mills must use cane cut farther from the mill to operate and must, therefore, have more investment in transportation infrastructure to operate efficiently. At any point after the beginning of the harvest, a large mill will have more cane in transit than will a smaller

mill. Since cane loses usable sugar content as soon as it is cut or burned, more transit time means more recoverable sugar is lost before the cane ever arrives at the mill. Processing old cane means less crystalline sugar and more invert sugars and molasses. To manage a harvest with a minimum of lost time in a large Cuban sugar factory would have required a mix of cane varieties not available, planted in a cycle that was not feasible, harvested on a time schedule that could not be met, and delivered to the mill in a steady flow just sufficient to operate the plant at its rated hourly capacity. Managers of large factories in Cuba did not have sufficient logistical infrastructure to make their processing problems soluble under the existing economic structure.

Florida sugar factories can only be efficient at their very large size by having sufficient infrastructure to run the field and factory operations in strict lockstep. To duplicate the degree of planning built into the huge Florida sugar factories like Clewiston, Bryant, and Okeelanta, Cuba's factories will have to operate with a longer time horizon. Since optimum performance requires that future cane planting, gestation, ratooning, harvesting and processing must be planned with a long view of five years or more, Transition II will be an extraordinarily long process for larger mills. While the large mills are getting back to rational operations, it may be wise to put the early emphasis on the smaller mills. Eventually, those smaller mills will be combined with other mills or phased out. But during transition, the best course may be to stabilize the industry first among the small and then later among the large mills. When Transition II begins, the experienced small mill managers will be able to solve production problems with more modest increments in inputs. Managers of large mills will also have good ideas of reasonable Transition II paths, but those paths will be more expensive and will require the Cuban people to wait longer before there are any tangible results.

VISUALIZING THE RELATIONSHIP BETWEEN SIZE AND MANAGERIAL RETENTION

Revolution during Transition I radically altered the fundamental industrial structure of the Cuban sugar industry. That restructuring can be visualized by comparing three-dimensional wireframe models fitted to data on lost time, factory size, and grinding days for the years 1956 and 1966. In a sense the visual models are "industry prints" analogous to finger prints that identify individuals. Industry prints for successive years for the same industry usually have similar patterns. Stochastic shocks to the industry will distort the pattern visibly and offer clues as to how the managers adjusted theiroperations to adapt to the shock.

Figure 1 shows a characteristic prerevolutionary pattern for the year 1956, using a wireframe fitted to actual Cuban data by the distance-weighted scatterplot smoothing technique. Most mills cluster between 60 and 110 grinding days, with mill sizes between 1800 and 8000 metric tons of daily capacity, and with lost time between 2 and 12 percent. The flat open pattern over most of the geometric figure indicates that large mills did not tend to do worse than smaller mills and that mills could operate within a broad

range of operating days without experiencing excessive lost time.

Figure 2 shows how radically different the situation was in 1966, after years of revolution and neglect of the sugar industry. The smallest factories clearly did better and the large mills did visibly worse. Although a trough of relatively superior performance for each size class can be seen between 50 and 100 days, no mill with capacity greater than 8000 tons did better than the worst mill with capacity of less than 3000 tons. Moreover, the 5 percent lost time that was typical of mills before the revolution (Figure 1) was only achieved by some of the smallest mills after the revolution (Figure 2).

Figure 3 represents the factories in 1967 that had lost all their managers. The wireframe has the same basic structure as the 1966 data for all mills (Figure 2), except that it has been fitted only to mills under 11,000 tons because results for one mill were missing in 1967. The pattern shows that lost time increased with mill size over a broad range of days of grinding.

Figure 1. Lost Time, Factory Size, and Grinding Days, 1956

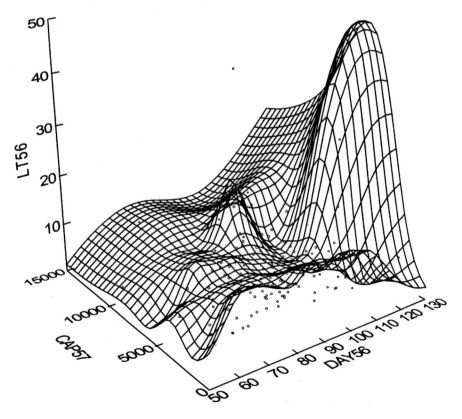

Figure 2. Lost Time, Factory Size, and Grinding Days, 1966

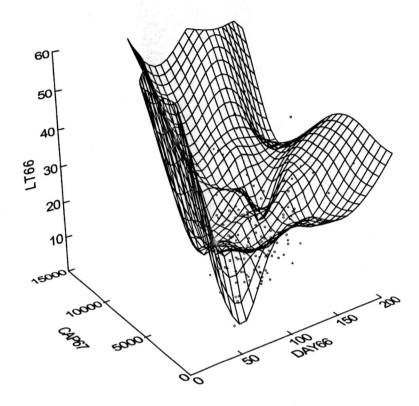

Figure 3. Lost Time, Factory Size, and Grinding Days, 1967
Mills Losing all Experienced Managers

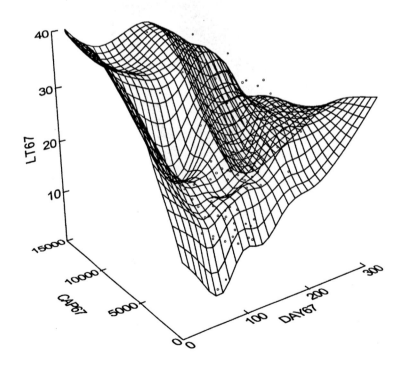

Figure 4. Lost Time, Factory Size, and Grinding Days, 1967
Mills Retaining Some Experienced Managers

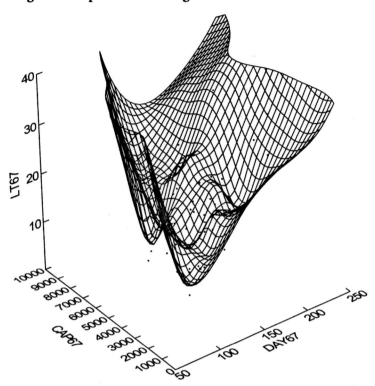

That implies that with all experienced managers gone, only the small mills were able to perform with acceptable levels of lost time. The general openness of the structure implies that, without any experienced managers, size of mill was a more important determinant of factory performance than was the number of grinding days.

Figure 4 represents the factories in 1967 that retained some pre-revolutionary managers. The cloud of small mills below the wireframe indicates that many small mills were doing well in ways that could not be explained by variation in mill size and days of grinding. A deep, well-defined trough of optimality between about 90 and 150 days of grinding indicates that experienced managers were able to reduce the "penalty" on large mill performance.

What were experienced managers doing in 1967 that their less experienced counterparts were not doing? Comparing Figures 3 and 4, it is clear that experienced managers knew better what day operations should begin on and did a better job of coordinating the agricultural and industrial operations. Although

Figures 3 and 4 offer no proof, it is likely that mills with experienced managers did not have the flat pattern of pre-revolutionary Cuban mills because politicians did not allow managers of the revolutionary period to set a terminal date on the harvest.

A rule of thumb in the international sugar industry is that grinding should begin on the first day that the marginal cost of produced sugar drops below the anticipated price, and should continue until the last day before marginal cost rises above price (Guise and Ryland, 1969). The logic behind the algorithm is that beginning too early has the mill grinding cane with too low a sugar content, while continuing too late in the season has the mill grinding cane with too great a content of invert sugars. Either grinding too early or too late will increase the unit cost of the high-value crystalline sugarthat is the primary output. When politicians decide how much cane will be planted and cut, even experienced managers will have trouble avoiding poor mill performance. Figure 4 indicates that experienced managers avoided the tendency for large mills to do worse than smaller mills under a socialist regime by more carefully controlling the beginning and end of the harvest. Small mills could more easily be "engineered" to operate well—large mills at the center of more complex enterprises required more experienced judgment to accompany the "engineering." Even though Cuban policy of the mid-1960s viewed marginal cost as a capitalist artifact irrelevant to socialist production, the experienced managers must have had marginal costs in mind when they planned the harvests. Contrasting Figure 4 to Figures 1 and 3, graphically shows that one of the biggest penalties Cuba paid for forcing its factory managers out of the country was the tendency for larger mills to do worse than smaller mills.

AVOIDING TRANSITION I MISTAKES IN TRANSITION II

The success of Transition II will, in part, be dependent on avoiding the mistakes of Transition I. Among the biggest mistakes that the emerging Cuban leadership could make would be hostility toward the managers who are now operating Cuba's sugar factories. Associating the existing managers with socialism and encouraging them to seek other employment will delay successful transition and increase transition costs by impairing efficiency. A listing of some of the mistakes in Cuba's last transition should point the new Cuban leaders away from policies that caused the extraordinarily high loss of experienced managers in the early years of Transition I.

1. Financial and executive management positions were eliminated.

2. Value of management was disparaged. Managers were viewed as parasites (Mesa-Lago, 1971, p. 513). Managers were viewed as getting away with something in their comfortable offices. Transition I politicians believed that only the masses toiled and did "real" work.

3. Management pay differentials were eliminated in the name of equity (Mesa-Lago, 1981, p. 150).

4. All pay scales were compressed. "In some cases, managers earned less than unskilled subordinates" (Roca, 1986, p. 165).

5. The principle of unity of command was undermined as politicians made economic decisions (Bernardo, 1971, pp. 202-204). Roca's wonderful description of this was "microeconomic intromission" (Roca, 1986, p. 174).

6. Costs, prices, and money were disparaged as capitalist artifacts (Roca, 1981, p. 87).

7. Monetary incentives were disparaged. Moral incentives were believed to yield better results than monetary rewards.

8. The sugar industry was viewed as suspect because of its association with hard and seasonal work, slavery, and exploitation (*sucraphobia*) (Pérez-López, 1991, p. 75).

9. Sugar factories were used as employment providers rather than as economic organizations. The result, according to Fidel Castro (1973) was that "...if we asked a lot of sugar mill workers how many workers there were in the mill under capitalism and how many there are now, it could be demonstrated that we use many more men than the capitalists, to run the mills less efficiently than the capitalists" (Hagelberg, 1974, p. 161). This practice has continued to the present day (Blanco, 1996, p. 259).

10. Viewed as "dead wood" compared to politically correct revolutionaries, experienced managerswere expected to become politicians (Guevara in Tablada, 1989, p. 213).

11. Che Guevara's system of budgetary finance and its successors subjected managers to accountability without authority to make decisions (Roca, 1986, p. 160).

12. Che Guevara's *consolidado* system eliminated enterprise autonomy, substituting national management for local management (Brunner, 1977, p. 31; Edquist, 1985, p. 31; Guevara in Tablada, 1989, p. 114).

13. Political operatives were given jobs that required technical and managerial skill without consultation with managers. That practice continues in Cuba (Catañeda and Montalván, 1994, p. 192).

Mesa-Lago uses the phrase "replacing technocrats with loyal but incompetent revolutionaries" (Mesa-Lago, 1981, pp. 29, 35). See also Bernardo, 1971, pp. 202-204.

14. Repression made "voice" to improve factory practice a more costly path than "exit" (Hirschman, 1970, p. 40).

Auty (1972, p. 12) suggests that "... differences in managerial ability ...[are] ...responsible for sizeable differences in costs" in the sugar industry. The ample evidence of the worth of competent, experienced management should guide Transition II Cuba to reform radically the training, evaluation, compensation, and retention of managers.

REFERENCES

Ahlfeld, Helmut, ed., *F. O. Lichts World Sugar Sweetener Yearbook 1990*, Ratzeburg, F. O. Licht, 1990.

Alonso, José F. and Lago, Armando. "A First Approximation of the Foreign Assistance Requirements of a Democratic Cuba," *Cuba In Transition—Volume 3*, Washington, ASCE, 1993, pp. 168-219.

Alvarez, José and Peña Castellanos, Lázaro, "The Transformation of the State Extensive Growth Model in Cuba's Sugarcane Agriculture," *Cuba In Transition—Volume 5*, Washington, ASCE, 1995, pp. 348-362.

Arrow, Kenneth, "The Economics of Learning By Doing," *Review of Economic Studies,* Vol. 29 (1962), pp. 155-173.

Auty, R. M., "The Sugar Industry of Demarara, 1930-65: Some Problems in Identifying Scale Economies," *Journal of Tropical Geography*, 34 (June 1972).

Bernardo, Roberto M., "Managing and Financing the Firm," in *Revolutionary Change in Cuba*, Carmelo Mesa-Lago editor, University of Pittsburgh Press, 1971.

Blanco, Alfredo. "The 1995-1996 Sugar Zafra: Results and Implications—The Machinery Sector," In *Cuba in Transition—Volume 6*, Washington, ASCE, 1996, pp. 253-259.

Brunner, Heinrich *Cuban Sugar Policy from 1963 to 1970*, Pittsburgh, University of Pittsburgh Press, 1977.

Catañeda, Rolando H. and Montalván, George Plinio, "Cuba 1990-1994: Political Intransigence versus Economic Reform," in *Cuba In Transition—Volume 4*, Washington, ASCE, 1994, pp. 181-208.

Eatwell, John, ed. *The New Palgrave: A Dictionary of Economics*, New York, Stockton Press, 1987.

Edquist, Charles, *Capitalism, Socialism, and Technology: a Comparative Study of Cuba and Jamaica*, London, Zed Books, 1985.

Germinsky, Robert A., "Louisiana Cane Mill Solves Tramp Iron Problem," *Sugar y Azúcar* (June 1989).

Guevara, Ernesto "Che," quoted in Carlos Tablada, *Economics and Politics in the Transition to Socialism*, Sydney, Pathfinder, 1989.

Guise, J. W. B. and Ryland, G. J. "Production Scheduling and Allocation: A Normative Decision Model for Sugar Milling," *Australian Journal of Agricultural Economics*, (June 1969), pp. 8-25.

Hagelberg, G. B., *The Caribbean Sugar Industries*, Antilles Research Program, Yale University, 1974.

Hirschman, A. O., *Exit, Voice, and Loyalty: Responses to Decline in Firms, Organizations and States*, Cambridge, Harvard University Press, 1970.

Lazonick, William and Brush, Thomas, "The 'Horndal Effect' in Early U.S. Manufacturing," *Explorations In Economic History*, 22 (1985), pp. 53-96.

Mesa-Lago, Carmelo, "Present and Future of the Revolution" in *Revolutionary Change in Cuba*, Mesa-Lago, ed., University of Pittsburgh Press, 1971.

Mesa-Lago, Carmelo, *The Economy of Socialist Cuba*, Albuquerque, University of New Mexico Press, 1981.

Meyers, Fred I., ed., *The Gilmore Manual Azucarero De Cuba 1958*, New Orleans, 1958.

Ministerio de la Industria Azucarera (MINAZ), *Manual Azucarero De Cuba 1971*, La Habana, Instituto Cubano del Libro, 1972.

Payne, John Howard. *Unit Operations in Cane Sugar Production*, New York, Elsevier Scientific Publishing Company, 1982.

Pedraza, Silvia. "Cuba's Refugees: Manifold Migrations," *Cuba In Transition—Volume 5*, Washington, ASCE, 1995, pp. 311-329

Pérez-López, Jorge. *Sugar and the Cuban Economy: An Assessment.* Research Institute for Cuban Studies, University of Miami, 1987.

Pérez-López, Jorge. *The Economics of Cuban Sugar*, Pittsburgh, University of Pittsburgh Press, 1991.

Radell, Willard W. "Comparative Performance of Large Cuban Sugar Factories in the 1984 'Zafra'," *Cuban Studies*, volume 17 (1987), pp. 141-155.

Roca, Sergio, "Cuban Economic Policy in the 1970s: The Trodden Paths," in Irving L. Horowitz, ed. *Cuban Communism*, 4th edition, New Brunswick, Transaction Books, 1981.

Roca, Sergio, "State Enterprises in Cuba Under the New System of Planning and Management (SDPE)," *Cuban Studies*, volume 16 (1986).

Romeu, Jorge Luis, "More on the Statistical Comparison of Cuban Socioeconomic Development," *Cuba In Transition—Volume 5*, Washington, ASCE, 1995, pp. 293-301.

Sanguinetty, Jorge A., "Evaluation of Changes in Economic Policy in Cuba," *Cuba In Transition—Volume 5*, Washington, ASCE, 1995, pp. 21-23.

AN EMPIRICAL STUDY OF INCOME AND PERFORMANCE INCENTIVES ON A CUBAN SUGARCANE CPA

Frederick S. Royce, William A. Messina, Jr. and José Alvarez

This paper presents findings of a case study of a sugarcane-farming cooperative (*cooperativa de producción agropecuaria*, CPA) located in the province of Havana, Cuba. Although the internal dynamics of specific Cuban cooperative farms have been examined by Cuban researchers, the results of their studies are not readily available in the United States.[1] A principal purpose of this paper is therefore to provide, in a form accessible to the U.S. academic community, insights into certain aspects of the management of Cuban cooperative farms. Since the data on which the study is based was collected at a single sugarcane-producing cooperative, the conclusions should be only tentatively applied to Cuban sugarcane cooperatives in general, and even more cautiously related to cooperatives that specialize in other crops.

Data, or evidence, was collected from four main sources: (a) interviews with cooperative members, especially, but not exclusively, those on the board of directors; (b) examination of documents created by, or about the co-op; (c) review of cooperative archives such as member lists, maps, and receipts; and (d) direct observation of work, decision making, relations between members and leaders and other aspects of co-op life over a four-week period of study.

Beginning on August 6, 1995, the lead author's four weeks at the cooperative were divided among three of the farm's four major administrative areas.[2] The first week was spent alongside the board member in charge of overall production (*jefe de producción*), who was also the acting president, while the president himself was on vacation. The following week was dedicated to working with the agronomist, who directs operations specifically for sugar cane. The third week began at the co-op's machine repair shop, spending time with the member in charge of co-op machinery (*jefe de maquinaria*), the shop foreman and the mechanics. Towards the end of that week, and during the fourth week, the investigation moved into the cooperative administrative offices. There, open-ended interviews with the cooperative's economic officer alternated with copying of data from cooperative records. After leaving the cooperative, three days were spent at a training center for cooperative members, where a month-long course for the agronomists from nearly 100 cooperatives was in progress. This contact with members of cooperatives from all corners of Cuba provided an excellent opportunity to place the experiences at "Amistad Cuba-Laos" into a larger perspective. Finally, on a brief vis-

---

1. An exception is the ongoing work of Carmen Diana Deere et al (1992, 1994 and 1995).

2. The department not examined was "Procurement." While this function is vital, especially in times of input shortages, its operations are principally oriented outward, while the focus of this research was on cooperative internal dynamics. In any case, the procurement "jefe" was on vacation during the entire research period, as was also the cooperative president. It was known that August was a vacation month in Cuba, so the research trip was originally scheduled for June and July (when harvest was completed and co-op members would have time for meetings, discussions and interviews). However, in spire of applying months in advance for the necessary documents, both the Cuban visa and the U.S. Treasury Department travel license were delayed until mid-July.

457

it to Cuba in June of 1996, the lead author was able to spend a day visiting another sugarcane cooperative in Ciego de Avila province, and later, a few hours at the "Amistad Cuba-Laos" cooperative, clarifying some points and taking photographs.[3]

Overall, the "Amistad Cuba-Laos" farm was found to be a highly mechanized, well organized, on-going operation, with basic planning and accounting systems in place. The cooperative leadership appeared to be open to the adoption of new technologies, and sugarcane yields, which plummeted as a result of severe input shortages in the early 1990s, were recovering somewhat as inputs became more available. On the other hand, work quality and intensity appear to be below potential, in part due to an incentive system that had not evolved to meet the country's changing economic conditions. The authors hope that the analysis presented in this paper can ultimately contribute to an improved understanding of an extremely important Cuban institution: the agricultural production cooperative.

AGRICULTURAL PRODUCTION COOPERATIVES IN CUBA

What is an Agricultural Production Cooperative?

Edward Reed (1977:360) has described the agricultural production cooperative as a farm where,

> the land and major capital items are held in joint ownership by the farm workers themselves, the bulk of the land is collectively cultivated, and any profits of the enterprise are shared by the cooperative members. Ideally, as joint owners, members of production cooperatives participate in the decision-making process concerning all aspects of production, distribution and investment. Thus, this type of group farm is distinguished from the state farm, where workers are wage employees of the state, and forms of cooperation where farmers cultivate their individual plots while carrying out some operations jointly.

According to Cuban law,[4]

> the agricultural production cooperative is a voluntary association of small farmers who join forces in collective agricultural production, of a socialist nature, that is based on the pooling of their lands and other means of production. . . . The agricultural production cooperative is an economic and social organization, whose management enjoys autonomy from the state. Its activities are carried out in the interests of society as a whole, in accordance with internal cooperative democracy and the shared labor of its members, and in conformity with the Unified Plan of Socio-Economic Development.

First Period of Cooperative Formation

Since the Cuban revolution of 1959, there have been three periods during which the government has promoted the formation of agricultural production cooperatives. The first period, from 1959 through 1963, saw the formation of three types of cooperatives. The earliest, called simply "agricultural cooperatives," were established on large non-sugarcane farms or ranches, which had been expropriated during the first months of the revolution (Bianchi 1964:105). Between May 1959 and May 1960, 881 of these agricultural production cooperatives, mostly in the size range of 200 to 300 hectares, were organized. This first co-op experience was short-lived, however. In January of 1961 these cooperatives were merged into the centrally managed network of state farms. Meanwhile, in June of 1960 similar cooperatives were established on the "administration lands" of large sugarcane plantations.[5] Within two months over 600 of these "sugarcane cooperatives" were established, and in May 1961, 622 cooperatives, with a total of 122,000 members controlled 809,000 hectares of land (Bianchi 1964:108).

Like the "agricultural cooperatives," the "sugarcane cooperatives" were to be a brief institutional interlude on the road to a centrally managed agriculture.

---

3. In addition, since the summer of 1994, the co-authors have visited a number of cane and non-cane UBPCs and CPAs, including "Amistad Cuba-Laos."

4. Chapter 1, Articles 4 and 5 of Ley 36, July 22, 1982 (Asamblea Nacional del Poder Popular 1982). Reaffirmed by Decree 159, September 20, 1990 (Consejo de Ministros 1990).

5. Administration lands are those fields managed directly by the sugarcane mill administration, as opposed to those lands leased to, or owned by, independent cane farmers.

After only two harvests, in August 1962, the National Congress of Sugarcane Cooperatives voted almost unanimously to transform their cooperatives into state farms (Domínguez 1978:448; Dumont 1970:48; Bianchi 1964:107-108). The National Association of Small Farmers (Asociación Nacional de Agricultores Pequeños, ANAP) in 1961 initiated a somewhat more enduring effort at cooperative agricultural production.[6] Between May of that year and May 1962, ANAP organized 229 "agrarian societies." These cooperatives differed from those previously discussed in three major ways. First, they were composed of small farmers who pooled their land in order to work it collectively, sharing draft animals and implements (Martín Barrios 1987:53). Second, they were much smaller than either the agricultural or sugarcane cooperatives: the average size of the 345 agrarian societies reported in August 1963 was 137 hectares, with an average membership just under 13 farmers.[7] Finally, the agrarian societies were more democratic, with members electing their own authorities, whereas the government appointed managers to the agricultural and sugarcane cooperatives (Bianchi 1964:106, 127). Although over 500 agrarian societies were organized in 1962 and 1963, these cooperatives failed to generate much interest among the small farmers (Regalado 1979:197). By late 1967 only 126 remained, and four years later, the count had dropped to 41 (Domínguez 1978:449; Martín Barrios 1987:74).

Second Period of Cooperative Formation

The second period of cooperative formation spanned the years 1977 through 1983. The "agricultural production cooperatives" (cooperativas de producción

agropecuaria or CPA) organized during this period were fundamentally very similar to the earlier agrarian societies, though usually larger.[8] Since the cooperative selected for this case study is a CPA, this period will receive a more thorough treatment than the other two.

As a result of the agrarian reform law of 1959, small, independent farmers came to own about 30 percent of Cuba's farmland (Zimbalist and Eckstein 1987:8). Throughout the late 60s and early 70s, the Cuban government utilized various pressures and incentives to integrate these private farmers into the state's agricultural planning, production and distribution system, which was a centerpiece of the planned economy (Zimbalist and Eckstein 1987:9). As a result, during this period many peasant farms were either leased or sold to the state.[9] Beginning in 1975, however, the government began changing official policy towards peasant farmers. The new policy led to a gradual, voluntary process of attracting farmers into agricultural production cooperatives of their own making, rather than into state owned farms (Deere et al. 1992:120; Zimbalist and Eckstein 1987:13).

The practical task of organizing the CPAs was carried out by the small producer association, ANAP. Beginning in the early 60s, ANAP's membership was gradually organized into mutual aid groups and "credit and service cooperatives" (cooperativas de crédito y servicios or CCS).[10] This organized, small farmer base proved to be fertile ground for the creation of production cooperatives, over 1000 of which were constituted between 1977 and 1980 (Martín Barrios 1987:154). A good deal of the long-term success of this effort seems to have been due to the emphasis

---

6. Since 1961 the ANAP has been the officially sanctioned representative of Cuba's private agricultural producers.

7. The totals reported in Martín Barrios (1987:53) are 4,429 members and 47,319 hectares (3,526 *caballerías*). It is not stated whether this is total land area, or agricultural lands only. In 1965, Sergio Aranda reported 270 agrarian societies encompassing 40,193 hectares (2,995 *caballerías*) and just over 3,200 farmers (Aranda 1958:158).

8. It may be confusing that the specific name given to the co-ops, "agricultural production cooperatives," is the same as the generic name. To reduce the possibility of confusion, we will use the Spanish acronym "CPA."

9. Even leaders of ANAP, the small farmer organization, apparently felt that their membership would gradually disappear, as peasants opted out of private farming. Interview with Mavis Alvares (July 1995), founding member of ANAP, and presently Director of Development Projects of that organization.

10. "The Credit and Service Cooperatives ... enable the sharing of irrigation and other installations, services and productive means, as well as collective arrangements for credit, even though the land, tools and production of each farm remain private" (Comité Estatal de Estadísticas 1989:178).

placed on persuasion, rather than coercion. By pooling their lands, and working collectively, each farmer would no longer be tied to a particular, often isolated, plot of ground. Cooperatives would bring member families together, often closer to towns or villages, and permit access to electricity, improved housing, schools, and medical care. This new form of production would be based on machinery, to lighten the farmer's burden, and to increase productivity. Cooperatives provided for paid vacations and retirement pensions, benefits which small farmers had never known. And in any case, those who entered the cooperatives could, to some extent, "have their cake, and eat it too," since each member would be gradually paid off by the cooperative for the land he or she "contributed" (Deere et al 1992:121; Ghai et al 1988:70-83).

During the late 1970s in Cuba, new departures in the economic, political, and even technological spheres seemed to bode well for these relatively autonomous, democratic, profit-making cooperatives. Coincident with the launching of the CPAs, a new system of economic planning known as the SDPE (Sistema de Dirección y Planificación de la Economía) was being implemented throughout Cuba. In contrast to official economic practice since the early 1960s, the new system emphasized the need for cost calculations, self-financing, profit sharing and enterprise autonomy (Fuller 1992:97; Zimbalist and Brundenius 1989:127). Meanwhile, the political space available to the citizenry was expanded somewhat through the incorporation of secret balloting into the local elections known as "poder popular" or people's power (Pérez-Stable 1993:123). Finally, in 1977, the same year in which the first CPAs were formed, the first Cuban sugarcane combine-harvester factory began production (Sims et al. 1993: 68). Together with the ubiquitous Soviet tractors, these harvesters came to represent the advantages of the large-scale operations permitted by production cooperatives (Edquist 1985:133).

Throughout the first few years of CPA development, a typical cooperative would comprise less than 30, socially homogeneous members. Thereafter, due to the entry of new members, and to a tendency to amalgamate smaller cooperatives into fewer, larger units, the average membership size grew to around 50, where it has remained (Deere et al 1992: 123,133).[11] The social origins of the membership also became more diverse, with new members increasingly from the ranks of landless agricultural laborers, skilled workers (mechanics, welders) and professionals (accountants, agronomists). Although the presence of a core of former small farmers and their family members remains a very important characteristic of the CPAs today, the tendency appears to be for the cooperatives to become numerically dominated by the other groups mentioned.

In 1983, there were 1,474 CPAs, with an average of 637 hectares, and 51 members, per cooperative (Deere et al 1992:123). By 1995, there were 1160 CPAs, averaging 641 hectares and 54 members. This total of 62,257 members farmed 743,000 agricultural hectares, or about 11 percent of Cuba's agricultural lands (Oficina Nacional de Estadísticas 1996). In spite of the gradual decline in numbers, the CPA has proved to be a much more successful model for cooperatives than were any of the previous attempts.

Third Period of Cooperative Formation

The most recent period of cooperative formation, from September 1993 through early 1995, constitutes a reversal of the early 1960s policies that converted the agricultural and sugarcane cooperatives to state farms. By the early 1990's, the large, inefficient state managed farms had become increasingly untenable, and soon the relatively more efficient CPA would provide the organizational model for an extensive agrarian reform (Deere 1995:14; Figueroa 1995:14, 15). This process of transformation of state farms into cooperatives, called "basic units of cooperative production" (unidades básicas de producción

---

11. The specific importance of the sugarcane combine-harvesters in convincing members of small cooperatives to merge into larger cooperatives was confirmed by the lead author's interviews with founding members of the "Antonio Maceo" CPA and the "Amistad Cuba-Laos" CPA of Havana province in August of 1985, and of the "Revolución de Etiopía" CPA in Ciego de Avila province, in June of 1996.

cooperativa or UBPCs), began in September of 1993, and unfolded very rapidly during the following year and a half. By the end of 1995, there were a total of 2807 UBPCs, 1288 in sugarcane, and 1519 in other crops and livestock. These farms, with a total membership of 271,810, occupied 3,151,500 hectares, or approximately 47 percent of Cuba's agricultural lands (Oficina Nacional de Estadísticas 1996).

While the UBPCs were patterned after the CPA model, they differ in a number of important ways. For example, while the CPAs were formed by small farmers pooling their lands, the UBPCs were established on lands still owned by the state with open-ended, rent-free usufruct granted to the cooperative and with membership comprised of former state farm workers (Deere 1995:14). Also, while CPA members are enrolled in the National Association of Small Farmers, the UBPC members remain in the Agricultural, Livestock and Forestry Workers' Syndicate. Finally, because of the connection between the former state farms and the CAI (Complejo Agro-Industrial), UBPCs typically have less autonomy than CPAs (Alvarez and Messina 1996).

THE "AMISTAD CUBA-LAOS" COOPERATIVE

According to a document developed by the Cuban Ministry of Sugar (MINAZ-ANAP 1983), the "Amistad Cuba-Laos" CPA was formally founded on December 9, 1980, with 134 hectares (10 *caballerías*) of land, and 18 members. On April 15, 1983, the original "Amistad Cuba-Laos" merged with the nearby "Antonio Maceo Grajales" CPA. That same year, the cooperative reached 809 hectares (60.3 *caballerías*) and 71 members. At the time of the study in August 1995, the cooperative possessed a total of 1188 hectares (88.5 *caballerías*), with the following distribution:

- 876 hectares (65.3 *caballerías*) in sugarcane;

- 39 hectares (2.9 *caballerías*) food crops for members;

- 39 hectares (2.9 *caballerías*) livestock, mostly milk cows for member consumption;

- 234 hectares (17.4 *caballerías*) area not useable for agriculture (areas for houses, buildings, access roads, drainage ditches and especially hillsides).

There were 88 members in August 1995 and 96 in June of 1996. The cooperative is highly mechanized, with the following machinery:

- 28 wheel tractors (MTZ-80 and JUMZ);

- 4 track-type tractors (DT-75);

- 4 sugarcane combine-harvesters (KTP-2); and

- 2 medium-duty trucks.

Figure 1 illustrates the organization of authority within the cooperative. Each of the four "departments" is presided over by an officer called a "jefe." The shaded boxes indicate the position held by each of the nine members of the executive council, which includes two "staff" positions: agronomist ("ingeniero agrónomo") and mechanization expert ("ingeniero mecanizador"). Each of these staff individuals has functional authority over a vital activity, as shown by the dotted lines.

Sugarcane Production at the CPA "Amistad Cuba-Laos"

During the "Special Period in Peacetime" the "Amistad Cuba-Laos" cooperative has seen substantial decreases in sugarcane production (see Table 1), accompanied by increases in costs of production (an issue outside the scope of this paper). Taken together, these trends have resulted in lower member incomes, and reduced opportunities for investments by the cooperative.

An interesting trend in Table 1, is the cooperative's reduction of harvested area over the past 10 years. Most of that reduction in area occurred before the initiation of the Special Period in 1990. At the same time, co-op agricultural yields increased substantially into the first year of the Special Period, enabling the co-op to achieve in 1990-91 the largest harvest of its history. These trends are in contrast to the trends in Cuba as a whole, where the land area harvested was maintained, as average yields fell from 1989 onward. All of this suggests an intensification of sugarcane cultivation by the cooperative from the late 1980s,

Figure 1. "Amistad Cuba-Laos" CPA Organizational Diagram

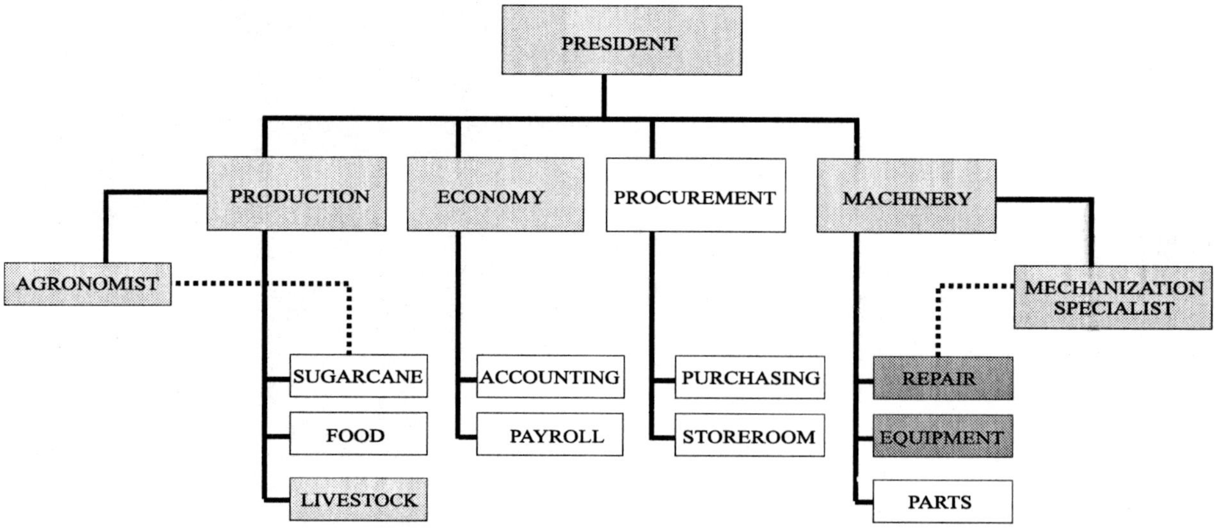

until well into the Special Period. Higher yields, accompanied by a large drop in area harvested, may indicate that the intensification rested in large measure upon longer growing cycles. However, as the economic problems associated with the Special Period progressed, the cooperative's production plummeted, with results paralleling the national average in 1992-93. In that year, cane production for the cooperative and the nation fell by 37 percent and 34 percent respectively, compared to the previous year's harvest.[12]

Member Incomes

Members received a variety of material benefits as a result of their affiliation with the cooperative. Each of these, whether received in cash or in-kind, is considered here as a type of income.

Advance: Although the advance (*adelanto*) received by a cooperative member every two weeks is apparently similar in amount to the wage received by a hired worker, it is important to recognize that they are not synonymous. A wage is paid by an owner to a worker; since the members are all owners, they share

profits or surplus rather than wages. However, since the farm's surplus can only be determined after the annual harvest, an advance is provided for members to live on between harvests.

The advance was nearly always expressed in an amount "per day." In activities with defined work standards, or norms (*normas de trabajo*), the daily amount received by a specific member could vary with the degree of completion of the norm. In general, norms existed for both manual and mechanized field work, but not for machine maintenance or office work.[13]

Where they existed, the norms could be applied in a variety of ways. For example, manual fieldwork usually was performed by groups and the norm determined how much area the group should complete during the course of the work day. The foreman (who supervised and worked alongside the others) made sure the pace was adequate to finish the job. The presence of a supervisor, combined with the fact that the work of each was apparent to all, seemed to

---

12. During visits in 1994, 1995 and 1996, the authors observed that the "Amistad Cuba-Laos" co-op always had standing cane after the harvest. This is in contrast to most Cuban cane UBPCs, which during the "special period" often cut all their cane (including immature cane) each year.

13. The range of advance-based earning differences among the members is not large. In August of 1995, tractor drivers earned 8 pesos per day, and field hands earned 7 to 7.5. The nine members of the co-op executive council are each paid an amount equal to the average of the five highest paid members for each period.

Table 1. Indicators of Sugarcane Production: CPA "Amistad Cuba-Laos" and Cuba

| | Area Harvested | | Can Produced | | Yield | |
	Co-op hectares	Cuba 1000 ha	Co-op 1000 mt	Cuba million mt	Co-op metric tons per hectare	Cuba metric tons per hectare
1986-87	837.4	1366.0	52.6	70.7	63.8	48.0
1987-88	735.4	1305.0	35.9	67.5	50.2	51.7
1988-89	671.0	1355.0	46.0	73.9	68.5	54.5
1989-90	591.8	1427.0	47.9	74.4	80.9	52.0
1990-91	612.0	1443.0	55.0	71.1	89.7	49.1
1991-92	556.9	1461.0	47.1	65.4	84.7	44.7
1992-93	519.4	1219.0	29.8	42.9	57.4	35.3
1993-94	522.0	1283.6	22.7	43.0	43.7	33.5
1994-95	476.4	1177.3	25.4	33.2	53.4	28.2
1995-96	520.7	1276.9	30.8	41.5	59.2	32.5

Source: Cuba, Alvarez and Peña 1995: 29, 81 and various sources based on data from Ministry of Sugar (MINAZ), Havana. Cooperative through 1995, cooperative records; co-op figures for 1995-96 estimated by co-op agronomist. Figures are as reported in records, and may vary slightly from calculated values

Table 2. Per Member Annual Advance and Surplus, from Sample (Pesos)

| | Year Ending July | | | | | | | | | | | |
	1984	1985	1986	1987	1988	1989	1990	1991	1992	1993	1994	1995
Mean Advance	1835	2174	2372	2439	2365	2498	2747	2726	2765	2647	2669	2525
Mean Surplus	1516	1525	1726	1740	981	1824	2747	3372	2049	646	366	1350
Surplus as % of Advance	83%	70%	73%	71%	41%	73%	100%	124%	74%	24%	14%	53%

Source: "Registro de Utilidades Amistad Cuba-Laos." Sample of 8 members randomly selected from among current members who had joined the co-op prior to 1983-84 fiscal year.

minimize outright slacking. Under this "collective" application of norms, each group member received the same pay. As an alternative, the foreman had the option of keeping track of each individual's output for the day. Here, the advance would vary from member to member within the same work group. Although both systems were used, the latter requires more complicated record keeping and was less frequently applied, at least to manual field labor. Individual output was more often the measure for mechanized tasks, particularly for the harvest, as described later in this paper. Evidently, a link exists between the work performed and the advance, although the strength of that link can vary considerably.

Surplus: Each year, after the harvest is sold, the cooperative allocates 50 percent of surplus (*excedente*) to be divided among the membership. The portion of surplus assigned to each member was based solely on days worked during the year, without regard to either the nature or quality of the work. A day spent hoeing out weeds earned precisely the same amount of surplus as a day directing the sugarcane harvest. For most members, in most years, the income from surplus distributed has been smaller, and sometimes much smaller, than the income from advances (Table 2).

The distribution of surplus created a direct connection between the efficiency of the collective, and the income of each member. Furthermore, the criterion for distribution rewarded those who work, or at least were present during working hours. There was, however, a less tangible connection between surplus income, and the quality and intensity of work, than was the case with advance income, which varied according to the fulfillment of work norms.

Food Crop Allotment: During 1995, the "Amistad Cuba-Laos" cooperative dedicated 39 hectares (2.9 *caballerías*) to the production of food crops, and another area of similar size to grazing animals, mainly milk cows. The production from this 8 percent of the farm's agriculturally productive lands was mostly destined for consumption by the cooperative membership (*autoconsumo*).[14] Food crop production, and the livestock operation were each organized as stable work groups. The supervisors of each of these areas were individuals with particular expertise, and those who work in these areas did not generally work in sugarcane, with the occasional exception of participating in the harvest.

Production from the food crop area represented a very important part of the income received by each cooperative member. Each week during the 1994-95 fiscal year an average allotment of 25 pounds of root crops, 12 pounds of rice and 22 pounds of vegetables was supplied to each member, apparently regardless of family size. For the majority of members who resided close to the cooperative, the food is delivered door-to-door. This is an important detail, since most members lived some distance from the local market where similar items could be purchased and transportation to and from shopping would be a problem. The milk herd provided 1.5 liters of milk per day per member.[15] The members paid a nominal fee for this food, which was only rarely as high as 10 percent of the free market value (without considering home delivery!). The only requirement for receiving a full allotment was membership in the cooperative; the amount of food received bore no relation to days worked, much less to work norms.[16]

Individual Family Plots: The 1994-95 fiscal year was the second year that the "Amistad Cuba-Laos" cooperative had assigned land to each member for family rice production. This rice was produced in rotation with sugarcane, in a field chosen because of its poor drainage. The co-op planted the rice area as a unit, by machine, and each member was assigned a specific "strip," 14 rows wide, of the 525-meter long field. The rows were 30 cm apart, so the standard area was 4.2 meters by 525 meters, or 0.22 hectares. Once planted and assigned, the rice plot was the responsibility of the individual member. Work (i.e. weeding and harvesting) on the plot was allowed only during one's free time. Of course the co-op member's family may have had more time to work the plot, although the distance from residential areas (several kilometers) was a limitation. Members sometimes organized after-work trips from the co-op staging area, to the rice field, with a co-op tractor and trailer. The previous year, a number of members with contiguous plots arranged among themselves to rent a rice harvester (which the "Amistad Cuba-Laos" cooperative did not own).

According to the agronomist, a well tended, fertilized plot should yield about 2000 pounds of rice, or perhaps 1300 pounds without fertilizer.[17] Fertilizer was quite scarce, and the cooperative does not have a fertilizer allotment for this purpose, so little was applied. The harvested rice was "hulled" using co-op machinery, at no charge to the individual. The final product belonged exclusively to the individual member, and the co-op did not retain any portion in exchange for the use of land, or machinery used in land preparation, planting, and transportation.

---

14. The details of *autoconsumo* distribution are arranged within the co-op, and had nothing to do with whatever quota of food ws also available through the state-issued ration book.

15. One interviewee claimed that the original contributors of land received 2 liters per day. This was the only evidence of an overt perquisite for the "landed founders" noted, although there may well be others.

16. For comparison, the residents of the City of La Habana only receive five pounds of rice per person per month through the ration system and must purchase additional quantities at relatively high prices in the agricultural markets. Furthermore, only those on special diets and children under seven years of age can obtain milk in the City of La Habana, with an allotment of one liter per day (when it is available).

17. Production could be considerably less, depending on the effort invested. One member contacted after the harvest said that she had done little or no weeding, and harvested 490 pounds of rice, before hulling.

The individual plots were one way of channeling family labor towards direct improvement of the family standard of living. Interestingly, a visit to the individual rice area found over half the plots nearly overrun with weeds. Although some were meticulously attended, overall, these family plots appeared considerably less well cared for than the collective food-producing areas of the co-op. The co-op leadership seemed to look upon this as a learning experience, to be continued, modified or abandoned, depending on member response and results.

Backyard Pig Raising: Prior to the collapse of the Cuba's eastern bloc trading partners, the cooperative was able to purchase sufficient feed for animals to regularly provide members with pork and chicken from its own production. At the time of this research, feed was no longer available in sufficient quantities to maintain livestock operations on the previous scale, so at that time the cooperative was breeding pigs in order to provide each member with a piglet, at about nine-month intervals. The member then raised the pig in a backyard pen, using table scraps, residue from banana plants, or other sources of food. Although the implications of this "take home" policy on neighborhood sanitation were problematic, as a solution to the animal feed shortage, it worked well. As with the individual rice plots, a suitable combination of collective and individual activities and inputs appeared to be evolving, in response to changing economic conditions.

Quantitative Comparison of Income Sources

One way of comparing these various non-monetary portions of family income is to express each using the common denominator of market value. Most of the in-kind items were available at the near-by Bauta agricultural market and the lowest estimated or observed market prices were used to generate conservative values for comparison.[18]

Table 3 summarizes and compares the relative magnitude of each income component already described, for an average cooperative member. Even using a conservative methodology for estimating the value of food provided, the cash income received by the average member, 3,507 pesos (from advances and distribution of surplus at the end of the year), was only a quarter of the estimated 14,282 peso value of all (cash plus non-cash) income.

Table 3. Per Member Income Equivalent in Pesos, July 1994 - June 1995 Period

Income Component	Amount	Percentage of Total
Advance on Profits	2,236	16%
End of Year Profits	1,271	9%
Food Crops Allotment	6,075	43%
Individual Plot Production	2,000	14%
Patio Pigs	2,700	19%
Total	14,282	100%

Source: Royce 1996: 162.

It is not unreasonable to assume that this apparently unbalanced situation is largely the result of two factors: 1) low prices paid by the State for sugar; and 2) the relative scarcity of food during the Special Period. As the amount of food available through the rationing system decreased in the 1990's, the price of food available through market (including black-market) channels increased and hence the value of food crop allotments and other similar programs to CPA members increased correspondingly. The value of monetary income was probably further diminished by the reduced availability of inexpensive consumer goods

18. It is widely recognized that prices at the Cuban agricultural markets during this period were not fixed in any way by the government (Pastor and Zimbalist 1995:18; Deere 1995:16-17). There was a tax of 5 percent in La Habana, 15 percen elsewhere (Pérez and Torres 1996). The government did attempt to exert some downward pressure on market prices by either directly selling products below the going rate, or by encouraging co-ops to do so. This appears to have been the case at "Amistad Cuba-Laos," which according to those responsible for selling a small amount of co-op production at the market, regularly prices its offerings about 20 percent below the general price. Since no study of prices at the Bauta market was available, the lead author collected prices during a visit to the market. The cooperative members who handled sales at the market also provided their estimates, and finally, prices were compared to those appearing in a survey done in La Habana markets (Deere et al 1997).

from Soviet or Eastern European origin, and their replacement by more costly items, often for sale only in U.S. Dollars.

Income as a Work Incentive

Each of these five income sources bears a specific relation to work motivation for cooperative members.

- "Advance" was usually based strictly on days worked, and to a lesser extent, on comparing work completed to work norms. It was the only income category tied (at least sometimes) to the quality and intensity of work within the cooperative.

- "End of Year Surplus" was the only category directly related to the farm's profitability. Since surplus was distributed according to days worked, no element of work quality or intensity entered into the calculation of each member's share.

- "Food Crop Allotment," the largest single category of income received by members, was distributed solely on the basis of membership, regardless of the level of responsibility, quality, intensity or any other aspect of the work performed.

- "Individual Plot Production" depended on the quality and intensity of work, but work within the family, and not within the cooperative. All co-op members were eligible for plots.

- "Backyard Pig Raising" depended on the piglets supplied by the co-op, for which the criterion was simply cooperative membership.

Only in the case of the "advance" was there any direct relation between work quality, and income, and only "end of year surplus" varied directly with farm profitability. All other income sources depended solely on membership. Strictly speaking, a member need not even have shown up for work, yet would

have remained eligible for these benefits. Additionally, this in-kind, membership-based incentive system severely limited income differentiation, or rewards, within the cooperative according to either the nature and requirements of a particular job, or job performance.

In order for these non-monetary, yet very substantial portions of income to serve any direct motivational purpose, the condition of membership itself needed to be strictly linked to some minimal indicator of productive activity. At the very least, this implied a credible threat of expulsion for work absenteeism.

The cooperative records indicated the date of entry of each new member, and the date of exit for those leaving. A reason for leaving was also generally included, although the level of detail included was inconsistent. Even assuming some errors or omissions, Table 4 indicates a clear trend.

The pronounced shift from "Resignation" to "Expulsion" (*baja*) probably indicates that the cooperative was indeed utilizing expulsion as a form of discipline to a much greater extent in recent years. Unfortunately, the use of expulsion as a usual form of labor discipline within a cooperative may engender problems of its own. If cooperative functioning is enhanced both by the sense of ownership possessed by each member, and by the existence of social solidarity among members (Prychitko and Vanek 1996:xv; Romero Valcárcel et al 1994:42; Bonfiglio 1986:187), and if, as seems probable, both the ownership and solidarity are undermined by expulsions, then the frequent use of expulsion as a method of eliciting work discipline may be fundamentally incompatible with cooperative forms of production.[19]

The Harvest

The sugarcane harvest itself was the most developed example of payment (of the wage-like "advance") according to norms. This is because it was the one ma-

---

19. Another issue raised indirectly by Table 4 is the high rate of turnover among membership. High turnover was especially marked among male members who entered without land. Between the co-op's inception and 1995, 179 landless men entered, and 119 also left during the same period. Some data indicate that this level of turnover may not have been typical of CPAs in general (Deere et al 1992:Table 4, p. 131).

Table 4. Reasons for Leaving "Amistad Cuba-Laos" Cooperative, Selected Years

	Resignations		Explusions		Retirements		Other		Unknown		Total	
1984	5	100%	0	0%	0	0%	0	0%	0	0%	5	100%
1986	12	86%	0	0%	0	0%	1	7%	1	7%	14	100%
1987	1	20%	2	40%	1	20%	1	20%	0	0%	5	100%
1988	4	44%	2	22%	1	11%	2	22%	0	0%	9	100%
1993	0	0%	22	88%	3	12%	0	0%	0	0%	25	100%
1994	0	0%	11	85%	1	8%	1	8%	0	0%	13	100%

Source: "Lista Consolidada de Socios de Cooperativa 'Amistad Cuba-Laos.'"

jor operation where output was always measured, and officially recorded (for payment by the sugar mill to the co-op). Each wagonload was weighed, with a receipt is issued which included the wagon number. Based on this documentation from the cane receiving station, the cooperative developed its own documentation in order to assign each wagon-load to the work group responsible for harvesting and moving that output.

Not all members were needed to participate directly in the harvest; those chosen to "go to the harvest" (*ir a la zafra*) appeared to consider it an honor, or at least an opportunity to earn increased monetary income through extra workdays and by exceeding the norms. The selection was said to be based on good work and especially on low absenteeism. Members with more seniority also tended to participate. Whatever criteria were used by the cooperative executive board, the list of those who implement the harvest had to be submitted to the general assembly for approval. Some specialized workers, like the combine drivers, invariably take part. Although this research was not conducted during the harvest months, it was apparent from many interactions with co-op members that the usual enthusiasm, and even mystique which agriculturists reserve for the harvest was alive and well at "Amistad Cuba-Laos."

The role of the "record keeper" (*computador*) was described as vital to determining the output of each work group. This member maintained a record of the movements of each of the 32 trailers circulating from the fields to weighing/receiving station, and back. Each trailer was hauled alongside a combine harvester that filled it with harvested, chopped cane. When

full, the trailer was hauled to a staging area, where it was hooked with two other trailers and towed to the receiving station. At the receiving station, the driver was given a receipt showing the weight of cane unloaded from each trailer. The receipts would later be matched up with each of the combine and tractor drivers who handled the trailer, and the amount of cane shown would be added to the day's total for each operator.

Detailed tables of norms were consulted to evaluate the daily performance of those involved in the harvest. Although the tables referred directly to the amount harvested by the combine, the norms for other machine operators were easy to derive: for each combine, there were two tractors that haul trailers as they are filled (*movedores*). The norm for the operators of each of these two tractors was one half the norm for the combine. There were five other tractors (*tiradores*), which hauled the full trailers, three-at-a-time, from the staging area to the receiving station and back empty. Since these five operators served all four combines, the norm for each of them was the combine norm multiplied by four, and then divided by five. In this fashion, most of the participants in the harvest had the satisfaction of knowing precisely their own (and each others') productivity. Central to the process were the combine drivers, who each aspired to harvest a million *arrobas* (11,502 metric tons) of cane in a season. Prior to the Special Period, "millionaire" status brought a material reward, such as a motorcycle, in addition to the social status. Usually, individuals from each harvest job category were selected as outstanding workers, and received recognition for their efforts. As a group, the members of "Amistad Cuba-Laos" were proud that they had, on

467

various occasions, won recognition as the best harvest team (*pelotón*) in Havana province. Overall, the compensation for harvest activities was a good example of payment based on work done, rather than on membership alone.

The Repair Shop

Repairs and maintenance of agricultural machinery were carried out within the cooperative's shop structure. Open on three sides, the shop was well lighted (during the day) and had excellent ventilation. Its concrete floor and high, pitched roof could accommodate six tractors and two harvesters at the same time. There was an area for welding, and another for secure storage for technical manuals, tools, supplies and spare parts. The staff consisted of about ten mechanics, welders and helpers, a fuel dispatcher, an administrator and a technical supervisor. The precise number of workers varied throughout the year, since some shop helpers and other machine operators are not always attached to the shop.

While mention of the harvest brought a smile to the face of nearly any co-op member, reference to the mechanical repair shop was likely to cause a look of concern. Of course, as work environments, these two situations could not have been any less similar. The harvest was a glorious battle, with a precise beginning and ending, and a sweet victory when the co-op's planned harvest was met or exceeded. The shop was an unending series of guerrilla skirmishes against aging machinery, with victory impossible, and defeat unthinkable.

Related to the inherent differences between the activities of the harvest and the shop, there is another difference. Among all major co-op activities, the harvest produced the most complete record of individual and group productivity, while the shop produced hardly any record linking people to work performance. It should be noted that the problem was not one of individual versus collective tasks: shop work by a given mechanic was as "individual" as any performed at the cooperative, while "individual" performance within the harvest was heavily conditioned by the coordinated functioning of the work group. Nor was this a problem of basic organization. The critical role of machinery in the farm's productive process, the scar-

city and high cost of spare parts and replacement machines, and the reporting requirements of the CAI (Complejo Agro-Industrial), each underscored the importance of achieving and maintaining an acceptable level of shop organization. In fact, the shop worked according to a post-harvest plan for major repairs, tracked maintenance periods through machine fuel consumption, and maintained a well-organized store room for spare parts. Missing, however, was precisely the element that made the harvest stand out—thorough record keeping. There was no way, beyond remembering, to know who performed a specific repair, on what date, and how much shop-time was involved.

Observations and interviews in the shop revealed poor morale, and generalized "free riding" in the form of low quality and quantity of work. Neither the low levels of work, nor low morale could be justified either by inadequate knowledge and skills among the workers, or by poor working conditions. Rather, the problem was motivational, probably related to the excessively egalitarian payment system already discussed, and compounded by the relative difficulty (though certainly not impossibility) of applying norms to maintenance and repair work.

This was not in any way an inevitable situation. The repair shop personnel possessed sufficient technical knowledge and experience to develop a performance-based system of rewards and sanctions, based on complete machine repair records. The goal of such a system would be to link each job to a specific mechanic, as well as account for the hours worked each day. The data collected would eventually form the basis of developing the shop's own set of norms for time spent on common repairs. Within the observed shop environment, there is no question that the implementation of such a system would require a good measure of leadership. The large question is, if such a system of accountability were implemented, to what extent might the problematic work ambiance of the repair shop be replaced by harvest-like smiles and productivity?

SUMMARY AND CONCLUSIONS

This paper presents partial results of four weeks of fieldwork at the sugarcane CPA "Amistad Cuba-

Laos" conducted in 1995. At that time, the cooperative was in its 15th year of operation, and seemed to be recovering from the most difficult years of the Special Period.

Members received income from five sources: "wage" (or more precisely, advance on surplus), end of year surplus, food crop allotment, individual family plots, and backyard pig raising. Only in the case of the wage was there any direct relation between work quality and income, and only "end of year surplus" varied directly with farm profitability. All other income sources depended solely on membership. Since these "other" sources comprised the bulk of all income, the system of payment and incentives was dominated by non-performance related elements.

The preponderance of non-performance related income almost certainly had a negative effect on work motivation. The analysis of very different working environments within the cooperative suggests that improved linking of individuals or small workgroups to their own productive results could significantly improve work motivation. This approach would minimize the need to resort to potentially destructive expulsions, which recently has been the motivational factor used by the cooperative for alleviating the problem. If sense of ownership and solidarity enhance cooperative functioning and, as seems probable, both feelings are undermined by expulsions, then the frequent use of expulsions may be fundamentally incompatible with cooperative forms of production.

At the other extreme one finds the sugarcane harvest as the most developed example of payment according to the norm performed. Granted, the nature of the process allowed the participants to have the satisfaction of knowing precisely their own (and each others') productivity, and of the material and moral rewards involved in the process. This example contrasted sharply with the situation found in the repair shop because of the very nature of the work performed and the way it was conducted. A constant cause of concern (where poor morale and "free riding" were generalized), this unit maintained hardly any record linking people to work performance. The situation, however, could be partially solved through the establishment of a good system of record keeping. Examples for accomplishing this goal are given in the main text of this paper. The question posed in that section still remains: if such a system were implemented, to what extent might the problematic work ambiance of the repair shop be replaced by the more satisfactory situation prevailing in the annual harvest? The answer to this and the other questions posed in this section rest on the cooperative leadership and the members at large.

Although the members of the CPAs originally were small landowners, many entering later have not brought land with them. At the CPA examined in this study, the August 1995 membership consisted of 21 land contributors, and 67 who entered without land. To the extent that this situation is typical of the sugarcane CPAs, it points out an important convergence in the nature of the membership between the CPAs and UBPCs.

Never in Cuba has there been a period of greater commitment to cooperative production than the one initiated in late 1993 with the decision to reorganize the state agricultural sector along the lines of the existing agricultural production cooperatives. In 1995, close to one-half million members of 6,621 agricultural production cooperatives (CPAs), credit and service cooperatives (CCSs) and basic units of cooperative production (UBPCs) were producing on 4.8 million hectares, which represents nearly three-quarters of Cuba's total agricultural land area (Oficina Nacional de Estadisticas 1996). The importance of the current cooperative movement deserves more attention from scholars studying the Cuban situation.

REFERENCES

Alvarez, José, and Lázaro Peña Castellanos. *Preliminary Study of the Sugar Industries in Cuba and Florida Within the Context of the World Sugar Market.* International Working Paper IW95-6. Gainesville, Florida: IFAS, University of Florida, 1995.

Alvarez, José, and William A. Messina, Jr. "Cuba's New Agricultural Cooperatives and Markets: Antecedents, Organization, Early Performance and Prospects." *Cuba in Transition—Volume 6.* Washington: Association for the Study of the Cuban Economy, 1996.

Aranda, Sergio. *La Revolución Agraria en Cuba.* México: Siglo Veintiuno Editores, 1968.

Asamblea Nacional del Poder Popular. "Ley No. 36: Ley de Cooperativas Agropecuarias." *Gaceta Oficial* 63 (July 22, 1982).

Bianchi, Andrés. "Chapter 3. Agriculture: Post Revolutionary Development." *Cuba: The Economic and Social Revolution*, ed. Dudly Seers, Andrés Bianchi, Richard Jolly and Max Nolff. Chapel Hill, North Carolina: University of North Carolina Press, 1964.

Bonfiglio, Giovanni. "Gestión Empresarial y Cooperativas Agrarias de la Costa." *Perú: El Problema Agrario en Debate*, ed. Seminario Permanente de Investigación Agraria (SEPIA). Lima, Perú: Seminario Permanente de Investigación Agraria (SEPIA), 1986.

Comité Estatal de Estadísticas. *Anuario Estadístico de Cuba 1989.* La Habana: Editorial Estadística, 1991.

Consejo de Ministros. "Decreto No. 159: Reglamento General de las Cooperativas de Producción Agropecuaria." *Gaceta Oficial* 8 (September 20, 1990), 15-28.

Deere, Carmen Diana. "The New Agrarian Reforms." *NACLA Report on the Americas* 29(2) (Sept/Oct 1995): 13-17.

Deere, Carmen Diana, Mieke Meurs, and Niurka Pérez. "Toward a Periodization of the Cuban Collectivization Process: Changing Incentives and Peasant Response." *Cuban Studies* 22 (1992): 115-149.

Deere, Carmen Diana, Niurka Pérez, and Ernel Gonzáles. "The View from Below: Cuban Agriculture in the 'Special Period in Peacetime.'" *The Journal of Peasant Studies* 21(2) (January 1994): 194-234.

Deere, Carmen Diana, Niurka Pérez, and Cary Torres. "Random Survey in Havana Markets of 'Alta Habana,' 'Marianao,' and 'El Egido,' January 18, 1995; June 10, 1995 and January 6, 1996." To be published as a table in "Reforming Cuban Agriculture," *Development and Change*, forthcoming in Fall 1997.

Domínguez, Jorge I. *Cuba: Order and Revolution.* Cambridge, Massachusetts: Belknap Press of Harvard University, 1978.

Dumont, René. *Cuba: Socialism and Development.* New York: Grove Press, 1970.

Edquist, Charles. *Capitalism, Socialism and Technology: A Comparative Study of Cuba and Jamaica.* London: Zed Books, Ltd., 1985.

Figueroa, Víctor M. *La Reforma de la Tenencia de la Tierra en Cuba y la Formación de un Nuevo Modelo Mixto de Economía Agrícola.* Universidad Central de Las Villas, Cuba, 1995. 33 pages.

Fuller, Linda. *Work and Democracy in Socialist Cuba.* Philadelphia: Temple University Press, 1992.

Ghai, Dharam, Cristobal Kay, and Peter Peek. *Labour and Development in Rural Cuba.* New York: St. Martin's Press, 1988.

Martín Barrios, Adelfo. *La ANAP: 25 Años de Trabajo.* La Habana: Editora Política, 1987.

MINAZ-ANAP, Delegación La Habana. *Programa de Desarrollo Perspectivo de la Cooperativa de Producción Agropecuaria "Amistad Cuba-Laos."* Segunda etapa del plan rector CPA modelo. La Habana, 1983.

Oficina Nacional de Estadísticas. *Estadísticas Agropecuarias 1995*. Ciudad de La Habana, Septiembre 1996.

Pastor, Manuel Jr., and Andrew Zimbalist. "Cuba's Economic Conundrum." *NACLA Report on the Americas* 29(2) (Sept/Oct 1995): 7-12.

Pérez Rojas, Niurka, and Cary Torres Vila. *La Apertura de los Mercados Agropecuarios: Impacto y Valorizaciones*. Paper presented at Latin American Studies Association Conference, September 1995. Rural Research Team. La Habana: University of Havana Faculty of Philosohpy and History; Department of Sociology, 1995. 25 pages.

Pérez-Stable, Marifeli. *The Cuban Revolution*. New York: Oxford University Press, Inc., 1993.

Prychitko, David L., and Jaroslav Vanek. *Producer Cooperatives and Labor-Managed Systems: Theory*. Cheltenham, UK: Edward Elgar Publishing, Ltd., 1996.

Reed, Edward P. "Introducing Group Farming in Less Developed Countries: Some Issues." *Cooperative and Commune*, ed. Peter Dorner. Madison, Wisconsin: University of Wisconsin, 1977.

Regalado, Antero. *Las Luchas Campesinas en Cuba*. La Habana: Editorial Orbe, 1979.

Romero Valcárcel, Lázaro, Prisco Barroso Fernández, and Ramón Díaz Menéndez. "Vías para el Perfeccionamiento de la Actividad Socioeconómica de la UBPC '9 de Abril.'" *Colectivos Laborales de Nuevo Tipo, Resumen de Investigaciones Sobre las UBPC*, ed. Polo Científico de Humanidades. La Habana: Universidad de La Habana, 1994.

Royce, Frederick S. "Cooperative Agricultural Operations Management on a Cuban Sugarcane Farm: '. . . and Everything Gets Done Anyway.'" Master of Science Thesis. Gainesville: University of Florida, 1996.

Sims, Brian G., Raymundo Ventot, and Alberto Rivera. "Cooperatives as a Solution to Small Farm Mechanization Problems in Cuba." *Agricultural Mechanization in Asia, Africa and Latin America* 24(4) (1993): 63-72.

Zimbalist, Andrew, and Claes Brundenius. *The Cuban Economy: Measurement and Analysis of Socialist Performance*. Baltimore, MD: Johns Hopkins University Press, 1989.

Zimbalist, Andrew, and Susan Eckstein. "Patterns of Cuban Development: The First Twenty Five Years." *World Development* 15(1) (1987): 5-22.

PROPERTY RIGHTS, TECHNOLOGY, AND LAND DEGRADATION: A CASE STUDY OF SANTO DOMINGO, CUBA

Héctor Sáez

This paper explores environmental-economic issues in the agricultural sector. It presents a case-study of the Municipality of Santo Domingo, in the province of Villa Clara. The goal of this paper is to explore the way in which property rights and technological packages promote and undermine the long-term ecological-economic viability of farming land in the area.

I chose this municipality on the basis of the sensitivity of plant ecosystems to environmental stress.[1] The paper examines two state farms, two cooperatives, and three family farms. These units are compared in terms of their efforts to prevent resource degradation problems and engage in conservationist activities. The experience of family farmers suggests that a reduction in the size of large farms in Cuban agriculture, and a recasting of their incentive structure and technologies away from those of large-scale state farms, can have a positive effect in terms of natural-resource conservation.

The productivity of state farms in the area declined in both the sugar and non sugar sector even before the Special Period (DPPF 1988:9; Martínez 1993). The degradation of natural resources, particularly soils and tree cover, helps to explain these declines in productivity and output. On the other hand family

farms seemed to have been maintained or increased their productivity during the same period. No data was available to assess productivity trends for the agricultural cooperative sector.

Table 1 illustrates the output of state farms in Santo Domingo between 1983 and 1993, valued at current prices. The Manacas state farm (Empresa de Cultivos Varios Manacas, or ECV Manacas) reached its peak level of output for this period in 1985, with a value of production equal to 3,340,500 pesos. By 1990, its production had decreased to 2,227,600 pesos, a 33% reduction from its 1985 level. After the "Special Period" set in, agrochemical inputs became very scarce, and by 1993, the value of the state farm's output had fallen to 1,551,100 pesos, or less than half of its 1985 level. Table 2 shows the decline of output of the Manacas state farm by crop groups.

Most of the reduction in the farm's output occurred before the onset of the "Special Period." Moreover, according to the director of the Manacas state farm, due to the importance of this enterprise in producing vegetables for the region the Ministry of Agriculture (MINAGRI) tried hard to shield it from the fertilizer and pesticide scarcities associated with the "Special Period," by prioritizing the farm in the allocation of

---

1. This municipality was one of the three chosen by the Cuba team of the MacArthur Foudation funded comparative project "Rural Transformation in Socialist Societies." The Cuba team, to which I belonged, also chose the municipality of Güines in Havana province, and Majibacoa in the eastern province of Las Tunas. Whereas Güines represents an area with the best resource endowment, where agricultural development occurred early on, Majibacoa represents an area with a poor resource endowment and was a late comer to agricultural development. Santo Domingo represents "the middle of the road" in terms of the historical development of plantation agriculture in Cuba, and in terms of its natural resource endowment.

Table 1. Value of Agricultural Output Sold, in the Mixed Crop, Sugar, and Cattle Sectors (thousands of current pesos)

Items	Non Sugar	Meat and Dairy	Sugar	Sugar	Sugar
Empresa	ECV[a] Manacas	EP Cascajal	26 de Julio	Washington	C. Baliño
1983	1,992.9	6,794.1	—-	—-	—-
1984	1,992.9	6,794.1	—-	—-	—-
1985	3,340.5	6,449.2	3,626.4	15,783.1	7,214.0
1986	3,062.8	5,782.2	3,130.1	13,300.0	6,308.3
1987	2,091.0	5,367.1	3,045.6	9,844.4	4,005.1
1988	2,927.7	5,372.2	3,213.9	14,651.1	6,729.8
1989	2,626.1	5,164.2	2,923.8	12,185.6	5,019.4
1990	2,227.6	5,760.5	3,836.4	13,522.2	7,418.8
1991	2,378.4	3,973.0	3,284.5	12,633.4	5,342.4
1992	1,958.9	3,324.5	2,997.1	11,644.6	5,650.5
1993	1,551.1	2,409.9	1,070.3	10,041.8	5,038.6

Source: Informe de Economía Municipal, OME, Santo Domingo, (various years); and Tabla de Trabajo y Salario, OME, Santo Domingo, 1991, 1992, 1993. As reported by Rural Research Group of the University of La Habana.

a. Includes the ECV Cascajal, formed in 1991, which previously belonged to the ECV Manacas.

Table 2. Output of the Manacas State Farm by Crop Group, 1985-1991 (quintals)

Year	Viandas[a]	Vegetables	Citrus	Fruits[b]	Other	Total
1985	143,816	330,248	117,640	5,721	4,013	601,438
1986	111,971	296,663	92,888	12,709	6,089	520,320
1987	110,486	157,794	92,820	22,330	4,987	388,417
1988	90,193	244,206	98,973	16,571	3,642	453,585
1989	121,704	171,992	61,731	11,195	13,082	379,704
1990	73,905	164,057	78,359	23,619	16,694	356,634
1991	61,518	109,213	60,362	19,208	2,853	253,154

Source: Registro de Datos Históricos, Empresa Cultivos Varios Manacas, Santo Domingo. Reported by the Rural Research Group of the University of La Habana.

a. Tubers, roots and plantains
b. Non-citrus fruits.

these inputs (Yera 1993). However, as I show below, the MINAGRI did little to halt the degradation of the farm's soils. On the contrary, its production strategy intensified the use of natural resources, without setting up a program of natural-resource conservation.

A similar argument can be made in the case of sugar agro-industrial complexes (CAI). Santo Domingo's sugar production peaked in 1985 with a value of output equal to 26,621,500 pesos. Despite the national efforts to increase sugar production, prompted by

Cuba's external debt crisis during the late 1980s, Santo Domingo's sugar output trended downward from 1985 on. And while output bounced back in 1988 and 1990, the downward trend prevailed. In 1989, the value of sugar output was 20,128,000 pesos, or 24% less than in 1985. By 1993 sugar production had decreased to 16,150,700 pesos, or 39% less than in 1985. The production of milk and meat also suffered from significant reductions before the onset of the "Special Period." The value of output of the EP Cascajal (producers of meat and dairy products) stood at 6,794,100 pesos in 1983. By 1989, it had fallen to 5,760,500, for a 15% decrease. By 1991, the value of milk and meat production had gone down to 3,973,000, or 41% less than in 1983. By 1993, it had collapsed to 2,409,900, or 65% less than in 1983.

Clearly, without subsidized Soviet inputs, Santo Domingo could not return to the pre-crisis levels of output. Notably, this was not the case in the small farmer sector. Table 3 presents data on the sales of this sector to the state, disaggregated by crop groups. According to several farmers interviewed and to the official data available, the output of private farmers in Santo Domingo <u>increased</u> between 1990 and 1993, despite the widespread scarcity in agrochemical inputs and fuel, and before the opening of produce markets in 1994. After an initial decline, the total value of sales from family farmers to the state grew from 71,473 pesos in 1990 to 101,443 pesos in 1993, for a 42% increase. While the opening of produce markets in 1994 would enhance private incentives to produce, output increases were recorded even before the opening of markets. An important question is, how can private farmers maintain and increase production in the face of widespread chemical-input scarcities? The answer given in this paper is that the small-scale production technologies used by small farmers as well as their private incentives make small farmers willing and able to invest in natural resource conservation.

STATE FARMS

Natural-resource conservation was not a goal of state enterprises, and while managers had a de jure duty to conserve natural resources, this was not enforced. For example, failing to fulfill the productive plan may have resulted in the dismissal of the enterprise's director, no such penalty existed for failing to conserve natural resources. The failure to structure similar incentives for resource conservation had negative consequences with respect to conservation decisions.

At the Manacas State Farm little importance was paid to even the most basic and inexpensive anti-erosive measures: plowing perpendicular to the slope, the construction of barriers at the margin of irrigation canals, and the use of cover crops (Yera 1993). To be sure, changes in the spatial distribution of dif-

ferent crops and reduced tillage had been used in different sectors of the enterprise. Since the "Special Period" began in 1990, the MINAGRI experimented with the use of alternative fertilizers such as organic matter, humus, and sugar cane ashes. Soil amendments were used only if they fostered short-run productivity. Yet since their short-run productivity increases are small, low tech, alternative practices were not sufficiently supported by state farms; they were often perceived as costly conservation measures that compete with "real" production activities.

Table 3. Santo Domingo's Private Farmer Sales to the State (quintals)

	1990	1991	1992	1993
Total	71,473	67,674	67,796	101,443
Tubers & Roots	5,562	2,732	15,073	31,234
Vegetables	44,951	40,369	31,251	58,131
Rice	76	775	506	35
Corn	746	1,658	1,404	1,252
Plantains	7	6,462	13,492	8,155
Citrus[a]	2,189	2,545	2,986	2,308
Fruits[b]	17,942	13,233	2,904	296
Beans	15	22	58	32
Milk[c]	n.a.	243.2	190.3	305.3
Pork (kg)	n.a.	2,271	n.a.	n.a.
Meat (kg)	n.a.	437	7,228	815

Source: As reported by Rural Research Group of the University of Havana

a. Citrus Fruits
b. Non-Citrus Fruits
c. Thousand liters

State farms were created to produce a specific product or set of products. The Manacas state enterprise was specifically created to produce vegetables, particularly tomatoes, because of the success of tomato production in the area before 1959. But this productive specialization was imposed from above in an inflexible way and served as an obstacle for conservation. In the case of the Manacas farm, tomato monocropping led to the persistence of nematodes in the soil, with a crippling effect on productivity. Crop rotation (with nitrogen-fixating varieties)and fallow periods were necessary, particularly in areas planted with tomatoes. Yet the state control over the output-mix and the technology used impeded the revamping of rotation patterns.

Given that the main responsibility of this enterprise was to produce tomatoes, enterprise managers always allocated the most fertile plots to that crop. The most modern irrigation systems were in place in these fields. Further, these fields were cultivated all year round.

The Manacas state enterprise was among the first in the province to engage in the intensive use of traditional irrigation in the early days of the revolution (ENPA 1986:9). Traditional irrigation systems waste much water, foster soil erosion and the silting of canals, and require much maintenance work. According to Yera (then director of the Manacas Enterprise), traditional irrigation has taken a heavy toll upon the enterprise's topsoil. Much runoff is generated by this water-intensive method, resulting in erosion and leaching. Given the subsoil conditions that prevail in the area, irrigation tends to worsen flooding problems.

MINAGRI officials at the provincial level, as well as enterprise administrators, identified deficiencies in irrigation as one of the main causes of the low productivity of inputs in the Manacas enterprise. In 1986, the MINAGRI set out to increase the areas under irrigation in the Manacas enterprise and to transform the outdated irrigation systems there. However, both of the systems promoted erosion and led to inflexible land use patterns which impeded environmentally-sound crop rotation schemes.

The Volshanka irrigation machines that were installed require that furrows follow the longest side of the field. But because of the design and distribution of fields in this enterprise, the longest side of the field often coincided with the direction of the slope. Therefore, the use of this irrigation technology increased the sensitivity of the agricultural system to erosion: by eliminating furrows that are perpendicular to the slope it increases the amount of runoff generated and its erosive force. On the other hand the DDA mechanized sprinklers made irrigation work very difficult and required that workers be trained to use them. Furthermore, routine irrigation activities

may have created sizable erosion problems. Yet given the relatively low wages and the lack of well developed self-provisioning schemes, the labor force at the Manacas state enterprise was very unstable. Even the chiefs of irrigation frequently quit. Therefore, at any given time, many of the workers handling irrigation equipment had little training and experience. Thus, the workers managing irrigation technologies and water resources may actually contribute to erosion, waterlogging, and water waste.

Irrigation systems in the enterprise have generated an additional problem. The construction of irrigation canals and other infrastructure investments impose a rigid land use pattern. Those areas where irrigation systems are in place, which comprise 70% of the cultivated land, were used very intensely, often without fallow periods. Irrigation systems also limit the kinds of crops that the enterprise decided to plant in each area, and thus the choice set for crop rotation. Tomatoes were almost exclusively planted in areas where machine-based irrigation was in place. The fact that tomatoes were planted in the same (irrigated) fields led to the persistence of nematodes, a pest that severely reduced tomato yields.

Resource conservation could have been pursued by careful performance of the soil preparation tasks. However state control reduced the enterprises' space for decision making, and limited their ability to face environmental stress and shocks. Decisions came from the MINAGRI and often disregarded the conditions of the soil, climate, and the state of infrastructure-works. The provincial MINAGRI or MINAZ specified deadlines for planting and harvesting all fields. If the soil was too dry soil preparation led to eolic erosion; and if it was more humid than required, it resulted in soil compaction.

Due to the pressures put on workers to plant larger areas and to catch up with piled-up work, pre-planting soil preparation was sometimes carried out very quickly. Poor soil preparation had adverse consequences for soil fertility, humidity, and structure.

From the point of view of most of the decision makers of the Manacas state farm and the "26 de Julio" sugar complex, inadequate drainage was the main obstacle to increases in productivity. Several factors determine the occurrence of flooding, which affects much of the agricultural areas in Santo Domingo. First, the existence of a hard layer of clay (hard pan at a depth of 20 to 50 cms.) does not readily permit water to travel deep underground. Second, the water table is very close to the surface in many places. Third, while the original vegetation may serve as a sponge, absorbing water during rainy periods and releasing it during dry periods, the area is severely deforested. Fourth, drainage problems have been worsened by increases in irrigation, and by the hardening of the soil due to the use of heavy agricultural equipment (i.e. soil compaction).

Soil compaction is a pervasive problem in Cuba, and is caused by the use of heavy equipment. Their constant use hardens the soil, reducing its capacity to absorb water, which, in turn, contributes to waterlogging. The hardened soil reduces the plant's root growth. Deep subsoiling may solve the problem, but subsoiling equipment is not widely available. Furthermore, subsoiling requires large expenditures of scarce fuel.

The decision not to tackle the problem of flooding in Santo Domingo is based in part on the large amount of resources required by the "high-technology" model of farming and its lack of an ecological framework. The agricultural ministries classify the problems into seemingly unrelated compartments: according to Remo Pérez (1992), a soil technician with the MINAGRI in Villa Clara, "[i]n lowlands the important thing is flooding, in mountains, erosion. In Santo Domingo, instead of soil conservation we need to deal with drainage... "

The soil specialist classifies the soil as poor, focusing on one problem in the abstract (flooding) and dismissing other problems as minor in comparison. Solving "the main problem" in this case would require a large investment that the state cannot currently afford. As a consequence, provincial officials do nothing about flooding and erosion at the Manacas farm. Two changes in the mid-level bureaucrat's perception of land degradation, within the organic framework of an alternative farming model, could

bring about a very different strategy to deal with the problem.

First, they need to understand that flooding, erosion, the persistence of pests, and other problems are all related to one another. Second, the poor quality of the soils is directly associated with erosion and leaching because both processes reduce the amount of organic matter and minerals in these soils. Moreover, the notion that flatlands are not prone to erosion is a myth. Sheet erosion is pervasive in this type of (sandy) soil (Febles and Durán 1988). Furthermore, a study conducted by researchers at the National Soil Institute of Cuba showed that this area is highly prone to leaching through the dissolution of mineral nutrients in the soil (González, et al. 1991).

To solve the problem of nutrient loss, chemical fertilization is supposed to be carried out according to tests performed by the Soils and Fertilizers office of the provincial MINAGRI, which schedules tests for different areas every year. However, fertility tests are few and far between, the number of plots tested is small, and their distribution is so irregular that no solid conclusions may be derived about fertility conditions (Fundora, O. 1993). The MINAGRI claims that testing is crucial for the allocation of scarce fertilizers but, ultimately, technicians made their decisions regarding the composition and quantity of fertilizers to be applied in each field without adequate data. Because of the sheer size of the enterprises and the scarcity of workers, state farming did not afford many alternatives.

Awareness is crucial for the design and enforcement of rules and technologies that may promote sustainability in resource use. Different perceptions of land degradation problems also seem to permeate the MINAZ in this area. Top administrators in the CAI "26 de Julio" do not recognize erosion to be a problem; they too believe flat soils are not erodible. However, some mid-level managers are aware of the erosion problem. About 50% of the arable land of the CAI "26 de Julio" consists of highly erodible sandy soil (the same type present in the Manacas state farm). Erosion is a problem in places where irrigation is used. Camilo Cárdenas, production chief of the second brigade, admitted that conservation has never been a priority; "I have tried to call attention to the erosion problem, but we have a small amount of time to plant and great pressure to harvest. Some things are accomplished; we have ploughed against the slope" (Cárdenas 1993). The vague soil-conservation directives issued by the MINAZ did not structure any incentives for compliance nor monitoring and enforcement mechanisms.

Cárdenas pointed out some of the limitations that made it difficult to carry out anti-erosive measures, even if information of the problem was adequate. First, Cárdenas confirmed the lack of concern about erosion and the perception, by planners and managers, that relatively flat-sloped soils are not erodible (Cárdenas 1993). Second, the farming technology used limited the institutional resilience of state farms to deal with land degradation. For example, large harvesting combines require long furrows (otherwise the combines would make many turns, thus complicating their maneuverability). However, just as in the Manacas enterprise, whether the longest side of the field coincides with the direction of the slope was not taken into consideration. If furrows are aimed towards the slope, irrigation or rain water moves with greater speed, thus increasing its erosive force. Conservation tillage, which lessens soil erosion and the loss of nutrients, is not an option because of the employment of heavy equipment. Third, he pointed out that most, if not all, of the tasks performed are aimed at increasing output; conservation was not a priority, but maximizing output was.

In sum, the evidence presented suggests that state farms did a poor job of protecting the environment in agriculture. The strategy of agricultural modernization at all costs, imposes a "high-technology" production paradigm which results in severe environmental degradation, and which demands "high-technology" solutions. For a while, short run productivity gains associated with agricultural modernization made up for the productivity losses associated with environmental degradation. This limited the environmental awareness of workers, managers and planners, who in addition have no incentives to seek information regarding degradation nor to pass it along. Neither workers nor managers and administrators have incentives to tackle resource degradation problems.

INDIVIDUAL FARMS

Private property rights and access to social services give small farmers the incentives to invest in conserving natural resources. Yet property rights and the safety net cannot explain why farmers choose specific production technologies that enhance their resource base. In this section I look at both incentives and technologies that help small farmers protect the environment.

Private farmers retained control over their land and productive process at the "expense" of their limited access to chemical and mechanical inputs and to economies of scale in production. Along with credit, equipment and extension services are made available through service cooperatives (the Cooperativas de Crédito y Servicios or CCS). During the first thirty years of the revolution, family farmers gained access to mechanical inputs such as small tractors, turbines, and to a low but consistent supply of chemical inputs such as fertilizers and pesticides.

Small farms belong to the families, one member of which, usually the male head of household or "independent peasant," controls most production decisions as well as the appropriation and distribution of the surplus. The land can only be sold to the state, or bequeathed to the peasant's children. This is an important rule because it virtually eliminates the incentive to produce by running down natural resources and then selling it for an alternative use. Small farmers can also transfer their land to a cooperative and become a member. These private property rights are curtailed by the state's control of various aspects of family production. The state controls small farmer's access to, and prices of, chemical and mechanical inputs, equipment, fuel and credit.

While private property rights, including access to stable marketing outlets, support the development of small farms, state limits on these rights curtail them. State officials dictate part of the output mix and its part of its distribution and suggest production techniques, and further limit the access to inputs and credit if the farmer does not comply. Failing to comply with the state productive plans can also result in fines.

Case Studies

Fernando García Cairo, a 65 year old peasant, farmed the land for thirty years at Paradero de Alvarez, Santo Domingo, and was a beneficiary of the first law of agrarian reform. His multicrop production takes place on 7.5 has. and includes peppers, tomatoes, beans, corn, cucumbers, and different kinds of squash.[2] Multicropping patterns reduce the farm's sensitivity (e.g. to pests) and increases its resiliency by maintaining fertility. Crop variety spreads his risk of crop failure. He has some fowl birds and two oxen, but has no cows or horses. His knowledge does not come exclusively from experience. Having learned to read during the literacy campaigns of the 1960s, he developed a passion for books about soils and farming (García Cairo, 1993). If available, he makes use of small amounts of chemical fertilizers and pesticides.

A four inch turbine pumps water from underground and is used to irrigate all of his land with small aspersors or with traditional methods. The soils on García's farm are sandy and hilly, making them extremely prone to erosion. Small farmers are well aware that irrigation on their land could wash away the soil. In order to minimize erosion, he divided the farm into blocs by digging small canals that follow the direction of the slope (perpendicular to the furrows) and created planting beds. Water is poured on the canal on the superior part of the planting bed. This system maximizes the land surface exposed to the irrigation water, possibly leading to greater erosion if irrigation is not performed carefully. But he irrigates slowly and carefully, which maximizes the absorption of water and minimizes runoff, and thus erosion.

García constantly rotates his crops, avoids planting crops that might allow pests to persist, uses nitrogen-fixating crops, as well as plants that serve as green-manure. His rotation and intercropping patterns are intimately associated with his fertilizer and pest-control needs. García has used urea and chicken manure as fertilizer since 1987, but he can only secure limited quantities (enough for 1 hectare a year). The application of chicken manure requires a very labor intensive process of soil preparation. Because of its strength, fields treated with chicken manure are left idle for about two years. According to García, fields treated with chicken manure do not need fertilizer for up to five years thereafter. Other small farmers also fertilize with *cachaza*, decomposed sugar cane, crop residues, and tree debris.

One such farmer who uses organic fertilizers is Francmacio Pérez Chavez. Francmacio lives on a farm he inherited from his father with his family. His brother's family, and his daughters, sons in law, and grandchildren live in a two-story house and two one-story houses at the edge of the small farm. His father was a beneficiary of the first law of agrarian reform; the land had been taken over in 1957 by one of the sugar companies in Santo Domingo and was subsequently expropriated and redistributed to his family, which numbers twenty people. Most family members help sporadically on the farm. He has a 1½ inch turbine, no tractor, three cows, two oxen, and one horse.

Pérez Chávez produces more than forty products on less than three hectares of land. His rotation sequence is based upon planting a nitrogen-fixating crop (e.g. beans) or one which leaves large amounts of residues (e.g. rice), before planting a demanding crop (e.g. corn). He uses both an alley distribution, with crops planted in between lines of trees, and a mosaic pattern, with fruit trees on one quadrant, animals on another, annual crops on another, and vegetables on yet another. A dirt road divides the farm into two halves with fences made of cacti.

Cropping patterns which combine lines of trees with vegetables and grain patches are found on many small farms, albeit with differences in crops and tree combinations. Some farmers emphasize fruit trees.

---

2. In 1992 García sold more than eight hundred quintals of tomato, chile, cucumber and squash to Acopio, the state procurement agency.

One of the farmers interviewed, Jacinto Pérez, specializes in fruits, some of which are very hard to find elsewhere. This farm started as a producer of mangos and oranges. However, after planting, farmers have to wait a minimum of eight years for the trees to mature and produce commercially. In the meantime, Jacinto's father, the original owner, experimented with grafting and sold plantlets of locally improved varieties of mangos, oranges, and avocados. In 1995 the selection included oranges,[3] mango, avocado, lemon, *mamoncillo*, tamarind, *marañón*, *red mamey*, *mamey Santo Domingo*, *caimito*, *fruta bomba*, *pomarosa*, *chirimoya*, *anón*, *guanábana*, prunes, guavas, grapefruits, tangerines, plantains, and coconuts, as well as wood trees such as *júcaro*, *guásima*, *guamá*, eucalyptus, mahogany, and others.

The twenty-seven hectare farm was inhabited by twelve family members, six of whom help in the farm sporadically, and four (two men and two women), who work on the farm on a daily basis. Just as in Francmacio's case, the main household is where Jacinto lives. Here is where organization of production, negotiations with state officials, and surplus appropriation take place, led by him.

Jacinto has a six-inch oil-powered turbine which was not been in use between 1993 and 1995 for lack of fuel. His tractor, however, was used often and plays an important role in tilling between the mango trees. Among other tasks, the tractor was used to mix the soil with organic debris, improving its humidity and fertility.

Private production and appropriation of the surplus allows small farmers to be flexible to the vagaries of weather and state policies. In order to produce food crops that became scarce through the state allocation system after the beginning of the "Special Period," both Francmacio and Jacinto cleared new patches by cutting or trimming trees. Francmacio pruned every other tree line and planted yucca, rice, and other food crops between the mango trees. Jacinto cleared a half hectare and planted corn, pumpkins, sweet po-

tatoes, and rice. He also increased the number of cows, pigs and fowl on the farm.

Besides changing his technology of production, Francmacio has experimented with products which he did not produce before, such as wheat and peanuts. The scarcity of cooking oil associated with the "Special Period" prompted him to plant peanuts from which he extracts more than thirty pounds of oil, three times a year. He also produced two quintals of wheat. Because of his experience working in the state's industrial sector, Francmacio was able to design and build a simple grinding machine in his friend's shop, which he now uses to grind everything from wheat to sugar cane. This machine allows him to grind the ingredients to produce *gofio* (a snack made from ground wheat), and animal feed from rice chaff, peanut hull, and mango seeds.

Private Rights and Small-Scale Technology

Private property rights allow and encourage small farmers to experiment and develop technologies that are uniquely suited to the specific characteristics of particular fields (e.g. planting beds and grafting). Small farmers appropriate their own surplus, consume part of it, and transfer part of it to the state. They also share it with their neighbors and extended families, or exchange some of it for valued goods. Control over the surplus (as well as the relatively high degree of autonomy in decision making, the security provided by their productive unit, and the transferability of their assets to their children), gives small farmers ample reward and reason to maintain the long-run sustainability of their resource base.

Their limited access to modern inputs prompted small farmers to further develop traditional, "organic" methods. Small farmers utilize numerous techniques and produce a wide variety of output combinations, while using less chemicals, machinery, and equipment per unit of arable land, and more labor than state farms and cooperatives. Small farmers attempt to maintain and increase the value of their natural resources in several ways. They increase local biodiversity by planting assorted crops and plant va-

---

3. Jacinto has four varieties of oranges: *agria* (bitter), *chinas*, *nevo*, and *valencia*.

rieties. With time, biological diversity and intercropping in "alley" and "mosaic" patterns results in feedback effects between plants, predators and pests. Furthermore, individual farmers carry out labor-intensive, anti-erosion measures. The high labor-to-land ratios increase the productivity of these systems, and the small number of resource users on each farm allow for the enforcement of sustainable resource-use norms. Small farmers have an intimate knowledge of their land and the interaction between crops, soils, fertilizers, pests, and pesticides. They are keenly aware of the processes of land degradation and diligently engage in activities aimed at restoring and protecting soil fertility. Their agricultural systems exhibit high resiliency, allowing them to adapt to cumulative stresses and sudden shocks upon the sensitive ecosystems of Santo Domingo.

PRODUCTION COOPERATIVES (CPAS)

The government's movement towards the formation of production cooperatives, which began in 1977, aimed to increase output by modernizing peasant production and to increase state control over the country's output mix and its distribution. The incentives for small farmers to pool their land and labor included preferential access to credit to buy capital inputs at subsidized prices and retirement benefits (Deere, Meurs and Pérez 1992:121).

Cooperatives combine state and group control with peasant farming culture, resulting in productive systems that exhibit some characteristics of both modern and traditional farming. In general, cooperatives exhibit higher degrees of mechanization, use of chemicals, irrigation equipment, and productive specialization per unit of land, than individual producers, but less so than state farms.

In terms of their institutional arrangement, cooperatives are structured as a common-property regime. As such, the land and other productive assets are owned by cooperative members and the surplus product is appropriated collectively. Cooperative members can transfer their membership to their children, and thus the right to belong to the cooperative. The main production decisions are made collectively at monthly meetings led by the internally-elected council. Whereas self-provisioning schemes were introduced in state farms during the "Special Period," cooperatives have always (since their creation) produced for their own consumption, in addition to selling the bulk of their output to the state. Much of the production of meat, vegetables, plantains, and tubers is sold to cooperative members for self-provisioning. Just as in the case of individual farmers, these rights motivate cooperative members to protect their natural resources.

However, the range of cooperative property rights is limited by the cooperative's relationship with the state agricultural ministries. The state controls the allocation of inputs and credit to the CPAs, and has a heavy hand in determining the technology of production. The state also controls the prices of output and contracts the amounts to be sold to the state, and can pressure cooperatives to make certain investments.

The "Mariana Grajales" CPA

Most of the original members of this CPA were once individual farmers who pooled their land to join the cooperative. On the other hand, three of the main managers previously worked for the state sector before joining the CPA. The cooperative's stock of cattle has grown consistently, going from 100 in 1987 to 864 head in 1992, to more than 980 in 1995. In 1993, this CPA cultivated 323 hectares of land, with the remaining 957 hectares dedicated to cattle production.

The CPA's production Chief, Ernesto Sutil, calculated that 90% of their area is sandy soil. There are some good soils in the Mordazo area (carbonated-dark and red-ferralitic soils) but are extremely prone to flooding (Sutil 1993). The "Mariana Grajales" is located in, what an official from the National Enterprise for Agricultural and Cattle Projects (ENPA) described as, a geological "drain" or lowlands that are prone to severe flooding (Choy 1993). Several creeks pass through the CPA which, in periods of intense rain, flood several areas of the cooperative. To deal with their flooding problems, they have built canals surrounding their main fields. These canals help both by collecting the water that comes from outside of the cooperative, and by draining its own fields. According to Sutil, solving the drainage problem would allow for more production and for more people to join the cooperative.

The cooperative exhibited some of the practices associated with small, alternative farming namely, the use of organic fertilizers, and innovative soil preparation and rotation techniques. Some fields in the plantain area have been improved with chicken manure, produced in their own chicken compound. Around 135 hectares are rotated between cattle ranching and cropping. Crop residues are left in the tilled fields, increasing the potassium contents of the soil and improving its structure. Corn is planted in areas where potatoes are grown to fixate nitrogen. Animal traction is routinely used in the CPA. In 1992, the cooperative had eleven teams of oxen and eight tractors.

While soil preparation procedures in the cooperative are similar to those in state farms, the cooperative has developed norms to prepare the soil in innovative ways in some areas. In fields of low soil depth, crops are planted in mounds (for plantains) or in humps (for potatoes) that are made of topsoil. These techniques also help crops survive waterlogging, especially in areas where hardpan is present in the subsoil. According to Menéndez (1993), these techniques have notably improved the production of plantains.

The "Mariana Grajales" CPA is a good example of the control and limits imposed by the relationship between cooperatives and the central government in Cuba. In an attempt to acquire the equipment and infrastructure needed to increase production, CPA leaders sought to join the "campaign for the 100,000 quintals." In exchange for state investment, inputs, and technical assistance associated with this campaign, the CPA submitted itself more fully to the production targets, infrastructural design, and directives of the Ministry of Agriculture. Several departments of the Ministry of Agriculture, namely the ENPA, Soils and Fertilizers, Plant Health, and the municipal office of the Ministry, crafted a five-year plan for development of this CPA. The plan lays out specialization and rotation schemes by area, and the kinds of infrastructure investments required.

The most important infrastructural investment in the plan is the installation of Fregat machines to irrigate fifty hectares of land for sixteen hours per day. Since there had been problems with Fregat machines in the ECV Manacas, the Ministry of Agriculture undertook 50% of the investment costs. Thanks to this new irrigation system, the cooperative can plant three crops a year in the areas benefited. The crops planted in these areas are potato, plantain, cucumber, pumpkin, rice, and sweet potato. Potato yields increased from between 75 and 150 quintals per hectare in 1986 to 535 quintals per hectare in 1992, much of it due to the irrigation equipment. The average (national) returns are between 300 and 335 quintals per hectare.

However, the MINAGRI had not provided the technical assistance and resources needed to carry out the circular draining system of canals that goes along with Fregat irrigation. In 1993 the CPA still had a traditional drainage system based upon simple canals. As a result of the Fregat machines and the lack of adequate drainage, the affected fields became more prone to flooding, and the productive system more sensitive to rain. Drainage is a key component of the project, for it could prevent the worsening flooding and waterlogging, and thus is very important for soil conservation.

ENPA officials admit that this irrigation technology may worsen erosion and drainage problems, but the responsibility for conservation is placed solely in the hands of workers. ENPA officials emphasize that irrigators must be very disciplined in following the technical specifications and water application norms; in order for the Fregat system to work it must be properly managed. The solution, however, resulted in another degradation problem. Whereas by 1995 a circular drainage system had been finished, this required changing the direction of the furrows, which now follow the heading of the slope and which has lead to soil erosion. In addition, because of the limited amount of water that may be extracted from wells, in 1992 the state authorized increases in the extraction of water from underground sources for the crops projected in the plan only (and not for self-provisioning crops).

It is clear that the state exerts a great deal of control over the CPA. Moreover, because of the changes towards modern farming methods, these cooperativists face problems that they did not have as family farmers (e.g., persistent pest problems). Yet the cooperative maintains many aspects of the family-farm culture in the context of a systematic cooperative system. Giraldo Pérez is quick to point out that CPA members work for themselves and that this autonomy makes a difference; "People here work with interest and, because there is love for the land and the cooperative, things are done well. If there are pests it is quickly discovered and dealt with. The cadres and workers have responsibilities and the liberty to make decisions. This power leads to success" (G. Pérez 1993).

The "Nelson Veitía" CPA

With 613 hectares, the CPA "Nelson Veitía" has half the land area of the "Mariana Grajales" and fifty four members. It had 300 hectares of grazing land, 242 hectares planted in tubers and legumes, and four hectares of trees. Agricultural production in this cooperative has characteristics of both the alternative and the modern farming models. Whereas only one of the founding members had a tractor before the formation of the cooperative, by 1993 the cooperative had six tractors. Still, soil preparation with heavy equipment is kept to a minimum. Relay cropping and some inter-cropping were used to maintain soil fertility. The "Nelson Veitía" exhibits more agro-diversity than the "Mariana Grajales."

The cooperative's irrigation infrastructure includes two small dams, five turbines, one deep water well with a pump, a system of tubes and canals, and other equipment. There have been saline intrusions in some of their wells, probably due to the heavy extraction of water by state farms in the area and to the damming of the Alacranes river, which reduces the recharge in underground wells in the area. The CPA uses portable sprinklers and sometimes traditional irrigation. This cooperative also has urgent flooding and drainage problems.

The dark soils of this CPA are better than the sandy soils that prevail in the rest of the municipality. The cooperative has more than 500 hectares of dark soils, 54 hectares of sandy soils and 15 hectares of red soils. Dark soils are more fertile than other soils in the area

and are therefore used constantly. Notwithstanding this, the MINAGRI regards the "Nelson Veitía" as a low-productivity cooperative. Some members interviewed argue that the cooperative has not received sufficient state support. In part as a consequence of its low profitability, cooperative members feel compelled to use the most productive areas more intensely. In addition, farming methods have changed greatly since the cooperative was formed. While there is some intercropping and crop rotation, the farm's layout is a far cry from the mosaic and alley patterns found in individual farms. There is no emphasis on agroforestry. Rather, the cooperative was slowly moving towards monocropping, yet it faced difficult pest-problems and *marabú* infestations.

Interestingly, the MINAGRI has not aggressively searched for ways to deal with pest problems in this cooperative in an integrated way. And in 1993 the coop had no access to biological pest controls produced in state-sponsored laboratories but rather, it relied on chemical pesticides with little success. CPA members are concerned that pest problems increasingly limit what they can produce. Because of pest problems, the CPA agreed with the MINAGRI to limit production of cucumbers and pumpkins and not to produce onions in 1992. Cooperative members wonder whether it would be in their best interest to stick to cattle ranching. Cattle production is less complex and would increase their profitability and the stability of output and earnings. However, it can have a negative impact upon the soil, a fact not explicitly considered by the members interviewed.

The "Nelson Veitía" still produced multiple crops; some are produced in intercropping patterns, but not in the "mosaic" or multiple-patch layouts that are typical of small farms. Some fields are set aside and used as pastures for horses and some crops are rotated, however Navias admits that crop rotations, along with soil preparation and conservation activities, are not carried out in a systematic way. Moreover, while CPA members are not too concerned with soil degradation, some forms of degradation are evident. As in the rest of Santo Domingo, flooding affects the "Nelson Veitía" and is partly the result of deforestation. Yet while more than half of the cooperative's area is used for raising cattle, less than 1% of the area is planted with trees.

SUMMARY AND CONCLUSIONS

Agricultural ecosystems in Santo Domingo are very sensitive as they change easily and drastically after human intervention. However, they exhibit high resilience, as they respond favorably to soil amendments, appropriate humidity, fallow periods, small scale reforestation and polycropping.

State farms in Santo Domingo conformed to the modern model of farming. They were large farms that base their productivity on monocropping, chemical pesticides, fertilizers, use of heavy tilling equipment, modern irrigation equipment and no fallow periods. State farms make little use of intercropping, agroforestry, crop rotation, and other alternative technologies. Alternative fertilizers are used but their supplies are limited by the reluctance of administrators to assign more workers and resources to their production.

The use of modern farming technologies in the context of state agriculture led to resource degradation in Santo Domingo. The heavy use of fertilizers in the area is responsible for water contamination with nitrate. Large-scale use of traditional irrigation led to erosion and leaching, and modern irrigation systems have only contributed to these trends. The use of heavy equipment has led to soil compaction and has prevented basic anti-erosive measures. Monocropping has fostered erosion and pest problems, and has made fields more prone to flooding.

Inevitably, resource degradation reduces overall productivity, which compels enterprise managers and state officials to try to improve upon the modern techniques used, with more heavy equipment and infrastructure. State farms were understaffed, due to the lack of attractive worker incentives. The lack of an adequate number of steady workers meant that crops did not receive the attention that they needed. To counter this, state farms planted larger areas which reduced labor inputs per unit of land. As a result of this and the degradation of the resource base, total output stagnated. Managers had very limited awareness and sought no information about the de-grading impact of their productive practices. Instead, they perceive the resource base as naturally poor.

Small farmers' agricultural systems take advantage of restorative potential of the resource base and are therefore very resilient. They have the incentives to spend long hours in the fields, where they constantly monitor and gather information on the condition of plant, tree, soil and water resources. In general, small farmers exhibited more awareness of degradation problems than did cooperative members. Small-farmers have greater incentives to seek and use information about their resource base. CPA members emphasized the importance of chemical fertilizers and drainage works over the integration of production and conservation activities.

Labor-intensive, small-farming techniques combine modest amounts of agrochemicals, small tractors, and irrigation equipment, with traditional methods. As a result, they generate proportionally less pollution and soil degradation by compaction, salinization and acidification than large-modern farms. Small farms in Cuba promote biodiversity, as they produce more than thirty agricultural and livestock products each, and dozens of different sub-species. They employ a variety of productive techniques in agrosilvi-pastural patterns. Monocropping makes no sense for them. All private producers interviewed experiment with different technologies. They have ample space for experimentation, as their families have access to nearby schools and medical doctors, they appropriate their own surplus, and the farm's output has secure, stable markets and prices. These conditions enable the farmer to administer and control production and invest his time and effort in the development of the farm.

Cooperatives possess more machinery and irrigation equipment, they use a greater amount of chemicals, and have a higher degree of specialization than individual producers. Many cooperative members seem to be convinced that the net benefits of adopting modern inputs are high. State farms, however, are more advanced in this sense. On the other hand, cooperatives make more use of alternative fertilizers, pesticides, and tilling techniques than state farms do. In general, CPAs develop rotation schemes that best suit their soils and output mix. CPAs are no longer formed mainly by former individual farmers, as many former state-farm technicians and field workers have joined them and, in some cases occupy administrative and managerial positions. This interaction facilitates the merging of modern and traditional farming techniques.

Judging by the characteristics of each form of organization of production, the productive system of small farms are less sensitive and more resilient than those of cooperatives and state farms (the latter displaying the highest sensitivity and lowest resilience of the three). In terms of their institutional arrangements, the evidence presented here suggests that small farmers have incentives and use technologies that enable sustainable resource management.

REFERENCES

Alvarez, J. and Ricardo A. Puerta (1994). " State Intervention in Cuban Agriculture: Impact on Organization and Performance." *World Development* 22(11), 1663-1675.

Anonymous (1993). Sub Director, CAI "26 de Julio," Santo Domingo.

Anonymous (1995). Cooperative Member, CPA "Nelson Veitía," Santo Domingo.

Cárdenas, Camilo (1993). Chief of Brigade # 2, CAI "26 de Julio," Santo Domingo.

Deere, Carmen Diana (1995). "Towards a Reconstruction of Cuba's Agrarian Transformation: 1900-1989." Paper prepared for the Congress "Agrarian Questions," Wageningen Agricultural University, The Netherlands, May 22-24, 1995.

Deere, Carmen Diana, Mieke Meurs, and Niurka Pérez (1992). "Toward a Periodization of the Cuban Collectivization Process: Changing Incentives and Peasant Response." *Cuban Studies/ Estudios Cubanos* (22)115-149.

Dirección Provincial de Planificación Física (DPPF) (1988). "Plan Director del Municipio de Santo Domingo." Santa Clara (mimeo).

ENPA (1986) Directive Plan for the ECV Manacas. *Plan Director de la ECV Manacas*. MINAGRI. Santa Clara.

Febles, José M. and José L. Durán (1988). *Manual de Erosión y Conservación de Suelos*. La Habana.

Fundora, Jorge Luis (1993). Chief of the Department of Technology, CAI "26 de Julio." Santo Domingo.

Fundora, Onelio (1993). Professor of Soil Chemistry at the Instituto Técnico. Santo Domingo.

García Cairo, Fernando (1993). Private Farmer. Santo Domingo.

González, Juan E., Alina Fundora, Ramón Ysa, Gabriel Guerra, Osmay Peña, Raúl Marzán (1991). "Origen de la Diferenciación Textural Mediante la Caracterización de la Mineralogía de los Suelos y sus Rásgos Pedológicos Esenciales," Instituto de Suelos Código 18 RI 92, Forma de Aprobación: Grupo Experto 436 Acta (3).

MINAGRI (1993). *Trabajo de Riego y Viales en la Empresa de Cultivos Varios Manacas*. Santa Clara: Ministerio de Agricultura.

Martínez, Lilian (1993). Chief of Soils and Fertilizers. CAI "26 de Julio," Santo Domingo.

Menéndez, Serafín (1993). Member, CPA "Mariana Grajales," Santo Domingo.

Núñez, Lupo (1995). "Evolución de la Organización Empresarial Agropecuaria en la Cuba Revolucionaria." Paper presented at the XIX International

Congress of the Latin American Studies Association, Washington, D.C., September 28-30.

Navias, Homero (1992). President of the CPA "Nelson Veitía," Santo Domingo.

Pérez, Jacinto (1993). Private Farmer. Santo Domingo.

Pérez, Francmacio (1995). Private Farmer. Santo Domingo.

Pérez, Remo (1993). Director. Office of Soils and Fertilizers. MINAGRI. Santa Clara.

Sutil, Ernesto (1993). Production Chief. CPA "Mariana Grajales," Santo Domingo.

Yera, Cristóbal (1993). Director of the Manacas State Farm, Santo Domingo.

COMMENTS ON

"Property Rights, Technology and Land Degradation: A Case Study of Santo Domingo, Cuba" by Sáez

José Alvarez

Reading the article by Professor Sáez, which I received as an 84-page chapter of his dissertation, has been a long but rewarding experience. If I had to summarize my reaction in just one sentence, the following would be very appropriate: a well researched, documented, written, impressive and devastating paper. This piece adds considerably to the growing wealth of information developed lately in the area of resource conservation and degradation in Cuba.

Since my comments can not address the wide range of topics covered by the author, I have decided to focus in one of my favorite issues: differences in productivity between the state and non-state sectors. At the 1993 ASCE meetings, Ricardo Puerta and I presented a paper, which was later revised and published in *World Development*, discussing statistical results on productivity differences between the state and non-state sectors and some obvious reasons for such differences. In addition to confirming, with data from the municipality of Santo Domingo, the failure of the state extensive growth model applied in agriculture during the 1980s—well before the establishment of the Special Period (SP) in September of 1990—the paper by Professor Sáez adds another dimension that, to my knowledge, has not been documented before in the literature.

After presenting data on increasing private sector output in contrast with declining trends in state farms during the SP, the author asks the following question: "How can private farmers maintain and in-crease production in the face of widespread chemical-input scarcities?" And he continues:

> The evidence presented ... shows that, in the case of Santo Domingo, private family farmers have conserved and developed their natural resource base, which allowed them to respond to the economic crisis. On the other hand, the state failed to foster resource conservation. The decline of output in state farms is explained in part by the degradation of natural resources in the area.

The article contains a long list of examples on the trade-offs between production and conservation practices in state farms. ("Conservation is not a priority, but maximizing output is.") Cultural practices that increase production (MINAGRI's main objective) rather than those that conserve resources are chosen by state managers. It is like reading René Dumont's accounts of the continuous mistakes made in the early years of the revolution. And this is still happening more than 30 years later! On the other hand, as you will read in the original paper, the author enumerates not only the reasons but also the procedures used by non-state farmers for resource conservation.

Given the success of non-state farmers on higher productivity ("All individual producers interviewed argued that small, individual farming is more productive than state farming in Santo Domingo") due in part to crop rotation, selective use of organic and commercial fertilizers, intercropping, fallow periods, and many other easy practices, one wonders about the current state of affairs after the establishment of the Basic Units of Cooperative Production (UBPCs). Since the bulk of this research was conducted before their creation, it would be interesting to know the UBPCs' approach to resource conservation—an attractive topic for further research.

One final thought comes to mind. Most of us know about the numerous environmental laws and regulations enacted by the Cuban government. According to Professor Sáez, however, those related to agricultural production and several others are not enforced in the municipality of Santo Domingo. The new environmental law approved by the National Assembly of People's Power at the end of July 1997 appears to be comprehensive and complements previous legislation. It is our hope that strict enforcement will follow for the benefit of those living on the island and the future generations of Cubans.

THE ENVIRONMENT AND THE CUBAN TRANSITION

Sergio Díaz-Briquets and Jorge F. Pérez-López[1]

Actions and neglectful policies of Cuba's socialist government over nearly four decades will leave a legacy of environmental disruption that future governments will have to reckon with. We have argued elsewhere (Díaz-Briquets and Pérez-López, forthcoming) that the environmental disruptions that have occurred in socialist Cuba were not merely the result of the process of transformation from rural to urban, modern societies. Indeed, we have shown that there were systemic reasons for the disruption, among them government control of the means of production, a tendency toward gigantism, central planning that focused on quantity of output rather than on quality or on how it was produced, a development model that emphasized heavy industrialization and lack of public participation in decision making.

Anticipated changes that will move Cuba in the direction of a market-oriented, multi-party system by themselves will not bring about an immediate improvement in the underlying environmental situation. Two experts on environmental issues in former socialist countries transitioning to market economies have stated:

> Based on our observations in Russia and Ukraine, and on extensive discussions with experts in those countries, we believe that real progress on environmental problems in the countries of the former Soviet Union will lag until there are substantial and far-ranging reforms in basic economic, legal, and social institutions. We do not deny that some targeted technical assistance could produce substantial improvements in en-

vironmental quality and quality of life for individuals affected by the assistance. Without basic institutional reforms, however, it is doubtful that these countries will have the capacity to continue the progress made possible by foreign assistance and to generate substantial environmental improvement on their own (Toman and Simpson 1994, p. 74).

The first part of the paper summarizes the major environmental problems that will be faced by a post-socialist Cuba. The second part discusses institutional reforms that are essential to attain meaningful progress to improve the environment. The paper closes with a discussion of technical and economic assistance that may be available to a democratic, free market Cuba to conserve and improve the environment.

THE SOCIALIST ENVIRONMENTAL LEGACY

Water

Clean water is one of the most basic needs of any society. Clean water is essential for consumption by the population, for industrial processes, to sustain aquatic life in rivers and streams, and to provide recreation opportunities for the population.

Streams, rivers and surface waters in socialist Cuba have been severely polluted by runoff from fields heavily treated with fertilizers, pesticides, and herbicides as well as by untreated effluents from cities, industrial plants—sugar mills, plants producing sugar by-products, food processing plants, etc.—and open pit mining operations. The pollution of surface wa-

---

1. This paper presents strictly the views of the authors.

ters has been so intense that toxic substances have penetrated some of the country's largest aquifers.

Socialist Cuba's fixation with irrigation resulted in very high rates of extraction of underground water, and there is evidence to conclude that, in at least some parts of the country, an extensive dam construction program may have interfered with the natural recharge of aquifers. As a result, groundwater levels have dropped and, in some instances, sea water has penetrated aquifers, thereby increasing the salinity of underground reserves.

During the special period, lack of import capacity caused a reduction in imports of fertilizers and pesticides and in the rate in which these inputs were used in agriculture. This has led some observers to posit that an "organic farming" revolution has occurred in Cuba, one that should be emulated by other countries. To be sure, the economic crisis of the 1990s indeed decreased Cuba's imports of fertilizers, pesticides, and other chemical products, with a positive impact on the environment. Lack of fuel, likewise, has interfered with the ability to pump water from underground stores. However, how genuine and long lasting will be the shift in agricultural techniques away from chemicals and energy-intensive practices is questionable. Since 1994, Cuba has been borrowing funds abroad to finance the purchase of fertilizers, pesticides, parts for its agricultural machinery, and fuel in order to return to its input-intensive production mode for its sugar and tobacco crops.

Soils

Cuba's agricultural model has severely affected soils, bringing about degradation that in many instances will take decades to reverse. The drive to increase land under cultivation resulted in the clearing of low-quality soils prone to severe erosion by wind and rain. In some instances it also led to the loss of forested areas and ground cover, making certain regions more vulnerable to flooding during heavy rains. The excessive use of heavy mechanical equipment resulted in the compaction of many soils.

The very intensive use of irrigation without adequate drainage has brought about salinization and waterlogging, rendering some of the affected lands unus-

able for agricultural production, or severely constraining their productivity. These problems are concentrated in the eastern portion of the country, but are also present in the southern coastal regions of western Cuba (Pinar del Río, La Habana, and Matanzas provinces) as well as in Ciego de Avila province, where salt water intrusions are reported to be severe.

Strip mining has also affected soils in the eastern portion of the country. Nickel-containing laterites in the northern coast of Holguín province have been subject to strip mining for many years. Reclamation has been ignored altogether or has lagged far behind.

Forests

Reforestation is one of the few areas in which Cuba's socialist government has made a significant positive contribution to the environment. Contrary to the worldwide trends in deforestation, Cuba's area covered by forests has increased appreciably, from 14% in 1959 to 18.2% in 1989. At the same time that overall forested area was increasing, however, a substantial reduction of old forests was occurring as a result of the expansion of cultivated areas. Major tree losses also occurred as traditional agroforestry practices were largely abandoned when vast-scale state farms and agricultural cooperatives were created during the drive to establish the socialist agricultural development model. During the economic crisis, there has been an alarmingly high rate of instances of cutting down of tree cover and forests for lumber and to make charcoal, since oil-based cooking fuels have been in very short supply.

Natural Habitat/Biodiversity

Forests, coastal and inland wetlands, and coral reefs are among the most important ecosystems that provide natural habitats for Cuban species. Loss of old forests has affected watersheds and habitats, as has the introduction of non-native species (García Azuero 1994, p. 1A). Pollution of bays and coastal areas resulting from agricultural runoff and effluents from industrial plants has adversely affected the marine habitat, including coral reefs. There are also some reports that coral reefs are being extracted to use the calcium carbonate they contain in nickel processing operations.

During the special period, the Cuban government has focused on the tourism industry as a source of scarce foreign exchange. Substantial investments have been made in the development of tourism facilities, some of them involving construction of hotels and other infrastructure projects that affect very fragile environmental ecosystems, particularly those that until recently were largely untouched by development projects. Examples of this type of infrastructure construction are the *pedraplenes* constructed in the Sabana-Camagüey archipelago, that include the 24-kilometer causeway between Turiguanó and Cayo Coco, the 43-kilometer causeway linking Jigüey, Cayo Cruz and Cayo Romano, and the 48-kilometer causeway between Caibarién and Cayo Santa María.

Air

Airborne emissions from industry and transportation constitute significant environmental problems in socialist Cuba. Carbon dioxide emissions—mostly from electric power plants and industrial facilities fueled by oil and oil products—are a source of concern, particularly in the areas surrounding the source of the emissions. During the special period, Cuba has increasingly turned to domestic or low-quality imported oil to reduce the oil import bill; these grades of oil, rich in sulphur, have aggravated the nation's air pollution problems, offsetting reductions in other sources of air pollution resulting from the contraction in economic activity. Oil refineries and cement and nickel plants emit huge amounts of dust and particulant matter into the atmosphere, damaging air quality. Because of its geography and prevailing wind patterns, Cuba is fortunate in that the concentration of pollutants over the country dissipates rapidly. However, the toxic plumes contribute to general atmospheric pollution in the area surrounding Cuba, reaching as far as Mexico and the continental United States.

Automobile emissions present less of an environmental problem in Cuba compared to other countries because of the relatively low density of automobiles per capita in the island. However, the Cuban stock of automobiles are heavy polluters: they are of quite old vintage, a large portion predating use of catalytic converters, and are in a state of disrepair.

In comparison to Poland and other Central European nations where pollution from coal-burning heavy industry and electric power plants poisoned entire regions, environmental damage in Cuba is less severe. Nevertheless, remediation of environmental damage in the form of salinization and soil erosion associated with excessive irrigation, pollution of rivers, bays and coastal waters, and unreclaimed areas that have been strip mined, are significant trouble spots that will be expensive and time consuming to remediate.

- Scientist José Oro (Remos 1996, p. 11A) estimates that remediation costs could range between $2 billion and $3 billion if standards similar to those recommended by the United States Environmental Protection Agency were to be achieved. Soil desalinization will cost between $600 and $800 million, removing chemical pollutants between $600 and $700 million, and removing other water residues between $800 and $900 million. These remediation efforts will have to be sustained over a multi-year period.

- Cuban scientists estimate that cleanup of the Almendares river in the city of La Habana alone will cost upward of $20 million ("Sanear el Almendares" 1996).

- Many more millions of dollars will have to be spent expanding and upgrading the country's poorly maintained sanitary infrastructure and in protecting the natural environment in coastal regions damaged by poorly designed water development projects and by international tourism centers. The cost of reducing salt concentrations in coastal aquifers infiltrated by sea water is unknown but likely to be considerable.

It has been estimated that the cost of cleanup and restoration of the Everglades and Florida Bay in South Florida, an ecosystem comparable to some of those damaged in south central Cuba, will eventually reach $5 billion ("The 50-Year War" 1997, p. 14). Although it is impossible to predict with precision the size of Cuba's environmental remediation bill, it can be assumed that it will be in the billions of dollars.

INSTITUTIONAL DEVELOPMENT

It is essential during Cuba's transition to set into motion a domestic process that results in: (1) effective environmental laws and regulations; (2) credible and effective institutions to manage environmental policies; (3) suitable structures of private ownership; (4) devolution of government authority; and (5) adequate public participation in decision-making (Kabala 1992, p. 13).

Legal Framework

Socialist Cuba lacks adequate general environmental legislation as well as sector-specific laws and regulations to deal with environmental problems associated with individual industries. The general environmental law, Law No. 33 of 1980, is typical of environmental laws of socialist countries in the 1970s. These laws were premised on the intrinsic harmony between socialist economic development and protection of the environment. Their emphasis is on the "rational use" of natural resources, with environmental disruption defined as the deviation from rational use. The severe environmental damage that occurred in the socialist countries—despite the existence of this type of environmental laws—is clear evidence of their lack of effectiveness in protecting the environment.

In the early stages of their transition to market-oriented economies, Central European nations began to overhaul existing environmental laws and regulations. For example, in the early 1990s (WRI 1992, p. 72):

- Poland passed legislation enacting a comprehensive national environmental policy that, among others, set specific targets for air emissions and established a system of incentives for pollution control equipment. Poland also approved strict automobile emission standards that required catalytic converters and unleaded gasoline.

- Hungary passed laws requiring firms building or expanding plants to submit environmental impact assessments before receiving construction permits; requiring all vehicles to undergo annual emission inspections; and offered tax incentives to vehicles with catalytic converters. The government also devised a new tax or fee system to stem the further degradation of air and water resources and a freedom of information act that would allow public access to government data and allow the government to publish material on polluting enterprises.

- Czechoslovakia drafted a general environmental law that anticipated command-and-control laws and environmental taxes; gave citizens the right to obtain information about the environment and required companies to provide it; allowed citizens to claim rights under the environmental laws in court; and required environmental impact assessments before the initiation of any construction activity, use of natural resources, or production of products.

An essential first step during the transition is for Cuba to enact a new set of environmental laws (including regulations, standards and norms) that are realistic and provide an effective framework for environmental protection.[2] Laws and standards need to be realistic or risk contributing to cynicism and perpetuating inefficient practices.[3] General laws should separate out promotional and regulatory activities. Among the principles that might be included in such laws are requiring environmental impact assessments before granting permits for construction activity beyond some threshold value or in environmentally sensitive locations, requiring that automobiles be equipped with pollution abatement devices, and making information about the environment available to the public. To avoid the rush to design all-encompassing laws with little flexibility, it might be preferable to implement realistic interim regulations and to

---

2. According to the Cuban press, the National Assembly of People's Power approved a new general environmental law in July 1997. The text of the law was not available at the time of this writing.

3. Poland, for instance, may have set air quality standards that are too strict and cannot be met by most cities of the world. See Ackermann (1991, p. 10).

delay passage of major legislation until there has been an effective national dialogue on these issues (Ackermann 1991, p. 10).

Application

Environmental agencies in socialist Cuba are weak. Regulatory authorities lack autonomy from the central government and enforcement capacity. Not only are environmental laws and regulations non-specific—which makes them difficult to enforce—but enforcement lines of authority are unclear and there is uncertainty about who is to be held responsible for environmental damage. Moreover, bureaucratic units are responsible for ensuring their own compliance with environmental laws, with conflicts of interest often arising since those responsible for attaining production goals are also responsible for overseeing and enforcing environmental regulations. In several documented cases, economic needs have overridden environmental concerns. Bureaucratic reshuffling in 1994 that moved the main environmental protection agency, Comisión Nacional para la Protección del Medio Ambiente y Conservación de los Recursos Naturales (COMARNA), to the Ministry of Science, Technology and Environment does not seem to have significantly affected that agency's autonomy or enforcement capacity.

For over three decades, Cuba's socialist government has actively worked to eliminate the market-oriented institutions that existed in Republican Cuba and to supplant them with institutions that support a centrally-directed economy. During the transition, Cuban policy makers must begin to rebuild an institutional framework for the market that will promote competition, promote efficient economic management and control, create and regulate factor markets, devise and implement a tax system, and protect the environment. Institution-building is an expensive and time-consuming undertaking, however, as it takes considerable investment of money and time to develop the human resources necessary to make these institutions carry out their mandates effectively (Pérez-López 1994, pp. 296-298).

Clearly, environmental laws and regulations that are not backed by a strong institutional structure and sufficient enforcement resources have little value.

Monitoring and inspection systems must be credible—to the government as well as to the private sector and the general public. To be credible, they have to be independent of entities that own the resources being monitored or whose role it is to promote production. It is common in many countries—not only in socialist countries—for the public sector to own the most polluting industries. Environmental disruption in the former Soviet Union and the old communist countries of Eastern Europe clearly demonstrates that the public sector is notoriously bad at policing itself: "Being both poacher and gamekeeper does not work, especially when public agencies are responsible for such essential but massive tasks as wastewater treatment or solid waste disposal" (World Bank 1992, p. 84).

Institution-building in the environmental protection area is a slow, costly and difficult process. It requires well-trained technical personnel and professional managers with job security—to prevent them from being dismissed when their actions do not please powerful interests—as well as adequate financing. Cuba must meet the challenge of beginning to build these institutions during the transition in order to be able to set the bases for meaningful improvement of the environmental situation in the mid and longer term.

Private Property

In socialist Cuba, nearly all of the country's productive resources are owned and operated by the state. The only exception is the agricultural sector, where 5-8 % of farm land is under the control of individuals. As with state enterprises throughout the socialist world, Cuban state enterprises lack defined property rights that spur work effort and profit making in market economies. They have little incentive to use inputs efficiently and to limit pollution. They operate under a "soft budget constraint" which allows cost increases to be passed on, and under which industries could rely on government to bail them out rather than lose the enterprises' production or create unemployment (WRI 1992, p. 5). Environmental fines are weakly enforced and ultimately the state pays the fines levied, as they are part of the budgets of enterprises.

A precondition for authentic environmental protection under a market framework is a pattern of ownership of resources that allows economic actors to internalize the economic benefits of gains in efficiency in production processes. This means, among other considerations, strict budgetary constraints on producers and the elimination of subsidies that distort the price signals received by producers (Kabala 1992, p. 13).

During the transition, Cuba must proceed rapidly to curb the state's role in the economy by (1) turning over to the private sector productive resources it currently controls, i.e., privatize; and (2) creating the basis for the establishment of new private enterprises. While privatization runs it course and private enterprises grow in number and significance, prices of energy and natural resources (including water) must rise to stem overconsumption and begin the process of internalizing pollution control costs. Similarly, subsidies to enterprises must be curbed or eliminated, particularly those to the most blatant polluters, which may have to be closed even if this means loss of jobs.

Decentralization

Cuba's economic decisionmaking process is extremely rigid, with most decisions regarding nature of investments, location, technology, etc., made from the top, in accordance with a national plan developed by the central government. Provincial and local government authorities are weak and underfunded and play a very marginal role in economic decisions that affect the environment.

In the 1970s, Cuba adopted a system of government called People's Power (*Poder Popular*) which created government institutions at three levels: municipal, provincial, and national. Enterprises were made subordinate to the level that was served by their output or at which they were deemed to have the most importance. For example, enterprises whose output was deemed to be of national importance, such as sugar mills, nickel mining complexes, tourism facilities, were considered as national enterprises, subordinate to the appropriate sectoral ministry of the central government. Enterprises whose output served a region were considered to be the jurisdiction of Provincial Organs of People's Power. Since very little production is made only for the municipality in which it is made, enterprises under the jurisdiction of Municipal Organs of People's Power are mostly those engaged in retail trade (pharmacies, candy shops, cafeterias, movie theaters, etc) or in providing services to the population (health, education, sports, culture, and communal services such as parks and sanitation) (Malinowitz 1997).

Because provincial and municipal enterprises are subject to the principle of "double subordination"— subordination to the provincial government and to a national ministry in the case of provincial enterprises, and to the provincial government and to the municipal government in the case of municipal enterprises—they have very little impact on making economic decisions even with regard to industries that are nominally under their jurisdiction. Amaro (1996, p. 267) sums up the situation as follows:

> Local self-government is ruled out in Cuba. The 1992 Constitution is clear about the endorsement of centralism when it states that Cuba has a socialist economy (Article 14) with a comprehensive central plan. It also states that "decisions taken by higher state organs are mandatory on lower ones" (Article 68(d)) and "lower state organs are responsible to higher ones and have to report to them about their management" (Article 68(e)). An Executive Council composed of the President of the State Council (Fidel Castro himself) and Ministers appointed by him, may decide matters which are the competence of the Ministers' Cabinet (Article 97). The Cabinet may revoke decisions of subordinated administrative organs accountable to the Municipal Assembly.

During the transition, as central planning is eliminated and a private sector begins to emerge as a result of newly-created enterprises and privatization, provincial and local authorities should be given a more prominent role in determining the location of investments and plans to control environmental disruption.

Public Participation

It is not an overstatement to say that Cuba has been more effective in preventing public participation in decisionmaking than any other socialist society, with the possible exception of North Korea. The controls on the formation and operation of independent organizations has extended to environmental groups. As a result, the public has not been availed of mechanisms to express its views on policy decisions that affect the environment and public education and general public understanding and appreciation of environmental issues has lagged.

Independent environmental movements emerged in Eastern Europe in the 1970s. Government restrictions on public discussion and speech severely affected their ability to express environmental concerns and educate the public on environmental matters. These groups relied primarily on underground journals to transmit whatever information they could obtain on environmental conditions in their country. In 1980, however, the Polish Ecological Club—the first fully independent environmental group in the region—was created in Krakow. A coalition of trade unions, scientists, members of the Polish Ecological Club, and the press were successful in convincing the Polish State Ministry of Metallurgy to close down the Skawine aluminum works, a heavy emitter of toxic fluoride emissions, located near Krakow (WRI 1992, p. 60). Environmental movements played an important role in toppling communist governments in Eastern Europe in 1989-90 (WRI 1992, p. 60).

A new trend in Cuba in the 1990s is the establishment of "non-governmental organizations" (NGOs) to represent citizens in nearly all areas of society. By 1994, approximately 2,200 such organizations had been registered with the Ministry of Justice. Whether these organizations represent "autonomous citizen groups capable of laying the ground work for civil society" and therefore can be considered as NGOs in the traditional sense of the term or they are rather government creations, a "mechanism to funnel funds to the bankrupt state sector" is a matter of disagreement among analysts (Gunn 1995, p. 1). Some proponents of the latter view refer to these organizations as GONGOs—government-operated non-governmental organizations—to highlight that they are creatures of the state and lack independence from it. Raúl Castro's 1996 address to the Central Committee of the Cuban Communist Party (1996, p. 32) left

little doubt of where the Cuban government stands on NGOs:

> Our concept of civil society is not the same as they refer to in the United States. Rather, it is our own Cuban socialist civil society, encompassing our strong mass organizations, namely the CTC (Central Organization of Cuban Trade Unions), the CDRs (Committees for the Defense of the Revolution), the FMC (Federation of Cuban Women), the ANAP (National Association of Small Farmers), the FEU (Federation of University Students) and FEEM (Federation of Students in Intermediate Education) and the Pioneers. There are also social groups which, as is known, include veterans, economists, lawyers, journalists, artists and writers, as well as other NGOs which operate within the law and do not attempt to undermine the economic, political and social system freely chosen by our people. Even though they have their own characteristics and terminology, in conjunction with the revolutionary state, they pursue the common objective of building socialism.

In the environmental area, the leading Cuban-style NGO is *Pro-Naturaleza*, an organization created in April 1993 reportedly having more than 5,000 members nationwide. According to Gunn (1995, p. 2), *Pro-Naturaleza* is sponsored by the Ministry of Science, Technology and Environment; most of the leadership of the organization is employed at the Ministry; and it is housed rent-free within the Ministry. Although *Pro-Naturaleza* has not received any state funds, the membership funds it collects are insufficient to pay for a secretary and a researcher, and it has asked the Ministry to cover the salaries, with the request that this donation not be used to "encroach on the organization's independence." Gunn gives examples of *Pro-Naturaleza*'s independence and acquiescence to the state: in 1993, the organization's "citizen complaint" facility followed up a report by a resident of Santa Cruz del Norte regarding the cutting down of trees for firewood by workers of a sugar mill and obtained action by the local authorities to provide the workers with kerosene so that they would not have to cut trees for cooking fuel; a citizen complaint about effluents from a state slaughterhouse that were polluting a river did not lead to any positive response, as *Pro-Naturaleza* readily accepted the enterprise's argument that no funds were available to purchase equipment to address the problem (Gunn 1995, p. 7).

During the transition to a multi-party market economy, Cuba should stimulate public participation and environmental education. Public involvement and participation augments resources that are available for environmental protection. Environmental education informs the environmental debate, increasing the likelihood that it will result in positive policies. The World Bank (1992a, p. 85) has put the imperative for environmental education very succinctly: "ignorance is an important cause of environmental damage and a serious impediment to finding solutions."

RESOURCES TO IMPROVE THE ENVIRONMENT

In a market economy, the private sector—and private investment—can carry out many of the functions that are the responsibility of the state in socialist societies and that require the expenditure of public resources, e.g., build and operate energy-efficient power plants, extract and refine minerals, reclaiming land and minimizing water and air pollution. Nevertheless, a market-oriented post-socialist Cuban government will face many competing demands on the resources it will have available to deal with public policy challenges. In addition to environmental problems, future Cuban governments will face challenges such as a large external debt, outdated plant and equipment, and crumbling infrastructure.

Cuban state enterprises, as their counterparts in other socialist countries, are notorious for their disregard for the environment. Some of the worst offenders among these enterprises may have to be shut down at once, thereby creating losses in employment and production. Small businesses and foreign investment will hopefully create new sources of employment to absorb those workers who are dislocated from state enterprises. It will be essential to require environmental impact assessments for all new investments and a mechanism to take them into account in decision making to avoid adding to the already-existing environmental problems.

Mitigation of the most serious environmental problems that post-socialist Cuba will face will require a great deal of resources. The bulk of those resources will have to be generated internally. However, some external assistance is available to deal with some of the challenges and to improve environmental management.

Multilateral Assistance

Given budget constraints of most governments, there are very few resources available for foreign aid for conservation projects that have more than local significance. Thus, national efforts tend to be financed by local resources while multilateral support is concentrated on cross-border global issues. An example of the latter is the Global Environmental Facility (GEF), a fund created in 1991 and administered by the World Bank, whose purpose is to provide grants to deal with four major cross-border environmental problems: 1) loss of biodiversity; 2) global warming; 3) pollution of international waters; and 4) emission of chlorofluorocarbons (CFCs) (World Bank 1992b, p. 45). In 1996, there were 11 GEF grants under implementation in Latin America and the Caribbean, 6 supporting biodiversity conservation, 3 targeted at climate change, and 2 at international water initiatives ("Latin America" 1996, p. 23).

Multilateral institutions such as the World Bank and the Inter-American Development Bank are actively involved in: 1) supporting countries as they seek to reform their environmental management, including mitigating accumulated problems; and 2) factoring environmental concerns into new investments. As of mid-1996, the World Bank's active environmental portfolio stood at $11.5 billion for 153 projects in 62 countries, which leveraged an additional $14.5 billion from other sources for total investment in the environment of $26 billion (Steer 1996b, p. 5). Cuba is not currently a member of either the World Bank or the Inter-American Development Bank, and therefore not eligible to receive their technical and financial assistance, but a post-socialist Cuba would logically seek to become part of the multilateral financial institutions and to benefit from such association.[4]

Bilateral Assistance

Bilateral foreign assistance may also be available to post-socialist Cuba to deal with environmental problems. An obvious source of foreign assistance for environmental protection and reclamation during the transition will be the U.S. Agency for International Development (USAID). USAID environmental resources are limited, however, and are being mostly assigned to the "management of natural resources used by the marginal poor, and the management of watersheds which provide clean and dependable water sources for urban populations," under the agency's strategic objective of offering "improved protection of selected LAC [Latin America and Caribbean] parks and protected areas representing a variety of ecosystems" (USAID 1995, p. 20). In light of these priorities, USAID environmental assistance could be expected to be primarily available for the protection of natural habitats, including perhaps the reclamation of formerly forested areas damaged by open pit mining operations, and less so for the reclamation of agricultural soils damaged by inappropriate agricultural practices or to restore the quality of water bodies adversely affected by mismanagement. Many other donor countries, however, have environmentally-oriented bilateral assistance programs, but there is intense competition for this aid, since the demand vastly exceeds the supply.

A sobering consideration is that the document issued by the President of the United States in early 1997 outlining foreign assistance that might be available to support a democratic transition in Cuba does not single out the environment as a priority. However, envisioned processes that build "essential democratic institutions, both in the government and in civil society," and establish "policy, institutional, and legal reforms necessary to stimulate the domestic private sector, meet the long-term social needs of the population, attract foreign investment, meet conditions for lending from international financial institutions and otherwise lay the basis for economic recovery" (*Support for a Democratic* 1997, p. 4) are supportive of environmental objectives.

Project Specific Assistance

An expert on Cuba-U.S. relations has proposed that the United States should assist socialist Cuba financially and technically in the completion of the Juraguá nuclear power plant, thereby allowing the island to ease its electricity shortages during the special period and at the same time addressing United States' concerns about the safety of the plant (Smith 1995). In a meeting with U.S. energy and environmental experts[5] in February 1996, President Castro stated that the future of the Juraguá nuclear power plant was a "very complex question." He indicated that he looked forward to the day nuclear reactors would become "20th-century pyramids, like those in Egypt." Moreover, Castro indicated he was open to better ideas on how to proceed regarding the Juraguá plant, a reference to potential assistance from Western nations to abandon its construction (Rohter 1996, p. A6).

Uncertainty about the quality of construction of the Juraguá plant makes it highly unlikely that the facility will ever by completed. In a post-socialist Cuba, however, there is the possibility that the United States, other countries, and international organizations might be willing to assist Cuba in building either a safe Western-designed nuclear power plant or efficient thermoelectric plants in return for razing the Juraguá reactors, removing once and for all the possibility of a nuclear accident at this site.

There is precedent for the United States and other countries stepping in to assist financially-strapped countries in return for eliminating nuclear plants that are deemed to be dangerous because of the likelihood of nuclear accidents or their potential to produce fis-

---

4. Requirements for Cuba's membership in the International Monetary Fund, a prerequisite for joining the World Bank and a step that would ease entry into the Inter-American Development Bank, are given in Pujol (1991).

5. The U.S. delegation was led by Michael L. Kennedy, chairman of Citizens Energy Corporation, a Boston-based nonprofit company that promotes the development of alternative energy sources, and by Robert F. Kennedy, Senior Staff Attorney for the Natural Resources Defense Council, and environmental NGO. The two Kennedys are nephews of President John F. Kennedy.

sionable materials for nuclear weapons. After reunification, Germany shut down unsafe nuclear power plants in East Germany, and Western Europe and the United States have been assisting Central European countries in phasing out the more dangerous nuclear power plants in the region.

In March 1993, North Korea announced that it intended to withdraw from the nuclear Non-Proliferation Treaty (NPT) to protest pressure from the international community to allow inspection of certain nuclear facilities suspected of being used to produce nuclear weapons (Smith 1993). Subsequently, North Korea agreed to "suspend" its withdrawal from the NPT and entered into negotiations with the United States. These discussions ultimately resulted in an agreement, known as the "Agreed Framework," whereby North Korea agreed to "freeze" its nuclear power program in return for foreign assistance to replace its graphite reactors (which lend themselves to the production of weapons-grade materials) with light-water reactors and interim energy supplies. The Korean Peninsula Energy Development Organization (KEDO), an international consortium of member countries led by the United States, Japan, and South Korea, was created to finance and supply two light-water reactors to North Korea at a cost of about $4 billion, with North Korea expected to repay the loan interest-free over an extended period of time (Smith 1994; U.S. General Accounting Office, 1996).

SUMMARY AND IMPLICATIONS

In its post-socialist transition, Cuba must inevitably deal with the environmental legacy of nearly four decades of socialist development policies. The effects of these policies, while apparently not as adverse as in the former Eastern European communist countries and the Soviet Union, warrant serious concern, particularly in the agriculture and mining sectors. At present, there is also growing concern about the environmental consequences resulting from the rapidly growing tourism industry.

The Cuban nation will face a herculean task as it begins to reshape it most basic political and economic institutions to adapt to a market economy. The task is no less demanding regarding the environment since balancing the economic needs of the population and protecting nature will require the development of an appropriate legal framework consistent with private property rights, the decentralization of political power, and growing public participation in the country's governance.

To some extent Cuba will have the advantage of learning from others, as it will be able to draw on the accumulated experience of many other countries that have experimented with diverse approaches to achieve sustainable development, both in the developed and the developing worlds. Many lessons have been learned. Environmental problems can not be resolved overnight, but much can be accomplished by the careful setting of priorities and assignation of financial resources. A post-socialist Cuba will also have access to the technical and financial resources of the international community for environmental remediation purposes. With the right regulatory framework, including proper economic incentives, the country will be able to enlist as well the private sector in managing the natural environment to the benefit of current and future generations.

REFERENCES

Ackerman, Richard. 1991. "Environment in Eastern Europe: Despair or Hope?" *Transition* 2:4 (April) 9-11.

Amaro, Nelson. 1996. "Decentralization, Local Government and Citizen Participation in Cuba." In *Cuba in Transition—Volume 6*, pp. 262-282. Washington: Association for the Study of the Cuban Economy.

Castro, Raúl. 1996. "Maintaining Revolutionary Purity." Excerpts from a report presented to the

Central Committee of the Cuban Communist Party, March 23, 1996. In *Cuba: Political Pilgrims and Cultural Wars*, pp. 31-37. Washington: The Free Cuba Committee of Freedom House.

Díaz-Briquets, Sergio, and Jorge F. Pérez-López. Forthcoming. *The Environmental Legacy of Socialism in Cuba*.

Environmental Protection and Foreign Aid: Institutional Reform. 1984. Report of the Second Seminar on International Environmental Issues. Medford, Massachusetts: Tufts University Department of Urban and Environmental Policy.

García Azuero, Francisco. 1994. "Crisis en Cuba amenaza el medio ambiente." *El Nuevo Herald* (17 February): 1A, 6A.

Gunn, Gillian. 1995. *Cuba's NGOs: Government Puppets or Seeds of Civil Society*. Cuban Briefing Paper Series No. 7. Washington: Center for Latin American Studies, Georgetown University.

Kavala, Stanley J. 1992. *Environment and Development in the New Eastern Europe*. Occasional Paper No. 3. Middlebury, Vermont: Geonomics Institute.

"Latin America and Caribbean Region." 1996. *Environment Matters* (Fall) 20-23.

Malinowitz, Stanley. 1997. "Public and Private Services and the Municipal Economy in Cuba." *Cuban Studies* 27.

Parenteau, Patrick. 1997. "Promoting Exchange of Environmental Law and Policymaking Experience: Some Observations on the Evolution of Environmental Law." In *The Environment in U.S.-Cuba Relations: Recommendations for Cooperation*, pp. 31-39. Washington: Inter-American Dialogue.

Pérez-López, Jorge F. 1994. "Economic and Financial Institutions to Support the Market." In *Cuba in Transition—Volume 4*, pp. 292-302. Washington: Association for the Study of the Cuban Economy.

Pujol, Joaquín P. 1991. "Membership Requirements in the IMF: Possible Implications for Cuba." In *Cuba in Transition*, pp. 91-102. Miami: Florida International University.

Remos, Ariel. 1996. "Grave la polución soterrada." *Diario Las Américas* (25 May):1A, 11A.

Rohter, Larry. 1996. "A Kennedy-Castro Talk Touched by History." *The New York Times* (19 February) A1, A6.

"Sanear el Almendares costaría $20 millones." 1996. *El Nuevo Herald* (16 May) 1B.

Steer, Andrew. 1992a. "The Principles of the New Environmentalism." *Finance & Development* 33:4 (December) 4-7.

Steer, Andrew. 1992b. "The Year in Perspective." *Environment Matters* (Fall) 4-7.

Support for a Democratic Transition in Cuba. 1997. Report of the President of the United States. Washington (28 January).

"The 50-Year War on the Everglades." 1997. *The New York Times* (20 April) 14.

Toman, Michael A., and R. David Simpson. 1994. "Environmental Policies, Economic Restructuring, and Institutional Development in the Former Soviet Union." In Michael A. Toman, editor, *Pollution Abatement Strategies in Central and Eastern Europe*, pp. 73-80. Washington: Resources for the Future.

U. S. Agency for International Development (USAID). 1995. *LAC Regional Program Strategy for FY 1996-FY 2000 and Action Plan for FY 1996-FY 1997*. Washington: U.S. Agency for International Development.

U.S. General Accounting Office. 1996. *Implications of the U.S./North Korean Agreement on Nuclear Issues*. GAO/RCED/NSIAD-97-8. Washington: General Accounting Office.

World Bank. 1992. *Development and the Environment—World Development Report 1992*. Washington: Oxford University Press.

World Resources Institute (WRI). 1992. *World Resources 1992-93*. New York: Oxford University Press.

Appendix A:
AUTHORS AND DISCUSSANTS

JOSE D. ACOSTA had a long career at the Organization of American States, where he was both a tax policy economist and a lawyer. He retired in 1989 as Director of the Department of General Legal Services, Secretariat of Legal Affairs, after serving as a Principal Economist in the joint tax program OAS/IDB/ECLA. He has a Doctorate of Law from the Universidad de la Habana and did graduate work in economics at the Universidad de Villanueva and at The George Washington University. He was a Senior Partner at Bufete de Machado in La Habana and a Professor of Law and Economics at the Universidad de Villanueva, La Habana.

JOSE ALVAREZ is Professor, Food and Research Economics Department, Institute of Food and Agricultural Sciences, University of Florida, where he works as the Area Economist at the Everglades Research and Education Center, Belle Glade, Florida. He has been traveling to Cuba in the past few years as one of the principal investigators in two grants from the John D. and Catherine T. MacArthur Foundation to study Cuban agriculture and the potential economic impact on the agricultural economies of Florida and Cuba after the lifting of the U.S. economic embargo. He earned a B.A. in Economics (1971) and M.S. (1974) and Ph.D. (1977) in Food and Resource Economics all from the University of Florida.

UVA DE ARAGON is Acting Director of the Cuban Research Institute, Florida International University. She has published 9 books of poetry, short stories and essays, among them *El caimán ante el espejo: Un ensayo de interpretación de lo cubano* (Miami: Ediciones Universal, 1994) and *Alfonso Hernández-Catá: Un escritor cubano, salamantino y universal* (Salaman-

ca: Universidad Pontificia de Salamanca, 1996), and has received several literary awards in the United States, Latin America and Europe. A seasoned journalist, she writes a weekly column for *Diario las Américas*. She received her Ph.D. in Spanish and Latin American Literature from the University of Miami.

ROGER R. BETANCOURT is Professor of Economics at the University of Maryland-College Park. He has been a Visiting Professor and Scholar at the University of Washington and at INSEAD (Fountainbleau, France). He received his Ph.D. from the University of Wisconsin-Madison..

TEO A. BABUN, JR. Is President of Cuba-Caribbean Development Co., Ltd. He is an Electrical Engineer and Business Management graduate of Michigan Technological University. He is the author of *Cuba Sea & Air Transportation*, a report dealing with infrastructure issues in Cuba and of *Cuba Infrastructure & Opportunities*, a report dealing with ten key industries in Cuba. His most recent project is *The Business Guide to Cuba*, published by the Miami Herald Publishing Co.

RICHARD N. BROWN is Economist, U.S. Department of Agriculture, Economic Research Service, Washington, D.C. He is a specialist on Caribbean Basin agricultural production and trade and related issues and has been the USDA coordinator on a series of cooperative research agreements with the University of Florida's International Agricultural Trade and Development Center studying Cuba's agricultural sector.

JULIE MARIE BUNCK is Assistant Professor, Department of Political Science, University of Louisville. She is the author of *Fidel Castro and the Quest for Revolutionary Culture in Cuba* and co-author of *Law, Power and the Sovereign State* (both Pennsylvania State University Press). She spent seven months in Vietnam in 1995.

NESTOR CARBONELL CORTINA is Vice President of PepsiCo, with global responsibility for government, institutional and external affairs. Forced into exile in 1960, he represented the Cuban Revolutionary Council before the OAS and coordinated the diplomatic strategy which led to the expulsion of the Castro regime from the inter-American system. He holds a Doctor of Law degree from the Universidad de Villanueva (La Habana) and an LLM degree from Harvard. He is the author of several books and publications on Cuba, including *El Espíritu de la Constitución de 1940, And the Russians Stayed,* and *Por la Libertad de Cuba: Una Historia Inconclusa.*

RODOLFO A. CARRANDI is currently an international consultant specializing in financial aspects of development projects. He worked for the Inter-American Development Bank from 1961 to 1989. Prior to that, he was an official of the BANFAIC in Cuba.

ROLANDO H. CASTAÑEDA is currently a Senior Operations Officer working with Chile and Perú at the Inter-American Development Bank (IDB), where he has held different positions since 1974. Before joining the IDB, he worked as an economist at the Organization of American States; the Rockefeller Foundation at the University of Cali, Colombia; the University of Puerto Rico at Río Piedras; and the Puerto Rico Planning Board. He holds an M.A. and is a Ph.D. candidate at Yale University, concentrating in monetary policy and econometrics.

YOSEM E. COMPANYS graduated from Yale University in 1996 with a B.A. degree in Economics. His research has concentrated on financial sector reform in Cuba.

NICOLAS CRESPO is the founder and President of The Phoenix Hospitality and Consulting Corporation and Latin America Hospitality and Consulting. The firm provides consulting services to the Hospitality Industry in a variety of fields. Previously Mr.

Crespo held positions as Vice President Development for Latin America and the Caribbean for Holiday Inns, Inc. and Senior Vice President Latin America and the Caribbean for The Sheraton Corporation. Mr. Crespo is a graduate in Commercial Sciences from the Universidad de la Habana. His last employment in Cuba was as Controller of the then Havana Hilton Hotel.

LARRY DALEY is Professor in the Department of Horticulture, Oregon State University, Corvallis, Oregon, specializing in Plant Germplasm Biochemistry and Biophysics. Earlier in his career, he held teaching positions at the University of North Texas and at East Texas State University. Born in England, Daley lived in Cuba from 1948 to 1961 in the family lands between the Guamá and Bayamo rivers in Oriente Province. During the revolution, he fought as a soldier in an assault battalion of Column 1 in the Sierra Maestra. He resigned from the rebel army in January 1959 and arrested by the government in April 1961; he was allowed to leave Cuba after mediation by the British Embassy and has not returned since then. He attended the Universidad de la Habana (Ingeniería Agronómica), University of Florida, Purdue University, and the University of California at Riverside, receiving his Ph.D. in Biochemistry and Biophysics as the University of California at Davis. He also conducted postdoctoral studies at Queens University in Canada, the University of Georgia, and the Boyce Thomson Institute in Yonkers, New York.

SERGIO DIAZ-BRIQUETS is a Vice President of Casals and Associates, a Washington-based consulting firm. He was Research Director of the Congressional Committee for the Study of International Migration and Cooperative Economic Development, and earlier held appointments with the International Development Research Centre, Population Reference Bureau, and Duquesne University. He has published numerous articles and books dealing with Cuba and is co-author of *The Environmental Legacy of Socialism in Cuba* (forthcoming). He received a Ph.D. in Demography from the University of Pennsylvania.

MAIDA DONATE-ARMADA is currently a counselor for "at risk" students in Miami, a program of the Cuban American National Council, Inc. She recently completed the book *Suicide in Miami and Cuba* (forthcoming from the Cuban American National Council). Prior to coming to the United States in 1993, she held a number of positions, including Director of Research of the Instituto Cubano de la Demanda Interna. She earned B.A.s in History and Sociology and a Ph.D. in Psychology from the Universidad de la Habana.

ALEJANDRO FERRATE is an associate in Shaw Pittman Potts & Trowbridge's Corporate and Energy Groups. He concentrates on international business transactions, Latin American business development, and special projects, including the firm's Cuba Project. Mr. Ferraté has published several law review articles on foreign investment and privatization in Latin America. He received a B.A. degree from Roanoke College (1991) and J.D. degree from George Mason School of Law (1995).

RENE GOMEZ MANZANO, an attorney, is President of the *Corriente Agramontista*. He is a member of the Cuban Dissidence Task Group, which issued the document *La patria es de todos* (*The Homeland Belongs to Us All*), for which he was jailed by the Cuban Government together with Vladimiro Roca, Félix Bonne Carcassés and Martha Beatriz Roque Cabello. Gómez Manzano was in jail in Cuba at the time his paper was presented at ASCE's Seventh Annual Meeting.

GERARDO GONZALEZ is Professor of Economics at the Universidad Interamericana, Puerto Rico. He is an specialist on economic and international relations of Cuba and the Caribbean. His articles have appeared in specialized journals in Latin America, the United States and Europe. He is the author of *The Caribbean and the Foreign Policy of Cuba* (Dominican Republic, 1991) and co-author of *Popular Participation and Development in Cuban Municipalities* (Venezuela, 1994).

MIGUEL GONZALEZ-PANDO attended graduate school at Harvard University. Since 1973, he has been a faculty member at Florida International University, where he directs the Cuban Living History Project. He is the author of several books and documentaries on the Cuban exile experience.

ERNESTO HERNANDEZ-CATA is currently Deputy Director of the African Department, International Monetary Fund (IMF). Previously, he served as Deputy Director of the IMF's Western Hemisphere Department and of the European II Department (in charge of relations with Russia and other states of the former Soviet Union) and held other positions at the IMF and at the Board of Governors of the Federal Reserve System. He received a License from the Graduate Institute of International Studies in Geneva (1967) and M.A. (1970) and Ph.D. (1974) in economics from Yale University.

ARTIMUS KEIFFER is Assistant Professor, Geography Department, Indiana University Purdue University at Indianapolis.

JUAN J. LOPEZ is Assistant Professor of Political Science, University of Illinois at Chicago. He specializes in Latin American politics and political economy of development. He has published on Argentinean politics and political economy of development. His current research includes the politics of economic development in Latin America, transition to democracy in Cuba, and democratic governability in Latin America. He earned a Ph.D. in Political Science from the University of Chicago.

ALBERTO LUZARRAGA is a Cuban banker and lawyer with more than 30 years of varied international experience in the commercial and investment banking business. During his career he has held high positions with the Chase Manhattan Bank and American Express Bank in New York and Continental Bank. In his latest position, Mr. Luzárraga was Chairman of the Board of Continental Bank International in New York and developed the program for investment in privatized companies. Mr. Luzárraga currently heads his own firm, the Amerinvest Group, a company specialized in equity investments. He holds a Ph.D. in Civil Law from the Universidad de Villanueva (La Habana) and an MBA from the University of Miami.

MANUEL MADRID-ARIS is an engineer and economist. He is currently an international economic and

501

environmental consultant specializing in Latin America. He is also an Associate Researcher at the NIAD Center, University of California, Los Angeles. He holds an Engineering degree from the Universidad Técnica Santa María de Chile and a Ph.D. in Political Economy and Public Policy from the University of Southern California.

ALBERTO MARTINEZ-PIEDRA is Professor of Economics at the Catholic University of America. He was U.S. Representative to the Economic and Social Council of the Organization of American States with the rank of Personal Ambassador (1982-84), U.S. Ambassador to Guatemala (1984-87) and Special Assistant on Latin American Affairs to the U.S. Mission to the United Nations (1987-88). His research interests include ethics in business and economics, economic development and history of economic thought. He received a degree in Political Economy at the Universidad Complutense de Madrid (1957) and a Ph.D. in Economics from Georgetown University (1962).

WILLIAM A. MESSINA, JR., is Executive Coordinator, International Agricultural Trade and Development Center (IATDC), Department of Resource Economics, Institute of Food and Agricultural Sciences, University of Florida. Mr. Messina is also the principal investigator and project director of IATDC's comprehensive research initiative to study Cuba's agricultural sector and the potential impact on the agricultural economies of Florida, Cuba and the United States of the lifting of the U.S. embargo funded by the John D. and Catherine T. MacArthur Foundation and the U.S. Department of Agriculture. He holds a B.S. in Agricultural Economics from Cornell University (1976) and an M.S. in Food and Resource Economics from the University of Florida (1989).

GEORGE PLINIO MONTALVAN is currently an international economic and management consultant working principally with Inter-American Development Bank. He was previously Chief Economist at the Organization of American States and conducted research at the Brookings Institution. He edited several volumes of *Cuba in Transition*, the papers and proceedings of ASCE's annual meeting, and is the author of numerous publications, among them *Latin America: The Hardware and Software Markets* (INTERSOL, 1991) and *Promoting Investment and Exports in the Caribbean* (Organization of American States, 1989). He holds a B.A. and M.A. and is a Ph.D. candidate in economics from The George Washington University.

SANTOS NEGRON DIAZ is President of Ecoplan, Inc., a recently established firm engaged in economic analysis and strategic planning located in Puerto Rico. Before retiring from public service in August 1995, he was Vice President and Director of the Office of Economic Analysis and Research of the Government Development Bank of Puerto Rico (1989-1995), Director of the Economic and Social Planning Area of the Puerto Rico Planning Board (1987-1989) and Professor of Economics Planning at the University of Puerto Rico, Rio Piedras Campus. He is the author of *Análisis de la Literatura Sobre la Situación de la Sociedad Post Industrial* (Puerto Rican Chapter of the Club of Rome, 1995) and of the forthcoming *Ensayos Económicos de Dos Décadas*.

LORENZO L. PEREZ is Assistant Director of the Western Hemisphere Department, International Monetary Fund (IMF). Previously, he served in the IMF's Exchange and Trade Relations Department and the European Department, and held positions at the U.S. Department of the Treasury and the U.S. Agency for International Development. He received a Ph.D. in economics from the University of Pennsylvania.

JORGE F. PEREZ-LOPEZ is an international economist with the Bureau of International Labor Affairs, U.S. Department of Labor. He is the author of *Cuba's Second Economy: From Behind the Scenes to Center Stage* (Transaction Publishers, 1995) and co-author of *The Environmental Legacy of Socialism in Cuba* (forthcoming). He received a Ph.D. in Economics from the State University of New York at Albany.

SATURNINO LUCIO II is one of the founders of the law firm Lucio, Mandler, Croland, Bronstein, Garbett, Stiphany & Martinez, Miami, Florida. He graduated from Harvard College (B.A. *Magna Cum Laude,* 1976) and Harvard Law School (J.D. *Cum*

Laude, 1979). His practice consists of domestic and international corporate law, finance, mergers and acquisitions; federal and state bank regulation and lending; offshore and inbound investment (including privatizations and debt/equity swaps), contracting, distribution, trade, countertrade and licensing; and federal, state and foreign tax planning.

JOSEPH M. PERRY is Professor of Economics and Chairperson of the Department of Economics and Geography at the University of North Florida, where he has been a faculty member since 1971. He was previously a member of the economics faculty of the University of Florida. Dr. Perry received his Ph.D. in Economics from Northwestern University in 1966, after completing undergraduate studies at Emory University and Georgia State University. His recent research has focused on regional economic development, with specific reference to Central American and Caribbean nations, and their trade relationships with the United States.

ENRIQUE S. PUMAR is an Adjunct Professor in the Graduate International Relations Program, Department of Politics, Catholic University, and a Senior Policy Analyst at EDS Government Consulting Group.

WILLARD RADELL is Professor of Economics at Indiana University of Pennsylvania, where he teaches managerial economics. His Ph.D. dissertation (1980) at the University of Illinois was titled "Scale Effects of Seasonal Production in the U.S. Raw Cane Sugar Industry." His papers have appeared in *The Journal of Developing Areas, Cuban Studies, World Development, Scholars,* and *Industrial Crisis Quarterly.*

MARTHA BEATRIZ ROQUE CABELLO is Director, Instituto Cubano de Economistas Independientes (ICEI), La Habana, Cuba. She is a member of the Cuban Dissidence Task Group, which issued the document *La patria es de todos (The Homeland Belongs to Us All),* for which she was jailed by the Cuban Government together with Vladimiro Roca, René Gómez Manzano and Félix Bonne Carcassés. Roque Cabello was in jail in Cuba at the time her paper was read at ASCE's Seventh Annual Meeting.

JAMES E. ROSS is Courtesy Professor and Program Advisor, International Agricultural Trade and Development Center (IATDC), Department of Food and Resource Economics, Institute of Food and Agricultural Science, University of Florida. Dr. Ross is retired from the U.S. Department of Agriculture's Foreign Agricultural Service and has been involved in IATDC's research initiative on Cuban agriculture since its inception.

FREDERICK S. ROYCE is Graduate Research Associate, Department of Agricultural and Biological Engineering, University of Florida. Mr. Royce holds B.S. and M.S. degrees in Agricultural Operations Management from the University of Florida and has extensive work experience in Central America and the Caribbean. He has conducted a total of eight weeks of intensive field research in Cuba.

HECTOR SAEZ is Assistant Professor of Economics at Wagner College, Staten Island, New York.

JULIA SAGEBIEN is an Associate Professor at the School of Business Administration, Dalhousie University, Halifax, Nova Scotia, Canada. She has lectured extensively on the subject of Canada-Cuba commercial relations and has acted on an advisory capacity to the Canadian Government. Her articles have appeared in journals such as *Cuban Studies* and *Business Quarterly.*

JORGE A. SANGUINETTY is founder and President of DevTech Systems, Inc., a Washington, D.C.-based international and domestic economic consulting firm. He has over 30 years' experience in research, teaching, management and consulting in economic policy design and implementation at the macro and sectorial levels. He received a Ph.D. in economics from the City University of New York.

CARLOS SEIGLIE is a Professor of Economics at Rutgers University, Newark, New Jersey.

MAURICIO SOLAUN is a Professor of Latin American social and political institutions at the University of Illinois. He served as U.S. Ambassador to Nicaragua from September 1977 to February 1979, the first Cuban-American to serve as U.S Ambassador. Among his published books are *Sinners and Heretics:*

503

The Politics of Military Intervention Latin America, Discrimination with Violence: Miscegenation and Racial Conflict in Latin America and *Politics of Compromise: Coalition Government in Colombia.* He holds degrees in law, economics and sociology from the Universidad de Villanueva, Cuba, Yale University and the University of Chicago, respectively.

JEFFREY W. STEAGALL is Associate Professor of Economics and Director of the International Business Studies Program at the University of North Florida. He received his Ph.D. in Economics from the University of Wisconsin at Madison in 1990. His undergraduate studies were completed at St. Norbert College. Dr. Steagall is an international trade and finance specialist, with a particular interest in the trade relationships of developing countries.

CHARLES SUDDABY is currently associated with The Economics Planning Group of Canada. He has spent considerable time in Cuba conducting economic research and authored the first comprehensive report on the island's tourism industry in 1994. Since then, he has completed other assignments relating to the structure and performance of the industry, including studies of proposed new hotel rooms. In addition to his work in Cuba, Mr. Suddaby has provided consulting expertise to lenders, developers and operators of tourism facilities throughout the Caribbean, as well as elsewhere in the world.

RICARDO L. TEJADA is currently an international economist with The World Bank working on rural financial reform in Latin America. Prior to that, he was Special Assistant to the Chief Economist at the United States Department of Labor and worked with the Organization for Economic Cooperation and Development on matters related to the economic transition of Central and Eastern Europe. He holds an M.A. from the Fletcher School of Law and Diplo-macy (1995) and a B.A. in International Economics from the American University of Paris (1990).

MATIAS F. TRAVIESO-DIAZ is a partner in Shaw Pittman Potts & Trowbridge, a 250-lawyer firm with offices in Washington, D.C., New York City and Northern Virginia. He has published a book on the changes that will be required in Cuba's legal system during its free-market transition entitled *The Laws and Legal System of a Free-Market Cuba* (Quorum Books, 1996) and numerous law review articles, papers and newspaper columns on matters related to Cuba's transition to a free-market democratic society. The recipient of B.S. (1966) and M.S. (1967) degrees in Electrical Engineering from the University of Miami, he earned a Ph.D. in Electrical Engineering from the Ohio State University (1971) and a J.D. degree from Columbia Law School (1976).

MARIA C. WERLAU is Owner/President of Orbis, S.A., incorporated in Chile, operating in the United States as Orbis International. The firm provides diverse consulting services related to multinational business and international relocation in Latin America. A former Second Vice-President of the Chase Manhattan Bank, N.A., she holds a B.S. in Foreign Service from Georgetown University and a Masters in International Relations from the Universidad de Chile.

LOUIS A. WOODS is Professor of Geography and Economics at the University of North Florida, where he has been a faculty member since 1972. Dr. Woods received his Ph.D. in Geography from the University of North Carolina at Chapel Hill in 1972, after completing undergraduate studies in Geography at Jacksonville University. He completed postgraduate work in Economics at East Carolina University. His recent research has focused on the determinants of regional economic development, and the constraints imposed by environmental concerns.

Appendix B:
ACKNOWLEDGEMENTS

We want to take this opportunity to acknowledge the continued financial support provided to ASCE's activities by the following sponsoring members:

Acosta, José D.	Law and Economics Consultant	Miami, FL
Alonso, José F.	USIA (Retired)	Washington, DC
Amaro, Nelson R.	U. del Valle de Guatemala	Guatemala
Asón, Elías R.	Empresas Fonalledas	San Juan, PR
Batista-Falla, Agustín	Neder Finanz NV	Paris, France
Betancourt, Roger	University of Maryland	College Park, MD
Botifoll, Luis J.	Republic National Bank	Coral Gables, FL
Cueto, Guillermo	CUBAWORLD SERVICES, INC.	Miami, FL
Delgado, Natalia, Esq.	Jenner & Block	Chicago, IL
Domínguez, Julio P.	Great Eastern Bank of Florida	Miami, FL
Espinosa, Juan Carlos	University of Miami	Coral Gables, FL
Falk, Pamela S.	City University of New York	New York, NY
Fernández, Carlos J.	KPMG Peat Marwick	Miami, FL
Fernández-Morrell, Andrés	Popular Leasing	San Juan, PR
Freer, Robert E. Jr., Esq.	Freer & McGarry	Washington, DC
García-Aguilera Hamshaw, Carolina	C&J Investigations	Miami, FL
Gayoso, Antonio	World Council of Credit Unions	Washington, DC
Giral, Juan A.	Consultant	Washington, DC
Gutiérrez, Alfredo	Morgan Guaranty	Sao Paulo, Brazil
Hernández-Catá, Ernesto	International Monetary Fund	Washington, DC
Linde, Armando	International Monetary Fund	Washington, DC
López, Roberto I.	Citromax Corporation	Tampa, FL
Luis, Luis R.	Scudder, Stevens & Clark	Boston, MA
Luzárraga, Alberto	Cuban American Research Group	Summit, NJ
Miranda, José E.	Kelly Tractor Co.	Miami, FL
Morris, Roy	Carr, Morris & Graekk, P.C.	Washington, DC
O'Connell, Richard	Private Investor	Paris, France
Padial, Carlos M.	Padial & Associates, Inc.	Baton Rouge, LA
Palomares, Carlos	CITIBANK, Florida	Miami, FL
Pérez, Lorenzo	International Monetary Fund	Washington, DC
Pérez-López, Jorge	U.S. Department of Labor	Washington, DC
Perry, Joseph M.	University of North Florida	Jacksonville, FL

505

Pino, Jorge E.	META	Miami, FL
Pino Cros, Fidel	Fidel Pino & Associates	Mayaguez, PR
Pinon, Jorge R.		
Reich, Ambassador Otto	RMA International Inc.	Arlington, VA
Roca, Rubén	The Rouse Company	Columbia, MD
Rodríguez, José Luis	Trans-Tech-Ag Corp.	Fort Lauderdale, FL
Rodríguez, Ricardo	Smith Barney	New York, NY
Sánchez, Federico F.	Interlink Group	San Juan, PR
Sánchez, Nicolás	College of the Holy Cross	Worcester, MA
Sanguinetty, Jorge	Development Technologies Inc.	Miami, FL
Seiglie, Carlos & Diana	Rutgers University	Newark, NJ
Sirven, José	Holland & Knight	Miami, FL
Vallejo, Jorge I.	Vallejo & Vallejo	San Juan, PR
Vega, Juan Antonio Sr.	Latin Finance, Inc.	Coconut Grove, FL
Werlau, María Cañizares	Orbis, S.A.	Chatham, NJ

ASCE also gratefully acknowledges the generous contributions of the following corporate sponsors of the Seventh Annual Meeting:

Citibank Florida
Cuban Studies Association
DevTech Systems, Inc.
Sergio Diaz-Briquets, Casals & Associates
Oscar Echevarria, U.S. Investment Corporation

Freer & McGarry Law Firm
Kelly Tractor Co.
North-South Center of the University of Miami
Enrique Oliver, Yield Development
Shaw, Pittman, Potts & Trowbridge

ASSOCIATION FOR THE STUDY OF THE CUBAN ECONOMY MEMBERSHIP AND CONTACT INFORMATION

Inquiries regarding the Association may be addressed to:

Steven R. Escobar
Secretary, ASCE
11929 Oden Court
Rockville, MD 20852
Escobars@aol.com

ASCE's fiscal year runs from July 1 to June 30. Members in good standing will receive copies of ASCE's Newsletter and of *Cuba in Transition*, the papers and proceedings of the Annual Meetings of the Association (see information in the copyright page for ordering previous volumes), as well as other communications for the year in which they are members in good standing.

Annual membership fees are:

Institutional Members and Sponsors $100 or more
Regular Members $ 45 ($55 outside the U.S.)
Students $20 ($30 outside the U.S.)

To become a member of ASCE, please submit a check payable to ASCE in the amount required for the type of membership desired, along with the following information:

- Name
- Occupation and Title
- Home and Business Addresses (please indicate preferred mailing address)
- Home and Business Telephone Numbers, Fax Numbers and E-mail Addresses

Mail check and membership information to:

Association for the Study of the Cuban Economy
c/o Ivette M. Barbeite, Treasurer
9890 S.W. 70 Street
Miami, FL 33173

ASSOCIATION FOR THE STUDY OF THE CUBAN ECONOMY

The Association for the Study of the Cuban Economy (ASCE) is a non-political, non-partisan, professional association whose main objectives are to promote interest in the study of the Cuban economy in its broadest sense, and to encourage economic scholarship by Cuban Americans and other persons interested in furthering ASCE's purposes. Of special interest to ASCE is the study of economic and business development issues, legal reform, and social and environmental problems associated with the transition of Cuba to a free-market democracy. Membership is open to all scholars, teachers, students, institutions and other professional individuals interested in the study of the Cuban economy and society.

ASCE was incorporated in the State of Maryland, U.S.A., on August 7, 1990. ASCE is a nonprofit corporation registered as such with the Internal Revenue Service of the United States of America. Donations and gifts are deductible for tax purposes as established under Section 509(a)(2) of the Internal Revenue Code. ASCE is affiliated with the American Economic Association and the Allied Social Science Associations.

The 1996-1998 ASCE Executive Committee members are:

President:	Antonio Gayoso
Immediate Past President:	Armando Lago
Treasurer:	Ivette Barbeite
Secretary:	Steven R. Escobar

At-Large Executive Committee Members:

José D. Acosta	Ernesto Hernández-Catá
Sergio Díaz-Briquets	Luís Locay
Juan Carlos Espinosa	Lorenzo Pérez